ESSENTIALS
OF PSYCHOLOGY

SECOND EDITION

ESSENTIALS
OF PSYCHOLOGY

SPENCER A. RATHUS

Department of Psychology
St. John's University
Jamaica, N.Y.   11439

Holt, Rinehart and Winston, Inc.
New York   Chicago   San Francisco   Philadelphia
Montreal   Toronto   London   Sydney   Tokyo

Publisher   Susan Driscoll
Acquisitions Editors   Heidi Udell, Eve Howard
Developmental Editor   Laura Pearson
Senior Project Manager   Françoise Bartlett
Design Supervisors   Judy Allan, Robert Kopelman
Production Manager   Annette Mayeski
Text Design   Ed Butler
Photo Researcher   Cheryl Mannes
Cover Design   Joan Peckolick

Library of Congress Cataloging-in-Publication Data

Rathus, Spencer A.
   Essentials of psychology.

   Bibliography: p.
   Includes indexes.
   1. Psychology.   I. Title.
BF121.R33   1989   150   88-12817

ISBN 0-03-022954-5

Printed in the United States of America

9 0 1 2   069   9 8 7 6 5 4 3 2 1

Holt, Rinehart and Winston, Inc.
The Dryden Press
Saunders College Publishing

For Françoise Bartlett

Voltaire, the French man of letters, once apologized to a friend for writing such a long letter. He had not the time, he lamented, to write a briefer one. Now that *Psychology,* the parent of this book, has undergone a number of revisions, I have had the time to focus on the *Essentials of Psychology.* Doing so was a very special challenge. Not only did *Essentials* have to be comprehensive enough to cover the basic areas of psychology; space was also needed for the pedagogical features that have facilitated learning and, in this edition, for a new chapter-length appendix on applied psychology.

In short, *Essentials* is not a carved-out version of the larger book. It has integrity and literary merit of its own. There are even instances in which *Essentials* amplifies the subject matter.

WHAT'S NEW IN THIS EDITION

The second edition of *Essentials* turns out to be a very new book. The language, of course, has profited from feedback from readers of the first edition; it has been honed to better foster understanding and motivate students. And of course there has been a thorough updating: the results of literally hundreds of new research studies have been incorporated. But there are more "essential" changes:

Chapter 1: "What Is Psychology?" New discussion of psychology's place among the behavioral sciences and new sections on the history of psychology and the scientific method.

Chapter 2: "Biology and Behavior." Amplified discussion of neurotransmitters, the endocrine system, and heredity.

Chapter 3: "Sensation and Perception." New sections on color vision, the skin senses, and nativist versus empiricist approaches to sensation and perception.

Chapter 4: "Learning and Memory." New coverage of taste aversion, prepared conditioning, applications of classical and operant conditioning, eyewitness testimony, and cue-dependent memory.

Chapter 5: "Language, Thought, and Intelligence." A new chapter that includes coverage of language and language development, exploring the biological, learning-theory, and cognitive approaches to understanding language development; new coverage of race and social class differences in intelligence; and expanded coverage of research on the determinants of intelligence.

Chapter 6: "Motivation and Emotion." New sections on theories of motivation, on sleep and dreams, and on theories of emotional development.

Chapter 7: "Developmental Psychology." New sections on theories of sex-typing, including the biological, psychodynamic, social-learning, cognitive-developmental, and gender-schema approaches; the information-processing theory of cognitive development; and Ainsworth's stages of attachment.

Chapter 8: "Personality: Theory and Measurement." New sections on Karen Horney's psychodynamic theory and George Kelly's phenomenological theory of personal constructs, and complete revision of the section on social-learning theory.

Chapter 9: "Abnormal Behavior." New sections on the cognitive model of abnormal behavior; and on panic disorder, post-traumatic stress disorder, depersonalization disorder, and the eating disorders of anorexia nervosa and bulimia nervosa labeled according to the DSM-III-R.

Chapter 10: "Methods of Therapy." Expanded coverage of cognitive therapy methods, of the physiological bases of the efficacy of various kinds of chemotherapy, and of the various kinds of ECT.

Chapter 11: "Social Psychology." New sections on the A–B problem, "low-balling," possible explanations for the behavior of participants in the Milgram studies of obedience, group decision-making schemes, and "groupthink."

Appendix A: "Health Psychology." New coverage of this relevant topic.

Illustration program. Use of full color and dynamic new illustrations in Chapter 2, "Biology and Behavior," Chapter 3, "Sensation and Perception," and Chapter 7, "Developmental Psychology."

Built-in study guide. A brand-new, built-in, chapter-by-chapter, self-scoring student study guide that will make the academic material more accessible to the student, and at lower cost.

Essentials continues to make clear the many meanings of psychology. Psychology touches almost every aspect of our lives, and I sought to emphasize this relevance. Yet psychology remains a science with strict rules for determining what is truth and what is fiction. Psychology also includes guidelines for determining what is acceptable as evidence. And so, *Essentials* is also a recounting of the ongoing human endeavor to replace superstition with science, and to place logic and facts before folklore, common sense (which some refer to as "common nonsense"), and the emotional appeal.

FEATURES OF THIS EDITION

The features of the second edition include the following:

Coverage

Essentials of Psychology is a comprehensive and balanced textbook, a straight-forward introduction to the basic research areas of psychology: physiological psychology, sensation and perception, learning and cognition, language, motivation and emotion, and personality and social psychology. With that knowledge as a base, the text also explores the evolving applications of psychology in the areas of human growth and development, sex roles and sex differences, intelligence and its assessment, abnormal behavior, methods of therapy, and health psychology.

No introductory survey can pursue every area of psychology in depth. For this reason, *Essentials* is succinct in presentation. A number of areas are combined to receive single-chapter coverage: "Sensation and Perception" (Ch. 3); "Learning and Memory" (Ch. 4); "Language, Thought, and Intelligence" (Ch. 5); "Motivation and Emotion" (Ch. 6); and "Personality: Theory and Measurement" (Ch. 8).

Clear, concise coverage of these topics permits inclusion elsewhere of topics that immediately touch students' lives. For example, sleep and dreams, obesity, homosexuality, pornography, and forcible rape are discussed in Chapter 6 ("Motivation and Emotion"). Chapter 7 ("Developmental Psychology") includes thorough coverage of adult development and its challenges. Sexual dysfunctions and substance abuse are covered in Chapter 9 ("Abnormal Psychology"). Techniques for self-control are explored in Chapter 10 ("Methods of Therapy"). Applications in the areas of physical health are covered in Appendix A.

Writing Style

It matters little how comprehensive and rigorous an introductory psychology textbook is if students do not read it. And so, *Essentials of Psychology* was written deliberately with the needs of the students in mind. *Essentials* maintains an engaging and motivating quality but avoids frivilousness and condescension. I have tried to present even the most abstract, difficult concepts in energetic, accessible prose.

Essentials was also written explicitly for the instructor who requires a textbook that is

comprehensive and balanced

rigorous

accurate and up-to-date

clearly written

interest arousing

applied as well as theoretical

well-illustrated and visually appealing

succinct

Built-In Self-Scoring Student Study Guide

Essentials also contains a brand-new, built-in, chapter-by-chapter, self-scoring student study guide that promotes learning and is economical. The study guide contains the following seven features:

Chapter Outlines   Each chapter begins with an outline that helps organize the subject matter for the student.

Pretests ("Truth or Fiction?" Sections)   Pretests follow the chapter outlines. These series of true/false items stimulate student interest by challenging their own preconceptions about psychology and accumulated centuries of "common knowledge" and folklore. In this way students are primed for rigorous scientific discussion of issues that have previously received biased and unscientific consideration.

Running Glossary   Research shows that most students do not make use of a glossary in the back of a book. And so the technical terms in *Essentials* are defined on the pages on which they appear in the text. An added advantage is that ready access to definitions helps students maintain their concentration on the chapter; they need not flip back and forth between different sections of the book.

To amplify this study-guide feature, definitions are presented in two or more chapters, as needed. In this way, instructors are given flexibility in the order of reading assignments, and students are reminded of the meanings of terms. All technical terms are boldfaced on the pages on which they appear. Moreover, these terms are listed in the subject index, and the pages on which they are defined are boldfaced in the index, allowing students to readily locate definitions.

"Truth or Fiction Revisited" Sections   These end-of-chapter sections help provide psychological closure. Now that students have had the opportunity to read about psychological theory and research, they are ready to be reminded of their initial responses to the chapter pretests (the "Truth or Fiction?" sections). Students receive feedback about whether erroneous impressions have been dispelled, and are reminded once more that psychology is a science.

Chapter Reviews   Chapter reviews recap the material in a logical step-by-step manner. Care was taken to include in them as many technical terms as possible.

Exercises   These are designed to help students consolidate their learning. Often these are matching exercises, as in matching names of psychologists with the theoretical views they espouse. In Chapters 2 and 3 we offer students diagrams of anatomical illustrations within the text, giving them the opportunity to label the essential parts.

Posttests   Most psychology instructors use multiple-choice tests in their assessment of students. For this reason, the final study-guide element of each chapter is a 25-item multiple-choice test. These tests provide students with a numerical measure of their knowledge of the chapter and, perhaps, a reasonably accurate basis for predicting their performance on their instructors' quizzes and tests.

Illustrations

As the author of the second edition of *Essentials of Psychology*, I am particularly proud of its new illustration program. There are new drawings throughout the text, and Chapters 2 and 3 ("Biology and Behavior," "Sensation and Perception") particularly shine with enlarged, full-color illustrations that can dramatically enhance student comprehension of difficult topics.

Figure captions are extensive where needed, to reinforce the explanatory power of the illustrations themselves.

Applications

Essentials of Psychology makes psychology relevant to students' own lives by emphasizing psychological theory, research, *and* applications. While the text avoids deceivingly simple answers to complex human problems, it offers information about how psychological principles and research has been applied in such areas as

methods of fear reduction

biofeedback training

methods of weight control

rape prevention

polygraphs (lie detectors)

effects of day care

coping with child abuse

cognitive and behavioral self-control strategies

Type A behavior

psychological hardiness

compliance with medical instructions and procedures

pain management

methods of coping with insomnia

methods of cutting down and quitting smoking

Questionnaires

The Greek philosopher Socrates is credited with having said "Know thyself" and innovating the method of introspection, or looking inward. *Essentials* contains several questionnaires that students can use under the guidance of their instructors to enhance their self-knowledge:

The Social-Desirability Scale

The Remote Associates Test

Sensation-Seeking Scale

The Love Scale

The Rathus Assertiveness Schedule

Are You Type A or Type B?

Locus of Control Scale

"60 Minutes" Inserts

Essentials includes five inserts based on the "60 Minutes" television program. These inserts recount episodes that deal with psychologically related issues. A videotape of these five segments is available to instructors who adopt the textbook and can be ordered through the local Holt, Rinehart and Winston representative. The "60 Minutes" segments are:

"King of the Jungle"

"Talk to the Animals"

"Depo-Provera"

"By Reason of Insanity"

"Hypnosis"

THE ANCILLARIES

The needs of today's instructors and students demand a full and broad array of ancillary materials to make teaching and learning more effective. *Essentials of Psychology* is accompanied by a complete, convenient, and carefully conceived package:

For the Student

Essentials features a comprehensive built-in study guide at no additional cost to the student. The study guide includes chapter outlines, a running glossary of key terms, pre- and posttests, "Truth or Fiction?" and "Truth or Fiction Revisited" sections, end-of-chapter reviews, and extensive exercises.

For the Instructor

The *Essentials of Psychology* ancillary package includes a number of support materials to promote effective teaching: An Instructor's Manual that includes Learning Objectives, Teaching Strategies, Expanded Chapter Outlines, Demonstrations, Suggested Readings, and Films—all closely integrated with text; a Whole Psychology Catalog that contains handouts, demonstrations, experiments, and transparency masters; a set of transparency acetates; slides; a comprehensive Test Bank that includes 120 multiple-choice items per chapter, organized by Learning Objectives; a Computerized Test Bank available on Apple or IBM; "60 Minutes" videotapes; and PSYCHLEARN, a computerized set of activity disks (Apple or IBM) consisting of five units: Schedules of Reinforcement, Short-Term Memory, Reaction Time Experiment Lab, Personality Test, and Cooperation and Competition. For more information about the ancillaries, please contact your local Holt, Rinehart and Winston representative or regional office.

ACKNOWLEDGMENTS

The discipline of psychology owes its progress and its scientific standing to experts who conduct research in many different areas. Similarly, *Essentials of Psychology* owes a great deal of its substance and form to my colleagues, who provided expert suggestions and insights at various stages in its development. My sincere thanks to the following:

John Benson, Texarkana College

Ervin L. Betts, Norwalk Community College

Richard L. Cahoon, Cape Cod Community College

Albert Cohoe, Ohio Northern University

Philip W. Compton, Ohio Northern University

Bridget Coughlin, Hocking Technical Institute

James R. Council, North Dakota State University

R. Scott Ditsel, Tiffin University

George J. Downing, Gloucester County College

Barbara Engler, Union County College

Mary Farkas, Lansing Community College

Barry Fish, Eastern Michigan University

Ajaipal S. Gill, Anne Arundel Community College

Brian Gladue, North Dakota State University

John N. Goodwin, School of the Ozarks

Charles S. Grunder, University of Maine

Barbara Gryzlo, Illinois Technical College

John R. Haig, Philadelphia College of Textiles and Science

Tom Hailen, Northwestern College

George Hampton, University of Houston

James E. Hart, Edison State Community College

Kathryn Jennings, College of the Redwoods

Grace Leonard, University of Maine—Augusta

Kenneth LeSure, Cuyahoga Community College—Metro Campus

Peter C. Murrell, Milwaukee Area Technical College

Carroll S. Perrino, Morgan State University

Richard L. Port, University of Pittsburgh

Valda Robinson, Hillsborough Community College

John Roehr, Hudson Valley Community College

Laurie M. Rotando, Westchester Community College

David L. Salmond, Vincennes University

Keith Schirmer, Kellogg Community College

Linda Schwandt, Western Wisconsin Technical Institute

Joe M. Tinnin, Richland College

Carol Vitiello, Kirkwood Community College

Ann Weber, University of North Carolina

Kenneth N. Wildman, Ohio Northern University

Michael Witmer, Skagit Valley College

Cecelia K. Yoder, Oklahoma City Community College

David Zehr, Plymouth State College

The publishing professionals at Holt, Rinehart and Winston are a particularly able group of individuals, and many of them have become good friends over the years.

On numerous occasions over the past several years, I have presented Fran Bartlett, Senior Project Manager, with "typo"-ridden manuscripts and mysterious-looking floppy diskettes; and each time, without fail, she has managed to have these items converted into beautiful bound books. Fran coordinates the activities of many editors and other professionals, at Holt and elsewhere, in order to create her magic, and I am very fortunate to have her on my side.

Others at Holt also participated in bringing this project to fruition. They include Laura Pearson, the Developmental Editor, who coordinated and distilled the ideas of my professional peers. Heidi Udell is to be credited for the brave concept of creating the built-in study guide. Robert Kopelman and Judy Allan directed the art program for the book. Annette Mayeski ably supervised the production of the text. Cheryl Mannes brought imagination to the task of photo research. Brian Ellerbeck, Editorial Assistant, patiently and professionally handled a multitude of administrative tasks. Geri Badler, Marketing Manager, is to be credited for the marketing and promotion of the book. Finally, I'd like to thank the management team at Holt: Dave Dusthimer, President; Ted Buchholz, Editor-in-Chief; John Howard, Vice President, Sales; Ed Hunter, Director of Marketing; and the Holt sales representatives for their continued belief in and support of my books.

S.A.R.

CONTENTS IN BRIEF

1 WHAT IS PSYCHOLOGY?   1

2 BIOLOGY AND BEHAVIOR   42

3 SENSATION AND PERCEPTION   93

4 LEARNING AND MEMORY   143

5 LANGUAGE, THOUGHT, AND
   INTELLIGENCE   189

6 MOTIVATION AND EMOTION   230

7 DEVELOPMENTAL PSYCHOLOGY   276

8 PERSONALITY: THEORY AND
   MEASUREMENT   321

9 ABNORMAL BEHAVIOR   358

10 METHODS OF THERAPY   396

11 SOCIAL PSYCHOLOGY   434

APPENDIX A: HEALTH PSYCHOLOGY   478

APPENDIX B: STATISTICS   506

APPENDIX C: ANSWER KEY FOR
   QUESTIONNAIRES   520

REFERENCES   R-1

INDEXES   I-1

C O N T E N T S

Preface   *vii*

CHAPTER 1   WHAT IS PSYCHOLOGY?   1

Pretest: Truth or Fiction?   **1**
WHAT IS PSYCHOLOGY?   2
  The Goals of Psychology   3
WHAT PSYCHOLOGISTS DO   4
  Clinical, Community, and Counseling
    Psychologists   5
  School and Educational Psychologists   6
  Developmental Psychologists   6
  Personality, Social, and Environmental
    Psychologists   6
  Experimental Psychologists   8
  Psychologists in Industry   8
  Emerging Fields   9
WHERE PSYCHOLOGY COMES FROM:
  A BRIEF HISTORY   9
  Structuralism   10
  Functionalism   11
  Behaviorism   12
  Gestalt Psychology   13
  Psychoanalysis   15
HOW TODAY'S PSYCHOLOGISTS VIEW
  BEHAVIOR   16
  The Biological Perspective   16
  The Cognitive Perspective   18
  The Humanistic Perspective   19
  The Psychoanalytic Perspective   20
  Learning-Theory Perspectives   20

HOW PSYCHOLOGISTS STUDY BEHAVIOR   21
  The Scientific Method   22
  The Naturalistic-Observation Method   22
  The Experimental Method   24
  The Survey Method   27
  The Testing Method   29
  The Case-Study Method   29
  The Correlational Method   31
ETHICS IN PSYCHOLOGICAL RESEARCH
  AND PRACTICE   32
  Research with Human Subjects   33
  The Use of Deception   33
  Research with Animal Subjects   35

Truth or Fiction Revisited   **36**
Chapter Review   **36**
Exercise   **38**
Posttest   **39**

CHAPTER 2   BIOLOGY AND
BEHAVIOR   42

Pretest: Truth or Fiction?   **42**
NEURONS   43
  The Makeup of Neurons   44
  A Psychological Controversy: Do We Lose
    Brain Cells as We Grow Older?   47
  The Neural Impulse   47
  The Synapse   49
  Neurotransmitters   49
  Neuropeptides   51

THE NERVOUS SYSTEM 52
The Central Nervous System 53
The Peripheral Nervous System 59
THE CEREBRAL CORTEX 61
The Geography of the Cerebral Cortex 61
Thought, Language, and the Cortex 62
Divided-Brain Experiments:When Two
Hemispheres Stop Talking to One Another 66
Electrical Stimulation of the Brain 66
THE ENDOCRINE SYSTEM 69
The Pituitary Gland 70
The Pancreas 72
The Thyroid Gland 72
The Adrenal Glands 72
The Testes and the Ovaries 73
HEREDITY 74
Genes and Chromosomes 75
Genetics and Behavior Genetics 76
Mitosis and Meiosis 76
Identical and Fraternal Twins 77
Dominant and Recessive Traits 79
Chromosomal and Genetic Abnormalities 79
Genetic Counseling and Prenatal Testing 81
Experiments in Selective Breeding 83
Genetics and the Future 84

Truth or Fiction Revisited 86
Chapter Review 87
Exercises 89
Posttest 90

**CHAPTER 3   SENSATION AND
PERCEPTION** 93
Pretest: Truth or Fiction? 93
BASIC CONCEPTS IN SENSATION AND
PERCEPTION 95
Absolute Threshold 95
Difference Threshold 96
Signal-Detection Theory 97
Sensory Adaptation 97
VISION 98
Light 98
The Eye: Our Living Camera 100
COLOR VISION 105
Psychological Dimensions of Color: Hue,
Brightness, and Saturation 105
Complementary versus Analogous Colors 107

Theories of Color Vision 110
Color Blindness 111
VISUAL PERCEPTION 111
Perceptual Organization 111
Perception of Movement 115
Depth Perception 116
Perceptual Constancies 120
Visual Illusions 122
HEARING 124
Pitch and Loudness 124
The Ear 126
Locating Sounds 128
Perception of Loudness and Pitch 128
Deafness 129
SMELL 129
Some Recent Studies in Olfaction:
"The Nose Knows" 130
TASTE 131
THE SKIN SENSES 132
Touch and Pressure 132
Temperature 133
Pain 134
KINESTHESIS 135
THE VESTIBULAR SENSE 135

Truth or Fiction Revisited 136
Chapter Review 136
Exercises 139
Posttest 141

**CHAPTER 4   LEARNING AND
MEMORY** 143
Pretest: Truth or Fiction? 143
CLASSICAL CONDITIONING 145
Stimuli and Responses in Classical
Conditioning: US, CS, UR, and CR 146
Extinction and Spontaneous Recovery 147
Generalization and Discrimination 149
Applications of Classical Conditioning 150
OPERANT CONDITIONING 152
Edward L. Thorndike and the Law of Effect 152
B. F. Skinner and Reinforcement 153
Schedules of Reinforcement 159
Applications of Operant Conditioning 161
COGNITIVE LEARNING 163
Learning by Insight 164
Latent Learning 164
Observational Learning 165

MEMORY   165
  The Structure of Memory   166
  Sensory Memory   167
  Short-Term Memory   167
  Long-Term Memory   171
  Forgetting   174
  Why People Forget   177
  Some Methods for Improving Memory   179
  The Biology of Memory: From Engrams to
    Epinephrine   180

  Truth or Fiction Revisited   **182**
  Chapter Review   **182**
  Exercise   **184**
  Posttest   **185**

CHAPTER 5   LANGUAGE, THOUGHT,
AND INTELLIGENCE   189
Pretest: Truth or Fiction?   **189**
ON LANGUAGE AND APES: GOING APE
  OVER LANGUAGE?   190
  Properties of Human Language: Semanticity,
    Productivity, and Displacement   192
THE BASICS OF LANGUAGE   193
  Phonology   193
  Morphology   193
  Syntax   194
  Semantics   194
PATTERNS OF LANGUAGE DEVELOPMENT   195
  Prelinguistic Vocalizations   195
  Development of Vocabulary   196
  Development of Syntax   198
  Toward More Complex Language   198
THEORIES OF LANGUAGE DEVELOPMENT   200
  Learning-Theory Views   200
  Nativist Views   201
  Cognitive Views   202
  Putting It All Together   202
LANGUAGE AND THOUGHT   203
  The Linguistic-Relativity Hypothesis   203
PROBLEM SOLVING   204
  Stages in Problem Solving   205
  Mental Sets   206
  Functional Fixedness   207
  Creativity in Problem Solving   208
INTELLIGENCE   209
  Theories of Intelligence   210
  Measurement of Intelligence   213

  Social-Class, Racial, and Ethnic Differences in
    Intelligence   218
  The Testing Controversy   218
  The Determinants of Intelligence: Where Do
    IQ Scores Come From?   220

  Truth or Fiction Revisited   **224**
  Chapter Review   **224**
  Exercise   **226**
  Posttest   **227**

CHAPTER 6   MOTIVATION AND
EMOTION   230
Pretest: Truth or Fiction?   **230**
MOTIVES, NEEDS, DRIVES, AND
  INCENTIVES   231
THEORETICAL PERSPECTIVES ON
  MOTIVATION   232
  Instinct Theory   232
  Drive-Reduction Theory   233
  Humanistic Theory   233
  Evaluation   234
PHYSIOLOGICAL DRIVES   234
  Hunger   235
  Obesity   236
  Thirst   239
  Sleep   240
  Sex   244
STIMULUS MOTIVES   250
  Sensory Stimulation and Activity   250
  Exploration and Manipulation   251
  The Search for Optimal Arousal   253
SOCIAL MOTIVES   255
  The Need for Achievement   256
  The Need for Affiliation   258
EMOTION   258
  Emotional Development   260
  Expression of Emotions   261
  The Facial-Feedback Hypothesis   263
  Theories of Emotion   266

  Truth or Fiction Revisited   **270**
  Chapter Review   **270**
  Exercise   **272**
  Posttest   **273**

CHAPTER 7   DEVELOPMENTAL PSYCHOLOGY   276

Pretest: Truth or Fiction?   276
CONTROVERSIES IN DEVELOPMENTAL PSYCHOLOGY   277
  Does Development Reflect Nature or Nurture?   278
  Is Development Continuous or Discontinuous?   278
PRENATAL DEVELOPMENT   278
  The Germinal Stage   279
  The Embryonic Stage   279
  The Fetal Stage   281
PHYSICAL DEVELOPMENT   282
  Childhood   282
  Adolescence   285
PERCEPTUAL DEVELOPMENT   286
COGNITIVE DEVELOPMENT   287
  Jean Piaget's Cognitive-Developmental Theory   288
  Information-Processing Approaches to Cognitive Development   294
  Lawrence Kohlberg's Theory of Moral Development   295
ATTACHMENT   297
  Stages of Attachment   298
  Theoretical Views of Attachment   298
  The Effects of Day Care   301
  Child Abuse: When Attachment Fails   302
SEX TYPING   302
  Sex Differences   303
  On Becoming a Man or a Woman: Theoretical Views   304
ADULT DEVELOPMENT   308
  Young Adulthood   309
  Middle Adulthood   310
  Late Adulthood   311

Truth or Fiction Revisited   314
Chapter Review   314
Exercises   316
Posttest   318

CHAPTER 8   PERSONALITY: THEORY AND MEASUREMENT   321

Pretest: Truth or Fiction?   321
PSYCHODYNAMIC THEORIES   322
  Sigmund Freud's Theory of Psychosexual Development   322
  Carl Jung   329
  Alfred Adler   329
  Karen Horney   330
  Erik Erikson   331

TRAIT THEORIES   332
  Gordon Allport   332
  Raymond Cattell   333
  Hans Eysenck   333
  Evaluation of Trait Theories   335
LEARNING THEORIES   336
  Behaviorism   336
  Social-Learning Theory   337
  Evaluation of Learning Theories   341
PHENOMENOLOGICAL THEORIES   342
  Carl Rogers's Self Theory   342
  George Kelly's Psychology of Personal Constructs   344
MEASUREMENT OF PERSONALITY   345
  Objective Tests   346
  Projective Tests   349
  Evaluation of Measures of Personality   350

Truth or Fiction Revisited   352
Chapter Review   352
Exercise   354
Posttest   355

CHAPTER 9   ABNORMAL BEHAVIOR   358

Pretest: Truth or Fiction?   358
DEFINING ABNORMAL BEHAVIOR   359
MODELS OF ABNORMAL BEHAVIOR   362
  The Demonological Model   362
  The Medical Model: Organic and Psychoanalytic Versions   362
  The Social-Learning Model   363
  The Cognitive Model   364
ANXIETY DISORDERS   365
  Phobias   365
  Panic Disorder   366
  Generalized Anxiety Disorder   366
  Obsessive-Compulsive Disorder   366
  Post-Traumatic Stress Disorder   367
  Theoretical Views   367
DISSOCIATIVE DISORDERS   368
  Psychogenic Amnesia   368
  Psychogenic Fugue   368
  Multiple Personality Disorder   368
  Depersonalization Disorder   369
  Theoretical Views   369
SOMATOFORM DISORDERS   370
  Conversion Disorder   370
  Hypochondriasis   370

EATING DISORDERS 371
Anorexia Nervosa 371
Bulimia Nervosa 371
Theoretical Views 372
MOOD DISORDERS 372
Major Depression 372
Bipolar Disorder 372
Theoretical Views 373
SCHIZOPHRENIA 374
Types of Schizophrenia 376
Theoretical Views 376
PERSONALITY DISORDERS 378
The Antisocial Personality 378
SEXUAL DISORDERS 379
Transsexualism 379
Paraphilias 380
Sexual Dysfunctions 382
PSYCHOACTIVE SUBSTANCE-USE
DISORDERS 383
Substance Abuse and Dependence 383
Causal Factors in Substance Abuse and
Dependence 383
Depressants 384
Stimulants 386
Hallucinogenics 387

Truth or Fiction Revisited 389
Chapter Review 389
Exercises 391
Posttest 392

CHAPTER 10   METHODS OF THERAPY 396
Pretest: Truth or Fiction? 396
HISTORICAL OVERVIEW 397
Asylums 397
Mental Hospitals 398
The Community Mental-Health Movement 398
INSIGHT-ORIENTED THERAPIES 399
Psychoanalysis: Where Id Was, There Shall
Ego Be 400
Person-Centered Therapy: Removing
Roadblocks to Self-Actualization 403
Transactional Analysis: I'm OK—You're OK—
We're All OK 405
Gestalt Therapy: Getting It All Together 406
Cognitive Therapy: "As a Man Thinketh,
So Is He" 407
BEHAVIOR THERAPY: ADJUSTMENT IS
WHAT YOU DO 410
Systematic Desensitization 410

Aversive Conditioning 411
Operant Conditioning 413
Assertiveness Training 414
Self-Control Techniques 416
Behaviorally Oriented Sex-Therapy Methods 419
Evaluation of Behavior Therapy 420
GROUP THERAPY 420
Encounter Groups 421
Family Therapy 421
Evaluation of Group Therapy 422
BIOLOGICAL THERAPIES 422
Chemotherapy 422
Electroconvulsive Therapy 424
Psychosurgery 425

Truth or Fiction Revisited 427
Chapter Review 428
Exercises 429
Posttest 431

CHAPTER 11   SOCIAL PSYCHOLOGY 434
Pretest: Truth or Fiction? 434
ATTITUDES 436
The A–B Problem 436
Origins of Attitudes 437
Changing Attitudes through Persuasion 437
Balance Theory 441
Cognitive-Dissonance Theory 442
Prejudice 444
SOCIAL PERCEPTION 446
Primacy and Recency Effects:
The Importance of First Impressions 446
Attribution Theory 447
Body Language 450
INTERPERSONAL ATTRACTION 451
Physical Attractiveness: How Important Is
Looking Good? 452
Attitudinal Similarity 455
The "Romeo and Juliet Effect" 455
Reciprocity: If You Like Me, You Must Have
Excellent Judgment 456
Propinquity: Simply Because You're Near Me,
I Must Be Attracted to You 456
Playing Hard to Get: "I Only Have Eyes for You" 456
SOCIAL INFLUENCE 456
Obedience to Authority 457
The Milgram Studies: Shocking Stuff at Yale 457
Conformity 460
Seven Line Judges Can't Be Wrong: The Asch
Study 461

Factors Influencing Conformity 462
GROUP BEHAVIOR 463
Social Facilitation 463
Group Decision Making 464
Polarization and the Risky Shift 465
Groupthink 466
Mob Behavior and Deindividuation 466
Helping Behavior and the Bystander Effect:
Some Watch While Others Die 468

Truth or Fiction Revisited **470**
Chapter Review **471**
Exercise **472**
Posttest **474**

APPENDIX A   HEALTH PSYCHOLOGY   478
Pretest: Truth or Fiction? 478
HEALTH PSYCHOLOGY 479
STRESS AND STRESSORS 479
Daily Hassles and Life Changes: "Going
through Changes" 479
Hassles versus Life Changes 480
Life Changes and Illness 481
Pain and Discomfort 482
Anxiety 482
Frustration 483
Conflict 484
Type A Behavior 485
PSYCHOLOGICAL FACTORS IN ILLNESS 486
General-Adaptation Syndrome 487
Psychoneuroimmunology: The Link Between
the GAS and Illness 488
Headaches 489
Ulcers 490
Hypertension 490
Asthma 490
Cancer 490
PSYCHOLOGICAL HARDINESS 492
PSYCHOLOGICAL INVOLVEMENT IN
TREATMENT OF HEALTH PROBLEMS 493
Physician–Patient Interactions 493
Compliance with Medical Instructions and
Procedures 493
PAIN MANAGEMENT 493
Accurate Information 496

Distraction and Fantasy 496
Coping with Irrational Beliefs 496
Social Support 496
PSYCHOLOGICAL TREATMENT OF
INSOMNIA 496
Progressive Relaxation, Biofeedback Training,
and Autogenic Training 497
Challenging Irrational Ideas about Sleeping 498
Stimulus Control 498
Establishing a Regular Routine 498
Fantasy 498
PSYCHOLOGICAL METHODS FOR CUTTING
DOWN AND QUITTING SMOKING 498
Methods for Quitting Cold Turkey 499
Methods for Cutting Down 499

Truth or Fiction Revisited **502**
Appendix A Review **502**
Exercise **503**
Posttest **503**

APPENDIX B   STATISTICS   506
Pretest: Truth or Fiction? 506
DESCRIPTIVE STATISTICS 507
The Frequency Distribution 507
Measures of Central Tendency 509
Measures of Variability 510
THE NORMAL CURVE 512
THE CORRELATION COEFFICIENT 513
The Scatter Diagram 513
INFERENTIAL STATISTICS 515
Statistically Significant Differences 516
Samples and Populations 518

Truth or Fiction Revisited **519**

APPENDIX C   ANSWER KEYS FOR
QUESTIONNAIRES   520

References R-1
Name Index I-1
Subject Index

FEATURES

QUESTIONNAIRES

The Social-Desirability Scale   30

The Remote Associates Test   209

The Sensation-Seeking Scale   252

The Love Scale   264

The Rathus Assertiveness Schedule   416

Are You Type A or Type B?   486

Locus of Control Scale   494

60 MINUTES

King of the Jungle   34

Talk to the Animals   192

Depo-Provera   249

By Reason of Insanity   360

Hypnosis   497

WHAT IS PSYCHOLOGY?

OUTLINE

PRETEST: TRUTH OR FICTION?
WHAT IS PSYCHOLOGY?
  The Goals of Psychology
WHAT PSYCHOLOGISTS DO
  Clinical, Community, and Counseling Psychologists
  School and Educational Psychologists
  Developmental Psychologists
  Personality, Social, and Environmental Psychologists
  Experimental Psychologists
  Psychologists in Industry
  Emerging Fields
WHERE PSYCHOLOGY COMES FROM:
A BRIEF HISTORY
  Structuralism
  Functionalism
  Behaviorism
  Gestalt Psychology
  Psychoanalysis
HOW TODAY'S PSYCHOLOGISTS
VIEW BEHAVIOR
  The Biological Perspective

  The Cognitive Perspective
  The Humanistic Perspective
  The Psychoanalytic Perspective
  Learning-Theory Perspectives
HOW PSYCHOLOGISTS STUDY BEHAVIOR
  The Scientific Method
  The Naturalistic-Observation Method
  The Experimental Method
  The Survey Method
  The Testing Method
  The Case-Study Method
  The Correlational Method
ETHICS IN PSYCHOLOGICAL RESEARCH
AND PRACTICE
  Research with Human Subjects
  The Use of Deception
  Research with Animal Subjects
TRUTH OR FICTION REVISITED
CHAPTER SUMMARY
EXERCISE
POSTTEST

PRETEST: TRUTH OR FICTION?

Psychology is the study of the mind.

Psychologists attempt to control behavior.

Some psychologists measure the effectiveness of TV commercials.

Other psychologists serve as expert witnesses in court.

Still other psychologists guide people into eating more healthful diets.

TV commercials must be likable if they are to influence us to buy the advertised products.

A book on psychology, whose contents are similar to those of the book you are now holding in your hands, was written by Aristotle more than 2,000 years ago.

The Greek philosopher Socrates suggested a research method that is still used in psychology today.

Some psychologists look upon our strategies for solving problems as "mental programs" that are operated by our "personal computers," or brains.

Only people use tools.

Alcohol causes aggression.

You could survey 20 million Americans and still not predict accurately the outcome of a presidential election.

Psychologists would not be able to carry out certain research studies without deceiving participants concerning the purposes and methods of the studies.

What Does Michelangelo's *David* Suggest about Human Nature?   "What a piece of work is man!" wrote William Shakespeare. Psychologists agree. Psychologists use the scientific method to study the observable behavior and mental processes of this most complex and subtle of creatures. Michelangelo's *David*, pictured here, captures the awesome beauty and power of human beings.

WHAT IS PSYCHOLOGY?

"What a piece of work is man!" wrote William Shakespeare. "How noble in reason! how infinite in faculty! in form, in moving, how express and admirable! in action how like an angel! in apprehension how like a god! the beauty of the world! the paragon of animals!"

You probably had no trouble recognizing yourself in Shakespeare's description—"noble in reason," "admirable," godlike in understanding, head and shoulders above all other animals. That's you to a "t," isn't it? But human behavior is greatly varied, and much of it is not so admirable. And a good deal of human behavior, even familiar behavior, is rather puzzling. Consider these examples:

> **Psychology** The science that studies observable behavior and mental processes.

Most adults on crowded city streets will not stop to help a person lying on the sidewalk, or to help a lost child. Why?

While most of us watch television, ride a bicycle, jog, or go for a swim, some people seek excitement by driving motorcycles at breakneck speed, skydiving, or taking "uppers." Why?

Most adults who overeat know that they are probably jeopardizing their health. Yet they continue their hazardous habit. Why?

Some children seem capable of learning more in school than others. Their teachers scan their records and find that more capable children usually have higher scores on intelligence tests. But what is intelligence? How is intelligence measured? Why do some people have, or seem to have, more of "it" than others?

A rapist or murderer claims to have committed his crime because another "personality" living in him took over, or because a dog prompted him with "mental messages." What is wrong with such people? What can be done about it?

Human behavior has always fascinated other human beings. Sometimes we are even "surprised at ourselves." Psychologists, like other people, are intrigued by the mysteries of behavior and make an effort to answer questions such as we have posed. But while most people try to satisfy their curiosity about behavior in their spare time, or through casual observations, psychologists make the study of behavior their lifework.

Psychology is a scientific approach to the study of behavior. Topics of interest to psychologists have included the workings of the nervous system, perception, learning and memory, language, intelligence, growth and development, personality, abnormal behavior, ways of treating abnormal behavior, and the behavior of individuals in social settings, such as groups and organizations.

As a science, psychology brings carefully controlled methods of observation, such as the survey and the experiment, to bear on its subject matter whenever possible. Most psychologists are interested primarily in human behavior, yet many of them focus much or all of their research on the behavior of animals ranging from rats and pigeons to flatworms and gorillas. Some psychologists believe that research findings about lower animals can be applied to humans. Others argue that people are so distinct from other animals that we can only learn about people by studying people. As with many such controversies, both views hold much truth. For instance, laboratory studies of the nerve cells of animals such as the squid have given us much insight into the workings of the nerve cells of people. But only by studying people can we understand the purely human inventions of morality, values, and romantic love. Yet many psychologists study the behavior of lower animals simply because they enjoy doing so. They are under no obligation to justify their interests on the basis of applicability to people.

Psychologists agree that psychology is the science of **behavior,** but they do not all agree on what behavior is. Some psychologists limit their definition to *overt* or observable behavior—for example, to activities like pressing a lever; turning left or right; eating and mating; or even involuntary body functions such as heart rate, dilation of the pupils of the eyes, blood pressure, or emission of a certain brain wave. All these behaviors can be measured by simple observation or by laboratory instruments. Other psychologists extend the definition of behavior to include mental processes such as images, concepts, thoughts, dreams, and emotions. The difficulty in studying mental processes is that they are private events that cannot be fully verified through use of laboratory instruments. Sometimes they are assumed to be present merely on the basis of the **self-report** of the person experiencing them. However, psychologists have found that mental processes often can be at least partially verified by laboratory instruments. Dreams, for instance, are most likely to occur when certain brain waves are being emitted (see Chapter 6). Strong emotions are usually accompanied by increases in heart rate and breathing (see Chapter 6). In this way psychologists who study mental processes can often tie them to a number of observable behaviors. This link allows them to verify self-reports with some confidence.

The Goals of Psychology

Psychology, like other sciences, seeks to describe, explain, predict, and control the events it studies. Thus, psychology seeks to describe, explain, predict, and control observable behavior and mental processes.

Psychologists attempt to describe and explain behavior in terms of psychological concepts such as learning, motivation, emotion, intelligence, personality, and attitudes. For example, we may describe learning as a process in which behavior changes as a result of experience. We can be more specific and also describe instances of learning in which children memorize the alphabet through repetition or acquire gymnastic skills through practice, in which their performance gradually approximates desired behavior. We may explain learning in terms of rules or principles that govern learning. We might explain the trainer's use of words like fine and good as "reinforcers" that provide the gymnast with "feedback," or "knowledge of results."

When possible, descriptive terms and concepts are interwoven into **theories.** Theories are related sets of statements about events. Theories are based on certain assumptions about behavior, and they allow us to derive explanations and predictions. Many psychological theories combine statements about psychological concepts (such as learning and motivation), behavior (such as eating or problem solving), and anatomical structures or biological processes. For instance, our responses to drugs such as alcohol and marijuana reflect the biochemical actions of these drugs and our psychological expectations or beliefs about them.

A satisfactory psychological theory must allow us to predict behavior. For instance, a satisfactory theory of hunger will allow us to predict when people will eat and not eat. A broadly satisfying, comprehensive theory should have a wide range of applicability. A broad theory of hunger might apply to human beings and lower animals, to normal-weight and overweight people, and to people who have been deprived of food for differing lengths of time. If our observations cannot be adequately

Behavior The observable actions and mental processes of people and lower animals.

Self-report A subject's testimony about his or her own thoughts, feelings, or behaviors.

Theory A formulation of relationships underlying observed events.

explained by or predicted from a given theory, we should consider revising or replacing that theory.

In psychology many theories have been found to be incapable of explaining or predicting new observations. As a result they have been revised extensively. For example, the theory that hunger results from stomach contractions may be partially correct for normal-weight individuals, but it is inadequate as an explanation for feelings of hunger among the overweight. In Chapter 6 we shall see that stomach contractions are only one of many factors, or **variables,** involved in hunger. Contemporary theories also focus on biological variables, such as fat cells and brain structures, and situational variables, such as the presence of other people who are eating and the time of day.

The notion of controlling behavior is controversial. Some people erroneously think that psychologists seek ways to make people do their bidding—like puppets dangling on strings. This could not be farther from the truth. Psychologists are committed to belief in the dignity of human beings, and human dignity demands that people be free to make their own decisions and choose their own behavior. Psychologists are learning more all the time about the various influences on human behavior, but they apply this knowledge only upon request and in ways they believe will be helpful to an individual or an institution. Later in this chapter you will see that ethical standards prevent psychologists from using any method in research or practice that might harm or injure an individual.

The remainder of this chapter provides an overview of psychology and psychologists. You will see that psychologists have diverse interests and fields of specialization. We shall discuss the history of psychology and the major perspectives from

which today's psychologists view behavior. Then we shall explore methods psychologists use to test their theoretical assumptions and gather new information about behavior.

WHAT PSYCHOLOGISTS DO

Psychologists share a keen interest in behavior, but in other ways they may differ markedly. Some psychologists engage primarily in basic research, or **pure research.** Pure research has no immediate application to personal or social problems and has thus been characterized as research for its own sake. Other psychologists engage in **applied research,** which is designed to find solutions to specific personal or social problems. Although pure research is spurred onward by curiosity and the desire to know and to understand, today's pure research frequently enhances tomorrow's way of life. For example, pure research in learning and motivation with lower animals early in the century has found widespread applications in today's school systems. Pure research into the workings of the nervous system has enhanced knowledge of disorders such as epilepsy, Parkinson's disease, and Alzheimer's disease.

Many psychologists do not engage in research at all. They are concerned with applying psychological knowledge to help individuals change their behavior so that they can be more effective in meeting their goals. A number of psychologists are also engaged primarily in teaching. They disseminate psychological knowledge in classrooms, seminars, and workshops. Figure 1.1 shows that a large percentage of psychologists are employed by colleges and universities, but some of these psychologists counsel students rather than teach.

Many psychologists are involved in all the activities just described: research, **consultation,** and teaching. For example, professors of psychology usually conduct pure or applied research and consult with individuals or industrial clients as well as instruct in the classroom. Full-time researchers may be called on to consult with industrial clients and to organize seminars or workshops in which they help others acquire some of their skills. Practitioners, such as clinical and industrial psychologists, may also engage in research—which is usu-

---

Variable A condition that is measured or controlled in a scientific study. A variable can vary in a measurable manner.

Pure research Research conducted without concern for immediate applications.

Applied research Research conducted in an effort to find solutions to particular problems.

Consultation The provision of professional advice or services.

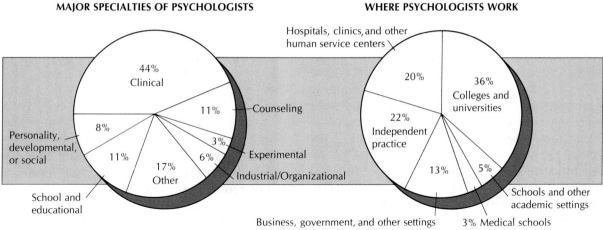

MAJOR SPECIALTIES OF PSYCHOLOGISTS

44%
Clinical

11% Counseling

8%

3%

Personality, developmental, or social

11%

6% Experimental

17% Other

Industrial/Organizational

School and educational

WHERE PSYCHOLOGISTS WORK

Hospitals, clinics, and other human service centers

20%

36% Colleges and universities

22% Independent practice

13%

5%

Schools and other academic settings

Business, government, and other settings

3% Medical schools

Figure 1.1. What Are the Specialties and Work Settings of Psychologists? A recent survey of doctoral-level psychologists by the American Psychological Association (Stapp. Tucker, & VandenBos, 1985) indicated that 44 percent identified themselves as clinical psychologists (see first chart). The single largest group of psychologists works in colleges and universities, while large numbers also work in independent practice and in hospitals. clinics, and other human-service settings (see second chart).

ally applied—and teach in the classroom or workshop. Unfortunately for psychologists who teach, conduct research, and also carry on a practice, research into expanding the week to 250 hours does not look promising.

Let us now explore some of the specialties of psychologists. Although psychologists tend to wear more than one hat, most of them carry out their functions in the following fields.

What Do Clinical Psychologists Do? Clinical psychologists are trained to evaluate problems through structured interviews and psychological tests. They help their clients resolve problems through techniques such as psychotherapy and behavior therapy.

Clinical, Community, and Counseling Psychologists

Clinical psychologists specialize in helping people who are behaving abnormally adjust to the demands of life. Their clients' problems may range from severe anxiety or depression to sexual dysfunctions to loss of goals in life. Clinical psychologists are trained to evaluate problems through structured interviews and psychological tests. They help their clients resolve their problems and change maladaptive behavior through the techniques of **psychotherapy** and **behavior therapy.** Clinical psychologists may work in institutions for the mentally ill or mentally retarded, in outpatient clinics, in college and university clinics, or in private practices.

As you can see in Figure 1.1, clinical psychologists comprise the largest subgroup of psychologists. So it is not surprising that most lay people think of clinical psychologists when they hear the

Psychotherapy The systematic application of psychological knowledge to the treatment of problem behavior.

Behavior therapy Application of principles of learning to the direct modification of problem behavior.

term *psychologist*. Many clinical psychologists divide their time among clinical practice, teaching, and research.

Community psychologists are similar to clinical psychologists in their training and functions. However, they more often work in community agencies—such as community mental-health centers—and they tend to focus on the prevention as well as the treatment of abnormal behavior. They consult with community organizations to develop ways of educating the public about personal and social problems, such as drug abuse and child abuse. They also study ways in which community systems—such as the educational system and the welfare system—interact in an effort to enhance communication and provide individuals with help.

Counseling psychologists, like clinical psychologists, use interviews and tests to define their clients' problems. Clients of counseling psychologists typically have adjustment problems but do not behave in seriously abnormal ways. These problems may include difficulty in making academic or vocational decisions, difficulty in making friends in college, marital or family conflicts, physical handicaps, or the adjustment problems of an offender who is returning to the community from prison. Counseling psychologists use various counseling methods to help clients clarify their goals and find ways of surmounting obstacles so that they can meet their goals. Counseling psychologists are often employed in college and university counseling and testing centers. They are also found in rehabilitation agencies.

School and Educational Psychologists

School psychologists are employed by school systems to help identify and assist students who encounter problems that interfere with learning. These range from social and family problems to emotional disturbances and learning disabilities such as **dyslexia.** School psychologists define students' problems through interviews with teachers, parents, and students themselves; through psychological tests such as intelligence and achievement tests; and through direct observation of student behavior in the classroom. They consult with

Dyslexia Severely impaired reading ability.

teachers, school officials, parents, and other professionals in an effort to help students overcome obstacles to learning. They help make decisions about placement of students in special education and remediation programs.

Educational psychologists, like school psychologists, are concerned with optimizing classroom conditions to facilitate learning. But they usually focus on improvement of course planning and instructional methods for a school system rather than on the identification of and assistance to children with learning problems.

Educational psychologists often are also more concerned than school psychologists about theoretical issues relating to learning, measurement, and child development. They are more likely to engage in pure and applied research and to hold faculty posts in colleges and universities. Educational psychologists who hold academic posts are likely to engage in research into how variables such as motivation, personality, intelligence, rewards and punishments, and teacher expectations influence learning. Some educational psychologists specialize in preparing standardized tests, such as the Scholastic Aptitude Tests (SATs).

Developmental Psychologists

Developmental psychologists study the changes—physical, emotional, cognitive, and social—that occur in people throughout the life span. They attempt to sort out the relative influences of heredity (nature) and the environment (nurture) on growth and to learn the causes of developmental abnormalities.

Developmental psychologists conduct research on a wide variety of issues, such as the effects of maternal use of aspirin or heroin on an unborn child, the value of breast-feeding as compared with bottle feeding, children's concepts of space and time, adolescent sexual behavior, and factors that help the elderly adjust to retirement.

Personality, Social, and Environmental Psychologists

Personality psychologists attempt to define human traits; to determine influences on human thought

Table 1.1 Divisions of the American Psychological Association

General Psychology	Psychopharmacology
Teaching of Psychology	Psychotherapy
Experimental Psychology	Psychological Hypnosis
Evaluation and Measurement	State Psychological Association Affairs
Physiological and Comparative Psychology	Humanistic Psychology
Developmental Psychology	Mental Retardation
Society of Personality and Social Psychology	Population and Environmental Psychology
Society for the Psychological Study of Social Issues	Psychology of Women
Psychology and the Arts	Psychologists Interested in Religious Issues
Clinical Psychology	Child, Youth, and Family Services
Consulting Psychology	Health Psychology
Society for Industrial and Organizational Psychology	Psychoanalysis
Educational Psychology	Clinical Neuropsychology
School Psychology	Psychology-Law Society
Counseling Psychology	Psychologists in Independent Practice
Psychologists in Public Service	Family Psychology
Military Psychology	Society for the Psychological Study of Lesbian and Gay Issues
Adult Development and Aging	Society for the Psychological Study of Ethnic Minority Issues
Division of Applied Experimental & Engineering Psychologists	Media Psychology
Rehabilitation Psychology	Exercise and Sport Psychology
Consumer Psychology	
Theoretical and Philosophical Psychology	
Experimental Analysis of Behavior	
History of Psychology	
Community Psychology	

This evolving list reflects the diversity of interests among psychologists, as well as areas of social concern and individual specialties. Many psychologists are active in several divisions.

processes, feelings, and behavior; and to explain both normal and abnormal patterns of behavior. They are particularly concerned with human issues such as **anxiety,** aggression, **sex typing,** and learning by observing others. Other topics of interest to personality psychologists include **repression,** as a way in which we defend ourselves from feelings of anxiety and guilt, and the effects of television violence.

Social psychologists are primarily concerned with the nature and causes of individuals' thoughts, feelings, and overt behavior in social situations. Whereas personality psychologists tend to look within the person for explanations of behavior, social psychologists tend to focus on social or external influences. The fact of the matter, of course, is that behavior is influenced from within and from without. Both avenues of research are valid.

Social psychologists have historically focused on topics such as attitude formation and attitude change, interpersonal attraction and liking, sex roles and **stereotypes,** obedience to authority, conformity to group norms, and group decision-making processes. Social psychologists, like personality psychologists, study the problem of human aggression.

Environmental psychologists are closely related to social psychologists. However, instead of focusing on how people behave in social situations, environmental psychologists study the ways in which behavior influences and is influenced by the

Anxiety A psychological state characterized by tension and apprehension, foreboding, and dread.

Sex typing The process through which people acquire a sense of being male or being female and the traits considered typical of each.

Repression In personality theory, an automatic tendency to eject anxiety-provoking thoughts, images, or impulses from awareness.

Stereotype A fixed, conventional idea about a group.

How Have Laboratory Rats Contributed to the Advance of Psychological Knowledge?   This fellow may look like just one more rat to you, but he and his fellow rodents have participated in countless experiments. Experimental psychologists conduct research into fundamental psychological processes, such as the functions of the nervous system, sensation and perception, learning and memory, thinking, language, motivation, and emotion.

physical environment. Like social psychologists, environmental psychologists are concerned with the effects of crowding on the behavior of city dwellers. Environmental psychologists study ways in which buildings and cities can be designed to better serve human needs. They also investigate the effects of extremes of temperature, noise, and air pollution on people and lower animals.

Experimental Psychologists

Psychologists in all specialties may conduct experimental research. However, those called experimental psychologists conduct research into fundamental processes relevant to all other specializations. These include the functions of the nervous system, sensation and perception, learn-

---

Job sharing Sharing of a full-time job by two or more workers.

Flextime A flexible work schedule that attempts to meet worker as well as company needs.

---

ing and memory, thinking, language, motivation, and emotion, to name only a few.

Experimental psychologists are more likely than other psychologists to engage in basic or pure research. Still, their findings are often applied by other specialists in psychological practice. Pure research in motivation, for example, has helped clinical and counseling psychologists devise strategies for helping people with weight problems. As noted earlier, pure research in learning and memory has helped school and educational psychologists improve learning conditions in the schools.

Psychologists in Industry

Industrial and organizational psychology are closely related fields. Industrial psychologists focus on the relationships between people and work, whereas organizational psychologists study the behavior of people in organizations (such as business organizations) and how organizations may function more efficiently. However, many psychologists are trained in both areas, and both industrial and organizational psychologists are employed by business firms to improve working conditions, enhance productivity, and—if they have counseling skills—work with employees who encounter problems on the job. They assist in the processes of hiring, training, and promotion. They devise psychological tests to help determine whether job applicants have abilities, interests, and traits that predict successful performance of certain job responsibilities. They help with the innovation of concepts such as **job sharing** and **flextime,** and their research skills equip them to evaluate the results. They also conduct research concerning the motivation to work, job satisfaction, the psychological and physical well-being of employees, and ways of making technical systems—such as automobile dashboards and computer keyboards—more "user friendly."

Industrial psychology is a rapidly expanding specialization. Businesses have been learning that psychological expertise can help them increase productivity while at the same time decrease employee turnover and absenteeism.

Consumer psychologists study the behavior of consumers in an effort to predict and influence their behavior. Their functions include advising

Will You Remember the Jeans or the Model?
Consumer psychologists study human behavior in an attempt to predict and influence our behavior as consumers. For example, consumer psychologists have found that if ads are too sexy, they may indeed catch the eye; however, the viewer may not be able to recall the name of the product. Does this photo of Brooke Shields in her Calvins help viewers recall the brand of jeans, or do they just remember Brooke Shields?

store managers how to lay out the aisles of a supermarket to increase impulse buying and how to arrange window displays to draw in customers. They also devise strategies for making newspaper ads and television commercials more effective. Interestingly, they have found that while some ads may catch the eye, such as the photo of Brooke Shields above, you may remember the photo but forget the product when the ad is too sexy (La-Chance et al., 1978; Schultz, 1978). Consumer psychologists have also found that it doesn't matter whether a commercial is likable or annoying; what is important is that the viewer remember the product (Baron & Byrne, 1987). Many TV viewers hate the "Tastes great!–Less filling!" commercials, but they remember Miller Lite Beer.

Emerging Fields

There are many other fields and subfields in psychology today. The behavior problems that affect children can be very different from those encountered by adults; child clinical psychologists assess these problems and work with parents, teachers, and the children themselves to overcome or adjust to them.

Health psychologists engage in research into the ways in which stress and other psychological factors can contribute to and influence the courses of diseases ranging from high blood pressure and heart problems to diabetes and cancer. Health psychologists also work with clients to help them discontinue harmful habits and engage in more healthful lifestyles; for example, they help clients to start exercising, to lose weight, and to stop or cut down smoking and alcohol intake.

Forensic psychologists apply psychological expertise within the criminal justice system. They may serve as expert witnesses in the courtroom, testifying about the competence of defendants to stand trial or describing mental disorders and how they may influence criminal behavior. Psychologists are employed by police departments to assist in the selection of stable applicants; to counsel officers on how to cope with stress; and to train police in the handling of suicide threats, hostage crises, family disputes, and a host of other human problems.

Psychologists are continually finding new areas in which to apply their knowledge and skills.

WHERE PSYCHOLOGY COMES FROM: A BRIEF HISTORY

Psychology is as old as history and as modern as today. Although theoretical developments and research seem to change dramatically the face of contemporary psychology every few years, the outline for this textbook could have been written by the Greek philosopher Aristotle, who lived from 384

Who Is Wilhelm Wundt?

to 323 B.C. One of Aristotle's works was called *Peri Psyches,* which translates as "About the Psyche." *Peri Psyches,* like this book, began with a history of psychological thought and historical perspectives on the nature of the mind and behavior. Given his scientific approach, Aristotle made the case that human behavior was subject to rules and laws, just as was the behavior of the stars and of the seas. Then Aristotle delved into his subject matter topic by topic: personality, sensation and perception, thought, intelligence, needs and motives, feelings and emotion, and memory. This book reorganizes these topics somewhat, but each is here.

There are many other contributors from ancient Greece. Democritus, for instance, suggested at about 400 B.C. that we could think of behavior in terms of a body and a mind. (Contemporary psychologists prefer to talk about the interaction of physiological and cognitive processes.) Democritus also pointed out that our behavior was influenced by external stimulation, and he was one of the first to raise the issue of whether there is such a thing as free will or choice.

Introspection An objective approach to describing one's mental content.

Structuralism The school of psychology that argues that the mind consists of three basic elements—sensations, feelings, and images—which combine to form experience.

Objective Of known or perceived objects rather than existing only in the mind; real.

Subjective Of the mind; personal; determined by thoughts and feelings rather than by external objects.

Plato (ca. 427–347 B.C.), the disciple of Socrates, recorded Socrates' advice "Know thyself," which has remained a sort of motto of psychological thought ever since. Socrates claimed that we could not gain reliable self-knowledge through our senses because the senses do not perfectly reflect reality. The senses are even known to give rise to illusions, as we shall see in Chapter 3. Since the senses provide imperfect knowledge, Socrates suggested that we should rely on processes such as rational thought and **introspection** to gain self-knowledge. Socrates can also be said to have stressed the importance of social psychology by pointing out how people are social creatures who are deeply influenced by one another.

If we had time, we could trace psychology's roots to more distant thinkers than the ancient Greeks, and we could trace its development through the great thinkers of the Renaissance. But let us now consider psychology's beginnings as a laboratory science in the 19th century.

Structuralism

Most historians set the birth of psychology as a science in the year 1879, when Wilhelm Wundt (1832–1920) established the first psychological laboratory in Leipzig, Germany.

Wundt, like Aristotle, claimed that the mind was a natural event and could be studied scientifically, just as light, heat, and the flow of blood. Wundt used the method of introspection, recommended by Socrates, to try to discover the basic elements of experience. When presented with various sights and sounds, he and his colleagues tried to look inward as objectively as possible to describe their sensations and feelings.

Wundt and his students—among them Edward Bradford Titchener, who brought Wundt's methodology to Cornell University—founded the school of psychology known as **structuralism.** Structuralism attempted to define the makeup of conscious experience, breaking it down into **objective** sensations, such as sight or taste, and **subjective** feelings, such as emotional responses, will, and mental images (for example, memories or dreams). Structuralists believed that the mind functioned by creatively combining the elements of experience.

Another of Wundt's American students was G. Stanley Hall (1844–1924), whose main interests included the psychological developments of childhood, adolescence, and old age. Hall is usually credited with originating the discipline of child psychology, and he also founded the American Psychological Association.

Functionalism

Toward the end of the nineteenth century, William James (1842–1910), brother of the novelist Henry James, adopted a broader view of psychology that focused on the relationships between conscious experience and behavior. James described his views in the first modern psychology textbook, *The Principles of Psychology,* published in 1890 by Henry Holt and Company, the corporate ancestor of Holt, Rinehart and Winston, publisher of the book you now hold in your hands. In *Principles,* which became known to students as the "Jimmy," James argued that the stream of consciousness is fluid and continuous. His experiences with introspection assured him that experience cannot be broken down into basic units as readily as the structuralists maintained.

James was also one of the founders of the school of **functionalism,** which dealt with overt behavior as well as consciousness. The U.S. philosopher and educator John Dewey (1842–1910) also contributed to functionalist thought. Functionalism addressed the ways in which experience permits us to function more adaptively in our environments and used behavioral observation in the laboratory to supplement introspection. The structuralists tended to ask, "What are the parts of psychological processes?" But the functionalists tended to ask, "What are the purposes (functions) of overt behavior and mental processes? What difference do they make?"

Dewey and James were influenced by the English naturalist Charles Darwin's (1809–1882) theory of evolution. Earlier in the 19th century, Darwin had argued that organisms with adaptive features survive and reproduce, whereas those without them are doomed to extinction. This doctrine is known as the "survival of the fittest." It suggests that as the generations pass, organisms

Who Is William James?

whose behavior and physical traits (weight, speed. coloring, size, etc.) are best suited to their environments are most likely to survive until reproductive age and to transmit these traits to future generations.

Functionalists adapted Darwin's view to behavior and proposed that more adaptive behavior patterns are learned and maintained. Less adaptive behavior patterns tend to drop out, to be discontinued. The "fittest" behavior patterns survive. Adaptive actions tend to be repeated and become **habits.** In *Principles'* chapter on habit, James wrote that "habit is the enormous flywheel of society." Habit, in other words, largely supplies the power that keeps things going from day to day.

The formation of habits is seen in acts such as lifting forks to our mouths and turning doorknobs. These acts require our full attention at first. If you don't believe this, stand by with paper towels and watch a baby's first efforts at self-feeding. But through repetition, self-feeding responses become automatic, or habitual. The multiple acts involved in learning to drive a car also become habitual through repetition. We can then carry them out without much attention at all, freeing ourselves to focus on other matters, such as our witty conversation and the tasteful sounds emanating from the radio. The concept of learning by repetition is also basic to the behavioral tradition.

Functionalism The school of psychology that emphasizes the uses or functions of the mind rather than the elements of experience.

Habit A response to a stimulus that becomes automatic with repetition.

Who Is John B. Watson?

Behaviorism

Think of placing a hungry rat in a maze. It meanders down a pathway that comes to an end, and it can then turn left or right. If you consistently reward the rat with food for turning right at this choice-point, it will learn to turn right when it arrives there, at least when it is hungry. But what does the rat *think* when it is learning to turn right? "Hmm, last time I was in this situation and turned to the right, I was given some food. Think I'll try that again"?

Does it seem ridiculous to try to place yourself in the "mind" of a rat? So it seemed to John Broadus Watson (1878–1958), the founder of U.S. **behaviorism.** But Watson was asked to consider this question as a requirement for his doctoral degree, which he received from the University of Chicago in 1903. Functionalism was abroad in the land and dominant at the University of Chicago at the time, and functionalists were concerned with

the stream of consciousness as well as overt behavior. Watson bridled at the introspective efforts of the functionalists to study consciousness—especially the consciousness of lower animals. He asserted that if psychology were to be a natural science, such as physics or chemistry, it must limit itself to observable, measurable events or behavior. It must not concern itself with "elements of consciousness" that were accessible only to the organism experiencing them.

Watson agreed with the functionalist focus on the importance of learning, however, and suggested that psychology address the learning of measurable **responses** to environmental **stimuli.** He pointed to the laboratory experiments being conducted by Ivan Pavlov in Russia as a model. Pavlov had found that dogs will learn to salivate when a bell is rung, if ringing the bell has been repeatedly associated with feeding. Pavlov explained the salivation in terms of the laboratory conditions, or **conditioning,** that led to it—not in terms of the imagined mental processes of the dogs. Moreover, the response that Pavlov chose to study, salivation, was a public event that could be measured by laboratory instruments. It was absurd to try to determine what a dog, or person, is thinking. Watson went to Johns Hopkins University in 1908, where behaviorism took root and soon became firmly planted in U.S. psychology.

Harvard University psychologist B. F. Skinner took up the behaviorist call and introduced the concept of **reinforcement** to behaviorism. Organisms, Skinner maintained, learn to behave in certain ways because they have been reinforced for doing so. He demonstrated that laboratory animals

---

Behaviorism The school of psychology that defines psychology as the study of observable behavior and studies relationships between stimuli and responses.

Response A movement or other observable reaction to a stimulus.

Stimuli Plural of *stimulus*. (1) A change in the environment that leads to a change in behavior (a response). (2) A form of physical energy, like light or sound, that impinges on the sensory receptors.

Conditioning A simple form of learning in which responses become associated with stimuli.

Reinforcement 6A stimulus that follows a response and increases the frequency of the response.

Who Is B. F. Skinner?

Figure 1.2. How Is Reinforcement Used to Train Animals? In the photo on the left, we see how our feathered gift to city life has earned its keep in many behavioral experiments on the effects of reinforcement. Here the pigeon pecks the blue button because pecking this button has been followed (reinforced) by the dropping of a food pellet into the cage. In the photo on the right, Magic Raccoon shoots a basket. Behaviorists teach animals complex behaviors, such as shooting baskets, by first reinforcing approximations to the goal (or target behavior). As time progresses, closer approximations are demanded before reinforcement is given.

would carry out various simple and complex behaviors because of reinforcement. They will peck buttons (Figure 1.2) or turn in circles, then climb ladders and push toys across the floor (see Barnabus the Rat in Chapter 4). Many psychologists adopted the view that, in principle, one could explain complex human behavior as the summation of instances of learning through reinforcement.

Who Is Max Wertheimer?

Gestalt Psychology

In the 1920s, another school of psychology was quite active in Germany: **Gestalt psychology.** In the 1930s, the three founders of the school, Max Wertheimer (1880–1943), Kurt Koffka (1886–1941), and Wolfgang Köhler (1887–1967), left Europe to escape the Nazi threat. They carried on their work in the United States, giving further impetus to the U.S. ascendance in psychology.

Wertheimer and his colleagues focused on perception, and on how perception influences thinking and problem solving. In contrast to the behaviorists, Gestalt psychologists argued that one cannot hope to understand human nature by focusing on overt behavior alone. In contrast to the structuralists, they claimed that one cannot explain human perceptions, emotions, or thought

Gestalt psychology The school of psychology that emphasizes the tendency to organize perceptions into wholes, to integrate separate stimuli into meaningful patterns.

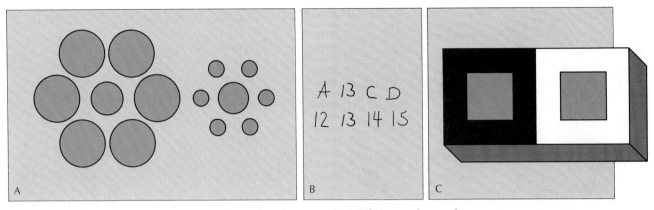

(A) Are the dots in the center of the configuration the same size? Why not take a ruler and measure their diameters?

(B) Is the second symbol in each line the letter B or the number 13?

(C) Which of the blue squares is brighter?

Figure 1.3. How Does Context Influence Perception?   Gestalt psychologists have shown that our perceptions depend not only on our sensory impressions but also on the context of our impressions. They argue that human perception cannot be explained in terms of basic units, because we tend to interpret our perceptions of things as wholes, in terms of the contexts in which they occur. You will interpret a person's running in your direction very differently depending on whether you are on a deserted street at night or at a track in the morning.

processes in terms of basic units. Perceptions were *more* than the sums of their parts; Gestalt psychologists saw our perceptions as wholes that give meaning to parts.

Gestalt psychologists illustrated how we tend to perceive separate pieces of information as integrated wholes, including the contexts in which they occur. As an example, note Figure 1.3. The dots in the centers of the configurations at the left are the same size, yet we may perceive them as being of different sizes because of the contexts in which they appear. The gray squares in the figure at the right are equally bright, but they may look different because of their differing backgrounds. The second symbol in each line in the center figure is identical. But in the top row we may perceive it as a B, and in the bottom row as the number 13. The symbol has not changed, only the context in

Insight In Gestalt psychology, the sudden reorganization of perceptions, allowing the sudden solution of a problem.

which it appears. In *The Prince and the Pauper,* Mark Twain dressed a peasant boy as a prince, and the kingdom bowed to him. Do clothes sometimes make the man, or woman?

Gestalt psychologists believed that learning could be active and purposeful, not merely responsive and mechanical, as in Pavlov's experiments. Wolfgang Köhler and the others demonstrated that much learning, especially in learning to solve problems, is accomplished by **insight,** not by mechanical repetition. Köhler was marooned by the World War I on one of the Canary Islands, where the Prussian Academy of Science kept a colony of apes, and his research on the island gave him, well, insight into the process of learning by insight.

Consider the chimpanzee in Figure 1.4. At first the ape is unsuccessful in reaching for bananas hanging from the ceiling. Then it suddenly piles the boxes atop one another and climbs them to reach the bananas. It seems that the chimp has experienced a sudden reorganization of the mental elements that represent the problem—that is,

Figure 1.4. What Is the Role of Insight in Learning? At first the chimpanzee cannot reach the bananas hanging from the ceiling. After some time has passed, it suddenly piles the boxes on top of one another to reach the fruit, behavior suggestive of a "flash of insight." Gestalt psychologists argue that behavior is often too complex to be explained in terms of learning mechanical responses to environmental stimulation.

has had a "flash of insight." Köhler's findings suggest that we often manipulate the mentally represented elements of problems until we group them in such a way that we believe we shall be able to reach our goal. The manipulations may take quite some time in a sort of mental trial and error. But once the proper grouping has been found, we seem to perceive it all at once.

Have you ever sat pondering a problem for quite a while, and then suddenly the solution has appeared? Did it seem to "come out of nowhere"? In a flasn? Was it difficult at that point to understand how it could have taken so long?

Psychoanalysis

Psychoanalysis, the school of psychology founded by Sigmund Freud, differs from the other schools in its background and approach. Psychoanalytic theory, more than the others, has invaded the popular culture, and you may already be familiar with a number of its concepts.

Think of TV crime shows for a moment. Every year on at least one show, a mentally unbalanced person goes on a killing spree. At the show's conclusion a psychiatrist explains that the killer

Who Is Sigmund Freud?

> **Psychoanalysis** The school of psychology that emphasizes the importance of unconscious motives and conflicts as determinants of human behavior.

was "unconsciously" doing away with his own mother or father. Or perhaps a friend has tried to "interpret" a slip of the tongue you made, or asked you what you thought might be the symbolic "meaning" of a dream.

The notions that people are driven by deeply hidden impulses and that verbal slips and dreams represent unconscious wishes largely reflect the influence of one man, Sigmund Freud (1856–1939), a Viennese physician who fled to England in the 1930s to escape Nazi tyranny. In contrast to the academic psychologists, who conducted research mainly in the laboratory, Freud gained his understanding of human thoughts, emotions, and behavior through clinical interviews with his patients. He was astounded at how little insight his patients seemed to have into their motives. Some patients justified the most abominable behavior with absurd explanations. Others, by contrast, seized the opportunity to blame themselves for nearly every misfortune that had befallen the human species.

Freud came to believe that hidden impulses, especially primitive sexual and aggressive impulses, were more influential than conscious thought in determining human behavior. Freud thought that most of the mind was unconscious, consisting of a seething cauldron of conflicting impulses, urges, and wishes. People were motivated to gratify these impulses, ugly as some of them were, but at the same time people were motivated to regard themselves positively. Thus, they would often delude themselves about their own motives.

Freud devised a method of psychotherapy called psychoanalysis. Psychoanalysis aims to help patients gain insight into many of their deep-seated conflicts and to find socially acceptable ways of expressing wishes and gratifying needs. Psychoanalytic therapy is a long-term process that can last several years, as we shall see in Chapter 10.

Today we no longer find psychologists who describe themselves as structuralists or functionalists. Although the school of Gestalt psychology gave birth to current research approaches in perception and problem solving, few would consider themselves Gestalt psychologists. So, too, are there relatively few "traditional" behaviorists or psychoanalysts. As we shall see in the following section, many contemporary psychologists in the behaviorist tradition look on themselves as social-

learning theorists, and most psychoanalysts consider themselves neoanalysts as opposed to traditional "Freudians." Still, the historical traditions of psychology find expression in many contemporary fields and schools of psychology.

HOW TODAY'S PSYCHOLOGISTS VIEW BEHAVIOR

To understand the various perspectives from which today's psychologists view behavior, let us use the example of the continuing human problem of violence. It turns out that for violence, there's no place like home. Consider the following statistics:

Half of all U.S. wives have been physically assaulted by their husbands at least once.

In a given year, 16 of every 100 couples have conflicts that involve biting, kicking, punching, or worse.

Each year more than a million U.S. children are brought to the attention of authorities as victims of child abuse.

We know to avoid dark streets and alleyways and not to frequent unknown bars. We know that the world at large is a violent place, with open warfare and guerrilla conflict. But for many U.S. residents, the most dangerous place is home. In *Behind Closed Doors: A Survey of Family Violence in America*, Murray Strauss and his colleagues (1979) estimate that as many as 8 million U.S. residents are assaulted by family members each year.

Psychologists tend to view problems such as human violence and aggression from a variety of perspectives, or broad psychological theories. There are at least five major perspectives in contemporary psychology: the biological, cognitive, humanistic, psychoanalytic, and learning theory. Let us look at each of them to see what they have to say about human nature. We also note what each perspective suggests about the origins and control of human aggression.

The Biological Perspective

Psychologists assume that our thoughts, fantasies, dreams, and mental images are made possible by the nervous system, and especially by that central part of the nervous system we call the brain. Biologically oriented psychologists seek links between measurable events in the brain—such as the "firing" of brain cells—and mental processes. They have used techniques such as electrical stimulation of certain sites in the brain to show that these areas are involved in a wide range of emotional and behavioral responses—for example, mating behavior and aggression. Electrical stimulation of parts of the brain prompts innate, or "built-in," behavior patterns in many animals.

Psychologists who focus on biological **determinants** of behavior also study the influences of hormones and genes. For instance, the **hormone** prolactin stimulates not only production of milk in rats but also maternal behavior. In lower animals, sex hormones channel mating behavior into stereotypical masculine or feminine behavior patterns. In people, hormones seem to play a somewhat subtler role.

Genes are the basic units of heredity. Psychologists are vitally interested in the extent of genetic influences on human traits and behaviors such as intelligence, abnormal behaviors, criminal behaviors, and even the tendency to become addicted to substances such as alcohol and **morphine.** Identical twins (who share the same genetic endowment) are more likely than fraternal twins (who are no more closely related than other brothers and sisters) to share such broad personality traits as sociability, emotionality, and level of activity. In Chapter 5 we shall see that the degree to which intelligence reflects heredity (nature) or environmental influences (nurture) is a hotly debated issue, with political implications.

The Biological Perspective and Aggression

Numerous biological structures appear to be involved in aggression. One is the brain structure called the *hypothalamus*. In response to certain environmental stimuli that have been called "releasers," many lower animals show apparently inborn, or instinctive, aggressive reactions. The hypothalamus appears involved in this inborn reaction pattern; and electrical stimulation of part of the hypothalamus, just as do environmental "releasers," triggers aggressive behaviors and **rage responses** in a number of lower animals. People, whose

Can Rage Be Induced by Electrical Stimulation of the Brain?   Biological psychologists use electrical stimulation of the brain (ESB) and other techniques to learn what parts of the brain are linked to such behaviors as mating and aggression. The monkey in this photo is exhibiting a rage response, not because the other monkey in the cage has provoked him but because certain areas within his brain are receiving electrical stimulation.

brains are more complex, appear to have other brain structures that act to inhibit, or moderate, possible inborn response patterns.

Sociobiology   The offshoot of the biological perspective called **sociobiology** became popular in the 1970s. Sociobiology views the gene as the "ultimate unit of life," or the "hereditary units . . . which either fail or prosper as a result of [natural]

Determinants Factors that set limits.

Hormone A chemical substance that promotes development of body structures and regulates various body functions.

Genes The basic building blocks of heredity.

Morphine A narcotic derived from opium that produces feelings of well-being.

Rage response Stereotypical aggressive behavior that can be brought forth in lower animals by electrical stimulation of the brain.

Sociobiology A biological theory of social behavior that assumes that the primary purpose of behavior is to ensure the transmission of an organism's genes from generation to generation.

selection" (Leak & Christopher, 1982, pp. 313–314). Sociobiology argues that the underlying purpose of animal behavior is to contribute as many genes as possible to the next generation. More aggressive individuals are usually more likely to survive to maturity and to reproduce. Therefore, whatever genes are linked to aggressive behavior might be more likely to be transmitted to the following generation. This view is thought to apply to people as well as to lower animals, although our intelligence—our capacity to outwit other species—may be a more central factor in our survival.

Sociobiological theory also attempts to explain **altruism** among animals and people—for example, why some animals (e.g., some monkeys and apes) will sacrifice themselves (say, by attacking a leopard that has broken into a colony of monkeys) so that the remainder of the colony has time to flee from the predator. From the sociobiological perspective, altruistic behavior is basically selfish. Sociobiologists argue that the self-sacrificing animal shares a large gene pool with relatives in the colony, and so the act of self-sacrifice actually increases the chances that one's genes will survive.

Sociobiology has been severely attacked on various grounds. Many scientists argue that it is absurd to suggest that genes can harbor anything akin to an "intent" to be transmitted. Sociobiology also seems to suggest that aggressiveness is natural and desirable. Thus, efforts to control aggression can be seen as doomed to failure and even morally questionable because they interfere with the natural order of things.

But do not confuse sociobiology with the biological perspective in general. Although the role of sociobiology remains controversial, the biological perspective makes regular vital contributions to our understanding of behavior and to human welfare, as we shall see in later chapters.

Altruism Selflessness; unselfish concern for the welfare of others.

Cognitive Having to do with mental processes such as sensation and perception, memory, intelligence, language, thought, and problem solving.

Information processing The ways in which knowledge is perceived, stored, and retrieved.

The Cognitive Perspective

Cognitive psychologists study mental processes— how we perceive and mentally represent the outside world, how we go about solving problems, how we dream and daydream. Cognitive psychologists, in short, attempt to study all those things we refer to as the *mind*.

The cognitive tradition has clear roots in Socrates' advice "Know thyself" and in Socrates' suggested method of looking inward (introspection) to find truth. We also find cognitive psychology's roots in structuralism, functionalism, and Gestalt psychology, each of which, in its own way, addressed issues that are still of interest to cognitive psychologists.

Cognitive-Developmental Theory   Today the cognitive perspective has many faces. For instance, Swiss psychologist Jean Piaget's (1896–1980) innovative study of the intellectual or cognitive development of children has inspired thousands of research projects by developmental and educational psychologists. The focus of this research is to learn how children and adults mentally represent and reason about the world.

Information Processing   Psychologists have always been influenced in their thinking by the physical sciences of the day. And so many cognitive psychologists are influenced by the concepts of computer science. Computers process information to solve problems. Information is first fed into the computer (input). Then it can be stored (e.g., placed in a "long-term memory" on a floppy disk or hard disk). At some point the information is retrieved from storage by using the proper code or index, and it is placed in "memory" (or "working memory") where it is manipulated according to certain programs and an answer is derived (output).

Some cognitive psychologists focus on **information processing** in people—the processes by which information is perceived (input), stored (in long-term memory), retrieved from storage, placed in (working) memory, and manipulated in order to solve problems (output). You may even hear of our strategies for solving problems being referred to as "mental programs" or "software." In this world of computer metaphor, our brains are translated into the "hardware" that "runs" our mental programs. Our brains, that is, become *very* personal computers. When these psychologists talk about the cognitive development of children, they are likely to talk in terms of the size of the child's working memory at a given age and of the number of programs a child can run simultaneously.

The Cognitive Perspective and Aggression

Cognitive psychologists assert that our behavior is influenced by our values, by our perceptions of our situations, and by choice. For example, people who believe that aggression is necessary and justified, as in wartime, are likely to act aggressively. People who believe that a particular war or act of aggression is unjust, or who oppose aggression under all circumstances, are less likely to behave aggressively.

Cognitively oriented psychologists also focus on the ways in which our thoughts **mediate** behavior, or come between environmental events and our overt responses to them. For example, aggressive adolescents are frequently biased in their processing of social information: They perceive other people to be more aggressive than they are (Lochman, 1987), and they assume that other people intend them ill when they do not (Dodge & Frame, 1982; Jurkovic, 1980). Similarly, some rapists, particularly men who rape their dates, tend to misread women's wishes (e.g., Lipton et al., 1987).

Psychologists in the behaviorist tradition argue that cognitions are not directly observable and that cognitive psychologists do not place adequate emphasis on the situational determinants of behavior. Cognitive psychologists counter that human behavior cannot be understood without reference to cognition.

The Humanistic Perspective

Humanistic psychology is a recent school strongly related to Gestalt psychology and cognitive in flavor. Humanism stresses the human capacity for self-fulfillment and the central roles of human consciousness, self-awareness, and the capacity to make choices. Consciousness is seen as the unifying force underlying our personalities. Because of its focus on consciousness and self-awareness, humanistic psychology is also labeled **phenomenological.** Humanistic psychology considers the person's experience, as perceived by the person, the most important event in psychology.

In the previous section it was mentioned that there is an ongoing debate in psychology about whether we are free to choose or whether our behavior is determined by external factors. John Watson's behaviorism was a deterministic stance that assumed that our behavior reflected the summation of the effects of the stimuli impinging upon us. The humanistic approach of U.S. psychologists such as Carl Rogers (1902–1986), Rollo May (born 1909), and Abraham Maslow (1916–1972) asserts that we are basically free to determine our own behavior. To humanists, freedom is a source of both pride and great responsibility. Humanistic psychologists suggest that we are engaged in quests to discover our personal identities and the meanings of our lives.

The goals of humanistic psychology have been more applied than academic. Humanistic psychologists have been involved in devising ways to help people "get in touch" with their feelings and realize their potentials. Humanistic psychology reached the peak of its popularity in the 1970s with encounter groups, gestalt therapy, meditation, and a number of other methods that have been referred to, collectively, as the Human Potential Movement.

The Humanistic Perspective and Aggression

Humanistic psychologists are generally optimistic about human nature. They do not see aggression as an inevitable state of affairs but rather as a defensive reaction to frustrations imposed on us by people who, for their own reasons, do not want us to develop into what we are capable of being. Humanistic psychotherapists have sought to help

Mediate To go between.

Humanistic psychology The school of psychology that assumes the existence of the self and emphasizes the importance of consciousness and self-awareness.

Phenomenological Having to do with the experience of perceiving the world.

clients get in touch with their true motives and potentials and have encouraged them to express their genuine feelings. The faith is that when people are truly free to choose their own directions in life and express their own feelings, they do not choose violence.

Critics, including those in the behaviorist tradition, insist that psychology must be a natural science and address itself to observable events. They argue that our experiences are subjective events that are poorly suited to objective observation and measurement. Humanists such as Carl Rogers (1985) may agree that the observation methods of humanists have sometimes been less than scientific, but they argue that subjective human experience remains vital to the understanding of human nature. Rogers would have us improve the research methods used to study humanistic concepts rather than remove humanistic theory from serious scientific consideration.

The Psychoanalytic Perspective

Contemporary followers of Freud are likely to consider themselves neoanalysts. Neoanalysts such as Karen Horney, Erich Fromm, and Erik Erikson tend to focus less on the roles of unconscious sexual and aggressive impulses in human behavior and more on conscious choice and self-direction. In this sense they are more humanistic than Freud was, a point that will be elaborated in Chapter 8.

The Psychoanalytic Perspective and Aggression
Freud believed that aggressive impulses were an inevitable result of the frustrations of daily life. Children (and adults) would normally desire to vent aggressive impulses on other people, including parents, because even the most attentive parents could not meet all their children's demands immediately. Yet children, also fearing

their parents' retribution and loss of love, would come to repress most aggressive impulses. Still, aggressive impulses might be expressed toward the parents in other ways, or they might be expressed toward strangers later in life.

In his later years Freud became so despondent about the mass slaughter in World War I and other human tragedies that he also proposed the existence of a death instinct, **Thanatos.** Thanatos was the ultimate expression of what Freud saw as the unconscious human wish to return to the stress-free days prior to birth. Not a very pretty picture of human nature.

Research has been somewhat hard on the psychoanalytic perspective. Still, psychoanalysts claim, with some justification, that their views have not been tested adequately in the laboratory.

Learning-Theory Perspectives

Many psychologists today study the effects of experience on behavior. Learning, to them, is the essential factor in describing, explaining, predicting, and controlling behavior. However, there are different kinds of learning, and some of them have a role for consciousness and self-awareness, whereas others do not, as we see in the behavioral and the social-learning perspectives.

The Behavioral Perspective
John B. Watson was a **radical behaviorist.** Behaviorism for him was a philosophy of life as well as a broad guideline for psychological research. Not only did Watson despair of measuring consciousness and mental processes in the laboratory; he also denied their influence on behavior in his private conversations.

Learning, for Watson and his followers, is exemplified by experiments in conditioning. The results of conditioning are explained in terms of external laboratory procedures and not what changes have occurred within the organism. Behaviorists do not attempt to find out what an organism has come to "know" through learning.

The Social-Learning Perspective
Social-learning theorists appear to comprise the largest group of learning theorists today. Albert Bandura

---

Thanatos In psychoanalytic theory, the death instinct.

Radical behaviorist A person who believes that mind and consciousness do not exist.

Social-learning theory A school of psychology in the behaviorist tradition that includes cognitive factors in the explanation and prediction of behavior.

of Stanford University and other social-learning theorists see themselves as within the behaviorist tradition because of their strong focus on the role of learning in human behavior. However, they also return to their functionalist roots in the sense that they perceive a major role for cognition. Behaviorists emphasize the importance of environmental influences and focus on the learning of habits through repetition and reinforcement. Social-learning theorists, by contrast, suggest that people are capable of modifying or creating their environments, and they emphasize the importance of intentional learning by observing others. Conditioning may be mechanical in theory, but observational learning is not. Through observational learning we are theorized to acquire a storehouse of possible responses to life's situations. Social-learning theorists are also humanistic in that they believe that our expectations and values play a role in determining whether we shall do the things we have learned how to do.

Learning-Theory Perspectives and Aggression

From the behavioral perspective, learning is acquired through principles of reinforcement. Organisms that are reinforced for aggressive behavior become more likely to behave aggressively in similar situations. From the social-learning perspective, aggressive skills are acquired predominantly by observing others. However, social-learning theorists find roles for consciousness and choice. They believe that we are not likely to act aggressively unless we also believe that aggression is appropriate for us under the circumstances.

The social-learning perspective in a sense integrates the behavioral, cognitive, and humanistic perspectives. Some psychologists believe that the future of psychology will see continued efforts to integrate these approaches. The behaviorist tradition, they assert, has served its historic purpose of highlighting some of the nonscientific excesses that have characterized cognitive and humanistic efforts to explore the "stream of consciousness." But no approach that diminishes the roles of human values and personal choice can be adequate to explain the complexity and richness of human behavior. On the other hand, B. F. Skinner (1987) indicts cognitive psychology and humanistic psychology as two of the "obstacles" in the path of

Who Is Albert Bandura?

psychology's development as a true science of behavior.*

Historic traditions and theoretical perspectives encourage psychologists to focus on various psychological questions and issues in their research. Their research findings are also made meaningful by integrating them with existing perspectives or, when existing perspectives fall short, by creating new perspectives that will encompass them. In the next section, we survey the methods that today's psychologists use in their investigation of behavior.

HOW PSYCHOLOGISTS STUDY BEHAVIOR

Do only people use tools? Does alcohol cause aggression? What are the effects of aspirin and alcohol on the fetus? What are the effects of divorce on children? Does pornography trigger crimes of violence?

Many of us have expressed opinions on questions such as these at one time or another, and different psychological theories also suggest a number of possible answers. But psychology is an **empirical** science. Within an empirical science, as-

*The third obstacle, according to Skinner, is psychotherapy, because psychotherapy addresses what clients think and feel as well as what they do.

> **Empirical** Emphasizing or based on observation and experiment.

sumptions about the behavior of cosmic rays, chemical compounds, cells, or people must be supported by evidence. Strong arguments, reference to authority figures, even tightly knit theories are not adequate as scientific evidence. Scientific evidence is obtained by means of the **scientific method.**

The Scientific Method

There are four basic steps to the scientific method:

Step 1: Formulating a Research Question

The first step is formulation of a research question. Our daily experiences, psychological theory, even folklore all help generate questions for research. Daily experience in using day-care centers may motivate us to conduct research into whether day care influences development of social skills or the bonds of attachment between children and their mothers.

Step 2: Developing a Hypothesis

The second step is the development of a **hypothesis.** A hypothesis is a specific statement about behavior that is tested through research.

One hypothesis about day care might be that preschoolers placed in day care will acquire greater social skills in relating to peers than preschoolers who are cared for in the home.

Step 3: Testing the Hypothesis

The third step is testing the hypothesis. Psychologists test the hypothesis through carefully controlled methods of observation, such as the naturalistic-observation method and the experiment.

For example, we could introduce day-care and non-day-care children to a new child in a college child-research center and observe how each group fares with the new acquaintance.

Step 4: Drawing Conclusions about the Hypothesis

The fourth step is drawing conclusions. Finally, psychologists draw conclusions about the accuracy of their hypotheses on the basis of their research findings. When findings do not bear out their hypotheses, they may modify the theories from which the hypotheses were derived. Research findings often suggest new hypotheses and, consequently, new studies.

In our research on day care, we would probably find that day-care children show somewhat greater social skills than children cared for in the home, as we shall see in Chapter 7.

Let us now consider the major research methods used by psychologists: the naturalistic-observation method, the experimental method, the survey method, the testing method, the case-study method, and the correlational method.

The Naturalistic-Observation Method

The next time you go to McDonald's or Burger King for lunch, look around. Pick out slender people and overweight people and observe whether they eat their burgers and fries differently. Do the overweight eat more rapidly? Chew less frequently? Leave less food on their plates? This is precisely the type of research psychologists have recently used to study the eating habits of normal-weight and overweight people. In fact, if you notice some mysterious people at McDonald's peering out over sunglasses and occasionally tapping the head of a mostly concealed microphone, perhaps they are recording their observations of other people's eating habits—even as you watch.

This method of scientific investigation is called **naturalistic observation.** Psychologists and other scientists use it to observe behavior in the field, or "where it happens." They try to avoid interfering with the behaviors they are observing by using **unobtrusive** measures. Jane Goodall has observed the behavior of chimpanzees in their natural environment to learn about their social behavior, sexual behavior, use of tools, and other facts of chimp life. Her observations have shown us that (1) we were

---

Scientific method A four-step method for obtaining scientific evidence in which a hypothesis is formed and tested.

Hypothesis An assumption about behavior that is tested through research.

Naturalistic observation A scientific method in which organisms are observed in their natural environments.

Unobtrusive Not interfering.

Figure 1.5. What Is the Naturalistic-Observation Method? Jane van Lawick Goodall has used the naturalistic-observation method with chimpanzees, quietly observing them for many years in their natural environments. In using this method, scientists try to avoid interfering with the animals or people they observe, even though this sometimes means allowing an animal to be mistreated by other animals or to die from a curable illness. We learn from Goodall that tools are used by primates other than human beings. The chimp in the left-hand photo is using a stick as a tool to poke around in a termite hill for food. Goodall's observations have also taught us that not only humans use kissing as a social greeting (see right-hand photo). Male chimps have even been observed greeting females by kissing their hands. Very European?

incorrect to think that only people use tools; and (2) kissing, as a greeting, is used by **primates** other than humans. But don't conclude that using tools or kissing are inborn, or **instinctive,** behaviors among primates. Chimps, like people, can learn from experience. It may be that they learned how to use tools and to kiss. The naturalistic-observation method provides descriptive information but is not the best method for determining the causes of behavior.

Other scientists have observed the Tasaday, a recently discovered primitive tribe in the Philippine Islands. Aggressive behavior is unknown among the Tasaday. It would be romantic to conclude that aggressive behavior results from the effects of civilization, especially since other primitive tribes are quite aggressive. Still, the findings on the Tasaday show that aggression is not universal among human beings and may not be inevitable.

There are many problems with the naturalistic-observation method. For instance, sometimes we see what we want to see. Kissing behavior among chimps seems to serve a social function similar to human kissing, but "kissing" by the kissing gourami, a tropical fish, seems to be a test of strength. We must be cautious in our interpretations.

Primates An order of mammals including people, apes, and monkeys.
Instinctive Inborn, natural, unlearned.

We must also be certain that the animals or people we are observing represent the target **population,** such as citizens of the United States (rather than southern California "Yuppies" or members of the middle class). Visitors from space who encountered only the Tasaday would gain an erroneous impression of the human potential for violence.

Finally, it is difficult to determine the causes of behavior through naturalistic observation. After visiting a few bars near the college where I teach, you might conclude, as you duck to avoid the flying ashtrays and chairs, that alcohol causes aggressive behavior. There is little doubt that aggression often accompanies drinking, but you will soon learn that alcohol may not cause aggression—at least among college males who are social drinkers.

The Experimental Method

Most psychologists would agree that the preferred method for answering research questions, such as whether alcohol causes aggression, is the experimental method. In an **experiment** a group of participants receives a **treatment,** such as a dosage of alcohol. The participants, also called **subjects,** are then observed carefully to determine whether the

Population A complete group of organisms or events.

Experiment A scientific method that seeks to discover cause-and-effect relationships by introducing independent variables and observing their effects on dependent variables.

Treatment In experiments, a condition received by participants so that its effects may be observed.

Subjects Participants in a scientific study.

Independent variable A condition in a scientific study that is manipulated so that its effects may be observed.

Intoxication Drunkenness.

Dependent variable A measure of an assumed effect of an independent variable.

Experimental subjects Subjects receiving a treatment in an experiment.

Control subjects Experimental participants who do not receive the experimental treatment but for whom all other conditions are comparable to those of experimental subjects.

treatment influences their behavior. In another example, environmental psychologists have varied room temperatures and the background levels of noise to see whether these treatments have an effect on subjects' behavior.

Experiments are used whenever possible in contemporary psychological research because they allow psychologists to control directly the experiences of animals and people to determine the effects of a treatment.

A psychologist may theorize that alcohol leads to aggression because it reduces fear of consequences or because it generally energizes the activity levels of drinkers. He or she may then hypothesize that the treatment of a specified dosage of alcohol will lead to increases in aggression.

Independent and Dependent Variables   In an experiment to determine whether alcohol causes aggression, experimental subjects would be given a quantity of alcohol and its effects would be measured. Alcohol would be considered an **independent variable.** The presence of an independent variable is manipulated by the experimenters so that its effects may be determined. The independent variable of alcohol may be administered at different levels, or doses, from none or very little to enough to cause **intoxication.**

The measured results or outcomes in an experiment are called **dependent variables.** The presence of dependent variables presumably depends on the independent variables. In an experiment to determine whether alcohol influences aggression, aggressive behavior would be a dependent variable. Other dependent variables of interest in an experiment on the effects of alcohol might include sexual arousal, visual-motor coordination, and performance on intellectual tasks such as defining words or numerical computations.

Experimental and Control Groups   Ideal experiments use experimental and control subjects, or experimental and control groups. **Experimental subjects** receive the treatment, whereas **control subjects** do not. Every effort is made to ensure that all other conditions are held constant for both experimental and control subjects. In this way we can be confident that experimental outcomes reflect the treatments, not chance factors or chance fluctuations in behavior.

In an experiment concerning the effects of alcohol on aggression, experimental subjects would be given alcohol, and control subjects would not. In a complex experiment, different experimental groups might receive (1) different dosages of alcohol and (2) different types of social provocations.

Blinds and Double Blinds

One experiment on the effects of alcohol on aggression (Boyatzis, 1974) reported that men at parties where beer and liquor were served acted more aggressively than control subjects at parties where only soft drinks were served. But we must be cautious in interpreting these findings because the experimental subjects *knew* that they had drunk alcohol, and the control subjects *knew* that they had not. And so aggression that appeared to result from alcohol might not have reflected drinking per se; instead, it might have reflected subjects' expectations about the effects of alcohol. There is reason to be suspicious because people tend to "act in stereotyped ways" when they think that they have been drinking alcohol (Marlatt & Rohsenow, 1981). For instance, men will become less anxious in social situations, more aggressive, and more sexually aroused—even though they have drunk only a **placebo** such as tonic water.

A placebo, sometimes referred to as a "sugar pill," often results in the behavior that people expect. Physicians have been known to give sugar pills to demanding but healthy patients, and many patients who receive placebos report that they feel better. When subjects in psychological experiments are given placebos such as tonic water, but they think that they have drunk alcohol, we can conclude that changes in their behavior stem from their beliefs and expectations about alcohol.

Well-designed experiments control for the possible effects of expectations by creating conditions under which the subjects are unaware of, or **blind** to, the treatment they have received. But researchers may also have expectations. They may, in effect, be "rooting for" a certain treatment. For instance, tobacco-company executives may wish to show that cigarette smoking is harmless. For this reason it is useful if the people measuring the ex-

perimental outcomes are also unaware of who has received the treatment. Studies in which both subjects and experimenters are unaware of who has received the treatment are called **double-blind studies.**

Double-blind studies are used in medicine as the standard method of determining the usefulness of new drugs. The drug and the placebo are made up to look and taste the same. Subjects are assigned to the new drug or to the placebo at random. Neither the subjects who take the drugs, the people who hand them out, nor the people who measure the subjects' progress know who has received the drug and who has received the placebo. After the final measurements of progress are made, an impartial panel determines whether the outcomes differed for people who took the drug and the placebo.

In one carefully controlled study on the effects of alcohol, Alan Lang of the University of Wisconsin and his colleagues (1975) pretested a highball of vodka and tonic water to determine that it could not be discriminated by taste from tonic water alone. They recruited as subjects college men who described themselves as social drinkers. Some subjects received vodka and tonic water; others received tonic water only. Of subjects who received vodka, half were misled into believing that they had drunk tonic water only (Figure 1.6). Of subjects receiving tonic water only, half were misled into believing that their drink contained vodka. And so subjects were blind to the treatment they received. Experimenters who measured aggressive responses were also blind concerning which subjects had received vodka.

The research team found that men who believed that they had drunk vodka responded more aggressively to a provocation than men who believed that they had drunk tonic water only. The actual content of the drink was immaterial. That

Placebo A bogus treatment that has the appearance of being genuine.

Blind In experimental terminology, unaware of whether one has received a treatment.

Double-blind study A study in which neither the subjects nor the persons measuring results know who has received the treatment.

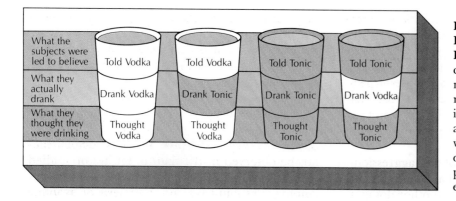

Figure 1.6. What Were the Experimental Conditions in the Lang Study? The taste of vodka cannot be discerned when vodka is mixed with tonic water. For this reason, it was possible for subjects in the Lang study on the effects of alcohol to be kept "blind" as to whether or not they had actually drunk alcohol. Blind studies allow psychologists to control for the effects of subject expectations.

is, men who had actually drunk alcohol acted no more aggressively than men who had drunk tonic water only. The results of the Lang study differ dramatically from those reported by Boyatzis, perhaps because the Boyatzis study did not control for the effects of expectations or beliefs about alcohol.

Is it possible that alcohol does not cause aggression? That centuries of folklore have been in error? Quite possible. Alcohol is a depressant drug, which means that it decreases the activity of the nervous system. High doses of alcohol can lead to a stupor, even to passing out. Why should such a substance cause aggressive outbursts? Now, in depressing the nervous system, alcohol may also decrease fear of the consequences of aggressive behavior. But still, most people do not act aggressively when they drink, and lowered fear of consequences does not directly cause aggressive behavior.

So what do we make of it? Why does belief that one has drunk alcohol increase aggression, whereas alcohol itself may not? Perhaps alcohol gives one a certain social role to play in our culture—the role of the uninhibited social mover. Perhaps alcohol also provides an excuse for aggressive or other antisocial behavior. After all, the drinker can always claim, "It wasn't me, it was the alcohol." How will you respond the next time someone says, "It was the alcohol"?

Sample Part of a population.

Generalize To go from the particular to the general; to extend.

Infer Draw a conclusion.

Psychology is an empirical science. Centuries of folklore may stimulate research into certain topics, but folklore is not acceptable evidence within science.

Generalizing from Experimental Results
Many factors must be considered in interpreting the results of experiments. In the Lang study, the subjects represented a **sample** of male college students who were social drinkers—that is, they tended to drink at social gatherings at which alcohol was available. In the discussion of the naturalistic-observation method, it was noted that we need to be certain that the sample under study represents the target population. Whom do male college students represent, other than themselves? To whom can we extend, or **generalize,** the results?

For one thing, the results may not extend to women, not even college women. College men also tend to fall within a certain age range (about 18 to 22) and are more intelligent than the general population. We cannot be certain that the findings extend to older men of average intelligence, although it seems reasonable to **infer** that they do. The social drinkers in the Lang study may also differ biologically and psychologically from alcoholics, who have difficulty controlling their drinking. Nor can we be certain that college social drinkers represent people who do not drink at all.

There is a quip in psychology that experiments tend to be run with "rats, sophomores, and soldiers." Why? Because these subjects have been readily available. Still, science is a conservative enterprise, and scientists are cautious about generalizing experimental results to populations other than those from which their samples were drawn.

Operational Definitions   Our ability to generalize experimental results also relates to the operational definitions of the independent and dependent variables. The **operational definition** of a variable is limited to the methods used to create or measure that variable.

In the Lang study on alcohol and aggression, alcohol was operationally defined as a certain dose of vodka. Other types of drinks and other dosages of vodka might have had different effects. Aggression was operationally defined as selecting a certain amount of electric shock and administering it to another student participating in a psychological experiment. College men might behave differently when they drink in other situations—for example, when they are insulted by a supporter of an opposing football team or are threatened outside a bar. Still, some psychologists argue that subjects in a laboratory may assign a meaning to the laboratory setting and their actions that makes them comparable to the real-life situation (e.g., Berkowitz & Donnerstein, 1982).

Does it sound as if we are speaking from both corners of our mouth? As if we're praising the Lang study, on the one hand, but telling you not to believe it on the other? Not quite. The Lang study has been **replicated** to some degree with subjects other than college men and other dosages of alcohol. We can also say, with some justification, that only studies that control for the effects of expectations should receive our attention.

The Survey Method

In the good old days, when being "sound as a dollar" was a sign of good health, one had to wait until the wee hours of the morning to learn the results of local and national elections. Throughout the evening and early morning hours, suspense would build as ballots from distant neighborhoods and states were tallied. Nowadays one is barely settled with an after-dinner cup of coffee on election night when the news-show computer cheerfully announces (computers do not, of course, have emotions or make "cheerful" announcements, but they certainly seem rather smug at times) that it has examined the ballots of a "scientifically selected sample" and then predicts the next president of the United States. All this may occur with less than 1 percent of the vote tallied.

Just as computers and pollsters predict election results and report national opinion on the basis of scientifically selected samples, psychologists conduct **surveys** to learn about behavior that cannot be observed in the natural setting or studied experimentally. Psychologists making surveys may employ questionnaires and interviews or examine public records. By distributing questionnaires and analyzing answers with a computer, psychologists can survey many thousands of people at a time.

In the late 1940s and early 1950s Alfred Kinsey of Indiana University and his colleagues published two surveys of sexual behavior, based on interviews, that shocked the nation: *Sexual Behavior in the Human Male* (1948) and *Sexual Behavior in the Human Female* (1953). Kinsey reported that masturbation was virtually universal in his sample of men at a time when masturbation was still widely thought to impair physical or mental health. He also reported that about one woman in three still single at age 25 had engaged in premarital intercourse.

The survey was the appropriate method for attaining these data, since Kinsey wished to learn what was happening in the United States rather than to study the causes of sexual behavior in depth. And if Kinsey had tried to use the naturalistic-observation method, he and his colleagues might have been tossed into jail as Peeping Toms.

In addition to compiling self-reports of behavior, surveys are also used to learn about people's opinions, attitudes, and values. For example, more recent surveys concerning sex have found that during the 1970s people were less likely to condemn masturbation and premarital intercourse than were people in Kinsey's era (Hunt, 1974).

Operational definition A definition of a variable in terms of the methods used to create or measure it.

Replicate Repeat or duplicate.

Survey A scientific method in which large samples of people are questioned.

"Would you say Attila is doing an excellent job, a good job, a fair job, or a poor job?"

Interviews and questionnaires are not fool-proof, of course. People may inaccurately recall their behavior or purposefully misrepresent it. Some people try to ingratiate themselves with their interviewers by answering in what they perceive to be the socially desirable direction. The Kinsey studies all relied on male interviewers, for example, and it has been speculated that women interviewees might have been more open and honest with women interviewers. Similar problems may occur when interviewers and those surveyed are from different racial or socioeconomic backgrounds. Other people may falsify attitudes and exaggerate problems to draw attention to themselves, or just to try to foul up the results.

The *Literary Digest* Survey: A Case Study in the Importance of Random Sampling

You recall President Landon, don't you? Elected in

1936, he defeated the incumbent president, Franklin D. Roosevelt? If this sounds wrong, it may be because it is wrong. Roosevelt defeated Landon in a landslide of about 11 million votes. Still, the *Literary Digest,* a popular magazine of the day, had predicted a Landon victory.

The *Digest,* you see, had phoned the voters it surveyed. Today telephone sampling is a widely practiced and reasonably legitimate technique. But the *Digest* poll was taken during the Great Depression, when U.S. citizens who had telephones were decidedly higher in socioeconomic status than those without them. Citizens at higher income levels are also more likely to vote Republican, and Alf Landon was heading the Republican ticket. No surprise, then, that the overwhelming majority of the people sampled said that they would vote for Landon.

The principle involved here is that survey samples must accurately *represent* the population they are intended to reflect. One way to achieve a representative sample is by means of **random sampling.** In a random sample, each member of a population has an equal chance of being selected to

Random sample A sample drawn such that every member of a population has an equal chance of being selected.

participate. Researchers can also use a **stratified sample,** which is drawn so that known subgroups in the population are represented proportionately in the sample. For instance, 12 percent of the U.S. population is black. Thus, a racially stratified sample would be 12 percent black. As a practical matter, a large randomly selected sample will show reasonably accurate stratification. In any event an appropriately selected random sample of 1,500 people will represent the general U.S. population reasonably well. But a haphazardly drawn sample of 20 million might not.

The Kinsey studies on sexual behavior did not adequately represent blacks, poor people, the elderly, and other groups. Large-scale magazine surveys of sexual behavior run by *Redbook* (Tavris & Sadd, 1977) and *Cosmopolitan* (Wolfe, 1981) asked readers to fill out and return questionnaires. Although many thousands of readers responded, did they represent the general U.S. population? Probably not. They may have represented only a subgroup of readers of those magazines who were willing to fill out candid questionnaires about their sexual behavior. For each of her three popular reports on sexual behavior and male–female relationships, Shere Hite (1976, 1981, 1987) distributed about 100,000 survey questionnaires, but her returns were only 3,000 (1976), 7,000 (1981), and 4,500 (1987). Do the people who returned her questionnaires represent the general population, or even the people who received them? What do you think?

The Testing Method

Psychologists also use psychological tests, such as intelligence, aptitude, and personality tests, to measure various traits and characteristics among a population. There is a wide range of psychological tests, and they measure traits ranging from verbal ability and achievement to anxiety, depression, the need for social dominance, musical aptitude, and vocational interests.

Psychological test results, like the results of surveys, can also be distorted by respondents who answer in a socially desirable direction or attempt to exaggerate problems. For these reasons some commonly used psychological tests have items built into them called **validity scales.** Validity scales are sensitive to misrepresentations and alert the psychologist when test results may be deceptive.

Because of validity problems, many psychologists prefer to observe behavior directly when possible.

The Case-Study Method

Sigmund Freud developed psychoanalytic theory largely on the basis of **case studies,** or carefully drawn biographies of the lives of individuals. In the case study, the psychologist studies one or a few individuals in depth, seeking the factors that contribute to patterns of behavior. Freud studied some patients for several years, meeting with them many times a week.

Of course there are bound to be gaps in memory when people are interviewed. People may also distort their pasts because of social desirability and other factors. Interviewers may also have certain expectations and subtly encourage their subjects to fill in gaps in ways that are consistent with their theoretical perspectives. Psychoanalysts have been criticized, for example, for guiding their patients into viewing their own lives from the psychoanalytic perspective (e.g., Bandura, 1986). No wonder that many patients provide "evidence" consistent with psychoanalytic theory. But interviewers of any theoretical viewpoint can indirectly prod their subjects into producing what they want to hear.

When doing a case study, it is useful to have regular access to the person being studied, as Freud did with his patients. But case studies of prominent historical figures have also been carried out—powerful political leaders such as Napoleon and Hitler, great artists such as Michelangelo and Vincent van Gogh, and ingenious scientists such as Leonardo da Vinci and Madame Curie. The goals

---

Stratified sample A sample drawn such that known subgroups within a population are represented in proportion to their numbers in the population.

Validity scales Groups of test items that suggest whether or not the test results are valid (measure what they are supposed to measure).

Case study A carefully drawn biography that may be obtained through interviews, questionnaires, and psychological tests.

Questionnaire

The social-desirability scale

Do you say what you think, or do you tend to misrepresent your beliefs to earn the approval of others? Do you answer questions honestly, or do you say what you think other people want to hear?

Telling others what we think they want to hear is making the socially desirable response. Falling prey to social desirability may cause us to distort our beliefs and experiences in interviews or on psychological tests. You can complete the following test devised by Crowne and Marlowe (1960) to gain insight into whether you have a tendency to produce socially desirable responses. Read each item and decide whether it is true (T) or false (F) for you. Try to work rapidly and answer each question by placing a checkmark (√) in the blank beneath T or F. Then see the scoring key in Appendix C to interpret your answers.

T____   F____

1. Before voting I thoroughly investigate the qualifications of all the candidates.
2. I never hesitate to go out of my way to help someone in trouble.
3. It is sometimes hard for me to go on with my work if I am not encouraged.
4. I have never intensely disliked anyone.
5. On occasions I have had doubts about my ability to succeed in life.
6. I sometimes feel resentful when I don't get my way.
7. I am always careful about my manner of dress.
8. My table manners at home are as good as when I eat out in a restaurant.
9. If I could get into a movie without paying and be sure I was not seen I would probably do it.
10. On a few occasions, I have given up something because I thought too little of my ability.
11. I like to gossip at times.

are usually to discover the factors that led to the dominant traits of these figures. The researcher reconstructs traits and motives from the figure's writings, public and private records, and possibly, interviews with people who have known the figure.

Case studies are also used to investigate rare occurrences, as in the case of "Genie." Genie's father locked her in a small room at the age of 20 months and kept her there until she was discovered at the age of 13½ (Curtiss, 1977). Her social contacts were limited to her nearly blind mother, who entered the room only to feed her, and to beatings at the hands of her father. No one spoke to her throughout this period. After her rescue, Genie's language development followed the normal sequence, as outlined in Chapter 5, suggesting the universality of this sequence. But Genie did not reach normal proficiency in language use, also suggesting that there may be a "sensitive period" for learning language in early childhood.

The case study is also used in psychological consultation. Psychologists learn what they can about individuals, agencies, and businesses so that they can suggest ways in which these clients can more effectively meet their challenges. Psychologists base their suggestions on laboratory research whenever possible, but psychological practice is also sometimes an art in which psychologist and client agree that a suggestion or a treatment has been helpful on the basis of the client's self-report.

The case study can be used quite scientifically in clinical practice if the psychologist repeatedly

_____   _____   12. There have been times when I felt like rebelling against people in authority even though I knew they were right.

_____   _____   13. No matter whom I'm talking to, I'm always a good listener.

_____   _____   14. I can remember "playing sick" to get out of something.

_____   _____   15. There have been occasions when I have taken advantage of someone.

_____   _____   16. I'm always willing to admit it when I make a mistake.

_____   _____   17. I always try to practice what I preach.

_____   _____   18. I don't find it particularly difficult to get along with loudmouthed, obnoxious people.

_____   _____   19. I sometimes try to get even rather than forgive and forget.

_____   _____   20. When I don't know something I don't mind at all admitting it.

_____   _____   21. I am always courteous, even to people who are disagreeable.

_____   _____   22. At times I have really insisted on having things my own way.

_____   _____   23. There have been occasions when I felt like smashing things.

_____   _____   24. I would never think of letting someone else be punished for my wrong-doings.

_____   _____   25. I never resent being asked to return a favor.

_____   _____   26. I have never been irked when people expressed ideas very different from my own.

_____   _____   27. I never make a long trip without checking the safety of my car.

_____   _____   28. There have been times when I was quite jealous of the good fortune of others.

_____   _____   29. I have almost never felt the urge to tell someone off.

_____   _____   30. I am sometimes irritated by people who ask favors of me.

_____   _____   31. I have never felt that I was punished without cause.

_____   _____   32. I sometimes think when people have a misfortune they only got what they deserved.

_____   _____   33. I have never deliberately said something that hurt someone's feelings.

Source: D. P. Crowne and D. A. Marlowe, A new scale of social desirability independent of pathology, _Journal of Consulting Psychology_, 1960, _24_, p. 351, Table 1. Copyright 1960 by the American Psychological Association. Reprinted by permission.

---

applies and removes a treatment, attempts to control for variables such as client expectations, or takes repeated measures through behavioral observations, psychological tests, or structured interviews (Hayes, 1981; Kazdin, 1981). If the treatment leads to consistent changes in the client, it may be concluded that these are not chance fluctuations in behavior. But this approach is unlikely to be used in clinical practice. Some "treatments," such as helping a client gain insight into the meaning of events that occurred prior to the age of 5, cannot be repeatedly applied then removed. Also, how can the psychologist who helps clients quit smoking, lose weight, or resolve sexual problems reinstate these problems—even with the intention of reversing them a second time—to determine whether treatment has been effective?

The case study looks for relationships between variables within individuals or within small groups. The correlational method seeks out relationships between variables among larger groups.

The Correlational Method

Are people with higher intelligence more likely to do well in school? Are people with a stronger need for achievement likely to climb higher up the corporate ladder? Are we more or less likely to behave aggressively as the temperature soars through 80 and 90 degrees Fahrenheit?

In **correlational research,** psychologists investigate whether one kind of behavior or trait is related to, or correlated with, another. Consider the variables of intelligence and academic performance. Numerous studies report **positive correlations** between intelligence and achievement. This means that by and large the higher people score on intelligence tests, the better their academic performance is likely to be. In these studies, the variables of intelligence and academic performance are assigned numbers, such as intelligence test scores and academic averages. These numbers are mathematically related and expressed as a **correlation coefficient.***

In Chapter 5 you will see that the scores attained on intelligence tests are positively correlated with overall academic achievement.

The correlations between aggression and temperature are not so straightforward. There is a positive correlation between temperature and aggression as the numbers rise through the 70s and the low 80s Fahrenheit. However, past this point, the evidence becomes mixed.†

Some studies reported in Appendix A suggest that the rates of crimes of violence continue to rise with the temperature. Other studies, such as those reported by the U.S. Riot Commission (1968), suggest that there is a **negative correlation** between

*The mathematics of the correlation coefficient are discussed in Appendix B.
†See Baron and Byrne (1987) for a review.

Correlational research A scientific method that studies the relationships between variables.

Positive correlation A relationship between variables in which one variable increases as the other also increases.

Correlation coefficient A number ranging from +1.00 to −1.00 that expresses the strength and direction (positive or negative) of the relationship between two variables.

Negative correlation A relationship between two variables in which one variable increases as the other decreases.

Ethical Moral; referring to one's system of deriving standards for determining what is moral.

---

temperature and aggression once we reach the 90 degrees Fahrenheit. That is, when the heat is really on, to coin a phrase, we tend to become less active. In the case of the negative correlation, as one variable (in this case, temperature) increases in value, the other variable (in this case, aggression) decreases in value.

Another example of a negative correlation is found in the relationships between stress and health. As we shall see in Appendix A, it seems that as the amount of stress affecting us increases, the functioning of our immune systems is impaired. As a result, we become prone to illnesses, and our health declines.

Correlational research may suggest but does not show cause and effect. For instance, it may seem logical that intelligence makes it possible for children to profit from education, but research has also shown that education contributes to higher scores on intelligence tests. Preschoolers placed in Head Start programs do better later on intelligence tests than agemates who did not have this experience. The relationship between intelligence and academic performance may not be so simple as you might have thought. Motivation and adjustment to school also enter the picture by contributing to both academic performance and scores on tests, such as intelligence tests.

Despite the inability of correlational research to place clear "cause" and "effect" labels on variables, correlational research does point the way to profitable experimental research. That is, if there were no correlation between intelligence and achievement, there would be little purpose in running experiments to determine causal relationships.

To properly study behavior, psychologists must not only be skilled in the uses and limitations of various kinds of research methods. They must also adhere to ethical guidelines that govern the treatment of human and animal participants in research, as we shall see in the following section.

ETHICS IN PSYCHOLOGICAL RESEARCH AND PRACTICE

Psychologists adhere to **ethical** standards to ensure that they do not undertake research methods or treatments that are harmful to subjects or clients (American Psychological Association, 1981). However, some exceptions may be necessary, as we shall see.

Research with Human Subjects

Human subjects must provide **informed consent** before they participate in research programs. Having a general overview of the research and the opportunity to choose not to participate apparently gives subjects a sense of control and decreases the stress of participation (Dill et al., 1982).

Psychologists treat the records of research subjects and clients as **confidential.** They do not divulge the names of participants in research and in therapy unless participants specifically request that they do so.

Ethical standards tend to limit the types of research that psychologists may conduct. For example, how can we determine whether early separation from one's mother impairs social development? One research direction is to observe the development of children who have been separated from their mothers from an early age. But it is difficult to draw conclusions from such research because the same factors that led to the separation, such as family tragedy or irresponsibility, instead of the separation itself, might have led to the observed outcomes.

Scientifically, it would be more sound to run experiments in which children are purposefully separated from their mothers at an early age and compared with children who are not. Psychologists would not seriously consider such research because of ethical standards. However, experiments in which infants are purposefully separated from mothers have been run with lower animals, as we shall see below.

The Use of Deception

Some psychological experiments cannot be run without deceiving their human subjects. But the use of deception raises ethical issues. Before we explore these issues, let us first return briefly to the Lang (Lang et al., 1975) study on alcohol and aggression. In that study, the researchers had to

(1) misinform subjects about the beverage they had drunk; and (2) mislead subjects into believing that they were giving other participants electric shock when they were actually only pressing switches on a console. (Pressing switches was the operational definition of aggression in the study.)

In the Lang study, students who believed they had drunk vodka were more aggressive than students who believed they had not. The actual content of the beverages was immaterial. But this study could not have been run without deceiving the subjects. Foiling their expectations or beliefs was crucial to the experiment, and the potential benefits of the research may well outweigh the possible harmful effects of the deceptions.

Still, some psychologists are invariably opposed to deception. Diana Baumrind (1985) argues that deception not only harms research subjects but also the reputation of psychology and society at large. In a study that supports Baumrind's views, students who participated in experiments in which they were deceived afterward regarded psychologists as less trustworthy than did students who were not (Smith & Richardson, 1983). Baumrind argues that deception might eventually cause the public to lose trust in expert authorities.

In any event, many research endeavors continue to rely on deception (Adair et al., 1985). The code of ethics of the American Psychological Association requires that research participants who are deceived be **debriefed** to help eliminate any harmful effects, and the incidence of debriefing has increased in recent years (Adair et al., 1985). After the Lang study was over, the subjects were informed of the deceptions and of the rationale for them. Students who had actually drunk alcohol were given coffee and a **breathalyzer** test so that

---

Informed consent The term used by psychologists to indicate that a person has agreed to participate in research after receiving information about the purposes of the study and the nature of the treatments.

Confidential Secret; not to be disclosed.

Debrief To receive information about a just-completed procedure.

Breathalyzer A device that measures the quantity of alcohol in the body by analyzing the breath.

60 Minutes

King of the Jungle

When you were a child, you may have been told that the lion was the king of the jungle. However, in the "60 Minutes" segment "King of the Jungle," we and not lions are portrayed as the kings of the jungle because of our domination over lower animals. One aspect of our domination is expressed in our use of animal subjects in research. And as noted by correspondent Ed Bradley,

In the name of science, animals have been drugged, shocked, radiated, castrated. Cats have had their eyelids sewn shut so scientists could study vision deprivation. Monkeys have had electrodes implanted in their brains. Rabbits have had chemicals and drugs put in their eyes to determine the damage caused. Primates have sustained head injuries so their behavioral changes could then be observed.

This "60 Minutes" segment addresses questions such as: Is it ethical to harm animals for the sake of science and the well-being of people? How much pain can we inflict on animals to find the answers to such human problems as obesity and diabetes?

Supporters of the use of animals argue that many major advances in medicine and psychology over the past century could not have taken place without laboratory animals (Gallup & Suarez, 1985). Dr. Frances Conley, the brain surgeon, claims that the "study of tumors going to the brain from another site in the body would be stopped" if animals could no longer be used in research. Research with animal subjects has also benefited people in areas such as behavioral medicine, rehabilitation or neuromuscular disorders, development of drugs, coping with stress and pain, and the survival of premature infants.

Actress Gretchen Wyler, head of the California chapter of the Fund for Animals, counters,

I believe some day this will be looked on as the "horse and buggy" days of medical research. We live in a computer age right now, computer models, mathematical models, cell culture, tissue culture—all sorts of alternatives that could be available. I think it's an insult

Who Is "King of the Jungle"?   Now and then psychologists and other scientists must do animals some harm if they are to answer research questions that may yield important benefits for people. Justifying such harm is a major ethical dilemma.

to the intelligence of our species to say that we are still vivisecting animals to find cures for diseases.

Dr. Norman Shumway, the heart-transplant surgeon, answers that the "computer will only respond to the information that one gives it, and what we're looking for are the responses we can't anticipate, and those are the ones that will be derived from animal work." The debate over the subjecting of animals to harm in scientific research will go on.

the researchers could be sure they were sober when they left the laboratory.

Psychologists use deception only when research cannot be run without it. As with other ethical dilemmas, deception is used when the psychologist believes that the benefits will outweigh potential harm.

Research with Animal Subjects

Researchers frequently turn to animals to conduct research that cannot be carried out with humans. For example, experiments on the effects of early separation from the mother have been done with monkeys and other animals. As you will see in Chapter 7, such research has helped psychologists investigate the formation of parent-child bonds of attachment.

Experiments with infant monkeys highlight some of the dilemmas faced by psychologists and other scientists when they contemplate research with people or animals that has or may have harmful effects. Psychologists and biologists who study the workings of the brain have destroyed sections of the brains of laboratory animals to learn how these areas influence behavior. For instance, as you

will see in Chapter 6, a **lesion** in one part of a brain structure will cause a rat to overeat. A lesion elsewhere will cause the rat to go on a crash diet. Psychologists generalize to people from experiments such as these in the hope that we may find solutions to persistent human problems, such as obesity.

But as noted in the nearby box, "King of the Jungle," psychologists must still face the ethical dilemma of subjecting animals to harm. By and large, psychologists follow the principle that they should do so only when they believe that the eventual benefits to people of their research justify the harm done to animals (Rollin, 1985). Still, tradition and law suggest that "there is a limit to the amount of pain an animal should endure in the name of science" (Larson, 1982).

Psychologists are human, of course, and capable of making errors. Occasionally human and animal research participants may be exposed to more harm than anticipated. But generally speaking, psychologists make every effort to minimize the possible harmful effects of their research.

Lesion An injury that results in impaired behavior or loss of a function.

TRUTH OR FICTION REVISITED

Psychology is the study of the mind. False. Whereas psychology may be translated from its Greek roots as the study of the soul or mind, scientific psychology is defined as the study of behavior. Some psychologists restrict their definition of behavior to observable behavior; others include mental processes—thoughts, images, and dreams.

Psychologists attempt to control behavior. True. The goals of psychology include the description, explanation, prediction, and control of behavior. However, as explained, psychologists also believe in the dignity of other people and do not attempt to foster behavior that is harmful or opposed to the desires of the individual.

Some psychologists measure the effectiveness of TV commercials. True. They are called consumer psychologists.

Other psychologists serve as expert witnesses in court. True. Forensic psychologists may testify about the competence of defendants to stand trial and also about psychological factors that may influence criminal behavior.

Still other psychologists guide people into eating more healthful diets. True. Psychology is found in the worlds of academia, business, law, and health. Health psychologists—along with clinical and counseling psychologists—may help clients with problems in weight control and smoking and with stress-related problems that have an impact on physical illness.

TV commercials must be likable if they are to influence us to buy the advertised products. False. It is important that the information about products in TV commercials be *remembered,* not that the commercials be likable.

A book on psychology, whose contents are similar to those of the book you are now holding in your hands, was written by Aristotle more than 2,000 years ago. True. The name of the book was *About the Psyche,* and it was written in the fourth century B.C. It included topics such as sensation and perception, development, intelligence, thought, personality, and motivation and emotion.

The Greek philosopher Socrates suggested a research method that is still used in psychology today. True. It is called *introspection.*

Some psychologists look upon our strategies for solving problems as "mental programs" that are operated by our "personal computers," or brains. True. They are cognitive psychologists involved in the study of information processing. Their approach has been influenced by the concepts of computer science.

Only people use tools. False. Naturalistic-observation methods have found that chimpanzees and other animals also use tools.

Alcohol causes aggression. False. But people who drink may act aggressively because of their beliefs about the effects of alcohol.

You could survey 20 million Americans and still not predict accurately the outcome of a presidential election. True. It is most important that a sample represent the population it is meant to represent. If the sample is not representative, sample size is immaterial.

Psychologists would not be able to carry out certain research studies without deceiving participants concerning the purposes or methods of the studies. True. The Lang study on the effects of alcohol is an example.

Chapter Review

Psychology is defined as the study of behavior. However, some psychologists limit their definition of behavior to observable behavior, such as muscular responses or measurement of heart rate, and others include mental processes, such as images, concepts, thoughts, and dreams.

Psychology seeks to describe, explain, predict, and control behavior. Behavior is explained through psychological theories, which are sets of statements that involve assumptions about behavior. Theories are revised, as needed, to accommodate new observations.

Some psychologists engage in basic or pure research; others engage in applied research. Clinical psychologists help people who are behaving abnormally adjust to the demands of life by means of psychotherapy and behavior therapy. Community psychologists focus on prevention as well as treatment of abnormal behavior. Counseling psychologists work with individuals who have adjustment problems but do not show seriously abnormal behavior. School psychologists assist students with problems that interfere with learning. Educational psychologists are more concerned with theoretical issues concerning human learning.

Developmental psychologists study the changes that occur throughout the life span. Personality psychologists try to define human traits and study influences on our thought processes, feelings, and behaviors. Social psychologists study behavior in social situations.

Experimental psychologists conduct research into basic psychological processes, such as sensation and perception, learning and memory, and motivation and emotion. Industrial psychologists focus on the relationships between people and work. Organizational psychologists study the behavior of people in organizations.

Wilhelm Wundt established the first psychological laboratory in 1879 and founded the school of structuralism, which focused on the structure of experience. William James founded the school of functionalism, which dealt with observable behavior as well as conscious experience, and focused on the importance of habit.

John B. Watson founded the school of behaviorism, which argued that psychology must limit itself to observable behavior. Behaviorism focused on learning by conditioning, and B. F. Skinner introduced the concept of reinforcement as an explanation of how learning occurs.

Gestalt psychology focused on perception and learning by insight.

Sigmund Freud founded psychoanalytic theory, according to which people are driven by hidden impulses and distort reality in order to protect themselves from anxiety.

The five major perspectives in contemporary psychology include the biological, cognitive, humanistic, psychoanalytic, and learning-theory perspectives. Biologically oriented psychologists study the links between behavior and biological events, such as the firing of cells in the brain and the release of hormones. Cognitive psychologists study the ways in which we perceive and mentally represent the world. Humanistic psychologists stress the importance of experience and assert that people have the freedom to make choices. Contemporary psychoanalysts generally follow Freud's views, but focus less on the roles of unconscious sexual and aggressive impulses and see people as more capable of making conscious choices. Watson and his literal followers are referred to as radical behaviorists. Social-learning theorists also find roles for observational learning, expectations, and values in explaining human behavior.

Theory may lead to predictions, or hypotheses about behavior that psychologists confirm or disconfirm hypotheses through empirical research. The scientific method consists of four steps: forming a research question, developing a hypothesis, testing the hypothesis, and drawing conclusions about the hypothesis.

The naturalistic-observation method studies behavior where it happens—in the "field."

Experiments are used to seek cause and effect. In experiments, psychologists observe the effects of independent variables on dependent variables. Experimental subjects are given a treatment, whereas control subjects are not. Blinds and double blinds may be used to control for the effects of the expectations.

In the survey method, psychologists may use interviews or questionnaires to learn about behavior that cannot be observed directly. It is important to use random or stratified samples in order to accurately represent the population one is surveying.

Psychologists also use psychological tests, such as intelligence, aptitude, and personality tests, to measure various traits and characteristics among a population.

Case studies are carefully drawn biographies of the lives of individuals.

Correlational research shows relationships between variables, but cannot determine cause and effect.

Ethical standards of psychologists are designed to protect subjects from harm. Records of human behavior are kept confidential so that the names of participants in research and treatment will not be divulged. Human subjects are given a general overview of research in which they participate so that they can give informed consent prior to participating.

Exercise

Names to Know

Directions: *The names of a number of persons who are important to psychology are placed in the first column. Schools of psychology and other identifying information are placed in the second column. Place the letter of the item that is best associated with the person in the blank space to the left of the person's name. Answers are given in the answer key.*

_____ 1. Aristotle	A. Humanistic perspective
_____ 2. Plato	B. Behaviorism
_____ 3. Wolfgang Köhler	C. Gestalt psychology
_____ 4. Gustav Theodor Fechner	D. Differentiated between body and mind
_____ 5. Erik Erikson	E. Psychoanalytic perspective
_____ 6. Edward B. Titchener	F. Author, *Elements of Psychophysics*
_____ 7. Abraham Maslow	G. Structuralism
_____ 8. B. F. Skinner	H. Founder of American Psychological Association
_____ 9. Charles Darwin	I. Introspection
_____ 10. Carl Rogers	J. Social-learning theory
_____ 11. Socrates	K. Functionalism
_____ 12. John B. Watson	L. Cognitive perspective
_____ 13. Wilhelm Wundt	

_____ 14. Jean Piaget   M. Author, *Peri Psyches*
_____ 15. Ivan Pavlov   N. Said "Know thyself"
_____ 16. Max Wertheimer   O. Theory of evolution
_____ 17. G. Stanley Hall   P. Disciple of Socrates
_____ 18. Kurt Koffka
_____ 19. Sigmund Freud
_____ 20. Karen Horney
_____ 21. Democritus
_____ 22. William James
_____ 23. Albert Bandura
_____ 24. John Dewey

Answer Key to Exercise

1. M	**7.** A	**13.** G, I	**19.** E
2. P	**8.** B	**14.** L	**20.** E
3. C	**9.** O	**15.** B	**21.** D
4. F	**10.** A	**16.** C	**22.** K
5. E	**11.** I, N	**17.** H	**23.** J
6. G	**12.** B	**18.** C	**24.** K

Posttest

Directions: For each of the following, select the choice that best answers the question or completes the sentence.

1. If you wanted to run a study in which you learned about another person's _____, you would have to rely on that person's self-report.

   (a) heart rate, (b) mental images, (c) emission of a brain wave, (d) muscular responses.

2. Applied research is best described as research undertaken

   (a) with human beings, (b) with lower animals, (c) to find solutions to specific problems, (d) for its own sake.

3. The largest number of psychologists are _____ psychologists.

   (a) counseling, (b) clinical, (c) personality, (d) industrial/organizational.

4. If you knew someone who was having an adjustment problem, you would be best-advised to refer that person to a(n) _____ psychologist.

   (a) educational, (b) developmental, (c) personality, (d) counseling.

5. If you were to read an article comparing the values of breast-feeding and bottle feeding, it would probably report research that had been carried out by _____ psychologists.

   (a) clinical, (b) personality, (c) developmental, (d) school.

6. _____ psychologists are most directly concerned with the prevention of abnormal behavior.

   (a) Community, **(b)** Clinical, **(c)** Personality, **(d)** School.

7. Industrial/organizational psychologists are most likely to be consulted to

   (a) assist in the processes of hiring and promotion, **(b)** help workers make educational decisions, **(c)** treat workers showing abnormal behavior, **(d)** investigate the political and social attitudes of workers.

8. The earliest author of a book about psychology is

   (a) Democritus, **(b)** Darwin, **(c)** Sophocles, **(d)** Aristotle.

9. Who published *Elements of Psychophysics* in 1860?

   (a) G. Stanley Hall, **(b)** Wilhelm Wundt, **(c)** Gustav Theodor Fechner, **(d)** Edward Bradford Titchener.

10. Which of the following schools of psychology originated in Germany?

    (a) Functionalism, **(b)** Structuralism, **(c)** Behaviorism, **(d)** Psychoanalysis.

11. Who argued that the mind, like light or sound, was a natural event?

    (a) Carl Rogers, **(b)** Sigmund Freud, **(c)** B. F. Skinner, **(d)** Wilhelm Wundt.

12. The school of psychology that focused most directly on perceptual processes is

    (a) psychoanalysis, **(b)** behaviorism, **(c)** humanistic psychology, **(d)** Gestalt psychology.

13. Who founded the American Psychological Association?

    (a) William James, **(b)** Edward Bradford Titchener, **(c)** G. Stanley Hall, **(d)** John B. Watson.

14. _____ is a neoanalyst.

    (a) Carl Rogers, **(b)** Erik Erikson, **(c)** Albert Bandura, **(d)** Jean Piaget.

15. Biological psychologists have evoked rage responses in lower animals by means of

    (a) electrical stimulation of the brain, **(b)** food deprivation, **(c)** sleep deprivation, **(d)** placing them in frustrating mazes.

16. Social-learning theorists differ from radical behaviorists in that social-learning theorists

    (a) believe that people are driven by unconscious urges, **(b)** consider people's values in predicting their behavior, **(c)** focus on the role of reinforcement in behavior, **(d)** focus on the role of learning in behavior.

17. According to the text, the first step of the scientific method is

    (a) running an experiment, **(b)** selecting a sample, **(c)** formulating a research question, **(d)** developing a hypothesis.

18. Secretly observing diners at a fast-food restaurant to determine how frequently they take bites is an example of the

    (a) experimental method, (b) case-study method, (c) survey method, (d) naturalistic-observation method.

19. If you were to run an experiment on the effects of temperature on aggressive behavior, aggressive behavior would be the

    (a) hypothesis, (b) dependent variable, (c) treatment, (d) independent variable.

20. In the Lang experiment on alcohol and aggression, the condition that led to the most aggressive behavior was

    (a) drinking tonic water only, (b) drinking vodka and tonic water, (c) belief that one had drunk tonic water only, (d) belief that one had drunk vodka and tonic water.

21. The results of the *Literary Digest* survey illustrate the importance of _____ in research.

    (a) random sampling, (b) control subjects, (c) carefully stated hypotheses, (d) using blinds.

22. An operational definition of behavior

    (a) may refer to self-report or to observable behavior, (b) refers to observable behavior only, (c) refers to self-report of behavior only, (d) can generalize to any population.

23. Kinsey used _____ as the operational definition of sexual behavior in his research.

    (a) laboratory observations of sexual behavior, (b) reports of former lovers of the subjects, (c) interview data, (d) psychological test data.

24. A _____ sample is one in which every member of a population has an equal chance of being selected.

    (a) biased, (b) chance, (c) random, (d) probability.

25. The development of psychoanalytic theory depended largely on the

    (a) case-study method, (b) naturalistic-observation method, (c) survey method, (d) psychological testing method.

Answer Key to Posttest

1. B	8. D	14. B	20. D
2. C	9. C	15. A	21. A
3. B	10. B	16. B	22. A
4. D	11. D	17. C	23. C
5. C	12. D	18. D	24. C
6. A	13. C	19. B	25. A
7. A			

BIOLOGY AND BEHAVIOR

OUTLINE

PRETEST: TRUTH OR FICTION?
NEURONS
  The Makeup of Neurons
  A Psychological Controversy: Do We Lose Brain
    Cells as We Grow Older?
  The Neural Impulse
  The Synapse
  Neurotransmitters
  Neuropeptides
THE NERVOUS SYSTEM
  The Central Nervous System
  The Peripheral Nervous System
THE CEREBRAL CORTEX
  The Geography of the Cerebral Cortex
  Thought, Language, and the Cortex
  Divided-Brain Experiments
  Electrical Stimulation of the Brain
THE ENDOCRINE SYSTEM
  The Pituitary Gland

The Pancreas
The Thyroid Gland
The Adrenal Glands
The Testes and the Ovaries
HEREDITY
  Genes and Chromosomes
  Genetics and Behavior Genetics
  Mitosis and Meiosis
  Identical and Fraternal Twins
  Dominant and Recessive Traits
  Chromosomal and Genetic Abnormalities
  Genetic Counseling and Prenatal Testing
  Experiments in Selective Breeding
  Genetics and the Future
TRUTH OR FICTION REVISITED
CHAPTER REVIEW
EXERCISES
POSTTEST

PRETEST: TRUTH OR FICTION?

Some cells in your body stretch all the way down your back to your big toe.

We lose brain cells as we grow older.

Messages travel in the brain by means of electricity.

Our bodies produce natural pain killers that are more powerful than morphine.

The human brain is larger than that of any other animal.

Many men who are paralyzed below the waist can still achieve erection and ejaculate.

Fear can give you indigestion.

If a surgeon were to stimulate a certain part of your brain electrically, you might swear in court that someone had stroked your leg.

A routine operation for a certain disorder involves splitting the brain down the middle.

Rats will learn to do things that result in a "reward" of a burst of electricity in the brain.

Some people grow into "giants" because of "glands."

Athletes have used growth hormone and steroids in an effort to build up their muscle mass.

With so many billions of people in the world, you are bound to have a "double" somewhere, even if you are not an identical twin.

If both parents have brown eyes, the children invariably have brown eyes.

Blacks are at high risk for sickle-cell anemia.

You can learn the sex of your child several months before it is born.

We can "see" a fetus by bouncing sound waves off it in the womb.

Inventors are applying for patents on new life forms.

According to one theory, our universe began with a "big bang" that sent countless atoms and other particles hurtling at fantastic speeds into every corner of space. For 15 to 20 billion years, galaxies and solar systems have been condensing from immense gas clouds, sparkling for some eons, then winking out. Human beings have only recently evolved on an unremarkable rock circling an average star in a typical spiral-shaped galaxy.

Since the beginning of time, the universe has been in flux. Change has brought life and death and countless challenges. Some creatures have adapted successfully to these challenges and continued to evolve. Others have not met the challenges and have become extinct, falling back into the distant mists of time. Some have left fossil records. Others have disappeared without a trace.

At first human survival on planet Earth required a greater struggle than it does today. We fought predators like the leopard. We foraged across parched lands for food. We might have warred with creatures very much like ourselves—creatures who failed to meet the challenges of life and whose bones are now being unearthed on digs in Africa. Yet we prevailed. The human species has survived and continues to pass on its unique characteristics from generation to generation through genetic material whose complex chemical codes are only now being cracked.

Yet what is passed on from generation to generation? The answer is biological, or **physiological,** structures. There is no evidence that we can inherit thoughts or ideas or images or plans. But we inherit physiological structures and biological processes that serve as the material base for our observable behaviors, our emotions, and our cognitions—our thoughts, images, and plans.

Just how our mental processes and observable behaviors are linked to physiological structures is the fascinating question being answered piece by piece by a group of psychologists referred to as **biological psychologists** or **physiological psychologists.** Through systematic probing of the brain and other structures, biological psychologists in recent years have been seemingly on the threshold of exciting discoveries. Biological psychologists today are unlocking the mysteries of

1. *Neurons.* Neurons are the building blocks of the nervous system. There are billions of neurons in the body, all transmitting messages of one kind or another.

2. *The nervous system.* Neurons combine to form the various structures of the nervous system. The nervous system has subdivisions that are responsible for muscle movement, perception, automatic functions such as breathing and the secretion of hormones, and psychological phenomena such as thoughts and feelings.

3. *The cerebral cortex.* The cerebral cortex is the large, wrinkled mass inside your head that you think of as your brain. Actually, it is only one part of the brain—the part that is the most characteristically human.

4. *The endocrine system.* Through secretion of hormones, the endocrine system controls functions ranging from growth in children to production of milk in nursing women.

5. *Heredity.* Within every cell of your body there are about 100,000 genes. These complex chemical substances determine just what type of creature you are, from the color of your hair to your body temperature and the fact that you have arms and legs rather than wings or fins.

NEURONS

Let us begin our journey in a fabulous forest of nerve cells that can be visualized as having branches, trunks, and roots very much like trees. As in other "forests," many of these nerve cells ("trees") are next to one another. But unlike other forests, these "trees" sometimes lie end to end; their "roots" are intertwined with the "branches" of many nerve cells, or other "trees" below. Messages can be transmitted from nerve cell to nerve cell, or "tree" to "tree." Nerve cells communicate through chemical substances, called **neurotransmitters,** that are released by the "branches" of one

Physiological Having to do with the biological functions and vital processes of organisms.

Biological psychologists Psychologists who study the relationships between life processes and behavior.

Physiological psychologists Same as biological psychologists.

Neurotransmitters Chemical substances involved in the transmission of neural messages from one neuron to another.

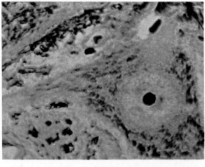

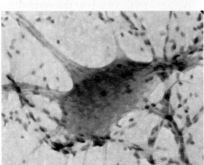

FIGURE 2.1. What Are Neurons?
Neurons take different forms in
different parts of the nervous
system. *Above left:* the large cell
body belongs to a motor neuron
(multipolar) from the gray matter
in the spinal cord. *Above right:*
pyramidal neurons in the cerebral
cortex. *Left:* a large multipolar
neuron from the myenteric
(intestinal) plexus.

and taken up by the "roots" of the next. Neurotransmitters cause chemical changes in the receiving nerve cell such that the message travels along
its "trunk," is translated back into neurotransmitters in its "branches," and then travels through the
small spaces between nerve cells to be received by
the "roots" of yet other nerve cells.

Each "tree" in this forest is a nerve cell, or
neuron, that transmits and coordinates messages
in the form of neural impulses (Figure 2.1). We
are born with about 12 billion neurons, which is
all that we shall ever have. The nervous system also
contains billions of **glial cells,** which outnumber
the neurons by about a ratio of ten to one (Arms
& Camp, 1987). Glial cells nourish neurons, direct
their growth, and remove waste products from the

nervous system. But neurons occupy center stage
in the nervous system. The messages transmitted
by neurons somehow account for phenomena
ranging from perception of an itch from a mos-
quito bite and the coordination of a skier's vision
and muscles to the composition of a concerto and
the solution of an algebraic equation.

The Makeup of Neurons

Neurons vary according to their functions and
their location. Some in the brain are a fraction of
an inch in length; others in the legs are several feet
long. But every neuron is a single nerve cell with
a number of common features: a cell body, or
soma, dendrites, and axon (Figure 2.2). The cell
body is enclosed by the cell membrane and contains the nucleus of the cell. The cell body uses
oxygen to create energy to carry out the work of
the cell. From a few to several hundred short fibers, or **dendrites,** extend from the cell body to
receive incoming messages from up to 1,000 adjoining neurons. In the analogy of the neuron and
a tree, dendrites serve as the roots. Each neuron

Neuron A nerve cell.

Glial cells Cells that produce myelin and engage in
housekeeping chores for neurons.

Soma A cell body.

Dendrites Rootlike structures attached to the soma of
a neuron that receive messages from other neurons.

has one **axon** that extends trunklike from the cell body. Axons are very thin, but they might be quite short or extend for several feet if they are carrying messages from the toes to the spinal cord. Like tree trunks, axons too might branch and extend in different directions. Axons end in smaller branching structures that are aptly named **terminals.** At the tips of the axon terminals are swellings called **knobs.** Neurons carry messages in one direction only, from the dendrites or cell body through the axon to the axon terminals. The messages are then transmitted from the terminal knobs to other neurons, to muscles or to glands.

As the child matures, the axons of neurons grow in length and the dendrites and axon terminals proliferate, creating vast interconnected networks for the transmission of complex messages. The number of glial cells also increases as the nervous system develops, contributing to the dense appearance of the structures of the nervous system.

Myelin   Many neurons are wrapped tightly with white, fatty **myelin sheaths.** Myelin actually consists of the membranes of the type of glial cell called the **Schwann cell.** The membranes of Schwann cells expand and wrap repeatedly around the axons of neurons. The high fat content of the Schwann cells insulates the axon from electrically charged atoms, or ions, found in the fluids that encase the nervous system. In this way, leakage of the electric current along the axon is minimized, and messages are conducted more efficiently. Myelin does not uniformly coat the surface of an axon. It is missing at points called **nodes of Ranvier.** Because of the insulation provided by myelin, neural messages, or impulses, travel rapidly from node to node.

The term **myelination** refers to the process by which Schwann cells insulate neurons. Myelination is not complete at birth. It is part of the maturation process that leads to the abilities to crawl and walk during the first year after birth. Babies are not physiologically "ready" to engage in activities involving visual-motor coordination until the coating process has reached a certain level. In the disease multiple sclerosis, myelin is replaced with a hard fibrous tissue that throws off the timing of nerve impulses and in this way interferes with muscular control. If neurons that control breathing are afflicted, the person can die from suffocation.

Afferent and Efferent Neurons   If someone steps on your big toe, the sensation is registered by receptors or sensory neurons near the surface of your skin. Then it is transmitted to the spinal cord and brain through **afferent neurons,** which are perhaps two to three feet long. In the brain, subsequent messages might be buffeted about by associative neurons that are only a few thousandths of an inch long. You experience the pain through this process and perhaps entertain some rather nasty thoughts about the perpetrator who is now apologizing and begging for understanding. Long before you arrive at any logical conclusions, however, motor neurons, or **efferent neurons,** will have sent messages back to your toe and foot so that you have withdrawn them and begun an impressive hopping routine. Other efferent neurons might have stimulated glands, so that by now your heart is pounding, you are sweating, and the hairs on the backs of your arms have become erect! Being a sport, you might say, "Oh, it's nothing." But considering all the neurons involved, it really was something, wasn't it?

Axon A long, thin part of a neuron that transmits messages to other neurons from branching structures called terminals.

Terminals Small structures at the tips of axons.

Knobs Swellings at the ends of terminals. Also referred to as *bulbs* or *buttons.*

Myelin sheath A fatty coating that encases and insulates axons, facilitating transmission of neural impulses.

Schwann cell A type of glial cell that wraps around the axons of neurons to form myelin.

Node of Ranvier A noninsulated segment of a myelinated axon.

Myelination The process by which the axons of neurons acquire myelin coatings.

Afferent neurons Neurons that transmit messages from sensory receptors to the spinal cord and brain. Also called sensory neurons.

Efferent neurons Neurons that transmit messages from the brain or spinal cord to muscles and glands. Also called motor neurons.

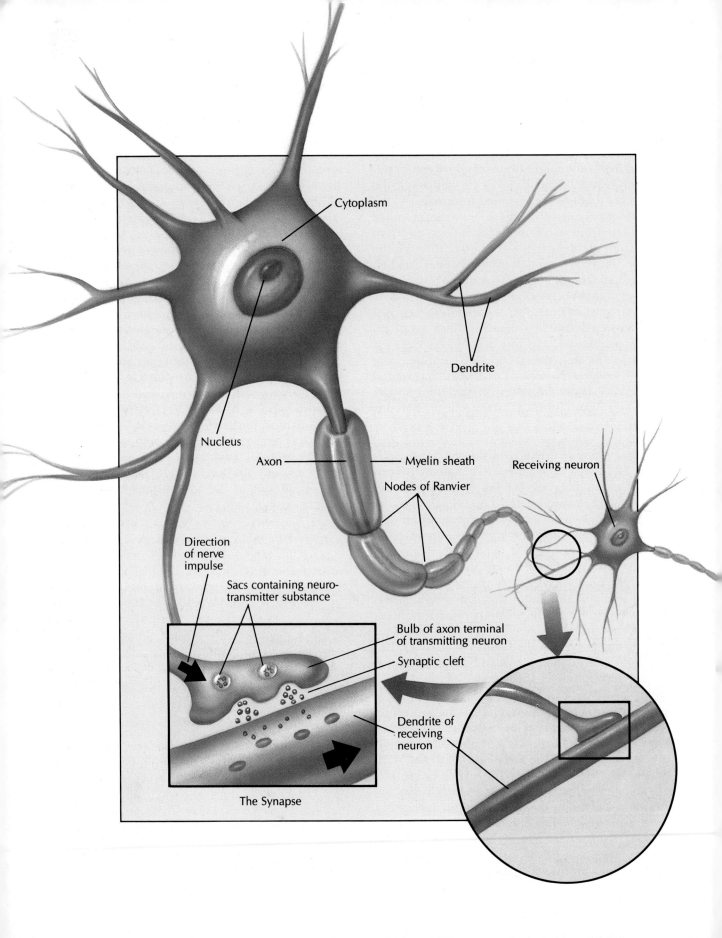

Cytoplasm

Dendrite

Nucleus

Axon — Myelin sheath

Nodes of Ranvier

Receiving neuron

Direction
of nerve
impulse

Sacs containing neuro-
transmitter substance

Bulb of axon terminal
of transmitting neuron

Synaptic cleft

Dendrite of
receiving
neuron

The Synapse

In case you think that afferent and efferent neurons will be hard to distinguish because they sound pretty much the SAME to you, simply remember that they are the "SAME." That is, Sensory = Afferent, and Motor = Efferent. But don't tell your professor I let you in on this **mnemonic** device.

A Psychological Controversy: Do We Lose Brain Cells as We Grow Older?

I've waited awhile, but now I'll come out with it. Although you have many billions of neurons, almost all of them were present at birth, and they have probably been dying off at the rate of several thousand a day. Yes, the brain and other parts of the nervous system grew larger as you matured, but this growth has been largely due to the development of existing neurons through myelination, the proliferation of dendrites and axon terminals, and an increase in the number of glial cells.

No doubt about it, you're losing some cells. But don't despair: We probably have more cells than we need. And many brain functions seem to be duplicated in different groups of cells. If you started with, say, 12 billion neurons and were losing 10,000 a day, or 3 million a year, it would take a while to make a dent.

Yet Marian Diamond (1978) of the University of California maintains that we have no basis for affixing any number to the daily loss of brain cells.

FIGURE 2.2 How Do Neurons Conduct and Transmit "Messages"? "Messages" enter neurons through dendrites, are transmitted along the trunklike axon, and then are sent through axon terminals to muscles, glands, and other neurons. A neuron relays its message to another neuron across a junction called a synapse, which consists of an axon terminal from the transmitting neuron, a dendrite of the receiving neuron, and a small gap between the neurons referred to as the synaptic cleft. Axon terminals contain sacs of chemicals called neurotransmitters. Neurotransmitters are released by the transmitting neuron into the synaptic cleft, and many of them are taken up by receptor sites on the dendrites of the receiving neuron. Some neurotransmitters (called excitatory) influence receiving neurons in the direction of firing; others (called inhibitory) influence them in the direction of *not* firing. To date, a few dozen possible neurotransmitters have been identified.

She claims that no reports of loss of brain cells have been supported by adequate research methodology. And she warns that one sinister effect of theorizing that we lose vast numbers of brain cells as we age is that it seems to justify tossing elderly workers onto the scrap heap of forced retirement.

Diamond and her colleagues decided to do a careful study on brain-cell counts. Rats journey through the life cycle more rapidly than we slowpoke humans, and so the researchers compared the numbers of cells in rats' brains at the ages of 26 days (weaning), 41 days (onset of puberty), 108 days (young adulthood), and 650 days (old age).

The brains were cut into thin slices and stained so that neurons could be differentiated under the microscope from glial cells. The greatest decrease in neurons and glial cells occurred prior to 108 days, or young adulthood. Decreases at later ages were trivial by comparison. We must be cautious in generalizing from rats to people, but these findings suggest that intellectual deficits found in some elderly people might have little if anything to do with loss of brain cells.

Diamond also reports that rats raised in enriched environments—with ladders, mazes, tunnels, and many companions—developed thicker cerebral **cortices** with larger numbers of glial cells than rats raised in plain cages with fewer companions. The same thickening of the cerebral cortex occurred in rats who were first placed in enriched environments at the advanced age of 766 days. In other words, neurological development in response to experience can take place even in very old age—at least with rats and probably with humans (Diamond, 1984). Not only does the brain shape our experience. Experience to some degree can also shape the brain, apparently at any age.

The Neural Impulse

In the late 1700s, Italian physiologist Luigi Galvani engaged in a shocking experiment in a rainstorm. While his neighbors had the sense to remain indoors, Galvani and his wife were out on the porch connecting lightning rods to the heads of dissected frogs whose legs were connected by wire to a well

---

Cortices Plural of *cortex*.

of water. When lightning blazed above, the frogs' muscles contracted repeatedly and violently. This is not a recommended way to prepare frogs' legs—Galvani was demonstrating that the messages (**neural impulses**) that travel along neurons are electrical in nature.

Neural impulses travel between 2 (in nonmyelinated neurons) and 225 miles an hour (in myelinated neurons). This speed is not impressive when compared with that of an electric current in a toaster oven or a lamp, which can travel at the speed of light—over 186,000 miles per second. But distances in the body are short, and a message will travel from a toe to the brain in perhaps one-fiftieth of a second.

An Electrochemical Process   Neural impulses travel by an electrochemical process. Chemical changes take place within neurons that cause an electric charge to be transmitted along their lengths. In a resting state, when a neuron is not being stimulated by its neighbors, there are relatively greater numbers of positively charged sodium ions ($Na+$) and negatively charged chloride

($Cl-$) ions in the body fluid outside the neuron than in the fluid within the neuron. Positively charged potassium ($K+$) ions are more plentiful inside. This difference in electrical charge **polarizes** the neuron with a negative **resting potential** of about -70 millivolts in relation to the body fluid outside the cell membrane.

When an area on the surface of the resting neuron is adequately stimulated by other neurons, the cell membrane in the area changes its **permeability** to allow sodium ions to enter. As a consequence, the area of entry becomes positively charged or **depolarized** with respect to the outside (Figure 2.3). The permeability of the cell membrane changes again, allowing no more sodium ions to enter.

The inside of the cell at the disturbed area is now said to have an **action potential,** or positive charge, of about $+40$ millivolts. Inner change causes the next section of the cell to become permeable to sodium ions, while at the same time sodium ions are being pumped out of the area of the cell previously affected, which then returns to its resting potential. In this way the neural impulse is transmitted continuously along an axon that is not myelinated. Because the impulse is created anew as it progresses, its strength does not change.

The conduction of the neural impulse along the length of a neuron is what is meant by "firing." A neuron "fires" in less than one-thousandth of a second. In firing, it "attempts" to transmit the "message" to other neurons, muscles, or glands. However, other neurons will not fire unless the incoming messages combine to reach an adequate **threshold.** A weak message might cause a temporary shift in electrical charge at some point along the cell membrane of a neuron; but this charge will dissipate if the neuron is not stimulated to threshold.

A neuron might transmit several hundred such messages a second. Yet in accord with the **all-or-none principle,** each time a neuron fires it transmits an impulse of the same strength. Neurons fire more frequently when they have been stimulated by larger numbers of other neurons.

For a thousandth of a second or so after firing, a neuron enters an **absolute refractory period,** during which it will not fire in response to stimulation from other neurons. Then, for another few

---

Neural impulse The electrochemical discharge of a nerve cell, or neuron.

Polarize To ready a neuron for firing by creating an internal negative charge in relation to the body fluid outside the cell membrane.

Resting potential The electrical potential across the neural membrane when it is not responding to other neurons.

Permeability The degree to which a membrane allows a substance to pass through it.

Depolarize To change the resting potential of a cell membrane from about -70 millivolts to zero.

Action potential The electrical impulse that provides the basis for the conduction of a neural impulse along an axon of a neuron.

Threshold The point at which a stimulus is just strong enough to produce a response.

All-or-none principle The fact that a neuron fires an impulse of the same strength whenever its action potential is triggered.

Absolute refractory period A phase following firing during which a neuron's action potential cannot be triggered.

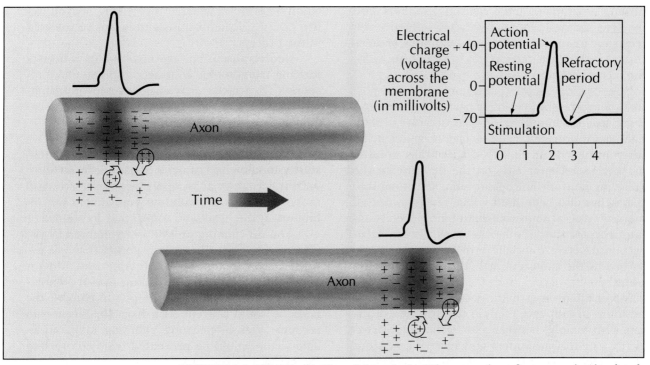

FIGURE 2.3 What Is the Neural Impulse?   When a section of a neuron is stimulated by other neurons, the cell membrane becomes permeable to sodium ions so that an action potential of about +40 millivolts is induced. This action potential is transmitted along the axon. Eventually the neuron fires (or fails to fire) according to the all-or-none principle.

thousandths of a second, the neuron is said to be in a **relative refractory period,** during which it will fire but only in response to stronger-than-usual messages. The refractory period is a time of recovery: The chemical balance is restored to the resting potential. When we realize that such periods of recovery might take place hundreds of times per second, it seems a rapid recovery and a short rest indeed.

The Synapse

A neuron relays its message to another neuron across a junction called a **synapse.** A synapse consists of a "branch," or axon terminal, from the transmitting neuron; a "root," or dendrite, of a receiving neuron; and a small fluid-filled gap between the neurons that is called the synaptic cleft (see Figure 2.2). The neural impulse is electrical, but it does not jump across the synaptic cleft like a spark. Instead, when a nerve impulse reaches them, axon terminals release chemicals into the synaptic cleft like a myriad of ships being cast off into the sea.

Neurotransmitters

In the knobs at the tips of the axon terminals are sacs or synaptic vesicles that contain chemicals called neurotransmitters. When a neural impulse reaches the axon terminal, the vesicles release

Relative refractory period A phase following the absolute refractory period during which a neuron will fire in response to stronger-than-usual messages.

Synapse A junction between the terminal knobs of an axon and the dendrites or soma of another neuron.

varying amounts of these neurotransmitters into the synaptic cleft. From there they influence the receiving neuron. If adequate quantities of neurotransmitters are released by transmitting cells, the receiving neuron will also fire.

As of today, some three dozen different possible neurotransmitters have been identified, and there may be hundreds of them (Snyder, 1980). Each neurotransmitter has its own chemical structure, and each can fit into a specifically tailored harbor, or **receptor site,** on the dendrite of the receiving neuron. The analogy of a key fitting into a lock has also been used. Once released, not all molecules of a neurotransmitter find their ways into receptor sites of other neurons. "Loose" neurotransmitters are usually broken down or reabsorbed by the axon terminal (a process called "reuptake").

Some neurotransmitters act to excite receiving neurons, to influence them in the direction of firing. The synapses between axon terminals with excitatory neurotransmitters and receiving neurons are called **excitatory synapses.** Other neurotransmitters inhibit receiving neurons; that is, they influence them in the direction of not firing. The synapses between axon terminals with inhibitory neurotransmitters and receiving neurons are called **inhibitory synapses.** Neurons may be influenced by neurotransmitters that have been released by 1,000 other neurons. The additive stimulation determines whether a receiving neuron will fire and which neurotransmitters will be released in the process.

Neurotransmitters are involved in processes ranging from muscle contraction to emotional response. Excesses or deficiencies of neurotransmitters have been linked to diseases and abnormal behavior.

Acetylcholine   **Acetylcholine** (ACh) is a neurotransmitter that controls muscle contractions. ACh is excitatory at synapses between nerves and muscles that involve voluntary movement but inhibitory at the heart and some other locations.

The functioning of ACh is highlighted by the effects of curare. Curare is a poison that was extracted from plants by South American Indians and used in hunting. If an arrow tipped with curare pierced the skin and the poison entered the body, it would prevent ACh from lodging within receptor sites in neurons, resulting in paralysis. The victim would be prevented from contracting the muscles used in breathing and would die from suffocation. Botulism, a disease that stems from food poisoning, prevents the release of ACh and has the same effect as curare.

ACh is also normally prevalent in a part of the brain called the **hippocampus,** a structure involved in the formation of memories. When the ACh available to the brain decreases, memory formation is impaired. **Alzheimer's disease** is associated with progressive deterioration of neurons that produce ACh and is characterized by gradual impairment of memory and other cognitive functions, such as the capacity for abstract thought.

Dopamine   **Dopamine** is primarily an inhibitory neurotransmitter. Dopamine is involved in voluntary movements, learning and memory, and emotional arousal. Deficiencies of dopamine are linked to Parkinson's disease, a disorder in which patients progressively lose control over their muscles. They come to show muscle tremors and jerky, uncoordinated movements. The drug L-Dopa, a substance that the brain converts to dopamine, helps slow the progress of Parkinson's disease.

The mental disorder schizophrenia (see Chapter 9) has also been linked to dopamine. Schizophrenic individuals may have more receptor sites

---

Receptor site A location on a dendrite of a receiving neuron tailored to receive a neurotransmitter.

Excitatory synapse A synapse that influences receiving neurons in the direction of firing by increasing depolarization of their cell membranes.

Inhibitory synapse A synapse that influences receiving neurons in the direction of not firing by encouraging changes in their membrane permeability in the direction of the resting potential.

Acetylcholine A neurotransmitter that controls muscle contractions. Abbreviated *ACh.*

Hippocampus A part of the *limbic system* of the brain that is involved in memory formation.

Alzheimer's disease A progressive disorder characterized by loss of memory and other cognitive functions.

Dopamine A neurotransmitter that is involved in Parkinson's disease and appears to play a role in schizophrenia.

for dopamine in an area of the brain that is involved in emotional responding. For this reason, they may *overutilize* the dopamine that is available in the brain, leading to hallucinations and disturbances of thought and emotion. The phenothiazines, a group of drugs used in the treatment of schizophrenia, are thought to work by blocking the action of dopamine—by locking some dopamine out of these receptor sites (Snyder, 1984). Not surprisingly, phenothiazines may have Parkinson-like side effects, which are usually then treated by additional drugs, adjustment of the dose of phenothiazine, or switching to another drug.

Norepinephrine   **Norepinephrine** is produced at many sites in the body. It is chemically similar to the hormone epinephrine, which we shall discuss later in the chapter. Norepinephrine acts both as a neurotransmitter and a hormone. Norepinephrine, like epinephrine, speeds up the heartbeat and other body processes. Norepinephrine is involved in general arousal, learning and memory, and eating. Excesses and deficiencies of norepinephrine have been linked to mood disorders (see Chapter 9).

The stimulants cocaine and amphetamines ("speed") facilitate the release of dopamine and norepinephrine, and also impede their re-uptake by the synaptic vesicles that release them. As a result, there are excesses of these neurotransmitters in the nervous system, vastly increasing the firing of neurons and leading to a persistent state of high arousal. The stimulant caffeine, found in coffee, is thought to prevent reabsorption of these neurotransmitters by blocking the action of the enzymes that break them down. Until the caffeine has been removed from the system, we may encounter "coffee nerves."

Serotonin   **Serotonin** is also primarily an inhibitory transmitter, involved in emotional arousal and sleep. Deficiencies of serotonin have been linked to anxiety, mood disorders, and insomnia. The drug LSD (see Chapter 9) decreases the action of serotonin and may also influence the utilization of dopamine. With LSD, "two no's make a yes." By inhibiting an inhibitor, brain activity increases, in this case frequently leading to hallucinations.

Why Are Marathon Races So Popular?   Why have thousands of people taken up long-distance running? Running, of course, promotes cardiovascular conditioning, firms the muscles, and helps us to control weight. But long-distance running may also induce the so-called runner's high by stimulating the release of endorphins—naturally occurring substances that are similar in function to the narcotic morphine.

Neuropeptides

Jogging and running are popular not only because running promotes cardiovascular conditioning, firms the muscles, and helps control weight. There are also psychological effects, including enhanced feelings of self-competence and the so-called "runner's high."

Endorphins   "Runner's high" may be caused by the release of chains of amino acids called **endorphins.** Endorphins are members of a family of

---

Norepinephrine A neurotransmitter whose action is similar to that of the hormone *epinephrine,* and which may play a role in depression.

Serotonin A neurotransmitter, deficiencies of which have been linked to affective disorders, anxiety, and insomnia.

Endorphins Neurotranmitters that are composed of amino acids and are functionally similar to morphine.

chemicals known as **neuropeptides** (Krieger, 1983). The word *endorphin* is the contraction of *endogenous morphine. Endogenous* means "developing from within." Endorphins, then, are similar to the narcotic morphine in their functions and are produced by our own bodies. They occur naturally in the brain and in the bloodstream.

Endorphins have effects that are similar to those of morphine (Bolles & Faneslow, 1982). Endorphins act like inhibitory neurotransmitters. They lock into receptor sites for chemicals that transmit pain messages to the brain. Once the endorphin "key" is in the "lock," pain-causing chemicals cannot transmit their (unwelcome) messages. There are a number of endorphins. Beta-endorphin is many times as powerful as morphine, molecule for molecule (Snyder, 1977).

Endorphins also play a role in regulating respiration, hunger, memory, sexual behavior, blood pressure, mood, and body temperature.

Enkephalins   **Enkephalins** are one specific type of endorphins and, as such, also occur naturally in the brain. The word *enkephalin* derives from roots meaning "in" and the Greek *kephale,* meaning "head." Enkephalins share the pain-relieving effects of endorphins but may be somewhat weaker and shorter-acting.

There you have it—a fabulous "forest" of neurons in which billions upon billions of vesicles are pouring neurotransmitters into synaptic clefts at any given time, when you are involved in strenuous activity, now as you are reading this page, even as you are passively watching television. This microscopic picture is repeated several hundred

---

Neuropeptides A group of compounds formed from amino acids (peptides) that function as neurotransmitters.

Enkephalins Types of endorphins that are weaker and shorter-acting than beta-endorphin.

Nerve A bundle of axons from many neurons.

Nuclei Plural of *nucleus.* A group of neural cell bodies found in the brain or spinal cord.

Ganglia Plural of *ganglion.* A group of neural cell bodies found elsewhere in the body other than the brain or spinal cord.

Central nervous system The brain and spinal cord.

---

times every second. The combined activity of all these neurotransmitters determines which messages will be transmitted and which will not. Your experience of sensations, your thoughts, and your psychological sense of control over your body are very different from the electrochemical processes we have described. Yet somehow these many electrochemical events are responsible for your psychological sense of yourself and of the world.

THE NERVOUS SYSTEM

There was a time during my childhood when it seemed to me that it was not a very good thing to have a "nervous" system. For instance, if your system were not so nervous, you might be less likely to jump at strange noises.

At some point I learned that a nervous system was not a system that was nervous but a system of nerves that were involved in thought processes, heartbeat, visual-motor coordination, and so on. I also learned that the human nervous system was more complex than that of any other animal and that our brains were larger than those of any other animal. Now this last piece of business is not exactly true. A human brain weighs about three pounds, but elephant and whale brains may be four times as heavy. Still, our brains comprise a greater part of our body weight than do those of elephants or whales. Our brains weigh about one-sixtieth of our body weight. Elephant brains weigh about one-thousandth of their total weight, and whale brains a paltry one-ten-thousandth of their weight. So if we wish, we can still find figures to make us proud.

The brain is only one part of the nervous system. A **nerve** is a bundle of axons. The cell bodies of these neurons are not considered part of the nerve. The cell bodies are gathered into clumps called **nuclei** in the brain and spinal cord and **ganglia** elsewhere.

The nervous system consists of the brain, the spinal cord, and nerves linking them to receptors in the sensory organs and effectors in the muscles and glands. As shown in Figure 2.4, the brain and spinal cord make up what we refer to as the **central nervous system.** The sensory (afferent) neurons, which receive and transmit messages to the brain

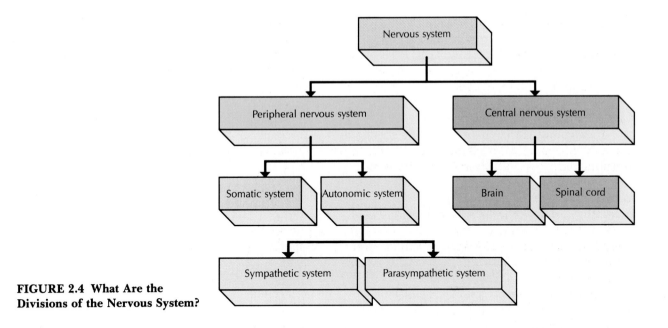

FIGURE 2.4 What Are the Divisions of the Nervous System?

and spinal cord, and the motor (efferent) neurons, which transmit messages from the brain or spinal cord to the muscles and glands, make up the **peripheral nervous system.**

Let us examine the nature and functions of the central and peripheral nervous systems.

The Central Nervous System

The central nervous system consists of the spinal cord and the brain.

The Spinal Cord The **spinal cord** is a column of nerves about as thick as a thumb. It transmits messages from receptors to the brain and from the brain to muscles and glands throughout the body (Figure 2.5). The spinal cord is also capable of some "local government" of responses to external stimulation through **spinal reflexes.** A spinal reflex is an unlearned response to a stimulus that may involve only two neurons—a sensory (afferent) neuron and a motor (efferent) neuron. In some reflexes a third neuron, called an **interneuron,** transmits the neural impulse from the sensory neuron through the spinal cord to the motor neuron (Figure 2.6).

The spinal cord includes both gray matter and white matter. The **gray matter** consists of nonmyelinated neurons. Some of these nonmyelinated neurons are involved in spinal reflexes; others send impulses to the brain. The **white matter** is composed of bundles of longer, myelinated (thus whitish) axons that carry messages back and forth to and from the brain. As you can see in Figure 2.6, a cross section of the spinal cord shows the gray matter, which includes cell bodies, to be dis-

---

Peripheral nervous system The part of the nervous system consisting of the somatic nervous system and the autonomic nervous system.

Spinal cord A column of nerves within the spine that transmits messages from sensory receptors to the brain and from the brain to muscles and glands throughout the body.

Spinal reflex A simple unlearned response to a stimulus that may involve only two neurons.

Interneuron A neuron that transmits a neural impulse from a sensory neuron to a motor neuron.

Gray matter In the spinal cord, the nonmyelinated neurons and neural segments that are involved in spinal reflexes.

White matter In the spinal cord, myelinated axon bundles that carry messages from and to the brain.

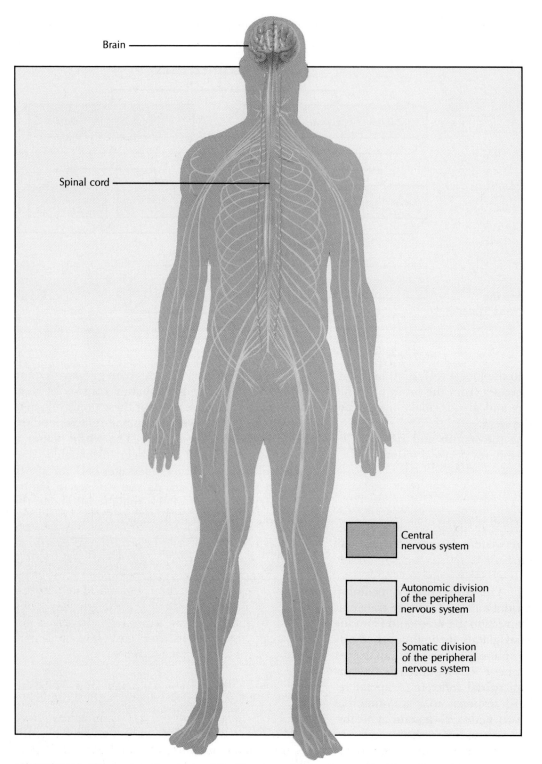

Brain

Spinal cord

Central
nervous system

Autonomic division
of the peripheral
nervous system

Somatic division
of the peripheral
nervous system

FIGURE 2.5 Where Are the Parts of the Nervous System Located?   Note from this
back view that the spinal cord is protected by a column of bones called vertebrae. The
brain is protected by the skull.

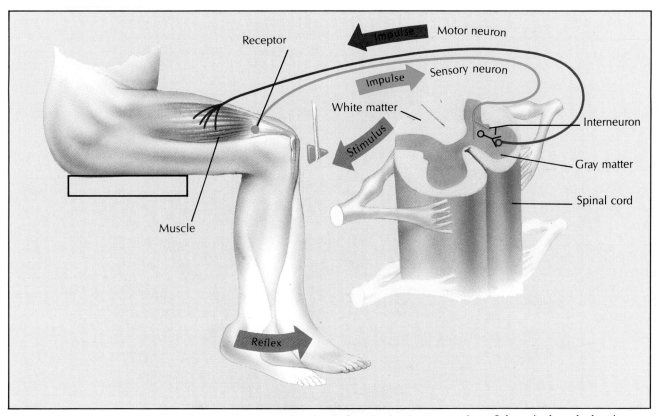

FIGURE 2.6 What Is the Reflex Arc? A cross-section of the spinal cord, showing a sensory neuron, interneuron, and motor neuron—a combination involved in many spinal reflexes.

tributed in something of a butterfly-shaped pattern.

We engage in many reflexes. We blink in response to a puff of air. We swallow when food accumulates in the mouth. A physician may tap the leg below the knee to see if we will show the knee-jerk reflex, a sign that the nervous system is operating adequately. Urinating and defecating are reflexes that occur in response to pressure in the bladder and the rectum. Parents typically spend a number of weeks or months in toilet training infants, or teaching them to involve their brains in the process of elimination. Learning to inhibit these reflexes makes civilized interaction possible.

Although sexual response in humans is rarely fully mechanical, we can respond sexually on a reflexive level. Some men and women have spinal cord injuries that prevent genital sensations from reaching the brain. But genital stimulation in many instances can still lead to reflexes of sexual arousal and orgasm (Comarr, 1970; Money, 1960). In experiments with dogs in which messages were prevented from reaching the brain by way of the spinal cord, the animals have achieved erection, shown pelvic thrusting, and ejaculated (Hart, 1967). Many men paralyzed below the waist have similarly achieved erection and ejaculated in response to genital stimulation, although they have not experienced sexual sensations. In this way, even paralyzed people often have sexually active relationships and become parents.

The Brain Every show has a star, and the brain is the undisputed star of the human nervous system. The size and shape of your brain are responsible for your large, delightfully rounded head. In all the animal kingdom, you (and about 5 billion other human beings) are unique because of the capacities for learning and thought made possible by the human brain.

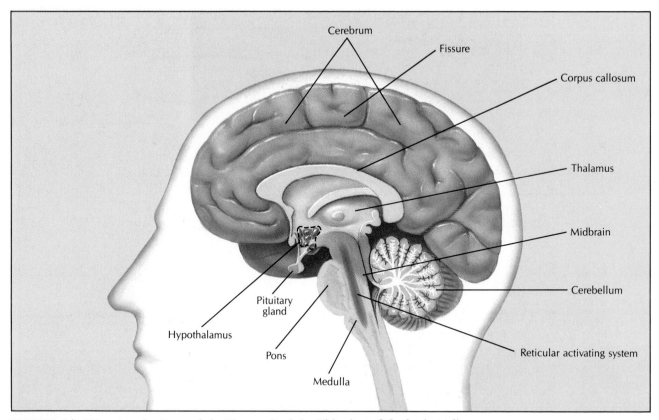

Cerebrum

Fissure

Corpus callosum

Thalamus

Midbrain

Cerebellum

Reticular activating system

Medulla

Pons

Hypothalamus

Pituitary
gland

FIGURE 2.7 What Are the Parts of the Human Brain?   This view of the brain, split
top to bottom, labels some of the most important structures.

Let us look at the brain, as shown in Figure 2.7. We shall begin with the back of the head, where the spinal cord rises to meet the brain, and work our way forward. The lower part of the brain, referred to as the hindbrain, consists of three major structures: the medulla, the pons, and the cerebellum.

Many nerves that connect the spinal cord to higher levels of the brain pass through the **medulla.** The medulla regulates vital functions such as heart rate, blood pressure, and respiration. The

medulla also plays a role in sleep, sneezing, and coughing. The **pons** is a bulge in the hindbrain that lies forward of the medulla. *Pons* is the Latin word for "bridge," and the pons is so named because of the bundles of nerves that pass through it. The pons transmits information concerning body movement and is also involved in functions related to attention, sleep and alertness, and respiration.

Behind the pons lies the **cerebellum,** which means "little brain" in Latin. The two hemispheres of the cerebellum are involved in maintaining balance and in controlling motor (muscle) behavior. Injury to the cerebellum may lead to lack of motor coordination, stumbling, and loss of muscle tone.

The **reticular activating system** (RAS) begins in the hindbrain and ascends through the region of the midbrain into the lower part of the forebrain. The RAS is vital in the functions of attention, sleep, and arousal. Injury to the RAS may

Medulla An oblong-shaped area of the hindbrain involved in heartbeat and respiration.

Pons A structure of the hindbrain involved in respiration.

Cerebellum A part of the hindbrain involved in muscle coordination and balance.

Reticular activating system A part of the brain involved in attention, sleep, and arousal.

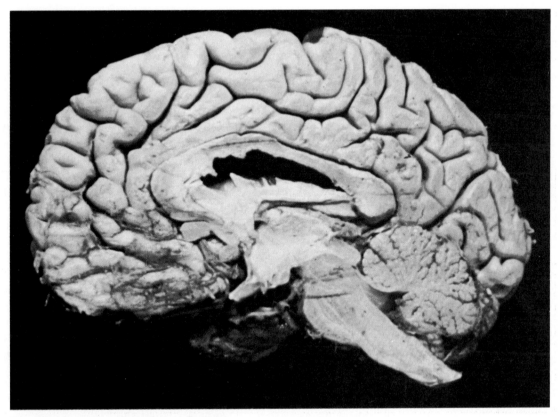

The Human Brain, Split Top to Bottom.

leave an animal **comatose.** Stimulation of the RAS causes it to send messages to the cortex, making us more alert to sensory information. Electrical stimulation of the RAS awakens sleeping animals, and certain drugs called central-nervous-system depressants, such as alcohol, are thought to work in part by lowering RAS activity.

Sudden loud noises will stimulate the RAS and awaken a sleeping animal or person. But the RAS may become selective, or acquire the capacity to play a filtering role, through learning. It may allow some messages to filter through to higher brain levels and awareness while screening others out. For example, the parent who has primary responsibility for child care may be awakened by the stirring sounds of an infant, whereas louder sounds of traffic or street noise are filtered out. The other parent, by contrast, may usually sleep through even loud cries. But if the first parent must be away for several days, the second parent's RAS may

quickly acquire sensitivity to noises produced by the child. This sensitivity may rapidly fade again when the first parent returns.

Also located in the midbrain are areas involved in vision and hearing. These include the area that controls eye reflexes such as dilation of the pupils and eye movements.

Five major areas of the front-most part of the brain, or forebrain, are the thalamus, the hypothalamus, the limbic system, the basal ganglia, and the cerebrum.

The **thalamus** is located near the center of the brain. It consists of two joined lobes that have egg or football shapes. The thalamus serves as a relay

Comatose In a coma, a state resembling sleep from which it is difficult to be aroused.

Thalamus An area near the center of the brain involved in the relay of sensory information to the cortex and in the functions of sleep and attention.

station for sensory stimulation. Nerve fibers from our sensory systems enter from below; the information carried by them is then transmitted to the cerebral cortex by way of fibers that exit from above. For instance, the thalamus relays sensory input from the eyes to the visual areas of the cerebral cortex. The thalamus is also involved in controlling sleep and attention, in coordination with other brain structures, including the RAS.

The **hypothalamus** is a tiny collection of nuclei located beneath the thalamus and above the pituitary gland. The hypothalamus is about the size of a pea and weighs only four grams, yet it is vital in the control of body temperature, the concentration of fluids, the storage of nutrients, and various aspects of motivation and emotion. Experimenters learn many of the functions of the hypothalamus by implanting electrodes in various parts of it and observing the behavioral effects when a current is switched on. In this way it has been found that the hypothalamus is involved in hunger, thirst, sexual behavior, caring for offspring, and aggression. Among lower animals, stimulation of various areas of the hypothalamus can trigger stereotyped behaviors, such as fighting, mating, or nest building. The hypothalamus is just as important to people, but our responses to messages from the hypothalamus are less stereotyped and are influenced by cognitive functions such as thought and choice.

The hypothalamus, along with parts of the thalamus and other structures make up the **limbic system.** The limbic system lies along the inner edge of the cerebrum and is fully evolved in mammals only. It is involved in memory and in the drives of hunger, sex, and aggression. A part of the limbic system is sometimes removed in an effort to control **epilepsy,** or seizures that stem from sudden neural discharges. People whose operations have damaged the hippocampus can retrieve old memories but cannot permanently store new information. As a result, they may reread the same newspaper day in and day out, without recalling that they have read it before, or have to be perpetually reintroduced to people they have met just hours earlier (Squire, 1986). Destruction of an area of the limbic system called the **amygdala** leads monkeys and other mammals to show docile behavior (Carlson, 1986). Destruction of another area of the limbic system, the **septum,** leads some mammals to show a rage reaction at the slightest provocation.

And so it seems that the hypothalamus and other parts of the limbic system provide a system of "checks and balances." The amygdala and the septum allow us to inhibit some of the stereotyped behaviors prompted by the hypothalamus. As a result, we have the opportunity to profit from experience and thought; we are less likely to automatically flee or attack in response to a threat.

The **basal ganglia** are buried beneath the cortex to the front of the thalamus. The basal ganglia are involved in the control of postural movements and the coordination of the limbs. The degeneration of a group of neurons that regulate the basal ganglia has been linked to Parkinson's disease, in which people walk with a clumsy, shuffling gait and find it difficult to initiate movement.

The **cerebrum** is the crowning glory of the brain. Only in human beings does the cerebrum comprise such a large proportion of the brain (Figure 2.7).

The surface of the cerebrum is wrinkled, or convoluted, with ridges and valleys. This surface is the **cerebral cortex.** The convolutions allow a great deal of surface area to be packed into the

---

Hypothalamus A bundle of nuclei below the thalamus involved in body temperature, motivation, and emotion.

Limbic system A group of structures involved in memory and motivation that form a fringe along the inner edge of the cerebrum.

Epilepsy Temporary disturbances of brain functions that involve sudden neural discharges.

Amygdala A part of the limbic system that apparently facilitates stereotyped aggressive responses.

Septum A part of the limbic system that apparently restrains stereotyped aggressive responses.

Basal ganglia Ganglia located between the thalamus and cerebrum that are involved in motor coordination.

Cerebrum The large mass of the forebrain, which consists of two hemispheres.

Cerebral cortex The wrinkled surface area ("gray matter") of the cerebrum.

brain. We shall explore the cerebral cortex in depth later in the chapter.

Valleys in the cortex are called **fissures.** A most significant fissure almost divides the cerebrum in half.* The hemispheres of the cerebral cortex are connected by the **corpus callosum** (Latin for "thick body" or "hard body"), a thick fiber bundle. Later we shall see that severing the corpus callosum is not life threatening and leads to some interesting behavior.

The Peripheral Nervous System

The peripheral nervous system consists of sensory and motor neurons that transmit messages to and from the central nervous system. Without the peripheral nervous system, our brains would be isolated from the world: They would not be able to perceive it, and they would not be able to act on it. The two main divisions of the peripheral nervous system are the somatic nervous system and the autonomic nervous system.

The Somatic Nervous System
The **somatic nervous system** consists of our sensory (afferent) and motor (efferent) neurons. It transmits messages about sights, sounds, smells, temperature, body positions, and so on to the central nervous system. As a result we can experience the beauties and the horrors of the world, its physical ecstasies and agonies. Messages from the brain and spinal cord to the somatic nervous system control purposeful body movements, such as raising a hand, winking, or running; breathing; and movements that we hardly attend to—movements that maintain our posture and balance.

The Autonomic Nervous System
Autonomic means "automatic." The **autonomic nervous system** (ANS) regulates the glands and **involuntary** activities such as heartbeat, digestion, and dilation of the pupils of the eyes—even as we sleep.

*I was going to note that this fissure runs from front to back, under the line covered by Mr. T's Mohawk hairstyle, but my editor persuaded me to omit this pedagogical aid.

The ANS has two branches or divisions, the **sympathetic** and the **parasympathetic.** These branches have largely opposing effects; when they work at the same time, their effects can be something of an averaging out of their influences. Many organs and glands are stimulated by both branches of the ANS (Figure 2.8). In general, the sympathetic division is most active during processes that involve the spending of body energy from stored reserves, such as in a fight-or-flight response to a predator or when you find out that your mortgage payment is going to be increased. The parasympathetic division is most active during processes that replenish reserves of energy, as during eating (Levitt, 1981). For instance, when we are afraid, the sympathetic division of the ANS accelerates the heart rate. But when we relax, it is the parasympathetic division that decelerates the heart rate. The parasympathetic division stimulates digestive processes, but the sympathetic branch inhibits digestive activity. Since the sympathetic division predominates when we feel fear or anxiety, fear or anxiety can lead to indigestion.

The autonomic nervous system is of particular interest to psychologists because its activities are linked to various emotions, such as anxiety and love. Some of us appear to have overly reactive sympathetic nervous systems; in the absence of

Fissures. Valleys.

Corpus callosum A thick fiber bundle that connects the hemispheres of the cortex.

Somatic nervous system The divison of the peripheral nervous system that connects the central nervous system with sensory receptors, muscles, and the surface of the body.

Autonomic nervous system The division of the peripheral nervous system that regulates glands and involuntary activities like heartbeat, respiration, digestion, and dilation of the pupils. Abbreviated *ANS.*

Involuntary Automatic, not consciously controlled.

Sympathetic The branch of the ANS that is most active during emotional responses that spend the body's reserves of energy, such as fear and anxiety.

Parasympathetic The branch of the ANS that is most active during processes that restore the body's reserves of energy, like digestion.

AUTONOMIC NERVOUS SYSTEM

Parasympathetic Branch

Sympathetic Branch

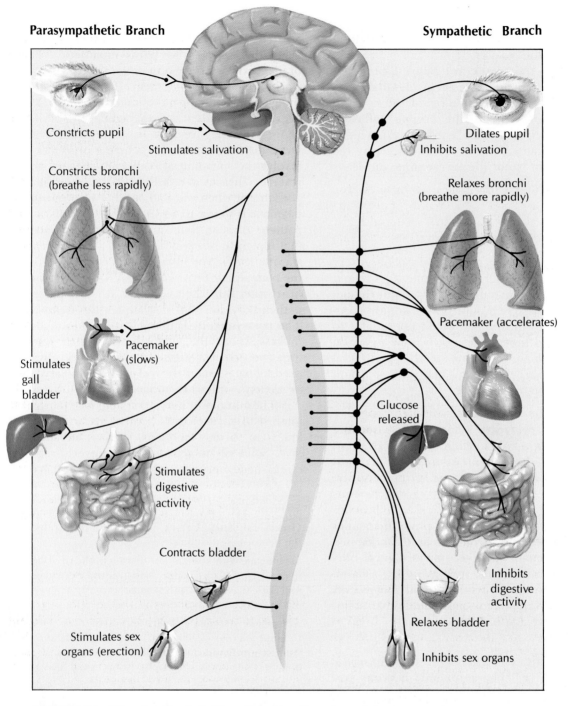

Constricts pupil

Stimulates salivation

Constricts bronchi
(breathe less rapidly)

Stimulates
gall
bladder

Pacemaker
(slows)

Stimulates
digestive
activity

Contracts bladder

Stimulates sex
organs (erection)

Dilates pupil
Inhibits salivation

Relaxes bronchi
(breathe more rapidly)

Pacemaker (accelerates)

Glucose
released

Inhibits
digestive
activity

Relaxes bladder

Inhibits sex organs

FIGURE 2.8. What Are the Activities of the Two Branches of the Autonomic Nervous System (ANS)?   The parasympathetic branch of the ANS generally acts to replenish stores of energy in the body. It is connected to organs by nerves that originate near the top and bottom of the spinal cord. The sympathetic branch is most active during activities that expend energy. Its neurons collect in clusters or chains of ganglia along the central portion of the spinal cord. The two branches of the ANS frequently have antagonistic effects on the organs they service.

outside threats our bodies respond as though we were faced with great danger. In Chapter 9 we shall see that psychologists are exploring the role of the sympathetic nervous system in anxiety disorders.

THE CEREBRAL CORTEX

Just where is that elusive piece of business you think of as your "mind"? Thousands of years ago it was not generally thought that the mind had a place to hang its hat within the body. It was common to assume that the body was inhabited by demons or souls that could not be explained in terms of substance at all. After all, if you look inside a human being, the biological structures you find do not look all that different in quality from those of many lower animals. So it seemed to make sense that those qualities that made us distinctly human—thinking, planning, talking, dreaming, composing—were unrelated to substances that you could actually see, feel, and weigh on a scale.

Some ancient Egyptians attributed control of the human being to a little person, or **homunculus,** who dwelled within the skull and regulated our behavior. The Greek philosopher Aristotle thought that the soul had set up living quarters in the heart. After all, serious injury to the heart could be said to cause the soul to take flight from the body. As noted by B. F. Skinner (1987), to be undecided about something in ancient Greece was to have "a divided heart." Skinner goes on to note that phrases such as the following show that modern English is still influenced by the view of the heart as the seat of will, thought, hunger, and joy: "deep in one's heart," "to know something by heart," "to look into someone's heart," and "to have a change of heart."

Through a variety of accidents and research projects, we have come to recognize that "mind," or consciousness, dwells essentially within the brain, largely in the cerebral cortex. Different sorts of body injuries have distinct effects. It has become increasingly apparent that injuries to the head can lead to impairments of consciousness and awareness, such as loss of vision and hearing, general confusion, or loss of memory. Experiments in stimulating or destroying specific areas in animal brains and human brains* have also shown that certain areas of the brain are associated with specific types of sensations or activities.

From the perspective of biological psychologists, the mind is a manifestation of the brain. Without the brain, there is no mind. Within the brain lies the potential for self-awareness and purposeful activity. Somehow the brain gives rise to mind. Whether thought is then self-initiated, merely responsive to external stimulation, or reflects an ongoing interaction between people and the environment is a hotly debated issue in psychology. But it is generally agreed that for every **phenomenological** event, such as a "thought" or a "feeling," there are accompanying, underlying neurological events.

When you realize that a neuron may fire hundreds of times a second, and that thoughts may involve the firing of millions or billions of neurons, you can understand that it will never become practical to try to explain a thought in terms of the firing of a particular combination of neurons. Still, biological psychologists, and many others, assume that the mind is generally based on the substance of the brain. All this adds to the fascination of the work of biological psychologists.

We have seen that sensation and muscle activity involve many parts of the nervous system. But the essential human activities of thought and language involve the hemispheres of the cerebrum.

The Geography of the Cerebral Cortex

Each of the hemispheres of the cerebral cortex is divided into four parts or lobes, as shown in Figure

*Experiments are not intended to harm people, but local injuries are sometimes unavoidable in operations that are intended to save life or cure certain disorders.

Homunculus Latin for "little man." A homunculus within the brain was once thought to govern human behavior.

Phenomenological Having to do with subjective, conscious experience.

2.9. The **frontal lobe** lies in front of the central fissure, and the **parietal lobe** lies behind it. The **temporal lobe** lies below the side, or lateral, fissure, across from the frontal and parietal lobes. The **occipital lobe** lies behind the temporal lobe and behind and below the parietal lobe.

When light strikes the retinas of the eyes, neurons in the occipital lobe fire and we "see." Direct artificial stimulation of the occipital lobe also produces visual sensations. You would "see" flashes of light if neurons in the occipital region of the cortex were stimulated with electricity, even if it were pitch black or your eyes were covered. The hearing or auditory area of the cortex lies in the temporal lobe along the lateral fissure. As we shall see in Chapter 3, sounds cause structures in the ear to vibrate. Messages are relayed to the auditory area of the cortex, and when you hear a noise, neurons in this area are firing.

Just behind the central fissure in the parietal lobe lies an area of **sensory cortex,** in which the messages received from skin senses all over the body are projected. These sensations include warmth and cold, touch, pain, and movement. Neurons in different parts of the sensory cortex fire, depending on whether you wiggle your finger or raise your leg. And if a brain surgeon were to stimulate the proper area of your sensory cortex with a small probe known as a "pencil electrode," you might testify in court that someone had touched your arm or leg. Figure 2.9 shows that our faces and heads are overrepresented on this cortex as compared with, say, our trunks and legs. Overrepresentation is one of the reasons that our faces and heads are more sensitive to touch than other parts of the body.

Many years ago it was discovered that patients with injuries to one hemisphere of the brain would show sensory or motor deficits on the opposite side of the body below the head. Experimentation since that time has made it clear that sensory and motor nerves cross in the brain and elsewhere. The left hemisphere controls functions on, and receives inputs from, the right side of the body. The right hemisphere controls functions on, and receives inputs from, the left side of the body.

The **motor cortex** lies in the frontal lobe, just across the valley of the central fissure from the sensory cortex. Neurons in the motor cortex fire when we move certain parts of our body. If a surgeon were to stimulate a certain area of the right hemisphere of the motor cortex with a pencil electrode, you would raise your left leg. Raising the leg would be sensed in the sensory cortex, and you might have a devil of a time trying to figure out whether you had "intended" to raise that leg!

Thought, Language, and the Cortex

Areas of the cerebral cortex that are not primarily involved in sensation or motor activity are called **association areas.** Association areas make possible the breadth and depth of human learning, thought, memory, and language.

Association areas, for example, involve memory functions required for simple problem solving. Monkeys with **lesions** in certain association areas have difficulty remembering which of a pair of cups holds food when the cups have been screened off from them for a few seconds (Bauer & Fuster, 1976; French & Harlow, 1962). Stimulation of many association areas with pencil electrodes during surgery sometimes stimulates recall of memories vividly (Penfield, 1969).

Some association areas are involved in the integration of sensory information. Certain neurons in the visual area of the occipital lobe fire in re-

---

Frontal lobe The lobe of the cerebral cortex that lies to the front of the central fissure.

Parietal lobe The lobe that lies just behind the central fissure.

Temporal lobe The lobe that lies below the lateral fissure, near the temples of the head.

Occipital lobe The lobe that lies behind and below the parietal lobe and behind the temporal lobe.

Sensory cortex The section of cortex in which tactile sensory stimulation is projected. It lies just behind the central fissure in the parietal lobe.

Motor cortex The section of cortex that lies in the frontal lobe, just across the central fissure from the sensory cortex. Neural impulses in the motor cortex are linked to muscular responses throughout the body.

Association areas Areas of the cortex involved in learning, thought, memory, and language.

Lesion An injury that results in impaired behavior or loss of a function.

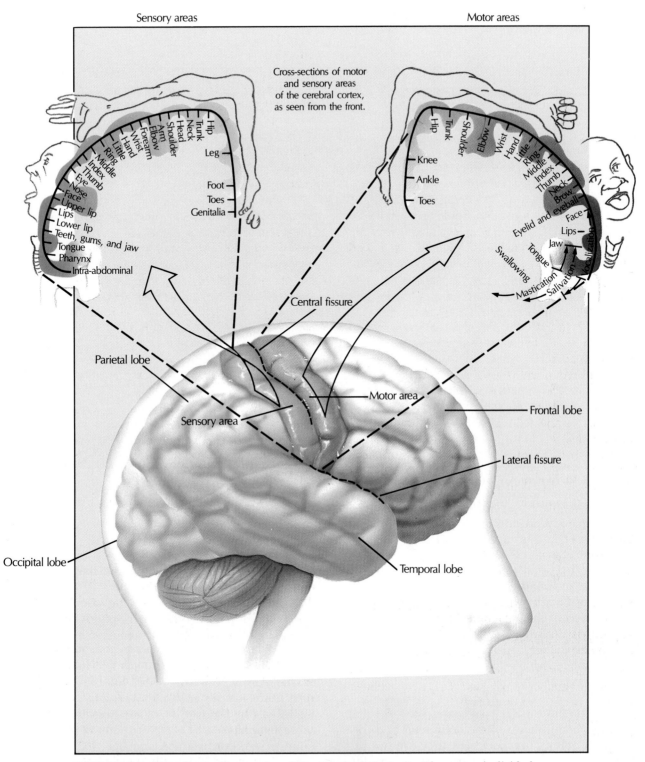

FIGURE 2.9. What Is the Geography of the Cerebral Cortex? The cortex is divided into four lobes: frontal, parietal, temporal, and occipital. The visual area of the cortex is located in the occipital lobe. The hearing or auditory cortex lies in the temporal lobe. The sensory and motor areas face each other across the central fissure. What happens when surgeons stimulate areas of the sensory or motor cortex during operations?

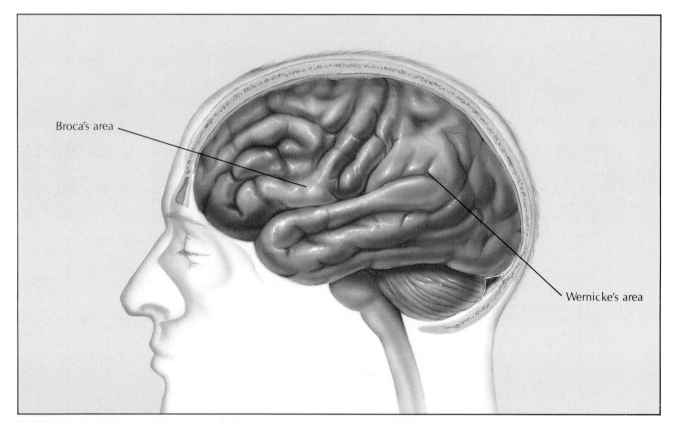

FIGURE 2.10. Where Are Broca's and Wernicke's Areas Located in the Cerebral Cortex?   The two areas of the dominant cortex most involved in speech are Broca's area and Wernicke's area. Damage to either area can produce a characteristic aphasia—that is, a predictable disruption of the ability to understand or produce language.

sponse to the visual presentation of vertical lines. Others fire in response to presentation of horizontal lines. Although one group of cells may respond to one aspect of the visual field and another group of cells may respond to another, association areas "put it all together." As a result, you see a box or an automobile or a road map, and not a confusing array of verticals and horizontals.

Language Functions   In many ways the left and right hemispheres of the brain tend to duplicate each other's functions, but they are not entirely equal. For the 90 percent of us who are right-handed, the left hemisphere contains language

functions and dominates. For about half the people who are left-handed—the other 10 percent—the right hemisphere contains language functions and is dominant. The left hemisphere thus contains language functions for about 95 percent of us.

Within the dominant (usually left) hemisphere of the cortex, the two areas most involved in speech are Broca's area and Wernicke's area (see Figure 2.10). Damage to either area is likely to cause an **aphasia,** that is, a disruption of the ability to understand or produce language.

Broca's area is located in the frontal lobe, near the section of the motor cortex that controls the muscles of the tongue and throat and of other areas of the face that are used when speaking. When Broca's area is damaged, people speak slowly and laboriously, with simple sentences—a

Aphasia Impaired ability to comprehend or express oneself through speech.

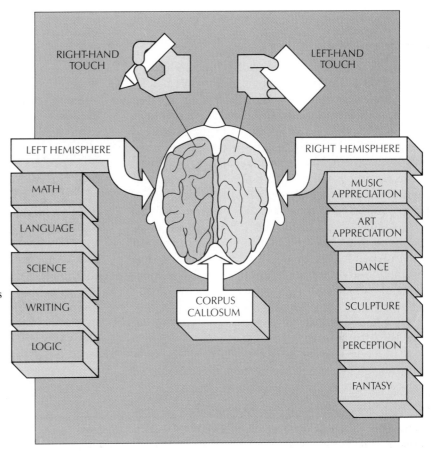

FIGURE 2.11. What Are Some of the "Specializations" of the Left and Right Hemispheres of the Cerebral Cortex?   This diagram exaggerates the "left-brain–right-brain" notion. It seems to be true that the dominant (usually left) hemisphere is somewhat more involved in intellectual undertakings that require logic and problem solving, while the nondominant (usually right) hemisphere is relatively more concerned with decoding visual information, esthetic and emotional responses, and imagination. However, each hemisphere has some involvement with logic and with creativity and intuition.

pattern termed **Broca's aphasia.** In more severe cases, their comprehension and use of proper syntax may be seriously impaired (Schwartz et al., 1980).

Wernicke's area lies in the temporal lobe near the auditory cortex. This area appears to be involved in the integration of auditory and visual information. Broca's area and Wernicke's area are connected by nerve fibers. People with damage to Wernicke's area may show **Wernicke's aphasia,** in which they usually speak freely and with proper syntax. However, their abilities to comprehend other people's speech and to think of the proper words to express their own thoughts is impaired (Gardner, 1978). And so Wernicke's area seems essential to understanding the relationships between words and their meanings.

"Left Brain," "Right Brain"?   In recent years it has become popular to speak of people as being either "left brained" or "right brained." The notion is that the hemispheres of the brain are involved in very different kinds of intellectual and emotional functions and responses, along the lines suggested in Figure 2.11. According to this view, people whose "left brains" are dominant would be basically logical and intellectual, whereas people whose "right brains" are dominant would be intuitive, creative, and emotional. Those of us fortunate enough to have our "brains" in balance would presumably have the best of it—the capacity for logic combined with emotional richness.

Broca's aphasia A language disorder characterized by slow, laborious speech.

Wernicke's aphasia A language disorder characterized by difficulty comprehending the meaning of the spoken language.

Like other popular ideas, the "left brain–right brain" notion is exaggerated. Research does suggest that the dominant (usually the left) hemisphere is somewhat more involved in intellectual undertakings that require logic and problem solving, understanding syntax, associating written words with their sounds, the general comprehension and production of speech, and mathematical computation (Levy, 1985). The nondominant (usually right) hemisphere is relatively more concerned with decoding visual information, aesthetic and emotional responses, imagination, understanding metaphors, and creative mathematical reasoning.

Despite these differences, it would be erroneous to think that the hemispheres of the brain act independently, or that some people are "left brained" and others are "right brained." The functions of the left and right hemispheres overlap to some degree, and the hemispheres tend to respond simultaneously as we focus our attention on one thing or another.

Biological psychologist Jerre Levy (1985) summarizes left-brain and right-brain similarities and differences as follows:

1. The hemispheres are similar enough so that each can function quite well independently, but not as well as they function in normal combined usage.
2. The left hemisphere does seem to play a special role in understanding and producing language while the right hemisphere does seem to play a special role in emotional response.
3. Both hemispheres are involved in logic.
4. Creativity and intuition are not confined to the right hemisphere.
5. Both hemispheres are educated at the same time, even when instruction is intended to "appeal" to the right hemisphere (as in music) or the left (as in a logic class).

Divided-Brain Experiments: When Two Hemispheres Stop Talking to One Another

A number of patients suffering from severe cases

of epilepsy have undergone **split-brain operations,** in which the corpus callosum is severed. The purpose of the operation is to try to confine epilepsy to one hemisphere of the cerebral cortex, rather than allow one hemisphere to agitate the other by transmitting a "violent storm of neural impulses" (Carlson, 1986). These operations do seem to help epilepsy patients. People who undergo them can be thought of as winding up with two brains, yet under most circumstances their behavior remains perfectly normal. But some of the effects of two hemispheres that have stopped talking to one another can be rather intriguing.

Gazzaniga (1972, 1983, 1985) has shown that split-brain patients whose eyes are closed may be able to describe verbally an object, such as a key, that they hold in one hand, but they cannot do so when they hold the object in the other hand. As shown in Figure 2.12, if a split-brain patient handles a key with his left hand behind a screen, **tactile** impressions of the key are projected into the right hemisphere, which has little or no language ability. Thus he will not be able to describe the key. If it were held in his right hand, he would have no trouble describing it because sensory impressions would be projected into the left hemisphere of the cortex, which contains language functions. To further confound matters, if the word *ring* is projected into the dominant (left) hemisphere while the patient is asked what he is handling, he will say "ring," not "key."

However, this discrepancy between what is felt and what is said occurs only in split-brain patients. As noted earlier, most of the time the hemispheres work together, even when we are playing the piano or are involved in scientific thought.

In case you have ever wondered whether other people could make us play the piano or engage in scientific thinking by "pressing the right buttons," let us consider some of the effects of electrical stimulation of the brain.

Split-brain operation An operation in which the corpus callosum is severed, usually in an effort to control epileptic seizures.
Tactile Of the sense of touch.

Electrical Stimulation of the Brain

Some years ago, José Delgado astounded the scientific world by stepping into a bullring armed only with a radio transmitter, a cape, and, perhaps,

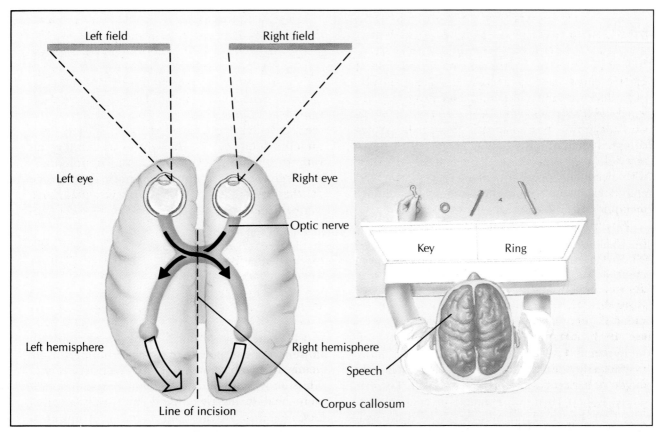

FIGURE 2.12. What Are Some of the Behavioral Effects of a Divided Brain? In the drawing on the left, we see that visual sensations in the left visual field are projected in the occipital cortex of the right hemisphere. Visual sensations from the right visual field are projected in the occipital cortex in the left hemisphere. In the divided-brain experiment diagrammed on the right, a subject with a severed corpus callosum handles a key with his left hand and perceives the written word *key* with his left eye. The word "key" is projected in the right hemisphere. But speech is usually a function of the left (dominant) hemisphere. The written word "ring," perceived by the right eye, is projected in the left hemisphere. So, when asked what he is handling, the divided-brain subject reports "ring," not "key."

crossed fingers (Figure 2.13). As he described his experiment in *Physical Control of the Mind* (1969), Delgado implanted a radio-controlled electrode in the limbic system of a "brave bull"—a variety bred to respond with a raging charge when it sees any human being. When Delgado pressed a button on the transmitter, sending a signal to a battery-powered receiver attached to the bull's horns, an electrical impulse went into the bull's brain and the animal ceased his charge. After several repetitions, the bull no longer attempted to charge Delgado.

During the 1950s, James Olds and Peter Milner (Olds, 1969) accidentally discovered (how many important discoveries are made by accident!) that electrical stimulation of an area of the hypothalamus of a rat would increase the frequency of whatever the rat was doing at the time (Figure 2.14). Rats would also rapidly learn to do things, such as pressing a lever (Figure 2.14), that would result in more stimulation. Rats, in fact, will stimulate themselves in this area repeatedly, up to 100 times a minute and over 1,900 times an hour. For

FIGURE 2.13. Can Brave Bulls Be Tamed by Electrical Stimulation of the Brain?
Brave bulls are dangerous animals that will attack an intruder in the arena. Even in full charge, however, a bull can be stopped abruptly by radio-triggered electrical stimulation of the brain. After several stimulations, there is a lasting inhibition of aggressive behavior.

this reason, Olds and Milner labeled this area of the hypothalamus the rat's "pleasure center."

Since these early days, ESB has been used with people to address a number of problems. For example, Robert Heath of Tulane University claims that ESB has helped some severely disturbed schizophrenia patients (Valenstein, 1978). Cancer or trauma patients suffering unrelenting pain have used ESB to block pain messages in the spinal cord before they reach the brain (Restak, 1975).

But psychologist Elliot Valenstein (1978) is not quite so impressed by the potential of ESB. He notes, for example, that the bull in the Delgado demonstration did not actually have its aggressive tendencies eliminated by ESB. Instead, the electrical impulses caused the bull to circle to the right. The bull might have become confused, not pacified.

Also, ESB-provoked behavior does not perfectly mimic natural behavior. Behavior brought about by ESB is stereotyped and compulsive. For example, an animal whose "hunger" has been prodded by ESB may eat one type of food only. And ESB in the same site may produce different effects on different occasions. On one occasion a rat may eat when receiving ESB. On another, it may drink. ESB may not be as predictable as had been thought.

The sites for producing pleasant or unpleasant sensations in people may vary from person to person and from day to day. As Valenstein notes, "The impression that brain stimulation in humans can repeatedly evoke the same emotional state, the same memory, or the same behavior is simply a myth. The brain is not organized into neat compartments that correspond to the . . . labels we as-

FIGURE 2.14. What Is the "Pleasure Center" of the Brain? A rat with an electrode implanted in a section of the hypothalamus that has been termed the "pleasure center" of the brain learns to press a lever in order to receive electrical stimulation.

sign to behavior" (1978, p. 31). I find that thought comforting.

In our discussion of the nervous system, we have described naturally occurring chemical substances that facilitate or inhibit the transmission of neural messages—neurotransmitters. Let us now turn our attention to other naturally occurring chemical substances that influence behavior—hormones. We shall see that some hormones also function as neurotransmitters.

THE ENDOCRINE SYSTEM

Here are some things you may have heard about hormones and behavior. Are they truth or fiction?

- Some obese people actually eat very little, and their excess weight is caused by "glands."
- A boy whose growth was "stunted" began to catch up with his agemates after receiving injections of "growth hormone."
- A woman who becomes anxious and depressed just before menstruating is suffering from "raging hormones."
- Women who "pump iron" frequently use hormones to achieve the muscle definition that is needed to win body-building contests.
- People who receive injections of adrenalin often report that they feel "as if" they are about to experience some emotion, but they're not sure which one.

Let us consider each of these items. The obese may often attribute their weight problems to glands, but much of the time they simply eat too much. Growth hormone, a secretion of the **pituitary gland,** can promote growth. Women may become somewhat more anxious or depressed at the time of menstruation, but the effects of hormones have been exaggerated, and women's response to menstruation reflects their attitudes as well as biological changes. It is an "open secret" that many top women (and men) bodybuilders use steroids, hormones that are produced by the **adrenal cortex,** along with human growth hormone, to achieve the muscle mass and definition sought by judges in competition (Leerhsen & Abramson, 1985). Steroids and growth hormone promote resistance to stress and muscle growth in both men

and women. Finally, adrenalin, a hormone produced by the **adrenal medulla,** does generally arouse people and thereby heighten general emotional responsiveness. In Chapter 6 you will see that the specific emotion to which this arousal is attributed depends in part on the person's situation.

Ductless Glands   The body contains two types of glands: glands with **ducts** and glands without ducts. A duct is a passageway that carries substances to specific locations. Saliva, sweat, and tears (the name of a new rock group?) all reach their destinations by ducts. Psychologists are more likely to show interest in the substances secreted by ductless glands because of their behavioral effects (see the summary in Table 2.1). The ductless glands make up the **endocrine system,** and they secrete substances called **hormones** (from the Greek *horman,* meaning "to stimulate" or "to excite").

Hormones are released directly into the bloodstream. Hormones, like neurotransmitters,* have specific receptor sites. And so, although they are poured into the bloodstream and circulate throughout the body, they only act on hormone receptors in certain locations. For example, certain hormones released by the hypothalamus influence only the pituitary gland. Some hormones released by the pituitary influence the adrenal cortex, others influence the testes and ovaries, and so on.

Let us now examine the functions of several glands of the endocrine system.

*Recall that some hormones, such as norepinephrine, also function as neurotransmitters.

Pituitary gland The gland which secretes growth hormone, prolactin, antidiuretic hormone, and others.

Adrenal cortex One of the two adrenal glands located above the kidneys. It produces steroids.

Adrenal medulla The adrenal gland that produces adrenalin.

Duct Passageway.

Endocrine system Ductless glands that secrete hormones and release them directly into the bloodstream.

Hormone A substance secreted by an endocrine gland that regulates various body functions.

Table 2.1   An Overview of Some Major Glands of the Endocrine System

GLAND	HORMONE	MAJOR EFFECTS
Hypothalamus	Releasing Hormones	Regulates secretions of the pituitary gland
Pituitary		
Anterior lobe	Growth hormone	Causes growth of muscles, bones, and glands
	Adrenocorticotropic hormone (ACTH)	Regulates adrenal cortex
	Thyrotrophin	Causes thyroid gland to secrete thyroxin
	Follicle-stimulating hormone	Causes formation of sperm and egg cells
	Luteinizing hormone	Causes ovulation, maturation of sperm and egg cells
	Prolactin	Stimulates production of milk
Posterior lobe	Antidiuretic hormone (ADH)	Inhibits production of urine
	Oxytocin	Stimulates uterine contractions during delivery and release of milk during nursing
Pancreas	Insulin	Enables body to metabolize sugar; regulates storage of fats
	Glucagon	Increases levels of sugar and fats in blood
	Somatostatin	Regulates secretion of insulin and glucagon
Thyroid	Thyroxin	Increases metabolic rate
Adrenal		
Cortex	Steroids (e.g., cortisol)	Increase resistance to stress; regulate carbohydrate metabolism
Medulla	Adrenalin (Epinephrine)	Increases metabolic activity (heart and respiration rates, blood sugar level, etc.)
	Noradrenalin (Norepinephrine)	Raises blood pressure, acts as neurotransmitter
Testes	Testosterone	Promotes growth of male sex characteristics
Ovaries	Estrogen	Regulates menstrual cycle
	Progesterone	Promotes growth of female reproductive tissues; maintains pregnancy
Uterus	(Several)	Maintain pregnancy

The Pituitary Gland

The pituitary gland lies just below the hypothalamus (see Figure 2.15). It is so central to the body's functioning that it has been referred to as the "master gland." But today we know that the hypothalamus regulates much pituitary activity. Much hormonal action helps the body maintain steady

---

Negative feedback Descriptive of a system in which information that a quantity (e.g., of a hormone) has reached a set point suspends action of the agency (e.g., a gland) that gives rise to that quantity.

---

states, as in fluid levels, blood sugar levels, and so on. These steady states are achieved by mechanisms that measure current levels and signal glands to release appropriate regulatory chemicals when these levels deviate from optimal. The maintenance of steady states requires systems in which information is fed back to glands as needed. This type of system is referred to as a **negative feedback** loop. That is, when the required level of a hormone has been secreted, the gland is signaled to stop. With a negative feedback system in effect, even the "master gland" must serve a master the hypothalamus. In turn the hypothalamus, as we

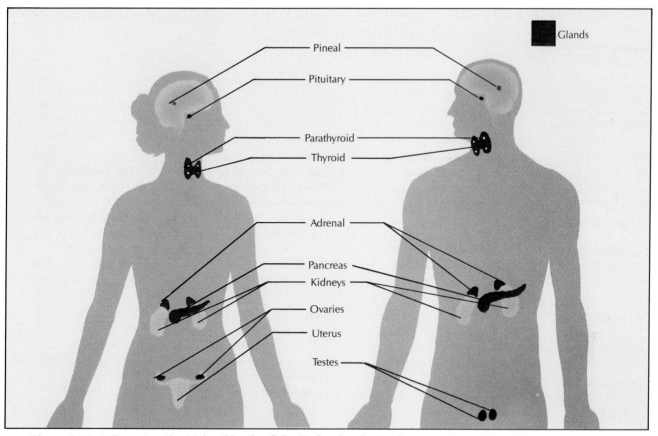

Glands

Pineal
Pituitary
Parathyroid
Thyroid
Adrenal
Pancreas
Kidneys
Ovaries
Uterus
Testes

Figure 2.15. Where Are the Major Glands of the Endocrine System?

shall see in Chapter 6, is responsive to information received from many sources throughout the body.

The anterior (front) and posterior (back) lobes of the pituitary gland produce or secrete many hormones, some of which are listed in Table 2.1. **Growth hormone** regulates the growth of muscles, bones, and glands. An excess of growth hormone can lead to *acromegaly,* a condition in which people may grow two to three feet taller than they would normally. Wrestler "André the Giant," who is over seven feet tall and weighs in at nearly 500 pounds, secreted extremely high levels of growth hormone as a child. In recent years, professional athletes have injected growth hormone as adults to increase their muscle mass, combining it with anabolic steroids, discussed later.

Children whose growth patterns seem abnormally slow often catch up to their agemates when growth hormone is administered by a physician. A

recently discovered substance, growth-hormone releasing factor (or hGRF), is produced by the hypothalamus and causes the pituitary to produce growth hormone (Taylor, 1985).

Prolactin largely regulates maternal behavior in lower mammals, such as rats, and stimulates production of milk in women. Transfusion of blood from a new mother rat to another female rat will cause the recipient to display typical mothering behaviors.

When the fluid level of the body is low, the hypothalamus stimulates the pituitary gland to se-

Growth hormone A pituitary hormone that regulates growth.

Prolactin A pituitary hormone that regulates production of milk and, in lower animals, maternal behavior.

crete **antidiuretic hormone,** which is abbreviated *ADH* and also referred to as *vasopressin.* ADH increases the reabsorption of urine in order to conserve fluid.

Oxytocin stimulates labor in pregnant women. Obstetricians may induce labor or increase the strength of uterine contractions during labor by injecting pregnant women with oxytocin.

Adrenocorticotrophic hormone (ACTH) is released by the pituitary in response to corticotrophin-releasing hormone (CRH), which is produced by the hypothalamus. ACTH acts on the adrenal cortex, causing it to release a number of hormones, including **cortisol,** which helps the body respond

---

Antidiuretic hormone A pituitary hormone that inhibits the production of urine. Abbreviated *ADH.*

Oxytocin A pituitary hormone that stimulates labor.

Adrenocorticotrophic hormone A pituitary hormone that regulates the adrenal cortex. Abbreviated *ACTH.*

Cortisol A hormone (steroid) produced by the adrenal cortex that helps the body cope with stress by counteracting inflammation and allergic reactions.

Pancreas A gland behind the stomach whose secretions influence the blood sugar level.

Insulin A pancreatic hormone that stimulates the metabolism of sugar.

Glucagon A pancreatic hormone that increases the levels of sugar and fat in the blood.

Hyperglycemia A disorder caused by excess sugar in the blood.

Hypoglycemia A disorder caused by too little sugar in the blood.

Syndrome A cluster of symptoms characteristic of a disorder.

Thyroxin The thyroid hormone that increases metabolic rate.

Metabolism In organisms, a continuous process that converts food into energy.

Hypothyroidism A condition caused by a deficiency of thyroxin and characterized by sluggish behavior and a low metabolic rate.

Cretinism A condition caused by thyroid deficiency in childhood and characterized by mental retardation and stunted growth.

Hyperthyroidism A condition caused by excess thyroxin and characterized by excitability, weight loss, and insomnia.

---

to stress by fighting inflammation and allergic reactions.

The Pancreas

The **pancreas** is influential in controlling the level of sugar in the blood and the urine through the hormones **insulin** and **glucagon.** One form of diabetes (diabetes mellitis) is characterized by excess sugar in the blood **(hyperglycemia)** and in the urine, a condition that can lead to coma and death. Diabetes stems from inadequate secretion or utilization of insulin. People who do not secrete enough insulin of their own may need to inject this hormone daily in order to control diabetes.

The condition **hypoglycemia** is characterized by too little sugar in the blood. Symptoms of hypoglycemia include shakiness, dizziness, and lack of energy, a **syndrome** that is easily confused with anxiety. Many people have sought help for anxiety and learned through a series of blood tests that they are actually suffering from hypoglycemia. This disorder is generally controlled through dietary restrictions.

The Thyroid Gland

Thyroxin, produced by the thyroid gland, affects the body's **metabolism,** or rate of using oxygen and producing energy. Some people who are overweight are suffering from a condition known as **hypothyroidism,** which results from abnormally low secretions of thyroxin. Deficiency of thyroxin can lead to **cretinism** in children, a disorder characterized by stunted growth and mental retardation. Adults who secrete too little thyroxin may feel tired and sluggish and may put on weight. People who produce excesses of thyroxin may develop **hyperthyroidism,** a disorder characterized by excitability, insomnia, and weight loss.

The Adrenal Glands

The adrenal glands, located above the kidneys, have an outer layer, or cortex, and an inner core, or medulla. The adrenal cortex is regulated by the pituitary hormone, ACTH, and secretes hormones known as **steroids.** Steroids (cortisol is one) increase resistance to stress; promote muscle development; and cause the liver to release stored sugar, making energy available for emergencies. Anabolic steroids (synthetic versions of the male sex hormone testosterone) have been used—frequently along with growth hormone—to enhance athletic prowess. Unfortunately, a number of athletes who have used growth hormone and steroids, such as nine-time world-champion weight lifter Larry Pacifico, have developed heart problems, such as blocked arteries. Anabolic steroids also have psychological effects. They increase self-esteem, the sex drive, and one's energy level (Taylor, 1985). However, they may also cause sleep disturbances and be linked with depression and apathy when discontinued.

Adrenalin, also known as epinephrine, is secreted by the adrenal medulla. It acts on the sympathetic branch of the ANS and on the RAS to arouse the body in preparation for threats and stress. Adrenalin is also involved in general emotional arousal.

The Testes and the Ovaries

If it were not for the secretion of the male sex hormone **testosterone** about six weeks after conception, we would all develop into females. Testosterone is produced by the testes, and a few weeks following fertilization of an ovum, it stimulates prenatal differentiation of male sex organs. During puberty it promotes the growth of muscle and bone and the development of **primary** and **secondary sex characteristics.** Primary sex characteristics are directly involved in reproduction, such as the growth of the penis and of the sperm-producing ability of the testes. Secondary sex characteristics, such as growth of the beard and deepening of the voice, differentiate the sexes but are not directly involved in reproduction.

Testosterone is maintained at fairly even levels by the hypothalamus, pituitary gland, and testes. Low blood levels of testosterone signal the hypothalamus to produce gonadotropin-releasing hormone (GnRH). GnRH, in turn, signals the pituitary to secrete luteinizing hormone (LH), which stimulates the testes to secrete testosterone and fol-

licle-stimulating hormone (FSH), which causes sperm cells to develop. The negative feedback loop is completed as follows: High blood levels of testosterone signal the hypothalamus not to secrete GnRH, so that production of LH, FSH, and testosterone are suspended.

The ovaries produce **estrogen** and **progesterone.** Estrogen is a generic name for several female sex hormones that lead to development of female reproductive capacity and secondary sex characteristics, such as accumulation of fat in the breasts and hips. Progesterone also has multiple functions. It stimulates growth of the female reproductive organs and maintains pregnancy. As is the case with testosterone, estrogen and progesterone levels influence and are also influenced by GnRH, LH, and FSH. In women, FSH causes ova (egg cells) within follicles in the ovaries to ripen.

Hormonal Regulation of the Menstrual Cycle

Whereas testosterone levels remain fairly stable, estrogen and progesterone levels vary markedly and regulate the menstrual cycle. Following **menstruation**—the monthly sloughing off of the inner lining of the uterus—estrogen levels increase, lead-

Steroids Hormones produced by the adrenal cortex that increase resistance to stress and regulate carbohydrate metabolism.

Adrenalin A hormone produced by the adrenal medulla that stimulates sympathetic ANS activity. Also called *epinephrine.*

Testosterone A male sex hormone produced by the testes that promotes growth of male sexual characteristics and sperm.

Primary sex characteristics Physical traits that distinguish the sexes and are directly involved in reproduction.

Secondary sex characteristics Physical traits that differentiate the sexes but are not directly involved in reproduction.

Estrogen A generic term for several female sex hormones that promote growth of female sexual characteristics and regulate the menstrual cycle.

Progesterone A female sex hormone that promotes growth of the sexual organs and helps maintain pregnancy.

Menstruation The monthly shedding of the lining of the uterus by women who are not pregnant.

ing to the development of an ovum (egg cell) and growth of the inner lining of the uterus. The ovum is released by the ovary when estrogens reach peak blood levels.* Then the inner lining of the uterus thickens in response to secretion of progesterone, gaining the capacity to support an embryo if fertilization should occur. If the ovum is not fertilized, estrogen and progesterone levels drop suddenly, triggering menstruation once more.

Women and PMS: Does Premenstrual Syndrome Doom Women to Misery?
For several days prior to and during menstruation, the stereotype has been that "raging hormones" doom women to irritability and poor judgment—two facets of premenstrual syndrome (PMS). Do women show behavioral and emotional deficits prior to and during menstruation? The evidence is mixed.

Psychologist Judith Bardwick (Bardwick, 1971; Ivey & Bardwick, 1968) found women's moods to be most positive halfway through their menstrual cycles (during release of an ovum). But a number of women show significant levels of anxiety, depression, and fatigue for two to three days before menstruating (Money, 1980). British investigator Katharina Dalton (1972, 1980) reported that women are more likely to commit suicide or crimes, call in sick at work, and develop physical and emotional problems before or during menstruation.

There is evidence showing a link between hormone levels and mood in women. Paige (1971) studied women whose hormone levels were kept rather even by birth-control pills and others whose hormone levels varied naturally throughout the cycle. She found that women whose hormone levels fluctuated appeared to show somewhat greater anxiety and hostility prior to and during menstruation. However, they did not commit crimes or wind up on mental wards. Other studies suggest that even among women who report premenstrual syndrome, the symptoms are most often mild, although a small percentage of women may have symptoms that are strong enough to interfere with their functioning (Keye, 1983).

We must note also that women may be responding to negative cultural attitudes toward menstruation as well as to menstrual symptoms themselves (Brooks-Gunn & Ruble, 1980; Sherif, 1980). Women who do not share highly traditional cultural attitudes—including attitudes about the debilitating nature of menstruation—are less likely to show mood changes throughout the different phases of the menstrual cycle (Paige, 1973).

However, some hormonal changes at the time of menstruation can cause some very real and painful problems. For instance, prostaglandins, which cause uterine contractions, may in some women cause painful cramping. In such cases prostaglandin-inhibiting drugs such as Motrin and Indocin show promise in helping women (Rathus, 1983). Unfortunately, the medical establishment has often treated women's menstrual complaints as hysterical, and so many women have not received the help that is available.

In sum, (1) hormone levels seem to exert some influence over mood shifts in women, but most often these shifts are minor; (2) much of the evidence indicating that women show performance deficits prior to and during menstruation is unreliable; (3) traditional views of (perfectly harmless) menstrual flow as polluting may contribute to any problems women may encounter; but (4) some women have very real menstrual discomfort, such as menstrual cramping, and these problems need to be treated medically.

HEREDITY

Spend a moment or two reflecting on some facts of life:

- People cannot breathe underwater (without special equipment).
- People cannot fly (again, without some rather special equipment).
- Fish cannot learn to speak French or do an Irish jig even if you raise them in enriched environments and send them to finishing school (which is why we look for tuna that tastes good, not for tuna with good taste).

---

*About one day prior to the releasing of an ovum, there is a surge of luteinizing hormone (LH) from the pituitary. LH is found in the urine as well as in the bloodstream, and a number of ovulation-predicting kits rely on measurement of changing LH levels.

• Chimpanzees and gorillas can use sign language but cannot speak.

People cannot breathe underwater or fly (without oxygen tanks, airplanes, or other devices) because of the structures they have inherited. Fish are similarly limited by their **heredity,** or the biological transmission of traits and characteristics from one generation to another. Because of their heredity, fish cannot speak French or do a jig. Chimps and gorillas are capable of understanding and expressing some concepts through American sign language and other nonverbal symbol systems. However, these apes have shown no ability to speak, even though they can make sounds and have voice boxes in their throats somewhat similar to ours. They have probably failed to inherit humanlike speech areas of the cerebral cortex.

Genes and Chromosomes

Genes are the basic building blocks of heredity. They are the biochemical materials that regulate the development of traits. Some traits, such as blood type, are transmitted by a single pair of genes—one of which is derived from each parent. Other traits, referred to as **polygenic,** are determined by complex combinations of genes.

Chromosomes, the rod-shaped genetic structures found in the nuclei of the body's cells, each consist of more than 1,000 genes. A normal human cell contains 46 chromosomes, which are organized into 23 pairs.

We have about 100,000 genes in our cells. Chromosomes consist of large, complex molecules of deoxyribonucleic acid (DNA), which has several chemical components. Genes occupy various segments along the length of chromosomes. As you can see in Figure 2.16, DNA takes the form of a double helix, similar in appearance to a twisting ladder. In all living things, the sides of the "ladder" consist of alternating segments of phosphate (P) and a simple sugar (S). The "rungs" of the ladder are attached to the sugars and consist of one of two pairs of bases, either *adenine* with *thymine* (A with T) or *cytosine* with *guanine* (C with G). The sequence of the rungs is the genetic code that will cause the unfolding organism to grow arms or wings, skin or scales.

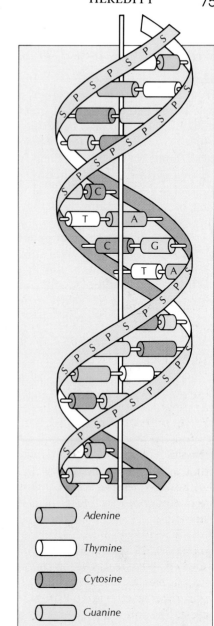

Adenine

Thymine

Cytosine

Guanine

FIGURE 2.16. What Does the Double Helix of DNA Look Like?

Heredity The tranmission of traits from one generation to another through genes.

Genes The basic building blocks of heredity, which consist of deoxyribonucleic acid.

Polygenic Determined by several genes.

Chromosomes Rodlike structures consisting of genes which are found in the nuclei of the body's cells.

Genetics and Behavior Genetics

Heredity, or the biological transmission of traits from one generation to another, plays a significant role in the determination of traits we consider human and nonhuman. The biological structures we inherit at once make our behaviors possible and place limits on them. The field within the science of biology that studies heredity is called **genetics.** **Behavior genetics** is concerned with the transmission of structures and traits that give rise to patterns of behavior.

Research suggests that genetic influences are a factor not only in physical traits such as height, race, and eye color but also in personality traits such as **extraversion** (Loehlin et al., 1982), **neuroticism** (Scarr et al., 1981), fearfulness and shyness (Daniels & Plomin, 1985; Kagan, 1984; Plomin, 1982), dominance and aggressiveness (Goldsmith, 1983), and antisocial behavior (Mednick, 1985).

The sets of traits specified by our genetic codes are referred to as our **genotypes.** But we are

also influenced by environmental factors such as nutrition, learning, exercise, and unfortunately, accident and illness. Our actual traits at any time are our **phenotypes.** Our traits, as expressed, represent the interaction of genetic and environmental influences.

Behavior geneticists are attempting to sort out the relative importance of **nature** (heredity) and **nurture** (environmental influences) in the development of various behavior patterns. Psychologists are especially interested in the roles of nature and nurture in intelligence (Plomin & DeFries, 1980), abnormal behavior patterns such as schizophrenia, and social problems such as sociopathy and aggression.

Genetics The branch of biology that studies heredity.

Behavior genetics The study of the genetic transmission of structures and traits that give rise to behavior.

Extraversion A trait in which a person directs his or her interest to persons and things outside the self. Sociability.

Neuroticism A trait in which a person is given to anxiety, tension, and emotional instability.

Genotype The sum total of our traits as inherited from our parents.

Phenotype The sum total of our traits at a given time, as inherited from our parents and influenced by environmental factors.

Nature In behavior genetics, heredity.

Nurture In behavior genetics, environmental influences on behavior, such as nutrition, culture, socioeconomic status, and learning.

Mitosis The process of cell division by which the identical genetic code is carried into new cells in the body.

Mutation Sudden variations in the genetic code that usually occur as a result of environmental influences.

Meiosis A process of reduction division in which sperm and ova are formed that each contain 23 chromosomes instead of 46.

Mitosis and Meiosis

We all begin life as a single cell that divides again and again. There are two types of cell division: *mitosis* and *meiosis.* **Mitosis** is the cell-division process by which growth occurs and tissues are replaced. Through mitosis, the identical genetic code is carried into each new cell in the body: The chromosomal strands of DNA "unzip" (see Figure 2.17). One side of the "ladder" and one of the two elements of each "rung" remain in the nucleus of each new cell after division takes place. The double helix is then rebuilt in each cell: Each incomplete rung combines with the appropriate base from the chemicals within the cell (that is, G with C, A with T, etc.) to form a complete ladder. As a consequence the genetic code is identical in every cell unless **mutations** occur through radiation or other environmental influences.

Sperm and ova are produced through **meiosis,** or reduction division. In meiosis, the 46 chromosomes within the nucleus first divide into 23 pairs. When the cell divides, one member of each pair goes to each newly formed cell. As a consequence, each new cell contains only 23 chromosomes, not 46. And so a cell that results from meiosis has half the genetic material of one that results from mitosis.

Through reduction division, or meiosis, we receive 23 chromosomes from our fathers' sperm cells and 23 chromosomes from our mothers' ova. When a sperm cell fertilizes an ovum, the chromosomes form 23 pairs (Figure 2.18). Twenty-two

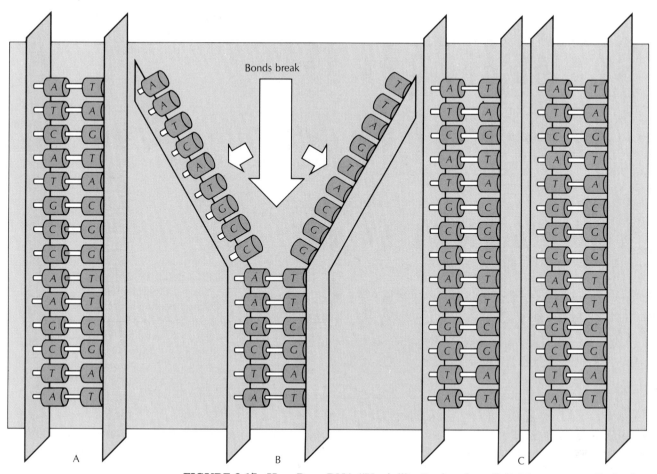

FIGURE 2.17. How Does DNA "Unzip"? During the cell-division process of mitosis, chromosomal strands of DNA "unzip." One side of the "ladder" and one element of each "rung" remain in each new cell following division. The double helix is then rebuilt in each new cell, as each incomplete rung combines with the appropriate base from the chemicals within the cell.

of the pairs contain **autosomes,** which are chromosomes that look alike and possess information concerning the same set of traits. The 23rd pair consists of **sex chromosomes,** which determine our sex. We all receive an X sex chromosome (so called because of the "X" shape) from our mothers. If we also receive an X sex chromosome from our fathers, we develop into females. If we receive a Y sex chromosome (named after the "Y" shape) from our fathers, we develop into males.

Identical and Fraternal Twins

The fertilized ovum that carries genetic messages from both parents is called a **zygote.** Now and then

a zygote divides into two cells that separate, so that each develops into an individual with the same genetic makeup. These persons are known as identical, or **monozygotic (MZ) twins.** The possible

Autosomes Chromosomes that look alike and possess information concerning the same sets of traits. One autosome is received from the father and the corresponding autosome is received from the mother.

Sex chromosomes The twenty-third pair of chromosomes which determine sex and, in the case of males, do not look alike.

Zygote A fertilized egg cell.

Monozygotic twins Identical, or MZ, twins. Twins who develop from a single zygote, thus carrying the same genetic instructions.

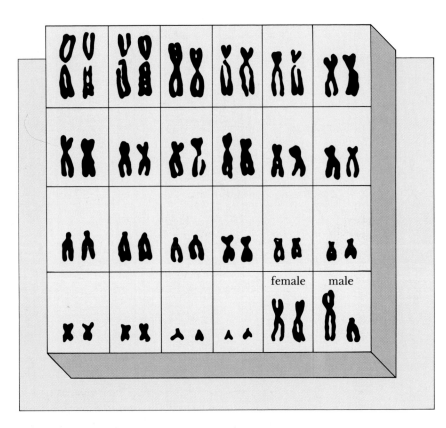

FIGURE 2.18. What Is the Normal Complement of Chromosomes? People normally have 23 pairs of chromosomes. Sex is determined by the 23rd pair of chromosomes. Females have two X sex chromosomes, whereas males have an X and a Y sex chromosome.

combinations of traits that can result from the coming together of so many thousands of genes is, practically speaking, unlimited. The chances that two people will show completely identical traits, with the exception of MZ twins (or triplets, quadruplets, etc.), are essentially nil.

If the woman releases two ova in the same month, and they are both fertilized, they develop into fraternal, or **dizygotic (DZ) twins,** and are related as are other brothers and sisters. Identical, or MZ, twins are important in the study of the relative influences of heredity and environment because differences between MZ twins are the re-

sult of environmental influences (of nurture, not nature).

MZ twins look alike and are closer in height than DZ twins. Classic research shows that MZ twin sisters begin to menstruate one to two months apart, whereas DZ twins begin to menstruate about a year apart (Petri, 1934). MZ twins resemble one another more strongly than DZ twins on traits such as general irritability and sociability, persistence in performing cognitive tasks, verbal and spatial skills, and perceptual speed (DeFries et al., 1987; Floderus-Myrhed et al., 1980; Matheny, 1983; Scarr & Kidd, 1983). MZ twins show more similarity than DZ twins in their early signs of attachment, such as smiling, cuddling, and expression of fear of strangers (Scarr & Kidd, 1983). MZ twins are also more likely than DZ twins to share behavioral problems such as **autism** (Ritvo et al., 1985), sleepwalking, **enuresis,** even nail-biting (Bakwin, 1970, 1971a, 1971b). In Chapter 9 we shall also see that MZ twins show a greater **concordance** rate for likelihood of becoming dependent on alcohol and other drugs.

Dizygotic twins Fraternal, or DZ, twins. Twins who develop from separate zygotes.

Autism A childhood disorder marked by problems such as failure to relate to others, lack of speech, and intolerance of change.

Enuresis Lack of bladder control at an age by which control is normally attained.

Concordance Agreement.

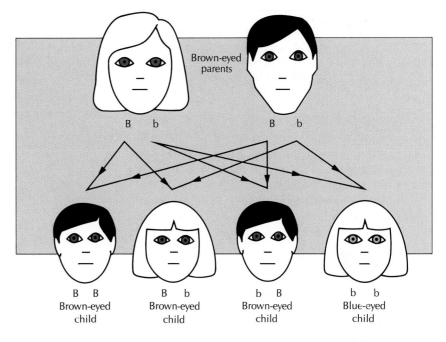

FIGURE 2.19. How Are Dominant and Recessive Traits Transmitted? Two brown-eyed parents each carry a recessive gene for blue eyes. Their children have an equal opportunity of receiving genes for brown eyes and blue eyes. In such cases, 25 percent of the children show the recessive trait—blue eyes. The other 75 percent show the dominant trait—brown eyes. But two of three who show brown eyes carry the recessive trait for transmittal to future generations.

Brown-eyed parents

B b   B b

B B
Brown-eyed child

B b
Brown-eyed child

b B
Brown-eyed child

b b
Blue-eyed child

Dominant and Recessive Traits

Traits are determined by pairs of genes. Each member of a pair of genes is called an **allele.** When both alleles for a trait, such as hair color, are the same, the person is said to be **homozygous** for that trait. When the alleles for a trait differ, the person is **heterozygous** for that trait. Some traits result from an "averaging" of the genetic instructions carried by the parents. When the effects of both alleles are shown, there is said to be incomplete or codominance.

Many genes carry **dominant traits,** whereas many others carry **recessive traits.** When a dominant allele is paired with a recessive allele, the dominant allele appears in the offspring. Brown hair, for instance, is dominant over blond hair. So if one parent carries genes for only brown hair, and the other for only blond hair, the children will have brown hair.* Brown eyes are similarly dominant over blue eyes, and brown-eyed persons may carry recessive genes for blue eyes (see Figure 2.19).

*An exception would occur if the children also inherit a gene for albinism, in which case their hair and eyes would be colorless.

If the recessive gene from one parent should combine with the recessive gene from the other, the recessive trait will be shown. In the example given in Figure 2.19, the child will have blond hair. Brown eyes are similarly dominant over blue eyes, and brown-eyed persons may carry recessive genes for blue eyes. Approximately 25 percent of the offspring of parents who each carry a gene for brown and blue eye color will have blue eyes.

Chromosomal and Genetic Abnormalities

There are a number of diseases that reflect chromosomal or genetic abnormalities. Some chromosomal disorders stem from abnormalities in the au-

Allele Each member of a pair of genes.
Homozygous Having two identical alleles for a trait.
Heterozygous Having two different alleles.
Dominant trait In genetics, a trait that is expressed.
Recessive trait In genetics, a trait that is not expressed when the genes involved are paired with dominant genes, but they are transmitted to future generations and expressed if paired with other recessive genes.

tosomes (such as Down syndrome). Others reflect disorders in the sex chromosomes (as in XYY syndrome). Some genetic abnormalities, such as phenylketonuria, are caused by a single pair of genes, whereas others are caused by combinations of genes.

Chromosomal Abnormalities   When we do not have the normal complement of 46 chromosomes, physical and behavioral abnormalities may result. The risk of chromosomal abnormalities rises with the age of the parents (Hook, 1981).

In **Down syndrome** (formerly referred to as Down's syndrome), the 21st pair of chromosomes has an extra, or third, chromosome. Down syndrome is thought to be caused by faulty division of the 21st pair of chromosomes during meiosis. Although this syndrome is usually attributed to the mother, fathers are responsible for it in about 25 percent of cases.

Persons with Down syndrome show a downward-sloping fold of skin at the inner corners of the eyes. They also show a characteristic round face; protruding tongue; and broad, flat nose. They are mentally retarded and may suffer from respiratory problems and malformations of the heart. Most Down-syndrome persons die by middle age. By this time they are also prone to memory loss and childish emotions that stem from a form of senility (Kolata, 1985).

An extra Y sex chromosome is associated with heightening of male secondary sex characteristics in men labeled "supermales." XYY males are somewhat taller than average and develop heavier beards. They are often mildly retarded, especially in language development. At one point it was speculated that XYY syndrome was linked to aggressive criminal behavior, but evidence for this assertion is poor.

Other sex chromosomal abnormalities include Klinefelter's syndrome, Turner's syndrome, and the XXX "superfemale" syndrome. Each of these is associated with mild mental retardation and fertility problems.

Genetic Abnormalities   Other disorders have been attributed to genes.

The enzyme disorder **phenylketonuria** (PKU) is transmitted by a recessive gene and affects about one child in 14,000. When both parents are **carriers** of the recessive gene, PKU is transmitted to about one child in four (as in Figure 2.19). One child in four will not carry the recessive gene. The other two, as their parents, will be carriers.

Children with PKU cannot metabolize the protein *phenylalanine*. As a consequence, it builds up in their bodies as phenylpyruvic acid and damages the central nervous system. The psychological results are mental retardation and emotional disturbance. We have no cure for PKU, but PKU can be detected in newborn children by blood or urine analysis. Children with PKU who are placed on diets low in phenylalanine within three to six weeks after birth develop normally. The children also receive protein supplements that compensate for the nutritional loss.

Huntington's chorea, the disease that afflicted folksinger Woodie Guthrie, is a fatal progressive degenerative disorder and a dominant trait. Physical symptoms include uncontrollable muscle movements. Psychological symptoms include personality change and loss of intellectual functioning. Because its onset is delayed until middle adulthood, many with the defect have borne children only to discover, years later, that they and their offspring will inevitably develop it.

Sickle-cell anemia and Tay-Sachs disease are caused by recessive genes. Sickle-cell anemia is most common among blacks and Hispanic Americans. Nearly one black in 10 and one Hispanic American in 20 is a carrier. In sickle-cell anemia, red blood cells take on a sickle shape and clump together, obstructing small blood vessels and decreasing the oxygen supply. Results can include jaundice, painful and swollen joints, pneumonia, and heart and kidney failure.

Down syndrome A chromosomal abnormality characterized by slanted eyelids and mental retardation and caused by an extra chromosome in the twenty-first pair.

Phenylketonuria A genetic abnormality in which phenylpyruvic acid builds up and leads to mental retardation.

Huntington's chorea A fatal genetic neurological disorder whose onset is in middle age.

Sickle-cell anemia A genetic disorder that impairs the blood's capacity to carry oxygen.

Tay-Sachs disease is a fatal degenerative disease of the central nervous system that mainly afflicts Jews of East European origin. About one in 25 U.S. Jews carries the recessive gene for the defect, so the chance that both members of a Jewish couple will carry the gene is about one in 625. Victims of Tay-Sachs disease gradually lose muscle control. They become blind and deaf, retarded and paralyzed, and die by the age of 5.

Some genetic defects, such as **hemophilia,** are carried on only the X sex chromosome. For this reason, they are called **sex-linked genetic abnormalities.** They also involve recessive genes. Females, each of whom contain two X sex chromosomes, are less likely than males to show sex-linked disorders because the disorders would have to be present in both of their sex chromosomes to be expressed. But sex-linked disorders are shown by the sons of female carriers, because the genetic instructions carried in their (single) X sex chromosomes are not canceled by opposing genetic instructions on their Y sex chromosomes.

Genetic Counseling and Prenatal Testing

In an effort to help parents avert predictable tragedies, **genetic counseling** is becoming widely used. In this procedure, information about a couple's ages and genetic backgrounds is compiled to determine whether their union may result in children with chromosomal or genetic problems. Some couples whose natural children would be at high risk elect to adopt.

Amniocentesis   Pregnant women may also confirm the presence of certain chromosomal and genetic abnormalities through **amniocentesis,** which is carried out about 14 to 15 weeks after conception (Figure 2.20). Fluid is withdrawn from the amniotic sac (also called the "bag of waters") containing the fetus. Sloughed-off fetal cells are then separated from amniotic fluid, grown in a culture, and examined microscopically.

Amniocentesis is commonly carried out with women who become pregnant past the age of 35 because the chances of Down syndrome increase dramatically as women and their partners approach or pass the age of 40. Amniocentesis can

What Is Genetic Counseling?   In genetic counseling, information about a couple's genetic backgrounds is examined to determine the possibility that their children may be genetically defective.

also detect the presence of sickle-cell anemia, Tay-Sachs disease, spina bifida, muscular dystrophy, and Rh incompatibility in the fetus.

Amniocentesis also permits parents to learn the sex of their unborn child through examination of the 23rd pair of chromosomes. But amniocentesis carries risks, and it would be unwise to have the procedure done solely for this purpose. If you were having an amniocentesis, would you want to know the sex of your unborn child, or would you prefer to wait?

Tay-Sachs disease A fatal genetic neurological disorder.

Hemophilia A gentic disorder in which blood does not clot properly.

Sex-linked genetic abnormalities Abnormalities due to genes found on the X sex chromosome, and thus more likely to be shown by male (who do not have an opposing gene) than female offspring.

Carriers Persons who carry and transmit the genes for a trait to future generations but who do not show the trait themselves.

Genetic counseling Counseling concerning the probability that a couple's children will have genetic abnormalities and what to do about it.

Amniocentesis A method for detecting the presence of genetic abnormalities in an unborn child by examining fluid drawn from the amniotic sac.

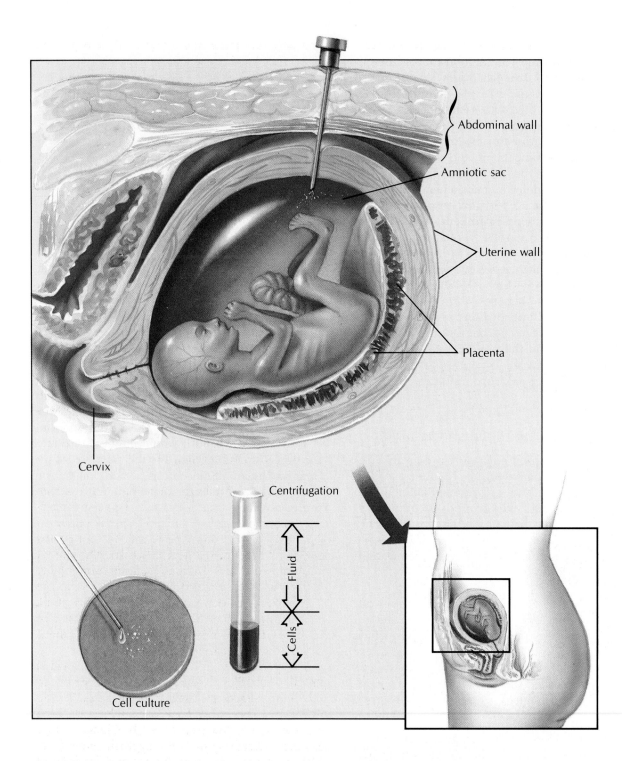

Abdominal wall

Amniotic sac

Uterine wall

Placenta

Cervix

Centrifugation

Fluid

Cells

Cell culture

FIGURE 2.20. What Is Amniocentesis?   This modern method for examining the chromosomes sloughed off by a fetus into amniotic fluid permits the prenatal identification of certain hereditary diseases. Amniocentesis also allows parents to learn the sex of their unborn child. Would you want to know?

(for example, ATTC rather than ATGC in a given segment of DNA) may cause inherited diseases such as sickle-cell anemia

Modifying the genetic codes of unborn children to prevent disease

Creating new wonder drugs from the materials that compose DNA

Some fear that increasing control of genetics will make possible future scenarios like that portrayed by Aldous Huxley in his still powerful 1932 novel *Brave New World*. Through a fictitious method called "Bokanovsky's Process," egg cells from parents who are identically suited for certain types of labor are made to "bud." From these buds up to 96 people with identical genetic makeups can be developed—filling whatever labor niches are required by society.

In the novel the director of a "hatchery" is leading a group of students on a tour. One student is foolish enough to question the advantage of Bokanovsky's Process:

"My good boy!" The Director wheeled sharply round on him. "Can't you see? Can't you see?" He raised a hand; his expression was solemn. "Bokanovsky's Process is one of the major instruments of social stability!"

Major instruments of social stability (wrote the student).

Standard men and women; in uniform batches. The whole of a small factory staffed with the products of a single Bokanovskied egg.

"Ninety-six identical twins working 96 identical machines!" The voice was almost tremulous with enthusiasm. "You really know where you are. For the first time in history." He quoted the planetary motto. "Community, Identity, Stability." Grand words. "If we could Bokanovskify indefinitely the whole problem would be solved."

Through Bokanovsky's Process we might be able to eliminate certain genetic disorders. We might even be able to lower the incidence of crime, aggression, and abnormal behaviors. But I ask those of you who think that all this might be a good idea to consider that from none of these "Bokanovskied" eggs would there emerge a Shakespeare, a Beethoven, or an Einstein. Perhaps we would avoid tyrants, but we would also be bereft of geniuses and individuals who might shape the world in ways we cannot foresee.

And those of you who think that genetic research ought to be stopped might consider that there is no such thing as bad knowledge—only bad use of knowledge.

TRUTH OR FICTION REVISITED

Some cells in your body stretch all the way down your back to your big toe. True. Some neurons span the length from your brain stem to your toes, whereas other neurons are only a few thousandths of an inch long.

We lose brain cells as we grow older. True. However, we have so many brain cells (neurons) that this loss probably has little or no influence on our abilities to learn, think, or remember.

Messages travel in the brain by means of electricity. True—up to a point. Messages (neural impulses) travel along the length of a neuron by means of an electrochemical process. However, messages are transmitted to other neurons by means of chemicals called neurotransmitters.

Our bodies produce natural pain killers that are more powerful than the narcotic morphine. True. They are called endorphins.

The human brain is larger than that of any other animal. False. Elephant and whale brains are larger, but our brains have a higher brain-to-body-weight ratio.

Many men who are paralyzed below the waist can still achieve erection and ejaculate. True. These sexual responses are reflexes that do not require input from the brain. But it is necessary that the appropriate section of the spine be intact.

Fear can give you indigestion. True. Fear stimulates (and is stimulated by) the sympathetic branch of the ANS, but digestion involves parasympathetic activity. These two branches of the ANS service many of the same organs and have largely opposing effects.

If a surgeon were to stimulate a certain part of your brain electrically, you might swear in court that someone had stroked your leg. True. Stimulation of areas of the sensory cortex leads to the perception of sensation in corresponding parts of the body.

A routine operation for a certain disorder involves splitting the brain down the middle. True. The disorder is epilepsy, and the operation involves severing the corpus callosum.

Rats will learn to do things that result in a "reward" of a burst of electricity in the brain. True. Electricity can apparently stimulate a so-called pleasure center in the hypothalamus of the rat.

Some people grow into "giants" because of "glands." True. The condition known as acromegaly is produced by an excess of growth hormone, which is secreted by the pituitary gland.

Athletes have used growth hormone and steroids to build up their muscle mass. True. Unfortunately, there are some harmful side effects.

With so many billions of people in the world, you are bound to have a "double" somewhere, even if you are not an identical twin. False. The number of possible combinations of genetic material is so vast that only identical twins can be "doubles," although some people, especially close relatives, may bear a resemblance to you.

If both parents have brown eyes, the children invariably have brown eyes. False. The parents may carry recessive genes for blue eyes, in which case the child has about a one-in-four chance of having blue eyes.

Blacks are at high risk for sickle-cell anemia. True. About one black in ten is a carrier of the disorder—as is about one Hispanic American in twenty.

You can learn the sex of your child several months before it is born. True. One method for doing so is amniocentesis.

We can "see" a fetus by bouncing sound waves off it in the womb. True. The sound waves used are ultrasound—higher in pitch than can be sensed by the human ear.

Inventors are applying for patents on new life forms. True. These life forms, mostly microscopic, are being created through genetic engineering.

Chapter Review

The nervous system contains billions of neurons and glial cells. Neurons transmit messages to other neurons by means of chemical substances called neurotransmitters, which travel across synapses. Glial cells nourish neurons and direct their growth. Neurons have a cell body, or soma; dendrites, which receive transmissions; and an axon, which extends trunklike from the cell body. Fatty, whitish myelin sheaths insulate, and facilitate conduction of messages along, many axons. Myelin is missing at the nodes of Ranvier. Sensory, or afferent, neurons transmit sensory messages to the central nervous system. Motor, or efferent, neurons conduct messages from the central nervous system that stimulate glands or cause muscles to contract.

Neural transmission is an electrochemical process. An electrical charge is conducted along an axon through a process that allows sodium ions into the cell and then pumps them out. The neuron has a resting potential of -70 millivolts, and an action potential of $+30$ to $+40$ millivolts.

Neurons fire according to an all-or-none principle. Neurons may fire hundreds of times per second. Firing is first followed by an absolute refractory period, during which neurons do not fire in response to further stimulation; then a relative refractory period, during which they will fire, but only in response to stronger-than-usual messages.

A synapse consists of an axon terminal from the transmitting neuron; a dendrite of a receiving neuron; and a small fluid-filled gap between them—the synaptic cleft. Excitatory synapses stimulate neurons to fire. Inhibitory neurons influence neurons in the direction of not firing.

Neurotransmitters are contained within synaptic vesicles in the knobs at the tips of the axon terminals. Each neurotransmitter can fit into a specific receptor site on the dendrite of the receiving neuron. Acetylcholine is the neurotransmitter that controls muscle contractions. Deficiencies of dopamine are linked to Parkinson's disease, and overutilization of dopamine is linked to schizophrenia. Deficiencies of norepinephrine are linked to depression. Deficiencies of serotonin are linked to anxiety, depression, and insomnia. Endorphins are the body's natural pain killers.

A nerve is a bundle of axons. The first major division of the nervous system is into the central and peripheral nervous systems. The brain and spinal cord make up the central nervous system. The peripheral nervous system is divided into the somatic and autonomic nervous systems. The somatic nervous system transmits sensory information about muscles, skin, and joints to the central nervous system and controls muscle activity from the central nervous system. The autonomic nervous system is subdivided into sympathetic and parasympathetic branches. The sympathetic division dominates in activities that expend the body's resources; the parasympathetic during processes that build the body's reserves, such as eating.

A spinal reflex may involve as few as two neurons: an afferent neuron and an efferent neuron. In the spinal cord, gray matter consists of small, nonmyelinated neurons that are involved in reflexes. White matter is composed of bundles of longer, myelinated axons that carry messages back and forth to and from the brain.

The hindbrain includes the medulla, which is vital in heartbeat, blood pressure, and respiration; the pons, which transmits information concerning movement and is also involved in attention and respiration; and the cerebullum, which is involved in maintaining balance and controlling motor behavior. The reticular activating system is vital in the functions of attention, sleep, and arousal.

Important structures of the forebrain include the thalamus, hypothalamus, limbic system, basal ganglia, and cerebrum. The thalamus serves as a relay station for sensory stimulation. The hypothalamus is vital in the control of body temperature, motivation, and emotion. The limbic system is involved in memory and in the drives of hunger, sex, and aggression. The basal ganglia are involved in posture and muscle coordination. The surface of the cerebrum is the cerebral cortex. The hemispheres of the cortex are connected by the corpus callosum.

The cerebral cortex is divided into the frontal, parietal, temporal, and occipital lobes. The visual cortex is in the occipital lobe; the auditory cortex in the temporal lobe. The sensory cortex lies in the parietal lobe; the motor cortex in the frontal lobe. Associative areas of the cortex are involved in learning, thought, memory, and language. Language areas of the cortex lie near the intersection of the frontal, temporal, and parietal lobes in the dominant hemisphere. The left hemisphere of the cortex seems to play a special role in understanding and producing language.

The endocrine system consists of ductless glands that secrete hormones, chemicals released directly into the bloodstream. Much hormonal action helps the body maintain steady states. The pituitary gland regulates the activities of many other glands. The pituitary secretes growth hormone; prolactin; antidiuretic hormone; oxytocin; and ACTH, which causes the adrenal cortex to release a number of hormones, including cortisol, which helps the body respond to stress.

The pancreas secretes insulin, which enables the body to metabolize sugar. The thyroid hormone thyroxin affects the body's metabolism. The adrenal cortex produces steroids; the adrenal medulla secretes adrenalin (also called epinephrine), which increases the metabolic rate and is involved in general emotional arousal. Sex hormones are responsible for prenatal sexual differentiation, and female sex hormones regulate the menstrual cycle.

Genes are the basic building blocks of heredity. Genes consist of DNA. A large number of genes make up each chromosome. People normally have 46 chromosomes, receiving 23 from the father and 23 from the mother. In mitosis, strands of DNA acid "unzip" and are rebuilt in each new cell. Sperm and ova are produced through reduction division, or meiosis.

Identical twins are formed from one zygote; fraternal twins from two. When dominant traits combine with recessive traits, the dominant traits are shown. Recessive traits are shown only if a recessive gene from one parent combines with a recessive gene from the other.

Down syndrome is caused by an extra chromosome on the 21st pair and is more common among children of older parents. "Supermale" syndrome, Klinefelter's syndrome, and Turner's syndrome are all caused by abnormal numbers of sex chromosomes. The genetic disorder phenylke-tonuria (PKU) leads to mental retardation, and is controlled by diet. Other genetic disorders include Huntington's chorea, sickle-cell anemia, Tay-Sachs disease, and hemophilia. Methods such as amniocentesis and ultra-sound permit parents to learn whether their children will have certain genetic abnormalities before they are born.

Experiments show that animals can be selectively bred to heighten the influence of many traits. Rats, for example, can be selectively bred for maze-learning ability.

In the future, genetic engineering may lead to the development of new vaccines; new methods of prenatal screening; and the direct modifi-cation of the genetic codes of unborn children, so that inherited diseases are prevented.

Exercises

Parts of the Brain

Directions: *Fill in the names of the parts of the brain on the lines. Check your answers against Figure 2.7 on page 56.*

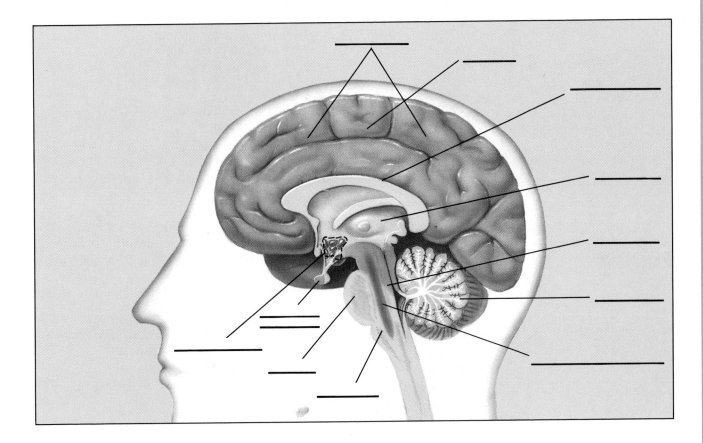

Major Glands of the Endocrine System

Directions: *Fill in the names of the glands of the endocrine system. Can you list the important hormones secreted by each gland and explain their functions? Check your answers against Figure 2.15 on page 71.*

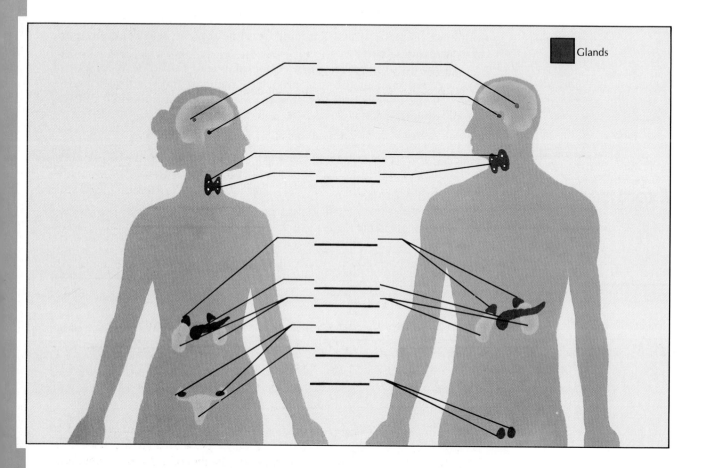

Glands

Posttest

Directions: *For each of the following, select the choice that best answers the question or completes the sentence.*

1. Neurons

   (a) transmit neural impulses, **(b)** support and nourish glial cells, **(c)** manufacture myelin, **(d)** are one kind of neurotransmitter.

2. The _____ of the neuron uses oxygen to create energy to carry out the work of the cell.

   (a) axon, **(b)** dendrite, **(c)** soma, **(d)** myelin.

3. Axons end in smaller, branching structures called

(a) synapses, (b) dendrites, (c) terminals, (d) myelin sheaths.

4. When the neuron is in a resting state, _____ ions are more common inside than in the body fluid outside the neuron.

   (a) sodium, (b) chlorine, (c) fluorine, (d) radon.

5. Motor neurons are otherwise known as

   (a) afferent neurons, (b) efferent neurons, (c) glial cells, (d) reflex arcs.

6. The small fluid-filled gap between neurons, across which neurotransmitters travel, is called the

   (a) synapse, (b) axon terminal, (c) dendrite, (d) synaptic cleft.

7. Which of the following is a neuropeptide?

   (a) Adrenalin, (b) Dopamine, (c) Myelin, (d) Endorphin.

8. A person you know begins to show symptoms such as hallucinations, delusions, and jumbling or confusion of thoughts. According to the research reported in the text, it is most likely that these symptoms are linked to _____ of dopamine.

   (a) excess production, (b) overutilization, (c) scarcity, (d) cyclical secretion.

9. In the brain and spinal cord, the cell bodies of neurons are gathered into clumps called

   (a) soma, (b) ganglia, (c) nuclei, (d) gray matter.

10. Which of the following structures is found in the hindbrain?

    (a) Pons, (b) Hypothalamus, (c) Limbic system, (d) Basal ganglia.

11. Destruction of an area of the limbic system called the _____ leads monkeys and other mammals to show docile behavior.

    (a) septum, (b) fovea, (c) amygdala, (d) guanine.

12. An elderly person you know is showing awkward movements and a shuffling gait. According to information presented in the text, this behavior pattern is most likely to reflect the loss of a group of neurons that regulate the

    (a) cerebellum, (b) motor cortex, (c) medulla, (d) basal ganglia.

13. When we are afraid, the _____ division of the ANS accelerates the heart rate.

    (a) somatic, (b) peripheral, (c) sympathetic, (d) parasympathetic.

14. The motor cortex lies in the _____ lobe.

    (a) frontal, (b) parietal, (c) temporal, (d) occipital.

15. A student participating in psychological research reports visual sensations although her eyes are closed and covered with dark material. She is probably receiving direct artificial stimulation of the _____ lobe.

    (a) frontal, (b) parietal, (c) temporal, (d) occipital.

16. The nondominant hemisphere of the cerebral cortex is usually relatively more involved with

    (a) understanding syntax, (b) decoding visual information, (c) problem solving, (d) associating written words with their sounds.

17. Concerning the left brain–right brain controversy, it is most accurate to note that

    (a) the sounds of speech evoke a response in the dominant hemisphere only, (b) the sounds of speech evoke a response in the nondominant hemisphere only, (c) creativity and intuition are confined to the nondominant hemisphere, (d) the hemispheres can function independently, but they function better in normal combined usage.

18. If you wanted to be able to reward a rat with a burst of electricity for engaging in a certain behavior, it would probably be most useful to implant the electrode into a section of the rat's

    (a) reticular activating system, (b) parietal lobe, (c) hypothalamus, (d) spinal cord.

19. Corticotropin-releasing hormone is produced by the

    (a) hypothalamus, (b) pituitary gland, (c) adrenal cortex, (d) adrenal medulla.

20. Glucagon is released by the

    (a) posterior lobe of the pituitary gland, (b) pancreas, (c) adrenal cortex, (d) adrenal medulla.

21. According to the text, _____ promotes growth of female reproductive tissues and maintains pregnancy.

    (a) estrogen, (b) prolactin, (c) growth hormone, (d) progesterone.

22. Which of the following is *not* known to contribute to the regulation of levels of testosterone?

    (a) Hypothalamus, (b) Pancreas, (c) Pituitary gland, (d) Testes.

23. In the rebuilding of strands of DNA, cytosine combines with

    (a) adenine, (b) cytosine, (c) guanine, (d) thymine.

24. Which of the following disorders is most likely to afflict blacks and Hispanic Americans?

    (a) Phenylketonuria, (b) Sickle-cell anemia, (c) Tay-Sachs disease, (d) Huntington's chorea.

Answers to Posttest

1. A	7. D	13. C	19. A
2. C	8. B	14. A	20. B
3. C	9. C	15. D	21. D
4. B	10. A	16. B	22. B
5. B	11. C	17. D	23. C
6. D	12. D	18. C	24. B

SENSATION AND PERCEPTION

OUTLINE

PRETEST: TRUTH OR FICTION?
BASIC CONCEPTS IN SENSATION
  AND PERCEPTION
  Absolute Threshold
  Difference Threshold
  Signal-Detection Theory
  Sensory Adaptation
VISION
  Light
  The Eye: Our Living Camera
COLOR VISION
  Psychological Dimensions of Color: Hue, Brightness,
    and Saturation
  Complementary versus Analogous Colors
  Theories of Color Vision
  Color Blindness
VISUAL PERCEPTION
  Perceptual Organization
  Perception of Movement
  Depth Perception
  Perceptual Constancies

  Visual Illusions
HEARING
  Pitch and Loudness
  The Ear
  Locating Sounds
  Perception of Loudness and Pitch
  Deafness
SMELL
  Some Recent Studies in Olfaction: "The Nose
    Knows"
TASTE
THE SKIN SENSES
  Touch and Pressure
  Temperature
  Pain
KINESTHESIS
THE VESTIBULAR SENSE
TRUTH OR FICTION REVISITED
CHAPTER REVIEW
EXERCISES
POSTTEST

PRETEST: TRUTH OR FICTION?

Sometimes we don't hear things because we don't want to hear them.

White sunlight is actually composed of all the colors of the rainbow.

On a clear, dark night you could probably see the light from a single candle burning 25 miles away.

If our eyes were sensitive to lights of slightly longer wavelengths, warmblooded animals would glow in the dark.

We all have blind spots in our eyes.

As we approach late adulthood, we become likely to need reading glasses, even if our visual acuity has been perfect at younger ages.

When we mix blue and yellow light, we get green light.

"Motion pictures" do not move at all.

We need two eyes to perceive depth.

The advertising slogan for the film *Alien* was accurate: "In space, no one can hear you scream."

A $500 machine-made violin will produce the same musical notes as a $200,000 Stradivarius.

People who listen to loud rock music are likely to suffer hearing loss.

The menstrual cycles of women who live together tend to become synchronized.

Onions and apples have the same taste.

The elderly find their food less flavorful than the young because of loss in the sense of taste.

We have no sensory receptors for perceiving hotness.

Rubbing or scratching a painful toe can help provide relief.

Five thousand years ago in China, give or take a day or two, an arrow was shot into the air. Where did it land? Ancient records tell us precisely where: in the hand of a fierce warrior and master of the martial arts.

As the story was told to me, the warrior had grown so fierce because of a chronic toothache. Incessant pain had ruined his disposition.

On one fateful day our hero watched as invading hordes assembled on surrounding hills. His troops were trembling, and he raised his arms in wild gestures in an effort to boost their morale in the face of the invaders' superior numbers. A slender wooden shaft lifted into the air from a nearby rise, arced, and then descended—right into the warrior's palm. His troops cringed and muttered among themselves, but our hero said nothing. Although he saw the arrow through his palm, he did not scream. He did not run. He did not even complain.

He was astounded. His toothache had vanished. His entire jaw was numb.

Meanwhile the invaders looked on—horrified. They, too, muttered among themselves. What sort of warrior could look upon an arrow through his hand with such indifference? Even with a growing smile? If this was the caliber of warrior in this village, they'd be better off traveling west and looking for a brawl in ancient Sumer or in Egypt. They sounded the retreat and withdrew.

Our warrior received a hero's welcome back in town. A physician offered to remove the arrow without a fee—a tribute to bravery. But our warrior would have none of it. The arrow had done wonders for his toothache, and he would permit no meddling. He had discovered already that if the pain threatened to return, he need only twirl the arrow and it would recede once more.

Acupuncture The ancient Chinese practice of piercing parts of the body with needles to deaden pain and treat illness.

Hypertension High blood pressure.

Sensation The stimulation of sensory receptors and the transmission of sensory information to the central nervous system.

Perception The process by which sensations are organized into an inner representation of the world.

But things were not so rosy on the home front. His wife was thrilled to find him jovial once more, but the arrow put a crimp in romance. When he put his arm around her, she was in dire danger of being stabbed. Finally she gave him an ultimatum: her or the arrow.

Placed in deep conflict, our warrior consulted a psychologist, who then huddled with the physician and the village elders. After much to-do, they asked the warrior to participate in an experiment. They would remove the arrow and replace it with a pin that the warrior could twirl as needed. If the pin didn't do the trick, they could always fall back on the arrow, so to speak.

To his wife's relief, the pin worked. And here, in ancient China, lay the origins of the art of **acupuncture**—the use of needles to relieve pain and treat a variety of ills ranging from **hypertension** to some forms of blindness.

I confess that this tale is not entirely accurate. To my knowledge, there were no psychologists in ancient China. (Their loss.) Moreover, the part about the warrior's wife is fictitious. But it is claimed that acupuncture, as a means for dealing with pain, originated in ancient China when a soldier was, in fact, wounded in a hand by an arrow and discovered that a chronic toothache had disappeared. The Chinese, historians claim, then set out to "map" the body by sticking pins here and there to learn how they influenced the perception of pain.

Control of pain is just one of the many issues that interest psychologists who study the closely related concepts of sensation and perception. **Sensation** is the stimulation of sensory receptors and the transmission of sensory information to the central nervous system (the spinal cord or brain). Sensory receptors are located in sensory organs like the eyes and ears and, as we shall see, in the skin and elsewhere in the body. The stimulation of the senses is mechanical; it results from sources of energy like light and sound or from the presence of chemicals, as in smell and taste.

Perception is not mechanical at all. Perception is the process by which sensations are organized and interpreted, forming an inner representation of the world. Perception involves much more than sensation. It involves learning and expectations and the ways in which we organize incoming information about the world. Perception is an active process through which we make sense of sensory stimulation. A human shape and a 12-inch ruler may stimulate paths of equal length among the sensory receptors in our eyes. But whether we interpret the human shape to be a foot-long doll or a full-grown person 15 to 20 feet away is a matter of perception.

In this chapter you will see that your personal map of reality—your ticket of admission to a world of changing sights, sounds, and other sources of sensory input—depends largely on the "five senses" of vision, hearing, smell, taste, and touch. We shall see, however, that touch is just one of several "skin senses," which also include pressure, warmth, cold, and pain. There are also other senses that alert you to your own body position without your having literally to watch every step you take. We shall explore the nature of each of these senses, and we shall find that highly similar sensations may lead to quite different perceptions in different people—or among the same people in different situations.

First let us explore some of the ways in which psychologists gather information about the processes of sensation and perception.

BASIC CONCEPTS IN SENSATION AND PERCEPTION

Before we begin our journey through the senses, let us consider a number of concepts that apply to all the senses: absolute threshold, difference threshold, signal-detection theory, and sensory adaptation. In doing so we shall see why we might be able to dim the lights gradually to near darkness, without people becoming aware of our mischief. We shall also see why we might grow unaware of the most savory aromas of delightful dinners.

Absolute Threshold

The weakest amount of a stimulus that can be told apart from no stimulus at all is called the **absolute threshold** for that stimulus. For example, the amount of physical energy required to activate the

visual sensory system is the absolute threshold for light. Beneath this threshold, detection of light is impossible (Haber & Hershenson, 1980).

Psychophysicists experiment to determine the absolute thresholds of the senses by presenting stimuli of progressively greater intensity. In the **method of constant stimuli,** researchers use sets of stimuli with magnitudes close to the expected threshold. The order of the stimuli is randomized. Subjects are asked to say yes if they detect a stimulus and no if they do not. Then the stimuli are repeatedly presented to the subjects. A subject's absolute threshold for the stimulus is the lowest magnitude of the stimulus that he or she reports detecting 50 percent of the time. Weaker stimuli may be detected, but less than 50 percent of the time. Stronger stimuli, of course, will be detected more than 50 percent of the time.

The relationship between the intensity of a stimulus (a physical event) and its perception (a psychological event) is **psychophysical.** That is, it bridges psychological and physical events.

As you can see in Table 3.1, absolute thresholds have been determined for the sense of vision, hearing, taste, smell, and touch. Naturally, there are individual differences in absolute thresholds. Some people, that is, are more sensitive to sensory stimuli than others. The same person may also differ somewhat in sensitivity to sensory stimuli from day to day or from occasion to occasion. In the section on signal-detection theory, we shall see that sensitivity reflects psychological as well as physical and biological variables.

If the absolute thresholds for the human senses differed significantly, our daily experiences would be unrecognizable. Our ears are particularly

---

Absolute threshold The minimal amount of energy that can produce a sensation.

Psychophysicist A person who studies the relationships between physical stimuli, like light or sound, and their perception.

Method of constant stimuli A psychophysical method for determining thresholds in which the researcher presents stimuli of various magnitudes and asks the subject to report detection.

Psychophysical Bridging the gap between the physical and psychological worlds.

Table 3.1   Absolute Detection Thresholds and Other Characteristics of Our Sensory Systems

SENSE	STIMULUS	RECEPTORS	ABSOLUTE THRESHOLD
Vision	Electromagnetic energy	Rods and cones in the retina	A candle flame viewed from a distance of about 30 miles on a clear, dark night
Hearing	Sound pressure waves	Hair cells on the basilar membrane of the inner ear	The ticking of a watch from about 20 feet away in a quiet room
Taste	Chemical substances dissolved in saliva	Taste buds on the tongue	About one teaspoon of sugar dissolved in two gallons of water (1 part in 2,000)
Smell	Chemical substances in the air	Receptor cells in the upper nasal cavity (the nose)	About one drop of perfume diffused throughout a small house (1 part in 500 million)
Touch	Mechanical displacement or pressure on the skin	Nerve endings located in the skin	The wing of a fly falling on a cheek from a distance of about 0.40 inch

Source: Adapted from Galanter (1962).

sensitive, especially to sounds low in **pitch.** If they were any more sensitive, we might hear the collisions among molecules of air. If our eyes were sensitive to lights of slightly longer wavelengths, we would perceive infrared light waves. As a result, animals who are warmblooded and thus give off heat—including our mates—would literally glow in the dark.

Difference Threshold

How much of a difference in intensity between two lights is required before you will detect one as being brighter than the other? The minimum required difference in the magnitude of two stimuli to tell them apart is their **difference threshold.** As

---

Pitch The highness or lowness of a sound, as determined by the frequency of the sound waves.

Difference threshold The minimal difference in intensity required between two sources of energy so that they will be perceived as different.

Weber's constant The fraction of the intensity by which a source of physical energy must be increased or decreased so that a difference in intensity will be perceived.

Just noticeable difference The minimal amount by which a source of energy must be increased or decreased so that a difference in intensity will be perceived.

---

is the case with the absolute threshold, psychologists have agreed to the criterion of a difference in magnitudes that can be detected 50 percent of the time.

Psychophysicist Ernst Weber discovered through laboratory research that the difference threshold for perceiving differences in the intensity of light is about 2 percent (actually closer to one-sixtieth) of their intensity. This fraction, one-sixtieth, is known as **Weber's constant** for light. It has also been called the **just noticeable difference** (jnd) for light, indicating that people can perceive a difference in intensity 50 percent of the time when the brightness of a light is increased or decreased by one-sixtieth. Remarkably, Weber's constant (1/60) for light holds whether we are comparing two quite bright or rather dull lights. However, it becomes inaccurate when we compare extremely bright or extremely dull lights.

As you can see in Table 3.2, Weber's research in psychophysics touched on many senses. He derived difference thresholds for different types of sensory stimulation.

A little math will show you the practical importance of these jnd's. Consider weightlifting. Weber's constant for noticing differences in lifted weight is one-fifty-third. Round it off to one-fiftieth. That means that one would probably have to increase the weight on a 100-pound barbell by about two pounds before the lifter would notice the difference. Now think of the one-pound dumbbells called Heavy Hands. Increasing the weight of each dumbbell by two pounds would be readily apparent to almost anyone because the increase would be threefold, not a small fraction. Yet the increase is still "only" two pounds. Return to our power lifter. When he is pressing 400 pounds, a two-pound difference is less likely to be noticeable than when he is pressing 100 pounds. This is because our constant two pounds has become a difference of only one-two hundredth.

The same principle holds for the other senses: Small changes are more apt to be noticed when we begin our comparisons with small stimuli. Some dieting programs suggest that dieters reduce calorie intake by "imperceptible" amounts on a daily or weekly basis. They eventually reach sharply reduced calorie-intake goals, but they may not feel so deprived during the reduction process.

Signal-Detection Theory

Our discussion so far has been rather "inhuman." We have written about perception of sensory stimuli as if we are simply switched on by certain amounts of external stimulation. This is not fully accurate. Although people are sensory instruments, they are influenced by complex patterns of psychological stimulation as well as external changes. **Signal-detection theory** has arisen as a response to the human elements in sensation and perception.

According to signal-detection theory, several factors determine whether people will perceive sensory stimuli (signals) or a difference between two signals. The intensity of the signal itself is just one factor. Another is the degree to which it can be distinguished from background **noise.** In other words, it is easier to hear a speech in a quiet room than in one where people are clinking silverware and glasses and engaging in competing conversations. The quality of the biological sensory system of the person is still another factor. Here we are concerned with the sharpness or acuteness of the individual's sensory system. We consider whether sensory capacity is fully developed or diminished because of illness or advanced years.

But signal-detection theory also considers the roles of psychological factors such as motivation, expectations, and learning. For example, the place in which you are reading this book may be abuzz with signals. If you are outside, perhaps there is a breeze against your face. Perhaps the shadows of passing clouds darken the scene now and then. If you are inside, perhaps there are the occasional clanks and hums of a heating system. Perhaps the odors of dinner are hanging in the air, or the voices from a TV set suggest a crowd in another room. Yet you are focusing your attention on this page (I hope), and so the other signals recede into the backdrop of your consciousness. Thus, one psychological factor in signal detection is the focusing or narrowing of attention to signals the person deems important. Because of training, an artist might notice the use of line or subtle colors that would go undetected by a lay person looking at the same painting. A book designer may notice subtle differences between typefaces among books, whereas a lay person would neither be motivated nor trained to attend to these differences.

And so, a combination of physical, biological, and psychological factors determine whether "signals" will be perceived.

Sensory Adaptation

There is a saying that the only thing that remains constant is change. It happens that our sensory

Table 3.2 **Weber's Constant for Various Sensory Discriminations**

SENSE	TYPE OF DISCRIMINATION	WEBER'S CONSTANT
Vision	Brightness of a light	1/60
Hearing	Pitch (frequency) of a tone	1/333
	Loudness of a tone	1/10
Taste	Difference in saltiness	1/5
Smell	Amount of rubber smell	1/10
Touch	Pressure on the skin surface	1/7
	Deep pressure	1/77
	Difference in lifted weights	1/53

Signal-detection theory The view that the perception of sensory stimuli involves the interaction of physical, biological, and psychological factors.

Noise (1) A combination of dissonant sounds. (2) Unwanted signals that interfere with perception of the signal being communicated.

systems are admirably suited to a changing environment. **Sensory adaptation** refers to the processes by which we become more sensitive to stimuli of low magnitude and less sensitive to stimuli relatively constant in magnitude.

Most of us are familiar with the process by which the visual sense adapts to lower intensities of light. When we first walk into a darkened movie theater we see little but the images on the screen. But as the minutes go on, we become increasingly sensitive to the faces of those around us and the inner features of the theater. The process of becoming more sensitive to stimulation is referred to as **sensitization,** or positive adaptation.

On the other hand, we become less sensitive to ongoing stimulation. Sources of light appear to grow dimmer as we adapt to them. In fact, if you were able to keep an image completely stable on the retinas of your eyes—which is virtually impossible to accomplish without a still image and stabilizing equipment—the image would fade within a few seconds and be very difficult to see. Similarly, at the beach we soon become desensitized to the lapping of the waves. When we live in the city, we become desensitized to traffic sounds except for the occasional backfire or accident. As you may have noticed from experiences with freshly painted rooms, disagreeable odors fade quite rapidly. The process of becoming less sensitive to stimulation is referred to as **desensitization,** or negative adaptation.

Sensory adaptation The processes by which organisms become more sensitive to stimuli that are low in magnitude and less sensitive to stimuli that are constant or ongoing in magnitude.

Sensitization The type of sensory adaptation in which we become more sensitive to stimuli that are low in magnitude. Also called *positive adaptation*.

Desensitization The type of sensory adaptation in which we become less sensitive to constant stimuli. Also called *negative adaptation*.

Visual capture The tendency of vision to dominate the other senses.

Light The part of the electromagnetic spectrum that stimulates the eye and produces visual sensations.

Visible light See *light*.

Prism A transparent triangular solid that breaks down visible light into the colors of the spectrum.

Let us now examine how each of the human sensory systems perceives signals from the outer (and inner) environments.

VISION

Our eyes are said to be our "windows on the world." We consider information from vision more essential than that from hearing, smell, taste, and touch. Studies in **visual capture** have shown, for example, that when we perceive a square object through lenses that distort it into a rectangle, we report the object to be a rectangle even when we can feel it with our hands (Rock & Victor, 1964). Because vision is our dominant sense, we consider blindness our most debilitating sensory loss. An understanding of vision requires discussion of the nature of light and of the master of the sensory organs, the eye.

Light

According to the Bible, in the beginning the **light** was set apart from the dark. The light was good, and the potential for evil lay in darkness. In almost all cultures light is a symbol of goodness and knowledge. We describe capable people as being "bright" or "brilliant." If we are not being complimentary, we label them as "dull." People who aren't "in the know" are said to be "in the dark." Just what is this stuff called light?

Visible light is the stuff that triggers visual sensations. Visible light is just one small part of a spectrum of electromagnetic energy (see Figure 3.1) that is described in terms of wavelengths. These wavelengths vary from those of cosmic rays, which are only a few trillionths of an inch long, to some radio waves that extend for many miles. Radar, microwaves, and X-rays are also forms of electromagnetic energy.

You have probably seen rainbows or light broken down into several colors as it filtered through your windows. Sir Isaac Newton, the British scientist, discovered that sunlight could be broken down into different colors by means of a triangular solid of glass called a **prism** (Figure 3.1). When I took introductory psychology, I was taught that I could remember the colors of the spectrum, from

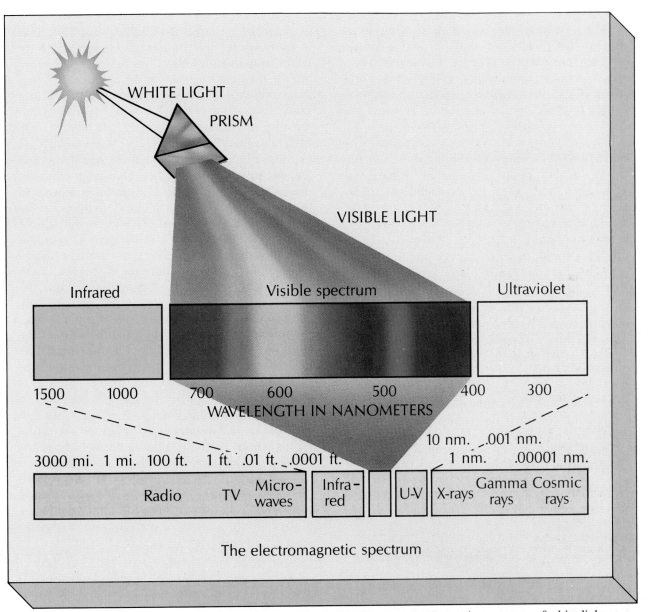

FIGURE 3.1. What Is the Visible Spectrum? By passing a source of white light, such as sunlight, through a prism, we break it down into the colors of the visible spectrum. The visible spectrum is just one part—and a narrow part indeed—of the electromagnetic spectrum. The electromagnetic spectrum also includes radio waves, microwaves, X-rays, cosmic rays, and many others. Different forms of electromagnetic energy have different wavelengths, which vary from a few trillionths of a meter to thousands of miles. Visible light varies in wavelength from about 400 to 700 nanometers. What is a nanometer? One *billionth* of a meter. (A meter = 39.37 inches.)

longest to shortest wavelengths, by using the mnemonic device *Mr. Roy G. Biv* (red, orange, yellow, green, blue, indigo, violet). I must have been a backward student because I found it easier to recall them in reverse order, using the meaningless acronym *vibgyor*.

The wavelength of visible light determines its color, or **hue.** The wavelength for red is longer than that for orange, and so on through the spectrum. Waves also have height, or **amplitude.** Light sources of greater amplitude are seen as brighter, or more intense.

The Eye: Our Living Camera

Consider that magnificent invention, the camera, which records visual experiences. In the camera, light enters an opening and is focused onto a sensitive surface, or film. Chemical reactions then take place on this surface that create a lasting impression of the image that entered the camera.

The eye—our living camera—is no less remarkable. Consider the major parts of the eye (Figure 3.2). As with a film or television camera, light enters through a narrow opening and is projected onto a sensitive surface. Light first passes through the transparent **cornea,** which covers the front of the surface of the eye. (The so-called white of the eye is composed of a hard protective tissue and is called the *sclera.*) The amount of light that passes through the cornea is determined by the size of the opening of the muscle called the **iris,** which is also the colored part of the eye. The opening in the iris is called the **pupil.** Pupil size adjusts automatically to the amount of light; you do not have to try purposefully to open the eye farther to see better under conditions of low lighting. The more intense the light, the smaller the opening. We similarly adjust the amount of light allowed into a camera according to its brightness. Pupil size is also sensitive to emotional response, as in being "wide-eyed with fear."

Once light passes through the iris, it encounters the **lens.** The lens adjusts or accommodates to the image by changing its thickness. Changes in thickness permit projection of a clear image of the object onto the retina—that is, they focus the light according to the distance of the object. If you hold a finger at arm's length, then slowly bring it toward your nose, you will feel tension in the eye as the thickness of the lens accommodates to keep the retinal image in focus (Haber & Hershenson, 1980). When people "squint" to bring an object into focus, they are adjusting the thickness of the lens. The lens in a camera does not accommodate to the distance of objects. Instead, to focus the light that is projected onto the film, the camera lens is moved farther away from or closer to the film.

The **retina** is like the film or image surface of the camera. But instead of being composed of film that is sensitive to light (photosensitive), the retina consists of photosensitive cells, or **photoreceptors,** called *rods* and *cones.* The retina (Figure 3.3) contains several layers of cells: the rods and cones, **bipolar cells,** and **ganglion cells.** All these cells are

---

Hue The color of light, as determined by its wavelength.

Amplitude Height

Cornea Transparent tissue forming the outer surface of the eyeball.

Iris A muscular membrane whose dilation regulates the amount of light that enters the eye.

Pupil The apparently black opening in the center of the iris, through which light enters the eye.

Lens A transparent body behind the iris that focuses an image on the retina.

Retina The area of the inner surface of the eye that contains rods and cones.

Photoreceptors Cells that respond to light.

Bipolar cells Neurons that conduct neural impulses from rods and cones to ganglion cells.

Ganglion cells Neurons whose axons form the optic nerve.

FIGURE 3.2. How Are the Human Eye and a Camera Alike?   In both the eye and a camera, light enters through a narrow opening and is projected onto a sensitive surface. In the eye, the photosensitive surface is the retina, and information about the changing images on the retina is transmitted to the brain. In a camera, the photosensitive surface is usually film, which captures a single image.

FIGURE 3.3 What Are the Parts of the Retina? After light travels through the vitreous humor of the eye, it moves through ganglion neurons and bipolar neurons to the photosensitive rods and cones. These photoreceptors then transmit sensory input back through the bipolar neurons to the ganglion neurons. The axons of the ganglion neurons form the optic nerve, which transmits sensory stimulation through the brain to the visual cortex of the occipital lobe.

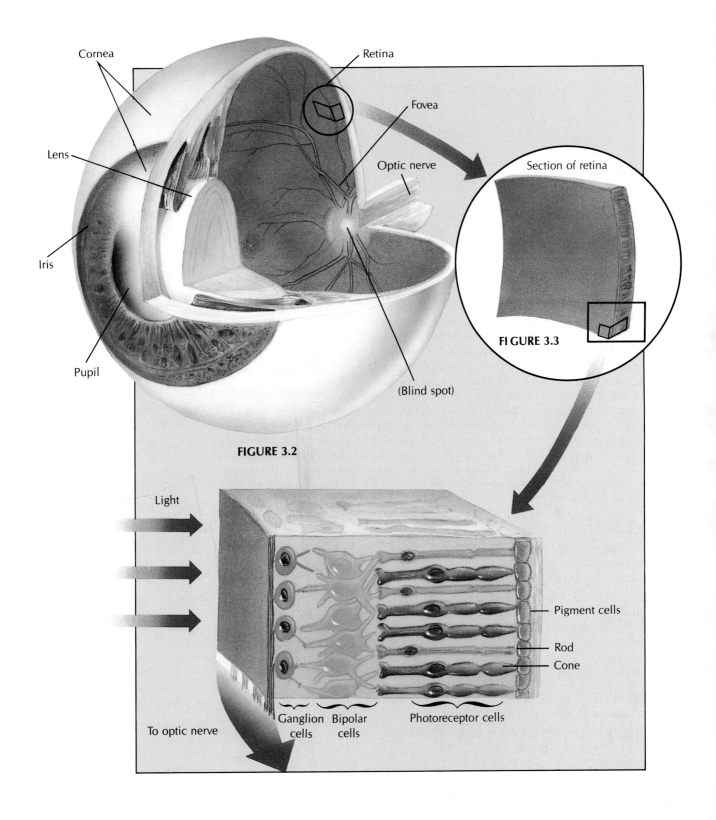

Cornea

Retina

Lens

Fovea

Iris

Optic nerve

Pupil

(Blind spot)

Section of retina

FIGURE 3.3

FIGURE 3.2

Light

Pigment cells

Rod

Cone

To optic nerve

Ganglion cells

Bipolar cells

Photoreceptor cells

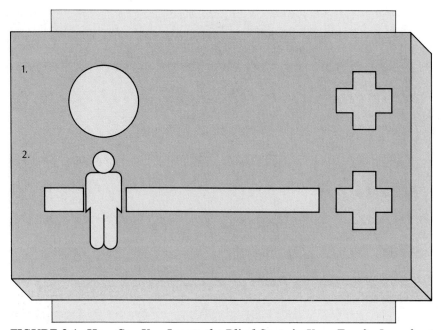

FIGURE 3.4. How Can You Locate the Blind Spots in Your Eyes?   In order to try a "disappearing act," first look at drawing 1. Close your right eye. Then move the book back and forth about one foot from your left eye while you stare at the plus sign. You will notice the circle disappear. When the circle disappears it is being projected onto the blind spot of your retina, the point at which the axons of ganglion neurons collect to form the optic nerve. Then close your left eye. Stare at the circle with your right eye and move the book back and forth. When the plus sign disappears, it is being projected onto the blind spot of your right eye. Now look at drawing 2. You can make this figure disappear and "see" the black line continue through the spot where it was by closing your right eye and staring at the plus sign with your left eye. When this figure is projected onto your blind spot, your brain "fills in" the line, which is one reason that we're not usually aware that we have blind spots.

neurons. Light travels past the ganglion cells and bipolar cells and stimulates the rods and cones. The rods and cones then send neural messages through the bipolar cells to the ganglion cells. The axons of the 1 million or so ganglion cells in our retinae form the **optic nerve.** The optic nerve conducts sensory input to the brain, where it is relayed to the visual area of the occipital lobe. Other neu-

rons in the retina make sideways connections at a level near the receptor cells and at another level near the ganglion cells. As a result of these lateral connections, many rods and cones funnel visual information into one bipolar cell, and many bipolar cells funnel information to one ganglion cell. Receptors outnumber ganglion cells by more than 100 to one.

The **fovea** is the most sensitive area of the retina (see Figure 3.2). Receptors there are more densely packed. The **blind spot,** by contrast, is insensitive to visual stimulation. The blind spot is the part of the retina where the axons of the ganglion cells congregate to form the optic nerve (Figure 3.4).

Optic nerve The nerve that transmits sensory information from the eye to the brain.

Fovea A rodless area near the center of the retina where vision is most acute.

Blind spot The area of the retina where axons from ganglion cells meet to form the optic nerve.

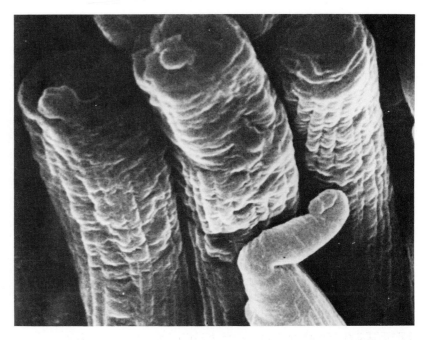

FIGURE 3.5. A Much (Much!) Enlarged Photograph of Several Rods and a Cone. Cones are usually upright fellows. However, the cone at the bottom right of this photo has been bent by the photographic process. You have more than 100 million rods and 6 million cones distributed across the retina of each eye. Only cones provide sensations of color. The fovea of the eye is populated by cones only, which are then distributed more sparsely as you work forward toward the lens. Rods, by contrast, are absent at the fovea and become more densely packed as you work forward.

Rods and Cones   **Rods** and **cones** are the photoreceptors in the retina (Figure 3.5). Over 100 million rods and 6 million cones are distributed across the retina. The fovea contains cones only. Cones then become more sparsely distributed as you work forward from the fovea toward the lens. Rods, by contrast, are absent at the fovea but distributed more densely as you approach the lens.

Rods are sensitive to the intensity of light only. They allow us to see in "black and white." Cones provide color vision. If you are a camera buff, you know that under conditions of extreme low lighting, it is possible to photograph a clearer image with black-and-white film than with color film. Rods, it happens, are also more sensitive than cones to light. Therefore, as the illumination grows dim, as during the evening and nighttime hours, objects appear to lose their color well before their outlines fade from view.

Light Adaptation   Have you ever entered a movie theater on a bright afternoon and had to feel your way to a seat by holding onto the backs of the chairs near the aisle? You may have thought at first that the theater was too dark. But after several minutes you were able to see other people clearly, even in the darkest recesses of the theater.

Adjusting to lower lighting is called **dark adaptation.**

Figure 3.6 shows the amount of light needed for detection as a function of the amount of time spent in the dark. The cones and rods adapt at different rates. The cones, which permit perception of color, reach their maximum adaptation to darkness in about ten minutes. The rods, which allow perception of light and dark only, are more sensitive and continue to adapt to darkness for up to about 45 minutes.

Adaptation to brighter lighting conditions takes place much more rapidly. When you emerge from the theater into the brilliance of the afternoon, you may at first be painfully surprised by the featureless blaze around you. The visual experience is not unlike turning the brightness of the TV set to maximum, in which case the edges of objects dissolve into light. But within a minute or

Rods Rod-shaped photoreceptors that are sensitive only to the intensity of light.

Cones Cone-shaped photoreceptors that transmit sensations of color.

Dark adaptation The process of adjusting to conditions of lower lighting by increasing the sensitivity of rods and cones.

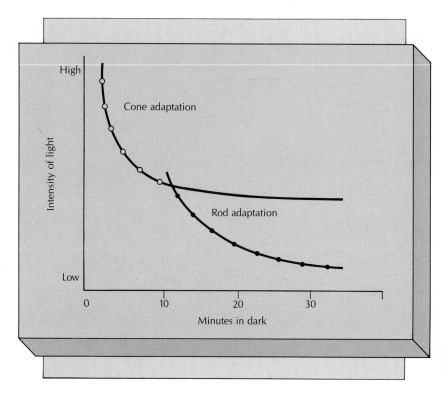

FIGURE 3.6. What Is Dark Adaptation? This illustration shows the amount of light necessary for detection as a function of the amount of time spent in the dark. Cones and rods adapt at different rates. Cones, which permit perception of color, reach maximum dark adaptation in about 10 minutes. Rods, which permit perception of dark and light only, are more sensitive than cones. Rods continue to adapt for up to about 45 minutes.

so of entering the street, the scene will have dimmed and objects will have regained their edges.

Visual Acuity   You may recall from geometry that an acute angle is a sharp angle. Your **visual acuity** is the sharpness of your vision—your ability to discriminate visual details.

A familiar means of measuring visual acuity is the Snellen Chart (Figure 3.7). If you were to stand 20 feet from the Snellen Chart and could only discriminate the E, we would say that your vision is "20/200." This would mean that you can see from a distance of 20 feet what a person with normal vision can discriminate from a distance of 200 feet.

Visual acuity Sharpness of vision.

Nearsighted Capable of seeing nearby objects with greater acuity than distant objects.

Farsighted Capable of seeing distant objects with greater acuity than nearby objects.

Presbyopia A condition characterized by brittleness of the lens.

In such a case you would be quite **nearsighted.** You would have to be unusually close to an object to discriminate its details. A person who could read the smallest line on the chart from 20 feet would have 20/15 vision and be somewhat **farsighted.** It is not unusual for eyes to differ somewhat in their visual acuity, although people tend to be generally nearsighted or farsighted when their vision is not normal.

You may have noticed that elderly people often hold newspapers or books at a distance. As you grow older, the lenses of the eyes become relatively brittle, making it more difficult to accommodate to, or focus on, objects. This condition is called **presbyopia,** from the Greek for "old man." The lens structure of elderly people with presbyopia differs from that of farsighted young people. Still, the effect of presbyopia in the elderly is to make it difficult to perceive nearby visual stimuli. People who had normal visual acuity in their youth typically find that they must use corrective lenses to read in old age. And people who were initially farsighted often suffer from headaches linked to eyestrain during the later years.

COLOR VISION

For most of us, the world is a place of brilliant colors. The blue-greens of the ocean, the red-oranges of the lowering sun, the deepened greens of June, the glories of rhododendron and hibiscus—color is a an emotional and aesthetic part of our everyday lives. In this section we explore psychological dimensions of color and then examine theories concerning how we manage to convert different wavelengths of light into perceptions of color.

How Early Can Children Perceive Color? Children can discriminate the colors of the spectrum early in infancy. Toy manufacturers usually make infants' toys in bright colors that catch the eye and are easy for parents to label.

Psychological Dimensions of Color: Hue, Brightness, and Saturation

The wavelength of light determines its color, or hue. The brightness of a color is its degree of lightness or darkness. The brighter the color, the lighter it is.

If we bend the colors of the spectrum into a circle, we create a color wheel, as in Figure 3.8. Yellow is the lightest color on the color wheel. As we work our way around from yellow to violet-blue, we encounter progressively darker colors.

Warm and Cool Colors Psychologically, colors on the green-blue side of the color wheel are considered cool; colors on the yellow-orange-red side are considered warm. Perhaps greens and blues suggest the coolness of the ocean and the sky, whereas things tend to burn red or orange. A room decorated in green or blue may seem more appealing on a hot day in July than a room decorated in red or orange.

When we look at a painting, warm colors seem to advance toward us, which explains, in part, why the oranges and yellows of Rothko's "Orange and Yellow" (Figure 3.9) seem to pulsate toward the observer. Cool colors seem to recede. Similarly the

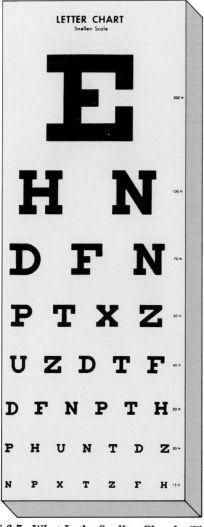

LETTER CHART
Snellen Scale

E   200 ft
H N   100 ft
D F N 70 ft
P T X Z 50 ft
U Z D T F 40 ft
D F N P T H 30 ft
P H U N T D Z 20 ft
N P X T Z F H 15 ft

FIGURE 3.7. What Is the Snellen Chart? The Snellen Chart and others like it are used to assess visual acuity.

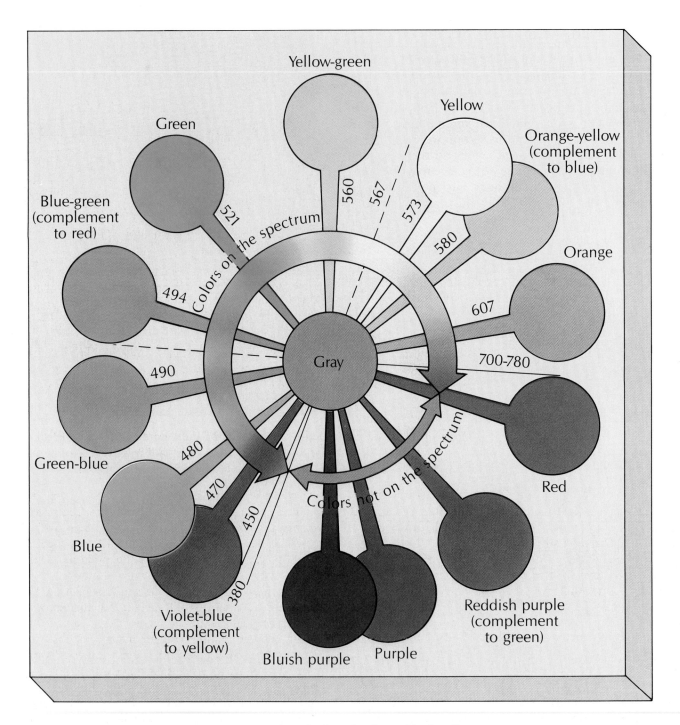

FIGURE 3.8. What Is the Color Wheel?   A color wheel can be formed by bending the colors of the spectrum into a circle and placing complementary colors across from one another. (A few colors between violet and red that are not found on the spectrum must be added to complete the circle.) When lights of complementary colors, such as yellow and violet-blue, are mixed, they dissolve into neutral gray. The afterimage of a color is also the color's complement.

(Left) **FIGURE 3.9. "Orange and Yellow."** Warm colors such as orange and yellow seem to advance toward the viewer, while cool colors such as blue and green seem to recede. The oranges and yellows of Rothko's painting seem to pulsate toward the observer.

(Right) **FIGURE 3.10. "Highway No. 2."** The "warm" Sunoco sign in d'Arcangelo's painting leaps out toward the viewer, while the "cool" blue sky recedes into the distance.

warm Sunoco sign in d'Arcangelo's "Highway No. 2" (Figure 3.10) leaps out toward the viewer, but the cool blue sky recedes into the distance.

The **saturation** of a color is its pureness. Pure hues have the greatest intensity, or brightness. The saturation, and thus the brightness, decreases when another hue or black, gray, or white is added.

Complementary versus Analogous Colors

Complementary Colors The colors across from one another on the color wheel are **complementary.** Red-green and blue-yellow are the major complementary pairs. If we mix complementary colors together, they dissolve into gray.

But wait! you say: Blue and yellow cannot be complementary because by mixing *pigments* of blue and yellow we create green, not gray. True, but

we are talking about mixing *light*, not pigment. Light is the source of all color. Pigments reflect and absorb different wavelengths of light selectively. The mixture of lights is an *additive* process, whereas the mixture of pigments is *subtractive* (see Figure 3.11).

Pigments attain their colors by absorbing light from certain segments of the spectrum and reflecting the rest. For example, we see most plant life as green because the pigment in chlorophyll absorbs most of the red, blue, and violet wavelengths of light. The remaining green is reflected. A red pigment absorbs most of the spectrum but reflects red. White pigments reflect all colors equally. Black pigments reflect very little light.

Saturation The degree of purity of a color.

Complementary Descriptive of colors of the spectrum that when combined produce white or nearly white light.

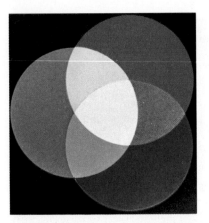

FIGURE 3.11. What Additive Color Mixtures Are Produced from the Lights of the Three Colors Red, Green, and Violet-Blue?   In the early 1800s, British scientist Thomas Young discovered that white light and all the colors of the spectrum could be produced by adding various combinations of lights of three colors and varying their intensities.

Afterimages   Before reading on, why don't you try a brief experiment? Look at the strangely colored American flag in Figure 3.14 for at least half a minute. Then look at a sheet of white or gray

In works of art, complementary colors placed next to one another clash, and there seems to be a pulsating where they meet. Note Richard Anusz-kiewicz's painting "Entrance to Green" (Figure 3.12). If you look at the picture from a foot or so away and allow your eyes to relax, you are likely to perceive vibrations in the areas where the lines separate the reddish and greenish colors.

Primary, Secondary, and Tertiary Colors
The pigments of red, blue, and yellow are the **primary colors**—those that we cannot produce by mixing pigments of other hues. **Secondary colors** are created by mixing pigments of the primary colors. The three secondary colors are orange (derived from mixing red and yellow), green (blue and yellow), and purple (red and blue). **Tertiary colors** are created by mixing pigments of primary and adjoining secondary colors, as in yellow-green and bluish-purple.

In his "Sunday Afternoon on the Island of La Grande Jatte" (Figure 3.13), French painter Georges Seurat molded his figures and forms from dabs of pure and complementary colors. Instead of mixing his pigments, he placed points of pure color next to one another. The sensations are of pure color from nearby (see detail, Figure 3.13), but from a distance the juxtaposition of pure colors creates the impression of mixtures of color.

Primary colors Colors that we cannot produce by mixing other hues.
Secondary colors Colors derived by mixing primary colors.
Tertiary colors Colors derived by mixing primary and adjoining secondary colors.

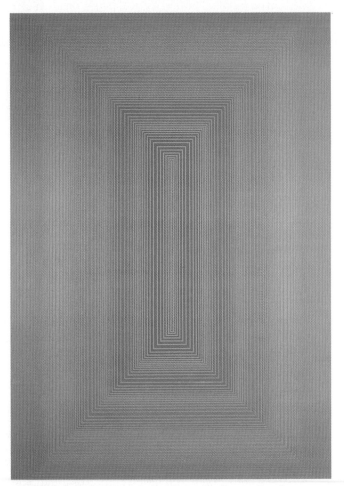

FIGURE 3.12. "Entrance to Green."   In works of art, there seems to be a pulsating where complementary colors come together. If you look at Anuszkiewicz's painting for a while from a foot or so away, you are likely to perceive vibrations where the red and green meet. So-called Op Art works rely on vibrations and other visual responses for their effect.

FIGURE 3.13. "Sunday Afternoon on the Island of La Grande Jatte." The French painter Seurat molded his figures and forms from dabs of pure and complementary colors. Up close, the dabs of pure color are visible. From afar, they create the impression of color mixtures.

paper. What has happened to the flag? If your color vision is working properly, and if you looked at the miscolored flag long enough, you should see a flag made up of the familiar red, white, and blue. The flag you perceive on the white sheet of paper is an **afterimage** of the first.

In afterimages, persistent sensations of color are followed by perception of the complementary color when the first color is removed. The phenomenon of afterimages has contributed to one of the theories of color vision, as we shall see later in the section.

Analogous Colors **Analogous** hues lie next to one another on the color wheel, forming families of colors like yellow and orange, orange and red, and green and blue. As we work our way around the wheel, the families intermarry, as blue with violet and violet with red. Works of art that use closely related families of color seem harmonious, for example, Rothko's "Orange and Yellow,"

Afterimage The lingering impression made by a stimulus that has been removed.

Analogous Similar or comparable colors.

FIGURE 3.14. Three Cheers for the . . . Green, Black, and Yellow? Don't be concerned. We can readily restore Old Glory to its familiar hues. Place a sheet of white paper beneath the book, and then stare at the center of the flag for 30 seconds. Then remove the book. You will see a more familiar image on the paper beneath. This is an afterimage. Afterimages such as this led Ewald Hering to doubt the trichromatic theory of color vision and to propose the opponent-process theory in its place. Both theories have received some empirical support.

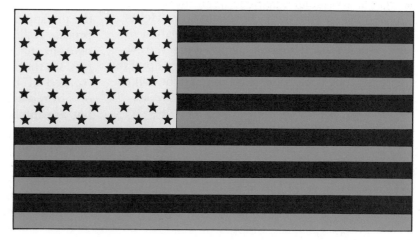

which draws on the color family containing analogous oranges and yellows.

Theories of Color Vision

Adults with normal color vision can discriminate up to 150 color differences across the visible spectrum (Bornstein & Marks, 1982). Different colors have different wavelengths. Although we can vary the physical wavelengths of light in a continuous manner, from shorter to longer, changes in color seem to be discontinuous, so that our perception of a color shifts suddenly from blue to green, even though the change in wavelength is smaller than that between two blues.

Our ability to perceive color depends on the eye's transmission of different messages to the brain when lights of different wavelengths stimulate the cones in the retina. Let us now consider two theories of how lights of different wavelengths are perceived as being of different colors: *trichromatic theory* and *opponent-process theory.*

Trichromatic Theory   **Trichromatic theory** is based on an experiment that was run by British scientist Thomas Young in the early 1800s. As in Figure 3.11, Young projected three lights of different colors onto a screen so that they partly overlapped. He found that he could create any color from the visible spectrum by simply varying the intensities of the lights. When all three lights fell on the same spot, they created white light, or the appearance of no color at all. The three lights manipulated by Young were red, green, and blue-violet.

German physiologist Hermann von Helmholtz saw in Young's discovery an explanation of color vision. Von Helmholtz suggested that the eye must have three different types of photoreceptors or cones. Some must be sensitive to red light, some

Trichromatic theory   The theory that color vision is made possible by three types of cones, some of which respond to red light, some to green, and some to blue.

Opponent-process theory   The theory that color vision is made possible by three types of cones, some of which respond to red or green light, some to blue or yellow, and some to the intensity of light only.

to green, and some to blue. We see other colors when two different types of color receptors are stimulated. The perception of yellow, for example, would result from the simultaneous stimulation of receptors for red and green. Trichromatic theory is also known as the Young-Helmholtz theory, after Thomas Young and Hermann von Helmholtz.

Opponent-Process Theory   In 1870, Ewald Hering proposed the **opponent-process theory** of color vision. Opponent-process theory also holds that there are three types of color receptors, but not red, green, and blue. Hering suggested that afterimages (as of the "American flag" shown in Figure 3.14) are made possible by receptors sensitive to red-green, blue-yellow, and lightness-darkness. A red-green cone could not transmit messages for red and green at the same time. Hering would perhaps have said that when you were staring at the green, black, and yellow flag for 30 seconds, you were disturbing the balance of neural activity. The afterimage of red, white, and blue would then have represented the eye's attempt to re-establish a balance.

Evaluation   Both theories of color vision may be partially correct (Hurvich, 1981). Methods for analyzing the sensitivity of single cones to lights of different wavelengths show that some cones are sensitive to blue, some to green, and some to yellow-red parts of the spectrum—consistent with trichromatic theory. But studies of the bipolar and ganglion neurons suggest that messages from the cones are transmitted to the brain and relayed by the thalamus to the occipital lobe in an opponent-process fashion (DeValois & Jacobs, 1984). Some neurons that transmit messages to the visual centers in the brain, for example, are excited or "turned on" by green light but inhibited or "turned off" by red light. Others can be excited by red light but are inhibited by green light. It may be that there is then a "neural rebound effect" that would help explain afterimages. With such an effect, a green-sensitive ganglion that had been excited by green light for half a minute or so might switch briefly to inhibitory activity when the light is shut off. As a result we would perceive, not sense, red.

These theoretical updates allow for the after-image effects with the green, black, and yellow flag, and are also consistent with Young's experiments in mixing lights of different colors.

Color Blindness

If you can discriminate the colors of the visible spectrum, you have normal color vision and are labeled a **trichromat.** This means that you are sensitive to red-green, blue-yellow, and light-dark. People who are totally colorblind are called **monochromats** and are sensitive to light-dark only. Total color blindness is quite rare.

Partial color blindness is more common—a sex-linked trait that strikes mostly males. The partially colorblind are called **dichromats.** They can discriminate only two colors, red and green, or blue and yellow, and the colors that are derived from mixing them. Figure 3.15 shows the types of tests that are used to diagnose color blindness. Also see Figure 3.16.

A dichromat might put on one red sock and one green sock but would not mix red and blue socks. Monochromats might put on socks of any color. They would not notice a difference so long as the socks did not differ in intensity, or brightness.

When we selectively breed cats and dogs, we are interested in producing coats of certain colors. But if cats and dogs bred human beings, they would not be concerned about our color because cats and dogs are monochromats.

VISUAL PERCEPTION

In perception, we organize or make sense of sensory impressions. Although visual sensations are caused by electromagnetic energy, visual perception also relies on our knowledge, expectations, and motivations.

For example, just what do you see in Figure 3.17? Random splotches of ink or a rider on horseback? If you perceive a horse and rider, it is not just because of the visual sensations provided by the drawing. Your perception also has something

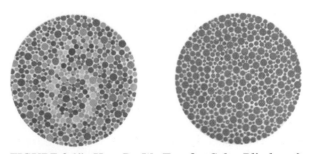

FIGURE 3.15. How Do We Test for Color Blindness? Can you see the numbers in these plates from a test for color blindness? A person with red-green color blindness would not be able to see the 6, and a person with blue-yellow color blindness would probably not discern the 12. (Caution: These reproductions cannot be used for actual testing of color blindness.)

to do with your general knowledge and your desire to fit incoming bits and pieces of information into familiar patterns.

The integration of disconnected shards of information into a meaningful whole reflects what Gestalt psychologists term the principle of **closure,** or the tendency to perceive a whole figure, even when there are gaps in sensory input. In perception the whole can be more than the sum of the parts.

Perceptual Organization

Gestalt psychologists noted consistencies in our integration of bits and pieces of sensory stimulation and attempted to formulate rules that governed these processes. Max Wertheimer, in particular, discovered many such rules. These rules make up the laws of **perceptual organization.** Let us examine a number of them.

Trichromat A person with normal color vision.

Monochromat A person who is sensitive to black and white only, and hence colorblind.

Dichromat A person who is sensitive to black-white and red-green or blue-yellow, and hence partially colorblind.

Closure The tendency to perceive a broken figure as complete or whole.

Perceptual organization The tendency to integrate perceptual elements into meaningful patterns.

FIGURE 3.16. How Do Color-Blind People and People with Normal Color Vision Perceive the Same Object? These pictures demonstrate how people with normal color vision and people with partial color blindness perceive the same scene. (Man Ray, "The Rope Dancer Accompanies Herself with Her Shadows." Museum of Modern Art, New York. Gift of G. David Thompson)

Figure-Ground Perception If you look out your window, you may see people, buildings, cars and streets, or perhaps grass, trees, birds, and clouds. The objects about you tend to be perceived as figures against backgrounds. Cars against the background of the street are easier to pick out than cars piled on each other in a junkyard. Birds against the sky are more likely to be perceived than, as the saying goes, birds in the bush. Figures are closer to us than their grounds.

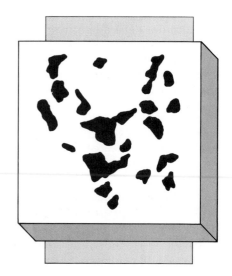

FIGURE 3.17. What Is Closure?
Meaningless splotches of ink or a horse and rider? This figure illustrates the Gestalt principle of closure.

FIGURE 3.18. Figure and Ground? How many animals and demons can you find in this Escher print? Do we have white figures on a black background or black figures on a white background? Figure-ground perception is the tendency to perceive geometric forms against a background.

When figure-ground relationships are **ambiguous,** or capable of being interpreted in different ways, our perceptions tend to be unstable, to shift back and forth. As an example, take a look at Figure 3.18—a nice leisurely look. How many people, objects, and animals can you find in this Escher print? If your eye is drawn back and forth, so that sometimes you are perceiving light figures on a dark background and then dark figures on a light background, you are experiencing figure-ground reversals. That is, a shift is occurring in your perception of what is figure and what is ground, or backdrop.

The Rubin Vase In Figure 3.19 we see a Rubin vase, one of psychologists' favorite illustrations of figure-ground relationships. Note that the figure-ground relationship in part A of the figure is ambiguous. There are no cues that suggest which area must be the figure. For this reason, our perception may shift from perceiving the vase then the profiles as the figure.

There is no such problem in part B. Since it seems that a vase has been brought forward against a ground, we are more likely to perceive the vase than the profiles. In part C we are again more likely to perceive the profiles than the vase. Why?

The Necker Cube The Necker cube (Figure 3.20) provides another example of how an ambiguous drawing can lead to perceptual shifts.

Hold page 114 at arm's length and stare at the center of the figure for 30 seconds or so. Relax your eyes. After a while you will notice a dramatic shift in your perception so that what was once a front edge is now a back edge, and vice versa. Again, the shift occurs because the drawing permits two interpretations.

Some Other Gestalt Rules for Organization
Our perceptions are also guided by rules or laws of *proximity, similarity, continuity,* and *common fate.*

Ambiguous Having two or more possible meanings.

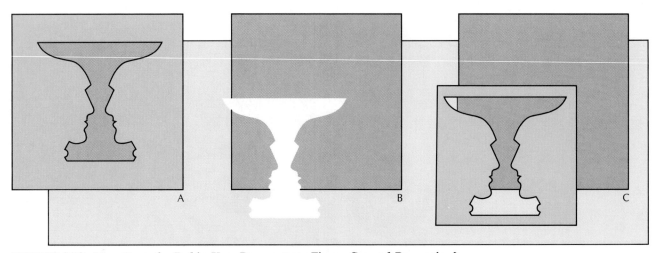

FIGURE 3.19. How Does the Rubin Vase Demonstrate Figure-Ground Perception?
A favorite drawing used by psychologists to demonstrate figure-ground perception.
Part *A* is ambiguous, with neither vase nor profiles clearly figure or ground. In *B*, the
vase is clearly the figure, and in *C*, the profiles are.

Verbally describe part A of Figure 3.21 without reading further. Did you say that part A consisted of six lines or of three groups of two (parallel) lines? If you said three sets of lines, you were influenced by the **proximity,** or nearness, of some of the lines. There is no other reason for perceiving them in pairs or subgroups: All lines are parallel and of equal length.

Now describe part B of the figure. Did you perceive the figure as a six-by-six grid, or as three columns of *x*'s and three columns of *o*'s? According to the law of **similarity,** we perceive similar objects as belonging together. For this reason, you may have been more likely to describe part B in terms of columns than rows or a grid.

What about part C? Is it a circle with two lines stemming from it, or is it a (broken) line that goes through a circle? If you saw it as a single (broken) line, you were probably organizing your perceptions according to the rule of **continuity.** That is, we perceive a series of points or a broken line as having unity.

According to the law of **common fate,** elements seen moving together are perceived as belonging together. A group of people running in the same direction appear unified in purpose. Birds that flock together seem to be of a feather.

FIGURE 3.20. How Does the Necker Cube Illustrate Perceptual Shifts? Ambiguity in the drawing of the cube makes perceptual shifts possible.

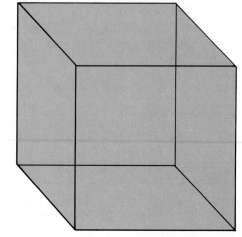

Proximity Nearness. The perceptual tendency to group together objects that are near one another.

Similarity The perceptual tendency to group together objects that are similar in appearance.

Continuity The tendency to perceive a series of points or lines as having unity.

Common fate The tendency to perceive elements that move together as belonging together.

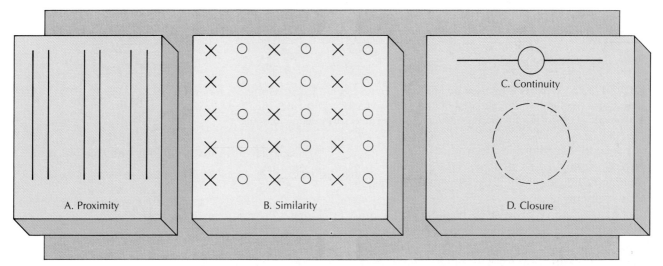

FIGURE 3.21. What Are Some Gestalt Laws of Perceptual Organization?

Part D of Figure 3.21 provides another example of the law of closure. The arcs tend to be perceived as a circle, or circle with gaps, not a series of arcs.

Perception of Movement

To understand how we perceive movement, recall what it is like to be on a train that has begun to pull out of the station while the train on the next track remains still. If your own train does not lurch as it accelerates, you might think at first that the other train is moving. You might not be certain whether your train is moving forward or the other train is moving backward.

The visual perception of movement is based on change of position relative to other objects. To early scientists, whose only instrument for visual observation was the naked eye, it seemed logical that the sun circled the earth. You have to be able to imagine the movement of the earth around the sun as seen from a theoretical point in outer space—you cannot observe it directly.

So, how do you determine which train is moving? One way is to look for objects you know are stable, like station platform columns, houses, signs, or trees. If you are stationary in relation to them, your train is not moving. You might also try to sense the motion of the train in your body.

We have been considering the perception of real movement. Psychologists also study types of apparent movement, or **illusions** of movement. These include the *autokinetic effect, stroboscopic motion,* and the *phi phenomenon.*

The Autokinetic Effect   If you were to sit quietly in a dark room and stare at a point of light projected onto the far wall, after a while it might appear that the light had begun to move, even if it remained quite still. The tendency to perceive a stationary point of light as moving in a dark room is called the **autokinetic effect.**

Stroboscopic Motion   In **stroboscopic motion,** the illusion of movement is provided by the presentation of a rapid progression of images of stationary objects (Beck et al., 1977). In a sense, a motion picture does not move at all. Motion pictures do not consist of images that move. Rather, the audience is shown 16 to 22 pictures, or frames,

---

Illusions Sensations that give rise to misperceptions.

Autokinetic effect The tendency to perceive a stationary point of light in a dark room as moving.

Stroboscopic motion A visual illusion in which the perception of motion is generated by a series of stationary images that are presented in rapid succession.

FIGURE 3.22. What Is Stroboscopic Motion?   In a motion picture, viewing a series of stationary images at the rate of about 16 to 22 per second provides the illusion of movement. This form of apparent movement is termed stroboscopic motion.

per second, like those in Figure 3.22. Each frame differs slightly from that preceding it. Showing them in rapid succession then provides the illusion of movement.

At the rate of at least 16 frames per second, the "motion" in a film seems smooth and natural. With fewer than 16 or so frames per second, the movement looks jumpy and unnatural. That is why slow motion is achieved by filming up to 100 or more frames per second. When they are played back at about 22 frames per second, movement seems slowed down, yet smooth and natural.

The Phi Phenomenon
Have you ever seen news headlines "wrapping around" a building or a huge electronic "scoreboard" in a sports stadium? When the hometeam scores, some scoreboards seem to shoot off fireworks. What actually happens is that a row of lights is switched on, then off. As the first row is switched off, the second row is switched on, and so on for dozens, perhaps hundreds, of rows. When the switching occurs rapidly, the **phi phenomenon** occurs: The on-off process is perceived as movement.

Like stroboscopic motion, the phi phenomenon is an example of apparent motion. Both stroboscopic motion and the phi phenomenon appear to occur because of the law of continuity. We tend to perceive a series of points as having unity, and

so the series of lights (points) is perceived as moving lines.

Depth Perception

Think of the problems you might have if you could not judge depth or distance. You might bump into other people, thinking them farther away than they are. An outfielder might not be able to judge whether to run toward the infield or the fence to catch a fly ball. You might give your front bumper a workout in stop-and-go traffic. Fortunately, both *monocular and binocular cues* help us perceive the depth of objects. Let us examine a number of them.

Monocular Cues   Now ponder the problems of the artist who attempts to portray three-dimensional objects on a two-dimensional canvas. Artists use **monocular cues,** or cues that can be perceived by one eye, to create an illusion of depth. These cues—including perspective, clearness, interposition, shadows, and texture gradient—cause certain objects to appear more distant from the viewer than others.

Distant objects stimulate smaller areas on the retina than nearby objects. The sensory input from them is smaller, even though they may be the same size. The distances between far-off objects also appear smaller than equivalent distances between nearby objects. For this reason, the phenomonen known as **perspective** occurs; that is, we tend to perceive parallel lines as coming closer, or converging, as they recede from us. However, as we shall see when we discuss *size constancy,* experience teaches us that distant objects that look small will be larger when they are close. In this way, their relative size also becomes a cue to their distance from us.

Phi phenomenon The perception of movement as a result of sequential presentation of visual stimuli.

Monocular cues Stimuli suggestive of depth that can be perceived with one eye only.

Perspective A monocular cue for depth based on the convergence (coming together) of parallel lines as they recede into the distance.

"I'll explain it to you, Stevie. It's called perspective."

The two engravings in Figure 3.23 represent impossible scenes in which the artists use principles of perspective to fool the viewer. In the engraving to the left, "Waterfall," note that the water appears to be flowing away from the viewer in a zigzag because the stream becomes gradually narrower (that is, lines that we assume to be parallel are shown to be converging) and the stone sides of the aqueduct appear to be stepping down. However, given that the water arrives at the top of the fall, it must actually somehow be flowing upward. However, the spot from which it falls is no farther from the viewer than is the collection point from which it appears to (but does not) begin its flow backward.

Again, distant objects look smaller than nearby objects of the same size. The paradoxes in the engraving to the right, "False Perspective," are made possible by the fact that more distant objects are not necessarily depicted as being smaller than nearby objects. Thus, what at first seems to be background suddenly becomes foreground, and vice versa.

The clearness of an object also suggests its distance from us. Experience shows us that we sense more details of nearby objects. For this reason, artists can suggest that certain objects are closer to the viewer by depicting them in greater detail. Note that the "distant" hill in the Hogarth engraving (Figure 3.23) is given less detail than the nearby plants at the bottom of the picture. Our perceptions are mocked when a man "on" that distant hill in the background is shown "conversing" with a woman leaning out a window in the middle ground. Note, too, how Vasarley uses clearness (crispness of line) to help provide a three-dimensional effect in "Chezt-Yord" (Figure 3.24).

We also learn that nearby objects can block our views of more distant objects. Overlapping, or **interposition,** is the placement of one object in

---

Interposition A monocular cue for depth based on the fact that a nearby object obscures vision of a more distant object behind it.

FIGURE 3.23. What Is Wrong with These Pictures?   In "Waterfall," to the left, how does Dutch artist M. C. Escher suggest that fallen water flows back upward, only to fall again? In "False Perspective," to the right, how did English artist William Hogarth use monocular cues for depth perception to deceive the viewer?

front of another. Experience encourages us to perceive partly covered objects as farther away than objects that shield parts of them (Figure 3.25). In the Hogarth engraving (Figure 3.23), which looks closer: the trees in the background (background?) or the moon sign hanging from the building (or is it buildings?) to the right? How does the artist use interposition to confound the viewer?

Additional information about depth is provided by **shadowing** and is based on the fact that opaque objects block light and produce shadows.

> **Shadowing** A monocular cue for depth based on the fact that opaque objects block light and produce shadows.
>
> **Texture gradient** A monocular cue for depth based on the perception that closer objects appear to have rougher (more detailed) surfaces.

Shadows and highlights give us information about the three-dimensional shapes of objects and about their relationships to the source of light. The left part of Figure 3.26 is perceived as a two-dimensional circle, but the right part tends to be perceived as a three-dimensional sphere because of the highlight on its surface and the shadow underneath. In the "sphere," the highlighted central area is perceived as closest to us, while the surface then recedes to the edges.

Another monocular cue is **texture gradient.** A gradient is a progressive change, and closer objects are perceived as having progressively rougher textures. How is texture gradient used in the Hogarth engraving (Figure 3.23)?

Motion Cues   If you have ever driven in the country, you have probably noticed that distant objects, such as mountains and stars, appear to move

FIGURE 3.24. "Chezt-Yord." How Does Op Artist Victor Vasarely use monocular cues for depth perception to lend this picture a three-dimensional quality?

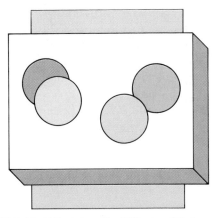

FIGURE 3.25. What Are the Effects of Interposition? The four circles are all the same size. Which circles appear closer? The complete circles or the circles with chunks bitten out of them?

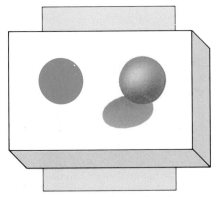

FIGURE 3.26. How Does Shadowing Serve as a Cue in the Perception of Depth?

along with you. Objects at an intermediate distance seem stationary, but nearby objects, such as roadside markers, rocks, and trees, seem to go by quite rapidly. The tendency of objects to seem to move backward or forward as a function of their distance is known as **motion parallax.** We learn to perceive objects that seem to move with us at greater distance.

Earlier we noted that nearby objects cause the lens to accommodate or bend more to bring them into focus. The sensations of tension in the eye muscles also provide a monocular cue to depth, especially when we are within about four feet of the objects.

Binocular Cues **Binocular cues,** or cues that involve both eyes, also help us perceive depth. Two binocular cues are *retinal disparity* and *convergence*.

Try a brief experiment. Hold your index finger at arm's length. Now gradually bring it closer, until it almost touches your nose. If you keep your eyes relaxed as you do so, you will see two fingers. An image of the finger will be projected onto the retina of each eye, and each image will be slightly different since the finger will be seen at different angles. The difference between the projected im-

Motion parallax A monocular cue for depth based on the perception that nearby objects appear to move more rapidly in relation to our own motion.

Binocular cues Stimuli suggestive of depth that involve simultaneous perception by both eyes.

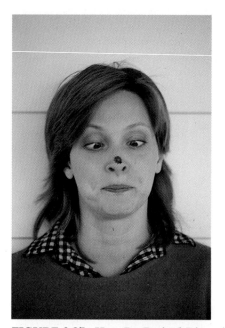

FIGURE 3.27. How Do Retinal Disparity and Convergence Serve as Cues for Depth?   As an object nears your eyes, you begin to see two images of it because of retinal disparity. If you maintain perception of a single image, your eyes must converge on the object.

ages is referred to as **retinal disparity** and serves as a binocular cue for depth perception (see Figure 3.27). Note that the closer your finger comes, the farther apart the "two fingers" appear. Closer objects have greater retinal disparity.

If we try to maintain a single image of the approaching finger, our eyes must turn inward, or converge on it, giving us a "cross-eyed" look. **Convergence** is associated with feelings of tension in

---

Retinal disparity A binocular cue for depth based on the difference of the image cast by an object on the retinas of the eyes as the object moves closer or farther away.

Convergence A binocular cue for depth based on the inward movement of the eyes as they attempt to focus on an object that is drawing nearer.

Size constancy The tendency to perceive an object as being the same size even as the size of its retinal image changes according to its distance.

Color constancy The tendency to perceive an object as being the same color even as lighting conditions change its appearance.

---

the eye muscles and provides another binocular cue for depth. The binocular cues of retinal disparity and convergence are strongest at near distances.

Perceptual Constancies

The world is a shifting display of visual sensations. What confusion would reign if we did not perceive a doorway to be the same doorway when seen from six feet as when seen from four feet. As we neared it, we might think that it was larger than the door we were seeking and become lost. Or consider the problems of the pet owner who recognizes his dog from the side, but not from above, because the shapes differ. Fortunately, these problems tend not to occur—at least with familiar objects—because of perceptual constancies.

The image of a dog seen from 20 feet occupies about the same amount of space on your retina as an inch-long insect crawling in the palm of your hand. Yet you would not perceive the dog or cat to be as small as the insect. Through your experiences you have acquired **size constancy,** or the tendency to perceive the same object as being the same size, even though the size of its image on the retina varies as a function of its distance. Experience teaches us about perspective, that the same object seen at a great distance will appear much smaller than when it is nearby. We *perceive* people to be the same size from great distances, although their sensory input stimulates fewer neurons on the retina.

We also have **color constancy,** or the tendency to perceive objects as retaining their color even though lighting conditions may alter their appearance. Your bright orange car may edge toward yel-

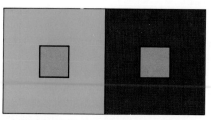

FIGURE 3.28. What Is Color Constancy?   The orange squares within the blue squares are the same hue, yet the orange within the dark blue square is perceived as purer. Why?

FIGURE 3.29. What Is Shape Constancy? When closed, this door is a rectangle. When open, the retinal image is trapezoidal. But because of shape constancy, we still perceive the door as rectangular.

low-gray as the hours wend their way through twilight to nighttime. But when you finally locate it in the parking lot you will still think of it as orange. You expect an orange car and still judge it "more orange" than the (faded) blue and green cars to either side. But it would be difficult to find it in a lot filled with yellow and red cars similar in size and shape.

Consider Figure 3.28. The orange squares within the blue squares are the same hue. However, the orange within the dark blue square is perceived as purer. Why? Again, experience teaches us that the pureness of colors fades as the background grows darker. Since the orange squares are equally pure, we assume that the one in the dark background must be more saturated; we would stand ready to perceive the orange squares as equal in pureness if the square within the darker blue field actually had a bit of black mixed in with it.

Similar to color constancy is **brightness constancy.** The same gray square is perceived as brighter when placed within a black background than when placed within a white background (see Figure 1.3 on p. 14). Again, consider the role of experience. If it were nighttime, we would expect gray to fade to near blackness. But the fact that the gray within the black square stimulates the eye with equal intensity suggests that it must be very much brighter than the gray within the white square.

We also perceive objects as maintaining their shapes, even if we perceive them from different angles so that the shape of the retinal image changes dramatically. This tendency is called **shape constancy.** You perceive the top of a coffee cup or a glass to be a circle, even though it is a circle when seen from above only. When seen from an angle, it is an ellipse. When seen on edge, the retinal image of the cup or glass is the same as that of a straight line. So why would you still describe the rim of the cup or glass as a circle? Perhaps for two reasons: One is that experience has taught you that the cup will look circular when seen from above. The second is that you may have labeled the cup as circular or round. Can you imagine the chaos if we described objects as they stimulated our sensory organs at the moment, rather than according to stable conditions?

In another example, a door is a rectangle only when viewed straight on (Figure 3.29). When we move to the side or open it, the left or right edge comes closer and appears larger, changing the retinal image to a trapezoid. Yet we continue to think of doors as being rectangles.

Brightness constancy The tendency to perceive an object as being just as bright even though lighting conditions change its intensity.

Shape constancy The tendency to perceive an object as being the same shape although the retinal image varies in shape as it rotates.

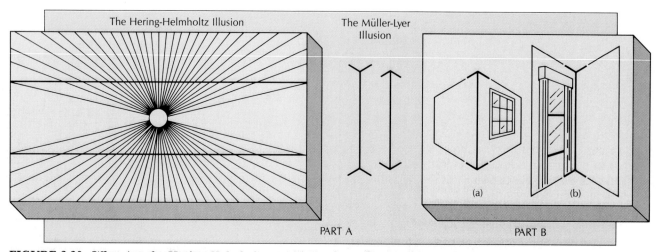

FIGURE 3.30. What Are the Hering-Helmholtz and Müller-Lyer Illusions?

Visual Illusions

The principles of perceptual organization make it possible for "our eyes to play tricks on us." Consider the Hering-Helmholtz and Müller-Lyer illusions (Figure 3.30, part A). In the Hering-Helmholtz illusion, the horizontal lines are straight and parallel. However, the radiating lines cause them to appear bent outward near the center. The two lines in the Müller-Lyer illusion are the same length, but the line on the left, with its reversed arrowheads, looks longer.

Let us try to explain these illusions. Because of experience and lifelong use of perceptual cues, we tend to perceive the Hering-Helmholtz draw-

ing as three-dimensional. Because of the tendency to perceive bits of sensory information as figures against grounds, we perceive the white area in the center as a circle in front of a series of radiating lines, all of which lies in front of a white ground. Next, because of our experience with perspective, we perceive the radiating lines as parallel. We perceive the two horizontal lines as intersecting the "receding" lines, and we know that they would have to appear bent out at the center if they were to be equidistant at all points from the center of the circle.

Experience probably compels us to perceive the vertical lines in the Müller-Lyer illusion as the corners of a room as seen from inside a house, at left, and outside a house, at right (see Figure 3.30, part B). In such an example, the reverse arrowheads to the left are lines where the walls meet the ceiling and the floor. We perceive the lines as extending toward us; they push the corner away from us. The arrowheads to the right are lines where exterior walls meet the roof and foundation. We perceive them as receding from us; they push the corner toward us. The vertical line to the left is thus perceived as farther away. Since both ver-

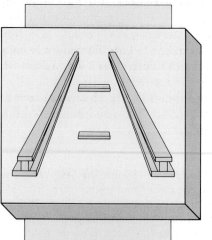

FIGURE 3.31. What Is the Ponzo Illusion?
The two horizontal lines in this drawing are equal in length, but the top line is perceived as longer. Can you use the principle of size constancy to explain why?

FIGURE 3.32. How Does the Principle of Size Constancy Explain This Illusion? In this drawing, the three cylinders are the same size, yet they appear to grow larger toward the top of the picture. Can you use the principle of size constancy to explain why?

tical lines stimulate equal expanses across the retina, the principle of size constancy encourages us to perceive the line to the left as longer.

Figure 3.31 is known as the Ponzo illusion. In this illusion, the two horizontal lines are the same length. But do you perceive the top line as being longer? The rule of size constancy may also afford insight into this illusion. Perhaps the converging lines again strike us as parallel lines receding into the distance, like the train tracks in the cartoon on page 117. If so, we assume from experience that the horizontal line at the top is farther "down" the "track"—farther away from us. And again, the rule of size constancy tells us that if two objects appear to be the same size, and one is farther away, the farther object must be larger. So we perceive the top line as larger.

Now that you are an expert on these visual illusions, look at Figure 3.32. First take some bets from friends concerning whether the three cylin-

ders are equal in height and width. Then get a ruler. Once you have made some money, however, try to explain why the cylinders to the right look progressively larger.

Now let us consider an illusion of movement. Figure 3.33, "Current," is an "optical art" picture by Bridget Riley. When you fix your gaze on any point in the picture, the surrounding areas seem to be in motion. "Current," like many other works of optical art, uses pictorial features to create the illusion of motion. In this case, the pictorial feature is a moiré pattern, in which nearly identical wavy lines are placed next to each other. It is nearly impossible to perceive the continuity of any one line in the picture. Instead, our gaze tends to hop back and forth from line to line. The hopping back and forth leads to the perception of vibrations in the lines, and hence movement.

Speaking of vibrations, the time has come to discuss a way in which we can sense vibrations in the air: hearing.

FIGURE 3.33. "Current." In this Op Art picture by Bridget Riley, the illusion of movement is created with a moiré pattern, in which nearly identical wavy lines are placed next to one another, inducing the perception of movement. (Museum of Modern Art, New York. Philip Johnson Fund)

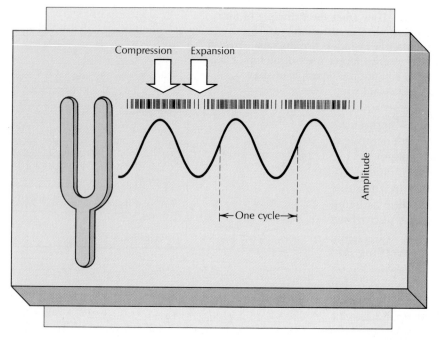

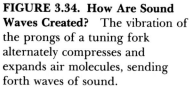

FIGURE 3.34. How Are Sound Waves Created? The vibration of the prongs of a tuning fork alternately compresses and expands air molecules, sending forth waves of sound.

HEARING

Consider the advertising slogan for the science fiction film *Alien:* "In space, no one can hear you scream." It's true. Space is an almost perfect vacuum, and hearing requires a medium, such as air or water, through which sound can travel.

Sound, or **auditory** stimulation, travels through the air like waves. Sound is caused by changes in air pressure that result from vibrations. These vibrations, in turn, can be created by a tuning fork, your vocal cords, guitar strings, or the clap of a book thrown down on a desk.

Figure 3.34 suggests the way in which a tuning fork creates sound waves. During a vibration back and forth, the right prong of the tuning fork moves to the right. In so doing, it pushes together, or compresses, the molecules of air immediately to the right. Then the prong moves back to the left, and the air molecules to the right expand. By vibrating back and forth, the tuning fork actually sends air waves in many directions. A cycle of

Auditory Having to do with hearing.
Hertz A unit expressing the frequency of sound waves. One Hertz, or *1 Hz*, equals one cycle per second.
Amplitude Height.

compression and expansion is considered one wave of sound. Sound waves can occur many times in one second. The human ear is sensitive to sound waves that vary from frequencies of 20 to 20,000 cycles per second.

Pitch and Loudness

Frequency The frequency of a sound, or the number of cycles per second, is expressed in the unit **Hertz**, abbreviated *Hz*. One cycle per second is one Hz. The greater the number of cycles per second (Hz), the higher the pitch of the sound. The pitch of women's voices is usually higher than those of men because women's vocal cords are usually shorter and thus vibrate at a greater frequency. The strings of a violin are shorter than those of a viola or bass viol. They vibrate at greater frequencies, and we perceive them as higher in pitch.

Amplitude The loudness of a sound is determined by the height, or amplitude, of sound waves. The higher the **amplitude** of the wave, the greater the loudness. Figure 3.35 shows records of sound waves that vary in frequency and amplitude. Frequency and amplitude are independent dimen-

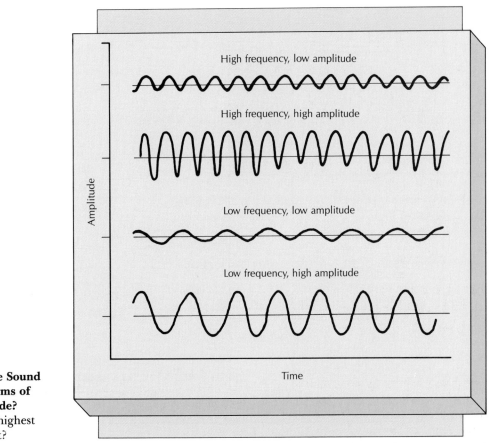

FIGURE 3.35. How Are Sound Waves Described in Terms of Frequency and Amplitude? Which sounds have the highest pitch? Which are loudest?

sions. Sounds both high and low in pitch can be either high or low in loudness.

The loudness of a sound is usually expressed in the unit **decibel,** abbreviated *dB,* which is named after the inventor of the telephone, Alexander Graham Bell. Zero dB is equivalent to the threshold of hearing. How loud is that? About as loud as the ticking of a watch 20 feet away in a very quiet room (see Table 3.1).

The decibel equivalents of many familiar sounds are shown in Figure 3.36. Twenty dB is equivalent in loudness to a whisper at five feet. Thirty dB is roughly the limit of loudness at which your librarian would like to keep your college library. You may suffer hearing damage if exposed to sustained sounds of 85 to 90 dB.

When musical sounds or tones of different frequency are played together, we also perceive a third tone that results from the difference in their frequencies. If the combination of tones is pleas-

ant, we say that they are in harmony, or **consonant** (from Latin roots meaning "together" and "sound"). Unpleasant combinations of tones are labeled **dissonant** ("the opposite of" and "sound"). The expression that something "strikes a dissonant chord" means that we find it disagreeable.

Overtones and Timbre   In addition to producing the specified musical note, instruments like the violin also produce a number of tones that are greater in frequency. These more highly pitched sounds are called **overtones.** Overtones result

Decibel A unit expressing the loudness of a sound. Abbreviated *dB.*

Consonant In harmony.

Dissonant Incompatible, discordant.

Overtones Tones of a higher frequency than those played that result from vibrations throughout a musical instrument.

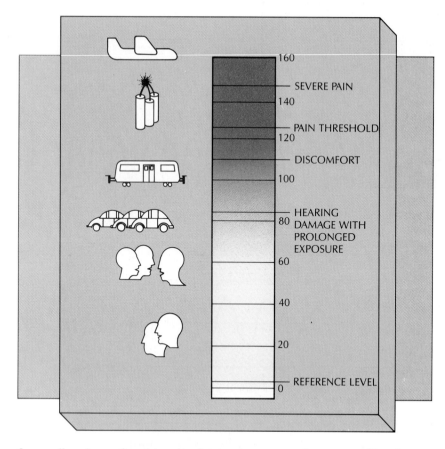

FIGURE 3.36. What Are the Decibel Ratings of Some Familiar Sounds?

from vibrations elsewhere in the instrument and contribute to the quality or richness—the **timbre**—of a sound. A $500 machine-made violin will produce the same musical notes as a $200,000 Stradivarius. But professional musicians require more expensive instruments because of the richness of their overtones—their timbre.

Noise   Noise is a combination of dissonant sounds. When you place a spiral shell to your ear, you do not hear the roar of the ocean. Rather, you hear the reflected noise in your vicinity. **White noise** consists of many different frequencies of sound. Yet white noise, this mixture, can lull us to sleep if the loudness is not too great.

Timbre The quality or richness of a sound.

White noise Discordant sounds of many frequencies, often producing a lulling effect.

Eardrum A thin membrane that vibrates in response to sound waves, transmitting the waves to the middle and inner ears.

Now let us turn our attention to the marvelous instrument that senses all these different "vibes": the human ear.

The Ear

The human ear is good for lots of things—catching dust, combing your hair around, hanging jewelry from, and nibbling. It is also admirably suited for sensing auditory stimulation, or hearing. It is shaped and structured to capture sound waves, to vibrate in sympathy with them, and to transmit all this business to the brain.

You have an outer ear, a middle ear, and an inner ear. The outer ear is shaped to funnel sound waves to the **eardrum** (see Figure 3.37), a thin membrane that vibrates in response to sound waves and thereby transmits them to the middle and inner ears. The middle ear contains the eardrum and three small bones, the hammer, the anvil, and the stirrup, which also transmit sound by

various perfumes on their breasts at bedtime. One perfume contained suspected pheromones. The couples tracked their sexual activity. One couple in five showed significantly more frequent sexual activity when they used the pheromone-laced perfume, although they did not know when the substance was being used. Pheromone-sensitive couples also engaged in sexual relations more frequently at the time of ovulation. And so, pheromones may play some role in the sex lives of people who are sensitive to them, even if they are unnecessary.

TASTE

Your cocker spaniel may jump at the chance to finish off your ice cream cones, but your Siamese cat may turn up her nose at this golden opportunity. Why? Dogs can perceive the taste quality of sweetness, as can pigs, but cats cannot (Dethier, 1978).

There are four primary taste qualities: sweet, sour, salty, and bitter. The "flavor" of a food involves its taste but is more complex. As noted earlier, apples and onions have the same taste—or the same mix of taste qualities—but their flavor is vastly different. After all, you wouldn't chomp into a nice cold onion on a warm day, would you? The flavor of a food depends on its odor, texture, and temperature, as well as its taste. If it were not for odor, heated tenderized shoe leather might just pass for your favorite steak.

Taste is sensed through **taste cells,** or receptor neurons that are located on **taste buds.** You have about 10,000 taste buds, most of which are located near the edges and back of your tongue. As noted in Figure 3.38, taste buds tend to specialize a bit. Some, for example, are more responsive to sweetness, whereas others react to several tastes. Receptors for sweetness lie at the tip of the tongue, and receptors for bitterness lie toward the back of the tongue. Sourness is sensed along the sides of the tongue, and saltiness overlaps the areas sensitive to sweetness and sourness (Figure 3.38). This is why people perceive a sour dish to "get them" at the sides of the tongue.

According to psychophysicist Linda Bartoshuk, we live in "different taste worlds" (Sheraton,

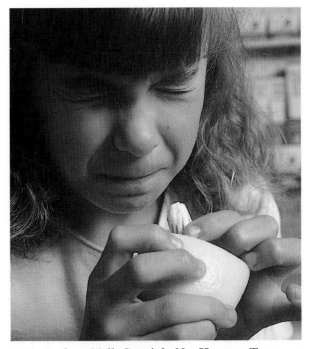

A Taste of . . . Well, Certainly Not Honey.   Tastes can lead to powerful emotional responses.

1984). Some of us, with a low sensitivity for the sweet taste, could require twice the sugar to sweeten our food as others who are more sensitive to sweetness. Others of us who claim to enjoy very bitter foods may actually be taste-blind to them. Sensitivities to different tastes apparently have a strong genetic component.

By eating hot foods and scraping your tongue, you regularly kill off many taste cells. But you need not be alarmed at this unintentional display of oral aggression. Taste cells are the rabbits of the sense receptors, reproducing at the rate of complete renewal every week or so.

The number of taste cells declines with age. However, Bartoshuk also found that strong taste intensities can be elicited from very small parts of the tongue (Turkington, 1985). It is more likely, according to Bartoshuk, that the "taste" loss asso-

Taste cells Receptor cells that are sensitive to taste.

Taste buds The sensory organs for taste. They contain taste cells and are located on the tongue.

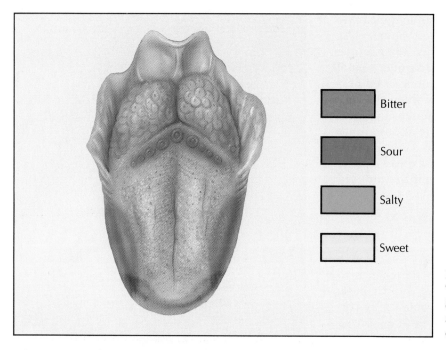

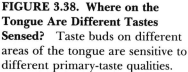

Bitter

Sour

Salty

Sweet

FIGURE 3.38. Where on the Tongue Are Different Tastes Sensed? Taste buds on different areas of the tongue are sensitive to different primary-taste qualities.

ciated with the elderly is actually due to a decline in the sense of smell. In any event, the elderly may spice their food more heavily than the young to enhance its flavor. Since food is less savory, the elderly may also eat less and become malnourished.

THE SKIN SENSES

Vision is usually the dominant sense, but 6-month-old infants are sometimes so engrossed with the feel of objects that they may better remember changes in temperature than changes in color (Bushnell et al., 1985). Of course, on a hot, humid July day, we may all pay more attention to an icy breeze than to a change in the color of a neighbor's beach umbrella.

Changes in temperature are just one type of event we sense by means of nerve endings in the skin. We know that the skin discriminates among many kinds of sensations—touch, pressure,

warmth, cold, and pain—but how it does so is not so clear. We apparently have distinct sensory receptors for pressure, temperature, and pain (Brown & Deffenbacher, 1979), but some nerve endings might also receive more than one type of sensory input.

Touch and Pressure

Sensory receptors located around the roots of hair cells appear to fire in response to touching the surface of the skin. You may have noticed that if you are trying to "get the feel" of a fabric or the texture of a friend's hair, you must move your hand over it (Loomis & Lederman, 1986). Otherwise, the sensations quickly fade. If you pass your hand over the skin and then hold it still, again sensations of touching will fade. This sort of "active touching" involves reception of information concerning not only touch per se but also pressure, temperature, and feedback from the muscles that are involved in movements of our hands.

Other structures beneath the skin are apparently sensitive to pressure. Different parts of the body are more sensitive to touch and pressure than others. Psychophysicists use methods such as the **two-point threshold** to assess sensitivity to pres-

Two-point threshold The least distance by which two rods touching the skin must be separated before the subject will report that there are two rods, not one, on 50 percent of occasions.

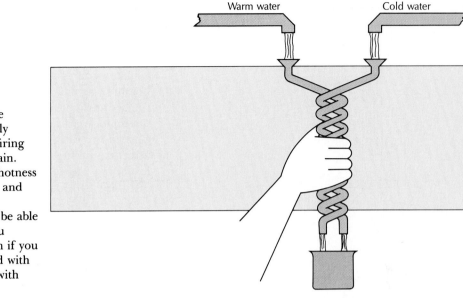

FIGURE 3.39. What Is Paradoxical Hotness? The perception of hotness usually relies on the simultaneous firing of receptors for cold and pain. However, we also perceive hotness when receptors for warmth and coldness are stimulated simultaneously. Would you be able to hold on to the coils if you perceived intense heat, even if you knew that one coil was filled with warm water and the other with cold water?

sure. This method determines the smallest distance by which two rods touching the skin must be separated before the (blindfolded) subject will report that there are two rods, not one. Our fingertips, lips, noses, and cheeks are more sensitive than our shoulders, thighs, and calves. That is, the rods can be closer together when they touch the lips than the shoulders but still be perceived as distinct.

The sense of pressure like the sense of touch undergoes rather rapid adaptation. You may have undertaken several minutes of strategic movements to wind up with your hand on the arm or leg of your date, only to discover that adaptation to this delightful source of pressure saps the sensation.

Temperature

The receptors for temperature are neurons just beneath the skin. When skin temperature increases, receptors for warmth fire. Decreases in skin temperature cause receptors for cold to fire.

Sensations of temperature are relative. When we are at normal body temperature, we might perceive the skin of another person as warm. But when we are feverish, the other person might seem cool to the touch. We also adapt to differences in temperature. When we walk out of an air-conditioned house into the desert sun, we at first feel

intense heat. Then the sensations of heat tend to fade (although we may still be made terribly uncomfortable by high humidity). Similarly, when we first enter a swimming pool, the water may seem cool or cold because it is below body temperature. But after a few moments an 85-degree-Fahrenheit pool might seem quite warm. In fact, we may tease the tentative newcomer for being overly sensitive.

Note that we have receptors that are sensitive to warmth and to coldness. However, sensations of hotness are *not* transmitted by rapid firing of warmth receptors—nor by firing of whole platoons of warmth receptors. Instead, in one of nature's unexpected twists, it turns out that so-called cold receptors fire not only when they are stimulated by objects below skin temperature but also when they are stimulated by objects above 45 degrees centigrade. Warmth receptors also fire in response to hot stimulation, so sensations of hotness rely on the simultaneous firing of receptors for cold and warmth. (In the case of actual burning, receptors for pain will also fire.)

A classic experiment showed that simultaneous firing of receptors for warmth and coldness are linked to sensations of hotness, regardless of the nature of the stimulus that is causing the cold receptors to fire. As shown in Figure 3.39, two coils were intertwined. Warm water was run through one of them, and cold water through the other.

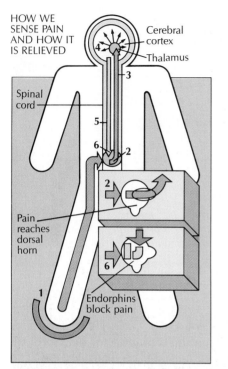

HOW WE SENSE PAIN AND HOW IT IS RELIEVED

Cerebral cortex

Thalamus

Spinal cord

Pain reaches dorsal horn

Endorphins block pain

FIGURE 3.40. How Do We Perceive Pain?   Pain originates at the point of contact, and the pain message to the brain is initiated by the release of prostaglandins, bradykinin, and substance *P*.

Yet people who grasped the coils simultaneously perceived heat so intense that they had to let go at once. Knowing that the heat was phony made no difference. Sensation was more convincing than knowledge. I'll bet my cash that you would let go of the coils on each trial, too.

Pain

Pain is a signal that something is wrong in the body. Pain is adaptive in the sense that it motivates us to do something about it. But for some of us, chronic pain—pain that even lasts once injuries or illnesses have cleared up—saps our vitality and the pleasures of everyday life.

As shown in Figure 3.40, pain originates at the point of contact, as with a stubbed toe. The pain message to the brain is initiated by the release of

Analgesic Giving rise to a state of not feeling pain, though fully conscious.

various chemicals, including prostaglandins, bradykinin (perhaps the most painful known substance), and the mysterious chemical called P (yes, *P* stands for "Pain"). Prostaglandins facilitate transmission of the pain message to the brain and heighten circulation to the injured area, causing the redness and swelling we call inflammation. Inflammation attracts white blood cells to the area to combat invading bacteria. **Analgesic** drugs such as aspirin and ibuprofen (Motrin, Medipren) work by inhibiting prostaglandin production.

The pain message is relayed from the spinal cord to the thalamus and then projected to the cerebral cortex, where the location and intensity of the damage become apparent.

Gate Theory   Simple remedies like rubbing and scratching the toe frequently help. Why? One possible answer lies in the so-called "gate theory" of pain, originated by Melzack (1980). From this perspective, only a certain amount of stimulation can be processed by the nervous system at a time. Rubbing or scratching the toe transmits sensations to the brain that, in a sense, compete for neurons. And so, a number of nerves are prevented from transmitting pain messages to the brain. The mechanism is analogous to shutting down a "gate" in the spinal cord. It is something like too many calls flooding a switchboard at once. The flood prevents any calls from getting through.

Endorphins   In response to pain, the brain triggers the release of endorphins (see Chapter 2). A number of people who have severe pain that cannot be relieved by available medical treatments have been found to have lower-than-normal concentrations of endorphins in their cerebrospinal fluid (Akil, 1978).

Acupuncture   Thousands of years ago the Chinese began mapping the body to learn where pins might be placed to deaden pain elsewhere. Much of the Chinese practice of acupuncture was unknown in the West, even though Western powers occupied much of China during the 1800s. But early in the 1970s, *New York Times* columnist James Reston underwent an appendectomy in China, with acupuncture the only anesthetic. He reported no discomfort.

Reston's evidence is anecdotal, of course. The question of whether acupuncture can be scientifically demonstrated to provide relief from pain has been controversial, but a number of studies have suggested that acupuncture can relieve pain in humans, such as chronic back pain (Price et al., 1984). There is also experimental evidence that acupuncture reduces perception of pain in cats and mice (Levitt, 1981).

In Appendix A we shall explore a number of psychological methods of pain management.

KINESTHESIS

Try a brief experiment. Close your eyes. Then touch your nose with your index finger. If you weren't right on target, I'm sure you came close. But how? You didn't see your hand moving, and you (probably) didn't hear your arm swishing through the air.

You were able to bring your finger to your nose through your kinesthetic sense, called **kinesthesis,** after the Greek words for "motion" *(kinesis)* and "perception" *(aisthesis).* When you "make a muscle" in your arm, the sensations of tightness and hardness in the arm are also made possible by kinesthesis. Kinesthesis is the sense that informs you about the position and motion of parts of your body. In kinesthesis, sensory information is fed back to the brain from sensory organs in the joints, tendons, and muscles.

Imagine going for a walk without kinesthesis. You would have to watch the forward motion of each leg to be certain you had raised it high enough to clear the curb. And if you had tried our brief experiment without the kinesthetic sense, you would have had no sensory feedback until you felt the pressure of your finger against your nose (or cheek, or eye, or forehead), and you probably would have missed dozens of times.

THE VESTIBULAR SENSE

Your **vestibular sense** informs you whether you are upright (physically, not morally). Sensory organs located in the **semicircular canals** (Figure 3.37) and elsewhere in the ears monitor your

What Is Kinesthesis? This dancer receives information about the position and motion of parts of her body through kinesthesis. She can intimately follow her own movements without visually observing herself.

body's motion and position in relationship to gravity. They tell you whether you are falling and provide cues to whether your body is changing speeds, as in an accelerating airplane or automobile.

In this chapter we have explored the sensory systems that permit us to gather information about the world. In the next chapter we shall see how information leads to learning and how we remember much of the information that we encounter.

Kinesthesis The sense that informs us about the positions and motion of parts of our bodies.

Vestibular sense The sense of equilibrium that informs us about our bodies' positions relative to gravity.

Semicircular canals Structures of the inner ear that monitor body movement and position.

TRUTH OR FICTION REVISITED

Sometimes we don't hear things because we don't want to hear them.   True. As explained by signal-detection theory, motivation is one of the psychological factors that influence perception.

White sunlight is actually composed of all the colors of the rainbow.   True. White light can be broken down into its components—the visible spectrum—by a prism.

On a clear, dark night you could probably see the light from a single candle burning 25 miles away.   True. This degree of brightness is well within the absolute threshold for light.

If our eyes were sensitive to lights of slightly longer wavelengths, warmblooded animals would glow in the dark.   True. Warmblooded animals give off heat, and heat is detected in the infrared portion of the electromagnetic spectrum.

We all have blind spots in our eyes.   True. It is at the spot where axons of ganglion cells gather to form the optic nerve.

As we approach late adulthood, we become more likely to need reading glasses, even if our visual acuity has been perfect at younger ages.   True. This is because of increased brittleness of the lens, or presbyopia.

When we mix blue and yellow light, we get green light.   False. By mixing blue and yellow light, we get gray light. We get green by mixing blue and yellow *pigments.*

"Motion pictures" do not move at all.   True. Stroboscopic motion—presentation of a series of still pictures—creates the illusion of movement.

We need two eyes in order to perceive depth.   False. There are several monocular (one-eyed) cues for depth perception.

The advertising slogan for the film Alien *was accurate: "In space, no one can hear you scream."*   True. Sound waves require a medium like air or water, and space is an almost perfect vacuum.

A $500 machine-made violin will produce the same notes as a $200,000 Stradivarius.   True. The difference in quality between the instruments lies in the rich overtones of the Stradivarius.

People who listen to loud rock music are likely to suffer hearing loss.   True. This kind of loss is referred to as stimulation deafness. (Stimulation deafness results from the loudness of the music, not the fact that it is rock music.)

The menstrual cycles of women who live together tend to be synchronized.   True. This occurs because of chemical substances that are sensed by smell.

Onions and apples have the same taste.   True. But their flavor, which includes their odor and other cues, is vastly different.

The elderly find their food less flavorful than the young because of loss in the sense of taste.   False. Loss in the sense of smell is the more likely culprit.

We have no sensory receptors for perceiving hotness.   True. The perception of extreme heat is brought about by the simultaneous stimulation of receptors for cold and warmth.

Rubbing or scratching a painful toe can help provide relief.   True. It seems that rubbing and scratching sends stimulation to the brain that competes with the pain messages and thus decreases their magnitude.

Chapter Review

Sensation refers to mechanical processes that involve the stimulation of sensory receptors (neurons) and the transmission of sensory information to the central nervous system. Perception is the active organization of sensations into a representation of the world.

The absolute threshold for a stimulus is the lowest intensity at which it can be detected. The minimum difference in intensity that can be discriminated is the difference threshold, which is expressed in a fraction called Weber's constant.

According to signal-detection theory, the detection of a signal is determined by the sensory stimuli themselves, the degree to which they can be distinguished from background noise, the biological sensory system of the person, and psychological factors such as motivation and attention. Sensory adaptation refers to the processes by which we become more sensitive to weak stimuli and less sensitive to strong stimuli.

Vision is our dominant sense. Visible light triggers visual sensations and is one part of a spectrum of electromagnetic energy, which is described in terms of wavelengths. The wavelength of visible light determines its color, or hue.

The eye senses and transmits visual stimulation to the occipital lobe of the cerebral cortex. Accommodation of the lens focuses light so that a clear image is projected onto the retina, which is composed of photoreceptors called rods and cones. Rods and cones send neural messages through the bipolar cells to ganglion cells, whose axons constitute the optic nerve.

Cones permit perception of color, whereas rods transmit sensations of light and dark only. Rods are more sensitive than cones to light and continue to adapt to darkness once cones have reached peak adaptation.

The brightness of a color is its lightness. The saturation of a color is its pureness. Yellows, oranges, and reds are considered warm colors, whereas blues and greens are considered cool.

Colors across from one another on the color wheel are termed complementary. The mixture of lights is an additive process. When we mix lights of complementary colors, they dissolve into gray. The afterimage of a color is its complement. The mixture of pigments is a subtractive process.

According to trichromatic theory, there are three types of cones, some sensitive to red, some to blue, and some to green light. Opponent-process theory proposes three types of color receptors: red-green, blue-yellow, and light-dark. People with normal color vision are called trichromats. People who can see light and dark only are called monochromats. Dichromats are more common, and they can discriminate only two colors: red and green or blue and yellow.

Gestalt rules of perceptual organization influence our grouping of bits of sensory stimulation into meaningful wholes. Rules of perceptual organization concern figure-ground relationships, proximity, similarity, continuity, common fate, and closure.

We perceive real movement by sensing motion across the retina and by sensing change of position of an object in relation to other objects. Illusions of movement include the autokinetic effect, stroboscopic motion, and the phi phenomenon. Depth perception involves monocular cues (perspective, clearness, interposition, shadowing, texture gradient, and motion parallax) and binocular cues (retinal disparity and convergence). Through experience we develop perceptual constancies; we learn to assume that objects retain their size, shape, brightness, and color despite their distance, their position, or changes in lighting conditions.

Sound waves alternately compress and expand molecules of the medium, creating vibrations. The human ear can hear sounds varying in frequency from 20 to 20,000 cycles per second. We can suffer hearing loss if exposed to protracted sounds of 85 to 90 dB or more.

The ear consists of an outer, middle, and inner ear. The eardrum transmits sound waves to the middle ear, which contains the bones, the hammer, anvil, and stirrup. The middle ear transmits sound waves to the inner ear, or cochlea. Within the cochlea are fluids that vibrate against the basilar membrane, to which the "command post of hearing," or organ of Corti, is attached. Hair cells on the organ of Corti respond to the vibrations of the basilar membrane and transmit sound to the brain by the auditory nerve.

Two major theories have been advanced to account for the perception of pitch: place theory and frequency theory. Duplicity theory suggests the view that pitch perception depends both on the place and frequency of neural response. There are three major types of deafness: conduction, sensory-neural, and stimulation deafness.

An odor is a sample of a number of molecules of a substance. Odors are detected by the olfactory membrane in each nostril.

There are four primary taste qualities: sweet, sour, salty, and bitter. Flavor involves not only the taste of food but also its odor, texture, and temperature. The receptor neurons for taste are called taste cells, and they are located in taste buds.

There are five skin senses: touch, pressure, warmth, cold, and pain. Receptors for pain are triggered by cold temperatures and also by temperatures of above 45 degrees centigrade. Pain originates at the point of contact and is transmitted to the brain by various chemicals, including prostaglandins, bradykinin, and substance P.

Kinesthesis is the sensing of body position and movement. Kinesthesis relies on sensory organs in the joints, tendons, and muscles. The vestibular sense tells us if we are in an upright position or changing speeds. The vestibular sense is housed primarily in the semicircular canals of the ears.

Exercises

Parts of the Eye

Directions: *Following is a drawing of the human eye. Can you label its parts and explain the function of each? Check your answers against Figure 3.2 on page 101.*

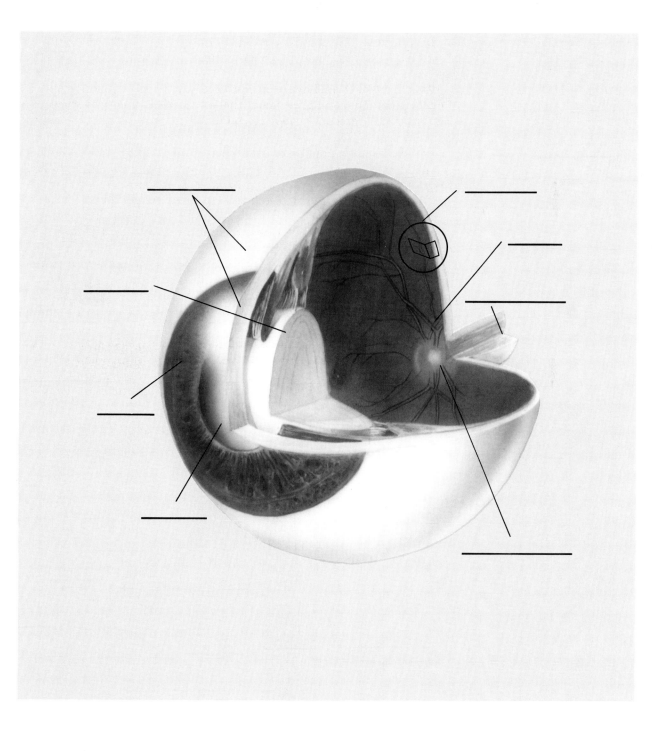

Parts of the Ear

Directions: *Following is a drawing of the human ear. Can you label its parts and explain the function of each? Check your answers against Figure 3.37 on page 127.*

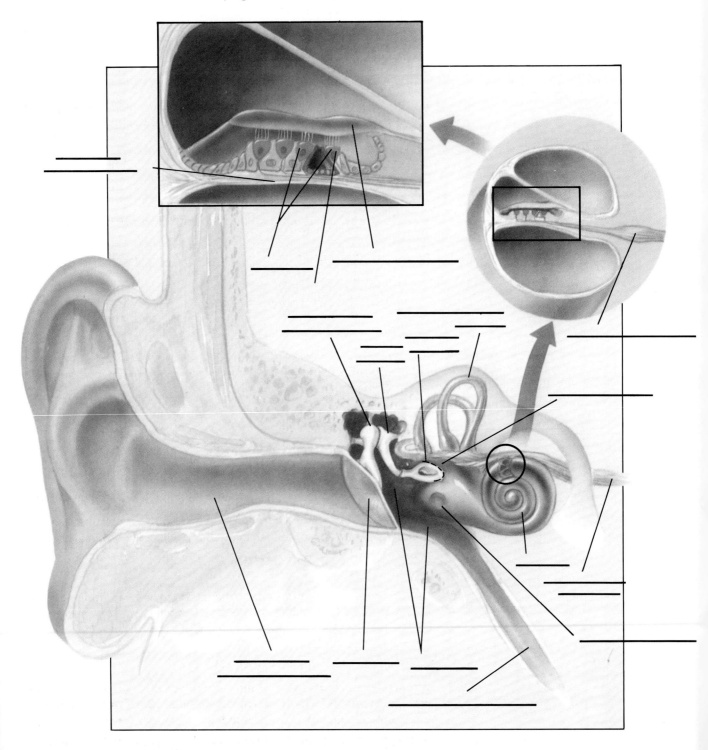

Posttest

Directions: *For each of the following, select the choice that best answers the question or completes the sentence.*

1. Perception is defined as the

   (a) stimulation of sensory receptors by physical energy, (b) organization of sensations into an inner map of the world, (c) transmission of sensory information to the brain, (d) formation of mental images.

2. The difference threshold for light is defined as the

   (a) difference in wavelengths between analogous hues, (b) amplitude divided by the wavelength, (c) smallest difference in intensity required to perceive a difference in intensity, (d) weakest amount of light the the average person can perceive.

3. Which of the following colors is longest in wavelength?

   (a) Red, (b) Yellow, (c) Indigo, (d) Green.

4. The amount of light that enters the eye is determined by the size of the

   (a) cornea, (b) lens, (c) retina, (d) pupil.

5. Rods and cones are both

   (a) bipolar cells, (b) ganglion cells, (c) photoreceptors, (d) color receptors.

6. You have normal color vision. You look at a sheet of paper that is colored yellow for about 30 seconds. Then you shift your gaze to a sheet of paper that is white. On this paper, you perceive the color

   (a) green, (b) blue, (c) gray, (d) red.

7. The Ponzo illusion can probably be explained by the

   (a) volley principle, (b) autokinetic effect, (c) phi phenomenon, (d) principle of size constancy.

8. The cue for depth perception that involves both eyes is

   (a) retinal disparity, (b) motion parallax, (c) perspective, (d) shape constancy.

9. The Rubin vase is used by psychologists to illustrate the principle of

   (a) shape constancy, (b) size constancy, (c) retinal disparity, (d) an ambiguous figure.

10. You look at a work of art that contains many colors. Some of these colors seem to leap out at you, whereas others seem to recede. The colors that appear to advance toward you are most likely to be _____ colors.

    (a) complementary, (b) analogous, (c) warm, (d) cool.

11. You see several birds flying in the same direction. It occurs to you that you assume these birds are going to the same place for the same reason. Your assumption illustrates the Gestalt principle of

    (a) shape constancy, (b) continuity, (c) similarity, (d) common fate.

12. The _____ is found in the inner ear.

(a) eardrum, (b) basilar membrane, (c) hammer, (d) stirrup.

13. The frequency of a sound is expressed in the unit

(a) waves, (b) dB, (c) Hz, (d) pitch.

14. Frequency theory breaks down for perception of pitch higher than

(a) 20 Hz, (b) 400 Hz, (c) 4,000 Hz, (d) 20,000 Hz.

15. Which of the following statements about deafness is accurate?

(a) Ringing in the ears probably means that hair cells have been damaged, (b) Prolonged exposure to loud noises can cause conduction deafness, (c) Conduction deafness occurs because of damage to the structures of the inner ear, (d) Hearing aids are frequently of help to people who suffer sensory-neural deafness.

16. Which of the following is a chemical sense?

(a) Smell, (b) Vision, (c) The vestibular sense, (d) Kinesthesis.

17. Research with pheromones suggests that

(a) there is really no such thing as a pheromone, (b) only lower animals are responsive to them, (c) they regulate sexual behavior in all animals, (d) most people are not responsive to them.

18. Receptors for _____ lie toward the back of the tongue.

(a) sweetness, (b) bitterness, (c) saltiness, (d) sourness.

19. The elderly probably spice their food heavily because of

(a) the loss of taste buds, (b) the loss of taste cells, (c) decline in the sense of smell, (d) decline in kinesthetic feedback.

20. Which of the following kinds of receptors fire in response to objects whose temperatures are above 45 degrees centigrade?

(a) Cold receptors only, (b) Warmth receptors only, (c) Hot receptors only, (d) Cold and warmth receptors.

21. Aspirin and acetaminophen probably reduce pain by

(a) shutting down a gate in the spinal cord, (b) locking into receptor sites for substance *P*, (c) inhibiting prostaglandin production, (d) attracting infection-fighting blood cells to the damaged area.

22. Kinesthetic sensory organs are found in all of the following *except*

(a) joints, (b) tendons, (c) muscles, (d) bones.

Answer Key to Posttest

1. B	**7.** D	**13.** C	**18.** B
2. C	**8.** A	**14.** C	**19.** C
3. A	**9.** D	**15.** A	**20.** D
4. D	**10.** C	**16.** A	**21.** C
5. C	**11.** D	**17.** D	**22.** D
6. B	**12.** B		

LEARNING AND MEMORY

OUTLINE

PRETEST: TRUTH OR FICTION?
CLASSICAL CONDITIONING
   Stimuli and Responses in Classical Conditioning:
      US, CS, UR, and CR
   Extinction and Spontaneous Recovery
   Generalization and Discrimination
   Applications of Classical Conditioning
OPERANT CONDITIONING
   Edward L. Thorndike and the Law of Effect
   B. F. Skinner and Reinforcement
   Schedules of Reinforcement
   Applications of Operant Conditioning
COGNITIVE LEARNING
   Learning by Insight
   Latent Learning

   Observational Learning
MEMORY
   The Structure of Memory
   Sensory Memory
   Short-Term Memory
   Long-Term Memory
   Forgetting
   Why People Forget
   Some Methods for Improving Memory
   The Biology of Memory: From Engrams
      to Epinephrine
TRUTH OR FICTION REVISITED
CHAPTER REVIEW
EXERCISE
POSTTEST

PRETEST: TRUTH OR FICTION?

Dogs can be trained to salivate when a bell is rung.

We can learn to change our behavior while we are sleeping.

Psychologists helped a young boy overcome fear of rabbits by having him eat cookies while a rabbit was brought nearer.

During World War II, a psychologist devised a plan for training pigeons to guide missiles to their targets.

You can "hook" people on gambling by allowing them to win some money in the early stages and then tapering off with the payoffs.

Punishment doesn't work.

Rats can be trained to climb a ramp, cross a bridge, climb a ladder, pedal a toy car, and do several other tasks—all in proper sequence.

Rats have been taught to raise or lower their heart rates in order to receive an interesting reward—a burst of electricity in the brain.

Psychologists successfully fashioned a method to teach an emaciated 9-month-old infant to stop throwing up.

We must make mistakes in order to learn.

Only people are capable of insight.

All our experiences are permanently imprinted on the brain so that proper stimulation can cause us to remember them exactly.

There is such a thing as a photographic memory.

There is no limit to the amount of information you can store in your memory.

We can remember some important events that took place as early as the age of 1 or 2.

We are more likely to recall happy events while we are feeling happy and sad events while we are feeling sad.

You can use tricks to improve your memory.

Rats were helped to remember their way through mazes by being injected with the poison strychnine.

A nasal spray can improve memory functioning.

In Aldous Huxley's futuristic novel, *Brave New World,* the Director of the Central London Hatchery and Conditioning Center is leading a group of visitors on a tour. The year is 632 A.F. (that is, after Ford, or 632 years after the birth of Henry Ford, the originator of many techniques of mass production in the twentieth century).

Five classes of people populate the London of the future—Alphas, Betas, Gammas, Deltas, and Epsilons. The Alphas are the brightest. Administrators are drawn from their rank. Epsilons are least intelligent and supply menial laborers. But Epsilons are happy. Selective breeding, oxygen deprivation prior to birth, and early learning or **conditioning** combine to lead them to want only what the central planners of the brave new world decree that they should have, and not to want what it is decreed they should not have. That, notes the Director, "is the secret of happiness and virtue—liking what you've got to do. All conditioning aims at that: making people like their unescapable social destiny."

The tour arrives at the Neo-Pavlovian Conditioning Rooms, where the visitors witness a demonstration of one step in the conditioning of Delta children. Deltas belong to the caste just above Epsilons, and also primarily supply laborers. The social destiny of Deltas requires them to be able to focus exclusively on their assigned physical labor and not on higher forms of human activity, such as reading or even the appreciation of beauty or nature.

"Set out the books," commands the Director.

In silence the nurses obeyed his command. Between the rose bowls the books were duly set out—a row of nursery quartos opened invitingly each at some gaily colored image of beast or fish or bird.

"Now bring in the children."

They hurried out of the room and returned in a minute or two, each pushing a kind of tall dumbwaiter laden, on all its four wire-netted shelves, with eight-month-old babies, all exactly alike (a Bokanovsky Group, it was evident) and all (since their caste was Delta) dressed in khaki.

"Put them down on the floor."

The infants were unloaded.

Conditioning A simple form of learning of associations between stimuli and responses.

"Now turn them so that they can see the flowers and books."

Turned, the babies at once fell silent, then [crawled] toward those clusters of sleek colors, those shapes so gay and brilliant on the white pages. . . . Small hands reached out uncertainly, touched, grasped, unpetaling the . . . roses, crumpling the . . . pages of the books. The Director waited until all were happily busy. Then, "Watch carefully," he said. And, lifting his hand, he gave the signal.

The Head Nurse, who was standing by a switchboard at the other end of the room, pressed down a little lever.

There was a violent explosion. Shriller and ever shriller, a siren shrieked. Alarm bells maddeningly sounded.

The children started, screamed; their faces were distorted with terror.

"And now," the Director shouted (for the noise was deafening), "now we proceed to rub in the lesson with a mild electric shock."

He waved his hand again, and the Head Nurse pressed a second lever. The screaming of the babies suddenly changed its tone. There was something desperate, almost insane, about the sharp spasmodic yelps to which they now gave utterance. Their little bodies twitched and stiffened; their limbs moved jerkily as if to the tug of unseen wires.

"We can electrify that whole strip of floor," bawled the Director in explanation. "But that's enough," he signalled to the nurse.

The explosions ceased, the bells stopped ringing, the shriek of the siren died down from tone to tone into silence. The stiffly twitching bodies relaxed, and what had become the sob and yelp of infant maniacs broadened out once more into a normal howl of ordinary terror.

"Offer them the flowers and the books again."

The nurses obeyed, but at the image of the roses, at the mere sight of those gaily colored images of pussy and cock-a-doodle-doo and baa-baa black sheep, the infants shrank away in horror; the volume of their howling suddenly increased.

"Observe," said the Director triumphantly, "observe."

Books and loud noises, flowers and electric shocks—already in the infant mind these couples were compromisingly linked; and after 200 repetitions of the same or a similar lesson would be wedded indissolubly. What man has joined, nature is powerless to put asunder.

"They'll grow up with what psychologists used to call an 'instinctive' hatred of books and flowers. Reflexes unalterably conditioned. They'll be safe from books and botany all their lives." The Director turned to his nurses. "Take them away again."

Still yelling, the khaki babies were loaded on to their dumbwaiters and wheeled out, leaving behind them the smell of sour milk and a most welcome silence.

Brave New World, fortunately, is a work of fiction, not of fact. But the Director's program for teaching Delta infants to cringe at the sight of books and flowers has a realistic ring. It is clearly consistent with what we know of **classical conditioning**—a simple form of learning in which an originally neutral stimulus comes to bring forth, or elicit, the response usually brought forth by another stimulus by being paired repeatedly with that other stimulus. In *Brave New World,* the Director repeatedly paired books and flowers with stimuli that elicited fear (loud noises and electric shocks). The result was that the children learned to respond to the books and flowers as if they were loud noises and electric shocks.

This type of classical conditioning described so vividly in *Brave New World* is more specifically termed **aversive conditioning.** In aversive conditioning a neutral stimulus is paired repeatedly with an aversive stimulus. Eventually, the previously neutral stimulus acquires aversive properties itself. *Brave New World* is a work of fiction and shows how the learning discoveries of psychologists may be perverted. But many psychologists today use aversive conditioning to help clients gain control over "bad habits," as we shall see in Chapter 10. For example, clients who want to stop smoking cigarettes may use the technique of rapid smoking, in which they inhale every six seconds, so that (previously desired) cigarette smoke takes on an aversive quality. Electric shock and nausea-producing drugs have also been used to help people gain control over problem drinking.

In this chapter we discuss learning and memory. We may as well admit at the outset that the very definition of **learning** stirs controversy in psychology. From a cognitive perspective, learning is *the process by which* experience leads to a relatively permanent change in behavior. Learning is *made evident* by behavioral change but is defined as an internal, and not directly observable, process. From a behaviorist perspective, learning *is* the change in behavior that stems from experience. Behaviorists, that is, define learning in terms of the measurable events or changes in behavior by which it is known. Let us be aware that there is a controversy about how to define *learning,* but it need not affect your study of the three major forms of learning discussed in the chapter: *classical conditioning, operant conditioning,* and *cognitive learning.*

Learning would do us little good if we could not remember what we had learned. For this reason, this chapter also discusses memory. We may define **memory** as the processes by which learning is maintained over the passage of time. Memory is actually a complex group of processes that do not all seem to operate according to the same set of rules. (When you have completed the chapter, you may think that we should speak of *memories,* not simply of *a* memory.) We shall attempt to sort out truth from fiction, myth from reality, in our study of memory. We shall see that we can use many strategies to improve memory, and that memory, like other cognitive processes, involves biological changes. In our exploration of this strange biology, we shall observe life in a goldfish bowl. We won't come to grips with why the chicken crossed the road, but we shall explain why the fish swam to the other side of the tank. We shall also learn, at long last, what makes the worm turn—or more precisely, what made a number of worms turn in the laboratories of certain psychologists.

CLASSICAL CONDITIONING

Classical conditioning was discovered by accident by Russian scientist Ivan Pavlov (1849–1936) while

Classical conditioning A simple form of learning in which one stimulus comes to evoke the response usually evoked by a second stimulus by being paired repeatedly with the second stimulus.

Aversive conditioning A type of classical conditioning in which a previously desirable or neutral stimulus acquires aversive (repugnant) properties by being paired repeatedly with an aversive stimulus.

Learning (1) The process by which experience leads to a relatively permanent change in behavior. (2) The behaviorist definition: a relatively permanent change in behavior that results from experience.

Memory Processes by which learning is maintained over time.

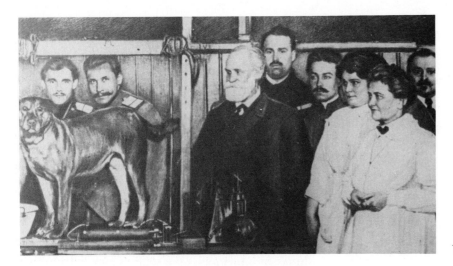

Who Is Ivan Pavlov?

he was trying to identify neural receptors in the mouth that triggered a response from the salivary glands. His efforts were hampered by the fact that the dogs often salivated at undesired times, as when a laboratory assistant inadvertently clinked a food tray.

Because of its biological makeup, a dog will salivate if meat is placed on its tongue. Salivation in response to meat is unlearned, a **reflex.** Reflexes are elicited by a certain range of stimuli. A **stimulus** may be defined as a change in the environment, such as dropping meat on the tongue or a traffic light changing from green to red. Reflexes are simple unlearned responses, but Pavlov found that reflexes can also be learned, or conditioned, through association. His dogs began salivating in response to clinking food trays because this noise had been paired repeatedly with the arrival of

food. The dogs would also salivate when an assistant entered the laboratory. Why? The assistant had brought in food.

Pavlov at first saw this uncalled-for canine salivation as an annoyance, an impediment to his research. But in 1901 he decided that his "problem" was worth looking into. He set about to show that he could train, or condition, his dogs to salivate when he wished and in response to any stimulus he chose. These trained salivary responses are **conditioned responses** (CRs).

Pavlov demonstrated conditioned responses by strapping a dog into a harness such as the one in Figure 4.1. When meat was placed on the dog's tongue, it salivated. He repeated the process several times, with one difference. He preceded the meat by half a second or so with the ringing of a bell on each occasion. After several pairings of meat and bell, Pavlov rang the bell but did *not* follow the bell with meat. Still the dog salivated. It had learned to salivate in response to the bell.

Stimuli and Responses in Classical Conditioning: US, CS, UR, and CR

In the demonstration just described, the meat is an unlearned or **unconditioned stimulus** (US). Salivation in response to the meat is an unlearned or **unconditioned response** (UR). The bell was at first a meaningless or neutral stimulus. It might have produced an **orienting reflex** in the dog because of its distinctness. But it was not yet associated with

---

Reflex A simple unlearned response to a stimulus.

Stimulus A change in the environment that leads to a change in behavior.

Conditioned response In classical conditioning, a learned response to a conditioned stimulus.

Unconditioned stimulus A stimulus that elicits a response from an organism without learning.

Unconditioned response An unlearned response to an unconditioned stimulus.

Orienting reflex An unlearned response in which an organism attends to a stimulus.

By means of the bell-and-pad method, children are taught to wake up in response to bladder tension. They sleep on a special sheet or pad. When they start to urinate, the water content of the urine causes an electrical circuit in the pad to be closed. Closing of the circuit triggers a bell or buzzer, and the child is awakened. Technically speaking, the bell is a *US* that wakes the child (waking up is the *UR*). By means of repeated pairings, stimuli that precede the bell become associated with the bell and also gain the capacity to awaken the child. What stimuli are these? The sensations of a full bladder. In this way, bladder tension (the CS) gains the capacity to awaken the child *even though the child is asleep during the classical conditioning procedure.*

The Story of Little Albert: A Case Study in the Classical Conditioning of Emotional Responses

In 1920, John B. Watson and his future wife, Rosalie Rayner, published an article describing their demonstration that emotional reactions such as fears could be acquired through classical conditioning. The subject of their demonstration was an unlucky lad by the name of Little Albert, who enjoyed playing with a laboratory rat.

Using a method that some psychologists have criticized as unethical, Watson startled Little Albert by clanging steel bars behind his head when he played with the rat. After seven pairings, Albert showed fear of the rat, even though clanging was suspended. Albert's fear generalized to objects similar in appearance to the rat, such as a rabbit and the fur collar on his mother's coat.

Somewhere there may be a gentleman in his 60s who cringes when he sees furry puppies or furry muffs protecting the hands of girls in winter and, of course, whenever rats are discussed on television.

Extinguishing and Counterconditioning of Fears

Behavior therapists have used principles of conditioning to derive several innovative methods for reducing fears.

Two behavioral methods for reducing fears are based on extinction. In one, **flooding,** the client is exposed to the fear-evoking stimulus until fear responses are extinguished. Albert, for example, might have been placed in close contact with a rat until his fears had become fully extinguished. In extinction, the CS (in this case, the rat) is presented repeatedly in the absence of the US (the clanging of the steel bars), until the CR (fear) is extinguished.

Although flooding is usually effective, it is unpleasant (when you are fearful of rats, being placed in a small room with one is not a holiday). For this reason, behavior therapists frequently prefer to use **systematic desensitization,** in which the client is exposed gradually to fear-evoking stimuli under circumstances in which he or she remains relaxed. Systematic desensitization will be described more fully in Chapter 10. Here let us note that systematic desensitization, like flooding, is highly effective; it takes longer to work than flooding, but the tradeoff is that it is not unpleasant.

In **counterconditioning,** a pleasant stimulus is paired repeatedly with a fear-evoking object, in this way counteracting the fear response. Eating sweets is a pleasant activity for most of us (sigh), and psychologists discovered early in the century that a rabbit could be gradually introduced into a room where a boy who feared rabbits was eating cookies (Jones, 1924). The pleasure from the cookies counteracted fear and apparently "rubbed off" on the rabbit, so that the animal could gradually be brought closer. In time the boy played with it.

Through classical conditioning we learn to associate stimuli, so that a simple, usually passive, response made to one is then made in response to the other. In the case of Little Albert, clanging noises were associated with a rat, so that the rat came to elicit the fear response brought forth by the noise. Let us now turn our attention to operant conditioning, in which organisms learn to engage

---

Flooding A fear-reduction technique in which fear-evoking stimuli (CSs) are presented continuously in the absence of actual harm so that fear responses (CRs) are extinguished.

Systematic desensitization A fear-reduction technique in which a hierarchy or fear-evoking stimuli are presented while the person remains relaxed.

Counterconditioning A fear-reduction technique in which pleasant stimuli are associated with fear-evoking stimuli, so that the fear-evoking stimuli lose their aversive qualities.

Who Is Edward L. Thorndike?

in certain behaviors because of their effects. After classical conditioning took place, Albert's avoidance of rats would be labeled *operant behavior.* Avoidance of rats would be a voluntary response that has desired effects—in this case, the reduction of fear. Similarly, the sight of a hypodermic syringe may elicit a fear response because a person once had a painful injection. But subsequent avoidance of injections is operant behavior. It has the effect of reducing fear.

OPERANT CONDITIONING

In **operant conditioning** an organism learns to engage in behavior because of its effects. Operant conditioning is also referred to as **instrumental conditioning,** or instrumental learning, because the learned behavior is *instrumental* in manipulating the environment.

We begin this section with the historic work of psychologist Edward L. Thorndike. Then we shall examine the more recent work of B. F. Skinner.

Operant conditioning A simple form of learning in which an organism learns to engage in behavior because it is reinforced.

Instrumental conditioning A term similar to *operant conditioning,* reflecting the fact that the learned behavior is *instrumental* in achieving certain effects.

Random trial-and-error Referring to behavior that occurs in a novel situation prior to learning what behavior is rewarded or reinforced.

Edward L. Thorndike and the Law of Effect

In the 1890s there was a mystery in Manhattan. Stray cats were disappearing from the streets and alleyways. Many of them, it turned out, were brought to the quarters of Columbia University doctoral student Edward Thorndike. Thorndike used them as subjects in experiments in learning by trial and error.

Thorndike placed the cats in so-called puzzle boxes. If the animals managed to pull a dangling string, a latch would be released, allowing them to jump out and reach a bowl of food.

When first placed in a puzzle box, a cat would try to squeeze through any opening and would claw and bite at the confining bars and wire. It would claw at any feature it could reach. Through such **random trial-and-error** behavior, it might take three to four minutes before the cat would chance on the response of pulling the string. Pulling the string would open the cage and allow the cat to reach the food. When placed back in the cage, it might again take several minutes for the

How Has B. F. Skinner Contributed to Our Knowledge of Operant Conditioning?

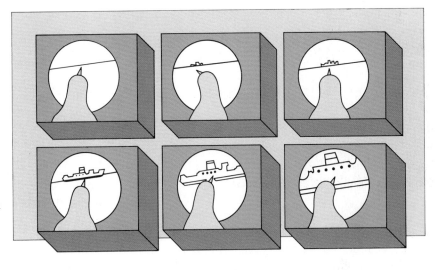

Figure 4.4. What Was Project Pigeon? During World War II, B. F. Skinner suggested training pigeons to guide missiles to their targets. In an operant conditioning procedure, the pigeons would be reinforced for pecking targets projected on a screen. Afterward, in combat, pecking at the on-screen target would keep the missile on course.

animal to pull the string. But as these trials were repeated, it would take progressively less time for the cat to pull the string. After seven or eight trials, it might pull the string immediately when placed back in the box.

The Law of Effect Thorndike explained the cat's learning to pull the string in terms of his **law of effect.** According to this law, a response (such as string pulling) is "stamped in" or strengthened in a particular situation (such as being inside a puzzle box) by a reward (escaping the box and eating). Rewards, that is, stamp in S–R (stimulus–response) connections. Punishments, by contrast, "stamp out" stimulus–response connections. Organisms would learn *not* to engage in punished responses. Later we shall see that the effects of punishment on learning are not so certain.

B. F. Skinner and Reinforcement

"What did you do in the war, Daddy?" is a question familiar to many who served during America's conflicts. Some stories involve heroism, others involve the unusual. When it comes to unusual war stories, few will top that of psychologist B. F. Skinner. For as he relates the tale in his autobiography, *The Shaping of a Behaviorist* (1979), one of Skinner's wartime efforts was "Project Pigeon."

During World War II Skinner proposed that pigeons be trained to guide missiles to their targets. In their training, the pigeons would be **reinforced** with food pellets for pecking at targets projected onto a screen (see Figure 4.4). Once trained, the pigeons would be placed in missiles. Pecking at similar targets displayed on a screen within the missile would correct the flight path of the missile, resulting in a "hit" and a sacrificed pigeon. But plans for building the necessary missile—for some reason called the *Pelican* and not the *Pigeon*—were scrapped. The pigeon equipment was too bulky, and as Skinner lamented, his suggestion was not taken seriously. Apparently the Defense Department concluded that Project Pigeon was for the birds.

Project Pigeon may have been scrapped, but the principles of learning Skinner applied to the project have found wide applications in operant conditioning. In operant conditioning an organism learns to *do* something because of its effects or consequences.

Law of effect Thorndike's principle that responses are "stamped in" by rewards and "stamped out" by punishments.

Reinforce To follow a response with a stimulus that increases the frequency of the response.

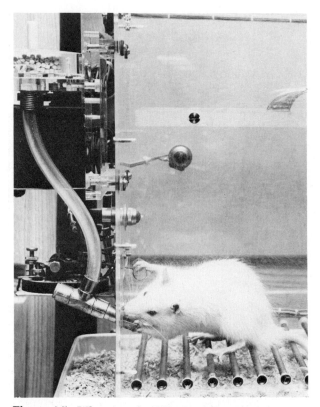

Figure 4.5. What Are the Effects of Reinforcement?
One of the stars of modern psychology, an albino laboratory rat, earns its keep in a Skinner box. The animal presses a lever because of reinforcement—in the form of food pellets—delivered through the spout of the feeder. The habit strength of this operant can be measured as the frequency of lever pressing.

This is **operant behavior,** behavior that operates on, or manipulates, the environment. In classical conditioning, involuntary responses such as salivation or eyeblinks are often conditioned. In operant conditioning, *voluntary* responses such as pecking at a target, pressing a lever, or many of the athletic skills required in playing tennis are acquired, or conditioned.

In operant conditioning, organisms engage in operant behaviors, also known simply as **operants,** that result in presumably desirable consequences such as food, a hug, an A on a test, attention, or social approval. Some children learn to conform their behavior to social codes and rules to earn the attention and approval of their parents and teachers. Other children, ironically, may learn to "misbehave," since misbehavior also results in attention from other people. Children may especially learn to be "bad" when their "good" behavior is routinely ignored.

Skinner Boxes and Cumulative Recorders

To study operant behavior efficiently, Skinner devised an animal cage dubbed the *Skinner box* (see Figure 4.5), in which conditions can be carefully controlled and laboratory animals can be carefully observed. The Skinner box is "energy-efficient"— in terms of the "energy" of the experimenter. In contrast to Thorndike's puzzle box, a "correct" response does not allow the animal to escape and thus have to be recaptured and placed back in the box.

The rat in Figure 4.5 was deprived of food and placed in a Skinner box with a lever at one end. At first it sniffed its way around the cage and engaged in **random trial-and-error behavior.** In random trial-and-error behavior, responses that meet with favorable consequences tend to occur more frequently; responses that do not meet with favorable consequences tend to be performed less frequently.

The rat's first pressing of the lever was accidental. However, because of this action a food pellet dropped into the cage. The food pellet increased the probability that the rat would press the lever again, and is thus said to have served as a reinforcement for the lever pressing.

Skinner further mechanized his laboratory procedure by making use of a **cumulative recorder,** as shown in Figure 4.6. The recorder provides a precise measure of operant behavior. The experimenter need not even be present to record correct responses. In the example used, the lever in the Skinner box is connected to the recorder, so that the recording pen moves upward with each

---

Operant behavior Voluntary responses that lead to reinforcement.

Operant The same as an operant behavior.

Random trial-and-error behavior Unplanned, random activity.

Cumulative recorder An instrument that records the frequency of an organism's operants (or "correct" responses) as a function of the passage of time.

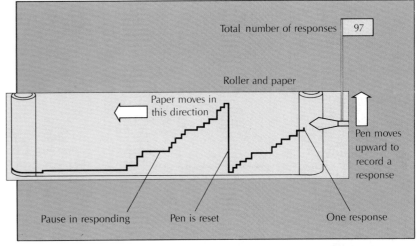

Figure 4.6. How Has the Cumulative Recorder Contributed to the Study of Operant Conditioning? In the cumulative recorder, paper moves continuously to the left while a pen automatically records each targeted response by moving upward. When the pen reaches the top of the paper, it is automatically reset to the bottom.

correct response. The paper moves continuously to the left at a slow but regular pace. In the sample record shown in Figure 4.6, lever pressings (which record correct responses) were at first few and far between. But after several reinforced responses, lever pressing came "fast and furious." When the rat is no longer hungry, the lever pressing will drop off and then stop.

The First "Correct" Response In operant conditioning, it matters little how the first response that is reinforced comes to be made. The organism can happen on it by chance, as in random trial-and-error learning. The organism can also be physically guided into the response. You may command your dog to "Sit!" then press its backside down until it is in a sitting position. Finally you reinforce sitting with food or a pat on the head and a kind word.

Animal trainers use physical guiding or coaxing to bring about the first "correct" response. People, of course, can be verbally guided into desired responses when they are learning tasks such as running a machine, spelling, or adding numbers. But they then need to be informed when they have made the correct response. Knowledge of results is often all the reinforcement that motivated people need to learn new skills.

Reinforcers Reinforcers increase the probability that an operant will be repeated. Any stimulus that

increases the probability that responses preceding it will be repeated serves as a reinforcer. Reinforcers include food pellets when an organism has been deprived of food, water when it has been deprived of liquid, the opportunity to mate, and the sound of a bell that has been previously associated with eating. (Yes, a CS can serve as a reinforcer.)

Skinner distinguished between positive and negative reinforcers. **Positive reinforcers** increase the probability that an operant will occur when they are applied. Food and approval usually serve as positive reinforcers. **Negative reinforcers** increase the probability that an operant will occur when they are *removed*. People often learn to plan ahead so that they need not fear that things will go wrong. Fear acts as a negative reinforcer, because *removal* of fear increases the probability that the behaviors preceding it (such as planning ahead or fleeing a predator) will be repeated.

Greater reinforcers prompt more rapid learning than lesser reinforcers. You will probably work much harder for $1,000 than for $10. (If not, get in touch with me—I have some chores that need to be taken care of.) With sufficient reinforcement,

---

Positive reinforcer A reinforcer that, when *presented*, increases the frequency of an operant.

Negative reinforcer A reinforcer that, when *removed*, increases the frequency of an operant.

operants become a **habit.** They show a high probability of recurrence in a certain situation.

We can also distinguish between primary and secondary, or conditioned, reinforcers. **Primary reinforcers** are effective because of the biological makeup of the organism. Food, water, adequate warmth (positive reinforcers), and pain (a negative reinforcer) all serve as primary reinforcers. **Secondary reinforcers** acquire their value through association with established reinforcers. For this reason they are also termed **conditioned reinforcers.** We may seek money because we have learned that it may be exchanged for primary reinforcers. Money, attention, social approval, all are conditioned reinforcers in our culture. We may be suspicious of, or not "understand," people who are not interested in money or the approval of others. Part of "understanding" others lies in being able to predict what they will find reinforcing (see Figure 4.7).

Extinction and Spontaneous Recovery in Operant Conditioning

Extinction in classical conditioning results from repeated presentation of the CS without the US, so that the CR becomes inhibited. In operant conditioning, extinction results from repeated performance of operant behavior without reinforcement. After a number of trials, the operant behavior also becomes inhibited (is no longer shown).

After some time has passed, however, an organism will usually again perform the operant when placed in a situation in which the operant had been previously reinforced. Spontaneous recovery of learned responses occurs in operant as well as classical conditioning. If the operant is reinforced at this time, it quickly regains its former strength.

Habit A learned response that shows a high frequency of recurrence under certain conditions.

Primary reinforcer An unlearned reinforcer.

Secondary reinforcer A stimulus that gains reinforcement value through association with established reinforcers.

Conditioned reinforcer Another term for a secondary reinforcer.

Reward A pleasant stimulus that increases the frequency of the behavior it follows.

Empirically By trial or experiment rather than by logical deduction.

Reinforcers versus Rewards and Punishments

Rewards, like reinforcers, are stimuli that increase the frequency of behavior. But rewards are also considered pleasant events. Skinner preferred the concept of reinforcement to that of reward because reinforcement does not suggest trying to "get inside the head" of an organism (person or lower animal) to guess what it would find pleasant or unpleasant. A list of reinforcers is arrived at **empirically,** by observing what sorts of stimuli will increase the frequency of the behavior. On the other hand, some psychologists use the term *reward* interchangeably with positive reinforcement.

Figure 4.7. What Are Secondary Reinforcers? Understanding other people includes being able to predict what they will find reinforcing. In this cartoon, Dagwood apparently finds money more reinforcing than the praise of his boss, Mr. Dithers.

Punishments are aversive events that suppress or decrease the frequency of the behavior they follow.* Punishment can rapidly suppress undesirable behavior and may be warranted in "emergencies," as when a child tries to run out into the street. But many learning theorists agree that punishment is usually undesirable, especially in rearing children, for reasons such as the following:

1. Punishment does not in and of itself suggest an alternative, acceptable form of behavior.

2. Punishment tends to suppress undesirable behavior only under circumstances in which its delivery is guaranteed. It does not take children long to learn that they can "get away with murder" with one parent, or one teacher, but not with another.

3. Punished organisms may withdraw from the situation. Severely punished children may run away, cut class, or drop out of school.

4. Punishment can create anger and hostility. Adequate punishment will almost always suppress unwanted behavior—but at what cost? A child may express accumulated feelings of hostility against other children.

5. Punishment may generalize too far. The child who is punished severely for bad table manners

may stop eating altogether. Overgeneralization is more likely to occur when children do not know exactly why they are being punished and when they have not been shown alternative, acceptable behaviors.

6. Punishment may be modeled as a way of solving problems or coping with stress. We shall see that one way that children learn is by observing others. Even though children may not immediately perform the behavior they observe, they may perform it later on, even as adults, when their circumstances are similar to those of the **model.**

7. Finally, children learn responses that are punished. Whether or not children choose to perform punished responses, punishment draws their attention to them.

It is usually preferable to focus on rewarding children for desirable behavior than to punish them for unwanted behavior. By ignoring their misbehavior, or by using **time out** from positive reinforcement, we can consistently avoid reinforcing children for misbehavior.

Discriminative Stimuli B. F. Skinner might not have been able to get his pigeons into the drivers' seats of missiles during the war, but he had no problem training them to respond to traffic lights. Try the following experiment for yourself.

Find a pigeon. Or sit on a park bench, close your eyes, and one will find you. Place it in a Skin-

---

*Recall that *negative reinforcers* are defined in terms of *increasing* the frequency of behavior, although the increase occurs when the negative reinforcer is *removed*. A punishment *decreases* the frequency of a behavior when it is *applied*.

1

2

"THIS IS A STICKUP!"

"THIS IS A STICKUP!"

3

4

"THIS IS A STICKUP!"

5

ner box with a button on the wall. Drop a food pellet into the cage whenever it pecks the button. (Soon it will learn to peck the button whenever it has not eaten for a while.) Now place a small green light in the cage. Turn it on and off intermittently throughout the day. Reinforce button pecking with food whenever the green light is on but not

when the light is off. It will not take long for this clever city pigeon to learn that it will gain as much by grooming itself or squawking and flapping around as it will by pecking the button when the light is off.

The green light is a **discriminative stimulus.** Discriminative stimuli are cues that indicate when an operant, such as pecking a button, will be reinforced, as with a food pellet.

As previously noted, operants that are not reinforced tend to become extinguished. For the pigeon in our experiment, pecking the button *when the light is off* becomes extinguished.

A moment's reflection will suggest many ways in which discriminative stimuli influence our behavior. Would you rather ask your boss for a raise when she is smiling or when she is frowning? Wouldn't you rather answer the telephone when it

Punishment An unpleasant stimulus that suppresses the behavior it follows.

Model An organism that engages in a response that is imitated by another organism.

Time out Removal of an organism from a situation in which reinforcement is available when unwanted behavior is shown.

Discriminative stimulus In operant conditioning, a stimulus that indicates that reinforcement is available.

is ringing? Do you think it is wise to try to get smoochy when your date is blowing smoke in your face or chugalugging a bottle of antacid tablets? An aspect of enhancing social skills is learning to interpret social discriminative stimuli (smiles, tones of voice, body language) accurately.

Schedules of Reinforcement

In operant conditioning, some responses are maintained by **continuous reinforcement.** You probably become warmer every time you put on heavy clothing. You probably become less thirsty every time you drink water. But if you have ever watched people throwing money down the maws of slot machines, or "one-armed bandits," you know that behavior can also be maintained by **partial reinforcement.**

Folklore about gambling is consistent with learning theory. You can get a person "hooked" on gambling by fixing the game to allow heavy winnings at first. Then you gradually space out the gambling behaviors that are reinforced until the gambling is maintained by very infrequent winning—or even no winning at all.

New operants or behaviors are acquired most rapidly through continuous reinforcement, or in some cases, through "one-trial learning" that meets with great reinforcement. So-called **pathological gamblers** often had a "big win" at the racetrack or casino or in the lottery in their late teens or early 20s (Greene, 1982). But once the operant has been acquired, it can be maintained by tapering off to a schedule of partial reinforcement.

There are four basic schedules of reinforcement. They are determined by changing either the *interval* of time that must elapse between correct responses before reinforcement is made available or the *ratio* of correct responses to reinforcements. If the interval that must elapse between correct responses before reinforcement becomes available is zero seconds, the reinforcement schedule is continuous. A larger interval of time, such as 1 or 30 seconds, is a partial-reinforcement schedule. A one-to-one (1:1) ratio of correct responses to reinforcements is a continuous-reinforcement schedule. A higher ratio, such as a 2:1 or 5:1 ratio, would be a partial-reinforcement schedule.

The four basic types of schedules of reinforcement are *fixed-interval, variable-interval, fixed-ratio,* and *variable-ratio* schedules.

In a **fixed-interval schedule,** a fixed amount of time, say one minute, must elapse between the previous and subsequent times that reinforcement is made available for correct responses. In a **variable-interval schedule,** varying amounts of time are allowed to elapse between making reinforcement available. In a three-minute variable-interval schedule, the mean amount of time that would elapse between reinforcement opportunities would be three minutes, but each interval might vary from, say, one to five or from two to four minutes.

With a fixed-interval schedule, an organism's response rate falls off after each reinforcement, then picks up as it nears the time when reinforcement will be dispensed. For example, in a one-minute fixed-interval schedule, a rat will be reinforced with, say, a food pellet for the first operant—for example, the first pressing of a lever—that occurs after a minute has elapsed. After each reinforcement the rat's rate of lever pressing slows down, but as the end of the one-minute interval draws near, lever pressing increases in frequency, as suggested by Figure 4.8. It is as if the rat has learned that it must wait a while before reinforcement will be made available. The resultant record on the cumulative recorder (Figure 4.8) shows a series of characteristic upward-moving waves or scallops, which is referred to as a *fixed-interval scallop.* In the case of the more unpredictable variable-

Continuous reinforcement A schedule of reinforcement in which every correct response is reinforced.

Partial reinforcement One of several reinforcement schedules in which not every correct response is reinforced.

Pathological gambler A person who gambles habitually, despite consistent losses.

Fixed-interval schedule A schedule in which a fixed amount of time must elapse between the previous and subsequent times that reinforcement is available.

Variable-interval schedule A schedule in which a variable amount of time must elapse between the previous and subsequent times that reinforcement is available.

FIXED-INTERVAL SCHEDULE

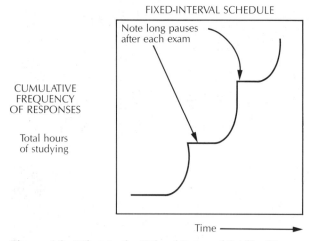

Note long pauses after each exam

CUMULATIVE
FREQUENCY
OF RESPONSES

Total hours
of studying

Time ⟶

Figure 4.8. What Is the "Fixed-Interval Scallop"?
Organisms who are reinforced on a fixed-interval schedule tend to slack off in responding after each reinforcement. The rate of responding then picks up as they near the time when reinforcement will again become available. The results on the cumulative recorder look like an upward-moving series of waves, or scallops.

interval schedule, the response rate is steadier but lower. If the boss calls us in for a weekly report, we will probably work hard to pull the pieces together just before the report, just as we might cram the night before a weekly quiz. But if the boss might call us in for a report on the progress of a project at any time (variable-interval schedule), we are likely to keep things in a state of reasonable readiness at all times. However, our efforts are unlikely to have the intensity they would in a fixed-interval (e.g., weekly) schedule. Similarly, we are less likely to cram for a series of unpredictable "pop quizzes" than for regularly scheduled

Fixed-ratio schedule A schedule in which reinforcement is provided after a fixed number of correct responses.

Variable-ratio schedule A schedule in which reinforcement is provided after a variable number of correct responses.

Shaping A procedure for teaching complex behaviors that at first reinforces approximations to the target behavior.

quizzes. But we are likely to do at least some studying on a regular basis.

In a **fixed-ratio schedule,** reinforcement is provided after a fixed number of correct responses have been made. In a **variable-ratio schedule,** reinforcement is provided after a variable number of correct responses have been made. In a 10:1 variable-ratio schedule, the mean number of correct responses that would have to be made before a subsequent correct response would be reinforced is 10, but the ratio of correct responses to reinforcements might be allowed to vary from, say, 1:1 to 20:1 on a random basis.

Fixed-ratio and variable-ratio schedules maintain a high response rate. With a fixed-ratio schedule, it is as if the organism learns that it must make several responses before being reinforced. It then "gets them out of the way" as rapidly as possible. Consider the example of piecework. If a worker must sew five shirts to receive a ten-dollar bill, he or she will be on a fixed-ratio (5:1) schedule and is likely to sew at a uniformly high rate, although there might be a brief pause following each reinforcement. With a variable-ratio schedule, reinforcement can come at any time. This unpredictability also maintains a high response rate. Slot machines tend to pay off on variable-ratio schedules, and players can be seen popping coins into their maws and pulling their "arms" with barely a pause. I have seen players who do not even pause to pick up their winnings. Instead, they continue to smoothly pop in the coins, whether from their original stack or from the winnings tray.

Shaping If you are teaching disco-type maneuvers to people who have never danced, do not wait until they have performed a perfect Latin hustle before telling them they're on the right track. The foxtrot will be back in style before they have learned a thing.

We can teach complex behaviors by **shaping,** or at first reinforcing small steps toward the behavioral goals. At first it may be wise to smile and say "Good" when a reluctant newcomer gathers the courage to get out on the dance floor, even if your feet get flattened by his initial clumsiness. If you are teaching someone to drive a car with a standard shift, at first generously reinforce the learner simply for shifting without stalling.

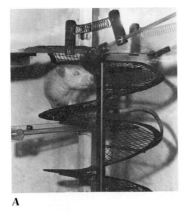

A

B

C

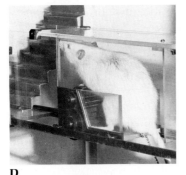

D

E

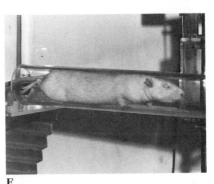

F

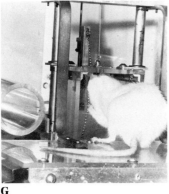

G

Figure 4.9. How Was Barnabus the Rat Shaped to Engage in a Complex Series of Behaviors? Psychologists at Columbia University (Pierrel & Sherman, 1963) shaped Barnabus to perform a complex behavioral chain by reinforcing each behavior in sequence. The sequence proceeded from last to first, so that each reward would trigger the next behavior in the chain. In these photos you see Barnabus (a) climb a spiral ramp, (b) cross a bridge, (c) climb a ladder, (d) pedal a toy car, (e) climb steps, (f) crawl through a tube, and (g) ride an elevator to return to the starting platform. Finally, Barnabus presses a lever to attain a food pellet (not shown). Complex behavior for a rat?

But as training proceeds, we come to expect more before dispensing reinforcement. We reinforce **successive approximations** to the goal. If you want to train a rat to climb a ladder, first reinforce it (with a food pellet) when it turns toward the ladder. Then wait until it approaches the ladder before using reinforcement. Then do not drop a food pellet into the cage until the rat touches the ladder. In this way the rat will reach the top of the ladder more quickly than if you had waited until the target behavior had first occurred by random trial and error. This method of shaping was used

to train one rat, Barnabus, to engage in the complex behavioral sequence shown in Figure 4.9.

Applications of Operant Conditioning

Brave New World showed us how a fictitious society abused the principles of learning to condition chil-

Successive approximations Behaviors that are progressively closer to a target behavior.

dren to want to fit into the niches deemed appropriate for them. But in the real world, operant conditioning is used every day in the **socialization** of young children. For example, parents and peers influence children to acquire "sex-appropriate" behavior patterns through the elaborate use of rewards and punishments. Parents also tend to praise their children for sharing with others and to punish them for being too aggressive.

Biofeedback Training

Biofeedback training (BFT) is based on principles of operant conditioning, and BFT has been an important innovation in the treatment of health-related problems over the past few decades. Through BFT, people and lower animals have learned to control autonomic responses to attain reinforcement.

In a landmark series of experiments on BFT, psychologist Neal E. Miller (1969) placed electrodes in the pleasure centers of rats' hypothalamuses. A mild burst of electricity in this center must be reinforcing because rats will learn to perform operants that result in shock. The heart rates of the rats were monitored. One group of rats received shock when their heart rates increased. Another group of rats received shock when their heart rates decreased. After a single 90-minute training session, rats altered their heart rates by as much as 20 percent in the direction for which they had been "rewarded." Other research with animals and humans has shown that organisms can gain control of **autonomic** functions such as blood pressure. They can also learn to improve their control over functions that are within the grasp of voluntary manipulation, such as muscle tension.

Socialization Guidance of people into socially desirable behavior by means of verbal messages and systematic use of rewards and punishments.

Biofeedback training A method for teaching control over body responses by providing an organism with a continuous flow of information about them.

Autonomic Automatic; of the autonomic nervous system.

Alpha waves Brain waves that are linked to feelings of relaxation.

Electroencephalograph An instrument that measures brain waves.

When people receive BFT, reinforcement is in the form of *information,* not electric current in the brain. Perhaps a "bleep" sound changes in pitch or frequency of occurrence to signal that they have modified the autonomic function in the desired direction. People, for example, can learn to emit **alpha waves** (and feel somewhat more relaxed) through feedback from an **electroencephalograph.** The "bleep" may increase in frequency whenever alpha waves are being emitted, and psychologists simply instruct clients to "make the bleep go faster." Through other instruments, people have learned to lower muscle tension, heart rate, blood pressure, and the amount of sweat in the palms of their hands. All these changes are relaxing.

BFT has also been used with accident patients who have lost neuromuscular control of various parts of the body. A "bleep" informs them when they have contracted a muscle or sent an impulse down a neural pathway. By concentrating on changing the bleeps, they also gradually regain voluntary control over the damaged function.

Behavior Modification in the Classroom

Adults frequently reinforce undesirable behavior in children by attending to them when they misbehave but ignoring them when they behave properly. The use of behavior modification in the classroom reverses this response pattern: Teachers pay attention to children when they are behaving appropriately and, when possible, ignore (avoid reinforcing) their misbehavior (Lahey & Drabman, 1981).

One study of behavior modification in the classroom was designed to change the behavior of three elementary school children who touched others, took others' property, turned around, made noise, and mouthed objects during lessons (Madsen et al., 1968). In this program, the teacher wrote out classroom rules on the blackboard, verbally guiding the children into appropriate responses. The children repeated them aloud. During the early part of training, the teacher left the rules visible while inappropriate behavior was ignored and appropriate behavior was praised. Targeted behavior rapidly decreased.

Among older children and adolescents, peer approval is often a more powerful reinforcer than teacher approval. Peer approval may maintain misbehavior, and ignoring misbehavior may only allow peers to become more disruptive. In such cases it may be necessary to separate troublesome children.

Teachers also frequently use time out from positive reinforcement to discourage misbehavior. In this method, children are placed in drab, restrictive environments for a specified time period, usually about 10 minutes, when they behave disruptively. When isolated, they cannot earn the attention of peers or teachers, and no reinforcing activities are present.

Programed Learning   B. F. Skinner has been instrumental in developing an educational practice called **programed learning.** Programed learning is based on the assumption that any complex task, involving conceptual learning as well as motor skills, can be broken down into a number of small steps. These steps can be shaped individually and combined in sequence to form the correct behavioral chain.

Programed learning does not punish errors. Instead, correct responses are reinforced. All children earn "100," but at their own pace. Programed learning also assumes that it is the task of the teacher (or program) to structure the learning experience in such a way that errors will not be made.

COGNITIVE LEARNING

Conditioning is a simple form of learning in which stimuli or responses become mechanically linked to certain situations. Although conditioning meets the scientific objective of explaining behavior in terms of public, observable events—in this case, laboratory conditions—many psychologists believe that conditioning cannot explain all instances of learned behavior, even in laboratory rats. They have turned to **cognitive learning** in order to describe and explain additional findings. Cognitive learning, in contrast to conditioning, is not a mechanical process. The defining feature of cognitive learning is that it modifies one's mental representation of the environment, even when it occurs in rats and apes. In our discussion of cognitive learning, we shall review a number of classic studies that

Figure 4.10. How Have Gestalt Psychologists Demonstrated the Role of Insight in Learning? Gestalt psychologist Wolfgang Köhler ran experiments with chimpanzees which suggest that not all learning is mechanical. This chimp must retrieve a stick outside the cage and attach it to a stick he already has before he can retrieve the distant circular object. While fiddling with two such sticks, Sultan, another chimp, seemed to suddenly recognize that the sticks can be attached. This is an example of learning by insight.

show why psychologists needed to develop principles of cognitive learning.

During World War I, as noted in Chapter 1, German Gestalt psychologist Wolfgang Köhler became convinced that not all forms of learning could be explained by mechanical conditioning when one of his chimpanzees, Sultan, "went bananas." Sultan had learned to use a stick to rake in bananas placed outside his cage. But now Herr Köhler (pronounced *hair curler*) placed the banana beyond the reach of the stick. He gave Sultan two bamboo poles that could be fitted together to make a single pole long enough to retrieve the delectable reward. The setup was similar to that shown in Figure 4.10.

Programed learning A method of learning in which complex tasks are broken down into simple steps, each of which is reinforced. Errors are not reinforced.

Cognitive learning Learning that involves mental representation, or a cognitive map, of the world.

As if to make this historic occasion more dramatic, Sultan at first tried to reach the banana with one pole. When he could not do so, he returned to fiddling with the sticks. Köhler left the laboratory after an hour or so of frustration (his own as well as Sultan's). An assistant was assigned the thankless task of observing Sultan. But soon afterward Sultan happened to align the two sticks as he fiddled. Then, in what seemed a flash of inspiration, Sultan fitted them together and pulled in the elusive banana.

Köhler was summoned to the laboratory. When he arrived the sticks fell apart, as if on cue. But Sultan regathered them, fit them firmly together, and actually tested the strength of the fit before retrieving another banana.

Learning by Insight

Köhler was impressed by Sultan's rapid "perception of relationships" and used the term **insight** to describe it. He noted that such insights were not learned gradually through reinforced trials. Rather they seemed to occur "in a flash" when the elements of a problem had been arranged appropriately. Sultan also proved himself immediately capable of stringing several sticks together to retrieve various objects, not just bananas. This seemed no mechanical generalization. It appeared that Sultan understood the principle of the relationship between joining sticks and reaching distant objects.

Psychologists in the United States soon demonstrated that not even the behavior of rats was as mechanical as most behaviorists suggested. E. C. Tolman (1948), a University of California psychologist, showed that rats behaved as if they had acquired **cognitive maps** of mazes. Although they would learn many paths to a food goal, they would typically choose the shortest. But if the shortest path was blocked, they would quickly switch to an-

other. The behavior of the rats suggested that they learned *places in which reinforcement was available,* not a series of mechanical motor responses.

Bismarck, one of University of Michigan psychologist N. R. F. Maier's laboratory rats, provided further evidence for learning by insight (Maier & Schneirla, 1935). Bismarck had been trained to climb a ladder to a tabletop where food was placed. On one occasion Maier used a mesh barrier to prevent Bismarck from reaching his goal. But as shown in Figure 4.11, a second ladder to the table was provided. The second ladder was in clear view of the animal. At first Bismarck sniffed and scratched and made every effort to find a path through the mesh barrier. Then Bismarck spent some time washing his face, an activity that apparently signals frustration in rats. Suddenly Bismarck jumped into the air, turned, ran down the familiar ladder, around to the new ladder, up the new ladder, and then claimed his just desserts.

It is difficult to explain Bismarck's behavior in terms of conditioning. It seems that Bismarck suddenly perceived the relationships between the elements of his problem so that the solution occurred by insight. He seems to have had what Gestalt psychologists have termed an "Aha!-experience."

Latent Learning

Many behaviorists argue that organisms acquire only those responses, or operants, for which they are reinforced. However, E. C. Tolman showed that rats learn about their environments in the absence of reinforcement.

Tolman trained some rats to run through mazes for standard food goals, whereas other rats were permitted to explore the same mazes for several days without food goals or other rewards. The rewarded rats could be said to have found their ways through the mazes with fewer errors (fewer "wrong turns") on each trial run. But in a sense, the unrewarded rats had no correct or incorrect turns to make, since no response led to a reward.

After the unrewarded rats had been allowed to explore the mazes for 10 days, food rewards were placed in a box at the far end of the maze. The previously unrewarded explorers reached the food box as quickly as the rewarded rats after only

---

Insight In Gestalt psychology, a sudden perception of relationships among elements of the "perceptual field," permitting the solution of a problem.

Cognitive map A mental representation or "picture" of the elements in a learning situation, such as a maze.

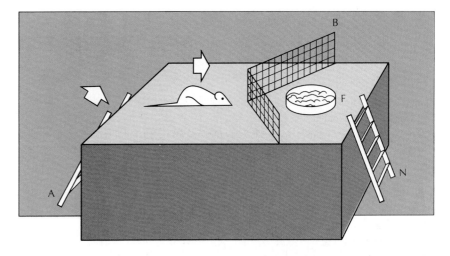

Figure 4.11. How Did Bismarck Use a Cognitive Map to Claim His Just Desserts? Bismarck has learned to reach dinner by climbing ladder *A*. But now the food goal (*F*) is blocked by a wire-mesh barrier (*B*). Bismarck washes his face for a while, but then, in an apparent flash of insight, runs back down ladder *A* and up new ladder *N* to claim his just desserts.

one or two reinforced trials (Tolman & Honzik, 1950).

Tolman concluded that rats learned about mazes in which they roamed even when they were unrewarded for doing so. He distinguished between learning and performance. Rats would acquire a cognitive map of a maze, and even though they would not be motivated to follow an efficient route to the far end, they would learn rapid routes from end to end, just by roaming about within the maze. But this learning might be hidden, or **latent,** until they were motivated to follow the rapid routes for food goals.

Observational Learning

How many things have you learned from watching other people in real life, in films, and on TV? From films and TV we may have gathered vague ideas about how to sky dive, ride surfboards, climb sheer cliffs, run a pattern to catch a touchdown pass in the Superbowl, and dust for fingerprints, even if we have never tried these activities.

Social-learning theorist Albert Bandura has run numerous experiments (e.g., Bandura et al., 1963) that show that we acquire operants by observing the behavior of others. We may need some practice to refine the skills we acquire by observation, but we can acquire the required knowledge by observation alone. We may also choose to allow these skills to lie latent. For example, we may not imitate aggressive behavior unless we are provoked

and believe that we are more likely to be rewarded than punished for it.

Observational learning may account for most human learning. It occurs when we as children observe parents cook, clean, or repair a broken appliance. Observational learning takes place when we watch teachers solve problems on the blackboard or hear them speak in a foreign language. Observational learning is not mechanically acquired through reinforcement. We can learn by observation without engaging in overt responses at all. It appears sufficient to pay attention to the behavior of others.

As noted at the beginning of the chapter, it would be of little use to discuss how we learn if we were not capable of remembering what we learn from second to second, from day to day, or in many cases, for a lifetime. Let us now turn our attention to the subject of memory. How do we remember things? How much can we remember? How can we improve our ability to remember?

MEMORY

Are you in a betting mood? I'll bet that I can show you how to memorize the lines and shapes that correspond to the numbers 1 through 9 in Figure

---

Latent Hidden or concealed.

Observational learning Acquiring expectations and operants by observing others.

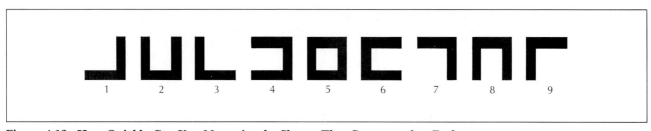

Figure 4.12. How Quickly Can You Memorize the Shapes That Correspond to Each Number, 1 to 9?   After you have pondered this question for a while, turn to Figure 4.13.

4.12—almost instantaneously. Look at them for a minute to see if you think you can do it. Then turn to Figure 4.13.

Memory is a most important area of investigation in psychology. Without memory—that is, the ability to store and retrieve information—learning would profit us little. There would be no point to reading this book, or any other, if you could not remember it. How well could you use a typewriter or a computer keyboard if you forgot the location of the keys after entering each character? What would life be like if you could not remember your name, your address, your family, your friends, and your minute-to-minute plans?

The Structure of Memory

Before the turn of the century, William James was intrigued by the fact that some memories were unreliable, "going in one ear and out the other," whereas others could be recalled for a lifetime:

The stream of thought flows on, but most of its elements fall into the bottomless pit of oblivion. Of some, no element survives the instant of their passage. Of others, it is confined to a few moments, hours, or days. Others, again, leave vestiges which are indestructible, and by means of which they may be recalled as long as life endures (1890).

Sensory memory The structure of memory first encountered by incoming information, in which sensory input, such as a visual stimulus, is maintained for only a fraction of a second.

Sensory register Another term for *sensory memory*.

James observed correctly that there were different types or structures of memory. Each holds impressions or "elements of thought" for different lengths of time. Many modern psychologists classify memory according to three such structures:

What Is Memory? Learning would profit us little if we could not remember what we had learned. As children mature and learn, they come to use more sophisticated strategies for storing and retrieving information.

sensory memory, short-term memory (STM), and long-term memory (LTM).

Sensory Memory

The world is a constant display of sights and sounds and other sources of sensory stimulation, but only some of these are remembered. Memory first requires that you pay attention to a stimulus or image, whether a new name, a vocabulary word, or an idea. Paying attention somehow separates it from all the stimuli you find irrelevant, and are less likely to retain. In experiments on memory, for example, 2-year-old boys are more likely to attend to and remember toys such as cars, puzzles, and trains, whereas 2-year-old girls are more likely to attend to and remember dolls, dishes, and teddy bears (Renninger & Wozniak, 1985). Even by this early age, children's patterns of attention have been shaped by sex-role expectations.

Note what happens when you perceive a visual stimulus and then turn away, such as this list of 10 letters:

THUNSTOFAM

After you turn away, the visual impression of the stimulus lasts for only a fraction of a second. This impression, or "trace," is said to "be in" what is referred to as **sensory memory,** or the **sensory register.** If the letters had been flashed on a screen for, say, one-tenth of a second, your ability to list them on the basis of sensory memory alone would be meager. The trace of their image would already have vanished, and you would probably recall only three or four of them.

Recollection of all 10 letters would depend on whether you had successfully transformed or **encoded** the list of letters into a form in which it could be processed further by memory. Later we shall see that one way of enhancing recall would be to read (or "mentally say") the list of letters as a word. Chances of recollection would have been further enhanced by repeating the "word" to yourself, or rehearsing it.

George Sperling (1960) demonstrated the existence of sensory memory in a series of classic experiments. In a typical procedure, three rows of numbers and letters like those that follow were flashed on a screen for about one-tenth of a second:

6 G R 2

V L 7 4

9 K 5 T

Viewers were asked what they had seen. On the average they remembered about three and a half numbers and letters. After that, presumably, the sensory image faded or decayed and no more numbers were remembered. But if Sperling pointed an arrow before, during, or after presentation at the row he wanted viewers to report, they were usually successful at recalling the entire row. Arrows pointed prior to the display facilitated recall most. Apparently they cued subjects to focus their attention on the "relevant" material.

Sperling found that if he delayed pointing the arrow for a few fractions of a second after the display, subjects were much less successful in reporting the target row. If he allowed a quarter of a second to elapse, the arrow did not aid recall at all. Apparently stimuli decay in the sensory register within that amount of time (see Figure 4.14).

Short-Term Memory

If you focus attention on a stimulus in the sensory register, you will tend to retain it in **short-term memory** for up to 30 seconds or so after the trace decays. In short-term memory the image tends to fade significantly after 10 to 12 seconds if it is not repeated or rehearsed (Keele, 1973). It is possible to focus on maintaining a visual image in the short-term memory (Fisher & Karsh, 1971), but it is more common to encode visual stimuli as sounds,

Encode To transform sensory input into a form that is more readily processed by memory.

Short-term memory The structure of memory that can hold a sensory stimulus for up to 30 seconds after the trace decays.

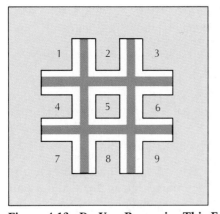

Figure 4.13. Do You Recognize This Familiar Grid?
The nine shapes in Figure 4.12 form this familiar tic-tac-toe grid when the numbers are placed inside them and they are arranged in numerical order, three shapes to a line. This method for recalling the shapes collapses nine chunks of information into one meaningful chunk. You encode them by thinking of the tic-tac-toe grid; then simply "read" the grid, shape by shape, numbering each one as you do so.

or auditory stimulation. Then the sounds can be rehearsed.

Encoding   Let us now return to the task of remembering the list of 10 letters shown at the beginning of this section. If you had coded them as the three-syllable word THUN-STO-FAM, you would probably have recalled them by mentally rehearsing (saying to yourself) the three-syllable "word" and then spelling it out from the sounds. Transforming a visual stimulus into sounds in order to remember it is known as using an **acoustic code**.

A few minutes later, if someone asked whether the letters had been upper case (THUN-STOFAM) or lower case (thunstofam), you might

Acoustic code   A code in which visual or other stimuli are transformed into sounds that may be rehearsed.

Acronym   A name composed of the initial letters of that which it represents.

Serial position effect   The finding that the first and last items in a series are more readily recalled than are intervening items.

not have been sure of the answer. You had used an acoustic code to help recall the list, and upper- and lower-case letters sound alike. When asked to list the letters, you might have said "s–t–o–w" rather than "s–t–o" since "stow" is an actual word that sounds like "sto."

A more elaborate way of coding the letters could have involved recognizing that they serve as an **acronym** for the familiar phrase "THe UNited STates OF AMerica." To recall the 10 letters, you would then have had to "picture" the phrase and "read aloud" the first two letters of each word. Since this phrase code is more complex than simply seeing the list as a single word, it might have taken you longer to recall (actually, to reconstruct) the list of 10 letters. But by using the phrase you would probably "remember" the list of letters longer. The phrase is meaningful, and thus more likely to be recalled than the meaningless "word" THUNSTOFAM.

THUNSTOFAM is not too difficult to remember. But what if the visual stimulus had been TBXLFNTSDK? This list of letters cannot be pronounced as it is. You would have had to have found a complex acronym in order to code these letters, and within a fraction of a second—most likely an impossible task. To aid recall you would probably have chosen to try to repeat or rehearse the letters rapidly, to read each one as many times as possible before the stimulus trace faded. You would have visualized each letter as you said it and tried to return to it before it decayed.

Auditory stimuli can be maintained longer in short-term memory than can visual stimuli (Keele, 1973). So you would probably try to use an acoustic code to remember the letters TBXLFNTSDK, rehearsing sounds. But in an effort to recall these letters, you might mistakenly report them as TVXLFNTSTK. This would be an understandable error since the incorrect V and T sound, respectively, like the correct B and D.

The Serial-Position Effect   Note that you would also be likely to recall the first and last letters in the series, T and K, more accurately than the others. Why? The tendency to recall more accurately the first and last items in a series is known as the **serial-position effect.** This effect may occur because we pay more attention to the first and last

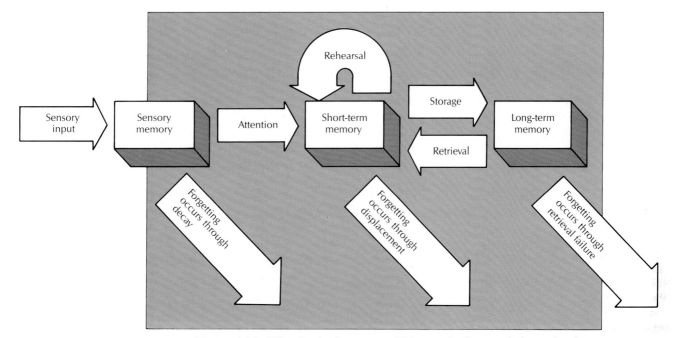

Figure 4.14. What Is the Structure of Memory? Sensory information impacts upon the sensory memory. If we attend to it, it is transferred to short-term memory (STM). Otherwise, the trace may decay. Once in STM, rehearsal stores the information in long-term memory (LTM), unless it is first displaced by other chunks of information. Once in LTM, memories may be retrieved through appropriate search strategies. But if the memory is organized poorly, or misfiled, it may be lost.

stimuli in a series. They serve as the visual or auditory boundaries for the other stimuli. It may also be that the first item is likely to be rehearsed more frequently (repeated more times) than any other item. The last item is likely to have been rehearsed most recently, and so least likely to have faded through decay.

Chunks of Information: Is Seven a Magic Number or Did the Phone Company Get Lucky?

Rapidly rehearsing 10 meaningless letters is not an easy task. With TBXLFNTSDK there are 10 **chunks** of information that must be maintained simultaneously in short-term memory. With THUNSTOFAM there are only three chunks to swallow at once—much easier on the digestion.

Psychologist George Miller (1956) noted that the average person was comfortable in digesting about seven integers at a time, the number of integers in a telephone number. (The three-digit area code prefix is usually recalled as a separate chunk of information.) Most people have little trouble recalling five chunks of information, as in a zip code. Some can remember nine, which is, for all but a few, an upper limit. So seven chunks, plus or minus one or two, is the "magic" number.

How, then, do children learn the alphabet, which is 26 chunks of information? How do they learn to associate letters of the alphabet with spoken sounds? The 26 letters of the alphabet cannot be spoken like a word or phrase. There is nothing about the shape of an *A* to indicate its sound. Nor does the visual stimulus *B* sound like a *B*. Children learning the alphabet and learning to associate letters (visual stimuli) with sounds do so by **rote.** It is mechanical associative learning that requires time and repetition. If you think that learning the al-

---

Chunk In memory theory, a discrete piece of information.

Rote A mechanical, routine way of doing something.

phabet by rote is a simple child's task, now that it is behind you, try learning the Russian or Hebrew alphabet.

If you had recognized THUNSTOFAM as an acronym for the first two letters of each word in the phrase "THe UNited STates OF AMerica," you would have reduced the number of chunks of information that have to be recalled. We could consider the phrase a single chunk of information, and the rule that we must use the first two letters of each word of the phrase as another chunk.

Reconsider Figures 4.12 and 4.13. In Figure 4.12 you were asked to learn nine chunks of visual information. Perhaps you could have used the acoustic codes "L" and "Square" for chunks three and five, but no obvious codes are available for the other seven chunks. But once you looked at Figure 4.13, you realized that you need only recall perhaps two chunks of information. One is the familiar tic-tac-toe grid. The other is the rule that each shape is the shape of a section of the grid, if read like words on a page (from upper left to lower right). The number sequence 1 through 9 presents no problem since you learned this series by rote many years ago and have rehearsed it in countless calculations since.

Interference in Short-Term Memory   Every time I have looked up a phone number and am trying to dial, rehearsing the number repeatedly, it is guaranteed that someone will ask me the time of day. Unless I say, "Just a minute!" and jot down the number on my cuff before I answer, it's back to the phone book again. Attending to new numbers, even briefly, impairs my ability to keep the phone number in short-term memory.

In an experiment with college students, Lloyd and Margaret Peterson (1959) showed how such interference can play havoc with short-term memory. They asked students to remember three-letter combinations, such as HGB, an easy three chunks

Displace In memory theory, to cause chunks of information to be lost from short-term memory by adding too many new items.

Eidetic imagery The capacity to remember visual sensory input, such as pictures, with exceptional clarity and detail. Also called *photographic memory*.

of information. Then they asked students to count backward from a number such as 181 by 3s (that is, 181, 178, 175, 172, and so on). The students were told to stop counting and to report the letter sequence after various brief intervals of time had passed, as shown in Figure 4.15. The percentage of combinations recalled accurately fell dramatically within just a few seconds. After 18 seconds of interference, the letter sequences had been **displaced** by counting in almost all of these bright young students.

Eidetic Imagery   Some people have short-term memories that are capable of storing many more than seven or nine chunks of information. Only about 5 percent of children tested are capable of what has been called photographic memory, or **eidetic imagery** (Haber, 1980). Even then this ability declines with age. These children can view a complex picture for 20 to 30 seconds, continue to observe a gray (neutral) background while the picture is removed, and then respond accurately to questions about details of the picture for many minutes (Haber, 1969). The accuracy of their responses suggests that they are still "seeing" the picture.

Figure 4.16 provides an example of a test of eidetic imagery. Children are asked to look at the first drawing in the series for 20 to 30 seconds, after which it is removed. The children then con-

Figure 4.15. How Does Interference Influence Memory?   The graph shows decrease in ability to recall three-letter combinations while counting backward for 18 seconds. Subjects in this experiment were bright college students.

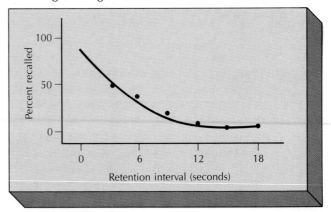

Figure 4.16. How Do Psychologists Test for Eidetic Imagery? Children look at the first drawing for 20 to 30 seconds, after which it is removed. Now the children look at a neutral background for several minutes. Then they are shown the second drawing. When asked what they see, children with the capacity for eidetic imagery report seeing a face. The face is seen only by children who retain the first image and fuse it with the second, thus perceiving the third image.

tinue to observe a neutral background. Several minutes later they are shown the drawing in the center. When asked what they see, many report "a face." A face would be seen only if the children had retained a clear image of the first picture and fused it with the second, so that they are in effect perceiving the third picture in Figure 4.16 (Haber, 1980).

Eidetic imagery appears remarkably clear and detailed. It seems to be essentially a perceptual phenomenon in which acoustic coding is not involved.

Long-Term Memory

Think of your **long-term memory** as a vast storehouse of information containing names, dates, places, what Johnny did to you in second grade, and what Susan said about you when you were 12. Psychologists are not certain how much of what you experience and think about becomes stored in long-term memory.

How Much of What We Experience or Think Is Stored in Long-Term Memory? Some psychologists argue that every perception and idea is stored permanently. The only question is whether we shall receive appropriate stimulation to help us retrieve this information. These psychologists often point to the work of neurosurgeon Wilder Penfield (1969). By electrically stimulating parts of the brain, some of his patients reported fairly vivid remembrance of things past.

Other psychologists such as Elizabeth Loftus (Loftus & Loftus, 1980; Loftus, 1983) note that the memories "released" by Penfield's probes were not perfectly detailed. Patients also seemed to recall more specifics of events that were important to them. We may be more likely to store permanently those perceptions and thoughts that are important or meaningful to us. We recall material better

Long-term memory The memory structure capable of relatively permanent storage.

when we pay more attention to it and encode it in a meaningful, rehearsable form.

How Accurate Are Long-Term Memories?

Loftus also notes that memories are distorted by biases and needs. For example, in memory tests that show pictures of a black man holding a hat and a white man carrying a razor, people often erroneously recall the razor as being in the hands of the black man.

The point here is that memory is not like the scanning of an old photograph. Instead, memory tends to be **reconstuctive** and less than fully accurate. Even the words we use in encoding our memories make a difference. In another study Loftus and Palmer (1974) showed subjects a film of a car crash and then asked them to fill out questionnaires that included a question about how fast the cars were going at the time. But the language of the question varied, so that some subjects estimated how fast the cars were going when they "hit" one another, and others estimated their speed when they "smashed" into one another. Subjects reconstructing the scene on the basis of the cue "hit" estimated a speed of 34 mph. Subjects who watched the same film but reconstructed the scene on the basis of the cue "smashed" estimated a speed of 41 mph!

Subjects in the same study were questioned again a week later: "Did you see any broken glass?" Since there was no broken glass shown in the film, yes answers were errors. Of subjects who had earlier been encouraged to encode the accident as one in which cars "hit" one another, 14 percent incorrectly answered yes. But 32 percent of the subjects who had encoded the cars as "smashing" into one another reported, incorrectly, that they had seen broken glass.

Reconstructive Based on piecing together of memory fragments with general knowledge and expectations, rather than a precise picture of the past.

Elaborative rehearsal A method for increasing the probability of recalling new information by relating it to already well-known material.

How Much Information *Can* Be Stored in Long-Term Memory?

There is no evidence for any limit to the amount of information that can be stored in long-term memory. New information may replace older information in the short-term memory, but there is no evidence that memories in long-term memory are lost by displacement. Long-term memories may last days, years, or for all practical purposes, a lifetime. From time to time it may seem that we have forgotten, or "lost," a memory in long-term memory, such as the names of elementary or high school classmates. But it is more likely that we simply cannot find the proper cues to help us retrieve the information. If it is lost, it usually becomes lost only in the same way as when we misplace an object but know that it is still somewhere in the house or apartment. We cannot retrieve it, but it is not eradicated or destroyed.

Transferring Information from Short-Term to Long-Term Memory

How is information transferred from short-term to long-term memory? By and large, the more often chunks of information are rehearsed, the more likely they are to be transferred to long-term memory (Rundus, 1971). But pure rehearsal, with no attempt to make information meaningful by linking it to past learning, is no guarantee of permanent storage (Craik & Watkins, 1973).

A more effective method is purposefully to relate new material to information that has already been solidly acquired. (Recall that the nine chunks of information in Figure 4.12 were made easier to reconstruct once they were associated with the familiar tic-tac-toe grid in Figure 4.13.) Relating new material to well-known material is known as **elaborative rehearsal** (Postman, 1975). For example, have you seen this word before?

FUNTHOSTAM

Say it aloud. Do you know it? If you had used an acoustic code alone to "memorize" THUNSTOFAM, the meaningless word you first saw on page 168, it might not have been easy to recognize FUNTHOSTAM as an incorrect spelling. But let us assume that you had coded (associated) THUNSTO-

FAM according to the phrase "The United States of America." Such a code would have involved the "meaning" of THUNSTOFAM and would thus have been an example of a **semantic code.** Then you would have been able to scan the spelling of the words in the phrase "The United States of America" to determine the correctness of FUN-THOSTAM. Of course, you would have found it incorrect.

You may recall that English teachers encouraged you to use new vocabulary words in sentences to help you remember them. Each new usage is an instance of elaborative rehearsal. You are building extended semantic codes that will help you retrieve their meanings in the future. When I was in high school, foreign-language teachers told us that learning classical languages "exercises the mind," so that we would understand English better. Not exactly. The mind is not analogous to a muscle that responds to exercise. But the meanings of many English words are based on foreign tongues. A person who recognizes that *retrieve* stems from roots meaning "again" *(re-)* and "find" *(trouver* in French) is less likely to forget that *retrieval* means "finding again" or "bringing back."

Before proceeding to the next section, let me ask you to cover the preceding paragraph. Now, which of the following words is correctly spelled: *retrieval* or *retreival?* The spellings sound alike, so an acoustic code for reconstructing the correct spelling would fail. But a semantic code, such as the spelling rule *"i before e except after c,"* would allow you to reconstruct the correct spelling: re-tr*ie*val.

Organization in Long-Term Memory   The storehouse of long-term memory is usually well organized. Items are not just piled on the floor or thrown into closets. We tend to gather information about rats and cats into a certain section of the warehouse, perhaps the animal or mammal section. We gather oaks, maples, and eucalyptus into the tree section.

As we develop, we tend to organize information according to a *hierarchical structure,* as shown in Figure 4.17. A **hierarchy** is an arrangement of items (or chunks of information) into groups or classes according to common or distinct features. As we work our way up the hierarchy shown in Figure 4.17, we find more encompassing, or **superordinate,** classes to which the items below belong. For example, all mammals are animals, but there are many types of animals other than mammals.*

When items are correctly organized in long-term memory, you are more likely to recall accurate information about them. For instance, do you remember whether whales breathe underwater? If you did not know that whales are mammals (or, in Figure 4.17, **subordinate** to mammals) or knew nothing about mammals, a correct answer might depend on some remote instance of rote learning. You might recall some details from a documentary on whales, for example. But if you *did* know that whales are mammals, you would be able to "remember" that whales do not breathe underwater by reconstructing information you know about mammals, the group to which whales are subordinate. Similarly, you might "remember" that whales, because they are mammals, are warm-blooded, nurse their young, and are a good deal more intelligent than, say, tunas and sticklebacks, which are fish.

Had you incorrectly classified whales as fish, you might have searched your memory and constructed the incorrect answer that they do breathe underwater.

*A note to biological purists: Figure 4.17 is not intended to reflect accurately phyla, classes, orders, and so on. Rather it shows how an individual's classification scheme might be organized.

Semantic code A code that is based on the meaning of material to be remembered.

Hierarchy A group of objects or events arranged according to rank or categories that represent common characteristics.

Superordinate Descriptive of a higher (including) class or category in a hierarchy.

Subordinate Descriptive of a lower (including) class or category in a hierarchy.

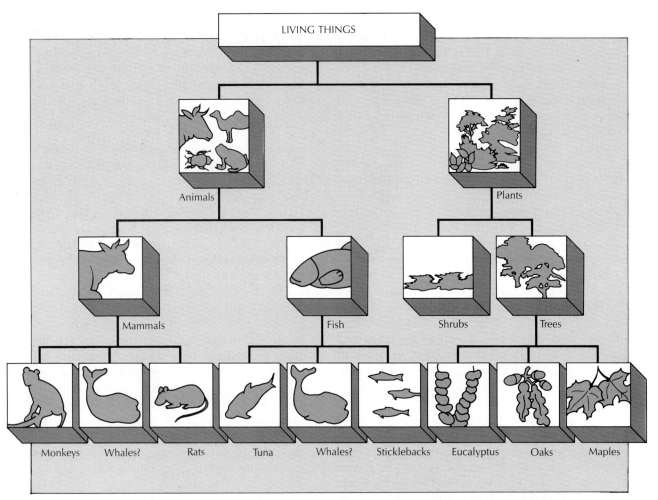

Figure 4.17. How Is Long-Term Memory Organized?   Where are whales filed in the hierarchical cabinets of your memory? Your classification of whales may influence your answers to these questions: Do whales breathe underwater? Are they warm-blooded? Do they nurse their young?

Forgetting

What do DAR, RIK, BOF, and ZEX have in common? They are all **nonsense syllables.** Nonsense syllables are meaningless syllables three letters in length. Their usage was originated by German psychologist Hermann Ebbinghaus (1850–1909), and they have been used by many psychologists to study memory and forgetting.

Nonsense syllables Meaningless syllables, three letters in length, used by psychologists to study memory.

Recognition In memory theory, the easiest memory task, identifying objects or events encountered before.

Since they are intended to be meaningless, remembering nonsense syllables should depend on simple acoustic coding and rehearsal, rather than on elaborative rehearsal, semantic coding, or other ways of making learning meaningful. Nonsense syllables provide a means of measuring simple memorization ability in studies of the three basic memory tasks of *recognition, recall,* and *relearning.* Studying these memory tasks has led to several conclusions about the nature of forgetting.

Recognition   There are many ways of measuring **recognition.** In one study of high school graduates, Harry Bahrick and his colleagues (1975) in-

Are whales warm-blooded or cold-blooded? Are whales mammals or fish? How have you categorized whales in the hierarchical structure of your own long-term memory?

terspersed photos of classmates with four times as many photos of strangers. Recent graduates correctly recognized persons who were former schoolmates 90 percent of the time, whereas subjects who had been out of school for 40 years recognized former classmates 75 percent of the time. But a chance level of recognition would have been only 20 percent (one photo in five was of an actual classmate), so that even older subjects showed rather solid long-term recognition ability.

In many studies of recognition, psychologists ask subjects to read a list of nonsense syllables. Then the subjects read a second list of nonsense syllables and indicate whether they recognize any of the syllables as having appeared on the first list. Forgetting is defined as failure to recognize a nonsense syllable that has been read before.

Recognition is the easiest type of memory task. This is why multiple-choice tests are easier than fill-in-the-blank or essay tests. We can recognize or identify photos of former classmates more easily than we can recall their names (Tulving, 1974).

Recall   Psychologists often use lists of pairs of nonsense syllables, called **paired associates,** to measure **recall,** a second memory task. A list of paired associates is shown in Figure 4.18. Subjects read through the lists, pair by pair. Later they are

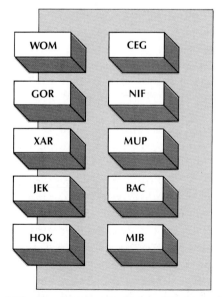

Figure 4.18. How Do Psychologists Use Paired Associates? Psychologists often use paired associates, like the above, to measure recall. Retrieving CEG in response to the cue WOM is made easier by an image of a WOMan smoking a "CEG-arette."

Paired associates Nonsense syllables presented in pairs in experiments that measure recall.

Recall Retrieval or reconstruction of learned material.

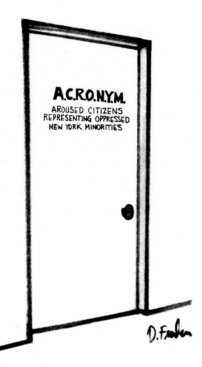

shown the first member of each pair and asked to recall the second. Recall is more difficult than recognition. In a recognition task, one simply indicates whether an item has been seen before or which of a number of items is paired with a stimulus (as in a multiple-choice test). But in a recall task, the person must retrieve a syllable, with another syllable serving as a cue.

Retrieval is made easier if the two syllables can be meaningfully linked, even if the "meaning" is stretched a bit. Consider the first pair of nonsense syllables in Figure 4.18. The image of a WOMan smoking a CEG-arette may make CEG easier to retrieve when the person is presented with the cue, WOM.

It is easier to recall vocabulary words from foreign languages if you can construct a meaningful link between the foreign and English words (At-

kinson, 1975). The *peso,* pronounced *pay-so,* is a unit of Mexican money. A link can be formed by finding a part of the foreign word, such as the *pe-* (pronounced *pay*) in *peso,* and construct a phrase such as "You pay with money." When you read or hear the word *peso* in the future, you recognize the *pe-* and retrieve the link or phrase. From the phrase, you then reconstruct the translation, "a unit of money."

A similar method for prompting recall involves the use of acronyms. As noted in our discussion of THUNSTOFAM, acronyms are words that are constructed from the first letter or letters of the chunks of material to be retrieved. In Chapter 2 we saw that the acronym SAME can help us recall that *s*ensory neurons are also called *a*fferent neurons, and *m*otor neurons are also termed *ef*ferent. In Chapter 3 we saw that the acronym ROY G. BIV can help us recall the colors of the visible spectrum.

Relearning: Is Learning Easier the Second Time Around?   **Relearning** is a third method of measuring retention. Do you remember having to learn all the state capitals in grade school? What were the capitals of Wyoming and Delaware? Even when we cannot recall or recognize material that had once been learned, we can relearn it more rapidly the second time, such as Cheyenne for Wyoming and Dover for Delaware. Similarly, as we go through our 30s and 40s we may forget a good deal of our high school French or geometry. But we could learn what took months or years much more rapidly the second time around.

Since time is saved when we relearn things we had once known, this method of measuring retention is also known as measuring **savings.** Quickly, now: What are the capitals of Wyoming and Delaware?

The Tip-of-the-Tongue Phenomenon: An Example of Cue-Dependent Forgetting
Have you ever been so close to recalling something that you felt it was "on the tip of your tongue"? But you still could not quite put your finger on it? This is a frustrating experience, such as reeling in a fish but having it drop off the line just before it breaks the surface of the water. Psychologists term

Relearning Another measure of retention. Material is usually relearned more quickly than it is learned initially.
Savings Another term for relearning.

this experience the **tip-of-the-tongue (TOT) phenomenon.** The TOT phenomenon appears to be an example of **cue-dependent forgetting.** That is, the information seems to be there, but the cue that could retrieve it is missing. As a result, the memory is inaccessible.

In one TOT experiment, Brown and McNeill (1966) defined some rather unusual words for students, such as *sampan,* which is a small riverboat used in China and Japan. Students were then asked to recall the words they had learned. Since the terms remained somewhat exotic and unelaborated,* students did not have well-developed cues for retrieving them. Students often had the right word "on the tips of their tongues," but many reported words similar in meaning, such as *junk, barge,* or *houseboat.* Other students reported words that sound similar, such as *Saipan, Siam, sarong,* and *sanching.*

Brown and McNeill concluded that our storage systems are indexed according to cues that include both the sounds and the meanings of words, according to both acoustic and semantic codes. By scanning words that are similar in sound and meaning to the word that is on the tip of the tongue, we often eventually find the right cue and retrieve the word for which we are searching.

State-Dependent Memory   Sometimes the cue for retrieving a memory is physiological or emotional rather than cognitive. Drugs, for example, alter our physiological response patterns. They can influence the production and uptake of neurotransmitters involved in learning and memory and can modify the general state of alertness of the body. It also happens that material that is learned "under the influence" of a drug may be most readily retrieved when the person is again under the influence of that drug (Overton, 1985).

Our moods may also serve as cues that aid the retrieval of memories. Feeling the rush of love may trigger images of other times when we had fallen in love. The grip of anger may prompt memories of frustration and rage. Gordon Bower (1981) ran

experiments in which happy or sad moods were induced in people by hypnotic suggestion and the subjects then learned lists of words. People who learned a list while in a happy mood showed better recall when a happy state was induced again. But people who had learned the list when a sad mood had been induced, showed superior recall when they were saddened again. Bower suggests that in day to day life, a happy mood influences us to focus on positive events. As a result we shall have better recall of these happy events in the future. A sad mood, unfortunately, leads us to focus on and recall the negative. Happiness may feed on happiness, but sadness under extreme circumstances can develop into a vicious cycle.

Why People Forget

When we do not attend to, encode, and rehearse sensory input, we may forget it through decay of the trace of the image. Material in short-term memory can be lost through displacement, as may happen when we try to remember several new names at a party.

According to **interference theory,** we also forget material in short-term and long-term memory because newly learned material interferes with it. The two basic types of interference are *retroactive interference* (also called *retroactive inhibition*) and *proactive interference* (also called *proactive inhibition*).

Retroactive Interference   In **retroactive interference** new learning interferes with the retrieval of old learning. A medical student may memorize

---

*Students, that is, had not had the opportunity to engage in elaborative rehearsal of the words—to use them in various contexts.

Tip-of-the-tongue phenomenon The experience of being unable to recall a word when we are certain that we know it.

Cue-dependent forgetting Forgetting because of lack of a relevant cue for retrieval of information.

Interference theory The view that we may forget material placed in memory because other learning interferes with its retrieval.

Retroactive interference The interference by new learning in ability to retrieve material learned previously.

the bones in the leg through rote repetition. Later he or she may find that learning the names of the bones in the arm makes it more difficult to retrieve the names of the leg bones, especially if the names are similar in sound or in relative location on each limb.

Proactive Interference

In **proactive interference** older learning interferes with the capacity to retrieve more recently learned material. High school Spanish may "pop in" when you are trying to retrieve college French or Italian words. All three are Romance languages, with similar roots and spellings. Old German vocabulary words would probably not interfere with your ability to retrieve more recently learned French or Italian because many German roots and sounds differ markedly from those of the Romance languages.

In terms of motor skills, you may learn how to drive a standard shift on a car with three forward speeds and a clutch that must be let up slowly after shifting. Later you learn to drive a car with five forward speeds and a clutch that must be released rapidly. For a while you make a number of errors on the five-speed car because of proactive interference. (Old learning interferes with new learning.) If you return to the three-speed car after driving the five-speed car has become "natural," you may stall it a few times. This is because of retroactive interference (new learning interfering with the old).

Repression

According to Sigmund Freud, we are motivated to forget painful memories and unacceptable ideas because they produce anxiety, guilt, and shame. (In terms of operant conditioning, anxiety, guilt, and shame serve as negative reinforcers. We learn to do that which is followed by their removal—in this case, not to think about

certain events and ideas.) In Chapter 9 we shall see that psychoanalysts believe that repression is at the heart of disorders such as **psychogenic amnesia.**

Childhood Amnesia

In his clinical investigations of patients' early experiences, Freud discovered that patients could not recall events that happened prior to the age of 3 and that recall was very cloudy through the age of 5. Freud labeled this phenomenon **childhood amnesia.** Many of us have the impression that we have vivid recollections of events during the first two or three years after birth, but studies in which attempts are made to verify these memories by interviewing independent older witnesses show that they are inaccurate (e.g., Sheingold & Tenney, 1982).

Childhood amnesia has nothing to do with the fact that the events are of the distant past. Those of us who are in our 30s, 40s, and older have many vivid memories of childhood events that occurred between the ages of 6 and 10, although they are many decades old. But 18-year-olds show steep declines in memory once they attempt to recall events earlier than the age of 6, even though these events are fewer than 18 years away (Wetzler & Sweeney, 1986).

Freud attributed childhood amnesia to the repression of the aggressive and sexual impulses that he believed young children had toward their parents. However, the events lost to childhood amnesia are not weighted in the direction of such "primitive" impulses; they include the most pedestrian, emotionally bland incidents. The effects of childhood amnesia are too broad, too nonselective, for Freud's hypothesis to hold water.

Childhood amnesia probably reflects the interaction of physiological and cognitive factors instead of psychoanalytic factors. For example, a structure of the limbic system (the hippocampus) that is involved in the storage of memories does not become mature until we are about 2 years old. Too, myelination of brain pathways is still occurring for the first several years after birth, contributing to the efficiency of memory functioning for the general processing of information. From a cognitive perspective, children usually cannot use language until about the age of 2. Since they are lacking language, they cannot label objects and events.

Proactive interference The interference by old learning in ability to retrieve material learned recently.

Psychogenic amnesia Amnesia thought to stem from psychological conflict or trauma.

Childhood amnesia Inability to recall events from prior to the age of 3.

Those early childhood memories we are so certain we can "see today" are probably reconstructed and mostly inaccurate. Or else they may stem from a time when we were much older than we thought we were.

Retrograde and Anterograde Amnesia

In **retrograde amnesia,** a source of trauma, such as a head injury or an electric shock, prevents people from remembering events that took place before the accident. In **anterograde amnesia,** there are memory lapses for the period following the traumatic event. In some cases it seems that the trauma interferes with all the processes of memory. Paying attention, the encoding of sensory input, and rehearsal are all impaired. A number of investigators have linked certain kinds of brain damage—as of the hippocampus—to certain kinds of amnesia, but their views remain somewhat speculative (Corkin et al., 1985; Squire et al., 1984).

Some perceptions and ideas must apparently be allowed to **consolidate** or rest undisturbed for a while if they are to be remembered (Gold & King, 1974). A football player who is knocked unconscious or a victim of an auto accident may be unable to recall events for several minutes prior to the trauma. The football player may not recall taking to the field. The accident victim may not recall entering the car.

Now that we have looked at how and why we forget, let us consider ways of improving our ability to remember.

Some Methods for Improving Memory

Who among us has not wished for a better memory from time to time? If we could remember more, we might earn higher grades, charm people with our stock of jokes, or even pay our bills on time. It was once believed that one's memory was fixed, that one had a good or poor memory and was stuck with it (Singular, 1982). But today psychologists have found that there are a number of ways in which we can all improve our memories, such as the following.

The Method of Loci

You might be better able to remember your shopping list if you imagine meat loaf in your navel or a strip of bacon draped over your nose. This is a meaty example of the **method of loci.** With this method you select a series of related images, such as the parts of your body or the furniture in your home. Then you imagine an item from your shopping list, or another list you want to remember, attached to each image.

By placing meat loaf or a favorite complete dinner in your navel, rather than a single item such as chopped beef, you can combine several items into one chunk of information. At the supermarket you recall the (familiar) ingredients for meat loaf and simply recognize whether or not you need each one.

Mediation

In the method of **mediation,** you link two items with a third that ties them together. What if you are having difficulty remembering that John's wife's name is Tillie? Laird Cermak (1978) suggests that you can mediate between John and Tillie as follows. Reflect that the *john* is a slang term for bathroom. Bathrooms often have ceramic *tiles. Tiles,* of course, sounds like *Tillie.* So it goes: John-bathroom-tiles-Tillie.

Mnemonics

In a third method of improving memory, **mnemonics,** chunks of information are combined into a format, such as an acronym, jingle, or phrase. Recalling the phrase "Every Good

---

Retrograde amnesia Failure to remember events that occur prior to physical trauma because of the effects of the trauma.

Anterograde amnesia Failure to remember events that occur after physical trauma because of the effects of the trauma.

Consolidation The fixing of information in long-term memory.

Method of loci A method of improving memory in which chunks of new material are related to a series of well-established or well-known images. (*Loci* is the plural of the Latin *locus,* meaning "place.")

Mediation A method of improving memory by linking two items with a third that ties them together.

Mnemonics A method of improving memory in which chunks of information are combined into a format like an acronym, jingle, or phrase.

Boy Does Fine" has helped many people remember the musical keys E, G, B, D, F.

How can you remember how to spell *mnemonics?* Simple—just be willing to grant "aMNesty" to those who cannot.

The Biology of Memory: From Engrams to Epinephrine

Early in this century most psychologists believed that **engrams** were responsible for memory. Engrams were hypothesized electrical circuits in the brain that corresponded to the memory trace—a neurological process that was somehow thought to parallel a perceptual experience. But biological psychologists such as Karl Lashley (1950) spent many fruitless years searching for these circuits or the parts of the brain in which they might be housed.

Still, contemporary psychologists have found evidence for the involvements of physiology and chemistry in learning and memory, including neurons, brain structures, and hormones such as epinephrine. Epinephrine not only generally stimulates bodily arousal and activity. It also strengthens memory when it is released into the bloodstream following instances of learning (Delanoy et al., 1982; Laroche & Bloch, 1982; McGaugh, 1983). The neurotransmitter acetylcholine (ACh) is also involved in memory. In Alzheimer's disease the brain cells that produce ACh degenerate, decreasing the amount of ACh available to the brain and, in particular, the hippocampus, which is vital in the formation of new memories.

Numerous studies of the biology of memory have also focused on the possible roles of so-called **memory molecules.** Let us examine a few experiments that are suggestive of the role of biology in memory.

Engram (1) An assumed electrical circuit in the brain that corresponds to a memory trace. (2) An assumed chemical change in the brain that accompanies learning. (From the Greek *en-*, meaning "in," and *gramma*, meaning "something that is written or recorded.")

Memory molecule Molecules whose chemical compositions are thought to change with experience, forming a chemical basis for memory.

The Worm Turns, *or*, How Some Worms Got Fed Up (Literally) with Learning   A flatworm has an unusual sex life. It has both male and female sex organs. When the pickings in the outside world don't look very promising, it may just mate with itself and produce more flatworms. The flatworm can also *regenerate*. If you cut it in half, the head part will grow a new tail, and more remarkably, the tail part will grow a new head, complete with a new brain.

In their efforts to locate memory functions in the flatworm, James McConnell and his colleagues (1959) devised a research program based on its ability to regenerate. Where would you think a flatworm's memory is located? Heads or tails?

To find out, the McConnell group conditioned some worms to scrunch up when a light was shone. Flatworms normally save "scrunching" for the stimulus of electric shock, but the researchers paired the light with shock. After repeated pairings, the light became a CS that elicited the response usually evoked by the shock (US). After conditioning, the worms were cut in half and given time to regenerate. As expected, the head part that grew a new tail scrunched up when a light was shone. But so did the tail part after a new head was regenerated! Memory of the light-shock association was not stored in the head alone.

In follow-up studies, the McConnell group fed chopped-up flatworms who had learned the light-shock association to other flatworms. The cannibal worms apparently got "fed up" with learning. They often scrunched up when the light was shone, even though they had not been conditioned to do so. In other experiments, flatworms were trained, by operant conditioning, to turn to the right or left at choice points in mazes. Then they were chopped up and fed to untrained worms. The untrained worms then learned to turn right or left (assuming that they were expected to turn in the same direction as their dinner) more rapidly than did untrained worms who had not been given this "brain food."

Where were memories stored in the worms that regenerated new heads? *What* did the cannibal worms eat that helped them learn mazes more rapidly than their fellows did? Additional studies by McConnell and his colleagues (1970) suggest that memories might have been stored and transmitted in molecules of **ribonucleic acid** (RNA). RNA is a protein, or amino acid, that is similar in structure to DNA. DNA, as noted in Chapter 2, is involved in the transmission of the genetic code from one generation of animals to another. The body's DNA is basically fixed, so that we don't suddenly become different people, but RNA is changeable.

The McConnell group transferred molecules of RNA from flatworms who had learned the light-shock association to untrained worms. The untrained worms then learned the light-shock association in fewer pairings than did worms who did not receive RNA.

Before you conclude that the best way to earn an A is to grind up your professor for dinner, we must note that McConnell's studies have not always been successfully replicated. For one thing, flatworms are not easy to condition. Also, similar experiments in transferring "memory molecules" between the brains of higher animals, such as mice and rats, have not led to the predicted results.

But other research on the possible role of proteins in learning and memory, in which scientists have experimentally manipulated protein formation, is also suggestive of the role of memory molecules.

Life in a Goldfish Bowl: The Consolidation of Learning   University of Michigan biochemist Bernard Agranoff taught goldfish that sometimes it is better to be left in the dark (Pines, 1975). He flashed a light and then the fish were given electric shock. The shock was turned off when the fish swam to the other side of the tank. After several trials the fish learned to swim to the other side of the tank whenever the light was flashed. This is an example of **avoidance learning:** By swimming across the tank the fish avoided the shock.

Agranoff found that he could interfere with the fishes' learning by injecting puromycin—a chemical that impairs the formation of neuropeptides in the brain—after the fish were taught to associate light and electric shock. They subsequently made no effort to swim across the tank when the light was shone.

Agranoff reasoned that the puromycin prevented consolidation of the fishes' learning. It had prevented the memory of the association from becoming fixed in long-term memory. If, on the other hand, Agranoff waited for an hour before injecting puromycin, the learning was apparently consolidated. The fish would swim to safety as soon as the light was shone.

At the University of California at Irvine, James McGaugh's research seems to serve as the mirror image of Agranoff's. McGaugh (McGaugh et al., 1980) injected strychnine into laboratory rats following conditioning. In large doses, strychnine is poisonous. In the smaller doses used by McGaugh, strychnine apparently promoted the formation of neuropeptides and helped the rats consolidate their learning of mazes. Here, too, the injection had to be given within an hour, while the new memories were apparently still being consolidated.

As noted earlier, current research into the chemistry of memory also involves hormones such as epinephrine. Another hormone that can play a role in memory is antidiuretic hormone (ADH). Volunteers have received a synthetic form of ADH, or **vasopressin,** through nasal sprays and have shown significant improvement in recall (McGaugh, 1983). Excess vasopressin, unfortunately, can have serious side effects, such as constriction of the blood vessels. But research into the effects of similar chemicals, which may have fewer side effects, is under way.

The Future of Learning and Memory   Research into the biology of memory is in its infancy, but what an exciting area of research it is. What would it mean to you if you could read for a half-hour to an hour, pop a pill, and cause your new learnings to become consolidated in long-term memory? You would never have to reread the material; it would be at your fingertips for a lifetime. It would save a bit of study time, would it not?

Ribonucleic acid A substance that is involved in transmitting genetic information, and possibly in memory formation. Abbreviated *RNA*.

Avoidance learning A conditioning procedure in which an organism learns to exhibit an operant that permits it to avoid an aversive stimulus.

Vasopressin Another term for *antidiuretic hormone*.

TRUTH OR FICTION REVISITED

Dogs can be trained to salivate when a bell is rung. True. Pavlov accomplished this by repeatedly pairing a bell with the presentation of meat to laboratory dogs.

We can learn to change our behavior while we are sleeping. True. In one example, the bell-and-pad method is used to condition children to wake up rather than urinate when their bladders are full.

Psychologists helped a young boy overcome fear of rabbits by having him eat cookies while a rabbit was brought nearer. True. This method is an example of counterconditioning of fears.

During World War II a psychologist devised a plan for training pigeons to guide missiles to their targets. True. B. F. Skinner proposed to accomplish this mission through operant conditioning.

You can "hook" people on gambling by allowing them to win some money in the early stages and then tapering off with the payoffs. True. Behavior can be maintained for quite a while on intermittent reinforcement schedules.

Punishment doesn't work. False. Strong enough punishments suppress unwanted behavior, but there are a number of drawbacks to punishment, as discussed in this chapter.

Rats can be trained to climb a ramp, cross a bridge, climb a ladder, pedal a toy car, and do several other tasks—all in proper sequence. True. The operant-conditioning methods that are used include shaping and chaining.

Rats have been taught to raise or lower their heart rates in order to receive an interesting reward—a burst of electricity in the brain. True. In these biofeedback experiments, the burst of electricity apparently stimulated a "pleasure center" in the animals' hypothalamuses.

Psychologists successfully fashioned a method to teach an emaciated 9-month-old infant to stop throwing up. True, they used avoidance-learning procedures.

We must make mistakes in order to learn. False. In programed learning, for example, it is possible to learn without making any errors.

Only people are capable of insight. False. Chimpanzees (such as Sultan) and rats (such as Bismarck) have also apparently demonstrated insight in problem solving.

All our experiences are permanently imprinted on the brain so that proper stimulation can cause us to remember them exactly. False. It seems that what we remember is a blend of truth and fiction, skewed by our biases and needs.

There is such a thing as a photographic memory. True. This phenomenon is called eidetic imagery and is found in about 5 percent of children. The capacity is lost by adulthood.

There is no limit to the amount of information you can store in your memory. This is true of long-term memory, as far as we know, although there are decided limits to short-term memory (around seven or so chunks of information).

We can remember important events that took place as early as the age of 1 or 2. False, despite the fact that some of us are convinced that we can. But we are probably recalling "reconstructed" (biased) memories or memories of events that occurred at later ages.

We are more likely to recall happy events while we are feeling happy and sad events while we are feeling sad. True. Research into state-dependent memory supports this view.

You can use tricks to improve your memory. True. The tricks are known as mnemonic devices, and they usually work by associating new information with well-known information.

Rats were helped to remember their way through mazes by being injected with the poison strychnine. True. A low dose of strychnine apparently promoted the formation of neuropeptides that are involved in consolidation of learning.

A nasal spray can promote memory functioning. True—when the spray contains a synthetic form of antidiuretic hormone (ADH).

Chapter Review

From a cognitive perspective, learning is defined as the process by which experience leads to relatively permanent changes in behavior. From a behavioral perspective, learning is the change in behavior that results from experience. Conditioning is a simple form of learning in which organisms learn to associate stimuli and responses. In aversive conditioning, a neutral stimulus is paired repeatedly with an aversive stimulus, so that the neutral stimulus acquires aversive properties.

Classical conditioning is defined as a simple form of learning in which an originally neutral stimulus comes to bring forth, or elicit, the response usually brought forth by another stimulus by being paired repeatedly with the other stimulus. A response to a US is called an unconditioned response (UR), and a response to a CS is termed a conditioned response (CR).

After a US–CS association has been learned, repeated presentation of the CS (e.g., a bell) without the US (meat) will extinguish the CR (salivation). But extinguished responses may show spontaneous recovery as a function of time that has elapsed since the end of the extinction process.

Thorndike originated the law of effect, which holds that responses are "stamped in" by rewards and "stamped out" by punishments. Skinner introduced the concept of reinforcement. In operant conditioning, an organism learns to emit an operant because it is reinforced. Initial "correct" responses may be performed by random trial and error, or by physical or verbal guiding.

Positive reinforcers increase the probability that operants will occur when they are applied. Negative reinforcers increase the probability that operants will occur when they are removed. Primary reinforcers have their value because of the biological makeup of the organism. Secondary reinforcers, such as money and approval, acquire their value through association with established reinforcers.

In operant conditioning, extinction results from repeated performance of operant behavior in the absence of reinforcement. Spontaneous recovery of learned responses can occur as a function of the passage of time following extinction.

Many learning theorists prefer treating children's misbehavior by ignoring it or using time out from reinforcement rather than punishment. Strong punishment will suppress undesired behavior. Punishment does not teach desirable behavior; suppresses undesired behavior only when it is guaranteed; may cause the organism to withdraw from the situation; can create anger and hostility; can lead to overgeneralization; and can serve as a model for aggression.

A discriminative stimulus indicates when an operant will be reinforced. Continuous reinforcement leads to most rapid acquisition of new responses, but operants are maintained most economically through partial reinforcement schedules—fixed ratio, fixed interval, variable ratio, and variable interval schedules.

Research in cognitive learning suggests that not all behavior can be explained through conditioning. Köhler showed that apes can learn through sudden reorganization of perceptual relationships, or insight. Tolman's work with rats suggests that they develop cognitive maps of the environment. Tolman's work in latent learning also found that organisms learn in the absence of reinforcement. Bandura and other social-learning theorists have shown that people can also learn by observing others.

Memory may be defined as the processes by which information is stored and retrieved. Memory may be divided into three "structures": sensory memory, short-term memory, and long-term memory. A stimulus is maintained in sensory memory only for a fraction of a second. The stimulus then decays unless it is attended to and encoded. Visual stimuli are usually encoded as sounds—that is, an acoustic code is used. Acoustic codes can be maintained by repetition, or rehearsal.

About seven chunks of information may be maintained in short-term memory at once. New chunks of information may displace older chunks that have not been transferred to long-term memory. Research has not found any limit to the amount of information that can be stored in long-term memory. Loss of long-term memories usually reflects inability to find cues that will enable us to retrieve desired information. Long-term memories are organized in a hierarchical structure.

Ebbinghaus used nonsense syllables in the study of memory and forgetting. Retention is tested through three types of memory tasks: recognition, recall, relearning.

The tip-of-the-tongue phenomenon is an example of cue-dependent forgetting. When the cue for retrieving a memory is physiological or emotional rather than cognitive, we may speak of a memory as being state-dependent.

According to interference theory, people forget because learning can interfere with retrieval of other learnings. Freud suggested that we also forget threatening or unacceptable material through repression. Freud also attributed childhood amnesia to repression, but critics note that the hippocampus is not mature until we are about 2 years old and that language helps children to remember because they can apply acoustic and semantic codes for objects and events once they have words for things. In retrograde amnesia, shock or other trauma prevents recently learned material from being recalled.

Early in the century, many psychologists thought that engrams were responsible for memory. Engrams were hypothesized electrical circuits in the brain that were thought to correspond to memory traces. Present research into the biology of memory focuses on the roles of RNA and neurotransmitters.

Exercise

Classical Versus Operant Conditioning

Directions: *Following are a number of terms that are used in discussions of conditioning. Some terms apply to classical conditioning, some to operant conditioning, and some to both. For each term place a checkmark in the appropriate blank space, or spaces, to show the type(s) of learning to which it applies. The answer key is given below.*

TERM	CLASSICAL CONDITIONING	OPERANT CONDITIONING
1. Discriminative stimulus	_____	_____
2. Unconditioned stimulus	_____	_____
3. Conditioned response	_____	_____
4. Extinction	_____	_____

5. Reinforcer _____ _____
6. Backward conditioning _____ _____
7. Generalization _____ _____
8. Instrumental conditioning _____ _____
9. Bell-and-pad method _____ _____
10. Biofeedback training _____ _____
11. Trial and error _____ _____
12. Stimulus _____ _____
13. Neutral stimulus _____ _____
14. Skinner box _____ _____
15. Operant _____ _____
16. Spontaneous recovery _____ _____
17. Shaping _____ _____
18. Cumulative recorder _____ _____
19. Conditional reflex _____ _____
20. Variable-ratio schedule _____ _____
21. Response _____ _____
22. Higher-order conditioning _____ _____
23. Successive approximations _____ _____
24. Programed learning _____ _____
25. Rewards and punishments _____ _____
26. Flooding _____ _____
27. Taste aversion _____ _____

Answer Key to Exercise

1. O	8. O	15. O	22. C
2. C	9. C	16. C, O	23. O
3. C	10. O	17. O	24. O
4. C, O	11. O	18. O	25. O
5. O	12. C, O	19. C	26. C
6. C	13. C	20. O	27. C
7. C, O	14. O	21. C, O	

Posttest

Directions: *For each of the following, select the choice that best answers the question or completes the sentence.*

1. Conditioning is best defined as a simple form of

(a) learning to engage in voluntary behavior, (b) acquiring expectations, (c) learning to associate stimuli and responses, (d) cognitive learning.

2. Which school of psychologists would define learning as a change in behavior that results from experience?

(a) Behaviorists, (b) Cognitive psychologists, (c) Gestalt psychologists, (d) Psychoanalysts.

3. In Pavlov's experiments, salivation in response to meat was a(n)

(a) CR, (b) CS, (c) UR, (d) US.

4. In using the bell-and-pad method for overcoming bedwetting, the sensations of a full bladder are the

(a) CR, (b) CS, (c) UR, (d) US.

5. Extinction in classical conditioning is defined as repeated presentation of the

(a) CR in the absence of the CS, (b) UR in the absence of the US, (c) CS in the absence of the US, (d) US in the absence of the CS.

6. In higher-order conditioning, a previously neutral stimulus comes to serve as a CS after being paired with a(n)

(a) CR, (b) CS, (c) UR, (d) US.

7. In the behavior therapy method of _____, a client is exposed to a fear-evoking stimulus at full force until the fear is extinguished.

(a) aversive conditioning, (b) systematic desensitization, (c) flooding, (d) counterconditioning.

8. Little Albert learned to fear rats as a result of

(a) clanging of steel bars in the presence of a rat, (b) observing a rat attack another animal, (c) being informed that rats carry certain harmful diseases, (d) being personally bitten by a rat.

9. Who originated the use of puzzle boxes?

(a) Ivan Pavlov, (b) John B. Watson, (c) B. F. Skinner, (d) Edward L. Thorndike.

10. According to the law of effect, _____ has the effect of stamping out stimulus-response connections.

(a) forgetting, (b) negative reinforcement, (c) extinction, (d) punishment.

11. Pain is an example of a

(a) primary positive reinforcer, (b) primary negative reinforcer, (c) secondary positive reinforcer, (d) secondary negative reinforcer.

12. A negative reinforcer

(a) increases the frequency of a response when it is applied, (b) decreases the frequency of a response when it is applied, (c) increases the frequency of a response when it is removed, (d) decreases the frequency of a response when it is removed.

13. Which of the following statements about punishment is *false*?

(a) Children learn responses that are punished, (b) Punishment increases the frequency of undesired behavior, **(c)** Punished children may withdraw from the situation, **(d)** Punishment may be modeled as a way of solving problems.

14. With a _____ schedule, an organism's response rate falls off after each reinforcement.

    (a) fixed-interval, **(b)** fixed-ratio, **(c)** variable-interval, **(d)** variable-ratio.

15. In the experiments with biofeedback training described in the text, Neal E. Miller trained rats to _____ by reinforcing them with a burst of electricity in the brain.

    (a) change their heart rates, **(b)** climb ladders and crawl through tubes, **(c)** press a lever, **(d)** emit alpha waves.

16. In using behavior modification in the classroom, teachers

    (a) pay attention to children when they are misbehaving, **(b)** pay attention to children when they are behaving correctly, **(c)** punish children when they are misbehaving, **(d)** reward children when they are misbehaving.

17. An experiment with Bismarck provided evidence for

    (a) classical conditioning, **(b)** operant conditioning, **(c)** learning by insight, **(d)** latent learning.

18. In order for observational learning to take place,

    (a) stimuli must be paired repeatedly, **(b)** a stimulus must elicit a response, **(c)** an organism must be reinforced, **(d)** an organism must watch another organism.

19. Visual impressions last for _____ in the sensory memory.

    (a) a fraction of a second, **(b)** a second, **(c)** several seconds, **(d)** several minutes or longer.

20. A parent knows that you are taking a psychology course and asks how he can teach his young child the alphabet. You respond by noting that children usually learn the alphabet by

    (a) mechanical associative learning, **(b)** use of elaborative rehearsal, **(c)** semantic coding, **(d)** chunking.

21. Information in short-term memory tends to be forgotten through

    (a) decay, **(b)** failure to use appropriate retrieval cues, **(c)** displacement, **(d)** retrograde amnesia.

22. Which of the following is an example of cue-dependent forgetting?

    (a) The serial-position effect, **(b)** The tip-of-the-tongue phenomenon, **(c)** Proactive interference, **(d)** Anterograde amnesia.

23. The easiest type of memory task is

    (a) recall, **(b)** recognition, **(c)** relearning, **(d)** savings.

24. According to the text, puromycin impairs consolidation of learning by

    (a) causing retrograde amnesia, **(b)** releasing strychnine into the bloodstream, **(c)** interfering with neuropeptide formation, **(d)** disorienting the organism.

25. Some physiological psychologists attribute childhood amnesia to immaturity of the

    (a) hypothalamus, **(b)** pons, **(c)** thalamus, **(d)** hippocampus.

Answers to Posttest

1. C	**8.** A	**14.** A	**20.** A
2. A	**9.** D	**15.** A	**21.** C
3. C	**10.** D	**16.** B	**22.** B
4. B	**11.** B	**17.** C	**23.** B
5. C	**12.** C	**18.** D	**24.** C
6. B	**13.** B	**19.** A	**25.** D
7. C			

LANGUAGE, THOUGHT, AND INTELLIGENCE

OUTLINE

PRETEST: TRUTH OR FICTION?
ON LANGUAGE AND APES
  Properties of Human Language

THE BASICS OF LANGUAGE
  Phonology
  Morphology
  Syntax
  Semantics

PATTERNS OF LANGUAGE DEVELOPMENT
  Prelinguistic Vocalizations
  Development of Vocabulary
  Development of Syntax
  Toward More Complex Language

THEORIES OF LANGUAGE DEVELOPMENT
  Learning-Theory Views
  Nativist Views
  Cognitive Views
  Putting It All Together

LANGUAGE AND THOUGHT
  The Linguistic-Relativity Hypothesis
PROBLEM SOLVING
  Stages in Problem Solving
  Mental Sets
  Functional Fixedness
  Creativity in Problem Solving
INTELLIGENCE
  Theories of Intelligence
  Measurement of Intelligence
  Social-Class, Racial, and Ethnic Differences in
    Intelligence
  The Testing Controversy
  The Determinants of Intelligence: Where Do IQ
    Scores Come From?
TRUTH OR FICTION REVISITED
CHAPTER REVIEW
EXERCISE
POSTTEST

PRETEST: TRUTH OR FICTION?

Chimpanzees and gorillas have been taught how to use sign language.

Crying is the child's earliest use of language.

Children babble only the sounds of their parents' language.

Deaf children do not babble.

To a 2-year-old, the word combinations "Go Mommy" and "Mommy go" have the same meaning.

Three-year-olds say "Daddy goed away" instead of "Daddy went away" because they *do* understand rules of grammar.

Children acquire grammar by imitating their parents.

The only way to solve a difficult problem is to keep plugging away at it.

It may be boring, but the most efficient way to solve a problem is to use the tried and tested formula.

Highly intelligent people are also creative.

Knowing what problem to tackle is an aspect of intelligent behavior.

Intelligence and *IQ* mean the same thing.

Two children can answer exactly the same items on an intelligence test correctly, yet one can be above average and the other below average in intelligence.

Japanese children attain higher IQ scores than U.S. children.

There is no such thing as an unbiased intelligence test.

High intelligence runs in families.

Head Start programs have raised children's IQs.

When I was in high school, I remember being taught that human beings differ from other creatures that ran, swam, or flew because we are the only ones to use tools and language. Then I learned that lower animals also use tools. Otters use rocks to open clam shells. Chimpanzees toss rocks as weapons and use sticks to dig out grubs for food.

In recent years, our exclusive claim to the use of language has also been questioned because chimps and gorillas have been taught to use **symbols** to communicate. Some make signs with their hands. Others use plastic symbols or press keys on a computer keyboard (see Figure 5.1).

Language is the communication of thoughts and feelings by means of symbols that are arranged according to rules of grammar. Language makes it possible for one person to communicate large amounts of knowledge to another and for one generation to communicate to another. According to **psycholinguist** Roger Brown, "The important thing about language is that it makes life experiences cumulative; across generations and within one generation, among individuals. Everyone can know much more than he [or she] could possibly learn by direct experience" (1970, p. 212).

Language provides many of the basic units of thought, and thought is central to intelligent behavior. Language is one of our great strengths. Other species may be stronger, run faster, smell more keenly, even live longer, but only we have produced literature, music, mathematics, and science. Language ability has made all this possible.

Symbol Something that stands for or represents another.

Language The communication of information by means of symbols arranged according to rules of grammar.

Psycholinguist A scientist who specializes in the study of the relationships between psychological processes and language.

American Sign Language The communication of meaning through the use of symbols that are formed by moving the hands and arms.

Telegraphic Referring to speech in which only the essential words are used, as in a telegram.

In this chapter we shall explore the interrelated cognitive processes of language, thought, and intelligence. We shall begin by surveying efforts to teach language to apes. This research is fascinating in its own right and affords insight into language development in humans. Next we shall discuss the structure of language, chronicle language development, and explore theories of language acquisition. This will prepare us for a discussion of how language and thought are intertwined in problem solving. Finally, we shall examine the concept of intelligence. As you may have gathered from publicity over IQ tests, the definition and measurement of intelligence are controversial issues.

ON LANGUAGE AND APES: GOING APE OVER LANGUAGE?

Some of us may know people who insist that their dogs understand every word they say, but when we look closely we find that the animals respond to their human owner's excitement and a few words or commands such as "Sit," "Lunchtime," or "Out" that have been paired repeatedly with certain acts or events. Nor has anyone had a talking pet cat, horse, or elephant. So the weight of human history made us skeptical of the first reports that chimpanzees had been taught to use symbols to communicate.

Washoe, a female chimp raised by Beatrice and Allen Gardner (1980), was one of the first primates who came to our notice. The Gardners and their assistants raised Washoe from the time she was 1 year of age. Instead of speaking to her, they used **American Sign Language** (ASL), the language of the deaf.

By the age of 5, Washoe could use more than 160 signs, including signs for actions (verbs), such as *come, gimme,* and *tickle;* signs for things (nouns), such as *apples, flowers,* and *toothbrush;* and signs for more abstract concepts, such as *more.* She could combine signs to form simple sentences. Washoe's brief sentences were largely **telegraphic,** like those of young children. Consider these two-word sentences: *More tickle, More banana,* and *More milk—* which doesn't sound like too bad a way to spend a lazy Sunday afternoon. As time passed Washoe signed longer sentences, such as *Please sweet drink, Come gimme drink* and *Gimme toothbrush hurry.*

Figure 5.1. How Do Apes Use Signs to Communicate? Operant conditioning was used to teach a chimp named Sarah to communicate by using plastic symbols. Psychologists reinforced Sarah for selecting the proper symbols, or for following instructions made with symbols. Here Sarah will follow directions to place the apple in the pail and the banana in the dish.

Washoe extended the meanings of many words to cover objects for which she had no words, a process called **overextension** that also characterizes children's language. During the second year, for example, children may overextend the word *doggy* to refer to many animals, such as dogs, horses, and cows.

Some observers believe that Washoe's communications showed failings by human standards. For example, we are not certain of the degree to which Washoe and other apes have attended to grammar, as shown by word order (Terrace et al., 1980). Washoe's words were frequently strung in haphazard combinations, but even the language productions of 1-year-old children tend to have reliable word order. Children appear to share an **intuitive** grasp of grammar, but apes might not. Still, in recent years Washoe and her companions have been observed spontaneously signing to one another, and some mother chimpanzees teach their infants to use signs to communicate (Bernstein, 1987; Fouts & Fouts, 1985).

Ann and David Premack (1975) taught another female chimp, Sarah, to communicate by arranging symbols on a magnet board (see Figure 5.1). Eventually Sarah learned simple telegraphic sentences like *Place orange dish*. Her word order was less sporadic than Washoe's. The Premacks consider their work with Sarah a demonstration of the role of operant conditioning in language learning. Sarah was reinforced for selecting the proper symbols to make a request and for following instructions communicated by symbols.

Still another chimp, Lana, was trained to communicate by means of a keyboard controlled by a computer (Savage-Rumbaugh & Rumbaugh, 1980). Lana learned to manipulate about 100 keys, each of which showed a different symbol. She would press various combinations of keys to communicate simple ideas and also tended to maintain a consistent word order.

Some of the most impressive claims for teaching language to an ape have been made by Francine (Penny) Patterson (1980). Patterson taught a gorilla, Koko, to use hundreds of signs, including signs for *friend, airplane, lollipop, belly button*, even *stethoscope*. Patterson also reports that Koko has produced some creative insults in ASL—for example, "You dirty toilet devil" and "Rotten stink." Koko, like children, has also created words (signs) of her own, such as tucking her index finger under her arm as a sign for thermometer (Patterson et al., 1987). Apes, like children, name objects. But

Overextension Using words in situations in which their meanings become extended, or inappropriate.

Intuitive The direct learning or knowing of something without conscious use of reason.

60 Minutes

Talk to the Animals

Since the mid-1960s psychologists have been employing sign language and other systems of symbols to, as the fictitious Dr. Doolittle did, "Talk to the Animals."

In the "60 Minutes" segment "Talk to the Animals," correspondent Morley Safer asks Penny Patterson, who has been teaching sign language to Koko and other gorillas, "Why bother?" Safer noted that people hearing of communicating with apes might say, "Interesting, but why?"

One answer to this question is that teaching sign language to apes has helped us teach retarded and brain-damaged people how to communicate.

But Patterson suggested that we need not justify our infant studies in communicating with apes in terms of their usefulness alone.

Patterson noted that apes

> have intrinsic value, the same as I would attribute to myself or you. And [by] studying them, we can understand another mind. It's as though we can look into a different consciousness. We don't have to wait for the extra-terrestrials to arrive; we've got something right here we can look at. . . . I feel that I'm privileged to know Koko, as I do, through language; that she's telling me, and maybe will tell me in the future, very important things about another form of life.

---

some **linguists** argue that Koko, like other apes, shows little understanding of grammar.

And so: Can apes really understand and produce language? To answer this question, we shall refer to some of the features of language.

Properties of Human Language: Semanticity, Productivity, and Displacement

According to Roger Brown (1973), three properties are used today to distinguish between human language and the communications systems of lower animals: *semanticity, productivity,* and *displacement.* **Semanticity** refers to the fact that words

serve as symbols for actions, objects, relational concepts (over, in, more, and so on), and other ideas.

Many species have systems of communication. Birds warn other birds of predators. They communicate that they have taken possession of a certain tree or bush through characteristic chirps and shrieks. The "dances" shown by bees inform other bees of the approximate direction and distance of a food source or of an invading enemy. But these communication patterns are innate and, in contrast to human language, largely unmodifiable by experience. They also lack semanticity. That is, specific sounds and—in the case of bees—waggles do not serve as symbols.

Productivity refers to the capacity to combine words into original sentences. An "original" sentence is one produced by the individual instead of being imitated. To produce original sentences, children must have a basic understanding of **syntax,** or the structure of grammar. Two-year-old children string signs (words) together in novel combinations, but questions have been raised about whether apes combine signs into original sentences (Terrace et al., 1980). Lana, for example, learned a number of standard sentences into which she could insert new verbs and nouns, but her productivity was limited.

Herbert Terrace of Columbia University has

Linguists Scientists who study the structure, functions, and origins of language.

Semanticity Meaning. The quality of language in which words are used as symbols for objects, events, or ideas.

Productivity The capacity to combine words into original sentences.

Syntax The rules in a language for placing words in proper order to form meaningful sentences.

concluded that apes cannot master the basics of grammar. Terrace (1980, 1987) also argues that what looks like spontaneous signing is actually signing for "a variety of concrete incentives"—that is, tricks to gain rewards. There are some exceptions, but apes generally use signs in the situations in which they have been taught to use them. What apes produce is very similar to what they have been taught to produce.

Displacement is the capacity to communicate information about events and objects in another time or place.* Language makes possible the efficient transmission of complex knowledge from one person to another and from one generation to another. Displacement permits parents to warn children of their own mistakes. Displacement allows children to tell their parents what they did in school.

In sum, if we use Brown's criteria for defining language, some critics argue that apes fall short. Still, Maratsos (1983) notes that Brown's strict criteria are relatively new on the scene. "Apes can probably learn to use signs to communicate meanings," Maratsos writes. "As this used to be the old boundary for language, it seems unfair to [now] raise the ante and say that [using signs to communicate meaning] is not really language" (1983, p. 771). But Maratsos adds that the questions of whether apes can use word order and other aspects of grammar in the way we do remain problematic to the supporters of apes.

We have not really answered the question of whether apes can use language. My apologies—the issue remains controversial. Nonetheless, our discussion of the language of apes affords insight into our facility with language.

THE BASICS OF LANGUAGE

ASL does not contain sounds because it is intended for use by deaf people. But the components of other languages do include sounds (*phonology*) and a number of other features: *morphology* (units of meaning), *syntax* (word order), and *semantics* (the meanings of words and groups of words).

*The word *displacement* has a different meaning in Sigmund Freud's psychoanalytic theory, as we shall see in Chapter 7.

Phonology

Phonology is the study of the basic sounds in a language. There are 26 letters in the English alphabet but a greater number of basic sounds or **phonemes.** These include the *t* and *p* in *tip*, which a psycholinguist may designate as the /t/ and /p/ phonemes. The *o* in *go* and the *o* in *gone* are different phonemes. They are spelled with the same letter, but they sound different. English speakers who learn French may be confused because /o/, as in the word *go*, has various spellings in French, including *o, au, eau,* even *eaux*.

Morphology

Morphemes are the smallest units of meaning in a language. A morpheme consists of one or more phonemes pronounced in a certain order. Some morphemes such as *dog* and *cat* function by themselves as words, but other morphemes must be combined to be used. The words *dogs* and *cats* each consist of two morphemes. Adding /z/ to *dog* makes the word plural. Adding /s/ to *cat* serves the same function.

An *ed* morpheme at the end of a regular verb places it in the past tense, as with *add* and *added* and with *subtract* and *subtracted*. A *ly* morpheme at the end of an adjective often makes the word an adverb, as with *strong* and *strongly* and *weak* and *weakly*.

Inflections   Morphemes such as *s* and *ed* tacked on to the ends of nouns and verbs are referred to as grammatical "markers," or **inflections.** Inflec-

---

Displacement The quality of language that permits one to communicate information about objects and events in another time and place.

Phonology The study of the basic sounds in a language.

Phoneme A basic sound in a language.

Morpheme The smallest unit of meaning in a language.

Inflections Grammatical markers that change the forms of words to indicate grammatical relationships such as number and tense.

tions change the forms of words to indicate grammatical relationships such as *number* (singular or plural) and *tense* (e.g., present or past). Languages have grammatical rules for the formation of plurals, tenses, and other inflections.

Syntax

Syntax concerns the customary arrangement of words in phrases and sentences in a language. It deals with the ways words are to be strung together, or ordered, into phrases and sentences. The precise rules for word order are the *grammar* of a language.

In English, statements usually follow the pattern *subject, verb,* and *object of the verb.* Note this example:

The young boy (subject) → has brought (verb) → the book (object).

The sentence would be confusing if it were written "The young boy *has* the book *brought.*" But this is how the sentence would be written in German. German syntax differs, and in German, a past participle ("brought") is placed at the end of the sentence, whereas the helping verb ("has") follows the subject. Although the syntax of German differs from that of English, children raised in German-speaking homes* acquire German syntax readily.

*No, homes do not really speak German or any other language. This is an example of idiomatic English; idioms like these are acquired readily by children.

> **Semantics** The study of the meanings of a language—the relationships between language and objects and events.

Semantics

The meanings of a language are the concern of **semantics.** Semantics is defined as the study of the relationship between language and the objects or events language depicts. As we just saw, words that sound (and are even spelled) alike can have different meanings, depending on their usage. Compare these sentences:

A rock sank the boat.
Don't rock the boat.

In the first sentence, *rock* is a noun and the subject of the verb *sank.* The sentence probably means that the hull of a boat was ripped open by an underwater rock, causing the boat to sink. In the second sentence, *rock* is a verb. The second sentence is usually used as a figure of speech in which a person is being warned not to change things—not to "make waves" or "upset the apple cart."

Or compare these sentences:

The chicken is ready for dinner.
The lion is ready for dinner.
The shark is ready for dinner.

The first sentence probably means that a chicken has been cooked and is ready to be eaten. The second sentence probably means that a lion is hungry, or about to devour its prey. Our interpretation of the phrase "is ready for dinner" reflects our knowledge about chickens and lions. Whether or not we expect a shark to be eaten or to do some eating might reflect our seafood preferences or how recently we had seen the movie *Jaws.*

Noam Chomsky differentiates between the *surface structure* and the *deep structure* of sentences.

The **surface structure** involves the superficial grammatical construction of the sentence. The surface structure of the "ready-for-dinner" sentences is the same. The **deep structure** of a sentence refers to its underlying meaning. The "ready-for-dinner" sentences clearly differ in their deep structure. "Make me a peanut butter and jelly sandwich" has an ambiguous surface structure, allowing different interpretations of its deep meaning—and the typical child's response: "Poof! You're a peanut butter and jelly sandwich!" Chomsky believes that children have an inborn tendency to grasp the deep structures of sentences.

Now that we have looked at the structure of language, we can better appreciate the "child's task" of acquiring language.

PATTERNS OF LANGUAGE DEVELOPMENT

Now that we have become familiar with the elements of language, let us trace language development in children. Children develop language in an invariant sequence of steps, as outlined in Table 5.1. We begin with the **prelinguistic** vocalizations of crying, cooing, and babbling.

Prelinguistic Vocalizations

Crying   Newborn children, as parents are well aware, have an unlearned but highly effective form of verbal expression: crying and more crying. Crying is a simple form of vocalizing that is accomplished by blowing air through the vocal tract. Although crying can be prolonged and vigorous and vary in pitch, there are no distinct, well-formed sounds.

Cooing   Crying is just about the only sound that infants make during the first month after birth. During the second month, babies also begin **cooing.** Cooing, like crying, is unlearned. Babies use their tongues when they coo, and so coos take on more articulated sounds than cries. Coos are often vowel-like, and may resemble repeated "oohs" and "ahs." Cooing appears linked to feelings of pleasure or positive excitement.

Parents soon learn that different cries and coos have different meanings and indicate different things: hunger, gas, or pleasure at being held

What Are the Functions of Crying?   Infant crying is a powerful communicator that helps determine whether a baby will become an abused or cherished child.

or rocked. Cries can be highly irritating, and psychologists are analyzing infants' cries as aids to diagnosing developmental disorders.

Remember that true language has *semanticity;* that is, sounds (or signs, in the case of ASL) are symbols. Cries and coos do not represent objects or events, and so they are prelinguistic. By about 8 months, cooing decreases markedly. By about the fifth or sixth month, children begin to babble.

Babbling   **Babbling** is the first vocalizing that sounds like human speech. Babbling children utter phonemes found in several languages, including

---

Surface structure The superficial grammatical construction of a sentence.

Deep structure The underlying meaning of a sentence.

Prelinguistic Prior to the development of language.

Cooing Prelinguistic, articulated vowel-like sounds that appear to reflect feelings of positive excitement.

Babbling The child's first vocalizations that have the sounds of speech.

the throaty German *ch*, the clicks of certain African tribes, and rolling *r*'s (Atkinson et al., 1970; McNeill, 1970). In their babbling, babies frequently combine consonants and vowels, as in "ba," "ga," and, sometimes, the much valued "dada." "Dada" at first is purely coincidental (sorry, you Dads), despite the family's jubilation over its appearance.

Babbling, like crying and cooing, appears inborn. For one thing, children from different cultures, where languages sound very different, all seem to babble the same sounds, including many that they could not have heard (Oller, 1981). For another, deaf children at first babble as much as children who can hear. But once uttered, babbling might produce sounds (or, in the case of deaf babies, vibrations in the throat) that are repeated because of their novelty.

Children seem to single out the types of phonemes used in the home within a few months. By the age of 9 or 10 months, these phonemes are repeated regularly. "Foreign" phonemes begin to drop out, so that there is an overall reduction in the variety of phonemes that infants produce. Even so, infants produce a greater diversity of sounds because of the ways in which they combine sounds. The babbling of deaf infants never approximates the sounds of the parents' language, and deaf children tend to lapse into silence by the end of the first year.

Development of Vocabulary

To understand vocabulary development, we must first distinguish between *receptive vocabulary* and *expressive vocabulary*. Children's **receptive vocabulary** consists of the words that they can understand, as demonstrated, for example, by following directions ("Where is your nose"). Children's **expressive vocabulary** consists of the words that they use in their speech. Receptive vocabulary growth out-

paces expressive vocabulary growth. At any given time, children can understand more words than they can use.

Now let us look at that exciting milestone—children's first words.

The Child's First Words(!)   Ah, that long-awaited first word! What a thrill! What a milestone! Sad to say, many parents miss this milestone. They are not quite sure when their infants utter their first word, often because the first word is not pronounced clearly or because pronunciation varies from usage to usage. *Ball* may be pronounced "ba," "bee," or even "pah" on separate occasions (Ferguson & Farwell, 1975).

Vocabulary acquisition is slow at first. According to Katherine Nelson (1973), it generally takes children three to four months to achieve a ten-word vocabulary after their first word is spoken. By about 18 months, children are producing nearly two dozen words, but as suggested in Table 5.1, they can understand simple commands using

5-8

"He has some teeth, but his words haven't come in yet."

Receptive vocabulary The extent of one's knowledge of the meanings of words that are communicated to one by others.

Expressive vocabulary The sum total of the words that one can use in the production of language.

Table 5.1 Milestones in Language Development

APPROXIMATE AGE	VOCALIZATION AND LANGUAGE
Birth	Cries.
12 weeks	Markedly less crying than at 8 weeks; when talked to and nodded at, smiles, followed by squealing-gurgling sounds usually called cooing, that is vowel-like in character and pitch-modulated; sustains cooing for 15–20 seconds.
16 weeks	Responds to human sounds more definitely; turns head; eyes seem to search for speaker; occasionally some chuckling sounds.
20 weeks	The vowel-like cooing sounds begin to be interspersed with more consonantal sounds; acoustically, all vocalizations are very different from the sounds of the mature language of the environment.
6 months	Cooing changing into babbling resembling one-syllable utterances; neither vowels nor consonants have very fixed recurrences; most common utterances sound somewhat like *ma, mu, da,* or *di.*
8 months	Reduplication (or more continuous repetitions) becomes frequent; intonation patterns become distinct; utterances can signal emphasis and emotions.
10 months	Vocalizations are mixed with sound play such as gurgling or bubble blowing; appears to wish to imitate sounds, but the imitations are never quite successful.*
12 months	Identical sound sequences are replicated with higher relative frequency of occurrence and words (*mamma* or *dadda*) are emerging; definite signs of understanding some words and simple commands ("Show me your eyes").
18 months	Has a definite repertoire of words—more than 3 but less than 50; still much babbling but now of several syllables with intricate intonation pattern; no attempt at communicating information and no frustration for not being understood; words may include items such as *thank you* or *come here,* but there is little ability to join any of the items into spontaneous two-item phrases; understanding is progressing rapidly.
24 months	Vocabulary of more than 50 items (some children seem to be able to name everything in environment); begins spontaneously to join vocabulary items into two-word phrases; all phrases seem to be own creations; definite increase in communicative behavior and interest in language.
30 months	Fastest increase in vocabulary with many new additions every day; no babbling at all; utterances have communicative intent; frustrated if not understood by adults; utterances consist of at least two words, although many have three or even five words; sentences and phrases have characteristic child grammar, that is, they are rarely verbatim repetitions of adult utterance; intelligibility is not very good yet, though there is great variation among children; seem to understand everything that is said to them.
3 years	Vocabulary of some 1,000 words; about 80 percent of utterances are intelligible even to strangers; grammatical complexity of utterances is roughly that of colloquial adult language, although mistakes still occur.
4 years	Language is well established; deviations from the adult norm tend to be more in style than in grammar.

*Here we are talking about imitating the sounds of speech. Infants of this age have already imitated the pitch of their parents' sounds quite well for a number of months. The ages in this table are approximations. Parents need not assume that their children will have language problems if they are somewhat behind. Source: Adapted from E. H. Lenneberg (1967). *Biological Foundations of Language.* New York: Wiley, pp. 128–130.

many more words at about 12 months. Many words are quite familiar, such as *no, cookie, mama, hi,* and *eat.* Others, like *allgone* and *bye-bye,* may not be found in the dictionary, but they function clearly as words.

Overextension

Young children try to talk about more objects than they have words for, and so they often extend the meaning of one word to refer to things and actions for which they do not have words. Eve Clark (1973, 1975) studied diaries of infants' language development and found that overextensions are generally based on perceived similarities in function or form between the original object or action and the new one to which the first word is being extended. She provides the example of the word *em,* which one infant originally used to designate a worm and which then became extended to include other small moving animals and objects such as insects and the head of waving grass.

Development of Syntax

Although children first use one-word utterances, these utterances appear to express the meanings found in complete sentences. Roger Brown (1973) calls brief expressions that have the meanings of sentences telegraphic speech. When we as adults write telegrams, we use principles of syntax to cut out all the "unnecessary" words. "Home Tuesday" might stand for "I expect to be home on Tuesday." Similarly, only the "essential" words are used in children's telegraphic speech—in particular, nouns, verbs, and some modifiers.

Let us consider the syntactic features of two types of telegraphic speech: the *holophrase* and *two-word utterances.*

Holophrases

Single words that are used to express complex meanings are called **holophrases.** For example, *mama* may be used by the child to signify meanings as varied as "There goes mama,"

"Come here, mama," and "You are mama." Similarly, *poo-cat* can signify "There is a pussycat," "That stuffed animal looks just like my pussycat," "I want you to give me my pussycat right now!" Most children readily teach their parents what they intend by augmenting their holophrases with gestures, intonations, and reinforcers.

Two-Word Utterances

Toward the end of the second year, children begin to use two-word sentences. In the sentence "That ball," the words *is* and *a* are implied. Several types of two-word utterances are used by young children and are listed in Table 5.2. Each shows a certain level of cognitive development and grasp of the syntax necessary to express an idea.

Two-word utterances seem to appear at about the same time in the development of all languages (Slobin, 1973). Also, the sequence of emergence of the types of two-word utterances (e.g., first, agent-action; then action-object, location, and possession) is the same in languages as diverse as English, Luo (an African tongue), German, Russian, and Turkish (Slobin, 1971, 1983). This apparently universal sequence suggests that innate processes govern language development.

Two-word utterances, although brief, show basic understanding of syntax. The child will say, "Sit chair" to tell a parent to sit in a chair, not "Chair sit." (Apes do not reliably make this distinction.) The child will say, "My shoe," not "Shoe my," to show possession. "Mommy go" means Mommy is leaving, whereas "Go Mommy" expresses the wish for Mommy to go away.

Toward More Complex Language

Between the ages of 2 and 3, children's sentence structure usually expands to include the words that were missing in telegraphic speech.

It is usually during the third year that children add an impressive array of articles *(a, an, the),* conjunctions *(and, but, or),* possessive and demonstrative adjectives *(your, her, that),* pronouns *(she, him, one),* and prepositions *(in, on, over, around, under, and through).* Their grasp of syntax is shown in language oddities such as *your one* instead of *yours,* and *his one* instead of, simply, *his.*

Holophrase A single word used to express complex meanings.

Table 5.2   Some Uses of Children's Two-Word Utterances

TYPE OF UTTERANCE	EXAMPLE	TYPE OF KNOWLEDGE SUGGESTED BY UTTERANCE
Naming, locating	That ball. Car there. See doggy.	Objects exist and they have names.
Negating	Milk allgone. No eat. Not doggy.	Objects may become used up or leave. People may choose *not* to do things.
Demanding, expressing desire	Want Mommy. More milk. Want candy.	Objects can be reinstated; quantities can be increased.
Agent-Action	Mommy go. Daddy sit. Doggy bark.	People, animals, and objects act or move.
Action-Object	Hit you.	Actions can have objects.
Agent-Object	Daddy car.	People do things to objects (although, in this two-word utterance, the action is not stated).
Action-Location	Sit chair.	A person (unstated) is engaging in an act in a place.
Action-Recipient	Give Mama.	An object (unstated) is being moved in relation to a person.
Action-Instrument	Cut knife.	An instrument is being used for an act.
Attribution	Pretty Mommy. Big glass.	People or objects have traits or qualities.
Possession	Mommy cup. My shoe.	People possess objects.
Question	Where Mommy? Where milk?	People can provide information when they are prompted.

Adapted from Slobin, 1972.

One of the more intriguing language developments is **overregularization.** To understand children's use of overregularization, let us first review the formation of the past tense and of plurals in English. We add *d* or *ed* phonemes to regular verbs and *s* or *z* phonemes to regular nouns. Thus, *walk* becomes *walked* and *look* becomes *looked*. *Pussycat* becomes *pussycats* and *doggy* becomes *doggies*. There are also irregular verbs and nouns. For example, *see* becomes *saw, sit* becomes *sat,* and *go* becomes *went. Sheep* remains *sheep* (plural) and *child* becomes *children.*

At first it seems that children learn a small number of these irregular verbs by imitating their parents. As noted by Stan Kuczaj (1977, 1978),

> **Overregularization** The application of regular grammatical rules for forming inflections (e.g., past tense and plurals) to irregular verbs and nouns.

2-year-olds tend to form them correctly—temporarily! Then they become aware of the syntactic rules for forming the past tense and plurals in English. As a result, they tend to make charming "errors" (Bowerman, 1982). Some 3- to 5-year-olds, for example, are more likely to say "I seed it" than "I saw it" and more likely to say "Mommy sitted down" than "Mommy sat down." They are likely to talk about the "gooses" and "sheeps" they "seed" on the farm and about all the "childs" they ran into at the playground. This tendency to regularize the irregular is what is meant by overregularization. Ironically, overregularization stems from accurate knowledge of grammatical rules—not from faulty language acquisition.

As language develops beyond the third year, children show increasing facility with the use of pronouns (such as *it* and *she*) and with prepositions (such as *in, before,* or *on*), which represent physical or temporal relationships among objects and events. Children's first questions are telegraphic and characterized by a rising pitch (which signifies a question mark in English) at the end. "More milky?" for example, can be translated into "May I have more milk?" or "Would you like more milk?" or "Is there more milk?"—depending on the context.

Pragmatics in language development refers to the practical aspects of communication. Children show pragmatism when they adjust their speech to fit the social situation. How many times have we heard children screaming rudely at one another, and then observed them standing still and carefully articulating "Yes sir," when dressed down by an adult? Children also say *please* more often when making requests of high-status people (Rice, 1982, 1984). Children also show pragmatism in their adoption of **motherese** when they are addressing a younger child. Four-year-olds' motherese shows brief sentences, high pitch, and precise articula-

tion, similar to the motherese of adults (Sachs & Devin, 1976; Tomasello & Mannle, 1985).

THEORIES OF LANGUAGE DEVELOPMENT

Countless billions of children have acquired the languages spoken by their parents and passed them down, with minor changes, from generation to generation. But how do children acquire language? In this section we discuss learning-theory, nativist, and cognitive views of language development.

Learning-Theory Views

Clearly there is a role for learning in language development. Children reared in English-speaking homes learn English, not Japanese or Russian. Learning theorists have explained language development in terms of imitation and reinforcement.

The Role of Imitation   From a social-learning perspective, parents serve as **models.** Children learn language, at least in part, by observation and imitation. It seems likely that many vocabulary words, especially nouns and verbs, including irregular verbs, are learned by imitation.

Recall that at first children repeat accurately the irregular verb forms they observe. This repetition can probably be explained in terms of modeling. But children later begin to overregularize irregular verb forms. These overregularizations are produced from knowledge of rules of syntax, not parroted through imitation. More generally, imitative learning does not explain how children can spontaneously utter phrases and sentences they have *not* observed (Rebok, 1987). Parents, that is, are unlikely to model utterances such as "bye-bye sock" and "allgone Daddy," but children do.

The Role of Reinforcement   In his landmark book, *Verbal Behavior,* B. F. Skinner outlined his view of the role of reinforcement in language development: "A child acquires verbal behavior when relatively unpatterned vocalizations, selectively reinforced, assume forms which produce appropriate consequences in a given verbal community" (Skinner, 1957, p. 31).

Pragmatics The practical aspects of communication. Adaptation of language to fit the social context.

Motherese Adaptation of language for use in speaking to young children, characterized by features such as repetition and high-pitched sounds.

Models In learning theory, persons who engage in behaviors that are imitated by others.

Skinner allows that prelinguistic vocalizations such as cooing and babbling may be inborn. But parents reinforce children for babbling that approximates the form of real words, such as *da*, which in English resembles *dog* or *daddy*. Children, in fact, do increase their babbling when it results in adults smiling at them, stroking them, and talking back to them.

As the first year progresses, children babble the sounds of their native tongues with increasing frequency. "Foreign" sounds tend to drop out. The behaviorist would explain this pattern of changing frequencies in terms of reinforcement (of the sounds of the adults' language) and extinction (of foreign sounds). An alternate (nonbehavioral) explanation is that children actively attend to the sounds in their linguistic environments and are intrinsically motivated to utter them.

From Skinner's (1957, 1983) perspective, children acquire an early vocabulary through shaping. Parents, that is, require that children's utterances come progressively closer to actual words before they are reinforced. Skinner views multiword utterances as complex stimulus–response chains that are also taught by shaping.

But if the reinforcement explanation were accurate, parents' selective reinforcement of their children's utterances would facilitate their learning of phonetics, syntax, and semantics. We do not have such evidence. For one thing, parents are more likely to reinforce their children for the accuracy, or "truth value," of their utterances than for their grammatical correctness (Brown, 1973). Parents, in other words, generally accept the syntax of their children's vocal efforts. The child who points down and says, "The grass is purple" is not likely to be reinforced, despite correct syntax. But the enthusiastic child who shows her empty plate and blurts out "I eated it all up!" is likely to be reinforced, despite overregularization of *to eat*.

Selective reinforcement of children's pronunciation, in fact, may backfire. Children whose parents reward proper pronunciation but correct poor pronunciation develop vocabulary *more slowly* than children whose parents are more tolerant in pronunciation (Nelson, 1973).

Learning-theory approaches also cannot account for the invariant sequences of language development and for children's spurts in acquisition.

Nativist Views

Earlier we noted that many psychologists question the ability of apes to grasp syntax. Now let us consider a related issue: Why can't apes *talk*—if only to reproduce words they have heard? Apes have structures in their throats that look similar to human vocal tracts. Psychologists have also maximized environmental influences by rearing apes with human families. Still, apes have never gained the ability to produce the sounds of language. Why not? Apes must lack *something else* that allows children to vocalize.

What children probably have, and apes do not, is a *native* capacity to speak. Children probably *bring something* to the observation and processing of language that apes do not. The view that innate or inborn factors cause children to attend to and acquire language in certain ways is termed the nativist view of language development (Maratsos, 1983). Perhaps children bring certain neurological "prewiring" that involves the speech areas (see Chapter 2) of the brain to language learning.

Psycholinguistic Theory: Is There a Language Acquisition Device?   According to **psycholinguistic theory**, language acquisition involves an interaction between environmental influences, such as exposure to parental speech and reinforcement, and an inborn tendency to acquire language (Chomsky, 1968, 1980). Evidence for an inborn tendency is found in the universality of human language abilities; in the regularity of the early production of sounds, even among deaf children; and in the invariant sequences of language development, regardless of which language the child is learning.

McNeill (1970) labeled this inborn tendency the **Language Acquisition Device** (LAD). He believed that the LAD is a prewiring of the nervous system that suits it to learn grammar.

Psycholinguistic theory The view that language learning involves an interaction between environmental influences and an inborn tendency to acquire language.

Language Acquisition Device In psycholinguistic theory, neural "prewiring" that facilitates the child's learning of grammar. Abbreviated *LAD*.

The Sensitive Period   Eric Lenneberg (1967) proposes that there is a **sensitive period** for learning language that begins at about 18 to 24 months and lasts until puberty. This "window" for language learning reflects the status of neural maturation. During the sensitive period, neural development (as in the differentiating of brain structures) provides a degree of plasticity that facilitates language learning.

Neural development also provides the basis for cognitive development. By 18 to 24 months, neural maturation permits the child to begin to entertain *preoperational thought,* as we shall see in Chapter 7, and to vastly accelerate the processes of acquiring words and stringing them together to express meaning. By the time people have reached sexual maturity, brain tissue has also reached adult levels of differentiation. Language learning can occur afterward but is more laborious (Elliot, 1981).

In the following section, we shall consider the relationships between language and thought, or cognition.

Cognitive Views

Cognitive views of language development focus on the relationships between cognitive development and language development. Cognitive theorists tend to hold a number of assumptions, including these:

1. Language development is made possible by cognitive analytical abilities (Bates & MacWhinney, 1982; Maratsos, 1983).
2. Children are active agents in language learning. Children's motivation for learning syntax and vocabulary grows out of their "desire to express meanings that conceptual development makes available to them" (Maratsos, 1983).

Jean Piaget believed that cognitive development precedes language development. Piaget

---

Sensitive period In linguistic theory, the period from about 18 months to puberty when the brain is thought to be particularly capable of learning language because of plasticity.

Concept A symbol that stands for a group of objects, events, or ideas that share common properties.

(1976) argued that children must first understand **concepts** before they can use words that describe the concepts. Children can learn the word *doggy* because they have already perceived the characteristics that distinguish dogs from other things.

The cognitive view of language development is not monolithic. Some theorists reverse the causal relationship and hold that children create cognitive classes in order to understand things that are labeled by words (Clark, 1973, 1983). The word can come before the meaning. When children hear the word *dog,* they strive to understand it by searching for characteristics that separate dogs from other things.

Most cognitive psychologists find something of value in each of these cognitive views (Greenberg & Kuczaj, 1982). In the early stages of language development, concepts often precede words, so that many of the infant's words describe classes that have already developed. But later on language is not merely the handmaiden of thought; language also influences thought.

Putting It All Together

A synthesis of the learning-theory, nativist, and cognitive views might be possible (Kuczaj, 1982; Maratsos, 1983; Rebok, 1987).

Learning plays an indispensable role in language development. Imitative learning explains, in part, why French children learn French and German children learn German. Moreover, young children apparently imitate their parents by correctly forming the past tense of some irregular verbs. Overregularization does not occur until knowledge of rules for forming the past tense emerges.

Adults (and older children) use "motherese" when they talk to young children. But young children also learn when their mothers use complex speech, suggesting that the children apply basic listening strategies that help them learn (Gleitman et al., 1984). The early use of such strategies brings us back to the nativist and the cognitive positions.

The nativist view holds, first, that "Language learning must build on a biological base that equips the organism for understanding and producing speech" (Rebok, 1987, p. 217). Children do attend to language—even complex sentences—in such a way that they pick out rules of grammar. By early childhood children are using grammatical rules to produce their own sentences; they are not just imitating models.

Cognitive development also appears to interact with language development. The infant's cognitive development makes early words meaningful. The word *doggy* is meaningful because the concept for dog exists. However, by about the age of 2 or so, most children also appear to strive to form new concepts because they hear new words. And so, there seems to come a time when cognitive development and language development stimulate each other.

While we as adults continue to struggle with complex concepts to explain language development, 1- and 2-year-olds go right on learning language all around us.

LANGUAGE AND THOUGHT

Theories of language development may be of little importance to a 20-month-old who has just polished off her plate of chocolate chip cookies and exclaims "Allgone!" In the previous section we were concerned with this question: How does the child come to say "Allgone" when she has finished her plate. Now let us ponder this question: What does her use of "Allgone" suggest about her thought processes? In other words, would the girl have *known* that there were no cookies left if she did not have a word to express this idea? Do you always think in words? Can you think *without* using language? Would you be able to solve problems without using words or sentences?

As noted, Jean Piaget (1976) believed that language reflects knowledge of the world but is not necessary to acquire much of this knowledge. It is possible to have the concepts of roundness or redness even when we do not know or use the words *round* or *red*.

The Linguistic-Relativity Hypothesis

Language may not be necessary for all thought, but according to the **linguistic-relativity hypothesis** proposed by Benjamin Whorf (1956), language structures the ways in which we perceive the world. Consider our perceptions of microcompu-

How Do We Explain the Origins of Language? How do innate, biological factors interact with experience so that children produce language?

ters. People who understand terms such as *640 K, megabyte,* and *RAM* can think about microcomputers with greater sophistication than people who do not.

According to the linguistic-relativity hypothesis, most English speakers' ability to think about snow might be rather limited when compared to that of the Eskimos. We have only a few words for snow, whereas the Eskimos have many words for snow, related, for example, to whether the snow is hard-packed, falling, melting, or covered by ice. When we think about snow, we have fewer words to choose from and might have to search for descriptive adjectives. Eskimos, however, can readily find a single word that describes a complex weather condition. It might then be easier for them to think about this variety of snow in relation to other aspects of their world.

In English we have hundreds of words to describe different colors, but those who speak Shona use only three words for colors. People who speak

---

Linguistic relativity hypothesis The view that language structures the way in which we view the world.

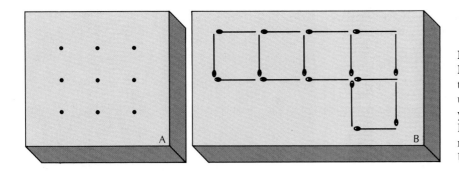

Figure 5.2. Can You Solve These Problems? Draw straight lines through all the points in Part A, using only four lines. Do not lift your pencil or retrace your steps. Move three matches in Part B to make four squares equal in size. Use all the matches.

Bassa use only two words for colors (Gleason, 1961), corresponding to light and dark. The Hopi Indians had two words for flying objects, one for birds and an all-inclusive word for anything else that may be found traveling through the air.

Does this mean that the Hopi were limited in their ability to think about bumblebees and airplanes? Are English speakers limited in their ability to think about skiing conditions? Are those who speak Shona and Bassa "colorblind" for practical purposes?

Probably not. People who use only a few words to distinguish colors seem to perceive the same color variations as people with dozens of words (Bornstein & Marks, 1982; Rosch, 1974). For example, the Dani of New Guinea, like the Bassa, have just two words for colors: *mola*, which refers to warm colors, and *mili*, which refers to cool colors. Still, tasks in matching and memory show that the Dani can discriminate the many colors of the spectrum when they are motivated to do so. English-speaking skiers, who are concerned about different skiing conditions, have developed a comprehensive special vocabulary about snow, including *powder, slush, ice, hard-packed,* and *corn snow,* that might enable them to communicate and think about snow with the facility of Eskimos. When a need to expand a language's vocabulary arises, the speakers of that language apparently have little difficulty in meeting the need.

Critics of the linguistic-relativity hypothesis argue that a language's vocabulary only suggests the range of concepts that the speakers of the language have traditionally found important. But people can make distinctions for which there are no words. Hopi Indians flying from New York to San Francisco nowadays would not think that they

are flying inside a bird or a bumblebee, even if they have no word for airplane.

Although language might not be necessary for all thought, it does help. In the section on problem solving, however, we shall see that our labels for things can sometimes impair our problem-solving abilities.

PROBLEM SOLVING

One of the pleasures I derived from my own introductory psychology course lay in showing friends the textbook and getting them involved in the problems in the section on problem solving. First, of course, I struggled with the problems myself. It's that time, now. And it's your turn. Get some scrap paper, take a breath, and have a go at the following problems. The answers will be discussed in the following pages, but don't peek. *Try the problems first.*

1. Provide the next two letters in the series for each of the following:

    a. ABABABAB??
    b. ABDEBCEF??
    c. OTTFFSSE??

2. Draw straight lines through all the points in part A of Figure 5.2, using only *four* lines. Do not lift your pencil from the paper or retrace your steps. (Answers are given in Figure 5.4.)

3. Move three matches in part B of Figure 5.2 to make four squares of the same size. You must use *all* the matches. (The answer is shown in Figure 5.4.)

4. You have three jars, A, B, and C, which hold the amounts of water, in ounces, shown in Table

5.3. For each of the seven problems in Table 5.3, use the jars in any way you wish to arrive at the indicated amount of water. Fill or empty any jar as often as you wish. How do you obtain the desired amount of water in each problem? (The solutions are discussed on pages 206–207.)

Stages in Problem Solving

If you are like most problem solvers, you used three steps to solve parts a and b of problem 1. First, you sought to define the elements of the problems by discovering the structure of the *cycles* in each series. Series *1a* has repeated cycles of two letters: *AB, AB,* and so on. Series *1b* may be seen as having four cycles of two consecutive letters: *AB, DE, BC,* and so on.

Then you tried to produce *rules* that governed the advance of each series. In series *1a,* the rule is simply to repeat the cycle. Series *1b* is more complicated, and different sets of rules can be used to describe it. One correct set of rules is that odd-numbered cycles *(1 and 3, or AB and BC)* simply repeat the last letter of the previous cycle (in this case *B*) and then advance by one letter according to the alphabet. The same rule applies to even-numbered cycles *(2 and 4, or DE and EF).*

Then you used your rules to produce the next letters in the series: *AB* in series *1a,* and *CD* in series *1b.* Finally, you evaluated the effectiveness of the rules by checking your answers against the solutions in the preceding paragraphs.

Question: What alternate sets of rules could you have found to describe these two series? Would you have generated the same answers from these rules?

Preparation, Production, and Evaluation

People tend to use three stages in solving problems, whether the problem concerns dieting, selecting a house, or moving matchsticks about to create a design. These stages include (1) preparation, (2) production, and (3) evaluation.

We prepare ourselves to solve a problem by familiarizing ourselves with its elements and clearly defining our goals. We prepare to solve high school algebra and geometry problems by outlining all the givens and trying to picture the

Table 5.3   Water Jar Problems

PROBLEM NUMBER	THREE JARS ARE PRESENT WITH THE LISTED CAPACITY (IN OUNCES)			OBTAIN THIS AMOUNT OF WATER
	JAR A	JAR B	JAR C	
1	21	127	3	100
2	14	163	25	99
3	18	43	10	5
4	9	42	6	21
5	20	59	4	31
6	23	49	3	20
7	10	36	7	3

For each problem, how can you use some combination of the three jars given, and a tap, to obtain precisely the amount of water shown?
Adapted from Abraham S. Luchins and Edith H. Luchins, *Rigidity of Behavior* (Eugene: University of Oregon Press, 1959), p. 109.

answers as best we can. Part of preparation is proper classification of the problem. "Does this problem involve a right triangle? Does it seem similar to problems I've solved by using the quadratic equation?"

In parts a and b of problem 1, the search for cycles and for the rules governing the cycles served as preparation for producing possible solutions.

Algorithms versus Heuristics   In solving problems, we sometimes turn to *algorithms* or *heuristic devices.* An **algorithm** is a specific procedure for solving a certain type of problem that will lead to the solution if it is used properly. Mathematical formulas, such as the quadratic equation, are examples of algorithms. They will yield correct answers to problems, *as long as the right formula is used.*

Consider anagram problems, in which we try to reorganize groups of letters into words. In seeing how many words we can make from *DWARG,* we can use the algorithm of simply listing every possible letter combination, using from one to all five letters, and then checking to see whether each result is, in fact, a word. The method is plodding, but it would certainly work.

Algorithm A systematic procedure for solving a problem that works invariably when applied correctly.

Heuristics are rules of thumb that help us simplify and solve problems. Heuristics, in contrast to algorithms, do not guarantee a correct solution to a problem, but when they work they tend to allow for more rapid solutions. A heuristic device for solving the anagram problem would be to look for letter combinations that are found in words and then to check the remaining letters for words that include these combinations. In *DWARG*, for example, we can find the familiar combinations *dr* and *gr*. We may then quickly find *draw*, *drag*, and *grad*. The drawback to this method, however, is that we might miss some words.

One type of heuristic device is the **means-end analysis,** in which we evaluate the difference between our current situations and our goals at various steps along the way, and then do what we can to reduce this discrepancy at each step. Let's say that you are lost, but you know that your goal is west of your current location and on the "other side of the tracks." A heuristic device would be to drive toward the setting sun (west), and at the same time, to remain alert for railroad tracks. If your road comes to an end and you must turn left or right, you can scan the distance in either direction for tracks. If you don't see any, turn right or left, but then, at the next major intersection, turn toward the setting sun again. Eventually you may get there. If not, you could use that most boring of algorithms: Ask people for directions until you find someone who knows the route.

Incubation   Let us return to the problems at the beginning of the section. How did you do with problem 1, part c, and problems 2 and 3? If you produced solutions that did not meet the goals, you may have become frustrated and thought, "The heck with it! I'll come back to it later." This attitude suggests a fourth stage of problem solving: **incubation.** An incubator warms chicken eggs for a while so that they will hatch. Incubation in problem solving refers to standing back from the problem for a while as some mysterious process in us seems to continue to work on it. Later, the answer may occur to us as "in a flash." Standing back from the problem might provide us with some distance from unprofitable but persistent mental sets.

Mental Sets

Let us return to problem 1, part c. To try to solve this problem, did you seek a pattern of letters that involved cycles and the alphabet? If so, it may be because parts a and b were solved by this approach.

The tendency to respond to a new problem with the same approach that helped solve earlier, similar-looking problems is termed a **mental set.** Mental sets usually make our work easier, but they can mislead us when the similarity between problems is illusory, as in part c of problem 1. But here is a clue: Part c is no alphabet series. Each of the letters in the series *stands* for something. If you can discover what they stand for (that is, discover the rule), you will be able to generate the ninth and tenth letters. (The answer is in Figure 5.4 on p. 208.)

Let us now have another look at the possible role of incubation in helping us get around hampering mental sets. Consider the seventh water-jar problem. What if we had tried all sorts of solutions involving the three water jars, and none worked? What if we were then to stand back from this water-jar problem for a day or two? Is it not possible that with a little distance we might suddenly recall a 10, a 7, and a 3—three elements of the problem—and realize that we can arrive at the correct answer by using only two water jars? Our solution might seem too easy, and we might check Table 5.3 cautiously to make certain that the numbers are there as remembered. Perhaps our incubation period would have done nothing more than unbind us from the mental set that the case 7 *ought* to be solved by the formula $B - A - 2C$.

Heuristics Rules of thumb that help us simplify and solve problems.

Means-end analysis A heuristic device in which we try to solve a problem by evaluating the difference between the current situation and the goal.

Incubation In problem solving, a hypothetical process that sometimes occurs when we stand back from a frustrating problem for a while and the solution "suddenly" appears.

Mental set The tendency to respond to a new problem with an approach that was successful with problems similar in appearance.

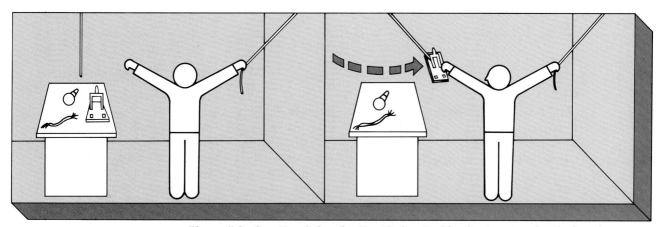

Figure 5.3. Can You Solve the Two-String Problem?   A person is asked to tie two dangling strings together, but he cannot reach them both at once. He is allowed to use any object in the room to help him—including a switch. He can solve the problem by tying the switch to one string and sending it swinging back and forth. Then he grabs the stationary string and catches the moving string when it swings his way. After removing the switch the strings are tied together. Functional fixedness could impede solution of the problem by causing the person to view the switch as electrical equipment only, and not as a weight.

While we are discussing mental sets and the water-jar problems, have another look at water-jar case number 6. The formula $B - A - 2C$ will solve this problem. Is that how you solved it? But note also that the problem could have been solved more efficiently by using the formula $A - C$. If the second formula did not occur to you, it may be because of the mental set you acquired from solving the first five problems.

Functional Fixedness

Functional fixedness may also impair our problem-solving efforts. For example, first ask yourself what a pair of pliers is. Is it a tool for grasping, a paperweight, or a weapon? A pair of pliers could function as any of these, but your tendency to think of it as a grasping tool is fostered by your experience with it. You have probably only used a pair of pliers for grasping things. Functional fixedness is the tendency to think of an object in terms of its name or its familiar usage. Functional fixedness can be similar to a mental set in that it can make it difficult for us to use familiar objects to solve problems in novel ways.

In a classic experiment in functional fixedness, Birch and Rabinowitz (1951) placed subjects in a room with electrical equipment, a switch and a relay, and asked them to solve the Maier two-string problem. In this problem, a person is asked to tie together two dangling strings. But as shown in Figure 5.3, they cannot be reached simultaneously.

In the experiment, either the switch or the relay can be used as a weight for one of the strings. If the weighted string is sent swinging, the subject can grasp the unweighted string and then wait for the weighted string to come his or her way. Subjects given prior experience with the switch as an electrical device were significantly more likely to use the relay as the weight. Subjects given prior experience with the intended function of the relay were significantly more likely to use the switch as a weight. Subjects given no prior experience with either device showed no preferences for using one or the other as the weight.

You may know that soldiers in survival training in the desert are taught to view insects and

Functional fixedness The tendency to view an object in terms of its name or familiar usage.

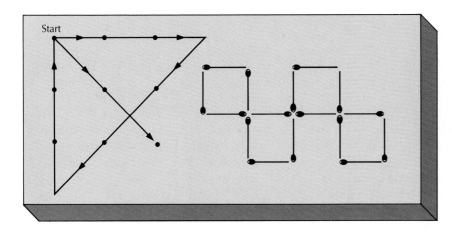

Figure 5.4. Answers to Problems on Page 204. For problem 1C, note that each of the letters is the first letter of the numbers one through eight. Therefore, the two missing letters are *NT*, for *n*ine and *t*en. The solutions to problems 2 and 3 are shown in this illustration.

snakes as sources of food rather than as pests or threats. But it would be understandable if you chose to show civilian functional fixedness for as long as possible if you were stuck in the desert.

Creativity in Problem Solving

A creative person may be more capable of solving problems to which there are no preexisting solutions, no tried and tested formulas.

Creativity is an enigmatic concept. According to Sternberg (1985), we tend to perceive creative people as

Being willing to take chances

Not accepting limitations; trying to do the impossible

Appreciating art and music

Being capable of using the materials around them to make unique things

Questioning social norms and assumptions

Being willing to take an unpopular stand

Being inquisitive

A professor of mine once remarked that there is nothing new under the sun, only novel combina-

Creativity The ability to generate novel solutions to problems.

Convergent thinking A thought process that attempts to narrow in on the single best solution to a problem.

Divergent thinking A thought process that attempts to generate multiple solutions to problems.

tions of old elements. To him, the core of creativity was the ability to generate novel combinations of existing elements.

My professor's view of creativity was similar to that of many psychologists—that creativity is the ability to make unusual, sometimes remote, associations to the elements of a problem, so that new combinations that meet the goals are generated. An essential aspect of a creative response is the leap from the elements of the problem to the novel solution (Amabile, 1983). A predictable solution is not particularly creative, even if it is difficult to arrive at.

In the two-string problem, the ability to associate a switch or a relay with the quality of weight rather than their intended electronic functions requires some creativity. Tying the switch or relay to the end of the string is a new combination of the familiar elements in the problem, one that meets the requirements of the situation.

Convergent Thinking and Divergent Thinking

According to Guilford (1959; Guilford & Hoepfner, 1971), creativity demands divergent thinking rather than convergent thinking. In **convergent thinking,** thought is limited to present facts as the problem solver tries to narrow thinking to find the best solution. In **divergent thinking,** the problem solver associates more fluently and freely to the various elements of the problem. The problem solver allows "leads" to run a nearly limitless course to determine whether they will eventually combine

Questionnaire

The Remote Associates Test

One aspect of creativity is the ability to associate freely to all aspects of a problem. As noted by psychologist Margaret Matlin, "Creative people can take far-flung ideas and combine them into new associations" (1983, p. 251). Following are items from the Remote Associates Test, which measures ability to find words that are distantly related to stimulus words. For each set of three words, try to think of a fourth word that is related to all three words. For example, the words *rough, resistance,* and *beer* suggest the word *draft* because of the phrases *rough draft, draft resistance,* and *draft beer.* The answers are given in the footnote.*

1.	charming	student	valiant
2.	food	catcher	hot
3.	hearted	feet	bitter
4.	dark	shot	sun
5.	Canadian	golf	sandwich
6.	tug	gravy	show
7.	attorney	self	spending
8.	arm	coal	peach
9.	type	ghost	story

*Answer to Remote Associates Test: (1) prince, (2) dog, (3) cold, (4) glasses, (5) club, (6) boat, (7) defense, (8) pit, (9) writer.

as needed. *Brainstorming* is a popular term for divergent thinking when carried out by a group.

Successful problem solving may require both divergent and convergent thinking. At first divergent thinking generates many possible solutions. Convergent thinking is then used to select the most probable solutions and to reject the others.

Factors in Creativity What factors contribute to creativity? Guilford (1959) noted that creative people show flexibility, fluency (in generating words and ideas), and originality. Getzels and Jackson (1962) found that creative schoolchildren tend to express rather than inhibit their feelings and to be playful and independent.

Intelligence and Creativity Intelligence and creativity sometimes, but not always, go hand in hand. Persons low in intelligence are often also low in creativity, but high intelligence is no guarantee of creativity (Crockenburg, 1972). However, it sometimes happens that people of only moderate intelligence excel in creativity, especially in fields like art and music.

INTELLIGENCE

What form of life is so adaptive that it can survive in desert temperatures of 120 degrees Fahrenheit, or Arctic climes of −40 degrees Fahrenheit? What form of life can run, walk, climb, swim, live underwater for months on end, and fly to the moon and back? I won't keep you in suspense any longer. We are that form of life. But our naked bodies do not allow us to adapt to these extremes of temperature. Brute strength does not allow us to live underwater or travel to the moon. Rather, it is our **intelligence** that permits us to adapt to these conditions and to challenge our physical limitations.

Intelligence According to David Wechsler, the "capacity . . . to understand the world [and] resourcefulness to cope with its challenges."

The term *intelligence* is familiar enough. At an early age we gain impressions of how intelligent we are compared to others. We associate intelligence with academic success, advancement on the job, and appropriate social behavior. Psychologists use intelligence as a **trait** that might explain—at least in part—why people do (or fail to do) things that are adaptive and inventive.

Despite our familiarity with the concept of intelligence, it cannot be seen, touched, or measured physically. And so intelligence is subject to various interpretations. In this section we shall discuss different ways of looking at intelligence. We shall see how intelligence is measured and discuss group differences in intelligence. Finally we shall examine the determinants of intelligence: heredity and the environment.

Theories of Intelligence

The meaning of *intelligence* is difficult to pin down (Green, 1981). Most psychologists agree that intelligence somehow provides the cognitive basis for academic achievement. Intelligence is usually perceived as underlying competence or learning ability, whereas achievement involves acquired competencies or performance. But psychologists disagree about the nature and origins of "underlying" competence or learning ability.

There are two broad approaches to understanding intelligence: factor and cognitive theories.

Factor Theories Many investigators have viewed intelligence as consisting of one or more mental abilities, or **factors.**

Trait A distinguishing characteristic that is presumed to account for consistency in behavior.

Factor A cluster of related items, such as those found on an intelligence test.

g Spearman's symbol for general intelligence, which he believed underlay more specific abilities.

s Spearman's symbol for *specific,* or *s, factors* that he believed accounted for individual abilities.

Primary mental abilities According to Thurstone, the basic abilities that make up intelligence.

Table 5.4 Louis Thurstone's Primary Mental Abilities

ABILITY	BRIEF DESCRIPTION
Visual and spatial abilities	Visualizing forms and spatial relationships
Perceptual speed	Grasping perceptual details rapidly, perceiving similarities and differences between stimuli
Numerical ability	Computing numbers
Verbal meaning	Knowing the meanings of words
Memory	Recalling information (words, sentences, etc.)
Word fluency	Thinking of words quickly (rhyming, doing crossword puzzles, etc.)
Deductive reasoning	Deriving examples from general rules
Inductive reasoning	Deriving general rules from examples

In 1904 British psychologist Charles Spearman suggested that the behaviors we consider intelligent have a common, underlying factor. He labeled this factor **g,** for "general intelligence." *G* represented broad reasoning and problem-solving abilities. Spearman supported this view by noting that people who excel in one area can usually excel in others. But he also noted that even the most capable people are relatively superior in some areas—whether music or business or poetry. For this reason, he suggested that specific, or **s** factors account for specific abilities. In his research on relationships among tests of verbal, mathematical, and spatial reasoning, Spearman repeatedly found evidence supporting the existence of *s* factors. The evidence for *g* was more limited.

U.S. psychologist Louis Thurstone (1938) believed that Spearman had oversimplified the concept of intelligence. Thurstone's research suggested the presence of nine specific factors, which he labeled **primary mental abilities** (see Table 5.4). Thurstone suggested that we might have high word fluency, enabling us to develop rapidly lists of words that rhyme yet not be efficient at solving math problems (Thurstone & Thurstone, 1963).

This view seems to make sense. Most of us know people who are "good at" math but "poor in" English, and vice versa. Nonetheless, some link

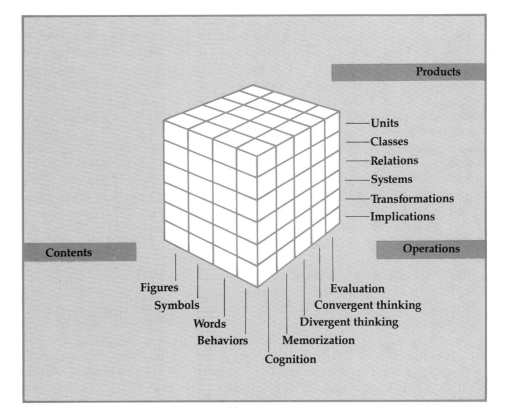

Figure 5.5. What Is Guilford's Structure-of-Intellect Model? With this model Guilford hypothesizes the existence of 120 factors in intelligence.

continues to seem to connect specific mental abilities.

The **structure-of-intellect** (SOI) **model** proposed by psychologist J. P. Guilford (1959) greatly expands the numbers of factors found in intellectual functioning. Guilford used a combination of factor analysis and logical reasoning to arrive at 120 factors in intellectual functioning. Each of the 120 factors consists of three elements, as shown in Figure 5.5:

1. Operations—the kinds of cognitive processing that are involved
2. Contents—the type of information that is processed
3. Products—the forms that the information takes

Guilford and his associates have developed test items to measure performance in many of the 120 factors. Consider the following examples:

1. Name as many objects as you can that are both white and edible.

2. Give as many sentences as you can that would fit into the form: W_____ c_____ s_____ d_____. [Example: "Workers can seldom deviate."]

The operation in each example is divergent thinking. The content of each example consists of words. However, the products differ. The products in the first example consist of single objects, or *units*. The products in example 2 consist of organized sequences of words, or *systems*.

Cognitive Theories   Cognitive theorists tend to view intelligence in terms of information processing. They focus on how information "flows" through us and is modified by us as we adapt to and act to change our environments. Two of these

Structure-of-intellect model Guilford's three-dimensional model of intelligence, which focuses on the operations, contents, and products of intellectual functioning.

cognitive theorists are Arthur Jensen and Robert Sternberg.

Jensen's concern has been to explain social-class differences in intelligence. He does so by hypothesizing the existence of two different levels of intelligence: Level I and Level II. Level I intelligence involves associative abilities, which are measured by tasks involving rote learning and memorization. One example would be memorizing a song. Another would be repeating a series of numbers that has been read aloud, such as 7–4–9–6–2–5. Still another would be associating letters and sounds, as in learning the alphabet. Level I skills are not strongly linked to school performance, as measured by academic grades (Rebok, 1987).

Level II intelligence involves conceptual abilities. It includes verbal ability, logical reasoning, and problem-solving skills. All these are related to cognitive learning and development. They are measured by items that require conceptual thinking ("How are good and bad alike?"), mathematical reasoning ("If two candy bars cost 25 cents, how many candy bars can you buy for one dollar?"), and general comprehension ("Why should pregnant women check with their doctors about the drugs they use?"). Level II skills correlate more strongly with academic grades than Level I skills do.

Jensen argues that all social classes possess adequate degrees of Level I intelligence. However, he controversially asserts that the middle and upper classes possess more Level II intelligence and that this difference accounts for their superior aca-

demic grades and performance in professional positions (Jensen, 1969, 1980, 1985).

Yale University psychologist Robert Sternberg (1985) constructed a three-level, or **triarchic,** model of intelligence. The three levels are *contextual, experiential,* and *componential.* Individual differences are found at each level. The **contextual level** concerns the environmental setting. It is assumed that intelligent behavior permits people to adapt to the demands of their environments. For example, keeping a job by "adapting" one's behavior to the requirements of one's employer is adaptive. But if the employer is making unreasonable demands, reshaping the environment (by changing the employer's attitudes) or selecting an alternate environment (finding a more suitable job) are also adaptive. On the **experiential level,** intelligent behavior is defined by the abilities to cope with novel situations and to process information automatically. The ability to quickly relate novel situations to familiar situations (to perceive the similarities and differences) fosters adaptation. Moreover, as a result of experience, we come to solve problems more rapidly. Intelligence and experience in reading permit the child to process familiar words more or less automatically and to decode new words efficiently. In sum, it is "intelligent" to profit from experience.

The **componential level** of intelligence consists of three processes: *metacomponents, performance components,* and *knowledge-acquisition components.* **Metacomponents** concern our awareness of our own intellectual processes. Metacomponents are involved in deciding what problem to solve, selecting appropriate strategies and formulas, monitoring the solution, and changing performance in the light of knowledge of results.

Performance components are the mental operations or skills used in solving problems or processing information. Performance components include encoding information, combining and comparing pieces of information, and generating a solution. Consider Sternberg's (1979) analogy problem:

Washington is to *one* as *Lincoln* is to (a) *five,* (b) *ten,* (c) *fifteen,* (d) *fifty?*

To solve the analogy, we must first correctly *encode* the elements—*Washington, one,* and *Lincoln*—by identifying them and comparing them to other in-

---

Triarchic Governed by three.

Contextual level Those aspects of intelligent behavior that permit people to adapt to their environment.

Experiential level Those aspects of intelligence that permit people to cope with novel situations and process information automatically.

Componential level The level of intelligence that consists of metacomponents, performance components, and knowledge-acquisition components.

Metacomponents Components of intelligence that are based on self-awareness of our intellectual processes.

Performance components The mental operations used in processing information.

formation. We must first encode *Washington* and *Lincoln* as the names of presidents,* and then try to combine *Washington* and *one* in a meaningful manner. Two possibilities quickly come to mind. Washington was the first president, and his picture is on the one dollar bill. We can then generate two possible solutions and try them out. First, what number president was Lincoln? Second, on what bill is Lincoln's picture found? (Do you need to consult a history book or peek into your wallet at this point?)

Knowledge-acquisition components are used in gaining new knowledge. These include encoding information (e.g., Roger Smith as the founder of Rhode Island or as the president of General Motors), combining pieces of information, and comparing new information with what is known.

Sternberg's model is complex, but it does a promising job of capturing what most investigators mean by intellectual functioning. David Wechsler, the originator of a series of widely used intelligence tests, described intelligence in terms that are simpler but, I think, consistent with Sternberg's view. Intelligence, wrote Wechsler, is the "capacity of an individual to understand the world [and the] resourcefulness to cope with its challenges" (1975, p. 139). Intelligence, to Wechsler, involves accurate representation of the world (which Sternberg discusses as encoding, comparing new information to old information, etc.) and effective problem solving (adapting to one's environment, profiting from experience, selecting the appropriate formulas and strategies, etc.).

Measurement of Intelligence

There may be disagreements about the nature of intelligence, but thousands of intelligence tests are administered by psychologists and educators every day.

In this section we first explore some basic characteristics of intelligence tests. We see that intelligence tests must be reliable and valid.

Characteristics of Intelligence Tests   Since important decisions are made on the basis of intelligence tests, they must be *reliable* and *valid*. Psy-

*There are other possibilities. Both are the names of memorials and cities, for example.

Table 5.5   Interpretations of Some Correlation Coefficients

CORRELATION COEFFICIENT	INTERPRETATION
+ 1.00	Perfect positive correlation, as between temperature in Fahrenheit and centigrade
+ 0.90	High positive correlation, adequate for test reliability
+ 0.60 to + 0.70	Moderate positive correlation, usually considered adequate for test validity
+ 0.30	Weak positive correlation, unacceptable for test reliability or validity
0.00	No correlation between variables (no association indicated)
− 0.30	Weak negative correlation
− 0.60 to − 0.70	Moderate negative correlation
− 0.90	High negative correlation
− 1.00	A perfect negative correlation

chologists use statistical techniques such as the *correlation coefficient* to assess reliability and validity.

A **correlation coefficient** is a number that indicates how strongly two or more things, such as height and weight or age and weight are related. Correlation coefficients vary from − 1.00 (a perfect negative correlation) to + 1.00 (a perfect positive correlation). For a test to be considered reliable, correlations between a group's test results on separate occasions should be positive and high—about + .90 (see Table 5.5).

The **reliability** of a measure is its consistency. A measure of height would not be reliable if a person appeared taller or shorter every time a meas-

---

Knowledge-acquisition components   Components used in gaining knowledge, such as encoding and relating new knowledge to existing knowledge.

Correlation coefficient   A number that indicates the direction (positive or negative) and strength of the relationship between two variables.

Reliability   Consistency.

Who Is Alfred Binet?

urement was taken. A reliable measure of intelligence, like a good tape measure, must yield similar results on different testing occasions.

There are different ways of showing a test's reliability, all of which rely on the correlation coefficient. One of the most commonly used is **test-retest reliability,** which is shown by comparing scores of tests taken on different occasions.

The **validity** of a test is the degree to which it measures what it is supposed to measure. To determine whether a test is valid, we see whether it actually predicts an outside standard, or external criterion. A proper standard, or criterion, for determining the validity of a test of musical **aptitude** is the ability to learn to play a musical instrument. Tests of musical aptitude, therefore, should correlate highly with the ability to learn to play a musical instrument. Most psychologists assume that intelligence is one of the factors responsible for academic success. For this reason, intelligence test

scores have frequently been correlated with school grades, which serve as one external standard, or criterion, to whether the test scores are valid. Other indexes of academic success include scores on achievement tests and teacher ratings of cognitive ability. Intelligence tests generally correlate from about $+0.60$ to $+0.70$ with school grades (Lavin, 1965; McCall, 1975; McClelland, 1973).

As noted in Table 5.5, a correlation of about $+0.60$ to $+0.70$ is generally considered adequate for purposes of assessing test validity. However, such a correlation does not approach a perfect positive relationship. This finding suggests that factors *other* than performance on intelligence tests contribute to academic and occupational success. Motivation to do well and one's general level of personal adjustment are two of them (Anastasi, 1983; Hrncir et al., 1985; Scarr, 1981).

By these standards, the Stanford-Binet Intelligence Scale (SBIS) and the Wechsler scales for children and adults have adequate reliability and validity.

The Stanford-Binet Intelligence Scale   The SBIS originated through the work of Frenchmen Alfred Binet and Theophile Simon early in this century. The French public school system sought an instrument that could identify children who were unlikely to profit from the regular classroom so that they could receive special attention. The Binet-Simon scale came into use in 1905. Since that time, it has undergone great revision and refinement.

Despite his view that many factors are involved in intellectual functioning, Binet constructed his test to yield a single overall score so that it could be more easily used by the school system. Binet also assumed that intelligence increased with age. And so, he included a series of age-graded questions, as in Table 5.6, and he arranged them in order of difficulty.

The Binet-Simon scale yielded a score called a **mental age,** or MA. The MA shows the intellectual level at which a child is functioning. A child with an MA of 6 is functioning, intellectually, like the average child aged 6. In taking the test, children earned "months" of credit for each correct answer. Their MA was determined by adding the years and months of credit they attained.

Test-retest reliability   A method for determining the reliability of a test by comparing (correlating) test takers' scores from separate occasions.

Validity   The degree to which a test measures what it is supposed to measure.

Aptitude   An ability or talent to succeed in an area in which one has not yet been trained.

Mental age   The accumulated months of credit that a person earns on the Stanford-Binet Intelligence Scale. Abbreviated *MA*.

Table 5.6   Some Test Items from the Stanford-Binet Intelligence Scale

LEVEL (YEARS)	ITEM	LEVEL (YEARS)	ITEM
2 years	1. Children show knowledge of basic vocabulary words by identifying parts of a doll such as the mouth, ears, and hair. 2. Children show counting and spatial skills along with visual-motor coordination by building a tower of four blocks to match a model.		old graveyard in Spain they have discovered a small skull which they believe to be that of Christopher Columbus when he was about ten years old. What is foolish about that?" 2. Children show fluency with words, as shown by answering the questions: "Tell me a number that rhymes with tree." "Tell me the name of a color that rhymes with head."
4 years	1. Children show word fluency and categorical thinking by filling in the missing words when they are asked: "Brother is a boy; sister is a _____?" "In daytime it is light; at night it is _____?" 2. Children show comprehension by answering correctly when they are asked questions such as: "Why do we have books?" "Why do we have houses?"	Adult	1. Adults show knowledge of the meaning of words and conceptual thinking by correctly explaining the differences between "poverty and misery," "laziness and idleness," and "character and reputation." 2. Adults show spatial skills by correctly answering the question: "What direction would you have to face so that your right hand would be to the north?"
9 years	1. Children can point out verbal absurdities, as in this question: "In an		

Source: L. M. Terman & M. A. Merrill (1973). *Stanford-Binet Intelligence Scales: 1973 Norms Edition.* Boston: Houghton Mifflin.

Louis Terman adapted the Binet-Simon scale for use with U.S. children. The first version of the *Stanford*-Binet Intelligence Scale (SBIS)* was published in 1916. The SBIS included more items than the original test and was used with children aged 2 to 16. The SBIS also yielded an **intelligence quotient (IQ)** rather than an MA. The current version of the SBIS is used with children from the age of 2 upward and with adults.

The IQ reflects the relationship between a child's mental age and actual age, or chronological age (CA). Use of this ratio reflects the fact that the same MA score has different implications for children of different ages. That is, an MA of 8 is an above-average score for a 6-year-old, but an MA of 8 is below average for a 10-year-old.

The IQ is computed by the formula IQ = (Mental Age/Chronological Age) × 100, or

$$IQ = \frac{MA}{CA} \times 100$$

According to this formula, a child with an MA of 6 and a CA of 6 would have an IQ of 100. Children who can handle intellectual problems as well as older children will have IQs above 100. Children who do not answer as many items correctly as other children of their age will attain MAs lower than their CAs, and their IQ scores will be below 100.

Since adults do not make gains in problem-solving ability from year to year in the same dramatic way children do, adults' IQ scores are derived by comparing their performances to those of other adults.

*The test is so named because Terman carried out his work at Stanford University.

Intelligence quotient (1) Originally, a ratio obtained by dividing a child's score (or "mental age") on an intelligence test by his or her chronological age. (2) Generally, a score on an intelligence test.

IQ Intelligence quotient.

Table 5.7 Subtests from the Wechsler Intelligence Scale for Children (WISC-R)

VERBAL SUBTESTS	PERFORMANCE SUBTESTS
1. *Information:* "What is the capital of the United States?" "Who was Shakespeare?"	1. *Picture Completion:* Pointing to the missing part of a picture.
2. *Comprehension:* "Why do we have zip codes?" "What does 'A stitch in time saves 9' mean?"	2. *Picture Arrangement:* Arranging cartoon pictures so that they tell a meaningful story.
3. *Arithmetic:* "If 3 candy bars cost 25 cents, how much will 18 candy bars cost?"	3. *Block Design:* Using multicolored blocks to copy pictures of geometric designs.
4. *Similarities:* "How are peanut butter and jelly alike?" "How are good and bad alike?"	4. *Object Assembly:* Putting pieces of a puzzle together so that they form a meaningful object.
5. *Vocabulary:* "What does canal mean?"	5. *Coding:* Rapid scanning for and drawing of symbols that are associated with numbers.
6. *Digit Span:* Repeating series of numbers presented orally by the examiner, forwards and backwards.	6. *Mazes:* Using a pencil to trace the correct route from a starting point to home.

Items for verbal subtests 1–5 are similar but not identical to items on the WISC. Consider the verbal similarities subtest for a moment. What are a couple of correct answers to question 4? Did you come up with (1) Both are found on a sandwich, and (2) Both are types of food? Do you think that one of these answers suggests a higher level of intellectual functioning than the other? Why? Note that in the coding subtest children are shown a series of symbols that are associated with numbers. Below are found lines of numbers with empty boxes for drawing in the correct symbol. In this time-limited subtest, the sooner the test-taker memorizes (learns by repeated association) the correct symbol for each number, the sooner he or she can stop scanning for symbols and concentrate on rapid drawing instead.

The Wechsler Scales David Wechsler developed a series of scales for use with children and adults. The Wechsler scales group test questions into a number of separate subtests (such as those shown in Table 5.7). Each subtest measures a different type of intellectual task. For this reason, the test shows how well a person does on one type of task (such as defining words) as compared with another (such as using blocks to construct geometric designs). In this way, the Wechsler scales highlight children's relative strengths and weaknesses, as well as measure overall intellectual functioning.

As you can see in Table 5.7, Wechsler described some of his scales as measuring *verbal* tasks, and others as assessing *performance* tasks. In general, verbal subtests require knowledge of verbal concepts, whereas performance subtests require familiarity with spatial-relations concepts. Wechsler's scales permit the computation of verbal and performance IQs.

Wechsler also introduced the concept of the **deviation IQ.** Instead of using mental and chronological ages to compute an IQ, Wechsler based IQ scores on how a person's answers compared with (or deviated from) those attained by people in the same age group. The average test result at any age level is defined as an IQ score of 100. Wechsler then distributed IQ scores so that the middle 50 percent of them would fall within the "broad average range" of 90 to 110.

As you can see in Figure 5.6, most IQ scores cluster around the average. Only 5 percent of the population have IQ scores of above 130 or below 70. Table 5.8 indicates the labels that Wechsler assigned to various IQ scores and the approximate percentages of the population who attain IQ scores at those levels.

Group Tests The SBIS and Wechsler scales are administered to one person at a time. This one-to-one ratio is optimal. It allows the examiner to facilitate performance (within the limits of the standardized directions) and to observe the test taker closely. Thus examiners are alerted to factors that impair performance, such as language difficulties, illness, or a noisy or poorly lit room. But large institutions with few trained examiners, such as the public schools and armed forces, have also

> **Deviation IQ** A score on an intelligence test that is derived by determining how far it deviates from the norm.

A Boy Takes the Block Design Subtest of an Individual Intelligence Test.

wished to estimate the intellectual functioning of their charges. They require tests that can be ad-

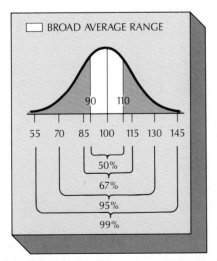

Figure 5.6. What Is the Approximate Distribution of IQ Scores? Wechsler defined the deviation IQ so that 50 percent of scores would fall within the broad average range of 90–110. This bell-shaped curve is referred to as a *normal curve* by psychologists. It describes the distribution of many traits, including height.

ministered simultaneously to large groups of people.

Group tests for children, first developed during World War I, were administered to 4 million children by 1921, a couple of years after the war had ended (Cronbach, 1975). At first these tests were heralded as remarkable instruments because of their easing of the huge responsibilities of

Table 5.8 Variations in IQ Scores

RANGE OF SCORES	PERCENT OF POPULATION	BRIEF DESCRIPTION*
130 and above	2	Very superior
120–129	7	Superior
110–119	16	Bright normal
100–109	25	High average
90–99	25	Low average
80–89	16	Dull normal
70–79	7	Borderline deficient
Below 70	2	Intellectually deficient

*According to David Wechsler.

school administrators. But as the years passed they came under increasing attack because many administrators relied on them completely to track children. They did not seek other sources of information about the children's abilities and achievements (Reschly, 1981).

Social-Class, Racial, and Ethnic Differences in Intelligence

There is a body of research suggestive of differences between social, racial, and ethnic groups. Lower-class U.S. children attain IQ scores some 10 to 15 points lower than those of middle- and upper-class children. Black children tend to attain IQ scores some 15 to 20 points lower than their **Caucasian** agemates (Hall & Kaye, 1980; Loehlin et al., 1975). In his analysis of the data from eleven major studies of black-white differences, Arthur Jensen (1985) concluded that these differences reflected different rates in processing information (Jensen's Level II functioning), rather than differences in specific knowledge, training, or skills (Level I functioning). As groups, Hispanic American and Native American children also score significantly below the Caucasian norms.

Several studies on IQ have confused the factors of social class and race because disproportionate numbers of blacks, Hispanic Americans, and Native Americans are found among the lower socioeconomic classes. But when we limit our observations to particular racial groups, we still find an effect for social class. That is, middle-class Caucasians outscore lower-class Caucasians. Middle-class blacks, Hispanic Americans, and Native Americans also all outscore lower-class members of their own racial groups.

Research has also discovered differences between Asians and Caucasians. Asian Americans, for example, frequently outscore Caucasian Americans on the math test of the Scholastic Aptitude Test. Students in China (Taiwan) and Japan also outscore Americans on standardized achievement tests in math and science (Stevenson et al., 1986). More than a decade ago, reports were published by British psychologist Richard Lynn (1977, 1982) that the Japanese (residing in Japan) attain higher IQ scores than Caucasian Britishers or Americans. The mean Japanese IQ was 111, which is 11 points higher than the U.S. average.

The findings concerning Asian and U.S. children have not gone undisputed. Harold Stevenson and his colleagues (1985) gave ten cognitive tasks along with reading and math achievement tests to children from Minneapolis, Minnesota; Taiwan; and Sendai, Japan. They selected 240 children in each of the first five school grades. Although the Asian children attained higher achievement scores than the Americans, their performance on the cognitive tasks was comparable.

The higher scores of Asian students might not reflect differences in underlying competence. They might reflect, instead, different values in the home, the school, or the culture at large. Lynn (1982) suggested that environmental factors such as intensive educational practices have motivated Japanese children to achieve more than their U.S. and European peers.

The differences in IQ scores between black children and Caucasian children in the United States have stimulated yet hotter disputes and have been studied with greater intensity. We shall discuss these differences in the broader contexts of the IQ testing controversy and the determinants of intelligence.

The Testing Controversy

I was almost one of the testing casualties. At 15 I earned an IQ test score of 82, three points above the track of the special education class. Based on this score, my counselor suggested that I take up bricklaying because I was "good with my hands." My low IQ, however, did not allow me to see that as desirable.

This testimony, offered by black psychologist Robert L. Williams (1974, p. 32), echoes the sentiments of many psychologists. A recent survey of psychologists and educational specialists by Mark Snyderman and Stanley Rothman (1987) found

Caucasian Descriptive of people whose ancestors came from Europe, North Africa, and the Middle East to North India. Usually referred to as "white people," although skin color actually varies from pale reddish white to olive brown.

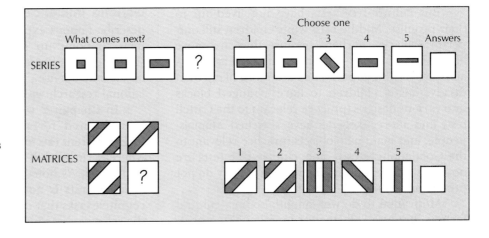

Figure 5.7. What Do Items from Raymond Cattell's Culture-Fair Intelligence Test Look Like? This figure shows a couple of examples from the test.

that the majority believe that intelligence tests are somewhat biased against blacks and members of the lower classes.

During the 1920s intelligence tests were misused to prevent the immigration of many Europeans and others into the United States (Kamin, 1982; Kleinmuntz, 1982). For example, test pioneer H. H. Goddard (1917) assessed 178 newly arrived immigrants at Ellis Island and claimed that "83 percent of the Jews, 80 percent of the Hungarians, 79 percent of the Italians, and 87 percent of the Russians were 'feeble-minded'" (Kleinmuntz, 1982, p. 333). Apparently it was of little concern to Goddard that these immigrants by and large did not understand English—the language in which the tests were administered.

Misuse of intelligence tests has led psychologists such as Leon Kamin to complain, "Since its introduction to America the intelligence test has been used more or less consciously as an instrument of oppression against the underprivileged—the poor, the foreign born, and racial minorities" (in Crawford, 1979, p. 664). Let us explore further some of the controversy concerning the use of both individual and group intelligence tests.

Intelligence tests, as pointed out by critics such as Robert Williams, measure traits that are required in modern, high-technology societies (Anastasi, 1983; Pearlman et al., 1980; Schmidt et al., 1981). The vocabulary and arithmetic subtests on the Wechsler scales, for example, clearly reflect achievements in language skills and computational ability. It is generally assumed that the broad

achievements measured by these tests reflect intelligence, but they might also reflect cultural familiarity with the concepts required to answer test questions correctly. In particular, the tests seem to reflect middle-class white culture in the United States (Garcia, 1981).

If scoring well on intelligence tests requires a certain type of cultural experience, the tests are said to have a **cultural bias.** Children reared in black neighborhoods could be at a disadvantage, not because of differences in intelligence, but because of cultural differences and economic deprivation. For this reason, psychologists such as Raymond B. Cattell (1949) and Florence Goodenough (1954) have tried to construct **culture-free** intelligence tests.

Cattell's Culture-Fair Intelligence Test evaluates reasoning ability through the child's ability to comprehend the rules that govern a progression of geometric designs, as shown in Figure 5.7. Goodenough's Draw-A-Person test is based on the premise that children from all cultural backgrounds have had the opportunity to observe people and note the relationships between the parts and the whole. Her instructions simply require children to draw a picture of a man or woman.

Cultural bias A factor that provides an advantage for test takers from certain cultural or ethnic backgrounds.

Culture-free Describing a test in which cultural biases have been removed.

How Are Monozygotic Twins Important in the Study of the Determinants of Intelligence? Monozygotic twins are important in the study of the origins of traits and behavior patterns. Because their genetic endowment is identical, any differences between them stem from environmental influences.

A third strategy for exploring genetic influences on intelligence is to compare the correlations between adopted children and their biological and adoptive parents. When children are separated from their biological parents at early ages, one can argue that strong relationships between their IQs and those of their natural parents reflect genetic influences. Strong relationships between their IQs and those of their adoptive parents might reflect environmental influences.

Several recent studies with 1- and 2-year-old children in Colorado (Baker et al., 1983), Texas (Horn, 1983), and Minnesota (Scarr & Weinberg, 1983) show a stronger relationship between the IQ scores of adopted children and their biological parents than between adopted children and their adoptive parents. The Scarr and Weinberg report concerns black children reared by white adoptive parents, and we shall return to its findings in the section on environmental influences on intelligence.

And so, there may be a genetic influence on intelligence. However, there is also probably an environmental influence.

Environmental Influences on Intelligence

One approach in studies on environmental influences on IQ focuses on the situational factors that determine IQ scores. Remember that an IQ is a score on a test. Thus in some cases, the testing situation itself can explain part of the social-class difference in IQ. In one study, the experimenters (Zigler et al., 1982) simply made children as comfortable as possible during the test. Rather than being cold and impartial, the examiner was warm and friendly and care was taken to see that the children understood the directions. As a result, the children's IQ scores were six points higher than those for a control group treated in a more indifferent manner, and disadvantaged children made relatively greater gains from the procedure.

Ironically, the studies of the rats selectively bred for maze-learning ability have also provided evidence for the importance of experience. Cooper and Zubek (1958) provided young rats descended from maze-bright and maze-dull parents with different early environments. Some rats from each group were reared in a dull, featureless environment. Others were reared in rat amusement parks with ramps, ladders, wheels, and toys. Rats reared in the impoverished environment did poorly on maze learning tasks in adulthood, regardless of their parentage. But rats reared in the "amusement park" later learned mazes relatively rapidly. An enriched early environment narrowed the gap between the performances of rats with maze-dull and maze-bright parents.

Developmental psychologist Lois Hoffman (1985) believes that the early home environment and styles of parenting also have an impact on IQ. Numerous studies have shown that the children of mothers who are emotionally and verbally responsive, who provide appropriate play materials, who are involved with their children, and who provide varied daily experiences during the early years attain higher IQ scores later on (Bradley & Caldwell, 1976; Elardo et al., 1975; Elardo et al., 1977; Gottfried, 1984). The extent of home organization and safety has also been linked to higher IQs at later ages and to higher achievement test scores during the first grade (Bradley & Caldwell, 1984).

Dozens of other studies support the view that the early environment of the child is linked to IQ scores and academic achievement. For example, Ronald McGowan and Dale Johnson (1984) found that good parent-child relationships and maternal encouragement of independence were both positively linked to Mexican-American children's IQ scores by the age of 3.

Government-funded efforts to provide preschoolers with enriched early environments have also led to intellectual gains. Head Start programs, for example, were instituted in the 1960s to enhance the cognitive development and academic skills of poor children. Children in these programs are exposed to letters and words, numbers, books, exercises in drawing, pegs and pegboards, puzzles, toy animals, and dolls, along with other materials and activities that middle-class children can usually take for granted. Studies of Head Start programs provide further evidence that environmental enrichment can enhance the learning ability of children (Darlington et al., 1980; Sprigle & Schaefer, 1985; Zigler & Berman, 1983). In a New York City study, adolescent boys who had participated in Head Start attained average SBIS IQ scores of 99. Boys similar in background, but without preschooling, earned an average SBIS score of 93 (Palmer, 1976). Children whose IQ scores were initially lowest made the greatest gains in these programs (Zigler & Valentine, 1979). In addition to positively influencing IQ scores, Head Start programs have also led to gains in knowledge of letters, numbers, vocabulary, and scores on achievement tests.

As noted earlier, the Minnesota adoption studies reported by Scarr and Weinberg suggest a genetic influence on intelligence. But the same studies (Scarr & Weinberg, 1976, 1977) also suggest a role for environmental influences. Black children who were adopted during the first year by white parents above average in income and education showed IQ scores some 15 to 25 points higher than those attained by black children reared by their natural parents (Scarr & Weinberg, 1976). Still, the adoptees' average IQ scores, about 109, remained somewhat below those of their

What Are Head Start Programs?   Preschoolers placed in Head Start programs have been shown to make dramatic increases in readiness for elementary school and in IQ scores.

adoptive parents' natural children—115 (Scarr & Weinberg, 1977). Even so, the adoptive early environment closed much of the IQ gap.

On Race and Intelligence: A Concluding Note

Many psychologists believe that heredity and environment interact to influence intelligence (Plomin & DeFries, 1980). Forty-five percent of Snyderman and Rothman's (1987) sample of 1,020 psychologists and educational specialists believe that black–white differences in IQ are a "product of both genetic and environmental variation, compared to only 15 percent who feel the difference is entirely due to environmental variation. Twenty-four percent of experts do not believe there are sufficient data to support any reasonable opinion, [and 1 percent] indicate a belief in an entirely genetic determination" (p. 141).

Perhaps we need not be concerned with "how much" of a person's IQ is due to heredity and how much is due to environmental influences. Psychology has traditionally supported the dignity of the individual. Thus it might be more appropriate for us to try to identify children *of all races* whose environments place them at risk for failure and to do what we can to enrich them.

TRUTH OR FICTION REVISITED

Chimpanzees and gorillas have been taught how to use sign language.   True. They have been taught to use ASL, the language of the deaf.

Crying is the child's earliest use of language.   False. Crying is an example of a *pre*linguistic vocalization.

Children babble only the sounds of their parents' language.   False. Children babble phonemes found in all languages.

Deaf children do not babble.   False. The emergence of babbling in deaf children suggests that babbling is inborn.

To a 2-year-old, the word combinations "Go Mommy" and "Mommy go" have the same meaning.   False. The different word order is consistently expressive of different meanings.

Three-year-olds say "Daddy goed away" instead of "Daddy went away" because they do *understand rules of grammar.*   True. They overregularize because they apply rules for forming the past tense to irregular verbs.

Children acquire grammar by imitating their parents.   False. It appears that children attend to language in such a way that they pick out rules of grammar and then apply them to produce their own sentences.

The only way to solve a difficult problem is to keep plugging away at it.   False. Sometimes it is more efficient to allow the elements of a problem to "incubate" for a while.

It may be boring, but the most efficient way to solve a problem is to use the tried and tested formula.   False. It might be more efficient to cast about for heuristic devices.

Highly intelligent people are also creative.   Not necessarily. Intelligence is only moderately related to creativity.

Knowing what problem to tackle is an aspect of intelligent behavior.   True. Sternberg refers to this aspect as a metacomponent of intelligence.

Intelligence and IQ *mean the same thing.*   False. Intelligence is a hypothetical trait, whereas an IQ is a score on a test.

Two children can answer exactly the same items on an intelligence test correctly, yet one can be above average and the other below average in intelligence.   True. Performance is considered in relation to age.

Japanese children attain higher IQ scores than U.S. children.   True.

There is no such thing as an unbiased intelligence test.   True, in the sense that school adjustment and motivation to perform well influence scores even on "culture-free" tests.

High intelligence runs in families.   Not necessarily. The evidence shows that high *IQs* run in families. But intelligence and IQ are not exactly the same thing.

Head Start programs have raised children's IQs.   True.

Chapter Review

Language is the communication of thoughts and feelings through symbols that are arranged according to rules of grammar. A number of apes have learned to communicate by means of American Sign Language and other signs; however, many psycholinguists question whether apes use signs as symbols and grasp grammar.

Language has the properties of semanticity, productivity, and displacement. The basic components of language include phonology, morphology, syntax, and semantics.

Newborn children cry and begin to coo by about 2 months. Babbling is the first kind of vocalization that has the sound of speech.

Children speak their first words at about a year, and their receptive vocabularies grow more rapidly than their expressive vocabularies. Young children show overextension of the meanings of words by using familiar words to refer to things for which they do not yet have words. Children's early utterances are telegraphic, although they show knowledge of grammar. The sequence of development of two-word utterances is invariant among children learning different languages, suggesting that there is a universal, innate tendency to develop language according to a preprogramed schedule. The "errors" made in overregularizing also indicate a grasp of the rules of grammar.

Learning theorists tend to explain language development in terms of imitation and reinforcement. The view that inborn factors cause children to attend to and acquire language in certain ways is the nativist view. According to psycholinguistic theory, language acquisition involves an interaction between environmental influences and inborn tendencies. McNeill labeled this inborn tendency the Language Acquisition Device. Lenneberg suggests that there is a sensitive period for learning language that begins during the second year and lasts until puberty. Cognitive theorists tend to believe that language development is made possible by cognitive analytical abilities and that children are active agents in language learning.

Thought is possible without language, but language facilitates thought. According to the linguistic-relativity hypothesis, language structures (and limits) the ways in which we perceive the world.

Problem solving involves stages of preparation, production, and evaluation. Algorithms are specific procedures for solving problems (such as formulas) that will work invariably, as long as they are applied correctly. Heuristics are rules of thumb that help us simplify and solve problems.

When we cannot find a solution to a problem, distancing ourselves from the problem sometimes allows the solution to incubate. Incubation may permit the breaking down of misleading mental sets.

Creativity is the ability to make unusual and sometimes remote associations to the elements of a problem to generate new combinations that meet the goals. There is only a moderate relationship between creativity and intelligence.

According to the text, there are factor theories and cognitive theories of intelligence. Spearman believed that a common factor, **g,** underlay all intelligent behavior, but that people also have specific abilities, or **s** factors. Thurstone suggested that there are several primary mental abilities. Guilford has proposed a structure-of-intellect model of 120 factors.

Arthur Jensen hypothesizes the existence of Level I and Level II intelligence. Robert Sternberg has constructed a three-level, or triarchic, model of intelligence. The three levels are contextual, experiential, and componential.

Intelligence tests must be reliable and valid. Reliability is the consistency of a test. Validity is the degree to which a test measures an external criterion, or that which it is supposed to measure. Validity studies typically correlate intelligence with measures of academic success.

Intelligence tests yield scores called intelligence quotients, or IQs. The Stanford-Binet Intelligence Scale originally derived IQ scores by dividing children's mental age scores by their chronological ages, then multiplying by 100. The Wechsler scales use deviation IQs, which are derived by comparing a person's performance to that of agemates. Wechsler scales contain verbal and performance subtests.

Lower-class children attain IQ scores some 10 to 15 points lower than those attained by middle- and upper-class children. A number of studies have found that Japanese and Chinese children attain higher IQ scores than U.S. children. The issue is whether social-class and racial differences reflect inborn or cultural factors.

Some psychologists argue that intelligence tests are culturally biased in favor of middle-class white children. As a consequence, efforts have been made to develop culture-fair or culture-free tests.

Research into the genetic determinants of intelligence tends to rely on kinship studies and studies of the intelligence of adoptees. The correlations of intelligence test scores of MZ twins average about +.90. There is a stronger relationship between the IQ scores of adopted children and their biological parents than there is with their adoptive parents.

Evidence for the importance of environmental factors stems from research into the effects of the early environment, including Head Start programs, and studies of adoptees. Children in Head Start programs make significant and lasting intellectual gains. Black children adopted before the age of 1 by white parents show higher IQ scores than those attained by black children reared by their natural parents.

It seems that genetic and environmental factors interact to influence intelligence.

Exercise

Names to Know

Directions: *In the first column are the names of some individuals who have had an impact on psychological thought and research. In the second column are names and concepts with which they are associated. Match the concepts in the second column with the names in the first by writing as many letters as apply to the left of the names. Check your answers against those in the key, given below.*

_____ 1. Alfred Binet	A. Apes and language
_____ 2. Noam Chomsky	B. Culture-free IQ test
_____ 3. Beatrice and Allen Gardner	C. Deviation IQ
	D. Determinants of intelligence
_____ 4. Arthur Jensen	E. **g**
_____ 5. Francine Patterson	F. Koko
_____ 6. Ann and David Premack	G. Linguistic-relativity hypothesis
	H. Measurement of intelligence
_____ 7. Duane Rumbaugh	I. Mental age
_____ 8. Sandra Scarr	J. Primary mental abilities
_____ 9. Charles Spearman	K. Language Acquisition Device
_____ 10. Louis Terman	L. **s**
_____ 11. Herbert Terrace	M. Sarah
_____ 12. Louis Thurstone	N. SBIS
_____ 13. David Wechsler	O. WAIS-R

_____ 14. Benjamin Whorf   P. Washoe
_____ 15. Florence Goodenough   Q. Word fluency
_____ 16. Robert Sternberg   R. Yerkish
_____ 17. J. P. Guilford   S. Psycholinguistic theory
_____ 18. David McNeill   T. Triarchic theory
_____ 19. Eric Lenneberg   U. Structure-of-intellect model
_____ 20. Raymond B. Cattell   V. Sensitive period
_____ 21. Sir Cyril Burt

Answer Key to Matching Exercise

1. H, I, N	**7.** A, R	**13.** C, H, O	**17.** H, U
2. S	**8.** D	**14.** G	**18.** K, S
3. A, P	**9.** E, L	**15.** B, H	**19.** S, V
4. D, H	**10.** H	**16.** T	**20.** B, H
5. A, F	**11.** A		**21.** D
6. A, M	**12.** H, J, Q		

Posttest

Directions: *For each of the following, select the choice that best answers the question or completes the sentence.*

1. According to the text, language is defined as the communication of thoughts and feelings through _____ that are arranged according to rules of grammar.

   (a) words, **(b)** sentences, **(c)** concepts, **(d)** symbols.

2. Washoe's production of sign language was deficient in that

   (a) no signs for actions were used, **(b)** word order was haphazard, **(c)** sentences were limited to two signs, **(d)** signs were unrelated to objects.

3. The Premacks consider their work with Sarah a demonstration of the role of _____ in language acquisition.

   (a) the language-acquisition device, **(b)** classical conditioning, **(c)** operant conditioning, **(d)** observational learning.

4. The smallest unit of meaning in a language is the

   (a) morpheme, **(b)** phoneme, **(c)** word, **(d)** concept.

5. The word *cats* consists of _____ morpheme(s).

   (a) no, **(b)** one, **(c)** two, **(d)** four.

6. The true meaning of the phrase "an English-speaking home" reflects the _____ of the phrase.

   (a) surface structure, **(b)** deep structure, **(c)** syntax, **(d)** inflections.

7. Which of the following is *not* a prelinguistic event?

   (a) the holophrase, **(b)** cooing, **(c)** babbling, **(d)** crying.

8. A parent knows that you are taking a psychology course and expresses concern to you that his 4-year-old child refers to the "gooses" and "sheeps" she saw on the farm. As an expert on language development, you state that the child's formation of the plural in this way probably suggests that

   (a) the language-acquisition device has not yet been activated, (b) parents or other children in the family speak this way, (c) learning does not play an important role in language acquisition, (d) language development is proceeding normally.

9. According to Eric Lenneberg,

   (a) Broca's area does not begin to develop until a child is 24 months old, (b) people have difficulty understanding the deep structure of sentences once they are adults, (c) people cannot learn language once they have outgrown the sensitive period, (d) brain-injured children often regain language ability because of plasticity of the brain.

10. According to the text, the three main stages of problem solving are

    (a) observation, analysis, and synthesis, (b) hypothesis formation, testing, and confirmation, (c) preparation, production, and evaluation, (d) analysis, research, and incubation.

11. According to the text, the incubation effect may be explained by

    (a) breakthrough of unconscious ideas into the conscious, (b) distancing problem solvers from persistent but unprofitable mental sets, (c) conscious searching for heuristic devices, (d) spontaneous means-end analysis.

12. Each of the following contributes to creativity *except* for

    (a) flexibility, (b) fluent thinking, (c) divergent thinking, (d) convergent thinking.

13. A friend says, "I keep on hearing all this stuff about IQs. What is an IQ, anyhow?" You clear your throat and note that your psychology textbook defines an *IQ* as

    (a) a personality trait, (b) word fluency, (c) the capacity to understand the world and the resourcefulness to cope with its challenges, (d) a score on an intelligence test.

14. According to the text, which of the following conceived of intelligence as a group of primary mental abilities?

    (a) Charles Spearman, (b) Louis Thurstone, (c) Louis Terman, (d) Alfred Binet.

15. Jensen's Level II intelligence consists of

    (a) word fluency, (b) experiential components, (c) conceptual abilities, (d) computational ability.

16. According to Sternberg, knowing what problem to tackle is an example of one of the _____ of intelligence.

(a) metacomponents, (b) contextual components, (c) metacognitions, (d) knowledge acquisition components.

17. An intelligence test constructed by ———————— yields a deviation IQ.

(a) Raymond Cattell, (b) Louis Terman, (c) David Wechsler, (d) Arthur Jensen.

18. According to Lynn's research, ———————— children attain the highest scores on intelligence tests.

(a) black U.S., (b) Hispanic American, (c) Caucasian U.S., (d) Japanese.

19. Which of the following statements about social-class differences in intelligence in the United States is most accurate?

(a) There are no social-class differences in intelligence, (b) Social-class differences in intelligence are found within racial groups, (c) There are social-class differences in associative abilities only, (d) Social-class differences are outgrown by the time children reach their teens.

20. Intelligence test scores tend to correlate about ———————— with school grades.

(a) +0.50 to +0.60, (b) +0.60 to +0.70, (c) +0.70 to +0.80, (d) +0.80 to +0.90.

21. Culture-fair tests have not lived up to their promise in that

(a) middle-class white children outperform blacks on them, (b) they do not have adequate test-retest reliability, (c) it has not been possible to standardize them, (d) test results do not correlate with performance on the Stanford-Binet or Wechsler scales.

22. A friend says, "We run experiments to find out everything else, so why can't we run experiments to find out exactly how much of a person's intelligence is due to heredity and how much is due to the environment?" You point out that we do not have experimental evidence concerning the genetic determinants of human intelligence because

(a) it would be unethical to breed people selectively, (b) it is theoretically impossible to separate the effects of heredity and the environment, (c) data from kinship and adoptee studies has been faked, (d) psychologists have not been able to agree on the definition of intelligence in humans.

Answer Key to Posttest

1. D	7. A	13. D	18. D
2. B	8. D	14. B	19. B
3. C	9. D	15. C	20. B
4. A	10. C	16. A	21. A
5. C	11. B	17. C	22. A
6. B	12. D		

MOTIVATION AND EMOTION

OUTLINE

PRETEST: TRUTH OR FICTION?
MOTIVES, NEEDS, DRIVES, AND INCENTIVES
THEORETICAL PERSPECTIVES ON
   MOTIVATION
  Instinct Theory
  Drive-Reduction Theory
  Humanistic Theory
  Evaluation
PHYSIOLOGICAL DRIVES
  Hunger
  Obesity
  Thirst
  Sleep
  Sex
STIMULUS MOTIVES

Sensory Stimulation and Activity
Exploration and Manipulation
The Search for Optimal Arousal
SOCIAL MOTIVES
  The Need for Achievement
  The Need for Affiliation
EMOTION
  Emotional Development
  Expression of Emotions
  The Facial-Feedback Hypothesis
  Theories of Emotion
TRUTH OR FICTION REVISITED
CHAPTER REVIEW
EXERCISE
POSTTEST

PRETEST: TRUTH OR FICTION?

One U.S. adult in five is obese.

Overweight people are more sensitive to stomach pangs than are normal-weight people.

Eating salty pretzels can make you thirsty.

Sleep becomes gradually deeper as we approach the middle of the night and then gradually lightens until we awaken in the morning.

People who sleep nine hours or more a night tend to be lazy and happy-go-lucky.

We tend to act out our forbidden fantasies in our dreams.

Stimulating male rats in a certain part of the brain causes them to engage in sexual foreplay.

Only men are sexually stimulated by hard-core pornography.

Homosexuals suffer from hormonal imbalances.

Any healthy woman can successfully resist a rapist if she really wants to.

"Getting away from it all" by going on a vacation from all sensory input for a few hours is relaxing.

If quarterbacks get too "psyched up" for a big game, their performance on the field may suffer.

A strong need to get ahead is the most powerful predictor of success in climbing the corporate ladder.

Misery loves company.

You may be able to fool a lie detector by squiggling your toes.

When is the last time you came face to face with a tarantula, a laser beam, or an alien from outer space? Actually, if you have been to a movie lately, it may not have been that long ago at all: *Aliens, Star Wars, Raiders of the Lost Ark, Romancing the Stone, First Blood, Star Trek, Close Encounters, Indiana Jones and the Temple of Doom, A View to a Kill, Superman, Conan, The Predator.* In adventure films characters such as Rambo, James Bond, and Indiana Jones have been pitted against snakes, tarantulas, alligators, mythical monsters, automatic rifles, knives, swords, helicopter gunships, nuclear weapons, laser beams, computers, crazed cultists, floods, hurricanes, blizzards, airplane crashes, shipwrecks, cosmic forces, international forces, occult forces—forces of every flavor and every size.

Most of us lead rather orderly lives, so how do we account for the huge success of these adventure films at the box office? What motivates us to flock to every film from *Gremlins* to *Goonies?*

We do not have the final answer to this question. But here are some speculations that have been advanced by psychologists, religious leaders, politicians, film critics, and your friendly neighborhood bartender:

Life is filled with vague anxieties and persistent pressures. Adventure films give us a temporary focus for our fears, anxieties, and frustrations.

Audiences can purge their aggressive impulses by enjoying conflicts in which other people are involved.

We are seeking coping strategies. We learn how to deal with our own frustrations and conflicts by observing the heroes and the heroines.

Adventure films make our own problems seem trivial.

Adventure films heighten awareness of the possibilities of life, giving us hope that we may someday find ourselves in exotic situations.

Most of us lead sedentary lives with uncomfortably low levels of arousal. Adventure films raise our arousal to more optimal levels, so that we feel full of vim and vigor.

Afterward, our dates may interpret their high levels of arousal from the movie as attraction to us.

We have an instinctive drive to throw away money.

We're grateful it's not happening to us.

Harrison Ford is cute.

They're fun.

The psychology of motivation is concerned with the *whys* of behavior. Why do we attend adventure films? Why do we eat and drink? Why do some of us ride motorcyles at breakneck speeds? Why do we try new things or strive to get ahead?

In this chapter we explore motivation and the closely related topic of emotion. Adventure films give rise to powerful emotional responses, and it may be that expectation of these responses partly motivates our visit to the theater.

Let us begin with a few basic definitions. Then we shall discuss various theoretical perspectives on motivation and conclude that each has its limitations. We shall explore physiological drives, stimulus motives, and social motives. Finally, we shall explore theories about how emotional responses add color to our lives.

MOTIVES, NEEDS, DRIVES, AND INCENTIVES

The word *motive* derives from the Latin *movere*, meaning "to move." **Motives** can be defined as hypothetical states within organisms that activate behavior and propel the organisms toward goals.

The term **need** has been used in at least two different ways by psychologists. We speak both of physiological needs and psychological needs. Certain physiological needs must be met if we are to survive. Such physiological needs include oxygen, food, drink, pain avoidance, proper temperature, and the elimination of waste products. Some physiological needs, such as hunger and thirst, are states of physical deprivation. For instance, when we have not eaten or drunk for a while, we develop needs for food and water. We speak of the body as having needs for oxygen, fluids, calories, vitamins, minerals, and so on.

Psychological needs include needs for achievement, power, self-esteem, social approval, and belonging, among others. Psychological needs differ from physiological needs in two important ways: First, psychological needs are not necessarily based

Motive A hypothetical state within an organism that propels the organism toward a goal.

Need A state of deprivation.

What Is a Fixed-Action Pattern?   In the presence of another male, the Siamese Fighting Fish assumes an instinctive threatening stance in which the fins and gills are extended. If neither threatening male retreats, there will be conflict.

on states of deprivation; a person with a strong need for achievement may have a history of consistent success. Second, psychological needs may be acquired through experience, or learned, whereas physiological needs reside in the physical basis of the organism.

Needs are said to give rise to **drives.** Depletion of food gives rise to the hunger drive, and depletion of liquids gives rise to the thirst drive. Physiological drives are the psychological counterparts of physiological needs. When we have gone without food and water our bodies may *need* these sub-

Drive A condition of arousal in an organism that is associated with a need.

Incentive An object, person, or situation perceived as capable of satisfying a need.

Instinct An inherited disposition to activate specific behavior patterns that are designed to reach certain goals.

Ethologist A scientist who studies the behavior patterns characteristic of different species.

Fixed-action pattern An instinct; abbreviated *FAP.*

stances; however, our *experience* of drives of hunger and thirst is psychological in nature. Drives arouse us to action. Our drive levels tend to increase with the length of time we have been deprived.

Our psychological needs for approval, achievement, and belonging also give rise to drives. We can be driven to get ahead in the world of business just as surely as we can be driven to eat. For many of us the drives for achievement and power consume our daily lives.

An **incentive** is an object, person, or situation perceived as capable of satisfying a need or as desirable for its own sake. Money, food, a sexually attractive person, social approval, and attention all can act as incentives that motivate behavior.

Let us now turn our attention to theoretical perspectives on motivation. We shall see that psychologists and others have spawned very different views of the motives that propel us.

THEORETICAL PERSPECTIVES ON MOTIVATION

Although psychologists agree that it is important to understand why people and lower animals do things, they do not agree about the nature of their motives. Let us have a brief look at three theoretical perspectives on motivation: instinct theory, drive reductionism, and self-actualization.

Instinct Theory

Animals are born with preprogramed tendencies to respond to certain situations in certain ways. Birds reared in isolation from other birds build nests during the mating season even though they have never observed another bird build a nest (or, for that matter, seen a nest). Siamese fighting fish reared in isolation assume stereotypical threatening stances and attack other males when they are introduced into their tanks.

Behaviors such as these are characteristic of particular species ("species-specific") and do not rely on learning. They are labeled **instincts**—inherited dispositions that activate specific behavior patterns that appear designed to reach certain goals.

Ethologists label instincts **fixed-action patterns** (or FAPs). FAPs occur in response to stimuli that ethologists refer to as **releasers.** As noted in Chapter 3, male members of many species are sexually aroused by pheromones secreted by females. Pheromones "release" the FAP of sexual response.

At the turn of the century, psychologists William James (1890) and William McDougall (1908) argued that people have various instincts that foster self-survival and social behavior. James asserted that we have social instincts such as love, sympathy, and modesty. McDougall catalogued 12 "basic" instincts, including hunger, sex, and self-assertion. Other psychologists put together longer lists.

The psychoanalyst Sigmund Freud also used the term *instincts* to refer to physiological needs within people. Freud believed that the instincts of sex and aggression give rise to *psychic energy,* which is perceived as feelings of tension. Tension motivates us to restore ourselves to a calmer, resting state. However, the behavior patterns we use to reduce the tension are largely learned. Freud's views coincide to some degree with those of a group of learning theorists who presented a drive-reduction theory of learning.

Drive-Reduction Theory

According to **drive-reduction theory,** as framed by psychologist Clark Hull at Yale University in the 1930s, rewards foster learning because they reduce drives. Hull argued that **primary drives** such as hunger, thirst, and pain trigger arousal (tension) and activate behavior. We learn responses that partially or completely reduce the drives. Through association, we also learn **acquired drives.** We may acquire a drive for money because money enables us to attain food, drink, and homes that protect us from predators and extremes of temperature. We might acquire drives for social approval and affiliation because other people, and their good will, also help us to reduce primary drives, especially when we are infants. In all cases, tension reduction is the goal.

Humanistic Theory

Humanistic psychologists, particularly Abraham Maslow, note that the instinct and drive-reduction theories of motivation are basically defensive. They suggest that behavior is mechanical and aimed toward survival and tension reduction. As a humanist, Maslow asserted that behavior is also motivated by the conscious desire for personal growth. Humanists note that people will tolerate pain, hunger, and many other sources of tension to achieve what they perceive as personal fulfillment.

Maslow believed that we humans are separated from lower animals by our capacity for **self-actualization,** or self-initiated striving to become whatever we believe we are capable of being. Maslow saw self-actualization as essential a human need as hunger.

Maslow (1970) organized human needs into a **hierarchy,** from physiological needs, such as hunger and thirst, through self-actualization (see Figure 6.1). He believed that our lives would naturally travel up through this hierarchy, as long as we did not encounter insurmountable social or environmental hurdles.

Maslow's needs hierarchy includes

1. *Physiological needs:* hunger, thirst, elimination, warmth, fatigue, pain avoidance, sexual release.
2. *Safety needs:* protection from the environment through housing and clothing, security from crime and financial hardship.
3. *Love and belongingness needs:* love and acceptance through intimate relationships, social groups, and friends. Maslow believed that in a generally well-fed society, such as ours, much frustration stemmed from failure to meet needs at this level.

Releaser In ethology, a stimulus that elicits a FAP.

Drive-reduction theory The view that organisms learn to engage in behaviors that have the effect of reducing drives.

Primary drives Unlearned, or physiological, drives.

Acquired drives Drives that are acquired through experience, or learned.

Self-actualization According to Maslow and other humanistic psychologists, self-initiated striving to become what one is capable of being. The motive to reach one's full potential, to express one's unique capabilities.

Hierarchy A group of objects arranged according to rank or class structure.

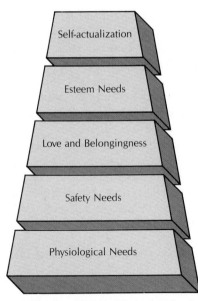

Figure 6.1. What Are the Needs in Maslow's Hierarchy? Maslow believed that we progress toward higher psychological needs once basic survival needs have been met. Where do you fit in this picture?

4. *Esteem needs:* achievement, competence, approval, recognition, prestige, status.
5. *Self-actualization:* fulfillment of our unique potentials. For many individuals, self-actualization involves needs for cognitive understanding (novelty, exploration, knowledge) and aesthetic needs (music, art, poetry, beauty, order).

Evaluation

Instinct theory has been criticized for yielding circular explanations of behavior. If we say that mothers love and care for their children because of a maternal instinct, and then we take maternal care as evidence for such an instinct, we have come full circle. But we have explained nothing. We have only repeated ourselves.

Instincts are also species-specific; that is, they give rise to stereotyped behaviors (FAPs) in all members of a species (or perhaps, they apply to all

Physiological drives Unlearned drives with a biological basis, such as hunger, thirst, and avoidance of pain.

male or to all female adults). There is so much variation in human behavior that it seems unlikely that much of it is instinctive.

Drive-reduction theory appears to apply in many situations involving physiological drives, such as hunger and thirst. But it runs aground when we consider evidence that we often act to increase, rather than decrease, the tensions acting on us. When hungry we might go to lengths to prepare a meal rather than snack, but the snack would reduce hunger as well. We drive fast cars, ride roller coasters, and parachute-jump for sport—activities that heighten rather than decrease arousal. We often shun tried and true ways of reducing drives because of the stimulation afforded by chancy, novel approaches. Other psychologists theorize the existence of "stimulus motives" that surmount the limitations of drive-reduction theory.

Critics of Maslow argue that there is too much individual variation for his hierarchy to apply to everyone. Some people whose physiological, safety, and love needs are met show little interest in achievement and recognition. Others seek distant, self-actualizing goals while exposing themselves to great danger. Some artists, musicians, and writers devote themselves fully to their art, even at the price of poverty.

In sum, no traditional view of motivation accounts fully for complex human behavior. Despite the lack of an integrated, satisfying theory of human motivation, there is a wealth of research concerning various types of motivated behavior. Let us first consider drives that arise from physiological needs.

PHYSIOLOGICAL DRIVES

Physiological needs give rise to **physiological drives**—aroused conditions within the organism that activate behavior that will reduce these needs. Because physiological drives are unlearned, they are also referred to as primary drives. Although sexual behavior allows survival of the species rather than survival of the individual, sex is also a primary drive.

Primary drives are inborn, but learning influences the *behavior* that satisfies them. Eating meat or fish, drinking coffee or tea, kissing lips or rubbing noses are all learned behavior patterns.

Homeostasis   Physiological drives operate largely according to principles of drive reduction. Mechanisms in the body are triggered when we are in a state of deprivation. These mechanisms then motivate us, through sensations such as hunger, thirst, and cold, to act to restore the balance. The body tendency to maintain a steady state is called **homeostasis.**

Homeostasis works much like a thermostat. When the room temperature drops below the set point, the heating system is triggered. The heat stays on until the set point is reached. The homeostatic systems of the body involve fascinating interactions between physiological and psychological processes.

In this section we shall explore the drives of hunger, thirst, and sex. We also explore the need for sleep.

Hunger

Most of us maintain remarkably constant weights over the years (Keesey, 1980). What body mechanisms regulate the hunger drive? What psychological processes are at work? Why do many of us continue to eat when we have already supplied our bodies with the needed nutrients?

The Mouth   Let us begin with the mouth—an appropriate choice since we are discussing eating. Chewing and swallowing provide some sensations of **satiety.** If they did not, we might eat for a long time after we had taken in enough food; it takes the digestive tract time to metabolize food and provide signals of satiety to the brain by way of the bloodstream.

In classic **sham** feeding experiments with dogs, a tube was implanted in the animals' throats, so that any food swallowed fell out of the body. Even though no food arrived at the stomach, the animals stopped feeding after a brief period (Janowitz & Grossman, 1949). However, they resumed feeding sooner than animals whose food did reach the stomach. Let us proceed to the stomach, too, as we seek further regulatory factors in hunger.

Stomach Contractions   An empty stomach will lead to stomach contractions, which we call hunger pangs, but these pangs are not as influential as had once been thought. People and animals whose stomachs have been removed will still regulate food intake to maintain a normal weight level. This finding led to the discovery of many other regulatory mechanisms, including blood sugar level, the hypothalamus, even receptors in the liver.

Blood Sugar Level   When we are deprived of food, the level of sugar in the blood drops. The deficit is communicated to the hypothalamus (see Chapter 2). The drop in blood sugar apparently indicates that we have been burning energy and need to replenish it by eating.

Experiments with the Hypothalamus: The Search for "Start-Eating" and "Stop-Eating" Centers in the Brain   If you were just reviving from a surgical operation, fighting your way through the fog of the anesthesia, food would probably be that last thing on your mind. But when you operate on rats and make a **lesion** in the **ventromedial nucleus** (VMN) of the hypothalamus, they will grope toward their food supplies as soon as their eyes open. Then they eat vast quantities of Purina Rat Chow or whatever else they can find.

The VMN might function like a stop-eating center in the rat's brain (Novin et al., 1976). If you electrically stimulate the VMN—that is, "switch it on"—a rat will stop eating until the current is turned off. When the VMN is lesioned, the rat becomes **hyperphagic.** It will continue to eat until it has mushroomed to about five times its normal

---

Homeostasis The tendency of the body to maintain a steady state.

Satiety The state of being satisfied; fullness.

Sham False, pretended.

Lesion An injury that results in impaired behavior or loss of a function.

Ventromedial nucleus A central area on the underside of the hypothalamus that appears to function as a stop-eating center.

Hyperphagic Characterized by excessive eating.

Figure 6.2. What Is a Hyperphagic Rat? This rodent winner of the basketball look-alike contest went on a binge after it received a lesion in the ventromedial nucleus (VMN) of the hypothalamus. It is as if the lesion pushed the "set point" for body weight up several notches, and the rat's weight is now about five times normal. But now it eats only enough to maintain its pleasantly plump stature, so you need not be concerned that it will eventually burst. If the lesion had been made in the lateral hypothalamus, the animal might become the "Twiggy" of the rat world.

weight (see Figure 6.2). Then it will level off its eating and maintain the higher weight. It is as if the set point of the stop-eating center has been raised to a higher level (Keesey & Powley, 1975; Powley, 1977).

VMN-lesioned rats are also more sensitive than normal rats to the taste of food. They will eat more food if sugar or fat is added, but they will eat less if the food is stale or bitter (Levitt, 1981).

Lateral hypothalamus An area at the side of the hypothalamus that appears to function as a start-eating center.

Aphagic Characterized by undereating.

The **lateral hypothalamus** might be a start-eating center in the rat's brain. If you electrically stimulate the lateral hypothalamus, the rat will start to eat. If you make a lesion in the lateral hypothalamus, the rat may stop eating altogether—that is, become **aphagic.** But if you force-feed an aphagic rat for a while, it will begin to eat on its own and level off at a relatively low body weight. You have lowered the rat's set point. It is like turning the thermostat down from, say, 70 degrees Fahrenheit to 40 degrees Fahrenheit.

Receptors in the Liver   Other research suggests that receptors in the liver are also important in regulating hunger (Friedman & Stricker, 1976; Schwartz, 1978). These receptors appear sensitive to the blood sugar level. In a state of food deprivation, blood sugar is low, and these receptors send rapid messages to the brain. After a meal the blood sugar level rises, and their rate of firing decreases.

Although many areas of the body work in concert to regulate the hunger drive, this is only part of the story. In human beings the hunger drive is more complex. Psychological as well as physiological factors play an important role, as we shall see in our discussion of the problem of obesity.

Obesity

We need food to survive, but food means more than survival to many of us. Food is a symbol of family togetherness and caring. We associate food with the nurturance of the parent-child relationship, with visits home at Thanksgiving. Friends and relatives offer food when we enter their homes. Saying no may be interpreted as a personal rejection. Bacon and eggs, coffee with cream and sugar, meat and mashed potatoes, all seem part of sharing U.S. values and agricultural abundance.

But many of us are paying the price of abundance—obesity:

Nearly 90 percent of U.S. residents consider themselves at least slightly overweight, and 35 percent want to lose at least 15 pounds (Toufexis et al., 1986).

One out of five U.S. adults is obese—that is, weighs more than 20 percent above the recommended weight (Wallis, 1985).

Eleven million U.S. adults are severely obese (Wallis, 1985), exceeding their desirable body weight by at least 40 percent.

About 30 percent of U.S. women and 16 percent of U.S. men were on diets in a recent year (Toufexis et al., 1986).

Within a few years, at least two-thirds of "successful" dieters regain every pound they have lost—and then some (Toufexis et al., 1986).

This nation idealizes slender heroes and heroines. For many of us who measure more-than-up to TV and film idols, food may have replaced sex as the central source of guilt. The obese also encounter more than their fair share of illnesses, including heart disease, arteriosclerosis, diabetes, gout, even certain types of cancer (Wallis, 1985).

Why do so many of us overeat? Is obesity a physiological problem, a psychological problem, or both? Research suggests that psychological and physiological factors both play a role in obesity.

On Fat Cells and Obese People

The efforts of obese people to maintain a slender profile might be sabotaged by microscopic units of life within their own bodies: **fat cells.** No, fat cells are not overweight cells. They are cells that store fat, or **adipose tissue.** Hunger might be related to the amount of fat stored in these cells. As time passes after a meal, the blood sugar level drops. Fat is then drawn from these cells to provide further nourishment. At some point, the hypothalamus is signaled of the fat deficiency in these cells, triggering the hunger drive.

People with more adipose tissue than others feel food-deprived earlier, even though they may be of equal weight. This might be because more signals are being sent to the brain. Obese people, and *formerly* obese people, tend to have more adipose tissue than people of normal weight. For this reason, many people who have lost weight complain that they are always hungry as they try to maintain normal weight levels. Psychologist Richard Keesey (1986) notes that displacing a person from his or her set point puts compensating metabolic forces into motion.

Moreover, fat cells metabolize food more slowly than muscle tissue, and some of us have more fat cells than others. That is, people of the same weight with a higher muscle-to-fat ratio will burn more calories. We inherit different numbers of fat cells, and so we may inherit a disposition toward becoming obese. But psychologist Kelly Brownell (1988) points out that "yo-yo dieting" also increases our body proportion of adipose tissue; when we regain lost weight, we tend to put on more fat and less muscle.

Internal and External Eaters: Out of Sight, Out of Mouth?

During the late evening news, just as I'm settling in for sleep, a Big Mac or frozen pizza ad assaults me from the TV set. Visions of juicy meat, gooey cheese, and drippy sauce threaten to do me in. My stomach growlings are all the evidence I need that hunger can be triggered by external stimuli, such as the sight of food, as well as by chemical imbalances in the body.

Although commercials might stir most of our appetites, the overweight seem more responsive than the normal-weight to external stimulation. People who respond predominantly to their own internal stimuli are referred to as **internal eaters.** Those who must be tied to the bedpost when they see a food commercial or catch a whiff of kitchen aromas are **external eaters.** Any of us might occasionally respond to an especially appealing incentive, such as a chocolate chip cookie (sorry, you externals). But external eaters are decidedly more swayed by external stimulation. Moreover, obese people are less likely to be swayed by external sources of stimulation than normal-weight people (Schachter & Gross, 1968; Stunkard, 1959).

Why are obese people more responsive than the normal-weight to external stimulation? Stanley Schachter (1971) observed similarities between the eating behavior of hyperphagic rats and obese people that led him to wonder whether many of the obese are troubled by faulty neural regulation of

---

Fat cells Cells that store fats.

Adipose tissue Containing animal fat.

Internal eaters People who eat predominantly in response to internal stimuli, such as hunger pangs.

External eaters People who eat predominantly in response to external stimuli, such as the sight or smell of food or the time of day.

What Are the Triggers of Hunger? Hunger can be initiated by external stimuli as well as by internal stimuli, such as a drop-off in the blood sugar level.

hunger because of problems, perhaps, in the hypothalamus.

Heavy people, like hyperphagic rats, are more sensitive than the normal-weight to the taste of food (Schachter, 1971; Schachter & Rodin, 1974). They eat relatively larger quantities of sweet foods, such as vanilla milkshakes, but lower quantities of bitter foods. Obese people also take larger mouthfuls, chew less, and finish their meals more rapidly than normal-weight people (LeBow et al., 1977; Marston et al., 1977).

But the faulty-neural-mechanism theory has not yet been directly supported as a factor in obesity in human beings. For the moment we can note only that the eating behavior of obese people resembles that of hyperphagic rats. It is also possible that early dietary habits promote the greater sensitivity to external cues found among the obese (Rodin & Slochower, 1976).

Other factors, such as emotional state, might also play a role in obesity. Dieting efforts might be impeded by negative emotional states such as depression (Baucom & Aiken, 1981; Ruderman, 1985) and anxiety (Pine, 1985).

But now, some good news for people who would like to lose a few pounds. Psychological research has led to a number of helpful suggestions for people who would like to lose some weight and keep it off. Following a self-help manual can be successful (Wing et al., 1982).

How to Lose Weight: A Brief Manual   There is no mystery about it. Successful weight-control programs do not involve fad diets. Instead, they tend to focus on (1) improving nutritional knowledge, (2) decreasing calorie intake, (3) exercise, and (4) behavior modification (Epstein et al., 1985; Israel et al., 1985; Stalonas & Kirschenbaum, 1985). Losing weight means burning more calories than you consume. You can accomplish that in part by eating less and by exchanging some high-calorie foods (such as ice cream and butter) for low-calorie foods (such as vegetables and diet margarine). Acquiring nutritional knowledge helps the individual select low-calorie healthful foods (such as vegetables, fruits, fish and poultry, and whole grain breads and cereals).

Why exercise? For many reasons. First, exercise burns calories (Epstein et al., 1984b). Dieting plus exercise is more effective than dieting alone (Epstein et al., 1984a). But there is another reason to exercise. As noted earlier, our metabolic rates tend to decrease when we diet as a compensatory measure (Apfelbaum, 1978; Polivy & Herman, 1985). This decrease can frustrate dieters severely. Many dieters complain they reach "plateaus" from which they cannot shed additional pounds, even though they eat very little. Exercise seems to help by maintaining the metabolic rate at higher levels throughout the day, even though we are restricting calories (Donahoe et al., 1984).

And so, here are a number of suggestions for losing weight. They are largely based on principles of behavior modification (see Chapter 10) and involve exercise and restricting calories:

Establish calorie-intake goals and heighten awareness of whether you are meeting them. Acquire a calorie-counting book and keep a diary of your calorie intake.

Use low-calorie substitutes for high-calorie foods. Fill your stomach with celery rather than cheese cake and burritos. Eat preplanned low-calorie snacks rather than binge on peanuts or ice cream.

Establish eating patterns similar to those of internal eaters. Take small bites. Chew thoroughly. Take a five-minute break between helpings. Ask yourself if you're still hungry. If not, stop eating.

Avoid sources of external stimulation (temptations) to which you have succumbed in the past. Shop at the mall with the Alfalfa Sprout, not the Gushy Gloppe Shoppe. Plan your meal before entering a restaurant and avoid ogling that tempting full-color menu. Attend to your own plate, not the sumptuous dish at the next table. (Your salad probably looks greener to them, anyhow.) Shop from a list, after dinner when you're no longer hungry. Don't be sidetracked by pretty packages (fattening things may come in them). Keep out of the kitchen. Study, watch television, write letters elsewhere. Keep fattening foods out of the house. Prepare only enough food to remain within your calorie-intake goals.

Exercise to burn more calories and maintain your pre-dieting metabolic rate. Reach for your mate, not your plate (to coin a phrase). Build exercise routines by a few minutes each week.

Reward yourself when you've met a weekly calorie-intake goal—but not with food. Imagine how great you'll look in that new swimsuit next summer.

Mentally rehearse solutions to problem situations. Consider how you will politely refuse when cake is handed out at the office party. Rehearse your next visit to parents or other relatives—the ones who tell you how painfully thin you look. Imagine how you'll politely refuse seconds and thirds, despite protestations.

Above all, if you slip from your plan for a day, do not catastrophize. Dieters are frequently tempted to binge, especially when they insist on viewing themselves rigidly as either perfect successes or complete failures (Polivy & Herman, 1985). Do not tell yourself you're a failure and then go on a binge. Consider the *weekly* trend, not just a day, and resume your strategies the next day. Even if you binge, resume the diet the next day.

Thirst

Our bodies need fluids as well as food in order to survive. We may survive without food for several weeks, but we will last only for a few days without water. It has been speculated that thirst is a stronger drive than hunger because animals who have been deprived of food and water will typically drink before eating when given the opportunity to do both. Critics of this view note that hungry animals must take in fluids to produce saliva and other digestive fluids before eating.

Physiological mechanisms maintain a proper fluid level in the body. When there is excess fluid, we are not likely to feel thirsty and our bodies form urine. When there is a fluid deficiency, we are likely to experience a thirst drive and our bodies are less likely to form urine.

Since we may experience thirst as dryness in the mouth and throat, it was once thought that receptors in the mouth and throat played a major role in determining thirst or satiety. But it seems that receptors in the kidney and hypothalamus play more central roles in regulating the thirst drive.

Regulation of Thirst in the Kidneys When the body is depleted of fluids, the flow of blood through the kidneys drops off. In response to this decreased flow of blood, the kidneys secrete the hormone **angiotensin.** Angiotensin, in turn, signals the hypothalamus of fluid depletion.

The Role of the Hypothalamus: On Shriveled Cells and Salty Pretzels

Osmoreceptors in the hypothalamus can also detect fluid depletion from changes that occur within the brain. The brain, like the rest of the body, becomes fluid-depleted. Fluid depletion causes the osmoreceptor cells to shrivel, which in and of itself may trigger thirst.

Another osmoreceptor signal involves the concentration of chemicals in body fluids. As the volume of water in the body decreases, the concentration of chemicals in the water, such as sodium (which combines with chlorine to make salt) increases. (Think of a pool of salt water evaporating in the sun. The salt does *not* evaporate, only the water, and the remaining water becomes increasingly salty. If all the water evaporated, there would be nothing left but a crust of salt.) An increasing concentration of salt can also signal the osmoreceptors that the body's water supply is falling.

In a classic experiment, an injection of a salt solution into a goat's hypothalamus triggered heavy intake of fluids, even though the goat had just drunk its fill (Andersson, 1971). Injection of salt-free water caused the animal *not* to drink, apparently by "fooling" the osmoreceptors into behaving as though there were a higher level of fluids throughout the body. Did you ever wonder why bartenders are usually happy to provide customers with "free" salty peanuts and salty pretzels? As the salt is dissolved into body fluids, the customer becomes thirsty again, even though he or she may also be making frequent trips to the bathroom in order to urinate.

The hypothalamus responds to signs of dehydration transmitted by osmoreceptors in at least two ways: (1) It signals the pituitary gland to secrete **antidiuretic hormone** (ADH). ADH causes the kidneys to reabsorb urine—a water-conservation measure. (2) The hypothalamus signals the cerebral cortex. As a result, we experience the thirst drive.

Our responses to thirst are varied and largely learned. Some of us go to the tap for water. Others brew coffee or tea. Still others prefer juice or a soft drink. The time of day, social custom, and individual preferences all play a role in deciding which fluids will be drunk.

External cues may also stimulate us to drink, as they can stimulate us to eat—even in the absence of internal cues for thirst. Watching someone squeeze an orange or hearing a cork pop can make us desire orange juice or champagne. We may also drink alcohol to earn the approval of drinking buddies or for whatever incentives the sensations of intoxication may provide.

Sleep

Sleep has always been a fascinating topic. After all, we spend about one-third of our adult lives sleeping. Most of us complain when we do not sleep at least six hours or so, but some people sleep for an hour or less a day and lead otherwise healthy and normal lives.

What happens during sleep? Why do we sleep? Why do we dream?

The Stages of Sleep

When I was an undergraduate, I learned that psychologists studied sleep by "connecting" people to the electroencephalograph (EEG), a device that measures the electrical activity of the brain. I had a gruesome image of people being "plugged in" to the EEG. Not so. Electrodes are simply attached to the scalp with tape or paste. A bit of soap and water, and you're as good as new.

The EEG provides some scrawls that show the frequency and strength of the electric currents of the brain (see Figure 6.3). During the deepest stage of sleep—or stage 4 sleep—there are only one to three cycles of this current each second. So the printouts in Figure 6.3 show what happens over a period of 15 seconds or so. During stage 4 sleep, the brain emits slow but strong delta waves. Delta waves reach relatively great height or amplitude,

---

Angiotensin A kidney hormone that signals the hypothalamus of bodily depletion of fluids.

Osmoreceptors Receptors in the hypothalamus that are sensitive to depletion of fluid.

Antidiuretic hormone A pituitary hormone that conserves body fluids by increasing the reabsorption of urine.

The waking state

Stage 1 sleep

Figure 6.3. What Are the Stages of Sleep? This figure illustrates typical EEG patterns for the stages of sleep. During REM sleep, EEG patterns resemble those of the lightest stage of sleep, stage 1 sleep. For this reason, REM sleep is often termed *paradoxical sleep*. As sleep progresses from stage 1 to stage 4, brain waves become slower and their amplitude increases. Dreams, including normal nightmares, are most vivid during REM sleep. More disturbing night terrors tend to occur during stage 4 sleep.

Stage 2 sleep

Stage 3 sleep

Stage 4 sleep

Rapid-eye-movement (REM) sleep

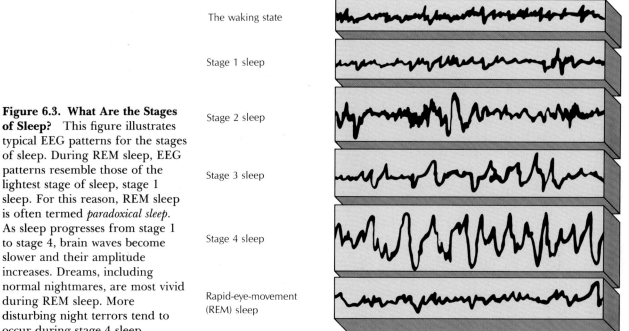

when compared with other brain waves. Their amplitude reflects their strength. The strength or energy of brain waves is expressed in the electric unit volts.

Figure 6.4 shows five stages of sleep: four stages of **non-rapid-eye-movement** (NREM) **sleep** and one stage of **rapid-eye-movement** (REM) **sleep.** When we close our eyes and begin to relax before going to sleep, our brains emit many alpha waves. Alpha waves are low-amplitude brain waves of about eight to twelve cycles per second. (Through biofeedback training, discussed in Chapter 4, people have been taught to relax by purposefully emitting alpha waves.)

As we enter stage 1 sleep, our brain waves slow down from the alpha rhythm and enter a pattern of theta waves. Theta waves have a frequency of four to six cycles per second and are accompanied by slow, rolling eye movements. The transition from alpha waves to theta waves may be accompanied by a **hypnagogic state,** during which we may experience brief hallucinatory, dreamlike images that resemble vivid photographs. These images may be somehow linked to creativity. Stage 1

sleep is the lightest stage of sleep. If we are awakened from stage 1 sleep, we may feel that we have not slept at all.

After 30 to 40 minutes of stage 1 sleep, we undergo a rather steep descent into sleep stages 2, 3, and 4 (see Figure 6.4). Stage 4 is the deepest stage of sleep, from which it is most difficult to be awakened. During stage 2, **sleep spindles** appear. These are rather short bursts of rapid brain waves of a frequency of 13 to 16 cycles per second. During stages 3 and 4, we produce the slower delta waves.

Non-rapid-eye-movement sleep. Stages of sleep 1 through 4.

Rapid-eye-movement sleep A stage of sleep characterized by rapid eye movements, which have been linked to dreaming.

Hypnagogic state The drowsy interval between waking and sleeping, characterized by brief, hallucinatory, dreamlike experiences.

Sleep spindles Short bursts of rapid brain waves that occur during stage 2 sleep.

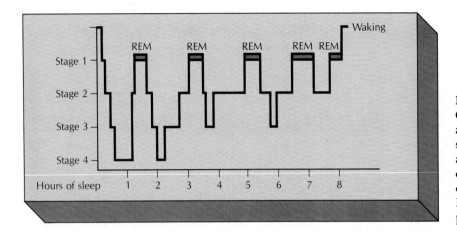

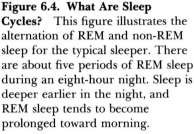

Figure 6.4. What Are Sleep Cycles? This figure illustrates the alternation of REM and non-REM sleep for the typical sleeper. There are about five periods of REM sleep during an eight-hour night. Sleep is deeper earlier in the night, and REM sleep tends to become prolonged toward morning.

After half an hour or so of stage 4 sleep, we begin a relatively rapid journey back upward through the stages until we enter REM sleep (Figure 6.4). REM sleep derives its name from the *rapid eye movements*, observable beneath our closed lids, that characterize this stage. During REM sleep we produce relatively rapid, low-amplitude brain waves that resemble those of light stage 1 sleep. REM sleep is also called paradoxical sleep. This is because the EEG patterns observed during REM sleep suggest a level of arousal similar to that of the waking state (Figure 6.4). However, we are difficult to awaken during REM sleep. If we are awakened during REM sleep, we report that we have been dreaming 80 percent of the time. (We report dreaming only about 20 percent of the time when awakened during NREM sleep.)

We tend to undergo five trips through the stages of sleep each night. These trips include about five periods of REM sleep. Our first journey through stage 4 sleep is usually longest. Sleep tends to become lighter as the night wears on. Our periods of REM sleep tend to become longer and, toward morning, our last period of REM sleep may last upward of half an hour.

Now that we have some idea of what sleep is like, let us examine the issue of *why* we sleep.

Functions of Sleep One outdated theory suggested that sleep allows the brain to rest and recuperate from the stresses of the day. But the EEG has shown that the brain is active all night long. Moreover, at least during REM sleep, brain waves are quite similar to those of light sleep and the waking state. So the power isn't switched off at night.

What of sleep and the rest of the body? Most researchers concur that sleep helps rejuvenate a tired body (Levitt, 1981). Most of us have had the experience of going without sleep for a night and feeling "wrecked" the following day. Perhaps the following evening we went to bed early to "get our sleep back." Research also suggests that increased physical exertion leads to a greater proportion of time spent in NREM sleep (Walker et al., 1978). Many proteins are synthesized during NREM sleep, and they might be linked to the restorative effects of sleep (Hartmann, 1973). However, no one has yet discovered a relationship between sleep and the restoration of specific chemical substances.

Some people sleep longer than others. Some seem to need only a few hours, whereas others would sleep away half the day if allowed to do so. Hartmann (1973) compared people who slept nine hours or more a night ("long sleepers") with people who slept six hours or less ("short sleepers"). He found that short sleepers tended to be more happy-go-lucky. They spent less time ruminating and were energetic, active, and relatively self-satisfied. The long sleepers were more concerned about personal achievement and social causes. They tended to be more creative and thoughtful but were also more anxious and depressed. Hartmann also found that we tend to need more sleep during periods of change and stress, such as a change of jobs, an increase in work load, or an episode of depression. So it may be that sleep helps us recover from the stresses of life.

Hartmann also found that long sleepers spend proportionately more time in REM sleep than do short sleepers. Subtracting the amount of REM sleep experienced by both types of sleepers dramatically closed the gap between them. Perhaps REM sleep is at least partially responsible for the restorative function. Since much REM sleep is spent in dreaming, it has been speculated that dreams may somehow promote recovery.

What are the effects of sleep deprivation? What will happen if you miss sleep for a night? For several nights? Carefully controlled experiments with people who remain sleepless for several consecutive days result in few serious disturbances. Most often, participants show temporary problems in attention, confusion, or misperception (Goleman, 1982). These cognitive lapses might reflect brief episodes of borderline sleep.

In some studies, animals or people have been deprived of REM sleep. With people, this deprivation is accomplished by monitoring EEG records and eye movements and waking subjects during REM sleep. Animals deprived of REM sleep learn more slowly and forget what they have learned more rapidly (Hartmann & Stern, 1972; Pearlman & Greenberg, 1973). Deprivation of REM sleep interferes with human memory—that is, the retrieval of information that has been learned earlier (Bloch et al., 1979; Cipolli & Salzarulo, 1978). People deprived of REM sleep tend to show *REM-rebound*. That is, they subsequently spend more time in REM sleep. They catch up.

As noted earlier, it is during REM sleep that we tend to dream. Let us now turn our attention to dreams, a mystery about which people have theorized for centuries.

Dreams Just what is the stuff of dreams? Dreams are a form of cognitive activity that occurs during sleep. Like vivid memories and daytime fantasies, dreams involve visual images in the absence of external visual stimulation. Some dreams are so realistic and well organized that we feel they must be real. Other dreams are disorganized and unformed.

Dreams are most vivid during REM sleep. Then they are most likely to have clear imagery and coherent plots, even if some of the content is fantastic. Plots are vaguer and images more fleeting during NREM sleep. You might dream every time you are in REM sleep. Therefore, if you sleep for eight hours and undergo five sleep cycles, you might have five dreams. Dreams tend to take place in "real time": Fifteen minutes of events fills about 15 minutes of dreaming. Your dream theater is quite flexible: You can dream in black and white and in full color.

According to Calvin Hall (1966), who has interviewed hundreds of dreamers and recorded the content of thousands of dreams, most dreams are simple extensions of the activities and problems of the day. Hall links dreams to life's stresses. If we are preoccupied with illness or death, sexual or aggressive urges, or moral dilemmas, we are likely to dream about them. The characters in our dreams are more likely to be friends and neighbors than spies, monsters, and princes.

Sigmund Freud theorized that dreams reflect unconscious wishes and urges. He argued that through dreams we express impulses that we would censor during the day. Moreover, the content of dreams symbolizes unconscious fantasized objects, such as genital organs. Freud also believed that dreams "protect sleep" by providing imagery that helps keep disturbing thoughts out of awareness. The view that dreams protect sleep has been challenged by the finding that disturbing events tend to be followed by related disturbing dreams—not protective imagery (Foulkes, 1971). Our behavior in dreams is also generally consistent with our waking behavior (Carrington, 1972; Cohen, 1973). Moralistic people usually do not run amok in dreams.

According to the **activation-synthesis model** proposed by J. Alan Hobson and Robert W. McCarley (1977), dreams reflect biological rather than psychological activity. A time-triggered mechanism in the pons stimulates three kinds of responses: One is *activation* of the reticular activating system (RAS), which arouses us, but not to the point of waking. The eye muscles also respond, showing the rapid eye movement associated with

Activation-synthesis model The view that dreams reflect stimulation of neural activity by the pons and automatic integration of this activity by the cerebral cortex.

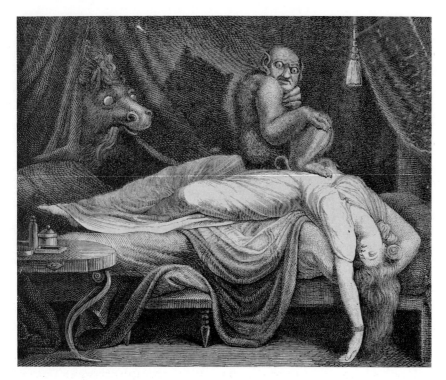

The Nightmare.   In some nightmares it seems as if we have a heavy weight on the chest, as of someone or something sitting there.

dreaming. A third is general inhibition of motor (muscular) activity, so that we don't thrash about as we dream; in this way, we save ourselves (and our bed partners) wear and tear. The RAS also stimulates neural activity in the parts of the cortex involved in vision, hearing, and memory. This activity is automatically *synthesized,* or put together, by the cerebral cortex. There is a strong tendency to dream about the day's events because the most current neural activity would be that which represented the events or concerns of the day.

Sex

People might be said to "hunger" or "thirst" for sex, but the sex drive differs from hunger and thirst in that sex might be necessary for the sur-

vival of the species but not for that of the individual (despite occasional claims to the effect "I'll simply *die* unless you . . .").

There are also similarities among the hunger, thirst, and sex drives. All three can be triggered by external cues as well as internal processes. The sex drive can be triggered by the thought of a loved one, a whiff of perfume, or a wink.

In Chapter 3 we noted that pheromones play a major role in sexual behavior among lower animals and might play a motivational role in the sexual behavior of some human beings. In this section, we focus on a number of issues concerning sexual motivation, including the organizing and activating influences of sex hormones and the issues involved in pornography, homosexuality, and forcible rape.

Organizing effects   The possible directional effects (i.e., heterosexual or homosexual) of sex hormones.

Activating effects   The arousal-producing effects of sex hormones.

Organizing and Activating Effects of Sex Hormones

Sex hormones not only promote sexual differentiation and regulate the menstrual cycle. They also have **organizing effects** and **activating effects** on sexual behavior. They predispose lower animals toward masculine or feminine mating patterns (an organizing effect). They also influence the sex drive and facilitate sexual response (activating effects).

Male rats who have been castrated at birth—and thus deprived of testosterone—make no effort to mate as adults. But when they receive *female* sex hormones in adulthood, they become receptive to the sexual advances of other males and assume female mating stances (Harris & Levine, 1965). Male rats who are castrated in adulthood also show no sexual behavior. But if they receive injections of testosterone, they resume male sexual behaviors.

Female mice, rats, cats, and dogs are receptive to males only during **estrus,** when female sex hormones are plentiful. The sex organs of female rodents exposed to large doses of testosterone in the uterus (because they share the uterus with many brothers or because of injections) become masculinized in appearance. These females are also predisposed toward masculine mating behaviors. If they are given testosterone as adults, they attempt to mount other females about as often as males do (Goy & Goldfoot, 1975). Prenatal testosterone might have "organized" the brain in the masculine direction, predisposing the rats toward masculine sexual behaviors in adulthood when "activated" by additional testosterone.

Testosterone is also important in the behavior of human males. Men who are castrated or given drugs that decrease the amount of androgens in the blood stream usually show gradual loss of sexual desire and of the capacities for erection and orgasm. Still, many castrated men remain sexually active for years, suggesting that for many people fantasies, memories, and other cognitive stimuli are as important as hormones in sexual motivation. Beyond minimal levels, there is no clear link between testosterone level and sexual arousal. For example, sleeping men are *not* more likely to have erections during surges in the testosterone level (Schiavi et al., 1977).

Unlike females of most other species, women are sexually responsive during all phases of the menstrual cycle, even during menstruation itself, when hormone levels are low, and even after **menopause.** But androgens may influence female as well as male sexual response. Women whose adrenal glands and ovaries have been removed (so that they no longer produce androgens) may gradually

lose sexual interest and the capacity for sexual response. An active and enjoyable sexual history seems to ward off loss of sexual capacity, suggestive of the importance of cognitive and experiential factors in human sexual motivation.

Pornography Since the late 1960s, when the Supreme Court ruled that prohibiting explicit sexual materials violated freedom of expression, pornography has been a boom industry in the United States. Some people complain that the availability of pornography has led to a breakdown in moral standards. Women's groups have argued that pornography inspires crimes of violence against women. In this section we review research bearing on two important questions concerning pornography: What are the effects of pornography? Does pornography inspire antisocial behavior?

In the 1960s, Congress created a presidential Commission on Obscenity and Pornography to review research on pornography and conduct its own studies. The commission concluded that married couples exposed to pornography reported feeling sexually aroused but were not motivated to try observed sexual activities that were "deviant" for them (Abelson et al., 1970). More recent studies with participants ranging from middle-aged couples to college students have attained similar results.

In a more recent study, undergraduates of both sexes were exposed to six pornographic films a week over a six-week period (Zillmann & Bryant, 1983). Generally speaking, the students became habituated to pornography, as shown by lessened sexual response to new pornographic films by the end of the study. The films included examples of sadomasochism and sex with animals, and by the end of the study, the students also showed less revulsion to these activities. Overexposure to deviant sex can apparently desensitize the viewer.

It is folklore that men are most sexually responsive to explicit, "hard-core" sexual materials and fantasies. Women, however, are considered

---

Estrus The periodic sexual excitement of many female mammals, during which they are receptive to sexual advances by males.

Menopause The cessation of menstruation.

What Are the Effects of Pornography? Does pornography trigger crimes of violence against women?

more romantic, and thus more likely to be sexually aroused by affectionate, "soft-core" themes. But psychologist Julia Heiman (1975) found that hard-core erotica is not for men only. She played audiotapes with romantic or sexually explicit content while college students' responses were measured by the **penile strain gauge** and the **vaginal photoplethysmograph.** She found that explicit sex, with or without romantic trappings, was sexually arousing to both women and men.

In recent years feminists and others have argued that pornography degrades women and supports stereotypes of women as submissive to the needs of men (Blakely, 1985). They have charged that materials that depict sexual and other types of violence against women encourages male viewers to abuse women. Experiments appear to support their concerns. That is, exposure to aggressive-

erotic films (films that depict forcible rape explicitly) may increase violence, even among normal college men (Donnerstein, 1980; Donnerstein & Linz, 1984; Malamuth et al., 1980).

A review of such research by the Attorney General's Commission on Pornography concluded, in 1986, that explicit sexual materials are a cause of violence against women. A follow-up workshop organized by the Surgeon General C. Everett Koop (1987) made three points about depictions of sexual *aggression:* (1) "Pornography that portrays sexual aggression as pleasurable to the victim increases the acceptance of the use of coercion in sexual relations"; (2) "Acceptance of coercive sexuality appears to be related to sexual aggression"; and (3) "In laboratory studies measuring short-term effects, exposure to violent pornography increases punitive behavior toward women" (p. 945).

As noted by Donnerstein and Linz (1987), the Attorney General's Report (1986) misses the point because commission members *did not separate the effects of explicit sexual materials from those of violent materials.* There is still no evidence that explicit sexual materials *in the absence of violence* stimulate antisocial behavior. Donnerstein and Linz assert that "It is not sex, but violence that is an obscenity in our society" (1986, p. 56). The same critique can

Penile strain gauge An instrument that measures size of erection.

Vaginal photoplethysmograph An instrument that measures sexual arousal in women as a function of blood pressure in the vaginal wall.

Why Have Homosexuals Demonstrated in Recent Years? During the past few decades, homosexuals have been vocal in their demands for equal protection under the law.

be made of Koop's (1987) remarks; that is, they do not distinguish between pornography and violent pornography. As a matter of fact, the only statement that Koop's (1987) workshop could agree on concerning the effects of nonviolent pornography on adults is that "Prolonged use of pornography increases beliefs that less common sexual practices are more common" (p. 945).

In sum, if legislation were to be considered to answer the legitimate concerns of women who argue against the availability of *violent* pornography, it might be that the Swedish approach of outlawing portrayals of *violence* rather than sexual behavior per se is more on target. The desire to curtail *nonviolent* pornography is based on moral, not scientific, grounds; research has failed to demonstrate that it has a harmful impact on adults. Moreover, Linz, Donnerstein, and Penrod (1987) argue that educational programs might be able to decrease many of the negative effects of sexual violence in the media. The question of what, if anything, should and can be done about pornography is a controversial issue that is likely to remain with us for some time to come. As the debate rages on, it is useful to separate moral issues from scientific issues, and moral judgments from scientific findings.

Homosexuality   **Homosexuality,** or a homosexual sexual *orientation,* is defined as erotic response to members of one's own sex. Sexual activity with member's of one's own sex is not in and of itself evidence of homosexuality since it may reflect limited sexual opportunities or even ritualistic cultural practices, as in the case of the New Guinean Sambia people. For instance, U.S. adolescent boys may masturbate one another while fantasizing about girls. Men in prisons may similarly turn to each other for sexual outlets. Sambian male youths engage exclusively in homosexual practices with older males since it is believed they must drink "men's milk" in order to achieve the fierce manhood of the headhunter (Money, 1987). But their behavior turns exclusively heterosexual once they reach marrying age.

Kinsey and his colleagues (1948, 1953) estimated that as many as 37 percent of the men and 13 percent of the women in his sample had had at

> **Homosexuality** A pattern of sexual behavior characterized by sexual response to, and formation of romantic relationships with, members of one's own sex.

least one homosexual encounter, whereas only about 4 percent of his male and 1 to 3 percent of his female subjects had a homosexual orientation. About 2 percent of the men and 1 percent of the women in a more recent survey reported a homosexual orientation (Hunt, 1974).

The causes of homosexuality are controversial. It was once thought that homosexuality might be genetically transmitted. Kallmann (1952) found a 100 percent **concordance** rate for homosexuality among the **probands** of 40 identical twins. However, more recent studies (e.g., Parker, 1964; McConaghy & Blaszczynski, 1980; Zuger, 1976) have failed to replicate Kallmann's findings. Psychologist John Money concludes that homosexuality is "not under the direct governance of chromosomes and genes" (1987, p. 384).

But what of sex hormones? Sex hormones influence the mating behavior of lower animals, and it was thought that gay males might be deficient in testosterone, whereas lesbians might have lower-than-normal levels of estrogen and higher-than-normal levels of androgens in their bloodstreams. However, recent studies do not show reliable differences in current hormone levels between heterosexuals and homosexuals (Feder, 1984).

Still, there are other ways in which sex hormones might be related to sexual orientation. Prenatal sex hormones not only cause differentiation of male and female sex organs; they also "masculinize" or "feminize" the brain in the ways that they direct the development of certain brain structures. It is possible that the brains of some gay males have been prenatally feminized and that the brains of some lesbians have been prenatally masculinized (Money, 1987). Even so, Money argues that prenatal hormonal influences would not induce "robotlike" sexual orientation in humans, and that socialization—or early learning experience—is also a determinant of homosexuality in humans.

The causes of human homosexuality are mysterious and complex. The current status of the research suggests that they might involve the interaction of prenatal hormonal influences and postnatal socialization experiences.

Concordance Agreement.
Proband The family member first studied or tested.

Forcible Rape Forcible rape is the seeking of sexual gratification against the will of another person. There are more than 90,000 reported cases of rape in the United States each year (Allgeier & Allgeier, 1984). Since it has been estimated that only one rape in five is reported, it may be that as many as 450,000 rapes take place in the United States each year. Nine percent of a sample of 6,159 women reported that they had given in to sexual intercourse as a result of threats or physical force (Koss et al., 1987). Up to 2 million instances of forced sex might occur within marriage each year.

If we add to these figures instances in which women are subjected to forced kissing and petting, the numbers grow more alarming. For example, nearly 70 percent of 282 women in one college sample had been assaulted (usually by dates and friends) at some time since entering college (Kanin & Parcell, 1977). At a major university, 40 percent of 201 male students surveyed admitted to using force to unfasten a woman's clothing, and 13 percent reported that they had forced a woman to engage in sexual intercourse (Rapaport & Burkhart, 1984). Forty-four percent of the college women in the Koss study (Koss et al., 1987) reported that they had "given in to sex play" because of a "man's continual arguments and pressure."

Why do men coerce women into sexual activity? Many social scientists argue that sexual motivation often has little to do with it. Rape, they argue, is more often a man's way of expressing anger toward, or power over, women (Groth & Birnbaum, 1979). In fact, many rapists have long records as violent offenders (Amir, 1971). With some rapists, violence also appears to enhance sexual arousal, so that they are motivated to combine sex with aggression (Quinsey et al., 1984).

Many social critics also assert that our culture socializes men into becoming rapists (Burt, 1980). Males, who are often reinforced for aggressive and competitive behavior, could be said to be asserting culturally expected dominance over women. Sexually coercive college males, as a group, are more likely to believe that aggression is a legitimate form of behavior than are noncoercive college males (Rapaport & Burkhart, 1984).

Women, on the other hand, may be socialized into the victim role. The stereotypical feminine role encourages passivity, nurturance, warmth,

60 Minutes

Depo-Provera

Are rapists in control of their own behavior? Should convicted rapists be thrown into prison?

One new treatment for rapists suggests that at least some rapists are not always in charge of their own behavior. And to the dismay of many rape victims, judges, and others, they are participating in experimental treatment programs rather than spending terms in prison.

As reported on a 60 Minutes segment by correspondent Ed Bradley, the experimental treatment is a drug called Depo-Provera, which has the effect of lowering testosterone levels in rapists. According to Dr. Fred Berlin of Johns Hopkins University Hospital, who was interviewed on the segment, many rapists are career criminals without a conscience, and drugs are not the answer for them. However—again according to Berlin—some rapists have unusually high levels of testosterone in their blood, and high levels of this hormone create intense sex drives that they have difficulty controlling.

Although conclusive findings are not yet in, a San Antonio rapist interviewed on the segment stated,

I'm not the monster [people] think I am. I'm a person with a problem. And if it's controllable, why put me in prison for five years and let me back out on the street with the same problem? And [Depo-Provera] reduces the sex drive to where I can change. With—with the drug, I have no sex drive.

Berlin did not explain why these men with high levels of testosterone raped strangers instead of engaging in more frequent sexual activity with wives or girlfriends—or why they chose rape over masturbation. Judge Tom Rickhoff, also interviewed, argued that rapists in this program should be sent to prison like other rapists. Why? Rickhoff argued,

[Prison] tells him that there is a punishment for crime. It forces him to recognize that he doesn't just have a psychological problem or a chemical problem in his body. His problem is he's raping people. . . . If he's going to get through life thinking he's got a chemical imbalance, what's to prevent him from going out and committing another violent rape? What's to prevent him is the punishment of confinement. That's why we have prisons, punishment.

Ed Bradley also asked a woman rape victim whether she thought that prison would do the rapist any good. She replied, "I'm sorry, Ed, but I'm not very much concerned with what's going to do *him* any good."

---

and cooperation. Women are often taught to sacrifice for their families and not to raise their voices. Thus a woman may be totally unprepared to cope with an assailant. She may lack aggressive skills and believe that violence is inappropriate for women. Mary Beth Myers and her colleagues (1984) found that rape victims are less dominant and self-assertive than nonvictims—that is, their behavior is more consistent with what society expects of women. Victimization is not a random process, and women who appear vulnerable are apparently more likely than others to be attacked (Myers et al., 1985).

Many people, including professionals who work with rapists and victims, believe a number of myths about rape. These include "Only bad girls get raped," "Any healthy woman can resist a rapist if she wants to," and "Women only cry rape when they've been jilted or have something to cover up" (Burt, 1980, p. 217). These myths tend to deny the impact of the assault and also to place blame on the victim rather than her assailant. They contribute to a social "climate" that is too often lenient toward rapists and unsympathetic toward victims.

In *The New Our Bodies, Ourselves*, The Boston Women's Health Book Collective (1984) lists a number of suggestions that women can use to lower the likelihood of rape: Establish signals and arrangements with other women in an apartment building or neighborhood. List only first initials in the telephone directory or on the mailbox. Use dead-bolt locks. Keep windows locked and obtain iron grids for first-floor windows. Keep entrances and doorways brightly lit. Have keys ready for the front door or the car. Do not walk alone in the dark. Avoid deserted areas.

Also, never allow a strange man into your apartment or home without checking his credentials. Drive with the car windows up and the door locked. Check the rear seat of the car before entering. Avoid living in an unsafe building. Do not pick up hitchhikers. Do not talk to strange men in the street. Shout "Fire!" not "Rape!" People crowd around fires but avoid scenes of violence.

STIMULUS MOTIVES

Physical needs give rise to the drives of hunger and thirst. In these cases, we are motivated to *reduce* tension or stimulation that impinges on us. In the case of **stimulus motives,** our goals are to *increase* the amount of stimulation impinging on us. Stimulus motives include sensory stimulation, activity, exploration, and manipulation of the environment.

Stimulus motives, like physiological motives, are generally considered innate. People might be motivated to seek the level of stimulation that produces an *optimal level of arousal*—that is, a general level of activity or motivation at which they feel their best and behave most effectively.

Some stimulus motives provide a clear evolutionary advantage. People and lower animals who are motivated to learn about and manipulate the environment are more likely to survive. Learning about the environment increases awareness of re-

Stimulus motives Motives to increase the stimulation impinging upon an organism.

Sensory deprivation Referring to a research method for systematically decreasing the amount of stimulation that impinges upon sensory receptors.

sources and of potential dangers, and manipulation can permit us to change the environment in beneficial ways. Learning and manipulation increase our chances of surviving until sexual maturity and of passing on whatever genetic codes may underlie these motives to future generations.

Sensory Stimulation and Activity

During the 1950s some lucky students at McGill University were paid $20 a day (which, with inflation, would be well above $100 today) for doing absolutely nothing. How would you like such "work"? Don't answer too quickly. According to the results of such experiments in **sensory deprivation,** which were run by Bexton, Heron, and Scott (1954), you might find it intolerable.

Student volunteers were placed in isolation booths. In these quiet cubicles, they were blindfolded, their arms were bandaged, and they could hear nothing but the dull, continuous hum of the air conditioning (Figure 6.5). With nothing to do, many students slept for a while. After a few hours of sensory-deprived wakefulness, most students felt bored and irritable. As time went on, they became increasingly uncomfortable. A number of them reported visual hallucinations, usually restricted to simple images of dots and geometric shapes (Zubek, 1973).

Many subjects quit during the first day despite the financial incentive and the desire to contribute to scientific knowledge. Those who remained found it temporarily difficult to concentrate on even the simplest problems after several days of sensory deprivation. All in all, the experimental conditions did not provide a relaxing vacation. Instead, they proved to be a nightmare of boredom and disorientation.

Some people seek higher levels of stimulation and activity than others. John is a "couch potato," content to sit by the TV set all evening; but Marsha doesn't feel right unless she's out on the tennis court or jogging. Cliff isn't content unless he has ridden his motorcycle over back trails at breakneck speeds, and Janet feels exuberance in the chest when she's catching the big wave or diving freefall from an airplane. One's preference for tennis, motorcycling, or skydiving will reflect one's geographical location, social class, and learning experiences. But it may just be that the levels of arousal at which we are comfortable would be too high or too low for other people. It may also be that these levels are determined to some degree by innate factors.

Exploration and Manipulation

Have you ever brought a dog or cat into a new home? At first they may show general excitement. New kittens are even known to hide under a couch

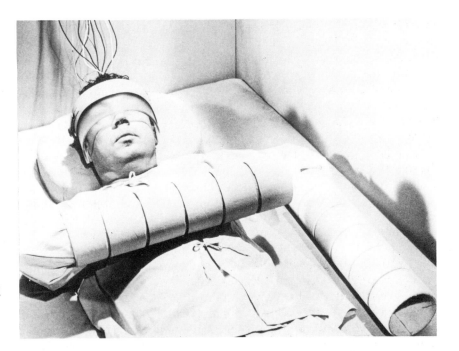

Figure 6.5. What Are Sensory Deprivation Experiments Like? He sees, hears, and touches "no evil"—nor anything else, for that matter. Experimental conditions such as these do not produce a restful vacation. Instead, volunteers become quickly bored and irritable, and many quit after only a few hours, despite financial incentives. Apparently we have strong motives for sensory stimulation.

Do We Have Innate Needs for Sensory Stimulation and Activity? Why do some people leap into the sky for sport? Perhaps they are trying to raise their body arousal to more stimulating levels.

Questionnaire

The sensation-seeking scale

Are you content reading or watching television all day? Or must you catch the big wave or bounce the bike across the dunes of the Mohave Desert? Psychologist Marvin Zuckerman (1980) has developed a number of sensation-seeking scales that measure the level of stimulation or arousal a person will seek and predict how well the person will fare in sensory-deprivation studies.

Zuckerman and his colleagues (1978) found four factors involved in sensation seeking: (1) seeking thrill and adventure, (2) disinhibition (that is, tendency to express impulses), (3) seeking of experience, and (4) susceptibility to boredom. Other studies show that people high in sensation seeking are less tolerant of sensory deprivation. Sensation seekers are also more likely to use drugs and become involved in sexual experiences, to be drunk in public, and to volunteer for high-risk activities and unusual experiments (Kohn et al., 1979; Malatesta et al., 1981; Zuckerman, 1974).

A shortened version of one of Zuckerman's scales follows. To gain insight into your own sensation-seeking tendencies, circle the choice, A or B, that best describes you. Then compare your answers to those in the answer key in Appendix C.

1. **A.** I would like a job that requires a lot of traveling.
   B. I would prefer a job in one location.
2. **A.** I am invigorated by a brisk, cold day.
   B. I can't wait to get indoors on a cold day.

or bed for a few hours. But then they will begin to explore every corner of the new environment. When placed in novel environments, many animals appear to possess an innate motive to engage in exploratory behavior.

Once familiar with the environment, lower animals and people appear motivated to seek **novel stimulation.** For example, when they have not been deprived of food for a great deal of time, rats will often explore unfamiliar arms of mazes rather than head straight for the section of the maze in which they have learned to expect food. Animals who have just **copulated** and thereby reduced their sex drives will often show renewed interest in sexual behavior when presented with a novel sex partner. Monkeys will learn how to manipulate gadgets for the incentive of being able to observe novel stimulation through a window (see Figure 6.6). Children will spend hour after hour manipulating the controls of video games for no apparent external reward.

The question has arisen whether people and animals seek to explore and manipulate the environment *because* these activities may help them reduce primary drives, such as hunger and thirst, or whether they will engage in these activities for their own sake. Many psychologists do believe that such stimulating activities are reinforcing in and of

Novel stimulation A hypothesized primary drive to experience new or different stimulation.

Copulate To engage in sexual intercourse.

3. **A.** I get bored seeing the same old faces.
   B. I like the comfortable familiarity of everyday friends.
4. **A.** I would prefer living in an ideal society in which everyone is safe, secure, and happy.
   B. I would have preferred living in the unsettled days of our history.
5. **A.** I sometimes like to do things that are a little frightening.
   B. A sensible person avoids activities that are dangerous.
6. **A.** I would not like to be hypnotized.
   B. I would like to have the experience of being hypnotized.
7. **A.** The most important goal in life is to live it to the fullest and experience as much as possible.
   B. The most important goal in life is to find peace and happiness.
8. **A.** I would like to try parachute-jumping.
   B. I would never want to try jumping out of a plane, with or without a parachute.
9. **A.** I enter cold water gradually, giving myself time to get used to it.
   B. I like to dive or jump right into the ocean or a cold pool.
10. **A.** When I go on a vacation, I prefer the comfort of a good room and bed.
    B. When I go on a vacation, I prefer the change of camping out.
11. **A.** I prefer people who are emotionally expressive even if they are a bit unstable.
    B. I prefer people who are calm and even-tempered.
12. **A.** A good painting should shock or jolt the senses.
    B. A good painting should give one a feeling of peace and security.
13. **A.** People who ride motorcycles must have some kind of unconscious need to hurt themselves.
    B. I would like to drive or ride a motorcycle.

themselves. Monkeys do seem to get a kick from "monkeying around" with gadgets (see Figure 6.7). They will learn how to manipulate hooks and eyes and other mechanical devices without any external incentives whatsoever (Harlow et al., 1950). Children will engage in prolonged play with "busy boxes"—boxes filled with objects that honk, squeak, rattle, and buzz. They seem to find manipulation of these gadgets pleasurable, even though manipulation does not result in food, ice cream, or even hugs from parents.

The Search for Optimal Arousal

Some drives, such as hunger and thirst, are associated with higher levels of **arousal** within an or-ganism. When we eat or drink to reduce these drives, we are also lowering the associated level of arousal. At other times we act to increase our levels of arousal, as in going to a horror film, engaging in athletic activity, or seeking a new sex partner.

How can we explain the apparently contradictory observations that people and lower animals sometimes act to reduce arousal and at other times act to increase arousal? Some psychologists attempt to reconcile these differences by suggesting that we are motivated to seek **optimal arousal**—that is, lev-

Arousal A general level of activity or motivation in an organism.

Optimal arousal The level of arousal at which we feel and function best.

Figure 6.6. Why Does Novel Stimulation Allure Us? People and many lower animals are motivated to explore the environment and seek novel stimulation. This monkey has learned to unlock a door for the privilege of viewing a model train.

els of arousal that are optimal for us as individuals at certain times of the day.

Our levels of arousal can vary from quite low (see Figure 6.8), as in when we are sleeping, to quite high, as when we are frightened or intensely angered. Psychologists also hypothesize that we each have optimal levels of arousal at which we are likely to feel best and function most effectively in various situations. People whose optimal levels of arousal are relatively low may prefer sedentary lives. People whose optimal levels of arousal are high may seek activities such as skydiving and motorcycling, intense problem solving (such as a difficult crossword puzzle), or vivid daydreaming. Psychologists Donald Fiske and Salvatore Maddi argue that people behave in ways that increase the

impact of stimulation when their levels of arousal are too low and decrease the impact of stimulation when their levels are too high (Maddi, 1980). The types of activity they will engage in also depend on such factors as needs for meaningfulness and for variety.

The Yerkes-Dodson Law   A former National Football League linebacker was reported to work himself into such a frenzy before a game that other players gave him a wide berth in the locker room. Linebacking is a relatively simple football job, requiring brute strength and something called "desire" more so than does, say, quarterbacking. This particular linebacker was no stronger than many others, but his level of arousal—or desire—helped his team reach the Superbowl on many occasions.

According to the **Yerkes-Dodson law** (see Figure 6.9), a high level of arousal increases performance on a relatively simple task, whether the task is linebacking or solving a series of simple math problems. When a task is complex it seems helpful to keep one's level of arousal at lower lev-

Yerkes-Dodson law The principle that a high level of motivation increases efficiency in the performance of simple tasks, whereas a lower level of motivation permits greater efficiency in the performance of complex tasks.

els. True, there are some complexities to the linebacker's job. Through experience, the linebacker must acquire the capacity to predict, or "read," the play. But the quarterback's job is more complicated. He must call the plays, sometimes change them at the line of scrimmage because of an unexpected defensive realignment, and "keep a cool head" as his receivers try to break into the open and defenders try to break through the offensive line and tackle him. Similarly, it is worthwhile to try to remain somewhat relaxed on the eve of a demanding (complex) "big test."

"Cool" linebackers and "hotheaded" quarterbacks don't fare well in the professional ranks. Instead, linebackers must "psych themselves up," and quarterbacks must "maintain their cool." Some linebackers convince themselves that the players on the opposing team represent the evil in the uni-

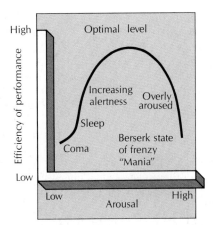

Figure 6.8. How Do Our Levels of Arousal Relate to Our Performance Efficiency? Our optimal levels of arousal may differ somewhat, but they tend to lie somewhere in between sleep and a state of panic. People whose optimal levels of arousal are high will seek more stimulation than people whose optimal levels are low.

verse; some quarterbacks approach their job with computerlike level-headedness.

What motivates people to get involved in contact sports such as football in the first place? Stimulus motives may be a part of the answer, but learned or social motives may also have a good deal to do with it, as we shall see in the next section.

SOCIAL MOTIVES

Money, achievement, social approval, power, aggression—these are examples of **social motives**. Social motives differ from primary motives in that they are acquired through social learning. But like physiological drives and stimulus motives, social motives arouse us and prompt goal-directed behavior.

Harvard University psychologist Henry Murray (1938) is one of the early researchers into social motives. He referred to social motives as psychological needs and compiled a list of 21, including needs for achievement, affiliation, aggression, au-

Figure 6.7. Do We Have an Innate Manipulation Drive? These young rhesus monkeys appear to monkey around with gadgets for the sheer pleasure of monkeying around. No external incentives or reinforcements are needed. Children similarly enjoy manipulating gadgets that honk, squeak, rattle, and buzz, even though the resultant honks and squeaks do not satisfy physiological drives such as hunger or thirst.

Social motives Learned or acquired motives.

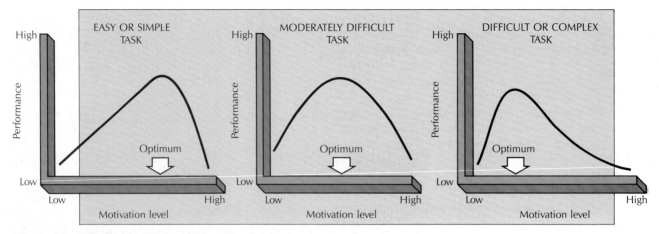

Figure 6.9. What Is the Yerkes-Dodson Law? An easy or simple task may be facilitated by a high level of arousal or motivation. A highly aroused 118-pound woman is reported to have lifted the front end of a two-ton Cadillac in order to rescue a child. But a complex task, such as quarterbacking a football team or attempting to solve a math problem, requires attending to many variables at once. For this reason, a complex task is usually carried out more efficiently at a lower level of arousal.

tonomy, dominance, nurturance, and understanding. Since we undergo different learning experiences, each of us may develop different levels of these psychological needs or give them different priorities. Let us now consider some findings concerning the needs for achievement and affiliation and the circumstances that give rise to them.

The Need for Achievement

We all know people who strive persistently to get ahead, to "make it," to earn vast sums of money, to invent, to accomplish the impossible. These people have a high need for achievement, abbreviated **n Ach.**

Psychologist David McClelland (1958), also of Harvard University, helped pioneer the assessment of *n Ach* through people's reported fantasies.

---

n Ach The need for achievement—to master, to accomplish difficult things.

Thematic Apperception Test A test devised by Henry Murray to measure needs through fantasy production.

One assessment method involves use of the **Thematic Apperception Test** (TAT), developed by Henry Murray. The TAT contains cards with pictures and drawings that are subject to various interpretations (see Chapter 8). Subjects are shown one or more TAT cards and asked to construct stories about the pictured theme—to indicate what led up to it, what the characters are thinking and feeling, and what is likely to happen.

One TAT card shows a boy with a violin (see Figure 6.10). The card itself is somewhat ambiguous: The boy may be staring into space, or his eyes may be almost closed. Consider two stories that could be told about this card:

Story 1: "He's upset that he's got to practice because his instructor is coming by and he hasn't yet learned his lesson for the week. But he'd rather be out playing with the other kids, and he'll probably sneak out to do just that."

Story 2: "He's thinking, 'Someday I'll be the world's greatest violinist. I'll be playing at Lincoln Center and the crowd'll be cheering.' He practices several hours every day."

There are formal standards that enable psychologists to derive *n Ach* scores from stories such as these, but in this case you need not be ac-

Figure 6.10. How Have Thematic Apperception Test Cards Been Used to Tap Fantasies in Personality Research? This is a Thematic Apperception Test card that is frequently used to measure the need for achievement. What is happening in this picture? What is the person thinking and feeling? What is going to happen? Your answers to these questions reflect your own needs as well as the content of the picture itself.

quainted with them to see that the second story suggests more achievement motivation than the first. McClelland (1985) has found that motives as measured by the TAT permit the prediction of long-term behavior patterns.

Behavior of Individuals with High *n* Ach Classic studies find that people with high *n* Ach earn higher grades than people of comparable learning ability but low *n* Ach. They are more likely to earn high salaries and be promoted than are low-*n*-Ach people with similar opportunities. They perform better at math problems and unscrambling anagrams, such as decoding RSTA into STAR, TARS, ARTS, or RATS.

McClelland (1965) found that 83 percent of high-*n*-Ach college graduates took positions characterized by risk, decision making, and the chance for great success, such as business management, sales, or businesses of their own making. Seventy percent of the graduates who chose nonentrepreneurial positions showed low *n* Ach. High-*n*-Ach individuals seem to prefer challenges and are willing to take moderate risks to achieve their goals. They see their fate as being in their own hands (McClelland et al., 1953). Workers with higher *n*

Ach are also more likely to find satisfaction on the job (Reuman et al., 1984).

A report by industrial psychologist Douglas Bray (1982) finds that factors similar to *n* Ach—including need for advancement and investment in one's work—are of moderate importance in predicting advancement through the managerial ranks at AT&T. But two other factors are more important: administrative skills and interpersonal skills. *N* Ach is an important element in success, but not the only factor.

Development of *n* Ach Mothers with high *n* Ach tend to encourage their children to think and act independently, whereas low-*n*-Ach mothers tend to be more protective and restrictive. Marion Winterbottom (1958) found that mothers of sons with high *n* Ach made more demands and imposed more restrictions on their sons during the early elementary school years than did mothers of sons with low *n* Ach. Even during the preschool years, the mothers of high-*n*-Ach sons demanded that they keep their rooms and possessions neat, that they make their own decisions concerning clothes, that they select their own friends, compete as needed, and undertake difficult tasks and persist at them. But mothers of high-n-Ach sons also showed warmth and praised their sons profusely for their accomplishments.

David McClelland and David Pilon (1983) studied n Ach among children whose parents' child-rearing practices had been studied 26 to 27 years earlier. It was found that high-n-Ach adults were more likely to have had parents who scheduled their feeding as infants (as opposed to allowing feeding on demand) and who were relatively demanding in their toilet-training practices.

In sum, it may be that children who develop high n Ach are encouraged to show independence and responsibility at early ages and that their parents respond warmly to their efforts.

The Need for Affiliation

The need for **affiliation,** abbreviated n Aff, prompts us to make friends, to join groups, and to prefer to do things with others rather than alone. Many rewards issue from affiliating with others, including praise and respect (Buss, 1983, 1986), attention, positive social stimulation, emotional support, and as we shall see, *social comparison* (Hill, 1987).

N Aff contributes to the social glue that creates families and civilizations. In this sense, it is certainly a healthful trait. Yet some people have such strong n Aff that they find it painful to make their own decisions or even to be by themselves for extended periods. Research by Stanley Schachter suggests that high n Aff may indicate anxiety, as when people "huddle together" in fear of some outside force.

The Schachter Studies on Anxiety and n Aff

In a classic experiment on the effects of anxiety on n Aff, Schachter (1959) manipulated subjects' anxiety by leading them to believe that they would receive either painful electric shocks (the high-anxiety condition) or mild electric shocks (the low-anxiety condition). Subjects were then asked to wait while the shock apparatus was supposedly being set up. Subjects could choose to wait alone or in a room with others. The majority (63 percent) of subjects who expected a painful shock chose to wait in a room with other people. Only one-third (33 percent) of the subjects who expected a mild shock chose to wait with others.

In a related experiment, Schachter found that "misery loves company," but only company of a special sort. Highly anxious subjects were placed in two social conditions. In the first, they could choose either to wait alone or with other subjects who would also receive painful shocks. Sixty percent of these subjects chose to affiliate, that is, to wait with others. In the second condition, highly anxious subjects could choose to wait alone or with people they believed were not involved with the study. In this second condition, no one chose to affiliate. Schachter concluded that misery loves company as long as the company is just as miserable.

Why did Schachter's subjects wish to affiliate only with people who shared their misery? Schachter explained their choice through the **theory of social comparison.** This theory holds that in an ambiguous situation—that is, a situation in which we are not certain about what we should do or how we should feel—we will affiliate with people with whom we can compare feelings and behaviors. Schachter's anxious recruits could compare their reactions with those of other "victims" but not with people who had no reason to feel anxious. His highly anxious subjects may also have resented uninvolved people for "getting away free."

Misery—whether it loves company or not—is one of the many human emotions. Let us now consider that most joyous and wrenching of psychological topics—emotion.

Affiliation Association or connection with a group.

Theory of social comparison The view that people look to others for cues about how to behave when they are in confusing or unfamiliar situations.

EMOTION

Emotions color our lives. We are green with envy, red with anger, blue with sorrow. The poets paint

Table 6.1 Components of Three Common Emotions

| | COMPONENTS | | |
EMOTION	PHYSIOLOGICAL	SITUATIONAL	COGNITIVE
Fear	Sympathetic arousal	Environmental threat	Belief in danger; desire to avoid
Anger	Sympathetic and parasympathetic arousal	Frustration or provocation	Desire to hurt provacateur
Depression	Parasympathetic arousal	Loss, failure, or inactivity	Thoughts of helplessness, worthlessness

Emotions have physiological, situational, and cognitive components.

a thoughtful mood as a brown study. Positive emotions such as love and desire can fill our days with pleasure, but negative emotions such as fear, depression, and anger can fill us with dread and make each day a chore.

An emotion can at once be a response to a situation (in the way that fear is a response to a threat) and have motivating properties (in the way that anger can motivate us to act aggressively). An emotion can also be a goal in and of itself. We may behave in ways that will lead us to experience joy or feelings of love.

An **emotion** is a state of feeling that has physiological, situational, and cognitive components. Although no two people experience emotions in exactly the same way, it is possible to make some generalizations. Fear, for example, involves predominantly **sympathetic** arousal (rapid heartbeat and breathing, sweating, muscle tension), the perception of a threat, and beliefs to the effect that one is in danger (see Table 6.1). Anger may involve both sympathetic and **parasympathetic** arousal (Funkenstein, 1955), a frustrating or provocative situation (such as an insult), and belief that the provocateur ought to be paid back. Depression usually involves predominantly parasympathetic arousal; a situational component of loss, failure, or inactivity; and cognitions of helplessness and worthlessness. Joy, grief, jealousy, disgust, embarrassment, liking—all have physiological, situational, and cognitive components.

Emotions and "Lie Detectors" The use of "lie detectors"—devices that are presented as being ca-

pable of distinguishing between truth and lies—highlights the link between autonomic arousal and emotion. The use of devices to sort out truth from lies actually has a lengthy, if not laudable, history. As told by Benjamin Kleinmuntz and Julian Szucko (1984, pp. 766–767),

The Bedouins of Arabia . . . until quite recently required conflicting witnesses to lick a hot iron; the one whose tongue was burned was thought to be lying. The Chinese, it is said, had a similar method for detecting lying: Suspects were forced to chew rice powder and spit it out; if the powder was dry, the suspect was guilty. A variation of this test was used during the Inquisition. The suspect had to swallow a "trial slice" of bread and cheese; if it stuck to the suspect's palate or throat he or she was not telling the truth.

These methods may sound primitive, even bizarre, but they are consistent with modern knowledge. Anxiety concerning being caught in a lie is linked to sympathetic arousal, and one sign of sympathetic arousal is lack of saliva, or dryness in the mouth. The emotions of fear and guilt are also linked to sympathetic arousal and, hence, dryness in the mouth.

Emotion A state of feeling that has physiological, situational, and cognitive components.

Sympathetic Of the sympathetic division of the autonomic nervous system.

Parasympathetic Of the parasympathetic division of the autonomic nervous system.

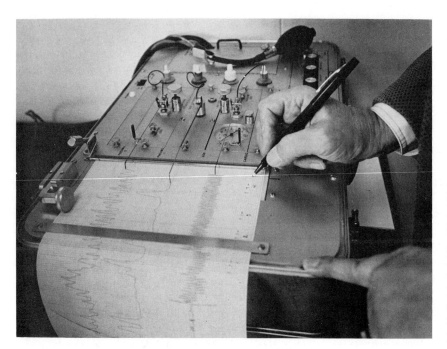

Figure 6.11. What Do "Lie Detectors" Detect? The polygraph monitors heart rate, blood pressure, respiration rate, and GSR (sweat in the palm of the hands). Is the polygraph sensitive to lying only? Is it foolproof? Because of the controversy surrounding these questions, many courts no longer admit polygraph evidence.

Modern-day lie detectors, or polygraphs (see Figure 6.11), monitor four indicators of sympathetic arousal while a witness or suspect is being examined: heart rate, blood pressure, respiration rate, and electrodermal response.

Supporters of the polygraph claim that they are accurate in more than 90 percent of cases (Podlesny & Raskin, 1977), but conflicting research suggests that polygraphs do not approach this high accuracy rate and that they are sensitive to more than lies (Kleinmuntz & Szucko, 1984; Lykken, 1981; Saxe et al., 1985; U.S. Congress, 1983). In one experiment, subjects were able to reduce the accuracy rate to 25 percent by thinking about exciting or disturbing events during the interview (Smith, 1971). In other studies, subjects have been yet more successful at poking holes in the accuracy rate. They dropped it to about 50 percent by biting their tongues (to produce pain) or pressing their toes against the floor (to tense muscles) while being interviewed (Honts et al., 1985).

As noted by Leonard Saxe and his colleagues at Boston University (1985), the fact of the matter is that "there is no such thing as a lie detector per se, [but] a number of approaches have been developed that are based on physiological measure-ment" (p. 355). Because of validity problems, results of polygraph examinations are no longer admitted as evidence in many courtrooms. Polygraph interviews are still often conducted in criminal investigations and in job interviews, but these practices are being questioned as well.

Emotional Development

There are a number of theories concerning the development of emotions. Basically they break down into two camps. The first, proposed originally by Katherine Bridges (1932), holds that we are born with a single emotion and that other emotions become differentiated as time passes. The second, proposed by Carroll Izard, holds that all emotions are present and adequately differentiated at birth. However, they are not shown all at once. Instead, they emerge in response to the child's developing needs and maturational sequences.

Bridges' and Sroufe's Theory   On the basis of her observations of babies, Bridges proposed that newborns experience one emotion—diffuse excitement. By 3 months, two other emotions have differentiated from this general state of excitement—a negative emotion (distress) and a positive emotion (delight). By 6 months, fear, disgust, and anger will have developed from distress. By 12 months elation and affection will have differentiated from delight. Jealousy develops from distress, and joy develops from delight—both during the second year.

Alan Sroufe (1979) has advanced Bridges' theory, focusing on the ways in which cognitive development may provide the basis for emotional development. Jealousy, for example, could not become differentiated without some understanding of the concept of possession. Anger usually results from situations in which our intentions are thwarted. For example, 7-month-old infants show anger when a biscuit is almost placed in their mouths and then removed (Stenberg et al., 1983). It may be that the development of concepts of intentionality (that is, the idea that people can do things "on purpose") and of rudimentary causality (the ability to perceive other people as the causes of frustration) precede the differentiation of anger.

Izard's Theory   Carroll Izard (1978, 1979, 1982) proposes that infants are born with discrete emotional states. However, the timing of their appearance is linked to the child's cognitive development and social experiences. For example, in one study, Izard and his colleagues (1983) claim that 2-month-old babies receiving inoculations showed distress, whereas older infants showed anger.

Izard's view may sound very similar to Sroufe's. After all, both are suggesting that there is an orderly unfolding of emotions such that they become more specific as time passes. However, in keeping with Izard's view, researchers have found that a number of different emotions appear to be shown by infants at ages earlier than those suggested by Bridges and Sroufe. In one study of the emotions shown by babies during the first three months, mothers reported that their babies showed the emotions of interest, joy, anger, surprise, and fear (Johnson et al., 1982). These figures are based on mothers' reports, and it is possible that the infants were actually showing more

diffuse emotions (Murphy, 1983). Perhaps the mothers were "reading" specific emotions "into" the babies based on their own knowledge of appropriate (adult) emotional reactions to the infants' situations. This is a problem that extends to Izard's interpretations of infants' facial expressions.

Izard (1979) claims to have found many discrete emotions at the age of 1 month by using his Maximally Discriminative Facial Movement Scoring System. Figure 6.12 shows some of the infant facial expressions that Izard believes are associated with the basic emotions of anger-rage, disgust, enjoyment-joy, fear-terror, interest-excitement, and sadness-dejection.

In sum, researchers seem to agree that a handful of emotions are shown by infants during the first few months. They agree that other emotions develop in an orderly manner. They agree that emotional development is linked to cognitive development and social experience. They do not agree on exactly when specific emotions are first shown or on whether discrete emotions are present at birth.

Expression of Emotions

Joy and sadness may be found in diverse cultures around the world, but how can we tell when other people are happy or despondent? It turns out that the expression of many emotions is also universal (Rinn, 1984). Smiling, for example, appears to be a universal sign of friendliness and approval (Ekman & Oster, 1979). Baring the teeth, as noted by Charles Darwin (1872) in the last century, may be a universal sign of anger. As the originator of the modern theory of evolution, Darwin believed that the universal recognition of facial expressions would have survival value. For example, facial expressions could signal the approach of enemies even in the absence of language.

Research by psychologist Paul Ekman and his colleagues also supports the universality of the facial expression of emotions. In one study, Ekman (1980) took a number of photographs of people posing the emotions of anger, disgust, fear, happiness, sadness, and surprise, similar to those

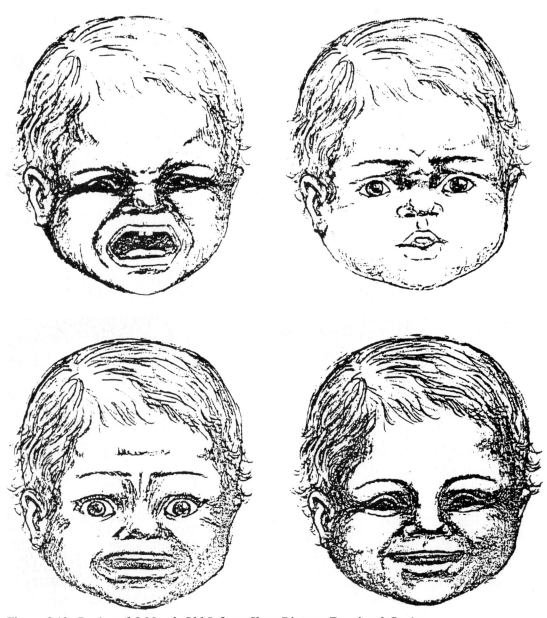

Figure 6.12. Do 1- and 2-Month-Old Infants Show Discrete Emotions? Or Are Emotions More Diffuse among Infants?   Drawings of the facial expressions of infants, as used in Izard's research.

shown in Figure 6.13, and asked subjects throughout the world to indicate what emotions they depicted. Subjects ranged from European college students to the Fore, an isolated tribe who dwell in the highlands of New Guinea. All groups, including the Fore, who had almost no contact with Western culture, correctly identified the emotions being portrayed. Moreover, even the Fore displayed fa-

miliar facial expressions when asked how they would respond if they were the characters in stories that called for basic emotional responses. Ekman and his colleagues (1987) obtained similar results in a study of ten cultures in which subjects were permitted to report that multiple emotions were shown by facial expressions. The subjects generally agreed on which two emotions were

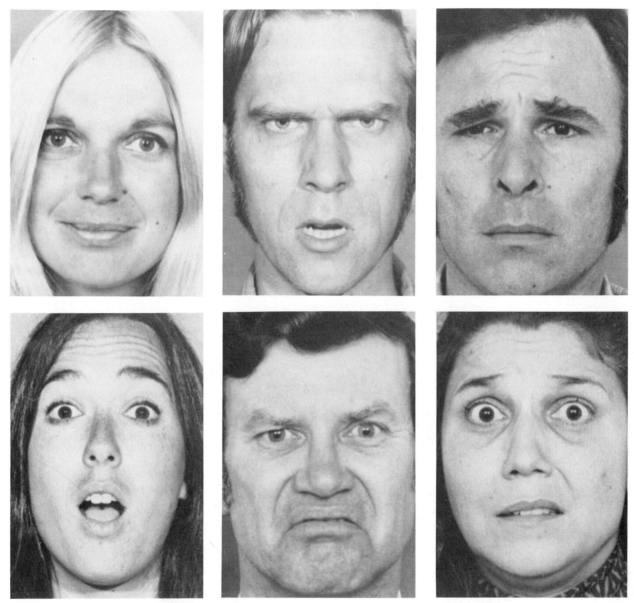

Figure 6.13. Is the Expression of Emotions Universal? Ekman's research suggests that there are several basic emotions, including those shown in these photographs, whose expression is recognized around the world.

being shown and as to which emotion was most intense.

The Facial-Feedback Hypothesis

We recognize that emotional states are *reflected* by facial expressions, but the **facial-feedback hypothesis** argues that the causal relationship between emotions and facial expressions can also work in the opposite direction. Inducing experimental subjects to smile, for example, leads them to report

Facial-feedback hypothesis The view that stereotypical facial expressions can contribute to stereotypical emotions.

Questionnaire

The love scale

What emotion makes the world go round? Love, of course.

Romantic love is a complex emotion involving strong feeling states, cognitions, and motivations (Hatfield, 1983; Sternberg & Grajek, 1984). According to psychologist Keith E. Davis (1985), love involves two clusters of feelings—a "passion cluster" and a "caring cluster." The passion cluster contains feelings of fascination, sexual desire, and exclusiveness (desire for an exclusive relationship with the loved one). The caring cluster includes championing the interests of the loved one, helping to the utmost, and when necessary sacrificing one's own interests. Romantic lovers also idealize one another—they magnify each other's positive features and overlook their flaws.

The love scale was developed at Northeastern University in Boston. To compare your own score (or scores, if you have been busy) with those of Northeastern University students, think of your dating partner (or partners) and circle the number that best shows how true or false the items are for you, according to the following code. Then compare your scores to those in Appendix C.

7 = definitely true
6 = rather true
5 = somewhat true
4 = not sure, or equally true and false
3 = somewhat false
2 = rather false
1 = definitely false

1. I look forward to being with (_____) a great deal.
definitely false   1   2   3   4   5   6   7   definitely true

more positive feelings (Kleinke & Walton, 1982; McCanne & Anderson, 1987) and to rate cartoons as more humorous (Laird, 1974, 1984). When subjects are induced to frown, they rate cartoons as being more aggressive (Laird, 1974, 1984). When subjects pose expressions of pain, they also rate electric shocks as more painful (Colby et al., 1977; Lanzetta et al., 1976). Modern-day findings seem reminiscent of the observations made by Charles Darwin more than a hundred years ago, "The free expression by outward signs of an emotion intensifies it. On the other hand, the repression, as far as possible, of all outward signs softens our emotions" (Darwin, 1872, p. 22).

What are the possible links between facial feedback and emotion? One link is arousal. Contracting facial muscles intensely, such as those used in signifying fear, heightens arousal (Zuckerman et al., 1981). Our perception of heightened arousal then leads to self-report of heightened emotional activity. Other links may involve changes in brain temperature and the release of neurotransmitters (Ekman, 1985; Zajonc, 1985). Kinesthetic feedback of the contraction of facial muscles may also induce us to perceive heightened emotional activation (McCaul et al., 1982).

But it should be noted that a number of psychologists remain skeptical of the facial-feedback

2. I find _____ to be sexually exciting.

definitely false   1   2   3   4   5   6   7   definitely true

3. _____ has fewer faults than most people.

definitely false   1   2   3   4   5   6   7   definitely true

4. I would do anything I could for _____.

definitely false   1   2   3   4   5   6   7   definitely true

5. _____ is very attractive to me.

definitely false   1   2   3   4   5   6   7   definitely true

6. I like to share my feelings with _____.

definitely false   1   2   3   4   5   6   7   definitely true

7. Doing things is more fun when _____ and I do them together.

definitely false   1   2   3   4   5   6   7   definitely true

8. I like to have _____ all to myself.

definitely false   1   2   3   4   5   6   7   definitely true

9. I would feel horrible if anything bad happened to _____.

definitely false   1   2   3   4   5   6   7   definitely true

10. I think about _____ very often.

definitely false   1   2   3   4   5   6   7   definitely true

11. It is very important that _____ care for me.

definitely false   1   2   3   4   5   6   7   definitely true

12. I am most content when I am with _____.

definitely false   1   2   3   4   5   6   7   definitely true

13. It is difficult for me to stay away from _____ for very long.

definitely false   1   2   3   4   5   6   7   definitely true

14. I care about _____ a great deal.

definitely false   1   2   3   4   5   6   7   definitely true

Total score for love scale: _____

---

hypothesis, or at least of the extent of its effects. Some critics note that whether or not modifying facial behavior activates emotional response, it has powerful effects on subjects' expectations. As a result, subjects' cognitions may play a major role—if not the major role—in self-reported changes of emotional state and in the other dependent variables measured in facial-feedback studies (e.g., ratings of cartoons). As an example, posing intense facial expressions might cause subjects to become highly involved in an experiment and to expect a heightened emotional response. If so, the emotion-evoking "mechanism" is cognitive, not facial-kinesthetic. In their experiment, McCanne and Anderson (1987) suppressed facial response and, as one consequence, decreased subjects' enjoyment of an experimental task. But the researchers admit that the lessened enjoyment might have resulted from distraction from the tasks at hand and not from the suppression of facial muscle activity itself. Another critic of the facial-feedback hypothesis recently analyzed a large body of research and concluded that the effects of modifying facial behavior on self-reported emotional response are small to moderate at best (Matsumoto, 1987).

In the following section we shall see that the facial feedback-hypothesis is related to the James-Lange theory of emotion.

Theories of Emotion

Emotions have physiological, situational, and cognitive components, but psychologists have disagreed about how these components interact to produce feeling states and actions. Some psychologists argue that physiological arousal is a more basic component of emotional response than cognition and that the type of arousal we experience strongly influences our cognitive appraisal and our labeling of the emotion (e.g., Izard, 1984; Zajonc, 1984). Other psychologists argue that cognitive appraisal and physiological arousal are so strongly intertwined that cognitive processes may determine the emotional response (e.g., Lazarus, 1984).

The so-called commonsense theory of emotions is that something happens (situation) that is cognitively appraised (interpreted) by the person and that the feeling state (a combination of arousal and thoughts) follows. For example, you meet someone new, appraise that person as delightful, and feelings of attraction follow. Or you flunk a test, recognize that you're in trouble, and feel down in the dumps.

However, historic and contemporary theories of how the components of emotions interact are at variance with the commonsense view. Let us consider a number of more important theories and see if we can arrive at some useful conclusions.

The James-Lange Theory

Just before the turn of the century, William James suggested that our emotions follow, rather than cause, our overt behavioral responses to events. This view was also proposed by a contemporary of James, the Danish physiologist Karl G. Lange. For this reason, it is referred to as the James-Lange theory of emotion.

According to James and Lange (see Figure 6.14, part A), certain external stimuli instinctively trigger specific patterns of arousal and action, such as fighting or fleeing. We then become angry *because* we act aggressively. We then become afraid *because* we run away. Emotions are simply the cognitive representations (or byproducts) of automatic physiological and behavioral responses.

Walter Cannon (1927) criticized the James-Lange assertion that each emotion has distinct physiological correlates. Cannon argued that the physiological arousal that accompanies emotion A is not so distinct from the arousal that accompanies emotion B as the theory asserts. We can also note that the James-Lange view ascribes a very meager function to human cognition; it denies the roles of cognitive appraisal, personal values, and personal choice.

The James-Lange theory may be mainly of historical interest today, but still it is of value. It suggests that by acting in a certain way we can induce desired emotional responses. Perhaps we can overcome the emotion of fear by somehow approaching, rather than running from, dreaded objects or situations. Perhaps we can overcome the emotion of depression by engaging in, rather than withdrawing from, activities that we normally enjoy, such as bicycling or attending concerts. Sound farfetched? These assumptions underlie many effective behavior-therapy practices that are currently used in clinics across the world. There is a kernel of truth in many outdated theories.

The Cannon-Bard Theory

Walter Cannon was not content to criticize the James-Lange theory. He (Cannon, 1927) and Philip Bard (1934) suggested that an event would trigger body responses (arousal and action) and the experience of an emotion simultaneously. As shown in Figure 6.14 (part B), when an event is perceived (processed by the brain), the brain stimulates autonomic and muscular activity (arousal and action) *and* cognitive activity (experiencing of the emotion). According to the Cannon-Bard theory, emotions *accompany* body responses. Emotions are not produced by body changes, as in the James-Lange theory.

The central criticism of the Cannon-Bard theory focuses on whether (1) body responses (arousal and action) and (2) emotions are actually stimulated simultaneously. For example, pain or the perception of danger may trigger arousal before we begin to feel distress or fear. Also, many of us have had the experience of having a "narrow escape" and then becoming aroused and shaky afterward, when we have finally had time to consider the damage that might have occurred.

What is needed is a theory that allows for an ongoing interaction of external events, physiolog-

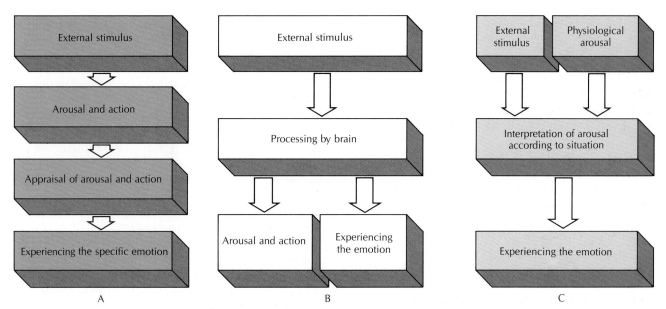

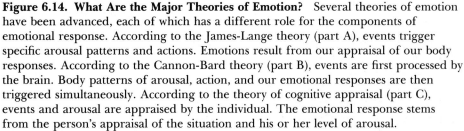

A   B   C

Figure 6.14. What Are the Major Theories of Emotion? Several theories of emotion have been advanced, each of which has a different role for the components of emotional response. According to the James-Lange theory (part A), events trigger specific arousal patterns and actions. Emotions result from our appraisal of our body responses. According to the Cannon-Bard theory (part B), events are first processed by the brain. Body patterns of arousal, action, and our emotional responses are then triggered simultaneously. According to the theory of cognitive appraisal (part C), events and arousal are appraised by the individual. The emotional response stems from the person's appraisal of the situation and his or her level of arousal.

ical changes (such as autonomic arousal and muscular activity), and cognitive activities.

The Theory of Cognitive Appraisal According to Stanley Schachter (1971) and a number of other psychologists, emotions have generally similar patterns of body arousal. The essential way in which they vary is along a weak-strong dimension that is determined by one's level of arousal. The label we *attribute* to an emotion largely depends on our cognitive appraisal of our situation. Cognitive appraisal is based on many factors, including our perception of external events and the ways in which other people seem to be responding to those events (see Figure 6.14, part C). Given the presence of other people, we engage in *social comparison* (see p. 258) to arrive at an appropriate response.

In a classic experiment, Schachter and Jerome Singer (1962) showed that arousal can be labeled

quite differently, depending on a person's situation. The investigators told subjects that their purpose was to study the effects of a vitamin on vision. Half the subjects received an injection of adrenalin, a hormone that increases autonomic arousal (see Chapter 2). A control group received an injection of an inactive **saline** solution. Subjects given adrenalin then received one of three "cognitive manipulations," as shown in Table 6.2. Group 1 was told nothing about possible emotional effects of the "vitamin." Group 2 was deliberately misinformed; group members were led to expect itching, numbness, or other irrelevant symptoms. Group 3 was informed accurately about the increased arousal they would experience.

Saline Containing salt.

Table 6.2   Injected Substances and Cognitive Manipulations in the Schachter-Singer Study

GROUP	SUBSTANCE	COGNITIVE MANIPULATION
1	Adrenalin	No information given about effects
2	Adrenalin	Misinformation given: itching, numbness, etc.
3	Adrenalin	Accurate information: physiological arousal
4	Saline solution	None

Source: Schachter & Singer, 1962.

After receiving injections and cognitive manipulations, subjects were asked to wait, in pairs, while the experimental apparatus was being set up. Subjects did not know that the person with whom they were waiting was a confederate of the experimenter. The purpose of the confederate was to model a response that the subject would believe resulted from the injection.

Some subjects waited with a confederate who acted in a happy-go-lucky manner. He flew paper airplanes about the room and tossed paper balls into a wastebasket. Other subjects waited with a confederate who acted angry, complaining about the experiment, tearing up a questionnaire, and departing the waiting room in a huff. As the confederates worked for their Oscars, real subjects were observed through a one-way mirror.

Subjects in groups 1 and 2 were likely to imitate the behavior of the confederate. Those exposed to the **euphoric** confederate acted jovial and content. Those exposed to the angry confederate imitated that person's complaining, aggressive ways. But groups 3 and 4 were less influenced by the behavior of the confederate.

Schachter and Singer concluded that groups 1 and 2 were in an ambiguous situation. They felt

arousal from the adrenalin injection but had no basis for attributing it to any event or emotion. Social comparison with the confederate led them to attribute their arousal either to happiness or anger, whichever was displayed by the confederate. Group 3 expected arousal from the injection with no particular emotional consequences. They did not imitate the confederate's display of happiness or anger because they were not in an ambiguous situation. Group 4 had no physiological arousal for which they needed an attribution, except perhaps for some induced by observing the confederate. Group 4 subjects also failed to imitate the confederate.

Now, happiness and anger are quite different emotions. Happiness is a positive emotion, and anger, for most of us, is a negative emotion. Yet Schachter and Singer suggest that any physiological differences between these two emotions are so slight that opposing cognitive appraisals of the same situation can lead one person to label arousal as happiness and another person to label arousal as anger. A supportive experiment suggests that it is similarly possible for people to confuse feelings of fear with feelings of sexual attraction (Dutton & Aron, 1974).

The Schachter-Singer view could not be farther removed from the James-Lange theory, which holds that each emotion has specific and readily recognized body sensations. The truth, it turns out, may lie somewhere in between.

In science it must be possible to attain identical or similar results when experiments are replicated. The Schachter and Singer study has been replicated with *different* results. For instance, in studies by Rogers and Deckner (1975) and Maslach (1978), subjects were less likely to imitate the behavior of the confederate and more likely to apply negative emotional labels to their arousal, even when exposed to a euphoric confederate.

Evaluation   What do we make of all this? As noted at the outset of our discussion of emotion, emotional responses are activated by physiological, situational, and cognitive factors. Recent research by Paul Ekman and his colleagues (1983) suggests that the patterns of arousal that lead us to believe we are experiencing certain emotions may be more

Euphoric Characterized by feelings of well-being, elation.

specific than suggested by Schachter and Singer but less specific than suggested by James and Lange. In any event, there are some reasonably distinct patterns of arousal, and these patterns are not fully exchangeable—although we may be confused about our feelings when patterns of arousal rise up in apparently inappropriate situations. This occurs because our situations, and our cognitive appraisals of our situations, are also influential in activating our emotional responses. And when our situations are ambiguous, we may be at least somewhat more likely to interpret them by social comparison.

In sum, it may be that there is no reason to insist that any particular component of an experience—physiological, situational, or cognitive—is more crucial than others in activating emotional response. Perhaps the most important thing to note is that people are thinking beings who gather information from all three sources in determining their behavioral responses and in pinpointing labels for their emotional responses. The fact that none of the theories we have discussed applies to all people in all situations is comforting. Our emotions are not quite so easily understood or manipulated as theorists have suggested.

TRUTH OR FICTION REVISITED

One U.S. adult in five is obese.   True. More than 30 million of us exceed our desirable body weight by at least 20 percent.

Overweight people are more sensitive to stomach pangs than are normal-weight people.   False. Normal-weight people are more sensitive to internal cues for hunger.

Eating salty pretzels can make you thirsty.   True. Increased concentrations of salt cause the hypothalamus to trigger the thirst drive.

Sleep becomes gradually deeper as we approach the middle of the night and then gradually lightens until we awaken in the morning.   False. Episodes of deep sleep are deepest early in the sleep cycle.

People who sleep nine or more hours a night tend to be lazy and happy-go-lucky.   False. "Long sleepers" are more anxious and ruminative than "short sleepers."

We tend to act out our forbidden fantasies in our dreams.   False. Most dreams are extensions of the events of the day.

Stimulating male rats in a certain part of the brain causes them to engage in sexual foreplay.   True. Much of the behavior of lower animals is instinctive and can be elicited by appropriate stimulation.

Only men are sexually stimulated by hard-core pornography.   False. Women are as well.

Homosexuals suffer from hormonal imbalances.   False. Reliable differences have not been found in hormone levels between homosexuals and heterosexuals.

Any healthy woman can successfully resist a rapist if she really wants to.   False. This is one of the myths that contributes to a social climate that supports rape.

"Getting away from it all" by going on a vacation from all sensory input for a few hours is relaxing.   False. Prolonged sensory deprivation is actually a disturbing experience.

If quarterbacks get too "psyched up" for a big game, their performance on the field may suffer.   True. The performance of complex tasks can suffer when we are very highly aroused.

A strong need to get ahead is the most powerful predictor of success in climbing the corporate ladder.   False. According to the Bray study, administrative and interpersonal skills were better predictors of getting ahead, at least at AT&T.

Misery loves company.   True, according to the Schachter study—at least when the company is also miserable.

You may be able to fool a lie detector by squiggling your toes.   True. Toe squiggling can cause arousal, and the "lie detector" measures arousal rather than lying per se.

Chapter Review

Motives are hypothetical states within organisms that activate behavior and direct organisms toward goals. A need is a state of physical deprivation. Needs give rise to psychological drives. An incentive is an object, person, or situation that is perceived as being capable of satisfying a need.

According to the instinct theory of motivation, animals are born with preprogramed tendencies to behave in certain ways in certain situations. According to the drive-reduction theory of motivation, rewards motivate behavior by reducing drives. Humanistic psychologists believe that people are motivated to strive consciously for personal fulfillment.

Physiological drives generally function according to the principle of homeostasis, which is the body's tendency to maintain a steady state. Hunger is regulated by several internal mechanisms, including stomach contractions, blood sugar level, receptors in the mouth and liver, and the responses of the hypothalamus.

We have four stages of NREM sleep, and one stage of REM sleep. Most dreams occur during REM sleep. Sleep appears to rejuvenate a tired body. Short sleepers are more happy-go-lucky than long sleepers. Most dreams are mundane. According to the activation-synthesis model, dreams reflect biological rather than psychological activity.

Sex hormones have organizing (directional) and activating (arousing) effects. Aggressive-erotic films heighten violence toward women, but heightened violence is a result of the aggressive content of these films—not the sex. Homosexuality is erotic response to members of one's own sex. Prenatal hormone levels and postnatal socialization might influence sexual orientation. Many social scientists argue that rapists use rape as a way of expressing anger toward women.

Stimulus motives prompt us to increase the stimulation impinging on us. People and many lower animals have needs for stimulation and activity, for exploration and manipulation. Studies in sensory deprivation show that lack of stimulation is aversive. We feel best and function most efficiently at our optimal levels of arousal. According to the Yerkes-Dodson Law, high levels of motivation facilitate performance on simple tasks but impede performance on complex tasks.

Social motives are acquired through social learning. Murray compiled 21 social motives, or psychological needs, including needs for achievement and affiliation. People with high n Ach attain higher grades and earn more money than people of comparable ability with lower n Ach. Anxiety tends to increase the need for affiliation.

An emotion is a state of feeling. Emotions motivate behavior but can also serve as responses to situations and as goals in themselves. Lie detectors, or polygraphs, assess sympathetic arousal rather than lies per se.

According to Bridges and Sroufe, we are born with one emotion and other emotions become differentiated as time passes. Izard proposes that infants are born with discrete emotional states.

The expression of many emotions appears to be universal. The posing of intense facial expressions to some degree heightens emotional response and induces emotions consistent with the expressions.

Psychologists do not agree on the relative importance of physiological arousal and cognitive appraisal in activating particular emotions. According to the James-Lange theory, emotions have specific patterns of arousal and action that are triggered by external events. The Cannon-Bard theory proposes that processing of events by the brain gives rise simultaneously to arousal, action, and the mental experience of the emotion. According to the theory of cognitive appraisal, emotions have largely similar patterns of arousal, and the emotion a person will feel reflects his or her appraisal of the situation. Research seems to suggest that patterns of arousal are more specific than suggested by the theory of cognitive appraisal but that cognitive appraisal plays an important role in determining our responses to events.

Exercise

Scientists and Concepts

Directions: *Here are a number of statements that express various concepts or positions in psychology. Below them are the names of a number of psychologists and other scientists discussed in Chapter 6. Write the number of the statement to the left of the name of the appropriate scientist. The answer key follows the exercise.*

1. When our levels of arousal are too low, we engage in activity that will elevate them. When our levels of arousal are too high, we engage in activity that will lower them.
2. Babies are born with one emotion—diffuse excitement—and other emotions become differentiated as they develop.
3. People have 12 basic instincts, including hunger, sex, and self-assertion.
4. Once people have met their lower-level needs, they naturally try to find personal fulfillment by actualizing their unique potentials.
5. When people are in an ambiguous situation, they tend to look to other people in the same situation for information on how they ought to act and feel.
6. The reason that people and lower animals find rewards to be pleasant is that rewards have the effect of reducing drives.
7. There are 21 important social motives or psychological needs, including the needs for achievement, affiliation, and nurturance.
8. External events trigger instinctive patterns of arousal and action such as fighting or fleeing. We then become angry *because* we fight, or we become afraid *because* we run away.
9. The instincts of hunger, sex, and aggression give rise to psychic energy, which is perceived as tension. This tension motivates us to find ways to restore ourselves to a calm, resting state.
10. The free expression by outward signs of an emotion intensifies it. On the other hand, the repression, as far as possible, of all outward signs softens our emotions.

_____ A. Charles Darwin
_____ B. Sigmund Freud
_____ C. Clark Hull
_____ D. William James
_____ E. Salvatore Maddi
_____ F. Abraham Maslow
_____ G. William McDougall
_____ H. Henry Murray
_____ I. Katherine Bridges
_____ J. Stanley Schachter

Answer Key to Exercise

A. 10	**D.** 8	**G.** 3	**I.** 2
B. 9	**E.** 1	**H.** 7	**J.** 5
C. 6	**F.** 4		

Posttest

Directions: *For each of the following, select the choice that best answers the question or completes the sentence.*

1. Physiological _____ are the psychological counterparts of physiological needs.

   (a) drives, **(b)** incentives, **(c)** responses, **(d)** behaviors.

2. Inherited dispositions that activate behavior patterns designed to reach specific goals are referred to as

   (a) motives, **(b)** drives, **(c)** instincts, **(d)** releasers.

3. Drive-reduction theory was framed by

   (a) William James, **(b)** Henry Murray, **(c)** Abraham Maslow, **(d)** Clark Hull.

4. Drive-reduction theory has the greatest difficulty explaining

   (a) sensation seeking, **(b)** the thirst drive, **(c)** the hunger drive, **(d)** avoidance of extreme cold.

5. When the ventromedial nucleus of a rat's hypothalamus is lesioned, the animal becomes

   (a) hyperglycemic, **(b)** hyperphagic, **(c)** hypoglycemic, **(d)** aphagic.

6. A friend has managed to lose 30 pounds but now complains that he is hungry "all the time." According to the text, obese and formerly obese people may be hungry more often than people who have always been normal in weight because of

   (a) a higher blood sugar level, **(b)** lack of adequate nutritional information, **(c)** more adipose tissue, **(d)** a lesion in the lateral hypothalamus.

7. When the body is depleted of fluids, angiotensin is secreted by the

   (a) liver, **(b)** kidneys, **(c)** hypothalamus, **(d)** osmoreceptors.

8. In a classic experiment, an injection of a(n) _____ solution into a goat's hypothalamus triggered heavy intake of fluids.

   (a) salt, **(b)** ADH, **(c)** calcium, **(d)** angiotensin.

9. The term *paradoxical sleep* refers to

   (a) the hypnagogic state, **(b)** the waking state, **(c)** REM sleep, **(d)** NREM sleep.

10. "Short sleepers" tend to be less _____ than "long sleepers."

    (a) self-satisfied, (b) active, (c) happy-go-lucky, (d) ruminative.

11. The sexual behavior of mice and cats differs from that of humans in that

    (a) sex hormones promote differentiation of sex organs in mice and cats but not in people, (b) sex hormones are involved in sexual motivation in mice and rats but not in people, (c) mice and rats are receptive to sexual advances during estrus only, (d) mice and rats are more sexually responsive to psychological stimuli than chemical stimuli.

12. Which of the following statements about pornography is *not* supported by research?

    (a) The sexual content of pornographic films stimulates violence against women, (b) Women are sexually responsive to hard-core pornographic films and stories, (c) Frequent exposure to pornographic films results in lessened sexual response to new pornographic films, (d) Overexposure to deviant sex can apparently desensitize the viewer to deviant practices.

13. Homosexuality is defined as

    (a) sexual preference for members of the opposite sex, (b) sexual response to members of one's own sex, (c) sexual activity with members of one's own sex, (d) sexual response to members of both sexes.

14. Participants in sensory-deprivation experiments reported all of the following *except*

    (a) boredom, (b) irritability, (c) hallucinations, (d) delusions.

15. High sensation seekers are less tolerant of _____ than other people.

    (a) high-risk activities, (b) sensory deprivation, (c) novel experiences, (d) sexual experiences.

16. A person's optimal level of arousal is

    (a) the level of arousal at which that person functions most efficiently, (b) equivalent to the greatest amount of stimulation that the person can tolerate, (c) equivalent to the smallest amount of stimulation that the person can tolerate, (d) the level of arousal that is associated with novel stimulation.

17. David McClelland assessed *n* Ach by using the

    (a) MMPI, (b) Rorschach inkblot test, (c) TAT, (d) California Psychological Inventory.

18. According to the text, the emotion of _____ involves predominantly sympathetic arousal.

    (a) depression, (b) anger, (c) acceptance, (d) fear.

19. A lie detector assesses all of the following body functions, with the *exception of*

    (a) blood pressure, (b) brain waves, (c) heart rate, (d) respiration rate.

20. According to Bridges and Sroufe, the first emotion felt by babies is

    (a) mild pleasure, (b) distress, (c) diffuse excitement, (d) joy.

21. Which of the following theorists proposes that cognitive development may provide the basis for emotional development?

    (a) Carroll Izard, (b) Charles Darwin, (c) Paul Ekman, (d) Alan Sroufe.

22. The text suggests that all of the following might provide links between facial feedback and emotional response, with the *exception of*

    (a) antidiuretic hormone, (b) kinesthetic feedback, (c) arousal, (d) release of neurotransmitters.

23. A person tries to get herself out of a state of depression by engaging in behaviors that were once enjoyable. This approach to overcoming depression is most consistent with a theory proposed by

    (a) William James, (b) Walter Cannon, (c) Carroll Izard, (d) Stanley Schachter.

24. Which of the following statements contradicts the theory of emotion proposed by Schachter and Singer?

    (a) Strong arousal is associated with stronger emotions, (b) Situations influence the experience of emotions, (c) In ambiguous situations, we may try to determine how we should feel by observing others in the same situation, (d) There are some reasonably distinct patterns of arousal that are not exchangeable.

Answer Key to Posttest

1. A	7. B	13. B	19. B
2. C	8. A	14. D	20. C
3. D	9. C	15. B	21. D
4. A	10. D	16. A	22. A
5. B	11. C	17. C	23. A
6. C	12. A	18. D	24. D

DEVELOPMENTAL PSYCHOLOGY

OUTLINE

PRETEST: TRUTH OR FICTION?

CONTROVERSIES IN DEVELOPMENTAL PSYCHOLOGY
Does Development Reflect Nature or Nurture?
Is Development Continuous or Discontinuous?

PRENATAL DEVELOPMENT
The Germinal Stage
The Embryonic Stage
The Fetal Stage

PHYSICAL DEVELOPMENT
Childhood
Adolescence

PERCEPTUAL DEVELOPMENT

COGNITIVE DEVELOPMENT
Jean Piaget's Cognitive-Developmental Theory
Information-Processing Approaches
Lawrence Kohlberg's Theory of Moral Development

ATTACHMENT
Stages of Attachment
Theoretical Views of Attachment
The Effects of Day Care
Child Abuse: When Attachment Fails

SEX TYPING
Sex Differences
On Becoming a Man or a Woman

ADULT DEVELOPMENT
Young Adulthood
Middle Adulthood
Late Adulthood

TRUTH OR FICTION REVISITED

CHAPTER REVIEW

EXERCISES

POSTTEST

PRETEST: TRUTH OR FICTION?

Fertilization takes place in the uterus.

Your heart started beating when you were a fifth of an inch long and weighed a fraction of an ounce.

If it were not for the secretion of male sex hormones a few weeks after conception, we would all develop as females.

Infants triple their birth weight by age 1 year.

Girls are capable of becoming pregnant after they have their first menstrual periods.

Early maturing boys are more popular than late maturing boys.

Newborn babies may look at one object with one eye and at another object with the other eye.

A 4-year-old may think that a row of five spread-out pennies has more pennies than a row of five bunched-up pennies.

The highest level of moral reasoning involves relying on our own views of what is right and wrong.

Infants who are securely attached to their mothers are more willing to leave their mothers to explore the environment.

Children placed in day care are more aggressive than children cared for in the home.

Child abusers have frequently been victims of child abuse themselves.

Girls are superior to boys in verbal abilities.

Fathers are more likely than mothers to help children with their math homework.

Girls do not like to play with guns.

A 2-year-old may know that he is a boy but think that he can grow up to be a "mommy."

Young adulthood is characterized by trying to "make" it in the career world.

Mothers suffer from the "empty-nest syndrome" when the youngest child leaves home.

Most elderly people are dissatisfied with their lives.

On a summerlike day in October, Elaine and her husband Dennis rush out to their jobs as usual. While Elaine, a buyer for a New York department store, is arranging for dresses from the Chicago manufacturer to arrive in time for the spring line, a very different drama is unfolding in her body. Hormones are causing a follicle (egg container) in one of her ovaries to rupture and release an egg cell, or ovum. Elaine, like other women, possessed from birth all the egg cells she would ever have. How this ovum was selected to ripen and be released this month is unknown. But for a day or so following **ovulation,** Elaine will be capable of becoming pregnant.

When it is released, the ovum begins a slow journey down a 4-inch-long **fallopian tube** to the **uterus.** It is within this tube that one of Dennis's sperm cells will unite with the egg.

Like many other couples, Elaine and Dennis engaged in sexual intercourse the previous night. But unlike most other couples, their timing and methodology were preplanned. Elaine had used a kit bought in a drug store to predict when she would ovulate. She had been chemically analyzing her urine for the presence of luteinizing hormone (LH). LH surges one to two days prior to ovulation, and the results suggested that Elaine would be most likely to conceive today.

When Elaine and Dennis made love, he ejaculated hundreds of millions of sperm, with about equal numbers of Y and X sex chromosomes. By the time of conception only a few thousand had survived the journey to the fallopian tubes. Several bombarded the ovum, attempting to penetrate. Only one succeeded. It carried a Y sex chromosome, and so the couple conceived a boy. The fertilized ovum, or **zygote,** is 1/175th of an inch long—a tiny stage for the drama yet to unfold.

Developmental psychologists would be pleased to study the development of Dennis and Elaine's new son from conception throughout his lifetime. There are several reasons for this: One approach to the explanation of adult behavior lies in the discovery of early influences and developmental sequences. One answer to the question of *why* we behave in certain ways lies in outlining the development of behavior patterns over the years. There is also interest in the effects of genetics, early interactions with parents and **siblings,** and

the school and the community on traits such as aggressiveness and intelligence.

Developmental psychologists also seek insight into the causes of developmental abnormalities. This avenue of research can contribute to children's health and psychological well-being. For instance, should pregnant women abstain from smoking and drinking? Is it safe for the **embryo** for pregnant women to take aspirin for a headache or tetracycline to ward off a bacterial invasion? Need we be concerned about placing our children in day care? What factors contribute to child abuse? Developmental psychologists are also concerned about issues in adult development. For example, what conflicts and disillusionments can we expect as we journey through our 30s, 40s, and 50s? The information acquired by developmental psychologists can help us make decisions about how we rear our children and lead our own lives.

Of course, there is another very good reason for studying development. Thousands of psychologists enjoy it. Let us now consider two of the many controversies within the field of developmental psychology. Then we shall chronicle development, beginning with the changes that occur prior to birth.

CONTROVERSIES IN DEVELOPMENTAL PSYCHOLOGY

We have seen throughout this text that psychologists see things in very different ways. Different views give rise to a number of controversies in developmental psychology as well.

Ovulation The releasing of an ovum from an ovary.

Fallopian tube A tube that conducts ova from an ovary to the uterus.

Uterus The hollow organ within females in which the unborn child develops.

Zygote A fertilized ovum.

Siblings Brothers and sisters.

Embryo The unborn child from the third through the eighth week following conception.

Does Development Reflect Nature or Nurture?

There is continuing interest in sorting out what human behavior is the result of nature and of nurture. What aspects of behavior originate in our genes—that is, nature—and are biologically "programed" to unfold in the child as long as minimal nutrition and social experience are provided? What aspects of behavior can be largely traced to environmental influences such as nutrition and learning—that is, nurture?

Psychologists seek the influences of nature in our genetic heritage, the functioning of the nervous system, and in the process of **maturation.** Psychologists seek the influences of nurture in our nutrition, cultural and family backgrounds, and opportunities to learn about the world, including early cognitive stimulation and formal education. The American psychologist Arnold Gesell (1880–1961) leaned heavily toward natural explanations of development, arguing that all areas of development are self-regulated by the unfolding of natural plans and processes. John Watson and other behaviorists leaned heavily toward environmental explanations.* But today nearly all researchers would agree that, broadly speaking, nature and nurture interact as children develop.

Is Development Continuous or Discontinuous?

Do developmental changes occur gradually (continuously) or in major qualitative leaps (discontinuously) that dramatically alter the ways in which we are structured and behave?

*Watson, of course, was focusing primarily on adaptive behavior patterns, whereas Gesell was focusing on many aspects of development, including physical and motor growth and development.

Maturation The orderly unfolding of traits, as regulated by the genetic code.

Stage A distinct period of life that is qualitatively different from other stages.

Puberty The period of early adolescence during which hormones spur rapid physical development.

Watson and other behaviorists view human development as a continuous process in which the effects of learning mount gradually, with no major sudden qualitative changes. Maturational theorists, by contrast, believe that there are periods of life during which development occurs so dramatically that we can speak of its occurring in **stages.** Maturational theorists point out that the environment, even when enriched, profits us little until we are mature enough, or ready, to develop. For example, newborn babies will not imitate their parents' speech, even when parents speak clearly and deliberately. Nor does aided practice in "walking" during the first few months notably advance development of independent walking.

Stage theorists such as Sigmund Freud (see Chapter 8) and Jean Piaget saw development as discontinuous. Both saw biological changes as the basis for psychological changes. Freud, as we shall see in Chapter 8, focused on the ways in which physical sexual developments might provide the basis for personality development. Piaget focused on the ways in which maturation of the nervous system permitted cognitive advances. Stage theorists see the sequences of development as invariant, although they expect individual differences in timing.

Aspects of physical development occur in stages. For example, from the age of 2 to the onset of **puberty,** children grow gradually larger. But then the adolescent growth spurt occurs, ushered in by hormones and characterized by rapid biological changes in structure and function (as in the development of the sex organs) as well as in size. And so, a new stage of life would appear to begin. But opinion is mixed as to whether psychological aspects of development such as cognitive development, attachment, and sex typing occur in stages.

Now let us turn to the developments that occur between conception and birth. Although they are literally "out of sight," our most dramatic biological changes occur within this short span of nine months.

PRENATAL DEVELOPMENT

During the months following conception, the single cell formed by the union of sperm and egg will multiply—becoming two, then four, then eight, and so on. By the time a **fetus** is ready to be born, it will contain more cells than there are stars in the Milky Way galaxy. Prenatal development is divided into three periods: the germinal stage (approximately the first two weeks), the embryonic stage (which lasts from two weeks to about two months after conception), and the fetal stage.

The Germinal Stage

The zygote divides repeatedly as it proceeds on its journey to the uterus. Three to four days are required for this journey. The ball-like mass of dividing cells wanders about the uterus for another three to four days before beginning to become implanted in the uterine wall. Implantation requires another week or so. The period from conception to implantation is called the **germinal stage,** or the **period of the ovum.**

Prior to implantation, the dividing ball of cells is nourished solely by the yolk of the original egg cell, and it does not gain in mass.

The Embryonic Stage

The embryonic stage lasts from implantation until about the eighth week of development. During this stage, the major body organ systems differentiate. Development follows two general trends—**cephalocaudal** and **proximodistal.** As you can note from the apparently oversized heads of embryos and fetuses at various stages of prenatal development (Figure 7.1), the growth of the head takes precedence over the growth of the lower parts of the body. If you also think of the body as containing a central axis that coincides with the spinal cord, the growth of the organ systems close to this axis (that is, *proximal*) takes precedence over the growth of the extremities (*distal* areas). Relatively early maturation of the brain and the major organ systems allows them to participate in the nourishment and further development of the unborn child.

During the third week after conception, the head and the blood vessels begin to form. During the fourth week, a primitive heart begins to beat and pump blood—in an organism that is one-fifth of an inch long. It will continue to beat without rest every minute of every day for perhaps 80 or 90 years. "Arm buds" and "leg buds" begin to appear toward the end of the first month. Eyes, ears, nose, and mouth begin to take shape. By this time, the nervous system, including the brain, has also begun to develop.

The upper arms and legs develop first, followed by the forearms and lower legs. Next come hands and feet, followed at 6 to 8 weeks by webbed fingers and toes. By the end of the second month the limbs are elongating and separated. The webbing is gone. The head has become rounded and the facial features have become distinct—all in an embryo about one inch long and weighing *one-thirtieth* of an ounce.

Hormones and Prenatal Sexual Differentiation

By about 5 to 6 weeks, when the embryo is only a quarter to a half an inch long, nondescript sex organs have been formed. By about the seventh week following conception, the genetic code (XY or XX) begins to assert itself, leading to changes in the internal and external sex organs. If a Y sex chromosome is present, testes will form and begin to produce **androgens,** which prompt further masculinization of the sexual organs.

In the absence of male sex hormones, the embryo will develop female sex organs. Female sex hormones are not needed to induce these changes.

The Amniotic Sac

The unborn child—embryo and fetus—develops within an **amniotic sac,** a protective environment in the mother's uterus. The

---

Fetus The unborn child from the third month following conception through childbirth.

Germinal stage The first stage of prenatal development in which the dividing mass of cells has not become implanted in the uterine wall.

Period of the ovum Another term for the *germinal stage.*

Cephalocaudal Proceeding from top to bottom.

Proximodistal Proceeding from near to far.

Androgens Male sex hormones.

Amniotic sac A sac within the uterus that contains the embryo or fetus.

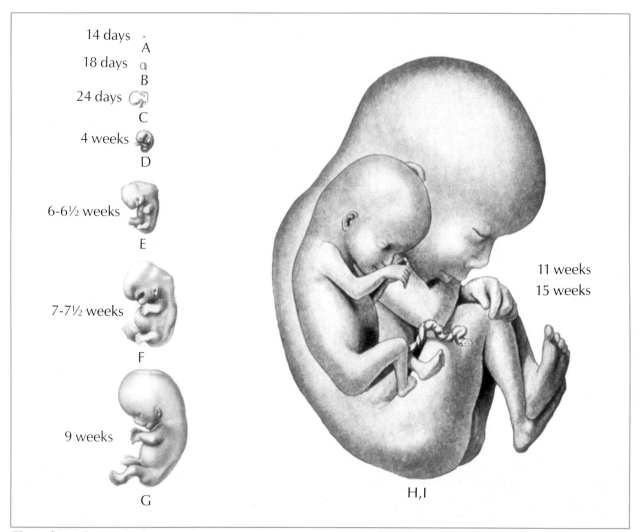

14 days
18 days
24 days
4 weeks
6-6½ weeks
7-7½ weeks
9 weeks
11 weeks
15 weeks

A
B
C
D
E
F
G
H, I

Figure 7.1 What Do Embryos and Fetuses Look Like at Various Stages of Development?

sac is surrounded by a clear membrane and contains amniotic fluid, in which the developing child is suspended. Amniotic fluid serves as a "shock absorber," preventing the child from being damaged by the mother's movements. It also helps maintain an even temperature.

Placenta A membrane that permits the exchange of nutrients and waste products between the mother and her developing child, but does not allow the maternal and fetal bloodstreams to mix.

Umbilical cord A tube between the mother and her developing child through which nutrients and waste products are conducted.

The Placenta   The **placenta** is a mass of tissue that permits the embryo (and later on, the fetus) to exchange nutrients and wastes with the mother. The placenta is unique in origin: It grows from material supplied both by mother and embryo. Toward the end of the first trimester it will have become a flattish, round organ about seven inches in diameter and one inch thick—larger than the fetus itself. The fetus is connected to the placenta by the **umbilical cord.** The mother is connected to the placenta by the system of blood vessels in the uterine wall.

Table 7.1 Possible Effects on the Fetus of Certain Agents during Pregnancy

AGENT	POSSIBLE EFFECT	AGENT	POSSIBLE EFFECT
Accutane	Malformation, stillbirth		
Alcohol	Mental retardation, addiction, hyperactivity, undersize	Paint fumes (substantial exposure)	Mental retardation
Aspirin (large doses)	Respiratory problems, bleeding		
Bendectin	Cleft palate? heart deformities?	PCB, dioxin, other insecticides and herbicides	Under study (possible stillbirth)
Caffeine (coffee, many soft drinks, chocolate, etc.)	Stimulates fetus; other effects uncertain	Progestin	Masculinization of female embryos, heightened aggressiveness?
Cigarettes	Undersize, premature delivery, fetal death		
Cocaine	Spontaneous abortion, neurological problems	Rubella (German measles)	Mental retardation, nerve damage impairing vision and hearing
Diethylstilbestrol (DES)	Cancer of the cervix or testes	Streptomycin	Deafness
Heavy metals (lead, mercury)	Hyperactivity, mental retardation, stillbirth	Tetracycline	Yellow teeth, deformed bones
		Thalidomide	Deformed or missing limbs
Heavy sedation during labor	Brain damage, asphyxiation	Vitamin A (large doses)	Cleft palate, eye damage
Heroin, morphine, other narcotics	Addiction, undersize	Vitamin D (large doses)	Mental retardation
Marijuana	Early delivery? Neurological problems? Birth defects?	X rays	Malformation of organs

A variety of chemical and other agents have been found to be harmful to the fetus, or are strongly implicated in fetal damage. Pregnant women are advised to consult their physicians about their diets, vitamin supplements, and use of any drugs including drugs available without a prescription.

Why Have Exercise Classes for Pregnant Women Become Popular? Years ago, the rule of thumb was that pregnant women were not to exert themselves. Today it is recognized that exercise is healthful for pregnant women, because it promotes cardiovascular fitness and increases muscle strength. Fitness and strength are assets during childbirth—and at other times.

The circulatory systems of mother and unborn child do not mix. A membrane in the placenta permits only certain substances to pass through. Oxygen and nutrients are passed from the mother to the embryo. Carbon dioxide and other wastes are passed from the child to the mother, where they are removed by the mother's lungs and kidneys. Unfortunately, a number of other substances can pass through the placenta. They include some microscopic disease organisms, such as those that cause syphilis, German measles, and **AIDS,** and some drugs, including aspirin, narcotics, alcohol, and tranquilizers (see Table 7.1).

The Fetal Stage

The fetal stage lasts from the beginning of the third month until birth. The fetus begins to turn

AIDS Acquired Immune Deficiency Syndrome.

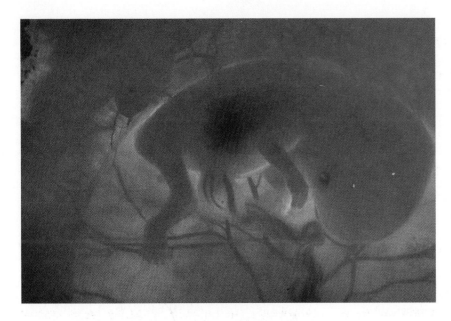

What Does a Human Fetus Look Like Halfway Through Pregnancy?   A fetus at about four and a half months.

and respond to external stimulation at about the ninth or tenth week. By the end of the third month, all the major organ systems have been formed (Arms & Camp, 1987). The fingers and toes appear fully formed. The eyes can be clearly distinguished, and the sex of the fetus can be determined visually.

The fourth through sixth months are characterized by maturation of fetal organ systems and dramatic gains in size. The fetus advances from one *ounce* to two *pounds* in weight and grows three to four times in length, from about four to 14 inches. Soft, downy hair grows above the eyes and on the scalp. The skin turns ruddy because of blood vessels that show through the surface. In the middle of the fourth month, the mother usually detects the first fetal movements and may suddenly feel that the baby is "alive." By the end of the sixth month, the fetus moves its limbs so vigorously that the mother may complain of being kicked. It opens and shuts its eyes, sucks its thumb, alternates between periods of wakefulness and sleep, and perceives light. It also turns somersaults, which can be clearly perceived by the mother.

During the seventh to ninth months, the organ systems of the fetus continue to mature. The heart and lungs become increasingly capable of sustaining independent life. The fetus gains about 5½ pounds and doubles in length. Newborn boys average about 7½ pounds and newborn girls about 7 pounds.

PHYSICAL DEVELOPMENT

Physical development is a complex process including gains in height and weight, maturation of the nervous system, development of bones and muscles, and the sex organs.

Childhood

Height and weight are two of the most obvious dimensions of physical growth. Children generally become taller and heavier as they grow older, and children's size has much to do with their self-concept and self-esteem. Young children literally "look up to" almost everyone else. With the exception of furniture and toys made for them, the artifacts of civilization seem designed for frustration.

The most dramatic gains in height and weight occur during prenatal development. Within nine months, children develop from a nearly microscopic cell to a **neonate** about 20 inches in length. Weight increases by a factor of billions.

During infancy dramatic gains continue. Babies usually double their birth weight in about five months and triple it by the first birthday. Their height increases by about 10 inches in the first year. Infants grow another four to six inches during the second year and gain about four to seven pounds.

Following the gains of infancy, boys and girls tend to gain about two to three inches a year until they reach the adolescent growth spurt. Weight gains also remain fairly even at about four to six pounds per year.

Many aspects of physical development are not so obvious as gains in height and weight, but they are just as important. In one example, the development of fine-motor skills at about the age of 4 coincides with myelination of the neural pathways that link the cerebellum to the cerebral cortex. Parts of the brain that enable children to sustain attention and screen out distractions become increasingly myelinated between the ages of about 4 and 7, readying the child to focus on schoolwork and to learn to read.

In one of the more fascinating aspects of the development of the nervous system, newborn babies show a number of automatic behavior patterns that are essential to survival—reflexes.

Reflexes   If soon after your birth you had been held gently, face down in comfortably warm water, you would not have drowned. Instead of breathing in, you would have exhaled slowly through the mouth and engaged in swimming motions.* This response is inborn, or innate, and just one of many **reflexes** with which children are born. Reflexes occur automatically, without thinking.

Many reflexes have survival value. The most basic reflex for survival is breathing. The breathing rate is regulated by the oxygen and carbon dioxide content of the blood and other body fluids. The breathing reflex works for a lifetime, although we can take conscious control of breathing when we choose to do so.

*I urge readers not to test babies for this reflex. The hazards are obvious.

At What Age Do Babies First Voluntarily Grasp Objects?

Since newborn children do not "know" that it is necessary to eat in order to live or to reduce feelings of hunger, it is fortunate that they have **rooting** and sucking reflexes. Neonates will turn their heads ("root") toward stimuli that prod or stroke the cheek, chin, or corners of the mouth. They will suck objects that touch their lips. Neonates reflexively withdraw from painful stimuli (the withdrawal reflex), and they draw up their legs and arch their backs in response to sudden noises, bumps, or loss of support while being held (the startle, or Moro, reflex). They reflexively grasp objects that press against the palms of their hands (the grasp, or palmar, reflex) and spread their toes when the soles of their feet are stimulated (the Babinski reflex). Babies also show sneezing, coughing, yawning, blinking, and many other reflexes. Elimination of wastes is also reflexive. Pediatricians largely learn about the adequacy of newborn children's neural functioning by testing their reflexes.

As children develop, their muscles and neural functions mature, and they learn to coordinate sensory and motor activity (Figure 7.2). Many re-

Neonate A newly born child.
Reflex A simple unlearned response to a stimulus.
Rooting The turning of an infant's head toward a touch, as by the mother's nipple.

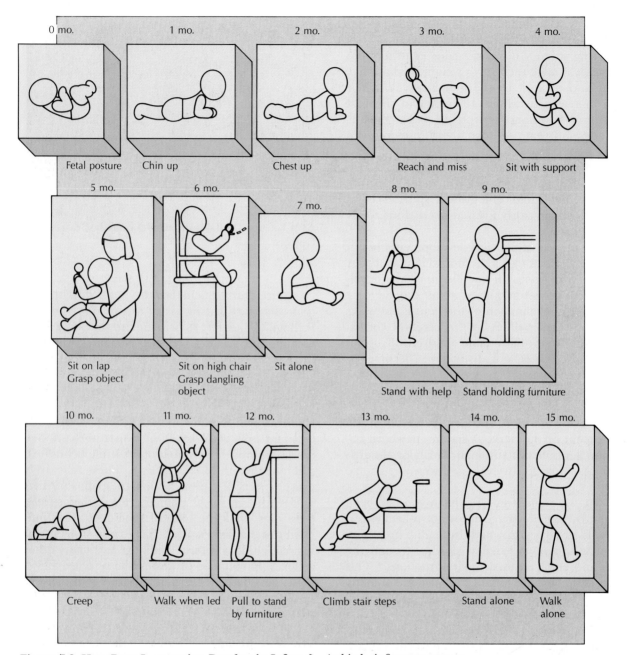

Figure 7.2 How Does Locomotion Develop in Infants? At birth, infants appear to be bundles of aimless "nervous energy." They have reflexive responses, but also engage in random muscular movements. Random movement is replaced by purposeful activity as they mature. Infants develop locomotion, or movement from place to place, in an orderly sequence of steps. Practice helps infants learn to coordinate muscles, but maturation is essential. During the first six months, cells in the motor and sensorimotor areas of the brain mature to allow activities like crawling and, later, walking. The times in the figure are approximate: An infant who is a bit behind may develop with no problems at all, and a slightly precocious infant will not necessarily become another Albert Einstein (or Rudolph Nureyev).

How Do Adolescents Differ from Young Children and from Adults?

flexes, such as the swimming reflex, drop out of their storehouse of responses, and many processes, such as the elimination of wastes, come under voluntary control.

Adolescence

In adolescence girls tend to spurt about 1½ years earlier than boys in height and weight. The spurts last between two and three years, with boys' spurts lasting about a half year longer than girls'. As a group, boys wind up several inches taller and many pounds heavier than girls. In boys, the muscle mass increases notably in weight, and there are gains in shoulder width and chest circumference.

At puberty pituitary hormones in boys stimulate the testes to increase the output of testosterone, causing the penis and testes to grow and pubic hair to appear. By age 13 or 14 erections become frequent and boys may ejaculate. Ejaculatory ability usually precedes the presence of mature sperm by at least a year, so that ejaculation is not evidence of reproductive capacity. Axillary, or underarm, hair appears at about 15. At 14 or 15 the voice deepens as the larynx, or voice box, grows.

In girls, pituitary secretions cause the ovaries to begin to secrete estrogen, which stimulates growth of breast tissue as early as 8 or 9. Estrogen promotes growth of fatty and supportive tissue in the hips and buttocks and widens the pelvis, rounding the hips. Small amounts of androgens produced by the adrenal glands, along with estrogen, stimulate growth of pubic and axillary hair. Estrogen and androgens work together to stimulate the growth of female sex organs. Estrogen production becomes cyclical in puberty and regulates the menstrual cycle. First menstruation, or **menarche,** usually occurs between 11 and 14. But girls cannot become pregnant until they begin to ovulate, about two years later.

Menarche is a "dividing time" for females in our society (Matlin, 1987). At menarche, girls come of age. A young girl might play football or lounge around in the home, even in the bedroom, of the boy next door. Now and then her father invites her to sit on his lap. But after menarche mothers often caution, "You're too big for that now."

Boys who reach physical and sexual maturity early are usually more popular and more likely to be leaders than late-maturing peers (Jones, 1957; Mussen & Jones, 1957). Their edge in sports and the admiration of peers boost their self-worth. But early maturation can hit some boys before they are psychologically prepared to live up to the expectations of others, such as athletic coaches who expect them to excel or peers who want them to fight their battles.

Menarche The beginning of menstruation.

The situation is somewhat reversed for girls. With their tallness and developing bustlines, early-maturing girls are conspicuous. Boys their own age may tease them, and older boys may try to pressure them into sexual activity (Simmons et al., 1983). Early-maturing girls are less poised and sociable than their late-maturing peers but appear to adjust by the high school years (Jones, 1958; Livson & Peskin, 1980).

PERCEPTUAL DEVELOPMENT

William James (1890) wrote that the newborn baby must sense the world as "one great booming, buzzing confusion." The neonate emerges from being suspended literally in a temperature-controlled environment to being—again, in James's words—"assailed by eyes, ears, nose, skin, and entrails at once." In this section we follow the perceptual development of the child and see that James, for all his eloquence, might have exaggerated the disorganization of the neonate.

Newborn children spend about 16 hours a day sleeping and do not have much opportunity to learn about the world. Still, it seems that they are capable of perceiving the world reasonably well soon after birth (Haber & Hershenson, 1980).

Vision   The **pupillary reflex** is present at birth. Infants may be able to discriminate most if not all of the colors of the visible spectrum by 2 to 3 months. By 4 months infants prefer red and blue to other colors (Bornstein & Marks, 1982; Fagan, 1980). Newborns can fixate on a light and within the first couple of days can follow, or track, a moving light with their eyes (McGurk et al., 1977). Estimates indicate that neonates' visual acuity is about 20/600 (Banks & Salapatek, 1981). But by 4 months or so, infants appear to focus on objects about as efficiently as adults do.

The visual preferences of infants are measured by the amount of time, termed fixation time, that they spend looking at one stimulus rather than another. Babies prefer stripes to featureless blobs and, by 8 to 12 weeks, curved lines

> **Pupillary reflex** The automatic adjusting of the irises to permit more or less light to enter the eye.

over straight lines. In classical studies run by Robert Fantz (1961), 2-month-old infants preferred visual stimuli that resembled the human face, as compared to newsprint, a bull's-eye, and featureless disks colored red, white, and yellow. In subsequent research (e.g., Haaf et al., 1983), babies have been shown facelike patterns that differ either according to the number of elements or the degree to which they are organized to match the human face. Five- to 10-week-old babies fixate longer on patterns that have high numbers of elements. The organization of the elements—that is, the degree to which they resemble the face—is less important. By the time infants are 15 to 20 weeks old, the organization of the pattern also becomes significant, and they look longer at patterns that are most facelike.

Infants generally respond to monocular and binocular cues for depth by the time they are able to crawl about (6 to 8 months or so), as well as have the good sense to avoid crawling off ledges and tabletops into open space (Campos et al., 1978). Note the setup (Figure 7.3) in the classic "visual cliff" experiment run by Walk and Gibson (1961). An infant crawls freely above the portion of the glass with a checkerboard pattern immediately beneath but hesitates to crawl over the portion of the glass beneath which the checkerboard has been dropped by about four feet. Since the glass alone would support the infant, this is a "visual" rather than an actual cliff.

Eight of ten infants studied by Walk and Gibson refused to venture onto the visually unsupported glass surface, even when their mothers beckoned repeatedly. Infants seemed interested, not distressed, when placed on the visually unsupported surface at the age of 55 days (several months before they can crawl), as suggested by decreases in heart rate (Campos et al., 1970).

Hearing   Fetuses respond to sounds months before they are born (Aslin et al., 1983). Normal neonates hear well unless their middle ears are clogged with amniotic fluid. In such cases, hearing typically improves dramatically within a few hours or days.

Most newborn infants will turn their heads toward unusual sounds and suspend other activities. Neonates normally respond to sounds of different duration, amplitude, and pitch. Three-day-old babies prefer their mothers' voices to those of other women (DeCasper & Fifer, 1980; Prescott & DeCasper, 1981). By the time they are born, children have had several months of "experience" in the uterus, and, for a good part of this time, they have been capable of sensing sounds. Since they are predominantly exposed to prenatal sounds produced by their mothers, learning may contribute to neonatal preferences.

Smell: The Nose Knows Early Neonates can discriminate distinct odors, such as those of onions and licorice. Infants breathe more rapidly and are more active when presented with powerful odors, and they will turn away from unpleasant odors as early as from 16 hours to 5 days of age (Rieser et al., 1976). Neonates, as can adults, can become habituated to even powerful odors. The nasal preferences of newborns are similar to those of older children and adults (Steiner, 1979).

The sense of smell, as the sense of hearing, may provide a vehicle for mother–infant recognition. Neonates respond to the odors of the mothers' breast secretions and underarms. Within the first week, nursing infants turn to look at their mothers' nursing pads (which can be discriminated only by the sense of smell) in preference to those of strange women (MacFarlane, 1977). By 15 days, nursing infants prefer their mothers' underarm odors to those of strange women (Cernoch & Porter, 1985).

Taste Shortly after birth infants show the ability to discriminate taste. They suck liquid solutions of sugar and milk but grimace and refuse to suck salty or bitter solutions. Infants can clearly discriminate sweetness on the day following birth. The tongue pressure of 1-day-old infants sucking on a nipple correlates with the amount of sugar in their liquid diet.

Touch Newborn babies are sensitive to touch. Many reflexes (rooting and sucking are two) are activated by pressure against the skin. Yet babies are relatively insensitive to pain, which may be adaptive considering the squeezing of the birth process. Sensitivity increases dramatically within a few days.

Figure 7.3 What Is the Visual Cliff? This young explorer has the good sense not to crawl out onto an apparently unsupported surface, even when Mother beckons from the other side. Rats, pups, kittens, and chicks also will not try to walk across to the other side. (So don't bother asking why the chicken crossed the visual cliff.)

The sense of touch is an extremely important avenue of learning and communication for babies. Not only do the skin senses provide information, but sensations of skin against skin also appear to provide feelings of comfort and security that may contribute to the formation of affectionate bonds between infants and caregivers, as we shall see in the section on attachment.

COGNITIVE DEVELOPMENT

When she was 2½, my daughter Allyn confused me when she insisted that I continue to play Billy Joel on the stereo. Put aside the issue of her taste in music. My problem stemmed from the fact that when she asked for Billy Joel, the name of the singer, she could be satisfied only by my playing the first song ("Moving Out") on the album. When

Table 7.2   Piaget's Stages of Cognitive Development

STAGE	APPROXIMATE AGE	DESCRIPTION
Sensorimotor	Birth to 2 years	Behavior suggests that child lacks language and does not use symbols or mental representations of objects in the environment. Simple responding to the environment (through reflexive schemes) draws to an end, and intentional behavior—such as making interesting sights last—begins. The child develops object permanence and acquires the basics of language.
Preoperational	2 to 7 years	The child begins to represent the world mentally, but thought is egocentric. The child does not focus on two aspects of a situation at once, and therefore lacks conservation. The child shows animism, artificialism, and objective moral judgments.
Concrete operational	7 to 12 years	The child shows conservation concepts, can adopt the viewpoint of others, can classify objects in series (e.g., from shortest to longest), and shows comprehension of basic relational concepts (such as one object being larger or heavier than another).
Formal operational	12 years and above	Mature, adult thought emerges. Cognition seems characterized by deductive logic, consideration of various possibilities before acting to solve a problem (mental trial and error), abstract thought (e.g., philosophical weighing of moral principles), and the formation and testing of hypotheses.

"Moving Out" ended and the next song, "The Stranger," began to play, she would insist that I play "Billy Joel" again. "That *is* Billy Joel," I would protest. "No! No!" she would insist, "I want Billy Joel!"

We went around in circles until it dawned on me that "Billy Joel," to her, symbolized the song "Moving Out," not the name of the singer. My daughter was conceptualizing *Billy Joel* as a *property* of a given song, not as the name of a person who could sing many songs. From the ages of 2 to 4, children tend to show confusion between symbols and the objects they represent. At their level of cognitive development, they do not recognize that words are arbitrary symbols for objects and events and that people could get together and decide to use different words for things. Instead, they tend to think of words as inherent properties of objects and events.

The developing thought processes of children—their cognitive development—is explored in this section. Cognitive functioning develops over a number of years, and children have many ideas about the world that differ markedly from those

of adults. Many of these ideas are charming but illogical. Swiss psychologist Jean Piaget (1896–1980) contributed significantly to our understanding of children's cognitive development.

Jean Piaget's Cognitive-Developmental Theory

Piaget hypothesized that children's cognitive processes develop in an orderly sequence of stages (1963). Piaget identified four major stages of cognitive development (see Table 7.2): *sensorimotor, preoperational, concrete operational,* and *formal operational.* We shall return to these periods in detail in the following pages.

Piaget regarded children as natural physicists who actively intend to learn about and manipulate their worlds. In the Piagetan view, children who squish their food and laugh enthusiastically are often acting as budding scientists. In addition to enjoying a response from parents, they are studying the texture and consistency of their food.

Piaget's Basic Concepts: Assimilation and Accommodation

Piaget described human thought or intelligence in terms of *assimilation* and *accommodation*. **Assimilation** is responding to a new stimulus through a reflex or existing habit. Infants, for example, usually try to place new objects in their mouths to suck, feel, or explore. Piaget would say that the child is assimilating a new toy to the sucking **scheme.** A scheme is a pattern of action or a mental structure that is involved in acquiring or organizing knowledge.

Accommodation is the creation of new ways of looking at the world. In accommodation, children transform existing schemes, or ways of organizing knowledge, so that new information can be incorporated. Children (and adults) accommodate to objects and situations that cannot be integrated into existing schemes. The ability to accommodate to novel stimulation advances as a result of both maturation and learning, or experience.

Newborn children merely assimilate environmental stimulation according to reflexive schemes, but true intelligence involves dealing with the world through a smooth, fluid balancing of the processes of assimilation and accommodation.

The Sensorimotor Stage

The newborn infant is capable only of assimilating novel stimulation to existing reflexes (or "ready-made schemes"), such as the rooting and sucking reflexes. But by the time an infant has reached the age of 1 month, it will show purposeful behavior by repeating pleasurable behavior patterns, such as sucking its hand. During the first month or so, infants apparently make no connection between stimulation perceived through different senses. Crude turning toward sources of auditory and olfactory stimulation has a reflexive look; it does not seem to be purposeful searching. But within the first few months the infant begins to coordinate vision with grasping, so that it simultaneously looks at what it is holding or touching.

A 3- or 4-month-old infant may become fascinated by its own hands and legs. It may become absorbed in watching itself open and close its fists. The infant becomes increasingly interested in acting upon the environment to make interesting results (such as the sound of a rattle) last. Behavior

Who Is Jean Piaget?

becomes increasingly intentional, purposeful. Between 4 and 8 months of age the infant explores cause-and-effect relationships, such as the thump that can be made by tossing an object or the way kicking can cause a hanging toy to bounce.

Prior to 6 months or so, out of sight is literally out of mind. Objects are not yet mentally represented. For this reason, as you can see in Figure 7.4, a child will make no effort to search for an object that has been removed or placed behind a screen. But by the ages of 8 to 12 months, infants develop **object permanence** and realize that objects removed from sight still exist and attempt to find them.

During the second year of life, children show interest in how things are constructed. It may be for this reason that they persistently touch and finger their parents' and their own faces. Toward the end of the second year, children begin to engage in mental trial and error before they try out overt behavior.

Assimilation According to Piaget, the inclusion of a new event into an existing schema.

Scheme According to Piaget, a hypothetical mental structure that permits the classification and organization of new information.

Accommodation According to Piaget, the modification of schemata so that information inconsistent with existing schemata can be integrated or understood.

Object permanence Recognition that objects removed from sight still exist.

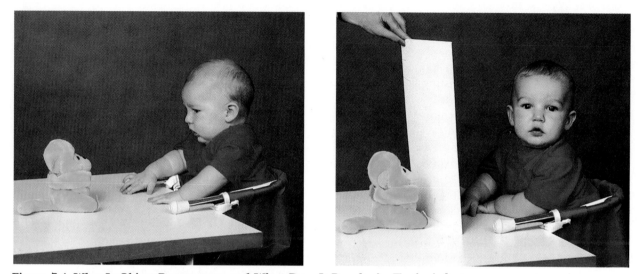

Figure 7.4 What Is Object Permanence, and When Does It Develop?   To the infant in these photographs, who is in the early part of the sensorimotor stage, out of sight is truly out of mind. Once a sheet of paper is placed between the infant and the toy elephant, the infant loses all interest in the toy. From evidence of this sort, Piaget concluded that the toy is not mentally represented.

Since the first stage of development is dominated by learning to coordinate perception of the self and of the environment with motor (muscular) activity, Piaget termed it the **sensorimotor stage.** The sensorimotor stage comes to a close at about the age of 2, with the acquisition of the basics of language.

Sensorimotor stage The first of Piaget's stages of cognitive development, characterized by coordination of sensory information and motor activity, early exploration of the environment, and lack of language.

Preoperational stage The second of Piaget's stages, characterized by illogical use of words and symbols, spotty logic, and egocentrism.

Egocentric According to Piaget, assuming that others view the world as one does oneself.

Animism The belief that inanimate objects move because of will or spirit.

Artificialism The belief that natural objects have been created by human beings.

The Preoperational Stage   The **preoperational stage** is characterized by children's early use of words and symbols to represent objects and the relationships among them. But be warned—any resemblance between the logic of children between the ages of 2 to 7 and your own often appears purely coincidental.

For one thing, preoperational children are decidedly **egocentric.** They cannot understand that other people do not see things as they do. They often perceive the world as a stage that has been erected for them. When asked, "Why does the sun shine?" they may respond, "To keep me warm." Or if you ask, "Why is the sky blue?" they may respond, " 'Cause blue's my favorite color." Preoperational children also show **animism:** They attribute life and intentions to inanimate objects, such as the sun and the moon. They show **artificialism,** the belief that environmental features like rain and thunder were made by people. Again, when asked why the sky is blue, 4-year-olds may answer, " 'Cause Mommy painted it." Examples of

Table 7.3 Examples of Preoperational Thought

TYPE OF THOUGHT	SAMPLE QUESTIONS	TYPICAL ANSWERS
Egocentrism	Why does it get dark out?	So I can go to sleep.
	Why does the sun shine?	To keep me warm.
	Why is there snow?	For me to play in.
	Why is grass green?	'Cause that's my favorite color.
	What are TV sets for?	To watch my favorite shows and cartoons.
Animism (Attributing life or intention to inanimate objects)	Why do trees have leaves?	To keep them warm.
	Why do stars twinkle?	Because they're happy and cheerful.
	Why does the sun move in the sky?	To follow children and hear what they say.
	Where do boats go at night?	They sleep like we do.
Artificialism (Assuming that natural events have been fashioned by people)	What makes it rain?	Someone emptying a watering can.
	Why is the sky blue?	Somebody painted it.
	What is the wind?	A man blowing.
	What causes thunder?	A man grumbling.
	How does a baby get in Mommy's tummy?	Just make it first. (How?) You put some eyes on it, put the head on (etc.).

egocentrism, animism, and artificialism are shown in Table 7.3.

To gain further insight into preoperational thinking, first consider these two problems: Imagine that you pour water from a tall, thin glass into a low, wide glass. Now, does the low, wide glass contain more than, less than, or the same amount of water as was in the tall, thin glass? I won't keep you in suspense. If you said the same (with possible minor exceptions for spillage and evaporation), you were correct. Now that you're rolling, here is the other problem. If you flatten a ball of clay into a pancake, do you wind up with more, less, or the same amount of clay? If you said the same, you are correct once more. To arrive at the correct answers to these questions, you must understand the law of **conservation:** Properties of substances such as mass, weight, and volume remain the same—or are *conserved*—when you change the shape or arrangement of substances.

Conservation requires the ability to think about, or **center,** on two aspects of a situation at once, such as height and width. But the boy in Figure 7.5, who is in the preoperational stage, focuses only on *one dimension at a time.* First he is shown two tall, thin glasses of water and agrees that they have the same amount of water. Then, as he watches, water is poured from one tall glass into a squat glass. Now he is asked which glass has more water. After mulling over the problem, he points to the tall glass. Why? When he looks at the glasses, he is "overwhelmed" by the tallness of the thinner glass. He focuses on the most apparent dimension of the situation only. He does not recognize that the gain in width in the new squat glass compensates for the loss in height.

If all this sounds rather illogical, that is because it is illogical—or to be precise, preoperational.

After you have tried the experiment with the water, try the following. Make two rows with five pennies each. In the first row, place the pennies about half an inch apart. In the second row, place the pennies two to three inches apart. Ask a 4- to 5-year-old child which row has more pennies. What will the child answer? Why?

Piaget (1962) found that the moral judgment of preoperational children is usually **objective.** In judging how guilty people are for their misdeeds, preoperational children center on the amount of

---

Conservation According to Piaget, recognition that properties of substances such as weight and mass remain constant even though their appearance may change.

Center According to Piaget, to focus one's attention.

Objective moral judgment According to Piaget, moral judgments that are based on the amount of damage done rather than on the motives of the actor.

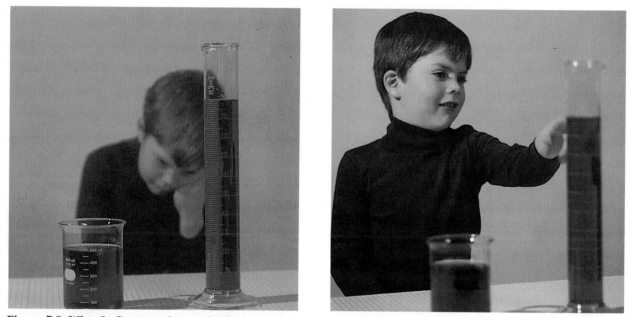

Figure 7.5 What Is Conservation, and When Does It Develop?   The boy in these photographs has agreed that the amount of water in two identical containers is equal. Then he watched as water from one container was poured into a tall, thin container. In the left-hand photograph, he is examining one of the original containers and the new container. When asked if he thinks that the amounts of water in the two containers are now the same, he says no. Apparently he is impressed by the height of the new container, and, prior to the development of conservation, he focuses on only one dimension of the situation at a time—in this case, the height of the new container.

damage done. Older children and adults, by contrast, usually focus on the intentions or motives of the wrongdoer.

To demonstrate objective moral judgments, Piaget would tell children stories about people and ask them which character was naughtier and why. Barry, for instance, is helping his mother set the table when he accidentally bangs the dining room door into a tray and breaks nine cups and six plates. Harmon breaks three cups as he sneaks into a kitchen cabinet to find forbidden cookies. Who

is naughtier, Barry or Harmon? The typical 4-year-old will say that Barry is naughtier. Why? He broke more china.

The Concrete Operational Stage   By about the age of seven, the child is entering the stage of **concrete operations.** In this stage, which lasts until about the age of 12, children begin to show adult logic. However, their logical thought, or operations, generally involve tangible objects and not abstract ideas. Concrete-operational children can center simultaneously on two dimensions or aspects of a problem. This attainment has implications for moral judgments, conservation, and other intellectual undertakings.

Children now become **subjective** in their moral judgments. They center on the motives of wrongdoers as well as the amount of damage done when assigning guilt. Concrete-operational children judge Harmon more harshly than Barry since

Concrete operational stage Piaget's third stage, characterized by logical thought concerning tangible objects, conservation, and subjective morality.

Subjective moral judgment According to Piaget, moral judgments that are based on the motives of the perpetrator.

Barry was trying to help his mother when he broke the plates and cups.

Concrete operational children show understanding of the laws of conservation. The boy in Figure 7.5, older, would say that the squat glass still has the same amount of water. If asked why, he might reply, "Because you can pour it back into the other one." An answer to this effect also suggests awareness of the concept of **reversibility**—recognition that many processes can be undone, so that relationships can be restored. Centering simultaneously on the height and the width of the glasses, he recognizes that the loss in height compensates for the gain in width.

Concrete operational children can conserve *number* as well as weight and mass. They recognize that there is the same number of pennies in each of the rows described earlier, even though one row may be spread out to look longer than the other.

Children in this stage are less egocentric. They acquire the abilities to take on the roles of others and view the world, and themselves, from other peoples' perspectives. They recognize that people see things in different ways because of different situations and different sets of values.

The Formal Operational Stage

The stage of **formal operations** is the final stage in Piaget's theory. It begins at about the time of puberty and is the stage of cognitive maturity. But some people do not reach it.

Formal operational children (and adults) think abstractly. They solve geometric problems about circles and squares without reference to what the circles and squares may represent in the real world. Children derive rules for behavior from general principles and can focus, or center, on many aspects of a situation at once in arriving at judgments and solving problems.

In a sense, it is during the stage of formal operations that people tend to emerge as theoretical scientists. They become aware that situations can have many outcomes, and they can think ahead, systematically "trying out" different possibilities.

Children in this stage can reason deductively, or draw conclusions about specific objects or people once they have been classified accurately. A new egocentrism can develop in which adolescents emotionally press for acceptance of their logic without recognition of the practical problems often weighed by adults. Consider this **syllogism:** "It is wrong to hurt people. Industry A occasionally hurts people (perhaps through pollution or economic pressures). Therefore, Industry A must be severely punished or dismantled." This thinking is logical. But by pressing for major changes or penalties, it may not weigh practical problems, such as resultant layoffs.

Evaluation of Piaget's Cognitive-Developmental Theory

Although Piaget's theory has led many psychologists to recast their concepts of children, it has also met with criticism (see Rathus, 1988, for a review). One issue has to do with the timing of Piaget's sequences. Piaget's methodology led him to underestimate the abilities of children. U.S. researchers have used different methods, and they have found, for example, that preschoolers are less egocentric and that children are capable of conservation at earlier ages than Piaget believed.

The most damaging criticism leveled at Piaget is that cognitive skills appear to develop more continuously than Piaget thought—not in general stages (Denney, 1972). Cognitive psychologist John Flavell (1982) argues that cognitive development is *"not* very stage-like" at all (Flavell, 1982, p. 17). Flavell admits that "later cognitive acquisitions build on or are otherwise linked to earlier ones, and in their turn similarly prepare the ground for later ones" (1982, p. 18). However, the "acquisitions" process may be gradual, not discontinuous.

Another issue is whether the sequences of development are invariant, as Piaget believed. It seems that they are.

In sum, Piaget's theoretical edifice has been rocked, but it has not been dashed to rubble. Though research continues to wear away at his

---

Reversibility According to Piaget, recognition that processes can be undone, that things can be made as they were.

Formal operational stage Piaget's fourth stage, characterized by abstract logical thought—deduction from principles.

Syllogism A form of reasoning in which a conclusion is drawn from two statements or premises.

timing and at his belief that the stages of cognitive development are continuous, his observations on the sequences of development appear to remain relatively inviolate.

Many psychologists regard Piaget as a towering figure in the study of cognitive development, but his approach is not the only one. There are many others, including information-processing approaches.

Information-Processing Approaches to Cognitive Development

Whereas Piaget viewed children as budding scientists, **information-processing** approaches view children (and adults) as similar to computer systems. Children, like computers, attain information ("input") from the environment, store it, retrieve and manipulate it, then respond to it overtly ("output"). One goal of the information-processing approach is to learn how children store, retrieve, and manipulate information—how their "mental programs" develop. Information-processing theorists also study the development of children's strategies for processing information.

Although there may be something to be gained from thinking of children as analogous to computers, children, of course, are not computers. Children are self-aware and capable of creativity and intuition.

Developments in Memory and Use of Cognitive Strategies   Many information-processing theorists focus on children's capacity for memory and their use of cognitive strategies, for example, the ways they focus their attention (Case, 1978; Case & Sandlos, 1980; Pascual-Leone, 1980; Pascual-Leone et al., 1978). They note, for example, that certain Piagetan tasks require several cognitive

strategies instead of one and that young children frequently fail at such tasks because they cannot hold many pieces of information in their short-term or working memories at once. Put another way, 3- and 4-year-old children can solve problems that have only one or two steps, whereas older children can retain information from early steps as they proceed to subsequent steps.

Some aspects of development that were thought by Piaget to reflect increasing capacity for the complexity and quality of thought may actually reflect an increasing capacity for storage and retrieval of information (Gelman & Baillargeon, 1983). Reconsider Piaget's study of children's moral reasoning in the story of the cups: Most 5-year-olds say that Barry is naughtier because he broke more cups, whereas 8-year-olds would usually consider Harmon naughtier because he was doing something wrong when he broke the cups. Piaget explained this age difference in terms of 5-year-olds' tendencies to focus on the amount of damage done instead of the intentions of the wrongdoer. But many 5-year-olds say that Barry is naughtier because they can *remember that he broke more cups but not all the details of the two stories.* When the stories are repeated, and effort is made to make sure that children remember them, even 5-year-olds frequently consider the intentions of the wrongdoer as well as the amount of damage done.

As noted in Chapter 4, stimuli are retained in short-term memory for up to 30 seconds or so after the trace of the stimulus decays. Ability to maintain information in short-term memory depends on cognitive strategies as well as basic capacity to continue to perceive a vanished stimulus. One cognitive strategy is encoding, for example, by transforming visual information into an **acoustic code.** Auditory stimuli can be maintained longer in short-term memory than visual stimuli. A simple way to convert visual information to an acoustic code is to label it. The sounds of the code can be rehearsed. Older children are more successful at recalling information, both because of improvements in the basic capacities of their short-term memories and because of their sophistication in employing strategies for enhancing memory (e.g., coding and rehearsal).

Information processing An approach to cognitive development that compares children to computers and deals with input, storage, retrieval, manipulation, and output of information.

Acoustic code A code in which visual or other sensory input is transformed into sounds that can be rehearsed.

The average adult can keep about seven chunks of information—plus or minus two—in short-term memory at a time. As measured by digit span (see Chapter 5), the typical 3-year-old can work on one chunk of information at a time. At the ages of 5 and 6, the typical child can recall two digits. The ability to recall series of digits improves throughout middle childhood, and 15-year-olds, like adults, can keep about seven chunks of information in short-term memory at once (Pascual-Leone, 1970).

Development of Selective Attention

Perhaps the initial cognitive strategy for solving problems is simply to attend to their elements. The ability to focus one's attention and screen out distractions advances steadily through middle childhood (Pick et al., 1975). Younger children (termed "preoperational" by Piaget) tend to focus their attention on one element of the problem at a time—a major reason that they lack conservation. Older children (termed "concrete" and "formal operational" by Piaget), by contrast, attend to multiple aspects of the problem at once, permitting them to conserve number, volume, and so on.

Pascual-Leone and Case suggest that children's problem-solving abilities improve because of (1) neurological developments that expand the working (short-term) memory and (2) growing automaticity in applying cognitive strategies. The younger child may have to count three sets of two objects each one by one to arrive at a total of six objects. The older child, with a larger working memory, familiarity with multiplication tables, and greater perceptual experience, is likely to arrive automatically at a total of six when three groups of two are perceived. Automaticity in adding, multiplying, and so on allow older children to solve math problems with several steps. Younger children, meanwhile, become lengthily occupied with individual steps, losing sight of the whole.*

Let us now turn our attention to Lawrence Kohlberg's theory of moral development and see how children process information that leads to judgments of right and wrong.

Lawrence Kohlberg's Theory of Moral Development

Psychologist Lawrence Kohlberg (1981) originated a theory to explain how children's cognitive development lays the groundwork for different styles of moral reasoning. Before we formally discuss Kohlberg's views, read the following tale used by Kohlberg (1969) in much of his research, and answer the questions that follow.

In Europe a woman was near death from a special kind of cancer. There was one drug that the doctors thought might save her. It was a form of radium that a druggist in the same town had recently discovered. The drug was expensive to make, but the druggist was charging ten times what the drug cost him to make. He paid $200 for the radium and charged $2,000 for a small dose of the drug. The sick woman's husband, Heinz, went to everyone he knew to borrow the money, but he could only get together about $1,000, which was half of what it cost. He told the druggist that his wife was dying and asked him to sell it cheaper or let him pay later. But the druggist said: "No, I discovered the drug and I'm going to make money from it." So Heinz got desperate and broke into the man's store to steal the drug for his wife.

What do you think? Should Heinz have tried to steal the drug? Was he right or wrong? As you can see from Table 7.4, the issue is more complicated than a simple yes or no. Heinz's story is an example of a moral dilemma in which a legal or social rule (in this case, laws against stealing) is pitted against a strong human need (Heinz's desire to save his wife). According to Kohlberg's theory, children and adults arrive at yes or no answers for different reasons. These reasons can be classified according to the level of moral development they reflect.

As a stage theorist, Kohlberg argues that the stages of moral reasoning follow an invariant sequence. Different children progress at different rates, and not all children (or adults) reach the highest stage. But children must go through stage 1 before they enter stage 2, and so on. According

*In Chapter 5 we saw that automaticity in processing information is an element in Robert Sternberg's (1985) theory of intelligence.

Table 7.4   Kohlberg's Levels and Stages of Moral Development

LEVELS	STAGES	ILLUSTRATIVE RESPONSES TO STORY OF HEINZ'S STEALING OF THE DRUG
Level I: Preconventional level	Stage I: Obedience and punishment orientation	It isn't really bad to take it—he did ask to pay for it first. He wouldn't do any other damage or take anything else, and the drug he'd take is only worth $200; he's not really taking a $2,000 drug.
	Stage 2: Naively egoistic orientation	Heinz isn't really doing any harm to the druggist, and he can always pay him back. If he doesn't want to lose his wife, he should take the drug because it's the only thing that will work.
Level II: Conventional level	Stage 3: "Good-boy orientation"	Stealing is bad, but this is a bad situation. Heinz isn't doing wrong in trying to save his wife; he has no choice but to take the drug. He is only doing something that is natural for a good husband to do. You can't blame him for doing something out of love for his wife. You'd blame him if he didn't love his wife enough to save her.
	Stage 4: Respect for authority and social order. Orientation to "doing duty" and to showing respect for authority	The druggist is leading a wrong kind of life if he just lets somebody die like that, so it's Heinz's duty to save her. But Heinz can't just go around breaking laws and let it go at that—he must pay the druggist back and he must take his punishment for stealing.
Level III: Postconventional level	Stage 5: Contractual legalistic orientation	Before you say stealing is wrong, you've got to really think about this whole situation. Of course, the laws are quite clear about breaking into a store. And, even worse, Heinz would know there are no legal grounds for his actions. Yet I can see why it would be reasonable for anybody in this situation to steal the drug.
	Stage 6: Conscience or principled orientation	Where the choice must be made between disobeying a law and saving a human life, the higher principle of preserving life makes it morally right—not just understandable—to steal the drug.

Source: R. J. Rest, "The Hierarchical Nature of Moral Judgment: The Study of Patterns of Comprehension and Preference with Moral Stages," *Journal of Personality,* 41 (1), 92–93. Copyright © 1974, by Duke University Press.

to Kohlberg, there are three levels of moral development and two stages within each level.

The Preconventional Level   In the **preconventional level,** which applies to most children

through about the age of 9, children base their moral judgments on the consequences of their behavior. For instance, stage 1 is oriented toward obedience and punishment. Good behavior is seen as that which involves obedience and allows one to avoid punishment.

In stage 2, good behavior is that which will allow people to satisfy their own needs and, sometimes, the needs of others. (Heinz's wife needs the drug; therefore, stealing the drug—the only way of attaining it—is not wrong.)

> **Preconventional level** According to Kohlberg, a period during which moral judgments are based largely on expectation of rewards or punishments.

The Conventional Level   In the **conventional level** of moral reasoning, right and wrong are judged by conformity to conventional (family, church, societal) standards of right and wrong. According to the stage 3 "good-boy orientation," it is good to meet the needs and expectations of others. During this stage moral behavior is seen as what is "normal"—that is, what the majority does. (Heinz should steal the drug because that is what a "good husband" would do. It is "natural" or "normal" to try to help one's wife. *Or,* Heinz should *not* steal the drug because "good people do not steal.")

In stage 4, moral judgments are based on rules that maintain the social order. Showing respect for authority and doing one's duty are valued highly. (Heinz must steal the drug; it would be his responsibility if he let her die. He would pay the druggist when he could.) Many people do not mature beyond the conventional level.

The Postconventional Level   In the **postconventional level,** moral reasoning is based on the person's own moral standards. In each instance, moral judgments are derived from personal values, not from conventional standards or authority figures. In stage 5's contractual, legalistic orientation, it is recognized that laws stem from agreed-upon procedures and that many rights have great value and should not be violated. But it is also recognized that there are circumstances in which existing laws cannot bind the individual's behavior. (Although it is illegal for Heinz to steal the drug, in this case it is the right thing to do.)

In stage 6's principled orientation, people choose their own ethical principles—such as justice, **reciprocity,** and respect for individuality. Behavior that is consistent with these principles is considered right. If a law is seen as unjust or as contradicting the rights of the individual, it is wrong to obey it.

Evaluation of Kohlberg's Theory   There is evidence that the moral judgments of children develop toward higher stages in sequence (Snarey et al., 1985), even though most children do not reach postconventional thought. Postconventional thought, when found, first occurs during adolescence.

Consistent with Kohlberg's theory, children do not appear to skip stages as they progress (Kohlberg & Kramer, 1969; Kuhn, 1976; White et al., 1978). When children are exposed to adult models who engage in a lower type of moral reasoning, they can be induced to express the patterns of judgment characteristic of the earlier stage (Bandura & McDonald, 1963). But children exposed to examples of moral reasoning above and below that of their own stage generally prefer the higher level of reasoning (Rest, 1976, 1983). Thus the thrust of moral development is from lower to higher stages, even if children can be sidetracked by social influences.

Kohlberg believed that the stages of moral development are universal, following the unfolding of innate sequences. However, stages 1 through 4 are found in about 90 percent of cultures studied around the world, and postconventional thought in only 64 percent (Snarey, 1987). Postconventional thinking is virtually absent in tribal and village societies. Critics have suggested that postconventional reasoning, especially stage 6 reasoning, may be more reflective of Kohlberg's philosophical ideals than of a natural stage of cognitive development. In recognition of this problem, Kohlberg (1985) virtually dropped stage 6 reasoning from his theory in recent years.

Let us now turn our attention from the cognitive realm to the emotional realm and observe the development of feelings of attachment between children and their caregivers.

ATTACHMENT

Attachment is a slippery concept. Parents and children do not tell one another, "I am attached to

---

Conventional level According to Kohlberg, a period during which moral judgments largely reflect social conventions. A "law and order" approach to morality.

Postconventional level According to Kohlberg, a period during which moral judgments are derived from moral principles and people look to themselves to set moral standards.

Reciprocity Mutual action.

Attachment The enduring affectional tie that binds one person to another.

you." They speak of feeling love for one another, not attachment. But the concept of attachment is of more scientific use because it is tied directly to overt behavior. According to Mary Ainsworth, one of the foremost researchers in the area of attachment, "Attachment may be defined as an affectional tie that one person or animal forms between himself and another specific one—a tie that binds them together in space and endures over time" (1973).

The behaviors that define attachment include (1) attempting to maintain contact or nearness and (2) showing anxiety when separated. Infants try to maintain contact with caregivers to whom they are attached. They engage in eye contact, pull and tug at them, ask to be picked up, and may even jump in front of them in such a way that they will be "run over" if they are not picked up!

Attachment is one measure of the quality of the care that children have received during infancy (Bretherton & Waters, 1985; Sroufe, 1985). **Securely attached** babies cry less frequently than **insecurely attached** babies. They are more likely to show affection toward their mothers, cooperate with them, and to use their mothers as a base for exploration. Securely attached children are more likely than insecure peers to be emotionally warm, socially mature, popular, enthusiastic, active, independent, and persistent (Frodi et al., 1985; LaFreniere & Sroufe, 1985; Sroufe, 1983).

Secure attachment A type of attachment characterized by positive feelings toward attachment figures and feelings of security.

Insecure attachment A negative type of attachment, in which children show indifference or ambivalence toward attachment figures.

Indiscriminate attachment Showing of attachment behaviors toward any person.

Initial-preattachment phase The first phase in forming bonds of attachment, characterized by indiscriminate attachment.

Attachment-in-the-making phase The second phase in forming bonds of attachment, characterized by preference for familiar figures.

Clear-cut-attachment phase The third phase in forming bonds of attachment, characterized by intensified dependence on the primary caregiver.

Stages of Attachment

John Bowlby (1980) is credited with first outlining phases in the development of attachment between infants and caregivers. His views have since been refined by Mary Ainsworth.

In one classic, cross-cultural study, Ainsworth (1967) traveled to Uganda, Africa, and observed infants who ranged in age from 2 to 14 months. She followed them over a nine-month period and tracked attachment behaviors, including maintaining contact with the mother, protesting when separated, and using the mother as a base for exploring the environment. At first the Ugandan infants showed **indiscriminate attachment.** That is, they clearly preferred being held or being with someone to being alone, but they showed no preferences for familiar caregivers. Specific attachment to the mother began to develop at about 4 months and grew intense by about 7 months. Fear of strangers, if it developed, followed by one or two months.

From studies such as these, Ainsworth (1978) identified three stages of attachment:

1. The **initial-preattachment phase,** which lasts from birth to about 3 months and is characterized by indiscriminate attachment.
2. The **attachment-in-the-making phase,** which occurs at about 3 or 4 months and is characterized by preference for familiar figures.
3. The **clear-cut-attachment phase,** which occurs at about 6 or 7 months and is characterized by intensified dependence on the primary caregiver—usually the mother.

Theoretical Views of Attachment

Attachment, like so many other behavior patterns, seems to develop as a result of the interaction between nature and nurture.

A Behavioral View of Attachment: Mothers as Reinforcers
Early in the century, behaviorists argued that attachment behaviors are learned through conditioning. Caregivers feed their infants and tend to their other physiological needs. And so infants associate their caregivers with gratification and learn to approach them in order to

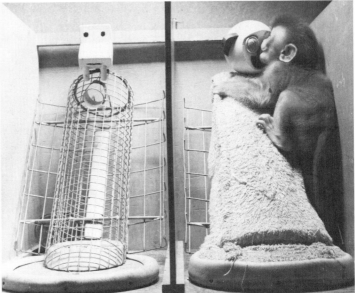

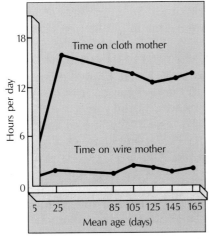

Figure 7.6 What Are the Roles of Feeding and Contact Comfort in the Development of Attachment in Infant Monkeys?
Although this rhesus monkey infant is fed by the "wire mother," it spends most of its time clinging to the soft, cuddly, "terrycloth mother." It knows where to get a meal, but contact comfort is apparently a more central determinant of attachment in infant monkeys (and infant humans?) than is the feeding process.

meet their needs. From this perspective, a caregiver becomes a conditioned reinforcer. The feelings of gratification that are associated with meeting basic needs generalize into feelings of security when the caregiver is present.

Harlow's View of Attachment: Mother as a Source of Contact Comfort Research by psychologist Harry F. Harlow cast doubt on the behaviorist view that attachment is learned mechanically. Harlow had noted that infant rhesus monkeys reared without mothers or companions became attached to pieces of cloth in their cages:

They maintained contact with them and showed distress when separated from them. He conducted a series of experiments to find out why (Harlow, 1959).

In one study, Harlow placed rhesus monkey infants in cages with two surrogate mothers, as shown in Figure 7.6. One "mother" was made from wire mesh from which a baby bottle was extended. The other surrogate mother was made of soft, cuddly terrycloth. Infant monkeys spent most of their time clinging to the cloth mother, even though "she" did not gratify the need for food (see Figure 7.6). Harlow concluded that monkeys—and perhaps humans—have a primary (unlearned) need for **contact comfort** that is as basic as the need for food. Gratification of the need for contact

Contact comfort A hypothesized primary drive to seek physical comfort from contact with another.

Figure 7.7 What Is Imprinting?   Quite a following? Konrad Lorenz may not look like Mommy to you, but these goslings became attached to him because he was the first moving object they perceived and followed. This type of attachment process is referred to as imprinting.

comfort, rather than food, might be why infant monkeys (and humans) cling to their mothers. Put another way, the path to a monkey's heart might be through its skin, not its stomach.

Imprinting: An Ethological View of Attachment

Ethologists note that for many animals attachment is an inborn fixed action pattern (FAP). The FAP of attachment, like other FAPs, is theorized to occur in the presence of a species-specific releasing stimulus and during a **critical period** of life.

A number of animals become attached to the first moving object they encounter. The unwritten rule seems to be, "If it moves, it must be mother." It is as if the image of the moving object becomes "imprinted" on the young animal, and so the formation of an attachment in this manner is called **imprinting.**

Critical period A period of time when a fixed action pattern can be elicited by a releasing stimulus.

Imprinting A process occurring during a critical period in the development of an organism, in which that organism responds to a stimulus in a manner that will afterward be difficult to modify.

Maternal-sensitive period A period of time during which a mother, because of hormone levels in the body, is theorized to be particularly disposed toward forming mother–infant bonds of attachment.

Ethologist Konrad Lorenz (1962, 1981) became well known when pictures of his "family" of goslings were made public (see Figure 7.7). How did Lorenz acquire his "following"? He was present when the goslings hatched, during their critical periods, and he allowed them to follow him. The critical period for geese and some other animals is bounded at the younger end by the age at which they first engage in locomotion and, at the older end, by the age at which they develop fear of strangers. The goslings followed Lorenz persistently, ran to him when frightened, honked with distress at his departure, and tried to overcome barriers between them. If you substitute crying for honking, it all sounds rather human.

If imprinting occurs with children, it cannot follow the mechanics that apply to waterfowl. Not all children develop fear of strangers. When they do, it occurs at about 6 to 8 months of age—*prior to* independent locomotion, or crawling, which usually occurs one or two months later. Human attachments also develop prior to and long after the middle of the first year of life.

Is There a "Maternal-Sensitive" Period? The Kennell and Klaus Studies

There might be no critical period for the development of attachment in humans, but physicians Marshall Klaus and John Kennell suggested that there might be a similar but weaker **maternal-sensitive period,** gov-

Why Has Day Care Become So Important? Since more than half of today's U.S. mothers are in the work force, day care is a major influence on the lives of millions of children. Parents are understandably concerned that their children will be provided with positive and stimulating experiences.

erned by hormones. In one study, Kennell and his colleagues (1974) randomly assigned a sample of new mothers and babies to standard hospital procedures or extended early contact. In the control condition, babies were whisked away to the nursery soon after birth and visited their mothers for half-hour feeding periods throughout the remainder of the stay. The experimental group of mothers and neonates spent five hours a day together throughout the hospital stay.

Two-year follow-ups suggested that extended early contact had benefits for mothers and children (Klaus & Kennell, 1976). Extended-contact mothers were more likely to cuddle, soothe, and enjoy their babies. Their babies outpaced controls in their physical and intellectual development. However, the Kennell and Klaus studies and others like them are fraught with methodological problems (Chess & Thomas, 1982; Lamb, 1982; Myers, 1984). For example, the extended-contact mothers knew that they were receiving special treatment. They were a group of poor, unwed mothers who received child-care training from the hospital staff during their extended early contact. Conceiving themselves to be special and staff training probably led to the benefits we have noted—not the extended early contact itself. In their more recent writings, Klaus and Kennell themselves have admitted that the period immediately following birth provides just one of many opportunities for attachment to develop between caregivers and infants.

In sum, attachment in humans appears to be a complex, continuous process. It includes learning in the broad sense of the term, as opposed to a limited, mechanistic-behaviorist sense, and the type of attachment that develops is related to the quality of the caregiver–infant relationship.

Let us now turn our attention to two important issues concerning attachment: the influences of day care and that distressing example of failed attachment—child abuse.

The Effects of Day Care

More than half of today's U.S. mothers spend the day on the job. This figure includes 41 percent of mothers of children in their first year (Klein, 1985). The ideals of the women's movement and financial pressures are likely to increase this number. When parents of young children both spend the day on the job, the children must be taken care of by others. As a consequence, 7 to 8 million U.S. preschool children are now placed in day-care centers (Trost, 1987). What are the effects of day care on parent–child bonds of attachment? On children's social development?

Studies of the effects of day care are encouraging. In their review of the literature, Jay Belsky and Laurence Steinberg (1978) concluded that day care has *not* been shown to interfere with mother–child bonds of attachment.

Day care seems to have positive and negative influences on children's social development. First, the positive: Infants with day-care experience are more peer-oriented and play at higher developmental levels. Day-care children are also more likely to share their toys (Belsky & Steinberg, 1978, 1979). Adolescent boys who had been placed in day care before the age of 5 were rated high in sociability and were liked by their peers (Moore, 1975). And so day care may stimulate interest in peers and help in the formation of social skills.

Now, the negative: A number of studies have compared 3- and 4-year-olds who had been in full-time day care for several years with agemates recently placed in day-care centers. The experienced children were more impulsive, more aggressive toward peers and adults, and more egocentric (Caldwell et al., 1970; Lay & Meyer, 1973; Schwartz et al., 1974). They were also less cooperative and showed less tolerance for frustration.

The negative characteristics found among children placed in day care suggest that many children do not receive the individual attention or resources they want. Placed in a competitive situation, many become more aggressive to attempt to meet their needs.

Even if day care usually fosters impulsivity and aggressiveness, these outcomes are not inevitable. Fewer children per caregiver and more toys would reduce competition. But two major obstacles stand in the way of having fewer children per caregiver: money and the scarceness of qualified personnel.

Child Abuse: When Attachment Fails

At least 625,000 children in the United States are neglected or abused by parents each year, and this figure is rising (Brown, 1983; National Center on Child Abuse and Neglect, 1982). A number of factors contribute to child abuse: situational stress (particularly unemployment), a history of child abuse in at least one of the parent's families of origin, acceptance of violence as a way of coping with stress, failure to become attached to the chil-

dren, and rigid attitudes about child rearing (Belsky, 1984; Milner et al., 1984; Rosenblum & Paully, 1984).

Stress is also created by crying infants themselves (Green et al., 1987; Murray, 1985). Infants who are already in pain of some kind, and relatively difficult to soothe, are ironically more likely to be abused (Frodi, 1981, 1985). Abusive mothers are also more likely than nonabusive mothers to assume that their children's stress-producing behavior is intentional, even when it is not (Bauer & Twentyman, 1985).

Sad to say, abused children show an alarming incidence of personal and social problems and abnormal behavior patterns. Maltreatment can disturb basic patterns of attachment: Abused children are less likely than nonabused agemates to venture out to explore the world (Aber & Allen, 1987). Abused children are more likely to be depressed and aggressive than nonabused children, even at preschool ages (Hoffman-Plotkin & Twentyman, 1984; Kazdin et al., 1985).

Child abuse is somewhat more likely to run in families. There is *no* evidence that women who were abused as children are more likely than other women to abuse their own children, but men who were abused are somewhat more likely to abuse their own children (Fisher, 1984). Why?

For one thing, their parents serve as violent role models. If children observe their parents using violence as a means of coping with stress and anger, they are less likely to learn to diffuse anger through techniques such as humor, verbal expression, reasoning, or even "counting to ten." Exposure to violence in their own homes may also lead some children to accept family violence as a norm.

SEX TYPING

When a friend's son Jason was 2 years old, he started talking about the things he would do when he grew up to be a "mommy." This took my friend back a bit. I suggested that perhaps no one had ever bothered to tell Jason that girls grow up to be "mommies" and boys grow up to be "daddies." My friend wisecracked that perhaps Jason was simply being democratic. After all, aren't we supposed to be able to grow up to be whatever we want to be?

At What Age Do Little Girls Realize They Will Grow Up to Be Women?

Actually, it wasn't democratic thinking that led Jason to think that he could grow up to be a woman. It was lack of **gender stability,** or knowledge that one's gender is a permanent feature. Development of gender stability is just one aspect of **sex typing,** or the process by which little girls (usually) grow up to act like women and little boys (usually) grow up to act like men.

Sex Differences

If the sexes were not clearly anatomically different, this book would never have come into being. But the extent to which the sexes differ in their behavior patterns and psychological traits remain open questions.

Differences in Cognitive Abilities   Psychological studies of sex differences find suggestions that females excel in verbal ability, whereas males excel in spatial relations and math abilities. Girls seem to acquire language somewhat faster than boys (Harris, 1977). Girls acquire additional words more rapidly, and their pronunciation is clearer (Nelson, 1973; Schachter et al., 1978). Female high school students exceed boys in spelling, punctuation, reading comprehension, solving verbal analogies (such as "Washington:one::Lincoln:?"), and solving anagrams (scrambled words).

Beginning in adolescence, boys usually outperform girls on tests of spatial abilty (Maccoby & Jacklin, 1974; Petersen, 1980). Boys and girls show similar math ability until late childhood. Boys begin to outperform girls at about the age of 12, and consistent sex differences appear at about 15 (Meece et al., 1982).

Although evidence continues to support the view that there are sex differences in cognitive abilities, three factors caution us not to attach too much importance to them. For one thing, they are *small* (Deaux, 1984; Hyde, 1981). Second, these sex differences are group differences. Variation in cognitive abilities is larger within, than between, the sexes. Third, the small differences that exist may only reflect cultural expectations and environmental influences. Even brief training in spatial-relations skills, for example, brings college women

Gender stability   The concept that gender is a permanent feature.

Sex typing   The processes by which children become aware of and adopt "masculine" or "feminine" preferences and behavior patterns.

Are There Sex-typed Mannerisms That Distinguish Girls from Boys?

up to the level of college men (Stericker & LeVesconte, 1982).

Differences in Play and School Activities
Boys and girls appear to develop stereotypical preferences for toys and activities by 18 to 36 months. Girls by these ages are more likely to play with soft toys and dolls and to dance. Boys are more likely to play with hard objects, blocks, and transportation toys (Fagot, 1974). Sex-typed preferences extend to school activities and team sports. Table 7.5 shows some of the results of a national survey of more than 2,000 children aged 7 to 11 (Zill, 1985).

Differences in Aggressiveness   Most studies show that males behave more aggressively than females (Maccoby & Jacklin, 1980; White, 1983).

Differences in Communication Styles: "He's Just a Chatterbox"   Despite the stereotype of women as gossips and "chatterboxes," in many situations males spend more time talking than women do. Males are more likely to introduce new topics and to interrupt (Brooks, 1982; Deaux,

1985; Hall, 1984). Boys dominate discussion in the classroom (Sadker & Sadker, 1985). As girls grow up, they appear to learn to let boys do the talking. Girls take a back seat to boys in mixed-sex groups (Haas, 1979; Hall, 1984). Yet females do seem more willing to reveal their feelings and personal experiences (Cozby, 1973). Females are less likely than males to curse—with the exception of women who are bucking sex-role stereotypes. Use of harsh language is considered a masculine trait.

There are also a number of sex-typed mannerisms found among girls and boys as young as 4 (Rekers et al., 1977). Girls, for example, are more likely than boys to show fluttering arms, bent elbows, and limp wrists.

And so, there are a number of behavioral differences between boys and girls. In the next section we shall consider theories and research concerning their development.

On Becoming a Man or a Woman: Theoretical Views

Like mother like daughter, like father like son—at least often, if not always. Why is it that little boys

Table 7.5   Rankings of Activities Favored by 7–11-Year-Old Boys and Girls

	BOYS	GIRLS
LOVE	1. Team sports	1. Going to parties
	2. Watching TV	2. Watching TV
	3. Caring for pets	3. Caring for pets
	4. Going to parties	4. Going to school
		5. Going to church
LIKE	5. Making things	6. Cooking
	6. Fixing things	7. Reading
	7. Going to school	8. Caring for kids
	8. Going to church	9. Team sports
	9. Boxing	10. Sewing
	10. Reading	11. Dancing
	11. Playing with guns	12. Playing with dolls
	12. Caring for kids	13. Making things
	13. Cooking	14. Fixing things
DON'T LIKE	14. Going to doctor	15. Going to doctor
	15. Dancing	16. Boxing
	16. Sewing	17. Playing with guns
	17. Playing with dolls	

Source: Zill, 1985.

How Do Parents Socialize Children into Assuming Sex-role Stereotypes?

(often) adopt stereotypical masculine behavior patterns? That little girls (often) grow up to behave like female stereotypes? Let us consider possible biological and psychological contributions to the development of sex differences in cognitive functioning, personality, and behavior.

Biological Influences   Biological views on sex typing focus on the role of sex hormones. For example, sex hormones are responsible for the in-utero differentiation of sex organs. Sex hormones in utero might also "masculinize" or "feminize" the brain by creating predispositions that are consistent with some sex-role stereotypes (Diamond, 1977; Money, 1977, 1987).

Sex hormones also spur sexual maturation during adolescence, and there are interesting suggestions that sexual maturation is linked to development of cognitive skills. Girls usually mature earlier than boys. Researchers have found that late maturers, whether boys or girls, show the "masculine pattern" of exceeding early maturers on math and spatial-relations tasks (Sanders & Soares, 1986; Sanders et al., 1982; Waber et al., 1985). Early-maturing boys exceed late-maturing boys in verbal skills and also show the "feminine pattern" of higher verbal than math or spatial-relations skills (Newcombe & Bandura, 1983). And so, early

maturation would seem to favor development of verbal skills, whereas late maturation might favor development of math and spatial-relations skills. Since girls usually mature earlier than boys, their verbal skills would usually be favored. The opposite would hold true for boys.

Let us now consider psychological views of sex typing.

Psychoanalytic Theory   Sigmund Freud explained sex typing in terms of **identification.** In psychoanalytic theory, identification is the process of incorporating within ourselves the behaviors and our perceptions of the thoughts and feelings of others. Freud believed that gender identity remains flexible until the resolution of the Oedipus or Electra complexes at about the age of 5 or 6. But the timing of sex typing in Freud's theory is not supported by research concerning the development of sex differences. Children display stereotypical sex-role behavior patterns by 18 to 36 months.

Identification (1) In psychoanalytic theory, incorporation within of the personality of another person. (2) In social-learning theory, a broad, continuous process of imitation during which children strive to become like role models.

What is the Role of the Parents in Sex-role Stereotyping?

Social-Learning Theory   Social-learning theorists explain sex typing in terms of observational learning, identification, and socialization.

Children learn much of what is considered masculine or feminine by observational learning, as suggested in an experiment by David Perry and Kay Bussey (1979). In this study, children learned how behaviors are sex typed by observing the *relative frequencies* with which men and women performed them. However, the adult role models expressed arbitrary preferences for one of each of 16 pairs of items—pairs such as oranges versus apples and toy cows versus toy horses—while 8- and 9-year-old boys and girls observed. Then the children were asked to show their own preferences. Boys selected an average of 14 of 16 items that agreed with the "preferences" of the men. Girls selected an average of only 3 of 16 items that agreed with the choices of the men.

Social-learning theorists view identification as a broad, continuous learning process in which children are influenced by rewards and punishments to imitate their parents—particularly the parent of the same sex—and same-sex adults in general (Bronfenbrenner, 1960; Kagan, 1964; Storms, 1979). In identification, as opposed to imitation, children not only imitate a certain behavior pattern. They also try to become broadly like the model.

Socialization also plays an important part in sex typing. Parents and others—even other children—provide children with messages about how they are expected to behave. They reward children

---

Socialization   In social-learning theory, guidance of children into socially desirable roles through instruction and rewards and punishments.

for behavior they consider sex-appropriate. They punish (or fail to reinforce) children for behavior they consider inappropriate. Girls, for example, are given dolls while they still sleep in cribs. They are encouraged to rehearse care-taking behaviors as preparation for traditional feminine adult roles.

Concerning the greater aggressiveness of boys, Maccoby and Jacklin note that

> Aggression in general is less acceptable for girls, and is more actively discouraged in them, by either direct punishment, withdrawal of affection, or simply cognitive training that "that isn't the way girls act." Girls then build up greater anxieties about aggression, and greater inhibitions against displaying it (1974, p. 234).

Girls frequently learn to respond to social provocations by feeling anxious about the possibility of acting aggressively, whereas boys are generally encouraged to retaliate (Frodi et al., 1977).

Social-learning theory has done an admirable job of outlining the situational factors that influence children's preferences for "sex-appropriate" toys and behavior patterns. The major criticisms of social-learning theory do not challenge the results of studies such as those reported in this section. Instead, they focus on theoretical issues, such as *How do reinforcers influence children?*

Let us now consider two cognitive-theory approaches to sex typing: cognitive-developmental theory and gender-schema theory.

Cognitive-Developmental Theory

Lawrence Kohlberg (1966) proposed a cognitive-developmental view of sex typing. Consistent with other aspects of cognitive-developmental theory, children are viewed as active participants in sex typing. Sex typing is seen as occurring in stages—discontinuously.

There is a role for rewards and punishments in cognitive theories. From the learning-theory perspective, rewards are seen as strengthening stimulus–response connections, but from the cognitive perspective, "rewards" give children information about when they are behaving in desirable ways. For this reason, even at the ages of 21 to 25 months, girls respond more positively to rewards from other girls. Boys at this age respond more positively to rewards from other boys (Fagot, 1985a). Rewards, that is, are most effective when

they have been processed in terms of the gender of the "rewarder"; their effects are not mechanical.

Although he sees a role for rewards, Kohlberg views the essential aspects of sex typing in terms of the emergence of three concepts: *gender identity*, *gender stability*, and *gender constancy*.

The first step in sex typing is attaining **gender identity.** Gender identity is one's knowledge that one is male or female. The origins of gender identity appear to lie in the initial labeling of the child as a boy or girl. Gender identity is so important to parents that they usually want to know if it's a boy or a girl before they begin to count fingers and toes. Most children acquire a firm gender identity by the age of 36 months (Marcus & Corsini, 1978; McConaghy, 1979; Money, 1977).

At around the age of 4 or 5, most children develop the concept of gender stability. They recognize that people retain their genders for a lifetime. Girls no longer believe they will grow up to be daddies, and boys no longer think they can become mommies. According to cognitive-developmental theory, the emergence of gender stability contributes to the organization of sex-typed behavior (Siegal & Robinson, 1987).

By the age of 7 or 8, most children develop the more sophisticated concept of **gender constancy** and recognize that gender does not change, even if people modify their dress or their behavior patterns. Gender is *conserved* despite rearrangement of superficial appearances. A woman who crops her hair short remains a woman.

A number of studies found that the concepts of gender identity, gender stability, and gender constancy do emerge in the order predicted by Kohlberg (Slaby & Frey, 1975). The order of emergence has been shown to be the same in cultures as different as those of the United States, Samoa, Nepal, Belize, and Kenya (Munroe et al., 1984).

According to cognitive-developmental theory, once children have established concepts of gender

Gender identity One's concept of being male or female.

Gender constancy The concept that gender remains the same despite superficial changes in appearance or behavior.

stability and constancy, they will be motivated to behave in ways that are consistent with their genders. Once girls understand that they will remain female, they will show a preference for "feminine" activities.

And so, cognitive-developmental theory has received some empirical support. As noted, the stages also appear to emerge in the order predicted by Kohlberg. But, as with psychoanalytic theory, there are problems with the ages at which sex-typed play emerges. Children prefer sex-typed toys and activities by 18 to 36 months (Huston, 1983), but gender stability and gender constancy remain some years away (Fagot, 1985b). Therefore, gender identity alone seems to provide a child with sufficient motivation to assume sex-typed behavior patterns.

Another cognitive view, gender schema theory, attempts to address this shortcoming.

Gender-Schema Theory: An Information-Processing View

Gender-schema theory holds that children use gender as one way of organizing their perceptions of the world (Bem, 1981, 1985; Martin & Halverson, 1981).

Gender-schema theory borrows elements from social-learning theory and from cognitive-developmental theory. As in social-learning theory, sex typing is viewed as largely learned from experience. Children learn "sex-appropriate" behavior patterns and which traits are relevant for them by observation.

Consider the example of strength and weakness. Children learn that strength is linked to the male sex-role stereotype and weakness to the female's. But they also learn that some traits, such as strong-weak, are more relevant to one gender than the other. In U.S. society, the strong-weak dimension is more relevant for boys than for girls. Bill will learn that the strength he displays in weight training or wrestling makes a difference in the way others perceive him. But most girls do not find this trait important in the eyes of others, unless they are competing in gymnastics, swimming, or other sports. Even so, boys are expected to compete in sports, and girls are not. Jane is likely to find that her gentleness and neatness are more important than strength in the eyes of others.

And so children learn to judge themselves according to the traits that are considered relevant to their genders. Their self-concepts become blended with the gender schema of their culture. The gender schema provides standards for comparison.

From the viewpoint of gender-schema theory, gender identity would be sufficient to prompt "sex-appropriate" behavior. As soon as children understand the labels of boy and girl, they have a basis for blending their self-concepts with the gender schema of their society. Children with gender identity will actively seek information concerning the gender schema. Their self-esteem will soon become wrapped up in the ways in which they measure up to the gender schema.

A number of recent studies support the view that children process information according to the gender schema (Cann & Newbern, 1984; List et al., 1983; Martin & Halverson, 1983). For example, they distort their memories so that they "recall" boys doing "masculine" things and girls doing "feminine" things.

In sum, brain organization and sex hormones may contribute to sex-typed behavior patterns. Social-learning theory does an excellent job of outlining the environmental factors that influence children to assume "sex-appropriate" behavior patterns. Cognitive-developmental theory views children as active seekers of information but may overestimate the roles of gender stability and gender constancy in sex typing. Gender-schema theory integrates the strengths of social-learning theory and cognitive-developmental theory and also highlights the ways in which children process information so as to blend their self-concepts with the gender schema of their culture.

Gender-schema theory The view that gender identity plus knowledge of the distribution of behavior patterns into "masculine" and "feminine" roles motivates and guides the sex typing of the child.

ADULT DEVELOPMENT

Human development continues through adulthood, with people showing shifting concerns and involvements. Psychologists have different

**What Trends Characterize
Development in Young
Adulthood?**

schemes for dividing the adult years, but we can use three broad categories without causing too much conflict: young adulthood (ages 20–40), middle adulthood (40–65), and late adulthood (65 and above).

Young Adulthood

Surveys show that U.S. adults in their 20s tend to be fueled with ambition as people strive to establish their pathways in life, to advance in the career world (Gould, 1975; Sheehy, 1976). Sheehy notes that during the 20s we often feel "buoyed by powerful illusions and belief in the power of the will [so that] we commonly insist . . . that what we have chosen to do is the one true course in life" (1976, p. 33). This "one true course" usually turns out to have many swerves and bends. As we develop, what seemed important one year can lose some of its allure in the next.

The Sheehy sample was overpopulated by professionals. Psychologists who have drawn more widely representative samples suggest that whereas men's development seems guided by needs for **individuation** and **autonomy,** women are more often guided by developing patterns of attachment and caring (Bardwick, 1980; Gilligan, 1982). In becoming adults men are likely to undergo a transi-

tion from restriction to control. Women, as a group, are relatively more likely to undergo a transition from being cared for to caring for others. Daniel Levinson found that many young, successful businesswomen differ from their male counterparts in that they do not have long-term goals: "They want to be independent but they are conflicted about ambition" (cited in Brown, 1987).

A study by Ravenna Helson and Geraldine Moane (1987) of the University of California found that between the ages of 21 and 27 women tend to take control over their own lives, accept the differences between romanticized visions of the way the world ought to be and the way it really is, and enlarge their psychological understanding of the people who are important to them.

The Challenge of the 30s   A number of researchers have noted that women frequently encounter a crisis that begins between the ages of 27 and 30 (Reinke et al., 1985). During the early 30s many women feel exploited by others, alone, weak, limited, and as if "I will never get myself together"

Individuation The process by which one separates from others and gains control over one's own behavior.
Autonomy Self-direction.

Up Against the Clock?   Many women delay childbearing because of careers and financial pressures. Lately there has been a baby boom among 30- to 40-year-olds who have decided to wait no longer.

(Helson & Moane, 1987). Concerns about nearing the end of the fertile years, opportunities closing down, and heightened responsibilities at home and work all make their contributions. Levinson notes, "By and large the image of a highly successful career woman is a single woman. But there is a flip side. The image of the single, childless career woman sitting alone by the fire at night is a powerful image today, one that is frightening to a lot of women, particularly businesswomen. Very few women get to their late 30s without strongly wanting to have children" (Brown, 1987).

Reassessments often occur during the late 20s and early 30s. People ask, "Where is my life going?" "Why am I doing this?" During the 30s we often find that the lifestyles we adopted during the 20s do not fit so comfortably as we had anticipated.

One response to the disillusionments of the 30s, according to Sheehy, "is the tearing up of the life we have spent most of our 20s putting together. It may mean striking out on a secondary road toward a new vision or converting a dream of 'running for president' into a more realistic goal. The single person feels a push to find a partner. The woman who was previously content at home with children chafes to venture into the world. The childless couple reconsiders children. And almost everybody who is married . . . feels a discontent" (1976, p. 34).

Levinson and his colleagues (1978) found that the second half of the 30s is characterized by settling down. At this time, many people feel a need to plant roots, to make a financial and emotional investment in their homes. Their concerns become more focused on promotion or tenure, career advancement, and long-term mortgages.

Middle Adulthood

Realizing that you're no longer as young as you used to be isn't easy. Sheehy (1976) writes that women enter midlife about five years earlier than men, at about 35 rather than 40. Entering midlife triggers a sense of urgency, of a "last chance" to do certain things.

What is so special about the mid-30s for women? Sheehy notes that

- 35 is the average age at which women send the youngest child off to school.
- 35 is the beginning of the so-called "age of infidelity."
- 35 is the average age at which married women reenter the work force.
- *34* is the average age at which divorced women get remarried.
- 35 is the age at which wives most frequently run away.
- 35 brings nearer the end of the childbearing years.

At some point between 35 and 45, most of us realize that life may be more than halfway over. There may be more to look back on than forward to. We'll never be president or chairperson of the board. We'll never play shortstop for the Dodgers or dance in the New York City Ballet. The middle-level, middle-aged businessperson looking ahead to another 10 to 20 years of grinding out accounts in a Wall Street cubbyhole may encounter severe depression. The housewife with two teenagers, an empty house from 8:00 to 4:00, and a 40th birthday on the way may feel that she is coming apart at the seams. Both are experiencing a **midlife crisis,** a feeling of entrapment and loss of purpose

Midlife crisis A crisis felt by many people at about age 40 when they realize that life may be halfway over and feel trapped in meaningless life roles.

that afflicts a number of middle-aged people. Some people are propelled into extramarital affairs at this time by the desire to prove to themselves that they are still attractive.

The early 40s mark a turning point for men (Levinson et al., 1978). Men in their 30s still think of themselves as older brothers to "kids" in their 20s. But at about 40, some marker event—illness, a change on the job, the death of a contemporary—leads men to realize that they are a full generation older than 20-year-olds. They mourn their own youth and begin to adjust to the specters of old age and death.

Until midlife, the men studied by the Levinson group were largely under the influence of **the Dream**—the overriding drive of youth to "become," to be the great scientist or novelist, to leave one's mark on history. At midlife we must come to terms with the discrepancies between the Dream and our achievements. Middle-aged people who free themselves from the Dream find it easier to enjoy the passing pleasures of the day.

But this discussion sounds unduly negative. During middle adulthood many of us have mastered our careers and retain the vitality to be highly productive. One study found that women at age 43 are more likely than women in their early 30s to feel confident, influence their communities, feel secure and committed, feel productive and effective, feel powerful, and extend their interests beyond their own families (Helson & Moane, 1987). During the middle years, many of us also take pleasure in continuing to nurture our children as they prepare for their own adulthoods. As we shall see in the next chapter, psychoanalyst Erik Erikson finds middle adulthood an opportunity to be generative in family life, at work, and in the larger community.

Another midlife issue centers around the so-called **empty-nest syndrome.** How do parents react when the last child leaves for college, gets married, or moves into an apartment? Do they feel a profound sense of loss, or do they heave a sigh of relief because they now have time for themselves? Findings are mixed.

As noted by Harbeson (1971), "many married women arrive at middle age without having looked and planned far enough ahead, and experience difficulties in making the transition from mother-

hood to socially useful occupations" (p. 139). But many women report increased marital satisfaction and positive personal changes such as greater mellowness, self-confidence, and stability when the children have left home (Reinke et al., 1985). Neither the "empty nest" nor menopause need be a negative or traumatic experience for women. A number of studies have found that middle-aged women show increased dominance and assertiveness, an orientation toward achievement, and greater influence in the worlds of politics and work (Serlin, 1980). It is as if they are cut free from traditional shackles by the knowledge that their childbearing years are behind them. Slightly more than half the U.S. women whose children have left the nest are now in the work force. Some have returned to college.

Late Adulthood

> Most people say that as you get old you have to give up things. I think you get old because you give up things.
> —Senator Theodore Francis Green, age 87,
> *Washington Post,* June 18, 1954

> How old would you be if you didn't know how old you was?
> —Satchel Paige, ageless baseball pitcher

> The true test of maturity is not how old a person is but how he reacts to awakening in the midtown area in his shorts.
> —Woody Allen, *Without Feathers*

Late adulthood begins at 65. One reason that developmental psychologists are concerned about the later years is the "demographic imperative" (Swensen, 1983). That is, more of us than ever before are 65 or older because of improved health care and knowledge of the importance of diet and exercise. Another reason for the increased interest in aging is the recognition that, in a sense, *all* development involves aging. A third reason for

---

The Dream Levinson's term for the overriding drive of youth to become someone important, to leave one's mark on history.

Empty-nest syndrome A sense of depression and loss of purpose felt by some parents when the youngest child leaves home.

How Do the Elderly Adjust to Retirement?

studying the later years is to learn how we can further promote the health and psychological well-being of the elderly.

A number of changes—some of them problematic—do occur in late adulthood. Changes in calcium metabolism lead to increased brittleness in the bones and heightened risk of breaks from accidents such as falls. The skin becomes less elastic, subject to wrinkles and folds. The senses become less acute. The elderly see and hear less acutely and may use more spice to flavor their food. The elderly require more time, or **reaction time,** to respond to stimuli. Elderly drivers need more time to respond to traffic lights, other vehicles, and changing road conditions. The elderly show some decline in general intellectual ability as measured by scores on intelligence tests. The drop-off is most acute on timed items, like those on many of the "performance" scales of the Wechsler Adult Intelligence Scale (see Chapter 5).

Although changes in reaction time, intellectual functioning, and memory are common, we understand very little about *why* they occur (Storandt, 1983). Loss of sensory acuity and of motivation might contribute to lower scores. Elderly psychologist B. F. Skinner (1983) argues that much of the fall-off is due to an "aging environment" rather than an aging person. That is, in many instances the behavior of elderly people goes unreinforced. Note that nursing home residents who are rewarded for remembering recent events show improved scores on tests of memory (Langer et al., 1979; Wolinsky, 1982).

In some cases, supposedly "irreversible cognitive changes" may also reflect psychological problems such as depression (Albert, 1981). Such changes are not irreversible. If the depression is treated effectively, intellectual performance may also improve.

However, the elderly often combine years of experience with high levels of motivation on the job. In these cases, forced retirement can be an arbitrary and painful penalty for no sin other than turning 65 or 70. According to Kimmel,

> Up to the age of 65 there is little decline in learning or memory ability; factors of motivation, interest, and lack of recent educational experience are probably more important in learning complex knowledge than age per se. Learning may just take a bit longer for the elderly and occur more at the individual's own speed instead of at an external and fast pace (1974, p. 381).

Despite changes that occur with aging, three of four adults aged 70 to 75 are generally satisfied with their lives (Neugarten, 1971). Similarly, 90 percent of the retired elderly rate their lives as

Reaction time The amount of time required to respond to a stimulus.

mostly good, and 75 percent rated their health as good or excellent (Hendrick et al., 1982).

Theories of Aging Although it may be hard to believe that it will happen to us, everyone who has so far walked the Earth has aged—which may not be a bad fate, considering the alternative. Why do we age? Various factors, some of which are theoretical, apparently contribute to aging.

Heredity plays a role. **Longevity** runs in families. People whose parents and grandparents lived into their 80s and 90s have a better chance of reaching these years themselves.

Environmental factors influence aging. People who exercise regularly appear to live longer. Disease, stress, obesity, and cigarette smoking can contribute to an early death.

There are several biological theories of aging. The **cellular-aging theory** suggests that the DNA within cells, which carries the genetic code of the individual, suffers damage from external factors (such as ultraviolet light) and random internal changes. As the person ages, the ability to repair DNA decreases. Damage and other changes eventually accumulate to the point where affected cells can no longer reproduce or serve their body functions. Another view is that waste products within cells eventually accumulate so that many cells are poisoned and no longer capable of functioning. These views are currently somewhat speculative.

On Death and Dying Death is the last great taboo. Psychiatrist Elisabeth Kübler-Ross comments on our denial of death in her book *On Death and Dying:*

We use euphemisms, we make the dead look as if they were asleep, we ship the children off to protect them from the anxiety and turmoil around the house if the [person] is fortunate enough to die at home, [and] we don't allow children to visit their dying parents in the hospitals (1969, p. 8).

From her work with terminally ill patients, Kübler-Ross found some common responses to news of impending death. She identified five stages of dying through which many patients pass: *denial, anger, bargaining, depression,* and *final acceptance.* Elderly people who suspect that death is approaching may undergo similar experiences.

In the denial stage, people feel, "It can't be me. The diagnosis must be wrong." Denial usually gives way to anger and resentment toward the young and healthy, and sometimes, toward the medical establishment—"It's unfair. Why me?" Then people may try to bargain with God to postpone death, promising, for example, to do good deeds if they are given another six months, another year. With depression come feelings of loss and hopelessness—grief at the specter of leaving loved ones and life itself. Ultimately an inner peace may come, a quiet acceptance of the inevitable. The "peace" does not resemble contentment; it is nearly devoid of feeling.

But reactions to impending death are varied. Robert Kastenbaum (1977) found little evidence that people undergo stages of dying as outlined by Kübler-Ross. Some people are reasonably accepting of it. Others are despondent. Still others are terrorized. Some people show a rapid shifting of emotions, ranging from rage to surrender, from envy of younger people to moments of yearning for the inevitable (Schneidman, 1976).

In any event, the final hours can pose a towering challenge, and inspirational works have been written about them. The U.S. poet William Cullen Bryant is best known for his poem "Thanatopsis," composed at 18. *Live,* wrote Bryant, so that

. . . when thy summons comes to join
The innumerable caravan that moves
To the pale realms of shade, where each shall take
His chamber in the silent halls of death,
Thou go not, like the quarry-slave at night,
Scourged to his dungeon, but, sustained and soothed
By an unfaltering trust, approach thy grave
Like one who wraps the drapery of his couch
About him, and lies down to pleasant dreams.

Bryant, of course, wrote "Thanatopsis" at 18, not 85. At that advanced age his feelings, his pen, might have differed. But literature and poetry, unlike science, need not reflect reality. They can serve to inspire and warm us.

Longevity A long span of life.

Cellular-aging theory The view that aging occurs because body cells lose the capacity to reproduce and maintain themselves.

TRUTH OR FICTION REVISITED

Fertilization takes place in the uterus.   False. Fertilization usually occurs in a fallopian tube.

Your heart started beating when you were a fifth of an inch long and weighed a fraction of an ounce.   True. It begins to beat within a month after conception.

If it were not for the secretion of male sex hormones a few weeks after conception, we would all develop as females.   True. Androgens stimulate differentiation of male sex organs.

Infants triple their birth weight by age 1 year.   True. Gains in height and weight are dramatic during the first year.

Girls are capable of becoming pregnant after they have their first menstrual periods.   False. Girls may not ovulate for more than a year after menarche.

Early maturing boys are more popular than late maturing boys.   True.

Newborn babies may look at one object with one eye and at another object with the other eye.   True. Their eyes do not yet converge on objects.

A 4-year-old may think that a row of five spread-out pennies has more pennies than a row of five bunched-up pennies.   True. Four-year-olds do not typically focus on two dimensions (length of row of pennies and number of pennies within a row) of an array simultaneously.

The highest level of moral reasoning involves relying on your own views of what is right and wrong.   True, according to Kohlberg's theory of moral development, in which postconventional thinking is viewed as the highest level.

Infants who are securely attached to their mothers are more willing to leave their mothers to explore the environment.   True. Secure attachment apparently provides a base for exploration.

Children placed in day care are more aggressive than children cared for in the home.   True. It may be that they learn to be aggressive because they compete for limited resources.

Child abusers have frequently been victims of child abuse themselves.   True for men. Perhaps their parents model aggression as a way of handling stress.

Girls are superior to boys in verbal abilities.   True, although the differences are small.

Girls do not like to play with guns.   True. There may be individual differences, but as a group, they do not.

A 2-year-old may know that he is a boy but think that he can grow up to be a "mommy."   True. Gender stability may not develop for another two years.

Young adulthood is characterized by trying to "make it" in the career world.   True. People in their 20s typically focus on trying to establish themselves.

Mothers suffer from the "empty-nest syndrome" when the youngest child leaves home.   False. Most mothers are well adjusted at this time of life, and many are first "coming into their own."

Most elderly people are dissatisfied with their lives.   False. At least 75 percent are quite content.

Chapter Review

There is controversy among developmental psychologists over the relative influences of nature and nurture and as to whether development is continuous or discontinuous—that is, occurs in stages. Gesell, Freud, and Piaget are stage theorists. Behaviorists emphasize the impact of nurture and view development as continuous.

Fertilization normally occurs in a fallopian tube. During the germinal stage of prenatal development, the zygote divides repeatedly and becomes implanted in the uterine wall. The major organ systems are formed during the embryonic stage, which lasts from the second through the eighth weeks following conception. The fetal stage lasts from the ninth week through birth and is marked by maturation of organ systems and gains in length and weight.

Physical development is characterized by cephalocaudal and proximodistal sequences. The adolescent growth spurt begins earlier in girls but lasts longer in boys. Reflexes make survival possible for neonates. As children develop, many reflexes drop out; some come under voluntary control. At puberty testosterone causes the male sex organs to grow. Estrogen causes the breasts and hips to grow. Early-maturing boys are usually more popular than late-maturing boys. Early-maturing girls are often teased and submitted to sexual pressures for which they are not prepared.

Neonates are nearsighted but visually track moving objects. Two-month-olds prefer viewing faces to colored disks, apparently because of their complex patterns. Infants usually show fear of depths by the time they can crawl. Neonates normally hear well and prefer their mothers' voices. The senses of smell and taste are well-developed at birth. Although newborns are sensitive to touch, they are relatively insensitive to pain.

Piaget viewed children as budding scientists who actively strive to understand the world. He defined intelligence as involving processes of assimilation and accommodation. Piaget proposed four stages of cognitive development: sensorimotor, which occurs prior to use of symbols and language; preoperational, which is characterized by egocentrism, animism, artificialism, inability to center on more than one aspect of a situation, and objective moral judgments; concrete operational, which is characterized by conservation, reversibility, and subjective moral judgments; and formal operational, which is characterized by abstract logic.

Information-processing approaches to cognitive development view development in terms of advances in the capacity of short-term memory, application of cognitive strategies for solving problems, and automaticity in processing information.

Kohlberg hypothesizes that moral judgments develop through three levels and two stages within each level. In the preconventional level, judgments are based on expectation of rewards or punishments. Conventional judgments reflect the need to maintain the social order. Postconventional judgments are derived from ethical principles, and the self is seen as the highest moral authority.

Attachment in children is measured by efforts to maintain closeness to caregivers and separation anxiety. Ainsworth theorizes three phases in the development of attachment; the initial-preattachment phase, the attachment-in-the-making phase, and the clear-cut attachment phase.

Behaviorists argue that children become attached to mothers through conditioning. Harlow's studies suggest that contact comfort is more important than feeding. Ethologists argue that animals show critical periods during which they will become imprinted on others. Kennell and Klaus argue for a maternal-sensitive period governed by hormones. There is no reliable evidence for critical periods (or weaker "maternal-sensitive" periods) for forming caregiver–infant bonds of attachment among humans.

Girls generally excel in verbal abilities, whereas boys generally excel in math and spatial-relations skills. Preferences for sex-typed toys develop by 18 to 36 months. Boys are usually more aggressive than girls.

Sex hormones may foster in-utero masculinization or feminization of the brain. The "masculine" pattern of cognitive skills is linked with late sexual maturation. Freud believed that gender identity remains flexible until the Oedipus or Electra complexes are resolved at 5 or 6. Social-learning theory explains sex typing in terms of observational learning, identification, and socialization. Cognitive-developmental theory views sex typing in terms of the emergence of gender identity, stability, and constancy. Gender-schema theory proposes that children use the gender schema of their society to organize their perceptions and that they blend their self-concepts with the gender schema.

Young adulthood is generally characterized by striving to advance in the career world. During their late 20s and 30s, many women encounter a life crisis concerning nearing the end of the optimal fertile years, closing opportunities, and heightened responsibilities. Some psychologists find that young men's development seems guided by needs for individuation, whereas young women are more often guided by shifting patterns of attachment.

Middle adulthood is a time of crisis and further reassessment for many people. Neither the "empty-nest syndrome" nor menopause need be traumatic events for women. Middle-aged women tend to show increased assertiveness and orientation toward achievement.

The elderly show less sensory acuity, and reaction time increases. Presumed cognitive deficits may reflect psychological problems or lack of motivation. Factors influencing longevity include heredity, exercise, diet, and maintenance of control. Kübler-Ross identifies five stages of dying among the terminally ill: denial, anger, bargaining, depression, and final acceptance. Research suggests that psychological reactions to dying are more varied than Kübler-Ross suggested.

Exercise

Stages of Prenatal Development

Directions: *Following are a number of events that take place during the three stages of prenatal development. In the blank space to the left of each event, write the letter A, B, or C to indicate the stage in which the event takes place:*

A = Germinal Stage
B = Embryonic Stage
C = Fetal Stage

_____ 1. Development of the amniotic sac
_____ 2. Completed formation of fingers and toes
_____ 3. Heart begins to beat
_____ 4. Mother senses movement of baby's limbs
_____ 5. Passage through fallopian tube
_____ 6. Beginning of sexual differentiation
_____ 7. Beginning of implantation in uterine wall
_____ 8. Soft, downy hair grows above the eyes and on the scalp
_____ 9. Development of the placenta
_____ 10. Division of the zygote into two cells

Answer Key to Exercise

1. B   4. C   7. A   9. B
2. C   5. A   8. C   10. A
3. B   6. B

Stages and Ages in Piaget's Theory

Directions: *List the names of each of Piaget's stages of cognitive development and the approximate ages during which they occur.*

	STAGE	APPROXIMATE AGES
1.	_____	_____
2.	_____	_____
3.	_____ _____	_____
4.	_____ _____	_____

Answer Key to Exercise

	STAGE	*APPROXIMATE AGES*
1.	Sensorimotor	Birth–2
2.	Preoperational	2–7
3.	Concrete operational	7–12
4.	Formal operational	12 and above

Events That Occur during Piaget's Stages of Development

Directions: *Following are a number of events that take place during Piaget's stages of cognitive development. In the blank space to the left of each event, write the letter A, B, C, or D in order to indicate the stage in which the event first takes place:*

A = Sensorimotor
B = Preoperational
C = Concrete operational
D = Formal operational

_____ 1. Artificialism
_____ 2. Subjective moral judgments
_____ 3. Abstract thinking
_____ 4. Object permanence
_____ 5. Children emerge as theoretical scientists
_____ 6. Animism
_____ 7. Conservation
_____ 8. Assimilation of novel stimulation to ready-made schemes
_____ 9. Objective moral judgments
_____ 10. Reversibility

Answer Key to Exercise

1. B	**4.** A	**7.** C	**9.** B
2. C	**5.** D	**8.** A	**10.** C
3. D	**6.** B		

Posttest

Directions: *For each of the following, select the choice that best answers the question or completes the sentence.*

1. Conception normally takes place in the

   (a) uterus, **(b)** fallopian tube, **(c)** ovary, **(d)** vagina.

2. Which of the following theoretical points of view places the least emphasis on the role of nature in human development?

   (a) Maturational theory, **(b)** Psychoanalytic theory, **(c)** Behaviorism, **(d)** Cognitive-developmental theory.

3. The embryonic period lasts from _____ until about the eighth week of prenatal development.

   (a) implantation, **(b)** conception, **(c)** ovulation, **(d)** the time the zygote reaches the uterus.

4. One organ is unique in that it develops from material supplied both by the mother and the embryo. It is the

   (a) umbilical cord, **(b)** placenta, **(c)** amniotic sac, **(d)** fallopian tube.

5. A pregnant woman wonders what types of agents can lead to premature delivery of her child. Research shows that premature delivery is most likely to stem from maternal use of _____ during pregnancy.

   (a) cigarettes, **(b)** aspirin, **(c)** diethylstilbestrol, **(d)** thalidomide.

6. There is a sudden noise in the nursery, and a newborn baby draws up his legs and arches his back in response. This response is an example of the _____ reflex.

   (a) Babinski, **(b)** palmar, **(c)** sphincter, **(d)** Moro.

7. According to the text, which of the following groups is most likely to be popular and admired by peers?

   (a) Early-maturing girls, **(b)** Early-maturing boys, **(c)** Late-maturing girls, **(d)** Late-maturing boys.

8. According to the text, the most damaging criticism leveled at Piaget is that

   (a) the sequence of stages varies from culture to culture, **(b)** not every child reaches the stage of formal operations, **(c)** cognitive skills may develop more continuously than he thought, **(d)** his research methods might have led him to underestimate the abilities of children.

9. According to Piaget, children first show object permanence during the

(a) sensorimotor period, (b) preoperational period, (c) concrete operational period, (d) formal operational period.

10. From the information-processing point of view, older children are likely to be more subjective in their moral judgments because

(a) they have developed the concept of reversibility, (b) they have previously developed the concepts of conservation of mass, weight, and volume, (c) they have more information in long-term storage, (d) they have greater capacity in short-term memory.

11. Which of the following stages of moral development comes earliest, according to Kohlberg?

(a) Good-boy orientation, (b) Contractual, legalistic orientation, (c) Naively egoistic orientation, (d) Obedience-and-punishment orientation.

12. Each of the following reflects an essential stage in the development of attachment, with the *exception of*

(a) preference for familiar figures, (b) intensified dependence on the primary caregiver, (c) fear of strangers, (d) indiscriminate attachment.

13. In Harlow's experiments, infant rhesus monkeys showed preference for surrogate mothers

(a) of their own species, (b) that were made from soft material, (c) that fed them, (d) that were present when they wanted to explore the environment.

14. A woman is concerned about having children of her own because she was abused as a child and has heard that child abuse "runs in families." Research concerning child abuse shows that

(a) child abuse is more likely to run in families for men than for women, (b) child abuse is more likely to run in families for women than for men, (c) the majority of men who have been abused abuse their own children, (d) the majority of women who have been abused abuse their own children.

15. Which of the following is not borne out by evidence?

(a) Girls show greater verbal skills, (b) Girls talk more than boys, (c) Boys show greater math skills, (d) Boys show greater spatial-relations skills.

16. Which of the following is most accurate concerning cognitive skills and timing of sexual maturation?

(a) Early-maturing boys exceed late-maturing boys in math and spatial-relations skills, (b) There is no connection between cognitive skills and timing of sexual maturation, (c) Early maturers, whether girls or boys, exceed late maturers on math and spatial-relations tasks, (d) Late maturers, whether girls or boys, exceed early maturers on math and spatial-relations tasks.

17. Sheehy labels the 30s the "Catch 30s" because

(a) the long bones make no further gains in length, (b) of disillusionments and reassessments, (c) women enter midlife at about age 35, (d) we reach the halfway point of the typical life span.

18. Research shows that middle-aged women

(a) frequently show increased dominance and assertiveness, (b) most often report decreased marital satisfaction, (c) cannot make the transition from motherhood to socially useful occupations, (d) come under the influence of the Dream.

19. According to the cellular-aging theory, the ability to repair _____ decreases as we age.

(a) the cell wall, (b) the myelin sheath, (c) DNA, (d) RNA.

Answer Key to Posttest

1. B	6. D	11. D	16. D
2. C	7. B	12. C	17. B
3. A	8. C	13. B	18. A
4. B	9. A	14. A	19. C
5. A	10. D	15. B	

PERSONALITY: THEORY AND MEASUREMENT

OUTLINE

PRETEST: TRUTH OR FICTION?
PSYCHODYNAMIC THEORIES
  Sigmund Freud's Theory of Psychosexual
    Development
  Carl Jung
  Alfred Adler
  Karen Horney
  Erik Erikson
TRAIT THEORIES
  Gordon Allport
  Raymond Cattell
  Hans Eysenck
  Evaluation of Trait Theories
LEARNING THEORIES

Behaviorism
Social-Learning Theory
Evaluation of Learning Theories
PHENOMENOLOGICAL THEORIES
  Carl Rogers's Self Theory
  George Kelly's Psychology of Personal Constructs
MEASUREMENT OF PERSONALITY
  Objective Tests
  Projective Tests
  Evaluation of Measures of Personality
TRUTH OR FICTION REVISITED
CHAPTER REVIEW
EXERCISE
POSTTEST

PRETEST: TRUTH OR FICTION?

The human mind is like a vast submerged iceberg, only the tip of which rises above the surface into awareness.

Biting one's fingernails or smoking cigarettes as an adult is a sign of conflict during very early childhood.

It is normal for boys to be hostile toward their fathers.

You have inherited mysterious memories that date back to ancient times.

People who show a strong drive for superiority are actually fighting feelings of inferiority that lie deep within them.

Psychologists have studied human personality by reading the dictionary.

Human behavior is largely consistent from situation to situation.

We may believe that we have freedom of choice, but our preferences and choices are actually forced on us by the environment.

We are more motivated to tackle difficult tasks if we believe that we shall succeed at them.

We all have unique ways of looking at ourselves and at the world outside.

Psychologists can determine whether a person has told the truth on a personality test.

Psychological tests can help you choose an occupation.

There is a psychological test made up of inkblots, and one of them looks something like a bat.

There is an ancient Islamic tale about the first time three blind men encounter an elephant. Each touches a different part of the elephant, but each is stubborn and claims that he alone has grasped the true nature of the beast. One grabbed the elephant by the legs and described it as firm, strong, and upright, like a pillar. To this the blind man who had touched the ear of the elephant objected. From his perspective, the animal was broad and rough, like a rug. The third man had become familiar with the trunk. He was astounded at the gross inaccuracy of the others. Clearly the elephant was long and narrow, he declared, like a hollow pipe.

Each of this trio had come to know the elephant from a different perspective. Each was blind to the beliefs of his fellows and to the real nature of the beast—not only because of his physical limitations, but also because his initial encounter had led him to think of the elephant in a certain way.

So it is that different ways of encountering people have led psychologists to view us from different perspectives. Various theories of human **personality** have been advanced. Because personality is not something that can be touched directly, theories of personality may differ as widely as the blind men's concepts of the elephant.

Nor do people agree on what the term *personality* means. Some equate personality with liveliness, as in, "She's got a lot of personality." Others characterize personality as made up of dominant traits, as in a "shy personality" or a "happy-go-lucky personality." Personality theorists define *personality* as the reasonably stable patterns of behavior, including thoughts and emotions, that distinguish people from one another (Mischel, 1986). These behavior patterns reflect a person's characteristic ways of adapting to the demands of life. Personality, therefore, deals with the ways in which people differ in behavior. Personality theories may include discussion of internal variables such as thoughts and emotions, as well as overt behavior.

Personality theories seek to explain how people develop distinctive patterns of behavior and to predict how people with certain patterns will respond to the demands of life. In this chapter we explore four major approaches to the study of personality: psychodynamic theories, trait theories, learning theories, and phenomenological theories. Then we discuss psychological methods of measuring personality.

PSYCHODYNAMIC THEORIES

There are several different **psychodynamic theories** of personality, but they have a number of things in common. Each teaches that personality is characterized by a dynamic struggle. Drives such as sex, aggression, and superiority come into conflict with laws, social rules, and moral codes. The laws and social rules become internalized. We make them parts of ourselves. After doing so, the dynamic struggle becomes a clashing of opposing *inner* forces. At a given moment our observable behaviors, as well as our thoughts and emotions, represent the outcome of these inner clashes.

Each psychodynamic theory also owes its origin to the thinking of Sigmund Freud.

Sigmund Freud's Theory of Psychosexual Development

Sigmund Freud was trained as a physician. Early in his practice, he was astounded that some people apparently experienced loss of feeling in a hand or paralysis of the legs in the absence of any medical disorder. These strange symptoms often disappeared once patients had recalled and discussed distressful events and feelings of guilt or anxiety that seemed to be associated with the symptoms. For a long time these events and feelings were hidden beneath the surface of awareness. Even so, they had the capacity to influence patients' behavior.

From this sort of clinical evidence, Freud concluded that the human mind was like an iceberg (Figure 8.1). Only the tip of an iceberg rises above the surface of the water, while the great mass of it

---

Personality The distinct patterns of behaviors, including thoughts and feelings, that characterize a person's adaptation to life.

Psychodynamic theory Sigmund Freud's perspective, which emphasizes the importance of unconscious motives and conflicts as forces that determine behavior.

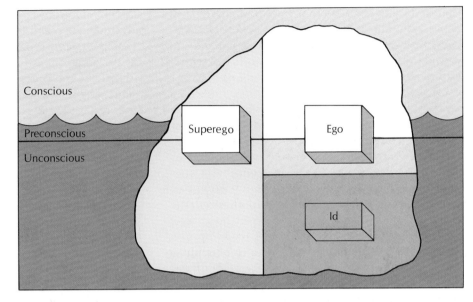

Figure 8.1. Why Can We Compare Freud's View of Human Personality to an Iceberg? According to psychoanalytic theory, only the tip of human personality rises above the surface of the mind into conscious awareness. Material in the preconscious can become conscious if we direct our attention to it, but unconscious material tends to remain shrouded in mystery.

darkens the deep. Freud came to believe that people, similarly, were only aware of a small number of the ideas and the impulses that dwelled within their minds. Freud argued that the greater mass of the mind, our deepest images, thoughts, fears, and urges, remained beneath the surface of conscious awareness, where little light illuminated

them. He labeled the region that poked through into the light of awareness the **conscious** part of the mind. He called the regions that lay below the surface the preconscious and the unconscious.

The **preconscious** mind contains elements of experience that are presently out of awareness but can be made conscious simply by focusing on them. The **unconscious** mind is shrouded in mystery. It contains biological instincts such as sex and aggression. Some unconscious urges cannot be experienced consciously because mental images and words could not portray them in all their color and fury. Other unconscious urges may be kept below the surface by **repression,** or the automatic ejection of anxiety-evoking ideas from awareness. Repression protects us from recognizing impulses we would consider inappropriate in light of our moral values.

The unconscious is the largest part of the mind. Here the dynamic struggle between biolog-

What Was Sigmund Freud's View of Personality? Freud taught that human personality is characterized by a dynamic struggle as basic physiological drives come into conflict with laws and social codes.

Conscious Self-aware.

Preconscious Capable of being brought into awareness by focusing of attention.

Unconscious In psychoanalytic theory, not available to awareness by simple focusing of attention.

Repression A defense mechanism that protects the person from anxiety by ejecting anxiety-evoking ideas and impulses from awareness.

ical drives and social rules is fierce. As drives seek expression, and internalized values exert counter-pressures, the resultant conflict can give rise to various psychological disorders and behavioral outbursts.

The Structure of Personality   When is a structure not a structure? When it is a mental or **psychic structure**—Freud's label for the clashing forces of personality. They could not be seen or measured directly, but their presence was suggested by observable behavior, expressed thoughts, and emotions. Freud hypothesized the existence of three psychic structures: the *id, ego,* and *superego.*

The **id** is present at birth. It represents physiological drives and is fully unconscious. Freud described the id as "a chaos, a cauldron of seething excitations" (1964, p. 73). Freud believed that con-

---

Psychic structure   In psychoanalytic theory, a hypothesized mental structure that helps explain different aspects of behavior.

Id   The psychic structure, present at birth, that represents physiological drives and is fully unconscious.

Pleasure principle   The governing principle of the id—the seeking of immediate gratification of instinctive needs.

Ego   The second psychic structure to develop, characterized by self-awareness, planning, and delay of gratification.

Reality principle   Consideration of what is practical and possible in gratifying needs.

Defense mechanism   In psychoanalytic theory, an unconscious function of the ego that protects it from anxiety-evoking material by preventing accurate recognition of this material.

Regression   A defense mechanism in which the person returns, under stress, to behavior characteristic of an earlier stage of development.

Rationalization   A defense mechanism in which the person finds self-deceptive justifications for unacceptable behavior.

Displacement   A defense mechanism in which ideas or impulses are transferred from a threatening or unsuitable object onto an acceptable object.

Superego   The third psychic structure, which functions as a moral guardian and sets forth high standards for behavior.

---

flicting emotions could dwell side by side in the id. In the id we could feel hatred for our mothers for failing to gratify immediately all our needs, even at the same time that we feel love for them. The id follows the **pleasure principle.** It demands instant gratification of instincts without consideration of law, social custom, or the needs of others.

The **ego** begins to develop during the first year of life, largely because not all of a child's demands for gratification can be met immediately. The ego "stands for reason and good sense" (Freud, 1964, p. 76), for rational ways of coping with frustration. It curbs the appetites of the id and makes plans that are in keeping with social convention, so that a person can find gratification yet avoid the disapproval of others. The id lets you know that you are starving. The ego creates the idea of walking to the refrigerator, heating up some tacos, and pouring a glass of milk. The ego is guided by the **reality principle.** It takes into account what is practical and possible, as well as what is urged. It is also the ego that provides the conscious sense of self.

Although most of the ego is conscious, some of its business is carried out unconsciously. For instance, the ego also acts as a watchdog or censor that screens the impulses of the id. When the ego senses that socially unacceptable impulses are rising into awareness, it may use psychological defenses to prevent them from surfacing. Repression is one such psychological defense, or **defense mechanism.** Other important defense mechanisms include *regression, rationalization,* and *displacement.* In **regression,** the individual, when under stress, returns to a form of behavior characteristic of an earlier stage of development, as in an adolescent who cries when forbidden to use the family car. **Rationalization** is the use of self-deceiving justifications for unacceptable behavior, as when a student blames her cheating on the teacher for leaving the room during a test. **Displacement** is the transfer of ideas and impulses from threatening or unsuitable objects to less threatening objects. Freud believed that children displace sexual urges toward parents onto people outside the family because, in part, of the incest taboo.

The **superego** develops throughout middle childhood, usually incorporating the moral standards and values of parents and significant

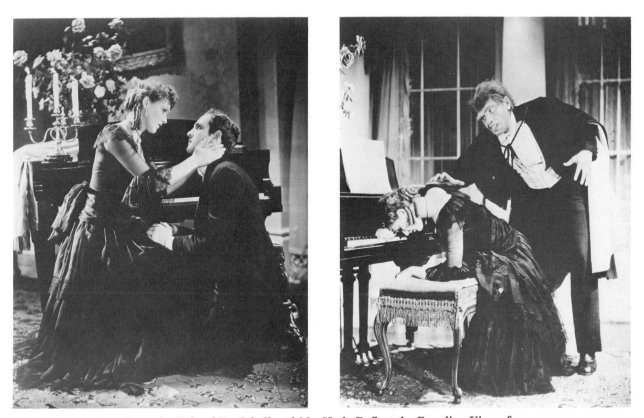

How Does the Tale of Dr. Jekyll and Mr. Hyde Reflect the Freudian View of Personality? Freud suggested that each of us is influenced by an id that demands instant gratification without regard for moral scruples and the needs of others. Robert Louis Stevenson had a dream in which a similar idea was expressed, and he developed it into the novel *Dr. Jekyll and Mr. Hyde*. In one film version of the tale, Dr. Jekyll, shown at left, is a loving, considerate person—suggestive of ego functioning. The monstrous Mr. Hyde, shown at right, is suggestive of the id. Stevenson's wife was horrified by the concept and destroyed an early version of the manuscript. But Stevenson was so enthralled by the idea that he rewrote the book.

members of the community through **identification.** The superego functions according to the **moral principle.** The superego can hold forth shining examples of an ideal self and also acts like the conscience, an internal moral guardian. Throughout life, the superego monitors the intentions of the ego and hands out judgments of right and wrong. It floods the ego with feelings of guilt and shame when the verdict is in the negative.

The ego hasn't an easy time of it. It stands between id and superego, braving the arrows of each. It strives to satisfy the demands of the id and the moral sense of the superego. The id may urge, "You are sexually aroused!" But the superego may

warn, "You're not married." The poor ego is caught in the middle.

From the Freudian perspective, a healthy personality has found ways to gratify most of the id's demands without seriously offending the superego. Most of the remaining demands of the id are contained or repressed.

Identification In psychoanalytic theory, the unconscious assumption of the behavior of another person.

Moral principle The governing principle of the superego, which sets moral standards and enforces adherence to them.

Are Children "Sexual"?   Freud stirred controversy within the medical establishment of his day by arguing that sexual impulses, and their gratification, were central factors in personality development, even among young children.

Stages of Psychosexual Development

Freud stirred controversy by arguing that sexual impulses, and their gratification, were central factors in personality development, even among children. Freud saw children's basic ways of relating to the world, such as sucking their mothers' breasts

Eros In psychoanalytic theory, the basic instinct to preserve and perpetuate life.

Libido (1) In psychoanalytic theory, the energy of Eros; the sexual instinct. (2) Generally, sexual interest or drive.

Erogenous zone An area of the body that is sensitive to sexual sensations.

Psychosexual development In psychoanalytic theory, the process by which libidinal energy is expressed through different erogenous zones during different stages of development.

Oral stage The first stage of psychosexual development, during which gratification is hypothesized to be attained primarily through oral activities.

and moving their bowels, as involving sexual feelings.

Freud believed that there was a major instinct to preserve and perpetuate life, which he termed **Eros.** Eros contained a certain amount of energy, which Freud labeled **libido.** This energy was psychological in nature and involved sexual impulses, so Freud considered it *psychosexual.* Libidinal energy would be expressed through sexual feelings in different parts of the body, or **erogenous zones,** as the child developed. To Freud, human development involved the transfer of libidinal energy from one zone to another. He hypothesized five stages of **psychosexual development:** oral, anal, phallic, latency, and genital.

During the first year of life, a child experiences much of its world through the mouth. If it fits, into the mouth it goes. This is the **oral stage.** Freud argued that oral activities such as sucking and biting bring the child sexual gratification as well as nourishment.

Freud believed that children would encounter conflicts during each stage of psychosexual development. During the oral stage, conflict would center around the nature and extent of oral gratification. Early **weaning** could lead to frustration. Excessive gratification, on the other hand, could lead an infant to expect it would automatically be handed everything in life. Inadequate or excessive gratification in any stage could lead to **fixation** in that stage, and the development of traits characteristic of that stage. Oral traits include dependency, gullibility, and optimism or pessimism.

Freud theorized that adults with an **oral fixation** could experience exaggerated desires for "oral activities," such as smoking, overeating, alcohol abuse, and nail biting. Like the infant whose very survival depends on the mercy of an adult, adults with oral fixations may be disposed toward clinging, dependent interpersonal relationships.

During the **anal stage,** sexual gratification is attained through contraction and relaxation of the muscles that control elimination of waste products. Elimination, which was controlled reflexively during most of the first year of life, comes under voluntary muscular control, even if such control at first is not reliable. The anal stage is said to begin in the second year of life.

During the anal stage, children learn to delay the gratification of eliminating as soon as they feel the urge. The general issue of self-control may become a source of conflict between parent and child. **Anal fixations** may stem from this conflict and lead to two sets of anal traits. So-called **anal-retentive** traits involve excessive use of self-control. They include perfectionism, a strong need for order, and exaggerated neatness and cleanliness. **Anal-expulsive** traits, on the other hand, "let it all hang out." They include carelessness, messiness, even **sadism.**

Children enter the **phallic stage** during the third year of life. During this stage the major erogenous zone is the phallic region (the **clitoris** in girls). Parent-child conflict is likely to develop over masturbation, which parents may treat with punishment and threats. During the phallic stage children may develop strong sexual attachments to the parent of the opposite sex and begin to view the same-sex parent as a rival for the other parent's affections. Boys may want to marry Mommy, and girls may want to marry Daddy.

Feelings of lust and jealousy are difficult for children to handle. So they remain unconscious, although their influence is felt through fantasies

about marriage and hostility toward the same-sex parent. Freud labeled this conflict in boys the **Oedipus complex,** after the legendary Greek king who unwittingly killed his father and married his mother. Similar feelings in girls give rise to the **Electra complex.** According to Greek legend, Electra was the daughter of King Agamemnon. She longed for him after his death and sought revenge against his slayers—her mother and her mother's lover.

The Oedipus and Electra complexes become resolved by about the ages of 5 or 6. Children then repress their hostilities toward, and identify with, the parent of the same sex. Identification leads to playing the social and sexual roles of the same-sex parent and internalizing that parent's values. Sex-

Weaning Accustoming the child not to suck the mother's breast or a baby bottle.

Fixation In psychoanalytic theory, arrested development. Attachment to objects of an earlier stage.

Oral fixation Attachment to objects and behaviors characteristic of the oral stage.

Anal stage The second stage of psychosexual development, when gratification is attained through anal activities.

Anal fixation Attachment to objects and behaviors characteristic of the anal stage.

Anal-retentive Descriptive of behaviors and traits that have to do with "holding in," or self-control.

Anal-expulsive Descriptive of behaviors and traits that have to do with unregulated self-expression, such as messiness.

Sadism Attaining gratification from inflicting pain on or humiliating others.

Phallic stage The third stage of psychosexual development, characterized by a shift of libido to the phallic region.

Clitoris An external female sex organ, which is highly sensitive to sexual stimulation.

Oedipus complex A conflict of the phallic stage in which the boy wishes to possess his mother sexually and perceives his father as a rival in love.

Electra complex A conflict of the phallic stage in which the girl longs for her father and resents her mother.

ual feelings toward the opposite-sex parent are repressed for a number of years. When they emerge during adolescence, they are displaced onto socially appropriate members of the opposite sex.

By the age of 5 or 6, Freud believed that children would have been in conflict with their parents over sexual feelings for several years. The pressures of the Oedipus and Electra complexes would motivate them to repress all sexual urges. In so doing they would enter the **latency stage,** a period of life during which sexual feelings would remain unconscious. They would use this period to focus on schoolwork. During the latency stage it would not be uncommon for children to prefer playmates of their own sex.

Freud wrote that we enter the final stage of psychosexual development, or **genital stage,** at puberty. Adolescent males again feel sexual urges toward their mothers, and adolescent females toward their fathers. But the **incest taboo** provides ample motivation for keeping these impulses repressed and displacing them onto other adults or adolescents of the opposite sex. But boys might still seek girls "just like the girl that married dear old Dad." Girls might still be attracted to men who resemble their fathers.

People in the genital stage prefer, by definition, to find sexual gratification through intercourse with a member of the opposite sex. In Freud's view, oral or anal stimulation, masturbation, and homosexual activity would all represent **pregenital** fixations and immature forms of sexual conduct.

Evaluation of Freud's Psychodynamic Theory

Freud's theory has had tremendous appeal. It is a rich theory, explaining many varieties of

---

Latency stage The fourth stage of psychosexual development, characterized by repression of sexual impulses.

Genital stage The mature stage of psychosexual development, characterized by preferred expression of libido through intercourse with an adult of the opposite sex.

Incest taboo The cultural prohibition against marrying or having sexual relations with a close blood relative.

Pregenital Characteristic of stages less mature than the genital stage.

---

human behavior and traits. But despite its richness, Freud's work has met with criticism.

Some followers of Freud, such as Erik Erikson, argued that Freud placed too much emphasis on human sexuality and neglected the importance of social relationships. Other followers, such as Alfred Adler and Erich Fromm, argued that Freud placed too much emphasis on unconscious motives. They assert that we consciously seek self-enhancement and intellectual pleasures. We do not only seek to gratify the dark demands of the id.

A number of critics note that "psychic structures" like the id, ego, and superego have no substance. They are little more than useful fictions, poetic ways to express inner conflict. It is debatable whether Freud ever attributed substance to the psychic structures. He, too, may have seen them more as poetic fictions than as "things." If so, his critics have the right to use other descriptive terms and write better "poems."

Sir Karl Popper (1985) argued that Freud's hypothetical mental processes fail as scientific concepts because they cannot be observed. Nor do they predict observable behavior with precision. They only "explain" behavior after the fact. For example, we can speculate that a client "repressed" (forgot about) an appointment because "unconsciously" he did not want to attend the session, but we cannot accurately predict when such "repression" will occur. Also, scientific propositions must be capable of being proven false. As noted by Popper, Freud's statements about mental structures are unscientific precisely because no imaginable type of evidence can disprove them; any behavior can be explained in terms of these hypothesized (but unobservable) "structures."

Nor have the stages of psychosexual development escaped criticism. Children begin to masturbate as early as the first year, not in the "phallic stage." As parents know from observing their children play "doctor," the latency stage is not so sexually latent as Freud believed. Freud's thinking concerning the Oedipus and Electra complexes is speculative.

As noted by philosopher Adolph Grünbaum (1985), Freud's method of gathering evidence from the clinical session is also suspect. Therapists may subtly influence clients to produce what they expect to find. Therapists may also fail to separate reported facts from their own interpretations.

Once we have catalogued our criticisms of Freud's views, what of merit is left? A number of things. Although we can fault the specifics of Freud's theory of development, Freud did point out that childhood experiences can have far-reaching effects on us. He noted that we have defensive ways of looking at the world, that our cognitive processes can be distorted by our efforts to defend ourselves against anxiety and guilt. If these ideas no longer impress us as innovative, it is largely because of the influence of Sigmund Freud.

A number of personality theorists are intellectual descendants of Sigmund Freud. Their theories, like Freud's, include roles for unconscious motivation, for motivational conflict, and for defensive responses to anxiety that involve repression and cognitive distortion of reality (Wachtel, 1982). In other respects, they differ markedly. We shall discuss the psychodynamic views of Carl Jung, Alfred Adler, Karen Horney, and Erik Erikson.

Carl Jung

Carl Jung (1875–1961) was a Swiss psychiatrist who had been a member of Freud's inner circle. He fell into disfavor with Freud when he developed his own psychodynamic theory—**analytical psychology.** Jung believed that we not only have a *personal* unconscious, which contains repressed memories and impulses, but also an inherited **collective unconscious,** which contains primitive images, or **archetypes,** reflections of the history of our species.

Archetypes include vague mysterious **mythical** images, as of the all-powerful God, the young hero, the fertile and nurturing mother, the wise old man, the hostile brother—even fairy godmothers, wicked witches, and themes of rebirth or resurrection. Archetypes remain unconscious, but Jung believed they influence our thoughts and emotions and render us responsive to cultural themes in stories and films. They are also somewhat accessible in dreams.

Jung saw the sexual instinct as only one of several important instincts. Jung also granted more importance to conscious motives than Freud did. He believed that one of the archetypes is a **Self,** a conscious, unifying force of personality that gives conscious direction and purpose to human

Who Is Carl Gustav Jung?

behavior. The Self strives to achieve a wholeness or fullness.

Ironically, the same Jung who insisted that importance must be attached to fully conscious functions went even further than Freud in constructing an involved, poetic inner life. Many of Jung's ideas cannot be verified through scientific study. They remain theoretical, even spiritual, speculation.

Alfred Adler

Alfred Adler (1870–1937), another follower of Freud, also believed that Freud had placed too much emphasis on sexual impulses. Adler believed that people are basically motivated by an **inferiority complex.** In some people feelings of inferi-

---

Analytical psychology Jung's psychoanalytic theory, which emphasizes the collective unconscious and archetypes.

Collective unconscious Jung's hypothesized store of vague racial memories.

Archetypes Basic, primitive images or concepts hypothesized by Jung to reside in the collective unconscious.

Mythical Descriptive of traditional, fictitious stories often intended to explain natural phenomena or human origins.

Self In analytical psychology, a conscious, unifying force to personality that provides people with direction and purpose.

Inferiority complex Feelings of inferiority hypothesized by Adler to serve as a central motivating force.

Who Is Alfred Adler?

ority may be based on physical problems, but Adler believed that all of us encounter them because of our small size as children and that they fuel a compensating **drive for superiority.** For instance, the English poet Lord Byron, with a crippled leg, became a champion swimmer. Adler as a child was crippled by rickets and suffered from pneumonia, and it may be that his theory developed in part from his own childhood striving to overcome repeated bouts of illness.

Adler, like Jung, believed that self-awareness plays a major role in the formation of personality. Adler spoke of a **creative self,** a self-aware aspect of personality that strives to overcome obstacles and develop the individual's potential. Because this potential is uniquely individual, Adler's views have been termed **individual psychology.**

Drive for superiority Adler's term for the desire to compensate for feelings of inferiority.

Creative self According to Adler, the self-aware aspect of personality that strives to achieve its full potential.

Individual psychology Adler's psychoanalytic theory, which emphasizes feelings of inferiority and the creative self.

Basic anxiety Horney's term for lasting feelings of insecurity that stem from harsh or indifferent parental treatment.

Basic hostility Horney's term for lasting feelings of anger that accompany basic anxiety but are directed toward nonfamily members in adulthood.

Karen Horney

Karen Horney (1885–1952) agreed with Freud that childhood experiences played a major role in the development of adult personality, but like many other neoanalysts, she believed that sexual and aggressive impulses took a back seat in importance to social relationships.

Horney, like Freud, also saw parent-child relationships as of paramount importance. Children are completely dependent, and when their parents treat them with indifference or harshness, they develop feelings of insecurity and what Horney terms **basic anxiety.** Children also resent neglectful parents, and Horney theorized that a **basic hostility** would accompany basic anxiety. Horney agreed with Freud that children would repress rather than express feelings of hostility toward their parents because of fear of reprisal and, just as important, fear of driving them away.

Later in life, basic anxiety and repressed hostility would lead to the development of one of three neurotic ways of relating to other people: moving toward others, moving against others, or moving away from them. Of course, it is healthful to relate to other people, but the neurotic person who moves toward others has feelings of insecurity and an excessive need for approval that render him or her compliant and overly anxious to please. People who move against others also are insecure, but they attempt to cope with their insecurity by asserting power and dominating social interactions. People who move away from others cope with their insecurities by withdrawing from social interactions. By remaining aloof from others, they

Who Is Karen Horney?

Table 8.1 Erik Erikson's Stages of Psychosocial Development

TIME PERIOD	LIFE CRISIS	THE DEVELOPMENTAL TASK
Infancy (0–1)	Trust vs. mistrust	Coming to trust the mother and the environment—to associate surroundings with feelings of inner goodness
Early childhood (2–3)	Autonomy vs. shame and doubt	Developing the wish to make choices and the self-control to exercise choice
Preschool years (4–5)	Initiative vs. guilt	Adding planning and "attacking" to choice, becoming active and on the move
Grammar school years (6–12)	Industry vs. inferiority	Becoming eagerly absorbed in skills, tasks, and productivity; mastering the fundamentals of technology
Adolescence	Identity vs. role diffusion	Connecting skills and social roles to formation of career objectives
Young adulthood	Intimacy vs. isolation	Committing the self to another; engaging in sexual love
Middle adulthood	Generativity vs. stagnation	Needing to be needed; guiding and encouraging the younger generation; being creative
Late adulthood	Integrity vs. despair	Accepting the timing and placing of one's own life cycle; achieving wisdom and dignity

Source: Erikson, 1963, pp. 247–269.

attempt to prevent themselves from getting hurt by them. The price, of course, is perpetual loneliness.

Erik Erikson

Erik Erikson also believed that Freud had placed undue emphasis on sexual instincts and taught that social relationships are more important. The general climate of the mother-infant relationship is more important than the details of the feeding process or sexual feelings that might be stirred by the mother's nearness.

For this reason, Erikson proposes stages of psycho*social* rather than psycho*sexual* development. Rather than labeling a stage after an erogenous zone, Erikson labeled stages after the traits that might be developed during that stage (Table 8.1). Each stage is named according to the possible outcomes, which are polar opposites. For example, the first stage of **psychosocial development** is the stage of trust versus mistrust because of the two possible major outcomes: (1) A warm, loving relationship with the mother (and **significant others**) during infancy may lead to a sense of basic trust in people and the world. (2) A cold, nongratifying relationship may lead to a pervasive sense of mistrust. Erikson believed that most of us would wind

Who Is Erik Erikson?

Psychosocial development Erikson's theory of personality and development, which emphasizes social relationships and eight stages of growth.

Significant others Persons who have a major impact on one's development, including parents, peers, and lovers.

Who Is Gordon Allport?

up with some combination of trust and mistrust—hopefully with more trust than mistrust.

Adolescent and Adult Development

Erikson extended Freud's five developmental stages to eight to include the changes in adulthood. For Erikson, the goal of adolescence is the attainment of ego identity, not genital sexuality. Adolescents who attain ego identity develop a firm sense of who they are and what they stand for. One aspect of ego identity is selection of a career, but ego identity extends to sexual, political, and religious beliefs and commitments. According to Erikson, adolescents who do not develop a firm sense of identity are especially subject to peer influences and short-sighted hedonism.

The establishment of intimate relationships is a central task of young adulthood. Young adults who have evolved a sense of who they are during adolescence are now ready to fuse their identities with others through relationships such as marriage and abiding friendships.

Generativity is the task of middle adulthood. Erikson describes it as including having children, productivity (as in work), and creativity (1983). Erikson assumes that middle-aged people are con-

Trait An aspect of personality that is inferred from behavior and assumed to give rise to behavioral consistency.

Cardinal trait Allport's term for pervasive traits that guide almost all of a person's behavior.

cerned about the welfare of the next generation, about making the world a better place.

The central task of late adulthood is maintaining our sense of who we are and what we stand for (ego integrity) in the face of declining physical functioning. The maintenance of integrity requires development of wisdom—wisdom to accept the limits of our own life spans and our places in the ebb and flow of history. Wisdom is more possible for those who have responded to the tasks of the first seven stages in generally positive ways.

One of the richer aspects of the psychodynamic theories is the way in which they account for the development of various traits. Let us now consider trait theories, which address traits from a different perspective.

TRAIT THEORIES

If asked to describe yourself, you would probably mention one or more of your **traits.** Traits are enduring elements of personality that are inferred from behavior and account for behavioral consistency. We use traits to describe others. If you describe a friend as "shy," it may be because you observed some social anxiety or withdrawal in early meetings. Similarly, you would probably predict consistent social anxiety and withdrawal for your "shy" friend and might be surprised if he or she acted assertively.

Gordon Allport

According to psychologist Gordon Allport (1937, 1961), traits are rooted in the nervous system. Allport considered them "neuropsychic" structures. Traits steer or guide people to behave consistently in various situations. For example, the trait of sociability may steer a person to invite friends when going out, to share confidences in letters, and to make others feel welcome at gatherings. A person who "lacks" sociability would behave differently in these situations.

Allport labeled traits according to the roles they play in directing behavior. In rare cases a trait—called a **cardinal trait**—may be so outstanding and pervasive that it steers virtually all aspects of a person's behavior. Allport (1937) offered examples of cardinal traits taken from historic and literary figures: Christlike, **Machiavellian, Napoleonic,** and **sadistic.**

Central traits define the outstanding characteristics of the person. They are the sort that might be mentioned in a letter of recommendation, such as "well groomed," "honest," and "hard working." **Secondary traits** are less influential and less noticeable. They do not generally guide the person's behavior. Instead, they occur in a small range of situations and govern a limited number of responses. Our total pattern of traits is termed our **personality structure.**

More than 50 years ago Allport and Odbert (1936) catalogued some 18,000 human traits from a search through word lists of the sort found in dictionaries. Some were physical traits, like short, white, and brunette. Others were behavioral traits, like shy and emotional. Still others were moral traits, like honest. This exhaustive list has served as the basis for personality research by many other psychologists.

Raymond Cattell

Some psychologists—Raymond Cattell (1965) is one—have used statistical techniques to reduce this universe of innumerable traits to smaller lists that show commonality in meaning. Cattell also distinguished between surface traits and source traits. **Surface traits** describe characteristic ways of behaving, that is, cleanliness, stubbornness, thrift, and orderliness. Such traits tend to form meaningful patterns that are suggestive of underlying traits.

Cattell refined the Allport catalogue by removing unusual terms and grouping the remaining traits into 16 central **source traits**—the underlying traits from which surface traits are derived. Cattell argued that psychological measurement of a person's source traits would enable us to predict his or her behavior in various situations. His research led him to suggest the existence of 16 source traits, including outgoing–reserved, affected by feelings–emotionally stable, submissive–dominant, serious–happy-go-lucky, timid–venturesome, sensitive–tough-minded, self-as-

Who Is Raymond Cattell?

sured–apprehensive, conservative–experimenting, controlled–uncontrolled, and relaxed–tense.

Hans Eysenck

British psychologist Hans J. Eysenck (1960; Eysenck & Eysenck, 1985) has focused much of his research on the relationships between two source traits: **introversion–extraversion** and emotional

Machiavellian Characterized by craftiness and deceitfulness in the attainment of one's goals. (After Italian statesman Niccolo Machiavelli.)

Napoleonic Governed by the needs for power and aggression.

Sadistic Attaining gratification by inflicting pain on others.

Central traits Outstanding, noticeable (but not necessarily all-pervasive) characteristics of a person.

Secondary traits Traits that appear in a limited number of situations and govern a limited number of responses.

Personality structure One's total pattern of traits.

Surface traits Cattell's term for characteristic, observable ways of behaving.

Source traits Cattell's term for underlying traits from which surface traits are derived.

Introversion A source trait characterized by intense imagination and the tendency to inhibit impulses.

Extraversion A source trait characterized by tendencies to be socially outgoing and to express feelings and impulses freely.

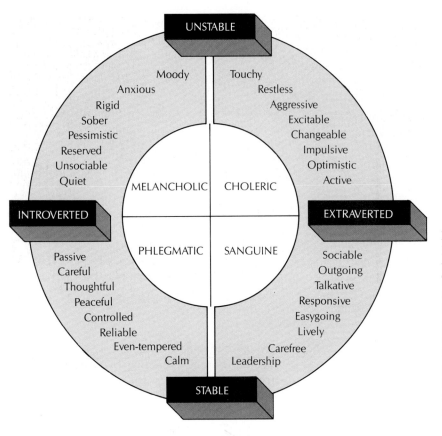

Figure 8.2. How Are Eysenck's Personality Dimensions Related to Galen's Four Personality Types? Various personality traits shown in the outer ring fall within the two major dimensions of personality suggested by Hans Eysenck. The inner circle shows how Galen's four major personality types—choleric, sanguine, phlegmatic, and melancholic—fit within Eysenck's modern dimensions.

stability–instability, otherwise called **neuroticism.** His research suggests that these basic traits are independent dimensions, and that our combinations of these traits place us along these dimensions. Figure 8.2 shows a number of surface traits (such as touchy and restless in the upper-right quadrant) and how they reflect combinations of the two basic source traits or personality dimensions.

Carl Jung was first to distinguish between introverts and extraverts. Eysenck added the dimension of neuroticism to introversion–extraversion, and he has catalogued a number of personality traits according to where they are "situated" along these dimensions (refer to Figure 8.2). For instance, an anxious person would be high both in introversion and neuroticism—that is, preoccupied with his or her own thoughts and emotionally unstable.

Eysenck notes that his scheme is reminiscent of that suggested by the Greek physician Galen, who lived from 129–199 A.D. Galen suggested that there are four basic personality types: choleric (quick-tempered), sanguine (warm, cheerful, confident), phlegmatic (sluggish, calm, cool), and melancholic (gloomy, pensive).

Who Is Hans Eysenck?

Neuroticism Eysenck's term for emotional instability.

How Do Extraverts Differ from Introverts? Extraverts are socially outgoing. Where do you place yourself along the personality dimension of introversion–extraversion?

Where would you place athletes and artists in terms of the dimensions of introversion–extraversion and neuroticism? Where would you place yourself?

Evaluation of Trait Theories

Trait theory has been criticized on several grounds. For one, it is more descriptive than explanatory. It focuses on describing traits rather than tracing their origins or investigating how they may be modified. The "explanations" provided by trait theory have been criticized as **circular explanations.** If we say that John failed to ask Marsha for a date *because* of shyness, we have contributed little to our understanding of the causes of John's behavior.

Allport argued that traits are *neuropsychic structures,* somehow embedded in the person's nervous system. Critics have argued that Allport failed to specify where and how these traits are embedded. On the other hand, a number of psychologists (e.g., Daniels & Plomin, 1985; DeFries et al., 1987; Scarr & Kidd, 1983) argue that basic traits such as activity level, emotional responsiveness, sociability, and impulsivity reflect strong genetic influences. As noted in Chapters 2 and 7, for example, the

patterns of their appearance seem clearly related to patterns of kinship.

A basic assumption of trait theory is that human behavior tends to be largely consistent from one situation to another. But research suggests that behavior varies more from situation to situation—at least for some people—than trait theory would allow (Bem & Allen, 1974; Mischel, 1977, 1986). People who are high in **private self-consciousness**—who carefully monitor their own behavior, even when others are not observing them—also try to show consistent behavior from situation to situation (Fenigstein et al., 1975; Scheier et al., 1978; Underwood & Moore, 1981). Other people show more variability in behavior.

On the other hand, longitudinal research has shown that a number of personality traits seem to possess remarkable stability over the years. James Conley (1984, 1985), for example, studied psychological tests taken by a sample of adults during the

Circular explanation An explanation that merely restates its own concepts instead of offering additional information.

Private self-consciousness The tendency to take critical note of one's own behavior, even when unobserved by others.

Behaviorism

At Johns Hopkins University in 1924, psychologist John B. Watson announced the battle cry of the **radical-behaviorist** movement:

> Give me a dozen healthy infants, well-formed, and my own specified world to bring them up in and I'll guarantee to take any one at random and train him to become any type of specialist I might suggest—doctor, lawyer, merchant-chief and, yes, even beggar-man and thief, regardless of his talents, penchants, tendencies, abilities, vocations, and the race of his ancestors (p. 82).

So it was that Watson sounded the behaviorist cry that situational variables, or environmental influences—not internal, person variables—are the significant shapers of human preferences and behaviors. The radical-behaviorist outlooks of John B. Watson and B. F. Skinner largely discard the notions of personal freedom, choice, and self-direction. Most of us tend to assume that our wants originate within us. But Skinner suggests that environmental influences, such as parental approval and social custom, shape us into *wanting* certain things and *not wanting* others. To Watson and Skinner, even our telling ourselves that we have free will is determined by the environment as surely as is our becoming startled at a sudden noise.

In his novel *Walden Two* Skinner (1948) describes a Utopian society in which people are happy and content because they are allowed to do as they please. However, they have been trained or conditioned from early childhood to engage in **prosocial** behavior and express prosocial attitudes. Because of their reinforcement histories, they *want* to behave in a decent, kind, and unselfish way. But they see themselves as free because society makes no effort to control them as adults.

Skinner elaborated his beliefs about people and society in *Beyond Freedom and Dignity* (1972). According to Skinner, adaptation to the environment requires acceptance of behavior patterns that ensure survival. If the group is to survive, it must construct rules and laws that will foster social harmony. Other people are then rewarded for following these rules and punished for disobeying them. Nobody is really free, even though we think of ourselves as coming together freely to establish the rules and as choosing to follow them.

Do Radical Behaviorists See People as Similar to R2D2 and C3PO of the *Star Wars* Film Series? Charming and entertaining, but rather mechanical when all is said and done?

1930s, during the 1950s, and again during the 1980s. Their scores on the traits of extraversion, neuroticism, and impulsiveness showed significant consistency across five decades.

LEARNING THEORIES

There are a number of learning-theory approaches to the understanding of personality. We shall focus on two of them: behaviorism and social-learning theory. Behaviorism is important for its historical significance and still has many followers. But today most learning-theory-oriented psychologists identify with social-learning theory.

Radical behaviorist A person who does not believe in "mind" or other mentalistic concepts.

Prosocial Behavior that is characterized by helping others and making a contribution to society.

Some object to radical-behaviorist notions because they degrade the importance of human consciousness and choice. Others argue that people are not so blindly ruled by pleasure and pain. People have rebelled against the so-called necessity of survival by choosing pain and hardship over pleasure or death over life. Many people have sacrificed their own lives to save those of others.

The radical-behaviorist defense might be that the apparent choice of pain or death is forced on the "altruist" as inevitably as conformity to social custom is forced on others. The altruist was also shaped by external influences, but those influences differed from those that affect most of us.

Social-Learning Theory

Social-learning theory is a contemporary view developed by Albert Bandura (1977, 1986) and other psychologists that focuses on the importance of learning by observation and on the role of cognitive activity in human behavior.

The Behavioral Approach Becomes Cognitive Social-learning theorists reject the radical behaviorist ideas of Watson and Skinner. They see people as influencing the environment, just as the environment influences them. Theorists such as Bandura, Walter Mischel (1986), and Julian B. Rotter believe that variables within the person must also be considered if human behavior is to be adequately explained and predicted.

Rotter (1972), for example, argues that behavior depends on the person's **expectancies** con-

Who Is Julian B. Rotter?

cerning the outcome of that behavior and the perceived or **subjective values** of those outcomes. However, his view remains a learning-theory view because expectancies and subjective values are thought to reflect the reinforcement history of the individual. As such, most expectancies change when experience changes. But **generalized expectancies** are broad expectations that reflect extensive learning and resist change. Their stability makes them the equivalent of "traits" within social-learning theory.

To social-learning theorists, people are self-aware and learn actively. People are not simply at the mercy of the environment. Instead, people seek to learn about their environments, and people modify and create environments to make reinforcers available.

Social-learning theorists also note the importance of rules and symbolic processes in learning. Children, for example, learn more effectively how to behave in certain situations when parents state the rules that are involved.

Who Is Walter Mischel?

Social-learning theory. A cognitively oriented learning theory in which observational learning, values, and expectations play major roles in determining behavior.

Expectancies Personal predictions about the outcomes of potential behaviors. "If-then" statements.

Subjective value The desirability of an object or event.

Generalized expectancies Broad expectations that reflect extensive learning and are relatively resistant to change.

Figure 8.3. Do Children Imitate Aggressive Models?   Children will imitate the behavior of adult models in certain situations, as shown in these pictures from a classic study by Albert Bandura and his colleagues. In the top row, an adult model strikes a clown doll. The next two rows show a boy and a girl imitating the aggressive behavior.

Observational Learning   In observational learning (also termed **modeling**) we acquire knowledge by observing others. Observational learning occurs even when the learner does not perform the learned behavior pattern and, therefore, is not directly reinforced. Observing others extends to reading about others or perceiving what they do and what happens to them in the visual media.

> **Model** In social-learning theory, an organism that exhibits behaviors that others will imitate, or acquire, through observational learning.
>
> **Person variables** In social-learning theory, determinants of behavior that lie within the person.

Our expectations stem from our observations of what happens to others as well as our own experiences. For example, teachers are more accepting of "calling out" in class from boys than from girls (Sadker & Sadker, 1985). As a result, boys frequently expect to be rewarded for calling out in class, whereas girls are more likely to expect to be reprimanded for not behaving in a "ladylike" manner. As suggested in Figure 8.3, children will imitate aggressive behavior observed on TV when they expect positive rather than negative outcomes as a result.

Let us now consider a number of the variables within persons (termed **person variables**) that account for individual differences in behavior in social-learning theory.

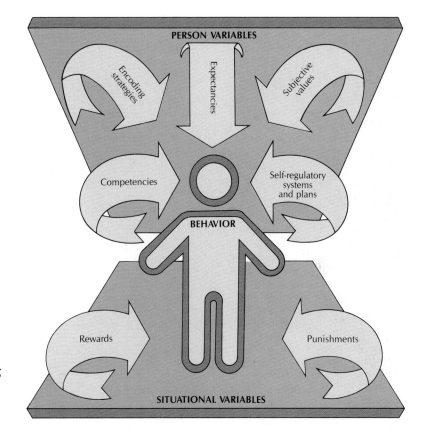

Figure 8.4. How Do Person and Situational Variables Influence Behavior, According to Social-Learning Theory? According to social-learning theory, person and situational variables interact to influence behavior.

What Are the Effects of Media Violence? With such an abundance of media violence in the U.S.A., the question might not be why some people imitate aggressive models but rather why so many do *not*.

Person Variables in Social-Learning Theory

Social-learning theorists view behavior as stemming from an ongoing interaction between person and **situational variables** (Figure 8.4). Person variables include competencies, encoding strategies, expectancies, subjective values, and self-regulatory systems and plans. Our discussion of these variables follows that of Walter Mischel (1986, pp. 308–312).

Competencies: What Can You Do? **Competencies** include knowledge of rules that guide conduct, concepts about ourselves and other people, and skills. Our abilities to use information ac-

---

Situational variables In social-learning theory, determinants of behavior that lie outside the person.

Competencies Knowledge and skills.

How Do Competencies Contribute to Performance?
There are great individual differences in our competencies, based on genetic variation, nourishment, differences in learning opportunities, and other environmental factors. What factors contribute to this girl's competencies in ballet?

tively to construct plans and plan overt behavior depend on our competencies.

Competencies include knowledge of the physical world, of cultural codes of conduct, and of the behavior patterns expected by others. They include academic skills such as reading and writing, athletic skills such as swimming and tossing a football properly, social skills such as knowing how to ask someone out on a date, job skills, and many others.

People's competencies differ, based on genetic variation, nourishment, differences in learning opportunities, and other environmental factors. Gen-

---

Encode Interpret; transform.

---

erally speaking, people do not perform well at given tasks unless they have the competencies needed to do so.

Encoding Strategies: How Do You See It?
Different people **encode** (symbolize or represent) the same stimuli in different ways, and their encoding strategies are an important factor in their overt responses. One person may encode a weather report of 97 degrees Fahrenheit and high humidity as a punitive forecast that will make construction work an aversive task. Another, planning to spend the day at the pool, is likely to have pleasant anticipations. Similarly, the person who missed the opportunity to buy IBM at $50 a share may encode a price of $120 as a symbol of a loss that will never be made up. A newcomer to the market may encode the price of $120 as a good buying opportunity based on projected earnings.

Our encoding of stimuli reflects our competencies (some of us may have strategies for encoding stock market prices, whereas others do not) and our experiences. Our encoding also reflects our abilities to respond positively to stimuli.

Expectancies: What Will Happen? Expectancies are "if-then" statements or personal predictions about the outcome (or reinforcement contingencies) of engaging in a response. The unique human abilities to manipulate symbols and to ponder events allow us to foresee potential consequences of behavior.

Expectancies are based on our observations of others and on our experiences in similar situations. Assume that we encountered pain by falling off a bicycle or pleasure from eating a piece of cake. Now we have the opportunity to ride a bicycle or eat another piece of cake. The associated pain or pleasure is symbolized as an image, such as a mental picture of scraping your hands and knees or of the deep chocolate flavor of the cake. The nature of the image (negative or positive) influences us either not to repeat (not to ride a bicycle recklessly) or to repeat (eat another piece of cake) the response. But the nature of the image is one influence among many—we may decide not to eat another piece of cake despite the pleasure it might afford. (And sometimes, alas, we do decide not to eat the cake.)

Competencies influence expectancies, and expectancies, in turn, influence motivation to perform. People who believe that they have the competencies required to perform effectively are more likely to try difficult tasks than people who do not believe that they can master them. Albert Bandura (1982) refers to beliefs that one can handle a task as **self-efficacy expectations.** As noted by Bandura and his colleagues Linda Reese and Nancy Adams,

In their daily lives people must make decisions about whether to attempt risky courses of action or how long to continue, in the face of difficulties, those they have undertaken. Social-learning theory posits that . . . people tend to avoid situations they believe exceed their coping capabilities, but they undertake and perform assuredly activities they judge themselves capable of managing. . . .

Self-judged efficacy also determines how much of an effort people will make and how long they will keep at a task despite obstacles or adverse experiences. . . . Those who have a strong sense of efficacy exert greater effort to master the challenges . . . (1982, p. 5).

Bandura (1986) also suggests that one of the helpful aspects of psychotherapy is that it frequently changes clients' self-expectancy expectations from "I can't" to "I can." As a result, clients are motivated to try out new—and more adaptive—patterns of behavior.

Subjective Values: What Is It Worth?   Because of our different learning experiences, we may each place a different value on the same outcome. What is frightening to one person may be enticing to another. What is slightly desirable to one may be irresistible to someone else. From the social-learning perspective, as contrasted to the behaviorist perspective, we are not controlled by stimuli; instead, stimuli have various meanings for us, and these meanings may influence us in various ways.

The subjective value of a particular stimulus or reward is related to direct or observational experience with it or similar rewards. If you became nauseated the last time you drank a glass of iced tea, its subjective value as an incentive may diminish, even on a hot day.

Self-Regulatory Systems and Plans: How Can You Achieve It?   Social-learning theory recognizes that one of the features of being human is that we tend to regulate our own behavior, even in the absence of observers and external constraints. We set goals and standards for ourselves, construct plans for achieving them, and congratulate or criticize ourselves, depending on whether we reach them.

Self-regulation amplifies our opportunities for influencing our environments. We can select the situations to which we expose ourselves; we can select the arenas in which we shall contend.

Evaluation of Learning Theories

Radical behaviorism has many shortcomings in its power to explain human behavior. First, behaviorism fails to explain how behaviors can be learned but not performed. Second, behaviorism views human behavior as the summation of so many instances of conditioning. But since all instances of conditioning could never be specified, this assertion must remain unsubstantiated.

Behaviorism also cannot describe or explain the richness of human behavior. We all have the experiences of thought, of complex inner maps of the world, and behaviorism in a sense deprives us of the right to search for ways to discuss scientifically what it means to us to be human. Behaviorism also seems at a loss to explain how it is that many of us will strive, against all hardships, to fulfill distant inner visions. If we only repeat behaviors that have been reinforced, how is it that we struggle—without reinforcers—to create new works and ideas? How is it that mathematicians and composers sit motionless for hours, then suddenly write new formulas and symphonies?

Critics of social-learning theory do not accuse its supporters of denying the importance of cognitive activity. But they might contend that social-learning theory has not derived satisfying statements about the development of traits and

Self-efficacy expectations Beliefs to the effect that one can handle a task.

Who Is Carl Rogers?

accounted for self-awareness. Social-learning theory—like its intellectual forebear, radical behaviorism—might also not always have paid sufficient attention to genetic variation in explaining individual differences in behavior.

Social-learning theorists seem to be working on these theoretical flaws. Today's social-learning theorists view people as active, not as mechanical reactors to environmental pressures (as Watson saw them). Cognitive functioning is an appropriate area of study for social-learning theorists (Bandura, 1986; Wilson, 1982). Mischel admits that "within . . . every individual there are structurally imposed limits on potential behavior" (1986, p. 305). In the area of abnormal behavior, social-learning theorists Gerald Davison and John Neale (1986) may speak for many of their fellows when they suggest that inherited or physiological factors often interact with situational stress to give rise to abnormal behavior.

Social-learning theory has also contributed to the formation of many strategies for helping people change maladaptive behavior. These strategies are collectively termed *behavior therapy,* and you will learn more about them in Chapter 10.

Phenomenological Having to do with conscious, subjective experience.

Gestalt In this usage, a quality of wholeness.

Innate Inborn; natural; unlearned.

Self-actualization In humanistic theory, the innate tendency to strive to realize one's potential.

PHENOMENOLOGICAL THEORIES

In this section we shall discuss two **phenomenological** approaches to personality: Rogers's self theory and Kelly's psychology of personal constructs. They have a number of things in common: Both propose that the personal experience of events is the most important aspect of human nature. Both propose that we as individuals are our own best experts on ourselves. Both propose that we have unique ways of looking at the world.

Carl Rogers's Self Theory

"My experience in therapy and in groups makes it impossible for me to deny the reality and significance of human choice. To me it is not an illusion that man is to some degree the architect of himself," wrote Carl Rogers (1974, p. 119). According to a survey of clinical and counseling psychologists (Smith, 1982), Rogers is the single most influential psychotherapist of recent years.

Rogers defines the self as an "organized, consistent, conceptual **gestalt** composed of perceptions of the characteristics of the 'I' or 'me' and the perceptions of the relationships of the 'I' or 'me' to others and to various aspects of life, together with the values attached to these perceptions" (1959, p. 200). Your self is your center of experience. It is your ongoing sense of who and what you are, your sense of how and why you react to the environment, and how you choose to act on the environment. Your choices are made on the basis of your values, and your values are also parts of your self.

To Rogers the sense of self is inborn, or **innate.** The self provides the experience of being human in the world. It is the guiding principle behind personality structure and behavior.

Self-Actualization
Humanistic personality theorists such as Rogers and Abraham Maslow believe that organisms are genetically programed to grow, unfold, and become themselves. This central tendency, termed **self-actualization,** is a characteristic of life itself. Self-actualization renders behavior organized, meaningful, and whole.

The Self-Concept and Frames of Reference

Our self-concepts are our impressions of ourselves and our evaluation of our adequacy. It may help to think of us as rating ourselves along various scales or dimensions, such as good–bad, intelligent–unintelligent, strong–weak, and tall–short.

Rogers states that we all have unique ways of looking at ourselves and the world, or unique **frames of reference.** It may be that we each use a different set of dimensions in defining ourselves, and that we judge ourselves according to different sets of values. To one person achievement–failure may be the most important dimension. To another person the most important dimension may be decency–indecency. A third person may not even think in terms of decency.

Self-Esteem and Positive Regard

Rogers assumes that we all develop a need for self-regard, or **self-esteem,** as we develop and become self-aware. Self-esteem at first reflects the esteem others hold us in. Parents help children develop self-esteem when they show them **unconditional positive regard**—accept them as having intrinsic merit regardless of their behavior at the moment. But when parents show children **conditional positive regard**—accept them only when they behave in a desired manner—they may learn to disown the thoughts, feelings, and behaviors that parents have rejected. Conditional positive regard may lead children to develop **conditions of worth,** to think that they are worthwhile only if they behave in certain ways.

Since each of us is thought to have a unique potential, children who develop conditions of worth must be disappointed in themselves. We cannot fully live up to the wishes of others and remain true to ourselves. But children in some families learn that it is bad to have ideas of their own, especially about sexual, political, or religious matters. When they perceive their parents' disapproval, they may come to see themselves as rebels and label their feelings as selfish, wrong, or evil. If they wish to retain a consistent self-concept, and self-esteem, they may have to deny many of their genuine feelings, or disown parts of themselves. In this way the self-concept becomes distorted. According to Rogers, anxiety often stems from partial perception of feelings and ideas that are inconsistent with the distorted self-concept. Since anxiety is unpleasant, we may deny that these feelings and ideas exist.

The Self-Ideal

Rogers also believes that we have mental images of what we are capable of becoming, or **self-ideals.** We are motivated to reduce the discrepancy between our self-concepts and our self-ideals. But as we undertake the process of actualizing ourselves, our self-ideals may gradually grow more complex. Our goals may become higher or change in quality. The self-ideal is something like a carrot dangling from a stick strapped to a burro's head. The burro strives to reach the carrot, as though it were a step or two away, without recognizing that its own progress also causes the carrot to advance. Rogers believes that the process of striving to meet meaningful goals, the good struggle, yields happiness.

Evaluation

Perhaps the most telling criticism of self theory is that the central concept of self-actualization cannot be proved or disproved. Like an id or a trait, a self-actualizing force cannot be observed or measured directly. Self-actualization, like trait theory, yields circular explanations for behavior. When we observe someone apparently engaged in positive striving, we gain little insight by attributing this striving to self-actualization. And when we observe someone who is not engaged in

---

Frame of reference One's unique patterning of perceptions and attitudes, according to which one evaluates events.

Self-esteem One's evaluation and valuing of oneself.

Unconditional positive regard A persistent expression of esteem for the value of a person but not necessarily an unqualified acceptance of all of the person's behaviors.

Conditional positive regard Judgment of another person's value on the basis of the acceptability of that person's behaviors.

Conditions of worth Standards by which the value of a person is judged.

Self-ideal A mental image of what we believe we ought to be.

Who Is George Kelly?

growth-oriented striving, it seems arbitrary to "explain" this outcome by suggesting that the self-actualizing tendency has been blocked or frustrated. It may simply be that self-actualization is an acquired need rather than an innate need and that it is found in some, but not all, of us.

Self theory, like learning theories, also has little to say about the development of traits and personality types. Self theory assumes that we are all unique but does not predict the sorts of traits, abilities, and interests we shall develop.

In Chapter 10 we shall see how Rogers's form of psychotherapy is designed to help each of us live up to our potential.

George Kelly's Psychology of Personal Constructs

Psychologists see themselves as attempting to gather accurate information about, and to predict the behavior of, others. But George Kelly (1955) noted with irony that psychologists too often act as though the "others"—that is, the people being studied—are victims of psychic forces, steered by traits, or shaped by environmental influences. Nonsense, said Kelly. The main thing to know about people—even experimental subjects!—is

---

Construe Interpret.

Personal construct A psychological dimension such as strong–weak according to which one evaluates experience.

---

that they all function as "scientists." It is human nature to try to understand one's own behavior and the behavior of others. It is human nature to try to find a way to interpret, categorize, and **construe** the world so that one can make accurate predictions about what will lead to what.

Personal Constructs   Kelly (1955, 1958) believed that people view their experiences in terms of their **personal constructs.** A personal construct is a psychological dimension according to which we categorize ourselves and others. Extraversion–introversion is a construct of importance to Jung and Eysenck. In Chapter 7 we saw that strong–weak is a construct of more relevance to males than females in our culture, according to the gender schema.

According to Freud, people are motivated to behave by basic instincts. According to the behaviorist, motives are external—reinforcers. According to Kelly, people are motivated to understand, anticipate, and control the events in their lives. They try to use constructs that allow them to anticipate and control events.

Alternate Constructions   To know the individual, wrote Kelly, we must learn how the individual categorizes and interprets experience—how the individual construes events. People construe the same event in different ways, as in the example offered by Walter Mischel:

A boy drops his mother's favorite vase. What does it mean? The event is simply that the vase has been broken. Yet ask the child's psychoanalyst and he may point to the boy's unconscious hostility. Ask the mother and she tells you how "mean" he is. His father says he is "spoiled." The child's teacher may see the event as evidence of the child's "laziness" and chronic "clumsiness." Grandmother calls it just an "accident." And the child himself may construe the event as reflecting his "stupidity" (1986, pp. 207–208).

Different ways of construing the same event—that is, alternate constructions of the event—can lead to different emotional reactions and different courses of action. In Chapter 9 we shall see that the boy's construction of the event as evidence of his "stupidity" could well be linked to depression. Whereas some psychoanalysts might wonder whether the dropping of the vase reflected unconscious motives, Kelly might try to point out to the boy that his way of construing the event is not *convenient* for him. Kelly did not believe that there is one absolute way of construing an event. Instead, he believed that when our constructions of events make us miserable and do not lead to productive behavior, we might do better to seek alternatives.

Role Playing   Psychoanalysts see our characters as formed by early life experiences. Trait theorists see our traits as generally stable and steering us to behave in similar ways in different situations. Some learning theorists view us as creatures of habit; others suggest that "generalized expectancies" might lead to stability in behavior in many situations. Kelly, by contrast, saw people as capable of continuous change, as capable of enacting different roles.

One avenue to change is playing another role—attempting to look at the world as through the eyes of a person with another set of beliefs. If we strive to see the world as through the eyes of another, perhaps our constructs will be loosened up and we will be able to generate more convenient ways of doing things.

Evaluation   It is difficult to evaluate Kelly's views. On the one hand, one could say that we have not heard much of them—at least in the terms Kelly used to state them—since Kelly's death in 1967 (Jankowitz, 1987). On the other hand, one could say that elements of Kelly's thinking have found their way into cognitive theories of abnormal behavior (see Chapter 9) and into cognitive-therapy approaches (see Chapter 10). As in the example of the boy who broke the vase, it has been shown that the ways in which we construe our failures and shortcomings are linked to our emotional responses.

Jankowitz (1987) notes that whereas the popularity of Kelly's theory is unclear in the United States, Kelly's views have had a major impact on industrial/organizational psychology in Britain. In one example, psychologists involved in market research have found it valuable to learn how consumers construe the value of different cosmetics and perfumes (Stewart & Stewart, 1982). In another, Eden and Sims (1981) identified values and beliefs (constructs) that would be helpful in certain corporate cultures and showed that new manage-

rial recruits profited from being exposed to these constructs as part of the recruitment and training process.

The psychology of personal constructs, like self theory, has little to say about the origins of traits and personality types. It remains to be seen whether Kelly's views continue to be discussed mainly for their historical importance or whether they enjoy a resurgence of popularity in their own right.

Now that we are familiar with a number of theories of personality, let us see how psychologists measure different aspects of personality.

MEASUREMENT OF PERSONALITY

Measures of personality are used to make important decisions, such as whether a person is suited for a certain type of work, for a particular class in school, or for a drug to reduce agitation. As part of their admissions process, graduate schools will often ask professors to rate prospective students on scales that assess traits like intelligence, emotional stability, and cooperation. Students may take tests of **aptitudes** and interests to gather insight into whether they are suited for certain occupations. It is assumed that students who share the aptitudes and interests of people who are well adjusted in certain positions are likely to be well adjusted themselves in those positions.

If you had wanted to learn about your personality early in the last century, an "expert" might have measured the bumps on your head with a **caliper.** This method, termed **phrenology,** was based on the erroneous belief that traits, abilities, and mental functions dwelled in specific places in the head and could be measured from the outside. Figure 8.5 shows a "map" of these functions, as used by many phrenologists.

Aptitude   A natural ability or talent.

Caliper   An instrument consisting of a pair of curved movable legs that is used to measure the diameter or thickness of an object.

Phrenology   The analysis of personality by measuring the shape and protuberances of the skull.

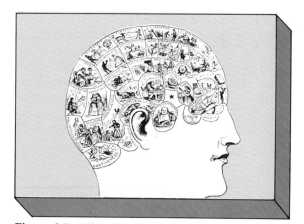

Figure 8.5. What Was Phrenology?

Today's personality measures are more scientific, if not more interesting. They take a sample of behavior, usually in the form of the self-report, to predict future behavior. Standardized interviews can be used, and psychologists even arrange for some routine interviews to be carried out by computer (Erdman et al., 1985). Some measures of personality are **behavior-rating scales,** which assess overt behavior in settings such as the classroom or mental hospital. With behavior-rating scales, trained observers usually check off each occurrence of a specific behavior within a certain time frame, say, a 15-minute period. Standardized objective and projective tests are used more frequently, and they shall be discussed in this section.

Behavior-rating scale A systematic means for recording the frequency with which target behaviors occur.

Objective tests Tests whose items must be answered in a specified, limited manner. Tests whose items have concrete answers that are labeled correct.

Standardized Given to a large number of respondents, so that data concerning the usual responses can be accumulated and analyzed.

Forced-choice format A method of presenting test questions that requires a respondent to select one of a number of possible answers.

Objective Tests

Objective tests present respondents with a **standardized** group of test items in the form of questionnaires. Respondents are limited to a specific range of answers. One test might ask respondents to indicate whether items are true or false for them. Another might ask respondents to select the preferred activity from groups of three.

Some tests have a **forced-choice format** in which respondents are asked to indicate which of two statements is more true for them or which of several activities they prefer. They are not given the option of answering "none of the above." Forced-choice formats are frequently used in interest inventories, which help predict whether one would be well adjusted in a certain occupation. The following item is similar to those found in interest inventories:

I would rather

a. be a forest ranger.
b. work in a busy office.
c. play a musical instrument.

A forced-choice format is also used in the Edwards Personal Preference Schedule, which measures the relative strength of social motives (such as achievement and affiliation) by pitting them against one another consecutively in groups of two.

The Minnesota Multiphasic Personality Inventory

The Minnesota Multiphasic Personality Inventory (MMPI) contains 566 items presented in a true-false format. The MMPI was intended to be used by clinical and counseling psychologists to help diagnose abnormal behavior problems (see Chapter 9), and it is the most widely used psychological test in the clinical setting (Lubin et al., 1985). Accurate measurement of clients' problems should point to appropriate treatment. In recent years the MMPI has also become the most widely used instrument for personality measurement in psychological research (Costa et al., 1985).

The MMPI has been given to thousands of individuals over the last few decades. This wide usage has permitted psychologists to compare the test records of clients with those of people who are known to have had certain problems. A similar test

Table 8.2 Commonly Used Validity and Clinical Scales of the MMPI

SCALE	ABBREVIATION	POSSIBLE INTERPRETATIONS
Validity Scales		
Question	?	Corresponds to number of items left unanswered
Lie	L	Lies or is highly conventional
Frequency	F	Exaggerates complaints, answers haphazardly
Correction	K	Denies problems
Clinical Scales		
Hypochondriasis	Hs	Expresses body concerns and complaints
Depression	D	Is depressed, pessimistic, guilty
Hysteria	Hy	Reacts to stress with physical symptoms, lacks insight
Psychopathic deviate	Pd	Is immoral, in conflict with the law, involved in stormy relationships
Masculinity/femininity	Mf	Has interests characteristic of stereotypical sex roles
Paranoia	Pa	Is suspicious, resentful
Psychasthenia	Pt	Is anxious, worried, high-strung
Schizophrenia	Sc	Is confused, disorganized, disoriented
Hypomania	Ma	Is energetic, active, easily bored, restless
Social introversion	Si	Is introverted, timid, shy, lacking self-confidence

record is suggestive of the presence of similar problems.

The MMPI is usually scored for the four **validity scales** and ten **clinical scales** described in Table 8.2. The validity scales indicate whether there is reason to believe that the test answers represent the client's thoughts, emotions, and behaviors. The validity scales in Table 8.2 assess different **response sets,** or biases in answering the questions. People with high L scores, for example, may be attempting to present themselves as excessively moral and well behaved. People with high F scores may be attempting to present themselves as bizarre or may be answering haphazardly. F-scale scores are positively correlated with conceptual confusion, hostility, presence of **hallucinations** and other unusual thought patterns (Smith & Gra-

ham, 1981). Many personality measures have some kind of validity scale. The clinical scales of the MMPI assess the problems shown in Table 8.2, as well as stereotypical masculine or feminine interests and introversion.

Validity scales Groups of test items that indicate whether a person's responses accurately reflect that individual's traits.

Clinical scales Groups of test items that measure the presence of various abnormal behavior patterns.

Response set A tendency to answer test items according to a bias—for instance, to make oneself seem perfect or bizarre.

Hallucinations Perceptions in the absence of sensory stimulation that are confused with reality.

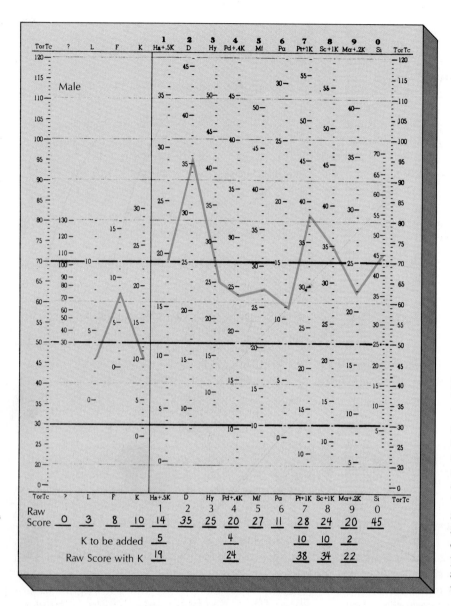

Figure 8.6. What Is Suggested by This MMPI Personality Profile? This profile was attained by a depressed barber. On this form, scores at the standard level of 50 are average for males, and scores above the standard score of 70 are considered abnormally high. The "raw score" is the number of items answered in a certain direction on a given MMPI scale. K is the correction scale. A certain percentage of the K-scale score is added onto several clinical scales to correct for denial of problems.

The MMPI scales were constructed empirically, on the basis of actual clinical data, rather than on the basis of psychological theory. A test-item bank of several hundred items was derived from questions often asked in clinical interviews. Here are some of the items that were used:

My father was a good man   T   F
I am very seldom troubled by headaches   T   F
My hands and feet are usually warm
enough   T   F

I have never done anything dangerous
for the thrill of it   T   F
I work under a great deal of tension   T   F

The items were administered to clients and psychiatric patients with known clinical symptoms such as depressive or schizophrenic symptoms. Items that successfully set apart people with these symptoms were included on scales named accordingly. Figure 8.6 shows the personality profile of a 27-year-old barber who consulted a psychologist because of depression and difficulty making decisions. The barber scored abnormally high on the Hs, D, Pt, Sc, and Si scales, suggestive of concern with body functions (Hs), persistent feelings of anxiety and tension (Pt), depression (D), insomnia and fatigue, and some difficulties relating to other people (Sc, Si). Note that the high Sc score does not in and of itself necessarily suggest that the barber is schizophrenic.

In addition to the standard validity and clinical scales, investigators of personality have derived many experimental scales, such as neuroticism, religious orthodoxy, assertiveness, substance-abuse, and even a measure of well-being (Costa et al., 1985; Johnson et al., 1984; Snyder et al., 1985). The MMPI remains a rich mine for unearthing elements of personality.

The California Psychological Inventory Another personality inventory, the California Psychological Inventory (CPI), is widely used in research to assess 18 dimensions of normal behavior, such as achievement, dominance, flexibility, self-acceptance, and self-control.

Occupational Tests Psychologists have devised a number of psychological tests that can be of help to high school and college students who are uncertain about their future occupations. Tests such as the Strong-Campbell Interest Inventory (SCII) and the Kuder Occupational Interest Survey (KOIS) are used to predict adjustment in various occupations.

The SCII is used from high school to adulthood and is the most widely used test in counseling centers (Lubin et al., 1985). Most items on the SCII require test takers to indicate whether they like, are indifferent to, or dislike items chosen from the following: occupations (e.g., actor/actress, architect), school subjects (algebra, art), activities (adjusting a carburetor, making a speech), amusements (golf, chess, jazz or rock concerts), and types of people (babies, nonconformists). The preferences of test takers are compared with those of people in various occupations. Areas of general interest (e.g., sales, science, teaching, agriculture) and specific interest (e.g., mathematician, guidance counselor, beautician) are derived from these comparisons.

The KOIS, like the SCII, is used from high school to adulthood. It consists of triads of activities, such as the following:

a. write a story about a sports event
b. play in a baseball game
c. teach children to play a game

For each triad, the test taker indicates which activities he or she would like most and least. The KOIS predicts adjustment in college majors as well as occupations.

Projective Tests

You may have heard that there is a personality test that asks people what a drawing or inkblot looks like and that they commonly answer "a bat." There are a number of such tests, the best known of which is the Rorschach inkblot test, named after its originator, Swiss psychiatrist Hermann Rorschach (1884–1922).

The Rorschach Inkblot Test The Rorschach test is a **projective test.** In projective techniques there are no clear, specified answers. People are presented with **ambiguous** stimuli, like inkblots or vague drawings, and may be asked to report what these stimuli look like to them or to tell stories about them. Since there is no concrete proper response, it is assumed that people *project* their own personalities into their responses. The meanings they attribute to these stimuli are assumed to reflect their personalities as well as the drawings or blots themselves.

Actually the facts of the matter are slightly different. There may be no single "correct" response to the Rorschach inkblot shown in Figure 8.7, but some responses would clearly not be in keeping with the features of the blot. Figure 8.7 could be a bat or a flying insect, the pointed face of an animal, the face of a jack-o'-lantern, or many other

Projective test A psychological test that presents ambiguous stimuli onto which the test taker projects his or her own personality in making a response.

Ambiguous Having two or more possible meanings.

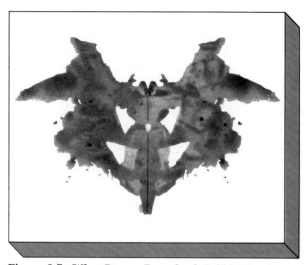

Figure 8.7. What Does a Rorschach Inkblot Look Like? What does this inkblot look like? What could it be?

things. But responses like "an ice cream cone," "diseased lungs," or "a metal leaf in flames" are not suggested by the features of the blot and may reflect personality problems.

The Rorschach inkblot test contains ten cards. Five are in black and white and shades of gray. Five use a variety of colors. Subjects are given the cards, one by one, and asked what they look like or what they could be. They can give no, one, or several responses to each card. They can hold the card upside down or sideways.

The Thematic Apperception Test   The Thematic Apperception Test (TAT) was developed in the 1930s by psychologist Henry Murray at Harvard University. It consists of drawings, like that shown in Figure 8.8, that are open to a variety of interpretations. Subjects are given the cards one at a time and asked to make up stories about them.

The TAT has been widely used in research in social motives as well as in clinical practice. In an experiment described in Chapter 6, need for achievement was assessed from subjects' responses to a card of a boy and a violin. The notion is that we are likely to some degree to be preoccupied with our needs and that our needs will be projected into our responses to ambiguous situations. The TAT is also widely used to assess attitudes toward

other people, especially parents, lovers, and spouses.

Evaluation of Measures of Personality

It seems clear that personality measures can provide useful information to help people make decisions about themselves and others. But in general, psychological tests should not be the sole criteria for making important decisions.

For example, single scales of the MMPI are reasonably accurate measures of the presence of a trait, like depression. But one could not justifiedly hospitalize a person for fear of suicide solely on the basis of a high D-scale score on the MMPI. Similarly, combinations of high MMPI scale scores seem to reflect certain clinical pictures in some populations but not in others. A typical study found that a combination of high scores on the D, Pt, and Sc scales was likely to suggest severe disturbance in college males but not college females (Kelley & King, 1979). There is also controversy about whether whites, blacks, and other racial groups score differently on the MMPI, so that special norms should be established for each group

Figure 8.8. What Does a Thematic Apperception Test Card Look Like? What is happening in this picture? What are the people thinking and feeling? How will the situation turn out?

(Bertelson et al., 1982; Butcher et al., 1983; Pritchard & Rosenblatt, 1980; Snyder et al., 1985). Interpretation of the MMPI is further clouded by the fact that abnormal validity scale scores do *not* necessarily invalidate the test for respondents who are highly disturbed.

The Rorschach inkblot test, for all its artistic appeal, has had major difficulties with validation. The TAT has been consistently shown to be a useful research tool, but its clinical validity has also met with criticism. Despite problems with projective techniques, they are used regularly. The Rorschach inkblot test, in fact, remained the most widely used test in psychiatric hospitals in the 1980s (Lubin et al., 1985).

Psychological tests should not be used as the sole means for making important decisions. But tests that are carefully chosen and interpreted may provide useful information for supplementing other sources of information in making decisions.

TRUTH OR FICTION REVISITED

The human mind is like a vast submerged iceberg, only the tip of which rises above the surface into awareness. Probably not. This statement is consistent with Freud's psychoanalytic theory, which proposes the existence of an unconscious psychic structure (the id) and a partly unconscious psychic structure (the ego). However, empirical evidence does not confirm the existence of these structures.

Biting one's fingernails or smoking cigarettes as an adult is a sign of conflict during very early childhood. Probably not. This statement is consistent with the psychoanalytic view that adult problems can reflect fixations during early stages of psychosexual development. But again, empirical evidence does not confirm this belief.

It is normal for boys to be hostile toward their fathers. Probably not. We have another statement consistent with Freud's views—in this case, his views concerning the Oedipus complex. However, Freud's views on the Oedipus complex are speculative.

You have inherited mysterious memories that date back to ancient times. Probably not. This statement is consistent with Jung's view that there exists a collective unconscious mind. However, empirical evidence does not confirm the existence of a collective unconscious.

People who show a strong drive for superiority are actually fighting feelings of inferiority that lie deep within them. Perhaps, perhaps not. This statement is consistent with Adler's views but unconfirmed by empirical evidence.

Psychologists have studied human personality by reading the dictionary. True. Allport, for example, used the dictionary to derive a preliminary list of personality traits.

Human behavior is largely consistent from situation to situation. Not necessarily. However, people high in private self-consciousness attempt to behave consistently.

We may believe that we have freedom of choice, but our preferences and choices are actually forced on us by the environment. Probably not. This statement is consistent with the behaviorist view that behavior, including preferences, is situationally determined, but social-learning theorists argue that people modify and create environments in addition to simply conforming to environmental demands.

We are more motivated to tackle difficult tasks if we believe that we shall succeed at them. True. Positive "self-efficacy expectations" motivate us to take on challenges.

We all have unique ways of looking at ourselves and at the world outside. Since all of us, with the exception of identical twins, are genetically unique, this assertion is probably accurate. It is also consistent with phenomenological theories of personality.

Psychologists can determine whether a person has told the truth on a personality test. Often, but not with certainty. Some tests, such as the MMPI, have validity scales that can suggest that test takers have not answered items accurately.

Psychological tests can help you choose an occupation. True. Tests such as the SCII help pinpoint where our occupational interests lie.

There is a psychological test made up of inkblots, and one of them looks something like a bat. True. It is the Rorschach inkblot test.

Chapter Review

Personality can be defined as the reasonably stable patterns of behavior that distinguish people. These behavior patterns characterize a person's ways of adjusting to the demands of life.

Psychodynamic theories view psychological forces as being in movement and in conflict. Freud labeled the clashing forces of personality psychic structures. His psychoanalytic theory assumes that we are driven largely by unconscious motives.

Freud hypothesized the existence of three psychic structures. The unconscious id represents psychological drives and operates according to the pleasure principle. The ego is the sense of self, or "I" and operates according to the reality principle. Defense mechanisms protect the ego from anxiety by repressing unacceptable ideas or distorting reality. The superego is the moral sense and operates according to the moral principle.

People undergo psychosexual development as psychosexual energy is tranferred from one erogenous zone to another. There are five stages of psychosexual development: oral, anal, phallic, latency, and genital. Conflicts develop at each stage and, if unresolved, can lead to fixations. Children are theorized to identify with the same-sex parent because of the Oedipus and Electra complexes.

In his analytical psychology, Jung proposed a collective unconscious mind and a conscious self. In his individual psychology, Adler proposed that people respond to inferiority complexes with compensating drives for superiority. Horney believed that children can develop basic hostility or basic anxiety if their parents mistreat them. Erikson highlights the importance of early social relationships and extends Freud's five developmental stages to eight.

Traits are personality elements that are inferred from behavior and account for behavioral consistency. According to Allport, cardinal traits dominate the personality, central traits define notable characteristics, and secondary traits govern a limited number of responses. According to Cattell, surface traits are characteristic ways of behaving, and source traits are underlying traits from which surface traits are derived. Eysenck focuses on the relationships between introversion–extraversion and neuroticism.

Watson, the founder of behaviorism, rejected notions of mind and personality altogether. He and Skinner discarded notions of personal freedom and argued that environmental contingencies can shape people into wanting to do the things that the physical environment and society requires of them. Social-learning theory has a cognitive orientation and focuses on the importance of learning by observation. Social-learning theorists believe that not only situational rewards and punishments but also person variables influence behavior. Person variables include competencies, encoding strategies, expectancies, subjective values, and self-regulatory systems and plans.

Rogers's phenomenological theory begins with the assumption of the existence of the self—an organized and consistent way in which a person perceives his or her "I" to relate to others and the world. The self will become actualized (develop its unique potential) when the person receives unconditional positive regard.

According to Kelly, all people function as scientists, attempting to explain and predict behavior. Kelly believed that to understand people, we must know how they construe events. Kelly argues that we are capable of making major changes in ourselves and our lives.

In personality measurement, psychologists take a sample of behavior in order to predict future behavior. Objective tests such as the MMPI present test takers with a standardized set of test items in the form of questionnaires. Respondents are limited to a specific range of answers. Projective tests such as the Rorschach and the TAT present ambiguous stimuli and permit the respondent a broad range of answers.

Exercise

Theorists and Concepts

Directions: *In the column to the left are the names of personality theorists. In the column to the right is a list of personality-theory concepts. Match the concept with the theorist by writing the letter(s) of the appropriate theorist(s) in the blank space to the left of the concept.*

A. Alfred Adler
B. Gordon Allport
C. Albert Bandura
D. Raymond Cattell
E. Erik Erikson
F. Hans Eysenck
G. Sigmund Freud
H. Karen Horney
I. Carl Jung
J. George Kelly
K. Carl Rogers
L. Julian Rotter
M. John B. Watson

_____ 1. Surface trait
_____ 2. Self
_____ 3. Generalized expectancies
_____ 4. Id
_____ 5. Neuropsychic structure
_____ 6. Psychosocial development
_____ 7. Frame of reference
_____ 8. Behaviorism
_____ 9. Inferiority complex
_____ 10. Personal constructs
_____ 11. Basic anxiety
_____ 12. Self-efficacy expectations
_____ 13. Introversion
_____ 14. Cardinal trait
_____ 15. Personality structure
_____ 16. Conditions of worth
_____ 17. Electra complex
_____ 18. Archetype
_____ 19. Creative self
_____ 20. Source trait
_____ 21. Person variables

Answer Key to Exercise

1. D	7. K	12. C	17. G
2. I, K, A	8. M	13. I, F	18. I
3. L	9. A	14. B	19. A
4. G	10. J	15. B	20. D
5. B	11. H	16. K	21. C, L
6. E			

Posttest

Directions: *For each of the following, select the choice that best answers the question or completes the sentence.*

1. Which of the following theorists has argued that we can make broad changes in our personalities?

   (a) Sigmund Freud, (b) John B. Watson, (c) Gordon Allport, (d) George Kelly.

2. Freud labeled the clashing forces of personality

   (a) repression and resistance, (b) the conscious and the unconscious, (c) defense mechanisms, (d) psychic structures.

3. According to psychoanalytic theory, the _____ follows the reality principle.

   (a) id, (b) ego, (c) superego, (d) libido.

4. According to psychoanalytic theory, the superego usually incorporates the standards of parents through

   (a) identification, (b) socialization, (c) conscious choice, (d) selective reinforcement.

5. John throws his clothing and books all over the floor, keeps his hair unkempt, and rarely cleans his room. According to psychoanalytic theory, John's behavior is suggestive of conflict during the _____ stage of psychosexual development.

   (a) genital, (b) oral, (c) phallic, (d) anal.

6. Which of the following theorists proposed the concept of "generalized expectancies" to account for consistency in behavior?

   (a) Walter Mischel, (b) Albert Bandura, (c) Julian Rotter, (d) B. F. Skinner.

7. Alfred Adler believed that people are basically motivated by

   (a) the collective unconscious, (b) hostility, (c) biological and safety needs, (d) an inferiority complex.

8. Karen Horney agreed with Freud that

   (a) some women suffer from penis envy, (b) there are eight stages of psychosocial development, (c) parent-child relationships are paramount in importance, (d) sexual impulses are more important than social relationships.

9. According to Erikson, the task of middle adulthood is

   (a) establishing intimate relationships, (b) generativity, (c) maintaining ego integrity, (d) attaining ego identity.

10. According to the text, which of the following theorists believed that a basic element of personality was the Self?

    (a) John B. Watson, (b) Carl Jung, (c) Sigmund Freud, (d) Hans J. Eysenck.

11. Gordon Allport looked upon traits as

    (a) archetypes, (b) basic instincts, (c) generalized expectancies, (d) neuropsychic structures.

12. Raymond Cattell hypothesized the existence of two types of traits: _____ traits and source traits.

    (a) surface, (b) cardinal, (c) secondary, (d) central.

13. The radical outlooks of John B. Watson and B. F. Skinner discarded all of the following notions, *with the exception of*

    (a) self-direction, (b) personal freedom, (c) learning, (d) choice.

14. _____ has argued for the inclusion of cognitive points of view within the learning-theory perspective.

    (a) B. F. Skinner, (b) Albert Bandura, (c) John. B. Watson, (d) Carl Jung.

15. One construction worker may interpret a weather report of 97 degrees Fahrenheit as punitive, whereas a vacationer at the pool may interpret the same report as pleasant. Within the framework of social-learning theory, the construction worker and vacationer may be said to interpret the same information in different ways because of different

    (a) subjective values, (b) personal constructs, (c) frames of reference, (d) encoding strategies.

16. Within the framework of social-learning theory, setting goals for ourselves and creating ways of attaining them are examples of

    (a) self-regulatory systems and plans, (b) competencies, (c) conditions of worth, (d) self-efficacy expectations.

17. According to Carl Rogers, the sense of self

    (a) is an archetype, (b) develops as a result of conditions of worth, (c) is innate, (d) develops once biological and safety needs have been met.

18. According to self theory, parents are likely to help their children develop self-esteem when they show them

    (a) conditional positive regard, (b) conditions of worth, (c) unconditional positive regard, (d) psychological congruence.

19. Which theorist has focused on the relationships between introversion–extraversion and neuroticism?

    (a) Carl Jung, (b) Hans J. Eysenck, (c) Raymond Cattell, (d) Karen Horney.

20. Which theorist extended Freud's five stages of development to eight?

    (a) Erik Erikson, (b) John B. Watson, (c) Alfred Adler, (d) Karen Horney.

21. Objective personality tests

    (a) all have forced-choice formats, (b) are easier to answer than projective tests, (c) limit respondents to a specific range of answers, (d) are less valid than projective personality tests.

22. The _____ is used to help diagnose abnormal behavior.

(a) Minnesota Multiphasic Personality Inventory, **(b)** California Psychological Inventory, **(c)** Edwards Personal Preference Schedule, **(d)** Strong/Campbell Interest Inventory.

Answer Key to Posttest

1. D	**7.** D	**13.** C	**18.** C
2. D	**8.** C	**14.** B	**19.** B
3. B	**9.** B	**15.** D	**20.** A
4. A	**10.** B	**16.** A	**21.** C
5. D	**11.** D	**17.** C	**22.** A
6. C	**12.** A		

ABNORMAL BEHAVIOR

OUTLINE

PRETEST: TRUTH OR FICTION?
DEFINING ABNORMAL BEHAVIOR
MODELS OF ABNORMAL BEHAVIOR
  The Demonological Model
  The Medical Model: Organic and Psychoanalytic
    Versions
  The Social-Learning Model
  The Cognitive Model
ANXIETY DISORDERS
  Phobias
  Panic Disorder
  Generalized Anxiety Disorder
  Obsessive-Compulsive Disorder
  Post-Traumatic Stress Disorder
DISSOCIATIVE DISORDERS
  Psychogenic Amnesia
  Psychogenic Fugue
  Multiple-Personality Disorder
  Depersonalization Disorder
SOMATOFORM DISORDERS
  Conversion Disorder
  Hypochondriasis

EATING DISORDERS
  Anorexia Nervosa
  Bulimia Nervosa
MOOD DISORDERS
  Major Depression
  Bipolar Disorder
SCHIZOPHRENIA
  Types of Schizophrenia
PERSONALITY DISORDERS
  The Antisocial Personality
SEXUAL DISORDERS
  Transsexualism
  Paraphilias
  Sexual Dysfunctions
PSYCHOACTIVE SUBSTANCE-USE DISORDERS
  Substance Abuse and Dependence
  Causal Factors in Substance Abuse and Dependence
TRUTH OR FICTION REVISITED
CHAPTER REVIEW
EXERCISES
POSTTEST

PRETEST: TRUTH OR FICTION?

A man shot the president of the United States in front of millions of television witnesses yet was found not guilty by a court of law.

In the Middle Ages innocent people were drowned to prove that they were not possessed by the Devil.

Some people are suddenly flooded with feelings of panic, even when there is no external threat.

Some people have irresistible urges to wash their hands—over and over again.

Stressful experiences can lead to recurrent nightmares.

Some people have not one but two or more distinct personalities dwelling within them.

People have lost the use of their legs or eyes under stress, even though there was nothing medically wrong with them.

Some college women control their weight by going on cycles of binge eating followed by vomiting.

It is abnormal to feel depressed.

Some people ride an emotional roller coaster, with cycles of elation and depression.

In some mental disorders, people see and hear things that are not actually there.

Stripteasers are exhibitionists.

Some people fail to enjoy sexual activity because they try too hard at it.

Alcohol is a stimulant.

Coca-Cola once "added life" through a powerful but now illegal stimulant.

Marijuana is the drug most frequently abused by adolescents.

The Ohio State campus lived in terror throughout the long fall of 1978. Four college women were abducted, forced to cash checks or obtain money with their instant-cash cards, and then raped. A mysterious phone call led to the arrest of a 23-year-old drifter, William, who had been dismissed from the Navy.

William was not the boy next door.

Several psychologists and psychiatrists who interviewed William concluded that ten personalities resided within him, eight male and two female (Keyes, 1982). His personality had been "fractured" by an abusive childhood. The personalities showed distinct facial expressions, vocal patterns, and memories. They even performed differently on personality and intelligence tests.

Arthur, the most rational personality, spoke with a British accent. Danny and Christopher were normal, quiet adolescents. Christene was a 3-year-old girl. It was Tommy, a 16-year-old, who had enlisted in the Navy. Allen was 18 and smoked. Adelena, a 19-year-old lesbian personality, had committed the rapes. Who had made the mysterious phone call? Probably David, aged 9, an anxious child personality.

The defense claimed that William was suffering from **multiple personality.** Several distinct personalities dwelled within him. Some were aware of the others; some believed that they were the sole occupant. Billy, the core personality, had learned to sleep as a child to avoid the abuse of his father. A psychiatrist asserted that Billy had also been "asleep," in a "psychological coma," during the abductions. Therefore Billy should be found innocent by reason of **insanity.**

On December 4, 1978, Billy was found not guilty by reason of insanity. He was committed to an institution for the mentally ill and released in 1984.

In 1982, John Hinckley, was also found not guilty of the assassination attempt on President Reagan by reason of insanity. Expert witnesses testified that he was suffering from **schizophrenia.** Hinckley, too, was committed to an institution for the mentally ill.

Multiple personality and schizophrenia are two types of abnormal behavior. In this chapter we first define abnormal behavior. Then we examine various explanations for, or "models" of, abnormal behavior. In our discussion of the demonological model, we shall see that if William had lived in Salem, Massachusetts, in 1692, just 200 years after Columbus set foot in the New World, he might have been hanged or burned as a witch. At that time most people assumed that abnormal behavior was caused by possession by the Devil. Nineteen people lost their lives that year in that colonial town for allegedly practicing the arts of Satan.

Then we discuss various patterns of abnormal behavior, including *anxiety disorders, dissociative disorders, somatoform disorders, eating disorders, mood disorders, schizophrenia, personality disorders, sexual disorders,* and *psychoactive substance abuse disorders.*

DEFINING ABNORMAL BEHAVIOR

What is meant by abnormal behavior? Just being different is not sufficient cause to label a person abnormal. There is only one president of the United States at a given time, yet that person is not considered abnormal (usually). Only one person holds the record for running or swimming the fastest mile. That person is different from you and me but is not abnormal.

For someone's behavior to be labeled abnormal, someone else must be *disturbed* by it—perhaps the person showing the behavior, a family member, a police officer, or a psychologist. If nobody is disturbed by the behavior, nobody will bother to label it abnormal. Behavior that meets one or more of the following criteria is likely to be labeled abnormal:

1. *Infrequent behavior.* Although rarity or statistical deviance is not sufficient for behavior to be labeled abnormal, it helps. Highly anxious or depressed people are not likely to be considered abnormal in a society in which nearly everyone is anxious or depressed.

Multiple personality A dissociative disorder in which a person appears to have two or more distinct personalities.

Insanity A legal term descriptive of a person judged to be incapable of recognizing right from wrong or of conforming his or her behavior to the law.

Schizophrenia A psychotic disorder characterized by loss of control of thought processes and inappropriate emotional responses.

60 Minutes

By Reason of Insanity

In the "60 Minutes" segment "By Reason of Insanity," correspondent Morley Safer noted that

Not guilty by reason of insanity is a verdict that's been controversial since it was first used in law a hundred and forty years ago. When John Hinckley was acquitted of charges of attempted murder after successfully using the insanity defense, the debate inside the legal and psychiatric communities heated up once again.

In pleading insanity, lawyers use . . . the M'Naghton rules, named after Daniel M'Naghton, a man in England who, in 1843, had delusions that the British prime minister, Sir Robert Peel, was persecuting him. In attempting to assassinate Sir Robert, he killed his secretary. M'Naghton was found not guilty by reason of insanity. Public outrage forced the court to issue reasons for its decision. These became the M'Naghton rules which, with a few modifications, are the standards used in American law today. The central principle is that the accused does not know what he is doing when the act is committed, or—if he does know—that he does not realize it is wrong.

You can readily see how this principle leads to problems. After all, we cannot *know* whether other people understand right from wrong or "know what they are doing" at any given moment. We can only observe what they do and listen to what they say, and then we must draw our own conclusions. In the typical insanity defense, defense attorneys employ experts as witnesses—psychologists or psychiatrists, who on the basis of interviews or previous acquaintance with the client, usually testify that the accused was insane at the time of the act. The prosecution presents conflicting testimony from other expert witnesses to the effect that the accused was sane at the time of the crime.

This type of back-and-forth "expert" testimony characterized the John Hinckley trial in 1982. Hinckley tried to assassinate President Ronald Reagan, claiming that he wished to impress movie actress Jodie Foster. The defense claimed that Hinckley was suffering from schizophrenia at the time and was therefore insane. He was portrayed as a "mental cripple" living in a "fantasy world." Influenced by the movie *Taxi Driver*, he had even sought young prostitutes on the streets of New York who seemed in need of help. (Jodie Foster had played a street prostitute in *Taxi Driver*, and she was "saved" by the movie's schizophrenic "hero.")

The prosecution then brought forth witnesses who testified that Hinckley was sane. Because well-trained professionals often have conflicting views about people's "mental states," which are private events, the public seems to be becoming somewhat skeptical of the insanity plea. Even some jury members who participated in the Hinckley decision were appalled that he had to be found not guilty. They argued that this was a case in which the presumption of innocence backfired; they would have had to prove "beyond a shadow of a doubt" that Hinckley was *sane* at the time of the crime in order to convict him—an impossible task. (Nowadays in many locales the burden of proof lies with the defense to prove insanity beyond a shadow of a doubt.)

Criminals who are found not guilty by reason of insanity are often committed to mental institutions rather than given concrete prison terms. They are eligible for release when they are no

---

2. *Socially unacceptable behavior.* Each society has standards or norms for acceptable behavior in a given context. In our society, walking naked is normal in a locker room but abnormal on a crowded boulevard. Similarly, what is abnormal for one generation can be normal for another. Living together without benefit of marriage was almost unheard of a generation ago but scarcely raises an eyebrow today.

3. *Faulty perception or interpretation of reality.* Our society considers it normal to be inspired by religious beliefs but abnormal to believe that God is

longer behaving abnormally. The possibility of release leads the public to fear that "sick" people will be walking the streets if they show no symptoms for a while. Also, in an Associated Press–NBC News poll, 87 percent of a sample of Americans said they feared that many murderers were using the insanity plea to avoid going to jail (Caplan, 1984).

The American Psychological Association (1984) has taken the position that social and political pressures for curtailment of the standards for the insanity plea should be resisted. Instead, the APA proposes a review of the scientific research on the appropriateness and effects of the insanity plea, and the conducting of new research, as needed. As noted by Rogers (1987), the public is not invariably concerned when obviously disturbed people are found not guilty by reason of insanity. The public's ire is aroused, instead, when morally repugnant people are found not guilty or when the victim is a well-known public figure, as in the case of Ronald Reagan.

Do Criminals Evade Responsibility for Their Behavior by Means of the Insanity Plea? Would-be Presidential assassin John Hinckley (left) is just one of the many who have evaded criminal responsibility through the insanity plea. The defense claimed that Hinckley was living in a fantasy world that involved actress Jodie Foster (right), who played a young prostitute in the film *Taxi Driver*.

literally speaking to you. "Hearing voices" and "seeing things" are considered **hallucinations.** Similarly, **ideas of persecution,** such as believing that the mafia or the CIA or the Communists are "out to get you," are considered abnormal (unless they *are* out to get you, of course).

Hallucination A sensory experience in the absence of sensory stimulation, in which there is confusion of imagined objects and events with reality.

Ideas of persecution Erroneous beliefs that one is being victimized or persecuted.

4. *Personal distress.* Anxiety, depression, exaggerated fears, and other psychological states cause personal distress and can be considered abnormal. But anxiety and depression may also be appropriate responses to one's situation, a real threat or a loss, for instance. In such cases they are not abnormal unless they persevere long after the source of distress has been removed or after most people would have adjusted.

5. *Self-defeating behavior.* Behavior that leads to misery rather than happiness and fulfillment may be considered abnormal. From this perspective, chronic drinking that interferes with work and family life and cigarette smoking that impairs health may be labeled abnormal.

6. *Dangerous behavior.* Behavior that is dangerous to the self or others is considered abnormal. People who threaten or attempt suicide may be considered abnormal, as may people who threaten or attack others.

MODELS OF ABNORMAL BEHAVIOR

There are a number of historical and contemporary views or models of abnormal behavior. They include the demonological, medical, social-learning, and cognitive models. The organic and psychoanalytic models are offshoots of the medical model.

The Demonological Model

Throughout human history, the **demonological model** has been the most widely believed model for explaining abnormal behavior. During the

---

Demonological model The view that explains abnormal behavior in terms of possession by evil spirits.

Possession According to superstitious belief, a psychological state induced by demons or the Devil in which a person exhibits abnormal behavior.

Retribution Deserved punishment for evildoing.

Exorcist A person who drives away evil spirits through means such as ritual prayers and beatings.

Medical model The view that abnormal behavior is symptomatic of mental illness.

Middle Ages and during the early days of American civilization along the rocky coast of Massachusetts, the demonological model was in full sway. It was generally believed that abnormal behavior was a sign of **possession** by agents or spirits of the Devil. Possession could stem from **retribution,** or God having the Devil possess your soul as punishment for your sins. Wild agitation and confusion were attributed to retribution. Possession was also believed to result from deals with the Devil in which people ("witches") traded their souls for earthly power or wealth. Witches were held responsible for unfortunate events, ranging from a neighbor's infertility to a poor crop.

In either case you were in for it. An **exorcist,** whose function was to persuade those spirits to find better pickings elsewhere, might pray at your side and wave a cross at you. If the spirits didn't call it quits, you might be beaten or flogged. If your behavior was still unseemly, there were other remedies, like the rack, which have powerful influences on behavior.

In 1484 Pope Innocent VIII ordered that witches be put to death. At least 200,000 accused witches were killed over the next two centuries. Europe was no place to practice strange ways. The goings-on at Salem were trivial by comparison.

There were ingenious "diagnostic" tests to ferret out possession. One was dunking the suspect under water. Failure to drown was interpreted as support by the Devil—in other words, possession. Then you were in real trouble.

The Medical Model: Organic and Psychoanalytic Versions

According to the **medical model,** abnormal behavior reflects an underlying illness, not evil spirits. The organic model and the psychoanalytic model are offshoots of the medical model.

Medical Model: Organic Version   In 1883 Emil Kraepelin published a textbook of psychiatry in which he defined the medical model. Kraepelin argued that there were specific forms of abnormal behavior, which within the medical model are often called mental illnesses. (See Table 9.1 for a list of many of the commonly used terms concerning abnormal behavior that reflect the widespread influence of the medical model.) Each mental illness had specific origins, which he assumed were physiological. The assumption that biochemical or physiological problems underlie mental illness is the heart of the **organic model.**

Kraepelin argued that each mental illness, just like each physical illness, was typified by its own cluster of symptoms, or **syndrome.** Each mental illness had a specific outcome, or course, and would presumably respond to a characteristic form of treatment, or therapy.

Contemporary supporters of the organic model point to various sources of evidence. For one thing, a number of mental disorders run in families and might therefore be transmitted from generation to generation by DNA. For another, imbalances in neurotransmitters and other chemicals produce behavioral effects like those found in disorders such as severe depression and schizophrenia, as we shall see later.

According to the organic model, treatment requires biological expertise and involves controlling or curing the underlying organic problem. The biological therapies discussed in Chapter 10 are largely based on the organic model.

Medical Model: Psychoanalytic Version

Sigmund Freud's psychoanalytic model argues that abnormal behavior is symptomatic of unconscious conflict of childhood origins—an underlying psychological rather than biological disorder. The abnormal behavior (or "symptoms") often reflect difficulty in repressing primitive sexual and aggressive impulses.

Within Freudian theory, **neurotic** behavior and anxiety stem from the leakage of primitive impulses. Anxiety represents the impulse itself and fear of what might happen if the impulse were acted on. In the case of **psychosis,** impulses are assumed to have broken through, so that behavior falls under the control of the id rather than the ego or superego. According to psychoanalytic theory, treatment (other than a sort of "Band-Aid" therapy) requires resolving the unconscious conflicts that underlie the abnormal behavior.

The medical model is a major advance over demonology. It led to the view that mentally ill people should be treated by qualified professionals

Table 9.1 Some Commonly Used Terms Concerning Abnormal Behavior That Are Derived from the Medical Model

Mental illness	Mental hospital
Mental health	Prognosis
Symptoms	Treatment
Syndrome	Therapy
Diagnosis	Cure
Mental patient	Relapse

rather than be punished. Compassion replaced hatred, fear, and persecution.

But there are problems with the medical model. For instance, the model suggests that the mentally ill, like the physically ill, may not be responsible for their problems and limitations. In the past, this view often led to hospitalization and suspension of responsibility (as in work and maintenance of a family life). Thus removed from the real world, the coping ability of the mentally ill often declined further. But today most adherents of the medical model encourage patients to remain in the community and maintain as much responsibility as they can.

The Social-Learning Model

From a social-learning point of view, abnormal behavior is not necessarily symptomatic of anything. Rather, the abnormal behavior is itself the problem. To a large degree, abnormal behavior is believed to be acquired in the same way normal behaviors are acquired—for example, through conditioning and observational learning. Why, then, do some people show abnormal behavior?

Organic model The view that abnormal behavior is symptomatic of underlying biochemical or physiological abnormalities.

Syndrome A cluster or group of symptoms suggestive of a particular disorder.

Neurotic Of neurosis. Neuroses are theorized to stem from unconscious conflict.

Psychosis A major disorder in which a person lacks insight and has difficulty meeting the demands of daily life and maintaining contact with reality.

One reason is found in situational variables; that is, their learning or reinforcement histories might differ from those of most of us. But differences in person variables such as competencies, encoding strategies, self-efficacy expectations, and self-regulatory systems might also make the difference.

A person who lacks social skills might never have had the chance to observe skillful models. Or it might be that a minority subculture reinforced behaviors that are not approved by the majority. Punishment for early exploratory behavior, or childhood sexual activity, might lead to adult anxieties over independence or sexuality. Inconsistent discipline (haphazard rewarding of desirable behavior and unreliable punishing of misbehavior) might lead to antisocial behavior. Children whose parents ignore or abuse them might come to pay more attention to their fantasies than to the outer world, leading to schizophrenic withdrawal and inability to distinguish reality from fantasy. Deficits in competencies, encoding strategies, and self-regulatory systems might heighten schizophrenic problems. Since social-learning theorists do not believe that behavior problems necessarily reflect organic or unconscious problems, they often try to change or modify them directly, as with behavior therapy (see Chapter 10).

The Cognitive Model

Cognitive theorists focus on the cognitive events—such as thoughts, expectations, and attitudes—that accompany and in some cases underlie abnormal behavior.

One cognitive approach to understanding abnormal behavior involves information processing. As noted in earlier chapters, information-processing theorists compare the processes of the mind to those of the computer and think in terms of cycles of input (based on perception), storage, retrieval, manipulation, and output of information. They view abnormal behavior patterns as disturbances

in the cycle. Disturbances might be caused by the blocking or distortion of input or by faulty storage, retrieval, or manipulation of information. Any of these can lead to lack of output or distorted output (e.g., bizarre behavior). Schizophrenic individuals, for example, frequently jump from topic to topic in a disorganized fashion, which information-processing theorists might explain as problems in manipulation of information.

Other cognitive theorists (Albert Ellis, 1977, 1987, is one) view anxiety problems as stemming from irrational beliefs and attitudes, such as perfectionism and overwhelming desire for social approval. Aaron Beck attributes many cases of depression to "cognitive errors," such as self-devaluation, interpretion of events in a negative light, and general pessimism (Beck et al., 1979). Some cognitive psychologists, as we shall see, attribute many cases of depression to cognitions to the effect that one is helpless to change things for the better.

Social-learning theorists such as Albert Bandura (1986) and Walter Mischel (1986) straddle the border between the behavioral and the cognitive. As noted, they place primary importance on encoding strategies, self-regulatory systems, and expectancies in explaining and predicting behavior. For example, expectancies that we will not be able to carry out our plans (low "self-efficacy expectations") sap motivation and lead to feelings of hopelessness—two aspects of depression (Bandura, 1982).

Many psychologists look to more than one model to explain and treat abnormal behavior. They are considered **eclectic.** For example, many social-learning theorists believe that some abnormal behavior patterns stem from biochemical factors or the interaction of biochemistry and learning. They are open to combining behavior therapy with drugs to treat problems such as schizophrenia and **bipolar disorder.** A psychoanalyst might also be eclectic. He or she might believe that schizophrenic disorganization reflects control of the personality by the id and argue that only long-term psychotherapy can help the ego achieve supremacy. But the psychoanalyst might still be willing to use drugs to calm agitation on a temporary basis.

Now let us consider the major categories of abnormal behavior, as compiled in the third edition (revised version) of the *Diagnostic and Statistical*

Eclectic Selecting from various systems or theories.

Bipolar disorder A disorder in which the mood alternates between two extreme poles (elation and depression). Also referred to as *manic-depression*.

What Is Anxiety? Where Does It Come From? Anxiety is characterized by nervousness, fears, feelings of dread and foreboding, and physical signs such as rapid heartbeat and sweating.

Manual of the Mental Disorders (DSM–III–R) by the American Psychiatric Association (1987). We shall refer to the DSM–III–R because it is the most widely used classification system in the United States. However, psychologists criticize the DSM–III–R on many grounds, such as adhering too strongly to the medical model. So our use of it is intended as a convenience, not an endorsement. In future years psychologists might publish their own system for classifying abnormal behavior patterns.

ANXIETY DISORDERS

Anxiety disorders are characterized by nervousness, fears, feelings of dread and foreboding, and signs of sympathetic overarousal that include rapid heartbeat, muscle tension, and shakiness. The anxiety disorders we shall consider include phobic, panic, generalized anxiety, obsessive-compulsive, and post-traumatic stress disorders.

Phobias

There are several types of phobias, including *simple phobia, social phobia,* and *agoraphobia.* According to the DSM–III–R, **simple phobias** are excessive, ir-rational fears of specific objects or situations. **Social phobias** are persistent fears of scrutiny by others and of doing something that will be humiliating or embarrassing. Stage fright and speech anxiety are examples of common social phobias.

One simple phobia is fear of elevators. Some people will not enter them, despite the hardships they suffer (such as walking up six flights of steps) as a result. Yes, the cable *could* break. The ventilation *could* fail. One *could* be stuck in midair waiting for repairs. But these problems are infrequent, and it does not make sense for most of us repeatedly to walk up flights of stairs to avoid them. Similarly, some people with phobias for hypodermic needles will not receive injections, even when they are the recommended treatment for serious illness. Injections can be painful, but most people with phobias for needles would gladly suffer a pinch that would cause even greater pain if it would help them fight illness. Other simple phobias include **claustrophobia** (fear of tight or enclosed places);

Simple phobia Persistent fear of a specific object or situation.

Social phobia An irrational, excessive fear of public scrutiny.

Claustrophobia Fear of tight, small places.

acrophobia (fear of heights); and fear of mice, snakes, and other "creepy-crawlies."

Phobias can seriously interfere with one's life. A person may know that a phobia is irrational yet still feel intense anxiety and avoid the phobic object or situation.

Fears of animals and imaginary creatures are common among children, and **agoraphobia** is among the most widespread phobias of adults (Mahoney, 1980). *Agoraphobia* is derived from Greek, meaning "fear of the marketplace," or of being out in open, busy areas. Persons with agoraphobia fear being in places from which it might be difficult to escape or in which help might be unavailable if they become distressed. In practice, people who receive this label are frequently afraid of venturing out of their homes, especially when they are alone. They find it difficult or impossible to hold jobs or to carry on a normal social life.

Panic Disorder

Panic disorder is an unexpected attack of intense anxiety that is not triggered by a specific object or situation. Panic sufferers experience symptoms such as shortness of breath, heavy sweating, trembling, and pounding of the heart (Anderson et al., 1984; Barlow et al., 1985; Norton et al., 1985). According to the DSM–III–R, there may also be choking sensations, nausea, numbness or tingling, flushes or chills, chest pain, and fear of dying, going crazy, or losing control. There is a stronger body component to the anxiety felt by people with

---

Acrophobia Fear of high places.

Agoraphobia Fear of open, crowded places.

Panic disorder Recurrent attacks of extreme anxiety in the absence of external stimuli that usually elicit anxiety.

Generalized anxiety disorder Feelings of dread and foreboding and sympathetic arousal of at least one month's duration.

Obsession A recurring thought or image that seems beyond control.

Compulsion An apparently irresistible urge to repeat an act or engage in ritualistic behavior, such as hand washing.

---

panic disorders than to that encountered by people with other anxiety disorders (Barlow et al., 1985). Panic attacks may last from a minute or two to an hour or more, and afterward victims usually feel exhausted.

Nearly half of us experience panic now and then (Norton & Rhodes, 1983), but the DSM–III–R diagnoses panic disorder when there have been four attacks in a four-week period or an attack has been followed by a month of dread of another attack. When we use these criteria, panic disorders affect only about 1 percent of the population (Meyers et al., 1984).

Generalized Anxiety Disorder

Generalized anxiety disorder is persistent anxiety of at least one month's duration. As in panic disorder, the anxiety cannot be attributed to a phobic object, situation, or activity. It seems free-floating. Symptoms may include motor tension (shakiness, inability to relax, furrowed brow, fidgeting, etc.); autonomic overarousal (sweating, dry mouth, racing heart, light-headedness, frequent urinating, diarrhea, etc.); feelings of dread and foreboding; and excessive vigilance, as shown by distractibility, insomnia, and irritability.

Obsessive-Compulsive Disorder

An **obsession** is a recurring thought or image that seems irrational and beyond control. Obsessions are so strong and frequent that they interfere with daily life. They may include doubts about whether one has locked the doors and shut the windows; impulses, such as the wish to strangle one's spouse; and images, such as one mother's recurrent fantasy that her children had been run over by traffic on the way home from school. In other cases, a 16-year-old boy found "numbers in my head" whenever he was about to study or take a test. A housewife became obsessed with the notion that she had contaminated her hands with Sani-Flush and that the contamination was spreading to everything she touched.

A **compulsion** is a seemingly irresistible urge to engage in an act, often repeatedly, such as lengthy, elaborate washing after using the bathroom. The impulse is frequent and forceful, interfering with daily life. Some men, called *exhibitionists,* report having the compulsion to expose their genitals to female strangers. The woman who felt contaminated by Sani-Flush engaged in elaborate hand-washing rituals. She spent three to four hours daily at the sink and complained, "My hands look like lobster claws."

Post-Traumatic Stress Disorder

Post-traumatic stress disorder (PTSD) is defined as intense and persistent feelings of anxiety and helplessness that are caused by a traumatic experience, such as a physical threat to oneself or one's family, destruction of one's community, or witnessing the death of another person. PTSD has troubled many Vietnam war veterans, victims of rape, and persons who have seen their homes and communities destroyed by natural disasters such as floods or tornadoes. PTSD may begin six months or more after the event.

The precipitating event is reexperienced through intrusive memories, recurrent dreams, and the sudden feeling that the event is actually recurring (as in "flashbacks"). Typically the sufferer attempts to avoid thoughts and activities associated with the traumatic event. He or she may also display sleep problems, irritable outbursts, difficulty concentrating, excessive vigilance, and a heightened "startle" response.

Theoretical Views

Psychoanalytic theory suggests that phobias symbolize conflicts of childhood origin. It explains generalized anxiety as persistent difficulty in maintaining repression of primitive impulses. Psychoanalysts view obsessions as the leakage of unconscious impulses and compulsions as acts that allow people to keep such impulses partly repressed.

From the learning-theory perspective, phobias are conditioned fears that might have been acquired in early childhood and whose origins are beyond memory. Avoidance of feared stimuli is reinforced by reduction of anxiety.

Seligman and Rosenhan (1984) suggest that we are genetically prepared to be conditioned to certain stimuli. This view is termed **prepared conditioning.** We do not inherit specific fears, but evolutionary forces favor the survival of individuals who are biologically *prepared* to acquire fears of large animals, snakes, heights, entrapment, sharp objects, and strangers. In laboratory experiments, people have been shown photographs of various objects and then been given electric shock (Hugdahl & Ohman, 1977; Ohman et al., 1976). Subjects have indeed acquired fear reactions to some stimuli (e.g., spiders and snakes) more readily than others (e.g., flowers and houses), as measured by sweating in response to subsequent showings of these stimuli. However, these experiments do not show that the subjects were *genetically* prepared to develop fear responses to stimuli such as snakes and spiders. Subjects also had years of experience in a society in which other people react negatively to these stimuli. Learning, not genetic factors, might have "prepared" subjects to fear them.

Social-learning theorists stress the role of observational learning in acquiring fears (Bandura et al., 1969). If parents squirm, grimace, and shudder at mice, blood, or dirt on the kitchen floor, children might encode these stimuli as awful and imitate their parents' behavior. Social-learning and cognitive theorists suggest that anxiety can be maintained by thinking that one is in a terrible situation and helpless to change it. Social-learning theorists suggest that obsessions and compulsions serve the purpose of diverting attention from more important and threatening issues, such as "What am I to do with my life?"

Cognitive theorists note that we also entertain thoughts that heighten and perpetuate anxiety (Meichenbaum & Jaemko, 1983), such as "I've got to get out of here" or "My heart is going to leap

Post-traumatic stress disorder A disorder that follows a psychologically distressing event outside the range of normal human experience, and which is characterized by symptoms such as intense fear, avoidance of stimuli associated with the event, and reliving of the event.

Prepared conditioning The view that people are biologically preprogramed to acquire fears of certain objects and situations.

out of my chest." Such thoughts heighten physical anxiety responses, interfere with planning, magnify the aversiveness of stimuli, motivate avoidance, and decrease self-efficacy expectations concerning the ability to control the situation. Belief that we shall not be able to handle a threat heightens anxiety (Bandura, 1981; Bandura et al., 1982), whereas belief that we are in control lessens it (Miller, 1980).

Organic factors might play a role in anxiety disorders. For one thing, anxiety disorders tend to run in families (Turner et al., 1987). In an adoptee study of adolescents and parents, Sandra Scarr and her colleagues (1981) found that **neuroticism** test scores of parents and their natural children correlated more highly than those of parents and adopted children—suggestive of a stronger role for heredity than environmental influences. A twin study found that the **concordance** rate for anxiety disorders is higher among pairs of identical than fraternal twins (Torgersen, 1983).

And so, a predisposition toward anxiety—perhaps in the form of a highly reactive autonomic nervous system—might be inherited. The "highly reactive nervous system" might take the form of certain overly sensitive chemical receptors in the brain. We believe that **benzodiazepines,** a class of drugs effective in reducing anxiety, work by "docking" at receptor sites for naturally occurring molecules that have been linked to anxiety (Costa, 1985). In this way they might block the action of chemicals that induce or compound anxiety reactions. People prone to anxiety disorders might have more sensitive receptor sites than other peo-

ple, and thus respond to anxiety-provoking substances more readily.

DISSOCIATIVE DISORDERS

The DSM–III–R lists four major **dissociative disorders:** *psychogenic amnesia, psychogenic fugue, multiple personality,* and *depersonalization.* In each case there is a disturbance in the normal functions of identity, memory, or consciousness that make the person feel whole.

Psychogenic Amnesia

In **psychogenic amnesia,** there is sudden inability to recall important personal information. Memory loss cannot be attributed to organic problems, such as a blow to the head or alcoholic intoxication. In the most common example, the person cannot recall events for a number of hours after a stressful incident, as in warfare or in the case of the uninjured survivor of an accident. In generalized amnesia, people forget their entire lives. Amnesia may last for hours or years. Termination of amnesia is also sudden.

Psychogenic Fugue

In **psychogenic fugue,** the person shows loss of memory for the past, travels suddenly from his or her home or place of work, and assumes a new identity. Either the person does not think about the past or reports a past filled with bogus memories that are not recognized as false. Following recovery, the events that occurred during the fugue are not recalled.

Multiple Personality Disorder

Multiple personality is the name given William's disorder, as described in the beginning of the chapter. In this disorder, two or more "personalities," each with distinct traits and memories, "occupy" the same person, with or without awareness of the others. Different personalities may even have different eyeglass prescriptions (American Psychiatric Association, 1987).

Neuroticism A personality trait characterized largely by persistent anxiety.

Concordance Agreement.

Benzodiazepines A class of drugs that reduce anxiety. Minor tranquilizers.

Dissociative disorders Disorders in which there are sudden, temporary changes in consciousness or self-identity.

Psychogenic amnesia A dissociative disorder marked by loss of memory or self-identity.

Psychogenic fugue A dissociative disorder in which one experiences amnesia, then flees to a new location and establishes a new life-style.

What Is Multiple Personality?   In the film *The Three Faces of Eve*, Joanne Woodward played three personalities in the same woman: the shy, inhibited Eve White (lying on couch); the flirtatious and promiscuous Eve Black (in dark dress); and a third personality ("Jane") who was healthy enough to accept her sexual and aggressive impulses and still maintain her sense of identity.

In the celebrated case that became the subject of the film *The Three Faces of Eve,* a timid housewife named Eve White harbored two other personalities: Eve Black, a sexually aggressive, antisocial personality, and Jane, an emerging personality who was able to accept the existence of her primitive impulses yet show socially appropriate behavior. Finally, the three faces merged into one: Jane.

Depersonalization Disorder

Depersonalization disorder is the persistent feeling that one is not real. Persons with the disorder may feel detached from their own bodies, as if they are observing their thought processes from the outside. Or they may feel that they are functioning on automatic pilot or as if in a dream.

Theoretical Views

According to psychoanalytic theory, dissociative disorders involve massive use of repression to prevent recognition of unacceptable impulses. In psychogenic amnesia and fugue, the person forgets a profoundly disturbing event or impulse. In mul-

Depersonalization disorder   Persistent or recurrent feelings that one is not real or is detached from one's own experiences or body.

tiple personality, people express unacceptable impulses through alternate personalities. In depersonalization, the person stands outside—removed from the turmoil within.

Social-learning theorists generally regard dissociative disorders as conditions in which people learn *not to think* about disturbing acts or impulses to avoid feelings of guilt and shame. Technically speaking, *not thinking about these matters* is negatively reinforced by *removal* of the aversive stimuli of guilt and shame.

Social-learning theory also suggests that many people come to role-play people with multiple personality through observational learning. This is not exactly the same thing as pretending or malingering because people can "forget to tell themselves" that they have assumed a role. Reinforcers are made available by role-playing individuals with multiple personality: Drawing attention to oneself and escaping responsibility for unacceptable behavior are two (Spanos et al., 1985; Thigpen & Cleckley, 1984). Films and TV shows like *The Three Faces of Eve* and *Sybil* have "provided detailed examples of the symptoms and course of multiple personality" (Spanos et al., 1985, p. 363).

One cognitive perspective explains dissociative disorders in terms of deployment of attention. Perhaps all of us are capable of dividing our awareness so that we become unaware, at least temporarily, of events that we usually focus more attention on. Perhaps the marvel is *not* that attention can be divided but that human consciousness normally integrates experience into a meaningful whole.

Somatoform disorders Disorders in which people complain of physical (somatic) problems although no physical abnormality can be found.

Conversion disorder A disorder in which anxiety or unconscious conflicts are "converted" into physical symptoms that often have the effect of helping the person cope with anxiety or conflict.

La belle indifférence A French term descriptive of the lack of concern sometimes shown by people with conversion disorders.

Hypochondriasis Persistent belief that one has a medical disorder despite lack of medical findings.

SOMATOFORM DISORDERS

In **somatoform disorders,** people show or complain of physical problems, such as paralysis, pain, or the persistent belief that they have a serious disease, yet no physical abnormality can be found. In this section we shall discuss two somatoform disorders: *conversion disorder,* and *hypochondriasis.*

Conversion Disorder

Conversion disorder is characterized by a major change in or loss of physical functioning, although there are no medical findings to support the loss.

If you lost the ability to see at night, or if your legs became paralyzed, you would show understandable concern. But some victims of conversion disorder show indifference to their symptoms, a remarkable feature referred to as **la belle indifférence.** Conversion disorder is so named because it appears to "convert" a source of stress into a physical problem. Instances are rare and of short duration, but their existence led the young Sigmund Freud to believe that subconscious processes were at work.

During World War II a number of bomber pilots developed night blindness. They could not carry out their nighttime missions, although no damage to the optic nerves was found. In rare cases, women with large families have become paralyzed in the legs, again with no medical findings.

Conversion disorder, like dissociative disorders, seems to serve a purpose. The "blindness" of the pilots may have afforded them temporary relief from stressful missions or allowed them to avoid the guilt of bombing civilian populations. The paralysis of a woman who prematurely commits herself to a large family and a life at home may prevent her from doing housework or from engaging in sexual intercourse and becoming pregnant again. She "accomplishes" certain ends without having to recognize them or make decisions.

Hypochondriasis

Persons with **hypochondriasis,** have the persistent belief that they are suffering from serious disease, although no medical evidence can be found. Sufferers often become preoccupied with minor physical sensations and maintain an unrealistic belief that something is wrong despite medical reassurance. "Hypochondriacs" may go from doctor to doctor, seeking the one who will find the causes of the sensations. Fear may impair work or home life.

There is also evidence that some hypochondriacs use their complaints as a self-handicapping strategy (Smith et al., 1983). That is, they are more likely to complain of feeling ill in situations in which illness can serve as an excuse for poor performance. In other cases, focusing on physical sensations and possible problems may serve the function of taking the person's mind off other life problems.

EATING DISORDERS

Eating disorders are characterized by gross disturbances in patterns of eating. The eating disorders we shall consider are *anorexia nervosa* and *bulimia nervosa*.

Anorexia Nervosa

There is a saying that you cannot be too rich or too thin. Excess money may be pleasant enough, but one certainly can be too thin, as in the case of **anorexia nervosa.** Anorexia is a life-threatening disorder characterized by refusal to maintain a healthful body weight, intense fear of being overweight, a distorted body image, and in females, **amenorrhea.** Anoretic persons usually weigh less than 85 percent of their expected body weight.

By and large, anorexia afflicts girls and young women. Nearly one in 200 school-aged girls has trouble gaining or maintaining weight (Crisp et al., 1976). Anoretic females outnumber anoretic males by estimates of 9:1 to 20:1. Onset is most often between the ages of 12 and 18.

Anoretic girls may be full height but weigh 60 pounds or less. They may drop 25 percent or more of their body weight in a year. Severe weight loss triggers amenorrhea. The girl's general health declines, and she may experience decreased heart rate, low blood pressure, constipation, dehydration, and a host of other problems (Kaplan &

Woodside, 1987). About 5 percent of anoretic girls die from weight loss.

In the typical pattern, girls notice some weight gain after menarche and decide that it must come off. However, dieting and, often, exercise continue at a fever pitch after the girls reach normal body weights, even after family and others have told them that they are losing too much. Anoretic girls almost always adamantly deny that they are wasting away. They may point to their fierce exercise regimens as proof. Their body images are distorted. Although others perceive them as "skin and bones," they sit before the mirror and focus on nonexistent pockets of fat.

Many anoretics become obsessed with food and are constantly "around it." They may engross themselves in cookbooks, take on the family shopping chores, and prepare elaborate dinners for others.

Bulimia Nervosa

Bulimia nervosa is defined as recurrent cycles of binge eating, especially of foods rich in carbohydrates*, and the taking of dramatic measures to purge the food. These measures include self-induced vomiting, fasting or strict dieting, use of laxatives, and vigorous exercise. As with anorexia, there is overconcern about body shape and weight. The disorder usually begins in adolescence or early adulthood and afflicts women more so than men by about a 10:1 ratio (American Psychiatric Association, 1987).

Bulimia is even more common than anorexia. It has been estimated to affect 5 percent of the population (Nagelman et al., 1983).

*For example, candy, cookies, cakes. Meats contain protein and fat and are of less interest to bulimic bingers.

Anorexia nervosa An eating disorder characterized by maintenance of an abnormally low body weight, intense fear of weight gain, a distorted body image, and in females, amenorrhea.

Amenorrhea Absence of menstruation.

Bulimia nervosa An eating disorder characterized by recurrent episodes of binge eating followed by purging.

Theoretical Views

It has been speculated that a number of eating disorders might reflect problems in the hypothalamus. For example, the neurotransmitter norepinephrine, when it acts on the ventromedial hypothalamus, stimulates animals to eat, with preference for carbohydrates (Kaplan & Woodside, 1987; Leibowitz, 1986; Mitchell & Eckert, 1987). The neurotransmitter serotonin, by contrast, appears to induce feelings of satiation, thereby suppressing the appetite, and particularly the desire for carbohydrates (Halmi et al., 1986; Kaplan & Woodside, 1987). And so a biological condition that would increase the impact of serotonin could have a negative impact on the desire to eat, as in anorexia. One could also speculate that a biological condition that decreased the impact of serotonin, which normally suppresses appetite for carbohydrates, could result in periodic carbohydrate binge eating, as found in bulimia. "Antidepressant" medications that work by increasing the quantities of norepinephrine and serotonin available to the brain have increased the appetite of some anoretic patients and controlled cycles of binge eating and vomiting in some bulimics (Halmi et al., 1986; Hughes et al., 1986; Walsh et al., 1984).

Psychological hypotheses concerning the origins of anorexia nervosa and bulimia nervosa have also been advanced. The frequent link between anorexia and menarche has led psychoanalysts to suggest that anorexia may represent an effort by the girl to remain prepubescent. Anorexia allows the girl to avoid growing up, separating from the family, and assuming adult responsibilities. Severe weight loss also prevents the rounding of the breasts and the hips. And so, some investigators hypothesize that anoretic girls are conflicted about their sexuality, and the possibility of pregnancy in particular.

An irrational fear of gaining weight might also reflect cultural idealization of the slender female.

Major depression A severe depressive disorder in which the person may show loss of appetite, psychomotor symptoms, and impaired reality testing.

Psychomotor retardation Slowness in motor activity and (apparently) in thought.

As noted by psychologists Janet Polivy and C. Peter Herman (1987), this cultural ideal has become so ingrained that dieting is the "norm" for U.S. women today! Women college students generally see themselves as heavier than the figure that is most attractive to males, and heavier, still, than the "ideal" female figure (Fallon & Rozin, 1985). College men actually prefer women to be heavier than women expect.

MOOD DISORDERS

Mood disorders are characterized by disturbance in expressed emotions. The disturbance generally involves depression or elation. We shall discuss two mood disorders: *major depression* and *bipolar disorder*.

Major Depression

Depression is the "common cold" of psychological problems, according to Seligman (1973)—the most common psychological problem we face. Depressed people may feel sad, blue, or "down in the dumps." They may complain of lack of energy, loss of self-esteem, difficulty concentrating, loss of interest in other people and usually enjoyable activities, pessimism, crying, and thoughts of suicide.

In addition to the symptoms that define depression in general, people with **major depression** may show poor appetite and significant weight loss, agitation or severe **psychomotor retardation,** inability to concentrate and make decisions, complaints of "not caring" anymore, and recurrent thoughts of death or suicide attempts.

Persons with major depression may also show impaired reality testing, or psychotic symptoms. These include delusions of unworthiness, guilt for imagined great wrongdoings, even ideas that one is rotting away from disease. There may also be hallucinations, as of the Devil administering just punishment or of strange sensations in the body.

Bipolar Disorder

In bipolar disorder, formerly known as manic-depression, there are mood swings from elation to depression. These cycles seem unrelated to external events. In the elated, or **manicky** phase, people might show excessive excitement or silliness, carrying jokes too far. They might show poor judgment, sometimes destroying property, and might be argumentative (Depue et al., 1981). Roommates might avoid them, finding them abrasive. Manicky people often speak rapidly ("pressured speech") and jump from topic to topic, showing **rapid flight of ideas.** It is hard to "get a word in edgewise." They might show extreme generosity by making unusually large contributions to charity or giving away expensive possessions. They might not be able to sit still or to sleep restfully.

Depression is the other side of the coin. Bipolar depressed people often sleep more than usual and are lethargic. People with major (or "unipolar") depression are more likely to show insomnia and agitation (Davison & Neale, 1986). Bipolar depressed individuals show social withdrawal and irritability.

Some persons with bipolar disorder attempt suicide "on the way down" from the elated phase of the disorder. They report that they will do almost anything to escape the depths of depression that lie ahead.

Theoretical Views

The causes of brief, "garden variety" depression are frequently situational. Depression is a normal reaction to loss or to exposure to unpleasant events such as marital discord, physical discomfort, incompetence, failure at work, and pressure at work (Coyne et al., 1987; Eckenrode, 1984; Lewinsohn & Amenson, 1978; Stone & Neale, 1984). There are many people, however, who recover from losses less readily than the rest of us.

Psychoanalytic Views
Psychoanalysts suggest various explanations for persistent depression. In one, depressed people are overly concerned about hurting others' feelings or losing their approval. As a result, they hold in rather than express feelings of anger. Anger becomes turned inward and is experienced as misery and self-hatred.

Social-Learning Views
Social-learning theorists note similarities in behavior between people who are depressed and laboratory animals who are not reinforced for instrumental behavior. Inactivity and loss of interest result in each. Lewinsohn (1975) theorizes that many depressed people lack skills that might lead to rewards. Some depressed people are nonassertive (Gotlib, 1984); others do have the social skills of nondepressed people, but they do not reinforce (credit) themselves as much for showing these skills (Gotlib, 1982).

Research has also found links between depression and **learned helplessness.** In one study, Seligman (1975) taught dogs that they were helpless to escape an electric shock by preventing them from leaving a cage in which they received repeated shocks. Later a barrier to a safe compartment was removed, allowing the animals a way out. But when they were shocked again, the dogs made no effort to escape. Apparently they had learned that they were helpless. Seligman's dogs were also, in a sense, reinforced for doing nothing. That is, the shock *eventually* stopped when the dogs were showing helpless behavior—inactivity and withdrawal. "Reinforcement" might have increased the likelihood of repeating their "successful behavior"—that is, doing nothing—in a similar situation. This helpless behavior resembles that of depressed people.

Cognitive Factors
Depressed people tend to construe stress and their own shortcomings in negative ways (Cochran & Hammen, 1985; Hammen et al., 1985; Persons & Rao, 1985). They tend to be self-critical (Zuroff & Mongrain, 1987), to attribute problems to factors that they are helpless to change (Lam et al., 1987), and to be generally pessimistic about the future (Alloy & Ahrens, 1987; Pyszczynski et al., 1987).

Seligman and his colleagues note that when things go wrong, we may think of the causes of failure as *internal* or *external, stable* or *unstable, global*

Manicky Elated, showing excessive excitement.

Rapid flight of ideas Rapid speech and topic changes, characteristic of manicky behavior.

Learned helplessness Seligman's model for the acquisition of depressive behavior, based on findings that organisms in aversive situations learn to show inactivity when their operants are not reinforced.

or *specific*. Let us explain these various **attributional styles** through the example of having a date that does not work out. An internal attribution involves self-blame, as in "I really loused it up," whereas an external attribution places the blame elsewhere (as in "Some couples just don't take to each other" or "She was the wrong sign"). A stable attribution ("It's my personality") suggests a problem that cannot be changed, whereas an unstable attribution ("It was the head cold") suggests a temporary condition. A global attribution of failure ("I have no idea what to do when I'm with people") suggests that the problem is quite large. A specific attribution ("I have problems making small talk at the very outset of a relationship") chops the problem down to a manageable size.

Research shows that depressed people are more likely than nondepressed people to attribute the causes of their failures to internal, stable, and global factors (Blumberg & Izard, 1985; Miller et al., 1982; Peterson et al., 1981; Pyszczynski & Greenberg, 1985; Raps et al., 1982; Seligman et al., 1979, 1984). Depressed people exaggerate the blame they deserve and view their problems as all but impossible to change. Is it any wonder that they are more likely than nondepressed people to feel helpless?

Organic Factors   Researchers are also searching for organic factors in the mood disorders. Mood swings tend to run in families, and there is a higher concordance rate for bipolar disorder among identical than fraternal twins (Klein et al., 1985; Smith & Winokur, 1983). A study of the Amish community in Pennsylvania traced the distribution of bipolar disorder among an extended family with a high incidence of the problem (Egeland et al., 1987). The researchers isolated a gene that was transmitted to children half the time and present in family members who showed bipolar disorder. But not all of those who had the gene displayed the disorder, and the severity of their symptoms varied. And so genetic factors might

create a disposition for bipolar disorder but not guarantee its appearance.

Perhaps the genetic vulnerability manifests itself in terms of the actions of neurotransmitters. Much research has focused on the role of the neurotransmitter norepinephrine. Martin Seligman (1975) and Jay Weiss (1982), for example, found that dogs who had learned helplessness showed a decrease in the amount of the norepinephrine available to the brain. Rats with lowered levels of norepinephrine show behavior similar to that of depressed people (Ellison, 1977). They are less aggressive than colony-mates and appear apathetic and withdrawn. They lie around listlessly in their burrows. Their appetites decrease and they lose weight.

And so, helplessness and inactivity are linked to low norepinephrine levels. The relationship might be a "vicious cycle": A depressing situation might lower norepinehrine levels, and low levels of norepinephrine might exacerbate depressive behavior. Manicky behavior, by contrast, appears to reflect excesses of norepinephrine.

Other researchers argue that the neurotransmitter serotonin also plays a role in mood disorders (e.g., Berger, 1978). It has been speculated that deficiencies in serotonin may create a general disposition toward mood disorders. A deficiency of serotonin *combined with* a deficiency of norepinephrine might be linked with depression. But a deficiency of serotonin combined with excessive levels of norepinephrine might produce manicky behavior. The relationships between the mood disorders and organic factors are complex and under intense study.

SCHIZOPHRENIA

Joyce was 19. Her boyfriend Ron brought her into the emergency room because she had slit her wrists. When she was interviewed, her attention wandered. She seemed distracted by things in the air, or something she might be hearing. It was as if she had an invisible earphone.

She explained that she had cut her wrists because the "hellsmen" had told her to. Then she seemed frightened. Later she said that the hellsmen had warned her not to reveal their existence. She had been afraid that they would punish her for talking about them.

Attributional style One's tendency to attribute one's behavior to internal or external factors, stable or unstable factors, etc.

The "Son-of-Sam Killer." David Berkowitz, the "Son-of-Sam Killer," smiles benignly upon his arrest in 1977. Does his response to arrest seem appropriate? Because of his inappropriate emotional responses and his claim that a dog had urged him to commit his crimes, many mental-health professionals considered him schizophrenic.

Ron told the psychiatrist that Joyce had been living with him for about a year. At first they had been together in a small apartment in town. But Joyce did not want to be near other people and had convinced him to rent a bungalow in the country. There she would make fantastic drawings of goblins and monsters during the days. Now and then she would become agitated and act as if invisible things were giving her instructions.

"I'm bad," Joyce would mutter, "I'm bad." She would begin to jumble her words. Ron would then try to convince her to go to the hospital, but she would refuse. Then the wrist-cutting would begin. Ron thought he had made the cottage safe by removing knives and blades. But Joyce would always find something.

Then Joyce would be brought to the hospital, have stitches put in, be kept under observation and medicated. She would explain that she cut herself because the hellsmen had told her she was bad and must die. After a few days she would deny hearing the hellsmen and insist on leaving the hospital.

Ron would take her home. The pattern continued.

When the doctor examined Joyce's wrists and heard that she believed she had been following the orders of "hellsmen," he began to suspect that she was suffering from schizophrenia. Schizophrenia touches every aspect of victims' lives. It is characterized by disturbances in (1) thought and language, (2) perception and attention, (3) motor activity, (4) mood, and (5) withdrawal and **autism.**

Schizophrenia is known primarily by disturbances in thought, which are from verbal and other overt behavior. Schizophrenic persons may show *loosening of associations.* Unless we are daydreaming or deliberately allowing our thoughts to "wander," our thinking is normally tightly knit. But schizophrenics often think in an illogical, disorganized manner. Their speech may be jumbled, combining parts of words or making rhymes in a meaningless fashion. Schizophrenics may also jump from topic to topic, conveying little useful information. Nor do they usually have insight that their thoughts and behavior are abnormal.

Schizophrenics often have **delusions,** for example, delusions of grandeur, persecution, or reference. In the case of delusions of grandeur, the person may believe he is Jesus or a person on a special mission, or he may have grand, illogical plans for saving the world. Delusions tend to be unshakable, despite disconfirming evidence. Persons with delusions of persecution may believe that

Autism Self-absorption. Absorption in daydreaming and fantasy.

Delusions False, persistent beliefs that are unsubstantiated by sensory or objective evidence.

they are sought by the Mafia, CIA, FBI, or some other group or agency. A woman with delusions of reference expressed the belief that national news broadcasts contained coded information about her. A man with such delusions complained that neighbors had "bugged" his walls with "radios." Other schizophrenics may have delusions to the effect that they have committed unpardonable sins, that they are rotting away from a hideous disease, or that they or the world do not exist.

The perceptions of schizophrenics often include hallucinations—imagery in the absence of external stimulation that the schizophrenic cannot distinguish from reality. Joyce believed she heard "hellsmen." Others may see colors or even obscene words spelled out in midair. Auditory hallucinations are most common.

Motor activity may become wild and excited or slow to a **stupor.** There may be strange gestures and peculiar facial expressions. Emotional responses may be flat or blunted or inappropriate—as in giggling at bad news. Schizophrenics tend to withdraw from social contacts and become wrapped up in their thoughts and fantasies.

There are different kinds, or types, of schizophrenia, and different symptoms are predominant with each type.

Types of Schizophrenia

The DSM–III–R lists three major types of schizophrenia: *disorganized, catatonic,* and *paranoid.*

Stupor A condition in which the senses and thought are dulled.

Disorganized schizophrenics Schizophrenics who show disorganized delusions and vivid hallucinations.

Catatonic schizophrenics Schizophrenics who show striking impairment in motor activity.

Waxy flexibility A symptom of catatonic schizophrenia in which persons maintain postures into which they are placed.

Mutism Refusal to talk.

Paranoid schizophrenia A type of schizophrenia characterized primarily by delusions—commonly of persecution—and by vivid hallucinations.

Disorganized Type **Disorganized schizophrenics** show incoherence; loosening of associations; disorganized behavior; disorganized delusions; and vivid, abundant hallucinations that are often sexual or religious. A 23-year-old female disorganized schizophrenic remarked, "I see 'penis.'" She pointed vaguely into the air before her. Asked to spell *pennis,* she replied irritatedly, "p–e–n–i–s." Apparently her social background was so inhibited that she had never heard the word for the male sex organ spoken aloud; and so she mispronounced it. Extreme social impairment is common among disorganized schizophrenics. They also often show silliness and giddiness of mood, giggling and speaking nonsensically. They may neglect their appearance and hygiene and lose control of their bladder and bowels.

Catatonic Type **Catatonic schizophrenics** show striking impairment in motor activity. It is characterized by slowing of activity into a stupor that may change suddenly into an agitated phase. Catatonic individuals may hold unusual, even difficult postures for hours, even as their limbs grow swollen or stiff. A striking symptom is **waxy flexibility,** in which they maintain positions into which they have been manipulated by others. Catatonic individuals may also show **mutism,** but afterward they usually report that they heard what others were saying at the time.

Paranoid Type **Paranoid schizophrenics** have systematized delusions and, frequently, related auditory hallucinations. They usually show delusions of grandeur and persecution, but they may also show delusions of jealousy, in which they believe that a spouse or lover has been unfaithful. They may show agitation, confusion, and fear and experience vivid hallucinations that are consistent with their delusions. The paranoid schizophrenic often constructs a complex or systematized delusion involving themes of wrongdoing or persecution.

Theoretical Views

Psychologists have investigated various factors that may contribute to schizophrenia.

Psychoanalytic Views   Psychoanalytic theorists view schizophrenia as the overwhelming of the ego by sexual or aggressive impulses from the id. The impulses threaten the ego and cause intense intrapsychic conflict. Under this threat the person regresses to an early phase of the oral stage in which the infant has not yet learned that it and the world are separate. Fantasies become confused with reality, giving birth to hallucinations and delusions. Primitive impulses may carry more weight than social norms.

Social-Learning Views   Social-learning theorists explain schizophrenia through conditioning and observational learning. From this perspective, people show schizophrenic behavior when it is more likely than normal behavior to be reinforced. This may occur when the person is reared in a socially nonrewarding or punitive situation; inner fantasies then become more reinforcing than social realities.

In the hospital, patients may learn what is "expected" of them by observing other patients. Hospital staff may reinforce schizophrenic behavior by paying more attention to patients who behave bizarrely. This view is consistent with folklore that the child who disrupts the class earns more attention from the teacher than the "good" child.

Critics note that many of us grow up in socially punitive settings but seem to show immunity to extinction of socially appropriate behavior. Others acquire schizophrenic behavior patterns without having had the opportunity to observe other schizophrenics.

Genetic Factors   Schizophrenia, like many other abnormal behavior patterns, runs in families. Children of schizophrenics have more difficulty in social relationships, more emotional instability, and less academic motivation than other children (Watt et al., 1982).

Schizophrenic persons constitute about 1 percent of the population, but children with two schizophrenic parents have about a 35 percent chance of becoming schizophrenic (Rosenthal, 1970). Twin studies also find a higher concordance rate for the diagnosis among pairs of identical twins than among pairs of fraternal twins (Davison & Neale, 1986). In studies of adoptees, the biological parents typically place the child at greater risk for schizophrenia than the adoptive parents—even though the child has been reared by the adoptive parents (Heston, 1966; Wender et al., 1974). Heredity might transmit biochemical factors such as those discussed in the following section.

The Dopamine Theory of Schizophrenia   Over the years numerous substances have been thought to play a role in schizophrenic disorders. Much of current theory and research focuses on the neurotransmitter **dopamine.**

The dopamine theory of schizophrenia evolved from observation of the effects of **amphetamines,** a group of stimulants. Researchers are confident that amphetamines act by increasing the quantity of dopamine in the brain. High doses of amphetamines lead to behavior that mimics paranoid schizophrenia in normal people, and even low doses exacerbate the symptoms of schizophrenics (Snyder, 1980). A second source of evidence for the dopamine theory lies in the effects of a class of drugs called **phenothiazines.** Research suggests that the phenothiazines, which are often effective in treating schizophrenia, work by blocking the action of dopamine receptors (Creese et al., 1978; Turkington, 1983).

It does not appear that schizophrenic persons produce more dopamine than others but that they *utilize* more of it (Davison & Neale, 1986). Why? It could be that they have a greater number of dopamine receptors in the brain or that their dopamine receptors are hyperactive (Lee & Seeman, 1977; Mackay et al., 1982; Snyder, 1984).

Future research may suggest that schizophrenia has multiple causes. Genetic factors might predispose some individuals to display schizophrenic symptoms in response to stressors. Other people might be so severely handicapped by genetic factors that they will develop schizophrenia under the most positive conditions.

Dopamine   A neurotransmitter implicated in schizophrenia.

Amphetamines   Stimulants whose abuse can trigger symptoms that mimic schizophrenia.

Phenothiazine   A member of a family of drugs that is effective in treating many cases of schizophrenia.

PERSONALITY DISORDERS

Personality disorders, like personality traits, are characterized by enduring patterns of behavior. Personality disorders, however, are inflexible and maladaptive. They impair personal or social functioning and are a source of distress to the individual or to others.

There are a number of personality disorders, including the *paranoid, schizotypal, schizoid,* and *antisocial personality disorders.* Persons with **paranoid personality disorder** interpret other people's behavior as deliberately threatening or demeaning. Although persons with the disorder do not show grossly disorganized thinking, they are mistrustful of others, and their social relationships suffer for it. They may be suspicious of co-workers and supervisors, but they can usually hold onto jobs.

Schizotypal personality disorder is characterized by pervasive peculiarities in thought, perception, and behavior, such as excessive fantasy and suspiciousness, feelings of being unreal, or odd usage of words (American Psychiatric Association, 1987, pp. 340–342). The bizarre psychotic behaviors that characterize schizophrenia are absent, and so this disorder is schizo*typal,* not schizophrenic. Because of their oddities, persons with the disorder are often maladjusted on the job.

The **schizoid personality disorder** is defined by indifference to social relationships and flatness in emotional responsiveness. Schizoid personalities are "loners" who do not develop warm, tender

---

Personality disorders Enduring patterns of maladaptive behavior that are a source of distress to the individual or others.

Paranoid personality disorder A disorder characterized by persistent suspiciousness but not the disorganization of paranoid schizophrenia.

Schizotypal personality disorder A disorder characterized by oddities of thought and behavior but not involving bizarre psychotic symptoms.

Schizoid personality disorder A disorder characterized by social withdrawal.

Antisocial personality disorder The diagnosis given a person who is in frequent conflict with society yet is undeterred by punishment and experiences little or no guilt and anxiety.

Table 9.2   Characteristics of the Antisocial Personality

Persistent violation of the rights of others
Irresponsibility
Lack of formation of enduring relationships or loyalty to another person
Failure to maintain good job performance over the years
Failure to develop or adhere to a life plan
History of truancy
History of delinquency
History of running away
Persistent lying
Sexual promiscuity
Substance abuse
Impulsivity
Inability to tolerate boredom
At least 18 years of age
Onset of antisocial behavior by age 15

Source: DSM–III–R (1987).

feelings for others. They have few friends and rarely get married. Some schizoid personalities do very well on the job, as long as continuous social interaction is not required. Hallucinations and delusions are absent.

The Antisocial Personality

Persons with **antisocial personality disorders** persistently violate the rights of others, show indifference to commitments, and conflict with the law. Cleckley (1964) notes that antisocial personalities often show a superficial charm and are at least average in intelligence. Perhaps their most striking feature, given their antisocial behavior, is their lack of guilt and low level of anxiety. They seem largely undeterred by punishment. Though they have usually received punishment from parents and others for their misdeeds, they continue their impulsive, irresponsible styles of life (see Table 9.2).

Theoretical Views   Various factors appear to contribute to antisocial behavior, including an antisocial father, parental lack of love and rejection during childhood, and inconsistent discipline.

Antisocial personalities tend to run in families. Studies of adoptees have found higher incidences of antisocial behavior among the biological than the adoptive relatives of persons with the disorder (Cadoret, 1978; Hutchings & Mednick, 1974; Mednick, 1985).

Some researchers have attributed antisocial personality disorder to an extra Y sex chromosome. So-called **supermales,** with an XYY sex chromosomal structure, were thought to have a predisposition toward aggressiveness and crime. Supermales as a group are somewhat taller and more heavily bearded than XY males, but only about 1.5 percent of male delinquents and criminals tested show the XYY structure (Rosenthal, 1970).

One promising avenue of research concerns the observation that antisocial personalities are unlikely to show guilt for their misdeeds or be deterred by punishment. It is suggested that low levels of guilt and anxiety reflect lower-than-normal levels of arousal, which, in turn, have at least a partial genetic basis (Lykken, 1957, 1982). Experiments on this issue show, for example, that antisocial subjects do not learn as rapidly as others equal in intelligence when the payoff is avoidance of impending electric shock. But when the levels of arousal of the antisocial subjects are increased by injections of adrenalin, they learn to avoid punishment as rapidly as others (Chesno & Kilmann, 1975; Schachter & Latané, 1964).

A lower-than-normal level of arousal would not guarantee the development of an antisocial personality. It might also be necessary that a person be reared under conditions that do not foster the self-concept of a person who abides by law and social custom. Punishment for deviation from the norm would then be unlikely to induce feelings of guilt and shame. The individual might be "undeterred" by punishment.

Before ending this section, we must note one further finding with antisocial personalities. The one form of punishment that does seem effective with many of them is loss of money (Schmauk, 1970). Do we need further evidence that antisocial personalities are not out of touch with reality?

SEXUAL DISORDERS

The DSM–III–R lists a number of sexual disorders, including *paraphilias* and *sexual dysfunctions*.

We shall also discuss the **gender-identity disorder** of transsexualism in this section. In a gender-identity disorder, one's assigned sex (as based on anatomic sex and recorded on the birth certificate) is inconsistent with one's gender identity (one's psychological sense of being male or being female). In the **paraphilias,** people show sexual arousal in response to unusual or bizarre objects or situations. **Sexual dysfunctions** are characterized by problems in becoming sexually aroused and reaching orgasm.

Transsexualism

About 30 years ago headlines were made when an ex-GI, now known as Christine Jorgensen, had a "sex-change operation" in Denmark. Since that time some 2,500 American transsexuals, including tennis player Dr. Renée Richards, have undergone sex-reassignment surgery. Sex-reassignment surgery does not implant reproductive organs of the opposite sex. Instead, it creates the appearance of the external genitals of the opposite sex—more successfully with male-to-female than female-to-male transsexuals. After these operations, transsexuals can engage in sexual activity and reach orgasm, but they cannot have children.

Transsexualism is the persistent feeling that one is of the wrong sex. They do not see themselves as homosexuals, even though they are sexually attracted to members of their own anatomic sex. This is because they see themselves as "trapped" inside a body of the wrong sex.

Supermale A male with XYY chromosomal structure.

Gender-identity disorder A disorder in which a person's anatomic sex is inconsistent with his or her gender identity.

Paraphilias Disorders in which people show sexual arousal in response to unusual or bizarre objects or situations.

Sexual dysfunctions Persistent problems in achieving or maintaining sexual arousal or in reaching orgasm.

Transsexualism A gender-identity disorder in which a person feels trapped in the body of the wrong sex.

What Is Transsexualism?   Physician Richard Raskin underwent sex reassignment surgery and became Renée Richards. For a while, Renée competed as a woman on the women's tennis circuit. More recently, Renée served as a coach to Martina Navratilova.

The causes of transsexualism are unclear. Socialization patterns might affect transsexuals who are reared by parents who had wanted children of the opposite sex and who thus encourage cross-sex dressing and patterns of play. But it is also possible that some transsexuals have been influenced by prenatal hormonal imbalances. The majority of transsexuals who undergo sex reassignment are pleased with the surgical results and relatively well adjusted (Abramowitz, 1986; Blanchard et al., 1985; Fleming et al., 1982).

> **Fetishism**   A variation of choice in sexual object in which a body part (like a foot) or an inanimate object (like an undergarment) elicits sexual arousal and is preferred to a person.
>
> **Transvestic fetishism**   Recurrent, persistent dressing in clothing worn by the opposite sex for purposes of sexual excitement.

Paraphilias

Paraphilias are characterized by sexual response to unusual objects or situations. The American Psychiatric Association (1987) uses the following diagnoses either when people act on these urges or when they are markedly distressed by them but do not act them out.

Fetishism   **Fetishism** is sexual response to an inanimate object, such as an article of clothing, or to a bodily part, such as the feet. Sexual gratification is often achieved through masturbating in the presence of the object. Fetishes for undergarments and for objects made of leather, rubber, or silk are not uncommon.

Transvestic Festishism   **Transvestic fetishism** is recurrent, persistent dressing by a heterosexual male in clothing usually worn by a woman in order to achieve sexual excitement. Transvestism may range from wearing a single female undergarment in private to sporting full dress at a transvestite club. Most transvestites are married, but they seek additional sexual gratification through dressing as women.

Pedophilia **Pedophilia** is actual or fantasized sexual activity with children as a preferred means of becoming sexually aroused. Most episodes are not coerced and involve exhibitionism or fondling rather than sexual intercourse.

Exhibitionism **Exhibitionism** is the repetitive act of exposing one's genitals to a stranger in order to surprise or shock, rather than sexually arouse, the victim. The exhibitionist is usually not interested in actual sexual contact with the victim. He may masturbate while fantasizing about or actually exposing himself.

Professional stripteasers and scantily clad swimmers do not fit the definition of exhibitionist. Both groups might seek to arouse sexually, but usually not to shock, observers. The major motive of the stripteaser might also be simply to earn a living.

Voyeurism **Voyeurism** is repetitive watching of unsuspecting strangers while they are undressing or engaging in sexual activity as the preferred or exclusive means of achieving sexual arousal. We may enjoy observing spouses undress, or even the nudity in an R-rated film, without being diagnosed as voyeurs. In voyeurism, the "victim" does not know that he or she is being watched, and the voyeur prefers looking to doing.

Sexual Masochism **Masochism** is named after the Austrian storyteller Leopold von Sacher-Masoch, who portrayed sexual satisfaction as deriving from pain or humiliation. The sexual masochist must receive pain or humiliation to achieve sexual gratification. It has been suggested that many masochists feel guilt about sex but can enjoy sex as long as they see themselves being appropriately punished for it.

Sexual Sadism **Sadism** is named after the infamous Marquis de Sade, a Frenchman who wrote stories about the pleasures of achieving sexual gratification by inflicting pain or humiliation on others. In sadism, the person may not be able to become sexually excited unless he inflicts pain on his partner.

Theoretical Views According to psychoanalytic theory, paraphilias are defenses against anxiety. The exhibitionist, for example, has unconscious castration anxiety. His victim's shock at his exposure reassures him that he does, after all, have a penis. Fetishism, pedophilia, and so on protect him from fear of failure in adult heterosexual relationships.

Rathus (1983) offers a social-learning view of fetishism and other paraphilias. First, a fantasized or actual event—such as becoming excited when a woman happens upon one who is urinating behind a bush—prompts the person to encode the unusual object or situation as sexually arousing. As a consequence, second, the person acquires the expectancy that the object or situation will increase the pleasure of sexual activity. As noted in the section on substance abuse, expectancies concerning an outcome can be more powerful predictors of behavior than the actual outcomes. Third, the object is used in actuality or fantasy to heighten sexual arousal. Fourth, recognition of the deviance of the fantasy or act might cause feelings of anxiety or guilt. These feelings, if not extreme, might enhance emotional arousal in the presence of the deviant object or activity. Heightened emotional response might then be *attributed* to the deviant object or activity. Fifth, orgasm reinforces the preceding behaviors and fantasies. Sixth, orgasm also confirms the stimulating properties attributed to

---

Pedophilia Sexual contact with children as the preferred source of sexual excitement.

Exhibitionism The compulsion to expose one's genitals in public.

Voyeurism Attainment of sexual gratification through secretly observing others undress or engage in sexual activity.

Masochism Attainment of sexual gratification by receiving pain or humiliation.

Sadism Attainment of sexual gratification by means of inflicting pain or humiliation on sex partners.

the deviant object or activity. Seventh, in cases in which a person is anxious about normal sexual relationships, the deviant object or activity might become the major or sole sexual outlet.

Sexual Dysfunctions

Many of us will be troubled by a sexual dysfunction at some time or other. Masters and Johnson (1970) estimated that at least half the marriages in this nation are sexually dysfunctional, and the incidence of sexual dysfunctions may be higher among single people.

Types of Psychosexual Dysfunctions
In **hypoactive sexual desire disorder,** the person shows lack of interest in sexual activity and frequently reports an absence of sexual fantasies.

In the female, sexual arousal is characterized by a lubricating of the vaginal walls that makes entry by the penis possible. Sexual arousal in the male is characterized by erection of the penis. Almost all women now and then have difficulty becoming or remaining lubricated. Almost all men have occasional difficulty attaining erection or maintaining an erection through intercourse. The diagnoses of **female sexual arousal disorder** and **male erectile disorder** are used when these problems are persistent or recurrent.

In **inhibited orgasm,** the man or woman, although sexually excited, is persistently delayed in reaching orgasm or does not reach orgasm at all. Inhibited orgasm is more common among women than men.

In **premature ejaculation** the male persistently ejaculates with minimal sexual stimulation, too soon to permit his partner or himself to enjoy sexual relations fully.

In **dyspareunia,** sexual intercourse is associated with recurrent pain in the genital region. **Vaginismus** is involuntary spasm of the muscles surrounding the vagina, making sexual intercourse painful or impossible.

Hypoactive sexual desire disorder Persistent or recurrent lack of sexual fantasies and of interest in sexual activity.

Female sexual arousal disorder Persistent or recurrent lack of sexual arousal.

Male erectile disorder Persistent or recurrent inability to attain or maintain erection.

Inhibited orgasm Persistent or recurrent delay in, or absence of, orgasm in a sexually excited person who has been engaging in sexually stimulating activity.

Premature ejaculation Persistent or recurrent ejaculation that occurs after minimal sexual stimulation and before the person wishes it.

Dyspareunia Persistent or recurrent pain during or after sexual intercourse.

Vaginismus Persistent or recurrent spasm of the muscles surrounding the outer part of the vaginal barrel, making entry difficult or impossible.

Performance anxiety Fear that one will fail, as at sexual relations, tending to make one a spectator to, rather than a participant in, one's own performance.

Causes of Sexual Dysfunctions
Perhaps 10 to 20 percent of sexual dysfunctions stem from disease. Hypoactive sexual desire, for example, can reflect diabetes and diseases of the heart and lungs. Fatigue can dampen sexual desire and inhibit orgasm. Depressants such as alcohol, narcotics, and tranquilizers can also impair sexual response.

Psychological causes include sex-negative attitudes, such as the belief that sex is a duty for women; physically or psychologically painful sexual experiences; a troubled relationship; communication problems; and lack of sexual knowledge and skill. In most cases physical and psychological factors lead to yet another psychological factor—**performance anxiety,** or fear of whether we shall be able to perform sexually. People with performance anxiety may focus on recollections of past failures and expectations of another disaster, rather than enjoy their erotic sensations and fantasies (Barlow, 1986). Sex therapy programs foster sexual competencies by enhancing sexual knowledge and encouraging sexual experimentation under circumstances in which performance anxiety is unlikely to be aroused.

PSYCHOACTIVE SUBSTANCE-USE DISORDERS

The world is a supermarket of **psychoactive** substances, or drugs. The United States is flooded with hundreds of drugs that distort perceptions and change mood—drugs that take you up, let you down, and move you across town. Some people use drugs because their friends do or because their parents tell them not to. Some are seeking pleasure, others are seeking inner truth.

Following a dropoff in popularity during the 1960s, alcohol has reasserted its dominance among drugs used on college campuses. Most college students have tried marijuana, and perhaps one in five smokes it regularly. Many take **depressants** to get to sleep at night and **stimulants** to get going in the morning. Heroin may literally be the opium of the lower classes. Cocaine was until recently the toy of the well-to-do; but price breaks have allowed it to find its way into the lockers of students. Despite laws, moral pronouncements, medical warnings, and an occasional horror story, drugs are very much with us.

We shall deal with some general issues in substance abuse and dependence and then turn our attention to specific drugs.

Substance Abuse and Dependence

The American Psychiatric Association considers use of a substance to be abusive when it is continued for a period of at least one month despite the fact that it is causing or compounding a social, occupational, psychological, or physical problem (1987, p. 169). If you are missing school or work because you are drunk, or "sleeping it off," your behavior fits the definition of **substance abuse.**

Substance dependence is more severe and is shown by signs such as increased use despite knowledge that the substance is interfering with one's life and despite desire to cut down. Dependence is also characterized by tolerance, frequent intoxication, and withdrawal symptoms (American Psychiatric Association, 1987, pp. 166–168). **Tolerance** is the body's habituation to a drug, so that with regular use higher doses are required to achieve similar effects. Dependence is physiological; there are characteristic withdrawal symptoms,

or an **abstinence syndrome,** when the level of use suddenly drops off. The abstinence syndrome for alcohol includes anxiety, tremors, restlessness, weakness, rapid pulse, and high blood pressure.

People who are *psychologically* dependent on a drug show signs of anxiety about doing without it that overlap abstinence syndromes. Thus they may believe that they are physiologically dependent on a drug when they are psychologically dependent.

Causal Factors in Substance Abuse and Dependence

There are many reasons for substance abuse and dependence. Just a handful include curiosity, conformity to peer pressure, rebelliousness, and escape from boredom or pressure (Brook et al. 1980; Conger & Petersen, 1984; Hollister, 1983, Kandel, 1980). Alcohol and other drugs have been used as excuses for problem behaviors such as aggression, sexual forwardness, and forgetfulness.

Psychoanalytic explanations propose that drugs help people control or express unconscious

---

Psychoactive Of a substance that has psychological effects.

Depressants Substances that decrease the activity of the nervous system and may also have relaxing, intoxicating, or euphoric effects.

Stimulants Substances that increase the activity of the nervous system and may also bolster self-confidence, self-esteem, and one's sense of well-being.

Substance abuse Continued use of a substance despite knowledge that it is hazardous or causes or compounds a social, occupational, psychological, or physical problem.

Substance dependence A pattern of usage characterized by factors such as tolerance, loss of control over use, frequent intoxication, and withdrawal symptoms.

Tolerance Habituation to a substance such that markedly increased dosages must be used to achieve the desired effects.

Abstinence syndrome A characteristic cluster of symptoms that results from sudden decrease in the level of usage of a substance.

Some Nonprescription Drugs.
From the time we are little children, we are bombarded with images of substances that alleviate pain, reduce anxiety and tension, and induce a state of euphoria.

needs and impulses. Alcoholism, for example, may reflect the need to remain dependent on an overprotective mother or the effort to reduce emotional conflicts or to cope with unconscious homosexual impulses.

Learning theorists suggest that first use of tranquilizing agents such as Valium and alcohol usually results from observing others or from a recommendation. But subsequent use may be reinforced by positive effects on one's mood and reduction of anxiety, fear, and tension. For the physiologically dependent, avoidance of withdrawal symptoms is also reinforcing. Children whose parents use drugs such as alcohol, tranquilizers, and stimulants are more likely to use drugs. Modeling increases their knowledge of drugs and shows them when to use them—for example, when they are anxious or depressed.

There is growing evidence that people can have a genetic predisposition toward physiological dependence on certain substances (Goodwin, 1985; Schuckit, 1987; Vaillant, 1982). The biological children of alcoholics who are raised by adoptive parents are more likely to develop alcohol-related problems than are the natural children of the adoptive parents (Goodwin, 1979; Goodwin et al., 1973). Alcoholics (and their children) frequently inherit greater tolerance of alcohol: They can drink more without getting drunk. College-age children of alcoholics show better muscular control and visual-motor coordination when they drink (Kolata, 1987).

Let us now consider the effects of some frequently used substances, including depressants, stimulants, and hallucinogenics.

Depressants

Depressant drugs act by slowing the activity of the central nervous system, although there are a number of other effects specific to each drug. In this section we consider the effects of alcohol, opiates and opioids, and barbiturates and methaqualone.

Alcohol   No drug has meant so much to so many as alcohol. Alcohol is our dinnertime relaxant, our bedtime sedative, our cocktail-party social facilitator. We celebrate holy days, applaud our accomplishments, and express joyous wishes with alcohol. The young assert their maturity with alcohol. The elderly use it to stimulate circulation in peripheral areas of the body. Alcohol kills germs on surface wounds. Some pediatricians even swab the painful gums of teething babies with alcohol.

No drug has been so abused as alcohol. Ten to 20 million U.S. residents are **alcoholics.** By contrast, 200,000 use heroin regularly, and 300,000 to 500,000 abuse sedatives. Heavy drinking has been linked to lower productivity, loss of employment, and downward movement in social status (Baum-Baicker, 1984; Mider, 1984; Vaillant & Milofsky, 1982).

As a depressant, alcohol slows the activity of the central nervous system. It also induces feelings of euphoria, although regular use over a year or more may contribute to feelings of depression (Aneshensel & Huba, 1983). Alcohol relaxes and deadens minor aches and pains. Alcohol also intoxicates: It impairs cognitive functioning, slurs the speech, and reduces motor coordination. Alcohol is clearly implicated in perhaps half of U.S. automobile accidents.

Drinkers may do things they would not do if sober because alcohol may impair the information processing needed to inhibit impulses (Hull et al., 1983; Steele & Southwick, 1985). That is, when intoxicated, people may be less able to foresee the negative consequences of misbehavior and may be less likely to recall social and personal standards.

As a food, alcohol is fattening. Yet chronic drinkers may be malnourished. Though high in calories, alcohol does not contain nutrients like vitamins and proteins. Heavy drinking has been linked to heart disease, high blood pressure, and brain damage. Even light drinking by a pregnant woman might be harmful to the embryo (see Rathus, 1988, for a review).

Opiates and Opioids

Opiates are a group of **narcotics** derived from the opium poppy. The opiates include morphine, heroin, codeine, demerol, and similar drugs whose major medical application is **analgesia.** Opiates appear to stimulate centers in the brain that lead to pleasure and to physiological dependence (Goeders & Smith, 1984; Ling et al., 1984). Opioids are similar to opiates in chemical structure and effect but are artificial (synthesized in the laboratory).

Heroin and morphine are powerful depressants that can provide a euphoric "rush." Users of heroin claim it is so pleasurable it can eradicate any thought of food or sex. Although regular users develop tolerance for heroin, high doses can cause drowsiness, stupor, altered time perception, and impaired judgment.

The opioid **methadone** has been used to treat dependence on heroin. Methadone is slower acting than heroin and does not provide the thrilling rush. Most people treated with it simply swap dependence on one drug for dependence on another. Because they are unwilling to undergo withdrawal symptoms or to contemplate a life-style devoid of drugs, they must be maintained indefinitely on methadone.

Barbiturates and Methaqualone

Barbiturates such as amobarbital, phenobarbital, pentobarbital, and secobarbital are depressants with a number of medical uses, including relief of anxiety and tension, deadening of pain, and treatment of epilepsy, high blood pressure, and insomnia. Barbiturates lead rapidly to dependence. Methaqualone, sold under the brand names Quaalude and Sopor, is a depressant similar in effect to barbiturates.

Psychologists generally oppose using barbiturates and methalqualone for anxiety, tension, and insomnia since they lead rapidly to dependence and do nothing to teach the individual how to alter disturbing patterns of behavior. Many physicians, too, have become concerned by barbiturates.

Alcoholics Persons who abuse alcohol.

Opiates A group of addictive drugs derived from the opium poppy that provide a euphoric "rush" and depress the nervous system.

Narcotics Drugs used to relieve pain and induce sleep.

Analgesia A state of not feeling pain, although one remains conscious.

Methadone An artificial narcotic that is slower acting than, and does not provide the euphoric rush of, heroin. By using methadone, heroin addicts can abstain from heroin without withdrawal symptoms.

Barbiturates A group of addictive depressants that are used to relieve anxiety or induce sleep.

Barbiturates and methaqualone are popular as street drugs because they relax the muscles and produce a mild euphoric state. High doses of barbiturates result in drowsiness, motor impairment, slurred speech, irritability, and poor judgment. A dependent person who is withdrawn abruptly may experience severe convulsions and die. High doses of methaqualone may cause internal bleeding, coma, and death. Because of additive effects, it is dangerous to mix alcohol and other depressants at bedtime, or at any time.

Stimulants

Stimulants act by increasing the activity of the nervous system. The other effects of stimulants vary somewhat from drug to drug, and some seem to contribute to feelings of euphoria and self-confidence.

Amphetamines
Amphetamines were first used by soldiers during World War II to help them remain alert through the night. Truck drivers have used them to drive through the night. But amphetamines have become more widely known through students who have used them for all-night cram sessions and through dieters who use them because they reduce hunger.

Amphetamines and a related stimulant, Ritalin (methylphenidate), increase self-control in hyperactive children, increase their attention span, decrease fidgeting, and lead to academic gains (Abikoff & Gittelman, 1985; Barkley et al., 1984; Kavale, 1982; Rapport, 1984; Whalen et al., 1987). The paradoxical calming effect of stimulants on hyperactive children may be explained by assuming that a cause of hyperactivity is immaturity of the cerebral cortex. Amphetamines might stimulate the cortex to exercise control over more primitive centers in the lower brain.

Called speed, uppers, bennies (for Benzedrine), and dexies (for Dexedrine), these drugs are often used for the euphoric "rush" they can produce, especially in high doses. Regular users may stay awake and "high" for days on end. Such highs must come to an end. People who have been on prolonged highs sometimes "crash," or fall into a deep sleep or depression.

People can become psychologically dependent on amphetamines, especially when they are using them to cope with depression. Tolerance develops rapidly, but opinion is mixed about whether they lead to physiological dependence. High doses may cause restlessness, hallucinations, paranoid delusions, insomnia, loss of appetite, and irritability.

Cocaine
No doubt you've seen commercials claiming that Coke adds life. Given its caffeine and sugar content, Coca-Cola should provide quite a lift. But Coca-Cola hasn't been "the real thing" since 1906. At that time the manufacturers discontinued use of the coca leaves from which the soft drink derived its name. Coca leaves contain cocaine, a stimulant that produces a state of euphoria, or high; reduces hunger; deadens pain; and bolsters self-confidence.

Cocaine is brewed from coca leaves as a "tea," breathed in ("snorted") in powder form, and injected into the vein ("shot up") in liquid form. Potent derivatives, "crack" and "bazooka," are less expensive because they are unrefined and more likely to be contaminated with poisonous substances such as heavy metals. Of course, users who "shoot up" drugs run the risk of being infected with the AIDS virus if they share needles.

Despite media claims that cocaine is addictive, there remains some question about whether it does cause physiological dependence. For example, it is not clear that there is a specific abstinence syndrome for cocaine (Van Dyke & Byck, 1982). However, Davison and Neale (1986) believe that research will uncover biochemical effects that induce dependence. On the other hand, there is no doubt that users can readily become psychologically dependent. Overdoses can lead to restlessness and insomnia, tremors, headaches, nausea, convulsions, hallucinations, delusions, and respiratory and cardiovascular collapse. "Normal" doses constrict blood vessels, heighten blood pressure, and can trigger angina (chest pains due to heart problems) and, now and then, heart attacks (Altman, 1988). Cocaine has been used as a local anesthetic for nearly 200 years and remains the anesthetic of choice for surgery on the nose and throat.

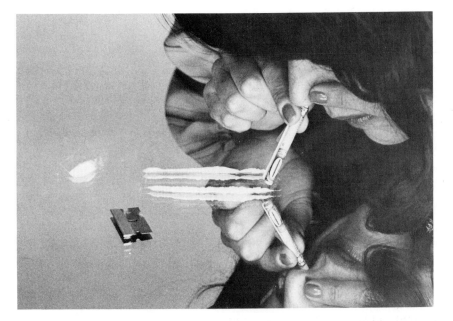

Why Do People Snort "Coke"?
Recent price breaks have
increased the availability of the
stimulant cocaine, and its potent
derivatives "crack" and "bazooka."

Hallucinogenics

Hallucinogenic drugs are so named because they
produce hallucinations—that is, sensations and
perceptions in the absence of external stimulation.
But hallucinogenic drugs may also have additional
effects, such as relaxing the individual, creating a
sense of euphoria, or in some cases, causing panic.
We shall focus on the effects of marijuana and
LSD.

Marijuana

Marijuana is produced from the *can-
nabis sativa* plant, which grows wild in many parts
of the world. Marijuana helps some people relax
and can elevate the mood. It also sometimes produces mild hallucinations, and so is classified as a
psychedelic or hallucinogenic drug. The major
psychoactive substance in marijuana is delta-9-
tetrahydrocannabinol, or THC.

In the 19th century, marijuana was used almost as aspirin is used today for headaches and
minor aches and pains. Today marijuana use and
possession are illegal in most states, but medical
applications are being explored. Marijuana decreases nausea and vomiting among cancer patients receiving chemotherapy (Grinspoon, 1987),
helps glaucoma sufferers by reducing fluid pressure in the eye, and may offer some relief from

asthma. But there are also causes for concern, as
noted in 1982 by the Institute of Medicine of the
National Academy of Sciences: Marijuana impairs
motor coordination and perceptual functions used
in driving and the operation of other machines. It
impairs short-term memory and slows learning.
Although it causes positive mood changes in many
people, there are also disturbing instances of anxiety and confusion and occasional reports of psychotic reactions. Marijuana increases the heart rate
up to 140 to 150 beats per minute and, in some
people, raises blood pressure. This rise in work-
load poses a threat to persons with cardiovascular
disorders.

The early stages of marijuana intoxication are
frequently characterized by restlessness, which
gives way to calmness. Fairly to highly intoxicated
smokers report heightened perceptions and increases in self-insight, creative thinking, and empathy. Strong intoxication is linked to perceiving
time as passing more slowly and to increased
awareness of body sensations, such as heartbeat.

Hallucinogenic Giving rise to hallucinations.
Psychedelic Causing hallucinations or delusions or
heightening perceptions.

Strong intoxication might also heighten sexual sensations. But strong intoxication also sometimes causes disorientation, nausea, and vomiting. Some people report that marijuana helps them socialize at parties. But friendliness may give way to self-absorption and social withdrawal as the smoker becomes higher (Fabian & Fishkin, 1981).

Marijuana's entire story has not yet been told.

LSD   LSD is the abbreviation for lysergic diethylamide acid, a synthetic hallucinogenic drug. Users of "acid" claim that it "expands consciousness" and opens new worlds. Sometimes people believe they achieved great insights while using LSD, but when it wears off they usually cannot apply or recall these discoveries.

As a powerful hallucinogenic, LSD produces vivid and colorful hallucinations, or "trips," that can be somewhat unpredictable. Some regular users have only "good trips." Others have one bad trip and swear off. Regular users who have had no bad trips argue that people with bad trips were

Flashbacks Distorted perceptions or hallucinations that occur days or weeks after LSD use but which mimic the LSD experience.

psychologically unstable prior to using LSD. Barber's review of the literature (1970) does suggest that psychotic symptoms are rare and usually limited to people with a history of psychological problems.

Some LSD users report **flashbacks**—distorted perceptions or hallucinations that occur long after usage. It has been speculated that flashbacks stem from chemical changes in the brain produced by LSD, but Heaton and Victor (1976) and Matefy (1980) found that users who have flashbacks are more oriented toward fantasy: They allow their thoughts to wander and enjoy focusing on internal sensations.

Other hallucinogenic drugs include mescaline (derived from the peyote cactus) and phencyclidine (PCP). Regular use of hallucinogenics may lead to tolerance and psychological dependence. But hallucinogenics are not known to lead to physiological dependence. High doses can induce frightening hallucinations, impaired coordination, poor judgment, mood changes, and paranoid delusions.

In this chapter we have described a number of abnormal behavior problems. In the next chapter we shall consider some of the methods of therapy that have been devised to help people deal with them.

TRUTH OR FICTION REVISITED

A man shot the president of the United States in front of millions of television witnesses yet was found not guilty by a court of law. True. The man's name is John Hinckley and he was found not guilty by reason of insanity.

In the Middle Ages innocent people were drowned to prove that they were not possessed by the Devil. True. It was believed that the Devil, or his agents, within people they "possessed," would not take kindly to drowning and would keep the person afloat.

Some people are suddenly flooded with feelings of panic, even when there is no external threat. True. They are said to have panic disorder.

Some people have irresistible urges to wash their hands—over and over again. True. They are said to have a compulsion.

Stressful experiences can lead to recurrent nightmares. True. Recurrent nightmares are one of the symptoms of post-traumatic stress disorder.

Some people have not one but two or more distinct personalities dwelling within them. Perhaps—we cannot be certain. There are many convincing case studies of multiple personality, but personalities are inferred from behavior, not observed directly. Therefore, our investigative methods do not absolutely rule out the possibility that people have convincingly faked multiple personality.

People have lost the use of their legs or eyes under stress, even though there was nothing medically wrong with them. True. They are said to have conversion disorder, in which stress is converted into loss or disturbance of a body function.

Some college women control their weight by going on cycles of binge eating followed by vomiting. True. Cycles of binge eating and purging define the disorder of bulimia.

It is abnormal to feel depressed. False. Depression is an appropriate response to a loss or failure.

Some people ride an emotional roller coaster, with cycles of elation and depression. True. They are said to have bipolar mood disorder.

In some mental disorders, people see and hear things that are not actually there. True. This occurs in schizophrenia, for example.

Stripteasers are exhibitionists. False. Exhibitionists attempt to surprise and shock their victims. Stripteasers attempt to make a living by sexually arousing their audiences.

Some people fail to enjoy sexual activity because they try too hard at it. True. "Trying too hard" is linked to performance anxiety, and performance anxiety can inhibit sexual response.

Alcohol is a stimulant. False. Alcohol is a depressant.

Coca-Cola once "added life" through a powerful but now illegal stimulant. True. The stimulant is cocaine.

Marijuana is the drug most frequently abused by adolescents. False. Alcohol is.

Chapter Review

Behavior is likely to be labeled abnormal when it is infrequent, socially unacceptable, involves faulty perception of reality, is dangerous, self-defeating, or personally distressing. Models for explaining abnormal behavior include the demonological model, which has been most prevalent throughout history; the medical model, with its organic and psychoanalytic versions; the social-learning model; and the cognitive model.

Anxiety disorders are characterized by motor tension, feelings of dread, and sympathetic overarousal. The anxiety disorders include irrational, excessive fears, or phobias; panic disorder, or sudden attacks of anxiety; generalized or "free-floating" anxiety; obsessive-compulsive disorders, in which people are troubled by intrusive thoughts or impulses to repeat some activity; and post-traumatic stress disorder, in which a stressful event is followed by persistent fears and intrusive thoughts about it. Psychoanalysts tend to view anxiety disorders as problems in maintaining repression of primitive impulses. Many learning theorists view phobias as conditioned fears. Biochemical factors that create a predisposition toward anxiety disorders might be inherited.

Dissociative disorders are characterized by a sudden temporary change in consciousness or self-identity and include psychogenic amnesia, psychogenic fugue, multiple personality, and depersonalization.

In somatoform disorders, people show or complain of physical problems, although no medical abnormality can be found. In conversion disorder, there is loss of a body function. Hypochondriacs insist that they are suffering from illnesses, although there are no medical findings.

Eating disorders include anorexia nervosa and bulimia nervosa. Anorexia is characterized by dramatic weight loss, distorted body image, and intense fear of being overweight. In bulimia nervosa, the individual engages in binge eating followed by purging, as by self-induced vomiting.

Mood disorders are characterized by disturbance in expressed emotions. Major depression is characterized by sadness, loss of interest, and feelings of worthlessness or guilt. In bipolar disorder there are mood swings from elation to depression and back. Research emphasizes the possible roles of learned helplessness, attributional styles, and neurotransmitters in depression.

Schizophrenia is characterized by disturbances in thought and language, such as loosening of associations and delusions; perception and attention, as found in hallucinations; motor activity, as shown by a stupor or by excited behavior; mood, as in flat or inappropriate emotional responses; and by withdrawal and autism. There are three major types of schizophrenia: disorganized, catatonic, and paranoid. There is a tendency for schizophrenia to run in families. Schizophrenics might utilize more dopamine than normal people do.

Personality disorders are inflexible, maladaptive behavior patterns that impair personal or social functioning and are a source of distress to the individual or others. Persons with antisocial personality disorders persistently violate the rights of others and conflict with the law but do not show guilt or shame and are largely undeterred by punishment.

Transsexualism is a gender-identity disorder in which the person feels trapped in the body of the wrong sex. Sexual disorders include paraphilias and sexual dysfunctions. In the paraphilias, people are sexually aroused by unusual or bizarre objects or situations. Sexual dysfunctions involve problems in becoming sexually aroused and reaching orgasm.

Psychoactive substance abuse is persistent use despite impairment of functioning or danger. Psychoactive substance dependence is inability to control use of a substance and is characterized by tolerance and withdrawal symptoms. Factors in substance abuse include curiosity, peer pressure, rebelliousness, modeling, and, perhaps, genetic predispositions.

Exercises

Major and Minor Categories of Abnormal Behavior

Directions: *In the first column are a number of types of abnormal behavior. In the second column are major categories of abnormal behavior. Write the letter signifying the appropriate major category of abnormal behavior in the blank space to the left of the type of abnormal behavior. Answers are given below.*

_____ 1. Conversion disorder
_____ 2. Panic disorder
_____ 3. Transvestic fetishism
_____ 4. Psychogenic fugue
_____ 5. Agoraphobia
_____ 6. Bipolar disorder
_____ 7. Exhibitionism
_____ 8. Obsessive-compulsive disorder
_____ 9. Schizotypal disorder
_____ 10. Catatonic schizophrenia
_____ 11. Multiple personality
_____ 12. Panic disorder
_____ 13. Hypochondriasis
_____ 14. Major depression
_____ 15. Psychogenic amnesia
_____ 16. Depersonalization
_____ 17. Post-traumatic stress disorder

A. Mood disorders
B. Anxiety disorders
C. Dissociative disorders
D. Personality disorders
E. Sexual disorders
F. Schizophrenia
G. Somatoform disorders

Answers to Exercise

1. G	6. A	10. F	14. A
2. B	7. E	11. C	15. C
3. E	8. B	12. B	16. C
4. C	9. D	13. G	17. B
5. B			

Symptoms and Disorders

Directions: *In the first column are a number of symptoms of types of abnormal behavior. In the second column are various diagnoses. Write the letter of the diagnosis in the appropriate blank space. Note that more than one type of abnormal behavior pattern may apply. Answers are given below.*

_____ 1. Waxy flexibility	A. Phobic disorder
_____ 2. Nervousness	B. Panic disorder
_____ 3. Elation	C. Generalized anxiety disorders
_____ 4. Free-floating anxiety	D. Obsessive-compulsive disorder
_____ 5. Vivid, abundant hallucinations	E. Psychogenic amnesia
	F. Multiple personality
_____ 6. Lack of guilt over misdeeds	G. Conversion disorder
	H. Hypochondriasis
_____ 7. Lack of energy	I. Anorexia nervosa
_____ 8. Suspiciousness	J. Major depression
_____ 9. La belle indifférence	K. Bipolar disorder
_____ 10. Sudden anxiety attacks	L. Disorganized schizophrenia
_____ 11. Compulsive behavior	M. Catatonic schizophrenia
_____ 12. Withdrawal	N. Paranoid schizophrenia
_____ 13. Weight loss	O. Paranoid personality
_____ 14. Delusions	P. Schizoid personality
_____ 15. Cross-dressing	Q. Antisocial personality
_____ 16. Pressured speech	R. Transsexualism
_____ 17. Physical complaints	S. Fetishism
_____ 18. Fear of public scrutiny	T. Transvestitism
_____ 19. Loose associations	U. Exhibitionism
_____ 20. Paranoid delusions	V. Bulimia nervosa
_____ 21. Giddiness	
_____ 22. Rapid flight of ideas	
_____ 23. Bingeing on carbohydrates	

Answer Key to Exercise

1. M	7. J, K	13. I, J	19. L, M, N
2. A, B, C, D, H, etc.	8. N, O	14. J, K, L, M, N	20. N
3. K	9. G	15. R, T	21. L
4. C	10. B	16. K	22. K
5. L	11. D, R, S, T, U	17. B, C, H, J	23. V
6. Q	12. L, M, N, P	18. A	

Posttest

1. According to the text, the _____ model has been the most prevalent model of abnormal behavior throughout history.

   (a) organic, **(b)** psychoanalytic, **(c)** cognitive, **(d)** demonological.

2. Some psychologists conceive of schizophrenia as a disorder that basically impairs the perception, storage, and retrieval of information. These psychologists may be said to be viewing schizophrenic behavior patterns in terms of the _____ model of abnormal behavior.

   (a) organic, **(b)** cognitive, **(c)** social-learning, **(d)** psychoanalytic.

3. Which of the following literally means "fear of the marketplace"?

   (a) claustrophobia, **(b)** agoraphobia, **(c)** acrophobia, **(d)** ailurophobia.

4. If we adhere to DSM–III–R standards for diagnosing panic disorder, we find that panic disorders affect about _____ percent of the population.

   (a) 1, **(b)** 5, **(c)** 25, **(d)** 40.

5. Jim complains that he has the seemingly irresistible urge to wash his hands repeatedly. Such a repetitive urge is termed a(n)

   (a) obsession, **(b)** compulsion, **(c)** neurosis, **(d)** psychosis.

6. Which of the following is *not* a dissociative disorder?

   (a) Depersonalization disorder, **(b)** Psychogenic amnesia, **(c)** Retrograde amnesia, **(d)** Psychogenic fugue.

7. Conversion disorder is so named because it appears to convert a

   (a) physical problem into a source of stress, **(b)** source of stress into a physical problem, **(c)** psychological problem into a source of stress, **(d)** social problem into a psychological problem.

8. Anoretic women

   (a) are never hungry, **(b)** worry that they are too thin, **(c)** fear that food will poison them, **(d)** have a distorted body image.

9. Bulimia nervosa is classified as a(n)

   (a) personality disorder, **(b)** eating disorder, **(c)** obsessive-compulsive disorder, **(d)** neurosis.

10. All the mood disorders involve

    (a) persistent depression, **(b)** rapid flight of ideas, **(c)** cycles of depression and elation, **(d)** a disturbance in expressed emotions.

11. Persons with _____ are most likely to show delusions of unworthiness.

    (a) paranoid schizophrenia, **(b)** disorganized schizophrenia, **(c)** antisocial personality disorder, **(d)** major depression.

12. Depressed people are *least* likely to make _____ attributions for their failures.

   (a) specific, (b) stable, (c) internal, (d) global.

13. Research into the biochemical correlates of abnormal behavior suggests that manicky people might have

   (a) abnormally low levels of serotonin and norepinephrine, (b) abnormally low serotonin and abnormally high norepinephrine, (c) abnormally high levels of serotonin and norepinephrine, (d) abnormally high serotonin and abnormally low norepinephrine.

14. The phenothiazines, which are often effective in treating schizophrenia, appear to work by

   (a) increasing utilization of dopamine, (b) blocking the action of dopamine receptors, (c) increasing the utilization of amphetamines, (d) blocking the action of amphetamine receptors.

15. Persons with antisocial personality disorder

   (a) are below average in intelligence, (b) tend to show XYY sex chromosomal structure, (c) were disciplined regularly as children, (d) are largely undeterred by punishment.

16. Persons with _____ seek sex reassignment.

   (a) transvestic fetishism, (b) transsexualism, (c) a sexual dysfunction, (d) a paraphilia.

17. Most episodes of pedophilia

   (a) involve fondling, (b) involve sexual intercourse, (c) are coerced, (d) show a gender-identity disorder.

18. According to psychoanalytic theory, paraphilias are defenses against

   (a) retribution, (b) obsessions and compulsions, (c) anxiety, (d) dominance by the id.

19. Which of the following problems is defined by recurrent pain in the genital region?

   (a) Vaginismus, (b) Inhibited orgasm, (c) Hypoactive sexual desire disorder, (d) Dyspareunia.

20. In inhibited orgasm, the individual

   (a) is not interested in sexual activity, (b) is interested in sexual activity but does not become sexually aroused, (c) becomes sexually aroused but has difficulty reaching orgasm, (d) reaches orgasm easily but does not enjoy it.

21. Substance dependence is set apart from substance abuse by

   (a) continued use over a period of at least one month, (b) a problem caused by the substance, (c) use of a larger than average quantity of the substance, (d) tolerance and withdrawal symptoms.

22. Which of the following has been shown to increase the attention span of hyperactive children?

(a) Barbiturates, **(b)** Ritalin, **(c)** Delta-9-tetrahydrocannabinol, **(d)** Methaqualone.

Answer Key to Posttest

1. D	**7.** B	**13.** B	**19.** D
2. B	**8.** D	**14.** B	**20.** C
3. B	**9.** B	**15.** D	**21.** D
4. A	**10.** D	**16.** B	**22.** B
5. B	**11.** D	**17.** A	
6. C	**12.** A	**18.** C	

METHODS OF THERAPY

OUTLINE

PRETEST: TRUTH OR FICTION?
HISTORICAL OVERVIEW
  Asylums
  Mental Hospitals
  The Community Mental-Health Movement
INSIGHT-ORIENTED THERAPIES
  Psychoanalysis
  Person-Centered Therapy
  Transactional Analysis
  Gestalt Therapy
  Cognitive Therapy
BEHAVIOR THERAPY
  Systematic Desensitization
  Aversive Conditioning
  Operant Conditioning

Assertiveness Training
Self-Control Techniques
Behaviorally Oriented Sex-Therapy Methods
GROUP THERAPY
  Encounter Groups
  Family Therapy
BIOLOGICAL THERAPIES
  Chemotherapy
  Electroconvulsive Therapy
  Psychosurgery
TRUTH OR FICTION REVISITED
CHAPTER REVIEW
EXERCISES
POSTTEST

PRETEST: TRUTH OR FICTION?

People in Merry Old England used to visit the local insane asylum for a fun night out on the town.

Many of the nation's homeless are people who have been discharged from mental hospitals.

The terms *psychotherapy* and *psychoanalysis* are interchangeable.

To be of significant help, psychotherapy must be undertaken for months, perhaps years.

If you were in traditional psychoanalysis, your major tasks would be to lie back, relax, and say whatever pops into your mind.

Some psychotherapists interpret clients' dreams.

Some psychotherapists encourage their clients to take the lead in the therapy session.

Other psychotherapists tell their clients precisely what to do.

Still other psychotherapists purposefully argue with clients.

You might be able to gain control over bad habits merely by keeping a record of where and when you practice them.

Lying around in your reclining chair and fantasizing can be an effective way of confronting your fears.

Smoking cigarettes can be an effective treatment for helping people to . . . stop smoking cigarettes.

Staff members in a mental hospital induced reluctant patients to eat by ignoring them.

Individual therapy is preferable to group therapy, for people who can afford it.

Drugs are never a solution to abnormal behavior problems.

There is a treatment for severe depression in which an electric current strong enough to induce seizures is passed through the head.

The originator of a surgical technique intended to reduce violence learned that it was not always successful—when one of his patients shot him.

Brad is having an uplifting experience—literally. Six people who minutes ago were perfect strangers have cradled him in their arms and raised him into midair. His eyes are closed. Gently they rock him back and forth and carry him about the room.

Brad is no paralyzed hospital patient. He has just joined an encounter group. He hopes to be able to learn to relate to other people as individuals, not as passing blurs on the street or as patrons asking him to cash payroll checks at the bank where he works as a teller. The group leader had directed that Brad be carried about to help him break down his defensive barriers and establish trust in others.

Brad had responded to a somewhat flamboyant ad in the therapy section of the classifieds in New York's *Village Voice*:

Come to life! Stop being a gray automaton in a mechanized society! Encounter yourself and others. New group forming. First meeting free. Call 212–555–0599. Qualified therapist.

Like many who seek personal help, Brad had little idea how to go about it. His group experience might or might not work out. For one thing, he has no idea about the qualifications of the group leader and did not know to ask. If he had answered other ads in the *Voice,* including some placed by highly qualified therapists, his treatment might have looked quite different. Brad could have been

Lying on a couch talking about anything that pops into his awareness and exploring the hidden meanings of a recurrent dream

Sitting face to face with a gentle, accepting therapist who places the major burden for what happens during therapy directly on Brad's shoulders

Listening to a frank, straightforward therapist insist that his problems stem from self-defeating attitudes and beliefs, such as an overriding need to be liked and approved of

Role playing the initiation of a social relationship, including smiling at a new acquaintance, making small talk, and looking the person squarely in the eye

The form of treatment, or psychotherapy, practiced by a psychologist or another helping professional is related to that practitioner's theory of personality or model of abnormal behavior. It

is not (or ought not to be) a matter of chance. In this chapter we shall explore the history of the treatment of abnormal behavior. Then we shall describe and evaluate several of the major current psychological treatment approaches, including *psychoanalysis, person-centered therapy, cognitive therapy, behavior therapy,* and *group therapy.* These are all forms of **psychotherapy.** After exploring various psychotherapies, we shall turn our attention to the *biological therapies* that are used with some of the more severe forms of abnormal behavior, such as schizophrenia and mood disorders. These include *drug therapy (chemotherapy), electroconvulsive shock therapy,* and *psychosurgery.*

HISTORICAL OVERVIEW

Ancient and medieval "treatments" of abnormal behavior often reflected the demonological model. They involved cruel practices such as exorcism and death by hanging or burning, as was practiced some 300 years ago. In Europe and the United States, some people who could not meet the demands of everyday life were also thrown into prisons. Others begged in city streets, stole produce and food animals from farms, or entered marginal societal niches occupied by prostitutes and petty thieves. A few might find their ways to monasteries or other retreats that offered a kind word and some support. Generally speaking, they died young.

Asylums

Asylums often had their origins in European monasteries. They were the first institutions meant primarily for the mentally ill. Their functions were human warehousing, not treatment. Asylums mushroomed in population until the daily stresses

---

Psychotherapy A systematic interaction between a therapist and a client that brings psychological principles to bear on influencing the client's thoughts, feelings, or behavior in order to help that client overcome abnormal behavior or adjust to problems in living.

Asylum An institution for the care of the mentally ill.

What Was St. Mary's of Bethlehem?
This historic insane asylum is the source of the word "bedlam."

created by noise, overcrowding, and unsanitary conditions undoubtedly heightened the problems they were meant to ameliorate. Inmates were frequently chained and beaten. Some were chained for decades.

The word *bedlam* is derived from the name of the London asylum St. Mary's of Bethlehem, which opened its gates in 1547. Here the unfortunate were chained, whipped, and allowed to lie in their own waste products. And here the ladies and gentlemen of the British upper class might go for a stroll on a lazy afternoon, to take in the sights. The admission for such amusement? One penny.

Humanitarian reform movements began in the eighteenth century. In Paris, Philippe Pinel unchained the patients at the asylum known as La Bicêtre. The populace was amazed that most patients, rather than running amok, profited from kindness and greater freedom. Many could later function in society once more. Reform movements were later led by the Quaker William Tuke in England and by Dorothea Dix in America.

Mental Hospitals

Mental hospitals gradually replaced asylums in the United States. In the mid-1950s, over a million people resided in state, county, Veterans Administration, or private facilities. Treatment, not warehousing, is the function of the mental hospital. Still, because of high patient populations and understaffing, many patients have received little attention. Even today, with somewhat improved conditions, it is not unusual for one psychiatrist to be responsible for the welfare of several hundred patients on a weekend.

The Community Mental-Health Movement

Since the 1960s, efforts have been made to maintain as many mental patients as possible in the community. The Community Mental-Health Centers Act of 1963 provided funds for creating hundreds of community mental-health centers, in which patients would be charged according to their ability to pay. These centers attempt to maintain new patients as outpatients, to serve patients from mental hospitals who have been released to the community, and to provide other services as listed in Table 10.1. Today, about 63 percent of the nation's chronically mental ill live in the community, not in the hospital (Morganthau et al., 1986).

But critics note that many mental patients who had resided in hospitals for decades were suddenly discharged to "home" communities that seemed

The Unchaining of Patients at La Bicêtre.   The unchaining of patients symbolizes a landmark in the humanitarian reform movement.

foreign and frightening. Many discharged patients do not receive adequate follow-up care in the community (Morganthau et al., 1986). Perhaps a third to a half of the nation's homeless are products of deinstitutionalization (Cordes, 1984; Fustero, 1984). Some former hospital inhabitants try to return to the protected world of the hospital and become trapped in a "revolving door" between the hospital and the community (Cordes, 1984).

The outlook for maintaining new patients in the community, rather than hospitalizing them, looks brighter. In a review of ten experiments in which seriously disturbed patients were randomly assigned either to hospitalization or to outpatient care, Kiesler (1982) did not find one case in which

**Table 10.1   Functions of the Community
                 Mental-Health Center**

Outpatient treatment
Short-term hospitalization
Partial hospitalization (e.g., patient sleeps in the
   hospital and works outside during the day)
Crisis intervention
Community consultation and education about
   abnormal behavior

The Community Mental-Health Centers Act provided funds for community agencies that attempt to intervene in mental-health problems as early as possible and to maintain mental patients in the community.

the outcomes of hospitalization were superior. The outpatient alternative was usually superior in terms of the patient's maintaining independent living arrangements, staying in school, and finding employment.

Let us now consider the types of therapy practiced today.

INSIGHT-ORIENTED THERAPIES

Many types of psychotherapy are based on the assumption that abnormal behavior can be remedied if people gain **insight** into their problems. Insight involves knowledge of the experiences that led to conflicts and maladaptive behavior. Insight also involves (1) efforts to identify and *label* feelings and conflicts that lie below conscious awareness and (2) ability to view objectively and to evaluate the appropriateness of one's own beliefs, attitudes, and thought processes. Insight-oriented therapies may vary in their methods, but they share the assumption that self-knowledge is required to change self-defeating behavior.

Insight In psychotherapy, knowledge of one's underlying motives or impulses.

Let us now examine the following insight-oriented psychotherapies: psychoanalysis, person-centered therapy, transactional analysis, Gestalt therapy, and cognitive therapy.

Psychoanalysis: Where Id Was, There Shall Ego Be

Canst thou not minister to a mind diseas'd,
Pluck out from the memory a rooted sorrow,
Raze out the written troubles of the brain,
And with some sweet oblivious antidote
Cleanse the stuff'd bosom of that perilous stuff
Which weighs upon the heart?

—Shakespeare, *Macbeth*

In this passage from *Macbeth*, Macbeth asks a physician to minister to Lady Macbeth after she has gone mad. In the play, her madness is in part caused by current events, namely her guilt for participating in murders designed to seat her husband on the throne of Scotland. But there are also hints of more deeply rooted and mysterious problems that might involve infertility.

If Lady Macbeth's physician had been a psychoanalyst, he might have asked her to lie down on a couch in a slightly darkened room. He would have sat just behind her and encouraged her to talk about anything that popped into her mind, no matter how trivial, no matter how personal. To avoid interfering with her self-exploration, he might have said little or nothing for session after session. That would have been par for the course. After all, **psychoanalysis** can extend for months, or even years.

Psychoanalysis is the clinical method devised by Sigmund Freud for plucking "from the memory a rooted sorrow," for digging "out the written troubles of the brain." Psychoanalysis is the method used by Freud and his followers to "cleanse . . . that perilous stuff which weighs upon the heart"—to provide insight into the conflicts presumed to lie at the roots of a person's problems. Psychoanalysis seeks to allow the client to express emotions and impulses theorized to have been dammed up by the forces of repression.

Freud was fond of saying, "Where id was, there shall ego be." In part he meant that psychoanalysis could shed light on the inner workings of the mind. But Freud did not believe we should become conscious of all conflicts and primitive impulses. Instead, he sought to replace impulsive and defensive behavior with coping behavior. He believed that impulsive behavior reflected the urges of the id. Defensive behavior, such as timidly avoiding confrontations, represented the ego's compromising efforts to protect the client from these impulses and the possibility of retaliation. Coping behavior would allow the client to express these impulses partially, but in socially acceptable ways. In so doing, the client would find gratification but avoid social and self-condemnation.

In this way a man with a phobia for knives might discover that he had been repressing the urge to harm someone who had taken advantage of him. He might also find ways to confront his antagonist verbally. A woman with a conversion disorder—paralysis of the legs—could see that her disability allowed her to avoid unwanted pregnancy without guilt. She might also realize her resentment at being pressed into a stereotypical feminine sex role and decide to expand her options.

Freud also believed that psychoanalysis permitted the client to spill forth the psychic energy theorized to have been repressed by conflicts and guilt. He called this spilling forth **abreaction,** or **catharsis**. Abreaction would provide feelings of relief.

Free Association   Early in his career as a therapist, Freud found that hypnosis allowed his clients to focus on repressed conflicts and talk about them. Hypnosis seemed an efficient way of breaking through to topics of which clients were unaware in the normal waking state. But Freud also found that many clients denied the accuracy of this material once out of the trance. Other clients found these revelations premature and painful.

Psychoanalysis Freud's method of psychotherapy.

Abreaction In psychoanalysis, expression of previously repressed feelings and impulses to allow the psychic energy associated with them to spill forth.

Catharsis Another term for *abreaction*.

What Happened Here? This is Freud's famed consulting room at Berggasse 19 in Vienna. Freud would sit in the chair by the head of the couch while a client free associated. The cardinal rule of free association is that no thought is to be censored, no matter how trivial or personal.

And so Freud turned to **free association**—a more gradual method of breaking down the walls of defense that blocked insight into unconscious processes.

In free association, the client is made comfortable, as by lying on a couch, and asked to talk about any topic that comes to mind. No thought is to be censored—that is the cardinal rule. Psychoanalysts ask their clients to wander "freely" from topic to topic, but they do not believe that the process *within* the client is fully free. Repressed impulses press for release. On a verbal level, they lead to a **compulsion to utter.** A client might begin to free associate with meaningless topics, but eventually the compulsion to utter will cause important repressed material to surface.

The ego persists, however, in trying to repress unacceptable impulses and threatening conflicts. As a result, clients might show **resistance** to recalling and discussing threatening ideas. Clients might claim, "My mind is blank" when they are about to entertain such a thought. They might accuse the analyst of being demanding or inconsiderate. They might "forget" their appointment when threatening material is due to be uncovered.

The therapist observes the dynamic struggle between the compulsion to utter and resistance. Through discreet remarks, the analyst subtly tips

---

Free association In psychoanalysis, the uncensored uttering of all thoughts that come to mind.

Compulsion to utter The urge to express ideas and impulses—in psychoanalytic theory, a reflection of seeking expression by impulses within the id.

Resistance The tendency to block the free expression of impulses and primitive ideas—a reflection of the defense mechanism of repression.

the balance in favor of uttering. A gradual process of self-discovery and self-insight ensues. Now and then the analyst offers an **interpretation** of an utterance, showing how it suggests resistance, or perhaps, the symbolic revelation of deep-seated feelings or conflicts.

Dream Analysis   Freud considered dreams the "royal road to the unconscious." The psychoanalytic theory of dreams holds that they are determined by unconscious processes as well as the remnants, or "residues," of the day. Unconscious impulses tend to be expressed in dreams as a form of **wish fulfillment.**

But unacceptable sexual and aggressive impulses are likely to be displaced onto objects and situations that reflect the era and culture of the client. These objects become **symbols** of the unconscious wishes. For example, long, narrow dream objects might be **phallic symbols,** but whether the symbol takes the form of a spear, rifle, "stick shift," or spacecraft partially reflects one's cultural background.

In psychoanalytic theory, the perceived content of the dream is called its shown content, or **manifest content.** Its presumed hidden or symbolic content is referred to as its **latent content.** A man might dream that he is flying. Flying is the manifest content of the dream. Psychoanalysts usually interpret flying as symbolic of erection, so issues concerning sexual potency might comprise the latent content of such a dream.

Freud often asked clients to jot down their dreams upon waking so that they could be interpreted during the psychoanalytic session.

Transference   Freud found that his clients responded not only to his appearance and behavior but also according to what they meant to clients. A young woman might see Freud as a father figure and displace, or transfer, her feelings toward her own father onto Freud. Another woman might view him as a lover and act seductively or suspiciously. Men also showed **transference.** A man might also view Freud as a father figure or, perhaps, a competitor. Freud discovered that he could transfer his feelings onto his clients—perhaps viewing a woman as a sex object or a young man as a rebellious son. He called this placing of clients into roles in his own life **countertransference.**

Transference and countertransference lead to unjustified expectations of new people and can foster maladaptive behavior. We might relate to our spouses as to our opposite-sex parents and demand too much (or too little) from them. Or we might accuse them unfairly of harboring wishes and secrets we attribute to our parents. We might not give new friends or lovers "a chance" when we have been mistreated by someone who played a similar role in our lives or our fantasies.

In any event, psychoanalysts are trained to be **opaque** concerning their own behavior and feelings, so that they will not encourage client transference or express their own feelings of countertransference. Then, when the client acts accusingly, seductively, or otherwise inappropriately toward the analyst, the analyst can plead not guilty of encouraging the client's behavior and can suggest that it reflects historical events and fantasies. In this way, transference behavior becomes grist for the therapeutic mill.

Analysis of client transference is an important element of therapy. It provides insight and encourages more adaptive social behavior. But it might take months or years for transference to de-

---

Interpretation An explanation of a client's utterance according to psychoanalytic theory.

Wish fulfillment A primitive method used by the id to attempt to gratify basic instincts.

Symbol A sign that stands for, or represents, something else.

Phallic symbol A sign that represents the penis.

Manifest content In psychoanalytic theory, the reported content of dreams.

Latent content In psychoanalytic theory, the symbolized or underlying content of dreams.

Transference In psychoanalysis, the generalization to the analyst of feelings toward a person in the client's life.

Countertransference In psychoanalysis, the generalization to the client of feelings toward a person in the analyst's life.

Opaque In psychoanalysis, descriptive of the analyst, who hides personal feelings.

velop fully and be resolved, which is one reason that psychoanalysis can be a lengthy process.

Modern Psychoanalytic Approaches
A number of psychoanalysts still adhere faithfully to Freud's protracted techniques. In recent years, however, briefer, less intense forms of psychoanalysis have been devised (Koss et al., 1986; Zaiden, 1982), making it possible for psychoanalysts to work with clients who cannot afford protracted therapy or whose schedules will not permit it. These psychoanalytically oriented therapies still focus on revealing unconscious material and on breaking through psychological defenses and resistance, but client and therapist usually sit face to face (as opposed to using a couch), and the therapist is more directive than the traditional psychoanalyst. Therapists frequently suggest productive behavior patterns as well as foster self-insight.

Evaluation of Psychoanalysis
Psychoanalysis is difficult to evaluate for several reasons. When possible, psychologists prefer to make evaluations on the basis of experimental evidence. But a sound experiment to evaluate psychoanalysis could require randomly assigning people seeking therapy to psychoanalysis and to a number of other therapies for comparison. A subject might have to remain in therapy for years to attain a "true" psychoanalysis, but the control subjects could not be kept in briefer forms of therapy for years. Moreover, some people want psychoanalysis per se rather than psychotherapy in general. It would not be ethical, or practical, to assign them randomly to other treatments or to a no-treatment control group (Basham, 1986; Parloff, 1986).

Self-insight and not behavioral change is the primary goal of psychoanalysis. As a matter of fact, many well-adjusted individuals undertake psychoanalysis in order to learn about themselves, not to "get better." Since each person's self-insights are to some degree unique, it might be impossible in principle to measure how much insight has been gained from psychoanalysis.

Psychoanalysts therefore claim, with some justification, that clinical judgment must be the basis for evaluating the effectiveness of analysis. Despite these evaluation problems, however, research into the effectiveness of psychoanalytically oriented therapies has been encouraging. Mary Lee Smith and Gene Glass, for example, analyzed the results of dozens of studies on psychoanalysis and concluded that people who receive psychoanalytically oriented therapy show greater well being, on the average, than 70 to 75 percent of those who are left untreated (Smith & Glass, 1977; Smith et al., 1981). There also seems to be a consensus that psychoanalysis is most effective with well-educated, highly verbal, and motivated clients (Luborsky & Spence, 1978). Psychoanalysis does not appear to be successful with psychotic disorders.

Despite the positive findings of Smith and Glass, critics of psychoanalysis, such as behavior therapist Joseph Wolpe (1985), assert that it has not been shown that the beneficial aspects of psychoanalysis can be attributed to the psychoanalytic method per se. There are common factors in many types of therapy, such as showing warmth, encouraging exploration, and combating feelings of hopelessness and helplessness (Klein & Rabkin, 1984; Rounsaville et al., 1987).

In any event, during the 1940s and 1950s, psychotherapy was almost synonymous with psychoanalysis. Few other approaches to psychotherapy had an impact on psychologists or on public awareness (Garfield, 1981, 1982). But today, according to a survey of clinical and counseling psychologists, only 14 percent of psychotherapists have a psychoanalytic orientation (Smith, 1982). Sigmund Freud, once the model for almost all therapists, is currently rated third in influence, following Carl Rogers and Albert Ellis, whom we shall discuss in the following pages. The largest group of psychotherapists (41 percent) consider themselves eclectic (Smith, 1982, p. 804).

Person-Centered Therapy: Removing Roadblocks to Self-Actualization

Person-centered therapy was originated by Carl Rogers (1951), the most influential psychotherapist

Person-centered therapy Carl Rogers's method of psychotherapy, which emphasizes the creation of a warm, therapeutic atmosphere that frees clients to engage in self-exploration and self-expression.

What Is Person-Centered Therapy? The qualities of the effective person-centered therapist include unconditional positive regard for clients, empathetic understanding, genuineness, and congruence.

in the Smith (1982) survey. Rogers believed that we have natural tendencies toward health, growth, and fulfillment and that abnormal behavior stems largely from roadblocks placed in the path of self-actualization. Because others show selective approval of us when we are young, we learn to disown the disapproved parts of ourselves. We don masks and façades to earn social approval. We might learn to be seen but not heard—not even heard, or examined fully, by ourselves. As a result we might experience stress and discomfort and the feeling that we—or the world—are not real.

Person-centered therapy aims to provide insight into parts of us that we have disowned so that we can feel whole. It stresses the importance of a warm, therapeutic atmosphere that encourages a client's self-exploration and self-expression. A therapist's acceptance of the client is thought to lead to the client's self-acceptance and self-esteem.

Unconditional positive regard Acceptance of the value of another person, although not necessarily acceptance of all of that person's behaviors.

Empathetic understanding Ability to perceive a client's feelings from the client's frame of reference.

Self-acceptance frees the client to make choices that foster development of his or her unique potential.

Person-centered therapy is nondirective. The client takes the lead, listing and exploring problems. The therapist reflects or paraphrases expressed feelings and ideas, helping the client to get in touch with deeper feelings and to follow the strongest leads in the quest for self-insight. The effective person-centered therapist also shows *unconditional positive regard, empathetic understanding, genuineness,* and *congruence.*

The therapist shows **unconditional positive regard** for clients. Clients are respected as important human beings with unique values and goals. They are provided with a sense of security that encourages them to follow their own feelings. Psychoanalysts might hesitate to encourage clients to express their impulses freely because of the fear that primitive sexual and aggressive forces might be unleashed. But person-centered therapists believe that people are basically *pro*social. If people follow their own feelings, rather than act defensively, they should not be abusive or *anti*social.

Empathetic understanding is shown by accurately reflecting the client's experiences and feelings. Therapists try to view the world through their clients' **frames of reference** by setting aside their own values and listening closely.

Whereas psychoanalysts are trained to be opaque, person-centered therapists are trained to show **genuineness.** Person-centered therapists are open about their feelings. Person-centered therapists must also be able to tolerate differentness because they believe that every client is different in important ways.

Person-centered therapists also try to show **congruence,** or a fit between their thoughts, feelings, and behavior. Person-centered therapists serve as models of integrity to their clients.

Evaluation of Person-Centered Therapy As with psychoanalysis, a number of the outcomes of person-centered therapy—heightened self-esteem, self-acceptance, and self-actualization—pose measurement problems for evaluators. Still, the analysis by Smith and Glass (1977) found that nearly 75 percent of the clients receiving person-centered therapy were better off than people who were untreated.

Like psychoanalysis, person-centered therapy seems most effective with well-educated, highly motivated, and verbal people (Abramowitz et al., 1974; Wexler & Butler, 1976). There is no evidence of effectiveness with psychotic disorders. Despite the influence of Carl Rogers, only about 9 percent of psychotherapists place themselves within the person-centered tradition (Smith, 1982, p. 804).

Transactional Analysis: I'm OK—You're OK—We're All OK

Transactional analysis (TA) is rooted in the psychoanalytic and humanistic traditions. According to Thomas Harris, author of *I'm OK—You're OK* (1967), many of us suffer from **inferiority complexes** of the sort described by psychoanalyst Alfred Adler. Although we are adults, we might still perceive ourselves as dependent children. We might think other people are OK but not see ourselves as OK. Within TA, I'm not OK—You're OK is one of four basic "life positions," or ways of perceiving relationships with others.

A major goal of TA is to help people adopt the life position I'm OK—You're OK, in which they accept others and themselves. Unfortunately, people tend to adopt "games," or styles of relating to others that are designed to confirm one of the unhealthy life positions: I'm OK—You're not OK, I'm not OK—You're OK, or I'm not OK—You're not OK.

Psychiatrist Eric Berne, the originator of TA and author of *Games People Play* (1976), described our personalities as containing three "ego states": **Parent, Child,** and **Adult.** The "parent" is a moralistic ego state. The "child" is an irresponsible and emotional ego state. The "adult" is a rational ego state. (These are three hypothesized *ego states,* or ways of coping. They do not correspond exactly to the concepts of id, ego, and superego.)

People tend to relate to each other as parents, children, or adults. A social exchange between two people is called a **transaction.** A transaction is said to fit, or be **complementary,** when a social exchange follows the same lines. In one type of complementary transaction, people relate as adults. But a transaction can also be complementary, even if upsetting, when two people relate as parent and child (Parent: "You shouldn't have done that." Child: "I'm sorry, I promise it won't happen

Frame of reference One's unique patterning of perceptions and attitudes, according to which one evaluates events.

Genuineness Recognition and open expression of the therapist's own feelings.

Congruence A fit between one's self-concept and behaviors, thoughts, and emotions.

Transactional analysis A form of psychotherapy that deals with how people interact and how their interactions reinforce attitudes, expectations, and "life positions." Abbreviated *TA.*

Inferiority complex Feelings of inferiority hypothesized by Alfred Adler to serve as a motivating force.

Parent In TA, a moralistic "ego state."

Child In TA, an irresponsible, emotional "ego state."

Adult In TA, a rational, adaptive "ego state."

Transaction In TA, an exchange between two people.

Complementary In TA, a transaction in which the ego states of two people interact harmoniously.

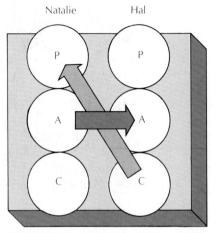

FIGURE 10.1. What Is a Crossed Transaction?
Natalie asks Hal, "Did you have a good time, tonight?"
Hal replies, "Why do you wanna know?"
Communication is thus broken off.

again"). Communication breaks down when the social exchange between the parties does not follow complementary lines (as in Figure 10.1). Note these examples:

NATALIE (adult to adult): Did you have a good time tonight?
HAL (child to parent): Why do you wanna know?

Or

BILL (adult to adult): Nan, did you see the checkbook?
NAN (parent to child): A place for everything and everything in its place!

TA is often used with couples who complain of communication problems. It encourages people to relate to each other as adults.

TA also attempts to put an end to game playing. The most commonly played marital game is "If It Weren't for You" (Berne, 1976). People who play this game marry domineering mates who prevent them from going into things they would not have the courage to do anyhow, such as taking a

Gestalt therapy Fritz Perls's form of psychotherapy, which attempts to integrate conflicting parts of the personality through directive methods designed to help clients perceive their whole selves.

more challenging job or moving to a new city. By playing "If It Weren't for You," they can blame their mates for their shortcomings and excuse their own timidity.

TA is one of the therapies that focus on the "here and now" rather than the past. It is assumed that we can change, despite our pasts, and that excessive focus on the past is a diversion. Berne (1976) noted that some clients play a psychoanalytically oriented game, which he termed "Archaeology." Archaeologists dig in the ruins of ancient civilizations. In this game, people dig into the ruins of their pasts to unearth the crucial event that will explain current problems. Why? Many of us focus on the adversity of early experiences when faced with the possibility of failure because a traumatic background might serve as an excuse for failure (DeGree & Snyder, 1985).

In therapy groups, Berne noted, some clients take advantage of the Freudian view that no thought is to be censored and play the game of "Self-Expression." They use vulgar language and paint a lurid scene; other group members play "liberated" roles and applaud their "honesty." Some of the other games people play have intriguing and reasonably self-explanatory titles:

- "Look How Hard I've Tried"
- "I'm Only Trying to Help You"
- "Why Does This Always Happen to Me?"
- "Now I've Got You, You Son of a Bitch!"
- "See What You Made Me Do"
- "You Got Me into This"
- "Kick Me"

Smith and Glass (1977) reported that people who receive TA are better off than about 72 percent of those who are untreated.

Gestalt Therapy: Getting It Together

Like psychoanalysis and person-centered therapy, **Gestalt therapy,** originated by Fritz Perls (1893–1970), aims to provide insight into how conflicting parts of the personality create distress. Perls used the term *Gestalt* to signify his interest in giving the conflicting parts of the personality an integrated shape. He wanted his clients to become aware of inner conflict, to live with rather than deny conflict, and to make productive choices despite fear.

Although Perls owes much to psychoanalytic theory, his form of therapy focuses on the present. In Gestalt therapy, clients heighten awareness of current feelings and behavior rather than explore the past. Perls believed, as Rogers, that people are free to make choices and to direct their growth; but unlike Rogers, Perls was highly directive. Gestalt therapists lead clients through planned experiences.

One technique for increasing awareness of internal conflict is the **dialogue.** Clients undertake verbal confrontations between opposing wishes and ideas. An example of these clashing personality elements is "top dog" and "underdog." One's top dog might conservatively suggest, "Don't take chances. Stick with what you have or you might lose it all." Your frustrated underdog might rise up and assert, "You never try anything. How will you ever get out of this rut if you don't take on new challenges?" Heightened awareness of the elements of conflict might clear a path toward resolution, perhaps through compromise.

Body language also provides insight into conflicting feelings. Clients might be instructed to attend to responses such as furrows in the eyebrow and facial tension when they express ideas they think they support.

To increase clients' understanding of opposing points of view, therapists might encourage them to argue in favor of ideas opposed to their own. They might also have clients role play people who are important to them to get more in touch with their points of view.

Whereas psychoanalytic theory views dreams as the "royal road to the unconscious," Perls saw the stuff of dreams as disowned parts of the personality. He would often ask clients to role play the elements in their dreams to get in touch with these parts. In *Gestalt Therapy Verbatim*, Perls—known to clients and friends alike as Fritz—describes a session in which a client, "Jim," is reporting a dream:

JIM: I just have the typical recurring dream which I think a lot of people might have if they have a background problem, and it isn't of anything I think I can act out. It's the distant wheel—I'm not sure what type it is—it's coming towards me and ever-increasing in size. And then finally, it's just above me and it's no

Who Is Fritz Perls?

height that I can determine, it's so high. And that's—
FRITZ: If you were this wheel, . . . what would you do with Jim?
JIM: I am just about to roll over Jim. (1971, p. 127)

Perls encourages Jim to undertake a dialogue with the wheel. Jim comes to see that the wheel represents fears about taking decisive action. Through this insight the "wheel" becomes more manageable in size, and Jim is able to use some of the "energy" that he might otherwise have spent in worrying to begin to take charge of his life.

Smith and Glass (1977) found that people who receive Gestalt therapy show greater well-being than about 60 percent of those who are untreated.

Cognitive Therapy: "As a Man Thinketh, So Is He"

Cognitive therapy is the newest form of therapy presented in this book. Cognitive therapists in general agree with Rogers that people are free to make choices and develop in accordance with their concepts of what they are capable of becoming. They also agree with Perls that it is appropriate for

---

Dialogue A Gestalt therapy technique in which clients verbalize confrontations between conflicting parts of their personality.

Cognitive therapy A form of therapy that focuses on how clients' cognitions (expectations, attitudes, beliefs, etc.) lead to distress and may be modified to relieve distress and promote adaptive behavior.

Who Is Albert Ellis?

clients to focus on the here and now, and they, too, are reasonably directive in their approaches.

I include cognitive therapy as an insight-oriented therapy because cognitive therapists focus on the beliefs, attitudes, and automatic types of thinking that create and compound our problems. Insight into clients' *current cognitions,* and not the distant past, is a primary goal of therapy. *Changing* these cognitions to reduce negative feelings, provide more accurate perceptions of the self and others, and orient the client toward solving problems in another goal.

Let us look at some specific cognitive-therapy approaches and methods.

Albert Ellis's Rational-Emotive Therapy   New York psychologist Albert Ellis is the founder of **rational-emotive therapy** and the second most influential psychotherapist in the Smith (1982) survey. Ellis (1977, 1987) notes that our beliefs about events, as well as the events themselves, fashion our reactions to them. Consider a case in which

one is upset about being fired from a job. It might appear that losing the job is responsible for the misery, but Ellis points out how beliefs about the loss compound misery. For example, the belief "There's nothing I can do about it" fosters helplessness. The belief "Losing this job means I'm worthless" is an exaggeration that might be based on perfectionism. The belief "My family will starve" is straightforward **catastrophizing.** Beliefs such as these compound misery, foster helplessness, and divert us from deciding what to do. Ellis proposes that we may harbor many of the following irrational beliefs and that they cause many of our interpersonal problems and anxieties. How many of these beliefs do you have? (Are you sure?)

Irrational Belief 1. You must have sincere love and approval almost all the time from the people who are important to you.

Irrational Belief 2. You must prove yourself thoroughly competent, adequate, and achieving.

Irrational Belief 3. Things must go the way you want them to, or else life is awful and horrible.

Irrational Belief 4. Other people must treat everyone fairly and justly, or else they are terrible and life is not worth living.

Irrational Belief 5. When there is danger or fear, you must be preoccupied with it.

Irrational Belief 6. Things should turn out better than they do, and it's awful when you don't find quick solutions to life's hassles.

Irrational Belief 7. Your emotional misery comes almost completely from external pressures that you have little or no ability to control. Unless these external pressures change, you must remain miserable.

Irrational Belief 8. It is easier to evade responsibilities and problems than to face them and show self-discipline.

Irrational Belief 9. Your past influenced you immensely and must therefore continue to determine your feelings and behavior today.

Irrational Belief 10. You can achieve happiness by inertia and inaction, or by just enjoying yourself from day to day.

Rational-emotive therapy Albert Ellis's form of cognitive psychotherapy, which focuses on how irrational expectations create anxiety and disappointment and encourages clients to challenge and correct these expectations.

Catastrophizing Exaggerating; blowing out of proportion.

Ellis points out that it is understandable that we would want the approval of others, but it is irrational to believe we cannot survive without it. It would be nice to be competent in everything we do, but it's unreasonable to expect it. Sure, it would be nice to serve and volley like a tennis pro, but most of us haven't the time or natural ability to perfect the game. Demanding self-perfection prevents us from going out on the courts on weekends and having fun. Belief 5 is a prescription for perpetual emotional upheaval. Beliefs 7 and 9 lead to feelings of helplessness and demoralization. Sure, Ellis might say, irrational beliefs may originate in childhood, but our own cognitive appraisal—here and now—causes the misery.

Rather than sitting back like the traditional psychoanalyst and occasionally offering an interpretation, Ellis actively urges clients to seek out irrational beliefs, which can be fleeting and hard to catch. He shows clients how their beliefs lead to misery and challenges them to change the beliefs.

Aaron Beck's Cognitive Therapy   Psychiatrist Aaron Beck (1976) also focuses on clients' cognitive distortions. He questions patients in a manner to encourage them to see the irrationality of their thinking—how, for example, minimizing accomplishments and assuming the worst will happen heightens feelings of depression. Beck, like Ellis, notes that cognitive distortions can be fleeting and automatic, difficult to detect. His therapy methods help clients pin them down.

In the discussion of depression in Chapter 9, it was noted that internal, stable, and global attributions of failure lead to feelings of helplessness and depression. Cognitive therapists alert clients to such cognitive distortions as a prelude to behavioral change.

Problem-Solving Training   Another cognitive-therapy approach, problem-solving training, encourages clients to use the stages of problem solving (see Chapter 5) to enhance control over their lives. Efficient problem solving involves studying all aspects of a problem (preparation), generating multiple solutions (production), trying them out, and evaluating their effectiveness (evaluation). Subjects receiving problem-solving training for preventing angry outbursts are encouraged to study sample provocations, to generate various behavioral solutions (alternatives to violence), and to try out and evaluate the most promising ones (e.g., Moon & Eisler, 1983). Subjects in the Moon and Eisler study learned to control their anger and respond to provocations with socially skillful (nonaggressive) behavior.

Evaluation of Cognitive Therapy   There is an increasing body of evidence that cognitive factors play a major role in behavior problems. They are particularly pertinent to feelings of anxiety and depression that are learned or acquired through experience. This is abundantly clear in phobias, where the client believes that a particular object or situation is awful and must be avoided, and in depressive reactions that are linked to internal, stable, and global attributions for failure. Cognitive approaches have yielded positive results with such problems. As an example, a study of methods for helping clients quit smoking showed that techniques that led clients to attribute cessation to *internal factors* resulted in longer abstinence from smoking than techniques that led clients to attribute cessation to external factors (Harackiewicz et al., 1987). Modification of Ellis's irrational beliefs has also been shown to decrease emotional distress (Lipsky et al., 1980; Smith, 1983). Reviews of the treatment literature have also found that cognitive-therapy clients show greater reduction of anxiety and depression than clients receiving traditional psychoanalytic or phenomenological treatments (Andrews & Harvey, 1981; Shapiro & Shapiro, 1982).

It should be noted that many theorists consider cognitive therapy to be a collection of techniques that belong within the province of behavior therapy, which is discussed in the following section. Some members of this group prefer the name "cognitive *behavior* therapy"; others argue that the term *behavior therapy* is broad enough to include cognitive techniques. However, there is a difference in focus. To behavior therapists, the purpose of dealing with cognitions is to change *overt* behavior. Cognitive therapists agree that cognitive change leads to overt change but assert that cognitive change is in and of itself a worthy goal.

BEHAVIOR THERAPY: ADJUSTMENT IS WHAT YOU DO

Behavior therapy—also called *behavior modification*—is the systematic application of principles of learning in the promotion of desired behavioral changes. As suggested in the section on cognitive therapy, behavior therapists incorporate cognitive processes in their theoretical outlook and cognitive procedures in their methodology (Wilson, 1982). For example, techniques such as *systematic desensitization, covert sensitization,* and *covert reinforcement* ask clients to focus on visual imagery. But behavior therapists insist that their methods be established by experimentation (Wolpe, 1985) and that therapeutic outcomes be assessed in terms of observable, measurable behavior.

Behavior therapists rely on principles of conditioning and observational learning. They help clients discontinue self-defeating behavior patterns, such as overeating, smoking, and phobic avoidance of harmless stimuli. They also help clients acquire adaptive behavior patterns, such as the social skills required to initiate relationships and to say no to insistent salespeople.

Behavior therapists help clients gain "insight" into maladaptive behavior in the sense of fostering awareness of the circumstances in which it occurs but not in the psychoanalytic sense of unearthing historic origins and symbolic meanings. Behavior therapists might also build warm, therapeutic relationships with clients, but they see the special efficacy of behavior therapy as deriving from specific learning-based procedures (Wolpe, 1985).

About 17 percent of the clinical and counseling psychologists surveyed by Smith (1982) labeled themselves behavioral or cognitive-behavioral in orientation—the largest group of therapists who identified with a specific orientation. Behavior therapists Joseph Wolpe and Arnold Lazarus were ranked fourth and fifth among the ten most influential psychotherapists (Smith, 1982, p. 807).

Let us look at a number of behavior-therapy techniques.

Systematic Desensitization

Adam has a phobia for receiving injections. His behavior therapist treats him as he reclines in a comfortable padded chair. In a state of deep muscular relaxation, Adam observes slides projected on a screen. A slide of a nurse holding a needle has just been shown three times, 30 seconds at a time. Each time Adam has shown no anxiety. So now a slightly more discomforting slide is shown: the nurse aiming the needle toward someone's bare arm. After 15 seconds our armchair adventurer notices twinges of discomfort and raises a finger as a signal (speaking might disturb his relaxation). The projector operator turns off the light, and Adam spends two minutes imagining his "safe scene"—lying on a beach beneath the tropical sun. Then the slide is shown again. This time Adam views it for 30 seconds before feeling anxiety.

Adam is undergoing **systematic desensitization,** a method originated by psychiatrist Joseph Wolpe (1958, 1973) for reducing phobic responses (Figure 10.2). Systematic desensitization is a gradual process. Clients learn to handle increasingly disturbing stimuli as anxiety to each one is counterconditioned. About 10 to 20 stimuli are arranged in a sequence, or hierarchy, according to their capacity to elicit anxiety. In imagination, or by being shown photos, the client travels gradually through this hierarchy, approaching the target behavior—ability to receive an injection without undue anxiety.

Wolpe developed systematic desensitization on the assumption that maladaptive anxiety responses, such as other behaviors, are learned or conditioned. He reasoned that they can be unlearned by counterconditioning, or by extinction (see Chapter 4). In counterconditioning, a response that is incompatible with anxiety is made to appear under conditions that usually elicit anxiety. Muscle relaxation is incompatible with anxiety. For this reason Adam's therapist is teaching Adam to

Behavior therapy Systematic application of the principles of learning to the direct modification of a client's problem behaviors.

Systematic desensitization Wolpe's method for reducing fears by associating a hierarchy of images of fear-evoking stimuli with deep muscle relaxation.

FIGURE 10.2. What Is Systematic Desensitization? In the systematic desensitization of fears, clients engage in deep muscle relaxation while the therapist presents a graduated series of fear-evoking stimuli.

experience relaxation in the presence of (usually) anxiety-evoking slides of needles.

Remaining in the presence of phobic imagery, rather than running from it, is also likely to enhance our self-efficacy expectations. Self-efficacy expectations are negatively correlated with levels of adrenalin in the bloodstream (Bandura et al., 1985). And so raising their self-efficacy expectations might help clients lower adrenalin levels to counteract nervousness and physical signs of anxiety.

The Symptom-Substitution Controversy Psychoanalysts have argued that phobias are symptoms of unconscious conflicts and that systematic desensitization of a "symptom" might only lead to the appearance of another symptom—that is, to **symptom substitution.** To behavior therapists, maladaptive behavior *is* the problem, not just a symptom of the problem. Evidence suggests that systematic desensitization is effective in more than 80 percent of cases (Paul, 1969a; Marks, 1982; Smith & Glass, 1977), and symptom substitution has not been found to be a problem.

Participant Modeling A behavioral alternative to systematic desensitization is **participant modeling,** which relies on observational learning. In this method, clients observe and then imitate people who do approach and cope with the objects or situations they fear. Bandura and his colleagues (1969) found that participant modeling worked as well as systematic desensitization, and more rapidly, in reducing fear of snakes (see Figure 10.3). Participant modeling, like systematic desensitization, is likely to increase self-efficacy expectations in coping with feared stimuli.

In any event, systematic desensitization is a largely "painless" way to confront fears.

Aversive Conditioning

You might have read or seen the filmed version of the futuristic Anthony Burgess novel, *A Clockwork Orange.* Alex, the antisocial "hero," finds violence and rape superb pastimes. When he is caught, he is given the chance to undergo an experimental

Symptom substitution The emergence of a second symptom when the first symptom is relieved.

Participant modeling A behavior-therapy technique in which a client observes and imitates a person who approaches and copes with feared objects or situations.

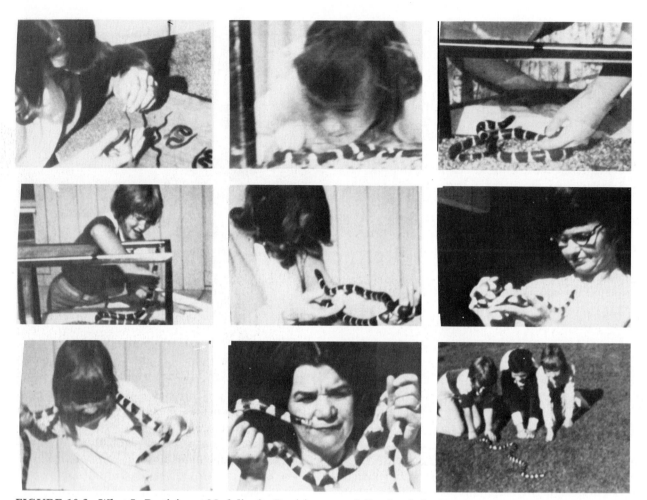

FIGURE 10.3. What Is Participant Modeling? Participant modeling is a behavior-therapy technique based on principles of observational learning. In this example, people with an aversion for snakes observe and then imitate people who are unafraid. Parents often try to convince young children that something tastes good by eating it in front of them and saying "Mmm!"

reconditioning program rather than serve a prison term. In this program, he watches films of violence and rape while he is vomiting as a result of a nausea-inducing drug. After his release, he feels ill whenever he contemplates violence. Unfortunately, Beethoven's music, which he had enjoyed,

accompanies the films and feelings of nausea. So Alex acquires an aversion for Beethoven as well.

In the novel, Alex undergoes a program of **aversive conditioning**—also called *aversion therapy*—which is actually used quite frequently today, although not in prisons. It is one of the more controversial procedures in behavior therapy. In aversive conditioning, painful or aversive stimuli are paired with unwanted impulses—such as desire for a cigarette or desire to engage in antisocial behavior—in order to make the goal less appealing. For example, in order to help people control alcohol

Aversive conditioning A behavior-therapy technique in which undesired responses are inhibited by pairing repugnant or offensive stimuli with them.

intake, tastes of different alcoholic beverages can be paired with drug-induced nausea and vomiting or with electric shock (Wilson et al., 1975).

Aversive conditioning has been used with some success in treating problems as divergent as paraphilias (Rathus, 1983), cigarette smoking (Lichtenstein, 1982; Walker & Franzoni, 1985), and retarded children's self-injurious behavior. In one large-scale study of aversive conditioning in the treatment of alcoholism, 63 percent of the 685 people treated remained abstinent for one year, and about a third remained abstinent for at least three years (Wiens & Menustik, 1983).

A number of aversive-conditioning techniques are used to help people quit smoking. In one, rapid smoking, the would-be quitter inhales every six seconds. Overexposure renders once-desirable cigarette smoke aversive. The quitter becomes motivated to avoid, rather than seek, cigarettes and stops smoking on a preplanned date. Many reports have shown a quit rate of 60 percent or higher at six-month follow-ups.

Rapid smoking is popular because it is effective and the apparatus is readily available—the quitter's own cigarettes. But in addition to producing discomfort, rapid smoking raises the blood pressure, decreases the blood's capacity to carry oxygen, and produces heart abnormalities, as shown by the electrocardiogram (Lichtenstein & Glasgow, 1977). Nevertheless, a two-year follow-up study of cardiac and pulmonary patients found no negative effects from rapid smoking (Hall et al., 1984). We must also consider the positive benefits of quitting for these patients.

What Is Aversive Conditioning?   In aversive conditioning, cravings for harmful stimuli, such as cigarette smoke, are broken by associating the harmful stimuli with aversive stimuli. As a result, the harmful stimuli take on aversive qualities. In an application of this method for quitting smoking, overexposure to once-desirable cigarette smoke makes smoke aversive rather than pleasurable.

Operant Conditioning

We tend to repeat behavior that is reinforced. Behavior that is not reinforced tends to become extinguished. Behavior therapists have applied these principles of operant conditioning with psychotic patients as well as clients with milder problems.

The staff at one mental hospital did not know how to encourage withdrawn schizophrenic patients to eat regularly. Ayllon and Haughton (1962) observed that the staff were exacerbating the problem by coaxing patients into the dining room, even feeding them. Increased staff attention apparently reinforced the patients for noncooperation. Some rules were changed. Patients who did not arrive at the dining hall within 30 minutes after serving were locked out. Staff could not interact with patients at mealtime. With uncooperative behavior no longer reinforced, patients quickly changed their eating habits. Patients were then required to pay one penny to enter the dining hall. Pennies were earned by interacting with other patients and showing other socially appropriate behaviors. These target behaviors also increased in frequency.

What Is Assertiveness Training? The behavior-therapy method of assertiveness training aims to decrease social anxiety and enhance social skills by having clients refine appropriate social behavior in the therapeutic setting.

Many psychiatric wards and hospitals now use **token economies,** in which tokens, like poker chips, must be used by patients to purchase TV time, extra visits to the canteen, or private rooms. The tokens are reinforcements for productive activities such as making beds, brushing teeth, and socializing. Whereas token economies have not eliminated all symptoms of schizophrenia, they have enhanced patients' activity and cooperation. Tokens have also been used successfully in programs designed to modify the behavior of children with conduct disorders. For example, Schneider and Byrne (1987) gave children tokens for helpful behaviors such as volunteering and removed tokens for behaviors such as arguing and inattention.

We can often use the operant-conditioning method of **successive approximations** in building good habits. Let us use a (not uncommon!) example: You wish to study three hours an evening but can only maintain concentration for half an hour. Rather than attempting to increase study time all at once, you could do so gradually, say by five minutes an evening. After every hour or so of studying, you could reinforce yourself with five minutes of people watching in a busy section of the library.

Assertiveness Training

Are you a person who can't say no? Do people walk all over you? Brush off those footprints and get some **assertiveness training!** Assertiveness training helps clients decrease social anxieties and is also used to optimize the functioning of individuals without problems.

Assertive behavior can be contrasted with both *nonassertive* (submissive) behavior and *aggressive* behavior. Assertive people express their genuine feelings, stick up for their legitimate rights, and refuse unreasonable requests. But they do not insult, threaten, or belittle. Assertive people also express positive feelings such as liking and love.

Token economy A controlled environment in which people are reinforced for desired behaviors with tokens (such as poker chips) that may be exchanged for privileges.

Successive approximations In operant conditioning, a series of behaviors that gradually become more similar to a target behavior.

Assertiveness training Behavior-therapy techniques that teach clients to express feelings, seek fair treatment, and improve social skills.

"Well, I'm sorry if my remarks hurt your feelings, but I think it's a little unfair of you to blame me. I said those things on the advice of a highly qualified therapist."

What's Wrong with This Cartoon?
It's true, of course, that psychologists of many theoretical persuasions encourage clients to express their feelings. However, "qualified" therapists also encourage clients to take responsibility for their own behavior—not to attribute their misdeeds to the suggestions of others.

Assertiveness training decreases social anxiety and builds social skills through techniques such as *self-monitoring, modeling,* and *behavior rehearsal.* In **self-monitoring,** the client keeps a record of upsetting social encounters in order to pinpoint instances of social avoidance, clumsiness, and feelings of frustration. The therapist **models** more effective social behavior and encourages the client to rehearse or practice this behavior as the therapist provides **feedback.** The therapist attends to the client's posture, facial expressions, and tone of voice as well as to the content of what is being said.

The therapist might also point out that various irrational beliefs can impede progress. Beliefs to the effect that it is awful to earn the disapproval of others or to fumble at the first few attempts at behavioral change are likely to increase, rather than decrease, social anxieties. Clients need to learn to reward themselves for small but consistent gains rather than condemn themselves for imperfection.

Assertiveness training is effective in groups. Group members can role play important people in the lives of other members, such as parents, spouses, or potential dates. The trainee then engages in **behavior rehearsal** with the role player.

Self-monitoring Keeping a record of one's own behavior to identify problems and record successes.

Model To engage in behaviors that are imitated by others.

Feedback In assertiveness training, information about the effectiveness of a response.

Behavior rehearsal Practice.

Questionnaire

The Rathus assertiveness schedule

How assertive are you? Do you stick up for your rights, or do you allow others to walk all over you? Do you say what you feel, or do you say what you think others want you to say? Do you start up relationships with attractive people, or do you shy away from them?

To see how assertive you are compared to other college students, take this self-report test of assertiveness. Then turn to Appendix C to calculate your score and compare it to those of a sample of 1,400 students drawn from campuses across the United States.

Directions: Indicate how well each item describes you according to this code:

  3 = very much like me
  2 = rather like me
  1 = slightly like me
  −1 = slightly unlike me
  −2 = rather unlike me
  −3 = very much unlike me

_____ **1.** Most people seem to be more aggressive and assertive than I am.*
_____ **2.** I have hesitated to make or accept dates because of "shyness."*
_____ **3.** When the food served at a restaurant is not done to my satisfaction, I complain about it to the waiter or waitress.
_____ **4.** I am careful to avoid hurting other people's feelings, even when I feel that I have been injured.*
_____ **5.** If a salesperson has gone to considerable trouble to show me merchandise that is not quite suitable, I have a difficult time saying no.*
_____ **6.** When I am asked to do something, I insist upon knowing why.
_____ **7.** There are times when I look for a good, vigorous argument.
_____ **8.** I strive to get ahead as strongly as most people in my position.
_____ **9.** To be honest, people often take advantage of me.*

Self-Control Techniques

Does it sometimes seem that mysterious forces are at work? Forces that delight in wreaking havoc with your New Year's resolutions and other efforts to take charge of bad habits? Just when you go on a diet, that juicy Big Mac stares at you from the TV set. Just when you resolve to balance your budget, that sweater goes on sale. Behavior therapists have developed a number of self-control techniques to help people cope with such temptations.

Functional analysis A systematic study of behavior in which one identifies the stimuli that trigger it and the reinforcers that maintain it.

Functional Analysis of Behavior   Behavior therapists first do a **functional analysis** of the problem behavior to determine the stimuli that

_____ **10.** I enjoy starting conversations with new acquaintances and strangers.

_____ **11.** I often don't know what to say to attractive persons of the opposite sex.*

_____ **12.** I will hesitate to make phone calls to business establishments and institutions.*

_____ **13.** I would rather apply for a job or for admission to a college by writing letters than by going through with personal interviews.*

_____ **14.** I find it embarrassing to return merchandise.*

_____ **15.** If a close and respected relative were annoying me, I would smother my feelings rather than express my annoyance.*

_____ **16.** I have avoided asking questions for fear of sounding stupid.*

_____ **17.** During an argument I am sometimes afraid that I will get so upset that I will shake all over.*

_____ **18.** If a famed and respected lecturer makes a comment which I think is incorrect, I will have the audience hear my point of view as well.

_____ **19.** I avoid arguing over prices with clerks and salespeople.*

_____ **20.** When I have done something important or worthwhile, I manage to let others know about it.

_____ **21.** I am open and frank about my feelings.

_____ **22.** If someone has been spreading false and bad stories about me, I see him or her as soon as possible and "have a talk" about it.

_____ **23.** I often have a hard time saying no.*

_____ **24.** I tend to bottle up my emotions rather than make a scene.*

_____ **25.** I complain about poor service in a restaurant and elsewhere.

_____ **26.** When I am given a compliment, I sometimes just don't know what to say.*

_____ **27.** If a couple near me in a theater or at a lecture were conversing rather loudly, I would ask them to be quiet or to take their conversation elsewhere.

_____ **28.** Anyone attempting to push ahead of me in a line is in for a good battle.

_____ **29.** I am quick to express an opinion.

_____ **30.** There are times when I just can't say anything.*

Source: Reprinted from Rathus (1973), pp. 398–406.

---

seem to trigger it and the reinforcers that seem to maintain it. In a functional analysis, you use a diary to jot down each instance of the behavior. You note the time of day, location, your activity (including your thoughts and feelings), and reactions (yours and others').

Functional analysis serves a number of purposes. For example, it makes you more aware of the environmental context of your behavior and can increase your motivation to change. In studies with highly motivated people, functional analysis alone has been found to increase the amount of time spent studying (Johnson & White, 1971) and talking in a therapy group (Komaki & Dore-Boyce, 1978) and to decrease cigarette consumption (Lipinski et al., 1975).

Brian used functional analysis to learn about his nail biting. Table 10.2 shows a few items from his notebook. He discovered that boredom and humdrum activities seemed to serve as triggers for

Table 10.2   Excerpts from Brian's Diary of Nail Biting for April 14

INCIDENT	TIME	LOCATION	ACTIVITY (THOUGHTS, FEELINGS)	REACTIONS
1	7:45 A.M.	Freeway	Driving to work, bored, not thinking	Finger bleeds, pain
2	10:30 A.M.	Office	Writing report	Self-disgust
3	2:25 P.M.	Conference	Listening to dull financial report	Embarrassment
4	6:40 P.M.	Living room	Watching evening news	Self-disgust

A functional analysis of problem behavior, like nail biting, increases awareness of the environmental context in which it occurs; spurs motivation to change; and in highly motivated people, might lead to significant behavioral change.

nail biting. He began to watch out for feelings of boredom as signs to practice self-control. He also made some changes in his life, so that he would feel bored less often.

There are a number of self-control strategies aimed at (1) the stimuli that trigger behavior, (2) the behaviors themselves, and (3) reinforcers.

Strategies Aimed at Stimuli That Trigger Behavior

Restriction of the stimulus field. Gradually exclude the problem behavior from more environments. For example, for a while first do not smoke while driving, then extend not smoking to the office. Or practice the habit only outside the environment in which it normally occurs. Psychologist J. Dennis Nolan's (1968) wife had tried to stop smoking several times—to no avail. Finally the Nolans applied restriction of the stimulus field by limiting her smoking to one place—a "smoking chair." The rule was that Ms. Nolan could smoke as much as she wanted to, but only in that chair. Also, smoking was the only activity permitted in the chair. The chair was set in a "stimulus-deprived" corner of the basement so that smoking would become dissociated from its usual triggers, such as watching television, reading, and conversing. Ms. Nolan's awareness of the details of her habit increased, and she had more opportunity to reflect on her reasons for cutting down. Her smoking fell off, and after a few weeks of humiliating trips to the basement, she quit altogether.

Avoidance of powerful stimuli that trigger habits. Avoid obvious sources of temptation. People who go window shopping often wind up buying more than windows. If eating at The Pizza Glutton tempts you to forget your diet, eat at home or at The Celery Stalk instead.

Stimulus control. Place yourself in an environment in which desirable behavior is likely to occur. Maybe it's difficult to lift your mood directly at times, but you can place yourself in the audience of that uplifting concert or film. It might be difficult to force yourself to study, but how about rewarding yourself for spending time in the library?

Strategies Aimed at Behavior

Response prevention. Make unwanted behavior difficult or impossible. Impulse buying is curbed when you shred your credit cards, leave your checkbook home, and carry only a couple of dollars. You can't reach for the strawberry cream cheese pie in your refrigerator if you have left it at the supermarket (that is, have not bought it).

Competing responses. Engage in behaviors that are incompatible with the bad habits. It is difficult to drink a glass of water and a fattening milkshake simultaneously. Grasping something firmly is a useful competing response for nail biting or scratching.

Chain breaking. Interfere with unwanted habitual behavior by complicating the process of engaging in it. Break the chain of reaching for a readily available cigarette and placing it in your mouth by wrapping the pack in aluminum foil and placing it on the top shelf in the closet. Rewrap the pack after taking one. Put your cigarette in the ashtray between puffs, or put your fork down between mouthfuls of dessert. Ask yourself if you really want more.

Successive approximations. Gradually approach targets through a series of relatively painless steps.

Increase studying by only five minutes a day. Decrease smoking by pausing for a minute when the cigarette is smoked halfway or by putting it out a minute before you would wind up eating the filter. Decrease your daily intake of food by 50 to 100 calories every couple of days, or else cut out one type of fattening food every few days.

Strategies Aimed at Reinforcements

Reinforcement of desired behavior. Why give yourself something for nothing? Make pleasant activities, like going to films, walking on the beach, or reading a new novel, contingent upon meeting reasonable, daily behavioral goals. Put one dollar away toward that camera or vacation trip each day you remain within your calorie limit.

Response cost. Heighten awareness of the long-term reasons for dieting or cutting down on smoking by punishing yourself for not meeting a daily goal or for practicing a bad habit. Make out a check to your most hated cause and mail it at once if you bite your nails or inhale that cheesecake.

"Grandma's method." Remember Grandma's method for inducing children to eat their vegetables? Simple: No veggies, no dessert. In this method, desired behaviors, like studying and brushing teeth, can be increased by insisting that they be done before you carry out a favored or frequently occurring activity. For example, don't watch television unless you have studied first. Don't leave the apartment until you've brushed your teeth.

Covert sensitization. Create imaginary horror stories about problem behavior. Psychologists have successfully reduced overeating and smoking by having clients imagine that they become acutely nauseated at the thought of fattening foods or that a cigarette is made from vomit. Some horror stories are not so "imaginary." Deliberately focusing on heart strain and diseased lungs every time you overeat or smoke, rather than ignoring these long-term consequences, might also promote self-control.

Covert reinforcement. Create rewarding imagery for desired behavior. When you have achieved a behavioral goal, fantasize about how wonderful you are. Imagine friends and family patting you on the back. Fantasize about the *Playboy* or *Playgirl* centerfold for a minute.

Behaviorally Oriented Sex-Therapy Methods

Behaviorally oriented sex therapists treat the sexual dysfunctions discussed in Chapter 9 by directly modifying problem sexual behavior. Treatment of most dysfunctions is enhanced by the cooperation of a patient sex partner, and so it might be useful to work on the couple's relationship before sex therapy itself is undertaken. But it is not considered necessary to gain insight into possible deep-seated roots of dysfunctions.

Sex therapy focuses on (1) reducing performance anxiety, (2) increasing self-efficacy expectations, and (3) enhancing sexual competencies (knowledge and skills). The sex therapists, often a male and female therapy team, educate the couple and guide them through sexual "homework" assignments. The sex-therapy pioneers Masters and Johnson (1970) have a standard two-week treatment format for couples in residence at their clinic. Other therapists find that the format need not be so rigid (Kaplan, 1974; Zilbergeld & Evans, 1980). Even "bibliotherapy"—or self-treatment based on self-help manuals—has been found helpful in some cases (e.g., Dodge et al., 1982).

Let us note some features of the Masters and Johnson therapy program that are used for all dysfunctions. The couple are asked to refrain from sexual activity while histories are taken and they receive physical examinations. Their first contact involves **sensate focus exercises,** in which they take turns giving and receiving pleasure without touching one another's genitals. In this way, physical interaction once more becomes pleasurable, and nothing is "demanded" of either partner. Neither partner feels he or she must become sexually aroused or reach orgasm, and so performance anxiety is countered. Erroneous ideas about sex are explored, and the couple is instructed in sexual anatomy and technique.

Methods then diverge according to the specific dysfunction. But some general concepts can be noted again. A gradual, nonpressured expansion

---

Sensate focus exercises Massage methods in which members of couples give one another pleasure without directly stimulating the genitals.

of sensate focus exercises to genital areas is helpful in treatment of hypoactive sexual desire, female sexual arousal disorder, male erectile disorder, and inhibited orgasm. Sexual pleasure and arousal are enhanced. Fears of failure—which lower self-efficacy expectations—are reduced.

Behaviorally oriented sex-therapy methods have revolutionized treatment of the sexual dysfunctions. Only 30 years ago no effective treatment for these problems was available. Today most of them can be reversed.

Evaluation of Behavior Therapy

Behavior therapy has provided a number of strategies for treating anxiety, mild depression, social-skills deficits, sexual disorders, and problems in self-control. Behavior therapists have also innovated treatments for phobias and sexual dysfunctions, for which there had not previously been effective treatments. Smith and Glass (1977) found that about 80 percent of those receiving behavior-therapy treatments, such as systematic desensitization and strategies for self-control, showed greater well-being than people who were untreated—as compared to percentages in the low to middle 70s for psychoanalytic and phenomenological approaches.

In analyses of studies that directly compare treatment techniques, behavior-therapy, psychoanalytic, and phenomenological approaches have been found about equal in overall effectiveness (Berman et al., 1985; Smith et al., 1980). However, psychoanalytic and phenomenological approaches seem to foster greater self-understanding, whereas behavior-therapy techniques (including cognitive-behavioral techniques) show superior results in problems such as phobias and sexual dysfunctions. Behavior therapy has also been effective in helping to manage institutionalized populations, including schizophrenics and the mentally retarded.

So it is not enough to ask which type of therapy is most effective. We must ask, instead, which type of therapy is most effective for a particular problem? What are its advantages? What are its limitations? Clients might successfully use systematic desensitization to overcome stage fright, as measured by actual ability to talk before a group of people. But if clients also want to know *why* they have stage fright, behavior therapy alone will not satisfy them.

GROUP THERAPY

When a psychotherapist has several clients with similar problems—whether stress management, adjustment to divorce, lack of social skills, or anxiety—it often makes sense to treat them in groups of six to twelve rather than conduct individual therapy. The methods and characteristics of the group will reflect the needs of the members and the theoretical orientation of the leader. In a psychoanalytic group, clients might interpret one another's dreams. In a person-centered group, they might provide an accepting atmosphere for self-exploration. Clients in a TA group might comment on the games played by others. Behavior-therapy groups might undergo joint desensitization to anxiety-evoking stimuli or model and rehearse social skills.

There are several advantages to group therapy:

1. Group therapy is economical, allowing several clients to be seen at once.
2. There is a greater fund of information and experience for clients to draw on.
3. Appropriate behavior receives the emotional support of the group rather than the therapist alone.
4. Group members who show improvement provide hope for others.
5. Group members can rehearse social skills with one another in a relatively nonthreatening atmosphere.

Still, many clients prefer individual therapy because they do not wish to disclose their problems to a group, are inhibited in front of others, or desire individual attention. It is the responsibility of the therapist to require that disclosures be kept confidential, to establish a supportive atmosphere, and to see that group members receive the attention they need.

Many types of therapy can be conducted either individually or in groups. Encounter groups

A Touching Exercise? Many groups use touching exercises to help members grow comfortable with one another. This encourages them to be open about feelings and to try out new, adaptive behavior patterns.

and family therapy can be conducted in group format only.

Encounter Groups

Encounter groups are not appropriate for treating serious psychological problems. Rather, they are intended to promote personal growth by heightening awareness of one's own needs and feelings and those of others. This goal is sought through intense confrontations, or encounters, between strangers. Like ships in the night, group members come together out of the darkness, touch one another briefly, then sink back into the shadows of one another's lives. But something is thought to be gained from the passing.

Encounter groups stress interactions among group members in the here and now. Discussion of the past might be outlawed. Interpretation is out. Expression of genuine feelings toward others is encouraged. When group members think that a person's social mask is phony, they might descend en masse to rip it off.

Professionals recognize that encounter groups can be damaging when they urge overly rapid disclosure of intimate matters or when several members attack one member in unison. Responsible

leaders do not tolerate these abuses and try to keep groups moving in growth-enhancing directions.

Family Therapy

In **family therapy,** one or more families constitute the group. Family therapy might be undertaken from various theoretical viewpoints. One is the systems approach, for which much credit is to be given family therapist Virginia Satir (1967). In Satir's method, the family system of interaction is studied and modified to enhance the growth of family members and of the family unit as a whole.

It is often found that family members with low self-esteem cannot tolerate different attitudes and behaviors from other family members. Faulty family communications also create problems. It is also not uncommon for the family to present an "identified patient"—that is, the family member who has

Encounter group A type of group that aims to foster self-awareness by focusing on how group members relate to each other in a setting that encourages open expression of feelings.

Family therapy A form of therapy in which the family unit is treated as the client.

the problem and is *causing* all the trouble. But family therapists usually assume that the identified patient is a scapegoat for other problems within and among family members. It is a sort of myth: Change the bad apple (identified patient) and the barrel (the family) will be functional once more.

The family therapist—who is often a specialist in this field—attempts to teach the family to communicate more effectively and to encourage growth and the eventual **autonomy** of each family member. In doing so, the family therapist will also show the family how the identified patient has been used as a focus for the problems of other members of the group.

There are many other types of groups: marathon groups, sensitivity-training groups, and psychodrama groups, to name just a few.

Evaluation of Group Therapy

An evaluation of group therapy must consider the intentions and goals of the various formats. Generally speaking, it is easiest to demonstrate the effectiveness of behavior-therapy groups because of the emphasis on measurable outcomes. Group desensitization, for example, works about as well as individual desensitization. A study of encounter groups suggests that they might hurt as many people as they help (Lieberman et al., 1973).

Generally speaking, people who desire a group experience should make certain that the leader is a qualified member of a helping profession and that their personal goals are consistent with group goals and methods.

BIOLOGICAL THERAPIES

In the 1950s Fats Domino popularized the song "My Blue Heaven." Fats was singing about the sky

and happiness. But today "blue heavens" is the street name for the ten-milligram dose of one of the more widely prescribed drugs in the world: Valium. The **minor tranquilizer** Valium became popular because it reduces anxiety and tension. The manufacturer also once claimed that people could not become addicted to Valium nor readily kill themselves with overdoses. Today Valium looks more dangerous. Some people who have been using high doses go into convulsions when use is suspended. And now and then someone dies from mixing Valium with alcohol, or someone shows unusual sensitivity to the drug.

Psychiatrists and other physicians prescribe Valium and other drugs as chemical therapy, or **chemotherapy,** for various forms of abnormal behavior. In this section we shall discuss chemotherapy, *electroconvulsive therapy,* and *psychosurgery,* three biological or medical approaches to treating abnormal behavior.

Chemotherapy

In this section we shall discuss minor tranquilizers, major tranquilizers, antidepressants, and lithium.

Minor Tranquilizers   Valium is only one of many (many) minor tranquilizers. Some of the others are Librium, Miltown, Atarax, Serax, and Equanil. These drugs are usually prescribed for outpatients who complain of anxiety or tension, although many people also use them as sleeping pills. Valium and other tranquilizers are theorized to depress the activity of parts of the central nervous system. The CNS, in turn, decreases sympathetic activity, reducing the heart rate, respiration rate, and feelings of nervousness and tension (Caplan et al., 1983).

With regular use, unfortunately, people begin to tolerate small doses of these drugs very quickly. Doses must be increased for the drug to remain effective. Some patients become embroiled in tugs-of-war with their doctors when the doctors become concerned about the doses they are using. Doctors typically want patients to cut down "for their own good," but patients resent them for getting them "started" with drugs and then playing moralists.

Autonomy Self-direction

Minor tranquilizer A drug that relieves feelings of anxiety and tension.

Chemotherapy The use of drugs to treat disordered behavior.

"It's no use, Marvin. We tried tenderness and we tried Valium and you're still impossible."

Major Tranquilizers Schizophrenic patients are likely to be treated with **major tranquilizers,** or "antipsychotic" drugs. Many of them, including Thorazine, Mellaril, and Stelazine, belong to the chemical class of **phenothiazines** and are thought to act by blocking the action of dopamine in the brain.

In most cases, major tranquilizers reduce agitation, delusions, and hallucinations (May, 1975; Watson et al., 1978). Major tranquilizers account in large part for the lessened need for various forms of restraint and supervision (padded cells, straitjackets, hospitalization, etc.) used with schizophrenic patients. More than any other single form of treatment, major tranquilizers have allowed hundreds of thousands of patients to lead largely normal lives in the community, to hold jobs and maintain family lives.

Unfortunately, blocking of dopamine action over the years can lead to a condition called **tardive dyskinesia,** whose symptoms are similar to those

Major tranquilizer A drug that decreases severe anxiety or agitation in psychotic patients or in violent individuals.

Phenothiazines A family of drugs that act as major tranquilizers and are effective in treating many cases of schizophrenic disorders.

Tardive dyskinesia A motor disorder linked with prolonged use of antipsychotic drugs.

of Parkinson's disease, including tremors and muscular rigidity (Calne, 1977; Jus et al., 1976; Levitt, 1981). Immediate side effects can usually be controlled by drugs that are used for Parkinsonism.

Antidepressants   There are two types of **antidepressant** drugs. Each type increases the brain concentrations of norepinephrine and serotonin in a different way. **Monoamine oxidase inhibitors** (MAO inhibitors) block the activity of an enzyme that breaks down norepinephrine and serotonin. Nardil and Parnate are examples of MAO inhibitors. **Tricyclic antidepressants** prevent reuptake of norepinephrine and serotonin by the axon terminals of the transmitting neurons. As a result, the neurotransmitters remain in the synaptic cleft for a greater amount of time, enhancing the probability that they will dock at receptor sites on receiving neurons. Tofranil and Elavil are examples of tricyclic antidepressants.

Antidepressants tend to alleviate the physical aspects of depression. For example, they tend to increase the patient's activity level and to reduce eating and sleeping disturbances (Lyons et al., 1985; Weissman et al., 1981). In this way patients might become more receptive to psychotherapy, which addresses the cognitive and social aspects of depression.

Lithium   In a sense, the ancient Greeks and Romans were among the first to use the metal lithium as a psychoactive drug. They would prescribe mineral water for patients with bipolar disorder. They had no inkling of why this treatment sometimes helped, but it might have been because mineral water contains lithium. A salt of the metal lithium (lithium carbonate), in tablet form, flattens out cycles of manicky behavior and depression for most sufferers, apparently by moderating the level of norepinephrine available to the brain.

Since lithium is more toxic than most drugs, the dose must be carefully monitored during early phases of therapy by repeated analysis of blood samples. It might be necessary for persons with bipolar disorder to use lithium indefinitely, just as a medical patient with diabetes must continue insulin to control the illness. Lithium has also been shown to have the side effects of impairing memory and depressing motor speed (Shaw et al., 1987).

Evaluation of Chemotherapy   There is little question that major tranquilizers, antidepressants, and lithium help many persons with severe psychiatric disorders. They enable thousands of formerly hospitalized patients to enter or return to the community and lead productive lives. Moreover, their potential for helping persons with eating disorders looks promising. Drug-related problems often concern their dosage and side effects.

Minor tranquilizers are frequently abused by overuse. Many people request them to dull the arousal that stems from anxiety-producing lifestyles or interpersonal problems. Rather than make the often painful decisions required to confront their problems and change their lives, they find it easier to pop a pill—at least for a while. Then the dosage must be increased if the drug is to remain effective, and substance dependence becomes a possibility. Another problem is that many family doctors find it easier to prescribe minor tranquilizers than to help patients examine their lives and change anxiety-evoking conditions. The doctor's lot is not eased by the fact that many patients want pills, not conversation.

Electroconvulsive Therapy

Electroconvulsive therapy (ECT) was introduced by Italian psychiatrist Ugo Cerletti in 1939 for use with psychiatric patients. Cerletti had noted that some slaughterhouses used electric shock to render animals unconscious. The shocks also produced convulsions, and Cerletti erroneously be-

---

Antidepressant Acting to relieve depression.

Monoamine oxidase inhibitors Antidepressant drugs that work by blocking the action of an enzyme that breaks down norepinephrine and serotonin.

Tricyclic antidepressants Antidepressant drugs that work by preventing reuptake of norepinephrine and serotonin by transmitting neurons.

Electroconvulsive therapy Treatment of disorders like major depression by passing an electric current (that causes a convulsion) through the head.

lieved, as did other European researchers of the period, that convulsions were incompatible with schizophrenia and other major disorders.

After the advent of major tranquilizers, the use of ECT was generally limited to treatment of people with major depression. The discovery of antidepressants limited the use of ECT even further—to patients who do not respond to these drugs. But even as a therapy of last resort, ECT is still used with about 60,000 to 100,000 people a year in the United States (Sackeim, 1985).

In ECT electrodes are attached to the temples and an electric current strong enough to induce unconsciousness and a seizure is passed between them. ECT patients typically receive one treatment three times a week for several weeks. Patients are usually put to sleep with a sedative prior to treatment. In the past, ECT patients flailed about wildly during the convulsions, sometimes breaking bones. Today they are given muscle-relaxing drugs, and convulsions are barely perceptible to onlookers. ECT is not given to patients with cardiovascular problems.

ECT is controversial for many reasons. First, many professionals are distressed by the thought of passing electric shock through the head and producing convulsions (even if they are suppressed by drugs). Second, there are the side effects. ECT disrupts recall of recent events. Although memory functioning usually seems near normal for most patients a few months after treatment, some patients appear to suffer permanent memory impairment (Roueche, 1980). Third, nobody knows *why* ECT works. Still, there is evidence that ECT brings many immobilized patients out of their depression when antidepressant drugs fail (Janicak et al., 1985). Also, memory impairment might be minimized by giving patients the lowest dose of electricity required to produce seizures and by applying the electrical current to one side of the head only (Sackeim et al., 1985).

Psychosurgery

Psychosurgery is more controversial than ECT. The best-known modern technique, the **prefrontal lobotomy,** has been used with severely disturbed patients. In this method, a picklike instrument is

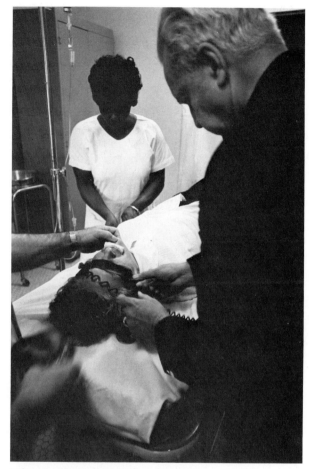

What Is Electroconvulsive Therapy? In ECT, electrodes are placed on each side of the patient's head, and a current is passed between them. Sufficient voltage induces a seizure. ECT is used mostly in cases of major depression where antidepressant drugs fail. ECT is quite controversial. Many observers find ECT barbaric, and there are negative side effects.

used to sever crudely the nerve pathways that link the prefrontal lobes of the brain to the thalamus. The prefrontal lobotomy was pioneered by the Portuguese neurologist Antonio Egas Moniz and was brought to the United States in the 1930s. It

Psychosurgery Surgery intended to promote psychological changes or to relieve disordered behavior.

Prefrontal lobotomy The severing or destruction of a section of the frontal lobe of the brain.

was performed on more than a thousand mental patients by 1950. Although the prefrontal lobotomy often reduces violence and agitation, it is not universally successful. One of Dr. Moniz's failures shot him, leaving a bullet lodged in his spine and causing paralysis in his legs.

The prefrontal lobotomy also has a host of side effects, including hyperactivity and distractibility, impaired learning ability, overeating, apathy and withdrawal, epileptic-type seizures, reduced creativity and, now and then, death. Because of these side effects, and because of the advent of major tranquilizers, the prefrontal lobotomy has been largely discontinued.

In recent years a number of more refined psychosurgery techniques have been devised for various purposes. Generally speaking, they focus on smaller areas of the brain and leave less damage in their wake than does the prefrontal lobotomy. As pointed out by Elliot Valenstein (1980), these operations have been performed to treat problems ranging from aggression to depression, psychotic behavior, chronic pain, and epilepsy. Follow-up studies of these contemporary procedures find that slightly more than half of them result in marked improvement (Corkin, 1980; Mirsky & Orzack, 1980). Moreover, no major neurological damage was attributable to these operations.

In sum, biological forms of therapy, particularly chemotherapy, seem desirable for major psychiatric disorders that do not respond to psychotherapy or behavior therapy alone. But common sense as well as research evidence suggest that psychological methods of therapy are preferable with problems such as anxiety, mild depression, and interpersonal conflict. No chemical can show a client how to change an idea or solve an interpersonal problem. Chemicals can only dull the pain of failure and put off the day when the client must deal with reality. ECT and psychosurgery should probably still be considered experimental, with use limited to severe cases in which all else fails.

TRUTH OR FICTION REVISITED

People in Merry Old England used to visit the local insane asylum for a fun night out on the town. True. People with severe disturbances were often chained and mistreated, and the public was frequently much amused.

Many of the nation's homeless are people who have been discharged from mental hospitals. True. Modern drugs have made it possible for many former hospital residents to assume productive lives in the community, but some persons discharged from the hospital do not receive adequate follow-up care and encounter difficulties.

The terms psychotherapy *and* psychoanalysis *are interchangeable.* False. Psychoanalysis is just one type of psychotherapy, the type originated by Sigmund Freud.

To be of significant help, psychotherapy must be undertaken for months, perhaps years. False. Psychoanalytic exploration is a lengthy process, but many briefer types of therapy are available.

If you were in traditional psychoanalysis, your major tasks would be to lie back, relax, and say whatever pops into your mind. True. The central method in a traditional psychoanalysis is free association.

Some psychotherapists interpret clients' dreams. True. Psychoanalysts and Gestalt therapists are two examples.

Some psychotherapists encourage their clients to take the lead in the therapy session. True. Psychoanalysts and person-centered therapists frequently use this approach.

Other psychotherapists tell their clients precisely what to do. True. Gestalt therapists, cognitive therapists, and behavior therapists may be highly directive, depending on the client's needs and situation.

Still other psychotherapists purposefully argue with clients. True. Certain methods in cognitive therapy, for example, involve convincing clients, through persuasive arguments, that their ways of interpreting events are irrational and self-defeating.

You might be able to gain control over bad habits merely by keeping a record of where and when you practice them. True. Self-monitoring of behavior has been shown to help highly motivated people increase the frequency of desired behaviors and decrease the frequency of unwanted behaviors.

Lying around in your reclining chair and fantasizing can be an effective way of confronting your fears. True. In the behavior-therapy technique of systematic desensitization, a client gradually travels through a hierarchy of fear-evoking stimuli, while remaining as relaxed as possible.

Smoking cigarettes can be an effective treatment for helping people to . . . stop smoking cigarettes. True. The specific technique is rapid smoking, in which the person inhales every six seconds.

Staff members in a mental hospital induced reluctant patients to eat by ignoring them. True. They used operant conditioning to extinguish uncooperative patient behavior.

Individual therapy is preferable to group therapy, for people who can afford it. Not necessarily. Some types of therapy, such as family therapy, can only be conducted in the group setting.

Drugs are never a solution to abnormal behavior problems. False. Drugs (or chemotherapy) are frequently helpful in disorders such as schizophrenia, major depression, and bipolar disorder.

There is a treatment for severe depression in which an electric current strong enough to induce seizures is passed through the head. True. It is called electroconvulsive therapy (ECT) and is used with some 60,000 depressed patients in the United States each year.

The originator of a surgical technique intended to reduce violence learned that it was not always successful—when one of his patients shot him. True. Antonio Moniz, the originator of the prefrontal lobotomy, was shot by a former patient.

Chapter Review

Ancient and medieval treatments of abnormal behavior, such as exorcism, often reflected the demonological model. The first institutions intended primarily for the mentally ill were asylums. Mental hospitals replaced asylums in the U.S.A. Today as many patients as possible are maintained in the community.

Many forms of psychotherapy, including psychoanalysis, person-centered therapy, TA, Gestalt therapy, and cognitive therapy primarily aim to foster insight. Behavior therapy, by contrast, helps clients substitute productive behavior for maladaptive behavior with or without benefit of self-insight.

Sigmund Freud's method of psychoanalysis attempts to shed light on unconscious conflicts that are presumed to lie at the roots of clients' problems. His major method is free association, in which no thought is to be censored. Repressed impulses are thought to seek release, leading to a compulsion to utter. Freud considered dreams the "royal road to the unconscious." Freud also found that people generalized feelings toward other men onto him, and he termed this generalization of feelings transference. Contemporary psychoanalytic approaches are briefer and less intense than Freud's.

Person-centered therapy was originated by Carl Rogers. It is a nondirective method that provides clients with a warm, accepting atmosphere that enables them to explore and overcome roadblocks to self-actualization. The characteristics shown by the person-centered therapist include unconditional positive regard, empathetic understanding, genuineness, and congruence.

Transactional analysis (TA) was originated by Eric Berne. TA focuses on people's life positions, such as I'm OK—You're not OK, and on how people play games to confirm unhealthy life positions. TA hypothesizes that there are three ego states (child, adult, and parent) and encourages clients to function according to their rational adult ego states.

Gestalt therapy, originated by Fritz Perls, provides directive methods designed to help clients integrate conflicting parts of the personality.

Cognitive therapists focus on the ways in which beliefs, attitudes, and automatic types of thinking create and compound clients' problems. Albert Ellis's rational-emotive therapy (RET) confronts clients with the ways in which self-defeating, irrational beliefs contribute to problems such as anxiety, depression, and hopelessness. Aaron Beck has focused on ways in which cognitive distortions heighten feelings of depression.

Behavior therapists use systematic desensitization to countercondition phobias; clients confront progressively more anxiety-evoking stimuli while they remain in a state of muscle relaxation. In aversive conditioning, undesired responses are made noxious by being paired with aversive stimuli. Through operant-conditioning methods, desired responses are reinforced and undesired responses are extinguished. Assertiveness-training methods include self-monitoring, modeling, and behavior rehearsal. In self-control methods, clients are taught how to manipulate the antecedents and consequences of their behavior.

Group therapy can be more economical than individual therapy, allowing several clients to be seen at once. Clients also profit from the experiences and support of other group members. Encounter groups heighten awareness of one's own feelings through intense confrontations with strangers. Family therapy uses a systems approach to boost family members' coping skills and self-esteem, and to promote the growth of each member.

Minor tranquilizers are usually prescribed for outpatients who complain of anxiety or tension. Major tranquilizers (antipsychotic drugs) reduce agitation, delusions, and hallucinations. Antidepressants are believed to work by increasing the amounts of the neurotransmitters norepinephrine and serotonin. Lithium helps flatten out the cycles of manicky behavior and depression found in bipolar affective disorder.

Electroconvulsive therapy (ECT) uses electric shock to produce convulsions. Since the advent of major tranquilizers, use of ECT has been generally limited to patients with major depression. ECT is controversial because it impairs memory and nobody knows why it works. The best-known psychosurgery technique is the prefrontal lobotomy, which has been used with severely disturbed patients. The prefrontal lobotomy has been discontinued because of the advent of major tranquilizers and because of side effects.

Exercises

Therapy Methods and Forms of Therapy

Directions: *In the first column are a number of therapy methods. In the second column are the types of therapy discussed in the text. Match the method to the type of therapy by placing the letter of the type of therapy in the blank space to the left of the method. Answers follow.*

THERAPY METHODS	TYPES OF THERAPY
_____ 1. Dialogue	A. Psychoanalysis
_____ 2. Assertiveness training	B. Person-centered therapy
_____ 3. Genuineness	C. Transactional analysis
_____ 4. Lithium	D. Gestalt therapy
_____ 5. Free association	E. Cognitive therapy
_____ 6. Restriction of the stimulus field	F. Behavior therapy
_____ 7. Analysis of "games"	G. Chemotherapy
_____ 8. Dream analysis	H. Psychosurgery
_____ 9. Prefrontal lobotomy	
_____ 10. Cognitive restructuring	
_____ 11. Empathetic understanding	
_____ 12. Phenothiazines	
_____ 13. Problem-solving training	

_____ 14. Interpretation
_____ 15. Aversive conditioning
_____ 16. Token economy
_____ 17. Challenging irrational
       beliefs
_____ 18. Showing congruence
_____ 19. Resolving transference
_____ 20. Analyzing social
       exchanges

Answer Key to Exercise

1. D	**6.** F	**11.** B	**16.** F
2. F	**7.** C	**12.** G	**17.** E
3. B	**8.** A, D	**13.** E	**18.** B
4. G	**9.** H	**14.** A	**19.** A
5. A	**10.** E	**15.** F	**20.** C

Names and Forms of Therapy

Directions: *In the left column are the names of people who have had an impact on methods of therapy. In the right column are the names of types of therapy. Match the name and the method by writing the letter that signifies the method in the blank space to the left of the name. Note that more than one letter can be associated with most names.*

NAME

_____ 1. Albert Bandura
_____ 2. Aaron Beck
_____ 3. Eric Berne
_____ 4. Ugo Cerletti
_____ 5. Albert Ellis
_____ 6. Sigmund Freud
_____ 7. Thomas Harris
_____ 8. Arnold Lazarus
_____ 9. Antonio Egas Moniz
_____ 10. Fritz Perls
_____ 11. Carl Rogers
_____ 12. Virginia Satir
_____ 13. Joseph Wolpe

TYPE OF THERAPY

A. Gestalt therapy
B. Chemotherapy
C. Psychosurgery
D. Transactional analysis
E. Behavior therapy
F. Person-centered therapy
G. Rational-emotive therapy
H. Psychoanalysis
I. Family therapy
J. Insight-oriented therapy
K. Biological therapy
L. Cognitive therapy
M. Participant modeling
N. Electroconvulsive therapy
O. Systematic desensitization

Answer Key to Exercise

1. E, M	**5.** G, J, L	**8.** E	**11.** F, J
2. J, L	**6.** H, J	**9.** C, K	**12.** I
3. D, J	**7.** D, J	**10.** A, J	**13.** E, O
4. K, N			

Posttest

1. Which of the following was a leader of the humanitarian reform movement in the United States?

    (a) Philippe Pinel, **(b)** Dorothea Dix, **(c)** Sigmund Freud, **(d)** William Tuke.

2. Behavior therapy is *not* considered an insight-oriented therapy because behavior therapists

    (a) are not concerned about establishing a close relationship with their clients, **(b)** combat demoralization, **(c)** are directive, **(d)** believe that adaptive behavioral changes can be fostered with or without benefit of insight.

3. A woman client complains to her therapist, "Who do you think you are—my father?" Sigmund Freud would probably consider this behavior an example of

    (a) transference, **(b)** reaction formation, **(c)** projection, **(d)** resistance.

4. Sigmund Freud remarked, "Where id was, there shall ego be." Freud meant that

    (a) all unconscious ideas should be made conscious, **(b)** feelings of guilt should be removed, **(c)** coping behavior should replace impulsive behavior, **(d)** defense mechanisms should be destroyed.

5. A person has a dream in which she is flying. According to Sigmund Freud, the perceived subject matter of a dream—in this case, flying—is its

    (a) manifest content, **(b)** objective content, **(c)** symbolic content, **(d)** latent content.

6. Congruence may be defined as

    (a) honesty in interpersonal relationships, **(b)** a fit between one's behavior and feelings, **(c)** ability to perceive the world from a client's frame of reference, **(d)** genuine acceptance of the client as a person.

7. Person-centered therapy seems to be most effective with _____ clients.

    (a) psychotic, **(b)** poorly motivated, **(c)** middle-class, **(d)** well-educated.

8. In transactional analysis, when two people relate to one another as adults, there is said to be a

    (a) crossed transaction, **(b)** confirmed exchange, **(c)** complementary transaction, **(d)** transference relationship.

9. According to Albert Ellis, the central factors in our problems are

    (a) genetic factors, **(b)** maladaptive habits, **(c)** unconscious conflicts, **(d)** irrational beliefs.

10. Which type of therapist is *not* likely to want clients to stick to issues in "the here and now"?

    (a) A Gestalt therapist, **(b)** An encounter group therapist, **(c)** A traditional psychoanalyst, **(d)** A behavior therapist.

11. Behavior rehearsal is most similar in meaning to

    (a) practice, **(b)** role playing, **(c)** modeling, **(d)** countertransference.

12. Carol is thrilled that after two months of sessions with a behavior therapist, her phobia for receiving injections no longer seems to exist. A friend, who also happens to be a psychoanalyst, confides to you that Carol should not be too surprised if she develops another problem because the technique of systematic desensitization can lead to

    (a) countertransference, **(b)** tolerance, **(c)** symptom substitution, **(d)** abreaction.

13. The technique called _____ is an example of aversive conditioning.

    (a) "Grandma's method," **(b)** restriction of the stimulus field, **(c)** operant conditioning, **(d)** rapid smoking.

14. Tom cut down on his cigarette intake by simply pausing between puffs. This technique is an example of

    (a) successive approximations, **(b)** chain breaking, **(c)** response prevention, **(d)** avoiding stimuli that trigger unwanted behavior.

15. Each of the following is an advantage of group therapy, *except that*

    (a) it relies on a systems approach, **(b)** it is economical, **(c)** there is a greater fund of information and experience for clients to draw on, **(d)** members can rehearse social skills with one another in a relatively unthreatening atmosphere.

16. According to the studies analyzed by Smith and Glass, the *least* effective form of therapy is

    (a) Gestalt therapy, **(b)** psychoanalysis, **(c)** cognitive therapy, **(d)** behavior therapy.

17. Which of the following methods is most likely to lead to hyperactivity and distractibility?

    (a) Prefrontal lobotomy, **(b)** Electroconvulsive therapy, **(c)** Antidepressant drugs, **(d)** Major tranquilizers.

18. Valium and other minor tranquilizers are thought to depress the activity of the _____, which in turn decreases sympathetic activity.

    (a) central nervous system, **(b)** parasympathetic nervous system, **(c)** adrenal glands, **(d)** heart.

19. Phenothiazines are thought to work by blocking the action of

    (a) acetylcholine, **(b)** norepinephrine, **(c)** dopamine, **(d)** serotonin.

20. The use of _____ might lead to symptoms like those of Parkinson's disease.

    (a) ECT, (b) the prefrontal lobotomy, (c) lithium, (d) Thorazine.

21. Lithium appears to work by moderating the level of _____ available to the brain.

    (a) acetylcholine, (b) norepinephrine, (c) dopamine, (d) serotonin.

Answer Key to Posttest

1. B	**7.** D	**13.** D	**18.** A
2. D	**8.** C	**14.** B	**19.** C
3. A	**9.** D	**15.** A	**20.** D
4. C	**10.** C	**16.** A	**21.** B
5. A	**11.** A	**17.** A	
6. B	**12.** C		

SOCIAL PSYCHOLOGY

OUTLINE

PRETEST: TRUTH OR FICTION?
ATTITUDES
  The A–B Problem
  Origins of Attitudes
  Changing Attitudes through Persuasion
  Balance Theory
  Cognitive-Dissonance Theory
  Prejudice
SOCIAL PERCEPTION
  Primacy and Recency Effects
  Attribution Theory
  Body Language
INTERPERSONAL ATTRACTION
  Physical Attractiveness
  Attitudinal Similarity
  The "Romeo and Juliet Effect"
  Reciprocity
  Propinquity

  Playing Hard to Get
SOCIAL INFLUENCE
  Obedience to Authority
  The Milgram Studies
  Conformity
  The Asch Study
  Factors Influencing Conformity
GROUP BEHAVIOR
  Social Facilitation
  Group Decision Making
  Polarization and the Risky Shift
  Groupthink
  Mob Behavior and Deindividuation
  Helping Behavior and the Bystander Effect
TRUTH OR FICTION REVISITED
CHAPTER REVIEW
EXERCISE
POSTTEST

PRETEST: TRUTH OR FICTION?

Religious people are likely to attend church regularly.

Admitting your product's weak points in an ad is the death knell for sales.

Most of us are swayed by ads that offer useful information, not by emotional appeals or celebrity endorsements.

People who are highly worried about what other people think of them are likely to be low in sales resistance.

We appreciate things more when we have to work hard for them.

We tend to divide the social world into "us" and "them."

First impressions have powerful effects on our social relationships.

We hold others responsible for their misdeeds but tend to see ourselves as victims of circumstances when our behavior falls short of our standards.

We tend to attribute our successes to our abilities and hard work but to attribute our failures to external factors such as lack of time or obstacles placed in our paths by others.

Waitresses who touch their patrons when making change receive higher tips.

Beauty is in the eye of the beholder.

College men prefer women to be thinner than college women expect.

People are perceived as more physically attractive when they are smiling.

Opposites attract: We are more likely to be drawn to people who disagree with our attitudes than to people who share them.

Most people would refuse to deliver painful electric shocks to an innocent party, even under powerful social pressure.

Many people are late to social gatherings because they are conforming to a social norm.

Bicycle riders and runners tend to move more rapidly in competition than when they are practicing alone.

Group decisions tend to represent conservative compromises of the opinions of the group members.

Nearly 40 people stood by and did nothing while a woman was being stabbed to death.

Candy and Stretch. A new technique for controlling weight gains? No, these are the names Bach and Deutsch (1970) give two people who have just met at a camera club that doubles as a meeting place for singles.

Candy and Stretch stand above the crowd—literally. Candy, an attractive woman in her early 30s, is almost 6 feet tall. Stretch is more plain-looking, but wholesome, in his late 30s, and 6 feet 5 inches.

Stretch has been in the group for some time. Candy is a new member. Let's listen in on them as they make conversation during a coffee break. As you will see, there are some differences between what they say and what they are thinking:

THEY SAY	THEY THINK
STRETCH: Well you're certainly a welcome addition to our group.	(Can't I ever say something clever?)
CANDY: Thank you. It certainly is friendly and interesting.	(He's cute.)
STRETCH: My friends call me Stretch. It's left over from my basketball days. Silly, but I'm used to it.	(It's safer than saying my name is David Stein.)
CANDY: My name is Candy.	(At least my nickname is. He doesn't have to hear Hortense O'Brien.)
STRETCH: What kind of camera is that?	(Why couldn't a girl named Candy be Jewish? It's only a nickname, isn't it?)
CANDY: Just this old German one of my uncle's. I borrowed it from the office.	(He could be Irish. And that camera looks expensive.)
STRETCH: May I? (He takes her camera, brushing her hand and then tingling with the touch.) Fine lens. You work for your uncle?	(Now I've done it. Brought up work.)
CANDY: Ever since college. It's more than being just a secretary. I get into sales, too.	(So okay, what if I only went for a year. If he asks what I sell, I'll tell him anything except underwear.)
STRETCH: Sales? That's funny. I'm in sales, too, but mainly as an executive. I run our department. I started using cameras on trips. Last time it was in the Bahamas. I took—	(Is there a nice way to say used cars? I'd better change the subject.) (Great legs! And the way her hips move—)
CANDY: Oh! Do you go to the Bahamas, too? I love those islands.	(So I went just once, and it was for the brassiere manufacturers' convention.)
STRETCH: I did a little underwater work there last summer. Fantastic colors. So rich in life.	(She's probably been around. Well, at least we're off the subject of jobs.)
CANDY: I wish I'd had time when I was there. I love the water.	(Look at that build. He must swim like a fish. I should learn. Well, I do. At the beach, anyway, where I can wade in and not go too deep.)

And so begins a relationship. Candy and Stretch have a drink and talk, sharing their likes and dislikes. Amazingly, they seem to agree on everything—from cars to clothing to politics. The attraction is very strong, and neither is willing to risk turning the other off by disagreeing.

They spend the weekend together and feel that they have fallen in love. They still agree on everything they discuss, but they scrupulously avoid one topic: religion. Their religious differences became apparent when they exchanged last names. But that doesn't mean they have to talk about it.

They also put off introducing each other to their parents. The O'Briens and the Steins are narrow-minded about religion. If the truth be known, so are Candy and Stretch. They narrow their relationships to avoid tension with one another, and as the romance develops, they feel progressively isolated from family and friends.

What happens in this tangled web of deception? Candy becomes pregnant. After some deliberation, and not without misgivings, the couple decide to get married. Do they live happily ever after? We cannot say—"ever after" hasn't arrived yet.

We do not have all the answers, but we have some questions. Candy and Stretch's relationship began with a powerful attraction. What is *attraction*? How do we determine who is attractive? Candy and Stretch pretended to share each other's attitudes? What are *attitudes*? Also, why were they so reluctant to disagree?

Candy and Stretch were both a bit prejudiced about religion. What is *prejudice*? Why didn't they introduce each other to their parents? Did they fear that their parents would want them to *conform* to their own standards? Would their parents try to *persuade* them to limit dating to people of their own religions? Would they *obey*?

And—as long as we're asking questions—what do you think might have happened if their parents had tried to break up the relationship? Would they have succeeded, or might Candy and Stretch, like the star-crossed lovers in *Romeo and Juliet,* have been pressed closer by family opposition?

Attraction, attitudes, prejudice, conformity, persuasion, obedience—these topics are the province of the branch of psychology called **social psychology.** Social psychologists study the nature and causes of our thoughts, feelings, and overt behaviors in social situations (Baron & Byrne, 1987). The social psychological topics we discuss in this chapter include attitudes, social perception, attraction, social influence, and group behavior.

ATTITUDES

Psychologists are a rather independent bunch, so it is not surprising to find different definitions of **attitudes.** Some view attitudes primarily as lasting cognitive evaluations (e.g., Petty & Cacioppo, 1986). Others consider attitudes to be feelings that have an evaluative, cognitive component. But most social psychologists today adhere to the **ABC**

model of attitudes, which views attitudes in terms of affect (feelings), behavior, and cognitions (Breckler, 1984). That is, attitudes are enduring systems of beliefs, feelings, and overt behavioral tendencies toward people, groups, religion and religious groups, politics, and so on.

Attitudes can change, but they tend to remain stable unless shoved a little. Most people do not change their religion or political affiliation without serious deliberation or in the absence of severe external pressure.

The A–B Problem

Our definition of attitude implies that our behavior is consistent with our beliefs and our feelings. When we are free to do as we wish, it often is. But as indicated by the term **A–B problem,** the link between attitudes (A) and overt behavior (B) tends to be weak. In their review of the literature, Ajzen and Fishbein (1977) found that global attitudes toward groups of people, politics, and religion (such as whether one is prejudiced toward blacks or whether one is a Republican or a Christian) do not predict specific behavior patterns very well. For example, knowing that James is a Republican does not guarantee that he will vote for Republicans across the board, or even that he will bother to vote. We would be better able to predict James's voting behavior if we knew whether he places party loyalty ahead of the qualities of individuals and if we knew how committed he was to expressing his political views, as by voting.

A number of factors influence the likelihood that we can predict behavior from attitudes:

1. *Specificity.* We can better predict specific behavior from specific attitudes than from global attitudes (Baron & Byrne, 1987). We can better predict church attendance by knowing people's attitudes toward the importance of regular church attendance than, more globally, whether they are Christian.

2. *Strength of attitudes.* Strong attitudes are more likely to determine behavior than weak attitudes (Fazio et al., 1982).

3. *Vested interest.* People are more likely to act on their attitudes when they have a vested interest in the outcome (Sivacek & Crano, 1982). People are

Social psychology The field of psychology that studies the nature and causes of individual thoughts, feelings, and overt behavior in social situations.

Attitude An enduring system of beliefs, feelings, and behavioral tendencies concerning people, objects, or ideas.

ABC model of attitudes The view that attitudes are composed of affect (feelings), behavioral tendencies, and cognitions.

A–B problem The issue of how well we can predict behavior on the basis of attitudes.

more likely to vote for (or against) unionization of their workplace, for example, when they believe that their job security depends on the outcome.

4. *Accessibility.* People are more likely to express their attitudes when they are accessible—that is, when they are brought to mind (Fazio, 1986; Fazio et al., 1986). This is why politicians attempt to "get out the vote" by media blitzes just prior to the election. It does politicians little good to have supporters who forget them on election day. Attitudes that have strong emotional impact are more accessible (Wu & Shaffer, 1987), which is one reason that politicians and TV evangelists strive to get their adherents "worked up" over the issues they wish to promote.

Candy and Stretch avoided discussing matters on which they differed. One motive might have been to avoid heightening the *accessibility* of their conflicting attitudes. By keeping them under the table, perhaps they would be less likely to act on them and go their separate ways. In the remainder of this section we shall discuss the origins of attitudes, persuasion, and a particularly troublesome type of attitude—prejudice. We shall see that just as Candy and Stretch were reluctant to express attitudes that might alienate each other, we may also be influenced to behave in ways that are inconsistent with our beliefs.

Origins of Attitudes

You were not born a Republican or Democrat. You were not born a Catholic or a Jew—although your parents may have practiced one of these religions when you came along. Political, religious, and other attitudes are learned.

Conditioning Conditioning may play a role in the acquisition of attitudes. Laboratory experiments have shown that attitudes toward national groups can be influenced simply by associating them with positive words (such as *gift* or *happy*) or negative words (such as *ugly* and *failure*) (Lohr & Staats, 1973). Parents often reinforce children for saying and doing things consistent with their own attitudes. Children may be shown approval for wearing Daddy's "No nukes" button or carrying Mommy's "My body is my own" placard.

Observational Learning Although attitudes formed through direct experience may be stronger and easier to recall (Fazio & Cooper, 1983), we also acquire attitudes from friends and the mass media. The approval or disapproval of peers molds adolescents to prefer short or long hair or blue jeans or preppy sweaters. Television shows us that body odor, bad breath, and the frizzies are dreaded diseases—and perhaps, that people who use harsh toilet paper are vaguely un-American.

Cognitive Appraisal Yet all is not so mechanical. Now and then we also evaluate information and attitudes on the basis of evidence. Research suggests that we may revise stereotypes on the basis of new evidence (Weber & Crocker, 1983). We are especially likely to examine our attitudes when we know that we shall have to justify them to people who may disagree with them (Tetlock, 1983).

Still, early attitudes tend to serve as cognitive "anchors." In this way, attitudes we hear of later are often judged in terms of how much they "deviate" from the first set. Accepting larger deviations appears to require greater adjustments in information processing (Quattrone, 1982). For this reason, perhaps, they are more likely to be resisted. Yet attitudes can be changed by persuasion.

Changing Attitudes through Persuasion

According to the **elaboration likelihood model,** there are at least two routes to persuading others to change attitudes—that is, two ways of responding to or elaborating persuasive messages (Petty & Cacioppo, 1986). The first, or central route, views elaboration and possible attitudinal change as resulting from careful consideration of arguments and evidence. The second, or peripheral route, involves elaboration of the objects of attitudes by associating them with positive or negative "cues." These cues include rewards (such as parental approval) and punishments (e.g., disapproval) and

---

Elaboration likelihood model The view that persuasive messages are evaluated (elaborated) on the basis of central and peripheral cues.

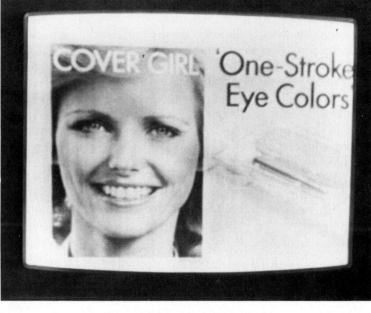

What Factors Contribute to the Persuasiveness of Messages? To the Persuasiveness of Communicators? Advertisers use both central and peripheral cues to sell their wares.

factors such as the trustworthiness and attractiveness of the communicator. Advertisements, which are a form of persuasive communication, also rely on central and peripheral routes. Some advertisments focus on the quality of the product (central route), whereas others attempt to associate the product with appealing images (peripheral route) (Fox, 1984). Ads for Total cereal, which emphasize its nutritional benefits, provide information about the quality of the product (Snyder & DeBono, 1985). So too do the "Pepsi challenge" taste-test ads, which claim that Pepsi tastes better than Coca-Cola. The Marlboro cigarette ads, by contrast, focus on the masculine, rugged image of the "Marlboro man" and offer no information about the product itself (Snyder & DeBono, 1985).

The success of most persuasive communications often relies on a combination of central and peripheral cues, such as speech content and voice quality (O'Sullivan et al., 1985). In this section we shall examine one central factor in persuasion—

that is, the nature of the message itself—and three peripheral factors: (1) the person delivering the message; (2) the context in which the message is delivered; and (3) the audience. We shall also examine two methods of persuasion used frequently, for example, by persons seeking charitable contributions and by salespersons: the foot-in-the-door technique and low-balling.

The Persuasive Message: Say What? Say How? Say How Often?   How do we respond when TV commercials are repeated until we have memorized every dimple on the actors' faces? Research suggests that familiarity breeds content, not contempt.

You might not be crazy about *zabulons* and *afworbus* at first, but Zajonc (1968) found that people began to react favorably toward these bogus Turkish words on the basis of repeated exposure. Political candidates who become highly familiar to the public through frequent TV commercials attain more votes (Grush, 1980). People respond more favorably to abstract art (Heingartner & Hall, 1974), classical music (Smith & Dorfman, 1975), even photographs of black people (Hamm et al., 1975) and of college students (Moreland & Zajonc, 1982) simply on the basis of repetition. Love for classical art and music may begin through exposure in the nursery—not the college appreciation course. The more complex the stimuli, the more likely it is that frequent exposure will have favorable effects (Saegert & Jellison, 1970; Smith & Dorfman, 1975). The one-hundredth repetition of a Bach concerto may be less tiresome than the one-hundredth repetition of a pop tune.

Two-sided arguments, in which the communicator recounts the arguments of the opposition in order to refute them, can be especially effective when the audience is at first uncertain about its position (Hass & Linder, 1972). Theologians and politicians sometimes expose their followers to the arguments of the opposition. By refuting them one by one, they give their followers a sort of psychological immunity to them. Swinyard found that two-sided product claims, in which advertisers admitted their product's weak points as well as highlighting its strengths, were most credible (in Bridgwater, 1982).

It would be nice to think that people are too sophisticated to be persuaded by an **emotional appeal.** However, grisly films of operations on cancerous lungs are more effective than matter-of-fact presentations for changing attitudes toward smoking (Leventhal et al., 1972). Films of bloodied gums and decayed teeth are also more effective than logical discussions for increasing toothbrushing (Dembroski et al., 1978). Fear appeals are most effective when they are strong, when the audience believes the dire consequences, and when the recommendations offered seem practical (Mewborn & Rogers, 1979).

Audiences also tend to believe arguments that appear to run counter to the personal interests of the communicator (Wood & Eagly, 1981). People may pay more attention to a whaling-fleet owner's claim than to a conservationist's that whales are becoming extinct. If the president of Chrysler or General Motors admitted that Toyotas and Hondas were superior, you can bet that we would prick up our ears.

The Persuasive Communicator: Whom Do You Trust?   Would you buy a used car from a person convicted of larceny? Would you attend weight-control classes run by a 350-pound leader? Would you leaf through fashion magazines featuring clumsy models? Probably not. Research shows that persuasive communicators show expertise (Hennigan et al., 1982), trustworthiness, attractiveness, or similarity to their audiences (Baron & Byrne, 1987).

Health professionals enjoy high status in our society and are considered experts. It is not surprising that toothpaste ads boast that their products have the approval of the American Dental Association.

Even though we are reared not to judge books by their covers, we are more likely to find attractive people persuasive. Corporations do not gamble millions on the physically unappealing to sell their products. Some advertisers seek out the perfect combination of attractiveness and plain, simple folksiness with which the audience can identify. Ivory Soap commercials sport "real" freshly scrubbed models.

Television news anchorpersons also enjoy high prestige. One study (Mullen et al., 1987) found that before the 1984 presidential election, Peter Jennings of ABC News had shown significantly more favorable facial expressions when reporting on Ronald Reagan than when reporting on Walter Mondale. Tom Brokaw of NBC and Dan Rather of CBS had not shown favoritism. The researchers also found that viewers of ABC News voted for Reagan in greater proportions than viewers of NBC or CBS News. It is tempting to conclude that viewers were subtly persuaded by Jennings to vote for Reagan. However, Sweeney and Gruber (1985) have shown that viewers do not simply absorb spongelike whatever the tube feeds them. Instead, they show **selective avoidance** and

Emotional appeal A type of persuasive communication that influences behavior on the basis of feelings that are aroused instead of rational analysis of the issues.

Selective avoidance Diverting one's attention from information that is inconsistent with one's attitudes.

selective exposure. They tend to switch channels when they are faced with news coverage that seems to run counter to their own attitudes, and they seek communicators whose attitudes coincide with their own. And so, whereas Jennings might have had an influence on his audience's attitudes toward Reagan, it might also be that Reaganites preferred Jennings to Brokaw and Rather.

The Context of the Message: "Get 'Em in a Good Mood"

You are too clever and insightful to allow someone to persuade you by buttering you up, but perhaps someone you know would be influenced by a sip of wine, a bite of cheese, and a sincere compliment. Seduction attempts usually come at the tail end of a date—after the Szechuan tidbits, the nouveau Fresno film, the disco party, and the wine that was sold at its time. An assault at the outset of a date would be viewed as . . . well, an assault. Experiments suggest that food and pleasant music increase acceptance of persuasive messages (Galizio & Hendrick, 1972; Janis et al., 1965).

It is also counterproductive to call your dates fools when they disagree with you—even though their views are bound to be foolish if they do not coincide with yours. Agreement and praise are more effective at encouraging others to accept your views (Baron, 1971; Byrne, 1971). Appear sincere, or else your compliments will look manipulative. It seems unfair to give out this information.

The Persuaded Audience: Are You a Person Who Can't Say No?

Why do some people have "sales resistance," whereas others enrich the lives of every door-to-door salesperson? It might be that people with high self-esteem and low social anxiety are more likely to resist social pressure (Santee & Maslach, 1982). However, Baumeister and Coving-ton (1985) challenge the view that persons with low self-esteem are more open to persuasion. Persons with high self-esteem may be persuaded as readily, but people with high self-esteem may be less willing to admit that others have persuaded them. Broad knowledge of the areas that a communicator is discussing also tends to decrease persuadability (Wood, 1982).

A study by Schwartz and Gottman (1976) reveals the cognitive nature of the "social anxiety" that can make it hard for some of us to say no to requests. Schwartz and Gottman found that people who comply with unreasonable requests are more likely to report such thinking as: "I was worried about what the other person would think of me if I refused," "It is better to help others than to be self-centered," or "The other person might be hurt or insulted if I refused." People who did not comply reported thoughts like "It doesn't matter what the other person thinks of me," "I am perfectly free to say no," or "This request is an unreasonable one" (p. 916).

The Foot-in-the-Door Technique

You might think that giving money to door-to-door solicitors for charity will get you off the hook. That is, they'll take the cash and leave you alone for a while. Actually, the opposite is true: The next time the organization mounts a campaign, they may call on generous you to go door to door! Giving an inch apparently encourages others to try to take a yard. They have gotten their "foot in the door."

To gain insight into the **foot-in-the-door technique,** consider a classic experiment by Freedman and Fraser (1966). In this study, groups of women received phone calls from a consumer group who asked whether they would allow a six-man crew to drop by their homes to inventory every product they used. It could take several hours to complete the chore. Only 22 percent of one group acceded to this rather troublesome request. But 53 percent of another group of women agreed to a visit from this wrecking crew. Why was the second group more compliant? The more compliant group had been phoned a few days earlier and had agreed to answer a few questions about the soap products they used. They had been primed for the second request. The caller had gotten his "foot in the door." The foot-in-the-door technique has also

---

Selective exposure Deliberate seeking of and attending to information that is consistent with one's attitudes.

Foot-in-the-door technique A method for inducing compliance in which a small request is followed with a larger request.

been shown to be effective in persuading people to make charitable contributions (Pliner et al., 1974) and to sign petitions (Baron, 1973).

The results of one study (Snyder & Cunningham, 1975) suggest that people who have acceded to a small request become more likely to accede to a larger one because they come to view themselves as the "type of person" who helps others by acceding to requests. Regardless of how the foot-in-the-door technique works, if you want to say no, it may be easier to do so (and stick to your guns) the first time a request is made rather than later. And organizations have learned that they can compile lists of persons they can rely upon.

Low-Balling

Have you ever had a salesperson promise you a low price for merchandise, committed yourself to buy at that price, and then had the salesperson tell you that he or she had been in error or that the supervisor had not agreed to the price? Have you then cancelled the order or stuck to your commitment?

You might have been a victim of **low-balling,** also called "throwing the low ball." In this method, you are persuaded to make a commitment on favorable terms, and the persuader then claims that he or she must revise the terms. Perhaps the car you agreed to buy for $9,400 did not have the automatic transmission and air conditioning you both thought it had. Perhaps the yen or the mark had just gone up against the dollar, and the price of the car had to be raised accordingly.

Low-balling is an aggravating technique, and there are few protections against it. One possibility is to ask the salesperson whether he or she has the authority to make the deal, and then have him or her write out the terms and sign the offer. Unfortunately, the salesperson might later confess to misunderstanding what you meant by "authority" to make the deal. Perhaps the best way to combat low-balling is to be willing to take your business elsewhere when the salesperson tries to back out of an arrangement.

Low-balling places us in conflict because one cognition is to the effect that we have made a commitment, and another cognition is to the effect that the terms have been altered—or perhaps that we are being "suckered." Let us examine the role of cognitive conflict further by considering the things

that happen when we perceive our own attitudes to be inconsistent or imbalanced.

Balance Theory

According to **balance theory,** we are motivated to maintain harmony among our perceptions, beliefs, and attitudes (Heider, 1958). When people we like share our attitudes, there is balance and all is well. It works the other way as well: If we like Peter Jennings and he expresses an attitude, our own cognitions will remain in balance if we agree with him. For this reason, we are likely to develop favorable attitudes toward unfamiliar objects that Jennings seems to endorse. If we dislike other people, we might not care very much about their attitudes. They may disagree with us, but this state of **nonbalance** leaves us indifferent (Newcomb, 1981).

But when someone you care about expresses a discrepant attitude, you are likely to be concerned. The relationship will survive if you like chocolate and your friend prefers vanilla, but what if the discrepancies concern important attitudes about religion, politics, or raising children? Now a state of **imbalance** exists. What if Peter Jennings, whom you like, reports favorably on an object you dislike? Now there is an uncomfortable state of imbalance. Consider the foot-in-the-door technique. If you have given to charity and are then asked to solicit from door to door for the same cause, your self-concept as "one who helps" and reluctance to go door to door might create a state of imbalance. Candy was Catholic and Stretch Jewish. Each was

Low-balling A method in which extremely attractive terms are offered to induce a person to make a commitment. Once the commitment is made, the terms are revised.

Balance theory The view that people have a need to organize their perceptions, opinions, and beliefs in a harmonious manner.

Nonbalance In balance theory, a condition in which persons whom we dislike do not agree with us.

Imbalance In balance theory, a condition in which persons whom we like disagree with us.

painfully aware of the imbalance in religious preferences. How did they handle the imbalance? At first they misperceived the other's preference. Later they tried to sweep it under the rug.

What else can people do to end a state of imbalance? We can try to convince others to change their attitudes. (Candy and Stretch could have asked each other to change religions.) Or we can change our feelings about the other person. (Candy or Stretch might have "realized" that the other was unworthy of their attention, after all.) Cognitive-dissonance theory, however, might suggest that Candy and Stretch's feelings for each other could grow even stronger as a result of discovering their religious differences, as we shall see.

Cognitive-Dissonance Theory

According to cognitive-dissonance theory, which was originated by Leon Festinger (Festinger, 1957; Festinger & Carlsmith, 1959), people dislike inconsistency. As with balance theory, we do not like to think that our attitudes (cognitions) are inconsistent. Nor do we like to think that our attitudes are inconsistent with our behavior. Awareness that two cognitions are dissonant, or that our cognitions and our behavior are inconsistent, is sufficient to motivate us to reduce the discrepancy. Cognitive dissonance is an unpleasant state (Fazio & Cooper, 1983) that is accompanied by heightened physiological arousal (Croyle & Cooper, 1983). Thus a physiological motive for eliminating cognitive dissonance might be to reduce our arousal to a more optimal level.

In the first and one of the best-known studies on cognitive dissonance, one group of subjects received $1 for telling someone else that a just-completed boring task was very interesting (Festinger & Carlsmith, 1959). A second group of subjects received $20 to describe the task positively. Both groups were paid to engage in **attitude-discrepant behavior**—that is, behavior that ran counter to

---

Attitude-discrepant behavior Behavior that runs counter to one's thoughts and feelings.

Effort justification The tendency to seek justification (reasons) for strenuous efforts.

---

their actual thoughts and feelings. After "selling" the task to others, the subjects were asked to rate their own liking for the task. Ironically, the group paid *less* rated the task as significantly more interesting. *Why?*

From a learning-theory point of view, this result would be confusing. After all, shouldn't we learn to like that which is highly rewarding? But cognitive-dissonance theory would predict this "less-leads-to-more effect" for the following reason: The cognitions "I was paid very little" and "I told someone that this task was interesting" are dissonant. You see, another concept in cognitive-dissonance theory is **effort justification,** and subjects in studies such as these are helped to justify their behavior by concluding that their attitudes might not have been as discrepant with their behavior as they had originally believed. The notion that we have greater appreciation for the things for which we must work hard is another example of effort justification.

Consider another situation. Cognitive dissonance would be created if we were to believe that our preferred candidate were unlikely to win the U.S. presidential election. One cognition would be that our candidate is better for the country or, at an extreme, would "save" the country from harmful forces. A second and dissonant cognition would be that our candidate does not have a chance to win. Research shows that in the presidential elections from 1952 to 1980, people by a four-to-one margin helped reduce such dissonance by expressing the belief that their candidate would win (Granberg & Brent, 1983). They frequently held these beliefs despite lopsided polls to the contrary. Among highly involved but poorly informed people, the margin of self-deception was still higher.

Concerning Candy and Stretch, cognitive-dissonance theory might predict that their discovery that they held different religious views might have *strengthened* rather than destroyed their relationship. Why? After finding out about the other's religion, each might have thought, "Stretch (Candy) must be *very* important to me if I can feel this way about him (her), knowing that he (she) is Jewish (Catholic)."

As another example of the ways in which dissonance can be created and reduced let us consider the kidnapping of newspaper heiress Patty Hearst.

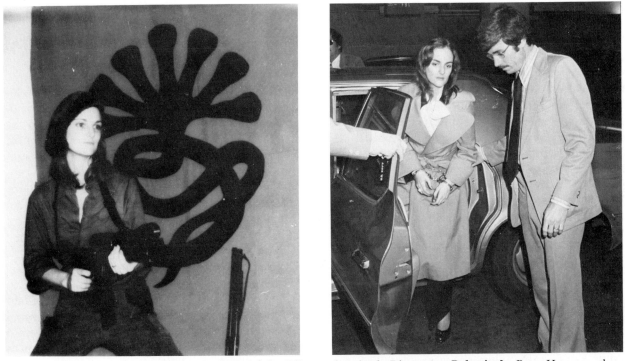

What Are Some of the Effects of Attitude-Discrepant Behavior?   Patty Hearst as the "urban guerrilla" Tania (left), and in manacles (right) on her way to testify in court. After her abduction by extremists, Patty was forced into attitude-discrepant revolutionary behavior. Engaging in antisocial acts such as armed robbery appears to have converted her self-identity from that of a typical (though wealthy) college student to that of a revolutionary. After her capture, her identity appeared to revert to that of Patty. Patty's experience raises a challenging question: How can any of us know where the influences of others end and our "real selves," or true identities, begin?

Can One's Self-Identity Be Converted Through Attitude-Discrepant Behavior? The Strange Case of Patty Hearst

In February 1974, newspaper heiress Patty Hearst, an undergraduate student at Berkeley, was abducted by a revolutionary group known as the Symbionese Liberation Army (SLA). Early messages from the SLA directed the Hearst family to distribute millions of dollars' worth of food to the poor if they wished their daughter to live. There was no suggestion that Patty was a willing prisoner.

But a couple of months later, SLA communiqués contained statements by Patty that she had willingly joined the group. Patty declared her revolutionary name to be Tania and sent a photograph in which she wore a guerrilla outfit and held a machine gun. She expressed contempt for her parents' capitalist values and called them pigs. But her family did not believe that Patty's attitudes had really changed. They had raised her for twenty years. She had been with the SLA for only two months. Surely her statements were designed to earn good treatment from her captors.

In April, Patty and other SLA members robbed a San Francisco bank. Patty was videotaped brandishing a rifle. She was reported to have threatened a guard. But, the Hearsts maintained, the rifle could have been unloaded. Patty might still have been acting out of fear of losing her life. Then Patty became involved in another incident. She acted as a cover for SLA members William and Emily Harris, firing an automatic rifle as they fled from a store they had robbed. Patty seemed unsupervised at the time.

Patty and the Harrises were captured in San Francisco late in 1975. At first Patty was defiant. She gave a revolutionary salute and identified herself as Tania. But once she was in prison, her identity appeared to undergo another transformation. She asked to be called Patty. At her trial she seemed quite remorseful. The defense argued that had it not been for the social influence of the SLA, Patty would never have engaged in criminal behavior or adopted revolutionary values. When President Jimmy Carter signed an order for Patty's early release from prison in 1979, he was operating under an admission from Patty's original prosecutors that they, too, believed that Patty would not have behaved criminally without being abducted by the SLA and experiencing dread in the days that followed.

How is it that a college undergraduate with typical American values came to express attitudes that were opposed to her lifelong ideals?

It may be that such conversions in identity can be explained through cognitive-dissonance theory. After Patty's kidnapping, she was exposed to fear and fatigue and forced into attitude-discrepant behavior. She had to express agreement with SLA values, engage in sexual activity with SLA members, and train for revolutionary activity. As long as she clung firmly to her self-identity as Patty, these repugnant acts created great cognitive dissonance. But by adopting the suggested revolutionary identity of Tania, Patty could look upon herself as "liberated" rather than as a frightened captive or criminal. In this way her cognitive dissonance would be reduced, and her behavior would no longer be so stressful. Supportive research shows that we do draw conclusions about our attitudes from our decisions to engage in particular behavior (Fazio et al., 1982; Nisbett & Ross, 1980).

And so, cognitive-dissonance theory leads to the hypothesis that we can change people's attitudes by getting them somehow to behave in a manner consistent with the attitudes we wish to promote. Research does show that people may indeed change attitudes when attitude-discrepant behavior is rewarded (Calder et al., 1973; Cooper, 1980). It is at once a frightening and promising concept. For instance, it sounds like a prescription for totalitarianism. Yet it also suggests that prejudiced individuals who are prevented from discriminating—who are compelled, for example, by open-housing laws to allow people from different ethnic backgrounds to buy homes in their neighborhoods—may actually become less prejudiced. In the following section, we shall turn our attention to the problems of prejudice and discrimination.

Prejudice

A few years ago Iowa schoolteacher Jane Elliot taught her all-white class of third graders some of the effects of prejudice. She divided the class into blue-eyed and brown-eyed children. The brown-eyed children were labeled inferior, made to wear collars that identified their group, and denied classroom privileges. After a few days of discrimination, the brown-eyed children lost self-esteem and earned poorer grades. They cried often and expressed the wish to stay at home.

Then the pattern was reversed. Blue-eyed children were assigned to the inferior status. After a few days they, too, learned how painful it is to be victims of discrimination. Weiner and Wright (1973) later found that making children victims of discrimination in this fashion led them to show less discrimination toward blacks. Why? Perhaps being discriminated against made the children more mindful of the sensitivities and feelings of members of outgroups. Unless we are encouraged to consider actively our attitudes toward others, we may automatically rely on previously conceived ideas, and these ideas are very often prejudiced (Langer et al., 1985).

Prejudice is an attitude toward a group that leads people to evaluate members of that group negatively. On a cognitive level, prejudice is linked to expectations that the target group will behave badly, in the workplace, say, or by engaging in criminal activity. On an affective level, prejudice is associated with negative feelings such as dislike or

Prejudice The belief that a person or group, on the basis of assumed racial, ethnic, sexual, or other features, will possess negative characteristics or perform inadequately.

What Is Stereotyping? How well is this child performing on her test? An experiment by Darley and Gross showed that our expectations concerning a child's performance on a test are linked to our awareness of that child's socioeconomic background.

hatred. Behaviorally, prejudice is associated with avoidance behavior, aggression, and as we shall see, discrimination. There is an interaction among our cognitions, affects, and behaviors.

As attitudes, prejudices act as cognitive filters through which we perceive the social world. Prejudices influence the processing of social information. In other words, when we observe the behavior of group members against whom we are prejudiced, we tend to pay special attention to, and to remember, instances of behavior that are consistent with our prejudices (Bodenhausen & Wyer, 1985; Dovidio et al., 1986; Fiske & Taylor, 1984). If you believe that Jews are cheap, you might be more likely to recall a Jew's negotiation of a price than a Jew's charitable donation. If you believe that Californians are "airheads," you might be more likely to recall TV images of surfing than of scientific conferences at Caltech and Berkeley.

Discrimination One form of negative behavior that results from prejudice is called **discrimination.** Many groups have been discriminated against from time to time in the United States. They include, but are not limited to, Jews, Catholics, blacks, Native Americans, Hispanic Americans, homosexuals, and women. Discrimination takes many forms, including denial of access to certain jobs, housing, even the voting booth. Many people

have forgotten that American blacks gained the right to vote several decades before it was obtained by American women.

Stereotypes Are Jews shrewd and ambitious? Are blacks superstitious and musical? Are men macho? If you believe such ideas, you are falling for a **stereotype**—a prejudice about a group that can lead us to interpret observations in a biased fashion. For example, sex-role stereotypes persist in U.S. society. As a result, men are generally perceived as assertive, dominant, aggressive, and independent, whereas women are generally perceived as gentle, compassionate, sensitive, and nurturant (Martin, 1987). These stereotypes at once tend to pressure men into socially combative roles and to limit women to supportive, dependent roles.

One experiment showed how social-class stereotypes can help advantaged children but influence teachers and other people to underrate the abilities of disadvantaged children. Subjects in the study watched videotapes of a girl taking an aca-

---

Discrimination The denial of privileges to a person or group on the basis of prejudice.

Stereotype A fixed, conventional idea about a group.

demic test. One group of subjects was told that she came from a high socioeconomic background, and as a consequence, they rated her performance as superior. Other subjects were told that she came from a low socioeconomic background. They watched the same videotape, but rated her performance as below grade level (Darley & Gross, 1983).

In further studies of stereotypes (Sagar & Schofield, 1980; Smedley & Bayton, 1978), whites viewed middle-class blacks as ambitious, intelligent, conscientious, and responsible, but saw *lower-class* blacks as ignorant, rude, dangerous, and self-pitying. Blacks shared whites' negative impressions of lower-class individuals of the other race. But blacks also negatively evaluated *middle-class* whites as biased, sly, and deceitful, even though they also considered middle-class whites conscientious and ambitious.

Despite the persistence of some stereotypes, white children in recent years seem more willing to work with and befriend blacks than they were during the 1960s (Moe et al., 1981).

Sources of Prejudice

The sources of prejudice are many and varied. Let us briefly consider several possible contributors:

1. *Assumptions of dissimilarity.* As we shall see later in the chapter, we are apt to be attracted to and like people who share our attitudes. In forming impressions of others, we are influenced by attitudinal similarity and dissimilarity as well as by race (Goldstein & Davis, 1972; Rokeach et al., 1960). People of different religions and races often have different backgrounds and values, giving rise to dissimilar attitudes. But even when people of different races share important values, they are likely to assume that they will not.

2. *Social conflict.* There is also a lengthy history of social and economic conflict between people of dif-

ferent races and religions. Conflict and competition lead to negative attitudes (Sherif, 1966).

3. *Authoritarianism.* Based on psychoanalytic theory and their interpretation of the **holocaust,** some social scientists (e.g., Adorno et al., 1950) have argued that racial and religious minorities serve as **scapegoats** for majority groups.

4. *Social learning.* As noted, children tend to acquire some attitudes from others, especially parents, through identification and socialization. Children often broadly imitate their parents, and parents often reinforce their children for doing so. In this way, prejudices are likely to be transferred from generation to generation.

5. *Information processing.* Another explanation of prejudice stems from the fact that people often divide the social world into two categories: "us" and "them." People also usually view those who belong to their own groups—the "ingroup"—more favorably than those who do not—the "outgroup" (Hemstone & Jaspars, 1982; Wilder & Thompson, 1980). Moreover, there is a tendency for us to assume that outgroup members are more alike in their attitudes and behaviors than members of our own groups (Park & Rothbart, 1982). Our relative isolation from outgroups does not encourage us to break down our stereotypes.

Let us now turn our attention to some of the factors involved in the formation of our impressions of other people.

SOCIAL PERCEPTION

Getting to know you,
Getting to know all about you. . . .

So goes the song from *The King and I.* How do we get to know other people, get to know all about them? In this section we shall explore some factors that contribute to **social perception:** primacy and recency effects, attribution theory, and body language. In the following section we shall explore the determinants of attraction to others.

Primacy and Recency Effects: The Importance of First Impressions

When I was a teenager, a young man was accepted or rejected by his date's parents the first time they were introduced. If he was considerate and made

---

Holocaust The name given the Nazi murder of millions of Jews during World War II.

Scapegoat A person or group upon whom the blame for the mistakes or crimes of others is cast.

Social perception A subfield of social psychology that studies the ways in which we form and modify impressions of others.

small talk, her parents would allow them to stay out past curfew, even to watch submarine races at the beach during the early morning hours. If he was boorish or uncommunicative, he was a cad forever. Her parents would object to him, no matter how hard he worked to gain their favor later on.

First impressions often make or break us. This is the **primacy effect.** As noted in Chapter 8, we infer traits from behavior. If we act considerately at first, we are labeled considerate. The trait of considerateness is used to explain and predict our future behavior. If after being labeled considerate, one keeps a date out past curfew, this behavior is likely to be seen as an exception to a rule—as justified by circumstances or external causes. But if at first one is seen as inconsiderate, several months of considerate behavior may be perceived as a cynical effort to "make up for it."

In a classic experiment on the primacy effect, Luchins (1957) had subjects read different stories about "Jim." The stories consisted of one or two paragraphs. One-paragraph stories portrayed Jim as friendly or unfriendly. These paragraphs were also used in the two-paragraph stories, but presented to different subjects in opposite order. Of subjects reading only the "friendly" paragraph, 95 percent rated Jim as friendly. Of those who read just the "unfriendly" paragraph, 3 percent rated him as friendly. Seventy-eight percent of those who read two-paragraph stories in the "friendly-unfriendly" order labeled Jim as friendly. But when they read the paragraphs in the reverse order, only 18 percent rated Jim as friendly.

How can we encourage people to pay more attention to more recent impressions? Luchins accomplished this by allowing time to elapse between presenting the paragraphs. In this way, fading memories allowed more recent information to take precedence. This is the **recency effect.** Luchins found a second way to counter first impressions: He simply counseled subjects to avoid snap judgments and to weigh all the evidence.

Attribution Theory

At the age of 3, one of my daughters believed that a friend's son was a boy because he *wanted* to be a boy. Since she was 3 at the time, this error in my daughter's **attribution** for the boy's gender is charming and understandable. But we shall see that we as adults also tend to exaggerate the role of conscious choice in other people's behavior.

An assumption about why people do things is called an attribution for behavior. Our inference of the motives and traits of others through the observation of their behavior is called the **attribution process.** We now focus on attribution theory, or the processes by which people draw conclusions about the factors that influence one another's behavior.

Attribution theory is very important because our attributions lead us to perceive others either as purposeful actors or as victims of circumstances.

Dispositional and Situational Attributions

When Patty Hearst was sent to prison, her sentence was harsh because the court believed that she had willfully chosen to break the law. The court, that is, had *attributed* Patty's behavior to internal factors—to her personality dispositions and to choice. The court may be said to have made a **dispositional attribution** for Patty's behavior. When President Carter ordered Patty Hearst's release, he was acting on the belief that Patty had been a victim of circumstances. He attributed Patty's behavior largely to external, situational factors. He may be said to have made a **situational attribution** for her behavior.

The fascinating aspect of the Patty Hearst case concerns Patty's attributions for her own behavior. In the early stages of her kidnapping, she was coerced into attitude-discrepant behavior and no

---

Primacy effect The tendency to evaluate others in terms of first impressions.

Recency effect The tendency to evaluate others in terms of the most recent impression.

Attribution A belief concerning why people behave in a certain way.

Attribution process The process by which people draw inferences about the motives and traits of others.

Dispositional attribution An assumption that a person's behavior is determined by internal causes, such as personal attitudes or goals.

Situational attribution An assumption that a person's behavior is determined by external circumstances, such as the social pressure found in a situation.

doubt attributed her participation to external, situational factors. But persistent coercion somehow led her to modify her self-identity, so that she became "radicalized." At that point she apparently attributed her behavior to internal, dispositional factors and might have wondered how she had been "duped" by U.S. society for all the years prior to her "awakening."

The Fundamental Attribution Error   If Patty Hearst came to attribute her radical behavior to internal factors, she was making an error in the attribution process. That is, she was attributing too much of her own behavior to internal factors. But we usually attribute too much of *other people's behavior* to internal factors. In fact, this bias in the attribution process is what social psychologists refer to as the **fundamental attribution error.** Apparently, when we observe the behavior of others, we focus excessively on their actions and too little on the contexts within which their actions take place. But we tend to be more aware of the networks of forces acting on ourselves.

One reason for the fundamental attribution error is that we tend to infer people's traits from their behavior. When we overhear a woman screaming at her husband in a supermarket, we tend to assume that she is impulsive and boisterous. We are usually not aware of the many things that her husband might have done to infuriate her. The fundamental attribution error is linked to another bias in the attribution process: the actor-observer effect.

The Actor-Observer Effect   When we see ourselves and others engaging in behavior that we do not like, we tend to see the others as willful but to perceive ourselves as victims of circumstances. The tendency to attribute the behavior of others to internal, dispositional factors and our own behavior to external, situational influences is called the **actor-observer effect** (Jellison & Green, 1981; Jones, 1979; Reeder, 1982; Safer, 1980).

Let us consider an example of the actor-observer effect. When parents and children argue about the children's choice of friends or dates, the parents infer traits from behavior and tend to perceive their children as stubborn, difficult, and independent. But the children also infer traits from behavior and may perceive their parents as bossy and controlling. Parents and children alike attribute the others' behavior to internal causes. That is, they make dispositional attributions about the behavior of others.

But how do the parents and children perceive themselves? The parents probably see themselves as forced into combat by their children's foolishness. If they become insistent, it is in response to their children's stubbornness. The children probably see themselves as responding to peer pressures and, perhaps, to sexual urges that may have come from within but do not seem "of their own making."*

The parents and the children both tend to see their own behavior as motivated by external factors. That is, they make situational attributions for their own behavior.

The Self-Serving Bias   There is also a **self-serving bias** in the attribution process. We are more likely to attribute our successes to internal, dispositional factors but our failures to external, situational influences (Baumgardner et al., 1986; O'Malley & Becker, 1984; Van der Plight & Eiser, 1983). When we have done well on a test or impressed a date, we are more likely to attribute these outcomes to our intelligence and charm. But when we fail, we are more likely to attribute them to bad luck, an unfairly difficult test, or our date's "bad mood."

Fundamental attribution error The tendency to assume that others act predominantly on the basis of their dispositions, even when there is evidence suggestive of the importance of their situations.

Actor-observer effect The tendency to attribute our own behavior to situational factors but to attribute the behavior of others to dispositional factors.

Self-serving bias The tendency to view one's successes as stemming from internal factors and one's failures as stemming from external factors.

---

*Psychologists, similarly, might speak of people in such a case as responding to the "inner environment."

Table 11.1 Factors Leading to Internal or External Attributions of Behavior

	INTERNAL ATTRIBUTION	EXTERNAL ATTRIBUTION
Consensus	Low: Few people behave this way.	High: Most people behave this way.
Consistency	High: The person behaves this way frequently.	High: The person behaves this way frequently.
Distinctiveness	Low: The person behaves this way in many situations.	High: The person behaves this way in few situations.

We are more likely to attribute behavior to internal, dispositional factors when it is low in consensus, high in consistency, and low in distinctiveness.

There are some exceptions to the self-serving bias. We are more likely to own up to our responsibility for our failures when we think that other people will not accept situational attributions (Reiss et al., 1981). And as noted in Chapter 9, depressed people are more likely than nondepressed people to attribute their failures to internal factors, even when dispositional attributions are not justified.

Another interesting bias in attribution is a sex difference in attributions for friendly behavior. Men are more likely than women to interpret a woman's friendliness toward men as a sign of promiscuity or seductiveness (Abbey, 1982). Traditional sex-role expectations apparently still lead men to believe that "decent" women are socially passive.

Factors Contributing to the Attribution Process: Consensus, Consistency, and Distinctiveness According to Harold Kelley (1979; Kelley & Michela, 1980), our attribution of behavior to internal or external causes can also be influenced by three factors: *consensus, consistency,* and *distinctiveness.* When few people act in a certain way—that is, when **consensus** is low—we are likely to attribute behavior to dispositional (internal) factors. Consistency refers to the degree to which the same person acts in the same way on other occasions. Highly consistent behavior can be attributed to dispositional or situational factors. Distinctiveness is the extent to which the person responds differently in different situations. If the person acts similarly in different situations, distinctiveness

is low and we are likely to attribute his or her behavior to dispositional factors.

Let us apply the criteria of consensus, consistency, and distinctiveness to a hypothetical situation adapted from Baron and Byrne (1987) involving a friend in a restaurant. She takes one bite of her blueberry cheese taco and calls loudly for the waiter. She argues that her food is inedible and demands that it be replaced. The question is whether she complained as a result of internal causes (e.g., because she is difficult to please) or external causes (i.e., because the food really is bad). Under these circumstances, we are likely to attribute her behavior to internal, dispositional causes: (1) No one else at the table is complaining, so consensus is low. (2) She has returned this dish on other occasions, so consistency is high. (3) She complains in other restaurants also, so distinctiveness is low (see Table 11.1).

But under the following circumstances, we are likely to attribute her behavior to external, situational causes: (1) Everyone else at the table is also complaining, so consensus is high. (2) She has returned this dish on other occasions, so consistency is high. (3) She usually does not complain at restaurants, so distinctiveness is high. Given these conditions, we are likely to believe that the blueberry cheese taco really was awful and our friend is justifiedly responding to the circumstances.

Consensus General agreement.

What Is Communicated by Body Language? By observing people's body language, we can frequently tell whether or not they like or dislike one another. What of this couple? What aspects of their nonverbal behavior provide cues about their attitudes and feelings?

Body Language

Body language is an important factor in our perception of others. At an early age we learn that the ways people carry themselves provide cues to how they feel and are likely to behave. You may have noticed that when people are "uptight," their bodies may also be rigid and straight-backed. People who are relaxed are more likely, literally, to "hang loose." It seems that various combinations of eye contact, posture, and distance between people provide broadly recognized cues to their moods and feelings toward their companions (Schwartz et al., 1983).

When people face us and lean toward us, we may assume that they like us or are interested in what we are saying. If we are privy to a conversation between a couple and observe that the woman is leaning toward the man but that he is sitting back and toying with his hair, we are likely to infer that he is not having any of what she is selling (Clore et al., 1975; DePaulo et al., 1978).

Touching also communicates. Women are more likely than men to touch other people when they are interacting with them (Stier & Hall, 1984). In one touching experiment, Kleinke (1977) showed that appeals for help can be more effective

when the distressed person engages in physical contact with people being asked for aid. A woman received more dimes for phone calls when she touched the person she was asking for money on the arm. In another experiment, waitresses received higher tips when they touched patrons on the hand or the shoulder while making change (Crusco & Wetzel, 1984).

In these experiments, touching was "noncontroversial"—usually gentle, brief, and occurring in familiar settings. But in another experiment, touching was introduced in a hospital prior to operations. In this experiment, women about to undergo operations reported lower anxiety and showed lower blood pressure when nurses explaining the procedures touched them on the arm (Whitcher & Fisher, 1979). But men who were touched as the procedures were being explained reported higher anxiety and showed elevated blood pressure. How do we account for this sex difference? Female patients may have interpreted touching as a sign of warmth, whereas male patients may have seen it as a threatening sign of the nurse's superior status in the hospital.

Body language can also be used to establish and maintain territorial control (Brown & Altman, 1981), as anyone who has had to step aside because

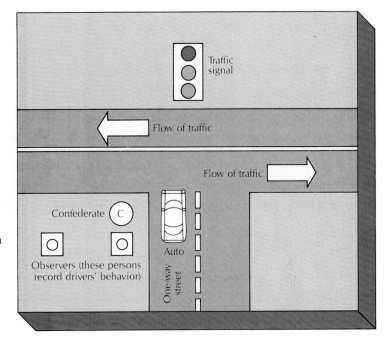

FIGURE 11.1. Diagram of an Experiment in Hard Staring and Avoidance. In the Greenbaum and Rosenfeld study, the confederate of the experimenter stared at some drivers and not at others. Those stared at drove across the intersection more rapidly once the light turned green. Why?

a football player was walking down the hall can testify. Werner and her colleagues (1981) found that players in a game arcade used touching as a way of signaling others to keep their distance. Solo players engaged in more touching than did groups, perhaps because they were surrounded by strangers.

Gazing and Staring: The Eyes Have It

We usually feel we can learn much from eye contact. When others "look us squarely in the eye," we may assume that they are assertive or open with us. Avoidance of eye contact may suggest deception or depression (Knapp, 1978; Siegman & Feldstein, 1977). In a study designed to validate a scale to measure romantic love, Rubin (1970) found that couples who attained higher "love scores" also spent more time gazing into each other's eyes.

Gazes are different, of course, from persistent "hard" stares. Hard stares are interpreted as provocations or signs of anger (Ellsworth & Langer, 1976). Adolescent males sometimes engage in "staring contests" as an assertion of dominance. The male who looks away first "loses."

In a series of field experiments, Phoebe Ellsworth and her colleagues (1972) subjected drivers stopped at red lights to hard stares from riders of motor scooters (see Figure 11.1). Recipients of the stares crossed the intersection more rapidly than nonrecipients when the light changed. Greenbaum and Rosenfeld (1978) found that recipients of hard stares from a man seated near an intersection also drove off more rapidly after the light turned green. Other research shows that recipients of hard stares show higher levels of physiological arousal than people who do not receive the stares (Strom & Buck, 1979). It may be that many of us rapidly leave situations in which we are stared at in order to achieve pleasant declines in arousal and avoid the threat of danger.

INTERPERSONAL ATTRACTION

Whether we are talking about a pair of magnetic toy animals or a couple in a singles bar, **attraction** is a force that draws bodies, or people, together. In social psychology, attraction has been defined as an attitude of liking or disliking (Berscheid, 1976). Factors such as physical appearance, atti-

Attraction In social psychology, an attitude of liking or disliking (negative attraction).

What Is the Role of Similarity in Attraction? According to the matching hypothesis, we tend to form relationships with people who are similar to ourselves in attractiveness. We also tend to be more attracted to people who possess similar attitudes, whether the relationship is a love relationship or a friendship.

tudinal similarity, family opposition, reciprocity, propinquity, and whether the other person seems "hard to get" all contribute to interpersonal attraction.

Physical Attractiveness: How Important Is Looking Good?

You might like to think that we are all so intelligent and sophisticated that we rank physical appearance low on the roster of qualities we seek in a date—below sensitivity and warmth, for example. But in experimental "Coke dates" and in commercial video-dating services, physical appearance has been the central factor in attraction and consideration of partners for future dates, sexual activity, and marriage (Byrne et al., 1970; Green et al., 1984; Hatfield & Sprecher, 1986).

What determines physical attractiveness? Are our standards fully subjective, or is there broad agreement on what is attractive?

It may be that there are no universal standards for beauty (Ford & Beach, 1951), but there are some common standards for physical attractiveness in our culture. Tallness is an asset for men in our culture, although college women prefer dates who are medium in height (Graziano et al., 1978). Tall women tend to be viewed less positively. Undergraduate women prefer their dates to be about six inches taller than they are, whereas undergraduate men, on the average, prefer women who are about four and a half inches shorter (Gillis & Avis, 1980).

Women generally prefer men with a V-taper, whose backs and shoulders are medium wide but whose waists, buttocks, and legs taper from medium thin to thin (Horvath, 1981; Lavrakas, 1975). Men, weaned on *Playboy* magazine perhaps, desire women with larger-than-average breasts, medium-width legs, and small to medium buttocks (Wiggins et al., 1968). Yet women with medium bust sizes are better liked than women with large or small busts. And speaking of the tendency to

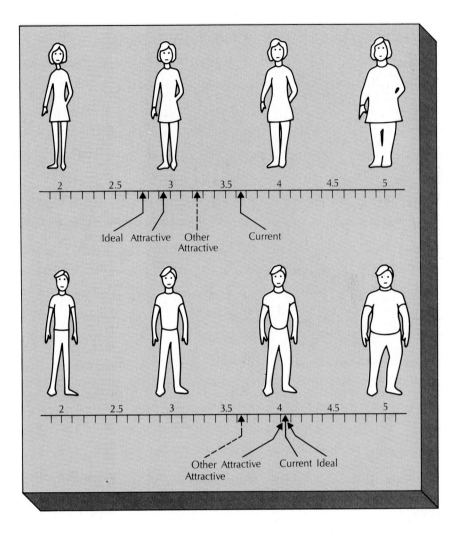

FIGURE 11.2. Can You Ever Be Too Thin? Research suggests that most college women believe that they are heavier than they ought to be. However, men actually prefer women to be a bit heavier than women assume they would like them to be.

overattribute other people's "behavior" to dispositional factors, consider a study of stereotypes of women with different bust sizes: It was found that women with large breasts are often viewed as less intelligent, competent, moral, and modest than women with smaller breasts (Kleinke & Staneski, 1980). Neither sex pays too much attention to the knees, ankles, or ears of the opposite sex (Nevid, 1984).

Both sexes perceive obese people as unattractive (Harris et al., 1982), but there remain some sex differences in perceptions of the most desirable body shape. Male college undergraduates as a group believe that their current physique is quite similar to the ideal male physique and to the physique women will find most attractive (Fallon & Ro-

zin, 1985). Women undergraduates, as noted in Chapter 9's discussion of anorexia nervosa, generally see themselves as heavier than the figure that is most attractive to males, and heavier still than the ideal female figure (Figure 11.2). But both sexes err in their estimates of the preferences of the opposite sex. Men prefer women to be heavier than women expect, and women prefer their men somewhat thinner than men expect.

An experiment at the University of Illinois found that the same people are perceived as being more attractive when they smile as compared to when they are posing sad faces (Mueser et al., 1984). So it may be that, as the song goes, there is ample reason to "put on a happy face" when you're looking for a date.

What Are the Stereotypes of Attractive People?
Today Christie Brinkley contributes to setting the standard for female beauty in our culture. Are attractive people more successful? Do they make better spouses and parents?

Even names have an influence on perceptions of attractiveness. In one experiment, photographs of women who had been rated equal in attractiveness were assigned various names (Garwood et al., 1980). They were then rated again, with the assigned names in view. Women given names such as Jennifer, Kathy, and Christine were rated significantly more attractive than women assigned names such as Gertrude, Ethel, and Harriet!

Stereotypes of Attractive People: Do Good Things Come in Pretty Packages?

By and large, we rate what is beautiful as good. We expect attractive people to be poised, sociable, popular, and mentally healthy; to be persuasive, hold prestigious jobs, be good parents, feel fulfilled, and even have stable marriages. Unattractive individuals are more likely to be evaluated as deviant, for example, as politically radical, as homosexual, or as having a mental disorder (Berscheid & Walster, 1974; Brigham, 1980; Dion et al., 1972; O'Grady, 1982; Unger et al., 1982). Less attractive college students are even more likely to rate themselves as prone toward developing problems such as mental disorders!

These stereotypes appear to have some basis in reality. For one thing, it does seem that more attractive individuals are less likely to develop mental disorders and that the disorders of unattractive individuals are more severe (e.g., Archer & Cash, 1985; Burns & Farina, 1987; Farina et al., 1986). Physical attractiveness is also positively correlated with educational achievement, occupational prestige, and income (Umberson & Hughes, 1984).

Attractive people are also seen as more self-centered and likely to have extramarital affairs (Dermer & Thiel, 1975). Yet even these "negative" assumptions have a positive side. After all, don't they mean that we think attractive people have more to be self-centered about and that their affairs reflect their greater sexual opportunities?

Attractive people are more likely to be found innocent of burglary and cheating in mock jury experiments. When found guilty, they are given less severe sentences (Efran, 1974). Perhaps we assume that more attractive people are less likely to need to resort to deviant behavior to achieve their goals. Even when they have erred, perhaps they will have more opportunity for personal growth and be more likely to change their evil ways.

The beautiful are also perceived as more talented. In one experiment, students rated essays as higher in quality when their authorship was attributed to a more attractive woman (Landy & Sigall, 1974).

The Matching Hypothesis: Who Is "Right" for You?

Have you ever refrained from asking out an extremely attractive person for fear of rejection? Do you feel more comfortable with someone who's a bit less attractive?

If so, you're not alone. Although we may rate highly attractive people as most desirable, we are more likely to try to construct relationships with and marry people who are similar to ourselves in attractiveness (Murstein & Christy, 1976). This tendency is predicted by the **matching hypothesis** (Berscheid et al., 1971). A major motivating factor is fear of rejection by more attractive people (Bernstein et al., 1983). For example, Shanteau and Nagy (1979) found that college women chose prospective dates who were moderately attractive but highly likely to accept the date, as opposed to more attractive men who were considered likely to reject them.

But the process of "settling" for someone other than the local Robert Redford or Cheryl Tiegs look-alike need not be an unhappy one. We tend to rate our mates as slightly more attractive than ourselves—as if we had somehow "gotten the better of the deal" (Murstein, 1972). We tend to idealize loved ones, but other explanations are also possible. By focusing on their positive features we may feel happier with our marriages. Too, we may be aware of our own struggles to present ourselves to the world each day but take our mates' appearance more or less for granted.

The matching hypothesis applies not only to physical attractiveness. We are also more likely to get married to people who are similar to us in their needs (Meyer & Pepper, 1977), personality (Buss, 1984; Lesnik-Oberstein & Cohen, 1984) and attitudes, as we shall see.

Attitudinal Similarity

It has been observed since ancient times that we tend to like people who agree with us (Jellison & Oliver, 1983). Birds of a feather, so to speak, flock together.

Byrne and his colleagues (1970) found that college students were most attracted to computer matchups who were physically appealing and expressed similar attitudes. Ratings of physically attractive dates with dissimilar attitudes approximated those of unattractive dates with similar attitudes. The more dogmatic we are, the more likely we are to reject people who disagree with us (Palmer & Kalin, 1985). Physical appeal and attitudes are both important determinants of whom we shall like and whom we shall dislike.

But there is also evidence that we may tend to *assume* that physically attractive people share our attitudes (Marks et al., 1981). Can this be a sort of wish-fulfillment? After all, from a balance-theory

perspective, when we and a person we like share attitudes toward third objects or situations, our cognitions are balanced. When physical attraction is very strong, as it was with Candy and Stretch, perhaps we like to think that the "kinks" in a relationship will be small or capable of being ironed out.

All attitudes are not necessarily equal. Men on computer dates at the University of Nevada were more influenced by sexual than religious attitudes (Touhey, 1972). But women were more attracted to men whose religious views coincided with their own. These findings suggest that women may have been less interested than men in a physical relationship but more concerned about creating a family with cohesive values. Recent studies show that attitudes toward religion and children are more important in mate selection than characteristics such as kindness and professional status (e.g., Buss & Barnes, 1986; Howard et al., 1987).

Similarity in tastes and distastes is also important in the development of relationships. For example, May and Hamilton (1980) found that college women rate photos of male strangers as more attractive when they are listening to music they prefer (in most cases, rock) as compared to music that they don't like (in this experiment, "avant-garde classical"). If a dating couple's taste in music does not overlap, one member may look more appealing at the same time that the second is losing appeal in the other's eyes, all because of what is on the stereo.

The "Romeo and Juliet Effect"

In the Shakespearean play, the young lovers Romeo and Juliet drew closer to each other against the bloody backdrop of a family feud. But that was literature. What about real life?

Psychologists sought an answer through a survey of dating and married couples at the University of Colorado (Driscoll et al., 1972). Student

---

Matching hypothesis The view that people tend to choose persons similar to themselves in attractiveness and attitudes in the formation of interpersonal relationships.

questionnaires suggested that parental opposition intensified feelings of love between couples during the first six to ten months of the relationship. But parental opposition did not affect feelings between married couples.

During the early stages of a relationship, parental opposition may intensify needs for security within a couple, so that they cling together more strongly. But for couples who have already made a strong commitment, as in a lengthy courtship or marriage, parental opposition may become irrelevant.

Reciprocity: If You Like Me, You Must Have Excellent Judgment

Has anyone told you how good-looking, brilliant, and mature you are? That your taste is refined? If so, have you been impressed by his or her fine judgment? When people praise us, we are more susceptible to the messages they are delivering. When we are admired and complimented, we tend to return these feelings and behaviors. This is **reciprocity.** We tend to reciprocate feelings of interest, respect, affection, and wanting to be together (Hays, 1984). Men tend to be attracted to women who engage them in conversation, maintain eye contact, and lean toward them while speaking, even when their attitudes are dissimilar (Gold et al., 1984). When people tell you that you are terrific, you may wonder why you didn't pay more attention to them before.

Propinquity: Simply Because You're Near Me

Why did Sarah Abrams walk down the aisle with Allen Ackroyd and not Danny Schmidt? Sarah and Danny actually had more in common. But Sarah and Al exchanged smoldering glances throughout 11th-grade English because their teacher had used an alphabetical seating chart. Danny sat diagonally across the room. Sarah, to him, was only a name called when attendance was taken.

Attraction is more likely to develop between people who are placed in frequent contact with one another. This is the effect of nearness, or **propinquity.** Students are more likely to develop friendships when they sit next to one another (Segal, 1974). Homeowners are most likely to become friendly with next-door neighbors, especially those with adjacent driveways (Whyte, 1956). Apartment dwellers tend to find friends among those who live nearby on the same floor (Nahemow & Lawton, 1975). Infants respond more positively to strangers after a number of meetings (Levitt, 1980). Adults report increased liking for a photograph of a stranger, simply as a result of being exposed to that picture several times (Moreland & Zajonc, 1982).

Playing Hard to Get: "I Only Have Eyes for You"

Elaine Walster and her colleagues (1973) recruited male subjects for an experiment in which they were given the opportunity to rate and select dates. They were given phony initial reactions of their potential dates to them and to the other men in the study. One woman was generally hard to get. She reacted indifferently to all the men. Another woman was uniformly easy to get. She responded positively to all male participants. A third showed the fine judgment of being attracted to the rater only. Men were overwhelmingly more attracted to this woman—the one who had eyes for them only. She was selected for dates 80 percent of the time.

Now that we have seen how our feelings of attraction are influenced by physical features, attitudinal similarity, and so on, let us consider the psychology of social influence.

SOCIAL INFLUENCE

Most of us would be reluctant to wear blue jeans to a funeral, to walk naked on city streets, or for that matter, to wear clothes at a nudist colony. Other people and groups can exert enormous pressure on us to behave according to their wishes

Reciprocity In interpersonal attraction, the tendency to return feelings and attitudes that are expressed about us.

Propinquity Nearness.

or according to group norms. **Social influence** is the area of social psychology that studies the ways in which people alter the thoughts, feelings, and behaviors of others. Earlier in the chapter we saw how attitudes can be changed through persuasion or by inducing attitude-discrepant behavior. In this section we shall describe a couple of classic experiments to show other ways in which people have influenced others to engage in destructive obedience and to conform to social norms.

Obedience to Authority

Richard Nixon resigned the presidency of the United States in August 1974. For two years the business of the nation had almost ground to a halt while Congress investigated the 1972 burglary of a Democratic party campaign office in the Watergate office and apartment complex. It turned out that Nixon supporters had authorized the break-in. Nixon himself might have been involved in the cover-up of this connection later on. For two years Nixon and his aides had been investigated by the press and by Congress. Now it was over. Some of the bad guys were thrown in jail. Nixon was exiled to the beaches of southern California. The nation returned to work. The new president, Gerald Ford, declared, "Our national nightmare is over."

But was it over? Have we come to grips with the implications of the Watergate affair?

According to Stanley Milgram (*APA Monitor*, January 1978), a prominent Yale University psychologist, the Watergate cover-up, like the Nazi slaughter of the Jews, was made possible through the compliance of people who were more concerned about the approval of their supervisors than about their own morality. Otherwise they would have refused to abet these crimes. The broad question is: How pressing is the need to obey authority figures at all costs?

The Milgram Studies: Shocking Stuff at Yale

Stanley Milgram also wondered how many of us would resist authority figures who made immoral requests. To find out, he ran a series of experiments at Yale University. In an early phase of his work, Milgram (1963) placed ads in New Haven newspapers for subjects for studies on learning and memory. He enlisted 40 men ranging in age from 20 to 50—teachers, engineers, laborers, salespeople, men who had not completed elementary school, men with graduate degrees. The sample was a cross section of the male population of this Connecticut city.

Let us suppose you had answered an ad. You would have shown up at the university for a fee of $4.50, for the sake of science and your own curiosity. You might have been impressed. After all, Yale was a venerable institution that dominated the city. You would not have been less impressed by the elegant labs, where you would have met a distinguished behavioral scientist dressed in a white laboratory coat and another newspaper recruit—like you. The scientist would have explained that the purpose of the experiment was to study the *effects of punishment on learning*. The experiment would require a "teacher" and a "learner." By chance you would be appointed the teacher, and the other recruit the learner.

You, the scientist, and the learner would enter a laboratory room with a rather threatening chair with dangling straps. The scientist would secure the learner's cooperation and strap him in. The learner would express some concern, but this was, after all, for the sake of science. And this was Yale University, was it not? What could happen to a person at Yale?

You would follow the scientist to an adjacent room from which you would do your "teaching." This teaching promised to be effective. You would punish the "learner's" errors by pressing levers marked from 15 to 450 volts on a fearsome looking console (Figure 11.3). Labels described 28 of the 30 levers as running the gamut from "Slight Shock" to "Danger: Severe Shock." The last two levers resembled a film unfit for anyone under age 17: They were rated simply "XXX." Just in case you had no idea what electric shock felt like, the scientist gave you a sample 45-volt shock. It stung. You pitied the fellow who might receive more.

Social influence The area of social psychology that studies the ways in which people influence the thoughts, feelings, and behavior of others.

FIGURE 11.3. What Is the "Aggression Machine"? In the Milgram studies on obedience to authority, pressing levers on the "aggression machine" was the operational definition of aggression.

Your learner was expected to learn word pairs. Pairs of words would be read from a list. After hearing the list once, the learner would have to produce the word that was paired with the stimulus word. He would do so by pressing a switch that would signify his choice from a list of four alternatives. The switch would light one of four panels in your room. If it was the correct panel, you would proceed to the next stimulus word. If not, you would deliver an electric shock. With each error, you would increase the voltage of the shock (Figure 11.4).

You would probably have some misgivings. Electrodes had been strapped to the learner's wrists, and the scientist had applied electrode paste to "avoid blisters and burns." You were also told that the shocks would cause "no permanent tissue damage," although they might be extremely painful. Still, the learner was going along, and after all, this was Yale.

The learner answered some items correctly and then made some errors. With mild concern you pressed the levers up through 45 volts. You had tolerated that much yourself. Then a few more mistakes were made. You pressed the 60-volt lever, then 75. The learner made another mistake. You paused and looked at the scientist. He was reassuring: "Although the shocks may be painful,

there is no permanent tissue damage, so please go on." Further errors were made, and quickly you were up to a shock of 300 volts. But now the learner was pounding on the other side of the wall! Your chest tightened and you began to perspire. Damn science and the $4.50, you thought. You hesitated and the scientist said, "The experiment requires that you continue." After the delivery of the next stimulus word, there was no answer at all. What were you to do? "Wait for five to ten seconds," the scientist instructed, "and then treat no answer as a wrong answer." But after the next shock, there was again that pounding on the wall! Now your heart was racing and you were convinced that you were causing extreme pain and discomfort. Was it possible that no lasting damage was being done? Was the experiment that important, after all? What to do? You hesitated again. The scientist said, "It is absolutely essential that you continue." His voice was very convincing. "You have no other choice," he said, "you *must* go on." You could barely think straight, and for some unaccountable reason you felt laughter rising in your throat. Your finger shook above the lever. What were you to do?

On Truth at Yale Milgram (1963, 1974) found out what most people would do. Of the 40 men in this phase of his research, only 5 refused to go beyond the 300-volt level, at which the "learner" first pounded the wall. Nine more "teachers" de-

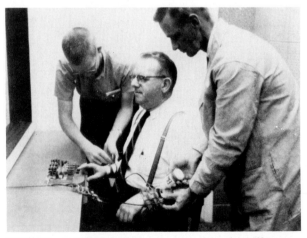

What Was the Role of the "Learner" in the Milgram Studies on Obedience to Authority?   This "learner" could be in for quite a shock.

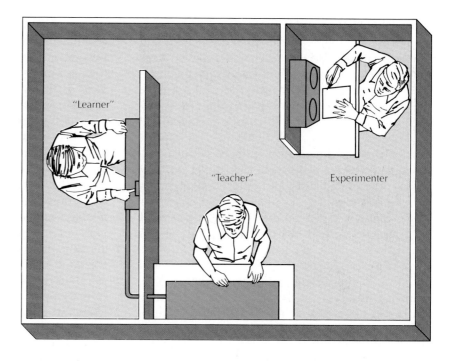

FIGURE 11.4. What Was the Experimental Set-Up in the Milgram Studies? When the "learner" makes an error, the experimenter prods the "teacher" to deliver a painful electric shock.

fied the scientist within the 300-volt range. But 65 percent of the participants complied with the scientist throughout the series, believing that they were delivering 450-volt, XXX-rated shocks.

Were these newspaper recruits simply unfeeling? Not at all. Milgram was impressed by their signs of stress. They trembled, they stuttered, they bit their lips. They groaned, they sweated, they dug their fingernails into their flesh. There were fits of laughter, though laughter was inappropriate. One salesperson's laughter was so convulsive that he could not continue with the experiment.

Milgram wondered if college students, heralded for independent thinking, would show more defiance. But a replication of the study with Yale undergraduates yielded similar results. What about women, who were supposedly less aggressive than men? Women, too, shocked the "learners"— and all this in a nation that values independence and the free will of the individual. Our "national nightmare" may not be over at all.

On Deception at Yale You are probably skeptical enough to wonder whether the "teachers" in the Milgram study actually shocked the "learners"

when they pressed the levers on the console. They didn't. The only real shock in this experiment was the 45-volt sample given to the "teachers." Its purpose was to lend credibility to the procedure.

The "learners" in the experiment were actually confederates of the experimenter. They had not answered the newspaper ads but were in on the truth from the start. "Teachers" were the only real subjects. They were led to believe that they were chosen at random for the teacher role, but the choosing was rigged so that newspaper recruits would always become teachers.

The Big Question: Why? We have shown that most people obey the commands of others, even when pressed to immoral tasks. But we have not answered the most pressing question: *Why?* Why did Germans "just follow orders" and commit atrocities? Why did "teachers" obey orders from the experimenter? We do not have all the answers, but we can offer a number of hypotheses:

1. *Socialization.* Despite the expressed U.S. ideal of independence, we are socialized to obey others (such as parents and teachers) from the time we are little children.

2. *Lack of social comparison.* In Milgram's experimental settings, experimenters showed command of the situation, whereas "teachers" (subjects) were on the experimenter's ground and very much on their own. Being on their own, they did not have the opportunity to compare their ideas and feelings with those of people in the same situation. And so they were less likely to have a clear impression of what to do. Ironically, in Nazi Germany, the average citizen was taught that all decent Germans revile Jews, blacks, and other "foreign" peoples. In Germany bigotry was the social norm.

3. *Perception of legitimate authority.* The phase of Milgram's research just described took place within the hallowed halls of Yale University. Subjects there might be overpowered by the reputation and authority of the setting. An experimenter at Yale might appear very much the legitimate authority figure—as might a government official or a high-ranking officer in the military. Further research showed that the university setting contributed to compliance but was not fully responsible for it. The percentage of subjects complying with the experimenter's demands dropped from 65 percent to 48 percent when Milgram (1974) replicated the study in a dingy storefront in a nearby town. At first glance this finding might seem encouraging. But the main point of the Milgram studies is precisely that most of us remain willing to engage in morally reprehensible acts at the behest of a legitimate-appearing authority figure. Hitler and his henchmen were the legitimate authority figures in Nazi Germany. The problem of acquiescence to authority figures remains.

4. *The foot-in-the-door technique.* The foot-in-the-door technique might also have contributed to the obedience of the "teachers" (Gilbert, 1981). That is, after they had begun the process of delivering graduated shocks to learners, perhaps they found it progressively more difficult to extricate themselves from the project. Soldiers, similarly, are first taught to obey unquestioningly in innocuous matters such as dress and drill. By the time they are ordered to risk their lives, they have been saluting smartly and following commands for quite some time.

5. *Inaccessibility of values.* Earlier in the chapter we saw that people are more likely to behave in ways that are consistent with their attitudes when their attitudes are readily available, or accessible. Moral values opposed to harming innocent people are attitudes. As noted in Chapter 6, we become subject to confused and conflicting thoughts and motives as our levels of arousal shoot up. As the subjects in the Milgram experiments became more and more aroused, their attitudes might have become less accessible. As a consequence, it might have become progressively more difficult for them to behave in ways that were consistent with their moral values.

6. *Buffers.* Social psychologist Daryl Bem (1987) also notes that several buffers decreased the immediate impact of the subjects' violence. "Learners" (confederates of the experimenter), for example, were in another room. When they were in the same room with "teachers"—that is, when subjects had full view of their victims—the compliance rate dropped from 65 to 40 percent. Moreover, when the subject was given the task of holding the "learner's" hand on the shock plate, the compliance rate dropped to 30 percent. In modern warfare, opposing soldiers tend to be separated by great distances. It is one thing to press a button to launch a missile or to aim a piece of artillery at a distant troop carrier or a distant ridge. It is another thing to hold the weapon to the throat of the victim.

And so, there are numerous theoretical explanations for obedience. Regardless of the exact nature of the forces that acted on the subjects in the Milgram studies, his research has alerted us to a real and present danger—the tendency of most people to obey an authority figure, even when the figure's demands contradict their own moral attitudes and values. It has happened before. Unhappily, unless we remain alert, it may happen again. Who are the authority figures in your life? How do you think you would have behaved if you had been a "teacher" in the Milgram studies? Are you sure?

In the section on conformity we describe another classic study, and you may try again to imagine how you would behave if you were involved in it.

Conformity

Earlier we noted that most of us would be reluctant to wear blue jeans to a funeral, to walk naked on

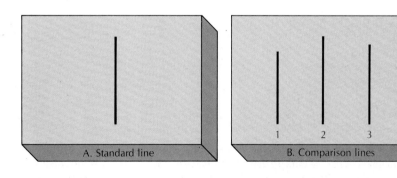

FIGURE 11.5. Cards Used in the Asch Study on Conformity.
Which line on the card at the right—1, 2, or 3—is the same length as the line on the card at the left? Line 2, right? But would you say "2" if you were a member of a group and six people answering ahead of you all said "3"? Are you sure?

A. Standard line

B. Comparison lines

city streets, or to wear clothes at a nudist colony. We are said to **conform** when we change our behavior to adhere to social norms. **Social norms** are widely accepted rules that indicate how we are expected to behave under certain circumstances (Moscovici, 1985). Rules that require us to whisper in libraries and to slow down when driving past a school are examples of explicit social norms. Other social norms are unspoken, or implicit (Zuckerman et al., 1983). One unspoken social norm is to face front in elevators. Another is to be "fashionably" late for social gatherings.

The tendency to conform to social norms is often a good thing. Many norms have evolved because they favor comfort and survival. But group pressure can also promote maladaptive behavior, as in pressure to wear coats and ties in summer in buildings cooled only, say, to 78 degrees Fahrenheit. At that high temperature the only motive for conforming to a dress code may be to show that we have been adequately socialized and are not threats to social rules.

Let us look at a classic experiment on conformity run by Solomon Asch in the early 1950s. Then we shall examine factors that promote conformity.

Seven Line Judges Can't Be Wrong: The Asch Study

Do you believe what you see with your own eyes? Seeing is believing, is it not? Not if you were a participant in the Asch (1952) study.

You would enter a laboratory room with seven other subjects for an experiment on visual discrimination. If you were familiar with psychology experiments, you might be surprised: There were

no rats and no electric-shock apparatus in sight, only a man at the front of a room with some cards with lines drawn on them.

The eight of you would be seated in a series. You would be given the seventh seat, a minor fact at the time. The man would explain the task. There was a single line on the card on the left. Three lines were drawn on the card at the right (Figure 11.5). One line was the same length as the line on the other card. You and the other subjects need only call out, one at a time, which of the three lines—1, 2, or 3—was the same length. Simple.

You would try it out. Those to your right spoke out in order: "3," "3," "3," "3," "3," "3." Now it was your turn. Line 3 was clearly the same length as the line on the first card, so you said "3." Then the fellow after you chimed in: "3." That's all there was to it. Then two other cards were set up in the front of the room. This time line 2 was clearly the same length as the line on the first card. The answers: "2," "2," "2," "2," "2," "2." Your turn again: "2," you said, and perhaps your mind began to wander. Your stomach was gurgling a bit. That night you would not even mind dorm food particularly. The fellow after you said, "2."

Another pair of cards was held up. Line 3 was clearly the correct answer. The six people on your right spoke in turn: "1," "1. . . ." Wait a second! ". . . 1," "1—" You forgot about dinner and studied the lines briefly. No, 1 was too short, by a good

Conform To change one's attitudes or overt behavior to adhere to social norms.

Social norms Explicit and implicit rules that reflect social expectations and influence the ways people behave in social situations.

What Was the Experimental Set-Up in the Asch Experiment in Conformity? The experimenter is at the right, and the unsuspecting subject is seated sixth from the left. All other "subjects" are actually in league with the experimenter.

half an inch. But "... 1," "1," and suddenly it was your turn. Your hands had quickly become sweaty and there was a lump in your throat. You wanted to say 3, but was it right? There was really no time and you had already paused noticeably: "1," you said, "1," the last fellow confirmed matter-of-factly.

Now your attention was riveted on the task. Much of the time you agreed with the other seven line judges, but sometimes you did not. And for some reason beyond your understanding, they were in perfect agreement, even when they were wrong—assuming that you could trust your eyes. The experiment was becoming an uncomfortable experience, and you began to doubt your judgment.

The discomfort in the Asch study was caused by the pressure to conform. Actually, the other seven recruits were confederates of the experimenter. They prearranged a number of incorrect responses. The sole purpose of the study was to see whether you would conform to the erroneous group judgments.

How many of Asch's subjects caved in? How many went along with the crowd rather than assert what they thought to be the right answer? Seventy-five percent. *Three of four agreed with the majority wrong answer at least once.*

What about you? Would you wear blue jeans if everyone else wore slacks and skirts? A number of more recent experiments (Wheeler et al., 1978) show that the tendency to conform did not go out with the Fabulous Fifties.

Factors Influencing Conformity

Several personal and situational factors prompt conformity to social norms. Personal factors include the desires to be liked by other members of the group and to be right (Insko, 1985), low self-esteem, high self-consciousness, social shyness (Krech et al., 1962; Santee & Maslach, 1982), gender, and familiarity with the task. Situational factors include group size and social support.

Gender There has been a great deal of controversy about whether women conform to social norms more so than men do. Old-fashioned stereotypes portray men as rugged individualists and women as "civilizing" influences, so it is not surprising that women have been generally perceived as more conformist. Experimental findings over the past several decades have at first glance tended to support this view. A sophisticated statistical analysis of the literature up through the middle 1970s, for example, suggested that women by and large were more conformist than men (Cooper, 1979).

On the other hand, there have been a number of studies suggestive that sex differences are complex and not quite so predictable. For example, an experiment run by Sandra Bem (1975) of Cornell University found that women who accept the sex-role stereotype of the passive, dependent female are more likely than men to conform. But other women can be as self-assertive and independent as men. Another fascinating experiment on sex differences was run by social psychologist Alice Eagly and her colleagues (1981). The Eagly group found that men conform to group opinions as frequently as women do when their conformity or independence will be private. But when their conformity would be made known to the group, they conform less often than women do, apparently because nonconformity is more consistent with the masculine sex-role stereotype of independence. Ironically enough, men may be motivated to act independently in order to conform to the male sex-role stereotype of rugged individualism.

Familiarity with Task Demands   Familiarity with the task at hand promotes self-reliance (Eagly, 1978). In one experiment, for example, Sistrunk and McDavid (1971) found that women were more likely to conform to group pressure on tasks involving identification of tools (such as wrenches) that were more familiar to men. But men were more likely to conform on tasks involving identification of cooking utensils, with which women, in our society, are usually more familiar.

Group Size   Situational factors include the number of people who hold the majority opinion and the presence of at least one other who shares the discrepant opinion. Probability of conformity, even to incorrect group judgments, increases rapidly as a group grows to five members. Then it increases at a slower rate up to eight members (Gerard et al., 1968; Wilder, 1977), at which point maximum probability of conformity is reached.

Social Support   But finding just one other person who supports your minority opinion is apparently enough to encourage you to stick to your

guns (Morris et al., 1977). In a variation of the Asch experiment, recruits were provided with just one confederate who agreed with their minority judgments (Allen & Levine, 1971). Even though this confederate seemed to have a visual impairment, as evidenced by thick glasses, his support was sufficient to lead actual subjects not to conform to incorrect majority opinions.

Studies in conformity highlight some of the ways in which we are influenced by groups. In the following section, we shall discuss other aspects of group behavior.

GROUP BEHAVIOR

To be human is to belong to groups. Families, classes, religious groups, political parties, circles of friends, bowling teams, sailing clubs, conversation groups, therapy groups—to how many groups do you belong? How do groups influence the behavior of individuals?

In this section we shall look at a number of aspects of group behavior: social facilitation, group decision making, mob behavior, and the bystander effect.

Social Facilitation

One effect of groups on individual behavior is **social facilitation,** or the effects on performance that result from the presence of others. Bicycle riders and runners tend to move more rapidly when they are members of a group. This effect is not limited to humans: Dogs and cats eat more rapidly when others are present. Even roaches run more rapidly when other roaches are present (Zajonc, 1980).

According to psychologist Robert Zajonc (1980), the presence of others influences us by increasing our levels of arousal, or motivation. When our levels of arousal are highly increased, our performance of simple, dominant responses is facili-

---

Social facilitation   The process by which a person's performance is increased when other members of a group engage in similar behavior.

Social Facilitation or Social Loafing?   Under what circumstances does working in a group facilitate performance? Under what circumstances does it promote social loafing?

tated, but our performance of complex, recently acquired responses may be impaired. For this reason, a well-rehearsed speech may be delivered more masterfully before a larger audience, but our performance in an offhand speech or at a question-and-answer session may be hampered by a large audience.

Social facilitation may be influenced by **evaluation apprehension** as well as level of arousal (Bray & Sugarman, 1980; Markus, 1981). Our performance before a group may be affected not only by the physical presence of others but also by our concern that they are evaluating our performance. When giving a speech, we may "lose our thread" if we become distracted by the audience and begin to focus too much on what they may be thinking of us (Seta, 1982). If we believe that we have begun to flounder, our evaluation apprehension may skyrocket, and as a consequence, our performance may deteriorate further.

The presence of others can also decrease performance when we are not acting *before* a group but are anonymous members *of* a group (Latané et al., 1979; Williams et al., 1981). Workers, for example, may "goof off" or engage in "social loafing" on humdrum tasks when they feel that they will not be found out and held accountable. There is then no evaluation apprehension. There may also be **diffusion of responsibilty** in groups. That is, each person may feel less responsibility to help because others are present. Group members may also reduce their efforts if an apparently capable member makes no contribution but tries to "ride free" on the efforts of other group members (Kerr, 1983). The belief that other group members are not likely to work as hard as oneself also contributes to social loafing (Jackson & Harkins, 1985).

Group Decision Making

In 1986 and 1987, President Ronald Reagan's popularity took a beating when it came out that he had authorized the sale of U.S. weapons to Iran to try to gain the release of U.S. hostages being held by pro-Iranian groups in Lebanon. This occurred at a time when the U.S. public was very hostile toward Iran. Reagan had also sworn he would never negotiate with terrorists and had branded Iran a "terrorist nation." The decision to "trade weapons for hostages" apparently resulted from heated discus-

Evaluation apprehension   Concern that others are evaluating our behavior.

Diffusion of responsibility   The spreading or sharing of responsibility for a decision or behavior among a group.

sions in the White House during which the secretaries of state and defense took one position, and the national security adviser took another position.

How do group decisions get made? Social psychologists have discovered a number of rules, or **social decision schemes,** that seem to govern group decision making (Baron & Byrne, 1987; Davis et al., 1984; Kerr & MacCoun, 1985; Vinocur et al., 1985). Note the following examples:

1. *The majority-wins scheme.* In this commonly used scheme, the group arrives at the decision that was initially supported by the majority. This scheme appears to guide decision making most often when there is no objectively correct decision. An example would be a decision about what car model to build when the popularity of various models has not been tested in the "court" of public opinion.

2. *The truth-wins scheme.* In this scheme, the group comes to recognize that one approach is objectively correct as more information is provided and opinions are discussed. For example, a group deciding whether to use SAT scores in admitting students to college would profit from information about whether these scores actually predict college success.

3. *The two-thirds majority scheme.* This scheme is frequently adopted by juries, who tend to convict defendants when two-thirds of the jury initially favors conviction.

4. *The first-shift rule.* In this scheme, the group tends to adopt the decision that reflects the first shift in opinion expressed by any group member. If a car-manufacturing group is equally divided on whether or not to produce a convertible, they may opt to do so after one group member initially opposed to the idea changes her mind. If a jury is deadlocked, the members may eventually follow the lead of the first juror to change his position.

Now let us consider whether group members are likely to make compromise decisions or to take relatively extreme viewpoints as a result of diverse initial positions.

Polarization and the Risky Shift

You might think that a group decision would be more conservative than an individual decision. After all, shouldn't there be an effort to compromise, to sort of "split the differences"? We might also expect that a few "mature" individuals would be able to balance the opinions of daredevils. But in general, groups seem not to work in these ways.

Consider the **polarization** effect. As an individual, you might recommend that your company risk $10,000 on a new product. Other company executives, polled individually, might risk similar amounts. But if you were gathered for a group decision, it is likely that you would recommend either an amount well above this figure or nothing at all (Myers & Lamm, 1976). This group effect is called polarization, or the taking of an extreme position. Yet if you had to gamble on which way the decision would go, you would do better to place your money on movement toward the higher sum—that is, to bet on a **risky shift.** Why?

One possibility is that a group member may reveal information the others had not been aware of and that this information clearly points in one direction or the other. With doubts removed, the group becomes polarized—moving decidedly in the appropriate direction. It may also be that social facilitation occurs in the group setting, and that increased motivation prompts more extreme decisions.

But why do groups tend to take greater, not smaller, risks than those that would be ventured by their members as individuals? One answer is diffusion of responsibility (Burnstein, 1983; Myers, 1983). If the venture flops, it will not be you alone to blame. Remember the self-serving bias: You can always say (and tell yourself) that the failure was, after all, a group decision. And if the venture pays off handsomely, you can attribute the outcome to your cool analysis and trumpet abroad your influential role in the group decision-making process.

Social decision schemes Rules for predicting the final outcome of group decision making on the basis of the initial positions of the members.

Polarization In social psychology, taking an extreme position or attitude on an issue.

Risky shift The tendency to make riskier decisions as a member of a group than as an individual acting independently.

Groupthink

A problem that sometimes arises in group decision making is called **groupthink.** Groupthink is usually instigated by a dynamic group leader. As noted by the originator of the term, Irving Janis (1982), groupthink is usually unrealistic and fueled by the perception of external threats to the group or to those the group wishes to protect. The perception of external threat heightens group cohesiveness and serves as a source of stress. When under stress, group members tend not to consider carefully all their options (Keinan, 1987). Flawed decisions are therefore a common outcome.

When the U.S. government sold weapons to Iran during the mid-1980s, profits from the sales were diverted—possibly illegally—to support the "contras," a group attempting to unseat the Sandinista government of the Central American country of Nicaragua. Although we do not know all the details of the plan to divert profits from the arms sales, it seems that the decision to do so was made by a small group including members of the National Security Council, such as Colonel Oliver North and Admiral John Poindexter, and, possibly, the director of the CIA, William Casey. Five characteristics of groupthink noted by Janis might all have played a role in this decision, which resulted in several indictments and a congressional investigation:

1. *Feelings of invulnerability.* The group might have believed that it was somewhat beyond the reach of the law because it was being carried out by powerful individuals close to the president. As reported during congressional testimony, group members might also have believed that they had not broken laws prohibiting aid to the contras.

2. *Group belief in its rightness.* The group apparently believed it was in the right because (1) it was carrying out the president's expressed desire to find ways to support the contras, and (2) it was arming the contras against a leftist government.

3. *The discrediting of information opposed to the group's decision.* At the time the group decided to divert

funds, the so-called Boland amendment to a congressional bill was in force, prohibiting the U.S. government from supporting the contras. The group apparently discredited the Boland amendment by (1) deciding that it was inconsistent with the best interests of the U.S.A., and (2) enlisting private citizens to divert profits from sales to the contras so that the U.S. government was not directly involved.

4. *Pressures on group members to conform.* Here we must be a bit more speculative. But it can be noted that North and Poindexter repeatedly testified that they were carrying out the expressed wishes of President Reagan (i.e., to help the contras), even though Reagan was unaware of the diversion of funds from arm sales to Iran. In this sense, they were conforming to the president's wishes. Moreover, most group members were convinced of the need to help the contras as a way of combating communism in the Western Hemisphere.

5. *Stereotyping of members of the outgroup.* The group apparently viewed persons who would oppose them as Communist "sympathizers"; "knee-jerk liberals"; and, in the case of the Congress that had voted for the Boland amendment, "slow-acting," "vacillating" (i.e., voting to aid the contras in one bill and prohibiting aid to the contras in another), and "irresolute."

These characteristics of the groupthink process apparently led the group to overestimate its power, to view itself as singlehandedly protecting the U.S.A. from the Communist threat in this hemisphere, and to make a decision that nearly brought the Reagan administration crashing down. The dynamics of this group apparently contributed to the distortion of information about the real political and legal world. In the next section we shall learn more about the importance of accurate information in the decision-making process.

Mob Behavior and Deindividuation

Gustave Le Bon (1960), the French social thinker, and savages. He branded mobs and crowds irrational, like a "beast with many heads." Mob actions like race riots and lynchings sometimes seem to operate on a psychology of their own. Do mobs elicit the beast in us? How is it that mild-mannered

---

Groupthink A process in which group members are influenced by cohesiveness and a dynamic leader to ignore external realities as they make decisions.

*"And now at this point in the meeting I'd like to shift
the blame away from me and onto someone else."*

people will commit mayhem as members of a mob? In seeking an answer, let us examine a lynching and the baiting type of crowd that often seems to attend threatened suicides.

The Lynching of Arthur Stevens

In *Social Learning and Imitation,* Neal Miller and John Dollard (1941) vividly described a southern lynching. Arthur Stevens, a black man, was accused of murdering his lover, a white woman, when she wanted to break up with him. Stevens was arrested and confessed to the crime. The sheriff feared violence and moved Stevens to a town 200 miles distant during the night. But his location was uncovered. The next day a mob of a hundred persons stormed the jail and returned Stevens to the scene of the crime.

Outrage spread from person to person like a plague bacillus. Laborers, professionals, women, adolescents, and law-enforcement officers alike were infected. Stevens was tortured, emasculated, and murdered. His corpse was dragged through the streets. Then the mob went on a rampage in town, chasing and assaulting other blacks. The riot ended only when troops were sent in to restore law and order.

Deindividuation

When we act as individuals, fear of consequences and self-evaluation tend to prevent antisocial behavior. But as members of a mob, we may experience **deindividuation,** a state of reduced self-awareness and lowered concern for social evaluation (Mann et al., 1982). Many factors lead to deindividuation, including anonymity, diffusion of responsibility, arousal due to noise and crowding (Zimbardo, 1969), and focus of individual attention on the group process (Diener, 1980). Individuals also tend to adopt the emerging norms and attitudes of the group (Turner & Killian, 1972). Under these circumstances, crowd members behave more aggressively than they would as individuals.

Deindividuation The process by which group members may discontinue self-evaluation and adopt group norms and attitudes.

Police know that mob actions are best averted early, by dispersing the small groups that may gather into a crowd. On an individual level, perhaps we can resist deindividuation by instructing ourselves to stop and think whenever we begin to feel highly aroused as group members. If we dissociate ourselves from such groups when they are in the formative process, we shall be more likely to retain critical self-evaluation and avoid behavior that we shall later regret.

The Baiting Crowd in Cases of Threatened Suicide

As individuals, we often feel compassion when we observe people who are so distressed that they are considering suicide. Why is it, then, that when people who are considering suicide threaten to jump from a ledge the crowd often baits them, urging them on?

Such baiting occurred in 10 of 21 cases of threatened suicide studied by Leon Mann (1981). Analysis of newspaper reports suggested a number of factors that might have prompted deindividuation among crowd members, all contributing to anonymity: The crowds were large. It was dark (past 6 P.M.). The victim and the crowd were distant from one another (with the victim, for example, on a high floor). Baiting by the crowd was also linked to high temperatures (the summer season) and a long duration of the episode, suggestive of stress and fatigue among crowd members.

Helping Behavior and the Bystander Effect: Some Watch While Others Die

In 1964 the nation was shocked by the murder of 28-year-old Kitty Genovese in New York City. Murder was not unheard of in the "Big Apple," but Kitty had screamed for help as her killer had repeatedly stabbed her. Nearly 40 neighbors had heard the commotion. Many watched. Nobody helped. Why? As a nation are we a callous bunch who would rather watch than help when others are in trouble? Penn State psychologist R. Lance Shotland notes that in the two decades since the mur-

Altruism Unselfish concern for the welfare of others.

der (Dowd, 1984), more than 1,000 books and articles have been written attempting to explain the behavior of bystanders in crises. According to Stanley Milgram, the Genovese case "touched on a fundamental issue of the human condition. If we need help, will those around us stand around and let us be destroyed or will they come to our aid?" (in Dowd, 1984).

What factors determine whether we help others who are in trouble?

The Helper: Who Helps?   Some psychologists (e.g., Hoffman, 1981) suggest that **altruism** is a part of human nature. In keeping with sociobiological theory (see Chapter 1), they argue that self-sacrifice will sometimes help guarantee that a close relative will succeed. In this way, self-sacrifice is actually "selfish" from a genetic point of view: It helps us perpetuate a genetic code similar to our own in future generations.

Most psychologists focus on the roles of a helper's mood and personality traits. By and large, we are more likely to help others when we are in a good mood (Berkowitz, 1987; Manucia et al., 1984; Rosenhan et al., 1981). Yet we may help others when we are miserable ourselves if our own problems work to increase our empathy or sensitivity to the plights of others (Batson et al., 1981; Thompson et al., 1980). People with a high need for approval may act "altruistically" to earn approval from others (Satow, 1975). People who are empathic, who can take the perspective of others, are also likely to help (Archer et al., 1981).

There are many other reasons why bystanders frequently do not come to the aid of others in distress. First, if bystanders do not fully understand what they are seeing, they may not recognize that an emergency exists. That is, the more ambiguous the situation, the less likely it is that bystanders will try to help (Shotland & Heinold, 1985). Second, the presence of others may lead to diffusion of responsibility, so that no one assumes responsibility for helping others (as we shall see in a following section). Third, if bystanders are not certain that they possess the competencies to take charge of the situation, they may also stay on the sidelines for fear of making a social blunder and being subject to ridicule (Pantin & Carver, 1982)—or for fear of getting hurt themselves.

Bystanders who believe that others "get" what they deserve may rationalize not helping by thinking that a person would not be in trouble unless this outcome was just (Lerner et al., 1975). A sense of personal responsibility increases the likelihood of helping. Such responsibility may stem from having made a verbal commitment to help (e.g., Moriarty, 1975) or from having been designated by others as responsible for carrying out a helping chore (Maruyama et al., 1982).

The Victim: Who Is Helped?   Although sex roles have been changing, it is traditional for men to help women in our society. Latané and Dabbs (1975) found that women were more likely than men to receive help, especially from men, when they dropped coins in Atlanta (a southern city) than in Seattle or Columbus (northern cities). The researchers explain this difference by noting that traditional sex roles persevere more strongly in the South.

Women are also more likely than men to be helped when their cars have broken down on the highway or they are hitchhiking (Pomazal & Clore, 1973). There may be sexual overtones to some of this "altruism." Women are most likely to be helped by males when they are attractive and when they are alone (Benson et al., 1976; Snyder et al., 1974).

As in the research on interpersonal attraction, similarity also seems to promote helping behavior. Poorly dressed people are more likely to succeed in requests for a dime with poorly dressed strangers, and well-dressed people are more likely to get money from well-dressed strangers (Hensley, 1981).

Situational Determinants of Helping: "Am I the Only One Here?"   It may seem logical that a group of people would be more likely to have come to the aid of Kitty Genovese than would a lone person. After all, a group could more effectively have overpowered her attacker. Yet research by Darley and Latané (1968) suggests that a lone

person may have been more likely to try to help her.

In their experiment, male subjects were performing meaningless tasks in cubicles when they heard a (convincing) recording of a person apparently having an epileptic seizure. When the subjects thought that four other persons were immediately available to help, only 31 percent made an effort to help the victim. But when they thought that no one else was available, 85 percent of them tried to offer aid. As in other areas of group behavior, it seems that diffusion of responsibility inhibits helping behavior in groups or crowds. When we are in a group, we are often willing to let George (or Georgette) do it. When George isn't around, we are more willing to help others ourselves.

Note that the bystanders in most studies on the bystander effect are strangers (Latané & Nida, 1981). Research shows that bystanders who are acquainted with victims are more likely to respond to the social norm of helping others in need (Rutkowski et al., 1983). After all, aren't we more likely to give to charity when asked directly by a coworker or supervisor in the socially exposed situation of the office, as compared to a letter received in the privacy of our own homes?

We are more likely to help others when we can clearly see what is happening (for instance, if we can see clearly that the woman whose car has broken down is alone) and when the environment is familiar to us (e.g., when we are in our home town rather than a strange city).

As this text draws to a close, let us hope that you have become persuaded that psychology is an attractive field of study. Let us hope that your first impressions of psychology led to positive attitudes and that these attitudes will prove resistant to change if you enroll in advanced courses in psychology. On the other hand, I do not want to urge compliance too strongly—your own attitudes and behavior need not conform to mine. After all, I'm not the one who is calculating your grade for this course.

TRUTH OR FICTION REVISITED

Religious people are likely to attend church regularly. Not necessarily. It is difficult to predict specific behavior, such as church attendance, from general attitudes, such as whether one is "religious."

Admitting your product's weak points in an ad is the death knell for sales. False. Admitting weaknesses while also stressing strengths can build credibility.

Most of us are swayed by ads that offer useful information, not by emotional appeals or celebrity endorsements. False. Emotional appeals are more effective than information presented matter-of-factly, and the appeal of the endorser often seems to rub off on the product.

People who are highly worried about what other people think of them are likely to be low in sales resistance. True. Focusing on the feelings of salespersons rather than on whether or not one needs a product makes it more difficult to refuse.

We appreciate things more when we have to work hard for them. True. According to the principle of effort justification, we would be seeking reasons to justify our labors, and these reasons would probably have something to do with the value of the goal.

We tend to divide the social world into "us" and "them." True. This tendency is one of the roots of prejudice.

First impressions have powerful effects on our social relationships. True. We tend to interpret subsequent behavior in terms of our first impressions.

We hold others responsible for their misdeeds but tend to see ourselves as victims of circumstances when our behavior falls short of our standards. True. This bias is the kernel of the fundamental attribution error—the tendency to underestimate the importance of the situation in making attributions of the behaviors of others.

We tend to attribute our successes to our abilities and hard work but to attribute our failures to external factors such as lack of time and obstacles placed in our paths by others. True. This bias in the attribution process is called the self-serving bias.

Waitresses who touch their patrons when making change receive higher tips. True. Brief, nonthreatening touches often elicit favorable behavior.

Beauty is in the eye of the beholder. False. There are some rather consistent cultural standards for beauty.

College men prefer women to be thinner than college women expect. False. College men actually prefer women to be somewhat heavier than college women expect.

People are perceived as more attractive when they are smiling. True.

Opposites attract: We are more likely to be drawn to people who disagree with our attitudes than to people who share them. False. Physical attraction and attitudinal similarity are the two most powerful contributors to the development of relationships.

Most people would refuse to deliver painful electric shocks to an innocent party, even under powerful social pressure. False. The great majority complied with an authority figure in the Milgram studies.

Many people are late to social gatherings because they are conforming to a social norm. True. People usually prefer guests to be somewhat late, perhaps because it gives them more time to get things organized.

Bicycle riders and runners tend to move more rapidly in competition than when they are practicing alone. True. This is an example of social facilitation.

Group decisions tend to represent conservative compromises of the opinions of the group members. False. Group decisions are usually riskier than the opinions of individual group members, probably because of diffusion of responsibility.

Nearly 40 people stood by and did nothing while a woman was being stabbed to death. True. We are more likely to help others when we believe we are the only ones available to do so.

Chapter Review

Social psychologists study the nature and causes of our thoughts, feelings, and overt behaviors in social situations.

Most social psychologists view attitudes as enduring systems of beliefs with affective, behavioral, and cognitive components. Factors that influence the likelihood that we can predict behavior from attitudes include attitudinal specificity, strength of attitudes, having a vested interest in the outcome of behavior, and accessibility of attitudes. Attitudes may be acquired through conditioning, observational learning, and cognitive appraisal.

According to the elaboration likelihood model, persuading people to change attitudes can take place through central and peripheral routes. Repeated messages generally "sell" better than messages delivered once. People show greater response to emotional appeals than to factual presentations. Persuasive communicators show expertise, trustworthiness, attractiveness, or similarity to the audience. According to the foot-in-the-door effect, people are more likely to accede to large requests after they have acceded to smaller requests.

According to balance theory, we are motivated to maintain harmony among our perceptions, beliefs, and attitudes. According to cognitive-dissonance theory, people dislike inconsistency between their attitudes and their behavior. Attitude-discrepant behavior apparently induces cognitive dissonance, which people can then reduce by changing their attitudes.

Prejudice is an attitude toward a group that includes negative evaluations, negative affect, and avoidance behavior or discrimination. Sources of prejudice include attitudinal dissimilarity, social conflict, social learning, authoritarianism, and the tendency to divide the social world into two categories: "us" and "them."

We often perceive others in terms of first impressions (primacy effect), although recent impressions (recency effect) can become important when time passes between observations. In making dispositional attributions, we attribute people's behavior to internal factors, such as their personality traits and decisions. In situational attributions, we attribute people's behavior to their circumstances or external forces. Biases in the attribution process include the fundamental attribution error, the actor-observer effect, and the self-serving bias. Our attribution of behavior is also influenced by the behavior's consensus, consistency, and distinctiveness.

People who feel positively toward one another position themselves close together and touch. Touching other people in a noncontroversial (e.g., brief, gentle) way appears to elicit favorable behavior. Gazing into another's eyes can be a sign of love; a "hard stare" is an aversive challenge.

We are more attracted to good-looking people. We tend to assume that attractive people are talented and unlikely to engage in criminal behavior. According to the matching hypothesis, we tend to seek dates and mates at our own level of attractiveness because of fear of rejection. Attitudinal similarity, propinquity, reciprocity, parental opposition, and playing hard-to-get can all enhance feelings of attraction.

Most people comply with the demands of authority figures, even when these demands seem immoral, as shown in the Milgram studies on obedience. Factors that heighten the tendency to obey include socialization, lack of social comparison, perception of legitimate authority, the foot-in-the-door technique, inaccessibility of values, and—in the Milgram studies—buffers between the actor and the victim.

People are said to conform when they change their behavior to adhere to social norms. People feel increasing pressure to conform to group norms and opinions as groups grow to eight persons. It was once believed that women are more likely to conform than men, but this stereotype is being called into question.

The presence of others may facilitate performance for reasons such as increased arousal and evaluation apprehension. However, when we are anonymous group members, task performance may fall off (social loafing may occur).

Group decisions appear to get made according to a number of social-decision schemes, such as the majority-wins scheme, the truth-wins scheme, the two-thirds-majority scheme, and the first-shift rule. Group decisions tend to be more polarized and risky than individual decisions. Groups are thought to make riskier decisions largely because of diffusion of responsibility.

Groupthink is an unrealistic and often disastrous decision-making process facilitated by a dynamic leader, group cohesiveness, perception of an external threat, feelings of invulnerability, group belief in its rightness, the discrediting of opposing information, pressure to conform, and stereotyping of members of the outgroup.

Emotional crowds may induce attitude-discrepant behavior through the process of deindividuation—a state of reduced self-awareness and lowered concern for social evaluation.

According to the bystander effect, people are unlikely to aid others in distress when they are members of crowds. Crowds diffuse responsibility. We are more likely to help when we think we are the only one available, have a clear view of the situation, and are not afraid of making a social blunder.

Exercise

Social Psychology Concepts and Examples

Directions: *In the first column are a number of concepts in social psychology. In the second column are instances of behavior that serve as examples of these concepts. Match the example with the appropriate concept by writing the letter of the example in the blank space to the left of the concept. Answers follow.*

CONCEPT	EXAMPLES
_____ 1. Prejudice	A. A person assumes that someone who bumped into him did so on purpose.
_____ 2. Bystander effect	
_____ 3. Cognitive dissonance	
_____ 4. Discrimination	B. A man does not ask a beautiful woman out for fear of rejection.
_____ 5. Conformity	
_____ 6. Dispositional attribution	

_____ 7. Emotional appeal
_____ 8. Foot-in-the-door technique
_____ 9. Matching hypothesis
_____ 10. Nonbalance
_____ 11. Primacy effect
_____ 12. Propinquity
_____ 13. Reciprocity
_____ 14. Evaluation apprehension
_____ 15. Effort justification
_____ 16. Risky shift
_____ 17. Situational attribution
_____ 18. Deindividuation
_____ 19. Diffusion of responsibility
_____ 20. Fundamental attribution error

C. A committee takes a greater gamble than any member would take acting alone.
D. A person asks a small favor to prepare someone to grant a larger favor later.
E. A new worker is late and the boss conceptualizes him as "a late person."
F. John blames his mood on the weather.
G. A person does not come to the aid of a crime victim because many people surround the victim.
H. Joan likes Jim more after he tells her that he likes her very, very much.
I. Patty Hearst's attitudes become radicalized after she is coerced into attitude-discrepant behavior.
J. A mob member forgets his own values and adopts the norms of the crowd.
K. A person is paid too little for his work and begins to think that his work has high intrinsic value.
L. A student wears blue jeans because "everyone" is wearing them.
M. An athlete runs faster because he is concerned that fellow racers are aware of his performance.
N. A man assumes that a woman will not be assertive in the business world.
O. The man in item N, above, chooses not to hire a woman.
P. A dentist shows photos of diseased gums to convince patients to improve their oral hygiene.
Q. A person falls in love with someone who works in the same office.
R. Jim disagrees with Joan, but Joan doesn't care since she is indifferent to Jim.

Answer Key to Exercise

1. N	**6.** A	**11.** E	**16.** C
2. G	**7.** P	**12.** Q	**17.** F
3. I, K	**8.** D	**13.** H	**18.** J
4. O	**9.** B	**14.** M	**19.** G
5. L	**10.** R	**15.** K	**20.** A

Posttest

Directions: *For each of the following, select the choice that best answers the question or completes the sentence.*

1. Which of the following most accurately expresses the relationship between attitudes and behaviors?

   (a) People behave in ways that are consistent with their general attitudes, **(b)** People usually change their attitudes so that they are consistent with their behavior, **(c)** There is no relationship between attitudes and behavior, **(d)** The relationships between attitudes and behavior are complex.

2. A salesperson agrees to sell you a car for a low price but must "check" with the manager first. The manager refuses to let the car go for the agreed-upon price and the salesperson must "reluctantly" ask you for a higher bid. Which technique is the salesperson using?

   (a) The foot-in-the-door technique, **(b)** The two-sided argument, **(c)** Evaluation apprehension, **(d)** Low-balling.

3. Which of the following is a central cue for persuading people to drink Coke or Pepsi?

   (a) Providing information about the taste of the drink, **(b)** Having a movie star deliver a television commercial, **(c)** Showing attractive, slender people drinking the soda, **(d)** Using a person with a fine voice to sell the product.

4. People tend to be easy to persuade when they

   (a) have high self-esteem, **(b)** focus on the needs and feelings of the persuader, **(c)** have low social anxiety, **(d)** focus on their own needs and feelings.

5. Mary and John like one another very much. However, they disagree on their choice of friends. According to the text, Mary and John are each in a state of

   (a) balance, **(b)** dissonance, **(c)** imbalance, **(d)** nonbalance.

6. Which of the following is a concept of cognitive-dissonance theory?

   (a) Diffusion of responsibility, **(b)** Evaluation apprehension, **(c)** Effort justification, **(d)** Imbalance.

7. One form of behavior that results from prejudice is called

(a) authoritarianism, (b) deindividuation, (c) attitude-discrepant behavior, (d) discrimination.

8. Which of the following represents an information-processing approach to explaining prejudice?

(a) Prejudiced people displace unconscious hostility onto the objects of their prejudice, (b) People tend to divide the social world into "us" and "them" and to assume that "they" are homogeneous, (c) Children acquire many attitudes from others, especially parents, by means of observational learning, (d) People who belong to outgroups are likely to be less similar to us in their attitudes than people who belong to our ingroup.

9. Which of the following statements reflects a clear dispositional attribution.

(a) "Something got the best of him," (b) "He did what he thought was right," (c) "He did it that way because of the weather," (d) "He could not refuse the money."

10. Attributing too much of other people's behavior to dispositional factors is called

(a) the fundamental attribution error, (b) the actor-observer effect, (c) internalization, (d) evaluation apprehension.

11. The central factor in attraction is

(a) playing hard to get, (b) reciprocity, (c) physical appearance, (d) propinquity.

12. Which of the following is true about standards for attractiveness in our culture?

(a) Tallness is an asset for women, (b) Women prefer their dates to be about the same height they are, (c) Women prefer their men somewhat heavier than men expect, (d) Men prefer their women somewhat heavier than women expect.

13. In their dating practices, people tend to ask out persons who are similar in attractiveness largely because of

(a) fairness, (b) fear of rejection, (c) balance theory, (d) evaluation apprehension.

14. Important experiments on obedience to authority were carried out by

(a) Stanley Milgram, (b) Solomon Asch, (c) Abraham Luchins, (d) John Dollard.

15. In the experiments on obedience to authority run at Yale University, who received electric shock?

(a) Learners, (b) Teachers, (c) Experimenters, (d) Confederates of the experimenters.

16. Fewer subjects obeyed the experimenter when the studies on obedience were shifted from Yale University to a dingy storefront. This lower compliance rate was probably due to

    (a) creation of fewer buffers between the subject and the confederate of the experimenter, (b) increased accessibility of personal values, (c) perception of the authority figure as less legitimate, (d) greater social comparison between subjects and the setting.

17. Conformity is defined as

    (a) obedience to authority, (b) deindividuation, (c) changing behavior to conform to social norms, (d) diffusion of responsibility.

18. When we are members of a group, we are most likely to engage in social loafing when

    (a) we experience evaluation apprehension, (b) our level of arousal increases, (c) we are anonymous, (d) the leader is an authority figure.

19. Groups are thought to make risky decisions because

    (a) needed information is rarely shared in the group process, (b) group members experience evaluation apprehension in regard to other group members, (c) strong group leaders tend to have their way, (d) responsibility for the decisions is diffused.

20. All of the following appear to lead to deindividuation, with the exception of

    (a) an explicit decision-making process, (b) anonymity, (c) diffusion of responsibility, (d) focusing of individual attention on the group process.

21. The case of Kitty Genovese illustrates

    (a) cognitive-dissonance theory, (b) group decision making, (c) the bystander effect, (d) the principle of social loafing.

22. Concerning the relationship between gender and conformity, Baron and Byrne argue that

    (a) men are more likely than women to conform, (b) women are more likely than men to conform, (c) the literature on gender and conformity is in such disarray that no conclusions are warranted, (d) there are no important differences between men and women in the tendency to conform.

23. Which of the following social decision schemes is used most often when there is no objectively correct decision?

    (a) The majority-wins scheme, (b) The truth-wins scheme, (c) The first-shift rule, (d) The two-thirds majority scheme.

24. Each of the following is a factor in fostering groupthink, with the *exception of*

    (a) group belief in its rightness, (b) a dynamic leader, (c) stereotyping of members of the outgroup, (d) feelings of vulnerability.

Answer Key to Posttest

1. D	8. B	14. A	20. A
2. D	9. B	15. B	21. C
3. A	10. A	16. C	22. D
4. B	11. C	17. C	23. A
5. C	12. D	18. C	24. D
6. C	13. B	19. D	
7. D			

HEALTH PSYCHOLOGY

OUTLINE

PRETEST: TRUTH OR FICTION?
HEALTH PSYCHOLOGY
STRESS AND STRESSORS
   Daily Hassles and Life Changes
   Hassles versus Life Changes
   Life Changes and Illness
   Pain and Discomfort
   Anxiety
   Frustration
   Conflict
   Type A Behavior
PSYCHOLOGICAL FACTORS IN ILLNESS
   The General-Adaptation Syndrome
   Psychoneuroimmunology: The Link Between the
     GAS and Illness?
   Headaches
   Ulcers
   Hypertension
   Asthma
   Cancer
PSYCHOLOGICAL HARDINESS
PSYCHOLOGICAL INVOLVEMENT IN
   TREATMENT OF HEALTH PROBLEMS

Physician–Patient Interactions
Compliance with Medical Instructions and
   Procedures
PAIN MANAGEMENT
   Accurate Information
   Distraction and Fantasy
   Coping with Irrational Beliefs
   Social Support
PSYCHOLOGICAL TREATMENT OF INSOMNIA
   Progressive Relaxation, Biofeedback Training, and
     Autogenic Training
   Challenging Irrational Ideas about Sleeping
   Stimulus Control
   Establishing a Regular Routine
   Fantasy
PSYCHOLOGICAL METHODS FOR CUTTING
   DOWN AND QUITTING SMOKING
   Methods for Quitting Cold Turkey
   Methods for Cutting Down
TRUTH OR FICTION REVISITED
APPENDIX REVIEW
EXERCISE
POSTTEST

PRETEST: TRUTH OR FICTION?

Too much of a good thing can make you ill.

Our blood pressure rises when we are under stress.

Stress can influence the course of cancer.

The belief that we can handle stress is linked to lower levels of adrenalin in the bloodstream.

Physicians' body language goes a long way toward determining whether they have a good "bedside manner."

Medical patients should be told as little as possible about their illnesses and why they are being given certain medicines.

Video games help children with cancer cope with the painful side effects of chemotherapy.

Many people have insomnia because they try too hard to get to sleep at night.

HEALTH PSYCHOLOGY

Health psychology studies the relationships between psychological factors (e.g., overt behavior, emotions, beliefs, and attitudes) and the prevention and treatment of physical illness (Rogers, 1983). For example, in recent years health psychologists have been exploring the ways in which

- Stress contributes to physical illnesses ranging from hypertension to ulcers to cancer.
- Behavior patterns (such as Type A behavior) contribute to high blood pressure and heart problems.
- Erroneous beliefs about insomnia can help keep us up at night.
- Belief in one's own self-efficacy can facilitate quitting smoking.
- Emotional responses toward illnesses (such as anger rather than passive acceptance) appears to help control the illness, as in the case of the spread of cancer (Levy et al., 1985).
- Operant conditioning (in the form of biofeedback training) can help accident victims regain control of limbs to which nerve pathways have been damaged.

In this section we shall consider a number of issues in health psychology: sources of stress; the body's response to stress; a number of stress-related physical illnesses (also referred to as psychosomatic or psychophysiological disorders); ways in which psychologists aid in the treatment of health problems, including stress management, treatment of insomnia, and treatment of cigarette smoking; and the management of pain.

STRESS AND STRESSORS

Did you know that too much of a good thing can make you ill? Yes, you might think that marrying Mr. or Ms. Right, finding a prestigious job, and moving to a better neighborhood all in the same year would propel you into a state of bliss. It might. But the impact of all these events, one on top of the other, could also lead to headaches, high blood pressure, and asthma. As pleasant as they may be, they all involve major life changes, and life changes are one source of **stress** (Holmes & Rahe, 1967).

In the science of physics, stress is defined as a pressure or force exerted on a body. Tons of rock pressing against the earth, one car smashing into another, a rubber band stretching—all are types of physical stress. Psychological forces, or stresses, also "press," "push," or "pull." We may feel "crushed" by the "weight" of a big decision, "smashed" by misfortune, or "stretched" to the point of "snapping."

In psychology, stress is the demand made on an organism to adapt, to cope, or to adjust. Some stress is necessary to keep us alert and occupied (Selye, 1980). But stress that is too intense or prolonged can overtax our adjustive capacity, dampen our moods (Eckenrode, 1984; Stone & Neale, 1984), and have harmful physical effects. Types of stress include daily hassles and life changes, pain and discomfort, anxiety, frustration, conflict, and Type A behavior.

Daily Hassles and Life Changes: "Going through Changes"

It is the "last" straw that will break the camel's back—so goes the saying. Similarly, stresses can pile atop each other until we can finally no longer cope. Some of these stresses are found in the form of daily "hassles"; others are life changes. Lazarus and his colleagues (1985) analyzed a scale that measures daily **hassles** and found that they could be grouped as follows:

Household hassles, such as preparing meals, shopping, and home maintenance

Health hassles, such as physical illness, concern about medical treatment, and the side effects of medication

Time-pressure hassles, such as having too many things to do, too many responsibilities, and not enough time

---

Health psychology The field of psychology that studies the relationships between psychological factors and the prevention and treatment of physical illness.

Stress The demand made on an organism to adjust.

Hassle A source of annoyance or aggravation.

Criticisms of the Holmes and Rahe Approach Although the links between life changes and illness may seem quite convincing, they are correlational and not experimental (Dohrenwend et al., 1982; Monroe, 1982). It may seem logical that the life changes caused the disorders, but the life changes were not manipulated experimentally, and rival explanations of the data are possible. One possibility is that people who are predisposed toward medical or psychological problems amass more life-change units. For example, before medical disorders are diagnosed, the disorders may contribute to sexual problems, arguments with one's spouse or in-laws, changes in living conditions and personal habits, changes in sleeping habits, and so on. So in many cases it may be that the physical and psychological problems precede rather than result from life changes (Dohrenwend et al., 1984; Dohrenwend & Shrout, 1985; Monroe, 1983).

Other aspects of the research into the relationship between life changes and illness have also been challenged. For instance, positive life changes may be less disturbing than negative life changes, even when their number of life-change units is high (Lefcourt et al., 1981; Perkins, 1982; Thoits, 1983). That is, a change for the better in the health of a family member is usually less stressful than a change for the worse—a change for the better is a change, but it is also less of a "hassle."

Another problem with the Holmes and Rahe approach is that different kinds of people respond to life stresses in different ways. People who are "easy-going" are less likely to become ill under stress than people who are hard-driving. Factors such as self-confidence and support from family members can also alleviate many of the potential effects of life stresses (Holahan & Moos, 1985).

A Role for Cognitive Appraisal The degree of stress linked to an event will also reflect the meaning the event has for the individual. Pregnancy, for example, can be a positive or negative life change, depending on whether one wants and is prepared to have a child. We cognitively appraise hassles and life changes (Lazarus et al., 1985). In responding to them, we take into account our values and goals, our beliefs in our coping abil-

ity, our social support, and so on. The same kind of event will be less taxing for people who have greater coping ability and support.

Still, life changes do require adjustments, and it seems wise for us to be aware of the hassles and life changes associated with our styles of life.

Pain and Discomfort

Pain and discomfort impair performance and coping ability. Athletes report that pain interferes with their ability to run, swim, and so forth, even when the source of the pain does not directly weaken them.

In an experiment on the effects of pain on performance, psychiatrist Curt Richter (1957) first recorded the amount of time rats could swim to stay afloat in a tub of water. In water at room temperature, most rats could keep their noses above the surface for about 80 hours. But when Richter blew noxious streams of air into their faces or kept the water uncomfortably hot or cold, the rats could remain afloat for only 20 to 40 hours. When the rats were traumatized before their dunking by having their whiskers noisily cropped off, some managed to remain afloat for only a few minutes. Yet the clipping itself had not weakened them. Rats that were allowed several minutes to recover from the clipping before being launched swam for the usual 80 hours. Psychologists also recommend that we space aggravating tasks or chores, so that discomfort does not build to the point where it compounds stress and impairs our performance.

Anxiety

Up-tight, shook up, jumpy, on edge, butterflies in the stomach—these are just some of the colorful expressions used to describe the unpleasant sensations we associate with anxiety. The relationship between anxiety and stress is a two-way street: Anxiety may be thought of as a general emotional response to stress, but anxiety is also a source of stress. Anxiety is also a source of motivation, which like other sources of motivation leads to goal-directed behavior—usually to reduce or eliminate the anxiety.

Figure A.1 What Are Frustration and Conflict? Part A is a model for frustration in which a person (*P*) has a motive (*M*) to reach a goal (*G*), but is frustrated by a barrier (*B*). Part B shows an approach–approach conflict, in which the person cannot approach two positive goals simultaneously. Part C is an avoidance–avoidance conflict, in which avoiding one undesirable goal requires approaching another undesirable goal. Part D shows an approach–avoidance conflict, in which the same goal has both positive and negative features. Part E is a model for a double approach–avoidance conflict, in which the various goals perceived by the individual have their positive and negative features.

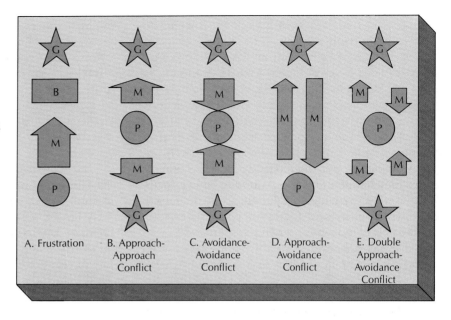

A. Frustration   B. Approach-Approach Conflict   C. Avoidance-Avoidance Conflict   D. Approach-Avoidance Conflict   E. Double Approach-Avoidance Conflict

As noted in Chapter 9, with some people anxiety is persistent and seems to take on the quality of a personality variable. Such people are frequently referred to as experiencing **trait anxiety.** With other people, anxiety attacks are swift and sudden, as in the case of panic disorder. These types of anxiety are likely candidates for having biological causes.

State anxiety, by contrast, refers to a temporary condition of arousal that is clearly triggered by a specific situation. We might experience state anxiety on the eve of a final exam, before a big date, on a job interview, or while waiting in the dentist's office. Different people experience state anxiety in different situations because events—such as learning to use a microcomputer or speaking before a group—have different meanings for us, based on our values and our learning histories.

But as noted in Chapter 9, anxiety can also stem from irrational beliefs and self-demands, such as those outlined by Albert Ellis. For example, perfectionists and people who are overly concerned about gaining the approval of others are likely to give themselves a good deal to be anxious about—and as a consequence, to heighten the stress impacting on them. Health psychologists therefore find themselves concerned with clients'

perfectionistic attitudes and excessive needs for approval, as well as with more theoretical issues.

Frustration

You may wish to play the line for the varsity football team, but you may weigh only 120 pounds or you may be a woman. You may have been denied a job or educational opportunity because of your ethnic background or favoritism. We all encounter **frustration,** the thwarting of a motive to attain a goal (see Figure A.1, Part A). Frustration is another source of stress.

Many sources of frustration are obvious. Adolescents are used to being too young to wear makeup, drive, go out, spend money, drink, or work. Age is the barrier that requires them to delay gratification. We may frustrate ourselves if our goals are set too high or if our self-demands are

Trait anxiety Anxiety as a personality variable, or persistent trait.

State anxiety A temporary condition of anxiety that may be attributed to a situation.

Frustration The thwarting of a motive.

irrational. Again, as Albert Ellis notes, if we try to earn other people's approval at all costs or insist on performing perfectly in all our undertakings, we doom ourselves to failure and frustration.

Anxiety and fear may also serve as barriers that prevent us from acting effectively to meet our goals. A high school senior who wishes to attend an out-of-state college may be frustrated by fear of leaving home. A young adult may not ask an attractive person out on a date because of fear of rejection. A woman may be frustrated in her desire to move up the corporate ladder by fear that co-workers, friends, and family may view her assertiveness as compromising her femininity.

Getting ahead is often a gradual process that demands the ability to live with some frustration and to delay gratification. Yet our **tolerance for frustration** may fluctuate. Stress heaped on stress can lower our tolerance, just as Richter's rats, stressed from their close shaves, sank quickly to the bottom of the tub. We may laugh off a flat tire on a good day. But if it is raining or if we have just waited for an hour in a gas line, the flat may seem like the last straw. People who have encountered frustration but learned that it is possible to surmount barriers or find substitute goals are more tolerant of frustration than those who have never experienced it or those who have experienced too much of it.

Conflict

Have you ever felt "damned if you did and damned if you didn't"? Regretted that you couldn't do two things, or be in two places, at the same time? Wanted to go to a film but had to study for a test? This is **conflict**—being torn in two or more directions by opposing motives. Conflict is frustrating and stressful. Conflict may also be looked at as a type of frustration in which the barrier to achieving a goal is an opposing impulse or motive. Psychologists often break conflicts down into four types.

An **approach-approach conflict** (Figure A.1, Part B) is the least stressful form of conflict. Here each of two goals is positive and within reach. You may not be able to decide between pizza or tacos, Tom or Dick, or a trip to Nassau or Hawaii. Conflicts are usually resolved by making decisions. People in conflict may **vacillate** until they make a decision, and afterward, there may be some regrets, especially if one's choice falls short of expectations.

An **avoidance-avoidance conflict** (Figure A.1, Part C) is more stressful because you are motivated to avoid each of two negative goals. However, avoiding one requires approaching the other. You may be fearful of visiting the dentist but also fear that your teeth will decay if you do not. You may not want to contribute to the Association for the Advancement of Lost Causes but fear that your friends will consider you cheap or uncommitted if you do not. Each goal is negative in an avoidance-avoidance conflict. When an avoidance-avoidance conflict is highly stressful and no resolution is in sight, some people withdraw from the conflict by focusing their attention on other matters or by suspending behavior altogether. For example, some highly conflicted people have refused to get out of bed in the morning and start the day.

The same goal can produce both approach and avoidance motives, as in the **approach-avoidance conflict** (Figure A.1, Part D). People and things have their pluses and minuses, their good points and their bad points. Cream cheese pie may be delicious, but oh, the calories! Why are so many attractive goals immoral, illegal, or fattening? Goals producing mixed motives may seem more attractive from a distance but more repulsive from nearby. Many couples repeatedly break up, then reunite. When they are apart and lonely, they may recall each other fondly and swear that they could make it work "the next time" if they got together again. But after they again spend time together, they may find themselves facing the same old ag-

---

Tolerance for frustration Ability to delay gratification, to maintain self-control when a motive is thwarted.

Conflict A condition characterized by opposing motives, in which gratification of one motive precludes gratification of the other.

Approach-approach conflict Conflict involving two positive but mutually exclusive goals.

Vacillate To move back and forth.

Avoidance-avoidance conflict Conflict involving two negative goals, with avoidance of one requiring approach of the other.

Approach-avoidance conflict Conflict involving a goal with positive and negative features.

gravations and think, "How could I have ever believed this so-and-so would change?"

The most complex form of conflict is the **double approach-avoidance conflict** (Figure A.1, Part E) in which each of two or more goals has its positive and negative aspects. Should you study on the eve of an exam or go to a film? "Studying's a drag, but I won't have to worry about flunking. I'd love to see the movie, but I'd just be worrying about how I'll do tomorrow." Should you take a job or go on for advanced training when you complete your college program? If you opt for the job, cash will soon be jingling in your pockets, but later you might wonder if you have the education to reach your potential. By furthering your education you may have to delay the independence and gratification that are afforded by earning a living, but you may find a more fulfilling position later on.

All forms of conflict entail motives that aim in opposite directions. When one motive is much stronger than the other—as when you feel "starved" and are only slightly concerned about your weight—it will probably not be too stressful to act in accordance with the powerful motive and, in this case, eat. But when each conflicting motive is powerful, you may encounter high levels of stress and confusion about the proper course of action. At such times you are faced with the need to make a decision, although making decisions can also be stressful, especially when there is no clear correct choice.

Type A Behavior

Many of us behave as though we were dedicated to the continuous creation of our own stress through the **Type A behavior** pattern. Type A people are highly driven, competitive, impatient, and aggressive (Holmes & Will, 1985; Matthews et al., 1982). They feel rushed and under pressure and keep one eye glued firmly to the clock. They are not only prompt, but frequently early, for appointments (Strahan, 1981). They eat, walk, and talk rapidly, and become restless when they see others working slowly (Musante et al., 1983). They attempt to dominate group discussions (Yarnold et al., 1985). Type A people find it difficult to surrender control or to share power (Miller et al., 1985; Strube & Werner, 1985). As a consequence, they are often reluctant to delegate authority in

the workplace, and in this way they increase their own workloads. Type A people also "accentuate the negative": they are merciless in their self-criticism when they fail at a task (Brunson & Matthews, 1981), and they seek out negative information about themselves in order to better themselves (Cooney & Zeichner, 1985).

Type A people find it difficult just to go out on the tennis court and bat the ball back and forth. They watch their form, perfect their strokes, and demand regular self-improvement. Albert Ellis's second irrational belief—that you must be perfectly competent and achieving in everything you undertake—seems to be their motto.

Type B people, by contrast, relax more readily and focus more on the quality of life. They are less ambitious, less impatient, and pace themselves. Type A's perceive time as passing more rapidly than do Type B's, and they work more quickly (Yarnold & Grimm, 1982). Type A's earn higher grades and more money than Type B's of equal intelligence (Glass, 1977). Type A's also seek greater challenges than Type B's (Ortega & Pipal, 1984).

A recent study of Type A women found that they, like their male counterparts, reach higher occupational levels than their Type B peers (Kelly & Houston, 1985). Their jobs are also more stressful and demanding than those held by Type B women. However, Type A and Type B women in this study did not differ in their marital adjustment or in the amount of time spent in leisure activities.

There is an irony in the Type A person's seeking of difficult challenges; Type A's respond to challenge with higher blood pressure than Type B's do (Holmes et al., 1984).

Until recently it was the gospel that Type A's were also at higher risk for heart attacks than Type B's, but evidence in support of this view seems currently in disarray. Numerous studies have found that Type A people are at greater risk for heart

---

Double approach-avoidance conflict Conflict involving two goals, each of which has positive and negative aspects.

Type A behavior Stress-producing behavior, characterized by hostility, perfectionism, and a sense of time urgency.

Questionnaire

Are you Type A or Type B?

Are you Type A or Type B? Type A's are ambitious, hard driving, and chronically discontent with their current achievements. Type B's, by contrast, are more relaxed, more involved with the quality of life.

The following checklist was developed from descriptions of Type A people by Friedman and Ulmer (1984), Matthews and her colleagues (1982), and Musante et al. (1983). The checklist will help give you insight into whether you are closer in your behavior patterns to the Type A or the Type B individual. Simply place a checkmark under the Yes if the behavior pattern is typical of you, and under the No if it is not. Try to work rapidly and leave no item blank. Then turn to the scoring key in Appendix C.

DO YOU: YES   NO

1. Strongly accent key words in your everyday speech?   _____ _____
2. Eat and walk quickly?   _____ _____
3. Believe that children should be taught to be competitive?   _____ _____
4. Feel restless when watching a slow worker?   _____ _____
5. Hurry other people to get on with what they're trying to say? _____ _____
6. Find it highly aggravating to be stuck in traffic or waiting for a seat at a restaurant? _____ _____
7. Continue to think about your own problems and business even when listening to someone else? _____ _____

---

disease than are Type B's (DeBacker et al., 1983; French-Belgian Collaborative Group, 1982; Haynes et al., 1980). But recent studies have found opposite results (Brody, 1988). Some researchers attribute these confused findings to the global nature of the Type A concept. They suggest that one or more components of the Type A pattern, such as hostility or cynicism (i.e., expecting the worst from people), is the actual risk factor for heart disease (Barefoot et al., 1982; Friedman & Booth-Kewley, 1987; Friedman et al., 1985; Shekelle et al., 1983).

Friedman and Ulmer (1984) report decreasing the risk for recurrent heart attacks among Type A men by helping them reduce their sense of time urgency, reduce their hostility, give up smoking, and eat low-fat diets. Health psychologists have also used techniques such as environmental engineering to help Type A people find a more relaxing way to get to and from work, relax before the day begins, and set aside some time for a hot bath, (noncompetitive!) exercise, or meditation.

PSYCHOLOGICAL FACTORS IN ILLNESS

Professionals interested in the impact of stress have learned that the body, under stress, is very much like a clock with an alarm system that does not shut off until its energy is dangerously depleted.

8. Try to eat and shave, or drive and jot down notes, at the same time?   ____ ____
9. Catch up on your work on vacations?   ____ ____
10. Bring conversations around to topics of concern to you?   ____ ____
11. Feel guilty when you spend time just relaxing?   ____ ____
12. Find that you're so wrapped up in your work that you no longer notice office decorations or the scenery when you commute?   ____ ____
13. Find yourself concerned with getting more *things* rather than developing your creativity and social concerns?   ____ ____
14. Try to schedule more and more activities into less time?   ____ ____
15. Always appear for appointments on time?   ____ ____
16. Clench or pound your fists, or use other gestures, to emphasize your views?   ____ ____
17. Credit your accomplishments to your ability to work rapidly?   ____ ____
18. Feel that things must be done *now* and quickly?   ____ ____
19. Constantly try to find more efficient ways to get things done?   ____ ____
20. Insist on winning at games rather than just having fun?   ____ ____
21. Interrupt others often?   ____ ____
22. Feel irritated when others are late?   ____ ____
23. Leave the table immediately after eating?   ____ ____
24. Feel rushed?   ____ ____
25. Feel dissatisfied with your current level of performance?   ____ ____

The General-Adaptation Syndrome

Hans Selye (1976) noted that the body's response to different stressors shows some similarities, whether the stressor is a bacterial invasion, a perceived danger, a major life change, an inner conflict, or a wound. For this reason he labeled the stress response the **general-adaptation syndrome** (GAS). The GAS consists of three stages: an alarm reaction, a resistance stage, and an exhaustion stage.

The **alarm reaction** is triggered by the impact of a stressor. It mobilizes or arouses the body in preparation for defense. It is characterized by a high level of activity of the sympathetic branch of the autonomic nervous system (see Table A.2). It provides more energy for muscular activity, which can be used to fight or flee from a source of danger, and at least temporarily, decreases the body's vulnerability to wounds. Perhaps the single most important component of the alarm reaction to health psychologists is the secretion of adrenalin, which is also referred to as a "stress hormone." The alarm reaction is inherited from a long-ago

General-adaptation syndrome Selye's term for a hypothesized three-stage response to stress. Abbreviated *GAS*.

Alarm reaction The first stage of the GAS, which is "triggered" by the impact of a stressor and characterized by sympathetic activity.

Table A.2   Components of the Alarm Reaction

Respiration rate increases
Heart rate increases
Blood pressure increases
Muscles tense
Blood shifts away from the skin
Digestion slows
Sugar is released from the liver
Adrenalin is secreted
Blood coagulability increases

The alarm reaction is triggered by various types of stressors. It is essentially defined by activity of the sympathetic branch of the autonomic nervous system, and it prepares the body to fight or flee from a source of danger.

time when many stressors were life-threatening. It was triggered by a predator at the edge of a thicket, by a sudden rustling in the undergrowth. Once the threat is removed, the body returns to a lower state of arousal.

Our ancestors lived in situations in which the alarm reaction would not be activated for long. They fought or ran quickly or, to put it bluntly,

Resistance stage The second stage of the GAS, characterized by prolonged sympathetic activity in an effort to restore lost energy and repair damage.

Exhaustion stage The third stage of the GAS, characterized by weakened resistance and possible deterioration.

Progressive relaxation A method for reducing muscle tension that involves alternate tensing and relaxing of muscle groups throughout the body.

Immune system The functions of the body that permit it to recognize and destroy harmful foreign agents, such as disease organisms.

Psychoneuroimmunology The field that studies the relationships between psychological factors and the functioning of the immune system.

Antigen A substance—such as a protein-containing substance from a disease organism—that can stimulate the body to mount an immune response against it.

Antibodies One of a class of proteins found in the blood that recognizes and destroys antigens, such as those of a bacterial invasion.

they died. Sensitive alarm reactions contributed to survival. Our ancestors did not spend 16 years in the academic grind or carry 30-year adjustable-rate mortgages. Contemporary pressures may activate our alarm systems for hours, days, or months at a time, so that highly sensitive systems may now be a handicap.

If the alarm reaction mobilizes the body and the stressor is not removed, we enter the adaptation stage, or **resistance stage,** of the GAS. Secretion of adrenalin is not so high as in the alarm reaction, but it is still greater than normal. In this stage the body attempts to restore lost energy and repair whatever damage has been done.

If the stressor is still not adequately dealt with, we may enter the final stage, or **exhaustion stage,** of the GAS. Continued stress at this time may lead to physical deterioration, to what Selye terms "diseases of adaptation"—from headaches and hives to allergies, ulcers, and heart disease—and, ultimately, to death.

Psychologists have found it helpful in reducing stress to focus on some of the body responses involved in the alarm reaction. For example, in the method of **progressive relaxation,** stressed clients learn systematically to lower the tension in muscle groups throughout the body. In this way, the heart and respiration rates are also brought down to more comfortable levels (Paul, 1966b).

Psychoneuroimmunology: The Link Between the GAS and Illness

Why does persistent arousal of the GAS lead to illness? One of the answers apparently lies in the GAS's effect on the body's **immune system.** Health psychologists along with biologists and medical researchers have recently been exploring a new field of study that addresses the relationships between psychological factors and the immune system: **psychoneuroimmunology** (Schindler, 1985).

The role of the immune system is to recognize and destroy foreign agents, or **antigens,** that invade the body (Arms & Camp, 1987). Various white blood cells within the body are responsible for taking on these foreign agents. One of their functions is the production of **antibodies,** or specialized proteins that combat antigens and prevent

What are the causes of headaches?

them from spreading throughout the body. Once antibodies to antigens have been formed, they remain in the bloodstream, so that future invasions are more efficiently repelled.

Research suggests that the persistent secretion of "stress hormones" impairs the functioning of the immune system by interfering, for example, with the formation of antibodies. As a consequence, susceptibility to various kinds of illnesses increases.

Let us now turn our attention to some of the many stress-related disorders. In some cases the immune system appears to be highly involved in succumbing to the disorder. Other disorders involve other factors. Most headaches, for example, reflect one of the less potentially harmful aspects of the GAS: muscle tension.

Headaches

Headaches are among the most common of the stress-related illnesses. Most headaches result from muscle tension. We are likely to contract muscles in the shoulders, neck, forehead, and scalp during the first two stages of the GAS. Persistent stress can lead to persistent muscle tension and persistent muscle-tension headaches.

Most other headaches, including the severe migraine headache, stem from changes in the blood supply to the head. These changes may be induced by barometric pressure, pollen, specific drugs, the chemical monosodium glutamate (MSG), which is often used to enhance the flavor of food, and red wines.

Regardless of the original source of the headache, we can unwittingly propel ourselves into a vicious cycle: Headache pain is a stressor that can lead us to increase, rather than relax, muscle tension in the neck and shoulders. In this way we may compound headache pain. Progressive relaxation, which focuses on decreasing muscle tension, has been shown to be highly effective in relieving the pain of muscle-tension headaches (Blanchard et al., 1985, 1987; Teders et al., 1984). Biofeedback training that alters the flow of blood to the head has been helpful in the treatment of migraine headache (Blanchard et al., 1980, 1982, 1985, 1987). People who are sensitive to MSG or red wine can ask that MSG be left out of their dishes and can switch to a white wine.

Why, under stress, do some of us develop ulcers, others develop hypertension, and still others suffer no body problems? In the following sections we shall see that there may be an interaction between stress and predisposing biological and psy-

What are the effects of meditation on hypertension?

chological differences between individuals (Davison & Neale, 1986; Walker, 1983).

Ulcers

Ulcers may afflict one person in ten and cause as many as 10,000 deaths each year in the United States (Whitehead & Bosmajian, 1982). People who develop ulcers under stress often have higher pepsinogen levels than those who do not (Weiner et al., 1957), and heredity may contribute to pepsinogen level (Mirsky, 1958). Research with laboratory rats suggests that intense approach-avoidance conflict may also contribute to ulcers (Sawrey et al., 1956; Sawrey & Weisz, 1956).

Hypertension

Hypertension may afflict 10 to 30 percent of Americans (Seer, 1979). It predisposes victims to

Meditation A psychological method in which a person becomes relaxed by narrowing his or her attention to a pleasant, repetitive stimulus, such as incense or a mantra.

other cardiovascular disorders such as arteriosclerosis, heart attacks, and strokes. Blood pressure rises in situations in which people must be constantly on guard against threats, whether in combat, in the workplace, or in the home. Blood pressure appears to be higher among blacks than whites, and also higher among both blacks and whites who tend to hold in, rather than express, feelings of anger (Diamond, 1982; Harburg et al., 1973).

Progressive relaxation has also been found helpful in the treatment of hypertension (Agras et al., 1983). **Meditation** is another psychological method for treating hypertension. In this method the client focuses on a pleasant stimulus, such as the odor of incense or a special word or "mantra" that is mentally repeated, and allows concerns of the day to be placed on the back burner. Meditation also seems to lower the blood pressure of many hypertensive individuals (Benson et al., 1973).

Asthma

Asthma is another disorder that has been linked to stress, although this link remains controversial. In one study, for example, efforts to induce asthma attacks in sufferers by subjecting them to stress led to a slightly decreased air flow but not to an actual attack (Weiss et al., 1976). Other evidence suggests that asthma sufferers can experience attacks in response to the suggestion that their air flow will become constricted (Luparello et al., 1971). In any event, in most cases the initial asthma attack follows on the heels of a respiratory infection (Alexander, 1981). Such evidence again suggests an interaction between the psychological and the physiological.

Cancer

In recent years, researchers have also begun to uncover links between stress and cancer. For example, a study of children with cancer by Jacob and Charles (1980) revealed that a significant percentage had encountered severe life changes within a year of the diagnosis, often involving the death of a loved one or the loss of a close relationship.

There are also numerous studies that connect stressful life events to the onset of cancer among adults. However, this research has been criticized in that it tends to be retrospective (Krantz et al., 1985). That is, cancer patients tend to be interviewed about events preceding their diagnoses and their psychological well-being prior to the onset of the disease. Self-reports are confounded by problems in memory and other inaccuracies. Moreover, as noted earlier in the chapter, the causal relationships in such research are clouded. For example, development of the illness might have precipitated many of the stressful events. Stress, in other words, might have been the result of the illness rather than the cause.

As in so many other areas of psychology, experimental research has been conducted with rats and other animals that could not be conducted with humans. In one type of study, animals are injected with cancerous cells or with viruses that cause cancer and then exposed to a variety of conditions, so that we can determine whether or not these conditions influence the likelihood that the animals' immune systems will be able to fend off the antigens. Such experiments with rodents suggest that once cancer has affected the individual, stress can influence its course. In one study, for example, rats were implanted with small numbers of cancer cells so that their own immune systems would have a chance to combat them successfully (Visintainer et al., 1982). Some of the rats were then exposed to inescapable shocks, whereas others were exposed to escapable shocks or to no shock. The rats exposed to the most stressful condition—the inescapable shock—were half as likely as the other rats to reject the cancer and two times as likely to die from it.

In a study of this kind with mice, Riley (1981) studied the effects of a cancer-causing virus that can be passed from mothers to offspring by nursing. This virus usually produces breast cancer in 80 percent of female offspring by the time they have reached 400 days of age. Riley placed one group of female offspring at risk for cancer in a stressful environment of loud noises and noxious odors. Another group was placed in a less stressful environment. At the age of 400 days, 92 percent of the mice under stressful conditions developed breast cancer, as compared to 7 percent of the con-

trols. Moreover, the high-stress mice showed increases in "stress hormone," which depresses the functioning of the body's immune system, and lower blood levels of disease-fighting antibodies. However, the "bottom line" in this experiment is of major interest: By the time another 200 days had elapsed, the "low-stress" mice had nearly caught up to their "high-stress" peers in the incidence of cancer. Stress appears to have hastened along the inevitable for many of these mice, but the ultimate outcomes for the high-risk rodents were not overwhelmingly influenced by stress. And so it may be that although stress influences the timing of the onset of certain diseases, such as cancer, genetic predispositions toward disease and the presence of powerful antigens will in many or most cases eventually do their damage.

Health psychologists have also found that the stressful feelings of depression and helplessness that often accompany the diagnosis of cancer can interfere with recovery among humans (Goldberg & Tull, 1984), perhaps by depressing the responsiveness of the patient's immune system. Hospitalization itself is highly stressful because it reduces the patient's sense of control over one's own fate (Peterson & Raps, 1984), and if handled insensitively, it might further depress the patient's own ability to fight illnesses.

Health psychologists are also investigating the role of chronic stress in inflammatory diseases, such as arthritis; premenstrual distress; digestive diseases, such as colitis; even metabolic diseases such as diabetes and hypoglycemia. If stress contributes to the onset or deadliness of cancer and other diseases, it is just possible that learning effective ways of reducing stress may be of some help to patients who are battling disease. For example, relaxation training, which counters many of the body's typical responses to stress, has been found generally effective in shoring up the immune systems of elderly people (Keicolt-Glaser et al., 1985). On the other hand, it has also been shown that cancer patients who respond to their disorder with anger rather than acceptance are apparently more effective at mobilizing their bodies' immune systems to control the spread of cancer (Levy et al., 1985).

The relationships among behavior patterns, attitudes, and illness are complex and under intense study. With some stress-related illnesses, it may be that stress determines whether or not the person will contract the disease at all. In others, it may be that an optimal environment merely delays the inevitable, or that a stressful environment merely hastens the onset of the inevitable. Then, too, in different illnesses stress may have different impacts on the patient's ability to recover. In the next section we shall see how a number of psychological factors, grouped under the name "psychological hardiness," appear to some degree to be able to buffer the effects of stress.

PSYCHOLOGICAL HARDINESS

Although we know that stress increases the risk of physical illness, we cannot predict, with certainty, how much stress will lead to illness. One reason, as noted earlier, is that some sources of stress, such as positive life changes, are less taxing than other sources of stress, such as negative life changes. Another is that the same source of stress, such as the arrival of a new family member, has different meanings for different people. Still another confounding factor is that some people apparently resist stress better than others do.

Some people resist stress better than others because of **psychological hardiness.** The research on psychological hardiness is indebted to Suzanne Kobasa, (1979) who studied business executives who resisted illness despite heavy loads of stress. She gave hardy and nonhardy executives a battery of psychological tests and found that the hardy executives differed from the nonhardy in three ways (Kobasa et al., 1982, pp. 169–170):

1. Hardy individuals were high in *commitment*. That is, they showed a tendency to involve themselves in, rather than experience alienation from, whatever they were doing or encountering.

Psychological hardiness A cluster of traits—commitment, challenge, and control—that reduce the impact of stress on the individual.

Locus of control The place (locus) to which an individual attributes control over the receiving of reinforcers—either inside or outside the self.

---

2. Hardy individuals were high in *challenge*. They believed that change rather than stability was normal in life. They appraised change as an interesting incentive to personal growth and not as a threat to security.

3. Hardy individuals were also high in perceived *control* over their lives. They felt and behaved as though they were influential rather than helpless in facing the various rewards and punishments of life. In terms suggested years ago by psychologist Julian Rotter (1966), psychologically hardy people tend to have an internal **locus of control.**

According to Kobasa, hardy people are more resistant to stress because they see themselves as *choosing* to be in their stress-producing situations. They also interpret the stress impacting upon them as making life more interesting and not simply compounding the pressures affecting them. Their activation of control allows them to regulate to some degree the amount of stress they will encounter at any given time (Maddi & Kobasa, 1984). Of the three aspects of psychological hardiness that help people resist stress, Hull and his colleagues (1987) suggest that commitment and control are the ones that make the difference.

Kobasa and Pucetti (1983) suggest that psychological hardiness helps by providing buffers between stressful life events and individuals. Buffering allows people the opportunity to draw on social supports (Ganellen & Blaney, 1984) and to use successful coping mechanisms, such as controlling what they will be doing from day to day. And Type A individuals who show psychological hardiness are more resistant to illness, including coronary heart disease, than Type A individuals who do not (Booth-Kewley & Friedman, 1987; Friedman & Booth-Kewley, 1987; Kobasa et al., 1983; Rhodewalt & Agustsdottir, 1984).

And so, stress need not necessarily be a prescription for illness. Important issues seem to be whether people *want* to be in their stressful situations and whether they see themselves as capable of exercising *control* over them. You may wish to take the nearby questionnaire on locus of control to see whether you tend to believe that you are in charge of your own life.

PSYCHOLOGICAL INVOLVEMENT IN TREATMENT OF HEALTH PROBLEMS

Just as health psychologists have been uncovering the links between stress and illness, they have also been participating in the prevention and treatment of health problems. In some cases, the research findings of health psychologists have been an invaluable aid to other professionals involved in the medical community and to patients. In the case of health problems in which medical training is not necessarily required—such as insomnia, weight control (see Chapter 6), and cigarette smoking—psychologists have increasingly been taking a primary role in treatment.

Let us first see how health psychologists have helped facilitate physician–patient interactions and ability to cope with medical treatments. Then let us see how pychologists have treated insomnia and helped people cut down and quit smoking.

Physician–Patient Interactions

Psychologists have found many ways in which physicians and patients can increase the effectiveness and satisfaction of their interactions. One area involves the so-called bedside manner of the physician. In an experiment to determine which aspects of a physician's nonverbal behavior contibuted to patients' satisfaction, Harrigan and Rosenthal (1983) manipulated behaviors such as leaning forward versus sitting back. It was found that patients evaluated physicians most positively when they leaned forward rather than sat back, nodded their heads in response to patients' verbalizations, and kept their arms open rather than folded.

Because of the anxiety they provoke, most people try not to think about the symptoms of illnesses when they first appear (Suls & Fletcher, 1985). By the time they visit the physician, they are frequently quite anxious. Anxiety during the physician–patient interview sometimes causes patients to forget to mention certain symptoms and to forget to ask questions that had been on their minds. Roter (1984) found that having patients take ten minutes before the visit with the physician to jot down concerns and questions led to more questions and greater satisfaction with the interview.

Compliance with Medical Instructions and Procedures

Psychologists have found that patients are more likely to comply with medical instructions when they believe that the instructions will work. Women, for example, are more likely to engage in breast self-examination when they believe that they will really be able to detect abnormal growths (Alagna & Reddy, 1984). Diabetes patients are more likely to use insulin regularly to control their blood sugar levels when they believe that their regimens will be of help (Brownlee-Duffeck et al., 1987).

Physicians often prescribe drugs and other treatment regimens without explaining to patients the purposes of the treatments and their possible complications. This approach can backfire. When it comes to taking prescribed drugs, patients frequently tend not to take them or to take them incorrectly (Haynes et al., 1979). Patients are particularly likely to discontinue medications when they encounter side effects, especially when they are unexpected. Therefore, specific instructions coupled with accurate information about potential side effects would appear to be most useful in inducing compliance (Baron & Byrne, 1987; Keown et al., 1984).

PAIN MANAGEMENT

Psychologists have been of major help in the management of pain. Pain is often an inevitable consequence of medical procedures, diseases, and injuries, although in some cases pain may be a learned response that is reinforced by medical attention (Berntzen & Götestam, 1987). Pain management has traditionally been a medical issue, with the main type of treatment being chemical, as in the use of analgesic drugs. But drugs are not always effective. Moreover, patients can develop tolerance for many analgesic drugs, such as morphine or demerol, so that increased doses are required to achieve the same effects. Because of limitations and problems such as these, health psychologists have increasingly focused their efforts on psychological methods for managing pain.

For example, when it is suspected that medical attention is reinforcing the reporting (and expe-

Questionnaire

Locus of control scale

Psychologically hardy people tend to have an internal locus of control. They believe that they are in control of their own lives. Persons with an external locus of control, by contrast, tend to see their fates as being out of their hands.

Are you more of an "internal" or more of an "external"? To learn more about your perception of your locus of control, respond to the following questionnaire developed by Nowicki and Strickland (1973).

Mark your responses to the questions on the answer sheet in the next column. When you are finished, turn to Appendix C to score your test.

		YES	NO
1.	Do you believe that most problems will solve themselves if you just don't fool with them?	____	____
2.	Do you believe that you can stop yourself from catching a cold?	____	____
3.	Are some people just born lucky?	____	____
4.	Most of the time do you feel that getting good grades meant a great deal to you?	____	____
5.	Are you often blamed for things that just aren't your fault?	____	____
6.	Do you believe that if somebody studies hard enough he or she can pass any subject?	____	____
7.	Do you feel that most of the time it doesn't pay to try hard because things never turn out right anyway?	____	____
8.	Do you feel that if things start out well in the morning it's going to be a good day no matter what you do?	____	____
9.	Do you feel that most of the time parents listen to what their children have to say?	____	____
10.	Do you believe that wishing can make good things happen?	____	____
11.	When you get punished does it usually seem it's for no good reason at all?	____	____
12.	Most of the time do you find it hard to change a friend's opinion?	____	____
13.	Do you think that cheering more than luck helps a team to win?	____	____
14.	Did you feel that it was nearly impossible to change your parents' minds about anything?	____	____
15.	Do you believe that parents should allow children to make most of their own decisions?	____	____
16.	Do you feel that when you do something wrong there's very little you can do to make it right?	____	____
17.	Do you believe that most people are just born good at sports?	____	____

18. Are most of the other people your age stronger than you are? ____ ____
19. Do you feel that one of the best ways to handle most problems is just not to think about them? ____ ____
20. Do you feel that you have a lot of choice in deciding who your friends are? ____ ____
21. If you find a four-leaf clover, do you believe that it might bring you good luck? ____ ____
22. Did you often feel that whether or not you did your homework had much to do with what kinds of grades you got? ____ ____
23. Do you feel that when a person your age is angry with you, there's little you can do to stop him or her? ____ ____
24. Have you ever had a good-luck charm? ____ ____
25. Do you believe that whether or not people like you depends on how you act? ____ ____
26. Did your parents usually help you if you asked them to? ____ ____
27. Have you felt that when people were angry with you it was usually for no reason at all? ____ ____
28. Most of the time, do you feel that you can change what might happen tomorrow by what you did today? ____ ____
29. Do you believe that when bad things are going to happen they are just going to happen no matter what you try to do to stop them? ____ ____
30. Do you think that people can get their own way if they just keep trying? ____ ____
31. Most of the time do you find it useless to try to get your own way at home? ____ ____
32. Do you feel that when good things happen they happen because of hard work? ____ ____
33. Do you feel that when somebody your age wants to be your enemy there's little you can do to change matters? ____ ____
34. Do you feel that it's easy to get friends to do what you want them to do? ____ ____
35. Do you usually feel that you have little to say about what you get to eat at home? ____ ____
36. Do you feel that when someone doesn't like you there's little you can do about it? ____ ____
37. Did you usually feel that it was almost useless to try in school because most other children were just plain smarter than you were? ____ ____
38. Are you the kind of person who believes that planning ahead makes things turn out better? ____ ____
39. Most of the time, do you feel that you have little to say about what your family decides to do? ____ ____
40. Do you think it's better to be smart than to be lucky? ____ ____

riencing) of pain, medical response can be decreased rather than increased. The shifting away from a medical response is most appropriate when the pain is not believed to be a sign that something requiring immediate medical attention is at work. Instead, the patient can be reinforced with, say, the attention and social approval of an occupational therapist for engaging in activities—such as gross or fine-motor activities—that have been hampered by the pain.

Accurate Information

Another psychological method for pain management is the provision of accurate and thorough information. As noted, most people try not to think about their symptoms (and their implications!) during the early phases of an illness. However, when it comes to administering painful or discomforting treatments, as with chemotherapy for cancer, knowledge of the details of the treatment, including how long the treatment will last and how much pain will be entailed, often helps patients cope—particularly patients who prefer to receive high levels of information in an effort to maintain control over their situations (Martelli et al., 1987). Accurate information even helps small children cope with painful procedures (Jay et al., 1983).

Distraction and Fantasy

Although it appears generally helpful for patients to have accurate and detailed explanations of painful procedures, psychologists have also been studying ways of minimizing discomfort once these procedures are underway. A number of such methods involve the use of distraction or fantasy. For example, patients can distract themselves from pain by focusing on environmental details, as by counting ceiling tiles, the hairs on the back of a finger, or describing the clothing of medical personnel or passersby (Kanfer & Goldfoot, 1966; McCaul &

Haugvedt, 1982). We are also less sensitive to pain when we try to recall lists of meaningless words (Farthing et al., 1984; Spanos et al., 1984). Studies with children ranging in age from 9 into their teens have found that playing video games diminishes the pain and discomfort of the side effects of chemotherapy (Kolko & Rickard-Figueroa, 1985; Redd et al., 1987).

In a similar vein, it is worth noting that a Norwegian study found that regularly scheduled analgesic drugs were more effective than on-demand drugs in the treatment of pain (Berntzen & Götestam, 1987). This outcome may seem puzzling, since on-demand analgesia places the patient in greater control of his or her treatment. However, the authors speculate that on-demand treatments can have the effect of encouraging patients to *focus on their pain,* that is, to seek changes in their sensations of pain rather than to think about other things.

Coping with Irrational Beliefs

Irrational beliefs about pain have been shown to heighten pain. For example, telling oneself that the pain is unbearable and will never cease increases discomfort, as found in a study relating knee pain and beliefs about pain (Keefe et al., 1987). Cognitive methods aimed at modifying irrational belief systems would also thus seem to be of promise.

Social Support

Supportive social networks also seem to help people cope with discomfort. And so, having friends visit the patient and encourage a return to health is as consistent with psychological findings as it is with folklore (Rook & Dooley, 1985).

PSYCHOLOGICAL TREATMENT OF INSOMNIA

Insomnia refers to three types of sleeping problems: difficulty in falling asleep (sleep-onset insomnia), difficulty in remaining asleep through the night, and awakening prematurely in the morning. Perhaps 30 million Americans suffer from insom-

> **Insomnia** A term for three types of sleeping problems: (1) difficulty in falling asleep ("sleep-onset insomnia"), (2) difficulty in remaining asleep, and (3) waking early.

60 Minutes

Hypnosis

In 1842 London physician W. S. Ward amputated a man's leg after using a rather unusual anesthetic: hypnosis. According to reports, the patient experienced no discomfort. Several years later operations were being performed routinely under hypnosis at the infirmary in London. Today hypnosis is used by thousands of professionals in pain management in dentistry, childbirth, even some forms of surgery.

Hypnosis is an altered state of consciousness that is induced by having people focus on repetitious stimuli, such as the voice of the hypnotist, and follow suggestions, frequently to the effect that their limbs are becoming warmer and heavier and that they are "going to sleep." They do not sleep during hypnosis, but they usually interpret these instructions as an invitation to become passive, follow directions, and adopt a what-will-happen-will-happen attitude. Moreover, suggestions that limbs are becoming warmer and heavier tend to have relaxing effects, as they encourage the flow of blood to the periphery of the body and decrease activity of the sympathetic branch of the autonomic nervous system (Pennebaker & Skelton, 1981). In any event, health psychologists, as other helping professionals, sometimes turn to hypnosis and related methods, such as relaxation training and guided imagery, in the management of pain (Moore & Chaney, 1985).

In the "60 Minutes" segment "Hypnosis," correspondent Dan Rather reported that psychologist Harold Wain hypnotized physician David Ramirez. Ramirez then underwent surgery on his nose, with no drugs. While Ramirez was fantasizing that he was lying beneath the warming sun on a beach in Puerto Rico, a doctor chiseled away at a deviated septum so that Ramirez would be able to breathe normally. After the operation Ramirez reported how his consciousness had been divided: "It's kind of funny to be lying there on the beach and have the surgeon saying, 'Well, this is the piece of the bone that was obstructing his breathing.'"

However, many patients who have been hypnotized report some pain during medical procedures (Barber et al., 1974). Others are adminis-

How does hypnosis help people manage pain?

tered analgesic (pain-relieving) drugs along with hypnotic suggestions. It also turns out that many internal organs are not particularly sensitive to pain—some, like the brain, register no pain at all. In such cases only a local anesthetic is required to deaden the pain of skin incisions. It is not surprising that hypnosis and a local anesthetic are a potent combination.

Remember, too, that anxiety and the expectation of pain can compound the pain experienced in any medical procedure. Witness the muscle tension and anxiety of many dental patients in the waiting room! Hypnosis can deeply relax individuals and encourage them to focus on pleasant imagery that distracts them from pain—just as video games distract many young cancer patients from the discomforting side effects of chemotherapy. A state of relaxation as induced by hypnotic procedures may also enhance the ability of the nervous system to produce endorphins, which are one of the body's natural ways of combatting pain.

nia (Clark et al., 1981), and millions of sleeping pills are downed each evening.

As a group, people who suffer from insomnia show higher levels of autonomic activity as they try to get to sleep and as they sleep (Haynes et al., 1981; Johns et al., 1971; Monroe, 1967). Persons with sleep-onset insomnia obtain higher anxiety scores on questionnaires and show more muscle tension in the forehead than nonsufferers (Haynes et al., 1974). Personality tests also find poor sleepers to be more depressed and ruminative than good sleepers, more concerned about physical complaints, and more shy and retiring (Freedman & Sattler, 1982; Marks & Monroe, 1976; Monroe & Marks, 1977). Insomnia comes and goes with many people, increasing during periods of anxiety and tension.

Insomniacs tend to compound their sleep problems through their efforts to force themselves to get to sleep (Kamens, 1980; Youkilis & Bootzin, 1981). Their concern heightens autonomic activity and muscle tension. You cannot force or will yourself to sleep. You can only set the stage for it by lying down and relaxing when you are tired. If you focus on sleep too closely, it will elude you. Yet millions go to bed each night dreading the possibility of sleep-onset insomnia.

The most common method for fighting insomnia in the United States is popping pills. Sleeping pills may be effective—for a while. They generally work by reducing arousal. At first lowered arousal may be effective in itself. Focusing on changes in arousal may also distract people from their efforts to *get* to sleep. Expectation of success may also help.

But there are problems with sleeping pills. First, people attribute their success to the pill and not to themselves, creating dependency on the pill rather than self-reliance. Second, as with analge-

sics, people develop tolerance for sleeping pills. With continued usage they must progressively increase the dose to achieve the same effects. Third, high doses of these chemicals can be dangerous, especially if mixed with an alcoholic beverage or two. Both sleeping pills and alcohol depress the activity of the central nervous system, and their effects are additive.

Fortunately, psychological methods for coping with insomnia have been recently developed. Some of these methods reduce tension directly, as with muscle-relaxation exercises. These exercises also involve cognitive elements that distract us from striving to get to sleep. We shall now discuss relaxation and other psychological methods for coping with insomnia.

Progressive Relaxation, Biofeedback Training, and Autogenic Training

Focusing on releasing muscle tension has been shown to reduce the amount of time needed to fall asleep and the incidence of waking during the night. It increases the number of hours slept and leaves us feeling more rested in the morning (Lick & Heffler, 1977; Weil & Gottfried, 1973). Perhaps the most commonly used method for easing muscle tension is progressive relaxation. Biofeedback training (Haynes et al., 1977) and autogenic training (Nicassio & Bootzin, 1974) have also been used successfully.

In **biofeedback training,** we receive a steady flow of information about the status of a body function. For example, a monitor of muscle tension can be connected to the forehead, so that greater tension results in faster or higher-pitched "bleeps" from an electronic console. We are then instructed to "make the bleeps go slower," and by so doing learn how to relax muscle tension in the forehead. Relaxation in the muscles of the forehead tends to generalize to muscles in the rest of the body. We can learn to lower blood pressure by getting feedback from a blood pressure cuff. We can learn how to emit (relaxing) alpha waves by means of feedback from an electroencephalograph (EEG).

In **autogenic training,** we reduce muscle tension by focusing on suggestions that our limbs are

Biofeedback training The systematic feeding back of information about a body function to an organism such that the organism can gain conscious control of that function.

Autogenic training A method for reducing tension that involves repeated suggestions to the effect that one's limbs are becoming warmer and heavier and that one's breathing is becoming regular.

growing warm and heavy and that our breathing is becoming regular. These methods also give us something on which to focus other than trying to fall asleep.

Challenging Irrational Ideas about Sleeping

You need not be a sleep expert to realize that convincing yourself that the day will be ruined unless you get to sleep *right now* will increase, rather than decrease, bedtime tensions. Sleep does seem to restore us, especially after physical exertion. But we often exaggerate the problems that will befall us if we do not sleep. Here are some beliefs that increase bedtime tension and some alternatives that may be of use to you:

EXAGGERATED BELIEF	ALTERNATIVE BELIEF
If I don't get to sleep, I'll feel wrecked tomorrow.	Not necessarily. If I'm tired, I can go to bed early tomorrow night.
It's unhealthy for me not to get more sleep.	Not necessarily. Some people do very well on only a few hours of sleep.
I'll wreck my sleeping schedule for the whole week if I don't get to sleep very soon.	Not at all. If I'm tired, I'll just go to bed a bit earlier. I'll get up about the same time with no problem.
If I don't get to sleep, I won't be able to concentrate on that big test tomorrow.	Possibly, but my fears may be exaggerated. I may just as well relax or get up and do something enjoyable for a while.

Stimulus Control

A number of methods are based on the principle of stimulus control, as defined in Chapter 10 (Bootzin & Nicassio, 1978; Morin & Azrin, 1987). In general, let your bed become the place where you sleep—not where you snack, do homework, and watch television. Also, don't plan or worry about tomorrow in bed. When you lie down for sleep, you may organize thoughts for the day for a few minutes, but then allow yourself to relax or

engage in fantasy. If an important idea comes to you, jot it down on a handy pad so that you won't lose it. But if thoughts persist, get up and follow them elsewhere. Let your bed be a place for relaxation and sleep—not your study. A bed—even a waterbed—is not a think tank.

Establishing a Regular Routine

Sleeping late can encourage sleep-onset insomnia. Set your alarm for the same time each morning and get up, regardless of how many hours you have slept. By sticking to a regular time for rising, you'll be indirectly encouraging yourself to get to sleep at a regular time as well.

Fantasy

Singer (1975) notes that fantasies or "daydreams" are almost universal and may occur naturally as we fall asleep. You can allow yourself to "go with" fantasies that occur at bedtime, or purposefully use fantasies to get to sleep. You may be able to ease yourself to sleep by focusing on a sun-drenched beach, with waves lapping on the shore, or on a walk through a mountain meadow on a summer day. You can construct your own "mind trips" and paint their details finely. With mind trips you conserve fuel and avoid lines at airports.

PSYCHOLOGICAL METHODS FOR CUTTING DOWN AND QUITTING SMOKING

All cigarette packs sold in the United States carry messages such as "Warning: The surgeon general has determined that cigarette smoking is dangerous to your health." Cigarette advertising has been banned on radio and television. In 1982, Surgeon General C. Everett Koop declared, "Cigarette smoking is clearly identified as the chief preventable cause of death in our society and the most important public health issue of our time."

In that year, 430,000 people would die from cancer, and the surgeon general's report argued that 30 percent of these deaths were attributable to smoking. Cigarette smoking can cause cancer of the lungs, larynx, oral cavity, and esophagus and may contribute to cancer of the bladder, pancreas, and kidneys. Cigarette smoking is also linked to death from heart disease, chronic lung and respiratory diseases, and other illnesses. Pregnant women who smoke risk miscarriage, premature birth, and birth defects. Once it was thought that smokers' ills tended to focus on men, but today women smokers have a 30 percent greater risk of dying from cancer than do women nonsmokers. Because of the noxious effects of second-hand smoke, smoking has been banished from many public places, like elevators. Many restaurants now reserve sections for nonsmokers. So it's no secret that cigarette smoking is dangerous.

Nicotine is the stimulant found in cigarettes. Nicotine stimulates discharge of the hormone adrenalin. Adrenalin creates a burst of autonomic activity, including rapid heart rate and release of sugar into the blood. Although there is considerable controversy about whether smokers develop physiological dependence on cigarettes, nicotine is apparently the agent that creates dependence. The controversy over physiological dependence stems from the fact that the withdrawal symptoms from smoking cigarettes (nervousness, drowsiness, energy loss, headaches, fatigue, irregular bowels, lightheadedness, insomnia, dizziness, cramps, palpitations, tremors, and sweating) mimic an anxiety state. However, Schachter (1977) has shown that regular smokers adjust their smoking in order to maintain fairly even levels of nicotine in their bloodstream. Thus we know that smokers will avoid drops in nicotine levels.

Evidence is mixed about whether it is more effective to cut down gradually or quit all at once. Going cold turkey (quitting all at once) is more effective for some smokers (Flaxman, 1978), but cutting down gradually is more effective for others (Glasgow et al., 1984). Although it is most healthful to quit smoking completely, some smokers, who were not able to quit, have nevertheless learned to reduce their cigarette consumption by at least 50 percent and to have stuck to their lower levels for up to two and a half years (Glasgow et al., 1983, 1985).

Methods for Quitting Cold Turkey

Psychologists have compiled suggestions such as the following for helping people quit smoking:

- Tell your family and friends that you're quitting—make a public commitment.
- Think of specific things to tell yourself when you feel the urge to smoke: how you'll be stronger, free of fear of cancer, ready for the marathon, and so on.
- Tell yourself that the first few days are the hardest—after that, withdrawal symptoms weaken dramatically.
- Remind yourself that you're "superior" to non-quitters.
- Start when you wake up, at which time you've already gone eight hours without nicotine.
- Go on a smoke-ending vacation to get away from places and situations in which you're used to smoking.
- Throw out ashtrays and don't allow smokers to visit you at home for a while.
- Don't carry matches or light other people's cigarettes.
- Sit in nonsmokers' sections of restaurants and trains.
- Fill your days with novel activities—things that won't remind you of smoking.
- Use sugar-free mints or gum as substitutes for cigarettes (don't light them).*
- Interpret withdrawal symptoms as a sign that you're winning and getting healthier. After all, you wouldn't have withdrawal symptoms if you were smoking.
- Buy yourself presents with all that cash you're socking away.

Methods for Cutting Down

Psychologists have compiled suggestions including the following for people who would rather try to cut down than quit altogether:

- Count your cigarettes to establish your smoking baseline.
- Set concrete goals for controlled smoking. For

---

*A nicotine gum is available that may be of use to some smokers who are heavily dependent on nicotine, especially when combined with behavioral techniques (Hall et al., 1985). The gum decreases withdrawal symptoms by providing a source of nicotine but does not contain hydrocarbons or carbon monoxide.

example, plan to cut down baseline consumption by at least 50 percent.

- Gradually restrict the settings in which you allow yourself to smoke.
- Get involved in activities where smoking isn't allowed or practical.
- Switch to a brand you don't like. Hold your cigarettes with your nondominant hand only.
- Keep only enough cigarettes to meet the (reduced) daily goal. Never buy more than a pack at a time.
- Use sugar-free candies or gum as a substitute for a few cigarettes each day.
- Jog instead of having a cigarette. Or walk, swim, or make love.
- Pause before lighting up. Put the cigarette in an ashtray between puffs. Ask yourself before each puff if you really want more. If not, throw the cigarette away.
- Put the cigarette out before you reach the end (no more eating the filter).
- Gradually lengthen the amount of time between cigarettes.
- Imagine living a prolonged, noncoughing life. Ah, freedom!
- As you smoke, picture blackened lungs, coughing fits, the possibilities of cancer and other lung diseases.

Using strategies such as these, many individuals have gradually cut down their cigarette consumption and eventually quit. It's true that there is a high relapse rate for quitters. Be on guard: We are most likely to relapse—that is, return to smoking—when we feel highly anxious, angry, or depressed (Shiffman, 1982). But when you are tempted, you can decrease the chances of relapsing by using almost any of the strategies just outlined (Hall et al., 1984; Shiffman, 1982, 1984), like reminding yourself of reasons for quitting, having a mint, or going for a walk. And also keep in mind a note of encouragement from Stanley Schachter (1982): Despite high relapse "rates," millions of Americans have quit and have been able to stay away from cigarettes permanently.

And so, psychologists have created an essential role for themselves in matters of health. They have added to our knowledge of the origins of disease, and they have assisted physicians and patients in relating to one another. Moreover, they have become primary caregivers in many health-related problems, such as insomnia, obesity, and smoking.

TRUTH OR FICTION REVISITED

Too much of a good thing can make you ill.   True. The accumulation of many life changes within a short period of time is stressful, and stress heightens the risk for medical illnesses.

Our blood pressure rises when we are under stress. True. Elevated blood pressure is one of the elements of the so-called general adaptation syndrome, which characterizes our response to stress.

Stress can influence the course of cancer. True. Stress exacerbates the course of cancer in laboratory animals and may have similar effects on people.

The belief that we can handle stress is linked to lower levels of adrenalin in the bloodstream. True. As a consequence the individual should feel less sympathetic ANS arousal.

Physicians' body language goes a long way toward determining whether they have a good "bedside manner." True. For example, physicians who lean toward patients and nod their heads in response to patients are rated more positively.

Medical patients should be told as little as possible about their illnesses and why they are being given certain medicines. False. Accurate information often encourages compliance with medical regimens.

Video games help children with cancer cope with the painful side effects of chemotherapy. True. The games distract them from unpleasant sensations.

Many people have insomnia because they try too hard to get to sleep at night. True. When people try to get to sleep, they raise their levels of arousal, and so sleep often eludes them.

Appendix Review

Health psychologists study the relationships between psychological factors and the prevention and treatment of physical illness.

Stress is the demand made on an organism to adjust. Sources of stress include daily hassles and life changes, pain and discomfort, anxiety, frustration, conflict, and Type A behavior. Holmes and Rahe found that people who accumulate 300 or more life-change units within a year are at high risk for physical illness, but their research is correlational, not experimental, and causal relationships are therefore clouded.

Pain and discomfort impair our abilities to perform. There are two types of anxiety: trait anxiety, which is persistent; and state anxiety, or a temporary condition of arousal that is triggered by a specific situation. Frustration is the thwarting of a motive to reach a goal. Stress decreases our tolerance for frustration. People in conflict are torn by opposing motives. Type A people are highly competitive and aggressive and have a sense of time urgency.

Selye noted that the body responds to stress by showing a general adaptation syndrome, which has alarm, resistance, and exhaustion stages. Alarm and resistance are characterized by secretion of adrenalin ("stress hormone") and activation of the body. Psychoneuroimmunologists note that the secretion of adrenalin, when prolonged, has depressing effects on the body's immune system, leaving the body prey to physical illnesses. The role of the immune system is to recognize and destroy foreign agents, called antigens.

Among the most common of the stress-related disorders are headaches, which stem most often from muscle tension. Persons who develop ulcers under stress frequently have higher pepsinogen levels than those who do not. Hypertension predisposes people to arteriosclerosis, heart attacks, and strokes. Asthma attacks frequently follow respiratory infections. Stress does not cause but seems to influence the course of cancer. Feelings of helplessness apparently impair the body's ability to fight cancer.

Psychologically hardy business executives are more capable of resisting the impact of stress than are less hardy executives. Kobasa found three factors involved in psychological hardiness: commitment, challenge, and control.

Health psychologists have found that physicians' body language influences ratings of their "bedside manners." Jotting down concerns and questions prior to the patient–physician interview increases patient satisfaction with the interview.

Patients are more likely to comply with medical instructions when they are given accurate and detailed information about the instructions and the rationales behind them. Patients are more likely to comply when they believe that compliance will be effective.

Psychological means for pain management include nonreinforcement of complaints of pain, accurate information about painful procedures, distraction and fantasy, challenging of patients' irrational beliefs about pain, and social support. Hypnosis may help patients manage pain by distracting attention.

Psychologists caution against using sleeping pills for insomnia because, with regular usage, tolerance for the pills increases. Psychological methods for treating insomnia include muscle relaxation techniques, biofeedback training, challenging irrational attitudes about sleeping, stimulus control, and use of fantasy.

Psychological methods for cutting down and quitting smoking include making a public commitment to stop, recognition that withdrawal symptoms are temporary, environmental changes, using substitutes, and avoiding catastrophizing lapses in self-control.

Exercise

Ranking Life-Change Units

Directions: Rank the following life-change units from most stressful (1) to least stressful (6). Check your answers against Table A.1.

_____ 1. Vacation
_____ 2. Marriage
_____ 3. Change in responsibilities at work
_____ 4. Divorce
_____ 5. Gain of a new family member
_____ 6. Death of a spouse

Posttest

Directions: *For each of the following, select the choice that best answers the question or completes the sentence.*

1. Which of the following life events involves the greatest number of life-change units, according to Holmes and Rahe?

   (a) Change in schools, (b) Personal injury or illness, (c) Vacation, (d) Change in sleeping habits.

2. All of the following are limitations of the Holmes and Rahe approach to explaining and measuring stress, *except that*

   (a) positive life changes may be less stressful than negative life changes, regardless of the life-change units accumulated, (b) the Holmes and Rahe research is correlational, not experimental, (c) different people respond to life stresses in different ways, (d) there is no evidence that large numbers of life-change units are correlated with medical illnesses.

3. _____ anxiety is a temporary condition of arousal that is clearly triggered by a specific situation.

   (a) Free-floating, (b) Neurotic, (c) State, (d) Trait.

4. Which of the following statements about conflict is accurate?

   (a) Goals producing mixed motives seem more attractive from a distance, (b) Goals producing mixed motives seem less attractive from a distance, (c) All goals seem more attractive from a distance, (d) No goals seem more attractive from a distance.

5. Type A people

   (a) are patient, (b) readily delegate responsibility to subordinates, (c) are more intelligent than Type B people, (d) are self-critical when they fail at a task.

6. The alarm reaction of the GAS is characterized by each of the following, *except for*

   (a) blood shifting toward the skin, (b) the heart rate increasing, (c) secretion of adrenalin, (d) blood coagulability increasing.

7. Antigens are

   (a) antibodies, (b) the basic units of the immune system, (c) foreign agents that invade the body, (d) chemical derivatives of stress hormone.

8. Which of the following predisposes victims to arteriosclerosis?

   (a) Ulcers, (b) Hypertension, (c) Asthma, (d) Headaches.

9. Psychologically hardy business executives

   (a) have an internal locus of control, (b) practice progressive relaxation twice a day, (c) have a stable, extraverted personality structure, (d) are Type B.

10. The following methods have been suggested by psychologists involved in pain management *except for*

(a) distraction and fantasy, (b) providing patients with accurate information about painful procedures, (c) reinforcement of complaints of pain, (d) relaxation methods.

11. Which of the following is *not* usually recommended by psychologists as a way of coping with insomnia?

(a) Sleeping pills, (b) Stimulus control, (c) Relaxation training, (d) Challenging irrational thoughts.

Answer Key to Posttest

1. B	**4.** A	**7.** C	**10.** C
2. D	**5.** D	**8.** B	**11.** A
3. C	**6.** A	**9.** A	

STATISTICS

OUTLINE

PRETEST: TRUTH OR FICTION?
DESCRIPTIVE STATISTICS
   The Frequency Distribution
   Measures of Central Tendency
   Measures of Variability
THE NORMAL CURVE

THE CORRELATION COEFFICIENT
   The Scatter Diagram
INFERENTIAL STATISTICS
   Statistically Significant Differences
   Samples and Populations
TRUTH OR FICTION REVISITED

PRETEST: TRUTH OR FICTION?

A person rated as a "10" is very attractive.

You could mathematically derive three very different figures for the average U.S. income, and each of them could be perfectly correct.

If we have a group of 30 men—20 of whom are 6 feet tall and 10 of whom are 5 feet 6 inches tall—the average height of the group is 6 feet.

Fifty percent of the U.S. population attains average IQ scores on the Wechsler intelligence scales.

Attaining a score of 200 on the Scholastic Aptitude Tests is not likely to impress a college admissions officer.

Students whose parents earn higher incomes attain higher scores on the Scholastic Aptitude Tests.

Men are significantly taller than women.

Imagine that some visitors from outer space arrive outside Madison Square Garden in New York City. Their goal this dark and numbing winter evening is to learn all they can about the inhabitants of planet Earth. They are drawn inside the Garden by lights, shouts, and warmth. The spotlighting inside rivets their attention to a wood-floored arena where the New York Apples are hosting the Cali-fornia Quakes in a brisky contested basketball game.

Our visitors use their sophisticated instruments to take some measurements of the players. Some surprising **statistics** are sent back to the planet of their origin: It appears that (1) 100 percent of Earthlings are male, and (2) the height of Earthlings ranges from six feet one inch to seven feet two inches.

Statistics is the name given the science concerned with obtaining and organizing numerical measurements or information. Our imagined visitors have sent home some statistics about the sex

> **Statistics** Numerical facts assembled in such a manner that they provide significant information about measures or scores.

and size of human beings that are at once accurate and misleading. They accurately measured the basketball players, but their small **sample** of Earth's **population** was quite distorted. Fortunately for us Earthlings, about half of us are female. And the **range** of heights observed by the aliens, of six feet one to seven feet two, is both restricted and too high. People vary in height by more than one foot and one inch. And our **average** height is not between six one and seven two but several inches below.

Psychologists, like our imagined visitors, are vitally concerned with measuring human as well as animal characteristics and traits—not just physical characteristics like sex and height but also psychological traits like intelligence, aggressiveness, anxiety, or self-assertiveness. By observing the central tendencies (averages) and variations in measurements from person to person, psychologists can state that some person is average or above average in intelligence or that another person is less assertive than, say, 60 percent of the population.

But psychologists, unlike our aliens, are careful in their attempts to select a sample that accurately represents the entire population. Professional basketball players do not represent the human species. They are taller, stronger, and more agile than the rest of us, and they make more shaving-cream commercials.

In this appendix we shall survey some of the statistical methods used by psychologists to draw conclusions about the measurements they take in research activities. First we shall discuss *descriptive statistics* and learn what types of statements we can make about the height of basketball players and some other human traits. Then we shall discuss the *normal curve* and learn why basketball players are abnormal—at least in terms of height. We shall explore *correlation coefficients* and provide you with some less-than-shocking news: More intelligent people attain higher grades than less intelligent people. Finally, we shall have a brief look at *inferential statistics* and see why we can be bold enough to say that the difference in height between basketball players and other people is not just a chance accident, or fluke. Basketball players are in fact *statistically significantly* taller than the general population.

DESCRIPTIVE STATISTICS

Being told that someone is a "10" is not very descriptive unless you know something about how possible scores are distributed and how frequently one finds a 10. Fortunately—for 10s, if not for the rest of us—one is usually informed that someone is a 10 on a scale of 1 to 10, and that 10 is the positive end of the scale. If this is not sufficient, one will also be told that 10s are few and far between—rather unusual statistical events.

This business of a scale from 1 to 10 is not very scientific, to be sure, but it does suggest something about **descriptive statistics.** We can use descriptive statistics to clarify our understanding of a distribution of scores, such as heights, test grades, IQs, or increases or decreases in measures of sexual arousal following drinking of alcohol. For example, descriptive statistics can help us to determine measures of central tendency, or averages, and to determine how much variability there is in the scores. Being a 10 loses some of its charm if the average score is an 11. Being a 10 is more remarkable in a distribution whose scores range from 1 to 10 than in one that ranges from 9 to 10.

Let us now examine some of the concerns of descriptive statistics: the *frequency distribution, measures of central tendency* (types of averages), and *measures of variability.*

The Frequency Distribution

A **frequency distribution** takes scores, or items of raw data, puts them into order, as from lowest to

---

Sample Part of a population.

Population A complete group from which a sample is selected.

Range A measure of variability; the distance between extreme measures of scores.

Average Central tendency of a group of measures, expressed as means, median, and mode.

Descriptive statistics The branch of statistics that is concerned with providing information about a distribution of scores.

Frequency distribution An ordered set of data that indicates how frequently scores appear.

highest, and groups them according to class intervals. Table B.1 shows the rosters for a recent California Quakes–New York Apples basketball game. The members of each item are listed according to the numbers of their uniforms. Table B.2 shows a frequency distribution of the heights of the players of both teams combined, with a class interval of one inch.

Table B.1   Rosters of Quakes vs. Apples at New York

CALIFORNIA			NEW YORK		
2	Callahan	6'-7"	3	Roosevelt	6'-1"
5	Daly	6'-11"	12	Chaffee	6'-5"
6	Chico	6'-2"	13	Baldwin	6'-9"
12	Capistrano	6'-3"	25	Delmar	6'-6"
21	Brentwood	6'-5"	27	Merrick	6'-8"
25	Van Nuys	6'-3"	28	Hewlett	6'-6"
31	Clemente	6'-9"	33	Hollis	6'-9"
32	Whittier	6'-8"	42	Bedford	6'-5"
41	Fernando	7'-2"	43	Coram	6'-2"
43	Watts	6'-9"	45	Hampton	6'-10"
53	Huntington	6'-6"	53	Ardsley	6'-10"

A glance at the rosters for a recent California Quakes–New York Apples basketball game shows you that the heights of the teams, combined, ranged from six feet one inch to seven feet two inches. Are the heights of the team members representative of those of the general male population?

It would also be possible to use three-inch class intervals, as in Table B.3. In determining how large a class interval should be, a researcher attempts to collapse that data into a small enough number of classes to ensure that they will appear meaningful at a glance but attempts also to maintain a large enough number of categories to ensure that important differences are not obscured.

Table B.3 obscures the fact that no players are six feet four inches tall. If the researcher feels that this information is extremely important, a class interval of one inch may be maintained.

Histogram A graphic representation of frequency distribution that uses rectangular solids.
Polygon A closed figure.

Table B.2   Frequency Distribution of Heights of Basketball Players, with a One-Inch Class Interval

CLASS INTERVAL	NUMBER OF PLAYERS IN CLASS
6-1 to 6-1.9	1
6-2 to 6-2.9	2
6-3 to 6-3.9	2
6-4 to 6-4.9	0
6-5 to 6-5.9	3
6-6 to 6-6.9	3
6-7 to 6-7.9	1
6-8 to 6-8.9	2
6-9 to 6-9.9	4
6-10 to 6-10.9	2
6-11 to 6-11.9	1
7-0 to 7-0.9	0
7-1 to 7-1.9	0
7-2 to 7-2.9	1

Figure B.1 shows two methods for representing the information in Table B.3 with graphs. Both in frequency **histograms** and frequency **polygons** the class intervals are typically drawn along the horizontal line, or X-axis, and the number of scores (persons, cases, or events) in each class is drawn along the vertical line, or Y-axis. In a histogram the number of scores in each class interval is represented by a rectangular solid, so that the graph resembles a series of steps. In a polygon the number of scores in each class interval is plotted as a point, and the points are then connected to form a many-sided geometric figure. Note that class intervals were added at both ends of the horizontal axis of the frequency polygon, so that the lines could be brought down to the axis to close the geometric figure.

Table B.3   Frequency Distribution of Heights of Basketball Players, with a Three-Inch Class Interval

CLASS INTERVAL	NUMBER OF PLAYERS IN CLASS
6-1 to 6-3.9	5
6-4 to 6-6.9	6
6-7 to 6-9.9	7
6-10 to 7-0.9	3
7-1 to 7-3.9	1

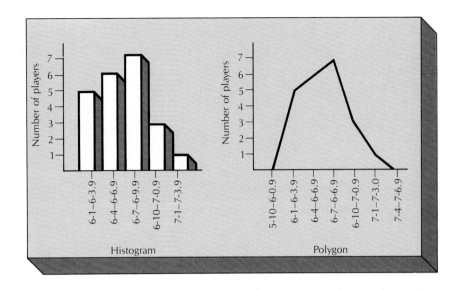

Figure B.1 Two Graphical Representations of the Data in Table B.3.

Measures of Central Tendency

There are three types of measures of central tendency, or averages: *mean, median,* and *mode.* Each tells us something about the way in which the scores in a distribution may be summarized by a typical or representative number.

The **mean** is what most people think of as the "average." The mean is obtained by adding up all the scores in a distribution and then dividing this sum by the number of scores. In the case of our basketball players it would be advisable first to convert all heights into one unit, such as inches (6′1″ becomes 73″, etc.). If we add all the heights in inches, then divide by the number of players, or 22, we obtain a mean height of 78.73″, or 6′6.73″.

The **median** is the score of the middle case in a frequency distribution. It is the score beneath which 50 percent of the cases fall. In a distribution with an even number of cases, such as the distribution of the heights of the 22 basketball players in Table B.2, the median is determined by finding the mean of the two middle cases. Listing these 22 cases in ascending order, we find that the eleventh case is 6′6″ and the twelfth case is 6′7″. Thus the median is (6′6″ + 6′7″)/2, or 6′6½″.

In the case of the heights of the basketball players, the mean and the median are similar, and either serves as a useful indicator of the central tendency of the data. But suppose we are attempting to determine the average savings of 30 families living on a suburban block. Let us assume that 29 of the 30 families have savings between $8,000 and $12,000, adding up to $294,000. But the thirtieth family has savings of $1,400,000. The mean savings for a family on this block would thus be $56,467. A mean can be greatly distorted by one or two extreme scores, and for such distributions the median is a better indicator of the central tendency. The median savings on our hypothetical block would lie between $8,000 and $12,000, and so would be more representative of the central tendency of savings. Studies of the incomes of American families usually report median rather than mean incomes just to avoid the distortions that would result from treating incomes of the small numbers of multimillionaires in the same way as other incomes.

The **mode** is simply the most frequently occurring score in a distribution. The mode of the data in Table B.1 is 6′9″ because this height occurs most often. The median class interval for the data

---

Mean A type of average calculated by dividing the sum of scores by the number of scores.

Median The score beneath which 50 percent of the cases fall.

Mode The most frequently occurring number or score in a distribution.

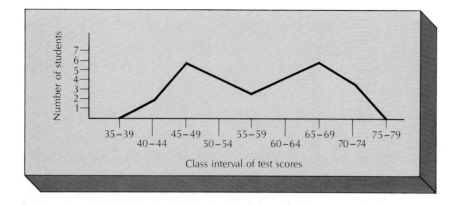

Figure B.2 Bimodal Distribution. This hypothetical distribution represents the scores of students on a test. The mode at the left represents the central tendency of students who did not study, and the mode at the right represents the mode of students who studied.

in Table B.3 is 6′6½″ to 6′9½″. In these cases the mode is somewhat higher than the mean or median height.

In some cases the mode is a more appropriate description of a distribution than the mean or median. Figure B.2 shows a **bimodal** distribution, or a distribution with two modes. In this hypothetical distribution of the test scores the mode at the left indicates the most common class interval for students who did not study, and the mode at the right indicates the most frequent class interval for students who did. The mean and median test scores would probably lie within the 55 to 59 class interval, yet use of that interval as a measure of central tendency would not provide very meaningful information about the distribution of scores. It might suggest that the test was too hard—not that a number of students chose not to study. One would be better able to visualize the distribution of scores if it is reported as bimodal. Even in similar cases in which the modes are not exactly equal, it might be more appropriate to describe a distribution as being bimodal or even multimodal.

Measures of Variability

Measures of variability of a distribution inform us about the spread of scores, or about the typical

distances of scores from the average score. Measures of variability include the *range* of scores and the *standard deviation.*

The **range** of scores in a distribution is defined as the difference between the highest score and the lowest score, and it is obtained by subtracting the lowest score from the highest score. The range of heights in Table B.2 is 7′2″ minus 6′1″, or 1′1″. It is important to know the range of temperatures if we move to a new climate so that we may anticipate the weather and dress appropriately. A teacher must have some understanding of the range of abilities or skills in a class in order to teach effectively. Classes of gifted students or slow learners are formed so that teachers may devise a level of instruction that will better meet the needs of all members of a particular class.

The range is an imperfect measure of variability because of the manner in which it is influenced by extreme scores. In our earlier discussion of the savings of 30 families on a suburban block, the range of savings is $1,400,000 to $8,000, or $1,392,000. This tells us little about the typical variability of savings accounts, which lie within a restricted range of $8,000 to $12,000. The standard deviation is a statistic that indicates how scores are distributed about a mean of a distribution.

The standard deviation considers every score in a distribution, not just the extreme scores. Thus the standard deviation for the distribution on the right in Figure B.3 would be smaller than that of the distribution on the left.

Note that each distribution has the same number of scores, the same mean, and the same range of scores. But the standard deviation for the distri-

Bimodal Having two modes.
Range The difference between the highest and the lowest scores in a distribution.

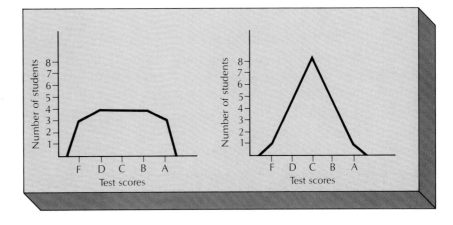

Figure B.3 Hypothetical Distributions of Student Test Scores Each distribution has the same number of scores, the same mean, and even the same range, but the standard deviation is greater for the distribution on the left because the scores tend to be farther from the mean.

bution on the right will be smaller than that of the distribution on the left because the scores tend to cluster more closely about the mean.

Table B.4   Hypothetical Scores Attained from an IQ Testing

IQ SCORE	d (DEVIATION SCORE)	d² (DEVIATION SCORE SQUARED)
85	15	225
87	13	169
89	11	121
90	10	100
93	7	49
97	3	9
97	3	9
100	0	0
101	−1	1
104	−4	16
105	−5	25
110	−10	100
112	−12	144
113	−13	169
117	−17	289

Sum of IQ scores = 1500   Sum of d² scores = 1426

$$\text{Mean} = \frac{\text{Sum of scores}}{\text{Number of scores}} = \frac{1500}{15} = 100$$

$$\text{Standard Deviation (S.D.)} = \sqrt{\frac{\text{Sum of } d^2}{\text{Number of scores}}}$$

$$= \sqrt{\frac{1426}{15}} = \sqrt{95.07} = 9.75$$

The **standard deviation** (S.D.) is calculated by the following formula:

$$\text{S.D.} = \sqrt{\frac{\text{Sum of } d^2}{N}}$$

where d equals the deviation of each score from the mean of the distribution, and N equals the number of scores in the distribution.

Let us find the mean and standard deviation of the IQ scores listed in column 1 of Table B.4. To obtain the mean, we add all the scores, attain 1500, and then divide by the number of scores (15) to obtain a mean of 100. We obtain the deviation score (d) for each IQ score by subtracting the score from 100. The d for an IQ of 85 equals 100 minus 85, or 15, and so on. Then we square each d and add these squares. The S.D. equals the square root of the sum of squares (1426) divided by the number of scores (15), or 9.75.

As an additional exercise, we can show that the S.D. of the test scores on the left (in Figure B.3) is greater than that for the scores on the right by assigning the grades points according to a 4.0 system. Let A = 4, B = 3, C = 2, D = 1, and F = 0. The S.D. for each distribution of test scores

Standard deviation A measure of the variability of a distribution attained by the formula

$$\sqrt{\frac{\text{Sum of } d^2}{N}}$$

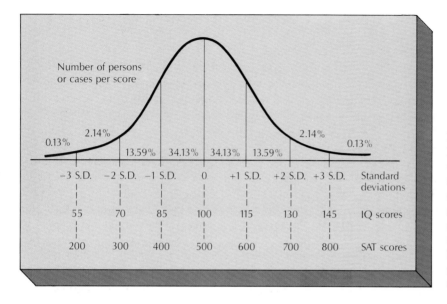

Number of persons
or cases per score

0.13%   2.14%   13.59%   34.13%   34.13%   13.59%   2.14%   0.13%

−3 S.D.	−2 S.D.	−1 S.D.	0	+1 S.D.	+2 S.D.	+3 S.D.	Standard deviations
55	70	85	100	115	130	145	IQ scores
200	300	400	500	600	700	800	SAT scores

Figure B.4 A Bell-shaped or Normal Curve   In a normal curve approximately 68 percent of the cases lie within a standard deviation (S.D.) from the mean, and the mean, median, and mode all lie at the same score. IQ tests and scholastic aptitude tests have been constructed so that distributions of scores approximate the normal curve.

is computed in Table B.5. The greater S.D. for the distribution on the left indicates that the scores in that distribution are more variable, or tend to be farther from the mean.

THE NORMAL CURVE

Many human traits and characteristics, such as height and intelligence, seem to be distributed in a pattern known as a normal distribution. In a **normal distribution** the mean, median, and mode all fall at the same data point or score, and scores cluster most heavily about the mean, fall off rapidly in either direction at first—as shown in Figure B.4—and then taper off more gradually.

The curve in Figure B.4 is bell-shaped. This type of distribution is also called a **normal curve.** It is hypothesized to reflect the distribution of variables in which different scores are determined by chance variation. Height is thought to be largely determined by chance combinations of genetic ma-

Normal distribution A symmetrical distribution in which approximately 68 percent of cases lie within a standard deviation of the mean.

Normal curve Graphic presentation of a normal distribution, showing a bell shape.

Table B.5   Computation of Standard Deviations for Test Score Distributions in Figure B.3

DISTRIBUTION AT LEFT			DISTRIBUTION AT RIGHT		
GRADE	d	d^2	GRADE	d	d^2
A (4)	2	4	A (4)	2	4
A (4)	2	4	B (3)	1	1
A (4)	2	4	B (3)	1	1
B (3)	1	1	B (3)	1	1
B (3)	1	1	B (3)	1	1
B (3)	1	1	C (2)	0	0
B (3)	1	1	C (2)	0	0
C (2)	0	0	C (2)	0	0
C (2)	0	0	C (2)	0	0
C (2)	0	0	C (2)	0	0
C (2)	0	0	C (2)	0	0
D (1)	−1	1	C (2)	0	0
D (1)	−1	1	C (2)	0	0
D (1)	−1	1	D (1)	−1	1
D (1)	−1	1	D (1)	−1	1
F (0)	−2	4	D (1)	−1	1
F (0)	−2	4	D (1)	−1	1
F (0)	−2	4	F (0)	−2	4

Sum of grades = 36   Sum of grades = 36
Mean grade = 36/18 = 2   Mean grade = 36/18 = 2
Sum of d^2 = 32   Sum of d^2 = 16
S.D. = $\sqrt{\dfrac{32}{18}}$ = 1.33   S.D. = $\sqrt{\dfrac{16}{18}}$ = 0.94

terial. A distribution of the heights of a random sample of the population approximates normal distributions for men and women, with the mean of the distribution for men a few inches higher than the mean for women.

Test developers traditionally assumed that intelligence was also randomly or normally distributed among the population. For that reason they constructed intelligence tests so that scores would be distributed as close to "normal" as possible. In actuality, IQ scores are also influenced by environmental factors and chromosomal abnormalities, so the resultant curves are not perfectly normal. Most IQ tests have means defined as scores of 100 points, and the Wechsler scales are constructed to have standard deviations of 15 points, as shown in Figure B.4. This means that 50 percent of the Wechsler scores fall between 90 and 110 (the "broad average" range), about 68 percent (or two of three) fall between 85 and 115, and more than 95 percent fall between 70 and 130—that is, within two S.D.s of the mean. The Stanford-Binet Intelligence Scale has an S.D. of 16 points.

The Scholastic Aptitude Tests (SATs) were constructed so that the mean scores would be 500 points, and an S.D. would be 100 points. Thus a score of 600 would equal or excel that of some 84 to 85 percent of the test takers. Because of the complex interaction of variables determining SAT scores, the distribution of SAT scores is not exactly normal either. The normal curve is an idealized curve.

THE CORRELATION COEFFICIENT

What is the relationship between intelligence and educational achievement? Between cigarette smoking and lung cancer in human beings? Between introversion and frequency of dating among college students? We cannot run experiments to determine whether the relationships between these variables are causal because we cannot manipulate the independent variable. For example, we cannot randomly assign a group of people to cigarette smoking and another group to nonsmoking. People must be permitted to make their own choices, and so it is possible that the same factors that lead people to choose to smoke may also lead to lung

cancer. However, the **correlation coefficient** may be used to show that there is a relationship between smoking and cancer. If a strong correlation is shown between the two variables, and we add supportive experimental evidence with laboratory animals who are assigned to conditions in which they inhale tobacco smoke, we wind up with a rather convincing indictment of smoking as a determinant of lung cancer.

The correlation coefficient is a statistic that describes the relationship between two variables. It varies from $+1.00$ to -1.00; therefore a correlation coefficient of $+1.00$ is called a perfect positive correlation, a coefficient of -1.00 is a perfect negative correlation, and a coefficient of 0.00 shows no correlation between variables. To examine the meanings of different correlation coefficients, let us first discuss the *scatter diagram*.

The Scatter Diagram

A **scatter diagram,** or scatter plot, is a graphic representation of the relationship between two variables. As shown in Figure B.5, a scatter diagram is typically drawn with an X-axis (horizontal) and Y-axis (vertical).

Let us assume that we have two thermometers. One measures temperature according to the Fahrenheit scale and one measures temperature according to the centigrade scale. Over a period of several months we record the temperatures Fahrenheit and centigrade at various times of the day. Then we randomly select a sample of eight Fahrenheit readings and jot down the corresponding centigrade readings, as shown in Figure B.5.

Figure B.5 shows a perfect positive correlation. One variable increases as the other increases, and the points on the scatter diagram may be joined to form a straight line. We usually do not

Correlation coefficient A number between -1.00 and $+1.00$ that indicates the degree of relationship between two variables.

Scatter diagram A graphic presentation showing the plotting of points defined by the intersections of two variables.

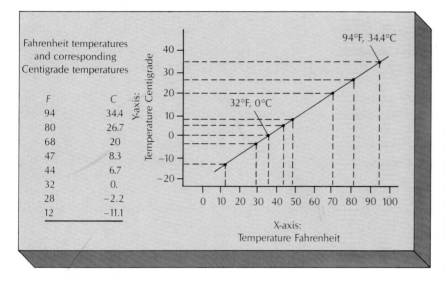

F	C
94	34.4
80	26.7
68	20
47	8.3
44	6.7
32	0.
28	−2.2
12	−11.1

Fahrenheit temperatures and corresponding Centigrade temperatures

Y-axis: Temperature Centigrade

94°F, 34.4°C

32°F, 0°C

X-axis: Temperature Fahrenheit

Figure B.5 A Scatter Diagram Showing the Perfect Positive Correlation Between Fahrenheit Temperatures and the Corresponding Centigrade Temperatures Scatter diagrams have X and Y axes, and each point is plotted by finding the spot where an X value and the corresponding Y value meet.

find variables forming a perfect positive (or perfect negative) correlation unless they are related according to a specific mathematical formula. The temperatures Fahrenheit and centigrade are so related (degrees Fahrenheit = 9/5 degrees centigrade + 32).

A positive correlation of about +0.80 to +0.90, or higher, between scores attained on separate testings is usually required to determine the **reliability** of psychological tests. Intelligence tests such as the Stanford-Binet Intelligence Scale and the Wechsler scales have been found to yield **test-retest reliabilities** that meet these requirements. Somewhat lower correlation coefficients are usually accepted as indicators that a psychological test is **valid** when test scores are correlated with scores on an external criterion. Figure B.6 shows a hypothetical scatter diagram that demonstrates the relationship between IQ scores and academic averages for children in grade school. The correlation coefficient that would be derived by mathematical formula would be between +0.60 and +0.70. Re-

Reliability Consistency.

Test-retest reliability Consistency of a test as determined by a comparison of scores on repeated testings.

Validity The degree to which a test measures what it is supposed to measure.

member that correlation does not show cause and effect. Figure B.6 suggests a relationship between the variables but cannot be taken as evidence that intelligence causes achievement.

Figure B.7 shows a scatter diagram in which there is a correlation coefficient of about 0.00 between the X and Y variables, suggesting that they are fully independent of each other. A person's scores on spelling quizzes taken in California ought to be independent of the daily temperatures in Bolivia. Thus we would expect a correlation coefficient of close to 0.00 between the variables.

Figure B.8 shows a scatter diagram in which there is a perfect negative correlation between two variables: As one variable increases, the other decreases systematically.

Correlations between 0.80 and 1.00 are considered very high (whether they are positive or negative). Correlations between 0.60 and 0.80 are high, between 0.40 and 0.60 moderate, from 0.20 to 0.40 weak, and between 0.00 and 0.20 very weak.

It cannot be overemphasized that correlation coefficients do not show cause and effect. For instance, a relationship between intelligence and academic performance could be explained by suggesting that the same cultural factors that lead some children to do well on intelligence tests also lead them to do well on academic tasks. According to this view, intelligence does not cause high aca-

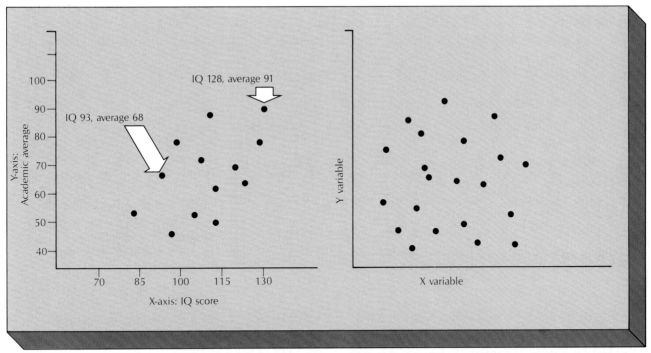

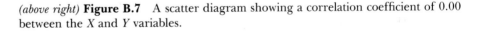

(above left) **Figure B.6 A Hypothetical Scatter Diagram Showing the Relationship between IQ Scores and Academic Averages** Such correlations usually fall between +0.60 and +0.70, which is considered an adequate indication of validity for intelligence tests, since such tests are intended to predict academic performance.

(above right) **Figure B.7** A scatter diagram showing a correlation coefficient of 0.00 between the *X* and *Y* variables.

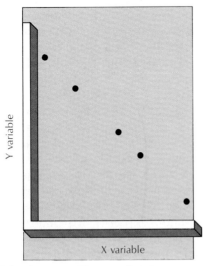

Figure B.8 A scatter diagram showing a correlation coefficient of −1.00 between the *X* and *Y* variables, or a perfect negative relationship.

demic performance. Instead, a third variable determines both intelligence and academic performance.

However, many psychologists undertake correlational research as a first step in attempting to determine causal relationships between variables. Correlation does not show cause and effect; but a lack of correlation between two variables suggests that it may be fruitless to undertake experimental research to determine whether they are causally related.

INFERENTIAL STATISTICS

In a study reported in Chapter 6 children enrolled in a Head Start program earned a mean IQ score of 99, whereas children similar in background who were not enrolled in Head Start earned a mean IQ

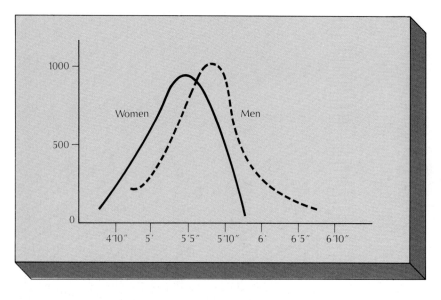

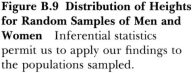

Figure B.9 Distribution of Heights for Random Samples of Men and Women Inferential statistics permit us to apply our findings to the populations sampled.

score of 93. Is this difference of six points in IQ significant, or does it represent chance fluctuation of scores? In a study reported in Chapter 1, subjects who believed they had drunk alcohol chose higher levels of electric shock to be applied to persons who had provoked them than did subjects who believed they had not drunk alcohol. Did the difference in level of shock chosen reflect an actual difference between the two groups of subjects, or could it have been a chance fluctuation? Inferential statistics help us make decisions about whether differences found between such groups reflect real differences or just fluctuations.

Figure B.9 shows the distribution of heights of a thousand men and a thousand women selected at random. The mean height for men is greater than the mean height for women. Can we draw the conclusion, or **infer,** that this difference in heights represents the general population of men and women? Or must we avoid such an inference and summarize our results by stating only that the sample of a thousand men in the study had a higher mean height than that of the sample of a thousand women in the study?

If we could not draw inferences about populations from studies of samples, our research findings would be very limited indeed—limited only to the specific subjects studied. However, the branch of statistics known as **inferential statistics** uses mathematical techniques in such a way that we can make statements about populations from which samples have been drawn, with a certain level of confidence.

Statistically Significant Differences

In determining whether differences in measures taken of research samples may be applied to the populations from which they were drawn, psychologists use mathematical techniques that indicate whether differences are statistically significant. Was the difference in IQ scores for children attending and those not attending Head Start significant? Did it represent only the children participating in the study, or can it be applied to all chil-

Infer To draw a conclusion, to conclude.

Inferential statistics The branch of statistics concerned with the confidence with which conclusions drawn about samples may be extended to the populations from which they were drawn.

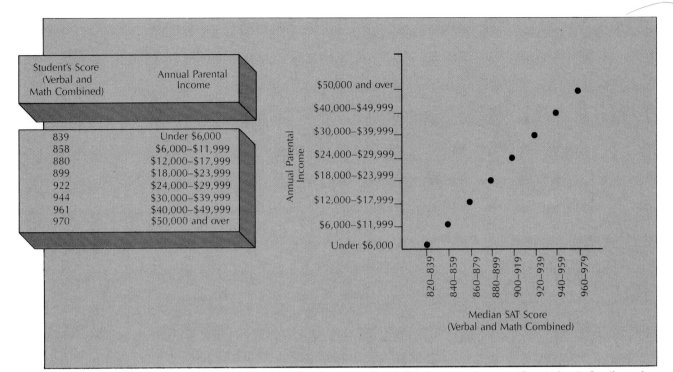

Student's Score (Verbal and Math Combined)	Annual Parental Income
839	Under $6,000
858	$6,000–$11,999
880	$12,000–$17,999
899	$18,000–$23,999
922	$24,000–$29,999
944	$30,000–$39,999
961	$40,000–$49,999
970	$50,000 and over

A scatter diagram showing the relationship between income of a student's family and the student's score on the Scholastic Aptitude Test (SAT) taken during 1980–1981. Scores are a combination of scores on the Verbal and Mathematics sub-tests, and may vary from 400 to 1600. Scores shown are for white students only. SAT scores predict performance in college. Note the strong positive correlation between SAT scores and parental income. Does the relationship show that a high-income family is better able to expose children to concepts and skills measured on the SAT? Or that families who transmit genetic influences that may contribute to high test performance also tend to earn high incomes? Correlation is *not* cause and effect. For this reason, the data cannot answer these questions.

dren represented by the sample? Is the difference between the height of men and the height of women in Figure B.9 statistically significant? Can we apply our findings to all men and women?

Psychologists use formulas involving the means and standard deviations of sample groups to determine whether group differences are statistically significant. As you can see in Figure B.10, the farther apart the group means are, the more likely it is that the difference between them is statistically significant. This makes a good deal of common sense. After all, if you were told that your neighbor's car had gotten one-tenth of a mile more per gallon of gasoline than your car had last year, you might assume that this was a chance differ-

ence. But if the differences were farther apart, say 14 miles per gallon, you might readily believe that this difference reflected an actual difference in driving habits or efficiency of the automobiles.

As you can see in Figure B.11, the smaller the standard deviation (a measure of variability) of the two groups, the more likely it is that the difference of the means is statistically significant. As an extreme example, if all women sampled were exactly 5′5″ tall, and all men sampled were exactly 5′10″, we would be highly likely to assume that the difference of five inches in group means is statistically significant. But if the heights of women varied from 2′ to 14′, and the heights of men varied from 2′1″ to 14′3″, we might be more likely to assume

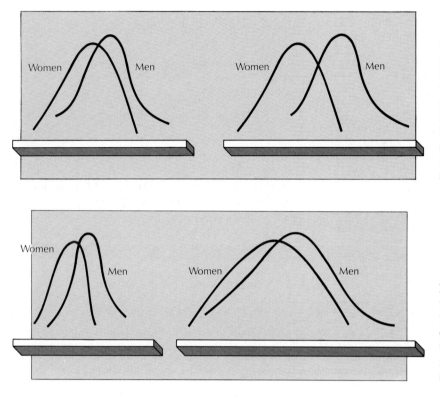

Figure B.10 Psychologists use group means and standard deviations in order to determine whether the difference between group means is statistically significant. The difference between the means of the groups on the right is greater and thus more likely to be statistically significant.

Figure B.11 The variability of the groups on the left is smaller than the variability of the groups on the right. Thus it is more likely that the difference between the means of the groups on the left is statistically significant.

that the five-inch difference in group means could be attributed to chance fluctuation.

Samples and Populations

Inferential statistics are mathematical tools that psychologists apply to samples of scores to determine whether they can generalize their findings to populations of scores. Thus they must be quite certain that the samples involved actually represent the populations from which they were drawn.

As you saw in Chapter 1, psychologists often use the techniques of random sampling and stratified sampling of populations in order to draw representative samples. If the samples studied do not accurately represent their intended populations, it matters very little how sophisticated the statistical techniques of the psychologist may be. We could use a variety of statistical techniques on the heights of the New York Apples and California Quakes, but none would tell us much about the height of the general population.

TRUTH OR FICTION REVISITED

A person rated as a "10" is very attractive. Not necessarily. We must know what the scale is (e.g., is it from 1 to 10 or from 10 to 100) and what a "10" is intended to indicate on that scale.

You could mathematically derive three very different figures for the average U.S. income, and each of them could be perfectly correct. True. There are three types of average—mean, median, and mode—and each can be a different number.

If we have a group of 30 men—20 of whom are 6 feet tall and 10 of whom are 5 feet 6 inches tall—the average height of the group is 6 feet. True, if the average we are speaking about is the mode—the most frequent height in the distribution.

Fifty percent of the U.S. population attains average IQ scores on the Wechsler intelligence scales. True. Wechsler defined the range from 90 to 110 as average on his scales, and because the standard deviation of scores attained on his tests is 15, 50 percent of the scores attained lie within this range.

Attaining a score of 200 on the Scholastic Aptitude Tests is not likely to impress a college admissions officer. True. Although the number 200 is twice as large as the number 100, which is an enviable performance on most tests, SAT scores generally vary from 200 to 800, so that 200 is about the poorest score that one could obtain.

Students whose parents earn higher incomes attain higher scores on the Scholastic Aptitude Tests. True. There is a strong positive correlation between the two variables.

Men are significantly taller than women. True. The difference in mean heights is large enough, considering the variability of the distributions of heights for men and women, that it is unreasonable to believe that it is a chance difference.

ANSWER KEYS FOR QUESTIONNAIRES

This appendix contains scoring keys, answer keys, and normative data for the various Questionnaires presented in the text.

Scoring Key for "The Social Desirability Scale" (Chapter 1, p. 30)

Place a check mark on the appropriate line of the scoring key each time your answer *agrees* with the one listed on the scoring key. Add the check marks and place the total number of check marks on the line marked "Total Score."

SCORING KEY

1. T _____	12. F _____	23. F _____
2. T _____	13. T _____	24. T _____
3. F _____	14. F _____	25. T _____
4. T _____	15. F _____	26. T _____
5. F _____	16. T _____	27. T _____
6. F _____	17. T _____	28. F _____
7. T _____	18. T _____	29. T _____
8. T _____	19. F _____	30. F _____
9. F _____	20. T _____	31. T _____
10. F _____	21. T _____	32. F _____
11. F _____	22. F _____	33. T _____

TOTAL SCORE _____

Interpreting Your Score. LOW SCORERS (0–8). About one respondent in six earns a score between 0 and 8. Such respondents answered in a socially *undesirable* direction much of the time. It may be that they are more willing than most people to respond to tests truthfully, even when their answers might meet with social disapproval.

AVERAGE SCORERS (9–19). About two respondents in three earn scores between 9 and 19. They tend to show an average degree of concern for the social desirability of their responses, and it may well be that their actual behavior represents an average degree of conformity to social rules and conventions.

HIGH SCORERS (20–33). About one respondent in six earns a score between 20 and 33. These respondents may be highly concerned about social approval and respond to test items in such a way as to avoid the disapproval of people who may read their responses. Their actual behavior may show high conformity to social rules and conventions.

Scoring Key for "The Sensation-seeking Scale" (Chapter 6, p. 252)

Since this is a shortened version of a questionnaire, no norms are available. However, the following answers are suggestive of sensation seeking:

1. A	5. A	8. A	11. A
2. A	6. B	9. B	12. A
3. A	7. A	10. B	13. B
4. B			

Norms for "The Love Scale" (Chapter 6, p. 264)

Table C.1 gives the scores of 220 undergraduate students at Northeastern University, aged between 19 and 24, with the largest single age group 21. Students were asked to indicate whether they were absolutely in love, probably in love, not sure, probably not in love, or definitely not in love. Scores of men and women in the five conditions did not differ, so they are lumped together. A number of students broke into arguments after taking the Love Scale: their love for one another "differed" by a couple of points! Please do not take scales like this too seriously. They are fun, but will not hold up in court as grounds for divorce. Rely on your feelings, not your scores.

Table C-1   Love-Scale Scores of Northeastern University Students

CONDITION	N*	MEAN SCORES
Absolutely in love	56	89
Probably in love	45	80
Not sure	36	77
Probably not in love	40	68
Definitely not in love	43	59

*N = Number of students.

Scoring Key for "The Rathus Assertiveness Schedule" (Chapter 10, p. 416)

Tabulate your score as follows: Change the signs of all items followed by an asterisk (*). Then add the 30 item scores. For example, if the response to an asterisked item was 2, place a minus (−) sign before the 2. If the response to an asterisked item was −3, change the minus sign to a plus sign (+) by adding a vertical stroke.

Scores on this test can vary from +90 to −90. Table B.2 will show you how your score compared with those of 764 college women and 637 college men from 35 campuses all across the United States. For example, if you are a woman and your score was 26, it exceeded that of 80 percent of the women in the sample. A score of 15 for a male exceeds that of 55–60 percent of the men in the sample.

Answer Key for "Are You Type A or B?" Questionnaire (Appendix A, p. 486)

Yesses suggest the Type A behavior pattern, which is marked by a sense of time urgency and constant struggle. In appraising your "type," you need not be overly concerned with the precise number of "yes" answers. As Friedman and Rosenman note, you will have little difficulty spotting yourself as "hard core" or "moderately afflicted" (1974, p. 85)—that is, if you are honest with yourself.

Scoring Key for the "Locus of Control Scale" (Appendix A, p. 494)

Credit yourself with one point each time your answer agrees with the answer on the scoring key below. Write the total number of answers in agreement in the box marked "Total Score."

SCORING KEY		
1. Yes _____	15. No _____	28. No _____
2. No _____	16. Yes _____	29. Yes _____
3. Yes _____	17. Yes _____	30. No _____
4. No _____	18. Yes _____	31. Yes _____
5. Yes _____	19. Yes _____	32. No _____
6. No _____	20. No _____	33. Yes _____
7. Yes _____	21. Yes _____	34. No _____
8. Yes _____	22. No _____	35. Yes _____
9. No _____	23. Yes _____	36. Yes _____
10. Yes _____	24. Yes _____	37. Yes _____
11. Yes _____	25. No _____	38. No _____
12. Yes _____	26. No _____	39. Yes _____
13. No _____	27. Yes '	40. No _____
14. Yes _____		

TOTAL SCORE _____

Interpreting Your Score. LOW SCORERS (0–8). About one respondent in three earns a score of from 0 to 8. Such respondents tend to have an internal locus of control. They see themselves as responsible for the reinforcements they attain (and fail to attain) in life.

AVERAGE SCORERS (9–16). Most respondents earn from 9 to 16 points. Average scorers may see themselves as partially in control of their lives. Perhaps they see themselves as in control at work, but not in their social lives—or vice versa.

HIGH SCORERS (17–40). About 15 percent of respondents attain scores of 17 or above. High scorers largely tend to see life as a game of chance, and success as a matter of luck.

REFERENCES

Abbey, A. (1982). Sex differences in attributions for friendly behavior. *Journal of Personality and Social Psychology, 42,* 830–838.

Abelson, H., Cohen, R., Heaton, E., & Slider, C. (1970). Public attitudes toward and experience with erotic materials. In *Technical reports of the commission on obscenity and pornography,* Vol. 6. Washington, DC: U.S. Government Printing Office.

Abikoff, H., & Gittelman, R. (1985). The normalizing effects of methylphenidate on the classroom behavior of ADDH children. *Journal of Abnormal Child Psychology, 13,* 33–44.

Abramowitz, C. V., Abramowitz, S. I., Roback, H. B., & Jackson, C. (1974). Differential effectiveness of directive and nondirective group therapies as a function of client internal-external control. *Journal of Consulting and Clinical Psychology, 42,* 849–853.

Abrams, D. B., & Wilson, G. T. (1983). Alcohol, sexual arousal, and self-control. *Journal of Personality and Social Psychology, 45,* 188–198.

Adair, J. G., Dushenko, T. W., & Lindsay, R. C. L. (1985). Ethical regulations and their impact on research practice. *American Psychologist, 40,* 59–72.

Adams, V. (1982, May). Mommy and I are one. *Psychology Today,* pp. 24–36.

Adelson, J. (1982, April). Still vital after all these years. *Psychology Today,* pp. 52–59.

Adolph, E. F. (1941). The internal environment and behavior: Water content. *American Journal of Psychiatry, 97,* 1365–1373.

Adorno, T. W., Frenkel-Brunswick, E., & Levinson, D. J. (1950). *The authoritarian personality.* New York: Harper.

Agras, W. S., Southam, M. A., & Taylor, C. B. (1983). Long-term persistence of relaxation-induced blood pressure lowering during the working day. *Journal of Consulting and Clinical Psychology, 51,* 792–794.

Akil, H. (1978). Endorphins, beta-LPH, and ACTH: Biochemical, pharmacological, and anatomical studies. *Advances in Biochemical Psychopharmacology, 18,* 125–139.

Akil, H., Mayer, D. J., & Liebeskind, J. L. (1976). Antagonism of stimulation-produced analgesia. *Science, 191,* 961–962.

Albert, M. S. (1981). Geriatric neuropsychology. *Journal of Consulting and Clinical Psychology, 49,* 835–850.

Alexander, A. B. (1981). Asthma. In S. N. Haynes & L. Gannon (Eds.), *Psychosomatic disorders: A psychophysiological approach to etiology and treatment.* New York: Praeger Books.

Allen, V. L., & Levine, J. M. (1971). Social support and conformity: The role of independent assessment of reality. *Journal of Experimental Social Psychology, 7,* 48–58.

Allgeier, A., & Byrne, D. (1973). Attraction toward the opposite sex as a determinant of physical proximity. *Journal of Social Psychology, 90,* 213–219.

Allgeier, E. R., & Allgeier, A. (1984). *Sexual interactions.* Lexington, MA: Heath.

Alloy, L. B., & Ahrens, A. H. (1987). Depression and pessimism for the future: Biased use of statistically relevant information in predictions for self versus others. *Journal of Personality and Social Psychology, 52,* 366–378.

Allport, G. W. (1937). *Personality: A psychological interpretation.* New York: Holt, Rinehart and Winston.

Allport, G. W. (1961). *Pattern and growth in personality.* New York: Holt, Rinehart and Winston.

Allport, G. W., & Odbert, H. S. (1936). Trait names: A psycholexical study. *Psychological Monographs, 47,* 2–11.

Altman, L. K. (1988, January 26). Cocaine's many dangers: The evidence mounts. *New York Times,* p. C3.

Amabile, T. M. (1982). Social psychology of creativity: A consensual assessment technique. *Journal of Personality and Social Psychology, 43,* 997–1013.

Amabile, T. M. (1983). The social psychology of creativity: A componential conceptualization. *Journal of Personality and Social Psychology, 45,* 357–376.

Amato, P. R. (1983). Helping behavior in urban and rural environments: Field studies based on a taxonomic organization of helping episodes. *Journal of Personality and Social Psychology, 45,* 571–586.

American Psychiatric Association. (1987). *Diagnostic and statistical manual of the mental disorders. (Third edition–Revised.)* (DSM–III–R.) Washington, DC: American Psychiatric Press, Inc.

American Psychological Association. (1981). Ethical principles of psychologists. *American Psychologist, 36,* 633–638.

American Psychological Association. (1984). Text of position on insanity defense. *APA Monitor, 15*(3), 11.

Amir, M. (1971). *Patterns in forcible rape.* Chicago: University of Chicago Press.

Anastasi, A. (1983). Evolving trait concepts. *American Psychologist, 38,* 175–184.

Andersson, B. (1971). Thirst—and brain control of water balance. *American Scientist, 59,* 408.

Andrews, G., & Harvey, R. (1981). Does psychotherapy benefit neurotic patients? *Archives of General Psychiatry, 38,* 1203–1208.

Aneshensel, C. S., & Huba, G. J. (1983). Depression, alcohol use, and smoking over one year: A four-wave longitudinal causal model. *Journal of Abnormal Psychology, 92,* 134–150.

Antill, J. K. (1983). Sex role complementarity versus similarity in married couples. *Journal of Personality and Social Psychology, 45,* 145–155.

APA *Monitor* (1978, February), p. 4.

APA *Monitor* (1978, January), pp. 5, 23.

Apfelbaum, M. (1978). Adaptation to changes in caloric intake. *Progress in Food and Nutritional Science, 2,* 543–559.

Archer, D., Iritani, B., Kimes, D. D., & Barrios, M. (1983). Face-ism: Five studies of sex differences in facial prominence. *Journal of Personality and Social Psychology, 45,* 725–735.

Archer, R. P., & Cash, T. F. (1985). Physical attractiveness and maladjustment among psychiatric patients. *Journal of Social and Clinical Psychology, 3,* 170–180.

Arkin, R. M., Detchon, C. S., & Maruyama, G. M. (1982). Roles of attribution, affect, and cognitive interference in test anxiety. *Journal of Personality and Social Psychology, 43,* 1111–1124.

Asarnow, J. R., Carlson, G. A., & Guthrie, D. (1987). Coping strategies, self-perceptions, hopelessness, and perceived family environments in depressed and suicidal children. *Journal of Consulting and Clinical Psychology, 55,* 361–366.

Asch, S. E. (1952). *Social psychology.* Englewood Cliffs, NJ: Prentice-Hall.

Athanasiou, R., Shaver, P., & Tavris, C. (1970). Sex. *Psychology Today, 4,* 39–52.

Atkinson, J., & Huston, T. L. (1984). Sex role orientation and division of labor early in marriage. *Journal of Personality and Social Psychology, 46,* 330–345.

Atkinson, K., MacWhinney, B., & Stoel, C. (1970). An experiment on recognition of babbling. In *Papers and reports on child language development.* Stanford, CA: Stanford University Press.

Atkinson, R. C. (1975). Mnemotechnics in second-language learning. *American Psychologist, 30,* 821–828.

Attorney General's Commission on Pornography: Final Report. (1986, July). Washington, DC: U.S. Department of Justice.

Averill, J. R. (1978). A constructivist view of emotion. In R. Plutchik & H. Kellerman (Eds.), *Theories of emotion.* New York: Academic Press.

Ayllon, T., & Haughton, E. (1962). Control of the behavior of schizophrenic patients by food. *Journal of the Experimental Analysis of Behavior, 5,* 343–352.

Azjen, I., & Fishbein, M. (1977). Attitude-behavior relations: A theoretical analysis and review of empirical research. *Psychological Bulletin, 84,* 888–918.

Azjen, I., & Fishbein, M. (1980). *Understanding attitudes and predicting social behavior.* Englewood Cliffs, NJ: Prentice-Hall.

Bach, G. R., & Deutsch, R. M. (1970). *Pairing.* New York: Peter H. Wyden.

Bachman, J. G., O'Malley, P. M., & Johnston, L. D. (1984). Drug use among young adults: The impacts of role status and social environment. *Journal of Personality and Social Psychology, 47,* 629–645.

Bagozzi, R. P. (1981). Attitudes, intentions, and behaviors: A test of some key hypotheses. *Journal of Personality and Social Psychology, 41,* 607–627.

Bahrick, H. P., Bahrick, P. O., & Wittlinger, R. P. (1975). Fifty years of memory for names and faces: A cross-sectional approach. *Journal of Experimental Psychology: General, 104,* 54–75.

Baker, L. A., DeFries, J. C., & Fulker, D. W. (1983). Longitudinal stability of cognitive ability in the Colorado adoption project. *Child Development, 54,* 290–297.

Bakwin, H. (1970, August 29). Sleepwalking in twins. *Lancet,* pp. 446–447.

Bakwin, H. (1971a). Enuresis in twins. *American Journal of Diseases of Children, 121,* 222–225.

Bakwin, H. (1971b). Nail-biting in twins, *Developmental Medicine and Child Neurology, 13,* 304–307.

Bandura, A. (1973). *Aggression: A social learning analysis.* Englewood Cliffs, NJ: Prentice-Hall.

Bandura, A. (1977). *Social learning theory.* Englewood Cliffs, NJ: Prentice-Hall.

Bandura, A. (1981). Self-referrant thought: A developmental analysis of self-efficacy. In J. H. Flavell & L. Ross (Eds.), *Social cognitive development: Frontiers and possible futures.* Cambridge, England: Cambridge University Press.

Bandura, A. (1982). Self-efficacy mechanism in human agency. *American Psychologist, 37,* 122–147.

Bandura, A. (1986). *Social foundations of thought and acton: A social-cognitive theory.* Englewood Cliffs, NJ: Prentice-Hall.

Bandura, A., Blanchard, E. B., & Ritter, B. (1969). The relative efficacy of desensitization and modeling approaches for inducing behavioral, affective, and cognitive changes. *Journal of Personality and Social Psychology, 13,* 173–199.

Bandura, A., Reese, L., & Adams, N. E. (1982). Microanalysis of action and fear arousal as a function of differential levels of perceived self-efficacy. *Journal of Personality and Social Psychology, 43,* 5–21.

Bandura, A., Ross, D., & Ross, S. A. (1963a). A comparative test of the status envy, and the secondary reinforcement theories of identificatory learning. *Journal of Abnormal and Social Psychology, 67,* 527–534.

Bandura, A., Ross, S. A., & Ross, D. (1963b). Imitation of film-mediated aggressive models. *Journal of Abnormal and Social Psychology, 66,* 3–11.

Banks, M. S., & Salapatek, P. (1983). Infant visual perception. In M. M. Haith & J. Campos (Eds.), *Handbook of child psychology, Vol. 2.* New York: Wiley.

Barber, T. X. (1970). *LSD, marihuana, yoga, and hypnosis.* Chicago: Aldine.

Barber, T. X., Spanos, N. P., & Chaves, J. F. (1974). *Hypnosis, imagination, and human potentialities.* New York: Pergamon Press.

Bard, P. (1934). The neurohumoral basis of emotional reactions. In C. A. Murchison (Ed.), *Handbook of general experimental psychology.* Worcester, MA: Clark University Press.

Bardwick, J. M. (1971). *Psychology of women: A study of biocultural conflicts.* New York: Harper & Row.

Bardwick, J. M. (1980). The seasons of a woman's life. In D. G. McGuigan (Ed.), *Women's lives: New theory, research, and policy.* Ann Arbor: University of Michigan, Center for Continuing Education of Women.

Barefoot, J. C., Dahlstrom, W. G., & Williams, R. B., Jr. (1983). Rapid communication, hostility, CHD incidence, and total mortality: a 25-year follow-up study of 225 physicians. *Psychosomatic Medicine, 45,* 59–63.

Barkley, R. A., Karlsson, J., Strzelecki, E., & Murphy, J. V. (1984). Effects of age and Ritalin dosage on the mother-child interactions of hyperactive children. *Journal of Consulting and Clinical Psychology, 52,* 750–758.

Barlow, D. H. (1986). Causes of sexual dysfunction: The role of anxiety and cognitive interference. *Journal of Consulting and Clinical Psychology, 54,* 140–148.

Barlow, D. H., Vermilyea, J., Blanchard, E. B., Vermilyea, B. B., DiNardo, P. A., & Cerny, J. A. (1985). The phenomenon of panic. *Journal of Abnormal Psychology, 94,* 291–297.

Barnes, M. L., & Buss, D. M. (1985). Sex differences in the interpersonal behavior of married couples. *Journal of Personality and Social Psychology, 48,* 654–661.

Barnett, R. C., & Baruch, G. K. (1985). Women's involvement in multiple roles and psychological distress. *Journal of Personality and Social Psychology, 49,* 135–145.

Baron, R. A. (1971). Behavioral effects of interpersonal attraction: Compliance with requests from liked and disliked others. *Psychonomic Science, 25,* 325–326.

Baron, R. A. (1973). The "foot-in-the-door" phenomenon: Mediating effects of size of first request and sex of requester. *Bulletin of the Psychonomic Society, 2,* 113–114.

Baron, R. A. (1983). *Behavior in organizations.* Boston: Allyn & Bacon.

Baron, R. A., & Byrne, D. (1987). *Social psychology: Understanding human interaction, 5th ed.* Boston: Allyn & Bacon.

Bar-Tal, D., & Saxe, L. (1976). Perceptions of similarly and dissimilarly physically attractive couples and individuals. *Journal of Personality and Social Psychology, 33,* 772–781.

Basham, R. B. (1986). Scientific and practical advantages of comparative design in psychotherapy outcome research. *Journal of Consulting and Clinical Psychology, 54,* 88–94.

Bates, E., & MacWhinney, B. (1982). A functionalist approach to grammatical development. In L. Gleitman & H. E. Wanner (Eds.), *Language acquisition: The state of the art.* Cambridge: Cambridge University Press.

Batson, C. D., Duncan, B. D., Ackerman, P., Buckley, T., Baucom, D. H., & Aiken, P. A. (1981). Effect of depressed mood on eating among obese and nonobese dieting and nondieting persons. *Journal of Personality and Social Psychology, 41,* 577–585.

Baucom, D. H., & Aiken, P. A. (1984). Sex role identity, marital satisfaction, and response to behavioral marital therapy. *Journal of Consulting and Clinical Psychology, 52,* 438–444.

Baucom, D. H., Besch, P. K., & Callahan, S. (1985). Relationship between testosterone concentration, sex role identity, and personality among females. *Journal of Personality and Social Psychology, 48,* 1218–1226.

Baucom, D. H., & Danker-Brown, P. (1983). Peer ratings of males and females possessing different sex role identities. *Journal of Personality Assessment, 44,* 334–343.

Bauer, R. H., & Fuster, J. M. (1976). Delayed-matching and delayed-response deficit from cooling dorsolateral prefrontal cortex in monkeys. *Journal of Comparative and Physiological Psychology, 90,* 293–302.

Bauer, W. D., & Twentyman, C. T. (1985). Abusing, neglectful, and comparison mothers' responses to child-related and non-child-related stressors. *Journal of Consult-*

ing and Clinical Psychology, 53, 335–343.

Baum-Baicker, C. (1984). Treating and preventing alcohol abuse in the workplace. *American Psychologist, 39,* 454.

Baumeister, R. F., & Covington, M. V. (1985). Self-esteem, persuasion, and retrospective distortion of initial attitudes. *Electronic Social Psychology, 1,* 1–22.

Baumgardner, A. H., Heppner, P. P., & Arkin, R. M. (1986). Role of causal attribution in personal problem solving. *Journal of Personality and Social Psychology, 50,* 636–643.

Baumrind, D. (1985). Research using intentional deception: Ethical issues revisited. *American Psychologist, 40,* 165–174.

Beatty, W. W. (1979). Gonadal hormones and sex differences in nonreproductive behavior in rodents: Organizational and activational influences. *Hormones and Behavior, 12,* 112–163.

Beauchamp, G. (1981). Paper presented to the Conference on the Determination of Behavior by Chemical Stimuli. Hebrew University, Jerusalem.

Beck, A. T. (1976). *Cognitive therapy and the emotional disorders.* New York: International Universities Press.

Beck, A. T., Rush, A. J., Show, B. F., & Emery, G. (1979). *Cognitive therapy of depression.* New York: Guilford Press.

Beck, J., Elsner, A., & Silverstein, C. (1977). Position uncertainty and the perception of apparent movement. *Perception and Psychophysics, 21,* 33–38.

Bell, A. P., Weinberg, M. S., & Hammersmith, S. K. (1981). *Sexual preference: Its development in men and women.* Bloomington, IN: University of Indiana Press.

Belsky, J. (1984). The determinants of parenting: A process model. *Child Development, 55,* 83–96.

Belsky, J., Gilstrap, B., & Rovine, M. (1984). The Pennsylvania infant and family development project, I: Stability and change in mother-infant and father-infant interaction in a family setting at one, three, and nine months. *Child Development, 55,* 692–705.

Belsky, J., & Steinberg, L. D. (1978). The effects of day care: A critical review. *Child Development, 49,* 929–949.

Belsky, J., & Steinberg, L. D. (1979, July–August). What does research teach us about day care? A follow-up report. *Children Today,* pp. 21–26.

Bem, D. J. (1987). Social influence. In R. L. Atkinson, R. C. Atkinson, E. E. Smith, & E. R. Hilgard, *Introduction to psychology, 9th ed.,* pp. 596–627. Orlando, FL: Harcourt Brace Jovanovich.

Bem, D. J., & Allen, A. (1974). On predicting some of the people some of the time: The search for cross-situational consistencies in behavior. *Psychological Review, 81,* 506–520.

Bem, S. L. (1974). The measurement of psychological androgyny. *Journal of Consulting and Clinical Psychology, 42,* 151–162.

Bem, S. L. (1975). Sex role adaptability: One consequence of psychological androgyny. *Journal of Personality and Social Psychology, 31,* 634–643.

Bem, S. L. (1981). Gender schema theory: A cognitive account of sex typing. *Psychological Review, 88,* 354–364.

Bem, S. L. (1985). Androgyny and gender schema theory: A conceptual and empirical integration. In T. B. Sonderegger (Ed.), *Nebraska symposium on motivation, 1984: Psychology and gender.* Lincoln, NE: University of Nebraska Press.

Bem, S. L., & Bem, D. J. (1973). Training the woman to know her place: The power of a nonconscious ideology. In L. S. Wrightsman & J. C. Brigham (Eds.), *Contemporary issues in social psychology,* 2d ed. Monterey, CA: Brooks/Cole.

Bem, S. L., & Lenney, E. (1976). Sex typing and the avoidance of cross-sexed behaviors. *Journal of Personality and Social Psychology, 33,* 48–54.

Bem, S. L., Martyna, W., & Watson, C. (1976). Sex typing and androgyny: Further explorations of the expressive domain. *Journal of Personality and Social Psychology, 34,* 1016–1023.

Bemis, K. M. (1978). Current approaches to the etiology and treatment of anorexia nervosa. *Psychological Bulletin, 85,* 593–617.

Benbow, C. P., & Stanley, J. C. (1983). Sex differences in mathematical reasoning ability: More facts. *Science, 210,* 1029–1030.

Benedict, R. (1934). *Patterns of culture.* Boston: Houghton Mifflin.

Bennett, D. (1985). Rogers: More intuition in therapy. *APA Monitor, 16*(10), 3.

Benson, P. L., Karabenick, S. A., & Lerner, R. M. (1976). Pretty pleases: The effects of physical attractiveness, race, and sex on receiving help. *Journal of Experimental Social Psychology, 12,* 409–415.

Berkowitz, L. (1987). Mood, self-awareness, and willingness to help. *Journal of Personality and Social Psychology, 52,* 721–729.

Berkowitz, L., & Donnerstein, E. (1982). External validity is more than skin deep: Some answers to criticisms of laboratory experiments. *American Psychologist, 37,* 245–257.

Berkowitz, W. R., Nebel, J. C., & Reitman, J. W. (1971). Height and interpersonal attraction: The 1960 mayoral election in New York City. Paper presented at the annual convention of the American Psychological Association. Washington, DC.

Berman, J. S., Miller, R. C., & Massman, P. J. (1985). Cognitive therapy versus systematic desensitization: Is one treatment superior? *Psychological Bulletin, 97,* 451–461.

Berne, E. (1976). *Games people play.* New York: Ballantine.

Bernstein, B. E. (1977). Effect of

menstruation on academic performance among college women. *Archives of Sexual Behavior, 6,* 289–296.

Bernstein, E. (1987). Reply to Terrace. *American Psychologist, 42,* 272–273.

Bernstein, W. M., Stephenson, B. O., Snyder, M. L., & Wicklund, R. A. (1983). Causal ambiguity and heterosexual affiliation. *Journal of Experimental Social Psychology, 19,* 78–92.

Berntzen, D., & Götestam, K. G. (1987). Effects of on-demand versus fixed-interval schedules in the treatment of chronic pain with analgesic compounds. *Journal of Consulting and Clinical Psychology, 55,* 213–217.

Berscheid, E. (1976). Theories of interpersonal attraction. In B. B. Wolman & L. R. Pomeroy (Eds.), *International Encyclopaedia of Neurology, Psychiatry, Psychoanalysis, and Psychology.* New York: Springer.

Berscheid, E., Dion, K., Walster, E., & Walster, G. W. (1971). Physical attractiveness and dating choice: A test of the matching hypothesis. *Journal of Experimental Social Psychology, 7,* 173–189.

Berscheid, E., & Walster, E. (1974a). A little bit about love. In T. L. Huston (Ed.), *Foundations of interpersonal attraction.* New York: Academic Press.

Berscheid, E., & Walster, E. (1974b). Physical attractiveness. In L. Berkowitz (Ed.), *Advances in Experimental Social Psychology,* Vol. 7. New York: Academic Press.

Berscheid, E., & Walster, E. (1978). *Interpersonal attraction.* Reading, MA: Addison-Wesley.

Bertelson, A. D., Marks, P. A., & May, G. D. (1982). MMPI and race: A controlled study. *Journal of Consulting and Clinical Psychology, 50,* 316–318.

Betz, N. E., & Hackett, G. (1981). The relationships of career-related self-efficacy expectations to perceived career options in college women and men. *Journal of Counseling Psychology, 28,* 399–410.

Bexton, W. H., Heron, W., & Scott, T. H. (1954). Effects of decreased variation in the sensory environment. *Canadian Journal of Psychology, 8,* 70–76.

Biglan, A., & Craker, D. (1982). Effects of pleasant-activities manipulation on depression. *Journal of Consulting and Clinical Psychology, 50,* 436–438.

Billings, A. G., Cronkite, R. C., & Moos, R. H. (1983). Social-environmental factors in unipolar depression: Comparisons of depressed patients and nondepressed controls. *Journal of Abnormal Psychology, 92,* 119–133.

Biran, M., & Wilson, G. T. (1981). Treatment of phobic disorders using cognitive and exposure methods: A self-efficacy analysis. *Journal of Consulting and Clinical Psychology, 49,* 886–899.

Birch, H. G., & Rabinowitz, H. S. (1951). The negative effect of previous experience on productive thinking. *Journal of Experimental Psychology, 42,* 121–125.

Birren, J. E. (1983). Aging in America: Roles for psychology. *American Psychologist, 38,* 298–299.

Blake, R. (1985). Neurohormones and sexual preference. *Psychology Today, 19*(1), 12–13.

Blakely, M. K. (1985). Is one woman's sexuality another woman's pornography? The question behind a major legal battle. *Ms, 13*(10), 37–47, 120–123.

Blanchard, E. B., Andrasik, F., Ahles, T. A., Teders, S. J., & O'Keefe, D. M. (1980). Migraine and tension headache: A meta-analytic review. *Behavior Therapy, 11,* 613–631.

Blanchard, E. B., Andrasik, F., Guarnieri, P., Neff, D. F., & Rodichok, L. D. (1987). Two-, three-, and four-year follow-up on the self-regulatory treatment of chronic headache. *Journal of Consulting and Clinical Psychology, 55,* 257–259.

Blanchard, E. B., Andrasik, F., Neff, D. F., Arena, J. G., Ahles, T. A., Jurish, S. E., Pallmeyer, T. P., Saunders, N. L., Teders, S. J., Barron, K. D., & Rodichok, L. D. (1982). Biofeedback and relaxation training with three kinds of headache: Treatment effects and their prediction. *Journal of Consulting and Clinical Psychology, 50,* 562–575.

Blanchard, R., Steiner, B. W., & Clemensen, L. H. (1985). Gender dysphoria, gender reorientation, and the clinical management of transsexualism. *Journal of Consulting and Clinical Psychology, 53,* 295–304.

Blank, M. (1974). Cognitive functions of language in the preschool years. *Developmental Psychology, 10,* 229–245.

Blittner, M., Goldberg, J., & Merbaum, M. (1978). Cognitive self-control factors in the reduction of smoking behavior. *Behavior Therapy, 9,* 553–561.

Bloch, V., Hennevin, E., & Leconte, P. (1979). Relationship between paradoxical sleep and memory processes. In M. A. B. Brazier (Ed.), *Brain mechanisms in memory and learning: From the single neuron to man.* New York: Raven Press.

Block, J. (1983). Differential premises arising from differential socialization of the sexes: Some conjectures. *Child Development, 54,* 1335–1354.

Bloom, L. (1975). Language development. In F. D. Horowitz (Ed.), *Review of Child Development Research, Vol. 4.* Chicago: University of Chicago Press.

Bloom, L., Lahey, L., Hood, L., Lifter, K., & Fiess, K. (1980). Complex sentences: Acquisition of syntactic connectives and the semantic relations they encode. *Journal of Child Language, 7,* 235–261.

Blumberg, S. H., & Izard, C. E. (1985). Affective and cognitive characteristics of depression in 10- and 11-year-old children. *Journal of Personality and Social Psychology, 49,* 194–202.

Bodenhausen, G. V., & Wyer, R. S. (1985). Effects of stereotypes on decision making and information-processing strategies. *Journal of Personality and Social Psychology, 48,* 267–282.

Bolles, R. C., & Faneslow, M. S. (1982). Endorphins and behavior. *Annual Review of Psychology, 33,* 87–101.

Booth-Kewley, S., & Friedman, H. S. (1987). Psychological predictors of heart disease: A quantitative review. *Psychological Bulletin, 101,* 343–362.

Borgida, E., & Campbell, B. (1982). Belief relevance and attitude-behavior consistency: The moderating role of personal experience. *Journal of Personality and Social Psychology, 42,* 239–247.

Bornstein, M. H., Kessen, W., & Weiskopf, S. (1976). The categories of hue in infancy. *Science, 191,* 201–202.

Bornstein, M. H., & Marks, L. E. (1982, January). Color revisionism. *Psychology Today,* pp. 64–73.

Boston Women's Health Book Collective (1984). *The new our bodies, ourselves.* New York: Simon & Schuster.

Bourne, L. E., Ekstrand, B. R., & Dominowski, R. L. (1971). *The psychology of thinking.* Englewood Cliffs, NJ: Prentice-Hall.

Bower, G. H. (1981). Mood and memory. *American Psychologist, 36,* 129–148.

Bowerman, M. F. (1982). Starting to talk worse: Clues to language acquisition from children's late speech errors. In S. Strauss (Ed.), *U-shaped behavioral growth.* New York: Academic Press.

Bowlby, J. (1973). Separation. *Attachment and Loss,* Vol. 2. New York: Basic Books.

Boyatzis, R. E. (1974). The effect of alcohol consumption on the aggressive behavior of men. *Quarterly Journal for the Study of Alcohol, 35,* 959–972.

Bradley, R. H., & Caldwell, B. M. (1976). The relation of infants' home environments to mental test performance at 54 months: A follow-up study. *Child Development, 47,* 1172–1174.

Bradley, R. H., & Caldwell, B. M. (1984). The relation of infants' home environments to achievement test performance in first grade: A follow-up study. *Child Development, 55,* 803–809.

Bray, R. M., & Sugarman, R. (1980). Social facilitation among interaction groups: Evidence for the evaluation-apprehension hypothesis. *Personality and Social Psychology Bulletin, 6,* 137–142.

Brazleton, T. B. (1970). Effects of prenatal drugs on the behavior of the neonate. *American Journal of Psychiatry, 126,* 95–100.

Breckler, S. J. (1984). Empirical validation of affect, behavior, and cognition as distinct components of attitude. *Journal of Personality and Social Psychology, 47,* 1191–1205.

Brent, E., & Granberg, D. (1982). Subjective agreement with the presidential candidates of 1976 and 1980. *Journal of Personality and Social Psychology, 42,* 393–403.

Briddell, D. W., & Wilson, G. T. (1976). Effects of alcohol and expectancy set on male sexual arousal. *Journal of Abnormal Psychology, 85,* 225–234.

Bridges, K. M. B. (1932). Emotional development in early infancy. *Child Development, 3,* 324–334.

Bridgwater, C. A. (1982, May). What candor can do. *Psychology Today,* p. 16.

Brigham, J. C. (1980). Limiting conditions of the "physical attractiveness stereotype": Attributions about divorce. *Journal of Research in Personality, 14,* 365–375.

Brim, O. G., & Kagan, J. (1980). *Continuity and change in human development.* Cambridge, MA: Harvard University Press.

Brody, J. (1988, January 14). "Type A" men fare better in heart attack study. *The New York Times,* p. B7.

Bronfenbrenner, U. (1960). Freudian theories of identification and their derivatives. *Child Development, 31,* 15–40.

Brooks, J. (1985). Polygraph testing: Thoughts of a skeptical legislator. *American Psychologist, 40,* 348–354.

Brooks, J., Ruble, D. N., & Clarke, A. E. (1977). College women's attitudes and expectations concerning menstrual-related changes. *Psychosomatic Medicine, 39,* 288.

Brown, B. B., & Altman, I. (1981). Territoriality and residential crime. In P. A. Brantingham & P. L. Brantingham (Eds.), *Urban crime and environmental criminology.* Beverly Hills, CA: Sage.

Brown, E. L., & Deffenbacher, K. (1979). *Perception and the senses.* Oxford: Oxford University Press.

Brown, P. L. (1987, September 14). Studying seasons of a woman's life. *The New York Times,* p. B17.

Brown, R. (1970). The first sentences of child and chimpanzee. In R. Brown (Ed.), *Psycholinguistics.* New York: Free Press.

Brown, R. (1973). *A first language: The early stages.* Cambridge, MA: Harvard University Press.

Brown, R., & McNeill, D. (1966). The tip-of-the-tongue phenomenon. *Journal of Verbal Learning and Verbal Behavior, 5,* 325–337.

Brownell, K. D. (1982). Obesity: Understanding and treating a serious, prevalent, and refractory disorder. *Journal of Consulting and Clinical Psychology, 50,* 820–840.

Brownell, K. D. (1988). Yo-yo dieting. *Psychology Today, 22*(1), 20–23.

Brownlee-Duffeck, M., Peterson, L., Simonds, J. F., Goldstein, D., Kilo, C., & Hoette, S. (1987). The role of health beliefs in the regimen adherence and metabolic control of adolescents and adults with diabetes mellitus. *Journal of Consulting and Clinical Psychology, 55,* 139–144.

Bruner, J. S. (1983). *Child's talk: Learning to use language.* New York: W. W. Norton.

Bruner, J. S., Goodnow, J. J., & Austin, G. A. (1956). *A study of thinking*. New York: Wiley.

Burns, G. L., & Farina, A. (1987). Physical attractiveness and self-perception of mental disorder. *Journal of Abnormal Psychology, 96,* 161–163.

Burnstein, E. (1983). Persuasion as argument processing. In M. Brandtstatter, J. H. Davis, & G. Stocker-Kreichgauer (Eds.), *Group decision processes*. London: Academic Press.

Burt, M. R. (1980). Cultural myths and supports for rape. *Journal of Personality and Social Psychology, 38,* 217–230.

Bushnell, E. W., Shaw, L., & Strauss, D. (1985). Relationship between visual and tactile exploration by 6-month-olds. *Developmental Psychology, 21,* 591–600.

Buss, A. H. (1983). Social rewards and personality. *Journal of Personality and Social Psychology, 44,* 553–563.

Buss, A. H. (1986). *Social behavior and personality*. Hillsdale, NJ: Erlbaum.

Buss, D. M. (1984). Toward a psychology of person-environment (PE) correlation: The role of spouse selection. *Journal of Personality and Social Psychology, 47,* 361–377.

Buss, D. M., & Barnes, M. (1986). Preferences in human mate selection. *Journal of Personality and Social Psychology, 50,* 559–570.

Buss, D. M., Gomes, M., Higgins, D. S., & Lauterbach, K. (1987). Tactics of manipulation. *Journal of Personality and Social Psychology, 52,* 1219–1229.

Butcher, J. N., Braswell, L., & Raney, D. (1983). A cross-cultural comparison of American Indian, black, and white inpatients on the MMPI and presenting symptoms. *Journal of Consulting and Clinical Psychology, 51,* 587–594.

Byrne, D. (1971). *The attraction paradigm*. New York: Academic Press.

Byrne, D., Baskett, G. D., & Hodges, L. (1971). Behavioral indicators of interpersonal attraction. *Journal of Applied Social Psychology, 1,* 137–149.

Cadoret, R. J. (1978). Psychopathology in adopted-away offspring of biologic parents with antisocial behavior. *Archives of General Psychiatry, 35,* 176–184.

Calder, B. J., Ross, M., & Inkso, C. A. (1973). Attitude change and attitude attribution: Effects of incentive, choice, and consequences. *Journal of Personality and Social Psychology, 25,* 84–99.

Calne, D. B. (1977). Developments in the pharmacology and therapeutics of Parkinsonism. *Annals of Neurology, 1,* 111–119.

Campbell, A. (1975). The American way of mating: Marriage si, children only maybe. *Psychology Today, 8,* 37–43.

Campos, J. J., Hiatt, S., Ramsey, D., Henderson, C., & Svejda, M. (1978). *The emergence of fear on the visual cliff*. In M. Lewis & L. Rosenblum (Eds.), *The origins of affect*. New York: Plenum Press.

Campos, J. J., Langer, A., & Krowitz, A. (1970). Cardiac responses on the visual cliff in prelocomotor infants. *Science, 170,* 196–197.

Cannon, D. S., & Baker, T. B. (1981). Emetic and electric shock alcohol aversion therapy. *Journal of Consulting and Clinical Psychology, 49,* 20–33.

Cannon, W. B. (1927). The James-Lange theory of emotions: A critical examination and an alternative theory. *American Journal of Psychology, 39,* 106–124.

Cannon, W. B. (1929). *Bodily changes in pain, hunger, fear, and rage*. New York: Appleton.

Caplan, L. (1984, July 2). The insanity defense. *The New Yorker,* pp. 45–78.

Caplan, P. J., MacPherson, G. M., & Tobin, P. (1985). Do sex-related differences in spatial abilities exist? A multilevel critique with new data. *American Psychologist, 40,* 786–799.

Carlson, N. R. (1986). *Physiology of behavior, 3rd ed.* Boston: Allyn & Bacon.

Carr, D. B., et al. (1981). Physical conditioning facilitates the exercise-induced secretion of beta-endorphins and beta-lipotropin in women. *New England Journal of Medicine, 305,* 560–563.

Cartwright, R. D. (1978). *A primer on sleep and dreaming*. Reading, MA: Addison-Wesley.

Cartwright, R. D., Lloyd, S., Nelson, J. B., & Bass, S. (1983). The traditional-liberated woman dimension: Social stereotype and self-concept. *Journal of Personality and Social Psychology, 44,* 581–588.

Cattell, R. B. (1949). *The culture-free intelligence test*. Champaign, IL: Institute for Personality and Ability Testing.

Cattell, R. B. (1965). *The scientific analysis of personality*. Baltimore: Penguin.

Cattell, R. B. (1973). Personality pinned down. *Psychology Today, 7,* 40–46.

Centor, A. (1982). Criminals and amnesia: Comment on Bower. *American Psychologist, 37,* 240.

Cermak, L. (1978). *Improving your memory*. New York: McGraw-Hill.

Chaiken, S., & Eagly, A. H. (1983). Communication modality as a determinant of persuasion: The role of communicator salience. *Journal of Personality and Social Psychology, 45,* 241–256.

Chesno, F. A., & Kilmann, P. R. (1975). Effects of stimulation intensity on sociopathic avoidance learning. *Journal of Abnormal Psychology, 84,* 144–151.

Chomsky, N. (1968). *Language and mind*. New York: Harcourt Brace World.

Chomsky, N. (1980). *Rules and representations*. New York: Columbia University Press.

Chouinard, G., Labonte, A., Fontaine, R., & Annable, L. (1983). New concepts in benzodiazepine therapy: Rebound anxiety and new indications for the more potent benzodiazepines. *Progress in Neuro-Psychopharmacology and Biological Psychiatry, 7,* 669–673.

Cipolli, C., & Salzarulo, P. (1978). Sleep and memory: Reproduction of syntactic structures previously evoked within REM-related reports. *Perceptual and Motor Skills, 46,* 111–114.

Clark, E. V. (1973). What's in a word? On the child's acquisition of semantics in his first language. In E. Moore (Ed.), *Cognitive development and the acquisition of language.* New York: Academic Press.

Clark, E. V. (1975). Knowledge, context, and strategy in the acquisition of meaning. In D. P. Dale (Ed.), *Georgetown University roundtable on language and linguistics.* Washington, DC: Georgetown University Press.

Clark, E. V. (1983). Meanings and concepts. In J. H. Flavell & E. M. Markman (Eds.), *Handbook of child psychology: Vol. 3. Cognitive development.* New York: Wiley.

Clark, M., Gosnell, M., Shapiro, D., & Hager, M. (1981, July 13). The mystery of sleep. *Newsweek,* pp. 48–55.

Cleckley, H. (1964). *The mask of sanity.* St. Louis: Mosby.

Cline, V. B., Croft, R. C., & Courrier, S. (1973). The desensitization of children to television violence. *Journal of Personality and Social Psychology, 27,* 360–365.

Clore, G. L., Wiggins, N. H., & Itkin, S. (1975). Gain and loss in attraction: Attributions from nonverbal behavior. *Journal of Personality and Social Psychology, 31,* 706–712.

Cochran, S. D., & Hammen, C. L. (1985). Perceptions of stressful life events and depression: A test of attributional models. *Journal of Personality and Social Psychology, 48,* 1562–1571.

Cohen, D. B. (1973). Sex-role orientation and dream recall. *Journal of Abnormal Psychology, 82,* 246–252.

Cohen, M. L., Garofalo, R., Boucher, R., & Seghorn, T. (1971). The psychology of rapists. *Seminars in Psychiatry, 3,* 307–327.

Colby, C. Z., Lanzetta, J. T., & Kleck, R. E. (1977). Effects of the expression of pain on autonomic and pain tolerance response to subject-controlled pain. *Psychophysiology, 14,* 537–540.

Comarr, A. E. (1970). Sexual function among patients with spinal cord injury. *Urologia Internationalis, 25,* 134–168.

Condiotte, M. M., & Lichtenstein, E. (1981). Self-efficacy and relapse in smoking cessation programs. *Journal of Consulting and Clinical Psychology, 49,* 648–658.

Conger, J. J., & Petersen, A. (1984). *Adolescence and youth: Psychological development in a changing world.* New York: Harper & Row.

Conley, J. J. (1984). Longitudinal consistency of adult personality: Self-reported psychological characteristics across 45 years. *Journal of Personality and Social Psychology, 47,* 1325–1333.

Conley, J. J. (1985). Longitudinal stability of personality traits: A multitrait-multimethod-multioccasion analysis. *Journal of Personality and Social Psychology, 49,* 1266–1282.

Connor, J. (1972). Olfactory control of aggressive and sexual behavior in the mouse. *Psychonomic Science, 27,* 1–3.

Conway, E., & Brackbill, Y. (1970). Delivery medication and infant outcome: An empirical study. *Monographs of the Society for Research in Child Development, 35*(4), 24–34.

Cooney, J. L., & Zeichner, A. (1985). Selective attention to negative feedback in Type A and Type B individuals. *Journal of Abnormal Psychology, 94,* 110–112.

Cooper, A. J. (1978). Neonatal olfactory bulb lesions: Influences on subsequent behavior of male mice. *Bulletin of the Psychonomic Society, 11,* 53–56.

Cooper, H. M. (1979). Statistically combining independent studies: A meta-analysis of sex differences in conformity research. *Journal of Personality and Social Psychology, 37,* 131–146.

Cooper, J. (1980). Reducing fears and increasing assertiveness: The role of dissonance reduction. *Journal of Experimental Social Psychology, 16,* 199–213.

Cooper, J., Zanna, M. P., & Goethals, G. R. (1974). Mistreatment of an esteemed other as a consequence affecting dissonance reduction. *Journal of Experimental Social Psychology, 10,* 224–233.

Cooper, R., & Zubek, J. (1958). Effects of enriched and restricted early environments on the learning ability of bright and dull rats. *Canadian Journal of Psychology, 12,* 159–164.

Cordes, C. (1984, February). The plight of homeless mentally ill. *APA Monitor,* pp. 1, 13.

Corkin, S. (1980). A prospective study of cingulotomy. In E. S. Valenstein (Ed.), *The psychosurgery debate.* San Francisco: W. H. Freeman.

Corkin, S., Cohen, N. J., Sullivan, E. V., Clegg, R. A., Rosen, T. J., & Ackerman, R. H. (1985). Analyses of global memory impairments of different etiologies. In D. S. Olton, E. Gamzu, & S. Corkin (Eds.), *Memory dysfunction.* New York: New York Academy of Sciences.

Costa, E. (1985). Benzodiazepine/GABA interactions: A model to investigate the neurobiology of anxiety. In A. H. Tuma & J. D. Maser (Eds.), *Anxiety and the anxiety disorders.* Hillsdale, NJ: Erlbaum.

Costa, P. T., Jr., & McCrae, R. R. (1985). Hypochondriasis, neuroticism, and aging: When are somatic complaints unfounded? *American Psychologist, 40,* 19–28.

Cowan, P. A. (1978). *Piaget with feeling.* New York: Holt, Rinehart and Winston.

Coyne, J. C., Kessler, R. C., Tal, M., Turnbull, J., Wortman, C. B., & Greden, J. F. (1987). Living with a depressed person. *Journal of Consulting and Clinical Psychology, 55,* 347–352.

Cozby, P. C. (1973). Self-disclosure: A literature review. *Psychological Bulletin, 79,* 73–91.

Craik, F. I. M., & Watkins, M. J. (1973). The role of rehearsal in short-term memory. *Journal of Verbal Learning and Verbal Behavior, 12,* 599–607.

Crawford, C. (1979). George Washington, Abraham Lincoln, and Arthur Jensen: Are they compatible? *American Psychologist, 34,* 664–672.

Creese, I., Burt, D. R., & Snyder, S. H. (1978). Biochemical actions of neuroleptic drugs. In L. L. Iversen, S. D. Iversen, & S. H. Snyder (Eds.), *Handbook of psychopharmacology,* Vol. 10. New York: Plenum Press.

Crockenburg, S. B. (1972). Creativity tests: A boon or boondoggle for children? *Review of Educational Research, 42,* 27–45.

Cronbach, L. J. (1975). Five decades of public controversy over mental testing. *American Psychologist, 30,* 1–14.

Crowe, R. R. (1974). An adoption study of antisocial personality. *Archives of General Psychiatry, 31,* 785–791.

Crowley, J. (1985). Cited in Zuckerman, D. (1985). Retirement: R & R or risky? *Psychology Today, 19*(2), 80.

Croyle, R. T., & Cooper, J. (1983). Dissonance arousal: Physiological evidence. *Journal of Personality and Social Psychology, 45,* 782–791.

Crusco, A. H., & Wetzel, C. G. (1984). The midas touch: The effects of interpersonal touch on restaurant tipping. *Personality and Social Psychology Bulletin, 10,* 512–517.

Cummings, N. A. (1979). Turning bread into stones: Our modern antimiracle. *American Psychologist, 34,* 1119–1129.

Curtiss, S. R. (1977). *Genie: A psycholinguistic study of a modern-day "wild child."* New York: Academic Press.

Dalton, K. (1972). *The menstrual cycle.* New York: Warner Books.

Dalton, K. (1980). Cyclical criminal acts in premenstrual syndrome. *Lancet, 2,* 1070–1071.

Daniels, D., & Plomin, R. (1985). Origins of individual differences in infant shyness. *Developmental Psychology, 21,* 118–121.

Darley, J. M., & Gross, P. H. (1983). A hypothesis-confirming bias in labeling effects. *Journal of Personality and Social Psychology, 44,* 20–33.

Darley, J. M., & Latané, B. (1968). Bystander intervention in emergencies: Diffusion of responsibility. *Journal of Personality and Social Psychology, 8,* 377–383.

Darlington, R. B., Royce, J. M., Snipper, A. S., Murray, H. W., & Lazar, I. (1980). Preschool programs and later school competence of children from low-income families. *Science, 208*(4440), 202–204.

Darwin, C. A. (1872). *The expression of the emotions in man and animals.* London: J. Murray.

Dauber, R. B. (1984). Subliminal psychodynamic activation in depression: On the role of autonomy issues in depressed college women. *Journal of Abnormal Psychology, 93,* 9–18.

Davis, J. H., Tindale, R. S., Nagao, D. H., Hinsz, V. B., & Robertson, B. (1984). Order effects in multiple decisions by groups: A demonstration with mock juries and trial procedures. *Journal of Personality and Social Psychology, 47,* 1003–1012.

Davison, G. C., & Neale, J. M. (1986). *Abnormal psychology,* 4th ed. New York: Wiley.

Davitz, J. R. (1969). *The language of emotion.* New York: Academic Press.

Deaux, K. (1976). *The behavior of men and women.* Monterey, CA: Brooks/Cole.

Deaux, K. (1984). From individual differences to social categories: Analysis of a decade's research on gender. *American Psychologist, 39,* 105–116.

DeBacker, G., et al. (1983). Behavior, stress, and psychosocial traits as risk factors. *Preventative Medicine, 12,* 32–36.

DeCasper, A. J., & Fifer, W. P. (1980). Of human bonding: Newborns prefer their mothers' voices. *Science, 208,* 1174–1176.

DeFries, J. C., Plomin, R., & LaBuda, M. C. (1987). Genetic stability of cognitive development from childhood to adulthood. *Developmental Psychology, 23,* 4–12.

DeGree, C. E., & Snyder, C. R. (1985). Adler's psychology (of use) today: Personal history of traumatic life events as a self-handicapping strategy. *Journal of Personality and Social Psychology, 48,* 1512–1519.

Delanoy, R. L., Merrin, J. S., & Gold, P. E. (1982). Modulation of long-term potentiation (LTP) by adrenergic agonists. *Neuroscience Abstracts, 8,* 316.

Delgado, J. M. R. (1969). *Physical control of the mind.* New York: Harper & Row.

Dembroski, T. M., Lasater, T. M., & Ramirez, A. (1978). Communicator similarity, fear-arousing communications, and compliance with health care recommendations. *Journal of Applied Social Psychology, 8,* 254–269.

Dement, W. (1972). Sleep and dreams. In A. M. Freedman & H. I. Kaplan (Eds.), *Human behavior: Biological, psychological, and sociological.* New York: Atheneum.

Dennis, M., Sugar, J., & Whitaker, H. A. (1982). The acquisition of tag questions. *Child Development, 53,* 1254–1257.

DePaulo, B. M., Rosenthal, R., Eisenstat, R. A., Rogers, P. L., & Finkelstein, S. (1978). Decoding discrepant nonverbal cues. *Journal of Personality and Social Psychology, 38,* 313–323.

Depue, R. A., Slater, J. F., Wolfstetter-Kausch, H., Klein, D., Goplerud, E., & Farr, D. (1981). A behavioral paradigm for identifying persons at risk for bipolar depressive disorder. *Journal of Abnormal Psychology, 90,* 381–438.

Dermer, M., & Thiel, D. L. (1975). When beauty may fail. *Journal of*

Personality and Social Psychology, 31, 1168–1176.

Dethier, V. G. (1978). Other tastes, other worlds. *Science, 201,* 224–228.

DeValois, R. L., & Jacobs, G. H. (1984). Neural mechanisms of color vision. In I. Darian-Smith (Ed.), *Handbook of physiology, Vol. 3.* Bethesda, MD: American Physiological Society.

Diamond, E. L. (1982). The role of anger and hostility in essential hypertension and coronary heart disease. *Psychological Bulletin, 92,* 410–433.

Diamond, M. (1977). Human sexual development: Biological foundations for social development. In F. A. Beach (Ed.), *Human sexuality in four perspectives.* Baltimore: Johns Hopkins University Press.

Diamond, M. (1978, September). Aging and cell loss: Calling for an honest count. *Psychology Today,* p. 126.

Diamond, M. (1984, November). A love affair with the brain. *Psychology Today,* pp. 62–73.

Diener, E. (1980). Deindividuation: The absence of self-awareness and self-regulation in group members. In P. Paulus (Ed.), *The psychology of group influence.* Hillsdale, NJ: Erlbaum.

Dill, C. A., Gilden, E. R., Hill, P. C., & Hanselka, L. L. (1982). Federal human subjects regulations: A methodological artifact. *Personality and Social Psychology Bulletin, 8,* 417–425.

Dimsdale, J. E., & Moss, J. (1980). Plasma catecholamines in stress and exercise. *Journal of American Medical Association, 243,* 340–342.

Dion, K. K., Berscheid, E., & Walster, E. (1972). What is beautiful is good. *Journal of Personality and Social Psychology, 24,* 285–290.

Dodge, K. A., & Frame, C. L. (1982) Social cognitive biases and deficits in aggressive boys. *Child Development, 53,* 620–635.

Dodge, L. J. T., Glasgow, R. E., & O'Neill, H. K. (1982). Bibliother-

apy in the treatment of female orgasmic dysfunction. *Journal of Consulting and Clinical Psychology, 50,* 442–443.

Dohrenwend, B. P., & Shrout, P. E. (1985). "Hassles" in the conceptualization and measurement of life stress variables. *American Psychologist, 40,* 780–785.

Dohrenwend, B. S., Dohrenwend, B. P., Dodson, M., & Shrout, P. E. (1984). Symptoms, hassles, social supports and life events: The problem of confounded measures. *Journal of Abnormal Psychology, 93,* 222–230.

Dohrenwend, B. S., Krasnoff, L., Askenasy, A. R., & Dohrenwend, B. P. (1982). The psychiatric epidemiology research interview life events scale. In L. Goldberger & S. Brenitz (Eds.), *Handbook of stress: Theoretical and clinical aspects.* New York: Free Press.

Dollard, J., Doob, L. W., Miller, N. E., Mowrer, O. H., & Sears, R. R. (1939). *Frustration and aggression.* New Haven, CT: Yale University Press.

Donahoe, C. P., Jr., Lin, D. H., Kirschenbaum, D. S., & Keesey, R. E. (1984). Metabolic consequences of dieting and exercise in the treatment of obesity. *Journal of Consulting and Clinical Psychology, 52,* 827–836.

Donnerstein, E. I. (1980). Aggressive erotica and violence against women. *Journal of Personality and Social Psychology, 39,* 269–277.

Donnerstein, E. I., & Linz, D. G. (1984). Sexual violence in the media: A warning. *Psychology Today, 18*(1), 14–15.

Donnerstein, E. I., & Linz, D. G. (1986). The question of pornography. *Psychology Today, 20*(12), 56–60.

Donnerstein, E. I., & Linz, D. G. (1987). *The question of pornography.* New York: The Free Press.

Doob, A. N., & Wood, L. (1972). Catharsis and aggression: The effects of annoyance and retaliation on aggressive behavior. *Journal of*

Personality and Social Psychology, 22, 236–245.

Dovidio, J. H., Evans, N., & Tyler, R. B. (1986). Racial stereotypes: The contents of their cognitive representations. *Journal of Experimental Social Psychology, 22,* 22–37.

Dowd, M. (1984, March 12). 20 years after the murder of Kitty Genovese, the question remains: Why? *The New York Times,* pp. B1, B4.

Doyne, E. J., Chambless, D. L., & Beutler, L. E. (1983). Aerobic exercise as treatment for depression in women. *Behavior Therapy, 14,* 434–440.

Driscoll, R., Davis, K. E., & Lipetz, M. E. (1972). Parental interference and romantic love. *Journal of Personality and Social Psychology, 24,* 1–10.

Dutton, D. G., & Aron, A. P. (1974). Some evidence for heightened sexual attraction under conditions of high anxiety. *Journal of Personality and Social Psychology, 30,* 510–517.

Eagly, A. H. (1974). Comprehensibility of persuasive arguments as a determinant of opinion change. *Journal of Personality and Social Psychology, 29,* 758–773.

Eagly, A. H. (1978). Sex differences in influenceability. *Psychological Bulletin, 85,* 86–116.

Eagly, A. H. (1983). Gender and social influence: A social psychological analysis. *American Psychologist, 38,* 971–981.

Eagly, A. H., & Carli, L. L. (1981). Sex of researchers and sex-typed communications as determinants of sex differences in influenceability: A meta-analysis of social influence studies. *Psychological Bulletin, 90,* 1–20.

Eagly, A. H., & Steffen, V. J. (1984). Gender stereotypes stem from the distribution of women and men into social roles. *Journal of Personality and Social Psychology, 46,* 735–754.

Eagly, A. H., Wood, W., & Chaiken, S. (1978). Causal inferences about communicators and their effect on opinion change. *Journal of Personality and Social Psychology, 36,* 424–435.

Eagly, A. H., Wood, W., & Fishbaugh, L. (1981). Sex differences in conformity: Surveillance by the group as a determinant of male conformity. *Journal of Personality and Social Psychology, 40,* 384–394.

Easterbrooks, M. A., & Goldberg, W. A. (1985). Effects of early maternal employment on toddler, mothers, and fathers. *Developmental Psychology, 21,* 774–783.

Ebbeson, E. B., & Bowers, J. B. (1974). Proportion of risky to conservative arguments in a group discussion and choice shift. *Journal of Personality and Social Psychology, 29,* 316–327.

Eckenrode, J. (1984). Impact of chronic and acute stressors on daily reports of mood. *Journal of Personality and Social Psychology, 46,* 907–918.

Eden, C., & Sims, D. (1981). Computerized vicarious experience: The future for management induction? *Personnel Review, 10,* 22–25.

Edwards, A. L. (1954). *Edwards personal preference schedule.* New York: Psychological Corporation.

Edwards, D. J. A. (1972). Approaching the unfamiliar: A study of human interaction differences. *Journal of Behavioral Sciences, 1,* 249–250.

Efran, M. G. (1974). The effect of physical appearance on the judgment of guilt, interpersonal attraction, and severity of recommended punishment in a simulated jury task. *Journal of Research in Personality, 8,* 45–54.

Egeland, J. A., Gerhard, D. S., Pauls, D. L., Sussex, J. N., Kidd, K. K., Allen, C. R., Hostetter, A. M., & Housman, D. E. (1987). Bipolar affective disorder linked to DNA markers on chromosome 11. *Nature, 325,* 783–787.

Ehrhardt, A. A., & Baker, S. W. (1975). Hormonal aberrations and their implications for the understanding of normal sex differentiation. In P. H. Mussen, J. J. Conger, and J. Kagan (Eds.), *Basic and contemporary issues in developmental psychology.* New York: Harper & Row.

Eibl-Eibesfeldt, I. (1974). *Love and hate: The natural history of behavior patterns.* New York: Schocken Books.

Eidelson, R. J., & Epstein, N. (1982). Cognition and relationship maladjustment: Development of a measure of dysfunctional relationship beliefs. *Journal of Consulting and Clinical Psychology, 50,* 715–720.

Eisdorfer, C. (1983). Conceptual models of aging: The challenge of a new frontier. *American Psychologist, 38,* 197–202.

Ekman, P. (1980). *The face of man.* Garland STPM Press.

Ekman, P. (1985). Cited in Bower, B. (1985, July 6). The face of emotion. *Science News, 128,* 12–13.

Ekman, P., Friesen, W. V., O'Sullivan, M., Chan, A., Diacoyanni-Tarlatzis, I., Heider, K., Krause, R., LeCompte, W. A., Pitcairn, T., Ricci-Bitti, P. E., Scherer, K., Tomita, M., & Tzavaras, A. (1987). Universals and cultural differences in the judgments of facial expressions of emotion. *Journal of Personality and Social Psychology, 53,* 712–717.

Ekman, P., Levenson, R. W., & Friesen, W. V. (1983). Autonomic nervous system activity distinguishes among emotions. *Science, 221,* 1208–1210.

Ekman, P., & Oster, H. (1979). Facial expressions of emotion. *Annual Review of Psychology, Vol. 30.* Palo Alto, CA: Annual Reviews.

Elardo, R., Bradley, R. H., & Caldwell, B. M. (1975). The relation of infants' home environments to mental test performance from 6 to 36 months: A longitudinal analysis. *Child Development, 46,* 71–76.

Elardo, R., Bradley, R. H., & Caldwell, B. M. (1977). A longitudinal study of the relation of infants' home environments to language development at age 3. *Child Development, 48,* 595–603.

Elkins, R. L. (1980). Covert sensitization treatment of alcoholism. *Addictive Behaviors, 5,* 67–89.

Elliot, A. J. (1981). *Child language.* Cambridge, MA: Cambridge University Press.

Ellis, A. (1977). The basic clinical theory of rational-emotive therapy. In A. Ellis & R. Grieger (Eds.), *Handbook of Rational–Emotive Therapy.* New York: Springer.

Ellis, A. (1985). Cognition and affect in emotional disturbance. *American Psychologist, 40,* 471–472.

Ellis, A. (1987). The impossibility of achieving consistently good mental health. *American Psychologist, 42,* 364–375.

Ellison, G. D. (1977). Animal models of psychopathology: The low-norepinephrine and low-serotonin rat. *American Psychologist, 32,* 1036–1045.

Ellsworth, P. C., Carlsmith, J. M., & Henson, A. (1972). The stare as a stimulus to flight in human subjects. *Journal of Personality and Social Psychology, 21,* 302–311.

Ellsworth, P. C., & Langer, E. J. (1976). Staring and approach: An interpretation of the stare as a nonspecific activator. *Journal of Personality and Social Psychology, 33,* 117–122.

Elman, J. B., Press, A., & Rosenkrantz, P. S. (1970, August). Sex roles and self-concepts: Real and ideal. Paper presented to the American Psychological Association, Miami.

Epstein, L. H., Wing, R. R., Koeske, R., & Valoski, A. (1984). Effects of diet plus exercise on weight change in parents and children. *Journal of Consulting and Clinical Psychology, 52,* 429–437.

Erdman, H. P., Klein, M. H., & Greist, J. H. (1985). Direct patient computer interviewing. *Journal of Consulting and Clinical Psychology, 53,* 760–773.

Erikson, E. H. (1963). *Childhood and society.* New York: Norton.

Erikson, E. H. (1975). *Life history and the historical moment.* New York: Norton.

Erikson, E. H. (1983, June). In Hall, E. A conversation with Erik Erikson. *Psychology Today,* pp. 22–30.

Eriksson, K. (1972). Behavior and physiological differences among rat strains specially selected for their alcohol consumption. *Annals of the New York Academy of Science, 197,* 32–41.

Erwin, J., Maple, T., Mitchell, G., & Willott, J. (1974). Follow-up study of isolation-reared rhesus monkeys paired with preadolescent cospecifics in late infancy: Cross-sex pairings. *Developmental Psychology, 6,* 808–814.

Estes, W. K. (1972). An associative basis for coding and organization in memory. In A. W. Melton & E. Martin (Eds.), *Coding processes in human memory.* Washington, DC: Winston.

Evans, R. I., Rozelle, R. M., Lasater, T. M., Demborski, T. M., & Allen, B. P. (1970). Fear arousal, persuasion, and actual versus implied behavioral change: New perspective utilizing a real-life dental hygiene program. *Journal of Personality and Social Psychology, 16,* 220–227.

Exline, R. V. (1972). Visual interaction: The glances of power and preference. In J. K. Cole (Ed.), *The Nebraska Symposium on Motivation,* Vol. 19. Lincoln, NE: University of Nebraska Press.

Eysenck, H. J. (1960). Classification and the problem of diagnosis. In H. J. Eysenck (Ed.), *Handbook of abnormal psychology.* London: Pitman.

Eysenck, H. J., & Eysenck, M. W. (1985). *Personality and individual differences.* New York: Plenum Press.

Fabian, W. D., Jr., & Fishkin, S. M. (1981). A replicated study of self-reported changes in psychological absorption with marijuana intoxication. *Journal of Abnormal Psychology, 90,* 546–553.

Fabricius, W. V., & Wellman, H. M. (1983). Children's understanding of retrieval cue utilization. *Developmental Psychology, 19,* 15–21.

Fagot, B. I. (1974). Sex differences in toddlers' behavior and parental reaction. *Developmental Psychology, 10,* 554–558.

Fagot, B. I. (1978). The influence of sex of child on parental reactions to toddler children. *Child Development 49,* 459–465.

Fagot, B. I. (1981). Male and female teachers: Do they treat boys and girls differently? *Sex Roles, 7,* 263–272.

Fagot, B. I. (1982). Adults as socializing agents. In T. M. Field (Ed.), *Review of human development.* New York: Wiley.

Fagot, B. I. (1985a). Beyond the reinforcement principle: Another step toward understanding sex role development. *Developmental Psychology, 21,* 1097–1104.

Fagot, B. I. (1985b). Changes in thinking about early sex role development. *Developmental Review, 5,* 83–98.

Fairbanks, L. A., McGuire, M. T., & Harris, C. J. (1982). Nonverbal interaction of patients and therapists during psychiatric interviews. *Journal of Abnormal Psychology, 91,* 109–119.

Fallon, A. E., & Rozin, P. (1985). Sex differences in perceptions of desirable body shape. *Journal of Abnormal Psychology, 94,* 102–105.

Fantz, R. L. (1961). The origin of form perception. *Scientific American, 204*(5), 66–72.

Farina, A., Burns, G. L., Austad, C., Bugglin, C. S., & Fischer, E. H. (1986). The role of physical attractiveness in the readjustment of discharged psychiatric patients. *Journal of Abnormal Psychology, 95,* 139–143.

Farmer, H. S. (1983). Career and homemaking plans for high school youth. *Journal of Counseling Psychology, 30,* 40–45.

Farthing, G. W., Venturino, M., & Brown, S. W. (1984). Suggestion and distraction in the control of pain: Test of two hypotheses. *Journal of Abnormal Psychology, 93,* 266–276.

Faust, M. S. (1977). Somatic development of adolescent girls. *Monographs of the Society for Research in Child Development, 42* (Whole #169).

Fazio, R. H. (1986). How do attitudes guide behavior? In R. M. Sorrentino & E. T. Higgins (Eds.), *The handbook of motivation and cognition: Foundation of social behavior.* New York: Guilford Press.

Fazio, R. H., Chen, J., McDonel, E. C., & Sherman, S. J. (1982). Attitude accessibility, attitude-behavior consistency, and the strength of the object-evaluation association. *Journal of Experimental Social Psychology, 18,* 339–357.

Fazio, R. H., & Cooper, J. (1983). Arousal in the dissonance process. In J. T. Cacioppo & R. E. Petty (Eds.), *Psychophysiology.* New York: Guilford Press.

Fazio, R. H., Sanbonmatsu, D. M., Powell, M. C., & Kardes, F. R. (1986). On the automatic activation of attitudes. *Journal of Personality and Social Psychology, 50,* 229–238.

Fazio, R. H., Sherman, S. J., & Herr, P. M. (1982). The feature-positive effect in the self-perception process: Does not doing matter as much as doing? *Journal of Personality and Social Psychology, 42,* 404–411.

Feder, H. H. (1984). Hormones and sexual behavior. *Annual Review of Psychology, 35,* 165–200.

Fein, G. G., Schwartz, P. M., Jacobson, S. W., & Jacobson, J. L. (1983). Environmental toxins and behavioral development: A new role for psychological research. *American Psychologist, 38,* 1188–1197.

Feldman, D. (1980). *Beyond universals in cognitive development.* Norwood, NJ: Ablex.

Felsenthal, N. (1976). *Orientations to mass communications.* Chicago: Science Research.

Feltz, D. L. (1982). Path analysis of the causal elements in Bandura's theory of self-efficacy and an anxiety-based model of avoidance behavior. *Journal of Personality and Social Psychology, 42,* 764–781.

Fenichel, O. (1945). *The psychoanalytic theory of the neuroses.* New York: Norton.

Fenigstein, A., Scheier, M. F., & Buss, A. H. (1975). Public and private self-consciousness: Assessment and theory. *Journal of Consulting and Clinical Psychology, 43,* 522–527.

Ferguson, C. A. & Farwell, C. (1975). Words and sounds in early language acquisition: English consonants in the first 50 words. *Language, 51,* 419–439.

Festinger, L. (1957). *A theory of cognitive dissonance.* Evanston, IL: Row, Peterson.

Festinger, L., & Carlsmith, J. M. (1959). Cognitive consequences of forced compliance. *Journal of Abnormal and Social Psychology, 58,* 203–210.

Findlay, M. J., & Cooper, H. M. (1983). Locus of control and academic achievement: A literature review. *Journal of Personality and Social Psychology, 44,* 419–427.

Fisher, D. F., & Karsh, R. (1971). Modality effects and storage in sequential short-term memory. *Journal of Experimental Psychology, 87,* 410–414.

Fisher, J. D., & Byrne, D. (1975). Too close for comfort: Sex differences in response to invasions of personal space. *Journal of Personality and Social Psychology, 32,* 15–21.

Fisher, W. A., & Byrne, D. (1978). Sex differences in response to erotica? Love versus lust. *Journal of Personality and Social Psychology, 36,* 117–125.

Fishman, S. M., & Sheehan, D. V. (1985). Anxiety and panic: Their cause and treatment. *Psychology Today, 19*(4), 26–32.

Fiske, S. T., & Taylor, S. E. (1984). *Social cognition.* Reading, MA: Addison-Wesley.

Fitch, G. (1970). Effects of self-esteem, perceived performance, and choice on causal attribution. *Journal of Personality and Social Psychology, 16,* 311–315.

Flaherty, J. F., & Dusek, J. B. (1980). An investigation of the relationship between psychological androgyny and components of self-concept. *Journal of Personality and Social Psychology, 38,* 984–992.

Flavell, J. H. (1982). Structures, stages, and sequences in cognitive development. In W. A. Collins (Ed.), *The concept of development: The Minnesota symposia on child psychology, Vol. 15.* Hillsdale, NJ: Erlbaum.

Flavell, J. H. (1985). *Cognitive development.* Englewood Cliffs, NJ: Prentice-Hall.

Flaxman, J. (1978). Quitting smoking now or later: Gradual, abrupt, immediate, and delayed quitting. *Behavior Therapy, 9,* 260–270.

Fleming, M. Z., MacGowan, B. R., Robinson, L., Spitz, J., & Salt, P. (1982). The body image of the postoperative female-to-male transsexual. *Journal of Consulting and Clinical Psychology, 50,* 461–462.

Floderus-Myrhed, B., Pederson, N., & Rasmuson, I. (1980). Assessment of heritability for personality based on a short form of the Eysenck Personality Inventory: A study of 12,898 twin pairs. *Behavior Genetics, 10,* 153–162.

Fodor, E. M., & Smith, T. (1982). The power motive as an influence on group decision making. *Journal of Personality and Social Psychology, 42,* 178–185.

Folkins, C. H., & Sime, W. E. (1981). Physical fitness training and mental health. *American Psychologist, 36,* 373–389.

Foulkes, D. (1971). Longitudinal studies of dreams in children. In J. Masserman (Ed.), *Science and psychoanalysis.* New York: Grune & Stratton.

Fouts, R. S., & Fouts, D. H. (1985). *Friends of Washoe, 4,* 3–8.

Fowler, R. D. (1985). Landmarks in computer-assisted psychological assessment. *Journal of Consulting and Clinical Psychology, 53,* 748–759.

Fox, S. (1984). *The mirror makers.* New York: Morrow.

Foy, D. W., Nunn, L. B., & Rychtarik, R. G. (1984). Broad-spectrum behavioral treatment for chronic alcoholics: Effects of training controlled drinking skills. *Journal of Consulting and Clinical Psychology, 52,* 218–230.

Franklin, D. (1984, October 20). Crafting sound from silence. *Science News, 126,* 252–254.

Freedman, J. L., & Fraser, S. C. (1966). Compliance without pressure: The foot-in-the-door technique. *Journal of Personality and Social Psychology, 4,* 195–202.

Freedman, J. L., Wallington, S. A., & Bless, E. (1967). Compliance without pressure: The effect of guilt. *Journal of Personality and Social Psychology, 7,* 117–124.

Freedman, R. R., & Sattler, H. L. (1982). Physiological and psychological factors in sleep-onset insomnia. *Journal of Abnormal Psychology, 91,* 380–389.

French, G. M., & Harlow, H. F. (1962). Variability of delayed-reaction performance in normal and brain-damaged rhesus monkeys. *Journal of Neurophysiology, 25,* 585–599.

French-Belgian Collaborative Group. (1982). Ischemic heart disease and psychological patterns: Prevalence and incidence in Belgium and France. *Advances in Cardiology, 29,* 25–31.

Freud, S. (1909). Analysis of a phobia in a five-year-old boy. In *Collected papers,* Vol. 3, translated by A. and J. Strachey. New York: Basic Books, 1959.

Freud, S. (1927). A religious experience. In *Standard edition of the complete psychological works of Sigmund Freud,* Vol. 21. London: Hogarth Press, 1964.

Freud, S. (1930). *Civilization and its*

discontents, translated by J. Strachey. New York: Norton, 1961.

Freud, S. (1933). New introductory lectures. In *Standard edition of the complete psychological works of Sigmund Freud*, Vol. 22. London: Hogarth Press, 1964.

Friedman, H. S., & Booth-Kewley, S. (1987). Personality, type A behavior, and coronary heart disease: The role of emotional expression. *Journal of Personality and Social Psychology, 53*, 783–792.

Friedman, M. I., & Stricker, E. M. (1976). The physiological psychology of hunger: A physiological perspective. *Psychological Review, 83*, 409–431.

Freidman, M., & Ulmer, D. (1984). *Treating Type A behavior and your heart*. New York: Fawcett Crest.

Friman, P. C., & Christopherson, E. R. (1983). Behavior therapy and hyperactivity: A brief review of therapy for a big problem. *The Behavior Therapist, 6*, 175–176.

Frodi, A. M. (1981). Contribution of infant characteristics to child abuse. *American Journal of Mental Deficiency, 85*, 341–349.

Frodi, A. M. (1985). When empathy fails: Infant crying and child abuse. In B. M. Lester & C. F. Z. Boukydis (Eds.), *Infant crying.* New York: Plenum Press.

Frodi, A. M., Macauley, J., & Thome, P. R. (1977). Are women always less aggressive than men? A review of the experimental literature. *Psychological Bulletin, 84*, 634–660.

Fromm, E. (1956). *The art of loving.* New York: Harper & Row.

Funkenstein, D. (1955, May). The physiology of fear and anger. *Scientific American.*

Fustero, S. (1984, February). Home on the street. *Psychology Today*, pp. 56–63.

Galanter, E. (1962). Contemporary psychophysics. In R. Brown et al. (Eds.), *New directions in psychology.* New York: Holt, Rinehart and Winston.

Galizio, M., & Hendrick, C. (1972). Effect of musical accompaniment on attitude: The guitar as a prop for persuasion. *Journal of Applied Social Psychology, 2*, 350–359.

Gallup, G. G., Jr., & Suarez, S. D. (1985). Alternatives to the use of animals in psychological research. *American Psychologist, 40*, 1104–1111.

Ganellen, R. J., & Blaney, P. H. (1984). Hardiness and social support as moderators of the effects of life stress. *Journal of Personality and Social Psychology, 47*, 156–163.

Garcia, J. (1981). The logic and limits of mental aptitude testing. *American Psychologist, 36*, 1172–1180.

Gardner, B. T., & Gardner, R. A. (1980). Two comparative psychologists look at language acquisition. In K. E. Nelson (Ed.), *Children's language, Vol. 2.* New York: Gardner Press.

Gardner, H. (1983). *Frames of mind: The theory of multiple intelligences.* New York: Basic Books.

Garfield, S. L. (1981). Psychotherapy: A 40-year appraisal. *American Psychologist, 36*, 174–183.

Garfield, S. L. (1982). Eclecticism and integration in psychotherapy. *Behavior Therapy, 13*, 610–623.

Garwood, S. G., Cox, L., Kaplan, V., Wasserman, N., & Sulzer, J. L. (1980). Beauty is only "name deep": The effect of first-name in ratings of physical attraction. *Journal of Applied Social Psychology, 10*, 431–435.

Gatchel, R. J., & Proctor, J. D. (1976). Effectiveness of voluntary heart rate control in reducing speech anxiety. *Journal of Consulting and Clinical Psychology, 44*, 381–389.

Gazzaniga, M. S. (1972). One brain—two minds? *American Science, 60*, 311–317.

Gazzaniga, M. S. (1983). Right hemisphere language following brain bisection: A 20-year perspective. *American Psychologist, 38*, 525–537.

Gazzaniga, M. S. (1985). The social brain. *Psychology Today, 19*(11), 29–38.

Gerard, H. B., Wilhelmy, R. A., & Conolley, E. S. (1968). Conformity and group size. *Journal of Personality and Social Psychology, 8*, 79–82.

Gerbner, G., & Gross, L. (1976). The scary world of TV's heavy viewer. *Psychology Today, 9*, 41–45.

Getzels, J. W., & Jackson, P. W. (1962). *Creativity and intelligence: Explorations with gifted students.* New York: Wiley.

Gibson, E. J., Owsley, C. J., & Johnston, J. (1978). Perception of invariants by five-month-old infants: Differentiation of two types of motion. *Developmental Psychology, 14*, 407–415.

Gilbert, S. J. (1981). Another look at the Milgram obedience studies: The role of the gradated series of shocks. *Personality and Social Psychology Bulletin, 7*, 690–695.

Gillen, B. (1981). Physical attractiveness: A determinant of two types of goodness. *Personality and Social Psychology Bulletin, 7*, 277–281.

Gilligan, C. (1982). *In a different voice.* Cambridge, MA: Harvard University Press.

Gillis, J. S., & Avis, W. E. (1980). The mate-taller norm in mate selection. *Personality and Social Psychology Bulletin, 6*, 396–401.

Gilovich, T. (1983). Biased evaluation and persistence in gambling. *Journal of Personality and Social Psychology, 44*, 1110–1126.

Glasgow, R. E., Klesges, R. C., Godding, P. R., & Gegelman, R. (1983). Controlled smoking, with or without carbon monoxide feedback, as an alternative for chronic smokers. *Behavior Therapy, 14*, 396–397.

Glasgow, R. E., Klesges, R. C., Godding, P. R., Vasey, M. W., & O'Neill, H. K. (1984). Evaluation of a worksite-controlled smoking program. *Journal of Consulting and Clinical Psychology, 52*, 137–138.

Glasgow, R. E., Klesges, R. C., Klesges, L. M., Vasey, M. W., & Gunnarson, D. F. (1985). Long-term effects of a controlled smoking program: A two and one-half year follow-up. *Behavior Therapy, 16,* 303–307.

Glass, D. C. (1977). *Stress and coronary-prone behavior.* Hillsdale, NJ: Erlbaum.

Gleason, H. A., Jr. (1961). *An introduction to descriptive linguistics,* rev. ed. New York: Holt, Rinehart and Winston.

Gleitman, L. R., Newport, E. L., & Gleitman, H. (1984). The current status of the motherese hypothesis. *Journal of Child Language, 11,* 43–79.

Goddard, H. H. (1917). Mental tests and the immigrant. *The Journal of Delinquency, 2,* 243–277.

Goeders, N. E., & Smith, J. E. (1983). Cortical dopaminergic involvement in cocaine reinforcement. *Science, 221,* 773–775.

Gold, J. A., Ryckman, R. M., & Mosley, N. R. (1984). Romantic mood induction and attraction to a dissimilar other: Is love blind? *Personality and Social Psychology Bulletin, 10,* 358–368.

Gold, P. E., & King, R. A. (1974). Retrograde amnesia: Storage failure versus retrieval failure. *Psychological Review, 81,* 465–469.

Goldberg, L. W. (1978). Differential attribution of trait-descriptive terms to oneself as compared to well-liked, neutral, and disliked others. *Journal of Personality and Social Psychology, 36,* 1012–1028.

Goldberg, S., & Lewis, M. (1969). Play behavior in the year-old infant: Early sex differences. *Child Development, 40,* 21–31.

Goldfoot, D. A., Essock-Vitale, S. M., Asa, C. S., Thornton, J. E., & Leshner, A. I. (1978). Anosmia in male rhesus monkeys does not alter copulatory activity with cycling females. *Science, 199,* 1095–1096.

Goldman, W., & Lewis, P. (1977). Beautiful is good: Evidence that the physically attractive are more socially skillful. *Journal of Experimental Social Psychology, 13,* 125–130.

Goldsmith, H. H. (1983). Genetic in-

fluences on personality from infancy to adulthood. *Child Development, 54,* 331–355.

Goldstein, M., & Davis, E. E. (1972). Race and belief: A further analysis of the social determinants of behavioral intentions. *Journal of Personality and Social Psychology, 22,* 345–355.

Goleman, D. J. (1978, November). Special abilities of the sexes: Do they begin in the brain? *Psychology Today,* pp. 48–120.

Goleman, D. J. (1982, March). Staying up. *Psychology Today,* pp. 24–35.

Goleman, D. J. (1985, January 15). Pressure mounts for analysts to prove theory is scientific. *The New York Times,* pp. C1, C9.

Goleman, D. J. (1987, November 24). Teen-age risk-taking: Rise in deaths prompts new research effort. *The New York Times,* pp. C1, C17.

Golub, S. (1976). The effect of premenstrual anxiety and depression on cognitive function. *Journal of Personality and Social Psychology, 34,* 99–104.

Goodhart, D. E. (1985). Some psychological effects associated with positive and negative thinking about stressful event outcomes. *Journal of Personality and Social Psychology, 48,* 216–232.

Goodwin, D. W. (1979). Alcoholism and heredity. *Archives of General Psychiatry, 36,* 57–61.

Goodwin, D. W. (1985). Alcoholism and genetics. *Archives of General Psychiatry, 42,* 171–174.

Goodwin, D. W., Schulsinger, F., Hermansen, L., Guze, S. B., & Winokur, G. A. (1973). Alcohol problems in adoptees raised apart from alcoholic biological parents. *Archives of General Psychiatry, 128,* 239–243.

Gordon, E. W., & Terrell, M. D. (1981). The changed social context of testing. *American Psychologist, 36,* 1167–1171.

Gormally, J., Sipps, G., Raphael, R., Edwin, D., & Varvil-Weld, D.

(1981). The relationship between maladaptive cognitions and social anxiety. *Journal of Consulting and Clinical Psychology, 49,* 300–301.

Gotlib, I. H. (1982). Self-reinforcement and depression in interpersonal interaction: The role of performance level. *Journal of Abnormal Psychology, 91,* 3–13.

Gotlib, I. H. (1984). Depression and general psychopathology in university students. *Journal of Abnormal Psychology, 93,* 19–30.

Gould, R. (1975). Adult life stages: Growth toward self-tolerance. *Psychology Today, 8,* 74–81.

Goy, R. W., & Goldfoot, D. A. (1976). Neuroendocrinology: Animal models and problems of human sexuality. In E. A. Rubenstein et al. (Eds.), *New directions in sex research.* New York: Plenum.

Goy, R. W., & McEwen, B. S. (1982). *Sexual differentiation of the brain.* Cambridge, MA: MIT Press.

Graham, J. (1977). *The MMPI: A practical guide.* New York: Oxford University Press.

Granberg, D., & Brent, E. (1983). When prophecy bends: The preference–expectation link in U.S. presidential elections. *Journal of Personality and Social Psychology, 45,* 477–491.

Graziano, W., Brothen, T., & Berscheid, E. (1978). Height and attraction: Do men and women see eye-to-eye? *Journal of Personality, 46,* 128–145.

Green, B. F. (1981). A primer of testing. *American Psychologist, 36,* 1001–1011.

Green, S. K., Buchanan, D. R., & Heuer, S. K. (1984). Winners, losers, and choosers: A field investigation of dating initiation. *Personality and Social Psychology Bulletin, 10,* 502–511.

Greenbaum, P., & Rosenfeld, H. M. (1978). Patterns of avoidance in response to interpersonal staring and proximity: Effects of bystanders on drivers at a traffic intersection. *Journal of Personality and Social Psychology, 36,* 575–587.

Greenberg, D. J., & Blue, S. Z. (1977). The visual-preference technique in infancy: Effect of number of stimuli presented upon experimental outcome. *Child Development, 48*(1), 131–137.

Greenberg, R., Pearlman, C., Schwartz, W. R., & Grossman, H. Y. (1983). Memory, emotion, and REM sleep. *Journal of Abnormal Psychology, 92,* 378–381.

Greene, J. (1982, September). The gambling trap. *Psychology Today,* pp. 50–55.

Gregory, R. L. (1973). *Eye and brain,* 2d ed. New York: World Universities Library.

Grinspoon, L. (1987, July 28). Cancer patients should get marijuana. *The New York Times,* p. A23.

Grossmann, K., Thane, K., & Grossmann, K. E. (1981). Maternal tactual contact of the newborn after various post-partum conditions of mother-infant contact. *Developmental Psychology, 17,* 158–169.

Groth, A. N., & Birnbaum, H. J. (1979). *Men who rape.* New York: Plenum.

Grünbaum, A. (1985). Cited in Goleman (1985).

Grush, J. E. (1980). The impact of candidate expenditures, regionality, and prior outcomes on the 1976 Democratic presidential primaries. *Journal of Personality and Social Psychology, 38,* 337–347.

Grush, J. E., & Yehl, J. G. (1979). Marital roles, sex differences, and interpersonal attraction. *Journal of Personality and Social Psychology, 37,* 116–123.

Guilford, J. P. (1959). Traits of creativity. In H. H. Anderson (Ed.), *Creativity and its cultivation.* New York: Harper & Row.

Guilford, J. P. (1967). *The nature of human intelligence.* New York: McGraw-Hill.

Guilford, J. P., & Hoepfner, R. (1971). *The analysis of intelligence.* New York: McGraw-Hill.

Haber, R. N. (1969). Eidetic images. *Scientific American, 220,* 36–55.

Haber, R. N. (1980, November). Eidetic images are not just imaginary. *Psychology Today,* pp. 72–82.

Haber, R. N., & Hershenson, M. (1980). *The psychology of visual perception.* New York: Holt, Rinehart and Winston.

Hall, C. S. (1966). *The meaning of dreams.* New York: McGraw-Hill.

Hall, C. S. (1984). "A ubiquitous sex difference in dreams" revisited. *Journal of Personality and Social Psychology, 46,* 1109–1117.

Hall, J. A., & Taylor, M. C. (1985). Psychological androgyny and the masculinity femininity interaction. *Journal of Personality and Social Psychology, 49,* 429–435.

Hall, R. G., Sachs, D. P. L., Hall, S. M., & Benowitz, N. L. (1984). Two-year efficacy and safety of rapid smoking therapy in patients with cardiac and pulmonary disease. *Journal of Consulting and Clinical Psychology, 52,* 574–581.

Hall, S. M., Rugg, D., Tunstall, C., & Jones, R. T. (1984). Preventing relapse to cigarette smoking by behavioral skill training. *Journal of Consulting and Clinical Psychology, 52,* 372–382.

Hall, S. M., Tunstall, C., Rugg, D., Jones, R. T., & Benowitz, N. (1985). Nicotine gum and behavioral treatment in smoking cessation. *Journal of Consulting and Clinical Psychology, 53,* 256–258.

Halmi, K. A., Eckert, E., LaDu, T. J., & Cohen, J. (1986). Treatment efficacy of cyproheptadine and amitriptyline. *Archives of General Psychiatry, 43,* 177–181.

Halperin, K. M., & Snyder, C. R. (1979). Effects of enhanced psychological test feedback on treatment outcome: Therapeutic implications of the Barnum effect. *Journal of Consulting and Clinical Psychology, 47,* 140–146.

Hamm, N. H., Baum, M. R., & Nikels, K. W. (1975). Effects of race and exposure on judgments of interpersonal favorability. *Journal of Experimental Social Psychology, 11,* 14–24.

Hammen, C., Marks, T., Mayol, A., & deMayo, R. (1985). Depressive self-schemas, life stress, and vulnerability to depression. *Journal of Abnormal Psychology, 94,* 308–319.

Hammen, C., & Mayol, A. (1982). Depression and cognitive characteristics of stressful life-event types. *Journal of Abnormal Psychology, 91,* 165–174.

Harackiewicz, J. M., Sansone, C., Blair, L. W., Epstein, J. A., & Manderlink, G. (1987). Attributional processes in behavior change and maintenance: Smoking cessation and continued abstinence. *Journal of Consulting and Clinical Psychology, 55,* 372–378.

Harbeson, G. E. (1971). *Choice and challenge for the American woman,* rev. ed. Cambridge, MA: Schenckman.

Harburg, E., Erfurt, J. C., Hauenstein, L. S., Chape, C., & Hare, R. D. (1980). *Personality and individual differences.* New York: Pergamon Press.

Harder, D. W., Gift, T. E., Strauss, J. S., Ritzler, B. A., & Kokes, R. F. (1981). Life events and two-year outcome in schizophrenia. *Journal of Consulting and Clinical Psychology, 49,* 619–626.

Hare-Mustin, R. T. (1983). An appraisal of the relationship between women and psychotherapy: 80 years after the case of Dora. *American Psychologist, 38,* 593–601.

Harlow, H. F. (1959). Love in infant monkeys. *Scientific American, 200,* 68–86.

Harlow, H. F. (1965). Sexual behavior in the rhesus monkey. In F. Beach (Ed.), *Sex and behavior.* New York: Wiley.

Harlow, H. F., & Harlow, M. K. (1966). Learning to love. *American Scientist, 54,* 244–272.

Harlow, H. F., Harlow, M. K., & Meyer, D. R. (1950). Learning motivated by a manipulation drive. *Journal of Experimental Psychology, 40,* 228–234.

Harlow, H. F., & Zimmermann, R. R. (1959). Affectional responses in the infant monkey. *Science, 130,* 421–432.

Harlow, M. K., & Harlow, H. F. (1966). Affection in primates. *Discovery, 27,* 11–17.

Harrell, T. W., & Harrell, M. S. (1945). Army General Classification Test scores for civilian occupations. *Educational and Psychological Measurement, 5,* 229–239.

Harris, G. W., & Levine, S. (1965). Sexual differentiation of the brain and its experimental control. *Journal of Physiology, 181,* 379–400.

Harris, M. B., Harris, R. J., & Bochner, S. (1982). Fat, four-eyed, and female: Stereotypes of obesity, glasses, and gender. *Journal of Applied Social Psychology, 12,* 503–516.

Harris, T. A. (1967). *I'm OK—You're OK.* New York: Harper & Row.

Harrison, A. A., & Saeed, L. (1977). Let's make a deal: An analysis of revelations and stipulations in lonely hearts advertisements. *Journal of Personality and Social Psychology, 35,* 257–264.

Hart, B. (1967). Sexual reflexes and mating behavior in the male dog. *Journal of Comparative and Physiological Psychology, 66,* 388–399.

Hartmann, E. L. (1973). *The functions of sleep.* New Haven, CT: Yale University Press.

Hartmann, E. L. (1981). The strangest sleep disorder. *Psychology Today, 15*(4), 14–18.

Hartmann, E. L., & Stern, W. C. (1972). Desynchronized sleep deprivation: Learning deficit and its reversal by increased catecholamines. *Physiology and Behavior, 8,* 585–587.

Harvey, J. H., Ickes, W. J., & Kidd, R. F. (Eds.) (1976). *New directions in attributional research,* Vol. 1. Hillsdale, NJ: Erlbaum.

Harvey, J. H., Ickes, W. J., & Kidd, R. F. (Eds.) (1978). *New directions in attributional research,* Vol. 2. Hillsdale, NJ: Erlbaum.

Hass, R. G., & Linder, D. E. (1972). Counterargument availability and the effects of message structure on persuasion. *Journal of Personality and Social Psychology, 23,* 219–233.

Hassett, J. (1978). Sex and smell. *Psychology Today, 11*(10), 40–42, 45.

Hatfield, E. (1983). What do women and men want from love and sex? In E. R. Allgeier & N. B. McCormick (Eds.), *Changing boundaries: Gender roles and sexual behavior.* Palo Alto, CA: Mayfield.

Hatfield, E., & Sprecher, S. (1986). *Mirror, mirror . . . The importance of looks in everyday life.* Albany, NY: SUNY at Albany Press.

Havighurst, R. J. (1972). *Developmental tasks and education,* 3d ed. New York: McKay.

Hayes, S. L. (1981). Single case design and empirical clinical practice. *Journal of Consulting and Clinical Psychology, 49,* 193–211.

Haynes, S. G., Feinlieb, M., & Kannel, W. B. (1980). The relationship of psychosocial factors to coronary heart disease in the Framingham study: III. Eight-year incidence of coronary heart disease. *Applied Journal of Epidemiology, 111,* 37–58.

Haynes, S. N., Adams, A., & Franzen, M. (1981). The effects of presleep stress on sleep-onset insomnia. *Journal of Abnormal Psychology, 90,* 601–606.

Haynes, S. N., Follingstad, D. R., & McGowan, W. T. (1974). Insomnia: Sleep patterns and anxiety level. *Journal of Psychosomatic Research, 18,* 69–74.

Haynes, S. N., Sides, S., & Lockwood, G. (1977). Relaxation instructions and frontalis electromyographic feedback intervention with sleep-onset insomnia. *Behavior Therapy, 8,* 644–652.

Haynes, S. N., Woodward, S., Moran, R., & Alexander, D. (1974). Relaxation treatment of insomnia. *Behavior Therapy, 5,* 555–558.

Hays, R. B. (1984). The development and maintenance of friendship. *Journal of Social and Personal Relationships, 1,* 75–98.

Heaton, R. K., & Victor, R. G. (1976). Personality characteristics associated with psychedelic flashbacks in natural and experimental settings. *Journal of Abnormal Psychology, 85,* 83–90.

Heiby, E., & Becker, J. D. (1980). Effect of filmed modeling on the self-reported frequency of masturbation. *Archives of Sexual Behavior, 9,* 115–122.

Heider, F. (1958). *The psychology of interpersonal relations.* New York: Wiley.

Heiman, J. R. (1975). The physiology of erotica: Women's sexual arousal. *Psychology Today,* pp. 90–94.

Heingartner, A., & Hall, J. V. (1974). Affective consequences in adults and children of repeated exposure to auditory stimuli. *Journal of Personality and Social Psychology, 29,* 719–723.

Helmreich, R. L., Spence, J. T., & Holahan, C. K. (1979). Psychological androgyny and sex-role flexibility: A test of two hypotheses. *Journal of Personality and Social Psychology, 37,* 1631–1644.

Helson, R., & Moane, G. (1987). Personality change in women from college to midlife. *Journal of Personality and Social Psychology, 53,* 176–186.

Hemstone, M., & Jaspars, J. (1982). Explanations for racial discrimination: The effects of group decision on intergroup attributions. *European Journal of Social Psychology, 12,* 1–16.

Hendrick, C., Wells, K. S., & Faletti, M. V. (1982). Social and emotional effects of geographical relocation on elderly retirees. *Journal of Personality and Social Psychology, 42,* 951–962.

Hendrick, S., Hendrick, C., Slapion-Foote, M. J., & Foote, F. H. (1985). Gender differences in sexual attitudes. *Journal of Personality and Social Psychology, 48,* 1630–1642.

Hennigan, K. M., Cook, T. D., & Gruder, C. L. (1982). Cognitive tuning set, source credibility, and the temporal persistence of attitude change. *Journal of Personality and Social Psychology, 42,* 412–425.

Hennigan, K. M., DelRosario, M. L., Heath, L., Cook, T. D., Wharton, J. D., & Calder, B. J. (1982). Impact of the introduction of television on crime in the United States. *Journal of Personality and Social Psychology, 42,* 461–477.

Hensley, W. E. (1981). The effects of attire, location, and sex on aiding behavior: A similarity explanation. *Journal of Nonverbal Behavior, 6,* 3–11.

Hersen, M., Bellack, A. S., Himmelhoch, J. M., & Thase, M. E. (1984). Effect of social skill training, amiltriptyline, and psychotherapy in unipolar depressed women. *Behavior Therapy, 15,* 21–40.

Heston, L. L. (1966). Psychiatric disorders in foster-home-reared children of schizophrenic mothers. *British Journal of Psychiatry, 112,* 819–825.

Hill, C. (1987). Affiliation motivation: People who need people . . . but in different ways. *Journal of Personality and Social Psychology, 52,* 1008–1018.

Hinshaw, S. P., Henker, B., & Whalen, C. K. (1984). Cognitive-behavioral and pharmacologic interventions for hyperactive boys: Comparative and combined effects. *Journal of Consulting and Clinical Psychology, 52,* 739–749.

Hirsch, J. (1975). Jensenism: The bankruptcy of "science" without scholarship. *Educational Theory, 25,* 3–28.

Hite, S. (1976). *The Hite report: A nationwide study on female sexuality.* New York: Macmillan.

Hite, S. (1981). *The Hite report on male sexuality.* New York: Knopf.

Hite, S. (1987). *Women and love, a cultural revolution in progress.* New York: Knopf.

Hobbs, N., & Robinson, S. (1982). Adolescent development and public policy. *American Psychologist, 37,* 212–223.

Hobson, J. A., & McCarley, R. W. (1977). The brain as a dream state generator: An activation-synthesis hypothesis of the dream process. *American Journal of Psychiatry, 134,* 1335–1348.

Hoffman, M. L. (1981). Is altruism part of human nature? *Journal of Personality and Social Psychology, 40,* 121–137.

Hoffmann-Plotkin, D., & Twentyman, C. T. (1984). A multimodal assessment of behavioral and cognitive deficits in abused and neglected preschoolers. *Child Development, 55,* 794–802.

Holahan, C. J., & Moos, R. H. (1985). Life stress and health: Personality, coping, and social support in stress resistance. *Journal of Personality and Social Psychology, 49,* 739–747.

Holmes, D. S. (1984). Meditation and somatic arousal reduction: A review of the experimental evidence. *American Psychologist, 39,* 1–10.

Holmes, D. S. (1985). To meditate or to simply rest, that is the question: A reply to the comments of Shapiro. *American Psychologist, 40,* 722–725.

Holmes, D. S., McGilley, B. M., & Houston, B. K. (1984). Task-related arousal of Type A and Type B persons: Level of challenge and response specificity. *Journal of Personality and Social Psychology, 46,* 1322–1327.

Holmes, D. S., & Will, M. J. (1985). Expression of interpersonal aggression by angered and non-angered persons with the Type A and Type B behavior patterns. *Journal of Personality and Social Psychology, 48,* 723–727.

Holmes, T. H., & Rahe, R. H. (1967). The social readjustment rating scale. *Journal of Psychosomatic Research, 11,* 213–218.

Horn, J. M. (1983). The Texas adoption project: Adopted children and their intellectual resemblance to biological and adoptive parents. *Child Development, 54,* 268–275.

Horney, K. (1967). *Feminine psychology.* New York: Norton.

Horton, D. L., & Turnage, T. W. (1976). *Human learning.* Englewood Cliffs, NJ: Prentice-Hall.

Horvath, T. (1981). Physical attractiveness: The influence of selected torso parameters. *Archives of Sexual Behavior, 10,* 21–24.

Howard, J. A., Blumstein, P., & Schwartz, P. (1987). Social or evolutionary theories: Some observations on preferences in mate selection. *Journal of Personality and Social Psychology, 53,* 194–200.

Howard, J. L., Liptzin, M. B., & Reifler, C. B. (1973). Is pornography a problem? *Journal of Social Issues, 29,* 133–145.

Hrncir, E. J., Speller, G. M., & West, M. (1985). What are we testing? *Developmental Psychology, 21,* 226–232.

Hsu, L. K. G. (1986). The treatment of anorexia nervosa. *American Journal of Psychiatry, 143,* 573–581.

Hugdahl, K., & Ohman, A. (1977). Effects of instruction on acquisition and extinction of electrodermal response to fear-relevant stimuli. *Journal of Experimental Psychology: Human Learning and Memory, 3,* 608–618.

Hughes, P. L., Wells, L. A., Cunningham, C. J., & Ilstrup, D. M. (1986). Treating bulimia with desipramine. *Archives of General Psychiatry, 43,* 182–186.

Hull, J. G. (1981). A self-awareness model of the causes and effects of alcohol consumption. *Journal of Abnormal Psychology, 90,* 586–600.

Hull, J. G., Levenson, R. W., Young, R. D., & Sher, K. J. (1983). Self-awareness-reducing effects of alcohol consumption. *Journal of Personality and Social Psychology, 44,* 461–472.

Hull, J. G., Van Treuren, R. R., & Virnelli, S. (1987). Hardiness and health: A critique and alternative approach. *Journal of Personality and Social Psychology, 53,* 518–530.

Humphreys, L. G. (1981). The primary mental ability. In M. P. Friedman, J. P. Das, & N. O'Connor (Eds.), *Intelligence and learning.* New York: Plenum.

Hurvich, L. M. (1981). *Color vision.* Sunderland, MA: Sinauer Associates.

Hutchings, B., & Mednick, S. A. (1974). Registered criminality in the adoptive and biological parents of registered male adoptees. In S. A. Mednick, F. Schulsinger, J. Higgins, & B. Bell (Eds.), *Genetics, environment, and psychopathology.* New York: Elsevier.

Huxley, A. (1939). *Brave new world.* New York: Harper & Row.

Hyde, J. S. (1981). How large are cognitive gender differences? *American Psychologist, 36,* 892–901.

Insko, C. A. (1985). Balance theory, the Jordan paradigm, and the Wiest tetrahedron. In L. Berkowitz (Ed.), *Advances in experimental social psychology.* New York: Academic Press.

Israel, A. C., Stolmaker, L., & Andrian, C. A. G. (1985). The effects of training parents in general child management skills on a behavioral weight loss program for children. *Behavior Therapy, 16,* 169–180.

Istvan, J., & Griffitt, W. (1978). Emotional arousal and sexual attraction. Unpublished manuscript, Kansas State University.

Ivey, M. E., & Bardwick, J. M. (1968). Patterns of affective fluctuation in the menstrual cycle. *Psychosomatic Medicine, 30,* 336–345.

Izard, C. E. (1978). On the development of emotions and emotion-cognition relationships in infancy. In M. Lewis & L. Rosenblum (Eds.), *The development of affect.* New York: Plenum.

Izard, C. E. (Ed.). (1982). *Measuring emotions in infants and children.* New York: Cambridge University Press.

Izard, C. E. (1984). Emotion-cognition relationships and human development. In C. E. Izard, J. Kagan, & R. B. Zajonc (Eds.), *Emotions, cognition, and behavior.* New York: Cambridge University Press.

Jackson, J. M., & Harkins, S. G. (1985). Equity in effort: An explanation of the social loafing effect. *Journal of Personality and Social Psychology, 49,* 1199–1206.

Jacobs, T. J., & Charles, E. (1980). Life events and the occurrence of cancer in children. *Psychosomatic Medicine, 42,* 11–24.

Jacobson, E. (1938). *Progressive relaxation.* Chicago: University of Chicago Press.

James, W. (1890). *The principles of psychology.* New York: Henry Holt and Company.

Jamison, K. K., & Akiskal, H. S. (1983). Medication compliance in patients with bipolar disorder. *Psychiatric Clinics of North America, 6,* 175–192.

Janicak, P. G., Davis, J. M., Gibbons, R. D., Ericksen, S., Chang, S., & Gallagher, P. (1985). Efficacy of ECT: A meta-analysis. *American Journal of Psychiatry, 142,* 297–302.

Janis, I. L. (1982). *Groupthink: Psychological studies of policy decisions and fiascoes, 2d ed.* Boston: Houghton Mifflin.

Janis, I. L., Kaye, D., & Kirschner, P. (1965). Facilitating effects of "eating while reading" on responsiveness to persuasive communications. *Journal of Personality and Social Psychology, 1,* 181–186.

Jankowicz, A. D. (1987). Whatever became of George Kelly? Applications and implications. *American Psychologist, 42,* 481–487.

Jannoun, L., Oppenheimer, C., & Gelder, M. (1982). A self-help treatment program for anxiety state patients. *Behavior Therapy, 13,* 103–111.

Janowitz, H. D., & Grossman, M. I. (1949). Effect of variations in nutritive density on intake of food in dogs and cats. *American Journal of Physiology, 158,* 184–193.

Jellison, J. M., & Green, J. (1981). A self-presentation approach to the fundamental attribution error: The norm of internality. *Journal of Personality and Social Psychology, 40,* 643–649.

Jellison, J. M., & Oliver, D. F. (1983). Attitude similarity and attraction: An impression management approach. *Personality and Social Psychology Bulletin, 9,* 111–115.

Johnson, J. H., Butcher, J. N., Null, C., & Johnson, K. N. (1984). Replicated item level factor analysis of the full MMPI. *Journal of Personality and Social Psychology, 48,* 105–114.

Johnson, J. T., Cain, L. M., Falke, T. L., Hayman, J., & Perillo, E. (1985). The "Barnum effect" revisited: Cognitive and motivational factors in the acceptance of personality descriptions. *Journal of Personality and Social Psychology, 49,* 1378–1391.

Johnson, J. T., & Judd, C. M. (1983). Overlooking the incongruent: Categorization biases in the identification of political statements. *Journal of Personality and Social Psychology, 45,* 978–996.

Johnson, P. B. (1981). Achievement motivation and success: Does the end justify the means? *Journal of Personality and Social Psychology, 40,* 374–375.

Johnson, S. M., & White, G. (1971). Self-observation as an agent of behavioral change. *Behavior Therapy, 2,* 488–497.

Johnston, L. D., Bachman, J. G., & O'Malley, P. M. (1982). Student drug use, attitudes, and beliefs, 1975–1982. DHHS Publication No. ADM 82-1260. Washington, DC: National Institute on Drug Abuse.

Jones, E. (1961). *The life and work of Sigmund Freud.* New York: Basic Books.

Jones, E. (1979). The rocky road from acts to dispositions. *American Psychologist, 34,* 107–117.

Jones, M. (1975). Community care for chronic mental patients: The need for a reassessment. *Hospital and Community Psychiatry, 26,* 94–98.

Jones, M. C. (1924). Elimination of children's fears. *Journal of Experimental Psychology, 7*, 381–390.

Julien, R. M. (1986). *A primer of drug action*, 2d ed. San Francisco: Freeman.

Jung, C. G. (1964). *Man and his symbols*. Garden City, NY: Doubleday.

Jurkovic, G. J. (1980). The juvenile delinquent as a moral philosopher: A structural-developmental perspective. *Psychological Bulletin, 88*, 709–727.

Jus, A., Pineau, R., Lachance, R., Pelchat, G., Jus, K., Pires, P., & Villeneuve, R. (1976). Epidemiology of tardive dyskinesia. *Diseases of the Nervous System, 37*, 210–214.

Kagan, J. (1964). Acquisition and significance of sex-typing and sex-role identity. In M. L. Hoffman & L. W. Hoffman (Eds.), *Review of child development research*, Vol. 1. New York: Russell Sage.

Kagan, J. (1972). The plasticity of early intellectual development. Paper presented at the meeting of the Association for the Advancement of Science, Washington, DC.

Kagan, J. (1984). *The nature of the child*. New York: Basic Books.

Kahn, E. (1985). Heinz Kohut and Carl Rogers: A timely comparison. *American Psychologist, 40*, 893–904.

Kahn, S., Zimmerman, G., Csikszentmihalyi, M., & Getzels, J. W. (1985). Relations between identity in young adulthood and intimacy at midlife. *Journal of Personality and Social Psychology, 49*, 1316–1322.

Kailish, R. A., & Reynolds, D. K. (1976). *Death and ethnicity: A psycho-cultural study*. Los Angeles: USC Press.

Kallmann, F. J. (1952). Comparative twin study on the genetic aspects of male homosexuality. *Journal of Nervous and Mental Disease, 115*, 283–298.

Kamens, L. (1980). Cognitive and attribution factors in sleep-onset insomnia. Unpublished doctoral dissertation, Southern Illinois University at Carbondale.

Kamin, L. J. (1973, May). Heredity, intelligence, politics, and psychology. Paper presented at the meeting of the Eastern Psychological Association, Washington, DC.

Kamin, L. J. (1982). Mental testing and immigration. *American Psychologist, 37*, 97–98.

Kandel, D. B. (1980). Drug and drinking behavior among youth. *Annual Review of Sociology, 6*, 235–285.

Kanfer, F., & Goldfoot, D. (1966). Self-control and tolerance of noxious stimulation. *Psychological Reports, 18*, 79–85.

Kanin, E. J., & Parcell, S. R. (1977). Sexual aggression: A second look at the offended female. *Archives of Sexual Behavior, 6*, 67–76.

Kanin, G. (1978). *It takes a long time to become young*. Garden City, NY: Doubleday.

Kaplan, A. S., & Woodside, D. B. (1987). Biological aspects of anorexia nervosa and bulimia nervosa. *Journal of Consulting and Clinical Psychology, 55*, 645–653.

Kaplan, R. M., & Singer, R. D. (1976). Television violence and viewer aggression: A reexamination of the evidence. *Journal of Social Issues, 32*, 35–70.

Karlins, M., Coffman, T. L., & Walter, G. (1969). On the fading of social stereotypes: Studies in three generations of college students. *Journal of Personality and Social Psychology, 13*, 1–16.

Kastenbaum, R. (1977). *Death, society, and human behavior*. St. Louis: Mosby.

Kavale, K. (1982). The efficacy of stimulant drug treatment for hyperactivity: A meta-analysis. *Journal of Learning Disabilities, 15*, 280–289.

Kazdin, A. E. (1981). Drawing valid inferences from case studies. *Journal of Consulting and Clinical Psychology, 49*, 183–192.

Kazdin, A. E., & Wilcoxin, L. A. (1976). Systematic desensitization and nonspecific treatment effects: A methodological evaluation. *Psychological Bulletin, 83*, 729–758.

Keating, C. F., Mazur, A., Segall, M. H., Cysneiros, P. G., Divale, W. T., Kilbride, J. E., Komin, S., Leahy, P., Thurman, B., & Wirsing, R. (1981). Culture and the perception of social dominance from facial expression. *Journal of Personality and Social Psychology, 40*, 615–626.

Keefe, F. J., Caldwell, D. S., Queen, K. T., Gil, K. M., Martinez, S., Crisson, J. E., Ogden, W., & Nunley, J. (1987). Pain coping strategies in osteoarthritis patients. *Journal of Consulting and Clinical Psychology, 55*, 208–212.

Keele, S. W. (1973). *Attention and human performance*. Santa Monica, CA: Goodyear.

Keesey, R. E. (1980). A set-point analysis of the regulation of body weight. In A. J. Stunkard (Ed.), *Obesity*. Philadelphia: W. B. Saunders Co.

Keesey, R. E., & Powley, T. L. (1975). Hypothalamic regulation of body weight. *American Scientist, 63*, 558–565.

Keinan, G. (1987). Decision making under stress: Scanning of alternatives under controllable and uncontrollable threats. *Journal of Personality and Social Psychology, 52*, 639–644.

Kelley, C. K., & King, G. D. (1979). Behavioral correlates of the 2-7-8 MMPI profile type in students at a university mental health center. *Journal of Consulting and Clinical Psychology, 47*, 679–685.

Kelley, H. H. (1973). The processes of causal attribution. *American Psychologist, 28*, 107–128.

Kelley, H. H. (1979). *Personal relationships: Their structure and processes*. Hillsdale, NJ: Erlbaum.

Kelley, H. H., & Michela, J. L. (1980). Attribution theory and research. *Annual Review of Psychology, 31*, 457–501.

Kelly, C. (1980, July 11). New NIDA studies document dramatic rise in drug abuse. *ADAMHA News*.

Kelly, G. A. (1955). *The psychology of personal constructs, Vols. 1 & 2*. New York: Norton.

Kelly, G. A. (1958). Man's construction of his alternatives. In G. Lindzey (Ed.), *Assessment of human motives*. New York: Holt, Rinehart and Winston.

Kelly, K. E., & Houston, B. K. (1985). Type A behavior in employed women: Relation to work, marital, and leisure variables, social support, stress, tension, and health. *Journal of Personality and Social Psychology, 48,* 1067–1079.

Kennell, J., Jerauld, R., Wolfe, H., Chesler, D., Kreger, N., McAlpine, W., Steffa, M., & Klaus, M. (1974). Maternal behavior one year after early and extended post-partum contact. *Developmental Medicine and Child Neurology, 16,* 172–179.

Kerr, N. L. (1983). Motivation losses in small groups: A social dilemma analysis. *Journal of Personality and Social Psychology, 45,* 819–828.

Kerr, N. L., & MacCoun, R. J. (1985). The effects of jury size and polling method on the process and product of jury deliberation. *Journal of Personality and Social Psychology, 48,* 349–363.

Kershner, J. R., & Ledger, G. (1985). Effect of sex, intelligence, and style of thinking on creativity: A comparison of gifted and average IQ children. *Journal of Personality and Social Psychology, 48,* 1033–1040.

Kesey, K. (1962). *One flew over the cuckoo's nest.* New York: Viking.

Keverne, E. B. (1977). Pheromones and sexual behavior. In J. Money & H. Musaph (Eds.), *Handbook of sexology.* Amsterdam: Excerpta Medica.

Keye, W. R. (1983). Update: Premenstrual syndrome. *Endocrine and Fertility Forum, 6*(4), 1–3.

Keyes, D. (1982). *The minds of Billy Milligan.* New York: Bantam Books.

Kiesler, C. A. (1982). Mental hospitalization and alternative care. *American Psychologist, 37,* 349–360.

Kihlstrom, J. F. (1980). Posthypnotic amnesia for recently learned material: Interactions with "episodic" and "semantic" memory. *Cognitive Psychology, 12,* 227–251.

Kimmel, D. C. (1974). *Adulthood and aging: An interdisciplinary developmental view.* New York: Wiley.

Kinsey, A. C., Pomeroy, W. B., & Martin, C. E. (1948). *Sexual behavior in the human male.* Philadelphia: W. B. Saunders Co.

Kinsey, A. C., Pomeroy, W. B., Martin, C. E., & Gebhard, P. H. (1953). *Sexual behavior in the human female.* Philadelphia: W. B. Saunders Co.

Klaus, M. H., & Kennell, J. H. (1978). In J. H. Stevens, Jr., & M. Mathews (Eds.), *Mother/child, father/child relationships.* Washington, DC: National Association for the Education of Young Children.

Klein, D. F., & Rabkin, J. G. (1984) Specificity and strategy in psychotherapy research and practice. In R. L. Spitzer & J. R. W. Williams (Eds.), *Psychotherapy research: Where are we and where should we go?* New York: Guilford Press.

Klein, D. N., & Depue, R. A. (1985). Obsessional personality traits and risk for bipolar affective disorder: An offspring study. *Journal of Abnormal Psychology, 94,* 291–297.

Klein, D. N., Depue, R. A., & Slater, J. F. (1985). Cyclothymia in the adolescent offspring of parents with bipolar affective disorder. *Journal of Abnormal Psychology, 94,* 115–127.

Kleinke, C. L. (1977). Compliance to requests made by gazing and touching experimenters in field settings. *Journal of Experimental Social Psychology, 13,* 218–223.

Kleinke, C. L., & Staneski, R. A. (1980). First impressions of female bust size. *Journal of Social Psychology, 110,* 123–134.

Kleinke, C. L., & Walton, J. H. (1982). Influence of reinforced smiling on affective responses in an interview. *Journal of Personality and Social Psychology, 42,* 557–565.

Kleinmuntz, B. (1982). *Personality and psychological assessment.* New York: St. Martin's Press.

Kleinmuntz, B., & Szucko, J. J. (1984). Lie detection in ancient and modern times: A call for contemporary scientific study. *American Psychologist, 39,* 766–776.

Knapp, M. L. (1978). *Nonverbal communication in human interaction.* New York: Holt, Rinehart and Winston.

Kobasa, S. C. (1979). Stressful life events, personality, and health: An inquiry into hardiness. *Journal of Personality and Social Psychology, 37,* 1–11.

Kobasa, S. C., Maddi, S. R., & Kahn, S. (1982). Hardiness and health: A prospective study. *Journal of Personality and Social Psychology, 42,* 168–177.

Kobasa, S. C., Maddi, S. R., & Zola, M. A. (1983). Type A and hardiness. *Journal of Behavioral Medicine, 6,* 41–51.

Kobasa, S. C. & Puccetti, M. C. (1983). Personality and social resources in stress resistance. *Journal of Personality and Social Psychology, 45,* 839–850.

Koffka, K. (1925). *The growth of the mind.* New York: Harcourt Brace Jovanovich.

Kohen, W., & Paul, G. L. (1976). Current trends and recommended changes in extended care placements of mental patients: The Illinois system as a case in point. *Schizophrenia Bulletin, 2,* 575–594.

Kohlberg, L. (1966). A cognitive-developmental analysis of children's sex-role concepts and attitudes. In E. E. Maccoby (Ed.), *The development of sex differences.* Stanford, CA: Stanford University Press.

Kohlberg, L. (1969). *Stages in the development of moral thought and action.* New York: Holt, Rinehart and Winston.

Kohlberg, L. (1981). *The philosophy of moral development: Moral stages and the idea of justice.* San Francisco: Harper & Row.

Köhler, W. (1925). *The mentality of apes.* New York: Harcourt Brace Jovanovich.

Kohn, P. M., Barnes, G. E., & Hoffman, F. M. (1979). Drug-use history and experience seeking among adult male correctional inmates. *Journal of Consulting and Clinical Psychology, 47,* 708–715.

Kolata, G. (1987, November 10). Alcoholism: Genetic links grow clearer. *The New York Times,* pp. C1, C2.

Kolko, D. J., & Rickard-Figueroa, J. L. (1985). Effects of video games on the adverse corollaries of chemotherapy in pediatric oncology patients: A single-case analysis. *Journal of Consulting and Clinical Psychology, 53,* 223–228.

Komacki, J., & Dore-Boyce, K. (1978). Self-recording: Its effects on individuals high and low in motivation. *Behavior Therapy, 9,* 65–72.

Koop, C. E. (1987). Report of the surgeon general's workshop on pornography and public health. *American Psychologist, 42,* 944–945.

Koss, M. P., Butcher, J. L., & Strupp, H. H. (1986). Brief psychotherapy methods in clinical research. *Journal of Consulting and Clinical Psychology, 54,* 60–67.

Koss, M. P., Gidycz, C. A., & Wisniewski, N. (1987). The scope of rape: Incidence and prevalence of sexual aggression and victimization in a national sample of higher education students. *Journal of Consulting and Clinical Psychology, 55,* 162–170.

Krantz, D. S., Grunberg, N. E., & Baum, A. (1985). Health psychology. *Annual Review of Psychology, 36,* 349–383.

Krech, D., Crutchfield, R. S., & Ballachey, E. L. (1962). *Individual in society.* New York: McGraw-Hill.

Krieger, D. T. (1983). Brain peptides: What, where, and why? *Science, 222,* 975–985.

Kübler-Ross, E. (1969). *On death and dying.* New York: Macmillan.

LaChance, C. C., Chestnut, R. W., & Lubitz, A. (1978). The "decorative" female model: Sexual stimuli and the recognition of advertisements. *Journal of Advertising.*

Lahey, B. B., & Drabman, R. S. (1981). Behavior modification in the classroom. In W. E. Craighead, A. E. Kazdin, & M. J. Mahoney (Eds.), *Behavior modification: Principles, issues, and applications,* 2d ed. Boston: Houghton-Mifflin.

Laird, J. D. (1974). Self-attribution of emotion: The effects of expressive behavior on the quality of emotional experience. *Journal of Personality and Social Psychology, 29,* 475–486.

Laird, J. D. (1984). The real role of facial response in the experience of emotion: A reply to Tourangeau and Ellsworth, and others. *Journal of Personality and Social Psychology, 47,* 909–917.

Lam, D. H., Brewin, C. R., Woods, R. T., & Bebbington, P. E. (1987). Cognition and social adversity in the depressed elderly. *Journal of Abnormal Psychology, 96,* 23–26.

Lamb, M. E. (1981). The development of father-infant relationships. In M. E. Lamb (Ed.), *The role of the father in child development.* New York: Wiley.

Landreth, C. (1967). *Early childhood.* New York: Knopf.

Landy, D., & Sigall, H. (1974). Beauty is talent: Task evaluation as a function of the performer's physical attractiveness. *Journal of Personality and Social Psychology, 30,* 299–304.

Lang, A. R., Goeckner, D. J., Adesso, V. J., & Marlatt, G. A. (1975). Effects of alcohol on aggression in male social drinkers. *Journal of Abnormal Psychology, 84,* 508–518.

Lang, A. R., Searles, J., Lauerman, R., & Adesso, V. J. (1980). Expectancy, alcohol, and sex guilt as determinants of interest in and reaction to sexual stimuli. *Journal of Abnormal Psychology, 89,* 644–653.

Langer, E. J., Bashner, R. S., & Chanowitz, B. (1985). Decreasing prejudice by increasing discrimination. *Journal of Personality and Social Psychology, 49,* 113–120.

Langer, E. J., Rodin, J., Beck, P., Weinman, C., & Spitzer, L.

(1979). Environmental determinants of memory improvement in late adulthood. *Journal of Personality and Social Psychology, 37,* 2003–2013.

Lansky, D., & Wilson, G. T. (1981). Alcohol, expectations, and sexual arousal. *Journal of Abnormal Psychology, 90,* 35–45.

Lanzetta, J. T., Cartwright-Smith, J., & Kleck, R. E. (1976). Effects of nonverbal dissimulation on emotional experience and autonomic arousal. *Journal of Personality and Social Psychology, 33,* 354–370.

Laroche, S., & Bloch, V. (1982). Conditioning of hippocampal cells and long-term potentiation: An approach to mechanisms of post-trial memory facilitation. In C. Ajmone Marsan & H. Matthies (Eds.), *Neuronal plasticity and memory formation.* New York: Raven Press.

Larson, C. C. (1982, January). Taub conviction revives centuries-old debate. APA *Monitor,* pp. 1, 12–13.

Lashley, K. S. (1950). In search of the engram. In *Symposium of the Society for Experimental Biology,* Vol. 4. New York: Cambridge University Press.

Latané, B., & Dabbs, J. M. (1975). Sex, group size, and helping in three cities. *Sociometry, 38,* 180–194.

Latané, B., & Nida, S. (1981). Ten years of research on group size and helping. *Psychological Bulletin, 89,* 308–324.

Latané, B., Williams, K., & Harkins, S. (1979). Many hands make light the work: The causes and consequences of social loafing. *Journal of Personality and Social Psychology, 37,* 822–832.

Lau, R. R., & Russell, D. (1980). Attributions in the sports pages. *Journal of Personality and Social Psychology, 39,* 29–38.

Lavin, D. E. (1965). *The prediction of academic performance: A theoretical analysis and review of research.* New York: Russell Sage.

Lavrakas, P. J. (1975, May). Female preferences for male physiques. Paper presented at the Midwestern Psychological Association, Chicago.

Layne, C. (1979). The Barnum effect: Rationality versus gullibility? *Journal of Consulting and Clinical Psychology, 47,* 219–221.

Lazar, I., & Darlington, R. (1982). Lasting effects of early education: A report from the Consortium of Longitudinal Studies. *Monographs of the Society for Research in Child Development, 47*(2–3), Serial No. 195.

Lazarus, R. S., DeLongis, A., Folkman, S., & Gruen, R. (1985). Stress and adaptational outcomes: The problem of confounded measures. *American Psychologist, 40,* 770–779.

Leak, G. K., & Christopher, S. B. (1982). Freudian psychoanalysis and sociobiology: A synthesis. *American Psychologist, 37,* 313–322.

LeBon, G. (1895). *The crowd.* New York: Viking, 1960.

LeBow, M. D., Goldberg, P. S., & Collins, A. (1977). Eating behavior of overweight and nonoverweight persons in the natural environment. *Journal of Consulting and Clinical Psychology, 45,* 1204–1205.

Lee, T., & Seeman, P. (1977). Dopamine receptors in normal and schizophrenic human brains. *Proceedings of the Society of Neurosciences, 3,* 443.

Lefcourt, H. M., Miller, R. S., Ware, E. E., & Sherk, D. (1981). Locus of control as a modifier of the relationship between stressors and moods. *Journal of Personality and Social Psychology, 41,* 357–369.

Leibowitz, S. F. (1986). Brain monoamines and peptides: Role in the control of eating behavior. *Federation Proceedings, 45,* 599–615.

Lenneberg, E. H. (1967). *Biological foundations of language.* New York: Wiley.

Lenneberg, E. H. (1969). On explaining language. *Science, 164,* 635–643.

Lerner, M. J., Miller, D. T., & Holmes, J. G. (1975). Deserving versus justice: A contemporary dilemma. In L. Berkowitz & E. Walster (Eds.), *Advances in Experimental Social Psychology,* Vol. 12. New York: Academic Press.

Lerner, R. M., & Gellert, E. (1969). Body build identification, preference, and aversion in children. *Developmental Psychology, 1,* 456–462.

Lesnik-Oberstein, M., & Cohen, L. (1984). Cognitive style, sensation seeking, and assortive mating. *Journal of Personality and Social Psychology, 46,* 112–117.

Leventhal, H. (1970). Findings and theory in the study of fear communication. In L. Berkowitz (Eds.), *Advances in Experimental Social Psychology,* Vol. 5. New York: Academic Press.

Leventhal, H., Watts, J. C., & Paogano, F. (1967). Effects of fear and instructions on how to cope with danger. *Journal of Personality and Social Psychology, 6,* 313–321.

Levinson, D. J., Darrow, C. N., Klein, E. B., Levinson, M. H., & McKee, B. (1978). *The seasons of a man's life.* New York: Knopf.

Levitt, M. J. (1980). Contingent feedback, familiarization, and infant affect: How a stranger becomes a friend. *Developmental Psychology, 16,* 425–432.

Levitt, R. A. (1981). *Physiological psychology.* New York: Holt, Rinehart and Winston.

Levy, J. (1985). Right brain, left brain: Fact and fiction. *Psychology Today, 19*(5), 38–44.

Levy, S. M., Herberman, R. B., Maluish, A. M., Schlien, B., & Lippman, M. (1985). Prognostic risk assessment in primary breast cancer by behavioral and immunological parameters. *Health Psychology, 4,* 99–113.

Lewinsohn, P. M. (1975). The behavioral study and treatment of depression. In M. Hersen, R. M. Eisler, & P. M. Miller (Eds.), *Progress in Behavior Modification,* Vol. 1. New York: Academic Press.

Lewinsohn, P. M., & Amenson, C. S. (1978). Some relations between pleasant and unpleasant mood-related events and depression. *Journal of Abnormal Psychology, 87,* 644–654.

Lewinsohn, P. M., & Graf, M. (1973). Pleasant activities and depression. *Journal of Consulting and Clinical Psychology, 41,* 261–268.

Lewinsohn, P. M., & Libet, J. (1972). Pleasant events, activity schedules, and depression. *Journal of Abnormal Psychology, 79,* 291–295.

Lichtenstein, E. (1982). The smoking problem: A behavioral perspective. *Journal of Consulting and Clinical Psychology, 50,* 804–819.

Lichtenstein, E., & Glasgow, R. E. (1977). Rapid smoking: Side effects and safeguards. *Journal of Consulting and Clinical Psychology, 45,* 815–821.

Lick, J. R., & Heffler, D. (1977). Relaxation training and attention placebo in the treatment of severe insomnia. *Journal of Consulting and Clinical Psychology, 45,* 153–161.

Lieberman, M. A., Yalom, I. D., & Miles, M. (1973). *Encounter groups: First facts.* New York: Basic Books.

Ling, G. S. F., MacLeod, J. M., Lee, S., Lockhart, S. H., & Pasternak, G. W. (1984). Separation of morphine analgesia from physical dependence. *Science, 226,* 462–464.

Linz, D., Donnerstein, E., & Penrod, S. (1987). The findings and recommendations of the attorney general's commission on pornography: Do the psychological "facts" fit the political fury? *American Psychologist, 42,* 946–953.

Lipinski, D. P., Black, J. L., Nelson, R. O., & Ciminero, A. R. (1975). Influence of motivational variables on the reactivity and reliability of self-recording. *Journal of Consulting and Clinical Psychology, 43,* 637–646.

Lipsky, M., Kassinove, H., & Miller, N. (1980). Effects of rational-emotive therapy, rational role reversal and rational-emotive imagery on the emotional adjustment of community mental health center patients. *Journal of Consult-*

ing and Clinical Psychology, 48, 366–374.

Lipton, D. N., McDonel, E. C., & McFall, R. M. (1987). Heterosocial perception in rapists. *Journal of Consulting and Clinical Psychology, 55,* 17–21.

Lloyd, C., Alexander, A. A., Rice, D. G., & Greenfield, N. S. (1980). Life events as predictors of academic performance. *Journal of Human Stress, 6,* 15–25.

Lochman, J. E. (1987). Self- and peer perceptions and attributional biases of aggressive and nonaggressive boys in dyadic interactions. *Journal of Consulting and Clinical Psychology, 55,* 404–410.

Loehlin, J. C., Willerman, L., & Horn, J. M. (1982). Personality resemblances between unwed mothers and their adopted-away offspring. *Journal of Personality and Social Psychology, 42,* 1089–1099.

Loftus, E. F. (1983). Silence is not golden. *American Psychologist, 38,* 564–572.

Loftus, E. F., & Loftus, G. R. (1980). On the permanence of stored information in the brain. *American Psychologist, 35,* 409–420.

Loftus, E. F., & Palmer, J. C. (1974). Reconstruction of automobile destruction: An example of interaction between language and memory. *Journal of Verbal Learning and Verbal Behavior, 13,* 585–589.

Lohr, J. M., & Staats, A. (1973). Attitude conditioning in Sino-Tibetan languages. *Journal of Personality and Social Psychology, 26,* 196–200.

Loomis, J. M., & Lederman, S. J. (1986). Tactual perception. In K. Boff, L. Kaufman, & J. Thomas (Eds.), *Handbook of perception and human performance, Vol. 1.* New York: Wiley.

Lorenz, K. Z. (1966). *On aggression.* New York: Harcourt Brace Jovanovich.

Lorenz, K. Z. (1981). *The foundations of ethology.* New York: Springer-Verlag.

Lott, B. (1981). A feminist critique of androgyny: Toward the elimina-

tion of gender attributions for learned behavior. In C. Mayo & N. M. Henley (Eds.), *Gender and nonverbal behavior.* New York: Springer.

Lott, B. (1985). The potential enhancement of social/personality psychology through feminist research and vice versa. *American Psychologist, 40,* 155–164.

Lubin, B., Larsen, R. M., Matarazzo, J. D., & Seever, M. (1985). Psychological test usage patterns in five professional settings. *American Psychologist, 40,* 857–861.

Luborsky, L., & DeRubeis, R. J. (1984). The use of psychotherapy treatment manuals: A small revolution in psychotherapy research style. *Clinical Psychology Review, 4,* 5–15.

Luborsky, L., & Spence, D. P. (1971). Quantitative research on psychoanalytic therapy. In A. E. Bergin & S. L. Garfield (Eds.), *Handbook of psychotherapy and behavior change: An empirical analysis.* New York: Wiley.

Luchins, A. S. (1957). Primacy-recency in impression formation. In C. I. Hovland (Ed.), *The order of presentation in persuasion.* New Haven, CT: Yale University Press.

Luparello, T. J., McFadden, E. R., Lyons, H. A., & Bleecker, E. R. (1971). Psychologic factors and bronchial asthma. *New York State Journal of Medicine, 71,* 2161–2165.

Lykken, D. T. (1957). A study of anxiety in the sociopathic personality. *Journal of Abnormal and Social Psychology, 55,* 6–10.

Lykken, D. T. (1981). *A tremor in the blood: Uses and abuses of the lie detector.* New York: McGraw-Hill.

Lykken, D. T. (1982, September). Fearlessness: Its carefree charm and deadly risks. *Psychology Today,* pp. 20–28.

Lyons, J. S., Rosen, A. J., & Dysken, M. W. (1985). Behavioral effects of tricyclic drugs in depressed inpatients. *Journal of Consulting and Clinical Psychology, 53,* 17–24.

Maccoby, E. E., & Feldman, S. S. (1972). Mother-attachment and stranger reactions in the third year of life. *Monographs of the Society for Research in Child Development, 37*(1).

Maccoby, E. E., & Jacklin, C. N. (1974). *The psychology of sex differences.* Stanford, CA: Stanford University Press.

Macfarlane, A. (1977). *The psychology of childbirth.* Cambridge, MA: Harvard University Press.

Mackay, A. V. P., Iversen, L. L., Rossor, M., Spokes, E., Arregio, A., Crease, I., & Snyder, S. H. (1982). Increased brain dopamine and dopamine receptors in schizophrenia. *Archives of General Psychiatry, 39,* 991–997.

Maddi, S. R. (1980). *Personality theories: A comparative analysis.* Homewood, IL: Dorsey Press.

Maddi, S. R., & Kobasa, S. C. (1984). *The hardy executive: Health under stress.* Homewood, IL: Dow Jones–Irwin.

Madsen, C. H., Becker, W. C., & Thomas, D. R. (1968). Rules, praise, and ignoring: Elements of elementary classroom control. *Journal of Applied Behavior Analysis, 1,* 139–150.

Mahoney, M. J. (1980). *Abnormal psychology.* New York: Harper & Row.

Maier, N. R. F., & Schneirla, T. C. (1935). *Principles of animal psychology.* New York: McGraw-Hill.

Maital, S. (1982). The tax-evasion virus. *Psychology Today, 16*(3), 74–78.

Malamuth, N. M. (1981). Rape fantasies as a function of exposure to violent sexual stimuli. *Archives of Sexual Behavior, 10,* 33–48.

Malamuth, N. M., Heim, N., & Feshbach, S. (1980). Sexual responsiveness of college students to rape depictions: Inhibitory or disinhibitory effects. *Journal of Personality and Social Psychology, 38,* 399–408.

Malatesta, V. J., Sutker, P. B., & Treiber, F. A. (1981). Sensation seeking and chronic public drunkenness. *Journal of Consulting and Clinical Psychology, 49,* 292–294.

Mandler, G. (1984). *Mind and body: The psychology of emotion and stress.* New York: Norton.

Mankiewicz, F., & Swerdlow, J. (1977). *Remote control.* New York: Quadrangle.

Mann, L. (1981). The baiting crowd in episodes of threatened suicide. *Journal of Personality and Social Psychology, 41,* 703–709.

Mann, L., Newton, J. W., & Innes, J. M. (1982). A test between deindividuation and emergent norm theories of crowd aggression. *Journal of Personality and Social Psychology, 42,* 260–272.

Manning, M. M., & Wright, T. L. (1983). Self-efficacy expectancies, outcome expectancies, and the persistence of pain control in childbirth. *Journal of Personality and Social Psychology, 45,* 421–431.

Manucia, G. K., Baumann, D. J., & Cialdini, R. B. (1984). Mood influences on helping: Direct effects or side effects? *Journal of Personality and Social Psychology, 46,* 357–364.

Maratsos, M. (1983). Some current issues in the study of the acquisition of grammar. In J. H. Flavell & E. M. Markman (Eds.), *Handbook of child psychology: Vol. 3. Cognitive development.* New York: Wiley.

Marks, G., Miller, N., & Maruyama, G. (1981). Effect of targets' physical attractiveness on assumption of similarity. *Journal of Personality and Social Psychology, 41,* 198–206.

Marks, I. M. (1982). Toward an empirical clinical science: Behavioral psychotherapy in the 1980s. *Behavior Therapy, 13,* 63–81.

Marks, P. A., & Monroe, L. J. (1976). Correlates of adolescent poor sleepers. *Journal of Abnormal Psychology, 85,* 243–246.

Markus, H. (1981). The drive for integration: Some comments. *Journal of Experimental Social Psychology, 17,* 257–261.

Marlatt, G. A., & Gordon, J. R. (1980). Determinants of relapse: Implications for the maintenance of behavior change. In P. O. Davidson & S. M. Davidson (Eds.), *Behavioral medicine: Changing health lifestyles.* New York: Brunner/Mazel.

Marlatt, G. A., & Rohsenow, D. J. (1981). The think-drink effect. *Psychology Today, 15*(12), 60–69.

Marston, A. R., London, P., Cohen, N., & Cooper, L. M. (1977). In vivo observation of the eating behavior of obese and nonobese subjects. *Journal of Consulting and Clinical Psychology, 45,* 335–336.

Martelli, M. F., Auerbach, S. M., Alexander, J., & Mercuri, L. G. (1987). Stress management in the health care setting: Matching interventions with patient coping styles. *Journal of Consulting and Clinical Psychology, 55,* 201–207.

Martin, C. L. (1987). A ratio measure of sex stereotyping. *Journal of Personality and Social Psychology, 52,* 489–499.

Maruyama, G., Fraser, S. C., & Miller, N. (1982). Personal responsibility and altruism in children. *Journal of Personality and Social Psychology, 42,* 658–664.

Maruyama, G., & Miller, N. (1975). *Physical attractiveness and classroom acceptance.* Social Science Research Institute Report no. 75–2, University of Southern California.

Maslach, C. (1978). Emotional consequences of arousal without reason. In C. E. Izard (Ed.), *Emotions and psychopathology.* New York: Plenum.

Maslow, A. H. (1963). The need to know and the fear of knowing. *Journal of General Psychology, 68,* 111–124.

Maslow, A. H. (1970). *Motivation and personality,* 2d ed. New York: Harper & Row.

Maslow, A. H. (1971). *The farther reaches of human nature.* New York: Viking.

Masters, W. H., & Johnson, V. E. (1970). *Human sexual inadequacy.* Boston: Little, Brown.

Masters, W. H., Johnson, V. E., & Kolodny, R. C. (1985). *Human sexuality,* 2d ed. Boston: Little, Brown.

Matefy, R. (1980). Role-playing theory of psychedelic flashbacks. *Journal of Consulting and Clinical Psychology, 48,* 551–553.

Matlin, M. (1983). *Cognition.* New York: Holt, Rinehart and Winston.

Matlin, M. (1987). *The psychology of women.* New York: Holt, Rinehart and Winston.

Matsumoto, D. (1987). The role of facial response in the experience of emotion: More methodological problems and a meta-analysis. *Journal of Personality and Social Psychology, 52,* 769–774.

Mattes, J. A., & Gittelman, R. (1983). Growth of hyperactive children on maintenance regimen of methylphenidate. *Archives of General Psychiatry, 40,* 317–321.

Matthews, K. A., Krantz, D. S., Dembroski, T. M., & MacDougall, J. M. (1982). Unique and common variance in structured interview and Jenkins Activity Survey measures of the Type A behavior pattern. *Journal of Personality and Social Psychology, 42,* 303–313.

May, J. L., & Hamilton, P. A. (1980). Effects of musically evoked affect on women's interpersonal attraction toward and perceptual judgments of physical attractiveness of men. *Motivation and Emotion, 4,* 217–228.

May, P. R. (1975). A follow-up study of treatment of schizophrenia. In R. L. Spitzer & D. F. Klein (Eds.), *Evaluation of psychological therapies.* Baltimore: The Johns Hopkins University Press.

McArthur, L. Z., & Resko, B. G. (1975). The portrayal of men and women in American film commercials. *Journal of Social Psychology, 97,* 209–220.

McAuliffe, K., & McAuliffe, S. (1983, November 6). Keeping up with the genetic revolution. *The New York Times Magazine,* pp. 40–44, 92–97.

McBurney, D. H., & Collings, V. (1977). *Introduction to sensation/perception.* Englewood Cliffs, NJ: Prentice-Hall.

McCann, I. L., & Holmes, D. S. (1984). Influence of aerobic exercise on depression. *Journal of Personality and Social Psychology, 46,* 1142–1147.

McCanne, T. R., & Anderson, J. A. (1987). Emotional responding following experimental manipulation of facial electromyographic activity. *Journal of Personality and Social Psychology, 52,* 759–768.

McCaul, K. D., & Haugvedt, C. (1982). Attention, distraction, and cold-pressor pain. *Journal of Personality and Social Psychology, 43,* 154–162.

McCaul, K. D., Holmes, D. S., & Solomon, S. (1982). Voluntary expressive changes and emotion. *Journal of Personality and Social Psychology, 42,* 145–152.

McCauley, C., Woods, K., Coolidge, C., & Kulick, W. (1983). More aggressive cartoons are funnier. *Journal of Personality and Social Psychology, 44,* 817–823.

McClearn, G. E., & DeFries, J. C. (1973). *Introduction to behavioral genetics.* San Francisco: Freeman.

McClelland, D. C. (1958). Methods of measuring human motivation. In J. W. Atkinson (Ed.), *Motives in fantasy, action, and society.* Princeton, NJ: Van Nostrand.

McClelland, D. C. (1965). Achievement and entrepreneurship: A longitudinal study. *Journal of Personality and Social Psychology, 1,* 389–392.

McClelland, D. C. (1979). Inhibited power motivation and high blood pressure in man. *Journal of Abnormal Psychology, 88,* 182–190.

McClelland, D. C., Alexander, C., & Marks, E. (1982). The need for power, stress, immune functions, and illness among male prisoners. *Journal of Abnormal Psychology, 91,* 61–70.

McClelland, D. C., Atkinson, J. W., Clark, R. A., & Lowell, E. L. (1953). *The achievement motive.* New York: Appleton.

McClelland, D. C., Davidson, R. J., Floor, E., & Saron, C. (1980). Stressed power motivation, sympathetic activation, immune function and illness. *Journal of Human Stress, 6*(2), 11–19.

McClelland, D. C., & Jemmott, J. B., III. (1980). Power, motivation, stress and physical illness. *Journal of Human Stress, 6*(4), 6–15.

McClelland, D. C., & Pilon, D. A. (1983). Sources of adult motives in patterns of parent behavior in early childhood. *Journal of Personality and Social Psychology, 44,* 564–574.

McClintock, M. K. (1971). Menstrual synchrony and suppression. *Nature, 229,* 244–245.

McClintock, M. K. (1979). Estrous synchrony and its mediation by airborne chemical communication. *Hormones and Behavior, 10,* 264.

McConaghy, M. J. (1979). Gender permanence and the genital basis of gender: Stages in the development of constancy of gender identity. *Child Development, 50,* 1223–1226.

McConaghy, N., & Blaszczynski, A. (1980). A pair of monozygotic twins discordant for homosexuality: Sex-dimorphic behavior and penile volume responses. *Archives of Sexual Behavior, 9,* 123–132.

McConnell, J. V., Jacobson, A. L., & Kimble, D. P. (1959). The effects of regeneration upon retention of a conditioned response in the planarian. *Journal of Comparative and Physiological Psychology, 52,* 1–5.

McConnell, J. V., Shigehisa, T., & Salive, H. (1970). Attempts to transfer approach and avoidance responses by RNA injections in rats. In K. H. Pribram & D. E. Broadbent (Eds.), *Biology of memory.* New York: Academic Press.

McDougall, W. (1908). *Social psychology.* New York: G. P. Putnam.

McFadden, D., & Wightman, F. L. (1983). Audition. *Annual Review of Psychology, 34,* 95–128.

McGaugh, J. L. (1983). Preserving the presence of the past: Hormonal influences on memory storage. *American Psychologist, 38,* 161–174.

McGaugh, J. L., Martinez, J. L., Jr., Jensen, R. A., Messing, R. B., & Vasquez, B. J. (1980). Central and peripheral catelcholamine function in learning and memory processes. In *Neural mechanisms of goal-directed behavior and learning.* New York: Academic Press.

McGowan, R. J., & Johnson, D. L. (1984). The mother-child relationship and other antecedents of childhood intelligence: A causal analysis. *Child Development, 55,* 810–820.

McGurk, H., Turnura, C., & Creighton, S. J. (1977). Auditory-visual coordination in neonates. *Child Development, 48,* 138–143.

McIntyre, K. O., Lichtenstein, E., & Mermelstein, R. J. (1983). Self-efficacy and relapse in smoking cessation: A replication and extension. *Journal of Consulting and Clinical Psychology, 51,* 632–633.

McNeill, D. (1970). The development of language. In P. H. Mussen (Ed.), *Carmichael's manual of child psychology,* Vol. 1, 3d ed. New York: Wiley.

Mead, M. (1935). *Sex and temperament in three primitive societies.* New York: Morrow.

Mednick, S. A. (1962). The associative basis of the creative process. *Psychological Review, 69,* 220–232.

Mednick, S. A. (1985). Crime in the family tree. *Psychology Today, 19*(3), 58–61.

Meer, J. (1985). Turbulent teens: The stress factors. *Psychology Today, 19*(5), 15–16.

Meichenbaum, D., & Jaremko, M. E. (Eds.). (1983). *Stress reduction and prevention.* New York: Plenum Press.

Mellstrom, M., Jr., Cicala, G. A., & Zuckerman, M. (1976). General versus specific trait anxiety measures in the prediction of fear of snakes, heights, and darkness. *Journal of Consulting and Clinical Psychology, 44,* 83–91.

Melzack, R. (1973). *The puzzle of pain.* New York: Basic Books.

Melzack, R. (1980). Psychological aspects of pain. In J. J. Bonica (Ed.), *Pain.* New York: Raven Press.

Melzack, R., & Scott, T. H. (1957). The effects of early experience on the response to pain. *Journal of Comparative and Physiological Psychology, 50,* 155–161.

Mendelson, J. H., Rossi, A. M., & Meyer, R. E. (Eds.) (1974). *The use of marihuana: A psychological and physiological inquiry.* New York: Plenum.

Meredith, N. (1984). The gay dilemma. *Psychology Today, 18*(1), 56–62.

Mewborn, C. R., & Rogers, R. W. (1979). Effects of reassuring and threatening components of fear appeals of physiological and verbal measures of emotion and attitudes. *Journal of Experimental Social Psychology, 15,* 242–253.

Meyer, J. P., & Pepper, S. (1977). Need compatibility and marital adjustment in young married couples. *Journal of Personality and Social Psychology, 35,* 331–342.

Meyers, J. K., et al. (1984). Six-month prevalence of psychiatric disorders in three communities. *Archives of General Psychiatry, 41,* 959–967.

Michael, R. P., Keverne, E. B., & Bonsall, R. W. (1971). Pheromones: Isolation of male sex attractants from a female primate. *Science, 172,* 964–966.

Mider, P. A. (1984). Failures in alcoholism and drug dependence prevention and learning from the past. *American Psychologist, 39,* 183.

Milgram, S. (1963). Behavioral study of obedience. *Journal of Abnormal and Social Psychology, 67,* 371–378.

Milgram, S. (1974). *Obedience to authority.* New York: Harper & Row.

Miller, G. A. (1956). The magical number seven, plus or minus two: Some limits on our capacity for processing information. *Psychological Review, 63,* 81–97.

Miller, I. W., Klee, S. H., & Norman, W. H. (1982). Depressed and non-depressed inpatients' cognitions of hypothetical events, experimental tasks, and stressful life events. *Journal of Abnormal Psychology, 91,* 78–81.

Miller, N. E. (1969). Learning of visceral and glandular responses. *Science, 163,* 434–445.

Miller, N. E., & Dollard, J. (1941). *Social learning and imitation.* New Haven, CT: Yale University Press.

Miller, P. H., Heldmeyer, K. H., & Miller, S. A. (1975). Facilitation of conservation of number in young children. *Developmental Psychology, 11,* 253.

Miller, S. M. (1980). Why having control reduces stress: If I can stop the roller coaster I don't want to get off. In J. Garber & M. E. P. Seligman (Eds.), *Human helplessness: Theory and research.* New York: Academic Press.

Miller, S. M., Lack, E. R., & Asroff, S. (1985). Preference for control and the coronary-prone behavior pattern. *Journal of Personality and Social Psychology, 49,* 492–499.

Mills, J., & Harvey, J. (1972). Opinion change as a function of when information about the communicator is received and whether he is attractive or expert. *Journal of Personality and Social Psychology, 21,* 52–55.

Milner, J. S., Gold, R. G., Ayoub, C., & Jacewitz, M. M. (1984). Predictive validity of the child abuse potential inventory. *Journal of Consulting and Clinical Psychology, 52,* 879–884.

Mirsky, A. F., & Orzack, M. H. (1980). Two retrospective studies of psychosurgery. In E. S. Valenstein (Ed.), *The psychosurgery debate.* San Francisco: W. H. Freeman.

Mirsky, I. A. (1958). Physiologic, psychologic, and social determinants in the etiology of duodenal ulcer. *American Journal of Digestive Diseases, 3,* 285–315.

Mischel, W. (1977). On the future of personality measurement. *American Psychologist, 32,* 246–254.

Mischel, W. (1986). *Introduction to personality.* New York: Holt, Rinehart and Winston.

Mitchell, J. E., & Eckert, E. D. (1987). Scope and significance of eating disorders. *Journal of Consulting and Clinical Psychology, 55,* 628–634.

Moe, J. L., Nacoste, R. W., & Insko, C. A. (1981). Belief versus race as determinants of discrimination: A study of Southern adolescents in 1966 and 1979. *Journal of Personality and Social Psychology, 41,* 1031–1050.

Money, J. (1960). Phantom orgasm in the dreams of paraplegic men and women. *Archives of General Psychiatry, 3,* 373–382.

Money, J. (1974). Prenatal hormones and posthormonal socialization in gender identity differentiation. In J. K. Cole & R. Dienstbier (Eds.), *Nebraska Symposium on Motivation.* Lincoln, NE: University of Nebraska Press.

Money, J. (1977). Human hermaphroditism. In F. A. Beach (Ed.), *Human sexuality in four perspectives.* Baltimore: The Johns Hopkins University Press.

Money, J. (1987). Sin, sickness, or status? Homosexual gender identity and psychoneuroendocrinology. *American Psychologist, 42,* 384–399.

Money, J., & Ehrhardt, A. (1973). *Man and woman, boy and girl.* Baltimore: The Johns Hopkins University Press.

Monroe, L. J., & Marks, P. A. (1977). MMPI differences between adolescent poor and good sleepers. *Journal of Consulting and Clinical Psychology, 45,* 151–152.

Monroe, S. M. (1982). Life events and disorder: Event-symptom associations and the course of disorder. *Journal of Abnormal Psychology, 91,* 14–24.

Monroe, S. M. (1983). Major and minor life events as predictors of psychological distress: Further issues and findings. *Journal of Behavioral Medicine, 6,* 189–205.

Monte, C. F. (1980). *Beneath the mask: An introduction to theories of personality.* New York: Holt, Rinehart and Winston.

Moon, J. R., & Eisler, R. M. (1983). Anger control: An experimental comparison of three behavioral treatments. *Behavior Therapy, 14,* 493–505.

Moore, J. E., & Chaney, E. F. (1985). Outpatient group treatment of chronic pain: Effects of spouse involvement. *Journal of Consulting and Clinical Psychology, 53,* 326–334.

Moos, R. (1968). The development of the Menstrual Distress Questionnaire. *Psychosomatic Medicine, 30,* 853.

Moreland, R. L., & Zajonc, R. B. (1982). Exposure effects in person perception: Familiarity, similarity, and attraction. *Journal of Experimental Social Psychology, 18,* 395–415.

Morganthau, T., Agrest, S., Greenberg, N. F., Doherty, S., & Raine, G. (1986, January 6). Abandoned: The chronic mentally ill. *Newsweek,* pp. 14–19.

Moriarty, T. (1975). Crimes, commitment, and the responsive bystander: Two field experiments. *Journal of Personality and Social Psychology, 31,* 370–376.

Morin, C. M., & Azrin, N. H. (1987). Stimulus control and imagery training in treating sleep-maintenance insomnia. *Journal of Consulting and Clinical Psychology, 55,* 260–262.

Morokoff, P. J. (1985). Effects of sex guilt, repression, sexual "arousability," and sexual experience on female sexual arousal during erotica and fantasy. *Journal of Personality and Social Psychology, 49,* 177–187.

Morris, N. M., & Udry, J. R. (1978). Pheromonal influences on human sexual behavior: An experimental search. *Journal of Biosocial Science, 10,* 147–157.

Morris, W. N., Miller, R. S., & Spangenberg, S. (1977). The effects of dissenter position and task difficulty on conformity and response conflict. *Journal of Personality, 45,* 251–256.

Moscovici, S. (1985). Social influence and conformity. In G. Lindzey & E. Aronson (Eds.), *Handbook of social psychology, Vol. 2.* New York: Random House.

Motowidlo, S. T. (1982). Sex role orientation and behavior in a work setting. *Journal of Personality and Social Psychology, 42,* 935–945.

Mueser, K. T., Grau, B. W., Sussman, S., & Rosen, A. J. (1984). You're only as pretty as you feel: Facial expression as a determinant of physical attractiveness. *Journal of Personality and Social Psychology, 46,* 469–478.

Mullen, B., Futrell, D., Stairs, D., Tice, D., Baumeister, R. F., Dawson, K., Riordan, C., Radloff, C., Kennedy, J., & Rosenfeld, P. (1987). Newscasters' facial expressions and voting behavior of viewers: Can a smile elect a president? *Journal of Personality and Social Psychology, 53,* in press.

Murray, H. A. (1938). *Explorations in personality.* New York: Oxford University Press.

Murstein, B. I. (1972). Physical attractiveness and marital choice. *Journal of Personality and Social Psychology, 22,* 8–12.

Murstein, B. I., & Christy, P. (1976). Physical attractiveness and marital adjustment in middle-aged couples. *Journal of Personality and Social Psychology, 34,* 537–542.

Musante, L., MacDougall, J. M., Dembroski, T. M., & Van Horn, A. E. (1983). Component analysis of the Type A coronary-prone behavior pattern in male and female college students. *Journal of Personality and Social Psychology, 45,* 1104–1117.

Myers, A. M., & Gonda, G. (1982). Utility of the masculinity-femininity construct: Comparison of traditional and androgyny approaches. *Journal of Personality and Social Psychology, 43,* 514–523.

Myers, D. G. (1983). Polarizing effects of social interaction. In H. Brandstatter, J. H. Davis, & G. Stocker-Kreichgauer (Eds.), *Group decision processes.* London: Academic Press.

Myers, D. G., & Lamm, H. (1976). The group polarization phenomenon. *Psychological Bulletin, 85,* 602–627.

Myers, M. B., Templer, D. I., & Brown, R. (1984). Coping ability of women who become victims of rape. *Journal of Consulting and Clinical Psychology, 52,* 73–78.

Myers, M. B., Templer, D. I., & Brown, R. (1985). Reply to Wieder on rape victims: Vulnerability does not imply responsibility. *Journal of Consulting and Clinical Psychology, 53,* 431.

Nadi, N. S., Nurnberger, J. I., Jr., & Gershon, E. S. (1984). Muscarinic cholinergic receptors on skin fibroblasts in familial affective disorder. *New England Journal of Medicine, 311,* 225–230.

Naffziger, C. C., & Naffziger, K. (1974). Development of sex role stereotypes. *Family Coordinator, 23,* 251–258.

Nahemow, L., & Lawton, M. P. (1975). Similarity and propinquity in a friendship formation. *Journal of Personality and Social Psychology, 32,* 205–213.

National Center on Child Abuse and Neglect Report (1982, January–February). *Children Today,* pp. 27–28.

National Institute of Mental Health (1982). Television and behavior: Ten years of scientific progress and implications for the eighties. Washington, DC: National Institute of Mental Health.

Neugarten, B. (1971, May). Grow old with me, the best is yet to be. *Psychology Today,* pp. 45–49.

Neugarten, B. (1982, May). Understanding psychological man. *Psychology Today,* pp. 54–55.

Nevid, J. S. (1984). Sex differences in factors of romantic attraction. *Sex Roles, 11*(5/6), 401–411.

Nevid, J. S., & Rathus, S. A. (1978). Multivariate and normative data pertaining to the RAS with the college population. *Behavior Therapy, 9,* 675.

Newcomb, T. M. (1971). Dyadic balance as a source of clues about interpersonal attraction. In B. I. Murstein (Ed.), *Theories of attraction and love.* New York: Springer.

Newcomb, T. M. (1981). Heiderian balance as a group phenomenon. *Journal of Personality and Social Psychology, 40,* 862–867.

Newcombe, N., & Bandura, M. M. (1983). The effect of age at puberty on spatial ability in girls: A question of mechanism. *Developmental Psychology, 19,* 215–224.

Newmark, C. S., Frerking, R. A., Cook, L., & Newmark, L. (1973). Endorsement of Ellis's irrational beliefs as a function of psychopathology. *Journal of Clinical Psychology, 29,* 300–302.

Newport, E. (1976). Motherese: The speech of mothers to young children. In N. J. Castellan, D. B. Pisoni, & G. R. Potts (Eds.), *Cognitive theory,* Vol. 2. Hillsdale, NJ: Erlbaum.

Nezu, A. M., & Ronan, G. F. (1985). Life stress, current problems, problem solving, and depressive symptoms: An integrative model. *Journal of Consulting and Clinical Psychology, 53,* 693–697.

Nicassio, P., & Bootzin, R. (1974). A comparison of progressive relaxation and autogenic training as treatments for insomnia. *Journal of Abnormal Psychology, 83,* 253–260.

Nisan, M. (1984). Distributive justice and social norms. *Child Development, 55,* 1020–1029.

Nisbett, R. E., & Ross, L. (1980). *Human inference: Strategies and shortcomings of social judgment.* Englewood Cliffs, NJ: Prentice-Hall.

Nolan, J. D. (1968). Self-control procedures in the modification of smoking behavior. *Journal of Consulting and Clinical Psychology, 32,* 92–93.

Noles, S. W., Cash, T. F., & Winstead, B. A. (1985). Body image, physical attractiveness, and depression. *Journal of Consulting and Clinical Psychology, 53,* 88–94.

Norton, G. R., Harrison, B., Hauch, J., & Rhodes, L. (1985). Characteristics of people with infrequent panic attacks. *Journal of Abnormal Psychology, 94,* 216–221.

Novin, D., Wyrwick, W., & Bray, G. A. (Eds.) (1976). *Hunger: Basic mechanisms and clinical implications.* New York: Raven Press.

Nowlis, G. H., & Kessen, W. (1976). Human newborns differentiate differing concentrations of sucrose and glucose. *Science, 191,* 865–866.

O'Grady, K. E. (1982). Sex, physical attractiveness, and perceived risk for mental illness. *Journal of Personality and Social Psychology, 43,* 1064–1071.

Ohman, A., Fredrikson, M., Hugdahl, K., & Rimmo, P. (1976). The premise of equipotentiality in human classical conditioning: Conditioned electrodermal responses to potentially phobic stimuli. *Journal of Experimental Psychology: General, 105,* 313–337.

Olds, J. (1969). The central nervous system and the reinforcement of behavior. *American Psychologist, 24,* 114–132.

Olds, J., & Milner, P. (1954). Positive reinforcement produced by electrical stimulation of the septal area and other regions of the rat brain. *Journal of Comparative and Physiological Psychology, 47,* 419–427.

O'Leary, K. D. (1980). Pills or skills for hyperactive children? *Journal of Applied Behavioral Analysis, 13,* 191–204.

O'Malley, M. N., & Becker, L. A. (1984). Removing the egocentric bias: The relevance of distress cues to evaluation of fairness. *Personality and Social Psychology Bulletin, 10,* 235–242.

Orme-Johnson, D. (1973). Autonomic stability and transcendental meditation. *Psychosomatic Medicine, 35,* 341–349.

Orne, M. T., Soskis, D. A., & Dinges, D. F. (1984). Hypnotically-induced testimony and the criminal justice system. In G. L. Wells & E. F. Loftus (Eds.), *Eyewitness testimony: Psychological perspectives.* New York: Cambridge University Press.

Ortega, D. F., & Pipal, J. E. (1984). Challenge seeking and the Type A coronary-prone behavior pattern. *Journal of Personality and Social Psychology, 46,* 1328–1334.

Osborn, D. K., & Endsley, R. C. (1971). Emotional reactions of young children to TV violence. *Child Development, 42,* 321–331.

O'Sullivan, M., Ekman, P., Friesen, W., & Scherer, K. (1985). What you say and how you say it: The contribution of speech quality and voice content to judgments of others. *Journal of Personality and Social Psychology, 48,* 54–62.

Overton, D. A. (1985). Contextual stimulus effects of drugs and internal states. In P. D. Balsam & A. Tomie (Eds.), *Context and learning.* Hillsdale, NJ: Erlbaum.

Pagel, M., & Becker, J. (1987). Depressive thinking and depression: Relations with personality and social resources. *Journal of Personality and Social Psychology, 52,* 1043–1052.

Paige, K. E. (1971). Effects of oral contraceptives on affective fluctuations associated with the menstrual cycle. *Psychosomatic Medicine, 33,* 515–537.

Paige, K. E. (1973, April). Women learn to sing the menstrual blues. *Psychology Today,* p. 41.

Palmer, D. L., & Kailn, R. (1985). Dogmatic responses to belief dissimilarity in the "bogus stranger" paradigm. *Journal of Personality and Social Psychology, 48,* 171–179.

Palmer, F. H. (1976). *The effects of minimal early intervention on subsequent IQ scores and reading achievement.* Report to the Education

Commission of the States, contract 13–76–06846, State University of New York at Stony Brook.

Pantin, H. M., & Carver, C. S. (1982). Induced competence and the bystander effect. *Journal of Applied Social Psychology, 12,* 100–111.

Park, B., & Rothbart, M. (1982). Perception of outgroup homogeneity and levels of social categorization: Memory for the subordinate attributes of in-group and outgroup members. *Journal of Personality and Social Psychology, 42,* 1051–1068.

Parker, N. (1964). Homosexuality in twins: A report on three discordant pairs. *British Journal of Psychiatry, 110,* 489–495.

Parloff, M. B. (1986). Placebo controls in psychotherapy research: A sine qua non or a placebo for research problems? *Journal of Consulting and Clinical Psychology, 54,* 79–87.

Parloff, M. B., Waskow, I. E., & Wolfe, B. E. (1978). Research on therapist variables in relation to process and outcome. In S. L. Garfield & A. E. Bergin (Eds.), *Handbook of psychotherapy and behavior change,* 2d ed. New York: Wiley.

Parron, D. L., Solomon, F., & Jenkins, C. D. (Eds.) (1982). *Behavior, health risks, and social disadvantage.* Washington, DC: National Academy Press.

Patterson, F. G. (1980). Innovative uses of language by a gorilla: A case study. In K. E. Nelson (Ed.), *Children's language, Vol. 2.* New York: Gardner Press.

Patterson, F. G., Patterson, C. H., & Brentari, D. K. (1987). Language in child, chimp, and gorilla. *American Psychologist, 42,* 270–272.

Paul, G. L. (1969a). Outcome of systematic desensitization II: Controlled investigations of individual treatment, technique variations, and current status. In C. M. Franks (Ed.), *Behavior therapy: Appraisal and status.* New York: McGraw-Hill.

Paul, G. L. (1969b). Physiological effects of relaxation training and hypnotic suggestion. *Journal of Abnormal Psychology, 74,* 425–437.

Pavlov, I. (1927). *Conditioned reflexes.* London: Oxford University Press.

Pearlman, C. A., & Greenberg, R. (1973). Posttrial REM sleep: A critical period for consolidation of shuttlebox avoidance. *Animal Learning and Behavior, 1,* 49–51.

Pearlman, K., Schmidt, F. L., & Hunter, J. E. (1980). Test of a new model of validity generalization: Results for job proficiency and training criteria in clerical occupations. *Journal of Applied Psychology, 65,* 373–406.

Peele, S. (1984). The cultural context of psychological approaches to alcoholism: Can we control the effects of alcohol? *American Psychologist, 39,* 1337–1351.

Pelham, W. E. (1983). The effects of psychostimulants on academic achievement in hyperactive and learning-disabled children. *Thalamus, 3,* 1–49.

Penfield, W. (1969). Consciousness, memory, and man's conditioned reflexes. In K. H. Pribram (Ed.), *On the biology of learning.* New York: Harcourt Brace Jovanovich.

Pennebaker, J. W., & Skelton, J. A. (1981). Selective monitoring of physical sensations. *Journal of Personality and Social Psychology, 41,* 213–223.

Perkins, D. (1982). The assessment of stress using life events scales. In L. Goldberger & S. Brenitz (Eds.), *Handbook of stress: Theoretical and clinical aspects.* New York: Free Press.

Perls, F. S. (1971). *Gestalt therapy verbatim.* New York: Bantam.

Perry, D. G., & Bussey, K. (1979). The social learning theory of sex differences: Imitation is alive and well. *Journal of Personality and Social Psychology, 37,* 1699–1712.

Persons, J. B., & Rao, P. A. (1985). Longitudinal study of cognitions, life events, and depression in psychiatric inpatients. *Journal of Abnormal Psychology, 94,* 51–63.

Peterson, C., Schwartz, S. M., & Seligman, M. E. P. (1981). Self-blame and depressive symptoms. *Journal of Personality and Social Psychology, 41,* 253–259.

Peterson, L. R., & Peterson, M. J. (1959). Short-term retention of individual verbal items. *Journal of Experimental Psychology, 58,* 193–198.

Petty, R. E., & Cacioppo, J. T. (1986). The elaboration-likelihood model of persuasion. In L. Berkowitz (Ed.), *Advances in experimental social psychology, Vol. 19.* New York: Academic Press.

Piaget, J. (1962). *The moral judgment of the child.* New York: Collier.

Piaget, J. (1963). *The origins of intelligence in children.* New York: Norton.

Piaget, J. (1971). *The construction of reality in the child.* New York: Ballantine.

Piaget, J. (1976). *The grasp of consciousness.* Cambridge, MA: Harvard University Press.

Pierrel, R., & Sherman, J. G. (1963, February). Train your pet the Barnabus way. *Brown Alumni Monthly,* pp. 8–14.

Pine, C. J. (1985). Anxiety and eating behavior in obese and nonobese American Indians and White Americans. *Journal of Personality and Social Psychology, 49,* 774–780.

Pines, M. (1975, October 26). Headstart. *New York Times Magazine.*

Pipp, S., Shaver, P., Jennings, S., Lamborn, S., & Fischer, K. W. (1985). Adolescents' theories about the development of their relationships with parents. *Journal of Personality and Social Psychology, 48,* 991–1001.

Pliner, P., Hart, H., Kohl, J., & Saari, D. (1974). Compliance without pressure: Some further data on the foot-in-the-door technique. *Journal of Experimental Social Psychology, 10,* 17–22.

Plomin, R. (1982). Quoted in Pines, M. Behavior and heredity: Links for specific traits are growing stronger. *New York Times*, June 29, 1982, pp. C1–C2.

Plomin, R., & DeFries, J. C. (1980). Genetics and intelligence: Recent data. *Intelligence, 4*, 15–24.

Plutchik, R. (1962). *The emotions: Facts, theories, and a new model.* New York: Random House.

Podlesny, J. A., & Raskin, D. C. (1977). Physiological measures and the detection of deception. *Psychological Bulletin, 84*, 782–799.

Polivy, J., & Herman, C. P. (1985). Dieting and binging: A causal analysis. *American Psychologist, 40*, 193–201.

Polivy, J., & Herman, C. P. (1987). Diagnosis and treatment of normal eating. *Journal of Consulting and Clinical Psychology, 55*, 635–644.

Pomazal, R. J., & Clore, G. L. (1973). Helping on the highway: The effects of dependency and sex. *Journal of Applied Social Psychology, 3*, 150–164.

Popper, K. (1985). Cited in Goleman (1985).

Postman, L. (1975). Verbal learning and memory. *Annual Review of Psychology, 26*, 291–335.

Powley, T. L. (1977). The ventromedial hypothalamic syndrome, satiety, and a cephalic phase hypothesis. *Psychological Review, 84*, 89–126.

Premack, A. J., & Premack, D. (1975). Teaching language to an ape. In R. C. Atkinson (Ed.), *Psychology in progress.* San Francisco: W. H. Freeman.

Prescott, P., & DeCasper, A. J. (1981). Do newborns prefer their fathers' voices? Apparently not. Paper presented to the meeting of the Society for Research in Child Development, Boston.

Press, A., et al. (1985, March 18). The war against pornography. *Newsweek*, pp. 58–66.

Prewett, M. J., van Allen, P. K., & Milner, J. S. (1978). Multiple electroconvulsive shocks and feeding and drinking behavior in the rat.

Bulletin of the Psychonomic Society, 12, 137–139.

Price, D. D., Rafii, A., Watkins, L. R., & Buckingham, B. (1984). A psychophysical analysis of acupuncture analgesia. *Pain, 19*, 27–42.

Pritchard, D., & Rosenblatt, A. (1980). Racial bias in the MMPI: A methodological review. *Journal of Consulting and Clinical Psychology, 48*, 129–142.

Pyszczynski, T., Holt, K., & Greenberg, J. (1987). Depression, self-focused attention, and expectancies for positive and negative future life events for self and others. *Journal of Personality and Social Psychology, 52*, 994–1001.

Qualls, P. J., & Sheehan, P. W. (1981). Imagery encouragement, absorption capacity, and relaxation during electromyographic feedback. *Journal of Personality and Social Psychology, 41*, 370–379.

Quattrone, G. A. (1982). Overattribution and unit formation: When behavior engulfs the person. *Journal of Personality and Social Psychology, 42*, 593–607.

Quinsey, V. L., Chaplin, T. C., & Upfold, D. (1984). Sexual arousal to nonsexual violence and sadomasochistic themes among rapists and non-sex-offenders. *Journal of Consulting and Clinical Psychology, 52*, 651–657.

Rabkin, J. G. (1980). Stressful life events and schizophrenia: A review of the literature. *Psychological Bulletin, 87*, 408–425.

Rapaport, K., & Burkhart, B. R. (1984). Personality and attitudinal characteristics of sexually coercive college males. *Journal of Abnormal Psychology, 93*, 216–221.

Rapport, M. D. (1984). Hyperactivity and stimulant treatment: *Abusus non tollit usum. The Behavior Therapist, 7*, 133–134.

Raps, C. S., Peterson, C., Reinhard, K. E., Abramson, L. Y., & Seligman, M. E. P. (1982). Attributional style among depressed patients. *Journal of Abnormal Psychology, 91*, 102–108.

Rathus, S. A. (1973). A 30-item schedule for assessing assertive behavior. *Behavior Therapy, 4*, 398–406.

Rathus, S. A. (1983). *Human sexuality.* New York: Holt, Rinehart and Winston.

Rathus, S. A. (1988). *Understanding child development.* New York: Holt, Rinehart and Winston.

Rathus, S. A., & Nevid, J. S. (1977). *Behavior therapy.* Garden City, NY: Doubleday.

Rathus, S. A., & Nevid, J. S. (1986). *Adjustment and growth: The challenges of life*, 3d ed. New York: Holt, Rinehart and Winston.

Rebok, G. W. (1987). *Life-span cognitive development.* New York: Holt, Rinehart and Winston.

Redd, W. H., Jacobsen, P. B., Die-Trill, M., Dermatis, H., McEvoy, M., & Holland, J. C. (1987). Cognitive/attentional distraction in the control of conditioned nausea in pediatric cancer patients receiving chemotherapy. *Journal of Consulting and Clinical Psychology, 55*, 391–395.

Reeder, G. D. (1982). Let's give the fundamental attribution error another chance. *Journal of Personality and Social Psychology, 43*, 341–344.

Reeder, G. D., Henderson, D. J., & Sullivan, J. J. (1982). From dispositions to behaviors: The flip side of attribution. *Journal of Research in Personality, 16*, 355–375.

Reeder, G. D., & Spores, J. M. (1983). The attribution of morality. *Journal of Personality and Social Psychology, 44*, 736–745.

Rehm, L. P. (1978). Mood, pleasant events, and unpleasant events. *Journal of Consulting and Clinical Psychology, 46*, 854–859.

Reich, J. W., & Zautra, A. (1981). Life events and personal causation: Some relationships with satisfaction and distress. *Journal of Personality and Social Psychology, 41*, 1002–1012.

Reinke, B. J., Holmes, D. S., & Harris, R. L. (1985). The timing of psychosocial changes in women's lives. *Journal of Personality and Social Psychology, 48,* 1353–1364.

Reis, H. T., Nezlek, J., & Wheeler, L. (1980). Physical attractiveness in social interaction. *Journal of Personality and Social Psychology, 38,* 604–617.

Reis, H. T., Senchak, M., & Solomon, B. (1985). Sex differences in the intimacy of social interaction. *Journal of Personality and Social Psychology, 48,* 1205–1217.

Reis, H. T., Wheeler, L., Spiegel, N., Kernis, M. H., Nezlek, J., & Perri, M. (1982). Physical attractiveness in social interaction: II. Why does appearance affect social experience? *Journal of Personality and Social Psychology, 43,* 979–996.

Reiss, M., Rosenfeld, P., Melburg, V., & Tedeschi, J. T. (1981). Self-serving attributions: Biased private perceptions and distorted public descriptions. *Journal of Personality and Social Psychology, 41,* 224–231.

Rempel, J. K., Holmes, J. G., & Zanna, M. P. (1985). Trust in close relationships. *Journal of Personality and Social Psychology, 49,* 95–112.

Renninger, K. A., & Wozniak, R. H. (1985). Effect of interest on attentional shift, recognition, and recall in young children. *Developmental Psychology, 21,* 624–632.

Reschly, D. J. (1981). Psychological testing in educational classification and placement. *American Psychologist, 36,* 1094–1102.

Rest, J. R. (1983). Morality. In P. H. Mussen, J. Flavell, & E. Markman (Eds.), *Handbook of child psychology, Vol. 3: Cognitive development.* New York: Wiley.

Restak, R. (1975, August 9). José Delgado: Exploring inner space. *Saturday Review.*

Rhodewalt, F., & Agustsdottir, S. (1984). On the relationship of hardiness to the Type A behavior pattern: Perception of life events versus coping with life events. *Journal of Research in Personality, 18,* 212–223.

Rice, B. (1979, September). Brave

new world of intelligence testing. *Psychology Today,* p. 27.

Richardson, D. C., Bernstein, S., & Taylor, S. P. (1979). The effect of situational contingencies on female retaliative behavior. *Journal of Personality and Social Psychology, 37,* 2044–2048.

Richter, C. P. (1957). On the phenomenon of sudden death in animals and man. *Psychosomatic Medicine, 19,* 191–198.

Ridon, J., & Langer, E. J. (1977). Long-term effects of control-relevant intervention with the institutionalized aged. *Journal of Personality and Social Psychology, 35,* 897–902.

Rieser, J., Yonas, A., & Wilkner, K. (1976). Radial localization of odors by human newborns. *Child Development, 47,* 856–859.

Riggio, R. E., & Woll, S. B. (1984). The role of nonverbal cues and physical attractiveness in the selection of dating partners. *Journal of Social and Personal Relationships, 1,* 347–357.

Riley, V. (1981). Psychoneuroendocrine influences on immunocompetence and neoplasia. *Science, 212,* 1100–1109.

Ringler, N., Kennell, J., Jarvella, R., Navojosky, B., & Klaus, M. (1975). Mother-to-child speech at two years—Effects of early postnatal contact. *Journal of Pediatrics, 86*(1), 141–144.

Rinn, W. E. (1984). The neuropsychology of facial expression: A review of the neurological and psychological mechanisms for producing facial expressions. *Psychological Bulletin, 95,* 52–77.

Rizley, R. (1978). Depression and distortion in the attribution of causality. *Journal of Abnormal Psychology, 87,* 32–48.

Robinson, M. H., & Robinson, B. (1979). By dawn's early light: Matutinal mating and sex attractants in a neotropical mantid. *Science, 205,* 825–826.

Rock, I., & Victor, J. (1964). Vision and touch: An experimentally

created conflict between the two senses. *Science, 143,* 594–596.

Rodin, J. (1976). Menstruation, reattribution, and competence. *Journal of Personality and Social Psychology, 33,* 345.

Rodin, J., & Slochower, J. (1976). Externality in the obese: The effects of environmental responsiveness on weight. *Journal of Personality and Social Psychology, 33,* 338–344.

Rogers, C. R. (1951). *Client-centered therapy.* Boston: Houghton Mifflin.

Rogers, C. R. (1959). A theory of therapy, personality and interpersonal relationships, as developed in the client-centered framework. In S. Koch (Ed.), *Psychology: A study of science,* Vol. 3. New York: McGraw-Hill.

Rogers, C. R. (1963). The actualizing tendency in relationship to "motives" and to consciousness. In M. R. Jones (Ed.), *Nebraska Symposium on Motivation.* Lincoln, NE: University of Nebraska Press.

Rogers, C. R. (1974). In retrospect: 46 years. *American Psychologist, 29,* 115–123.

Rogers, C. R., & Dymond, R. F. (Eds.) (1954). *Psychotherapy and personality change.* Chicago: University of Chicago Press.

Rogers, R. (1987). APA's position on the insanity defense: Empiricism versus emotionalism. *American Psychologist, 42,* 840–848.

Rogers, R. W. (1983). Preventive health psychology: An interface of social and clinical psychology. *Journal of Social and Clinical Psychology, 1,* 120–127.

Rogers, R. W., & Deckner, C. W. (1975). Effects of fear appeals and physiological arousal upon emotions, attitudes, and cigarette smoking. *Journal of Personality and Social Psychology, 32,* 222–230.

Rohsenow, D. J. (1983). Drinking habits and expectancies about alcohol's effects for self versus others. *Journal of Consulting and Clinical Psychology, 51,* 752–756.

Rollin, B. E. (1985). The moral status

of research animals in psychology. *American Psychologist, 40*, 920–926.

Rosch, E. (1974). Linguistic relativity. In A. Silverstein (Ed.), *Human communication: Theoretical perspectives*. New York: Halsted Press.

Rosenbaum, M., & Hadari, D. (1985). Personal efficacy, external locus of control, and perceived contingency of parental reinforcement among depressed, paranoid, and normal subjects. *Journal of Personality and Social Psychology, 49*, 539–547.

Rosenberg, M. S. (1987). New directions for research on the psychological maltreatment of children. *American Psychologist, 42*, 166–171.

Rosenberg, M. S., & Repucci, N. D. (1985). Primary prevention of child abuse. *Journal of Consulting and Clinical Psychology, 53*, 576–585.

Rosenhan, D. L. (1973). On being sane in insane places. *Science, 179*, 250–258.

Rosenhan, D. L., Salovey, P., & Hargis, K. (1981). The joys of helping. *Journal of Personality and Social Psychology, 40*, 899–905.

Rosenthal, D. M. (1980). The modularity and maturation of cognitive capacities. *Behavior and Brain Science, 3*, 32–34.

Rosenzweig, M. R. (1969). Effects of heredity and environment on brain chemistry, brain anatomy, and learning ability in the rat. In M. Manosovitz et al. (Eds.), *Behavioral genetics*. New York: Appleton.

Rotter, J. B. (1966). Generalized expectancies for internal versus external control of reinforcement. *Psychological Monographs, 80*(609).

Rotter, J. B. (1971). External control and internal control. *Psychology Today, 5*, 37–42, 58–59.

Rotter, J. B. (1972). Beliefs, social attitudes, and behavior: A social learning analysis. In J. B. Rotter, J. E. Chance, & E. J. Phares (Eds.), *Applications of a social learning theory of personality*. New York: Holt, Rinehart and Winston.

Rotter, J. B. (1975). Some problems and misconceptions related to the construct of internal versus external control of reinforcement. *Journal of Consulting and Clinical Psychology, 43*, 56–67.

Roueche, B. (1980). *The medical detectives*. New York: Truman Talley.

Rounsaville, B. J., Chevron, E. S., Prusoff, B. A., Elkin, I., Imber, S., Sotsky, S., & Watkins, J. (1987). The relation between specific and general dimensions of the psychotherapy process in interpersonal psychotherapy of depression. *Journal of Consulting and Clinical Psychology, 55*, 379–384.

Rubin, Z. (1970). Measurement of romantic love. *Journal of Personality and Social Psychology, 16*, 265–273.

Ruderman, A. J. (1985). Dysphoric mood and overeating: A test of restraint theory's disinhibition hypothesis. *Journal of Abnormal Psychology, 94*, 78–85.

Rundus, D. (1971). Analysis of rehearsal processes in free recall. *Journal of Experimental Psychology, 89*, 63–77.

Ruopp, R. (1979). *Children at the center*. Cambridge, MA: Abt Associates.

Ruppenthal, G. C., Arling, G. L., Harlow, H. F., Sackett, G. P., & Suomi, S. J. (1976). A ten-year perspective on motherless-mother monkey behavior. *Journal of Abnormal Psychology, 85*, 341–349.

Russell, J. A., & Mehrabian, A. (1977). Evidence for a three-factor theory of emotions. *Journal of Research in Personality, 11*, 273–294.

Rutkowski, G. K., Gruder, C. L., & Romer, D. (1983). Group cohesiveness, social norms, and bystander intervention. *Journal of Personality and Social Psychology, 44*, 545–552.

Rutter, M. (1979). Separation experiences: A new look at an old topic. *Pediatrics, 95*(1), 147–154.

Sackeim, H. A. (1985). The case for ECT. *Psychology Today, 19*(6), 36–40.

Sackeim, H. A., Portnoy, S., Neeley, P., Steif, B. L., Decina, P., & Malitz, S. (1985). Cognitive consequences of low dosage ECT. In S. Malitz & H. A. Sackeim (Eds.), *Electroconvulsive therapy: Clinical and basic research issues*. New York: Annals of the New York Academy of Science.

Sadalla, E. K., Kenrick, D. T., & Vershure, B. (1987). Dominance and heterosexual attraction. *Journal of Personality and Social Psychology, 52*, 730–738.

Sadker, M., & Sadker, D. (1985). Sexism in the schoolroom of the 1980s. *Psychology Today, 19*(3), 54–57.

Saegert, S. C., & Jellison, J. M. (1970). Effects of initial level of response competition and frequency of exposure to liking and exploratory behavior. *Journal of Personality and Social Psychology, 16*, 553–558.

Safer, M. A. (1980). Attributing evil to the subject, not the situation: Student reactions to Milgram's film on obedience. *Personality and Social Psychology Bulletin, 6*, 205–209.

Sagar, H. A., & Schofield, J. W. (1980). Racial and behavioral cues in black and white children's perceptions of ambiguously aggressive acts. *Journal of Personality and Social Psychology, 39*, 590–598.

Salapatek, P. (1975). Pattern perception in early infancy. In L. B. Cohen & P. Salapatek (Eds.), *Infant perception: From sensation to cognition*, Vol. 1. New York: Academic Press.

Sanders, B., & Soares, M. P. (1986). Sexual maturation and spatial ability in college students. *Developmental Psychology, 22*, 199–203.

Sanders, B., Soares, M. P., & D'Aquila, J. M. (1982). The sex difference on one test of spatial visualization: A nontrivial difference. *Child Development, 53*, 1106–1110.

Santee, R. T., & Maslach, C. (1982). To agree or not to agree: Personal dissent amid social pressure to conform. *Journal of Personality and Social Psychology, 42,* 690–700.

Sarbin, T. R., & Nucci, L. P. (1973). Self-reconstitution processes: A proposal for reorganizing the conduct of confirmed smokers. *Journal of Abnormal Psychology, 81,* 182–195.

Satir, V. (1967). *Conjoint family therapy.* Palo Alto, CA: Science and Behavior Books.

Satow, K. L. (1975). Social approval and helping. *Journal of Experimental Social Psychology, 11,* 501–509.

Savage-Rumbaugh, E. S., & Rumbaugh, D. M. (1980). Language analogue project I phase II: Theory and tactics. In K. E. Nelson (Ed.), *Children's language, Vol. 2.* New York: Gardner Press.

Savage-Rumbaugh, E. S., Rumbaugh, D. M., & Boysen, S. (1980). Do apes use language? *American Scientist, 68,* 49–61.

Savage-Rumbaugh, E. S., Rumbaugh, D. M., Smight, S. T., & Lawson, J. (1980). Reference: The linguistic essential. *Science, 210,* 922–924.

Sawrey, W. L., Conger, J. J., & Turrell, E. S. (1956). An experimental investigation of the role of psychological factors in the production of gastric ulcers in rats. *Journal of Comparative and Physiological Psychology, 49,* 457–461.

Sawrey, W. L., & Weisz, J. D. (1956). An experimental method of producing gastric ulcers. *Journal of Comparative and Physiological Psychology, 49,* 269–270.

Saxe, L., Dougherty, D., & Cross, T. (1985). The validity of polygraph testing: Scientific analysis and public controversy. *American Psychologist, 40,* 355–366.

Scarr, S. (1981a). Testing *for* children: Assessment and the many determinants of intellectual competence. *American Psychologist, 36,* 1159–1166.

Scarr, S. (1981b). *Race, social class, and individual differences in IQ.* Hillsdale, NJ: Erlbaum.

Scarr, S. (1985). An author's frame of mind. (Review of *Frames of mind,* by Howard Gardner). *New Ideas in Psychology, 3,* 95–100.

Scarr, S., & Kidd, K. K. (1983). Developmental behavior genetics. In M. Haith & J. Campos (Eds.), *Mussen handbook of child psychology.* New York: Wiley.

Scarr, S., Webber, P. L., Weinberg, R. A., & Wittig, M. A. (1981). Personality resemblance among adolescents and their parents in biologically related and adoptive families. *Journal of Personality and Social Psychology, 41,* 885–898.

Scarr, S., & Weinberg, R. A. (1976). IQ test performance of black children adopted by white families. *American Psychologist, 31,* 726–739.

Scarr, S., & Weinberg, R. A. (1977). Intellectual similarities within families of both adopted and biological children. *Intelligence, 1,* 170–191.

Scarr, S., & Weinberg, R. A. (1983). The Minnesota adoption studies: Genetic differences and malleability. *Child Development, 54,* 260–267.

Schachter, S. (1959). *The psychology of affiliation.* Stanford, CA: Stanford University Press.

Schachter, S. (1971a). *Emotion, obesity, and crime.* New York: Academic Press.

Schachter, S. (1971b). Some extraordinary facts about obese humans and rats. *American Psychologist, 26,* 129–144.

Schachter, S. (1982). Recidivism and self-cure of smoking and obesity. *American Psychologist, 37,* 436–444.

Schachter, S., & Gross, L. P. (1968). Manipulated time and eating behavior. *Journal of Personality and Social Psychology, 10,* 98–106.

Schachter, S., Kozlowski, L. T., & Silverstein, B. (1977). Effects of urinary pH on cigarette smoking. *Journal of Experimental Psychology: General, 106,* 13–19.

Schachter, S., & Latané, B. (1964). Crime, cognition, and the autonomic nervous system. In D. Levine (Ed.), *Nebraska Symposium on Motivation.* Lincoln, NE: University of Nebraska Press.

Schachter, S., & Rodin, J. (1974). *Obese humans and rats.* Washington, DC: Erlbaum/Halsted.

Schachter, S., & Singer, J. E. (1962). Cognitive, social, and physiological determinants of emotional state. *Psychological Review, 69,* 379–399.

Scheier, M. F., Buss, A. H., & Buss, D. M. (1978). Self-consciousness, self-report of aggressiveness, and aggression. *Journal of Research in Personality, 12,* 133–140.

Schiavi, R. C., et al. (1977). Luteinizing hormone and testosterone during nocturnal sleep: Relation to penile tumescent cycles. *Archives of Sexual Behavior, 6,* 97–104.

Schindler, B. A. (1985). Stress, affective disorders, and immune function. *Medical Clinics of North America, 69,* 585–597.

Schmauk, F. J. (1970). Punishment, arousal, and avoidance learning in sociopaths. *Journal of Abnormal Psychology, 76,* 443–453.

Schmidt, F. L., Hunter, J. E., & Pearlman, K. (1981). Task differences as moderators of aptitude test validity in selection: A red herring. *Journal of Applied Psychology, 66,* 161–185.

Schneider, B. H., & Byrne, B. M. (1987). Individualizing social skills training for behavior-disordered children. *Journal of Consulting and Clinical Psychology, 55,* 444–445.

Schotte, D. E., & Clum, G. A. (1982). Suicide ideation in a college population: A test of a model. *Journal of Consulting and Clinical Psychology, 50,* 690–696.

Schotte, D. E., & Clum, G. A. (1987). Problem-solving skills in suicidal psychiatric patients. *Journal of Consulting and Clinical Psychology, 55,* 49–54.

Schroeder, M. L., Schroeder, K. G., & Hare, R. D. (1983). Generalizability of a checklist for assessment of psychopathy. *Journal of Consulting and Clinical Psychology, 51,* 511–516.

Schuckit, M. A. (1987). Biological vulnerability to alcoholism. *Journal of Consulting and Clinical Psychology, 55,* 301–309.

Schulsinger, F. (1972). Psychopathy: Heredity and environment. *International Journal of Mental Health, 1,* 190–206.

Schultz, D. P. (1978). *Psychology and industry today.* New York: Macmillan.

Schwartz, M. (1978). *Physiological psychology.* Englewood Cliffs, NJ: Prentice-Hall.

Schwartz, R. M. (1982). Cognitive behavior modification: A conceptual review. *Clinical Psychology Review, 2,* 267–293.

Schwartz, R. M., & Gottman, J. M. (1976). Toward a task analysis of assertive behavior. *Journal of Consulting and Clinical Psychology, 44,* 910–920.

Schwarz, L. M., Foa, U. G., & Foa, E. B. (1983). Multichannel nonverbal communication: Evidence for combinatory rules. *Journal of Personality and Social Psychology, 45,* 274–281.

Scott, J. P., & Fuller, J. L. (1965). *Genetics and the social behavior of the dog.* Chicago: University of Chicago Press.

Seer, P. (1979). Psychological control of essential hypertension: Review of the literature and methodological critique. *Psychological Bulletin, 86,* 1015–1043.

Segal, M. W. (1974). Alphabet and attraction: An unobtrusive measure of the effect of propinquity in the field setting. *Journal of Personality and Social Psychology, 30,* 654–657.

Seligman, M. E. P. (1973). Fall into helplessness. *Psychology Today, 7,* 43–48.

Seligman, M. E. P., Abramson, L. Y., Semmel, A., & von Baeyer, C. (1979). Depressive attributional style. *Journal of Abnormal Psychology, 88,* 242–247.

Seligman, M. E. P., Kaslow, N. J., Alloy, L. B., Peterson, C., Tanenbaum, R. L., & Abramson, L. Y. (1984). Attributional style and depressive symptoms among children. *Journal of Abnormal Psychology, 93,* 235–238.

Seligman, M. E. P., & Rosenhan, D. L. (1984). *Abnormal psychology.* New York: W. W. Norton.

Selye, H. (1976). *The stress of life,* revised ed. New York: McGraw-Hill.

Selye, H. (1980). The stress concept today. In I. L. Kutash, L. B. Schlesinger, et al. (Eds.), *Handbook on stress and anxiety.* San Francisco: Jossey-Bass.

Senneker, P., & Hendrick, C. (1983). Androgyny and helping behavior. *Journal of Personality and Social Psychology, 45,* 916–925.

Serbin, L. A., Conner, J. M., Burchardt, C. J., & Citron, C. C. (1979). Effects of peer presence on sex typing of children's play behavior. *Journal of Experimental Child Psychology, 27,* 303–309.

Serlin, E. (1980). Emptying the nest: Women in the launching stage. In D. G. McGuigan (Ed.), *Women's lives: New theory, research, and policy.* Ann Arbor: University of Michigan, Center for Continuing Education of Women.

Seta, J. J. (1982). The impact of comparison processes on coactors' task performance. *Journal of Personality and Social Psychology, 42,* 281–291.

Shadish, W. R., Hickman, D., & Arrick, M. C. (1981). Psychological problems of spinal injury patients: Emotional distress as a function of time and locus of control. *Journal of Consulting and Clinical Psychology, 49,* 297.

Shanteau, J., & Nagy, G. (1979). Probability of acceptance in dating choice. *Journal of Personality and Social Psychology, 37,* 522–533.

Shapiro, D., & Goldstein, I. B. (1982). Behavioral perspectives on hypertension. *Journal of Consulting and Clinical Psychology, 50,* 841–859.

Shapiro, D. A., & Shapiro, D. (1982). Meta-analysis of comparative therapy outcome studies: A replication and refinement. *Psychological Bulletin, 92,* 581–594.

Shapley, R., & Enroth-Cugell, C. (1984). Visual adaptation and retinal gain controls. In N. Osborne & G. Chaders (Eds.), *Progress in retinal research, Vol. 3.* Oxford: Pergamon Press.

Shaw, E. D., Stokes, P. E., Mann, J. J., & Manevitz, A. Z. A. (1987). Effects of lithium carbonate on the memory and motor speed of bipolar patients. *Journal of Abnormal Psychology, 96,* 64–69.

Shaw, J. S. (1982). Psychological androgyny and stressful life events. *Journal of Personality and Social Psychology, 43,* 145–153.

Sheehy, G. (1976). *Passages: Predictable crises of adult life.* New York: Dutton.

Sheehy, G. (1981). *Pathfinders.* New York: Morrow.

Sheingold, K., & Tenney, Y. J. (1982). Memory for a salient childhood event. In U. Neisser (Ed.), *Memory observed: Remembering in natural contexts.* San Francisco: Freeman.

Shekelle, R. B., Gale, M., Ostfeld, A. M., & Paul, O. (1983). Hostility, risk of coronary heart disease, and mortality. *Psychosomatic Medicine, 45,* 109–114.

Sherif, M. (1966). *In common predicament: Social psychology of intergroup conflict and cooperation.* Boston: Houghton Mifflin.

Shiffman, S. (1982). Relapse following smoking cessation: A situational analysis. *Journal of Consulting and Clinical Psychology, 50,* 71–86.

Shiffman, S. (1984). Coping with temptations to smoke. *Journal of Consulting and Clinical Psychology, 52,* 261–267.

Shotland, R. L., & Heinold, W. D. (1985). Bystander response to arterial bleeding: Helping skills, the decision-making process, and differentiating the helping response. *Journal of Personality and Social Psychology, 49,* 347–356.

Siegler, R. S., & Liebert, R. M.

(1972). Effects of presenting relevant rules and complete feedback on the conservation of liquid quantity task. *Developmental Psychology, 7*, 133–138.

Siegman, A. W., & Feldstein, S. (Eds.) (1977). *Nonverbal behavior and communication.* Hillsdale, NJ: Erlbaum.

Silverstein, B. (1982). Cigarette smoking, nicotine addiction, and relaxation. *Journal of Personality and Social Psychology, 42*, 946–950.

Silverstein, B., Koslowski, L. T., & Schachter, S. (1977). Social life, cigarette smoking, and urinary pH. *Journal of Experimental Psychology: General, 106*, 20–23.

Singer, J. L. (1975). *The inner world of daydreaming.* New York: Harper & Row.

Singular, S. (1982). A memory for all seasonings. *Psychology Today, 16*(10), 54–63.

Sistrunk, F., & McDavid, J. W. (1971). Sex variable in conforming behavior. *Journal of Personality and Social Psychology, 17*, 200–207.

Skinner, B. F. (1938). *The behavior of organisms: An experimental analysis.* New York: Appleton.

Skinner, B. F. (1948). *Walden two.* New York: Macmillan.

Skinner, B. F. (1957). *Verbal behavior.* New York: Appleton.

Skinner, B. F. (1960). Pigeons in a pelican. *American Psychologist, 15*, 28–37.

Skinner, B. F. (1972). *Beyond freedom and dignity.* New York: Knopf.

Skinner, B. F. (1979). *The shaping of a behaviorist.* New York: Knopf.

Skinner, B. F. (1983). Intellectual self-management in old age. *American Psychologist, 38*, 239–244.

Skinner, B. F. (1987). Whatever happened to psychology as the science of behavior? *American Psychologist, 42*, 780–786.

Slade, M., & Biddle, W. (1982, October 31). Ideas and trends: Scientists find key to growth. *The New York Times,* p. E7.

Slater, E., & Shields, J. (1969). Genetic aspects of anxiety. In M. H. Luder (Ed.), *Studies of anxiety.* Ashford, England: Headley Brothers.

Slobin, D. I. (1971). *Psycholinguistics.* Glenville, IL: Scott, Foresman.

Slobin, D. I. (1973). Cognitive prerequisites for the development of grammar. In C. A. Ferguson & D. I. Slobin (Eds.), *Studies of child development.* New York: Holt, Rinehart and Winston.

Smedley, J. W., & Bayton, J. A. (1978). Evaluative race-class stereotypes by race and perceived class of subjects. *Journal of Personality and Social Psychology, 36*, 530–535.

Smith, B. M. (1971). *The polygraph in contemporary psychology.* San Francisco: Freeman.

Smith, C. P., & Graham, J. R. (1981). Behavioral correlates for the MMPI *F* scale and for a modified *F* scale for black and white psychiatric patients. *Journal of Consulting and Clinical Psychology, 49*, 455–459.

Smith, D. (1982). Trends in counseling and psychotherapy. *American Psychologist, 37*, 802–809.

Smith, D., King, M., & Hoebel, B. G. (1970). Lateral hypothalamic control of killing: Evidence for a cholinoceptive mechanism. *Science, 167*, 900–901.

Smith, G. F., & Dorfman, D. (1975). The effect of stimulus uncertainty on the relationship between frequency of exposure and liking. *Journal of Personality and Social Psychology, 31*, 150–155.

Smith, M. L., & Glass, G. V. (1977). Meta-analysis of psychotherapy outcome studies. *American Psychologist, 32*, 752–760.

Smith, M. L., Glass, G. V., & Miller, T. I. (1980). *The benefits of psychotherapy.* Baltimore: Johns Hopkins University Press.

Smith, R. E., & Winokur, G. (1983). Affective disorders. In R. E. Tarter (Ed.), *The child at psychiatric risk.* New York: Oxford University Press.

Smith, S. S., & Richardson, D. (1983). Amelioration of deception and harm in psychological research: The important role of debriefing. *Journal of Personality and Social Psychology, 44*, 1075–1082.

Smith, T. W. (1983). Change in irrational beliefs and the outcome of rational-emotive psychotherapy. *Journal of Consulting and Clinical Psychology, 51*, 156–157.

Smith, T. W., Snyder, C. R., & Perkins, S. C. (1983). The self-serving function of hypochondriacal complaints: Physical symptoms as self-handicapping strategies. *Journal of Personality and Social Psychology, 44*, 787–797.

Snarey, J. (1987). A question of morality. *Psychology Today, 21*(6), 6–8.

Snow, M. E., Jacklin, C. N., & Maccoby, E. E. (1983). Sex of child differences in father–child interaction at one year of age. *Child Development, 54*, 227–232.

Snyder, M., & Cunningham, M. R. (1975). To comply or not to comply: Testing the self-perception explanation of the "foot-in-the-door" phenomenon. *Journal of Personality and Social Psychology, 31*, 64–67.

Snyder, M., & DeBono, G. (1985). Appeals to image and claims about quality: Understanding the psychology of advertising. *Journal of Personality and Social Psychology, 49*, 586–597.

Snyder, M., Grether, J., & Keller, K. (1974). Staring and compliance: A field experiment on hitchhiking. *Journal of Applied Social Psychology, 4*, 165–170.

Snyder, M., Tanke, E. D., & Berscheid, E. (1977). Social perception and interpersonal behavior: On the self-fulfilling nature of social stereotypes. *Journal of Personality and Social Psychology, 35*, 656–666.

Snyder, S. H. (1977). Opiate receptors and internal opiates. *Scientific American, 236*, 44–56.

Snyder, S. H. (1980). *Biological aspects of mental disorder.* New York: Oxford University Press.

Snyder, S. H. (1984). Drug and neurotransmitter receptors in the brain. *Science, 224,* 22–31.

Sommer, R. (1969). *Personal space.* Englewood Cliffs, NJ: Prentice-Hall.

Sommers, S. (1981). Emotionality reconsidered: The role of cognition in emotional responsiveness. *Journal of Personality and Social Psychology, 41,* 553–561.

Sorce, J. F., Emde, R. N., Campos, J. J., & Klinnert, M. D. (1985). Maternal emotional signaling: Its effect on the visual-cliff behavior of 1-year-olds. *Developmental Psychology, 21,* 195–200.

Spanos, N. P., Radtke, H. L., & Dubreuil, D. L. (1982). Episodic and semantic memory in posthypnotic amnesia: A reevaluation. *Journal of Personality and Social Psychology, 43,* 565–573.

Spanos, N. P., Weekes, J. R., & Bertrand, L. D. (1985). Multiple personality: A social psychological perspective. *Journal of Abnormal Psychology, 94,* 362–376.

Spence, J. T., Helmreich, R., & Stapp, J. (1975). Ratings of self and peers on sex-role attributes and their relation to self-esteem and concepts of masculinity and femininity. *Journal of Personality and Social Psychology, 32,* 29–39.

Sperling, G. (1960). The information available in brief visual presentations. *Psychological Monographs, 74,* 498.

Sperry, R. W. (1974). Lateral specialization in the surgically separated hemispheres. In F. O. Schmitt & F. G. Worden (Eds.), *The neurosciences: Third study program.* Cambridge, MA: MIT Press.

Squire, L. R. (1986). Mechanisms of memory. *Science, 232,* 1612–1619.

Squire, L. R., Cohen, N. J., & Nadel, L. (1984). The medial temporal region and memory consolidations: A new hypothesis. In H. Weingartner & E. Parker (Eds.), *Memory consolidation.* Hillsdale, NJ: Erlbaum.

Staats, A. W., & Burns, G. L. (1981). Intelligence and child development: What intelligence is and how it is learned and functions. *Genetic Psychology Monographs, 104,* 237–301.

Stalonas, P. M., & Kirschenbaum, D. S. (1985). Behavioral treatments for obesity: Eating habits revisited. *Behavior Therapy, 16,* 1–14.

Stapp, J., Tucker, A. M., & VandenBos, G. R. (1985). Census of psychological personnel: 1983. *American Psychologist, 40,* 1317–1351.

Staub, E., Tursky, B., & Schwartz, G. (1971). Self-control and predictability: Their effects on reactions to aversive stimulation. *Journal of Personality and Social Psychology, 18,* 157–162.

Steck, L., Levitan, D., McLane, D., & Kelley, H. H. (1982). Care, need, and conceptions of love. *Journal of Personality and Social Psychology, 43,* 481–491.

Steele, C. M., & Southwick, L. L. (1985). Alcohol and social behavior I: The psychology of drunken excess. *Journal of Personality and Social Psychology, 48,* 18–34.

Steele, C. M., Southwick, L. L., & Critchlow, B. (1981). Dissonance and alcohol: Drinking your troubles away. *Journal of Personality and Social Psychology, 41,* 831–846.

Steinberg, L. D., Catalano, R., & Dooley, D. (1981). Economic antecedents of child abuse and neglect. Paper presented to the meeting of the Society for Research in Child Development, Boston.

Steiner, J. E. (1979). Facial expressions in response to taste and smell discrimination. In H. W. Reese & L. P. Lipsitt (Eds.), *Advances in child development and behavior,* Vol. 13. New York: Academic Press.

Steinmetz, J. L., Lewinsohn, P. M., & Antonuccio, D. O. (1983). Prediction of individual outcome in a group intervention for depression. *Journal of Consulting and Clinical Psychology, 51,* 331–337.

Stephan, C. W., & Langlois, J. H. (1984). Baby beautiful: Adult attributions of infant competence as a function of infant attractiveness. *Child Development, 55,* 576–585.

Stericker, A., & LeVesconte, S. (1982). Effect of brief training on sex-related differences in visual-spatial skill. *Journal of Personality and Social Psychology, 43,* 1018–1029.

Sternberg, R. J. (1979). Stalking the IQ quark. *Psychology Today, 13*(9), 42–54.

Sternberg, R. J. (1982, April). Who's intelligent? *Psychology Today,* pp. 30–39.

Sternberg, R. J. (1985). *Beyond IQ: A triarchic theory of human intelligence.* New York: Cambridge University Press.

Sternberg, R. J., Conway, B. E., Ketron, J. L., & Bernstein, M. (1981). People's conceptions of intelligence. *Journal of Personality and Social Psychology, 41,* 37–55.

Sternberg, R. J., & Grajek, S. (1984). The nature of love. *Journal of Personality and Social Psychology, 47,* 312–329.

Stevenson, H. W., Lee, S. Y., & Stigler, J. W. (1986). Mathematics achievement of Chinese, Japanese, and American children. *Science 231,* 693–699.

Stevenson, H. W., Stigler, J. W., Shin-Ying, L., Lucker, G. W., Kitamura, S., & Hsu, C. (1985). Cognitive performance and academic achievement of Japanese, Chinese, and American children. *Child Development, 56,* 718–734.

Stewart, V., & Stewart, A. (1982) *Business applications of repertory grid.* London: McGraw-Hill.

Stier, D. S., & Hall, J. A. (1984). Gender differences in touch: An empirical and theoretical review. *Journal of Personality and Social Psychology, 47,* 440–459.

Stipp, D. (1987, May 7). Breast-cancer risk may increase 40% with moderate alcohol use, studies say. *The Wall Street Journal,* p. 34.

Stock, M. B., & Smythe, P. M. (1963). Does undernutrition during infancy inhibit brain growth and subsequent intellectual development? *Archives of Disorders in Childhood, 38,* 546–552.

Stone, A. A., & Neale, J. M. (1984). Effects of severe daily events on mood. *Journal of Personality and Social Psychology, 46,* 137–144.

Storandt, M. (1983). Psychology's response to the graying of America. *American Psychologist, 38,* 323–326.

Storms, M. D. (1980). Theories of sexual orientation. *Journal of Personality and Social Psychology, 38,* 783–792.

Strahan, R. F. (1981). Time urgency, Type A behavior, and effect strength. *Journal of Consulting and Clinical Psychology, 49,* 134.

Strauss, M. A., Gelles, R., & Steinmetz, S. (1979). *Behind closed doors: A survey of family violence in America.* Garden City, NY: Doubleday.

Stretch, R. H. (1986). Posttraumatic stress disorder among Vietnam and Vietnam-era veterans. In C. R. Figley (Ed.), *Trauma and its wake: Vol. 2. Traumatic stress theory, research, and intervention.* New York: Brunner/Mazel.

Stretch, R. H. (1987). Posttraumatic stress disorder among U.S. army reservists: Reply to Nezu and Carnevale. *Journal of Consulting and Clinical Psychology, 55,* 272–273.

Strom, J. C., & Buck, R. W. (1979). Staring and participants' sex: Physiological and subjective reactions. *Personality and Social Psychology Bulletin, 5,* 114–117.

Strube, M. J., Berry, J. M., Goza, B. K., & Fennimore, D. (1985). Type A behavior, age, and psychological well being. *Journal of Personality and Social Psychology, 49,* 203–218.

Strube, M. J., & Werner, C. (1985). Relinquishment of control and the Type A behavior pattern. *Journal of Personality and Social Psychology, 48,* 688–701.

Stunkard, A. J. (1959). Obesity and the denial of hunger. *Psychosomatic Medicine, 1,* 281–289.

Sussman, N. M., & Rosenfeld, H. M. (1982). Influence of culture, language, and sex on conversational distance. *Journal of Personality and Social Psychology, 42,* 66–74.

Sweeney, P. D., & Gruber, K. L. (1984). Selective exposure: Voter information preferences and the Watergate affair. *Journal of Personality and Social Psychology, 46,* 1208–1221.

Swensen, C. H. (1983). A respectable old age. *American Psychologist, 38,* 327–334.

Symons, D. (1979). *The evolution of human sexuality.* New York: Oxford University Press.

Szucko, J. J., & Kleinmuntz, B. (1981). Statistical versus clinical lie detection. *American Psychologist, 36,* 488–496.

Taylor, C. B., Farquhar, J. W., Nelson, E., & Agras, D. (1977). Relaxation therapy and high blood pressure. *Archives of General Psychiatry, 34,* 339–343.

Taylor, S. P., & Epstein, S. (1967). Aggression as a function of the interaction of the sex of the aggressor and the sex of the victim. *Journal of Personality, 35,* 474–486.

Taylor, W. N. (1985). Super athletes made to order. *Psychology Today, 19*(5), 62–66.

Teders, S. J., Blanchard, E. B., Andrasik, F., Jurish, S. E., Neff, D. F., & Arena, J. G. (1984). Relaxation training for tension headache: Comparative efficacy and cost-effectiveness of a minimal-therapist-contact versus a therapist-delivered procedure. *Behavior Therapy, 15,* 59–70.

Télégdy, G. (1977). Prenatal androgenization of primates and humans. In J. Money & H. Musaph (Eds.), *Handbook of sexology.* Amsterdam: Excerpta Medica.

Terkel, J., & Rosenblatt, J. S. (1972). Humoral factors underlying maternal behavior at parturition: Cross transfusion between freely moving rats. *Journal of Comparative and Physiological Psychology, 80,* 365–371.

Terrace, H. S. (1980). *Nim: A chimpanzee who learned sign language.* New York: Knopf.

Terrace, H. S. (1987). Reply to Bernstein and Kent. *American Psychologist, 42,* 273.

Terrace, H. S., Petitto, L. A., Sanders, R. J., & Bever, T. G. (1980). On the grammatical capacity of apes. In K. E. Nelson (Ed.), *Children's language, Vol. 2.* New York: Gardner Press.

Tetlock, P. E. (1983). Accountability and complexity of thought. *Journal of Personality and Social Psychology, 45,* 74–83.

Thigpen, C. H., & Cleckley, H. M. (1984). On the incidence of multiple personality disorder. *International Journal of Clinical and Experimental Hypnosis, 32,* 63–66.

Thoits, P. A. (1983). Dimensions of life events as influences upon the genesis of psychological distress and associated conditions: An evaluation and synthesis of the literature. In H. B. Kaplan (Ed.), *Psychosocial stress: Trends in theory and research.* New York: Academic Press.

Thompson, W. C., Cowan, C. L., & Rosenhan, D. L. (1980). Focus of attention mediates the impact of negative affect on altruism. *Journal of Personality and Social Psychology, 38,* 291–300.

Thurstone, L. L. (1938). Primary mental abilities. *Psychometric Monographs, 1.*

Thurstone, L. L., & Thurstone, T. G. (1963). *SRA primary abilities.* Chicago: Science Research.

Tice, D. M., & Baumeister, R. F. (1985). Masculinity inhibits helping in emergencies: Personality does predict the bystander effect. *Journal of Personality and Social Psychology, 49,* 420–428.

Tobias, S. (1982, January). Sexist equations. *Psychology Today,* pp. 14–17.

Tolman, E. C., & Honzik, C. H. (1930). Introduction and removal of reward, and maze performance in rats. *University of California Publications in Psychology, 4,* 257–275.

Torgersen, S. (1983). Genetic factors in anxiety disorders. *Archives of General Psychiatry, 40,* 1085–1089.

Toufexis, A. (1982, March 8). Report from the surgeon general. *Time Magazine,* pp. 72–73.

Touhey, J. C. (1972). Comparison of two dimensions of attitude similarity on heterosexual attraction. *Journal of Personality and Social Psychology, 23,* 8–10.

Touhey, J. C. (1974). Effects of additional women professionals on ratings of occupational prestige and desirability. *Journal of Personality and Social Psychology, 29,* 86–89.

Tryon, R. C. (1940). Genetic differences in maze learning in rats. *Yearbook of the National Society for Studies in Education, 39,* 111–119.

Tucker, J. A., Vuchinich, R. E., & Sobell, M. B. (1981). Alcohol consumption as a self-handicapping strategy. *Journal of Abnormal Psychology, 90,* 220–230.

Turkington, C. (1983). Drugs found to block dopamine receptors. *APA Monitor, 14,* 11.

Turkington, C. (1984). Hormones in rats found to control sexual behavior. *APA Monitor, 15*(11), 40–41.

Turkington. C. (1985). Taste inhibitors. *APA Monitor, 16*(10), 3.

Turner, J. S., & Helms, D. B. (1983). *Life span development.* New York: Holt, Rinehart and Winston.

Turner, R. H., & Killian, L. M. (1972). *Collective behavior.* Englewood Cliffs, NJ: Prentice-Hall.

Turner, S. M. (1987). Psychopathology in the offspring of anxiety disorders patients. *Journal of Consulting and Clinical Psychology, 55,* 229–235.

Tversky, A., & Kahneman, D. (1974). Judgment under uncertainty: Heuristics and biases. *Science, 185,* 1124–1131.

Tzuriel, D. (1984). Sex role typing and ego identity in Israeli, Oriental, and Western adolescents. *Journal of Personality and Social Psychology, 46,* 440–457.

Ugwuegbu, D. C. E. (1979). Racial and evidential factors in juror attribution of legal responsibility. *Journal of Experimental Social Psychology, 15,* 133–146.

Umberson, D., & Hughes, M. (1984, August). The impact of physical attractiveness on achievement and psychological well-being. Paper presented at the meeting of the American Sociological Association, San Antonio.

Underwood, B., & Moore, B. S. (1981). Sources of behavioral consistency. *Journal of Personality and Social Psychology, 40,* 780–785.

Unger, R. K., Hilderbrand, M., & Madar, T. (1982). Physical attractiveness and assumptions about social deviance: Some sex-by-sex comparisons. *Personality and Social Psychology Bulletin, 8,* 293–301.

U.S. Congress (1983, November). *Scientific validity of polygraph testing: A research review and evaluation* (OTA-TM-H-15). Washington, DC: Office of Technology Assessment.

Vaillant, G. E. (1982). *The natural history of alcoholism.* Cambridge, MA: Harvard University Press.

Vaillant, G. E., & Milofsky, E. S. (1982). The etiology of alcoholism. *American Psychologist, 37,* 494–503.

Valenstein, E. S. (1978). Science-fiction fantasy and the brain. *Psychology Today, 12*(7), 28–39.

Valenstein, E. S. (1980). *The psychosurgery debate.* San Francisco: W. H. Freeman.

Valins, S. (1966). Cognitive effects of false heart-rate feedback. *Journal of Personality and Social Psychology, 4,* 400–408.

Vallis, M., McCabe, S. B., & Shaw, B. F. (1986, June). The relationships between therapist skill in cognitive therapy and general therapy skill. Paper presented to the annual meeting of the Society for Psychotherapy Research, Wellesley, MA.

Van der Pligt, J., & Eiser, J. R. (1983). Actors' and observers' attributions, self-serving bias, and positivity bias. *European Journal of Social Psychology, 13,* 95–104.

Van Dyke, C., & Byck, R. (1982). Cocaine. *Scientific American, 44*(3), 128–141.

Vestre, N. D. (1984). Irrational beliefs and self-reported depressed mood. *Journal of Abnormal Psychology, 93,* 239–241.

Visintainer, M. A., Volpicelli, J. R., & Seligman, M. E. P. (1982). Tumor rejection in rats after inescapable or escapable shock. *Science, 216*(23), 437–439.

Von Békésy, G. (1957, August). The ear. *Scientific American,* pp. 66–78.

Waber, D. P., Mann, M. B., Merola, J., & Moylan, P. M. (1985). Physical maturation rate and cognitive performance in early adolescence: A longitudinal examination. *Developmental Psychology, 21,* 666–681.

Wachtel, P. L. (1982). What can dynamic therapies contribute to behavior therapy? *Behavior Therapy, 13,* 594–609.

Walker, A. M., Rablen, R. A., & Rogers, C. R. (1960). Development of a scale to measure process changes in psychotherapy. *Journal of Clinical Psychology, 16,* 79–85.

Walker, B. B. (1983). Treating stomach disorders: Can we reinstate regulatory processes? In W. E. Whitehead & R. Holzl (Eds.), *Psychophysiology of the gastrointestinal tract.* New York: Plenum Press.

Wallis, C. (1985). Gauging the fat of the land. *Time,* February 25, 1985, p. 72.

Walsh, B. T., Stewart, J. M., Roose, S. P., Gladis, M. A., & Glassman, A. H. (1984). Treatment of bulimia with phenelzine: A double-blind, placebo-controlled study. *Archives of General Psychiatry, 41,* 1105–1109.

Walstedt, J. J., Geis, F. L., & Brown, V. (1980). Influence of television commercials on women's self-confidence and independent judgment. *Journal of Personality and Social Psychology, 38,* 203–210.

Walster, E., Aronson, E., & Abrahams, D. (1966a). On increasing the persuasiveness of a low prestige communicator. *Journal of Experimental Social Psychology, 2,* 325–342.

Walster, E., Aronson, E., Abrahams, D., & Rottman, L. (1966b). Importance of physical attractiveness in dating behavior. *Journal of Personality and Social Psychology, 4,* 508–516.

Walster, E., & Walster, G. W. (1978). *A new look at love.* Reading, MA: Addison-Wesley.

Walster, E., Walster, G. W., Piliavin, J., & Schmidt, L. (1973). "Playing hard to get": Understanding an elusive phenomenon. *Journal of Personality and Social Psychology, 26,* 113–121.

Walton, S. (1985). Girls and science: The gap remains. *Psychology Today, 19*(6), 14.

Watkins, M. J., Ho, E., & Tulving, E. (1976). Context effects on recognition memory for faces. *Journal of Verbal Learning and Verbal Behavior, 15,* 505–518.

Watson, J. B. (1913). Psychology as the behaviorist views it. *Psychological Review, 20,* 158–177.

Watson, J. B. (1924). *Behaviorism.* New York: Norton.

Watson, J. B., & Rayner, R. (1920). Conditioned emotional reactions. *Journal of Experimental Psychology, 3,* 1–14.

Watson, S. J., Berger, P. A., Akil, H., Mills, M. J., & Barchas, J. D. (1978). Effects of naloxone on schizophrenia: Reduction in hallucinations in a subpopulation of subjects. *Science, 201,* 73–76.

Watt, N. F., Grubb, T. W., & Erlenmeyer-Kimling, L. (1982). Social, emotional, and intellectual behavior among children at high risk for schizophrenia. *Journal of Consulting and Clinical Psychology, 50,* 171–181.

Weber, R., & Crocker, J. (1983). Cognitive processes in the revision of stereotypic beliefs. *Journal of Personality and Social Psychology, 45,* 961–977.

Wechsler, D. (1939). *The measurement of adult intelligence.* Baltimore: Williams & Wilkins.

Wechsler, D. (1975). Intelligence defined and undefined: A relativistic appraisal. *American Psychologist, 30,* 135–139.

Wegner, D. M. (1979). Hidden Brain Damage Scale. *American Psychologist, 34,* 192–193.

Weil, G., & Goldfried, M. R. (1973). Treatment of insomnia in an eleven-year-old child through self-relaxation. *Behavior Therapy, 4,* 282–294.

Weinberg, R. S., Yukelson, S., & Jackson, A. (1980). Effect of public and private efficacy expectations on competitive performance. *Journal of Sport Psychology, 2,* 340–349.

Weinberg, S. L., & Richardson, M. S. (1981). Dimensions of stress in early parenting. *Journal of Consulting and Clinical Psychology, 49,* 688–693.

Weiner, H., Thaler, M., Rieser, M. F., & Mirsky, I. A. (1957). Relation of specific psychological characteristics to rate of gastric secretion. *Psychosomatic Medicine, 17,* 1–10.

Weiner, M. J., & Wright, F. E. (1973). Effects of undergoing arbitrary discrimination upon subsequent attitudes toward a minority group. *Journal of Applied Social Psychology, 3,* 94–102.

Weiss, J. M. (1982, August). A model for the neurochemical study of depression. Paper presented to the American Psychological Association, Washington, DC.

Weissman, M., Klerman, C., Prusoff, B., Sholomkas, D., & Padin, N. (1981). Depressed outpatients: Results one year after treatment with drugs and/or interpersonal psychotherapy. *Archives of General Psychiatry, 18,* 51–55.

Wender, P. H., Rosenthal, R., Kety, S., Schulsinger, F., & Weiner, J. (1974). Cross-fostering: A research strategy for clarifying the role of genetic and experiential factors in the etiology of schizo-

phrenia. *Archives of General Psychiatry, 30,* 121–128.

Werner, C. M., Brown, B. B., & Damron, G. (1981). Territorial marking in a game arcade. *Journal of Personality and Social Psychology, 41,* 1094–1104.

West, M. A. (1985). Meditation and somatic arousal reduction. *American Psychologist, 40,* 717–719.

Wetzler, S. E., & Sweeney, J. A. (1986). Childhood amnesia. In D. C. Rubin (Ed.), *Autobiographical memory.* New York: Cambridge University Press.

Wexler, D. A., & Butler, J. M. (1976). Therapist modification of client expressiveness in client-centered therapy. *Journal of Consulting and Clinical Psychology, 44,* 261–265.

Whalen, C. K., Henker, B., Swanson, J. M., Granger, D., Kliewer, W., & Spencer, J. (1987). Natural social behaviors in hyperactive children: Dose effects of methylphenidate. *Journal of Consulting and Clinical Psychology, 55,* 187–193.

Wheeler, L., Deci, L., Reis, H., & Zuckerman, M. (1978). *Interpersonal influence.* Boston: Allyn & Bacon.

Whitcher, S. J., & Fisher, J. D. (1979). Multidimensional reaction to therapeutic touch in a hospital setting. *Journal of Personality and Social Psychology, 37,* 87–96.

White, G. L., Fishbein, S., & Rutstein, J. (1981). Passionate love and the misattribution of arousal. *Journal of Personality and Social Psychology, 41,* 56–62.

Whitehall, M. H., Gainer, H., Cox, B. M., & Molineaux, C. J. (1983). Dynorphin-A-(1-8) is contained within vasopressin neurosecretory vesicles in rat pituitary. *Science, 222,* 1137–1139.

Whitehead, W. E., & Bosmajian, L. S. (1982). Behavioral medicine approaches to gastrointestinal disorders. *Journal of Consulting and Clinical Psychology, 50,* 972–983.

Whorf, B. (1956). *Language, thought, and reality.* New York: Wiley.

Whybrow, P. C., & Prange, A. J. (1981). A hypothesis of thyroid-catecholamine-receptor interaction. *Archives of General Psychiatry, 38,* 106–113.

Whyte, W. W. (1956). *The organization man.* New York: Simon & Schuster.

Wiens, A. N., & Menustik, C. E. (1983). Treatment outcome and patient characteristics in an aversion therapy program for alcoholism. *American Psychologist, 38,* 1089–1096.

Wiggins, J. S., Wiggins, N., & Conger, J. C. (1968). Correlates of heterosexual somatic preference. *Journal of Personality and Social Psychology, 10,* 82–90.

Wilcoxon, L. A., Shrader, S. L., & Sherif, C. W. (1976). Daily self-reports on activities, life events, moods, and somatic changes during the menstrual cycle. *Psychosomatic Medicine, 38,* 399.

Wilder, D. A. (1977). Perception of groups, size of opposition, and social influence. *Journal of Experimental Social Psychology, 13,* 253–268.

Wilder, D. A., & Thompson, J. E. (1980). Intergroup contact with independent manipulations of ingroup and out-group interaction. *Journal of Personality and Social Psychology, 38,* 589–603.

Willerman, L. (1977). *The psychology of individual and group differences.* San Francisco: Freeman.

Williams, K., Harkins, S., & Latané, B. (1981). Identifiability as a deterrant to social loafing. *Journal of Personality and Social Psychology, 40,* 303–311.

Williams, R. L. (1974). Scientific racism and IQ: The silent mugging of the black community. *Psychology Today, 8*(5).

Williams, R. M., Goldman, M. S., & Williams, D. L. (1981). Expectancy and pharmacological effects of alcohol on human cognitive and motor performance: The compensation for alcohol effect. *Journal of Abnormal Psychology, 90,* 267–270.

Wilson, G. T. (1982). Psychotherapy process and procedure: The behavioral mandate. *Behavior Therapy, 13,* 291–312.

Wilson, G. T. (1987). Cognitive studies in alcoholism. *Journal of Consulting and Clinical Psychology, 55,* 325–331.

Wilson, G. T., & Lawson, D. M. (1978). Expectancies, alcohol, and sexual arousal in women. *Journal of Abnormal Psychology, 87,* 358–367.

Wilson, G. T., Lawson, D. M., & Abrams, D. B. (1978). Effects of alcohol on sexual arousal in male alcoholics. *Journal of Abnormal Psychology, 87,* 609–616.

Wilson, G. T., Leaf, R. C., & Nathan, P. E. (1975). The aversive control of excessive alcohol consumption by chronic alcoholics in the laboratory setting. *Journal of Applied Behavior Analysis, 8,* 13–26.

Wilson, R. S. (1983). The Louisville twin study: Developmental synchronies in behavior. *Child Development, 54,* 298–316.

Wilson, T. D., & Linville, P. W. (1982). Improving the performance of college freshmen: Attribution therapy revisited. *Journal of Personality and Social Psychology, 42,* 367–376.

Wing, R. R., Epstein, L. H., & Shapira, B. (1982). The effect of increasing initial weight loss with the Scarsdale diet on subsequent weight loss in a behavioral treatment program. *Journal of Consulting and Clinical Psychology, 50,* 446–447.

Wirtz, P. W., & Harrell, A. V. (1987). Effects of postassault exposure to attack-similar stimuli on long-term recovery of victims. *Journal of Consulting and Clinical Psychology, 55,* 10–16.

Witkin, H. A., Mednick, S. A., Schulsinger, F., Bakkestrom, E., Christiansen, K. O., Goodenough, D. R., Hirschhorn, K., Lundsteen, C., Owen, D. R., Philip, J., Rubin, D. B., & Stocking, M. (1976). Criminality in XYY and XXY men. *Science, 193,* 547–555.

Wittig, M. A. (1985). Metatheoretical dilemmas in the psychology of gender. *American Psychologist, 40,* 800–811.

Wolinsky, J. (1982, March). Responsibility can delay aging. *APA Monitor,* pp. 14, 41.

Wolpe, J. (1958). *Psychotherapy by reciprocal inhibition.* Stanford, CA: Stanford University Press.

Wolpe, J. (1973). *The practice of behavior therapy.* New York: Pergamon Press.

Wolpe, J. (1985). Existential problems and behavior therapy. *The Behavior Therapist, 8*(7), 126–127.

Wolpe, J., & Lazarus, A. A. (1966). *Behavior therapy techniques.* New York: Pergamon Press.

Wood, W. (1982). Retrieval of attitude-relevant information from memory: Effects on susceptibility to persuasion and on intrinsic motivation. *Journal of Personality and Social Psychology, 42,* 798–810.

Wood, W., & Eagly, A. H. (1981). Steps in the positive analysis of causal attributions and message comprehension. *Journal of Personality and Social Psychology, 40,* 246–259.

Woolfolk, R. L., & McNulty, T. F. (1983). Relaxation treatment for insomnia: A component analysis. *Journal of Consulting and Clinical Psychology, 51,* 495–503.

Wright, J. C., & Huston, A. C. (1983). A matter of form: Potentials of television for young viewers. *American Psychologist, 38,* 835–843.

Wu, C., & Shaffer, D. R. (1987). Susceptibility to persuasive appeals as a function of source credibility and prior experience with the attitude object. *Journal of Personality and Social Psychology, 52,* 677–688.

Yarnold, P. R., & Grimm, L. G. (1982). Time urgency among coronary-prone individuals. *Journal of Abnormal Psychology, 91,* 175–177.

Yarnold, P. R., Mueser, K. T., & Grimm, L. G. (1985). Interpersonal dominance of Type A's in group discussion. *Journal of Abnormal Psychology, 94,* 233–236.

Yost, W. A., & Nielson, D. W. (1985). *Fundamentals of hearing, 2d ed.* New York: Holt, Rinehart and Winston.

Youkilis, H. D., & Bootzin, R. R. (1981). A psychophysiological perspective on the etiology and treatment of insomnia. In S. N. Haynes & L. R. Gannon (Eds.), *Psychosomatic disorders.* New York: Praeger.

Zaiden, J. (1982). Psychodynamic therapy: Clinical applications. In A. J. Rush (Ed.), *Short-term psychotherapies for depression.* New York: Guilford Press.

Zajonc, R. B. (1965). Social facilitation. *Science, 149,* 269–274.

Zajonc, R. B. (1968). Attitudinal effects of mere exposure. *Journal of Personality and Social Psychology, Monograph Supplement 2,* Vol. 9, 1–27.

Zajonc, R. B. (1980). Compresence. In P. Paulus (Ed.), *The psychology of group influence.* Hillsdale, NJ: Erlbaum.

Zajonc, R. B. (1984). On the primacy of affect. *American Psychologist, 39,* 117–123.

Zajonc, R. B. (1985). Cited in Bower, B. (1985). The face of emotion. *Science News, 128,* 12–13.

Zamansky, H. S., & Bartis, S. P. (1985). The dissociation of an experience. *Journal of Abnormal Psychology, 94,* 243–248.

Zigler, E., Abelson, W. D., Trickett, P. K., & Seitz, V. (1982). Is an intervention program necessary to improve economically disadvantaged children's IQ scores? *Child Development, 53,* 340–348.

Zigler, E., & Berman, W. (1983). Discerning the future of early childhood intervention. *American Psychologist, 38,* 894–906.

Zigler, E., & Butterfield, E. C. (1968). Motivational aspects of change in IQ test performance of culturally deprived nursery school children. *Child Development, 39,* 1–14.

Zigler, E., & Valentine, E. (Eds.) (1979). *Project Head Start: A legacy of the war on poverty.* New York: Free Press.

Zillmann, D., & Bryant, J. (1983). Effects of massive exposure to pornography. In N. M. Malamuth & E. Donnerstein (Eds.), *Pornography and sexual aggression.* New York: Academic Press.

Zimbardo, P. G. (1969). The human choice: Individuation, reason, and order versus deindividuation, impulse, and chaos. In W. J. Arnold & D. Levine (Eds.), *Nebraska Symposium on Motivation,* Vol. 17. Lincoln, NE: University of Nebraska Press.

Zimbardo, P. G., Ebbesen, E. B., & Maslach, C. (1977). *Influencing attitudes and changing behavior.* Reading, MA: Addison-Wesley.

Zubek, J. P. (1973). Review of effects of prolonged deprivation. In J. E. Rasmussen (Ed.), *Man in isolation and confinement.* Chicago: Aldine.

Zuckerman, M. (1974). The sensation-seeking motive. In B. Maher (Ed.), *Progress in Experimental Personality Research,* Vol. 7. New York: Academic Press.

Zuckerman, M. (1980). Sensation seeking. In H. London & J. Exner (Eds.), *Dimensions of personality.* New York: Wiley.

Zuckerman, M., Eysenck, S., & Eysenck, H. J. (1978). Sensation seeking in England and America: Cross-cultural, age, and sex comparisons. *Journal of Consulting and Clinical Psychology, 46,* 139–149.

Zuckerman, M., Klorman, R., Larrance, D. T., & Spiegel, N. H. (1981). Facial, autonomic, and subjective components of emotion. *Journal of Personality and Social Psychology, 41,* 929–944.

Zuckerman, M., Miserandino, M., & Bernieri, F. (1983). Civil inattention exists—in elevators. *Personality and Social Psychology Bulletin, 9,* 578–586.

Zuger, B. (1976). Monozygotic twins discordant for homosexuality: Report of a pair and significance of the phenomenon. *Comprehensive Psychiatry, 17,* 661–669.

Zuroff, D. C., & Mongrain, M. (1987). Dependency and self-criticism: Vulnerability factors for depressive affective states. *Journal of Abnormal Psychology, 96,* 14–22.

Photo Credits

ates; page 454, Wide World Photos; page 458 (both), Estate of Stanley Milgram; page 464, © Ray Ellis/Photo Researchers, Inc.; page 467, © Maslin 1985/The New Yorker Magazine, Inc.

Appendix: page 480 (left), Alan Carey/ The Image Works, Inc.; (right), David Wells/The Image Works; page 489, © Will McIntyre/Photo Researchers, Inc.; page 490, Mike Button/EKM-Nepenthe; page 497, David Parker/Photo Researchers, Inc.

Copyright Acknowledgments

QUESTIONNAIRE (p. 30). Crowne, D. P., and Marlowe, D. "A New Scale of Social Desirability Independent of Pathology," *Journal of Consulting Psychology,* 1960, *24*:351, Table 1. Copyright 1960 by the American Psychological Association. Reprinted by permission of the author.

TABLE 3.1 (p. 96). Adapted from Galanter, E. "Contemporary Psychophysics." In R. Brown, et al. (eds.), *New Directions in Psychology.* New York, Holt, Rinehart and Winston, 1962.

QUESTIONNAIRE (p. 252). From Zuckerman, M. "Sensation Seeking." in London, H., and Exner, J. (eds.). *Dimensions of Personality.* Copyright © 1980 John Wiley and Sons, Inc. Reprinted by permission of John Wiley and Sons, Inc.

TABLE 6.2 (p. 268). From Schachter, S. and Sinter, J. E. "Cognitive, Social and Physiological Determinants of Emotional State," *Psychological Review,* 1962, 69:379–399. Copyright 1962 by the American Psychological Association. Reprinted by permission of the author.

TABLE 8.1 (p. 331). From Erikson, E. H. *Childhood and Society.* Copyright 1963 by W. W. Norton and Company, Inc. Reprinted by permission of the publisher.

CHAPTER INTRODUCTION (Chapter 4). Abridged from *Brave New World,* pp. 21–24, by Aldous Huxley. Copyright © 1960 by Aldous Huxley. Reprinted by permission of Harper & Row Publishers, Inc.

NAME INDEX

Abbey, A., 449
Abelson, H., 245
Abikoff, H., 386
Abramowitz, C. V., 405
Adair, J. G., 33
Adams, N., 341
Adler, A., 328–330, 353
Adorno, T. W., 446
Agranoff, B., 181
Agras, W. S., 490
Agustsdottir, S., 493
Ahrens, A. H., 373
Aiken, P. A., 238
Ainsworth, M., 298, 315
Akil, H., 134
Albert, M. S., 312
Alexander, A. B., 490
Allen, A., 335
Allen, V. L., 463
Allgeier, A., 248
Allgeier, E. R., 248
Alloy, L. B., 373
Allport, G. W., 332–333, 353
Altman, I., 450
Amabile, T. M., 208
Amenson, C. S., 373
Amir, M., 248
Anastasi, A., 214, 219
Anderson, J. A., 264, 265
Andersson, B., 240
Andrews, G., 409
Aneshensel, C. S., 385
Apfelbaum, M., 239
Archer, R. P., 454
Aristotle, 9–10, 61
Aron, A. P., 268
Asch, S. E., 461–462
Atkinson, K., 196
Atkinson, R. C., 176
Avis, W. E., 452
Ayllon, T., 413
Azrin, N. H., 498

Bach, G. R., 435
Bahrick, H. P., 174–175
Baker, L. A., 222
Bakwin, H., 78

Bandura, A., 20–21, 29, 165, 183, 337, 341, 342, 364, 367, 368, 411
Bandura, M. M., 305
Banks, M. S., 286
Barber, T. X., 388, 497
Bard, P., 266
Bardwick, J. M., 74, 309
Barkley, R. A., 386
Barlow, D. H., 366, 382
Barnes, M., 455
Baron, R. A., 9, 32, 436, 439, 440, 449, 465, 492
Bartoshuk, L., 131–132
Basham, R. B., 403
Bates, E., 202
Batson, C. D., 468
Baucom, D. H., 238
Bauer, R. H., 62
Bauer, W. D., 302
Baum-Baicker, C., 385
Baumeister, R. F., 440
Baumrind, D., 33
Bayton, J. A., 446
Beauchamp, G., 130
Beck, A. T., 364, 409, 428
Beck, J., 115
Bell, A. G., 125
Belsky, J., 301–302
Bem, D. J., 335, 360
Bem, S. L., 308, 463
Berkowitz, L., 27, 468
Berlin, F., 249
Berman, J. S., 420
Berman, W., 223
Berne, E., 405, 406, 428
Bernstein, E., 191
Bernstein, W. M., 455
Berntzen, D., 492, 496
Berscheid, E., 451, 454, 455
Bertelson, A. D., 351
Binet, A., 214
Birch, H. G., 207
Birnbaum, H. J., 248
Blakely, M. K., 246
Blanchard, E. B., 489
Blanchard, R., 380

Blaney, P. H., 493
Blaszczynski, A., 248
Bloch, V., 180, 243
Blumberg, S. H., 374
Bodenhausen, G. V., 445
Bolles, R. C., 52
Booth-Kewley, S., 485, 493
Bootzin, R. R., 498, 499
Bornstein, M. H., 110, 204, 286
Bosmajian, L. S., 490
Bowen, G. H., 177
Bowlby, J., 298
Boyatzis, R. E., 25, 26
Bradley, E., 34
Bradley, R. H., 222, 223
Bray, D., 257
Bray, R. M., 464
Breckler, S. J., 436
Brent, E., 442
Bridges, K. M. B., 260–261, 271
Brigham, J. C., 454
Bronfenbrenner, U., 306
Brooks-Gunn, J., 74
Brown, B. B., 450
Brown, E. L., 132
Brown, P. L., 309, 310
Brown, R., 177, 190, 192, 193, 198, 201
Brownell, K. D., 237
Brownlee-Duffeck, M., 492
Bryant, J., 245
Buck, R. W., 451
Burgess, A., 411
Burkhart, B. R., 248
Burns, G. L., 454
Burnstein, E., 465
Burt, C., 221
Burt, M. R., 248, 249
Buss, A. H., 258
Buss, D. M., 455
Bussey, K., 306
Butcher, J. N., 351
Butler, J. M., 405
Butterfield, E. C., 220
Byck, R., 386

Byrne, B. M., 414
Byrne, D., 9, 32n, 436, 439, 440, 449, 452, 455, 465, 492

Cacioppo, J. T., 436, 437
Cadoret, R. J., 379
Calder, B. J., 494
Caldwell, B. M., 222, 223
Calne, D. B., 424
Campos, J. J., 286
Canfer, F., 496
Cannon, W. B., 266
Carlsmith, J. M., 442
Carlson, N. R., 58, 66
Carver, C. S., 468
Cash, T. F., 454
Cattell, R. B., 219, 220, 333, 353
Cerletti, U., 424–425
Cermak, L., 179
Chaney, E. F., 497
Charles, E., 490
Chesno, F. A., 379
Chomsky, N., 194–195, 201
Christopher, S. B., 18
Christy, P., 454
Cipolli, C., 243
Clark, E. V., 198, 202
Clark, M., 498
Cleckley, H. M., 370, 378
Clore, G. L., 450, 469
Cochran, S. D., 373
Cohen, D. B., 243
Cohen, L., 455
Colby, C. Z., 264
Comarr, A. E., 55
Conger, J. J., 383
Conley, F., 34
Conley, J. J., 335
Connor, J., 130
Cooney, J. L., 485
Cooper, A. J., 130
Cooper, H. M., 463
Cooper, J., 437, 442, 444
Cooper, R., 222
Cordes, C., 399

Corkin, S., 179, 426
Costa, E., 368
Covington, M. V., 440
Coyne, J. C., 374
Cozby, P. C., 304
Craik, F. I. M., 172
Crawford, C., 219
Creese, I., 377
Crockenburg, S. B., 209
Crocker, J., 437
Cronbach, L. J., 217
Crowne, D. P., 30, 31
Croyle, R. T., 442
Crusco, A. H., 450
Cunningham, M. R., 441
Curtiss, S. R., 31

Dabbs, J. M., 469
Dalton, K., 74
Daniels, D., 76
Darley, J. M., 446, 469
Darlington, R. B., 223
Darwin, C., 11, 261, 264
Davis, E. E., 446
Davis, J. H., 465
Davison, G. C., 342, 373,
    377, 386, 490
Deaux, K., 303, 304
DeBacker, G., 485
DeBono, G., 438
DeCasper, A. J., 287
Deckner, C. W., 268
Deffenbacher, K., 132
DeFries, J. C., 76, 78, 84,
    223
DeGree, C. E., 406
Delanoy, R. L., 180
Delgado, J., 66–67
Dembroski, T. M., 439
Democritus, 10
DePaulo, B. M., 450
Depue, R. A., 373
Dermer, M., 454
Dethier, V. G., 131
Deutsch, R. M., 435
DeValois, R. L., 110
Dewey, J., 11
Diamond, E. L., 490
Diamond, M., 47, 305
Diener, E., 467
Dill, C. A., 33
Dion, K. K., 454
Dix, D., 398
Dodge, K. A., 19
Dodge, L. J. T., 419
Dohrenwend, B. P., 482
Dohrenwend, B. S., 482
Dollard, J., 467
Donahoe, C. P., Jr., 239

Donnerstein, E., 27
Donnerstein, E. I., 246, 247
Dore-Boyce, K., 417
Dorfman, D., 439
Dovidio, J. H., 445
Drabman, R. S., 162
Driscoll, R., 455
Dutton, D. G., 268

Eagly, A. H., 439, 464
Ebbinghaus, H., 174, 184
Eckenrode, J., 373, 479
Eckert, E. D., 372
Eden, C., 345
Efran, M. G., 454
Eisler, R. M., 409
Ekman, P., 261–262, 264,
    268
Elardo, R., 222
Elliot, A. J., 202
Ellis, A., 364, 403, 408–409,
    428, 483–485
Ellison, G. D., 374
Ellsworth, P. C., 451
Epstein, L. H., 238
Erdman, H. P., 346
Erikson, E., 20, 311, 328,
    329, 331–332, 353
Eriksson, K., 83
Eysenck, H. J., 333–334,
    344, 353

Fabian, W. D., 388
Fagot, B. I., 304, 307, 308
Fallon, A. E., 372, 453
Faneslow, M. S., 52
Fantz, R. L., 286
Farina, A., 454
Farthing, G. W., 496
Farwell, C., 196
Fazio, R. H., 436, 437, 442,
    444
Feder, H. H., 248
Feldstein, S., 451
Fenigstein, A., 335
Ferguson, C. A., 196
Festinger, L., 442
Fifer, W. P., 287
Fisher, D. F., 167
Fisher, J. D., 450
Fishkin, S. M., 388
Fiske, D., 254
Fiske, S. T., 445
Flavell, J. H., 293
Flaxman, J., 500
Fleming, M. Z., 380
Floderus-Myrhed, B., 78
Foulkes, D., 243
Fouts, D. H., 191

Fouts, R. S., 191
Fox, S., 438
Frame, C. L., 19
Franklin, D., 129
Fraser, S. C., 440
Freedman, J. L., 440
Freedman, R. R., 498
French, G. M., 62
Freud, S., 15, 16, 20, 29, 37,
    178, 184, 233, 243, 278,
    305, 315, 322–329, 344,
    353, 363, 370, 400–402,
    428
Friedman, H. S., 485, 493
Friedman, M. I., 236
Frodi, A. M., 298, 302, 307
Fromm, E., 20, 328, 329
Fuller, J. L., 84
Funkenstein, D., 259
Fuster, J. M., 62
Fustero, S., 399

Galen, 334
Galizio, M., 440
Gallup, G. G., Jr., 34
Galvani, L., 47–48
Ganellen, R. J., 493
Garcia, J., 219
Gardner, B. T., 190
Gardner, R. A., 190
Garfield, S. L., 403
Garwood, S. G., 454
Gazzaniga, M. S., 66
Genovese, K., 468, 469
Gerard, H. B., 463
Gesell, A., 278
Getzels, J. W., 209
Gilbert, S. J., 460
Gilligan, C., 309
Gillis, J. S., 452
Gittelman, R., 386
Glasgow, R. E., 413, 498
Glass, D. C., 485
Glass, G. V., 403, 405–407,
    411, 420
Gleason, H. A., Jr., 204
Gleitman, L. R., 202
Goddard, H. H., 219
Goeders, N. E., 385
Gold, J. A., 456
Gold, P. E., 179
Goldfoot, D., 496
Goldfoot, D. A., 130, 245
Goldsmith, H. H., 76
Goldstein, M., 446
Goleman, D. J., 243
Goodall, J., 22–23
Goodenough, F., 219
Goodwin, D. W., 384

Götestam, K. G., 492, 496
Gotlib, I. H., 373
Gottfried, M. R., 498
Gottman, J. M., 440
Gould, R., 309
Goy, R. W., 245
Granberg, D., 442
Graziano, W., 452
Green, J., 448
Green, S. K., 452
Greenbaum, P., 451
Greenberg, J., 374
Greenberg, R., 243
Greene, J., 159
Grimm, L. G., 485
Grinspoon, L., 387
Gross, L. P., 237
Gross, P. H., 446
Grossman, M. I., 235
Groth, A. N., 248
Gruber, K. L., 439
Grünbaum, A., 328
Grush, J. E., 439
Guilford, J. P., 208, 209,
    211, 225

Haber, R. N., 95, 100, 170,
    171, 286
Hall, C. S., 243, 304
Hall, G. S., 11
Hall, J. V., 439, 450
Hall, R. G., 413, 501
Halmi, K. A., 372
Hamilton, P. A., 455
Hamm, N. H., 439
Hammen, C. L., 373
Harackiewicz, J. M., 409
Harbeson, G. E., 311
Harkins, S. G., 464
Harlow, H. F., 62, 299, 315
Harris, G. W., 245
Harris, M. B., 453
Harris, T. A., 405
Hart, B., 55
Hartmann, E. L., 242, 243
Haugvedt, C., 496
Harvey, R., 409
Hass, R. G., 439
Hassett, J., 130
Hatfield, E., 452
Haughton, E., 413
Hayes, S. L., 31
Haynes, S. G., 485
Haynes, S. N., 498
Hearst, P., 442–444,
    447–448
Heath, R., 68
Heaton, R. K., 388
Heffler, D., 498

Heider, F., 441
Heiman, J. R., 246
Heingartner, A., 439
Heinold, W. D., 468
Helmholtz, H. von, 110
Helson, R., 309–311
Hemstone, M., 446
Hendrick, C., 313, 440
Hennigan, K. M., 439
Hensley, W. E., 469
Hering, E., 110
Herman, C. P., 239, 372
Hershenson, M., 95, 100, 286
Heston, L. L., 377
Hill, C., 258
Hite, S., 29
Hobson, J. A., 243
Hoepfner, R., 208
Hoffman, L., 222
Hoffman, M. L., 468
Hofman-Plotkin, D., 302
Holahan, C. J., 482
Holmes, D. S., 485
Holmes, T. H., 479–482
Honzik, C. H., 165
Horn, J. M., 222
Horney, K., 20, 329–331, 353
Horvath, T., 452
Houston, B. K., 485
Howard, J. A., 455
Hrncir, E. J., 214
Huba, G. J., 385
Hugdahl, K., 367
Hughes, M., 454
Hughes, P. L., 372
Hull, C., 233
Hull, J. G., 385, 493
Hurvich, L. M., 110
Hutchings, B., 379
Huxley, A., 85, 144
Hyde, J. S., 303

Israel, A. C., 238
Ivey, M. E., 44
Izard, C. E., 260, 261, 266, 374

Jacklin, C. N., 303, 304, 307
Jackson, J. M., 464
Jackson, P. W., 209
Jacobs, G. H., 110
Jacobs, T. J., 490
James, H., 11
James, W., 11, 37, 166, 233, 266, 269, 286
Janicak, P. G., 425
Janis, I. L., 440, 466

Jankowicz, A. D., 345
Janowitz, H. D., 235
Jaremko, M. E., 367
Jaspars, J., 446
Jellison, J. M., 439, 448, 455
Jensen, A., 212, 218, 220, 225
Johnson, D. L., 223
Johnson, J. H., 349
Johnson, S. M., 417
Johnson, V. E., 382, 419
Jones, E., 448
Jones, M. C., 151
Jorgensen, C., 379
June, C., 329, 334, 344, 353
Jurkovic, G. J., 19
Jus, A., 424

Kagan, J., 76, 306
Kalin, R., 455
Kallmann, F. J., 248
Kamens, L., 498
Kamin, L. J., 219
Kandel, D. B., 383
Kanin, E. J., 248
Kaplan, A. S., 371, 372
Karsh, R., 167
Kastenbaum, R., 313
Kavale, K., 386
Kazdin, A. E., 31
Keefe, F. J., 496
Keele, S. W., 167, 168
Keesey, R. E., 235–237
Kelley, C. K., 350
Kelley, H. H., 449
Kelly, G. A., 342, 344–345, 353
Kelly, K. E., 485
Kennell, J. H., 300–301, 315
Kerr, N. L., 464, 465
Keye, W. R., 74
Kidd, K. K., 78
Kiesler, C. A., 399
Killian, L. M., 467
Kilmann, P. R., 379
Kimmel, D. C., 312
King, G. D., 350
King, R. A., 179
Kinsey, A., 27–29, 247–248
Kirschenbaum, D. S., 238
Klaus, M. H., 300–301, 315
Klein, D. F., 403
Klein, D. N., 374
Kleinke, C. L., 264, 450, 453
Kleinmuntz, B., 219, 259, 260
Knapp, M. L., 451
Kobasa, S. C., 493, 503
Koffka, K., 13

Kohlberg, L., 295–297, 307, 308, 315
Köhler, W., 13–15, 163–164, 183
Kohn, P. M., 252
Kolata, G., 384
Kolko, D. J., 496
Komacki, J., 417
Koop, C. E., 246, 247, 499
Koss, M. P., 248, 403
Kraepelin, E., 362
Krantz, D. S., 491
Krech, D., 462
Krieger, D. T., 52
Kübler-Ross, E., 313, 316
Kuczaj, S., 198–199, 202

LaChance, C. C., 9
Lahey, B. B., 162
Laird, J. D., 264
Lam, D. H., 373
Lamm, H., 465
Landon, A., 28
Lang, A. R., 25–27, 33
Lange, K. G., 266, 269
Langer, E. J., 312, 451
Lanzetta, J. T., 264
Laroche, S., 180
Larson, C. C., 35
Lashley, K. S., 180
Latané, B., 379, 464, 469
Lavin, D. E., 214
Lavrakas, P. J., 452
Lawton, M. P., 456
Lazarus, A., 410
Lazarus, R. S., 479, 482
Leahy, D., 454
Leak, G. K., 18
LeBon, G., 466
LeBow, M. D., 238
Lederman, S. J., 132
Lee, T., 377
Lefcourt, H. M., 482
Leibowitz, S. F., 372
Lenneberg, E. H., 197n, 202
Lerner, M. J., 469
Lesnik-Oberstein, M., 455
LeVesconte, S., 304
Levine, J. M., 463
Levine, S., 245
Levinson, D., 309–311
Levitt, M. J., 456
Levitt, R. A., 135, 236, 242, 424
Levy, J., 66
Levy, S. M., 479, 491
Lewinsohn, P. M., 373
Lichtenstein, E., 413
Lick, J. R., 498

Lieberman, M. A., 422
Linder, D. E., 439
Ling, G. S. F., 385
Linz, D. G., 246, 247
Lipinski, D. P., 417
Lipsky, M., 409
Lipton, D. N., 19
Lochman, J. E., 19
Loehlin, J. C., 76
Loftus, E. F., 171, 172
Loftus, G. R., 171
Lohr, J. M., 437
Lloyd, C., 481
Loomis, J. M., 132
Lorenz, K. Z., 300
Lubin, B., 346, 349, 351
Luborsky, L., 403
Luchins, A. S., 447
Luparello, T. J., 490
Lykken, D. T., 260, 379
Lynn, R., 218
Lyons, J. S., 424

Maccoby, E. E., 303, 304, 307
MacCoun, R. J., 465
MacFarlande, A., 287
Mackay, A. V. P., 377
MacWhinney, B., 202
Maddi, S. R., 254, 493
Madsen, C. H., 162
Mahoney, M. J., 366
Maier, N. R. F., 164
Malamuth, N. M., 246
Malatesta, V. J., 252
Mann, L., 467, 468
Manucia, G. K., 468
Maratsos, M., 193, 201, 202
Marks, G., 455
Marks, I. M., 411
Marks, L. E., 110, 204, 286
Marks, P. A., 498
Markus, H., 464
Marlatt, G. A., 25
Marlowe, D. A., 30, 31
Marston, A. R., 238
Martelli, M. F., 496
Martin, C. L., 445
Maruyama, G., 469
Maslach, C., 268, 440, 462
Maslow, A. H., 19, 233, 234, 342
Masters, W. H., 382, 419
Matefy, R., 388
Matlin, M., 285
Matsumoto, D., 265
Matthews, K. A., 485
May, J. L., 455
May, P. R., 423

May, R., 19
McAuliffe, K., 84
McAuliffe, S., 84
McCanne, T. R., 264, 265
McCarley, R. W., 243
McCaul, K. D., 264, 496
McClearn, G. E., 84
McClelland, D. C., 256–258
McClintock, M., 130
McConaghy, M. J., 307
McConaghy, N., 248
McConnell, J. V., 180–181
McDavid, J. W., 463
McDougall, W., 233
McFadden, D., 129
McGaugh, J. L., 180, 181
McGowan, R. J., 223
McGurk, H., 286
McNeill, D., 196, 201, 225
Mednick, S. A., 76, 379
Meichenbaum, D., 367
Melzack, R., 134
Menustik, C. E., 413
Mewborn, C. R., 439
Meyer, J. P., 455
Meyers, J. K., 366
Michael, R. P., 130
Michela, J. L., 449
Mider, P. A., 385
Milgram, S., 457–460
Miller, G. A., 169
Miller, I. W., 374
Miller, N. E., 162, 467
Miller, S. M., 368, 485
Milner, J. S., 302
Milner, P., 67–68
Milofsky, E. S., 385
Mirsky, A. F., 426
Mirsky, I. A., 490
Mischel, W., 322, 335, 337,
    339, 342, 344, 364
Mitchell, J. E., 372
Moane, G., 309–311
Moe, J. L., 446
Money, J., 55, 74, 246, 247,
    305
Monroe, L. J., 498
Monroe, S. M., 482
Moon, J. R., 409
Moore, B. S., 335
Moore, J. E., 497
Moos, R. H., 482
Moreland, R. L., 439, 456
Morgenthau, T., 398, 399
Moriarty, T., 469
Morin, C. M., 498
Morris, N. M., 130
Morris, W. N., 463
Moscovici, S., 461

Mueser, K. T., 453
Mullen, B., 439
Murray, H. A., 255–256,
    271, 350
Murstein, B. I., 454, 455
Musante, L., 485
Myers, D. G., 465
Myers, M. B., 249

Nagy, G., 455
Nahemow, L., 456
Neale, J. M., 342, 373, 377,
    386, 479, 490
Nelson, K., 196, 201
Neugarten, B., 312
Nevid, J. S., 452
Newcomb, T. M., 441
Newcombe, N., 305
Newton, I., 98
Nicassio, P., 498, 499
Nida, S., 469
Nielson, D. W., 128
Nisbett, R. E., 444
Nolan, J. D., 418
Norton, G. R., 366

Odbert, H. S., 333
O'Grady, K. E., 454
Ohman, A., 367
Olds, J., 67–68
Oliver, D. E., 455
Ortega, D. F., 485
Orzack, M. H., 426
Oster, H., 261
O'Sullivan, M., 438
Overton, D. A., 177

Paige, K. E., 74
Palmer, D. L., 455
Palmer, F. H., 223
Palmer, J. C., 172
Pantin, H. M., 468
Parcell, S. R., 248
Park, B., 446
Parker, N., 248
Parloff, M. B., 403
Patterson, F. G., 191, 192
Paul, G. L., 411
Pavlov, I., 12, 145–146,
    148–150
Pearlman, C. A., 243
Pearlman, K., 219
Penfield, W., 62, 171
Pennebaker, J. W., 497
Pepper, S., 455
Perkins, D., 481, 482
Perls, F. S., 406–407, 428
Perry, D. G., 306
Persons, J. B., 373

Petersen, A., 383
Peterson, C., 374
Peterson, L. R., 170
Peterson, M. J., 170
Petty, R. E., 436, 437
Piaget, J., 18, 202, 203, 278,
    288–294, 315
Pilon, D. C., 258
Pine, C. J., 238
Pinel, P., 398
Pines, M., 181
Pipel, J. E., 485
Plato, 10
Plomin, R., 76, 223
Podlesny, J. A., 260
Polivy, J., 239, 272
Pomazal, R. J., 469
Popper, K., 328
Postman, L., 172
Powley, T. L., 236
Premack, A. J., 191
Premack, D., 191
Prescott, P., 287
Price, D. D., 135
Pritchard, D., 351
Puccetti, M. C., 493
Pyszcznski, T., 373, 374

Quattrone, G. A., 437
Quinsey, V. L., 248

Rabinowitz, H. S., 207
Rabkin, J. G., 403, 481
Rahe, R. H., 479–482
Ramirez, D., 497
Rao, P. A., 373
Rapaport, K., 248
Rapport, M. D., 386
Raps, C. S., 374
Raskin, D. C., 260
Rathus, S. A., 74, 293, 381,
    385, 413, 416–417
Rayner, R., 151
Rebok, G. Wa., 200, 202
Redd, W. H., 496
Reeder, G. D., 448
Reese, L., 341
Reinke, B. J., 309, 311
Reiss, M., 449
Rempel, J. K., 449
Renninger, K. A., 167
Reschly, D. J., 218
Rhodes, L., 366
Rhodewalt, F., 493
Richards, R., 379
Richardson, D., 33
Richter, C. P., 482, 484
Rickard-Figueroa, J. L., 496
Rickhoff, T., 249

Rieser, J., 287
Riley, V., 491
Rinn, W. E., 261
Robinson, B., 130
Robinson, M. H., 130
Rock, I., 98
Rodin, J., 238
Rogers, C. R., 19, 20, 342,
    353, 403–405, 407, 428
Rogers, R., 361
Rogers, R. W., 268, 439, 479
Rohsenow, D. J., 25
Rollin, B. E., 35
Rorschach, H., 349
Rosch, E., 204
Rosenblatt, A., 351
Rosenfeld, H. M., 451
Rosenhan, D. L., 367, 468
Rosenzweig, M. R., 83
Ross, L., 444
Rothbart, M., 446
Rothman, S., 218, 223
Rotter, J. B., 337, 493
Roueche, B., 425
Rounsaville, B. J., 403
Rozin, P., 372, 453
Rubin, Z., 451
Ruble, D. N., 74
Ruderman, A. J., 238
Rumbaugh, D. M., 191
Rundus, D., 172
Rutkowski, G. K., 469

Sackheim, H. A., 425
Sadker, D., 304
Sadker, M., 304
Saegert, S. C., 439
Safer, M. A., 448
Sagar, H. A., 446
Salapatek, P., 286
Salzarulo, P., 243
Sanders, B., 305
Santee, R. T., 440, 462
Satir, V., 421
Satow, K. L., 468
Sattler, H. L., 498
Savage-Rumbaugh, E. S., 191
Sawrey, W. L., 490
Saxe, L., 260
Scarr, S., 76, 78, 214, 222,
    223, 368
Schachter, S., 237, 238, 258,
    267–269, 379, 500, 501
Scheier, M. F., 335
Schiavi, R. C., 245
Schindler, B. A., 488
Schmauk, F. J., 379
Schmidt, F. L., 219
Schneider, B. H., 414

Schneirla, T. C., 164
Schofield, J. W., 446
Schuckit, M. A., 384
Schultz, D. P., 9
Schwartz, R. M., 65, 440
Schwartz, W., 236
Scott, J. P., 84
Seeman, P., 377
Seer, P., 490
Segal, M. W., 456
Seligman, M. E. P., 367, 373–374
Selye, H., 479, 487, 488, 502
Serlin, E., 311
Seta, J. J., 464
Shaffer, D. R., 437
Shakespeare, W., 2, 400
Shanteau, J., 455
Shapiro, D. A., 409
Shaw, E. D., 424
Sheehy, G., 309, 310
Sheingold, K., 178
Shekelle, R. B., 485
Sherif, M., 446
Shields, B., 9
Shiffman, S., 501
Shotland, R. L., 468
Shrout, P. E., 482
Shumley, N., 34
Siegman, A. W., 451
Sigall, H., 454
Simon, T., 214
Sims, D., 345
Singer, J. E., 267–268
Singer, J. L., 498
Sistrunk, F., 463
Skelton, J. A., 497
Skinner, B. F., 12–13, 21, 37, 61, 152–156, 158, 163, 200–201, 212, 336, 337, 353
Slobin, D. I., 198
Slochower, J., 238
Smedley, J. W., 446
Smith, B. M., 260
Smith, D., 403–405, 408, 410
Smith, G. F., 439
Smith, J. E., 385
Smith, M. L., 403, 405–407, 411, 420
Smith, R. E., 374
Smith, S. S., 33
Smith, T. W., 371, 409
Snyder, C. R., 406
Snyder, M., 438, 441

Snyder, S. H., 50–52, 377
Snyderman, M., 218, 223
Soares, M. P., 305
Socrates, 10, 18
Southwick, L. L., 385
Spanos, N. P., 370
Spearman, C., 210, 225
Spence, D. P., 403
Sperling, G., 167
Sprecher, S., 452
Squire, L. R., 58, 179
Sroufe, A., 260, 261, 271, 298
Staats, A., 437
Stalonas, P. M., 238
Staneski, R. A., 453
Steele, C. M., 385
Steinberg, L. D., 302
Stericker, A., 304
Stern, W. C., 243
Sternberg, R. J., 212, 213, 225
Stevens, A., 467
Stevenson, H. W., 218
Stewart, A., 345
Stewart, V., 345
Stier, D. S., 450
Stone, A. A., 373, 479
Storandt, M., 312
Strahan, R. F., 485
Stricker, E. M., 236
Strom, J. C., 451
Strube, M. J., 485
Stunkard, A. J., 237
Suarez, D. D., 34
Sugarman, R., 464
Sweeney, J. A., 178
Sweeney, P. D., 439
Swensen, C. H., 311
Szucko, J. J., 259, 260

Taylor, S. E., 445
Taylor, W. N., 71
Teders, S. J., 489
Tenney, Y. J., 178
Terman, L., 215
Terrace, H. S., 191–193
Tetlock, P. E., 437
Thiel, D. L., 454
Thigpen, C. H., 370
Thoits, P. A., 481, 482
Thompson, J. E., 446
Thompson, W. C., 468
Thorndike, E. L., 152–153
Thurstone, L. L., 210, 225

Thurstone, T. G., 210
Titchener, E. B., 10
Tolman, E. C., 164–165, 183
Torgersen, S., 368
Toufexis, A., 237
Touhey, J. C., 455
Tryon, R. C., 83
Tuke, W., 398
Turkington, C., 131, 377
Turner, R. H., 467
Turner, S. M., 368
Twain, M., 14
Twentyman, C. T., 302

Udry, J. R., 130
Umberson, D., 454
Underwood, B., 335
Unger, R. K., 454

Vaillant, G. E., 384, 385
Valenstein, E. S., 68–69, 426
Valentine, E., 223
Van Dyke, C., 386
Victor, J., 98
Victor, R. G., 388
Vinocur, A., 465
Visintainer, M. A., 491
Von Békésy, G., 128

Waber, D. P., 305
Wachtel, P. L., 329
Wain, H., 497
Walker, B. B., 490
Wallis, C., 237
Walsh, B. T., 372
Walster, E., 454, 456
Walton, J. H., 264
Ward, W. S., 497
Watkins, M. J., 172
Watson, J. B., 12, 19, 20, 37, 151, 278, 336, 337, 342, 353
Watson, S. J., 423
Watt, N. F., 377
Weber, E., 96
Weber, R., 437
Wechsler, D., 209, 212, 216
Weil, G., 498
Weinberg, R. A., 222, 223
Weiner, H., 490
Weiner, M. J., 444
Weiss, J. M., 374
Weissman, M., 424
Weisz, J. D., 490
Wender, P. H., 377

Werner, C., 485
Werner, C. M., 451
Wertheimer, M., 13, 111
Wetzel, C. G., 450
Wetzler, S. E., 178
Wexler, D. A., 405
Whalen, C. K., 386
Wheeler, L., 462
Whitcher, S. J., 450
White, G., 417
Whitehead, W. E., 490
Whorf, B., 203
Whyte, W. W., 456
Wiens, A. N., 413
Wiggins, J. S., 452
Wightman, F. L., 129
Wilder, D. A., 446, 463
Will, M. J., 485
Williams, R., 219
Williams, R. L., 218
Williams, R. M., 464
Wilson, G. T., 342, 410, 413
Wilson, R. S., 221
Wing, R. R., 238
Winokur, G., 374
Winterbottom, M., 257
Wolinsky, J., 312
Wolpe, J., 403, 410
Wood, W., 439, 440
Woodside, D. B., 371, 372
Wozniak, R. H., 167
Wright, F. E., 444
Wu, C., 437
Wundt, W., 10, 11, 37
Wyer, R. S., 445
Wyler, G., 34

Yarnold, P. R., 485
Yost, W. A., 128
Youkilis, H. D., 498
Young, T., 110, 111

Zaiden, J., 403
Zajonc, R. B., 264, 266, 438, 439, 456, 463
Zeichner, A., 485
Zigler, E., 220, 222, 223
Zillman, D., 245
Zimbardo, P. G., 467
Zubek, J., 222, 250
Zuckerman, M., 252, 264, 461
Zuger, B., 248

SUBJECT INDEX

Note: Terms in the running glossary are indicated by page numbers in boldface type.

A–B problem, **436**–437
ABC model of attitudes, **436**
Abnormal behavior, 342,
    358–395
  defining, 359–362
  models of, 362–365
  patterns of, 359, 365–388
  theoretical view of,
    367–368
  See also Therapy
Abnormalities
  chromosomal, 79–80
  genetic, 79–81, 377
Absolute refractory period,
  48
Absolute threshold, **95**–96
Abstinence syndrome, **383**
Accommodation, **289**
Accurate information, 496
Acetylcholine, **50,** 180
Achievement, need for,
  256–258
Acoustic code, **168,** 170, 174,
  177, **294**
Acquired drives, **233**
Acromegaly, 71
Acronym, **168,** 176
Acrophobia, **366**
ACTH, 72
Action potential, **48**
Activating effects, **244**–245
Activation-synthesis model,
  243–244
Activity, 250
Actor-observer effect, **448**
Acupuncture, **94,** 134–135
Adaptation, dark, **103**
Adenine, 75
Adipose tissue, **237**
Adolescence, 285–286, 332
Adrenal cortex, **69,** 70,
  72–73
Adrenal glands, 72–73
Adrenal medulla, **69,** 70, 72,
  73

Adrenalin, **73**
Adrenocorticotrophic
  hormone (ACTH), **72**
Adult (transactional analysis),
  405
Adult development,
  308–313, 332
Adulthood
  late, 309, 311–313
  middle, 309–311
  young, 309–310
Afferent neurons, **45**
Affiliation, **258**
Afterimage, 108–**109,** 111
Aggression, 76, 426
  alcohol and, 24–27, 33
  behavioral perspective and,
    21
  biological perspective and,
    17–18
  cognitive perspective and,
    19
  humanistic perspective
    and, 19–20
  psychoanalytic perspective
    and, 20
  sex differences and, 304,
    307
  social-learning perspective
    and, 21
  temperature and, 32
Aging, theories of, 313
Agoraphobia, **366**
AIDS, **281,** 386
Alarm reaction, **487,** 488
  components of the (table),
    488
Alcohol, 384–385
  aggression and, 24
  study on effects of, 24–27,
    33, 35
Alcoholics, **385**
Alcoholism, 384
Algorithm, **205**
All-or-none principle, **48**

Allele, **79**
Alpha waves, **162,** 241
Altruism, **18, 468**
Alzheimer's disease, **50,** 180
Ambiguity, **113**
Ambiguous, **349**
Amenorrhea, **371**
American Psychiatric
  Association, 365, 368,
  371, 378, 383
American Psychological
  Association, 33, 361
  code of ethics of, 33
  divisions of the, 7
  founding of, 11
American Sign Language,
  190, 191, 193, 195
Amnesia
  anterograde, **179**
  childhood, **178**–179
  psychogenic, **178**
  retrograde, **179**
Amniocentesis, **81**
Amniotic sac, **279**–280
Amphetamines, **377,** 386
Amplitude, **100,** 124–125
Amygdala, **58**
Anal-expulsive traits, **327**
Anal fixation, **327**
Anal-retentive traits, **327**
Anal stage, **327**
Analgesia, **134, 385**
Analogous colors, **109**–110
Analytical psychology, **229**
Androgens, 245, 248, **279**
Angiotensin, **240**
Animal subjects, research
  and, 34–35
Animism, **290,** 291
Anorexia nervosa, **371**
Anosmia, **130**
Answer keys for
  questionnaires, 520–522
Anterograde amnesia, **179**
Antibodies, **488**–489

Antidepressant, **424,** 425
Antidiuretic hormone, **72,**
  181, **240**
Antigen, **488**
Antisocial personality
  disorder, **378**–379
Anxiety, **7,** 426, 482–483
  basic, **330**
  state, **483**
  trait, **483**
Anxiety disorders, 359,
  365–368
Apes, language and,
  190–193, 201
Aphagic state, **236**
Aphasia, **64**–65
Approach-approach conflict,
  484
Approach-avoidance conflict,
  484–485, 490
Approximations, successive,
  161
Aptitude, **214, 345**
Aptitude tests, 6, 29
Archetypes, **329**
Are You Type A or Type B?
  (questionnaire), 486–487
Arousal, **253**
  optimal search for,
    253–255
Artificialism, **290,** 291
Asch Study, 461–462
Assertiveness training,
  414–415
Assimilation, **289**
Association areas, **62**
Asthma, 490
Asylums, **397**–398
Attachment, **297**–302
Attachment-in-the-making
  phase, **298**
Attitude, **436**–446
  changing, through
    persuasion, 437–441

defined, **436**
origins of, 437
Attitude-discrepant behavior, **442**–444
Attitudinal similarity, 455
Attraction, **451**–456
interpersonal, 451–456
Attribution, **447**
dispositional, **447**
situational, **447**
Attribution process, **447**
Attribution theory, 447–449
Attributional style, **374**
Auditory nerve, **128**
Auditory stimulation, 124
Authority, obedience to, 457–460
Autism, **78, 375**
Autogenic training, **498**–499
Autokinetic effect, **115**
Autonomic functions, **162**
Autonomic nervous system, **59**–61
Autonomy, **309, 422**
Autosomes, **77,** 79–80
Average, **507**
Aversion therapy, 412–413
Aversive conditioning, **145,** 411, **412,** 413
Avoidance-avoidance conflict, **484**
Avoidance learning, **181**
Axon, 43, **44,** 45
Axon terminals, **45,** 47

Babbling, **195**–197, 201
Backward conditioning, **147**
Baiting, 468
Balance theory, 441–442
Barbiturates, **385**–386
Basal ganglia, **58**
Basic anxiety, **330**
Basic hostility, **330**
Basilar membrane, **128**
Bedlam, origin of word, 398
Bedwetting, 150–151
Behavior, **3**
abnormal, *see* Abnormal behavior
adaptive, 11
assertive, 414
attitude-discrepant, **442**–444
biology and, 42–92
exploratory, 250–253
group, 463–469
helping, 468–469
self-control and, 416–420

strategies aimed at, 418–420
studying, 21–32
correlational method, 31–32
experimental method, 24–27, 35
naturalistic-observation method, 22–24, 27
scientific method, **22**
survey method, 27–29
testing method, 29
submissive, 414
views of, 16–21
behavioral perspective, 20, 21
biological perspective, 16–18
cognitive perspective, 18–19
psychoanalytic perspective, 20
social-learning perspective, 20–21
Behavior genetics, **76**
Behavior modification, 410
in the classroom, 162–163
Behavior-rating scale, **346**
Behavior rehearsal, **415**
Behavior therapy, 5, 266, 342, 409, **410**–420
evaluation of, 420
Behavioral perspective, 20, 21
aggression and, 21
Behavioral view of attachment, 298–299
Behaviorism, **12**–13, 20
personality and, 336–337, 341, 344
Benzedrine, 386
Benzodiazepines, **368**
Bimodal, **510**
Binet-Simon scale, 214–215
Binocular cues, 116, **119**–120
Biofeedback training, **162, 498**
Biological perspective, 16–18
aggression and, 17–18
Biological processes, 43
Biological psychologists, **43,** 61
Biology, behavior and, 42–92
Bipolar cells, **100,** 101
Bipolar disorder, **364,** 372–373, 424
theoretical views of, 373–374

Blind, **25**
Blind spot, **102**
Blood sugar level, 235–237
Body language, 207, 450–451
Botulism, 50
Brain, 52, 55–59
electrical stimulation of the, 66–69
hemispheres of the, 65–66
weight of the, 52
Brain cells, controversy over loss of, 47
Brainstorming, 209
Brave New World (Huxley), 85, 144–145, 161–162
Breathalyzer, **33**
Bridges' theory, 260–261
Brightness (of color), 105
Broca's aphasia, 64–**65**
Bulimia nervosa, **371**
Bystander effect, 468–469

California Psychological Inventory, 349
Caliper, **345**
Cancer, 490–491
Cannon-Bard theory (emotions), 266–267, 271
Cardinal trait, **332**–333
Carriers, **81**
Case study, **29,** 31
Case-study method, 29, 31
Catastrophizing, **408**
Catatonic schizophrenics, **376**
Catharsis, **400**
Caucasian, **218**
Cells
bipolar, **100,** 101
brain, controversy over loss of, 47
division of, 76–77
fat, **237**
ganglion, **100,** 101
glial, **44,** 45
taste, **131**
Cellular-aging theory, **313**
Center (in Piaget's theory), **291**
Central nervous system, **52,** 53–59
Central tendency, measures of, 509–510
Central traits, **333**
Cephalocaudal trend, **279**
Cerebellum, **56**
Cerebral cortex, 47, **58**–59, 61–62, 64–66

Cerebrum, **58**
Chemotherapy, **422**–424
evaluation of, 424
Child (transactional analysis), 405
Child abuse, 302
Child psychology, 11
Childhood, development during, 282–285
Childhood amnesia, **178**–179
Choice-point, **12**
Chromosomal abnormalities, 79–80
Chromosomes, **75**–77
Chunk of information, **169,** 170, 172, 173, 179, 295
Circular explanation, **335**
Classical conditioning, **145**–152
applications of, 150–152
Claustrophobia, **365**
Clear-cut-attachment phase, **298**
Clinical psychologist, 5–6, 9
Clinical scales, **347**
Clitoris, **327**
Closure, **111,** 115
Cocaine, 386
Cochlea, **128**
Cognitive appraisal, of hassles and life changes, 482
Cognitive appraisal theory (emotions), 267–268
attitudes and, 437
Cognitive development, 287–297
information processing and, **294**–295
Piaget's stages of (table), 288
and sex typing, 307–308
Cognitive-developmental theory, **18**
Cognitive-dissonance theory, 442–444
Cognitive learning, 145, **163**–165
Cognitive map, **164**
Cognitive model (abnormal behavior), 364–365, 373–374
Cognitive perspective, 18–19
aggression and, 19
Cognitive theories
of abnormal behavior, 367–368, 370, 373–374
of intelligence, 211–213

Cognitive theories, (*Cont.*)
  of language development, 202, 203
Cognitive therapy, **407**–409
  evaluation of, 409
Cold turkey, and quitting smoking, 500
Collective unconscious, **329**
Color, 105, 107–108
Color blindness, 111
Color constancy, **120**–121
Color vision, 103, 105–111
  theories of, 110–111
Color wheel, 105, 106
Comatose state, **57**
Common fate, 113–**114**
Community mental-health movement, 398–399
Community psychologists, 5, 6
Competencies, **339**–341
Complementary (transactional analysis), **405**
Complementary colors, **107**–108
Componential level, 212, **213**
Compulsion, **366**–367
Compulsion to utter, **401**
Concept, **202**
Concordance, **78, 248, 368**
Concrete operational stage (cognitive development), 288, **292**–293
Conditional positive regard, **343**
Conditioned reinforcer, **156**
Conditioned response, **146**–150, 156
Conditioned stimulus, **147**–151, 156
Conditioning, **12, 20, 144**
  attitudes and, 437
  aversive, **145**
  backward, **147**
  classical, **145**–152
  higher-order, **150**
  instrumental, **152**
  operant, 145, **152**–163
Conditions of worth, **343**
Conduction deafness, **129**
Cones, 100, 102, **103**
Confidentiality, **33**
Conflict, **484**–485
Conformity, 460, **461**–463
  factors influencing, 462–463
Congruence, **405**
Consciousness, 19, 21, **323**

Consensus, **449**
Conservation, **291**, 293
Consistency, 449
Consolidation, **179**
Consonance, **125**
Constancy
  brightness, **121**
  color, **120**–121
  perceptual, 120–121
  shape, **121**
  size, **120**
Constant stimuli, method of, **95**
Construe, **344**
Consultation, 4–5
Consumer psychologist, 8–9
Contact comfort, **299**–300
Contextual level, **212**
Contiguity, **150**
Continuity, 113–**114**
Continuous reinforcement, **159**
Control, locus of, **493**
Control subjects, **24**–25
Conventional level (moral development), **297**
Convergence, 119, **120**
Convergent thinking, **208**–209
Conversion disorder, **370**
Cooing, **195**, 201
Coping, 496
Copulation, **252**
Cornea, **100**
Corpus callosum, **59**, 66
Correlation coefficient, **32, 213, 513,** 514
Correlational method of studying behavior, 31–32
Correlational research, **32**
Cortices, **47**
Cortisol, **72**, 73
Counseling psychologist, 5, 6
Counterconditioning, **151**
Countertransference, **402**
Crack, 386
Creative self, **330**
Creativity, **208**
  intelligence and, 209
  in problem solving, 208–209
Cretinism, **72**
Critical period, **300**
Crying, 195, 197
Cue-dependent forgetting, 176, **177**
Culture bias, 219
Culture-free tests, 219–220

Cumulative recorder, **154**–155
Curare, 50
Curve, normal, **512**–513
Cytosine, 75

Dark adaptation, **103**
Day care, effects of, 301–302
Deafness, 129
Debriefing, **33**
Deception, use of, in psychological experiments, 33, 35
Decibel, **125**
Deep structure, 194, **195**
Defense mechanism, **324**
Deindividuation, 466, **467,** 468
Delta waves, 240–241
Delusions, **375**
Demonological model (abnormal behavior), **362,** 397
Dendrites, **44,** 45, 47
Deoxyribonucleic acid (DNA), 75
Dependent variable, **24**
Depersonalization disorder, **369,** 370
Depo-Provera, 249
Depolarization, **48**
Depressants, **383**–386
Depression, 364, 374, 424, 426
  major, 425
Depth perception, 116–120
Descriptive statistics, **507**
Desensitiziation, **98**
  systematic, **151**
Determinants, **17, 220**
Development
  adolescence, 285–286
  adult, 308–313
  childhood, 282–285
  cognitive, 287–297
  continuous, 278
  controversies over, 277–278
  discontinuous, 278
  infancy and, 283, 286–287
  intellectual, 291–293
  of locomotion, 283
  moral, 295–297
  perceptual, 286–287
  physical, 282–286
  prenatal, 278–282
  psychosexual, 326–328
  psychosocial, 331–332
  sensory, 286–287

theories of, 276–319
  visual, 286
Developmental psychologist, 6, 277
Developmental psychology, 276–319
  controversies in, 277–278
Deviation IQ, **216**
Dexedrine, 386
Diagnostic and Statistical Manual of the Mental Disorders, 364–366, 368, 376, 379
Diagram, scatter, **513**–515
Dialogue, **407**
Dichromats, **111**
Difference threshold, **96**–97
Diffusion of responsibility, **464,** 468
Discomfort, 482, 496
Discrimination, 149–150, **445**
Discrimination training, **150**
Discriminative stimulus, **158**–159
Disorders
  anxiety, 365–368
  bipolar, **364,** 372–374
  conversion, **370**
  depersonalization, **369**
  dissociative, **368**–370
  eating, 371–372
  gender-identity, **379**
  generalized anxiety, **366**
  mood, 372–374
  neurotic, **363**
  obsessive-compulsive, 366–367
  panic, **366**
  personality, 378–379
  phobic, **365**–366
  post-traumatic stress, **367**
  psychoactive substance use, 383–388
  sexual, 379–382
  sleep, 496, 498–499
  somatoform, **370**–371
Disorganized schizophrenics, **376**
Displacement
  in language, 192, **193**
  in memory, **170,** 177
  in personality, **324**
Dispositional attribution, **447**
Dissociative disorders, 368–370
  theoretical views of, 369–370
Dissonance, **125**
Distinctiveness, 449

Distraction, and pain, 496
Distribution
    frequency, **507**–508
    normal, **512**, 513
Divergent thinking, **208**–209, 211
Dizygotic (fraternal) twins, **78**, 220–221
DNA, 75, 76, 85, 181, 313
Dominant traits, **79**
Dopamine, **50**–51, **377**
Double approach-avoidance conflict, **485**
Double-blind study, **25**
Down syndrome, **80**
Dream, the, **311**
Dream analysis, 402
Dreams, 243–244, 407
    analysis of, 402
Drive-reduction theory, **233**, 234
    Drive for superiority, **330**
Drive(s), **232**
    acquired, **233**
    physiological, 232, **234**–250
    primary, **233**, 234
Duct, **69**
Ductless glands, 69–74
Duplicity theory, **129**
Dyslexia, **6**
Dyspareunia, **382**

Ear, 126–128
    structure of, 126–128
Eardrum, **126**
Eaters
    external, **237**–238
    internal, **237**–238
Eating disorders, 371–372
    theoretical views of, 372
Eclectic, **364**
Educational psychologist, 6
Effect, law of, **153**
Efferent neurons, **45**
Effort justification, **442**
Ego, **324**
Egocentrism, **290**, 291, 293
Eidetic imagery, **170**–171
Ejaculation, premature, **382**
Elaboration likelihood model, **437**
Elaborative rehearsal, **172**–174
Electra complex, 305, **327**, 328
Electrical stimulation of the brain, 66–69
Electrochemical process, 48

Electroconvulsive therapy, **424**–425
Electroencephalograph, **162**, 240, 242, 243
Embryo, **277**
Embryonic stage, **279**–281
Emotional appeal, **439**
Emotion(s), 230, 258, **259**–269
    components of three common (table), 259
    development of, 260–261
    expression of, 261–263
    theories of, 260–269
Empathetic understanding, **404**–405
Empiricism, **21**, 156
Empty-nest syndrome, **311**
Encoding, **167**, 168, 294, **340**
Encounter group, **421**
Endocrine system, 69–74
Endorphins, **51**–52, 134
Engram, **180**
Enkephalins, **52**
Enuresis, **78**
Environment
    intelligence and, 222–223
    longevity and, 313
Environmental psychologist, 6–8
Epilepsy, **58**, 66
Epinephrine, 51, 73, 180, 181
Erogenous zones, **326**
Eros, **326**
Estrogen, **73**, 74, 248
Estrus, **245**
Ethics, psychology and, 32–35
Ethologist, **232**, 300
Euphoria, **268**
Evaluation apprehension, **464**
Exaltolide, **130**
Excitatory synapse, **50**
Exhaustion stage, 487, **488**
Exhibitionism, **381**
Exorcist, **362**
Expectancies, **337**, 340–341
Experiential level, **212**–213
Experiment, **24**
Experimental method, 24–27, 32
Experimental psychologist, 8
Experimental subjects, **24**–25
Exploratory behavior, 250–253
Expressive vocabulary, **196**
External eaters, **237**–238

Extinction, 147–**148**, 151, 156, 158
Extroversion, **76**, 333–334
Eye, 100–104
    structure, 100–103

Facial-feedback hypothesis, **263**–265
Facilitation, social, **463**–464
Factor theories (of intelligence), 210
Fallopian tube, **277**
Family therapy, **421**–422
Fantasy
    and insomnia, 498
    and pain, 496
Farsightedness, **104**
Fat cells, **237**
Feedback, **415**
Female sexual arousal disorder, **382**, 420
Fetal stage, 281–282
Fetishism, **380**
Fetus, **279**, 281
    possible effects of certain agents on, 281
Figure-ground perception, 112–113
"Firing," of neurons, 48, 61, 62
Fissures, **59**
Fixation, **327**
    anal, **327**
    oral, **327**
Fixed-action pattern, **232**–234, 300
Fixed-interval schedule, **159**
Fixed-ratio schedule, **160**
Flashbacks, **388**
Flextime, **8**
Flooding, **151**
Follicle-stimulating hormone (FSH), 93
Foot-in-the-door technique, **440**–441
Forced-choice format, **346**
Forcible rape, 248–250
Forebrain, 57–59
Forensic psychologist, 9
Forgetting, 174–179
Formal operational stage (cognitive development), 288, **293**
Format, forced-choice, **346**
Fovea, **102**, 103
Frame of reference, **343**, **405**
Fraternal twins, 78
Free association, 400–401

Frequency distribution, **507**–508
Frequency of a sound, 124
Frequency theory, 128, **129**
Frontal lobe, **62**
Frustration, **483**–484
    tolerance for, **484**
Fugue, psychogenic, **368**, 369
Functional analysis, **416**–418
Functional fixedness, **207**–208
Functionalism, 11, 18
Fundamental attribution error, **448**

g (general intelligence), **210**
Ganglia, **52**
Ganglion cells, **100**, 101
Gate theory of pain, 134
Gender constancy, **307**–308
Gender identity, **307**–308
Gender-identity disorder, **379**
Gender-scheme theory, 308
Gender stability, **303**
General-adaptation syndrome, **487**
Generalization, 149, 158
    stimulus, **149**
Generalized anxiety disorder, **366**
Generalized expectancies, **337**
Generalizing from experimental results, 26–27
Genes, **17**, 75, 80
Genetic abnormalities, 79–81, 377
Genetic code, 76, 84–85
Genetic counseling, 81, 83
Genetic engineering, 84–85
Genetics, **76**
    behavior, **76**
    future and, 84–85
Genie case study, 31
Genital stage, **328**
Genotype, **76**
Genuineness, **405**
Germinal stage, **279**
Gestalt, **342**
Gestalt psychology, **13**–16, 18, 19, 111
Gestalt therapy, **406**–407
Gland(s)
    adrenal, **69**, 72–73
    ductless, 69–74

Gland(s), (Cont.)
  pituitary, **69**–72
  thyroid, **72**
Glial cells, **44,** 45, 47
Glucagon, **72**
Gonadotropin-releasing
  hormone (GnRH), 73
Grammar, 194, 203
Gray matter, **53**
Group behavior, 463–469
Group decision making,
  464–465
Group intelligence tests,
  217–218
Group therapy, 420–422
  evaluation of, 422
Groupthink, **466**
Growth hormone, **71**
Growth-hormone releasing
  factor (hGRF), 71
Guanine, 75

Habit, 11, **156**
Hallucination, **347, 361**
Hallucinogenics, **387**–388
Hassle, **479**–482
Head Start program, effects
  of, 32, 223, 515, 516
Headaches, 489–490
Health, stress and, 32
Health psychologist, 9, 491,
  492
Health psychology, 479–505
  treatment of health
    problems and, 492
Hearing, 124–129, 286–287
Helping behavior, 468–469
Helplessness, learned, **373**
Hemophilia, **81**
Heredity, 74, **75**–85
  intelligence and, 220–223
  longevity and, 313
Hering-Helmholtz illusion,
  122
Hertz, **124**
Heterozygous, **79**
Heuristics, 205, **206**
Hierarchy, **173, 233**
  of needs, 233–234
Higher-order conditioning,
  150
Hippocampus, **50**
Histogram, **508**
Holocaust, **446**
Holophrase, **198**
Homeostasis, **235**
Homosexuality, **247**–248
Homozygous, **79**
Homunculus, **61**

Hormone(s), **17, 69,** 74, 279
  antidiuretic, **72**
  growth, **71**
  prenatal sexual
    differentiation and,
    279
  sex, 305
Hospitals, mental, 398
Hostility, basic, **330**
Hue, **100,** 105
Human Potential Movement,
  19
Humanistic psychology,
  19–20
  aggression and, 19–20
Humanistic theory, 233
Hunger, 235–238, 252, 253
Huntington's chorea, **80,** 84
Hyperglycemia, **72**
Hyperphagic state, **235,** 237,
  238
Hypertension, **94,** 490
Hyperthyroidism, **72**
Hypnagogic state, **241**
Hypnosis, 400, 497
Hypoactive sexual desire
  disorder, **382,** 419
Hypochondriasis, **370**–371
Hypoglycemia, **72**
Hypothalamus, **17,** 57, **58,**
  70–73, 237, 240
Hypothesis, **22**
Hypothyroidism, **72**

Id, **324**
Ideas
  of persecution, **361**
  rapid flight of, **373**
Identical twins, 77, 78
Identification, **305, 325**
Identity, gender, **307**–308
Illness
  life changes and, 481–482
  psychological factors in,
    486–491
Illusions, **115**–116
Imagery, eidetic, **170**–171
Imbalance, **441**
Imitation (in learning
  language), 200, 202
Immune system, **488,** 489
Imprinting, **300**
Incentive, **232**
Incest taboo, **328**
Incubation, **206**
Independent variable, **24**
Indiscriminate attachment,
  298

Individual psychology, **330**
Individuation, **309**
Indocin, 74
Industrial psychologist, 8–9
Infancy, development
  during, 283, 286–287
Infer, **516**
Inference, **26**
Inferential statistics, 515,
  516, 518
Inferiority complex, **329**–330
Inflections, **193**–194
Information processing,
  18–19
Information processing
  (cognitive development),
  294–295, 308
Informed consent, **33**
Inhibited orgasm, **382,** 420
Inhibitory synapse, **50**
Initial-preattachment phase,
  298
Innateness, **342**
Insanity, **359,** 360–361
Insecure attachment, **298**
Insight, **14, 164, 399**
Insight-oriented therapies,
  399–409
Insomnia
  irrational ideas about, 499
  psychological treatment of,
    496, 498–499
Instinct, **23, 232**–234
Instrumental conditioning,
  152
Insulin, **72**
Intelligence, 76, 83, **209**–223
  achievement and, 32
  creativity and, 209
  determinants of, 220–223
  environmental influences
    on, 222–223
  ethnic differences in, 218
  genetic influences on,
    220–222
  heredity and, 220–223
  measurement of, 213–218
  race and, 218, 223
  social-class and, 218
  theories of, 210–213
Intelligence quotient (IQ),
  215 See also IQ
Intelligence tests, 29, 32
  characteristics of, 213–214
  controversy over, 218–220
  culturally biased, 219
  culture-free, 219–220
  differences in scores on,
    218

group, 217–218
  misuse of, 219
Interference theory, 170,
  177
  proactive, 177, **178**
  retroactive, **177**–178
Internal eaters, **237**–238
Interneuron, **53**
Interposition, **117**–118
Interpretation, **402**
Interval schedule
  fixed, **159**
  variable, 159–**160**
Interviews, 27–29
Intoxication, **24**
Introspection, **10**
Introversion, **333**–334
Intuition, **191**
Involuntary activities, **59**
IQ, **215,** 216, 514–516
  deviation, **216**
Iris, **100**
Irrational beliefs, coping
  with, **496**
Izard's theory, 261

James-Lange theory
  (emotions), 265, 266,
  271
Job sharing, **8**
Just noticeable difference,
  96–97

Kinesthesis, **135**
Klinefelter's syndrome, 80
Knobs, **44**
Knowledge-acquisition
  components, 212, **213**
Kuder Occupational Interest
  Survey, 349

L-Dopa, 50
La belle indifférence, 370
Language, **190**
  animals and, 190, 192
  apes and, 190–193, 201
  basics of, 193–195
  cerebral cortex and, 62,
    64–66
  patterns of development
    of, 195–200
  properties of human,
    192–193
  theories of development
    of, 200–203
  thought and, 203–204
Language Acquisition
  Device, **201**

Late adulthood, 309, 311–313
Latency stage, **328**
Latent content, **402**
Latent learning, 164
Lateral hypothalamus, **236**
Law of effect, **153**
Learned helplessness, **373**
Learning, 143–144, **145,** 146–165, 181
  avoidance, **181**
  cognitive, 145, **163**–165
  consolidation of, 179
  definitions of, **145**
  future of, 181
  by insight, **164**
  instrumental, **152**
  latent, 164
  language development and, 200–203
  misbehavior and, 154
  observational, **165**
  programmed, **163**
Learning-theory
  (abnormal behavior), 367, 384
  (language), 200–202
  (personality), 336–342, 345
"Left brain–right brain" notion, 65–66
Lens, **100,** 103
Lesion, 35, **62, 235,** 236
Level
  conventional, **297**
  postconventional, **297**
  preconventional, **296**
Libido, **306**
Librium, 422
Lie detectors, 259–260
Life-change units, **481**
  scale of (table), 481
Life changes, 479–482
  and hassles, 479–481
  and illness, 481–482
Light, **98**–100
  visible, **98**
Light adaptation, 103–104
Limbic system, 57, **58**
Linguist, **192**
Linguistic-relativity hypothesis, **203**–204
Literary Digest Survey (1936), 28
Lithium, 424
Lobe, 61–62
  frontal, **62**
  occipital, **62**
  parietal, **62**
  temporal, **62**

Lobotomy, prefrontal, **425**–426
Loci, method of, **179**
Locus of control, **493**
Locus of Control Scale (questionnaire), 494
Longevity, **313**
Long-term memory, **171**–173, 177
Loudness of a sound, 124–126, 128–129
Love Scale (questionnaire), 264
Low-balling, **441**
LSD, 51, 388
Luteinizing hormone (LH), 73, 277
Lynching, 467

Machiavellian trait, **333**
Major depression, **372**
Major tranquilizer, **423**–426
Male erectile disorder, **382,** 420
Manic-depression, 364, 372–373
Manicky behavior, **373,** 374, 424
Manifest content, **402**
Manipulation of the environment, 250–253
Marijuana, 387–388
Masochism, **381**
Masturbation, 27, 327
Matching hypothesis, 454–**455**
Maternal-sensitive period, **300**–301
Maturation, **278**
Mean, **509,** 517
Means-end analysis, **206**
Measures of central tendency, 509–510
Measures of variability, 510–512
Median, **509**
Mediation, **19, 179**
Medical instructions and procedures, 492
Medical model (abnormal behavior), 362–363
Meditation, **490**
Medulla, **56**
Meiosis, **76**–77
Memory, 143, **145,** 165–181
  biology of, 180–181
  defined, 166
  future of, 181
  improving, 179–180

information processing and, 18–19
  long-term, **171**–173
  photographic, 170
  reconstructive, **172**
  sensory, **166,** 167
  short-term, **167**–172, 177, 294–295
  state-dependent, 177
  structure of, 166–167
Memory molecules, **180,** 181
Menarche, **285**
Menopause, **245**
Menstrual synchrony, **130**
Menstruation, **73**–74
Mental abilities, primary, **210**
Mental age, **214**
Mental hospitals, 398
Mental set, **206**–207
Mescaline, 388
Metabolism, **72**
Metacomponents, **213**
Methadone, **285**
Metaqualone, 385–386
Method of constant stimuli, **95**
Method of loci, **179**
Midbrain, 56–57
Midlife crisis, **310**–311
Milgram studies at Yale, 457–460, 471, 472
Mind, 61
Minnesota Multiphasic Personality Inventory, 346–351
Minor tranquilizer, **422,** 424
Misbehavior, learning and, 154
Mitosis, **76**
Mnemonics, 47, **179**–180
Mob behavior, 466–468
Mode, **509**–510
Model, **158, 200, 415**
  cognitive (abnormal behavior), 364–365
  demonological (abnormal behavior), **362**
  medical (abnormal behavior), **362**–363
  organic (abnormal behavior), 362–**363**
  psychoanalytic, 363
  social-learning (abnormal behavior), 363–364
Modeling, **338, 415**
Monoamine oxidase inhibitors, **424**
Monochromats, **111**
Monocular cues, **116**–119

Monozygotic twins (identical), **77**–78, 220–221
Mood disorders, 372–374
Moral development theory, 295–297
Moral principles, **325**
Morpheme, **193**
Morphine, **17**
Mother
  as reinforcer, 298–299
  as source of contact comfort, 299–300
Motherese, **200,** 202
Motion parallax, **119**
Motivation, 230–258
  theoretical perspectives on, 232–234
Motives, **231**
  social, **255**–258
  stimulus, **250**–255
Motor cortex, **62**
Motrin, 74
Movement, perception of, 115–120
Müller-Lyer illusion, 122–123
Multiple personality, **359**
  disorder, 368–370
Mutation, **76**
Mutism, **376**
Myelin sheath, **45**
Myelination, **45,** 47
Mythical images, **329**

n Ach, **256**–258
n Aff, **258**
Napoleonic trait, **333**
Narcotics, **385**
Nativist views (of learning language), 201–203
Naturalistic-observation method of studying behavior, 22–24, 27
Nature, **76,** 78, 83, 278
Nearsightedness, **104**
Necker cube, 113
Need(s), **231**
  hierarchy of, 233–234
  physiological, 231
  psychological, 231–232
Negative adaptation, 98
Negative correlation, **32**
Negative feedback, **70,** 73
Negative reinforcer, **155,** 158n, 178
Neonate, **283,** 286, 287

Nerve, **52**
  auditory, **128**
  optic, **102**
Nervous system, 52–61
  autonomic, **59**–61
  central, **52**, 53–59
  peripheral, **53**, 59–61
  somatic, **59**
Neural impulse, 47, **48**, 49
Neurons, 43, **44**–52
  afferent, **45**
  efferent, **45**
  electrochemical process
    and, 48
  "firing" of, 48, 61, 62
  makeup of, 44–47
Neuropeptides, 51–**52**
Neurosis, **363**
Neuroticism, **76**, **334**, **368**
Neurotransmitters, **43**–44,
    49–51
Nicotine, 500
Nodes of Ranvier, **45**
Noise, **97**, 126
  white, **126**
Non-rapid-eye-movement
    sleep, **241**–243
Nonbalance, **491**
Nonsense syllables, **174**
Norepinephrine, **51**, 374,
    424
Normal curve, **512**–513
Normal distribution, **512**,
    513
Normative data, **480**–481
Novel stimulation, **252**
Nuclei, **52**
Nurture, **76**, 78, 83, 278

Obedience, to authority,
    457–460
  reasons for, 459–460
Obesity, 236–239
Object permanence, **289**
Objective moral judgment,
    291–292
Objective sensations, **10**
Objective tests, **346**
Observation, naturalistic,
    22–24, 27
Observational learning, **165**,
    338
  attitudes and, 437
Obsession, **366**
Occipital lobe, **62**
Occupational tests, 349
Odor, **129**–130

Oedipus complex, 305, **327**,
    328
Olfactory, **130**
Olfactory nerve, **130**
Opaque behavior, **402**
Operant, **154**
Operant conditioning, 145,
    152–163, 414
  applications of, 161–163
Operational definition, **27**
Opiates, **385**
Opioids, 385
Opponent-process theory,
    110
Optic nerve, **102**
Optimal arousal, **253**–254
Oral fixation, **327**
Oral stage (psychosexual
    development), **326**–327
Organ of Corti, **128**
Organic model (abnormal
    behavior), 362–**363**, 374
Organizing effects, **244**–245
Organizational psychologist,
    8
Orgasm, inhibited, **382**, 420
Orienting reflex, **146**
Osmoreceptors, **240**
Oval window, **128**
Ovaries, 73–74
Overextension, **191**, 198
Overregularization, **199**–200,
    202
Overtones, **125**–126
Ovulation, **277**
Oxytocin, **72**

Pain, 134–135, 482
  gate theory of, 134
Pain management, 492, 496
Paired associates, **175**
Pancreas, **72**
Panic disorder, **366**
Paranoid personality
    disorder, **378**
Paranoid schizophrenia, **376**
Paraphilias, **379**–382
  theoretical views of,
    381–382
Parasympathetic nervous
    system, **59**, 259
Parent (transactional
    analysis), 405
Parietal lobe, **62**
Parkinson's disease, 50, 424
Partial reinforcement, **159**
Participant modeling, **411**

Pathological gambler, **159**
Patient-physician
    interactions, 492
Pedophilia, **381**
Penile strain gauge, **246**
Perception, **94**
  basic concepts in, 95–98
  depth, 116–120
  figure-ground, 112–113
  of movement, 115–120
  visual, 111–123
Perceptual constancies,
    120–121
Perceptual organization,
    111–115
Performance anxiety, **382**
Performance components,
    213
Period of the ovum, **279**
Peripheral nervous system,
    53, 59–61
Permeability, **48**
Persecution, ideas of, **361**
Person-centered therapy,
    403–405
  evaluation of, 405
Person variables, **338**–339
Personal construct, **344**
Personality, 321, **322**–357
  antisocial, **378**–379
  measurement of, 322,
    345–351
  multiple, **359**
  paranoid, **378**
  schizoid, **378**
  structure of, 324–325, **333**
  theories, 322–345
Personality disorders,
    378–379
Personality psychologist, 6–7
Personality structure,
    324–325, **333**
Personality tests, 29,
    346–351
Perspective, **116**
Persuasion, changing
    attitudes through,
    437–441
Phallic stage, **327**
Phallic symbol, **402**
Phencyclidine, 388
Phenomenological theories
    (personality), **342**–345
Phenomenology, **19**, 61
Phenothiazines, 51, **377**, **423**
Phenotype, **76**
Phenylketonuria, **80**
Pheromones, **130**–131, 244
Phi phenomenon, **116**

Phobia
  simple, **365**
  social, **365**
Phoneme, **193**
Phonetics, 201
Phonology, **193**
Photoreceptors, **100**, 103
Phrenology, **345**
Physical attractiveness,
    452–454
Physician-patient
    interactions, 492
Physiological psychologist, **43**
Physiological structures, **43**
Pigment, 107
Pitch, **96**, 124–126, 128
Pituitary gland, **69**–72
Place theory, **128**, 129
Placebo, 25
Placenta, **280**–281
Pleasure principle, **324**
Polarization (in cells), **48**
Polarization (of attitudes),
    465
Polygenic traits, **75**
Polygon, **508**
Polygraph, 260
Pons, **56**
Ponzo illusion, 123
Population, **24**, **507**, 516, 518
Populations, samples and,
    518
Pornography, 245–247
Positive adaptation, 98
Positive correlation, **32**
Positive reinforcer, **155**
Possession, **362**
Postconventional level (moral
    development), **297**
Post-traumatic stress
    disorder, **367**
Pragmatics, **200**
Preconscious mind, **323**
Preconventional level (moral
    development), **296**
Prefrontal lobotomy,
    425–426
Pregenital stages, **328**
Prejudice, **444**–446
  sources of, 446
Prelinguistic vocalizations,
    195
Premature ejaculation, **382**
Premenstrual syndrome, **74**
Prenatal development,
    278–282
Prenatal sexual
    differentiation, 279
Prenatal testing, 81, 83

Preoperational stage (cognitive development), 288, **290–292**
thought in the (table), 291
Prepared conditioning, **367**
Presbyopia, **104**
Pressure, 132–133
Primacy effect, 446–**447**
Primary colors, **108**
Primary drives, **233**
Primary mental abilities, **210**
Primary reinforcer, **156**
Primary sex characteristics, **73**
Primate, **23**
Prism, **98**
Private self-consciousness, **335**
Proactive interference, 177, **178**
Proband, **248**
Problem solving, 204–209
creativity in, 208–209
functional fixedness, 207–208
mental set, 206–207
stages in, 205
Problem-solving training, 409, 426
Productivity, **192**
Progesterone, **73**, 74
Programmed learning, **163**
Progressive relaxation, **488**, 490, 498
"Project Pigeon," 153
Projective test, **349**
Prolactin, **71**
Propinquity, **456**
Prosocial behavior, **336**
Prostaglandins, 74, 134
Proximity, 113–**114**
Proximodistal trend, **279**
Psychedelic drug, **387**
Psychic structure, **324**
Psychoactive substance, **383**
Psychoactive substance use disorders, 383–388
causes of, 383–384
Psychoanalysis, **15**–16, **400**–403
evaluation of, 403
goals of, 400
modern approaches to, 403
Psychoanalytic perspective, 20, 29
aggression and, 20
Psychoanalytic theory, 305, 345, 367, 369–370, 373, 377, 383–384

Psychodynamic theory, **322**–332
Psychogenic amnesia, **178**, **368**, 369
Psychogenic fugue, **368**, 369
Psycholinguist, **190**
Psycholinguistic theory (of language learning), **201**–202
Psychological factors in illness, 486–491
Psychological hardiness, **493**
Psychological involvement, treatment of health problems and, 492
Psychological methods for cutting down and quitting smoking, 499–501
Psychological tests, 29
Psychological treatment of insomnia, 496, 498–499
Psychologists
biological, **43**, 61
clinical, 5–6, 9
community, 5, 6
consumer, 8–9
counseling, 5, 6
definition of, 2, 4
developmental, 6
educational, 6
environmental, 6–8
experimental, 8
forensic, 9
health, 9, 491, 492
industrial, 8–9
organizational, 8
personality, 6–7
physiological, **43**
school, 6
social, 6, 7
work of, 4–9
Psychology
analytical, **229**
child, 11
definition of, **2**–3
ethics and, 32–35
experimental, 8
Gestalt, **13**–15, 18, 19
goals of, 3–4
health, 479–505
history of, 9–16
humanistic, **19**–20
social, 434–477
Psychomotor retardation, 372
Psychoneuroimmunology, **488**

Psychophysical relationship, **95**
Psychophysicist, **95**
Psychosexual development, **326**–328
Psychosis, **363**
Psychosocial development, **331**–332
Psychosurgery, **425**–426
Psychotherapy, **5**, 16, **397**, 403
Puberty, **278**
Punishment, 153, 156, **158**
Pupil, **100**
Pupillary reflex, **286**
Pure research, **4**
Puzzle box, Thorndike's, 152–154

Questionnaires, 27–29
Answer keys for, 520–522
Are You Type A or Type B?, 486–487
Locus of Control Scale, 494–495
Love Scale, 264
Rathus Assertiveness Schedule, 416–417
Remote Associates Test, 209
Sensation-Seeking Scale, 252–253
Social-Desirability Scale, 30–31

Radical behaviorists, **20**, **336**, 341
Rage response, **17**
Random sample, **28**–29, 518
Random trial-and-error, **152**–153
Random trial-and-error behavior, **154**
Range, **507**, **510**
Rape, 248–250
forcible, 248–250
Rapid-eye-movement sleep, **241**–243
Rapid flight of ideas, **373**
Rathus Assertiveness Schedule (questionnaire), 416–417
Ratio schedule
fixed, **160**
variable, **160**
Rational-emotive therapy, **408**–409

Rationalization, **324**
Reaction time, **312**
Reality principle, **324**
Recall, 174, **175**–176
Recency effect, 446–447
Receptive vocabulary, **196**
Receptor site, **50**, 51
Recessive traits, **79**
Reciprocity, **297**, **456**
Recognition, 174–175
Reconstructive memory, **172**
Reflex(es), 54, **146**, **283**, 285
orienting, **146**
Refractory period
absolute, **48**
relative, **49**
Regard
conditional positive, **343**
unconditional positive, **343**, **404**
Regression, **324**
Reinforcement, **12**–13, **153**–156, 158–161
continuous, **159**
in learning leanguage, 200–201
partial, **159**
schedules of, 159–161
strategies aimed at, 419
Reinforcement, schedules of, 159–161
Reinforcers
conditioned, **156**
negative, **155**, 158n, 178
positive, **155**
primary, **156**
secondary, **156**
versus rewards and punishments, 156, 158
Relative refractory period, **49**
Relearning, 174, **176**
Releaser, **233**
Reliability, **213**–214, **514**
Remote Associates Test (questionnaire), 209
Replication, **27**
Representative sample, **28**, 518
Repression, **7**, 178, **323**
Research
animal subjects and, 34–35
applied, **4**
ethics and, 32–35
psychologists in, 8, 22–32
pure, **4**
resistance, **401**
Resistance stage, 487, **488**

Response, **12**
  conditioned, **146**–150, 156
  unconditioned, **146**–147,
    151
  voluntary, 154
Response set, **347**
Responsibility, diffusion of,
  464, 468
Resting potential, **48**, 49
Reticular activating system,
  56–58, 243, 244
Retina, **100**, 103
Retinal disparity, 119–**120**
Retribution, **362**
Retroactive interference,
  177–178
Retrograde amnesia, **179**
Reuptake, 50
Reversibility, **293**
Rewards, 153, **156**, 158
Ribonucleic acid, **181**
Risky shift, **465**
Rods, 100, 102, **103**
Role playing, 345, 370, 407
Rooting, **283**, 287
Rorschach inkblot test,
  349–351
Rote, **169**–170
Routine, regular, and
  insomnia, 499
Rubin vase, 113

s (specific factors), **210**
Sadism, **327**, 381
Saline solution, **267**
Sample, **26**, **507**, 516–517
  populations and, 518
  random, **28**–29, 518
  stratified, **29**, 518
Satiety, **235**
Saturation, **107**
Savings, **176**
Scales
  clinical, **347**
  validity, **29**, **347**
Scapegoat, **446**
Scatter diagram, **513**–515
Scheme, **289**
Schizoid personality
  disorder, **378**
Schizophrenia, 50–51, 76,
  359, 374–377
  causes of, 376–377
  dopamine and, 50–51, 377
  phenothiazines and, 51,
    377
  theoretical views of,
    376–377
  types of, 376

Schizotypal personality
  disorder, **378**
Scholastic Aptitude Tests
  (SATs), 6, 513
School psychologist, 6
Schwann cell, **45**
Scientific method, **22**
Secondary colors, **108**
Secondary reinforcer, **156**
Secondary sex characteristics,
  73
Secondary traits, **333**
Secure attachment, **298**
Selective avoidance, **439**–440
Selective breeding, 83–84
Selective exposure, **440**
Self, **329**
  creative, 330
Self-actualization, **233**, 234,
  342–344, 403–405
Self-concept, 343
Self-consciousness, private,
  335
Self-control techniques,
  416–420
Self-efficacy expectations,
  341
Self-esteem, **343**, 404, 405
Self-ideal, **343**
Self-monitoring, **415**
Self-regulation, 341
Self-report, **3**, 27, 31, 264,
  265
Self-serving bias, **448**–449
Self theory, 342–344
  evaluation of, 343–344
Semantic code, **173**, 174, 177
Semanticity, **192**
Semantics, **194**–195, 201
Semicircular canals, 127, **135**
Sensate focus exercises, **419**
Sensation, **94**
  basic concepts in, 95–98
  visual, 111
Sensation-Seeking Scale
  (questionnaire), 252–253
Sensitive period, **202**
Sensitization, **98**
Sensorimotor stage (cognitive
  development), 288–**290**
Sensory adaptation, 97–**98**
Sensory cortex, **62**
Sensory deprivation, **250**
Sensory memory, **166**, 167
Sensory-neural deafness, **129**
Sensory register, **166**, 167
Sensory stimulation, 250–251
Septum, **58**

Serial-position effect,
  168–169
Serotonin, **51**, 374, 424
Sex chromosomes, **77**, 80
Sex differences, 303–304
Sex drive, 244–250
Sex hormones, 244–245, 305
Sex-linked genetic
  abnormalities, **81**
Sex therapy, behaviorally
  oriented, 419–420
Sex typing, **7**, 302, **303**–308,
  462–463
Sexual disorders, 379–382
Sexual dysfunctions, **379**,
  382
Sexual masochism, **381**
Sexual response, 55
Sexual sadism, **381**
Shadowing, **118**
Sham, **235**
Shaping, **160**, 201
Short-term memory,
  167–172, 177, 204–295
Siblings, **277**
Sickle-cell anemia, **80**
Signal-detection theory, **97**
Significant others, **331**
Similarity, 113–**114**
  attitudinal, 455
Simple phobia, **365**
Situational attribution, **447**
Situational variables, **339**
Size constancy, 116, **120**
Skin senses, 132–135
Skinner box, 154
Sleep, 240–244
  disorders of, 496, 498–499
  functions of, 242–243
  non-rapid-eye-movement,
    241–242
  rapid-eye-movement,
    241–242
  stages of, 240–242
Sleep spindles, **241**
Sleeping, irrational ideas
  about, 499
Sleeping pills, 498
Sleepwalking, 78
Smell, 129–131, 287
Smoking
  as a danger to health,
    499–500
  psychological methods for
    cutting down and
    quitting, 499–501
Social comparison theory,
  258
Social decision schemes, **465**

Social-Desirability Scale,
  30–31
Social facilitation, **463**–464
Social influence, 456,
  457–463
Social-learning model
  (abnormal behavior),
  363–364, 367, 370, 373,
  377, 381–382
Social-learning theory,
  20–21, 306–308
  aggression and, 21
  personality and, **337**–342
Social motives, **255**–258
Social norms, **461**
Social perception, 446–451
Social phobia, **365**
Social psychologists, 6, 7
Social psychology, 434–477
  defined, **436**
Social support, 496
Socialization, **162**, 306–307
Sociobiology, **17**–18, 468
Sociopathy, 76
Soma, **44**
Somatic nervous system, **59**
Somatoform disorders,
  370–371
Sounds, locating, 128
Source traits, **333**
Spinal cord, 52, **53**–55
Spinal reflex, **53**
Split-brain operations, 66
Spontaneous recovery, 147,
  148, 156
Stage, **278**
Standard deviation, 510–**511**,
  517
Standardized tests, **346**
Stanford-Binet Intelligence
  Scale, 214–218, 514
State anxiety, **483**
State-dependent memory,
  177
Statistically significant
  difference, 516–517
Statistics, 506–519
  defined, **506**
  descriptive, **507**
  inferential, 515, **516**, 518
Stereotype, **7**, 445–446
  of attractive people, 454
Steroids, **73**
Stimulants, **383**, 386
Stimulation deafness, **129**
Stimulus, **12**, 146
  conditioned, **147**–149, 151,
    156
  discriminative, **158**–159

unconditioned, **146**–151, 156
Stimulus control, and insomnia, 499
Stimulus discrimination, **150**
Stimulus generalization, **149**
Stimulus motives, **250**–255
Stratified sample, **29,** 518
Stress, **479**–486
  health and, 32
Stressor, 479, 487, 489
Stroboscopic motion, **115**–116
Strong-Campbell Interest Inventory, 349
Sroufe's theory, 260, 261
Structuralism, **10**–11, 18
Structure-of-intellect model, **211**
Stupor, **376**
Subjective feelings, **10**
Subjective moral judgment, **292**–293
Subjective value, **337,** 341
Subjects, 24
  animal, 34–35
  control, **24**–25
  experimental, **24**–25
Subordinate concepts, **173**
Substance abuse, **383**
Substance dependence, **383**
Successive approximations, **161, 414,** 418–419
Suicide, baiting and, 468
Superego, **324**–325
Superfemale syndrome, 80
Supermale, **379**
Supermale syndrome, 80, **379**
Superordinate concepts, **173**
Surface structure, 194, **195**
Surface traits, **333**
Survey, **27**
Survey method of studying behavior, 27–29
Syllogism, **392**
Symbol, **190,** 191, **402**
Sympathetic nervous system, **59,** 61, 259
Symptom substitution, **411**
Synapse, **49**
  excitatory, **50**
  inhibitory, **50**
Synaptic cleft, 49, 51
Syndrome, **72, 364**
Syntax, **192,** 194, 201
  development of, 198
Systematic desensitization, **151, 410**–411

Tactile, **66**
Tardive dyskinesia, 423–424
Tasaday tribe, 23, 24
Taste, 131–132, 287
Taste aversion, **150**
Taste buds, **131**
Taste cells, **131**
Tay-Sachs disease, 80, **81**
Telegraphic speech, **190,** 198
Temperature, 133–134
  aggression and, 32
Temporal lobe, **62**
Terminals, **45,** 47
Tertiary colors, **108**
Test-retest reliability, **214, 514**
Testes, 73
Testing method, 29
Testosterone, **73,** 245, 248
Tests
  aptitude, 29
  controversy over, 218–220
  forced-choice format, **346**
  group, 217–218
  intelligence, *see* Intelligence tests
  objective, **346**
  personality, 29, 346–351
  projective, **349**
  psychological, 29
  reliability of, **514**
  Rorschach inkblot, 349–351
  Scholastic Aptitude, 6
  Thematic Apperception, **256**–257, 350–351
  validity of, **514**
Texture gradient, **118**
Thalamus, **57**–58
Thanatos, **20**
Thematic Apperception Test, **256**–257, 350–351
Theory, **3**–4
  of aging, 313
  attribution, 447–449
  balance, **441**–442
  Bridges', 260–261
  Cannon-Bard, 266–267, 271
  cellular aging, **313**
  cognitive appraisal (emotions), 267–268
  cognitive development, 287–297, 307–308
  cognitive dissonance, 442–444
  duplicity, **129**
  frequency, 128, **129**
  gate, 134

  gender-schema, 308
  interference, 170, 177–178
  Izard's, 261
  James-Lange (emotions), 265, 266, 271
  moral development, 295–297
  opponent-process, **110**
  phenomenological, 342–345
  place, **128,** 129
  psychoanalytic, 305
  self, 342–344
  signal-detection, **97**
  of social comparison, **258**
  social learning, **20**–21, 306–307
  Sroufe's, 260, 261
  trait, 332–336, 345
  trichromatic, **110**
  type, 485–486
  Young-Helmholtz, 110
Therapy, 363, 388
  attribution, 447–449
  aversion, 411–413
  balance, 441–442
  behavior, **5,** 266, 342, 409, **410**–420
  biological, 422–426
  chemotherapy, **422**–424
  cognitive, **407**–409
  cognitive-dissonance, 442–444
  electroconvulsive, **424**–425
  family, **421**–422
  Gestalt, **406**–407
  group, 420–422
  historical overview of, 397–399
  insight-oriented, 399–409
  methods of, 396, 433
  person-centered, **403**–405
  psychoanalytic, 400–403
  rational-emotive, **408**–409
  sex, behaviorally oriented, 419–420
  See also Psychotherapy
Theta waves, 241
Thinking
  convergent, **208**–209
  divergent, **208**–209, 211
Thirst, 239–240, 252, 253
Thought
  cerebral cortex and, 61, 62, 64
  language and, 203–204
Threshold, **48**
  absolute, **95**–96
  difference, **96**–97

Thymine, 75
Thyroid gland, 72
Thyroxin, **72**
Timbre, 125, **126**
Time out, **158**
Tip-of-the-tongue phenomenon, 176–**177**
Token economy, **414**
Tolerance, **383**
Tolerance for frustration, **484**
Touch, 132–135, 287
Training
  assertiveness, **414**–415
  autogenic, **498**–499
  biofeedback, **162, 498**
  discrimination, **150**
  problem-solving, 409, 426
Trait anxiety, **483**
Trait theory, 332–336, 345
Trait(s), **210, 332**
  cardinal, **332**–333
  central, **333**
  dominant, **79**
  Machiavellian, **333**
  Napoleonic, **333**
  recessive, **79**
  sadistic, **333**
  secondary, **333**
  source, **333**
  surface, **333**
Tranquilizers
  major, **423**–426
  minor, **422**
Transaction, **405**
Transactional analysis, 405–406
Transference, **402**–403
Transsexualism, **379**–380
Transvestic fetishism, **380**–381
Treatment, **24,** 31
Trial, **148**
Triarchic model of intelligence, 212
Trichromat, **111**
Trichromatic theory, **110**
Tricyclic antidepressants, 424
Turner's syndrome, 80
Twins
  dizygotic (fraternal), **78,** 220–221
  intelligence and, 220–221
  monozygotic (identical), **77,** 78, 220–221
Two-point threshold, **132**–133
Two-string problem, 207

Two-word utterances, 198, 199
Type A behavior, 479, 485–486, 493
Type B behavior, 485–486

Ulcers, 490
Ultrasound, **83**
Umbilical cord, **280**
Unconditional positive regard, **343, 404**
Unconditioned response, **146**–147, 151
Unconditioned stimulus, **146**–151, 156
Unconscious, **323**–324
collective, **329**
Unobtrusive observation, **22**
Uterus, **277**

Vacillation, **484**

Vaginal photoplethysmograph, **246**
Vaginismus, **382**
Validity, **214, 514**
Validity scales, **29, 347**
Valium, 384, 422
Variability, measures of, 510–512
Variable-interval schedule, 159–**160**
Variable-ratio schedule, **160**
Variables, **4**
dependent, **24**
independent, **24**
person, 338–**339**
situational, **339**
Vasopressin, **181**
Ventromedial nucleus, **235,** 236
Vestibular sense, **135**

Visible light, **98**
Vision, 98–111, 286
color, 103, 105–111
Visual acuity, **104**
Visual capture, **98**
Visual illusions, 122–123
Visual perception, 111–123
Vocabulary
development of, 196–198
expressive, **196**
receptive, **196**
Voyeurism, **381**

Waves
alpha, **162,** 241
delta, 240–241
theta, 241
Waxy flexibility, **376**
Weaning, **327**

Weber's constant, **96,** 97
Wechsler, scales, 214, 216–219, 312, 514
Weight, how to lose, 238–239
Wernicke's aphasia, **65**
White matter, **53**
White noise, **126**
Wish fulfillment, **402**

XXX syndrome, 80
XYY syndrome, 80, 379

Yerkes-Dodson law, **254**–255, 271
Young-Helmholtz theory, 110

Zygote, **77, 277**